Lecture Notes in Computer Science 4551

Commenced Publication in 1973
Founding and Former Series Editors:
Gerhard Goos, Juris Hartmanis, and Jan van Leeuwen

Julie A. Jacko (Ed.)

Human-Computer Interaction

Interaction Platforms and Techniques

12th International Conference, HCI International 2007
Beijing, China, July 2007
Proceedings, Part II

Springer

Volume Editor

Julie A. Jacko
Georgia Institute of Technology
and Emory University School of Medicine
901 Atlantic Drive, Suite 4100, Atlanta, GA 30332-0477, USA
E-mail: jacko@hsi.gatech.edu

Library of Congress Control Number: 2007929780

CR Subject Classification (1998): H.5.2, H.5.3, H.3-5, C.2, I.3, D.2, F.3, K.4.2

LNCS Sublibrary: SL 2 – Programming and Software Engineering

ISSN 0302-9743
ISBN-10 3-540-73106-7 Springer Berlin Heidelberg New York
ISBN-13 978-3-540-73106-1 Springer Berlin Heidelberg New York

Springer is a part of Springer Science+Business Media

springer.com

Printed in Germany

Typesetting: Camera-ready by author, data conversion by Scientific Publishing Services, Chennai, India
Printed on acid-free paper SPIN: 12077953 06/3180 5 4 3 2 1 0

Foreword

The 12th International Conference on Human-Computer Interaction, HCI International 2007, was held in Beijing, P.R. China, 22-27 July 2007, jointly with the Symposium on Human Interface (Japan) 2007, the 7th International Conference on Engineering Psychology and Cognitive Ergonomics, the 4th International Conference on Universal Access in Human-Computer Interaction, the 2nd International Conference on Virtual Reality, the 2nd International Conference on Usability and Internationalization, the 2nd International Conference on Online Communities and Social Computing, the 3rd International Conference on Augmented Cognition, and the 1st International Conference on Digital Human Modeling.

A total of 3403 individuals from academia, research institutes, industry and governmental agencies from 76 countries submitted contributions, and 1681 papers, judged to be of high scientific quality, were included in the program. These papers address the latest research and development efforts and highlight the human aspects of design and use of computing systems. The papers accepted for presentation thoroughly cover the entire field of Human-Computer Interaction, addressing major advances in knowledge and effective use of computers in a variety of application areas.

This volume, edited by Julie A. Jacko, contains papers in the thematic area of Human-Computer Interaction, addressing the following major topics:

- Graphical User Interfaces and Visualization
- Mobile Devices and Mobile Interaction
- Virtual Environments and 3D Interaction
- Ubiquitous Interaction
- Emerging Interactive Technologies

The remaining volumes of the HCI International 2007 proceedings are:

- Volume 1, LNCS 4550, Interaction Design and Usability, edited by Julie A. Jacko
- Volume 3, LNCS 4552, HCI Intelligent Multimodal Interaction Environments, edited by Julie A. Jacko
- Volume 4, LNCS 4553, HCI Applications and Services, edited by Julie A. Jacko
- Volume 5, LNCS 4554, Coping with Diversity in Universal Access, edited by Constantine Stephanidis
- Volume 6, LNCS 4555, Universal Access to Ambient Interaction, edited by Constantine Stephanidis
- Volume 7, LNCS 4556, Universal Access to Applications and Services, edited by Constantine Stephanidis
- Volume 8, LNCS 4557, Methods, Techniques and Tools in Information Design, edited by Michael J. Smith and Gavriel Salvendy
- Volume 9, LNCS 4558, Interacting in Information Environments, edited by Michael J. Smith and Gavriel Salvendy
- Volume 10, LNCS 4559, HCI and Culture, edited by Nuray Aykin
- Volume 11, LNCS 4560, Global and Local User Interfaces, edited by Nuray Aykin
- Volume 12, LNCS 4561, Digital Human Modeling, edited by Vincent G. Duffy

- Volume 13, LNAI 4562, Engineering Psychology and Cognitive Ergonomics, edited by Don Harris
- Volume 14, LNCS 4563, Virtual Reality, edited by Randall Shumaker
- Volume 15, LNCS 4564, Online Communities and Social Computing, edited by Douglas Schuler
- Volume 16, LNAI 4565, Foundations of Augmented Cognition 3rd Edition, edited by Dylan D. Schmorrow and Leah M. Reeves
- Volume 17, LNCS 4566, Ergonomics and Health Aspects of Work with Computers, edited by Marvin J. Dainoff

I would like to thank the Program Chairs and the members of the Program Boards of all Thematic Areas, listed below, for their contribution to the highest scientific quality and the overall success of the HCI International 2007 Conference.

Ergonomics and Health Aspects of Work with Computers

Program Chair: Marvin J. Dainoff

Arne Aaras, Norway
Pascale Carayon, USA
Barbara G.F. Cohen, USA
Wolfgang Friesdorf, Germany
Martin Helander, Singapore
Ben-Tzion Karsh, USA
Waldemar Karwowski, USA
Peter Kern, Germany
Danuta Koradecka, Poland
Kari Lindstrom, Finland
Holger Luczak, Germany
Aura C. Matias, Philippines
Kyung (Ken) Park, Korea
Michelle Robertson, USA
Steven L. Sauter, USA
Dominique L. Scapin, France
Michael J. Smith, USA
Naomi Swanson, USA
Peter Vink, The Netherlands
John Wilson, UK

Human Interface and the Management of Information

Program Chair: Michael J. Smith

Lajos Balint, Hungary
Gunilla Bradley, Sweden
Hans-Jörg Bullinger, Germany
Alan H.S. Chan, Hong Kong
Klaus-Peter Fähnrich, Germany
Michitaka Hirose, Japan
Yoshinori Horie, Japan
Richard Koubek, USA
Yasufumi Kume, Japan
Mark Lehto, USA
Jiye Mao, P.R. China
Fiona Nah, USA
Shogo Nishida, Japan
Leszek Pacholski, Poland
Robert Proctor, USA
Youngho Rhee, Korea
Anxo Cereijo Roibás, UK
Francois Sainfort, USA
Katsunori Shimohara, Japan
Tsutomu Tabe, Japan
Alvaro Taveira, USA
Kim-Phuong L. Vu, USA
Tomio Watanabe, Japan
Sakae Yamamoto, Japan
Hidekazu Yoshikawa, Japan
Li Zheng, P.R. China
Bernhard Zimolong, Germany

Human-Computer Interaction

Program Chair: Julie A. Jacko

Sebastiano Bagnara, Italy
Jianming Dong, USA
John Eklund, Australia
Xiaowen Fang, USA
Sheue-Ling Hwang, Taiwan
Yong Gu Ji, Korea
Steven J. Landry, USA
Jonathan Lazar, USA
V. Kathlene Leonard, USA
Chang S. Nam, USA
Anthony F. Norcio, USA
Celestine A. Ntuen, USA
P.L. Patrick Rau, P.R. China
Andrew Sears, USA
Holly Vitense, USA
Wenli Zhu, P.R. China

Engineering Psychology and Cognitive Ergonomics

Program Chair: Don Harris

Kenneth R. Boff, USA
Guy Boy, France
Pietro Carlo Cacciabue, Italy
Judy Edworthy, UK
Erik Hollnagel, Sweden
Kenji Itoh, Japan
Peter G.A.M. Jorna, The Netherlands
Kenneth R. Laughery, USA
Nicolas Marmaras, Greece
David Morrison, Australia
Sundaram Narayanan, USA
Eduardo Salas, USA
Dirk Schaefer, France
Axel Schulte, Germany
Neville A. Stanton, UK
Andrew Thatcher, South Africa

Universal Access in Human-Computer Interaction

Program Chair: Constantine Stephanidis

Julio Abascal, Spain
Ray Adams, UK
Elizabeth Andre, Germany
Margherita Antona, Greece
Chieko Asakawa, Japan
Christian Bühler, Germany
Noelle Carbonell, France
Jerzy Charytonowicz, Poland
Pier Luigi Emiliani, Italy
Michael Fairhurst, UK
Gerhard Fischer, USA
Jon Gunderson, USA
Andreas Holzinger, Austria
Arthur Karshmer, USA
Simeon Keates, USA
Zhengjie Liu, P.R. China
Klaus Miesenberger, Austria
John Mylopoulos, Canada
Michael Pieper, Germany
Angel Puerta, USA
Anthony Savidis, Greece
Andrew Sears, USA
Ben Shneiderman, USA
Christian Stary, Austria
Hirotada Ueda, Japan
Jean Vanderdonckt, Belgium
Gregg Vanderheiden, USA
Gerhard Weber, Germany
Harald Weber, Germany
Toshiki Yamaoka, Japan

George Kouroupetroglou, Greece
Jonathan Lazar, USA
Seongil Lee, Korea
Mary Zajicek, UK
Panayiotis Zaphiris, UK

Virtual Reality

Program Chair: Randall Shumaker

Terry Allard, USA
Pat Banerjee, USA
Robert S. Kennedy, USA
Heidi Kroemker, Germany
Ben Lawson, USA
Ming Lin, USA
Bowen Loftin, USA
Holger Luczak, Germany
Annie Luciani, France
Gordon Mair, UK
Ulrich Neumann, USA
Albert "Skip" Rizzo, USA
Lawrence Rosenblum, USA
Dylan Schmorrow, USA
Kay Stanney, USA
Susumu Tachi, Japan
John Wilson, UK
Wei Zhang, P.R. China
Michael Zyda, USA

Usability and Internationalization

Program Chair: Nuray Aykin

Genevieve Bell, USA
Alan Chan, Hong Kong
Apala Lahiri Chavan, India
Jori Clarke, USA
Pierre-Henri Dejean, France
Susan Dray, USA
Paul Fu, USA
Emilie Gould, Canada
Sung H. Han, South Korea
Veikko Ikonen, Finland
Richard Ishida, UK
Esin Kiris, USA
Tobias Komischke, Germany
Masaaki Kurosu, Japan
James R. Lewis, USA
Rungtai Lin, Taiwan
Aaron Marcus, USA
Allen E. Milewski, USA
Patrick O'Sullivan, Ireland
Girish V. Prabhu, India
Kerstin Röse, Germany
Eunice Ratna Sari, Indonesia
Supriya Singh, Australia
Serengul Smith, UK
Denise Spacinsky, USA
Christian Sturm, Mexico
Adi B. Tedjasaputra, Singapore
Myung Hwan Yun, South Korea
Chen Zhao, P.R. China

Online Communities and Social Computing

Program Chair: Douglas Schuler

Chadia Abras, USA
Lecia Barker, USA
Stefanie Lindstaedt, Austria
Diane Maloney-Krichmar, USA

Amy Bruckman, USA
Peter van den Besselaar, The Netherlands
Peter Day, UK
Fiorella De Cindio, Italy
John Fung, P.R. China
Michael Gurstein, USA
Tom Horan, USA
Piet Kommers, The Netherlands
Jonathan Lazar, USA
Isaac Mao, P.R. China
Hideyuki Nakanishi, Japan
A. Ant Ozok, USA
Jennifer Preece, USA
Partha Pratim Sarker, Bangladesh
Gilson Schwartz, Brazil
Sergei Stafeev, Russia
F.F. Tusubira, Uganda
Cheng-Yen Wang, Taiwan

Augmented Cognition

Program Chair: Dylan D. Schmorrow

Kenneth Boff, USA
Joseph Cohn, USA
Blair Dickson, UK
Henry Girolamo, USA
Gerald Edelman, USA
Eric Horvitz, USA
Wilhelm Kincses, Germany
Amy Kruse, USA
Lee Kollmorgen, USA
Dennis McBride, USA
Jeffrey Morrison, USA
Denise Nicholson, USA
Dennis Proffitt, USA
Harry Shum, P.R. China
Kay Stanney, USA
Roy Stripling, USA
Michael Swetnam, USA
Robert Taylor, UK
John Wagner, USA

Digital Human Modeling

Program Chair: Vincent G. Duffy

Norm Badler, USA
Heiner Bubb, Germany
Don Chaffin, USA
Kathryn Cormican, Ireland
Andris Freivalds, USA
Ravindra Goonetilleke, Hong Kong
Anand Gramopadhye, USA
Sung H. Han, South Korea
Pheng Ann Heng, Hong Kong
Dewen Jin, P.R. China
Kang Li, USA
Zhizhong Li, P.R. China
Lizhuang Ma, P.R. China
Timo Maatta, Finland
J. Mark Porter, UK
Jim Potvin, Canada
Jean-Pierre Verriest, France
Zhaoqi Wang, P.R. China
Xiugan Yuan, P.R. China
Shao-Xiang Zhang, P.R. China
Xudong Zhang, USA

In addition to the members of the Program Boards above, I also wish to thank the following volunteer external reviewers: Kelly Hale, David Kobus, Amy Kruse, Cali Fidopiastis and Karl Van Orden from the USA, Mark Neerincx and Marc Grootjen from the Netherlands, Wilhelm Kincses from Germany, Ganesh Bhutkar and Mathura

Prasad from India, Frederick Li from the UK, and Dimitris Grammenos, Angeliki Kastrinaki, Iosif Klironomos, Alexandros Mourouzis, and Stavroula Ntoa from Greece.

This conference could not have been possible without the continuous support and advise of the Conference Scientific Advisor, Prof. Gavriel Salvendy, as well as the dedicated work and outstanding efforts of the Communications Chair and Editor of HCI International News, Abbas Moallem, and of the members of the Organizational Board from P.R. China, Patrick Rau (Chair), Bo Chen, Xiaolan Fu, Zhibin Jiang, Congdong Li, Zhenjie Liu, Mowei Shen, Yuanchun Shi, Hui Su, Linyang Sun, Ming Po Tham, Ben Tsiang, Jian Wang, Guangyou Xu, Winnie Wanli Yang, Shuping Yi, Kan Zhang, and Wei Zho.

I would also like to thank for their contribution towards the organization of the HCI International 2007 Conference the members of the Human Computer Interaction Laboratory of ICS-FORTH, and in particular Margherita Antona, Maria Pitsoulaki, George Paparoulis, Maria Bouhli, Stavroula Ntoa and George Margetis.

Constantine Stephanidis
General Chair, HCI International 2007

HCI International 2009

The 13th International Conference on Human-Computer Interaction, HCI International 2009, will be held jointly with the affiliated Conferences in San Diego, California, USA, in the Town and Country Resort & Convention Center, 19-24 July 2009. It will cover a broad spectrum of themes related to Human Computer Interaction, including theoretical issues, methods, tools, processes and case studies in HCI design, as well as novel interaction techniques, interfaces and applications. The proceedings will be published by Springer. For more information, please visit the Conference website: http://www.hcii2009.org/

General Chair
Professor Constantine Stephanidis
ICS-FORTH and University of Crete
Heraklion, Crete, Greece
Email: program@hcii2009.org

Table of Contents

Part I: Graphical User Interfaces and Visualization

Part II: Mobile Devices and Mobile Interaction

Part V: Emerging Interactive Technologies

Part I

Graphical User Interfaces and Visualization

When Does a Difference Make a Difference? A Snapshot on Global Icon Comprehensibility

Sonja Auer[1] and Ester Dick[2]

[1] Siemens AG, Power Transmission & Distribution, Humboldtstr. 59, 90459 Nuremberg, Germany
Sonja.Auer@Siemens.com
[2] Siemens AG, Corporate Technology, Otto-Hahn-Ring 6, 81739 Munich, Germany
EsterDick@yahoo.com

Abstract. Global markets require global solutions, especially in user interface design. There are differences between cultures – but do those differences call for different icon designs? This paper provides a snapshot on icon comprehensibility in China, the US and Germany. The icon set was derived of an actual product to enable valid results. A web-based study with 135 participants from China, the US and Germany was conducted. Icon recognition rates among the Chinese participants were significantly lower than among US and German participants. Still, the mean rating for all three countries was above 69% and thus far removed from guesswork. Practical implications for global icon design are discussed based on these findings.

Keywords: Internationalization/Localization, Icon Evaluation, Icon Design, User Interface Design, Visual Design, Quantitative Empirical User Studies.

1 Motivation

In a world of growing globalization, the requirements for products are changing. Products are no longer made for a small homogeneous market but distributed all over the globe. Different markets may have differing needs. But many variants of the same product that may serve differing markets would multiply the product development costs. For reasons of economy, products are built on a common international denominator, allowing product transfer to many markets with only a minimum of localization effort.

Globalization has an impact on the product itself (e.g. functionality), but most of all on its user interface (UI). It's the UI that must support users regardless of their cultural background. The UI needs to "talk" and "listen" carefully to enable a smooth user experience. Today, most UIs are designed in Western countries (US, Europe), but need to be fit for the growing markets in China. The UI content is localized in terms of translation, date formats etc., though layout and icons are not changed. However, we know very little about how a UI that was built in the US or Europe work for Chinese users. Are there differences in understanding the UI? If so, what are the consequences? Do cultural differences call for different UI designs for US/European and Chinese users?

J. Jacko (Ed.): Human-Computer Interaction, Part II, HCII 2007, LNCS 4551, pp. 3–12, 2007.

2 Visual Perception and Cultural Differences

A theoretical framework from the field of perceptual psychology provides basic principles that can be applied to the design of visual displays. There are typically two approaches to perception, that both need to be taken into account, when designing user interfaces. The "bottom-up" approach to perception concentrates on the process of extracting information about the properties of a stimulus, thus the processing of sensory input. Marr [18] describes in his theory how the physical properties of the retinal picture are translated into conscious perception. The "top-down" approach emphasizes the active strategies that are intrinsic to the perceiver. Perception is a conscious experience. The observer interprets sensory data through e.g. previous knowledge, expectations, the context, or the cultural affiliation. Gestalt laws [23] and pattern recognition [1] are further examples of conceptually-driven processing of visual input. Only through simultaneous and interactive interplay of these two mechanisms visual perception is facilitated.

As we know from previous research, culture strongly influences human behavior, ethical values and patterns of social interpretation. Several concepts of culture have been constructed to understand and measure these influences [10, 11, 16, 26].

Hofstede [11] defined culture as "software of the mind" or "the collective programming of the mind that distinguishes the members of one group or category of people from another". This "software" or "programming" comprises essential patterns of thinking, feeling and acting. These patterns are programmed for a particular group and learned throughout lifetimes. Cultural differences manifest themselves in a culture's choices of symbols, heroes, rituals and values.

In the tradition of the Hofstede concept of culture especially, there are a number of studies focusing on specific cultural differences. Amongst others, there are studies investigating user-interface components in websites across countries [17], or research on how German and Chinese participants learn and work with mobile phones and how far they differ in learning and information gathering strategies [12]. Differences, for example between US and Asian participants, were found in cognitive style and the thinking process [22]. Furthermore, design preferences and attitudinal and behavioral consequences of satisfying or not satisfying such preferences have been examined [5].

In consequence of both theoretical concepts and empirical findings, cultural differences have to be taken into account for UI design. A good example may be the use of color schemes for web sites: as "colors have different connotations in different countries" [4], colors have to be used with care. Up to now, a large body of evidence related to cultural differences has been collected. To ease the development of UIs with an international audience, checklists for the design of UIs have been developed. They draw attention to local conventions, e.g. for date formats and currency formats, and to guidelines for graphical aspects such as the use of colors and icons. Refer to e.g. [7] for an extended specification.

2.1 Why Icons?

A picture says more than 1000 words. In a software context, icons (aka pictograms) are graphical symbols which represent underlying system functions, objects and processes in a pictorial manner. Compared to text buttons, icons are very economic and powerful tools: they provide a language-independent means of communicating with the user and therefore avoid localization efforts and translation errors [13]. Additionally, they reduce learning efforts for the user, are faster recognized on the screen and therefore support learning the handling of a new system [30]. Advantages and disadvantages are discussed in greater depth in [8, 24].

In an international context, icons are indispensable. But not all symbols are understood in the exact same manner worldwide [3, 7, 28]. When are icons appropriate for different cultures?

2.2 Culture and Icon Design

As icons represent real world objects and concepts, recognition and understanding of an icon depends on the cultural context.

The internationally valid ISO standard on icons defines general requirements and recommendations for icon design. [15]. Other guidelines [13, 14, 25] – as also developed by companies with a global audience such as Microsoft [20] or Sun [29] – give general recommendations for avoiding icons that might be offensive or misunderstood in some countries, e.g. numbers with special meanings, puns, flags, animals, taboos.

Beyond analyzing specific symbols, previous studies do not attempt to show that there is any cultural influence involved in understanding icons. Piamonte, Ohlsson & Abeysekera [21] compared icon comprehensibility between European and Asian users and found comparable hit rates. Smith & Siringo [27] investigated identifiability and attractiveness of icons in India, Turkey, Singapore and the US without finding significant discrepancies between countries.

Choong & Salvendy [3] assumed different cognitive styles and abilities between US and Chinese users because of differences in their language. The results supported their hypothesis.

3 Hypotheses

To investigate if we needed different icon sets for the US/European and the Chinese market, a study was set up with participants from the US, Germany and China. The icon set was derived of an actual product to provide a realistic snapshot on today's situation. Icon design was limited by product specific preconditions such as defined icon sizes and given color schemes. Nevertheless, the icons were not modified for the study, so that valid conclusions could be drawn for future products. Icons were designed carefully with respect to worldwide users. Based on these preconditions we assume from a practitioner's point of view that the icon set should work for users of all three nations.

Hypothesis 1: There should be no differences in the rate of recognition for US, Chinese and German participants.

Though icon design was based on the above-mentioned guidelines, there were some icons that might not be culture free (e.g., "i" for information, bug for "debug").

Hypothesis 2: The rate of recognition for a specific icon should be higher in one group when the icon is related to the language of that group (e.g. the US group should score a higher rate for the "debug" icon).

4 Method

The study was set up as a web based questionnaire that was accessible worldwide for anybody interested. The study was posted in several newsgroups, and additionally invitations were distributed by e-mail. Altogether, the study was online for two months. Though the study was open to everybody regardless of origin, the focus was on China, the US and Germany. Therefore, the study was available in three languages: English, Chinese and German.

4.1 Icon Comprehensibility

There are several methodologies for assessing the quality of icons [2, 13]. Methods vary in terms of the number of icons and meanings presented.

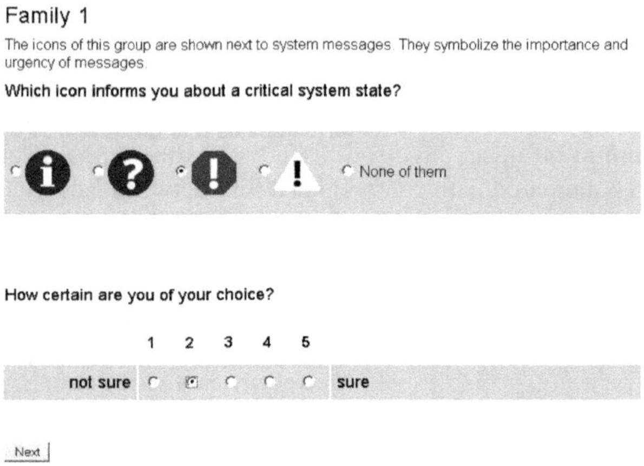

Fig. 1. Screenshot of the icon comprehensibility questionnaire

In this study, we wanted to achieve results with a high level of validity. The study setting was to represent the actual usage situation. But, as we wanted to draw conclusions for future icon design, the study was to concentrate on icons (not on a specific product or prototype). Therefore, we used the Multiple Index Approach for the evaluation of pictograms and icons [6]. The icons were presented in groups as they would appear in the real software, e.g. toolbar icons for settings or icons on a message bar. Figure 1 shows a screenshot of the icon presentation for the experiment. The user was a given toolbar of at least 4 icons and one function e.g. "Which icon would you use to undo your last action?" The user was asked to select the icon that represents the given function. We implemented two mechanisms to ensure overall result quality: firstly, icons within groups were presented in a random sequence to avoid effects of order; secondly, we showed more icons than there were functions, to prevent association by a process of elimination.

The study scope is to give a snapshot on icon comprehensibility based on today's actual conditions. Preconditions such as sizes, functions and compromises in icon metaphors were not changed for this study, so that conclusions could be drawn for future products designed in real-life conditions. We used a total set of 36 icons applicable for anybody working with computers and the internet. Examples of icons used are shown in Figure 2.

Fig. 2. Examples of icons: undo, redo, delete, zoom, chart, reset sort order

4.2 Participants

To assess variables that might influence the test results, each participant was asked to fill out a demographic profile containing information on age, gender, profession, country of current residence and country of birth, and a self-assessment of computer and internet experience.

Table 1. Participant profiles by country

Participants		US	China	Germany
Mean age in years		37.14	25.84	31.62
Age range in years		16 to 57	19 to 40	18 to 59
Gender: Female/Male		12/33	20/25	25/20
Experience: Computer/ Internet	Beginner	2/3	1/1	2/2
	Advanced	20/21	20/27	25/27
	Expert	23/21	24/17	18/16
Daily use: Computer/ Internet	< 2h/day	2/16	1/2	3/17
	2-6h/day	9/22	8/16	22/19
	> 6h/day	34/7	36/27	20/9

Out of a total of 283 participants, 238 were of US (including Canada), German or Chinese origin. the study disregarded the data of those who reported problems with correct display of the survey due to browser specifics or who reported a difference between their country of birth and country of current residence (N=1 for USA, N=1 for China, N=13 for Germany). As it was supposed that too many misses indicated either problems in the conduct of the survey or a lack of interest in filling in the complete survey properly, data was also excluded if the participant selected "none of these icons" for more than 36% of all icons or for more than 60% of icons from one icon family (N=2 for USA, N=9 for China, N=5 for Germany). To obtain equal group sizes, the sample for each country was randomly reduced to 45 participants from the US, Germany and China respectively. An overview of the participant profile for each country is given in Table 1.

5 Results

Each participant in this study was asked to select the corresponding icon for the given function. In the course of the experiment 28 functions were presented and thus the maximum score for one participant over all icons was 28. What is referred to as the mean hit rate per person is the percentage of correctly assigned items.

Each function was presented to all participants. What is referred to as the mean icon hit rate is the ratio between the number of correct hits and the total of 135 participants. According to their nationality, participants were assigned to one of three groups (China, Germany or the US).

To determine whether there were significant differences between users of different nationalities, analyses of variance (ANOVAs) were computed. If the prerequisites for the use of an ANOVA were not met, Greenhouse-Geisser corrected test values were recorded. Where there were significant differences, post hoc tests were performed to highlight the specific differences between the three nationalities in focus.

A repeated measures analysis of variance with the within-subject factor icon and the between-subject factor nationality was conducted. A significant main effect for the factor nationality was discovered ($F(2,132)=23.58$; $p<.001$). This result indicates that there are differences between participants from different home countries. Post hoc analysis showed significant differences between the Chinese sample and the two other samples (both $p<.001$). A second main effect for the factor icon ($F(18.10, 2388.99)=30.883$; $p<.001$) suggests that there are differences in the hit rates for the single icons. An interaction between icon and nationality ($F(36.197,2388.99) =4.09$; $p<.001$) shows differences regarding the hit rate between the nationalities depending on the specific icon. For further comparisons the mean hit rates per person were utilized.

Table 2. Mean hit rates in percent and standard deviations for all icon combinations, grouped by nationality

	All icons (N = 28)		**Culture-related (N = 5)**		**Culture-independent (N = 23)**	
	Mean in percent	**Std**	**Mean in percent**	**Std**	**Mean in percent**	**Std**
China	68.65	.11	47.56	.24	73.24	.12
Germany	78.81	.12	66.22	.24	81.55	.12
US	83.73	.09	86.22	.17	83.19	.10
Total	77.06	.12	66.67	.27	79.32	.12

In our choice of the material used we exercised great care. Still our goal was also to use a realistic set of icons that could be found within an authentic application. To assure that the results were not caused by single icons that contain some sort of language relatedness or draw on explicit cultural idiosyncrasies, we subdivided the complete icon set into two kinds of icons: culture-independent icons (N=23) and culture-related icons (N=5). Classification of icons was based on guidelines for international icon design [13, 14, 25]. Mean values for the hit rates in percent and standard deviations for all combinations are summarized in Table 2.

Icons were allocated to the group of culture-related icons according to the following principles. The initial letters of a function (as in the "Version Info" icon) serve as a cue for German and US participants, but not for Chinese participants. The "debug" icon should be helpful for US participants, but not for German or Chinese participants, because it follows an English wordplay. The status icons were included because they rely on color as an information transmitting element for one, and then also on shapes that may not be part of the signposting reality in a specific country. Using red as the semantic element for danger would not take account of research on cultural differences, e.g. [7].

As to the five culture-related icons we found significant differences between the three nationalities ($F(2,132)=36.09$; $p<.001$). Post hoc tests revealed that all groups differed regarding their mean hit rate for these icons (all $p<.001$). Apparently the icons that mainly depict US American culture or language lead to a reduced recognition rate in the Chinese subgroup, but also in the German subgroup, although to a lesser extent.

After removing the culture-related icons, an ANOVA was conducted with the remaining (culture-independent) icon set. Significant differences in the between-subject factor nationality ($F(2,32)=10.10$; $p<.001$) were found and a post hoc test showed that these differences can be ascribed to a lower mean recognition rate for Chinese participants (for China*Germany $p<.005$, for China*USA $p<.001$). So even with the exclusion of the culture-related icons the Chinese users still achieve the lowest hit rates. Hence the possible culture-relatedness of our icons cannot account for the differences between countries, although Chinese participants do benefit from the exclusion of these icons (see Figure 4).

When planning the study, we were aware that the icon recognition rates might be influenced by the participants' level of computer and internet literacy. Therefore we compared the self-rated classification as beginner, advanced or expert users. Participants of different nationalities did not differ in their rating either as computer users ($\chi^2(4,95\%)=2.12$; $p=.71$) or as internet users ($\chi^2(4,95\%)=2.74$; $p=.60$). The measured differences cannot be explained by different levels of computer literacy.

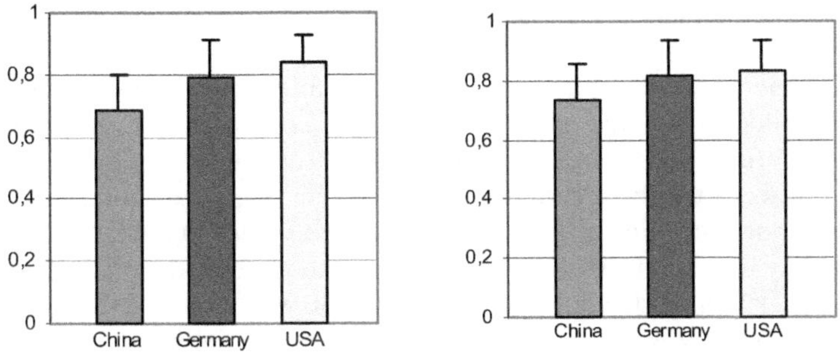

Fig. 4. Mean hit rates for a) all icons and b) language-independent icons

6 Discussion

The motivation to conduct this experiment was to give a snapshot on icon comprehensibility based on realistic conditions. Is there a need to design different sets of icons for US, China and Germany? In general, all participants achieved relatively high hit rates for the icons. With a span from 69% to 84% all three groups lay well above chance level. Still we found significantly lower hit rates for the Chinese group that could not be eliminated by excluding culture-related icons from the set. Thus, hypothesis 1 needs to be rejected: there are differences in the recognition rate between Chinese users and participants from the US or Germany.

Hypothesis 2 has to be retained: our analysis showed that, where we decided to include icons in our set that may have language dependencies, we had a drop in icon comprehensibility. Performance went down for Chinese and German users, but – as expected – not for the US participants.

The lower recognition rate for Chinese participants definitely needs further investigation. However, from a practitioner's point of view, the good overall hit rates from 69% to 84%, suggest that there is no need for over-hasty reaction. The icons tested could be used for an international audience, especially if the software uses tooltips in addition to icons. To be appropriate for professional applications, a set of icons needs to fulfill several criteria. It needs to be easy to understand and meaningful for the first part. Furthermore, as familiarity with the application in question progresses, the task of recognition becomes more and more important. The function that the user wants to trigger by clicking on the icon is often found by virtue of the fixed position of the icon, e.g. in a toolbar. That is to say, after the phase of initial exposure to the icon within the application, it's about positional consistency rather than icon comprehensibility [9, 17].

This study may allow us to draw conclusions about the first part in the "life" of an icon within a software application and the effects of culture on this phase. It does not give us any clue about the recognition of an icon after the user has worked with the software. The findings of a study by McDougall [19] can be summarized as follows: "good icons" are learned faster, but "bad icons" are learned as well at some point and then "work" just as well.

A second point of interest is the study's value for the scientific community. What is the reason for this result? Observed differences may not play a big role when the purpose is an economical process - but still they are there. Why do we find differences between the two Western cultures and Chinese culture?

The participants' age and level of familiarity with an icon might be an interfering variable. Younger users, as in the Chinese sample might have a disadvantage because they had less time to become acquainted with the computer and internet. .However, we could not find differences concerning the self-rated computer and internet proficiency between the three countries. Furthermore, the setup of the study as a web survey should guarantee that all participants were computer literate, at least to such an extent that they were able to take part. The methodological approach we used to collect our data is standardized. Nevertheless it is of Western origin and thus may lead to distortions. The only way for us to eliminate this suspicion was to clarify and verify the appropriateness of the approach with Chinese HCI professionals.

A possible bottom line to this experiment may be that the cultural background of the recipient of an icon (vs. the originator of the icon) actually plays a role in recognition performance, but is not the only factor. The underlying reasons for this difference are yet to be addressed in detail. But for practical purposes the reasons are of secondary importance. When designing a UI in a Western country for the Chinese market, one needs to be aware of the core fact that icon sets may be subject to lower recognition rates. The evaluation of icons should be an integral part of software development. Icons with low recognition rates may be reworked or localized. Localization of complete icon sets, though, is not appropriate as it multiplies effort for a minimum of improvement and may end up in even greater confusion.

7 Conclusion

Our first and foremost aim with this study was to gain a deeper understanding of today's comprehension and appraisal of icons in an international context. We found that there are significant differences, mainly between Chinese participants and participants from Western countries.

To support and explain these findings further research is certainly necessary. The use of different icon sets can lead to more differentiated results. Setting up a similar study, but with an icon set that was designed in China, could help to investigate whether the findings of this study can be applied to icon sets that are not of Western origin. Furthermore, a conclusion could be drawn as to whether the cultural background of the designer per se affects icon comprehensibility for the users of those icons (within an application). The use of new icons that are not known to any participant, on the other hand, could dispel the doubts regarding icon familiarity as an interfering factor. However, it is probably a rather foredoomed enterprise to "invent" icons for new functions and still remain within the framework of a realistic down-to-earth application that could be sold on an international market.

What does that mean for the actual design of icons for the global market? In all, when looking at the core recognition rates, we come to the conclusion that the differences in the hit rates do not justify the effort of designing country-specific icon sets for an application. Icons should be tested with users from the target audience and revised on the basis of the results. Single icons may be localized if needed.

References

1. Biederman, I.: Recognition-by-components: A theory of human image understanding. In: Psychological Review vol. 94, pp.115–147 (1987)
2. Boecker, M.: A Multiple Index Approach for the Evaluation of Pictograms and Icons. In: Computer Standards & Interfaces vol. 18(2), pp.107–115 (1996)
3. Choong, Y.Y., Salvendy, G.: Design of Icons for Use by Chinese in Mainland China. In: Interacting with Computers vol. 9(4), pp. 417–430 (1998)
4. Del Galdo, E.: Internationalization and Translation: Some Guidelines for the Design of Human-Computer Interfaces. In: Nielsen, J. (ed.) Designing User Interfaces for International Use, Elsevier, Amsterdam (1990)
5. Evers, V., Day, D.: The Role of Culture in Interface Acceptance. In: Proc. INTERACT 1997. Chapman and Hall pp. 260–267 (1997)

6. European Telecommunications Standards Institute (ETSI): ETR 070. Technical Report Human Factors (HF): The Multiple Index Approach (MIA) for the Evaluation of Pictograms. Valbonne (1993)
7. Fernandes, T.: Global Interface Design. AP Professional, Chestnut Hill (1995)
8. Gittins, D.: Icon-Based Human-Computer Interaction. In: International Journal of Human Machine Studies 24(6), 519–543 (1986)
9. Green, A.J.K., Barnard, P.J.: Iconic Interfacing: The Role of Icon Distinctiveness and Fixed or Variable Screen Locations. In: Proc. INTERACT 1990, pp. 457–462. Elsevier, Amsterdam (1990)
10. Hall, E.: The Hidden Dimension. Anchor Books/ Doubleday, New York (1990)
11. Hofstede, G.: Culture's Consequences: Comparing Values, Behaviors, Institutions, and Organizations across Nations, 2nd edn. McGraw-Hill, New York (2001)
12. Honold, P.: Learning How to Use a Cellular Phone: Comparison between German and Chinese Users. In: Technical Communication: Journal of the Society for Technical Communication 46(2), 196–205 (1999)
13. Horton, W.: The Icon Book. John Wiley & Sons, New York (1994)
14. Horton, W.: Designing Icons and Visual Symbols. In: Proc. CHI 1996, pp. 371–372. ACM Press, New York (1996)
15. International Organisation for Standardisation: ISO/IEC 11581:2000 Icons. Geneva (2000)
16. Jordan, P.: Designing Pleasurable Products: An Introduction to the New Human Factors. Taylor and Francis, London (2000)
17. Lansdale, M.W.: On the Memorability of Icons in an Information Retrieval Task. In: Behaviour & Information Technology vol. 7(2), pp. 131–152 (1988)
18. Marr, D.: Vision: The philosophy and the approach. W.H. Freeman, New York (1982)
19. McDougall, S.J.P., Curry, M.B., de Bruijn, O.: The Effects of Visual Information on Users' Mental Models: An Evaluation of Pathfinder Analysis as a Measure of Icon Usability. In: International Journal of Cognitive Ergonomics vol. 5(1), pp. 59–84 (2001)
20. Microsoft Official Guidelines for User Interface Developers and Designers: Localization. http://msdn.microsoft.com/library/default.asp?url=/library/en-us/dnwue/html/ch15d.asp
21. Piamonte, D.P., Ohlsson, K., Abeysekera, J.D.A.: Evaluation Telecom Icons among Asian Countries. In: Proc. HCI (1) 1997, pp. 169–172. Elsevier, Amsterdam (1997)
22. Rau, P.-L.P., Choong, Y.-Y., Salvendy, G.: A Cross-Cultural Study on Knowledge Representation and Structure in Human Computer Interfaces. In: International Journal of Industrial Ergonomics vol. 34, pp. 117–129 (2004)
23. Rock, I., Palmer, S.: The legacy of Gestalt Psychology. In: Scientific American vol. 263, pp. 84–90 (1990)
24. Rogers, Y.: Icons at the Interface: Their Usefulness. In: Interacting With Computers vol. 1, pp. 105–117 (1989)
25. Russo, P., Boor, S.: How Fluent is Your Interface? Designing for International Users. In: Proc. INTERCHI 1993, pp. 342–347. ACM Press, New York (1993)
26. Scarborough, J.: The Origins of Cultural Differences and their Impacts on Management. Greenwood Publishing Group, Westport (1998)
27. Smith, J.A., Siringo, M.P.: The Acceptability of Icons Across Countries. In: Proc. HCI (1) 1997, pp. 177–180. Elsevier, Amsterdam (1997)
28. Sukaviriya, P., Moran, L.: User Interface for Asia. In: Nielsen, J. (ed.) Designing User Interfaces for International Use, Elsevier, Amsterdam (1990)
29. Sun Guidelines: Planning for Internationalization and Localization. http://java.sun.com/products/jlf/ed2/book/HIG.Issues3.html
30. Wiedenbeck, S.: The Use of Icons and Labels in an End User Application Program: An Empirical Study of Learning and Retention. In: Behaviour and Information Technology vol. 2, pp. 68–82 (1999)

Interface and Visualization Metaphors

Vladimir Averbukh[1], Mikhail Bakhterev[1], Aleksandr Baydalin[1], Damir Ismagilov[2], and Polina Trushenkova[2]

[1] Inst. Math. Mech. 16. S. Kovalevskoi, Yekaterinburg. Russia. 620219
[2] Ural State University, 51. Lenina, Yekaterinburg, Russia. 620083
averbukh@imm.uran.ru, mike.bakhterev@gmail.com,
bajur@imm.uran.ru, idr_uz@mail.ru, trushenkova.p@gmail.com

Abstract. The paper is devoted to problems of computer metaphors,, such as Interface metaphor and Visualization metaphor. Interface metaphor is considered as the basic idea of likening between interactive objects and model objects of the application domain. A visualization metaphor is defined as a map establishing the correspondence between concepts and objects of the application domain under modeling and a system of some similarities and analogies. This map generates a set of views and a set of methods for communication with visual objects. Some positions of the metaphor theory are discussed. Concept of metaphor action is suggested.. "Formula" of metaphor is constructed. A set of examples of metaphor was analyzed. Aprioristic quality criteria of interface and visualization metaphors are suggested. These criteria allow evaluating as existing metaphors and to search for adequate metaphors for designing new specialized systems.

Keywords: Computer Metaphor, Visualization, Interface.

1 Introduction

This paper continues our researches of visualization metaphors that results have been published in [1-5], In turn these researches have been initiated by problems arising during processes of design and development of specialized visualization systems. Specificity of such systems frequently demands new methods of visualization and interaction that are adequate to the given task and concrete (possibly narrow) user's classes. The practice of design and development of specialized visualization systems shows necessity of specific metaphors, and a stage of metaphor searching and/or designing is a part of development process. Our goal is to design well the visual interactive systems, and choice of good (adequate) metaphors is the key to proper decisions.

Below some points of the metaphor theory are considered in connection with computer metaphors. The structural analysis of concrete metaphors is carried out. This analysis is necessary to understand the reasons of successes of one and failures of other visualization and visual interface metaphors. Studying of visualization object structures together with understanding of logic of metaphor choice and/or generation may help to formulate criteria of evaluations of cognitive component of visual systems.

J. Jacko (Ed.): Human-Computer Interaction, Part II, HCII 2007, LNCS 4551, pp. 13–22, 2007.

2 Related Works

The most part of literature on this theme reflects researches and development on interface metaphors. The important generalizing results contain in [8] where a today state of the interface metaphor theory and practice is described in detail. Metaphor is considered as use everyday and/or well known (often technical) realities. Thus the concept of visual interface metaphor is based on presentation new or unusual for an user phenomena by means of other phenomena, that are known to him of everyday life. These phenomena should have the same basic properties, as the phenomena, which they explain [15]. Thereby constraints of metaphor habitualness and completeness are brought forth [16].

In [7] problems of metaphor interpretation are given much attention. Interpretation problems are considered both for the designer of an interactive system and for its) user.

In [17] the ideas metaphor formalization are of an interest. Note, that the first works on formalization in this area have appeared in the beginning of 90th years. (See, for example, [12].)

Statement (and a partial decision) of problems of metaphor search automatic and semi-automatic metaphor generation are considered in [10] and [6].

As a rule, in the literature the concept of a visualization metaphor is not separated from the concept of human-computer interface metaphor. In turn our attention has been directed on visualization metaphors. Earlier we have been emphasized the difference between interface and visualization metaphors [1]. Now it is important to show not only the difference, but also the conceptual unity of these types of computer metaphors. The semiotic analysis of visual interface and examples of visualization may reveal in both cases the existence of sign systems as a basis of interactions and communications. On our opinion these sign systems are generated by computer metaphors. Some theoretical aspects of metaphor are considered in the next issue.

3 Computer Metaphors

The last decades metaphors are considered not only from traditional positions of philology, but also philosophies, logic, cognitive sciences, psychologies, and computer sciences. A basis of our consideration of metaphor conception is approaches to studying a scientific metaphor advanced by T. Kuhn, as well as the cognitive approach to metaphors, advanced by J. Lakoff. [11,13-14]

A role of a scientific metaphor in development of scientific disciplines is revealed and described (see, [11] and the detailed book [9]). Also there is well known by J. Lakoff and M. Johnson book [14] devoted to a role of metaphors in a modern society and its universal penetration into science, politics, daily activity and thinking of people.

The metaphor in this connection is considered as use of concepts and knowledge from one (source) area of human experience to understand better and to structure the phenomena and concepts another (target) domain that as a rule is more abstract.

Computer sciences, as well as all new scientific disciplines developed with active using of metaphors. The most known, for example, such as "memory" or "file" almost was lost links with initial concepts. The problems of computer metaphor become the topic of a large body of research. Further we consider two types of a computer metaphor - interface metaphor and visualization metaphor.

Interface metaphor is considered as the basic idea of likening between interactive objects and model objects of the application domain. Its role is to promote the best understanding of semantics of interaction, and also to determine the visual representation of dialog objects and a set of user manipulations with them.

Specificity of visualization, as independent discipline in frameworks of Computer Sciences, demands the distinction between visualization metaphors and interface metaphors. The concept of visualization metaphor is defined for generalization of metaphor using cases in all domains of Computer Visualization.

Let's define a visualization metaphor as a map establishing the correspondence between concepts and objects of the application domain under modeling and a system of some similarities and analogies. This map generates a set of views and a set of methods for communication with visual objects. We consider the metaphoricalness of any visualization.

This approach is substantially based on the concepts of semiotics. In terms of semiotics the metaphor is something dynamic, in contrast to a stable sign. We can describe a metaphor as the act or the process of a designation of one concept by means of a sign, traditionally connected to other concept. The visual interface uses regularly the language based on one or other sign system. Human-computer interaction in this connection may be described precisely as sign process. The analysis of examples shows, that visualization also may be described as sign process similarly to human-computer interaction. The choice of a metaphor is a choice of a sign system. This sign system is used to define the dialog language of interaction and/or visualization. Another function of a metaphor is to determine the context for a correct interpretation of language elements, and to reveal the sense of visual texts. Thus, interface and visualization metaphors provide understanding represented entities of the application domain, and also metaphors help to create new entities based on the internal metaphor logic.

Understanding of metaphors as mapping from source to target domains is incomplete in case of a visualization metaphor.

We offer more complex mechanism, which underlies functioning of metaphors. Our approach differs from others that in its frameworks the metaphor generates some independent metaphor domain at the expense of correspondence that puts to objects of target domain some objects from the source domain. And more exactly, structures and/or characteristics of objects from target domain are put in the correspondence structures and characteristics of objects from source domain. Cite an example of a classical metaphor LIFE IS A JOURNEY, where LIFE is target domain, and JOURNEY is source domain. Some structures of JOURNEY (beginning, ascent, descent, end, etc.) are considered in the given metaphor as a basis for the description of life structure. Similarly in other classical metaphor RICHARD - THE LION some lion qualities (for example, courage, but not tail, fangs, and claws) are transferred on a human being, who now becomes in frameworks of the metaphor domain.

An action of visualization metaphor consists of extractions of structures from target domain on the base of certain structures from source domain and transfer them in metaphor domain, which in this case has a visual nature. The visualization metaphor is mapping (more exactly operator) to certain visualization world, where unshaped objects get its visual presentations.

The use of metaphors should increase expressiveness of objects under investigation. To achieve it objects of target domain (with a set of structures, properties, and so on) are selected. As this takes place not all objects are chosen (and even not all their characteristic or structure elements), but only that, which are under interest most of all. Analogues for these objects (by way of structures, qualitative properties and so on) are searched in source domain. Further the following operation takes place. Object of target domain together with object from source domain are located in metaphorical domain, or more exact in doing so the metaphorical domain is generated. In this domain the investigated object now starts to function. (It is possible to consider, that it is already a new object of a new domain.) The metaphor domain gets autonomy from domains generated it. Many properties of its objects only mediately are connected (if at all are connected) to properties of source domain objects. There is a new logic of development metaphorical domain. So, for example, the use of the scientific metaphor of an electromagnetic field its intensity is studied. But it is obviously absent on a field of wheat. Thus, there is a projection of some target domain characteristics to source domain. And the task of metaphor completeness often may reduce quality of a metaphor.

There are questions - what are nature and structure of metaphor domain; how its generation is produced? The natural answer to them is connected to understanding of that the consideration of a metaphor as sign or as pair of signs is not fruitful. First of all the metaphor generates some sign system, that is integral sign set, in which existing internal relations between signs somehow map relations between designates. Our metaphor domain as a matter of fact is a sign system. In case of a metaphor the generation of a sign system is possible to consider as the adaptation of two metaphor operators, the basic: "Let A is similar to B" and the additional operator: "The following attributes /elements/characteristics of A are selected for assimilation to the following attributes /elements/characteristics of B" Where A is a source domain, and B is a target domain.

Other function of a metaphor is to define the context assisting to correct interpretation of elements of the given visualization language and to revealing of visual text meanings. Thus, a visualization metaphor is provided understanding of mapped entities of the application. Also a visualization metaphor participates in generation of new entities based on an internal logic of the metaphor.

4 Metaphor Analysis

Some different interface and visualization metaphors were analyzed. Among them popular desktop metaphor, room metaphor, and also metaphors used in highly specialized scientific and information visualization systems. We paid attention on genesis of metaphors, opportunities of data presentation and manipulation using concrete metaphors, potential properties of metaphorical objects, and also potential opportunities of user interpretation of these objects and manipulations with them. The purpose of analysis is to reveal structures of successful metaphors and to build a basis for comparison and evaluation of metaphors.

Let's define the concept “metaphor action”. This characteristic is constructed by answers to the following questions:

“How it is possible to represent the information by this metaphor?”

“What do properties of metaphorical objects take place?”

“What does actions or ideas result from user interaction (including seeing) with metaphorical objects?”

Some sort of metaphor action “formula” is constructed on the base of analysis of the well-known interface metaphors.

It is possible to construct a “formula” of metaphor actions.

The metaphor “formula” may include simplified descriptions of source and target domains, an idea of likening using in the metaphor and results of metaphor actions.

In the case of desktop metaphor the formula may be written as follows:

Source domain: Desk with folders containing documents (documents are structured, but folders may be disordered);

Target domain: Office automation system;

Idea of likening: “Folders with papers” = “structure of the data, a set of files”;

“Opening of a folder “ = “demonstration of file structures and/or files”;

“Processing of documents” = ”execution of functions, by means commands of the visual language”.

Result: The direct access to data structures by means manipulations of icons placed on the screen; calls of some [user] predetermined functions by means a visual dialog language.

Microsoft Windows uses the extended version of this metaphor.

Addition of source domain:

A desk is combined with control panel where starting buttons are placed.

Besides the “magic” idea is added: All actions within the framework of system are made by means of double click on icons.

Result: icons representing as data structures as programs calls.

There is also one more idea - opening of new windows when program executions are begun.

In other cases (for examples in case of room metaphor) we can’t write the full metaphor formula because there are not common application domain, successful .and generally used experience of its usage, and, that is there is not unities of target domain. However we shall result the review of properties of room metaphor. Realizations of this metaphor are characterized often by a combination of three-dimensional space of the room with bidimensionality of objects, placed on its “walls”', a “ceiling”' or a “floor”. Such combination on the one hand preserves principles of structural correspondence between model entities and visual objects, on the other - provides successful spatial placement of images.

Let's carry out the analysis of a room metaphor from two positions: the room metaphor itself and how it is possible to represent the information with its help.

The room metaphor possesses the following properties:

1. Ability to contain any objects inside itself.

The room not only represents separate object, but also is the container for others ones.

2. Restriction of a perception context. Objects inside a room are considered in a separation from “external worlds”.

3. Closeness. There are no any additional elements to use Room metaphor (excepting possible inner objects).

4. Inclusion in structure. It is possible "to build buildings of rooms", that is to consider set of rooms. Therefore the room may be an element of construction of some complex construction.

5. Naturalness of a metaphor. The room is natural metaphor, with presence of corresponding objects in the real world. Functionality and characteristics of real objects are transferred in the virtual world with only minor extended understanding.

The room metaphor was used to extend the possibility of desktop metaphor in office automation systems. But more effective in this case is using the combination of the main (desktop) metaphor and local metaphor reflecting as the specialization as user's mentality and labor experience. We use the idea of card file as local metaphor for municipal clerks. In this card file metaphor also some "magic" (automatic) operations are used to improve searching and ordering of documents. Thus, it is possible to characterize the complex metaphor "work with a card file placed on the desktop". This metaphor is natural for users. Also it is important the presence of structure in frameworks of the metaphor. The concept of a card file means structuring of the data. Use of this metaphor supports user mental models and has positive psychological effect. The user may be sure that she/he will find quickly the necessary information in structured repository. This metaphor (as well as real object) has organizing information functions. The card file metaphor allows using the concrete office automation system more effectively. This local metaphor structures as visual representation of programs, and user's operational activity. Explicit usage of the metaphor helps systematic designing of the interface.

In the majority of the specialized visualization systems the representations of abstract per se mathematical, program, information objects takes place. For a part of problems habitual views are used. However there are cases, when existing visualization methods are not applicable. Then it is necessary to search metaphorical source domain. Frequently this search is rather serious problem. Revealing of all components of metaphors in these cases is a difficult task. However there is our experience of search of new metaphors for scientific, information and software visualization systems [3]. For example the complex visualization metaphor was suggested to represent four-dimensional set resulted modeling of complex chemical processes [18].

5 Metaphor Structures and Analysis of Metaphor Generation

The analysis of results of metaphors and views transitions in different visualization domains has shown the presence of some regularity independent of visualized information nature. This regularity determines a success or a failure of visualization techniques. To achieve a success it is necessary the connection between the internal nature and structure of modelling objects (and the data corresponding to them) and internal mental structures of users. In this structure (so called "representative cognitive structures") his/her image of phenomena is mapped. Correspondents between model and cognitive structures are not arbitrary.

The person distinguishes any general logic in a picture, breaking it on set (perhaps enclosed) fragments, abstracting from minor elements. Thus, it is possible to speak about cognitive structures, structures of entities under analysis and structures of visual objects and images. When analysing a visual image interpretation proceeds in two phases. The elements interpreted according to the knowledge extracted from a dedicated domain are revealed. The information on interrelations between these elements is extracted (reconstructed) from the general visual image. Thus, a coherent adequate representation about visualized object is provided. That is the interpretation proceeds in part on the base of the visual image itself, and in part on the base of the analysis of its elements and their interpositions.

The information on element interrelations specifies the structure of a visualized object or more exact, our presentation about it. Process of visualization may be considered as construction of visual (geometrical) image on the basis of abstract representation about object. These abstract representations are model (object, the phenomenon, process under investigation), somehow connected with user cognitive structures describing a given entity. Visual images representing modelled entity, serve to create or extract by it cognitive structures. The purpose of researches in visualization domain is to create such techniques and principles, which will provide the extraction adequate cognitive structures on visual images. A process of interpretation is exactly the generation of cognitive structures on base of visual images. This process is inverse or more exactly dual to visualizations. As visualization principles the interpretation principles should exist.

Revealing of modelling (initial) object structure may reduce the complexity of development of a view representing this object. In this case the complex view may be developed as compound view. Therefore a criterion of views correctness is necessary. In this case construction of views may be based on such rule, that structure of the constructed visual image should not contradict to the structure of the initial entity. During the interpretation of visual objects there should not be relations absent in the initial entity. For example representation of the modelling entity with a bidimentional structure as 3D object may lead to wrong interpretation. Though often the increase of an image dimension are useful for better interposition of represented objects in a scene. While a reduction of dimension, as well as a reduction of all structures is not a mistake provided that the user (interpreter) is informed about it.

There is the question, why one metaphors (not only computer, but also literary or rhetorical) appear successful, despite of obvious discrepancy, and others, exact and detailed, are unsatisfactory? The answer we shall search considering the process of metaphor generation.

The goal here is to define relation between metaphor and target system of meanings, for which metaphor was formed. This relation might be expressed in the terms of "meanmarks". To define what meanmark is, let us consider the word "brave". The meaning of that word may be established through if-then (implication) relation of it to another words. The implication is important because it is base for reasoning, and metaphors help the process. For the word "brave" one may define outgoing implications. For instance, if A is "brave" then A is "not timid". This relation is denoted with ->, "brave" -> "not timid". Besides outgoing arrows every word has incoming ones.

So the following object emerges. I -> "brave" -> 0, where I is set of words implying "brave" and 0 is set of those which are implied by "brave" itself. Now the graph of such implications can be considered, and it is assumed here that the topology of graph's paths passing through node defines mean of that node. Meanmark is simple the label for node in such oriented graph. The graph may not be the graph of implication relations of words, it may depict any such relation.

Both metaphorical system of meanings and target system have such graphs which show how meanings are connected within them. According to that representation the correspondence between meanings at target system and meanings at metaphor can be established through homomorphism from target system meanmarks graph onto meanmarks graph of metaphor.

Let us consider example. If we want to illustrate the target system "King Richard is brave", firstly we must define meanmarks graph of that system. It is simple enough: Richard -> king, brave. But the meanmarks "king" and "brave" mean nothing without their language contexts: incoming and and outgoing implications in English's system of meanings. It is very difficult to find meanmarks in some graphs which will have the same topology of implications as "king": and "brave" in that system. So required metaphor should include both these meanmarks. We are looking now for "somebody" -> king, brave. And, of course "somebody" is "Lion:".

That is meanmarks graph is constructed. This graph may be superimposed on the similar graph, consisted of concepts of source domain. It is natural, that a set of meanmarks in this graph is distinct from source one, however its general structure is similar. Searching of a metaphor - is searching of the structure of interrelations which are similar to structure of interrelations in the target domain. Superimposing (not exact, not one to one) may be, that some of the bottom levels will be necessary to remove. But the additional level (absent in a target domain) may be appear. This second system of meanmarks with its interrelations is metaphor of an image considered originally. Interrelations between concepts in metaphorical system may be richer than in target one. Some interrelations may correspond to those arrows, which are present in the first set, but have not been noticed up in stage of metaphor construction. Here they may be obviously appreciable.

The suggested model may also help to describe how metaphor allows to establish new properties of target system.

Let's assume, that we have certain time sequence of values {X}. That is {X} is a set of elements with one linear discrete coordinate and some value. Problem of presentation of this sequence is raised. For example, let's transform these values into music notes with certain melody. It is possible because notes may be interpreted as values, and duration of music notes is always discrete. Then:

Melody -> time sequence of notes -> a set of elements with one linear discrete coordinate and a certain value.

Recognition {X} through a similar metaphor may lead to interesting conclusions. The sequence of notes has the special property - notes may compose (or not) to beautiful melodies. And if our way of formal transformation values {X} to notes may generate melody, that, probably, {X} has interesting properties, which may be found out by means of a metaphor.

The process of metaphor generation (metaphorization) first of all includes (may be implicit) analysis of target domain of the future metaphor. On a basis of the metaphor objects and its properties the hierarchical structure of object interrelations of target domain and their properties reveals. At the following stage a source domain and its main object are searched. Criteria of a choice are criteria of metaphor quality.

The success of a metaphor is connected first of all with structure of interrelations concepts in source domain and with an opportunity to understand relations in the target domain. The structural analysis of metaphors helps to construct criteria of metaphor quality.

6 Conclusion

Let's consider a set of requirements to a choice of metaphors and views.

The metaphor has to generate integral and systematic interface and/or visualization systems. It results an undesirability of the interface based on several fine metaphors describing details and components of dialog. This requirement means also necessity to conform as to others already existing computer metaphors, and to general ideas global metaphors.

Reduction of interpretation complexity is considered as a condition of “good” metaphor. Therefore direct interpretation of images is required, but decoding and interpretation of complex [visual] texts is considered as a source of failures.

Set of the criteria, imposed on initial and target domains in a process of metaphor generation includes:

- similarity of object properties in source and target domains,
- ability to visual presentation for object in the source domain,
- habitualness (recognition) of objects in the source domain,
- rich set of interrelations between objects in the source domain.

Also we may write criteria of generation for views based on metaphors. Among them such, as truthfulness, laconicalness, expressiveness, clearness.

Researching metaphors, views and their structures allows to analyze and evaluate existing design decisions and to project interactive visual systems with necessary properties.

References

1. Averbukh, V.L.: Visualization Metaphors. Programming and Computer Software 27(5), 227–237 (2001)
2. Averbukh V.L. Towards the Conceptions of Visualization Language and Visualization Metaphor. Proceedings of IEEE Symposia on Human Centric Computing Languages and Environments: September 5-7, Stresa, Italy. IEEE. 2001. pp. 390–391 (2001)
3. Averbukh, V.L.: Toward Theory of Computer Visualization. Computational Technologies (In Russian.) vol. 10(4), pp. 21–51 (2005)
4. Averbukh V.L. HCI Metaphor and Visualization Metaphor. What Theory Does We Need? In: The 16th International Conference on Computer Graphics and Applications GraphicCon'2006, July 1-5, Novosibirsk, Akademgorodok, Russia Conference Proceedings. (In Russian) pp. 262–268 (2006)

5. Bajdalin A., Ismagilov D. Structure Representation in Software Visualization Systems. In: The 16th International Conference on Computer Graphics and Applications GraphicCon'2006, July 1-5, Novosibirsk, Akademgorodok, Russia Conference Proceedings. (in Russian) pp. 271-274 (2006)
6. Barbosa S.D.J., de Souza C.S. Extending software through metaphors and metonymies. Proceedings of the 5th international conference on Intelligent user interfaces. January 09-12, New Orleans, Louisiana, United States. pp. 13–20 (2000)
7. Barr, P., Noble, J., Biddle, R.A: Semiotic Model of User-Interface Metaphor. Chapter in Virtual Distributed and Flexible Organisations. In: Edited proceedings of the Sixth International Workshop on Organisations Semiotics in Reading, UK. Kluwer Academic Publishers (2003). http://www.mcs.vuw.ac.nz/ chikken/research/papers/iwos2003/ barr_iwos2003.pdf
8. Blackwell. A.: The Reification of Metaphor as a Design Tool. ACM Transactions on Computer-Human Interaction (TOCHI) 13(4), 490–530 (December 2006)
9. Brown Th. L.: Making Truth: Metaphor in Science. Urbana Champaign. University of Illinois Press (2003)
10. Gazendam H.W.M.: Information System Metaphors (Groningen University, NL & Twente University, NL) http://www.econ.uba.ar/servicios/publicaciones/journal3/ontents/ HGazendam/methaphors.htm
11. Kuhn, T.: Metaphor in science. In: Ortony, A. (ed.) Metaphor and thought, pp. 533–542. Cambridge University Press, Cambridge (1979)
12. Kuhn, W., Frank, A.U: A Formalization of Metaphors and Image-Schemas in User Interfaces. Cognitive and Linguistic Aspects of Geographic Space, NATO ASI Series, 1991th edn. pp. 419–434. Kluwer Academic Publishers, Boston, MA (1991)
13. Lakoff, G.: The contemporary theory of metaphor. In: Ortony, A. (ed.) Metaphor and Thought, 2nd edn. pp. 202–251. Cambridge University Press, Cambridge (1993)
14. Lakoff, G., Johnson, M.: Metaphors we live by. University of Chicago Press, Chicago (1980)
15. Musil, S.: Monitoring Parallel Programs with INHOUSE http://www.ani.univie.ac.at/ani/ research/Monit.html
16. Richards, S., Barker, P., Banerji, A., Lamont, C., Manji, K.: The Use of metaphors in iconic interface design. Intelligent Tutoring Media 1994 5(2), 73–80 (1994)
17. Simoff, S.J.: Towards the development of environments for designing visualisation support for visual data mining. In: Proceedings International Workshop on Visual Data Mining, pp. 93-106 (2001)
18. Vasev, P.A., Pervalov, D.S.: One method of visualization of four-dimension sets. In: Proceedings of conference Supercomputing technologies in physical and chemical researches, Chernogolovka, Russia, (in Russian) pp. 32-36 (2001)

Displays Attentive to Unattended Regions: Presenting Information in a Peripheral-Vision-Friendly Way

Mon-Chu Chen[1] and Roberta L. Klatzky[1,2]

[1] Human-Computer Interaction Institute
[2] Department of Psychology
Carnegie Mellon University
Pittsburgh, PA, USA
{monchu,klatzky}@andrew.cmu.edu

Abstract. This study proposes that a visual attentive user interface should present information in a peripheral-vision-friendly way, rather than degrading the display resolution for unattended areas, as is sometimes practiced. It suggests that information presented in unattended areas could advantageously be perceived by our peripheral vision without compromising the primary task performance. The paper will discuss an empirical study in which several motion-based stimuli were examined on the periphery in a dual-task scenario. A proposed new design of GPS Navigation System design will then be described to demonstrate the concept of peripheral-vision-friendliness.

Keywords: Attentive User Interface, Peripheral Vision Friendly, Dual-Task Performance, Peripheral Visual Design, GPS Navigation System.

1 Introduction

To keep potential threats away from predators, our visual perception system has been evolved to continuously receive information from our periphery even when we are focusing on certain important matters. The central vision channel and peripheral channel work semi-independently and are sensitive to different visual elements to serve different purposes. A visual interface system should facilitate the distinction between two visual channels rather than shutting down possible interaction through unattended regions. This is very crucial as more devices are created and multi-tasking is inevitable. We believe that it has higher priority to better organize and properly deliver information through both central and peripheral vision channels than to focus solely on the attended regions to save computing power. Therefore, we propose to present information in a peripheral-vision-friendly way for unattended regions, as the traditional way has done for the attended region.

1.1 Visual Attentive User Interface

Visual attentive user interface (AUI) are developed mainly to lower the demands for rendering resources, a major concern in the field of computer graphics (Baudisch 03).

J. Jacko (Ed.): Human-Computer Interaction, Part II, HCII 2007, LNCS 4551, pp. 23–31, 2007.

For example, a gaze-contingent display (GCD) in a VR environment might present 3D graphics at different levels of details (LOD). By rendering the focused object at a higher degree of detail than the other objects in the environment, the system could manage the limited computing power more efficiently. The rationale comes from the nature of uneven visual acuity (VA) across the visual field in our vision system.

The density of photoreceptor cells is much higher in the macula, the center of the retina, than in the periphery. In addition, a large portion of our primary visual cortex (V1) is devoted to this small portion of our visual field (Goldstein 03). As a result, lowering the resolution of the unattended regions not only decreases the rendering power required by the system but also minimizes potential distractions to the users. This approach, however, works contrary to the human perceptual system, in that information in the periphery is degraded relative to the fovea; hence further degradation essentially eliminates potential peripheral contributions to visual information processing.

On the contrary, those unattended regions could be utilized to deliver information in a way that is perceivable by our peripheral vision. It could be some supplementary information to your current task, or a critical message that directs you to a more important task. Nevertheless, information has to be presented in a way users could process without directly looking at it in order to take advantage of the peripheral vision.

1.2 Convey Information Through Periphery

Normally a visual interface is designed with the assumption that the interface will be the user's single focus of attention. When multi-tasking, a user is forced to shift his/her eyes away from the primary task in order to perceive the information from the used-to-be-unattended secondary display. This is an existing problem to most visual interfaces no matter whether the resolution of unattended regions is degraded or not. By making visual elements perceivable by our peripheral vision, we could presumably save the switching cost.

Considering the biological difference between our central vision (favor color and details) and peripheral vision (favor motion and illumination), it is possible to tailor a visual interface sensitive to our peripheral vision system. In particular, motion has been proposed as a new dimension to expand the interface bandwidth in a complex system (Bartram 97). While our central vision has high acuity and excels at perceiving static displays with high spatial resolution, our peripheral vision is very sensitive to motion (i.e. has higher temporal resolution) (Paillard 85). Central and peripheral vision channels constitute two semi-independent visual information processes, which can work in parallel. Using motion, information could be easily processed by our peripheral vision with minimum effort. Hence, we argue that motion should be applied to convey information from peripheral visual field and that such information could be perceived without directly looking at it.

One example of this concept is Peripheral Vision Horizon Device (PHVD), which is designed for jet fighter cockpits to display the orientation of the aircraft. The system uses lasers to project an artificial horizontal line within the cockpit. The virtual horizon line will move as the aircraft moves in real time. A study showed that pilots performed better with this device than with traditional instruments, because pilots were aware the virtual horizon line through their peripheral vision with least efforts (Money 84). Peripheral Vision Horizon Device provides an excellent example of conveying information through peripheral vision. We believe the similar idea could be applied to general visual interface design, and more complex information could be delivered via peripheral vision channel.

1.3 Initiate Interaction from the Unattended

Another drawback of these types of visual AUIs or GCDs is that they only react to users passively, which could limit potential interactions. Shutting down the peripheral vision channel will eliminate the possibility of initiating interaction from those unattended regions. In fact, an unattended region (or display) could actively initiate contact, capture attention, or send messages, etc. This will be beneficial especially when the bandwidth of the central vision channel is mostly consumed.

A considerate and professional secretary would actively remove all possible distractions while making necessary information available, so that you can focus on the current task under the best conditions. When an interruption has to be made, the secretary would also know how to gently remind you without disturbing your current work. Likewise, in addition to presenting contents in a traditional way for the focused field of view, a visual display system should be able to deliver information passively as well as actively from the periphery in a user friendly way.

1.4 Peripheral-Vision-Friendly Interface

What we call a gentle reminder is an excellent example of the kind of design that would be peripheral-vision-friendly. It could notify the user that information is available, without distracting him or her from the central task. Thus it could provide an effective solution to the issue of limited attentional resources in accessing multiple devices simultaneously. Even after the user perceives the notification, he or she might decide not to react immediately, and the presence of the gentle reminder would not cause any irritation or interruption.

We define a peripheral-vision-friendly interface as one that is perceivable on the periphery, and with the minimum impact on an ongoing primary task. Putting non-essential devices on the periphery does not automatically make them perceivable by our peripheral vision, and even when perceivable, they might consume most of the attentional resources available, which is an unacceptable outcome. Currently there are several existing visual display devices designed specifically as peripheral displays [Matthews 03, van Dantzich 02]. However, there is a fundamental problem in that traditional interface design practices will not work well when translated from the focus of attention to the periphery. Therefore, new visual elements have to be created and tested to make sure that they are perceivable by our peripheral vision system.

Furthermore, perceiving the peripheral visual information should not take away our ability to maintain the primary task. The periphery-situated displays should minimally affect the primary performance, unless it is an emergency situation, where the purpose of the peripheral message is to stop the current task and switch to another more important one. In next section, we will report an empirical study which has tested a set of motion-based stimuli in terms of two factors of peripheral-vision-friendliness: peripheral perceivability and performance impact.

2 Empirical Evidence

To evaluate a peripheral visual display, we need to test it under a dual-task situation. That requires having subjects perceive peripheral displays for the secondary task while performing a primary task. In that way, we can measure the impact of introducing the peripheral visual display on the primary task. Designing peripheral displays is a relatively new endeavor. As a result, few conclusive studies have been reported. In general, however, people agree that motion from peripheral displays captures attention, and there are tradeoffs between performing the central task and getting information from the peripheral display. Inconsistent reports have been found with respect to the relationship between the performance of the primary task and the secondary task. Some researchers have found that peripheral displays that lead to equivalent performance on a secondary task have differential impact on a primary task (Maglio 00). In contrast, others suggest there are significant performance differences on a secondary task but few differences on the primary task across different peripheral display conditions (McCrickard 01).

One important factor in these discrepancies may be the type of task that is used to evaluate the performance. In particular, when a complex, cognitive task is used, performance reflects a large number of variables, measurement of which may be uncertain. For example, the primary task may include uncertain numbers of mouse actions, task switches, eye movements and so forth, which also contribute noise to performance measurement. When the primary task is of extended duration, it may be unclear what action is ongoing and where the gaze position is when the secondary task interrupts. In order to compare different peripheral displays with minimal contribution from complex cognitive factors and strategies, we should perform experiments consisting of a continuously demanding primary tracking task. Since attention shifting or dual task switching is not likely to occur, we could access of the direct impact from the secondary displays.

Another factor may be the design of the secondary display. A complex visual stimulus will certainly require more cognitive resources to process. The details and colors of the stimulus are hardly recognized. The selection of the stimuli is crucial for peripheral-vision-friendliness. The more cost a peripheral stimulus requires to process, the more processing resources are taken away from performing the primary task. As a result, the stimuli in our study were chosen for their nature of motion, being primitive and distinguishable in the early visual perception.

2.1 Dual-Task Experimental Design

In the primary task, subjects tracked several tracked points among multiple, identical randomly moving distractors. Research shows that typically people can successfully track 3 to 5 identical objects at the same time among other randomly moving objects (Pylyshyn 88). At a certain point, the tracked points ceased to move, and subjects' tracking performance was measured by asking them to identify the current target locations. In this demanding continuous task, subjects are occupied with the primary task from the beginning. Once shifting away from the center, subjects would be unable to keep track of the targets. We can assess the magnitude of any such shifts by determining whether performance on the central task declines, as the secondary task becomes more difficult.

The secondary task is to detect the onset of a change and to discriminate the type of a movement change on the periphery. That is, one of the non-target dots begins to move faster than others. The magnitude of this increase in speed is a variable in the experiments. Subjects are to respond as soon as they notice the onset of the change. We measure the reaction time and detection rate, which provide direct indices of secondary-task performance. We also assess whether this performance depends on the load of the primary task.

Subjects sat in front of a projection screen placed about 3 feet away. The screen was 3 feet high and 4 feet wide, making the widest visual angle approximately 53 deg. The tracked points were restricted to move within the center area, forcing the subject's gaze position centrally.

Four sets of experiments with different conditions and purposes have been conducted. The impact of introducing the secondary task has been measured. The performance in the secondary task was measured across various secondary display conditions. By varying the loads of both tasks, the performance interaction in dual-task situation was investigated. In addition to the secondary detection task, in some studies a discrimination task was also introduced to determine if the subjects could identify the type of the secondary display they detected. If so, this would demonstrate that the secondary display not only was detected, but that it carried information beyond the single bit constituting present vs. absent.

2.2 Fixed Monitoring Costs

The empirical results indicate, first, that the secondary task introduces a certain monitoring cost. However, the cost remained fixed across variations in secondary-task difficulty, as indexed by measures of secondary performance. The fixed monitoring cost of the secondary task opens the possibility that we can use secondary tasks of varying detectability without jeopardizing performance on the primary task. We can avoid secondary tasks that are so intrusive that they demand attention, as well as those that are so subtle as to be non-detectable at short latencies. The combination of high detectability without intrusiveness would constitute the "gentle reminder," a major role of peripheral visual displays.

2.3 Performance Independence

In addition, we found evidence for primary and secondary task independence. When varying the load of the secondary task (speed of secondary targets), the performance of the primary task remained the same. When we varied the load of the primary task (number of tracked points and distractors), the performance of the secondary task also did not change. Each task performance depends only on the load of the task itself (with the addition, for the primary task, of the monitoring cost introduced by the possibility of a secondary target). This independence of factors affecting the two tasks suggests that they have distinct processing components, which would minimize cross talk and interference from the peripheral display to the primary task (Stemberg 69).

These findings provide insights on how to design and evaluate a better peripheral display. It appears possible to optimize a peripheral display by maximizing the detection rate while minimizing the impact on the performance of the central task. Given the lack of impact of secondary-task difficulty and the ability of discriminating different secondary targets, the secondary task could then have more than a gentle alerting function. As the set goal for conveying information through periphery, a peripheral visual display indeed could provide more substantive information than a single alert.

2.4 Peripheral Perceivable Stimuli

In this set of experiments, we used change in the speed of a motion as the element of the peripheral display. While maintaining the same primary performance, the reaction time of the secondary task ranges from 0.64 to 2.13 seconds, and the detection rate ranges from 36% to 100% for various difficulty conditions of the secondary task. The results provide empirical evidence of successfully conveying signals through periphery (unattended regions of the whole display), while subjects focused on the primary task. Among this wide range of secondary display difficulty, there are those conditions with short reaction time and high detection rate. Those conditions, which share the same primary performance as others, will be potential candidates for presenting information through the peripheral vision channel.

Subjects could not only detect but also discriminate between motion-based secondary stimuli while attending to the primary task. This indicates that instead of merely being a notification, peripheral information could be informative without disrupting the level of primary task performance. By assigning meanings to different secondary displays subjects could discriminate, it is possible to convey more complicated information through periphery.

In another study (Chen 02), other types of change of motion were examined in a similar setting. In that study, subjects were asked to perform Wicken's tracking task as the primary task, and to detect motion changes on the periphery as the secondary task. An eye tracker was deployed to constantly monitor subjects' gaze position. Direction, frequency, size and frequency changes of a motion can also be easily perceived on the periphery with high detection rate and short reaction time. The results also support the principle of Performance Independence, which provides us more visual elements we could apply to design a peripheral vision friendly display. In the next section, we will describe a prototype of a GPS navigation system design based on the peripheral visual design concept.

3 Peripheral-Vision-Friendly Displays

There are several roles that the peripheral source could play. It could simply be informative, for example, indicating the passage of time, incoming messages, or an impending appointment. Depending on the situation, one might want the peripheral information to signal a switch of attention to the peripheral source. In that case, the system could actively adjust the input so that the previously central task is presented in a peripherally friendly way. This opens the possibility that differential rendering could be system-initiated and not just user-initiated. In our application, a gaze-contingent GPS navigation system, however, we focus on user-initiated changes.

3.1 GPS Navigation System

The GPS navigation system has become more powerful and popular, which significantly increases the safety concern in driving. Those complicated interface design requires more attention to process, which decreases the driving performance. Many efforts have been addressed to solve this problem. Among them, audio channel has been widely used, although driving direction given in audio form may be interfered by other sound sources and may not be preferred in a noisy or quiet situation. Others have tried to simplify the map and only show necessary information according to the context (Lee 05). This approach will decrease the processing time for accessing the navigation system, but the impact on the driving task due to task switching is still unavoidable.

Our design aims for reducing the switching cost by making driving direction perceivable on the periphery. We use motion changes, as suggested by the empirical study, to indicate when and where to make a turn. A driver then could perceive driving directions from the interface without directly looking at it. As a result, eye-gaze shifting between the road ahead and the display panel on the dashboard will no longer be necessary. If the driving direction could be successfully delivered through peripheral vision channel, it will make more attentional resource available for driving and increase safety.

3.2 Motion-Based, Gaze-Contingent Design

Our proposed design is a software-based solution. That means it can be applied to existing GPS navigation system without modifying any hardware component. The new system will have two different modes. The normal mode is like any other existing GPS navigation system, full of detailed information, which requires a driver's focus of attention to process all information. In the peripheral mode, the map information is replaced by a dot, which moves continuously.

The change of moving direction is used to indicate which direction the driver should turn to, while the change of the speed is used to notify the timing for making the turn. As the empirical study verified, these two types of change could be perceived well by our peripheral vision system, without impairing the performance of the primary task, in this case, the driving task.

The system is equipped with a web-cam based eye tracker. Depending on the driver's current eye-gaze position, the system will automatically switch to the normal mode when the display is attended, and to the peripheral mode when unattended. The system could also be switched between the two modes manually by the driver.

3.3 Peripheral Mode

When the driver focuses on the road ahead, which he/she should always do, the system will switch to the peripheral mode. In this mode, the dot moves continuously from the center to the direction where the driver should follow. When traveling forward, the dot moves upward till the top of the screen and then starts from the center again, forming a loop, at Cruising Speed. When no further driving direction is given, the motion should be gentle because of the constant moving speed and motion adaptation effect.

When a turning instruction should be given, the dot moves faster at the Signaling Speed, which is greater than Cruising Speed. The dot also changes the moving direction as well. As the previous study suggests, the change of the motion speed and direction will be picked up by the driver's peripheral vision without hurting the driving performance.

When approaching the intersection when the turn should be made, the dot gradually slows down to the Resting Speed, which is smaller than the Cruising Speed. Again, because of the change of the moving speed, the driver will have a reference to know how close he/she is to the intersection.

When making a turn, the moving direction of the dot will change in real time according to the bearing of the car and the destination direction. This will give the driver another reference to confirm whether the turn is correct or not. When finishing the turn, the dot moves upward at the Cruising Speed.

When approaching the destination, the dot will decrease the speed and eventually stops.

3.4 Future Works

Informal user tests show the motion-based interface in the peripheral mode can convey driving direction on the periphery. According to the empirical study, the visual elements we use to give turning instruction should not degrade the primary performance. However, we have not yet tested the interface design in a controlled experiment. We plan to conduct a quantitative study with a primary driving task to evaluate the effectiveness of the motion-based navigation system design. An eye-tracker will be deployed to record the gaze behavior.

The driving performance will be measured for both the normal display and peripheral display conditions. There will be no mode switching in this experiment. Important measurements will include the deviation from the center of the road, the correctness of the turn, and number of eye gaze on the navigation display.

4 Conclusions

The central and the peripheral vision channels of our vision system work together to help us perceive the external world. A display system should facilitate the nature of our visual perception system, rather than eliminating the communication between the unattended regions of the display and the users. We argue that a visual display should present information in a peripheral-vision-friendly way when unattended. A display qualified as peripheral-vision-friendly should be perceived without requiring a viewer's direct gaze. And such a display should impose minimum impact to the ongoing primary task.

We tested motion-based stimuli in a series of dual-task experiments, and found the facts of *Performance Independence*, *Fixed Monitoring Cost* and *Peripheral Perceivability* for the particular set of visual elements. We then applied those visual elements to design a GPS navigation system, which could continuously provide driving directions even when unattended. The direction and speed changes of a motion are used to indicate the direction and timing of a turn, which could be easily perceived on periphery without impairing the primary task. Another driving experiment is expected soon to further evaluate the peripheral-vision-friendliness in a more realistic setting.

Acknowledgments. Many thanks to Kaori Idemaru, who kindly provided valuable input during the preparation of this manuscript.

References

1. Bartram, L.: Can motion increase user interface bandwidth in complex systems?. In: IEEE International Conference on Systems, Man, and Cybernetics, IEEE, Orlando, FL, USA vol. 2 pp.1686–1692 (1997)
2. Baudisch, P., DeCarlo, D., Duchowski, A.T., Geisler, W.S.: Focusing on the essential: considering attention in display design. Communications of the ACM 46, 60–66 (2003)
3. Chen, M.-C., Fortes, F., Klatzky, R., Long, W.: Change Detection on Periphery and Dual-Task Performance. In: Human Factors and Ergonomics Society 46th Annual Meeting. HFES, Baltimore, MD, USA (2002)
4. Chen, M.-C.: Kinetic Pixels: Elements for Conveying Information Through Peripheral Visual Displays. In: 7th Asia-Pacific Conference on Computer Human Interaction, Taipei, Taiwan (2006)
5. Goldstein, E.B.: Sensation and Perception. Wadsworth Publishing Company (2001)
6. Lee, J., Forlizzi, J., Hudson, S.E.: Studying the effectiveness of MOVE: a contextually optimized in-vehicle navigation system. Conference on Human Factors in Computing Systems, pp. 571–580 (2005)
7. Maglio, P.P., Campbell, C.S.: Tradeoffs in displaying peripheral information. SIGCHI conference on Human factors in computing systems, Hague, Netherlands, pp. 241–248 (2000)
8. Matthews, T., Rattenbury, T., Carter, S., Dey, A.K., Mankoff, J.: A Peripheral Display Toolkit. University of California, Berkeley Technotes, UCB//CSD-03-1258. Intel Research (2003)
9. McCrickard, D.S., Catrambone, R., Stasko, J.T.: Evaluating animation in the periphery as a mechanism for maintaining awareness. Interact 2001: IFIP Conference on Human-Computer Interaction, Tokyo, Japan pp. 148–152 (2001)
10. Money, K.E.: Theory underlying the peripheral vision horizon device. NASA. Dryden Flight Research Center Peripheral Vision Horizon Display (PVHD) pp. 45–56 (1984)
11. Paillard, J., Amblard, B.: Static versus kinetic visual cues for the processing of spatial relationships. Brain Mechanism in Spatial Vision, pp. 367–385 (1985)
12. Pylyshyn, Z.W., Storm, R.W.: Tracking multiple independent targets: Evidence for a parallel tracking mechanism. Spatial Vision 3, 179–197 (1988)
13. Sternberg, S.: The discovery of processing stages: Extensions of Donders' method. Acta. Psychologica 30, 276–315 (1969)
14. van Dantzich, M., Robbins, D., Horvitz, E., Czerwinski, M.: Scope: Providing awareness of multiple notifications at a glance. In: International Conference of Advanced Visual Interfaces, Trento, Italy (2002)

Screen Layout on Color Search Task for Customized Product Color Combination Selection

Cheih-Ying Chen[1], Ying-Jye Lee[2], Fong-Gong Wu[3], and Chi-Fu Su[4]

[1] Department of Multimedia Design, Fortune Institute of Technology, No.1-10, Nwongchang Rd., Daliao Township, Kaohsiung County 831, Taiwan, R.O.C.
[2] Department of Cultural Business Development, National Kaohsiung University of Applied Sciences, 415 Chien Kung Road, Kaohsiung 807, Taiwan, R.O.C.
[3] Department of Industrial Design, National Cheng Kung University, 1, Ta-Hsueh Road, Tainan, Taiwan 70101, R.O.C.
[4] Department of Information Management, Fooyin University, 151, Chinhsueh Rd., Ta-liao, Kaohsiung, Taiwan, R.O.C.

Abstract. This article describes experimental investigations of the effects of color name displayed and screen layout on customized product color combination selection. In the experiment, 6 interface designs were developed by systematically varying with 2 factors (interface layout type and color name type) in order to explore the relations between the interface of the massive number of product color combinations and users' performance. Results from the experiment show the layout type of itemized color chips, which is divided into some items according to the customized color module parts of product, has the best grouping type for customized product color combination selection in search time by users. Besides, users view various color combinations for products directly with or without the aid of color names, it gets important whether displayed colors are correct or not as users make judgment and choices according to the product colors on the screen.

Keywords: Screen layout, Mass customization, Product color, Color name.

1 Introduction

Consumers prefer to choose products from the wide variety of styles that combine different colors and forms. Yun et al. (2003) regarded color as a product characteristic closely related to consumer impression of a product. Lai et al. (2006) demonstrated that the product color has a greater affect on product image than product form. They suggested providing consumers with various colors in addition to different product forms. Therefore, it is easier to vary product color than form when meeting individual consumer preference. Numerous products employ color changes in mass customization to create product variations and styles. Currently, many products allow consumers to customize color, such as sofas, system furniture, clothing, athletic shoes, cars, motorcycles, mobile phone, etc. However, the exhibition area can only show few samples and other color combinations can be seen in catalogs or by virtual images designed to allow consumers to choose product color via the Internet/Intranet. Kahn

J. Jacko (Ed.): Human-Computer Interaction, Part II, HCII 2007, LNCS 4551, pp. 32–40, 2007.

(1998) mentioned when the range of colors for customization is usually large, consumers often become confused and unable to choose colors. Wickens et al. (1997) addressed that the number of colors grows large for multicolor-coded displays, then the information may sometimes become clutter and hard to read. It is not surprising that customers feel lost and frustrated due to a large number of color combination options and the disorganized, disorder, and irrelevant screen layout when they surf the customized product information sphere. Therefore, an effective and efficient screen layout has to be designed to meet the needs of customers.

2 Methods

The experiment is aimed to explore the relations between the interface layout of customized product color combination selection and user performance, and takes the interface layout of the color combination of leathered sofas as an example. The experiment is designed to consider the variables influencing the screen layout involved in product color selection, including factors such as interface arrangement type and color name type. The factor regarding the interface layout type is mainly aimed at understanding whether different layouts of color combination arrangement will make any difference in users' performance when it comes to selecting color combination. Moreover, the use of color names enables people to categorize concepts and communicate with others (Lin et al., 2001). The tasks are all expected to be performed rapidly and accurately. Hornbæk (2006) classified the usability measures employed in the 180 studies into three groups including effectiveness, efficiency, and satisfaction measures. In the measures of effectiveness, quantify the number of errors users make either during the process of completing tasks. In the measures of efficiency, task completion time refers to measures of how long users take to complete tasks with the interface. In the measures of satisfaction, preference measures captures which interface users prefer using. Thus, search time and error rate were chosen as dependent variables in this experiment. However, besides operating effectiveness and efficiency, user subjective satisfaction is a vital index for screen layouts. This study thus further discusses subject performance in using interfaces, as well as their subjective satisfaction with those interfaces.

2.1 Participants

The participants from the same group/school were chosen to minimize individual difference. Thirty-six college students (evenly split between males and females) participated in the experiment. Moreover, the participants had all surfed the web for an average of four years.

2.2 Apparatus

2.2.1 Multimedia Computer

A multimedia computer was used to assist in the experiment. Furthermore, a high-resolution monitor (19") with a 1280(horizontal)*1024(vertical) pixel resolution and 75HZ refresh rate displayed the experiment stimuli (i.e. the experiment samples of interface layouts). All experiment stimuli were shown on the monitor in random order, and subjects were asked to perform specific experimental tasks.

2.2.2 Leather Sofa Deconstruction

Since most leathered sofas on the market are single-colored or dual-colored, the experiment divides a sofa into two module parts – the backrest and the sofa body –for purposes of color combination (see Fig. 1).

Using a focus group method, the five interior designers selected 12 popular colors (as shown in Table 1) often used in sofa-related industries. Image compositing technique was then applied to two randomly chosen colors to display the color combination on the backrest and sofa body, and then 144 (12×12) color combinations (including 12 single-colored and 132 dual-colored combinations) of the sofa image produced by image compositing technique. Descriptions and procedures with regard to image compositing technique can be found in the research conducted by Wu et al.(2003, 2004).

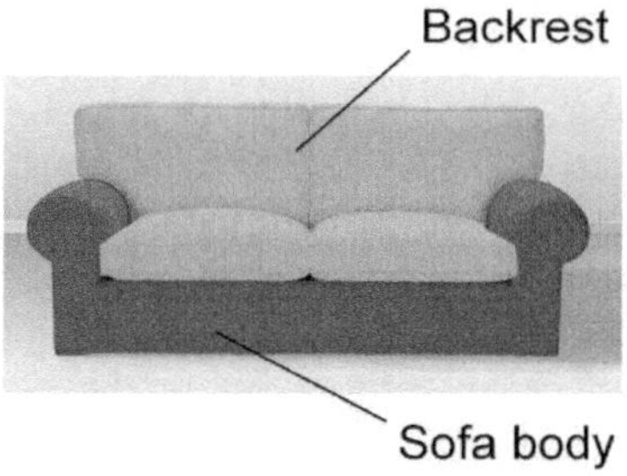

Fig. 1. Two components of the test sofa

Table 1. The 12 most popular sofa leather colors

Systematic color name	*L a b color space*	*Systematic color name*	*L a b color space*	*Systematic color name*	*L a b color space*	*Systematic color name*	*L a b color space*
White	L93, a1, b2	Pale Yellow	L90, a-1, b41	Light Blue	L78, a-17, b0	Dull Brown	L72, a5, b29
Red	L45, a46, b18	Yellow	L86, a7, b75	Blue	L38, a2, b-47	Dark Brown	L36, a7, b9
Orange	L69, a35, b54	Green	L37, a-13, b2	Purple	L31, a31, b-36	Grayish Black	L40, a0, b3

2.3 Experimental Design

In the experiment, the factors affecting the interface design of diverse color selection of customized products include color name (with two levels) and arrangement type (with three levels). All factors along with their corresponding levels are listed in Table 2. Therefore, the number of all factor-level combinations totals 6 (2*3=6), which is the same as the number of configuration combinations of interface layouts.

Table 2. Factors and levels for screen layouts of diverse customized product color combination selections

Factor	*Level*		
A: Color Name Type	A_1: no color name	A_2: systematic color name	
B: Interface Arrangement Type	B_1: color chip	B_2: product thumbnail	B_3: itemized color chip

2.3.1 Factor A: Color Name Type

When a screen layout contains too many colors, confusion can easily occur. Thus it can be helpful to utilize color names to present color information to users. The present experiment identifies two kinds of color names including product show without color names (A_1) and systematic color name (A_2) as aiding color display. This study employs PCCS color tone naming 12 color samples, see Table 1. Therefore, this study also intends to discuss whether color name affects usability of screen layout.

2.3.2 Factor B: Interface Arrangement Type

The experiments classified the arrangement types into three categories (as shown in Fig.2): the first arrangement type employs color chips (B_1) to display various product colors. This arrangement presents accurate information and provides a complete view of all of the 144 color combinations. The second arrangement type employed product thumbnails (B_2) to show various product colors, which are demonstrated to express product color and appearance of all 144 combinations. The third arrangement type employed itemized color chips (B_3), which are divided into different items according to the customized color module parts of the product. The website of NIKEiD is typical interface mployed itemized color chips to show various color combination. The sofa used involves backrest and sofa body, each item with 12 single-colored color chips. While clicking each one of the two itemized color chips, then the composite image of color combination is immediately shown on the screen.

2.4 Procedure

The experiment involved 6 interfaces. The experimental tasks for each interface include two topics: finding out sofas with specified color combinations and one questionnaire of the subjective satisfaction for interfaces. To avoid creating a learning effect, the participants performed the experimental tasks for the 6 interfaces in random order. The search time and error frequency were recorded during the experimental process.

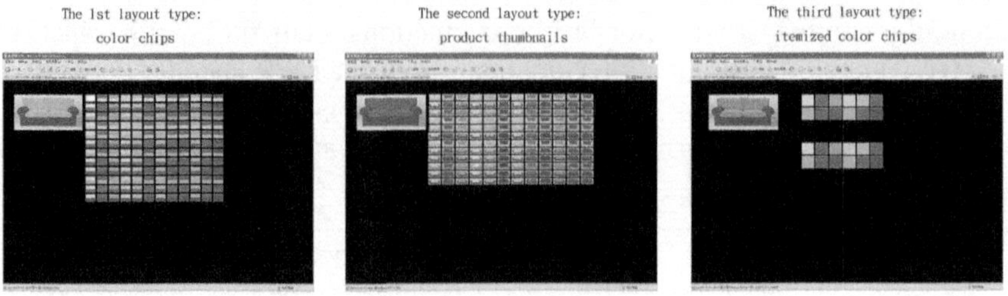

Fig. 2. Three interface Arrangement types

3 Results and Discussion

3.1 Analysis of Mean Search Time

The mean search time spent by each participant and error rate are listed in Table 3. The analysis of variance (ANOVA) is performed on the mean search time spent seeking sofa color combinations. Based on the ANOVA results listed in Table 4, the main effect of interface arrangement type significantly influence the mean search time. However, color name was found to be insignificant, indicating that there is no obvious difference between searching color combinations with or without color name. Table 5 lists the mean search time for each factor at different levels.

Table 3. Mean search time and error rate for 6 interfaces

Experiment No. (interface samples)	*Factor*		*Mean search time (sec)*	*Error rate (%)*
	A	B		
#01	1	1	12.133	0.167
#02	1	2	11.267	0.133
#03	1	3	7.233	0.133
#04	2	1	11.967	0.200
#05	2	2	13.233	0.167
#06	2	3	7.933	0.133

Regarding the main effect of interface arrangement type, table 5 shows that the mean search time for the arrangement type using itemized color chip (B_3: 7.58sec) is superiorto the arrangement of color chips (B_1: 12.05sec) and the arrangement of product thumbnails (B_2: 12.25sec). The interface arrangement type based on itemized color chip (B_3) includes 2 groups of single-colored color chips (i.e. the backrest and the sofa body) While clicking each one of the two itemized color chips, then the composite image of color combination is immediately shown on the screen. In that case, color

Table 4. ANOVA for mean search time

Source of variation	*Sum of squares*	*df*	*Mean square*	*F*	*p*
A (Color Name Type)	1.0417	1	1.0417	1.810	0.310765
B (Interface Arrangement Type)	27.8459	2	13.9230	24.190	0.039698*
Error	1.1511	2	0.5756		
Total	30.0387	5	15.5402		

*:$p<0.05$; **:p<0.01.

Table 5. Mean search time of each factor at different levels

Factor	*Level*				
A (Color Name Type)	A_1: (sec)	10.21	A_2: (sec)	11.04	
B (Interface Arrangement Type)	B_1: (sec)	12.05	B_2:12.25 (**sec**)		B_3:7.58 (**sec**)

*figures in ( ) represent mean search time, unit: sec.

chips are demonstrated to express precise color information and eliminate the complications associated with various color combinations. Therefore, itemized color chip (B_3) is simpler than 144 color chips (B_1) and 144 product thumbnails (B_2). The itemized color chip (B_3) is better arrangement type for large number color combinations.

3.2 Analysis of Error Rate

The error rate created by the subjects while searching for color combinations for sofas via the 6 interfaces (refer to Table 3) is tested by analysis of variance (ANOVA). From the ANOVA results listed in Table 6, no the main effect of cluster types is statistically

Table 6. ANOVA for error rate

Source of variation	*Sum of squares*	*df*	*Mean square*	*F*	*p*
A (Color Name Type)	0.000741	1	0.000741	4.00	0.183503
B (Interface Arrangement Type)	0.002593	2	0.001296	7.00	0.125000
Error	0.000370	2	0.000185		
Total	0.0037	5	0.0022		

*:$p<0.05$.

Table 7. Error rate at different levels of each factor

Factor	*Level*		
A (Color Name Type)	A_1: 0.14 (%)	A_2: 0.17(%)	
B (Interface Arrangement Type)	B_1:0.18(%)	B_2: 0.15(%)	B_3:0.13 (%)

*figures in (%) represent mean rate of error.

significant. The error rates of operation at different levels of each factor are listed in Table 7. This result demonstrates that color name type and interface arrangement type do not obviously influence error rate.

3.3 Analysis of User Subjective Satisfaction

When each subject has completes an assigned interface task, they must complete a questionnaire for that interface. The questionnaire includes items dealing with ease of use, ease of discrimination of product colors and preference, to which the subjects select sofa colors with the 6 interfaces. Table 8 lists the mean satisfaction degrees.

Regarding arrangement types, two items are clearly significant in operating the 6 interfaces (as listed in Table 9): 1.ease of use, 2.preference. From the mean of subjective satisfaction listed in Table 8: The mean of itemized color chips (B_3: easy of use, 4.42; preference, 4.45) exceed those of color chips (B_1: ease of use, 3.42; preference, 3.78) and product thumbnails (B_2: ease of use, 3.65; preference, 3.58); consequently, the layout of itemized color chips (B_3) is clearly superior. Users consider the arrangement type of itemized color chips to be easier to use, and thus prefer it, because in the color combinations involved in multi-colored sofas, an interface structured around two groups (each group involves the 12 colors) of color chips, for backrests and sofa bodies, is less confusing and easier to search. On the contrary, there are 144 color combinations in the arrangement type of color chips and product thumbnails. Consequently, numerous combinations appearing on the screen simultaneously create an impression of difficulty of use.

Table 8. All items for evaluating subjective satisfaction in correspondence to the mean assessment values for all factors with relative levels

Factor		*Items for Evaluating Subjective Satisfaction*		
		Ease of use	*Ease of discrimination*	*Preference*
A (Color Name Type)	A_1	3.79	3.92	3.98
	A_2	3.87	3.73	3.90
B (Interface Arrangement Type)	B_1	3.42	3.83	3.78
	B_2	3.65	3.70	3.58
	B_3	4.42	3.95	4.45

Table 9. Analysis of variance for subjective satisfaction

Factor	*Items for Evaluating Subjective Satisfaction*		
	Ease of use	*Ease of discrimination*	*Preference*
A (Color Name Type)	0.576341	0.173432	0.072827
B (Interface Arrangement Type)	0.036506*	0.283898	0.001795**

*:$P<0.05$; **:$p<0.01$.

Regarding color name type, no clearly significant existed among items (as listed in Table 9). In that case, whether the color names are added to the interface or not, there is no significant effect on the subjective satisfaction. In fact, when users are selecting color products, they mainly look at the colors themselves.

4 Conclusion

The experiment researches the relationship between the interface design of customized product color combination selection and user performance, and the results are reliable reference in designing screen layout for selecting color combinations for customized products. An interface should not create confusion and anxiety among users. A good interface design should aim to meet as many user needs as possible, while letting users find the information they require as fast as possible. It makes sense to recommend itemized color chip for arrangement type, which has the best search time performance and subjective satisfaction degree for easy of use, preference. Furthermore, it is suggested that product color combinations be grouped according to customized product module components, and then be displayed in the layout of itemized color chips. Such an arrangement can reduce the number of combinations of color chips displayed on the screen, and also meet the use efficiency for massive color combinations. Further, users can view various product color combinations directly on the screen with or without assistance from color names. Accordingly, whether the colors displayed on the screen are correct becomes quite important.

References

1. Yun, M.H., Han, S., Hong, S., Kim, J.: Incorporating user satisfaction into the look-and-feel of mobile phone design. Ergonomics 46(13-14), 1423–1440 (2003)
2. Lai, H.H., Lin, Y.C. Yeh, C.H., Wei, C.H.: User-oriented design for the optimal combination on product design. International Journal of Production Economics 100(2), 253–267 (2006)
3. Huffman, C., Kahn, B.E: Variety for sale: mass customization or mass confusion? Journal of Retailing 74(4), 491–513 (1998)

4. Wickens, C.D., Gordon, S.E., Liu, Y.: A introduction to human factors engineering. Lonfman (1997)
5. Lin, H., Luo, M.R., MacDonald, L.W.: Tarrant, A.W.S.: A cross-cultural colour-naming study. Part I: Using an unconstrained method. Color Research & Application 26(1), 40–60 (2001)
6. Hornbæk, K.: Current practice in measuring usability: Challenges to usability studies and research. International Journal of Human - Computer Studies 64(2), 79–102 (2006)
7. Wu, F.G., Lee, Y.J., Chen, C.H.: Evaluation of the Realistic Effect of Image Compositing to Assist in Curtain Selection. International Journal of Industrial Ergonomics 32(1), 1–12 (2003)
8. Wu, F.G., Lee, Y.J., Lin, M.C.: Using the fuzzy analytic hierarchy process on optimum spatial allocation. International Journal of Industrial Ergonomics 33(6), 553–569 (2004)

Experimental Comparison of Adaptive vs. Static Thumbnail Displays

Pilsung Choe[1], Chulwoo Kim[1], Mark R. Lehto[1], and Jan Allebach[2]

[1] School of Industrial Engineering, Purdue University, 1287 Grissom Hall, West Lafayette, In 47907-1287, USA
[2] School of Electrical and Computer Engineering, Purdue University, 1285 Electrical Engineering Building, West Lafayette, In 47907-1285, USA
{pchoe,kim218,lehto,allebach}@purdue.edu

Abstract. Keyword search is a very important method to find information on Web sites along with link-based browsing. How an information retrieval system displays search results is very important because users spend most of their time in finding, reading and understanding retrieved information. As an application of information retrieval systems, a self-help print quality troubleshooting system was introduced. As a method to show search results, displaying thumbnails is very useful in print defect diagnosis because users don't have to read and understand complex information in text. This study compared static thumbnail(s) and adaptive thumbnails to display search results to diagnose print defects. Results showed that the one thumbnail static display was worse in terms of user performance and preference. However there was no significant difference between the three thumbnails static display and the adaptive display although the three thumbnails static display was better than the adaptive display on average.

Keywords: Adaptive display, static display, thumbnail display, keyword search, search, information retrieval, diagnosis, troubleshooting, print defect diagnosis.

1 Introduction

Keyword search, also called information retrieval, is a very important method to find information on Web sites along with link-based browsing [5], [6], [9]. Keyword search is a process in which users enter queries into a search window to find the information that satisfies their needs. Although keyword search is very useful because users can quickly find information they need, it should be a supplementary tool of link-based browsing because it often returns inappropriate results and loses the important context present in the pages leading to the search results [2], [6]. Keyword search has a four-phase framework: The keyword formulation phase, the action phase, review of results, and the refinement phase [5], [9]. Of the four phases, the review of results is very important because users spend most of their time in finding, reading and understanding retrieved information. Therefore, interface design about how to display search results is very important. In addition, for users whose native language

J. Jacko (Ed.): Human-Computer Interaction, Part II, HCII 2007, LNCS 4551, pp. 41–48, 2007.

is not English, it is sometimes challenging to read through the search results and select relevant information. In this study, a self-help print quality diagnostic Web tool [1], [3], [7] based on the fuzzy Bayes model was considered as an application for the information retrieval. In this application, selecting a relevant print quality problem category is critical because print quality diagnosis requires users to follow complicated procedures. Therefore, if users choose an inappropriate print quality problem category as a result of the keyword search, they can easily become frustrated in diagnosing the print quality problems. This might have a bad effect on users' loyalty to products from the manufacturer of this particular printer. In order to avoid this kind of problem and to help users to easily identify a print quality problem, thumbnails to display print quality problems might be very helpful. Therefore, thumbnails display helps users to comfortably select a proper category of a print quality problem in the result of a keyword search.

This study investigated how to display thumbnails as a keyword search result on the self-help print quality diagnostic Web tool. Three different alternatives were evaluated: one thumbnail in the result page, three thumbnails in the result page, and adaptive numbers of thumbnails in the result page according to probabilities based on a fuzzy Bayes model. One thumbnail in the result page can help users diagnose print quality problems easily if the top hit rate is high, while it can cause disorientation if the top hit rate is low. An adaptive display can give flexibility in the number of thumbnails in result pages so that the users can see the results within a range of probabilities in one Web page. However, it can be confusing to see them because users cannot anticipate the number of thumbnails in the result page. Three thumbnails in the result page can have both the advantages and disadvantages of the two other alternatives. The evaluations were measured in terms of user performance and user preference while subjects used the self-help print quality diagnostic Web tool.

2 Method

2.1 Subjects

Nine engineering students at Purdue University participated in the experiment. The subjects were five males and four females with a mean age of 26. Four of the subjects were Koreans, two were from the US, two were Indian, and one was Chinese. Seven of them were familiar with troubleshooting on Web sites and six of them had some experience troubleshooting printer problems.

2.2 Experimental Design

A 3 x 3 Latin squares design was used in which subjects were assigned to three groups at random as summarized in Table 1 [10]. The two independent variables were display types and system accuracy. Display types had three levels, one thumbnail static display (a_1), three thumbnails static display (a_2), and adaptive display (a_3). System accuracy is a factor to represent how accurately the information system is showing the result of an entered query. In general, the more accurate the system is, the earlier the result is displayed. In this experiment, the system accuracy was designed to have three levels, first (b_1), middle (b_2), and last (b_3), which means that the system shows correct answers with the first, at the middle, and at the last thumbnail. Dependent variables were time to identify a print defect, number of pages viewed, and subjective ratings. Three print defects, white vertical lines on cyan background, vertical lines on magenta background, and vertical lines on yellow background were used for the experiment. Whole data for the experiment included nine defects, which were white vertical lines in cyan, magenta, yellow and black, and vertical lines or line segments in cyan, magenta, yellow, black and blank. The defects used for each subject and the order of each treatment per subject were counterbalanced to minimize learning effect.

Table 1. Experimental Design

	Display		
	Static Display		Adaptive Display (a_3)
Group	One thumbnail (a_1)	Three thumbnails (a_2)	
G_1 (sub. 1,2,3)	Last (b_3)	First (b_1)	Middle (b_2)
G_2 (sub. 4,5,6)	First (b_1)	Middle (b_2)	Last (b_3)
G_3 (sub. 7,8,9)	Middle (b_2)	Last (b_3)	First (b_1)

2.3 Experimental Apparatus

The experiment was conducted in the Purdue University School of Industrial Engineering Usability Laboratory. A computer (HP Compaq Presario SR1030NX) with a 19-inch LCD monitor (HP Pavillion F1903) was used. The Ishihara color test book [4], a consent form, a pretest questionnaire, and a post-evaluation form were prepared. In order to eliminate performance difference by different queries that subjects entered in the system, a dummy program was developed for the experiment. Regardless of what the subjects typed in the program, the result pages to display were fixed in advance. However, the search process was the same as a real diagnostic system so that subjects did not realize that they were using a dummy program. Figure 1 shows the program architecture. After subjects enter a query in the form, the system brings them to the thumbnail list page. The static display had one thumbnail or three thumbnails on the thumbnail list pages. Subjects could move forward and backward to see other thumbnails by clicking the "Prev" and the "Next" buttons. Three representative thumbnail sequences for the adaptive display were implemented as shown in Table 2. In Table 2, white parts are thumbnails on the second page, and black parts are thumbnails on the first and third pages. The adaptive display was designed to show thumbnails up to cumulative probability 60% at the first page, 95 % at the second page, and 100% at the third page. For example, from the table 1, sequence 1 had four thumbnails, four thumbnails, and one thumbnail at each thumbnail list page. By clicking one of thumbnails in the list, subjects could see a magnified picture and description of the defect. If the defect on the screen matched the defect on the printout, the subject clicked the "CHOOSE" button. Time and pages viewed were recorded with a commercial program, SpectorSoft.

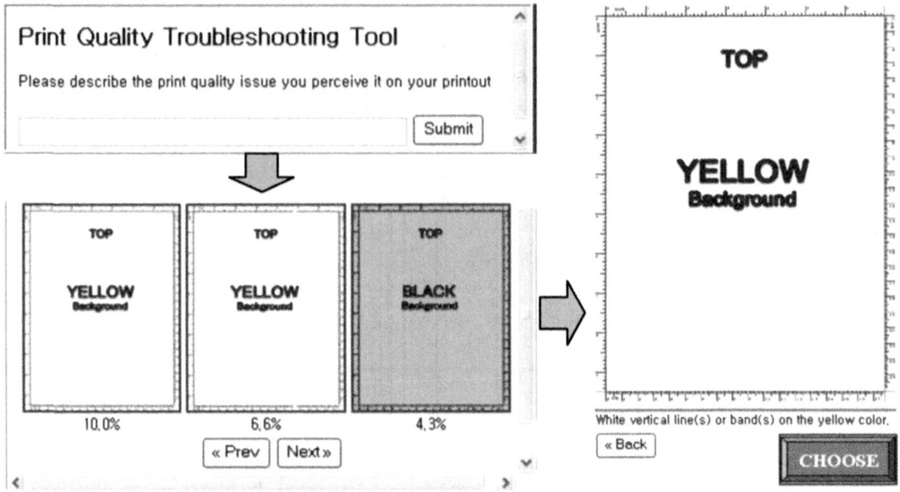

Fig. 1. Diagnostic process

Table 2. Three Representative Thumbnail Sequences for the Adaptive Display

Thumbnail Sequence	Likelihood of Correct Identification by Thumbnail								
	1st	2nd	3rd	4th	5th	6th	7th	8th	9th
Sequence 1	20.0%	16.9%	14.2%	12.0%	10.1%	8.5%	7.2%	6.1%	5.1%
Sequence 2	35.0%	23.0%	15.2%	10.0%	6.6%	4.3%	2.8%	1.9%	1.2%
Sequence 3	50.0%	25.1%	12.6%	6.3%	3.2%	1.6%	0.8%	0.4%	0.2%

2.4 Procedures

Prior to the experiment a colorblindness test was conducted because print defects in the experiment were highly related to colors. The Ishihara color test, which consists of a series of pictures of colored spots, was used to screen the colorblind subjects. A pretest questionnaire to collect subjects' demographic data was provided to the subjects at the beginning of the experiment. During the experiment, three printouts having three different defects were provided one by one based on the experimental design shown in Table 1. Subjects described each print defect and chose one matching the defect on a printout they had. During the trial, they were asked to identify correctly to collect time data independent of errors. After identifying each print defect, they were asked to rate the system that they used on four absolute 7-pt subjective rating scales. The values of the 7-pt scale were, respectively: (1) strongly disagree, (2) disagree, (3) slightly disagree, (4) neutral, (5) slightly agree, (6) agree, and (7) strongly agree. The absolute rating scales measured the extent to which subjects agreed or disagreed with the four following statements: (1) It was easy to identify the print defect using the diagnosis tool; (2) probability information below the thumbnails influenced your diagnosis; (3) the pages showing the thumbnails as a search result were clear and easy to understand; and (4) it is not difficult to navigate the diagnostic tool to diagnose the print defect. Statements 1 and 4 were identical questions to check subjects' internal consistency using Chronbach's alpha test. After finishing the three trials, they were asked to rate on 12 other 7-pt relative subjective rating scales [8] to compare user preference and ease of use of the three display types with the 12 following statements: (1) The static display with three thumbnails was easier to use than the static display with one thumbnail; (2) I prefer the static display with one thumbnail to the adaptive display; (3) the adaptive display was easier to use than the static display with three thumbnails; (4) I prefer the static display with three thumbnails to the static display with one thumbnail; (4) the adaptive display was easier to use than the static display with one thumbnail; (5) the static display with three thumbnails was more satisfactory than the adaptive display; (6) the static display with one thumbnail was more user-friendly than the static display with three thumbnails; (7) the adaptive display was more satisfactory than the static display with one thumbnail; (8) the static display with three thumbnails was more user friendly than the adaptive display; (9) the static display with one thumbnail was more satisfactory than the static display with three thumbnails; and (10) the static display with one thumbnail was more user friendly than the adaptive display. Statements (7) to (10) were additional questions of statements (1) to (6) to check subject internal consistency using Chronbach's alpha test.

3 Results

As shown in Table 3, the ANOVA results for time showed that system accuracy was significant ($p = 0.002$), at $\alpha = 0.05$, and display type was suggestively significant ($p = 0.059$) at $\alpha = 0.1$. The results also showed display type and system performance were suggestively significant ($p = 0.082$ for display type, $p = 0.057$ for system performance) for the number of pages viewed at $\alpha = 0.1$. However, there were no significant differences on absolute subjective ratings, ease of use and clearness. The Student-Newman-Keuls Test was conducted for multiple pair-wise comparisons as shown in Table 4. In term of the time, the one thumbnail static display was slower than the three thumbnails static or the adaptive display, and the last system accuracy was slower than the first or the middle system accuracy at $\alpha = 0.1$. Likewise, the one thumbnail static display and the last system accuracy had larger number of pages viewed. Although the three thumbnails static display was better on average in terms of time and number of pages viewed, they were not insignificant at $\alpha = 0.1$. Results showed that the subjects did not care much about the probability information below the thumbnail(s) for any display type. Table 5 summarizes the average relative subjective ratings and p-values from the t-test on each statement comparing the three displays. The three thumbnails static and the adaptive displays were better than the one thumbnail static display in terms of both preference and ease of use at $\alpha = 0.05$. Unlike the results of the absolute subjective ratings, subjects preferred the three thumbnails static display to the adaptive display at $\alpha = 0.1$. By the comments given after the experiment, the majority of subjects preferred conditions that allowed them to have an expectation of the content of the next pages, such as the number of thumbnails. Most subjects also insisted that the greater the number of thumbnails on each page, the better they could diagnose the problem. The Chronbach's alpha coefficients for all subjective ratings were over 0.85, and therefore subjects were considered internally consistent.

Table 3. ANOVA results

Dependent Variables	Source	DF	SS	MS	F value	Pr>F
Time	Display	2	477.9	238.9	3.81	0.059*
	Accuracy	2	1601.4	800.7	12.75	0.002**
	Display*Accuracy	4	453.5	113.4	1.81	0.204
Number of pages	Display	2	380.7	190.3	3.25	0.082*
	Accuracy	2	452.7	226.3	3.87	0.057*
	Display*Accuracy	4	123.3	30.8	0.53	0.719
Ease of use	Display	2	3.6	1.8	1.74	0.225
	Accuracy	2	2.9	1.5	1.39	0.292
	Display*Accuracy	4	3.7	0.9	0.89	0.505
Clearness	Display	2	2.9	1.4	1.08	0.375
	Accuracy	2	4.7	2.3	1.75	0.223
	Display*Accuracy	4	3.8	0.9	0.71	0.604

*: suggestively significant (p value<0.1), **: significant (p value<0.05).

Table 4. Student-Newman-Keuls Test Results

	Time (sec.)				Number of Pages Viewed			
Display type	SNK Grouping	Mean	N	Display	SNK Grouping	Mean	N	display
	A	25.778	9	1-thumbnail	A	14.556	9	1-thumbnail
	B	19.000	9	Adaptive	B	7.556	9	Adaptive
	B				B			
	B	15.667	9	3-thumbnails	B	5.889	9	3-thumbnails
System accuracy	SNK Grouping	Mean	N	Accuracy	SNK Grouping	Mean	N	Accuracy
	A	30.778	9	Last	A	15.111	9	Last
					B	6.778	9	First
	B	16.889	9	Middle	B			
	B				B	6.111	9	Middle
	B	12.778	9	First				

4 Discussion

An experiment was conducted to evaluate three display types, the one thumbnail static display, the three thumbnails static display, and the adaptive display showing thumbnails for print defect diagnoses. The results showed that the three thumbnails static and the adaptive displays were suggestively better in terms of time and number of pages viewed at $\alpha = 0.1$. In addition, the subjects also responded that the three thumbnails static and the adaptive displays were better than the one thumbnails static display in terms of preference and ease of use at $\alpha = 0.05$. However, the three

Table 5. Relative Subject Ratings of Displays

	Tasks	3-thumbnails >1-thumbnail	Adaptive >1-thumbnail	3-thumbnails > Adaptive
Preference	Mean	5.9	5.5	4.6
	$t(\alpha = 0.05, df = 8)$	1.86	1.86	1.86
	t_0	5.68	4.13	1.44
	p-value	0.00**	0.00**	0.09*
Ease of use	Mean	5.8	5.4	4.1
	$t(\alpha = 0.05, df = 8)$	1.86	1.86	1.86
	t_0	5.68	3.14	0.25
	p-value	0.00**	0.00**	0.4**

*: suggestively significant (*p* value<0.1), **: significant (*p* value<0.05).
1 (strongly disagree), 2 (disagree), 3 (slightly disagree), 4 (neutral), 5 (slightly agree), 6 (agree), 7 (strongly agree).

thumbnails static and the adaptive displays were not significantly different in terms of time, number of pages viewed, and subjective ratings although the three thumbnails static display was better than the adaptive display on average. Only in the aspect of preference, the three thumbnails static display was preferred at $\alpha = 0.1$. Considering the small subject number and reviewing subject comments, the three thumbnails static display is potentially recommended to show thumbnails as a result of query searches for print defect diagnoses. However, the static number of thumbnails at each page should be re-evaluated depending on applications or constraints such as a Web development standard for a company.

From this study, results showed that one thumbnail static display should be eliminated as an interface for thumbnail display. Therefore, more complicated comparisons between the three thumbnails static display and the adaptive display will be performed. In addition, in this study, only the three thumbnails static display was evaluated for multi-thumbnail static displays. In this respect, the number of thumbnails at each Web page should be re-evaluated in consideration of other applications.

References

1. Choe, P., Kim, C., Lehto, M.R., Lehto, X., Allebach, J.: Evaluating and improving a self-help technical support Web site: Use of focus group interviews. International Journal of Human-Computer Interaction 21(3), 333–354 (2006)
2. Diekema, A.R.: Translation events in cross-language information retrieval: Lexical ambiguity, lexical holes, vocabulary mismatch, and correct translations. Doctoral dissertation, Syracuse University (2003)
3. Kim, C., Choe, P., Lehto, M.R., Allebach, J.: Development of a web-based interactive self-help troubleshooting tool for print quality problems. International Conference on Human-Computer Interaction, Las Vegas, Nevada USA, (July 22-27, 2005) (2005)

4. Ishihara, S.: 1996. Ishihara's tests for colour-defficiency. 38 plates edition (2003)
5. Ma, L.: Search tools for internet2. Doctoral dissertation, Purdue University (2002)
6. Olston, C., Chi, E.H.: ScentTrails: Integrating browsing and searching on the web. ACM Transaction on Computer-Human Interaction 10(3), 177–197 (2003)
7. Park, H.J., Santos, H., Kim, C., Choe, P., Kumontoy, R., Low, K., Oldenberger, K., Ortiz, M., Lehto, X., Lehto, M., Allebach, J.P.: A Web-based self-diagnosis tool to solve print quality issues. In: Proceedings of NIP22 22nd International Conference on Digital Printing Technologies. Denver, CO, September 17-22, 2006, pp. 465–471 (2006)
8. Saaty, T.L.: Rank from comparisons and from ratings in the analytic hierarchy/network processes. European Journal of Operational Research 168(2), 557–570 (2006)
9. Shneiderman, B., Byrd, D., Croft, W.B.: Clarifying search: A user-interface framework for Text Searches. In: D-Lib magazine (January 1997) Accessed online on May 6, (2006) at: http://www.dlib.org/dlib/january97/retrieval/01shneiderman.html
10. Winer, B.J., Brown, D.R., Michels, K.M.: Statistical principles in experimental design, (3rd edn.) pp. 702–706. McGraw-Hill, New York (1991)

Improving Document Icon to Re-find Efficiently What You Need

Changzhi Deng[1], Mingjun Zhou[2], Feng Tian[2], Guozhong Dai[2], and Hong'an Wang[2]

[1] Laboratory of Human-Computer Interaction & Intelligent Information Processing
[2] Institute of Software, Chinese Academy of Sciences
P.O. Box 8718, Beijing, 100080, P.R. China
changzhi03@ios.cn
{zmj,tf,dgz,wha}@iel.iscas.ac.cn

Abstract. It is common that documents are represented by document icon in graphical user interfaces. The document icon facilitates user to retrieve documents, but it is difficult to distinguish the document from a collection of documents that user have accessed to. Our paper presents a document icon on which the users can add some subjective values and mark. Then we describe a system *ex-explorer* that users can browser and search the extent document icon. We found that it is easy to re-find the document on which users added some annotation or mark by themselves.

Keywords: document icon, annotation, mark, subjective value.

1 Introduction

It is more prevalent to represent a document by using an icon in graphical user interfaces. However, to re-find a document from current file system in GUI, the user has to know exactly what the document name or location is. If the user forgot that information, he/she had to open the document to browse one by one, which may be very time consuming. So it is very difficult to distinguish documents that been have been read from those have not that are represented by the same document icon (Fig 1). Specially, finding the important document from document collection required conscious effort to recall the context that it was previously used.

Fig. 1. Document icons in current GUI

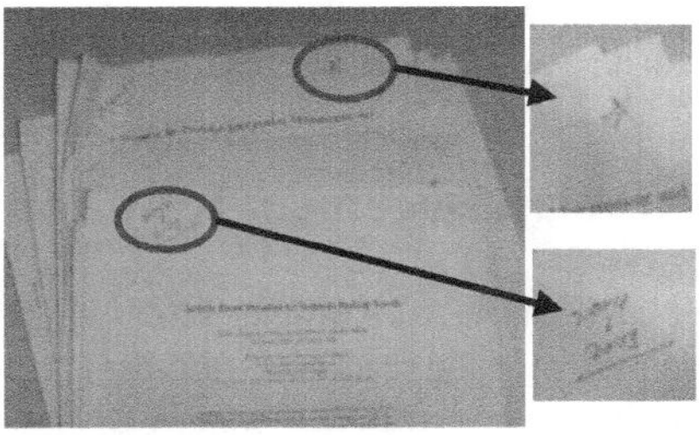

Fig. 2. Annotation on paper document cover

J. Jacko (Ed.): Human-Computer Interaction, Part II, HCII 2007, LNCS 4551, pp. 49–52, 2007.

In the real world, when we are reading or have read a paper document, we often annotate in the margin of its cover with pen. On the one hand, these annotations maybe is meaningful and reminded us to do something, and help us efficiently and conveniently re-find it. For example, we maybe annotate a symbol like star shape to represent the document is very important to us. If we need it in the future, we will quickly get it through visual searching [1]. On the other hand, the annotations can remind us what to do. For example, we annotate a date on document cover to represent the submission deadline for a proceeding. Therefore, the annotation is important additional information about paper-based documents for us to re-find and re-use them in the future.

In this paper we suggest that the document icon should be added some additional information by users and system and visualize them, which help users decrease the load on memory and facilitate re-finding the document needed. Therefore, the document isn't just represented by a static image, but an evolvement image with the interaction with the user. The additional information is divided two categories, both objective information and subjective information. The objective information refers to the metadata of a document, such as the document name, type, modified time and accessing times. Some literatures focus on how to visualize the objective values on document icon[2][3][4]. The subjective information includes the annotations and marks that are given to the digital document while the users are interacting with it.

2 Related Work

Though the icon is common component in GUI, there is a lack of focusing on document icon to facilitate the users re-find document. Lewis[2] researched about how to generate visually distinctive icon automatically and described the algorithm and discuss psychological and conceptual issues relating to icons, which facilitates users to retrieve documents. Unfortunately, the users had to remember a great number of the shapes of document icons.

To offer significant icon images which the users can assign to documents and enhance memory ability over time, Alain[5] brought forward a way to generate glyphs as document icons. It is maybe a good idea, but the idea is not implemented.

Previous work focused on how to visualize the objective information of a document in order to make it easy to retrieve the document for users, but they ignored the information that is about users' subjective information in interacting with a document. We investigate people why and how to make annotation on paper in real world, so we think the users can make annotation on document icon according the information in some context.

3 Design Document Icon

We design the document icon which is showed in figure 3. The document icon consists of four regions, including a region displaying document type, a region for annotation and mark, a region displaying times that the users have accessed to the document and a region for the document name.

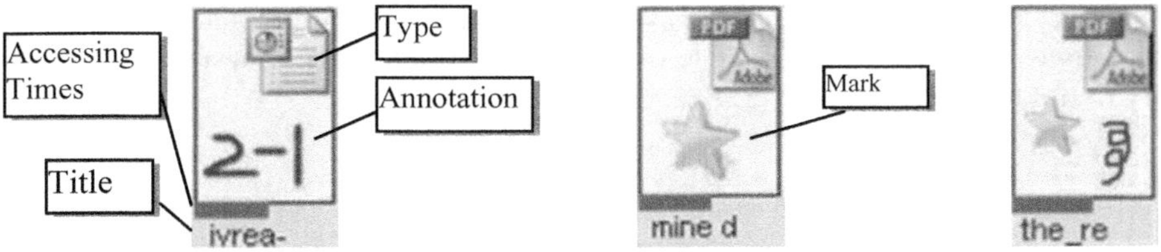

Fig. 3. Document Icon. (**Left**)Icon with annotation. (**Center**)Icon with mark. (**Right**)Icon with mark and annotation.

The objective information is acquired automatically from file system. Additionally, we record the interaction history, such as accessing times, and visualize it by the length of the column region, the more it is long, the more it is frequently accessed. The subjective information, annotation and mark on document icon, are meaningful for the users themselves, but possible meaningless for others. The users maybe annotate or mark one group document by the same ink symbol or mark. Through viewing these annotations or mark, the users search or review the document in the same context in which it was previously used.

4 Overview of Prototype *Ex-Explorer*

We developed a system named *Ex-Explorer* that offers users an interface for displaying and editing document icons (Figure 4). Current version Ex-Explorer consists of three vertical areas: a) Computer folder structure panel; b) Displaying document icon panel; c) Annotation and mark panel.

We use the tree widget to display the structure of computer folder. When users select a folder, the icons of documents in it are displayed in the middle region of *ex-explorer* interface. Users select document, click the "Add annotation" button, then pick ink color and annotate on the icon region. We can zoom in the document icon selected when users annotate. User also can drag existing mark from the mark list above any document icon to identify it. User can remove the existing annotation or mark on document icon. User may add more meaningful marks into mark list from local computer. Additional, user can zoom in or out the document icon through slipping a slide bar on the top of interface. User can classifies documents only by the same mark in current version.

5 User Feedback

To evaluate our designs we conduct an initial qualitative user study. The *ex-explorer* has been used by six students in our laboratory. After they used it three weeks, they gave us different feedbacks. Their positive comments are generalized as follows: It is very easy to distinguish the document the users have read according my annotation on document icon from one folder that there are lots of documents; It is very easy to annotate or mark on document icon; It is quick to local the document that the users need; It is very useful to group documents according to their mark; Their negative comments are as follows: It is too small area to annotate on document icon, and just for single annotation, the users can't annotate more; The users can't search their annotations; It should be to annotate or mark on the folder icon. These comments are very useful to improve it further.

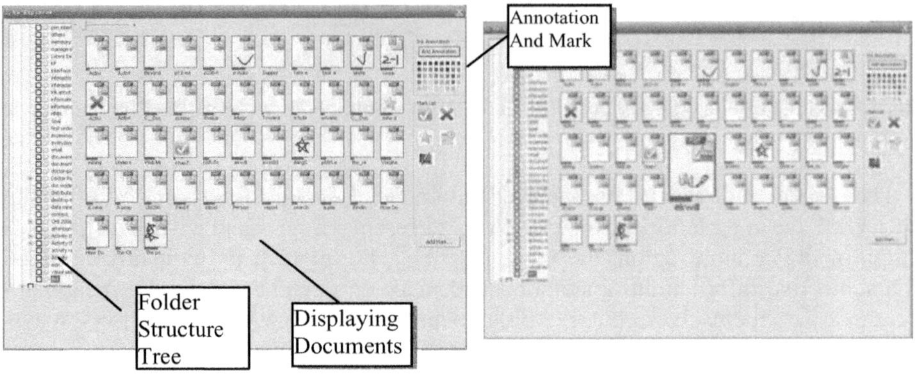

Fig. 4. Ex-explorer interface (**Left**)Browsing documents. (**Right**)Adding Annotation on document icon.

6 Conclusion and Future Work

The paper propose the document icon not only represents the static and objective attributes of document, but also the subjective information of users, which facilitates user re-finding and grouping documents. The users can annotate or mark on document icons randomly; meanwhile the annotations and marks can remind the users.

Future work is that we will provide the function that is to classify documents by the ink annotation including annotation color and annotation shape and complete those functions according to above users comments. Additionally, we will also provide different views for users to visually search documents like classical *resource explorer*.

References

1. Williams, E.: Visual Search: A Novel Psychophysics for Preattentive Vision, Masterthesis (1999)
2. Lewis, J.P., Rosenholtz, R., Fong, N., Neumann, U.: VisualIDs: Automatic Distinctive Icons for Desktop Interfaces. In: SIGGRAPH 2004 Conference Proceedings. ACM Trans. Graphics (2004)
3. Alain, D.M.G.: Vaillancourt Generated Glyphs as Memorable Desktop Icons for Documents. In: Proceedings of the, workshop on New paradigms in information visualization and manipulation,1998 (1998)
4. Everett, S.P., Byrne, M.D.: Unintended Effects: Varying Icon Spacing Changes Users Visual Search Strategy. In: Proceedings of CHI 2004, Vienna, Austria, pp. 24-29, (2004)
5. Alain, D.M.G.: Vaillancourt: Generated glyphs as memorable desktop icons for document. Workshop on New Paradigms in Information Visualization and Manipulation pp.10–12 (1998)

The Design of a Computer Mouse Providing Three Degrees of Freedom

Daniel Fallman, Anneli Mikaelsson, and Björn Yttergren

Umeå Design Research Group, Umeå Institute of Design,
Umeå University, SE-90187, Umeå, Sweden
{daniel.fallman,anneli.mikaelsson,bjorn.yttergren}@dh.umu.se

Abstract. We present the design process of designing and implementing a 3DOF mouse. First, we provide a review of the current literature in the field. Then we introduce a focus group workshop activity underlying the whole design process, pointing us towards graphical design applications and 3D modeling tools. Third, we present our prototype design process in some detail, especially denoting the important role we believe product semantics plays. We argue that 3DOF mice are most useful for small but precise rotation movements. If the extra degree of freedom provided by 3DOF mice over 2DOF mice is limited to such subtle manipulation tasks, we believe users might be more willing to accept them.

Keywords: 3D Interaction, input devices, multiple degree-of-freedom, 3DOF, computer mouse.

1 Introduction

With the advent of operating systems like Windows Vista and Apple Mac OS X, taking advantage of the impressive processing speed, memory capabilities, and hardware-accelerated graphics cards of today's desktop and notebook computers, the advanced three-dimensional graphics capabilities available to programmers are challenging interaction designers to keep up. Contemporary desktop computers are also increasingly being used for modeling, manipulating, and rendering three-dimensional representations of data and for moving around in three-dimensional worlds. Thus, the traditional two-dimensionality of graphical computer interfaces is currently being challenged in several ways.

To deal with the concept of using three dimensions instead of two in the design of computer interfaces, a number of new interface metaphors and new styles of interaction have been suggested and discussed within the field of Human-Computer Interaction, addressing the third dimension [3,4,15]. What appears quite remarkable however, especially as a contrast to the rapid hardware and software developments that have taken place within desktop computing since its dawn in the 1980s, is that the actual interaction techniques have changed very little. Most desktop computer users are still limited to a keyboard and a mouse. The computer mouse, for instance, whose basic design was conceived and prototyped in the 1960s, still limits the way it represents the user within the virtual desktop to a single point in a two-dimensional

J. Jacko (Ed.): Human-Computer Interaction, Part II, HCII 2007, LNCS 4551, pp. 53–62, 2007.

space. While mouse technology has in fact evolved rapidly over the last ten years or so—mainly by means of various vision-based technologies and wireless connectivity to the host computer—the mouse as a means of generating input to a computer is still inherently two-dimensional.

There have of course been many attempts to replace and improve the computer mouse in various ways, as will be discussed below, including two-handed input as well as devices providing up to six degrees of freedom. While sometimes providing interesting research results, they have however remained commercially unsuccessful.

In this paper, we will address the issue of multi-dimensional mice through a prototype design of a computer mouse providing three degrees of freedom. Particularly, we will approach the issue from three perspectives: from a hardware and software design perspective; from a physical design and product semantics perspective; and from a user-centered perspective.

1.1 Paper Overview

As noted above, the idea of a mouse providing three degrees of freedom is not entirely new. Hence, first, we will introduce and discuss some related work in the area. Second, partly based in previous work, we will present a straightforward way in which a working prototype of a wireless 3DOF mouse can be designed and implemented. We believe this implementation to be especially useful for testing, usability, and exploratory interaction design purposes, as it is easy to produce, cheap, reliable, wireless, easy to interface to existing desktop computer hardware, platform-independent, and depends solely on known hardware and software technologies.

Third, we will introduce and discuss what we regard as a number of pertinent product semantics issues concerning the physical design of 3DOF mice compared to those providing two degrees of freedom, exemplified by our physical design process. Fourth, based on the findings of a focus group workshop with expert users in the area of graphical design and 3D modeling and animation, we will introduce, discuss, and demonstrate the kind of interaction design made possible by using a 3DOF mouse, where we also draw extensively on and compare with previous work in the area.

2 The Computer Mouse: A Brief History

The traditional computer mouse, following Doug Engelbart's original design in the 1960s, provides two degrees of freedom, where a user can move the mouse sideways as well as forward and back in relation to one's body. The very first mice where bulky devices that used two gear-wheels perpendicular to each other, where the rotation of each wheel translated into motion along one axis. In the 1970s, Xerox PARC's Bill English invented ball mouse where the external wheels were replaced by a single ball that could rotate in any direction and where perpendicular wheels inside the mouse detected in their turn the motion of the ball. Early optical mice came about in the early 1980s. With no moving mechanical parts, these mice use light-emitting diodes and photodiodes to detect movement relative to the underlying surface. Today, surface-independent optical mice make us of an optoelectronic sensor to take consecutive pictures of the surface on which the mouse operates.

Thus, while mouse technology developed quite quickly, its usage has remained the same. Still today, the mouse is typically used in graphical computer applications to provide the user with a pointing device on a two-dimensional surface—precisely what was suggested by Engelbart in the 1960s. While improvements and more features have been suggested, little has happened to the original design, with one notable exception. Since the advent of the World Wide Web, the mouse wheel has become omnipresent and is today more or less an integral part of any mouse design.

2.1 Computer Mice Providing Multiple Degrees of Freedom

In this paper, we will specifically look at and discuss a possible further development of the basic computer mouse which would provide it with three degrees of freedom rather than just two. A 3DOF mouse is a computer mouse that is able to sense rotation along its vertical axis, i.e. yaw.

One of the earliest, exploratory examples of a means to track rotation by comparison of multiple sensors in the area of computer mouse design was the *Two-ball Mouse* [10,16]. This system has a very straightforward design, in which two traditional ball-based mice are put together and mechanically coupled inside a single box. A more recent design is the *3Style Mouse* [5], which differs from the design Two-ball Mouse by implementing a wireless connection to the host computer. In addition, the 3Style Mouse has a round shape, conveying no orientation of the mouse in terms of physical design. Thus, it needs to have an absolute orientation, which the authors argue is provided by magnetic solid state sensors acing as a compass. The cylindrical shape, and the absolute orientation which disconnects the yaw angle from up-down and left-right movements in relation to the user seems to make this design most appropriate for application areas such as controlling video streams, by the mouse taking the role of a jog wheel.

A third example of a 3DOF mouse is the *Yawing Mouse* [1]. The authors present a prototype design and an interaction technique based on the idea of a yawing mouse, i.e. a device that senses the yaw orientation specifically conceived for integral manipulation of 3D desktop windows in a three degrees-of-freedom space. Like the 3Style Mouse, the authors also deal with the fact that only relative orientation can be obtained with a device such as the Two-ball Mouse, and presents a mathematical solution with similarities to dead reckoning, whose accumulation of errors however makes its accuracy and thus usefulness clearly limited in practice. Unlike many other, more explorative approaches however, the authors also present a small formal usability study of their design. The results of their evaluation however show that when compared with the other mouse techniques, the performance gain was small.

Recently, Poston et al. [12] have argued for a system providing 3DOF using just a single optical mouse sensor, where computer vision algorithms analyze the low-resolution image as seen by the optical mouse sensor. The downside with such a solution might be that while in fact only one mouse sensor is needed, the amount of data that must be transferred between the mouse and the host computer to perform the image processing increases substantially, thus completely new hardware solutions are still needed.

A number of authors have presented computer mice variants which provide more than three degrees of freedom. The *Rockin' Mouse* [2] is a 4DOF mouse that sense relative standard position along the X and Y axis as well as tilting along both axes, showing at least a 30% performance gain in 3D positioning tasks. Other examples of input devices providing multiple degrees of freedom include the *Videomouse* [8] is a 6DOF device that uses video cameras and image processing for sensing movement in relation to a surface. Finally, the *Toolstone* [14] is a box-shaped device that senses position, orientation, and tilting through the use of magnetic trackers.

3 Focus Group Workshop

The bulk of the argument made and stances taken in this paper are based on the results of a workshop with a focus group of expert graphical design users from Umeå Institute of Design, Umeå University, Sweden. The six users taking part in the focus group activity are experts in graphical applications such as *Adobe Illustrator, Adobe Indesign, Adobe Photoshop,* and 3D tools like *Autodesk Maya* and *3ds Max*. In the workshop, we used probes in the form of low-fidelity prototypes that suggested a number of ways in which the rotational capability of the 3DOF mouse could influence and possibly enhance specific manipulations in such interfaces.

A number of new ideas sprung from the discussions that followed. Some of these ideas have been implemented and informally tested with members of the focus group as well as with other non-expert users. More formal usability testing is currently being conducted.

4 Hardware and Software Design and Implementation

To be able to try different physical designs and different kinds of interaction styles using a 3DOF mouse, we needed to design and implement a simple but functional hardware prototype. Early on, we decided to implement a simple, low-tech version that like the original Two-ball Mouse design [10] would calculate the differences in the relative movement of two mouse sensors. For a number of reasons that will be discussed later in this paper, we prefer this simple design to the various techniques of establishing absolute position that exist in the literature as introduced above.

To prototype the hardware in a straightforward way, we used two optical mouse sensors attached to the same physical body. For this purpose, we used two standard Belkin notepad mice, each containing a Cypress micro-controller and an ADNS-2610 optical mouse sensor, which is an optical sensor with a resolution of 400 CPI (Counts Per Inch) and a rate of motion of 12 inches per second. The sensor has a two-wire bus using a protocol that can be interfaced with ease to most micro-controllers. Using our own micro-controller to control the two sensors, we got rid of the two Cypress processors along with the casings, the buttons and the scroll wheels that were all part of the original mouse design.

We then designed a custom circuit to continually read the X and Y coordinates from both optical sensors and to send this information over a one-directional wireless radio link to the host computer. For this purpose, we used a AVR Atmega8 micro-controller and an ER400TS module to handle the radio transmission.

The yaw angle is calculated using the four relative coordinates: <X1, Y1> and <X2, Y2> acquired from the two optical mouse sensors. When the device is rotated, X1 and X2 increases/decreases according to the rotational direction. Therefore the yaw angle α can be expressed as S(X1 – X2), where S is a scaling constant effectively defining the relationship between physical mouse yawing and yawing on-screen. Calculation for the actual device positioning is defined as the mean of <X1, Y1> and <X2, Y2>, which by the way also enhances the precision of the mouse. The yaw resolution can be found using the following equation:

$$\frac{M_{cpi} 2\pi r}{360} = M_{yawres}$$

Here, M_{cpi} is the mouse sensor resolution, r is the distance between the sensors, and M_{yawres} is the resulting angular resolution. Utilizing mouse sensors with a modest 400 cpi and a two inches distance between its sensors equates to an angular resolution of nearly 14 counts per degree. This means that we get a total of 5040 steps in a 360 degrees rotation of the device. Such a high precision makes it feasible to map for example a +-15 degree device yaw to an on-screen yaw of +-180 degrees and still have an angular resolution of more than one count per degree. We will later argue that the high resolution provided could influence the way that rotation is implemented as a means of interaction.

5 Physical Design and Product Semantics

We argue that it is not only the hardware and software abilities of a 3DOF mouse that renders it useful for users, its product semantics are also important factors in having users understand the scope of a new product. The concept of product semantics has been developed by Krippendorff & Butter [9]. It can be defined as the study of symbolic qualities of man-made shapes in the cognitive as well as cultural context of their use. Traditional HCI has paid little interest in the physical qualities and design of products, focusing more on designing the virtual. If physical design has been denoted, it has most often been with regard to a particular design's ergonomics.

In areas such as industrial design, architecture, and graphical design however, there is a long-standing tradition of paying attention to and caring for product semantics when it comes to physical design. But product semantics is not only concerned with physical appearance; other aspects of artifacts that help shape people's meaning in relation to them are also part of the scope of product semantics, including how they feel, what materials they are made of and what those materials signify, the way they sound, color, texture, shape, etc. Product semantics argues that all products make a statement through their design, and that they because of this cannot appear neutrally in their contexts. Thus, a product tells us something about itself (and in some cases also about the person owning it). Through its physical design and its function, the product comes to express values that we interpret in relation to a certain social and cultural context.

At least four semantic functions of products can be distinguished [11]. First, the product describes its purpose, defines its task, its way of use, and the way it should be handled. Second, the product expresses values and qualities. Third, the product urges the user to react or handle in a specific way, e.g. to be careful or to be precise. Fourth, the product gestalt also operates to identify its origin, its nature and the product area to which it belongs. This connects new products with existing product ranges and with families of similar products.

These semantic functions allow the designer with the possibility to communicate a message through the product; to make the product comprehensible. Understanding how people 'read' unfamiliar products is crucial to the application of semantics in industrial design.

5.1 3DOF Mouse Product Semantics

In an explorative design process, we applied our experience and competence in industrial design to charge our 3DOF mouse prototype with material properties that would allow people to find meaning in it and understand its purpose, origin, values, and other qualities. In a first, very open form study phase, a number of shapes were explored and later reviewed by pen and paper sketching and joint design critique sessions [7].

Based on ideas from the extensive pen and paper sketching efforts, we designed a number of candidate models in Styrofoam, or expanded polystyrene, which is a common way of expressing physical 3D form within industrial design.

Fig. 1. A photo of a few of the styrofoam sketch models

Styrofoam modeling, on the one hand, can be regarded as a way of sketching in 3D, especially as carried out by a skilled product designer. On the other hand, such models embody a set of different properties that allow them to be approached and assessed differently than pen and paper sketches. First, they provide a more complete gestalt than a pen and paper model, in that their form for instance can be reviewed from every angle. Second, they are tangible which means that they, in this case, can actually be physically grabbed and handled like a mouse.

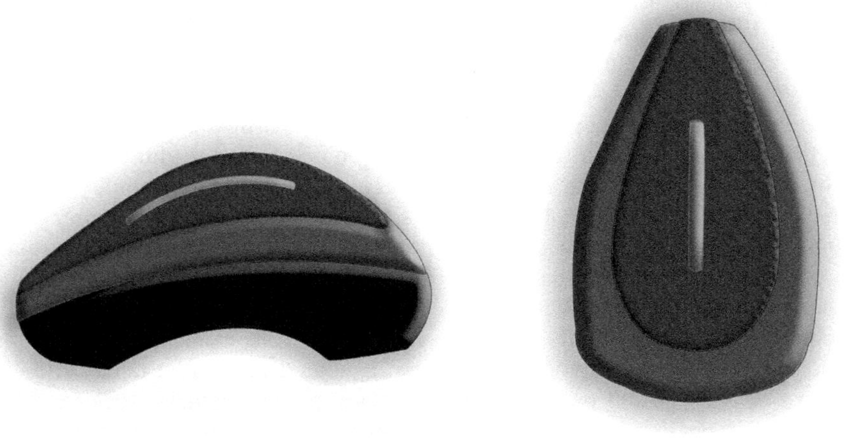

Fig. 2. The final form, side view (left) and top view (right)

Based on a number of styrofoam models and a number of design critique sessions, we decided to go on with one of the designs (see figure 2) and implement it.

The qualities we looked for in terms of product semantics were hence: first, that the 3DOF mouse should describes its purpose, defines its task, its way of use, and the way it should be handled. A typical computer mouse has a large, single bottom surface that rests on the underlying surface. In our design, the 3DOF mouse has two bottom surfaces, connected visually by an arch, which should give the user a visual clue as to its function. Second, when seen from above, a visual stroke goes from the rear end of the mouse towards the front end, suggesting a plane or a line that conceptually aligns with the rotation of the mouse. This suggests that the mouse does not control a point in two dimensions, but actually a line. Third, as the product gestalt also operates to identify its origin, its nature and the product area to which it belongs, we chose to retain a lot of the product semantics of existing computer mice—to allow users to conceptually connect the 3DOF mouse with an existing product family.

6 Discussion

One of the benefits of a 3DOF mouse compared to most 6DOF input devices is that it is not so much different from an ordinary mouse, which most computer users understands and appreciates. Also, the 3DOF mouse can rest on an underlying surface when in use, making it useable in practice for longer periods of time than for instance 6DOF input devices that typically has to be lifted up and manipulated without a surface on which to rest.

While the 6DOF input devices provides 'true' control in three dimensions, 3DOF mice can be regarded as more 'real' in terms of their usefulness in actual application situations [6]. A typical 3D modeling tool, such as Autodesk 3ds Max for instance, provide its user with four modeling surfaces, all depicting the current scene from four different perspectives: a side view, a top view, a front view, and a 3D view. It is actually only in one of these views, the 3D-view, that 6DOF manipulation has a real advantage. When the user is manipulating objects in the three other views, 3DOF is to prefer as it provides the user with stability and control due to the possibility of resting on an underlying surface.

Based on the focus group findings, we believe that compared to traditional 2DOF mice, the 3DOF mouse's extra freedom dimension is the most useful when working in the three other views, as the 3DOF mouse gives the user the possibility to perform rotation tasks (as well as scaling, zooming, and resizing) with great precision and without constantly having to change application mode [13], which is currently an time-consuming and annoying activity in 3D modeling.

The physical design and product semantics of a 3DOF mouse that we have explored and advocated in this paper is indeed different from some of the various shapes that have been promoted in the existing literature. For instance, Almeida & Cubaud's design [1] and the 3Style Mouse [5] propose a round, cylindrical design. From an ergonomics perspective for instance, they find some support in [17], who argues that the conventional mouse design, suggesting a whole hand grasp, may be problematic for 3DOF mice since it requires large muscle group which may lead to inefficient and straining movements. Rather, the authors argue, smaller devices that affords finger-tip grasp are better for quick and precise manipulations and a symmetrical shape better supports these small finger-movements yielding efficient rotation handling [1,17].

Notwithstanding the importance of ergonomics in design, we argue that wether or not rotation tasks are inefficient and straining also greatly depends on what kind of rotation tasks the user is performing. Based on our focus group discussions and the impressive precision that relational 3DOF mice, including our own prototype, are able to demonstrate in rotation tasks, we believe that the real strength of 3DOF are to be found in simple, relational 3DOF mice that look and operate like ordinary mice, but which when appropriate can provide its user access to yawing operations.

We understand that the a round, cylindrical design conveying no orientation through touch [cf. 1] is useful when conducting rotation handling requiring several rounds of rotation (such as jog wheels and volume controls). However, for such applications, the 3DOF mouse used also requires absolute positioning, for which no simple and precise technique exists that does not deteriorate over time and which does not require calibration. Based on focus group discussions, we argue that 3DOF mice on the contrary are most useful for small but precise rotation movements, such as fine-tuning the rotation of an object in 3ds Max; for perfectly aligning a curve in Adobe Illustrator; or for rotating the map view in Google Earth. If the extra degree of freedom provided by 3DOF mice over 2DOF mice is limited to such subtle manipulation tasks, we believe users might be more willing to accept them. We believe that it is the great precision in rotation tasks that is offered by 3DOF mice that should become emphasized, not how quickly one can perform the rotation.

The problem of relativity—that 'left' should mean left no matter how the mouse is rotated—that is suggested by both *the 3Style Mouse* [5] and by *the Yawing Mouse* [1] is still not solved by such a solution, but the effect in practice is of course much smaller. Hence, our design would also benefit from an improved solution to the problem of relativity in 3DOF mice. The solution argued by [1] is limited in that it builds solely on relative parameters in trying to make absolute claims, where errors quickly come to accumulate. The 3Style Mouse [5] on the other hand uses the earth's magnetic field (i.e. a compass) to keep track of the coordinate system. While no errors are accumulated, the downside with this technique is that it has a very slow updating frequency compared to the mouse sensor itself, which renders it not very appropriate for this application area. Combining these two techniques could provide a better solution to the problem of relativity, i.e. using [1]'s quick relative technique but continuously correct it by the means of the slower compass technique found in [5].

7 Conclusions

In this paper, we have presented some of the design processes involved in creating a 3DOF mouse. First, we have provided a review of the current literature in the field, discussing the limitations and possibilities that can be found in previous 3DOF, 4DOF, and 6DOF input devices. Second, we have introduced the focus group workshop activity that underlies the whole design process and which pointed us towards graphical design applications and 3D modeling tools.

Third, we have presented our prototype design process and the role we believe product semantics plays. In our design, the 3DOF mouse has two bottom surfaces, connected visually by an arch, signaling to the user a clue of its function. Second, when seen from above, a visual stroke goes from the rear end of the mouse towards the front end, suggesting a plane or a line that conceptually aligns with the rotation of the mouse, suggesting that the mouse does not control a point in two dimensions like a traditional mouse but actually a line. The round, cylindrical design conveying no orientation through touch that is proposed by other authors might be useful when conducting certain rotation tasks, such as when controlling jog wheels and volume controls. Based on our focus group discussions, we argue that 3DOF mice on the contrary are most useful for small but precise rotation movements. If the extra degree of freedom provided by 3DOF mice over 2DOF mice is limited to such subtle manipulation tasks, we believe users might be more willing to accept them. We believe that it is the great precision in rotation tasks that is offered by 3DOF mice that should become emphasized, not how quickly one can perform the rotation.

Acknowledgments. Thanks to Linda Bogren.

References

1. Almeida, R., Cubaud, P.: Supporting 3D Window Manipulation with a Yawing Mouse. In: Proc. of 4th Nordic Conference on Human-Computer Interaction (NordiCHI 2006), Oslo, Norway, pp. 477–480. ACM Press, New York (2006)
2. Balakrishnan, R., Baudel, T., Kurtenbach, G.: The Rockin'Mouse: Integral 3D Manipulation on a Plane. In: Proc CHI 1997, pp. 311–318. ACM Press, New York (1997)
3. Card, S., Robertson, G., York, W.: The WebBook and the Web Forager: An information workspace for the World-Wide Web. In: Proc. CHI 1996, pp. 111–117 ACM Press, New York (1996)
4. Chapuis, O., Roussel, N.: Metisse is not a 3D Desktop. In: Proc. UIST 2005, ACM Press, pp. 13–22. ACM Press, New York (2005)

5. Cylo 3Style Mouse Page. http://www.hifidesign.com.au/products.html/
6. Fallman, D.: Why Research-oriented Design Isn't Design-oriented Research. In: Proc. of Nordes: Nordic Design Research Conference, Copenhagen, Denmark (May 29-31, 2005)
7. Fallman, D.: Design-oriented Human–Computer Interaction. In: Proc. Conference on Human Factors in Computing Systems, CHI 2003, pp. 225–232. ACM Press, New York (2003)
8. Hinckley, K., Sinclair, M., Hanson, E., Szeliski, R., Conway, M.: The VideoMouse: a camera-based multidegree-of-freedom input device. UIST 1999, pp. 103–112. ACM, New York (1999)
9. Krippendorff, K., Butter, R.: Product semantics: Exploring the symbolic qualities of form, in Innovation: The Journal of the Industrial Designers Society of America (McLean, Va.: The Society) 3(2), 4–9 (1984)
10. MacKenzie, I.S., Soukoreff, W.R., Pal, C.: A two-ball mouse affords three degrees of freedom. In: Extended Abstracts of the CHI97 Conference on Human Factors in Computing Systems, pp. 303–304. ACM, New York (1997)
11. Monö, R.: Design for product understanding. Stockholm: Liber AB (1997)
12. Poston, T., Srikanth, M.: Computer Input Device Enabling Three Degrees of Freedom and Related Input and Feedback Methods, (2005) http://ssl.serc.iisc.ernet.in/m̃anohar/Research/Mushaca/SLA.htm
13. Raskin, J.: The Humane Interface. Addison-Wesley, London, UK (2000)
14. Rekimoto, J., Sciammarella, E.: ToolStone: effective use of the physical manipulation vocabularies of input devices. In: Proc. UIST 2000, pp. 109–117. ACM Press, New York (2000)
15. Robertson, G., van Dantzich, M., Robbins, D., Czerwinski, M., Hinckley, K., Risden, K., Thiel, D., Gorokhovsky, V.: The task gallery: a 3D window manager. In: Proc. CHI 2000, pp. 494–501. ACM Press, New York (2000)
16. Zhai, S., MacKenzie, I.S.: Teaching old mice new tricks: Innovations in computer mouse design. In: Proc. Ergon-Axia '98, pp. 80–83 (1998)
17. Zhai, S., Milgram, P., Buxton, W.: The influence of muscle groups on performance of multiple degree-of-freedom input. In: Proc. CHI 1996, pp. 308–315. ACM Press, New York (1996)

Facilitating Conditional Probability Problems with Visuals

Vince Kellen, Susy Chan, and Xiaowen Fang

DePaul University, School of Computer Science,
Telecommunications and Information Systems,
Chicago, IL, United States of America
{vkellen,schan,xfang}@depaul.edu

Abstract. In tasks such as disease diagnosis, interpretation of evidence in criminal trials and management of security and risk data, people need to process conditional probabilities to make critical judgments and decisions. As dual-coding theory and the cognitive theory of multimedia learning (CTML) would predict, visual representations (VRs) should aid in these tasks. Conditional probability problems are difficult and require subjects to build a mental model of set inclusion relationships to solve them. Evidence from neurological research confirms that mental model construction relies on visual spatial processing. Prior research has shown conflicting accounts of whether visuals aid in these problems. Prior research has also revealed that individuals differ in their ability to perform spatial processing tasks. Do visuals help solve these problems? Do visualization interface designers need to take into account the nuances of spatial processing and individual differences? This study uses a 3x2 factorial design to determine the relationship between subject's spatial abilities (high or low) and visual and text representations on user performance and satisfaction.

Keywords: Information visualization, Bayesian reasoning, conditional probabilities, dual-coding, cognitive theory of multimedia learning, mental models, individual differences, spatial ability.

1 Introduction

The medical, legal and security disciplines use Bayesian inference in many contexts that require many people who are naïve in Bayesian inference to make critical judgments and decisions involving disease diagnosis and treatment, interpretation of evidence in criminal and civil cases and the management of security data. Prior research has tangentially examined visual representations (VRs) in these Bayesian inference tasks involving conditional probabilities, usually to see how the VR facilitates teaching Bayes' theorem or to test specific theoretical claims made in prior research. Very little research has compared different VRs and their impact on naïve Bayesian subjects' performance and none have examined the role individual differences in spatial abilities play in this task. This research will examine three treatments of a conditional probability Bayesian inference task (text, and spatial and iconic VRs) and how differences in spatial ability affect subject performance with each of these representations.

J. Jacko (Ed.): Human-Computer Interaction, Part II, HCII 2007, LNCS 4551, pp. 63–71, 2007.

2 Prior Research

Information visualization techniques have been applied in a variety of domains. More recently, they have been integrated into general business applications [23], are finding its way to consumers via popular web sites (Peet's Coffee Selector, SmartMoney) that use visualization techniques, and are common in popular applications such as SPSS, SAS, Microsoft Outlook and Adobe Photoshop [25]. Citing several studies in the 1980s and the 1990s, Dull and Tegarden contend that visualization can improve problem-solving capabilities [7],[34]. Others propose that information visualization amplifies cognition through a knowledge crystallization process [4[. Some define information visualization as a process by which the visual presentation of information leads to a mental model, or cognitive map; a cyclical process of human activity creates and recreates this mental model [32]. Tufte [35] provides a compelling argument for proper data visualization to support decision-making in his retrospective analysis of the documents NASA engineers used to unsuccessfully convince NASA managers to scrub the doomed Challenger launch in January 1986. On the day of the launch, managers and engineers discussed canceling the launch due to unusually cold weather. Engineers familiar with the problem had correctly anticipated the problem – the now infamous O-rings would fail in the cold weather – but did not make an appropriate visual presentation of the data to management.

For Bayesian inference tasks involving processing conditional probabilities, most research has tangentially examined the use of VRs, usually to resolve other research problems. Over the past decade or so, researchers have engaged in a vigorous debate regarding the failure of subjects to properly solve Bayesian inference problems, with most of the debate concerning explanations for the apparent poor performance with textual presentations, including the role numeric format plays (e.g., natural frequencies versus probabilities) [11]; the varying performance levels at boundary conditions of the problem including manipulations of reference class size, prevalence, sensitivity and specificity rates [1]; explanations of performance based on theories of mental models [13] and the use of heuristics in judgment and decision making [14].

While researchers have examined the use of VRs in *teaching* Bayesian reasoning skills to students, only a few studies have focused on the use of VRs in Bayesian inference for naïve subjects. The list of textual and visual representations discussed or tested in the body of research includes: contingency tables [5] trees [22], frequency bars or "beam cut" diagrams [11], Euler circles [31], signal detection, probability curves [5], frequency grids [5], [11] and Bayesian boxes [3]. No research to-date has examined the role individual differences in spatial abilities plays in subject performance with conditional probability tasks.

One popular version of this problem, the "mammography problem," asks subjects to infer a probability to a medical disease problem [11]. Prior research indicates subject accuracy is typically poor for the text-only probability version of the problem [10], [11], [21], [30], [31] and in some cases accuracy can be improved with use of visuals [2] or have little or no impact [31]. Recent mental models research shows that visual processing, if engaged in text-versions of the problem, can impede reasoning [18].

The study of individual differences in cognitive abilities has a long history [33], [36]. Research into self reports of vividness of imagery and spatial abilities have conflicting results and explanations regarding the relationship between imagery and spatial abilities [8]. However, recent research provides some new insight clarifying prior conflicts. Subjects with low spatial abilities show an inclination towards constructing object or iconic VRs and have difficulty interpreting more abstract spatial VRs whereas subjects with high spatial abilities show an inclination towards constructing spatial or abstract VRs and a facility with interpreting more abstract spatial VRs [19], [20]. Imagery is not a unitary ability and may contain separate abilities reflecting the distinction between the "what" and the "where" pathways. The "what" pathway (the ventral stream) is crucial for the identification of objects and is sensitive to shape and color. The "where" pathway (the dorsal stream) is crucial for identifying spatial relations among objects and for visually guiding movements towards objects [15]. The dorsal and ventral streams are used not only for perception – processing external representations, but for mental imagery – constructing internal representations in the absence of external representations.

According to dual-coding theory [26], VRs should facilitate mental model construction by building referential connections between verbal and nonverbal representations of the same problem. These connections aid in accessing or encoding in long term memory. Dual coding theory, however, does not specify what kind of VR helps best [28]. Findings from mental models [17] and cognitive neuroscience research [16] suggests a distinction between a visual working memory for object imagery and a spatial working memory for spatial relations and mental model construction, also reflecting the "what" and the "where" pathways [29]. Conditional and relational reasoning tasks activate regions of the brain that make up the "where" pathway of spatial perception and working memory [18], [27], [17]. Because cognitive resources are finite, spatial activities can interfere with inference tasks in the "where" pathway when these tasks are performed concurrently [29].

CTML has a rich research track that explains subject learning (retention and transfer) via multimedia displays. However, no prior CTML research has focused on the conditional probabilities problem. Some prior CTML researched has examined the role of individual differences in spatial abilities on multimedia problems, but not in depth ([24]). According to the individual differences principle of CTML, multimedia displays help those with low domain knowledge and those with high spatial abilities. Subjects with high domain knowledge can solve problems without the aid of the VR. Subjects with high spatial abilities can accommodate more visual information within working memory and thus can make use of the VR [24]. Conditional probability problems are ones in which nearly all subjects have little prior knowledge in solving.

3 What Theoretical Model Prevails?

Interestingly, prior research into Bayesian inference and conditional probability problem solving has used both spatial and object VRs (hereafter referred to as iconic VRs) but without making a distinction between these two kinds of displays or measuring any linkage to differing spatial abilities. Spatial displays are more abstract representations of the relationships between sets of items without depicting individual items. Iconic displays use more concrete images to refer to specific items within a set, highlighting the use of shape and shading to make clear the distinction between kinds of items. Spatial displays are designed to take advantage of the "where" system and iconic displays are designed to take advantage of the "what" system. Figures 1 and 2 show the same conditional probability problem represented as a spatial and an iconic VR.

To help naïve subjects in solving this problem, what should interface designers do? The literature suggests different approaches.

First, as previously discussed, research into object and spatial visualizers suggests that the type of VR may matter; opposite their high-spatial counterparts, subjects with low spatial ability may not be able to effectively process spatial VRs [20]. High spatial subjects should do well with spatial VRs and low spatial subjects may do better with less abstract iconic VRs. Mental models research suggests that a spatial VR showing the relationships between the concepts would help reasoning and representations that contain irrelevant imagery details (iconic VRs), should impede reasoning [18].

However, the conditional probability problems used in our study are difficult and takes subjects several minutes to solve, despite the fact that it only involves two numbers and two basic mathematical operations (addition and division)., e.g., A / (A+B). Since subjects struggle to find a relevant strategy from long term memory, perhaps the type of VR should aid in referential processing between the verbal (text) and the visual coding. Dual coding theory suggests that a display with more concrete concepts would elicit better referential processing between the two codings and long-term memory. Also, if visual working memory is composed of two distinct parts (the "what" and the "where" system) that are used to both solve the problem (build an internal representation or mental model) and perceive the problem (by scanning the external representation and maintaining its properties in either visual system), should the display be mindful of cognitive overload of the "where" system? This suggests a second approach. An iconic VR should facilitate mental model construction without interfering with that construction.

Yet another possibility lurks. If the problem is difficult enough to solve, it may exhaust working memory resources. Any type of visual, including iconic displays, is likely to engage spatial processing and can thus interfere with solving the problem. Visual displays of any kind might be a form of task interference.

4 Hypotheses

Based on dual-coding theory and mental models research, while working with a spatial VR (an external representation) on a conditional probability problem, subjects must visually process explicit relations between concepts, thus activating the "where" pathway. Subjects need to maintain or rebuild this representation in visual working memory. While working with an iconic VR, subjects must process shape and texture more than spatial relations, thus activating the "what" pathway. Some activation of the "where" pathway may occur, but it should be less than with spatial VRs. Since this problem is novel and difficult, referential processing may not assist sufficiently with retrieval of strategies from long-term memory. With either spatial or iconic VRs, during mental model construction, subjects must alternate between constructing a mental model (an internal representation) of the problem and examining the VR (the external representation). Since a spatial VR and to a lesser extent an iconic VR must now compete for limited cognitive resources, in this case the "where" pathway, a spatial VR should be inferior to an iconic VR and both may be inferior to text. Users will likely find the using the visuals appealing or helpful are will be more likely to feel greater satisfaction with visuals regardless of their performance. Therefore, we hypothesize the following effects of the visualization of conditional probability problems:

H1. VRs will not generate more correct answers than textual representations
H2. Iconic VRs will generate more correct answers than spatial VRs
H3. VRs will result in a higher level of user satisfaction than textual representations

Based on the CTML research, subjects with high spatial ability, should perform better in all forms of representation in solving conditional probability problems (text, spatial or iconic VRs) and VRs (spatial or iconic) should benefit subjects with high spatial ability more so than subjects with lower spatial ability. Therefore, we hypothesize that:

H4. Users with higher spatial abilities generate more correct answers than subjects with lower spatial abilities under all three forms of representation (text, spatial or iconic VRs).

H5. VRs will have stronger effects for those users with high spatial abilities than users with low spatial ability.

Hypothesis H1 is supported by prior psychological research into conditional probability problems that shows if the problem text reveals the set relationships, visuals will not help. H2 is predicated on the split between "what" and "where" processing in visual working memory and use of the "where" pathway during mental model construction. Hypothesis H4 and H5 are supported in CTML research, specifically the individual differences principle.

5 Experiment Design

This research uses a between-subjects 2X3 factorial design to test the above hypotheses:

	Representation		
Spatial ability	Iconic	Spatial	Text
High			
Low			

There are two independent variables—spatial ability and representation. Spatial ability was measured by the paper folding tests from Ekstrom, French & Hardon [9]. High and low levels of spatial ability were determined by a median split of the paper folding test score. Representation is defined by three forms of presenting conditional probability problems – textual, iconic visual, and spatial visual. The conditional probability problems use frequency formats and a 'short' menu, which facilitate more normative answers than more complicated versions of these problems [11]. In keeping with CTML design principles, the VRs were presented in incremental, integrated displays in which the user can control the pace of the problem description, which is presented on the same screen as the visual treatment. Wordings of the problem were placed in the first person and made as simple as possible.

While all problems use the short frequency format which provides several advantages for subjects, we manipulated the text of the problems, where possible, to adopt a more natural perspective of asking the subject to imagine encountering a series of cases in the future and inferring an answer. We felt this more closely follows the natural frequency argument for facilitating solving these problems [11]. Because of these subtle textual manipulations consistent with CTML research, we expect subject performance to be somewhat better than other relevant studies. To compare with prior studies, the classic "mammography" version was included in the battery of problems.

Dependent variables are user performance and satisfaction. Performance was measured by accuracy (the number of correct answers). User satisfaction is measured by a 14-item questionnaire based to Davis' [6] technology acceptance model (TAM). In this model, perceived ease of use and perceived usefulness are two key determinants on user adoption of technology.

As of this writing the study is in the middle of data collection. A total of 200 subjects are being recruited from a Midwest university, classified as subjects of high and low spatial ability and randomly assigned to each of the three treatments. Subjects fill out a background questionnaire regarding their education level, prior skill in probabilities, age, gender and any visual impairment. Subjects then complete a timed paper folding test ([9]). Next, subjects received a brief explanation about the task, complete a battery of ten (10) conditional probability problems and a post-test survey designed to measure satisfaction.

We used a "write-aloud" process tracing protocol ([11]), in which the subjects' recorded notes, diagrams and calculations can be further analyzed. Consistent with Gigerenzer and Hoffrage [11], scoring of the correct answers follows a strict rounding criteria which allows for answers to be rounded up or down to the nearest integer, allowing for rounding being applied to intermediate steps or the final computational step. The combination of the rounding criteria and the process tracing data is used to score a correct answer. This eliminates simple math errors from disqualifying normatively correct processes.

We expect to complete this study and present the full data at the conference in July, 2007.

6 Problem Representations

A text version of the mammography problem>

Pretend you are a doctor with a breast-cancer specialty. Over the last four years, you have seen 1000 women who are at the age of forty for routine screening. 103 out of those 1,000 women did receive a positive mammogram in routine screening, thus exhibiting the symptoms of breast cancer. 8 of those women who had a positive mammography had breast cancer. If over the next few months you saw 200 additional forty-year-old women who already had positive mammographies in hand, how many would you expect to have breast cancer?

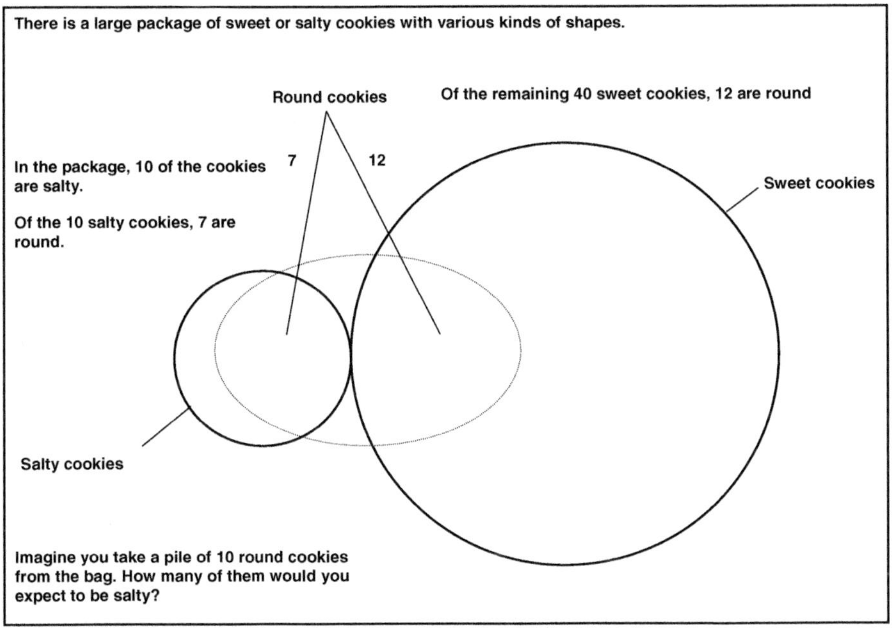

Fig. 1. A spatial VR

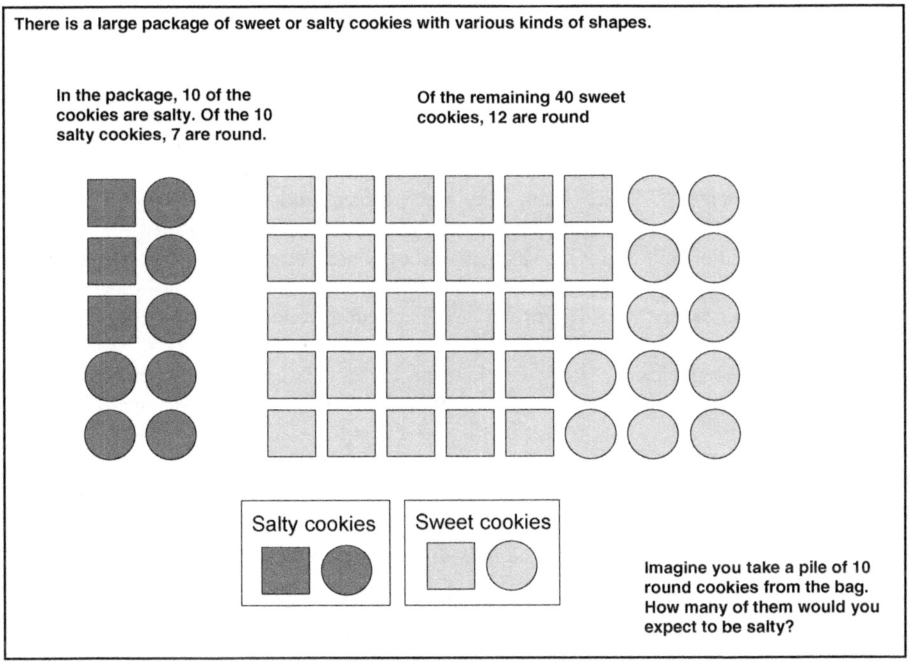

Fig. 2. An iconic VR

References

1. Brase, G.L.: Which statistical formats facilitate what decisions? The perception and influence of different statistical information formats. Journal of Behavioral Decision Making 15, 381–401 (2002)
2. Brase, G.L. (2006)
3. Burns, K.: Painting pictures to augment advice. AVI '04, pp. 344–349. ACM, New York (May 25-28, 2004)
4. Card, S.K., Mackinlay, J.D., Shneiderman, B.: Information Visualization: Using Vision to Think. Academic Press (1999)
5. Cole, W.G: Understanding Bayesian reasoning via graphical displays. In: CHI '89 Proceedings, pp. 381–386. ACM, New York (May 1989)
6. Davis, F.D.: Perceived usefulness, perceived ease of use and user acceptance of information technology. MIS Quarterly. pp. 319–340 (September 1989)
7. Dull, R.B., Tegarden, D.P.: A comparison of three visual representations of complex multidimensional accounting information. Journal of Information Systems 13, 117–131 (1999)
8. Dean, G.M., Morris, P.E.: The relationship between self-reports of imagery and spatial ability. British Journal of Psychology 94, 245–273 (2003)
9. Ekstrom, R.B., French, J.W., Harman, H.H.: Manual for kit of factor-referenced cognitive tests. Princeton: Educational Testing Service (1976)
10. Gigerenzer, G., Edwards, A.: Simple tools for understanding risks: from innumeracy to insight. BMJ 327, 741–744 (2003)
11. Gigerenzer, G., Hoffrage, U.: How to improve Bayesian reasoning without instruction: frequency formats. frequency formats. Psychological Review 102, 684–701 (1995)
12. Girotto, V., Gonzalez, M.: Solving probabilistic and statistical problems: a matter of information structure and question form. Cognition 78, 247–276 (2001)
13. Johnson-Laird, P.N., Legrenzi, P., Girotto, V., Legrenzi, M.S., Caverni, J.: Naïve probability: a mental model theory of extensional reasoning. Psychological Review 106(1), 62–88 (1999)
14. Kahneman, Daniel, Slovic, Paul, Tversky, Amos: Judgement Under Uncertainty: Heuristics and Biases. Cambridge University Press, Cambridge (1988)
15. Kastner, S., Ungerleider, L.G.: Mechanisms of visual attention in the human cortex. Annual Review of Neuroscience 23, 315–341 (2000)
16. Kossyln, S.M., Ganis, G., Thompson, W.L.: Neural foundations of imagery. Nature Review, Neuroscience 2(9), 635–642 (2001)
17. Knauff, M., Fangmeier, T., Ruff, C., Johnson-Laird, P.N.: Reasoning, models, images: behavioral measures and cortical activity. Journal of cognitive neuroscience 15(4), 559–573 (2003)
18. Knauff, M., Johnson-Laird, P.N.: Visual imagery can impede reasoning. Memory & Cognition. 30(3), 363–371 (2002)
19. Kozhevnikov, M., Hegarty, M., Mayer, R.E.: Revising the visualizer-verbalizer dimension: evidence for two types of visualizers. Cognition and Instruction 20(1), 47–77 (2002)
20. Kozhevnikov, M., Kossyln, S., Shephard, J.: Spatial versus object visualizers: a new characterization of visual cognitive style. Memory and Cognition 33(4), 710–726 (2005)
21. Kurzenhauser, S., Hoffrage, U.: Teaching Bayesian reasoning: An evaluation of a classroom tutorial for medical students. Medical Teacher 24, 516–521 (2002)

22. Martignon, L., Wassner, C.: Teaching decision making and statistical thinking with natural frequencies. ICOTS6 (2002)
23. Mirel, B.: Visualization for data exploration and analysis: a critical review of usability research. Technical Communication. Fourth Quarter 1998. pp. 491–509 (1998)
24. Mayer, R.E.: Multimedia Learning. The Psychology of Learning and Motivation 41, 85–139 (2002)
25. Plaisant, C.: The challenge of information visualization evaluation. AVI '04, ACM (May 25-28 2004)
26. Paivio, A.: Mental Representation: A Dual Coding Approach. Oxford University Press. New York (1990)
27. Ruff, C., Knauff, M., Fangmeier, T., Spreer, J.: Reasoning and working memory: common and distinct neuronal processes. Neuropsychologia 41, 1241–1253 (2003)
28. Schnotz, W., Bannert, M.: Construction and interference in learning from multiple representation. Learning and Instruction 13, 141–156 (2003)
29. Schnotz, W.: An integrated model of text and picture comprehension. In: Mayer, R.E. (ed.) The Cambridge Handbook of Multimedia Learning, Cambridge University Press, Cambridge (2005)
30. Sedlmeier, P.: How to improve statistical thinking: Choose the task wisely and learn by doing. Instructional Science 28, 227–262 (2000)
31. Sloman, S.A., Over, D., Slovak, L., Stibel, J.M.: Frequency illusions and other fallacies. Organizational Behavior and Human Decision Processes 91, 296–301 (2003)
32. Spence, R.: Information Visualization. Addison-Wesley (2001)
33. Stanovich, K.E., West, R.F.: Individual differences in reasoning: Implications for the rationality debate? Behavioral and Brain Sciences 23, 645–726 (2000)
34. Tegarden, D.P.: Business information visualization. Communications of the AIS. vol. 1(4) (January 1999)
35. Tufte, E.R.: Visual Explanations: Images and Quantities, Evidence and Narrative. Graphics Press (1997)
36. Woodcock, R.W.: New looks in the assessment of cognitive ability. Peabody Journal of Education 77(2), 6–22 (2002)

Interface Design Technique Considering Visual Cohesion-Rate by Object Unit

Chang-Mog Lee and Ok-Bae Chang

Division of Electronics and Information Engineering, Chonbuk National University, 664-14 1ga Duckjin-Dong Duckjin-Gu Jeonju, Jeonbuk, South Korea
{cmlee,okjang}@chonbuk.ac.kr

Abstract. With the application development environment rapidly changing, the design of an interface that supports the complex interactions between humans and computers is required. In addition, profound knowledge of various fields is required to cover the requirements of different customers. Therefore, in this paper, we suggest an interface design technique that considers the cohesion-rate in each objects of user interface. To accomplish this, specific and detailed models to embody the user interface are presented on the basis of the following classification: 1) event object model, 2) task object model, 3) transaction object model, 4) form object model. If this detailed modeling work is performed, the visual cohesion of the prototype user interface can be improved and, on this basis, even unskilled designers can construct an improved user interface. Moreover, the proposed method promotes the understanding of the business process and reduces the frequency of system development.

1 Introduction

With the rapid growth of the internet, the previous software environment evolved to the web based environment, and web applications emerged as a new paradigm. Along with this change, the user interface is also developing into software capable of high quality input/output and subject to a new set of rules. Jackob Nielsen reckoned that poor usability was behind the loss of billions of dollars caused by incorrect sales operations on the web [1]. It is estimated that 48% of the application code is applied to the user interface, and 50% of the implementation time is spent on the embodiment of the user interface when an application is developed [2]. Moreover, many studies have been conducted concerning the automatic creation of the user interface. The user interface supporting the complex interaction between humans and computers require very comprehensive and multi-faceted knowledge to collect the requirements of the customers and allow them to negotiate with each other.

Experts in various fields, such as graphics experts, requirement analysts, system designers, programmers, technical experts, social behavior experts, etc., are required to ensure a good user interface design [3]. However, it is not easy to involve so many experts in various fields in the design process. However, most of the studies conducted so far have concerned themselves with the issue of how to generate the interface. By contrast, there have been few studies that explored the method of creating the business events for the user interface. It is necessary to improve the comprehensibility

J. Jacko (Ed.): Human-Computer Interaction, Part II, HCII 2007, LNCS 4551, pp. 72–81, 2007.

of business tasks and the usability of the interface by clustering business events in such a way that they are semantically related one another [4, 5, 6]. Therefore, in this paper, we suggest interface design technique that applies visual cohesion-rate by object unit to design user interface of high quality. The use of Visual Cohesion (hereafter referred to as VC) in the design of a UI helps improve its quality by providing the designer or developer with a visual prototype prior to the embodiment of the system. Moreover, VC provides the standards needed to measure the appropriateness of the layout of the UI and its semantic contents. The rest of this paper is organized as follows. In section 2, describes the related works about this paper. Section 3 suggests the type of objects and the method of clustering which are necessary for the clustering of the business events in the UI based on their relevance. In section 4, the proposed object oriented design model and existing design models are compared by assessing their characteristics, and the UI of these design models is created to measure, compare and evaluate the VC. Finally in section 5, the findings of this study are discussed.

2 Related Works

2.1 Criteria for Measurement for UI Design

The criteria for the measurement of the UI includes those for the structural design, contents related design and task related design. The structural design is deemed to be the easiest, because its structure and layout are based on the simplicity of the UI structure. It does not have a clear enough theoretical principle to ensure the usability of the design and, indeed, is concerned very little with its usability [7]. Furthermore, it has been given a low priority in the design of UIs in general, and UI designers have considered it a practical matter that was burdensome [8]. Second, the criteria for the contents include the properties such as the function, operation, and meaning, etc, for users of the interface business events [9]. Third, the criteria for the task are based on practical or realistic tasks and scenarios that can be implemented by the UI. Various studies have been conducted to devise a set of criteria which can be applied to the design of the UI. The set of criteria used for the design is composed of 5 criteria, that is, the following VCs: 1) the basic efficiency that measures the expected efficiency of a task. 2) the task transparency that determines whether the design assures easy access to the properties. 3) the graphical uniformity of the UI layout, the uniformity of the layout that simplifies the complicity which measures to determine whether the regularity is configured simplistically. 4) the task consistency that determines whether the structure of the arrangement is appropriate to measure the expected frequency of the task and the difficulty (namely, the number of staff and length of the route) of the operation using the UI. 5) the VC that determines how much semantic relevance there is among the concepts related to the business event[10].

2.2 Criteria for VC

The VC of the UI is a new set of criteria which has been studied in relation to the UI contents, and is founded on the basis of the cohesion of the interface as defined using basic software engineering concepts. These criteria represent the VC of the UI based on the extension of the already well-established software engineering concepts, used to estimate the complexity of the UI, to its coherence. These criteria are based on the principle that semantically related elements in a large group of units can be combined, thereby promoting the understanding of each unit, reducing their inter-reliability and simplifying the overall structure[11, 12]. The VC includes the issue of how each unit is arranged and grouped, as well as the cohesion of the business events which appear in the programming unit. The interface will become easier to understand and use if the business events are grouped by their inter-relevance within the UI.

Constantine proposed an equation to estimate the VC [13]. This VC is represented by the ratio of the number of pairs related to visual business events to the number of business events. The summation of the VC in the form and dialogue box is the summation of the VC in the group of all levels.

$$VC = 100 \times \left(\frac{\sum_{\forall l} G_l}{\sum_{\forall l} N_l (N_l - 1)/2} \right) \quad \text{however, } G_l = \sum_{\forall i,j | i \neq j} R_{i,j}$$

N_l represents the number of business events in group l, $R_{i,j}$ represents the relevance between business event i and j in the same group (however, $0 \leq R_{i,j} \leq 1$)

$$VC = 100 \times \frac{\sum_{\forall f} G_f + \sum_{\forall t} G_t + \sum_{\forall r} G_r + \sum_{\forall p} G_p}{\sum_{\forall f} N_f (N_f - 1)/2 + \cdots + \sum_{\forall p} N_p (N_p - 1)/2}$$

($G_l = \sum_{\forall i,j | i \neq j} R_{i,j}$, f : business event object group, t : task object group, r : transaction object group, p : form object group)

Fig. 1. Equation to estimate the VC of object oriented design model

Fig. 1 shows the modified equation that is used to calculate the cohesion of multi-dimensional objects in a UI based on Constantine's cohesion calculation method. Because the cohesion has to be calculated for each object unit, the calculation method was defined to make it possible to calculate the VC by changing to object group. In general, subjective clustering is used to define the grouping, but the clustering of objects in this paper is based on the usability of business events, in order to ensure object oriented access. N_f represents the relevance of business event. N_t represents the relevance among business events. N_r symbolizes the relevance among business events in transaction object. N_p shows the relevance among business event groups. $R_{i,j}$ represents the semantic relevance(however, $0 \leq R_{i,j} \leq 1$) between the business events i and j in each group. If business events i and j are relevant, $R_{i,j}$. If no relevance exists, $R_{i,j} = 0$. VC calculated in this way leads to the estimation of the multi-dimensional VC and serves as the criteria to evaluate the quality of the UI [13].

In other words, the number of VCs increases if the grouping among relevant business events is good.

3 Interface Design by Classification

The object oriented model suggested in this paper is composed of 4 object models which can improve the VC of the UI, as shown in Fig. 2: 1) business event object, 2) task object, 3) transaction object, 4) form object model used to calculate the cohesion of the suggested object model and validate the improvement of cohesion compared to the existing design model. Therefore, the detailed objects of the UI are analyzed in terms of their similarity, relevance and transference of the business events in the UI in order to perform the clustering of the business events through the set of objects [14, 15]. This is because the visualization of objects patterned by clustering can lead to an improvement in the VC of the business events in the UI.

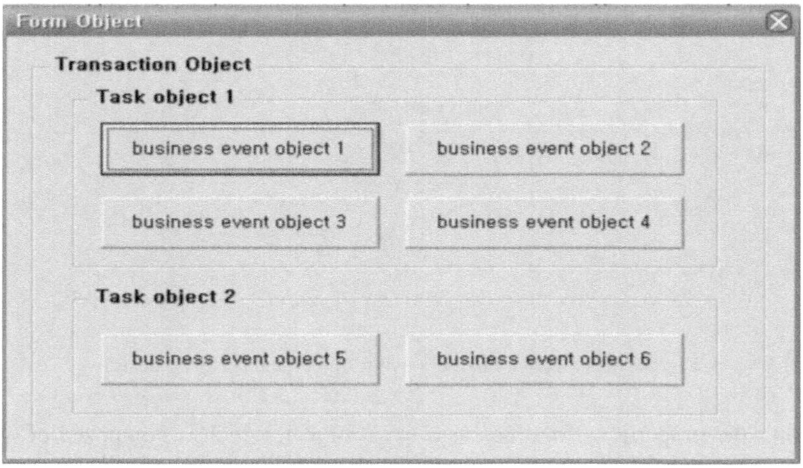

Fig. 2. Hierarchical structure of object oriented design model

3.1 Design of Business Event Object

The design of the business event object is the stage in which the object which represents the User Interface Business Event Object (hereafter referred to as UIBEO) is designed. The control pattern of the business event which comprises the transference data of the business event is designed in the UI. In other words, the designing operation of the business event includes the design of the business event controls, such as the radio buttons, combo boxes, check buttons, etc. The rules used to design the business event objects of the UIBEO are as follows.

<Rule 1> *the business event which has the number of instant limited to one business event is UIBEO.*

<Rule 2> *if the number of instance that can be fed to one business event is not regular, it is not the UIBEO.*

<Rule 3> *the item that can have the instance less than 7 at the maximum is the UIBEO that can use the radio button.*

<Rule 4> *the business event that can have over 8 instances is the UIBEO that can use the combo box.*

<Rule 5> *the item that can feed the instance of choice is the UIBEO that can use the check button.*

Fig. 3 shows the structure of the business event and the result of the design, according to the rules of business event object design.

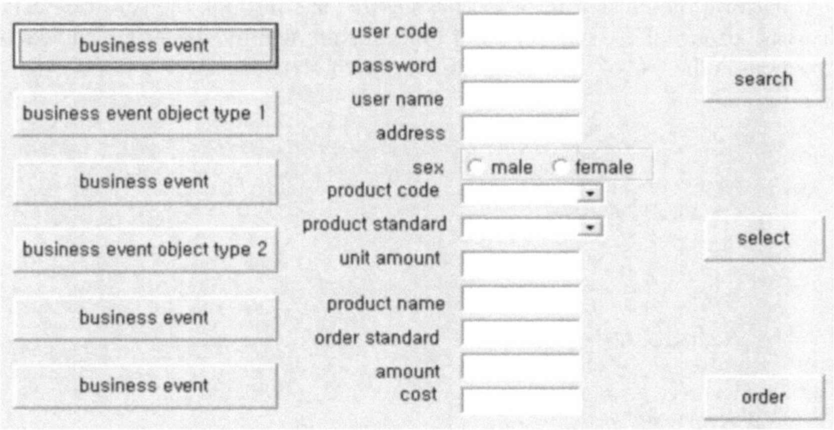

Fig. 3. Structures of business event object and result of design

It shows the properties of the business event object, which is composed of objects, product codes and an example of the product standard, in order to facilitate the understanding of the business event object. In other words, it is composed of radio buttons and product codes, whereas the product standard is designed using a combo box, showing that it is designed using business event objects capable of supporting users. This improves the cohesion of the business event by effectively modeling the function of the business event in the UI, and also enhances the reusability of instant data and functional cohesion within the UI.

3.2 Design of Task Object

The clustering of task objects is the design stage in which the objects that represent the User Interface Task Objects (hereafter referred to as UITO) are created. It is a clustering stage that enables the user to distinguish the set of task objects by modeling the block label composed of task units if there are more than 2 input or output business events which are transferred when the event occurs. The following is the rule related to the clustering of the set of task objects of the business event that is transferred to a task.

<Rule 1> *the business event which has the number of instant limited to one business event is UIBEO.*
<Rule 2> *the output UITO which has more than one record is the StringGrid bloc.*
<Rule 3> *the node which has more than one continual input business event is UITO.*
<Rule 4> *the node which has more than one continuous output business event is UITO.*

The business events are clustered and labeled by set of task objects in order to improve the communication cohesion and VC of the business event in the UI. Fig. 4 shows the structure of the task object and the result of the design. This provides the support needed to help users understand the business process composed of task units, thereby improving the VC and usability.

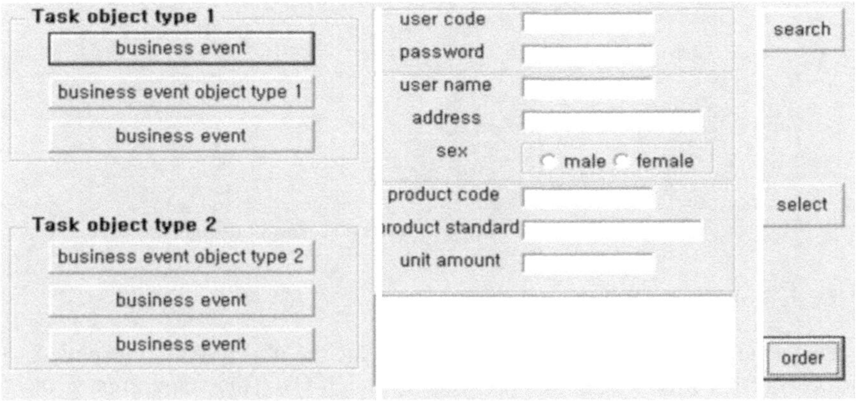

Fig. 4. Structure of task object and result of design

3.3 Design of Transaction Object

The design of the transaction object is the stage in which the object that represents the User Interface tRransaction Object (hereafter referred to as UIRO) is created. In other words, the UIRO is the clustering stage in which the group of business events composed of input-control-output events is grouped into the set of transaction objects. The transaction object is created by turning the request (input) and response (output) of the user into the block through one suite. The following is the rule used for clustering the set of transaction objects.

<Rule 1> *it is composed necessary of input task-button-output task, and the input task can be omitted if overlapping with the previous transaction.*
<Rule 2> *it can have more than one input task and output task.*
<Rule 3> *the input task is the beginning of UIRO, while the output task is the end of UIRO.*

The design of the transaction object, which is the stage in which the users are provided with the set of transaction objects, is the method of clustering the transaction objects that are grouped into 'task-control-output' tasks. This facilitates the understanding of the users by visualizing the transaction objects of the business events in the UI. In other words, it makes it easier for the users to understand the set of transactions in the Interface, by clustering the 'input task-control-output' tasks into one object unit for the sake of visualization. Fig. 5 shows the structure of the transaction object and the result of the design in the UI to promote the understanding of the transaction object.

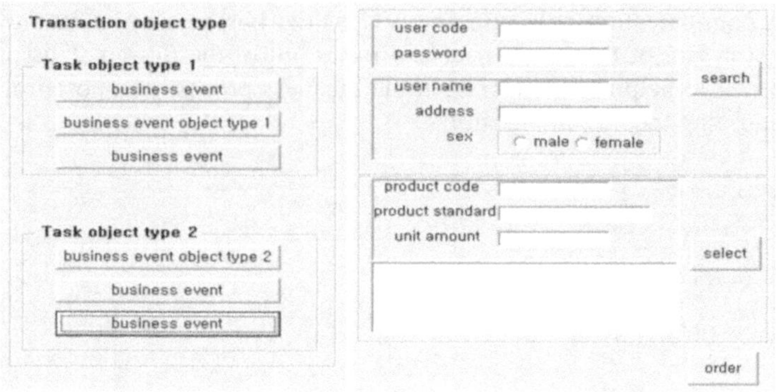

Fig. 5. Structure of transaction and result of design

3.4 Design of Form Object

The design stage of the form object serves to create the object that represents the User Interface Form Object (hereafter referred to as UIFO). This stage creates the form object by dividing the business events into the form in which they are presented in the UI. If the number of input/output business events exceeds 20 (criteria for human engineering) or the output form(or_state) is selected in more than one input and it is necessary to make the user clearly understand as in the case of Interrupt, it divides the objects into multiple forms. The following is the rule used for clustering the set of form objects.

<Rule 1> *the input/output objects exceed 20, and in case of different task, are divided into other form object.*
<Rule 2> *if the response to the demand is alternative, it is divided into different form object.*
<Rule 3> *if the result of event is Interrupt, it is divided into new form object.*
<Rule 4> *if it is the abstract object with same task though it exceeds 20 items, it cannot be divided into other form object.*
<Rule 5> *one task object can be divided into form object, and the transaction object gathers to become form object.*

The efficient design of the form provides the support needed to facilitate the development of the program and its maintenance/repair, by making it easy to understand the business process and reducing the complexity of the software. Fig. 6 shows the structure of the form object and the result of the design.

4 Evaluation of Proposed Model

The VCs of the designed models are compared and evaluated. The referenced design model used for the evaluation is designed in the form of a visual prototype of a non-functional screen layout, and the basic visual properties and business events were designed with the same number (of visual properties and business events) in order to

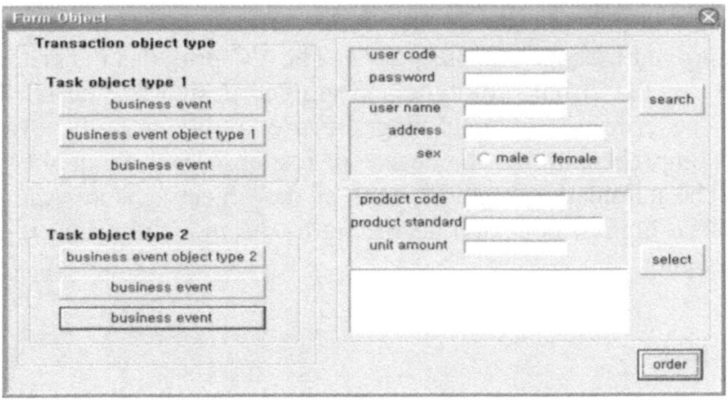

Fig. 6. Structure of form object and result of design

ensure the objective measurement of the result of this experiment. The equation used to calculate the VC in Fig. 1 was used to calculate the relevance and cohesion for the referenced design model which was designed in this way. Table 1 shows the outcome of the calculation of the relevance by pattern of this referenced design.

Table 1. Outcome of the calculation of relevance by referenced design model

Generalized design	$G_1=1, G_2=10, G_3=10, G_4=17$
	$N_1=2, N_2=5, N_3=5, N_4=16$
Structured design	$G_1=1, G_2=10, G_3=10, G_4=10, G_5=3, G_6=10, G_7=0$
	$N_1=2, N_2=5, N_3=5, N_4=5, N_5=3, N_6=5, N_7=6$
Object oriented design	$G_1=1, G_2=10, G_3=10, G_4=1, G_5=3, G_6=3, G_7=10, G_8=2, G_9=2, G_9=0$
	$N_1=2, N_2=5, N_3=5, N_4=2, N_5=3, N_6=3, N_7=5, N_8=3, N_9=3, N_{10}=3$

The number of instances of the product code and product standard were both assumed to be five.

The VC of the general design model was $N=4$, $N_1=2$, $N_2=5$, $N_3=5$, $N_4=16$, VC=27 was the lowest VC. The VC of the structured design model was N=7, and $N_1=2$, $N_2=5$, $N_3=5$, $N_4=5$, $N_5=3$, $N_6=5$, $N_7=6$, VC=74 was the intermediate level of VC. The VC of the object oriented design model was N=10 and $N_1=2$, $N_2=5$, $N_3=5$, $N_4=2$,

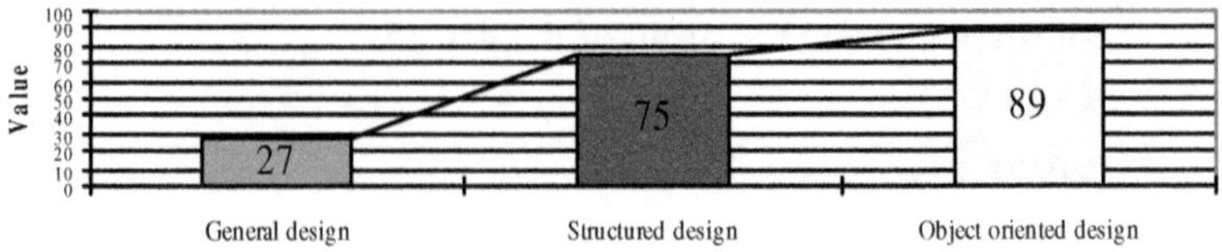

Fig. 7. Evaluation of VC of referenced design model

N_5=3, N_6=3, N_7=5, N_8=3, N_9=3, N_{10}=3, VC=89 was the highest VC. Therefore, the VC of the referenced design model can be compared as shown in Fig. 7.

It was found that the cohesion of the object oriented design model proposed in this paper was improved by approximately 14%. The VC provides the criteria for reviewing the quality of the visual prototype and graphic design for the UI. Moreover, the VC provides the criteria for forecasting the user preference, the evaluation of the easiness and comprehensibility, the degree of response, and the quality of the graphic layout [13]. The automatic graphic layout of the objects ensures the most efficient grouping and the highest cohesion according to the modeling rule, regardless of the skill of the designer.

5 Conclusion

In this paper, we suggest an interface design technique that considers the cohesion-rate by each object unit of user interface. To accomplish this, specific and detailed models to embody the user interface are presented on the basis of the following classification: 1) event object model, 2) task object model, 3) transaction object model, 4) form object model. Also, we studied the design rule and modeling technique of a UI that supports the user based on the improved VC. The findings of this study are as follows: First, the proposed method improves the VC by designing the objects of the UI on the basis of objects which are functional, consecutive and communicative. Second, it improves the user preference, easiness, comprehensibility, degree of response, and quality of the graphic layout on the basis of the improvement of the object based VC. Third, it improves the communicative, consecutive, and procedural cohesion of business events on the basis of the clustering of the UI objects. Fourth, it constitutes an object oriented designing method that can improve the comprehensibility of the business process and the usability of the UI on the basis of the visualization of the object pattern.

References

[1] Constantine, L.L., Lockwood, L.A.D.: Usage Centered Engineering for Web Applications. EEE Software 19(2), 42–50 March-April (2002)

[2] Lozano, M.D., Gonzalez, P., Ramos, I.:User Interface Specification and Modeling in an Object Oriented Environment for Automatic Software Development. In: Proceedings of the Technology of Object-Oriented Languages and Systems (TOOLS 34'00), pp. 373–381 (2000)

[3] Leszek, A.: Maciazek,Requirements Analysis and System Design, Addison Wesley, Mass (2001)
[4] Larry, L.: Constantine, Robert Biddle, and James Noble, Usage-centered Design and Software Engineering: Models for Integration, ICSE Workshop on SE-HCI 2003, pp. 106–113 (2003)
[5] Constantine, L.L., Lockwood, A.D.: Usage Centered Engineering for Web Applications. IEEE Software 19(2), 42–50 March-April (2002)
[6] Parush, A.: Whiteboard: Usability Design and Testing, ACM Interactions 8(5), 13–17 (2001)
[7] Harmelan, M.V.: Object Modeling an User Interface Design, Addison Wesley, Reading Mass (2001)
[8] Leszek, A.: Requirements Analysis and System Design. Addison Wesley, London, UK (2001)
[9] Bouillon, L., Limbourg, Q., Vanderdonckt, J., Michotte, B.: Reverse engineering of Web pages based on derivations and transformations. In: Proceedings of the Third Latin American Web Congress(LA-Web'05), pp. 3–14 (2005)
[10] Noble, J., Constantine, L.L: Interactive Design Metrics Visualization: Visual Metric Support for User Interface Design. In: Proceedings of the 6th Australian Conference on Computer-Human Interaction (OZCHI '96), pp. 213–220. IEEE Computer Society Press, Washington, DC, USA (1996)
[11] Robert, C.M.: The Interface Segregation Principle C++ Report (August 1996) http://www.objectmentor.com/resources/articles/dip.pdf
[12] Chidamber, S., Kemerer, C.: A Metrics Suite For Objected Oriented Design. IEEE Transaction on Software Engineering 20(6), 476–493 (1994)
[13] Constantine, L.L: Visual Coherence and Usability: A Cohesion Metric for Assessing the Quality of Dialogue and Screen Designs. In: Proceedings of the 6th Australian Conference on Computer-Human Interaction (OZCHI '96), pp. 115–121. IEEE Computer Society Press, Washington, DC, USA (1996)
[14] Knight, A., Dai, N.: Objects and the Web. IEEE Software 19(2), 51–59 (March-April 2002)
[15] Nerurkar, U.: Web User Interface Design, Forgotten Lessons. IEEE Software 18(6), 69–71 November-December (2002)

A Color Adjustment Method for Automatic Seamless Image Blending

Xianji Li and Dongho Kim

Department of Digital Media, Graduate School of Soongsil University
511 Sangdo-dong, Dongjak-gu, Seoul, Korea
{lixianji1120,dkim}@ssu.ac.kr

Abstract. In this paper we present a stable automatic system for image composition, which can well control the color difference between two images, and produce a seamless composite image with color continuity. This is a user-friendly system that reduces the user's manual tasks. We observe that Poisson image editing written by Perez et al. [8] blends well for seamless boundary automatically. However, the color of user-selected region can be changed after applying this method. So the object loses its original color tone after blending. To solve this problem, firstly we check out the case of object color being changed rapidly. It can be done by calculating color temperatures of two input images and comparing the white balance with each other. Next, a distance ratio rule is applied to controls the pixels included in the region between the user-selected boundary and object boundary.

Keywords: image composition, Poisson Image Editing, object color, color temperatures, distance ratio rule.

1 Introduction

Image processing is used widely by graphic designers and also used in other computer graphics field. A lot of researches have approached the field of image processing. In the image processing field, image composition is a process of creating a new image by pasting an object or region from the source image onto the target image. In general, there are no considerations of color adjustment for the image composition tasks that are done by automatic techniques.

Recently, Poisson image editing [8] using Poisson equation has been proposed as an effective approach for seamless composition, with which user can obtain results without visible discontinuity around the boundary [Figure 1-(c)].

We observe that Poisson image editing shows effectiveness only depending on seamless boundary, not color control. In this method, object color tone of the result is matched with target image tone. However, the results may not be acceptable in some cases because the object color tone changes too rapidly. In Figure 1 (d), after applying Poisson editing method, the dog in the source image loses not only its color but also its contrast. Importantly, the color of user-specified field in the result is not matched to the background. So there must be some methods to solve these problems.

J. Jacko (Ed.): Human-Computer Interaction, Part II, HCII 2007, LNCS 4551, pp. 82–91, 2007.

Fig. 1. Dog and flowers: (a) source image (b) Target image (c) User-selected and object boundary. (d) Result of Poisson editing (e) The result from manual cutting. (f) Result of our method. (g) Enlarged subimage in the belt region that matches both background and object.

In this paper, we propose a user-friendly method that solves the color changing problem. Here, we only give consideration to the case where the object region in the compound image needs to preserve its original color tone such as human image compositions.

Every digital image has its own color temperature. If the color temperatures of two images differ a lot, it means that the color tones of two images are much different. In this case the result of Poisson Image Editing may generate a new composite image whose object color is changed seriously. Before applying the method for preserving object color, we firstly calculate the color temperatures of the source image and the target image to estimate whether it is necessary to apply the ratio rule to preserve the object color of the source image.

Based on the color temperature measurement, if the composition requires the adjustment of color propagation, we employ our method to preserve object colors in image composition. We generate two types of compositing images, one is the result from Poisson Image Editing, and the other is from Poisson Image Editing processed with multiple boundaries. We define the external region of the object in the user-specified field as a belt region, where the distance ratio of every pixel is calculated. According to the ratio, every pixel in the belt region is blended by color information from two compositing images.

2 Related Works

In this section we describe some works related to image composition. Image matting, a similar task to image composition is a common way to extract an object from the source image to paste onto the target image naturally using alpha channel. It uses a trimap to estimate the alpha channel and the foreground color. There has been a lot of work on image matting [1] [10].

In image composition, multi-resolution spline technique[2] has been used to seamlessly blend two different images through the interpolation at different levels of Laplacian pyramids. Poisson image editing [8] blends two images through Poisson equations with user-selected field.

Image stitching in gradient domain [6] has been proposed to reduce the artifacts caused by manual alignment in stitch two images as in panorama.

Moreover, image cutting such as Grab Cut [9] and Lazy Snapping [7] can also be applied to image composition by cutting foreground region automatically from one image. Recently, detecting optical boundary algorithm named Drag and Drop Pasting [4] for Poisson image editing is based on these images cutting technique.

3 Checking Color Temperature Condition of the Image

This section explains the process about checking color tone condition of two images in order to determine the necessity of applying our new method when two images are blended by Poisson Image Editing.

Every digital image has its own color temperature value. It is determined when the scene is captured by the camera. In the different color temperature condition, the camera expresses the color tone differently. If the two images have different color tones, the color temperatures of the two images must be different. We estimate the color temperature of two images and compare the temperature value with each other in order to check whether the color tones of the two input images are similar.

In the RGB color system, the color information is not enough to describe the image property such as color temperature. We analyze the input image in CIE XYZ chromaticity coordinate to estimate the color temperature of the image. We convert the input image from RGB space to CIE XYZ space in order to get color chromaticity of image. Then, we can compute color temperature by CIE-chromaticity diagram.

$$\begin{bmatrix} X \\ Y \\ Z \end{bmatrix} = \begin{bmatrix} 0.43057 & 0.341550 & 0.178325 \\ 0.222015 & 0.706655 & 0.071330 \\ 0.020183 & 0.129553 & 0.939180 \end{bmatrix} \begin{bmatrix} R \\ G \\ B \end{bmatrix} \quad (1)$$

Next, we can get the representative chromaticity coordinate value (x_s, y_s). Here, X_{ave}, Y_{ave}, Z_{ave} is average value of the chromaticity XYZ from every pixel.

$$x_s = \frac{X_{ave}}{X_{ave} + Y_{ave} + Z_{ave}} \qquad y_s = \frac{Y_{ave}}{X_{ave} + Y_{ave} + Z_{ave}} \quad (2)$$

Fig. 2. Dogs: (a) Source image whose color temperature is 5900k (b) Target image whose color temperature is 5500k. (c) Target image whose color temperature is 5200k. (d) Poisson Image Editing result of the image-a and the image-b that the case when the difference value of color temperature is less than 500k. (e) Poisson Image Editing result of the image-a and image-c that the object color changed and the difference value of color temperature is more than 500k.

We use Robertson's method which defines 31 isotemperature lines to compute out the color temperatures by (x,y) chromaticity value of the image [12]. In this method, two neighboring lines connected with chromaticity values of the input image are found and the temperature is computed by interpolation method.

Using the proposed method above, two temperature values of the source image and target image are computed and compared with each other in other to check the necessity of applying the color ratio rule or not.

In the checking process, we don't need to compare the source image with the target image by the precise values of color temperature. We tested five dissimilar sets of image and found out the fact that the object color was not changed distinguishably when the difference of the color temperatures of the two images is less than 500k.

Shown as figure 2, the color temperature of the source image is 5900k. When the color temperature value of the target image is 5500k the object does not lose its own color. We can skip the next procedure in this case. But in the case of figure 2(c), the color temperature of target image is 5200k and the object color is changed in the result image after Poisson Image Editing. In this case, we apply our new blending method to solve the color changing problem.

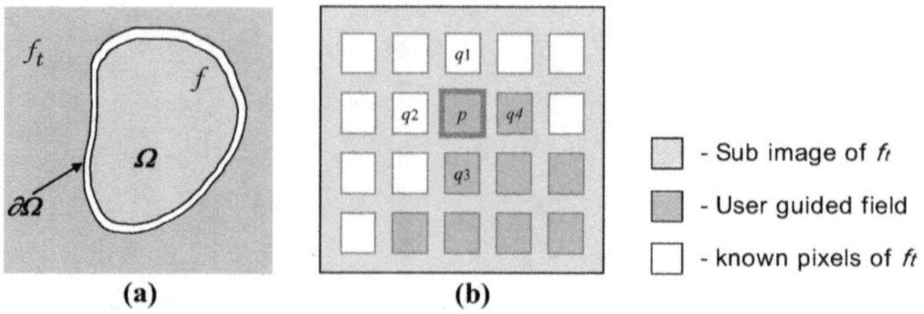

Fig. 3. Image interpolation (a) Unknown function f interpolates in domain Ω the destination image function f_t, based on the vector field of U. (b) P belongs to Ω and has four 4-connected neighboring pixels. White blocks are known pixels.

4 Blending with Object Color Preservation

We extract the case that the object color in the result image changes a lot when Poisson Image Editing method is applied to blend the images. If it is the case, it is needed to go through the step of our color preservation method in the composition process.

4.1 Poisson Image Editing

In this section we explain on Poisson image editing for interpolating the selected region.

Figure 3(a) shows the notations that blends user-selected region Ω. The vector field **V** is a user selected field from source image f_s. f is an unknown scalar function field among the exterior boundary $\partial\Omega$ of region Ω in the target image f_t.

This composition goes on with solving minimization problem of vector field variation. User-selected field U expressed as vector field $\mathbf{V} = \nabla$ U is settled on Ω region of target image with minimum color variation.

$$\min_f \iint_\Omega |\nabla f - \mathrm{v}|^2 \; with \; f|_{\partial\Omega} = f_t|_{\partial\Omega} \tag{3}$$

To solve equation 3 is to solve unknown function f at the boundary $\partial\Omega$. Vector field **V** is a gradient function of user-specified region U on the source image. It can be expressed as $\mathbf{V} = (u, v)$. ∇ is the gradient operator.

In equation 3, Poisson equation is applied for solving function f which satisfies equation 3. We denote it as more concise equation.

$$\Delta f = div\,\mathrm{v} \quad with\, f|_{\partial\Omega} = f_t|_{\partial\Omega} \tag{4}$$

Every pixel belongs to function f is called f_p. Pixel function f_p which satisfies equation 4 calculates pixel values in Ω by divergence method. In Figure 3(b), p is a pixel in the Ω region, (q_1, q_2, q_3, q_4) denote 4-connected neighbor pixels around p. $\mathbf{V}_p$ is vector field value of corresponding pixel p. Depending on equation 4 the following equation 5 is solved.

$$(f_{q1} - f_p) + (f_{q2} - f_p) + (f_{q3} - f_p) + (f_{q4} - f_p) = div\ \mathbf{v}_p \quad (5)$$

Shown as Figure 3(b), q_1 and q_2 are already known pixels around pixel p. Based from RGB color of q1, q_2, unknown pixel p is calculated by the divergence of $\mathbf{V}_P$. Every unknown pixel p is also applied to set values with the same method. The calculation goes on with sparse algebraic system which is useful to solve divergences problem.

Observing the solution of above algorithm, the pixel colors of the blending region are set from target image pixels colors at $\partial\Omega$. Because of that, the boundary of selected region can blend seamlessly. However, the object in blended region loses its original color and contrast as in Figure 1 (c).

In order to maintain object color, we need an effective method which can preserve the original color while blending boundary around the object field seamlessly.

4.2 Computation of Two Compositing Image Fields

In the process of image composition, the user can draw the boundary roughly outside the object. There is a gap region like a belt between the object boundary and the user-drawn boundary. We must blend this region seamlessly so that the region both matches the object field and external user-selected boundary field of the target image [Figure 1(f)].

There exist two different types of boundary in the U region. One is the user-drawn boundary defined as $\partial\Omega_u$, and the other is the object boundary defined as $\partial\Omega_{obj}$. Interactive segmentation techniques can be used in creating object boundary $\partial\Omega_{obj}$ once $\partial\Omega_u$ is given. In this paper, Ω_{obj} region is automatically computed by GrabCut [9] using Ω as initialization. Note that Ω is separated to Ω_u and Ω_{obj} fields in Figure 4.

Applying Poisson image editing, we first create the compositing image whose object field is changed [Figure 5 (b)]. The result from original Poisson image editing is defined as I_1.

Next we separate Ω region into two independent regions Ω_u and Ω_{obj}. Separated region Ω_u and Ω_{obj} are applied to Poisson method independently with different conditions. We retain the following color function:

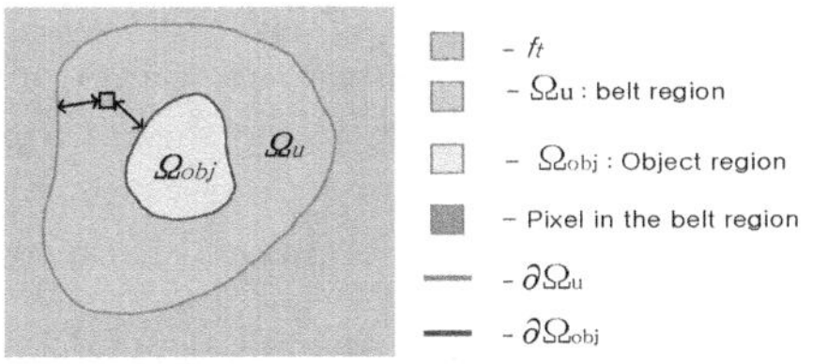

Fig. 4. Domain structure: User selected boundary domain Ω can separate to Ωobj and Ωu by $\partial\Omega obj$. We also call Ωu as belt region.

$$C_{start} = \begin{cases} C_{f_s} & \text{where } p(x,y) \subset \Omega_{obj} \\ C_{f_t} & \text{where } p(x,y) \subset \Omega_u \end{cases} \quad (6)$$

Fig. 5. Flowers (a) shows source and target images. (b)The result of Poisson composition named I_1. (c)The result based on two boundaries, defined as I_2. (d) Enlarged sub image of I_2 that is not seamless.

C_{start} is the basis color applied to the vector field. If pixel p lies on the Ωobj region, the starting color extracted from the source image on $\partial\Omega obj$ is settled on pixel p. Otherwise, we get starting color from target image on the $\partial\Omega u$. We define this special image as I_2 [Figure 5 (c)].

4.3 Color Blending Algorithm

This section continues to explain how to keep the object color with image I_1 and I_2. In Figure 5 (c), the object color of I_2 is preserved completely as source object. However, the belt region of result is not blended seamlessly blended with the background. We need prudent solution to create satisfying result.

Because I_2 keeps the original color of the source image, we just give attention to the belt region Ωu so as to compute the seamless composition. It is clear we recognized that I_1 is well matching to outside environment of target image, and I_2 is well preserving the object color from source image. Using these properties, we apply new interpolation scheme on the belt region Ωu.

First for every pixel p, minimum distance is computed from two boundaries:

$$\begin{aligned} D_{obj}(x,y) &= \min_{\mathrm{i,j}}(\mathrm{dist}(\mathrm{P_{obj}}(i,j), P(x,y))), where \mathrm{P_{obj}}(i,j) \in \partial\Omega_{obj} \\ D_u(x,y) &= \min_{\mathrm{i,j}}(\mathrm{dist}(\mathrm{P_u}(i,j), P(x,y))), where \mathrm{P_u}(i,j) \in \partial\Omega_u \end{aligned} \tag{7}$$

P(x, y) indicates the pixels in the belt region of interest. P_{obj} and P_u denote the pixels on the object boundary and the user-selected boundary. dist (p_1, p_2) is the distance between two pixels p_1 and p_2. Then D_{obj} and D_u are minimum values of the distance from P(x, y) to boundary pixels. We define the distance ratio as $\boldsymbol{r} = \boldsymbol{D}_u / (\boldsymbol{D}_{obj} + \boldsymbol{D}_u)$.

Every pixel in the belt region has its own distance ratio. The pixel closer to the user-drawn boundary than the object boundary is blended by color of I_1 with higher ratio and by color of I_2 with lower ratio. In order to blend by more smooth variation, we interpolate the ratio with the following function instead of normal ratio function [Figure 6].

$$R(\boldsymbol{r}) = (\sin(\pi \boldsymbol{r} - \pi/2) + 1)/2 \quad (8)$$

Final colors for the pixels in Ωu are computed as follows.

$$C_{O(x,y)} = (1 - R(r)) \cdot C_{I_1(x,y)} + R(r) \cdot C_{I_2(x,y)} \quad (9)$$

$C_{I1(x,y)}$ is the color from I_1 matched with background color tone, and $C_{I2(x,y)}$ is the color from I_2 matched with object color tone. Two colors for every pixel are blended with easeful ratio and generate an effective seamless belt region.

This solution takes well attention to the object colors in the source image, while generating more convincing results with proper colors.

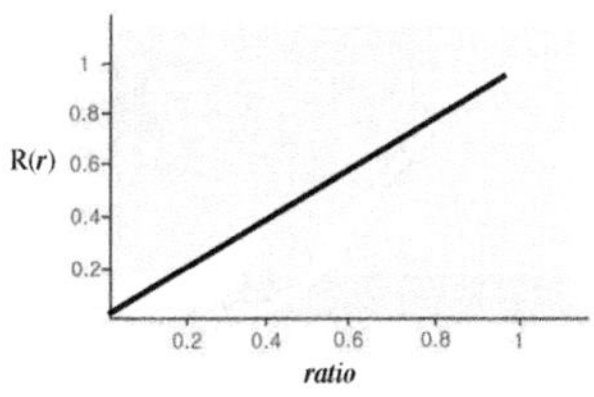

(a)

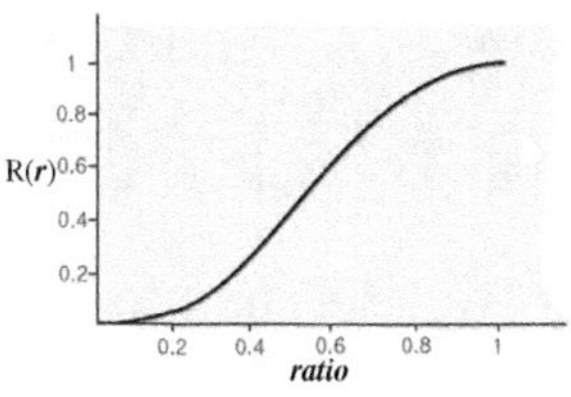

(b)

Fig. 6. Interpolation Curve of Distance Ratio (a) Linear interpolation with ***r*** (b) Ease-in ease-out interpolation of ***r***

5 Experimental Results

We applied Magic Blending method proposed in this paper on variety of source and target images whose object colors need to be preserved, and compared the results with Poisson image editing results.

Figure 1 shows result after pasting white dog from source image to the other image environment. (d) is the result of Poisson image editing. We can observe that the white dog change to green dog after processing. Using image (d) and (e), our method computes the blending result as in (f).

Figure 7 shows a result of human figure composition. Our method prevents the face color from being changed while Poisson editing does not.

In the figure 8, we can observe that the object loses its color and contrast in the result of Poisson Image Editing. The result image is unnatural because the color and contrast information are damaged.

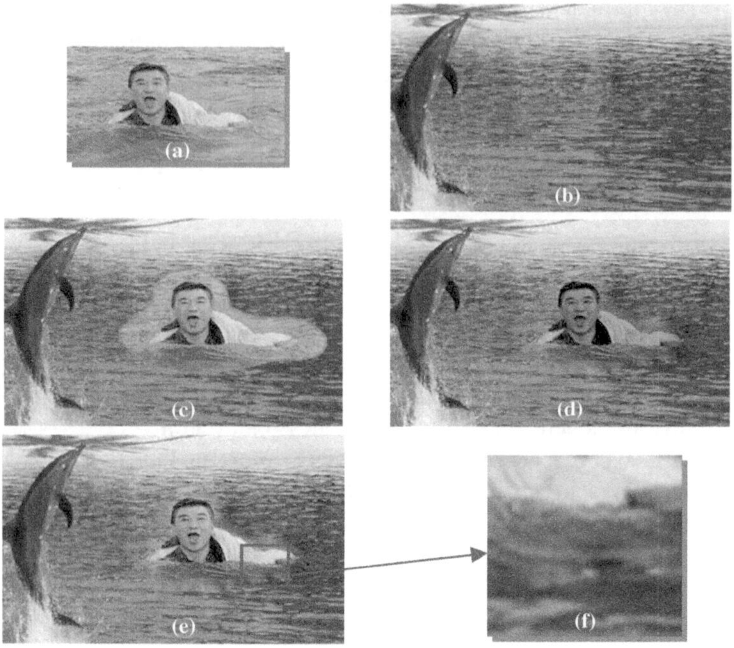

Fig. 7. Swimming: (a) Source image (b) Target image (c) Two types of boundaries (d) Poisson image composition where the face color is changed (e) The result of our method (f) Enlarged subimage of the belt region showing that colors are blended smoothly

Fig. 8. On the Lake: (a) Source image (b) Target image (c) The result of Poisson Image Editing. (d) The result of using our method.

6 Conclusion

This paper is about image composition for the case when preserving object color is needed. When we use existing techniques, changing all colors of compositing region after image composition sometimes makes objects to be non-realistic in the result image. Our method solved this problem of existing techniques. In this paper, using the color temperature value of two input images, we check the case that can apply our method. Then the color blending method is applied in order to preserve object color and make the belt region blending seamlessly.

In our method the users should draw a boundary line similar to the object shape around the object boundary; otherwise, the belt region of the result image maybe blended unnaturally. Imbalanced condition of belt region's thickness is not enough effective than common condition. We are planning to solve this problem as future research.

In addition, optimal boundary algorithm [4] may also be applied to our method in order to define better boundary conditions.

Acknowledgments. This work was supported by the Soongsil University Research Fund.

References

1. Berman, A., Vlahos, P., Dadourian, A.: Comprehensive method for removing from an image the background surrounding a selected object. U.S. Patent 6, 134, 345
2. Burt, P.J., Adelson,: multiresolution spline with application to image mosaics. In. ACM Transactions on Graphics 2, 217–236 (1983)
3. Ballester, C., Bertalmio, M., Caselles, V.: Filling-In by Joint Interpolation of Vector Fields and Gray Levels. AUGUST. IEEE TRANSACTIONS ON IMAGE PROCESSING vol. 10(8) (2001)
4. Jia, J., Tian, S., C.-K.: H.-Y.: Drag-and-Drop Pasting. In: ACM SIGGRAPH conference proceedings (2006)
5. Jia, J., Tang, -K.: Eliminating structure and intensity misalignment in image stitching. In: Proceedings of ICCV (2005)
6. Levin, A., Zomet, A., Peleg, S., Weiss, Y.: Seamless image stitching in the gradient domain. In: Pajdla, T., Matas, J(G.) (eds.) ECCV 2004. LNCS, vol. 3024, pp. 377–389. Springer, Heidelberg (2004)
7. Li, Y., Sun, J., Tang, C., Shum, H.: Lazy Snapping. April. ACM Transaction on Graphics vol. 23(3) (2004)
8. Perez, P., Gangnet, M., Blake, A.: Poisson image editing. In: Proceedings of ACM SIGGRAPH, pp. 313–318 (2003)
9. Rother, C., Kolmogorov, V., Blake, A.: grabcut - interactive foreground extraction using iterated graph cut. In: Proceedings of ACM SIGGRAPH, pp. 309–314 (2004)
10. Ruzon, M., Tomasi, C.: Alpha estimation in natural images. In: Proceedings of CVPR00 (2000)
11. Sun, J., Jia. J., Tang, C., Shum, H.: Poisson matting. In: Proceedings of ACM SIGGRAPH, pp. 315–321 (2004)
12. Wyszecki, G., Stiles, W.S.: Color Science: Concepts and Methods, Quantitative Data and Formulae. John Wiley & Sons, Inc. (1982)

Interactive Visual Decision Tree Classification

Yan Liu[1,*] and Gavriel Salvendy[2]

[1] Department of Biomedical, Industrial, and Human Factors Engineering, Wright State University, Dayton, OH 45435
[2] School of Industrial Engineering, Purdue University, West Lafayette, IN 47906
Department of Industrial Engineering, Tsinghua University, Beijing, P.R. China, 100084
yan.liu@wright.edu

Abstract. Data mining (DM) modeling is a process of transforming information enfolded in a dataset into a form amenable to human cognition. Most current DM tools only support automatic modeling, during which uses have little interaction with computing machines other than assigning some parameter values at the beginning of the process. Arbitrary selection of parameter values, however, can lead to an unproductive modeling process. Automatic modeling also downplays the key roles played by humans in current knowledge discovery systems. Classification is the process of finding models that distinguish data classes in order to predict the class of objects whose class labels are unknown. Decision tree is one of the most widely used classification tools. A novel interactive visual decision tree (IVDT) classification process has been proposed in this research; it aims to facilitate decision tree classification process regarding enhancing users' understanding and improving the effectiveness of the process by combining the flexibility, creativity, and general knowledge of humans with the enormous storage capacity and computational power of computers. An IVDT for categorical input attributes has been developed and experimented on twenty subjects to test three hypotheses regarding its potential advantages. The experimental results suggested that compared to the automatic modeling process as typically applied in current decision tree modeling tools, IVDT process can improve the effectiveness of modeling in terms of producing trees with relatively high classification accuracies and small sizes, enhance users' understanding of the algorithm, and give them greater satisfaction with the task.

Keywords: visual data mining, interactive modeling, model visualization, data visualization.

1 Introduction

The amount of data stored in corporate and scientific databases is exploding, far exceeding humans' abilities to capture and analyze without using powerful tools. Raw data by themselves, however, do not provide much information. Therefore, unless advanced knowledge discovery techniques are developed, organizations risk losing

[*] Corresponding author.

J. Jacko (Ed.): Human-Computer Interaction, Part II, HCII 2007, LNCS 4551, pp. 92–105, 2007.

much valuable information from the data they have collected and stored. Many people view data mining (DM) as a synonym for another widely used term, knowledge discovery in databases (KDD). A widely accepted definition of KDD is given in Fayyad et al [1], i.e., the non-trivial process of identifying valid, novel, potentially useful, and ultimately understandable patterns in data. Modeling is the crucial step in DM where information enfolded in a prepared dataset is transformed into a form amenable to human cognition [2]. During this process, selected DM algorithms are applied to the sampled preprocessed dataset in order to extract data patterns or build models.

Visual data mining (VDM) has become an active research area recently. VDM can be viewed as an integration of visualization and traditional DM techniques, such as visualizing raw data to help users discovering data characteristics, visualizing models obtained from modeling to enhance understanding of the derived patterns, and visualizing DM process during which models are induced. Many researchers have argued that visualization can be integrated with nonvisual techniques to greatly enhance the effectiveness and efficiency of a DM process [3, 4]. The accuracy of a model is only one measure that can be used to value its worth. The ability to interpret the model to domain experts and decision makers and the ease of implementation and maintenance are other important factors. Without proper visualization techniques, data mining models, although a reduced form of original data, may not give the desired insight to help humans understand the phenomena of interest [5]. However, visualization for DM modeling means more than representation; it should also be a means of involving users in the process of model construction. Through such involvement, users can gain a much better understanding of how the model is built in the context of the data samples and its applicability to their concerns. In addition, model construction can become more efficient when users take advantage of their background knowledge and pattern recognition ability to direct the learning of the algorithm when the situation warrants. Because some DM algorithms are highly susceptible to noise in the data, incorporating human background knowledge is a promising approach to avoiding overfitting and handling accuracy versus comprehensibility trade-offs in modeling [6]. Within these considerations, this paper aims to study how visualization techniques should be used to support DM modeling process. Since the applied visualization techniques depend on the selected modeling tools, this paper focuses on the decision trees classification, one of the most popular DM techniques. Classification is a process of finding models that distinguish data classes in order to predict the class of objects whose class labels are unknown.

The remainder of this paper is organized as follows. Section 2 gives a brief overview of the decision tree classification process. Section 3 reviews related research on visualization applied in decision trees classification. A proposed design of interactive visual decision tree (IVDT) classification is described in section 4. Section 5 describes an experiment that has been conducted to test three hypotheses apropos the proposed IVDT classification. Section 6 offers conclusions of this study.

2 Overview of Decision Trees Classification

As its name implies, a decision tree can be viewed a classifier in the form of a tree structure, in which each node is either a leaf node or decision node. All decision nodes have splits, testing the values of some functions of data attributes. Each branch from the decision node corresponds to a distinct outcome of the test. Each leaf node has a class label attached to it.

The most crucial issues in decision tree classification modeling are selecting the splits and determining the size of the tree. There are many goodness measures of splits which indicate their classification power, such as information gain [7] and Gini index of diversity [8]. An overly large tree is difficult for humans to understand and hence deteriorating its interpretability. In addition, a large tree can become fragmented, having many leaf nodes with few cases. Such leaf nodes are likely to be influenced by noise and thus causing overfitting problems when the tree captures both the target features and noise. Pruning is an often applied method for obtaining right-sized trees [9].

Although a variety of decision tree algorithms have been developed with different capabilities and requirements, most are variations of a core learning algorithm that employs a "greedy" top-down search through the space of possible decision trees, the most commonly used method for tree construction today. The basic strategy is as follows:

1. Start with an empty tree and the entire training set.
2. If all training samples at the current node *n* are of the same class *c*, then the node becomes a leaf node with *c*.
3. Otherwise, select the splitting attribute *s* that is the most useful in separating the samples into distinct classes based on some goodness measure of splits. This attribute becomes a decision node, and a branch is created for each distinct values of *s*, and the samples are partitioned accordingly.
4. The process is conducted recursively until the criterion of some stop rule is reached, such as all samples for *n* belong to the same class, no attribute can be further partitioned, or the improvement is not substantial enough to justify the further splitting.

3 Related Work on Visualization Support to Decision Trees Classification

This section focuses on reviews of previous research on visualization of decision trees and interactive decision trees classification.

3.1 Visualization of Decision Trees

A decision tree contains two kinds of information: the overall structure of the tree (such as the number of layers, decision nodes and leaf nodes, and relationships among nodes) and content information associated with each node and split (such as the number of records and distribution of the class attribute in each node). A number of visualization formats have been applied to represent trees or hierarchical information, such as outline views, node-link diagrams, tree-maps, tree-rings, and icicle-plots, illustrated in Fig. 1 in which each tree has 3 decision nodes and 4 leaf nodes (D_i and L_j represent ith decision node and jth leaf node, respectively).

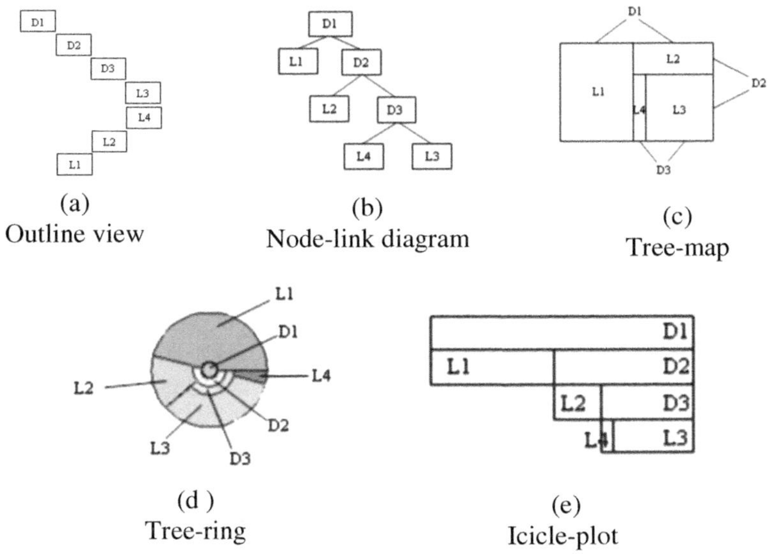

Fig. 1. Visual representations of decision trees (D_i and L_j represent ith decision node and jth leaf node, respectively)

The outline view of a tree is similar to the way in which files are organized in windows explorer, showing different levels of the tree through indention, as illustrated in Fig. 1(a). This representation is useful in revealing the hierarchical relationships among the nodes in the tree, but it is poor in demonstrating the overall structure of the tree such as its depth levels and the number of leaf nodes [10].

The node-link diagrams are probably the most popular and familiar tree structures and applied in most DM softwares [11, 12]. A major problem with the typical node-link diagrams is that they do not use the available space economically and thus are not suitable for displaying trees with large sizes.

Tree-maps and tree-rings are space-filling representations in that they make full use of the available display space. A tree-map is constructed via recursive subdivision of the initial rectangle horizontally and vertically, and the size of each sub-rectangle is proportional to the number of cases in its corresponding node [13]. Tree-rings map the hierarchies into circles with the most inner circle representing the root node, and the area of a circle segment is proportional to the frequency of its corresponding node [11].

The icicle-plot represents a tree node as a rectangle whose length is proportional to the number of cases associated with it [13]. There are no links between nodes, so this method is more space-efficient than the node-link diagrams.

Two experiments were conducted in Barlow and Neville [13] to compare the 2D node-link diagram, tree-map, tree-ring, and icicle-plot in terms of ease of identification of tree topology, ease of identification of node relationships, ease of identification of leaf sizes, and user preference. The experiment results suggested that the icicle-plot was superior to or as good as other representations in terms of the three identification tasks and user preference, and the tree-map was inferior to other representations in all these four aspects.

3.2 Interactive Decision Trees Classification

Several studies have been conducted on design of interactive decision tree classification. Ankerst et al. [15] and Ankerst et al. [16] constructed decision trees with univariate splits, in which data were visualized using circle segment pixel-based and bar pixel-based graphs, respectively. In these graphs, each segment or bar corresponded to an input attribute in which attribute values were sorted and mapped to pixels in a line-by-line fashion according to their orders; the color of a data point indicated its class label. They both supported n-ary (n>2) splits as well as binary splits. Ware et al. [17] and Poulet [18] produced bivariate decision trees and only binary splits were allowed in these two studies. In [17], a bar chart, similar to the one used in [16], was provided to help users select the two attributes to be visualized in the form of scatterplot, and the users chose split points by drawing a polyline or polygon in the scatterplot. In [18], a scatterplot matrix was used to assist users in selecting the two split attributes and the split regions were formed by drawing a straight line in the 2D space of the split attributes.

However, these studies, except [16], only dealt with continuous input attributes. Besides, none of them provided enough details of the experiments conducted to test their proposed design and no statistical analysis of the experimental results were reported.

4 Proposed Design of Interactive Visual Decision Tree Classification

Although categorical attributes were taken into consideration in [16], only binary splits were allowed in these attributes. Categorical data are often collected in social and behavior sciences, and visualization of these data remains a challenge. Within this context, therefore, a novel visual interactive decision tree classification for categorical input attributes is developed in this paper.

A dataset adapted from the German credit dataset in the Stalog database, retrieved from the University of California Irvine (UCI) machine learning repository [19], is used to illustrate the following discussions. Ten input attributes in the original dataset are chosen because of their relatively high correlation with "credit status" which is the target class attribute: "status of checking account", "duration", "credit history", "purpose", "credit amount", "savings account", "present employment", "property", "other installment", and "housing". The numeric attributes "duration" and "credit amount" in the original dataset are divided into four categories, and some categories of the "purpose" attribute in the original dataset are grouped because of their similarities in nature, which results in seven categories in the "purpose" attribute in the modified dataset.

In this paper, trees are visualized using the icicle plot structure, shown in Fig. 2, because of its several desirable merits stated in section 3.1, in particular, its familiarity to most users, ease of identification of tree topology, node relationships, and node sizes, and relative effectiveness in space usage. In Fig. 2, each node of the model is represented as a horizontal bar whose length is proportional to the number of records in it, and the exact number of records and percentage in the dataset that correspond to a node can be viewed by placing the mouse over its bar. If the entire dataset is divided into training and validation datasets for the purpose of evaluating the model, then information in both datasets is shown (the top row is for the training and the bottom row is for the validation). The numbers enclosed in the braces at the top of the bars are the split groups. The narrower horizontal bars underneath each node visualize the distribution of the class attribute. In Fig. 2, the green and red bars represent the good and bad credit customers, respectively. The length of each bar is proportional to the number of records in its corresponding class and the exact number of records and percentages in it can be viewed by placing the mouse over the bar.

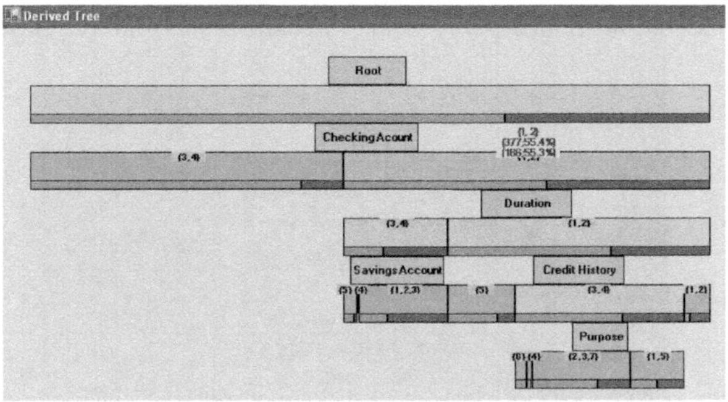

Fig. 2. Icicle plot representation of trees applied in the visual interactive decision tree classification process

Fig. 3 illustrates the data visualization approach employed in this study, which is a combination of two well-known visualization techniques: parallel coordinates [20] and mosaic displays [21]. Each attribute corresponds to a horizontal bar which is divided horizontally into sections, each for one category. The length of each section is proportional to the number of records in its associated category. The exact number and percentages of records in each category and its description can be viewed by placing the mouse over its section. Each section is further divided vertically into subsections, each for one class, and the height of each subsection is proportional to the number of records in its associated class. This strategy allows the user to quickly view how the distribution of the class attribute varies across categories in an attribute which indicates its classification power because more variations suggest higher classification power. The exact number and percentages of records in each class can be viewed by clicking its subsection.

In the IVDT process, the tree construction starts with the entire dataset and an empty tree with only the root node. The computer displays visualization of the current tree structure and distribution of the class attribute in the root node and visualization of data corresponding to the root node to help the user to decide whether the root node should be a leaf node or decision node. If it is a decision node, then the computer provides visualization of data corresponding to the node and goodness measures of

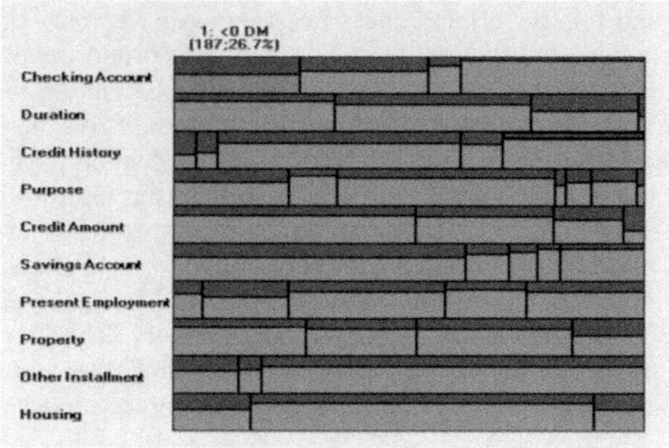

Fig. 3. Data visualization applied in the visual interactive decision tree classification process

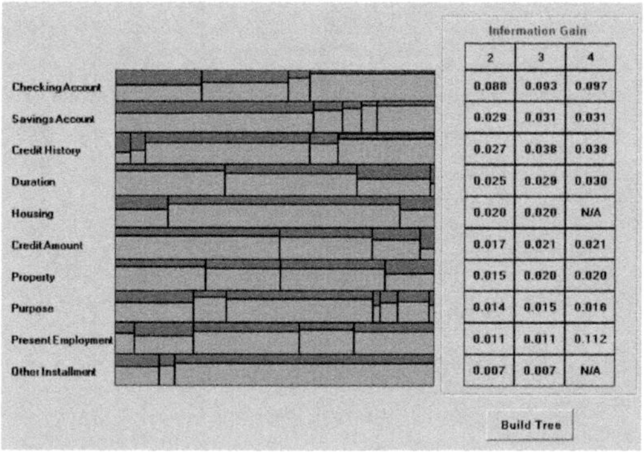

Fig. 4. Visualization of the data and the table of information gain of splits of the German Credit dataset

splits of the input attributes calculated by the applied algorithm to assist users to select a desirable split, as illustrated in Fig. 4. In Fig. 4, a table of information gain of splits is provided although other goodness measures, such as Chi-square and Gini index, could also be used. Each row of the table corresponds to its aligned attribute in the data visualization on the left and each column the number of branches in splits. The grouping in each split can be viewed by placing the mouse over its cell. The attributes are ordered by the information gain of their two-branch splits, with the ones with the highest information gain placed on the top. The purpose of showing the goodness measures of splits and sorting the attributes is to enable the user to quickly focus on the splits that have relatively large predictive power by releasing them from examining all attributes, and thus can reduce their mental load. Suppose the user decides to split the data into 2 branches using the "Status of Checking Account" attribute, the updated tree structure and distribution of the class attribute in the branches of the tree are visualized, through which the user evaluates whether the split is satisfactory. If not, the user can delete the added branches and go back to any previous step to make modifications as desired. If the user is satisfied with the selected split, then the same procedures applied in handling the root node are followed for the next node to be considered. This process continues till no more decision nodes need to be split. Then, the computer executes the tree pruning task if the user desires. The flow chart of the IVDT process can be found in Liu and Salvendy [22].

5 Experiment

An experiment was administered to test three hypotheses regarding the proposed IVDT by comparing it with the automatic approaches applied in current decision tree softwares.

5.1 Derivation of Hypotheses

Hypothesis I: Compared with the automatic decision tree classification, IVDT can improve the effectiveness of modeling

The present decision tree softwares allow very limited forms of guidance from users, and the common approach is to run the algorithm with parameters set at their default values. Such an approach forces the user to blindly explore a huge parameter space without clues and intuition about which parameters could give better results. In contrast, the proposed IVDT enables the involvement of the user to guide tree construction by providing them the insight to check the intermediary outcomes and select appropriate parameters.

Hypothesis II: Compared with the automatic decision tree classification, IVDT can improve understanding of the decision tree algorithm.

The use of visualization techniques and animations as education tools has been widely accepted. Visualization of the tree building and the intermediate results demonstrates how the tree is constructed using the applied algorithm and thus may help users to have a better understanding of the general mechanisms of the algorithm.

Hypothesis III: Compared with the automatic decision tree classification, IVDT gives users greater satisfaction with the task

Being more involved in the modeling process can increase users' trust in the derived model and give them a stronger sense of responsibility and achievement, which, in turn, according to Hackman and Oldman's job characteristic model [23], will bring them greater satisfaction.

5.2 Subjects

20 subjects, 10 males and 10 females with ages between 22 and 34, were recruited for this experiment; all of them are graduate engineering students. They all met the following qualifications: (a) had no knowledge of the decision tree algorithm previously, (b) were not color-blinded, and (c) had the capacity of conducting tasks on personal computers. They were randomly divided into two groups, 10 subjects for each type of decision tree classification process, the IVDT or automatic process.

5.3 Independent Variables

The independent variable in this experiment was the type of decision tree classification process, the IVDT or automatic process. The IVDT process has been presented in section 4. In the automatic process applied in current decision tree tools, users have little interaction with the system other than specifying some parameters before tree construction starts. For example, SAS Enterprise Miner [11], allows users to input the maximum number of branches in a split, minimum number of records in a decision node, minimum number of records in a leaf node, and the maximum number of layers in the tree, as well as the goodness measures of splits. Within this context, in the automatic process tested in the experiment, two interfaces were provided. The first interface was where the user input the four parameters of the maximum number of branches, minimum number of records in leaf nodes, minimum number of records in decision nodes, and maximum number of layers, assuming information gain was selected as the goodness of measures of splits so as to be consistent with the table of information gain used during the IVDT process in this experiment. After the parameters were entered, the derived tree was visualized in the second interface. Because the objective of this experiment was to test the potential benefits of having users more involved in the modeling process through visualizing the updated tree and corresponding data, in order to rule out the effects of the visual representation of decision trees on users' performance, the same icicle plot employed in the IVDT process was applied in the automatic modeling process.

5.4 Dependent Variables

There were three dependent variables in this experiment: effectiveness of modeling, understanding of the applied algorithm, and users' satisfaction with the task.

5.4.1 Effectiveness of the Modeling

Typical measures of effectiveness of tasks are time-to-completion and task outcomes [24]. However, because DM modeling is iterative and in order to eliminate possible effects of the task execution time on the other two dependent variables, task outcomes were used in this experiment as the measure of effectiveness of modeling. In this experiment, all subjects spent 20 minutes in deriving trees from each dataset (two datasets were used), and their best trees were utilized for testing the hypothesis.

Two important measures of tree quality are classification accuracy and tree size. Therefore, a measure of the effectiveness of decision tree classification (EDT), which took consideration of both classification accuracy and tree size, was defined in this experiment, following the Pessimistic Error Estimate applied to evaluate classification models [25]:

$$\text{EDT} = \frac{N_{correct} - k \cdot N_{Leaf}}{N} \quad . \tag{1}$$

where $N_{correct}$ is the number of correctly classified records, N_{leaf} is the number of leaf nodes, N is the total number of records, and k is the penalty for a leaf node. The value of k depends on applications. For instance, if accuracy is the only concern, then k is equal to zero and EDT is equal to the accuracy of the model. In this experiment, k was set to 0.5 and 2 in the German Credit dataset and DNA dataset, respectively, assuming the cost of a leaf node equals the gain of increase of accuracy by 0.2%. The two datasets will be described in section 5.6.

5.4.2 Understanding of Algorithms

A variety of approaches have been applied in measuring program comprehension. Dunsmore and Roper [26] classified the methods of measuring program comprehension into five groups: recall (or memorization) test, maintenance operation, dynamic/mental simulation tasks, static questions, and subjective ratings. A maintenance task usually takes the form of an addition, removal, or debugging. Dynamic/mental simulation tasks typically involve some kind of paper-based execution of the program via walkthrough or what-if questions. On the other hand, static questions usually include identification of variables and functions, labeling, syntactic grouping, etc. An experiment conducted in [26] indicated that the dynamic/mental simulation is the most reliable and easily controllable approach.

These approaches can also be applied to measure comprehension of an algorithm because understanding a computer program is to comprehend its functions, logic and process flow, the same as understanding how an algorithm derives models. Therefore, a questionnaire that consists of 7 questions – 2 static and 5 dynamic/simulation questions – was employed to measure understanding of the applied algorithm in this experiment.

5.4.3 Satisfaction with Task

Job Diagnostic Surve (JDS) [23] is a widely used instrument to study the effects of job characteristics on people. In this experiment, a modeling satisfaction questionnaire (MSQ) with 8 questions was developed by modification of the Hackman and Oldham's JDS: 2 questions for general satisfaction, 1 question for trust in results, 1 question for satisfaction with worthwhile accomplishment, 1 question for satisfaction with independent thought, 1 question for satisfaction with the amount of challenge, and 2 questions for satisfaction with the acquired knowledge.

5.5 Experiment Design

This experiment was of the one-way between-subject design in order to rule out learning effects. Each subject was randomly allocated to one type of decision tree classification process, IVDT or automatic, with 10 subjects for each type.

5.6 Procedure

Five steps were followed in the experiment: tutorial, training, practice, formal task, and post-study. At the beginning of the experiment, each subject was given the same tutorial of the decision tree classification algorithm. This tutorial was not intended to teach the subject the details of the algorithm, but to introduce its fundamental concepts so that he or she would be able to perform the modeling task. After the tutorial, each subject was asked to answer some questions regarding the knowledge learned from the tutorial in order to make sure he or she was ready to carry out the modeling task. After the tutorial, the subject was demonstrated the interfaces that would be used in the upcoming modeling tasks. The purpose of practice was to allow the subject to become familiar with the demonstrated interfaces. The dataset utilized for practice was a toy example and was not related to the formal tasks. During the formal task, two datasets were used. They were the DNA and German Credit datasets exercised for illustration of the data visualization and IVDT process described in section 4. The attributes of the German Credit dataset have been delineated in section 4. There were totally 1000 records in this dataset, which were randomly divided into two parts, one for training (700 records) and the other for validation (300 records). As recommended in the Stalog database, the DNA dataset consisted of 60 binary input attributes, and the class attribute had three classes. The DNA dataset was also tested in [16]. After the formal task, each subject filled out the algorithm understanding questionnaire and modeling satisfaction questionnaire.

5.7 Experimental Results

ANOVA was conducted to analyze the experimental results. In the following paragraphs of this section, groups 1 and 2 correspond to the IVDT and automatic processes, respectively.

5.7.1 Hypothesis I

Tables 1 and 2 summarize the experiment results for the German Credit and DNA datasets, respectively, as well as the result of C4.5, one of the most popular standard decision tree algorithms. German Credit and DNA datasets are social and scientific datasets, respectively, thus the accuracy of the former was relatively lower. From the tables, we can see that the automatic modeling and IVDT processes produced trees with comparable accuracy although the accuracy in the former process was a little higher. However, the number of leaf nodes of the trees generated from the IVDT process was less comparatively. Tables 2 and 3 also show that C4.5 produced trees with the highest accuracy yet with the largest number of leaf nodes as well. Therefore, we extended the trees generated from the IVDT process by applying C4.5 subsequently; the results are summarized in the "IVDT-C4.5" columns of Tables 2 and 3. It turned out that the accuracies of the expanded trees increased dramatically and exceeded those derived from C4.5. The right-most column of Table 3 shows the characters of the tree derived from PBC [16]. The accuracy of the PBC tree was much lower than that of the trees from other processes in the table, but the PBC tree was the smallest in size as well. Therefore, we reduced the sizes of the trees derived from the IVDT, so that their number of leaf nodes was the same as that of PBC-tree, and the results are shown in the last column of Table 3. From the table, we can see that the accuracy of the trees derived from the IVDT was significantly higher than that from PBC ($p=0.001$), increased by about 2%.

ANOVA results suggested that the EDT for IVDT was significantly higher than that for automatic modeling ($F=18.61$, $p=0.0004$ for the German Credit dataset; $F=23.91$, $p=0.0001$ for the DNA dataset).

Table 1. Summary of Decision Trees Derived from the German Credit Dataset

Measure	Process			
	IVDT	Automatic	C4.5	IVDT-C4.5
$N_{correct}$	231.8	232.1	237	243.9
Accuracy (%)	77.27%	77.37%	79.00%	81.30%
N_{leaf}	9.8	17.6	43	32.8
EDT (k=0.5)	75.63%	74.43%		

Table 2. Summary of Decision Trees Derived from the DNA Dataset

Measure	Process				
	IVDT	Automatic	C4.5	IVDT-C4.5	PBC*
$N_{correct}$	1112.4	1117.2	1121	1124.2	1058
Accuracy (%)	93.79%	94.20%	94.52%	94.79%	89.21%
N_{leaf}	26.3	35.8	41	35.8	18
EDT (k=2)	89.36%	88.16%			

* PBC is taken from [16].

5.7.2 Hypothesis II

First of all, the total scores of the algorithm understanding questionnaire were compared between subjects in the two groups. ANOVA results indicated that scores of subjects in the first group are significantly higher than those in the second group ($F=24.59$, $p<0.0001$), increased by about 3 points out of totally 9 points in average. Then, each question was compared individually between the two groups, and it was found that the differences between the two groups were significant in questions regarding the process flow of decision tree classification.

5.7.3 Hypothesis III

The cronbach alpha of the MSQ applied in this experiment was about 0.89. ANOVA was conducted to individually compare two groups regarding users' overall satisfaction, trust in the results, satisfaction with worthwhile accomplishment, satisfaction with independent thought, satisfaction with amount of challenge, and satisfaction with the gained knowledge. The results indicated that there were significant differences between the two groups in overall satisfaction ($F=23.47$, $p<0.0001$), trust in the result ($F=10.29$, $p=0.005$), satisfaction with independent thought and action ($F=17.19$, $p=0.001$), satisfaction with amount of challenge ($F=4.10$, $p=0.05$), and satisfaction with the gained knowledge ($F=17.19$, $p=0.0006$). Furthermore, regression analysis showed that the overall satisfaction was affected the most significantly by trust in results, satisfaction with the independent thought, and satisfaction with the gained knowledge.

6 Conclusions

A novel IVDT classification process have been proposed in this paper, with the aim of exploring humans' pattern recognition ability and domain knowledge to facilitate the knowledge discovery process. An experiment was administered to test three hypotheses regarding the potential merits of the proposed IVDT process, whose results suggested that compared to the automatic modeling process, IVDT process can improve the effectiveness of modeling, enhance users' understanding of the algorithm, and give them greater satisfaction with the task. However, it is not our argument that the visual interactive modeling process should replace its automatic counterpart. The automatic modeling takes much less time and thus may be favorable if users want to get an quick overview of the results, and then they can turn to the visual interactive modeling if simply manipulating parameters at the beginning of the modeling will not produce satisfactory results and/or they prefer to guide the model building process. The combination of IVDT and automatic algorithms, as demonstrated in the experiment, is also a promising strategy, especially in situations where classification accuracy is the primary concern but having users to manually select parameters for each intermediate step is very time-consuming and/or boring.

References

1. Fayyad, U., Piatetsky-Shapiro, G., Smyth, P.: From Data Mining to Knowledge Discovery: An Overview. In: Fayyad, U.M., Piatetsky-Shapiro, G., Smyth, P., Uthurusamy, R., Park, M. (eds.) Advances in Knowledge Discovery and Data Mining, pp. 1–36. AAAI Press, CA (1996)
2. Pyle, D.: Data Preparation for Data Mining. Morgan Kaufmann Publishers, CA, Seattle, Washington, USA (1999)
3. Ankerst, M., Keim, D.A., Kriegel, H.-P.: Circle Segments: A Technique for Visually Exploring Large Multidimensional Data Sets. In: Proceedings of IEEE Visualization 96, Hot Topic Session, San Francisco, CA (1996)
4. Kreuseler, M., Schumann, H.: A Flexible Approach for Visual Data Mining. IEEE Transactions on Visualization and Computer Graphics 8(1), 39–51 (2002)
5. Fayyad, U., Grinstein, G.G.: Introduction. In: Fayyad, U.M., Grinstein, G., Wierse, A. (eds.) Information Visualization in Data Mining and Knowledge Discovery, pp. 1–20. Morgan Kaufmann Publishers, CA, San Francisco (2002)
6. Domingos, P.: The Role of Occam's Razor in Knowledge Discovery. Data. Mining and knowledge discovery 3(4), 409–425 (1999)
7. Quinlan, J.R.: C 4.5 – Programs for Machine Learning. Morgan Kaufmann Publishers, CA, San Francisco (1993)
8. Breiman, L., Friedman, J., Olshen, R., Stone, C.: Classification and Regression Trees. Pacific Grove, Wadsworth, CA (1984)
9. Murthy, S.K.: Automatic Construction of Decision Trees from Data: A Multi-Disciplinary Survey. Data Mining and Knowledge Discovery 2(4), 345–389 (1998)
10. Helander, M.G.: Design of Visual Displays. In: Salvendy, G. (ed.) Handbook of Human Factors, pp. 507–548. John Wiley and Sons, NY (1987)
11. Enterprise, S.A.S.: Miner: Retrieved (May 15, 2006), from http://www.sas.com/technologies/ analytics/datamining/miner/
12. SPSS Answer Tree: Retrieved (May 15, 2006), from http://www.spss.com

13. Shneiderman, B.: Tree Visualization with Tree-Maps: 2D Space Filling Approach, ACM Transactions on graphics 11(1), 92–99 (1992)
14. Barlow, S.T., Neville, P.A.: Comparison of 2-D visualizations of hierarchies, In: IEEE Symposium on Information Visualization 2001, San Diego, CA pp. 131–138 (2001)
15. Ankerst, M., Elsen, C., Ester, M., Kriegel, H-P.: Visual Classification: An Interactive Approach to Decision Tree Construction. In: Proceedings of the 5th International Conference on Knowledge Discovery and Data Mining, pp. 392–397 (1999)
16. Ankerst, M., Ester, M., Kriegel, H.-P.: Towards an Effective Cooperation of the Computer and the User for Classification. In: Proc. 6th Int. Conf. on Knowledge Discovery and Data Mining (KDD '2000), Boston, MA, pp. 178–188 (2000)
17. Ware, M., Frank, E., Holmes, G., Hall, M., Witten, T.H.: Interactive Machine Learning: Letting Uses Build Classifiers. International Journal of Human Computer Studies 55(3), 281–292 (2001)
18. Poulet, F.: Cooperation between Automatic Algorithms, Interactive Algorithms and Visualization Tools for Visual Data Mining. In: The 6th European Conference on Principles and Practice of Knowledge Discovery in Databases, Helsinki, Finland, pp. 19–23 (2002)
19. Blake, C.L., Merz, C.J.: UCI Repository of Machine Learning Databases, Irvine, CA: University of California, Department of Information and Computer Science. Retrieved (May 15, 2006), from http://www.ics.uci.edu/ mlearn/MLRepository.html
20. Inselberg, A.: The Plane with Parallel Coordinates. The. Visual Computer 1(1), 69–97 (1985)
21. Friendly, M.: Visualizing Categorical Data. SAS Institute, NC (2001)
22. Liu, Y., Salvendy, G.: Design and Evaluation of Interactive Visual Decision Tree Classification. International Journal of Human-Computer Studies 65(2), 95–110 (2006)
23. Hackman, J.R., Oldham, G.R.: Development of the Job Diagnostic Survey. Journal of Applied Psychology 60(2), 159–170 (1975)
24. Novick, D.: What is Effectiveness? In: CHI '97 Workshop on HCI Research and Paractice Agenda Based on Human Needs and Social Responsibility, CHI '97, Atlanta, GA (1997)
25. Tan, P.-N., Steinbach, M., Kumar, V.: Introduction to Data Mining. Addison Wesley, Boston, MA (2005)
26. Dunsmore, A., Roper, M.: Comparative Evaluation of Program Comprehension Measures. Technical Report EFoCS 35-2000, Department of Computer Science, University of Strathclyde, Glasgow, UK (2000)

Anchored Maps: Visualization Techniques for Drawing Bipartite Graphs

Kazuo Misue

Department of Computer Science, University of Tsukuba
1-1-1 Tennoudai, Tsukuba, 305-8573 Japan
misue@cs.tsukuba.ac.jp

Abstract. A method of drawing anchored maps for bipartite graphs is presented. Suppose that the node set of a bipartite graph is divided into set *A* and set *B*. On an anchored map of the bipartite graph, the nodes in *A*, which are called "anchors," are arranged on the circumference, and the nodes in *B*, which are called "free nodes," are arranged at suitable positions in relation to the adjacent anchors. This article describes aesthetic criteria that are employed according to the purpose of drawing anchored maps and indices which are used to arrange the anchors so that they satisfy the criteria. It also shows an example of taking overviews of networks by using the developed technique.

Keywords: graph drawing, anchored map, bipartite graph, knowledge mining.

1 Introduction

Information with network structures (we call it "network information") can be seen in various fields of the real world. In some fields of research, some of the networks are the research objects such as communication networks and social networks. In recent years, the approach on large-scale networks is active. However, the problem that readability is low in drawing on the networks is not solved still enough. It is an critical problem we should challenge.

The purpose of this research is to develop visualization techniques to give overviews of networks with high readability for mining knowledge. We developed a drawing technique called "anchored map" [5] for the networks which are formalized as bipartite graphs to achieve the purpose. The node set of a bipartite graph is divided into two exclusive sets. Here, we call the nodes in one set "anchors," and the nodes in the other set "free nodes." Our technique arranges anchors on the circumference and arranges free nodes at suitable positions in relation to the adjacent anchors. The anchors are fixed on the circumference as their name suggests and give the effect like the coordinate system to increase readability of the network diagrams. The name "anchored map" was given by the author, but similar representation techniques were also used in some other tools, for example, Visual Who [1], which is a visualization tool for communities and SQWID [3], which is a WWW search tool.

In this article, we describe the technique for drawing anchored maps. First we explain the aesthetic criteria that are employed according to the map's purpose and a method to arrange anchors to fulfill the criteria. Then we propose indices which are

J. Jacko (Ed.): Human-Computer Interaction, Part II, HCII 2007, LNCS 4551, pp. 106–114, 2007.

used to arrange the anchors so that they satisfy the criteria and show some evaluation results of their effectiveness. As an example of usage of anchored maps, we show network diagrams which visualize relations between goods and time zones when the goods sold.

2 Anchored Maps of Bipartite Graphs

An anchored map restricts some nodes to certain positions, but leaves other nodes so they may be arranged freely. The restricted nodes are fixed like anchors, hence the terms "anchors" and "free nodes."

2.1 Bipartite Graphs

In this paper, we focus on networks which can be formalized as bipartite graphs. Suppose that $G=(A \cup B, E)$ is a bipartite graph. A and B are finite sets of vertices, and A and B are disjoint. E is a finite set of edges, and E is a subset of $A \times B$.

2.2 Expression Styles of Bipartite Graphs

Table 1. Matrix Style of a Bipartite Graph

	C1	C2	C3	C4	C5
m01	1	1			
m02	1			1	1
m03			1		1
m04	1	1		1	
m05	1		1	1	
m06	1	1			
m07			1		1
m08				1	1
m09	1	1		1	
m10		1	1		

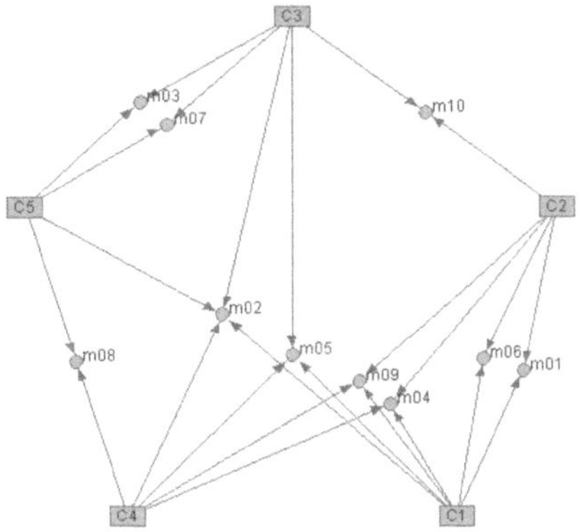

Fig. 1. Anchored-map Style of a Bipartite Graph

Table 1 and Fig. 1 show variations of expression styles of bipartite graphs. Virtual data is used as an example. Suppose that there is a bipartite graph that represents relationships between five communities (C1, ..., C5) and ten members (m01, …, m10). Table 1 shows the matrix representation. Each row corresponds to a community, and each column corresponds to a member. A "1" in a cell indicates that a member belongs to a community; for example, member m01 belongs to communities C1 and C2. This matrix cannot intuitively show relational structures because it is not visual.

Figure 1 shows the same bipartite graph shown in Table 1 in an anchored-map style. The communities are arranged on the vertices of a pentagon as anchors, and members are arranged at a suitable position to represent their relationship to the communities as free nodes. The distinction of the nodes is clear, and it is easy to see the relations between members.

2.3 Drawing Procedure of Anchored Maps

An anchored map is laid out in two steps:

(Step 1) Arrange anchors on the circumference at equal intervals. The size (i.e., radius) of the circumference is decided according to the size of the drawing area (i.e., window), and the order of the anchors on the circumference is decided.

(Step 2) Fix the anchors, and arrange the free nodes at the positions in which their relationships to the anchors are appropriately expressed.

The length of the circumference doesn't influence the quality of the layout; it influences only the size of the drawing. On the other hand, the order of the anchors has a large influence on the quality of the layout. We do not need to worry about routing of edges since the edges are drawn as straight line segments.

3 Aesthetic Criteria of Anchored Maps

We should provide aesthetic criteria of drawings of networks and develop drawing methods which follow the criteria to enable automatic drawing of networks. We employed the following aesthetic criteria for our anchored map drawing method.

(R1) Nodes are separated mutually more than the lowest distance.
(R2) Nodes connected to each other are laid out as closely as possible (minimize the total length of edges).
(R3) The number of crossings among edges is minimized.
(R4) Anchors connected to common free nodes are laid out as closely as possible.
(R5) Free nodes connected to common anchors are laid out as closely as possible. (Free nodes belonging to the same cluster are laid out as closely as possible; free nodes do not belong to the same cluster are not laid out closely).

The drawing rules (R1), (R2) and (R3) are also employed in many other drawing methods. We also judged them to be important in consideration of the adaptability to the purpose of drawing of anchored maps. The rules (R4) and (R5) are specific to the anchored maps. We show formal description of them in the following part of this section.

3.1 Preparation

Suppose that M is the number of anchors, that is, $M = |A|$. The anchors are arranged on the vertices of a regular M-gon (a polygon with M vertices). The vertices of the M-gon are labeled clockwise from 1 to M. It doesn't matter which vertex is chosen to be 1.

Suppose that $p(a)$ is the position of anchor a and that $A(f)$ is the set of anchors which connect to free node f, that is, $A(f) = \{a \in A \mid (a, f) \in E\}$.

3.2 (R4) Closeness of Anchors Connected to Common Free Nodes

Rule (R4) is to minimize $d(F)$ expressed by

$$d(F) = \sum_{f \in F} d(f) \tag{1}$$

Here, $d(F)$ represents closeness between anchors connected to free node *f*. Definition of $d(F)$ is described later.

Clockwise Distance. The "clockwise distance" between the *i*-th vertex and the *j*-th vertex is the number of vertices we meet when we trace the vertices of the *M*-gon from the *i*-th to the *j*-th clockwise. The clockwise distance l_M is defined as

$$l_M(i, j) = (j - i + M) \bmod M \tag{2}$$

Gap. We introduce a "gap" for every anchor connected to a certain free node. Suppose that *f* is a free node and $A' = \{a_1, a_2, \cdots, a_k\}$ is a set of anchors connected to *f*. Moreover, suppose that $a_1, \cdots, a_k$ have been sorted by the numbers of vertices of the *M*-gon. In other words, $p(a_s) < p(a_t)$ if $s < t$. The gap for each anchor is the clockwise distance between one node and the next node (the next of a_k is a_1). The gap $g(a_s)$ of node a_s is defined as

$$g(a_s) = l_M(p(a_s), p(a_{(s+1) \bmod M})) \tag{3}$$

Closeness of Anchors. When *k* anchors are connected with a certain free node *f*, a sequence of *k* gaps is obtained. Removing the maximum gap from the sequence leaves *k*-1 smaller gaps. The closeness of anchors is defined by the sum of powers of *k*-1 gaps and represented by $d(f)$. Suppose that *f* is a free node and $g_1, g_2, \ldots, g_{k-1}$ is the remainder sequence that excludes the maximum gap from the gap sequence of the anchors connected to *f*. The closeness of anchors connected to free node *f* is represented by $d(f)$ and is expressed as

$$d(f) = \sum_{i=1}^{k-1} g_i^q \tag{4}$$

For reason why the parameter q is introduced, please access [4].

Small $d(f)$ indicates that the anchors connected to the same free node should be arranged close to each other.

3.3 (R5) Closeness of Free Nodes Connected to Common Anchors

It is an intuitive and simple rule to make free nodes which connect to the same anchors close to each others. When there are two free node *f* and *g*, which connect to the same anchor set, the two free nodes should be arranged close to each other.

However, if there is another free node h, which connects to similar anchor set, we may want to place h a little closer to f and g than the other free nodes which connect completely difference anchors. So we defined similarity between two free nodes by using similarity of sets of anchors connect to the free nodes. The similarity of free nodes f and g is represented by $s(f,g)$ and is expressed as

$$s(f,g) = \frac{|A(f) \cap A(g)|}{|A(f) \cup A(g)|} \tag{5}$$

Rule (R5) can be formalized as to increase correlation between "similarities" and "distance," here similarities are similarities between free nodes and distance is Euclidean distance between the free nodes.

4 How to Decide the Order of Anchors

We employed numeric indices which can be used as replacement of aesthetic criteria (drawing rules) and conducted the experiment that evaluates the effectiveness of the indices. We have introduced an index in [4]. In this paper, we introduce other promised indices and show exhaustive evaluation results.

The distance between adjacent nodes (length of the edges) and the number of edge crossings are essentially influenced by the order of the anchors. However, these features are not deterministically decided from only the anchor order. The spring embedding in Step 2 and the initial positions of the free nodes also influence the distance. However, spring embedding has negligible influence compared with the influence of the anchor order.

4.1 Indices to Decide Anchor Order

The order of the anchors is the most critical for anchored maps. We can evaluate the goodness of a certain order only after the spring embedding has been processed for a certain anchor arrangement, but to do this for all the possible candidate orders would require too much computing time. Thus, we need an alternative index that is computable in a deterministic way and with a low computing cost.

As such the indices we considered to use drawing rules which can be evaluated before arranging anchors. Rules we considered are (R2), (R3) and (R4), and Penalty2, Penalty3 and Penalty4, which described in the followings, are indices correspond to the rules respectively.

(Penalty2) **Total length of edges** when all free nodes are placed at the barycenters of anchors connected to the free nodes (R2).

(Penalty3) **The number of crossings** among edges when all free nodes are placed at the barycenters of anchors connected to the free nodes (R3).

(Penalty4) **The distance along the circumference** between anchors connected to the same free nodes (R4).

We cannot use the drawing rules (R2) and (R3) as they are as indices because both two drawing rules can be evaluated only after the positions of free nodes has been decided. So, we use the values (edge lengths and number of crossings) which suppose that all free nodes are placed at the barycenters of anchors in definition of Penalty2 and Penalty3. Penalty4 is the same as the Penalty proposed in [4].

4.2 Evaluation of Indices

Table 2 shows the size of the five bipartite graphs used for the evaluation. Table 3 and Table 4 show summary of the evaluation results; Table 3 and Table 4 show the results of Penalty2 and Penalty4 respectively. Both tables show correlations of the penalty with drawing rules and ranks of optimal solution (order) for the indices concerning drawing rules. More precisely, ranks represent the rank of the best anchor order for the indices in all possible orders, that is, 181,440 (= (10-1)! / 2) combinations. There are three values at fields of (R2) and (R3) in the row of G1 in Table 4. It is because that there are three best orders for Penalty4. We had expected that Penalty2 was advantageous to (R2) and Panalty4 was advantageous to (R4). Moreover, we found that Penalty2 was effective for (R3) too.

Table 2. Size of the graphs used for the evaluation

	|A|	|B|	|E|
G1	10	16	65
G2	10	19	84
G3	10	40	182
G4	10	48	251
G5	10	98	473

5 Overview of Network Information

We show an example of overview of network information extracted from an actual database to explain the effectiveness of the anchored maps.

5.1 Database

A sales database is exploited. Table 5 shows a part of the database. One transaction is represented as one record, and one record has purchase date, time, customer name, goods name, goods category and price. We could not get any database of real shops, so we used a sales database managed in our laboratory. It is not a database of a real shop but the transactions in the database are real. We started to use the database in June 2006, and 2652 purchases are recorded for half a year until the end of 2006.

Various relations can be extracted from the database. For example, if we focus on the goods, we can extract relations goods and customers who bought the goods, relations goods and day when the goods was bought, and relations goods and time when the goods was bought. Besides, we can extract relations customers and day when the customers bought, and relations customers and time when the customers bought. Furthermore, we can extract relations customers who bought similar goods, and relations customers who bought at similar time.

Table 3. Evaluation Result of Penalty2

	Correlation with Rules			Ranks of Solutions		
	(r2)	(r3)	(r4)	(r2)	(r3)	(r4)
G1	0.9996	0.9359	0.8949	1	1	4
G2	0.9997	0.9463	0.8873	2	1	756
G3	0.9998	0.9763	0.8912	1	1	657
G4	0.9997	0.9709	0.8416	1	2	62
G5	0.9993	0.9916	0.9025	1	5	1

Table 4. Evaluation Relust of Penalty4

	Correlation with Rules			Ranks of Solutions		
	(r2)	(r3)	(r4)	(r2)	(r3)	(r4)
G1	0.8961	0.8315	1.0000	2,25,244	5,53,566	1
G2	0.8872	0.8240	1.0000	8	27	1
G3	0.8880	0.8592	1.0000	36	20	1
G4	0.8364	0.7969	1.0000	273	680	1
G5	0.9122	0.8954	1.0000	1	5	1

Table 5. Database of Sales (portion)

DATE	TIME	CUSTOMER	GOODS (in Japanese)	CATEGORY	PRICE
2006/6/2	22:32:24	Szyu	ホームラン軒鶏ガラ醤油	convenience food	100
2006/6/5	20:42:47	Masa	午後の紅茶ミルクティー	soft drink	100
2006/6/5	20:37:35	Naga	サッポロ一番塩らーめん	convenience food	100
2006/6/5	20:31:20	KSth	スーパーカップ1.5倍濃コクとんこつ	convenience food	100
2006/6/5	19:39:50	Yuki	昔ながらのソース焼きそば	convenience food	100
2006/6/5	17:59:05	Shuj	カップヌードルカレー	convenience food	100
2006/6/5	16:50:14	Mhro	爽健美茶	tea	100
2006/6/5	16:49:36	Mhro	コアラのマーチチョコレート	sweet	100
2006/6/5	15:09:38	Shuj	B lendy	coffee	100
2006/6/5	14:42:52	Jacq	深い味わい若武者	tea	100
2006/6/5	14:35:13	Snji	コカコーラ	soft drink	100
2006/6/5	13:39:50	Kazu	午後の紅茶ストレートティー	soft drink	100
2006/6/5	12:52:02	Naga	爽健美茶	tea	100
2006/6/5	12:36:17	Snji	爽健美茶	tea	100
2006/6/5	11:21:57	Mhro	午後の紅茶ミルクティー	soft drink	100

5.2 Overview by Using Anchored Maps

Fig. 2(a) shows networks which represent relations between goods and time zone when the goods were bought. Time zones are placed as 24 anchors. Time zone has cyclic order, so they placed in there proper order. From this map, we find at once that

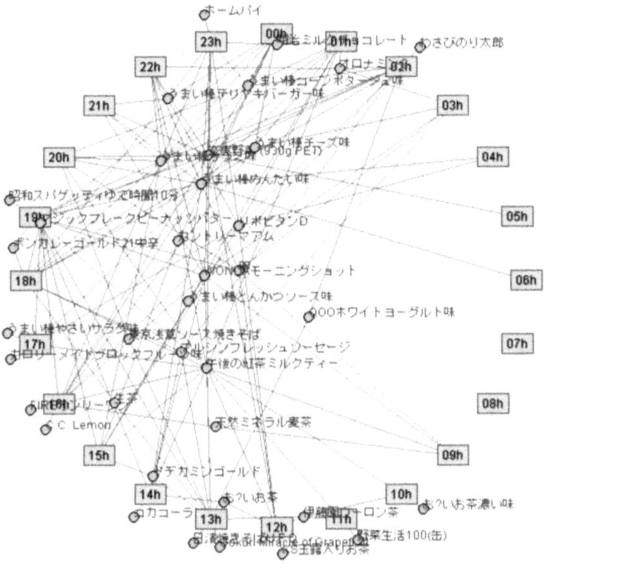

(a) 24 time zones are placed as anchors

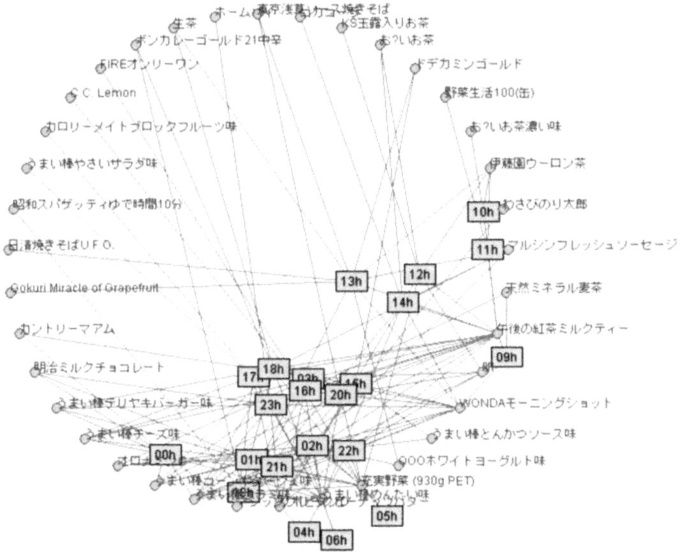

(b) Goods are placed as anchors

Fig. 2. Anchored Maps Showing Relations Goods and Time Zone

the activity of the students is very low in the morning. Furthermore, we find that food such as the curries and spaghettis were bought in specific time zone while the canned coffee and sweets were possibly not depend at specific time zone.

In Fig. 2(b), goods are placed as anchors. Goods have no proper orders, so we use the technique described in Section 4 to decide the order of anchors. We see the following clusters in the map.

(1) Early morning 1: 04h, 05h and 06h
(2) Early morning 2: 07h and 08h (no nodes = no activities)
(3) Morning: 09h, 10h and 11h
(4) Lunch time: 12h, 13h and 14h
(5) Evening ~ night: 15h ~ 03h

It might be possible to find such the clusters without the overview of the networks even by the clustering techniques that already exist. The advantage of overview of network information is that we can see grounds and the background that compose the clusters as some connecting lines between nodes. By using such the maps we can roughly observe the existence of the clusters at first. Then we understand the reason where those clusters exist by touching a virtual physical model of relations.

6 Conclusions

We explained an anchored map drawing technique which we developed to increase readability of network information. We proposed some indices to find good anchor orders effectively and explained effectiveness of the indices by using evaluation results. Moreover, we showed an example of overview of network information extracted from an actual database to illustrate capability of anchored maps at an early stage of observation of network information.

In the example we found some clusters of time zones from the viewpoint of activities of buying. If we would get more rich database we could find more useful relations and background of the relations; relations between goods and area, relations between goods and ages, relations between goods and occupation, and so on.

Acknowledgements. The author thanks Mr. Yu Suzuki and Mr. Hirohisa Miyazaki of the Interactive Programming Laboratory at the University of Tsukuba for their help in developing the sales database and in the experimental evaluation of the indices.

References

1. Donath, J.S.: Visual Who: Animating the affinities and activities of an electronic community, ACM Multimedia 95. In: Electronic Proceedings (1995)
2. Eades, P.: A Heuristic for Graph Drawing. Congressus Numerantium 42, 149–160 (1984)
3. McCrickard, S.D., Kehoe, C.: Visualizing Search Results using SQWID. In: Proceedings of the sixth International World Wide Web Conference (WWW6) (1997)
4. Misue, K.: Drawing Bipartite Graphs as Anchored Maps. In: Proceedings of Asia-Pacific Symposium on Information Visualization (APVIS 2006), pp. 169–177 (2006)
5. Misue, K., Watanabe, I.: Visualization of Keyword Association for Text Mining. In: IPJS SIG Technical Report, -FI-55-8, Information Processing Society of Japan, (in Japanese) pp. 65–72 (1999)

ParSketch: A Sketch-Based Interface for a 2D Parametric Geometry Editor

Ferran Naya[1], Manuel Contero[1], Nuria Aleixos[2], and Pedro Company[2]

[1] Polytechnic University of Valencia, Camino de Vera s/n,
46022 Valencia, Spain
[2] Universitat Jaume I, Avda. Sos Baynat s/n,
12071 Castellón, Spain
{fernasan,mcontero}@degi.upv.es,
{naleixos,pcompany}@emc.uji.es

Abstract. ParSketch is a software prototype to evaluate the usability and functionality of a sketching interface aimed at defining 2D parametric sections. Currently, ParSketch interprets strokes which can be recognized as geometry (line, arc, circle, ellipse, or composed entities that are automatically segmented into those basic entities), or graphic gestures representing constraints (dimension, parallel, perpendicular, tangent, concentric, horizontal or vertical). From the functionality point of view, ParSketch compares to current commercial parametric CAD applications, as it offers many of the features provided by such applications. A theoretical analysis of the efficiency component of usability is provided that justifies the potential capability of sketching interfaces to compete with classical WIMP applications. Finally, a usability study is presented, which makes special emphasis in the satisfaction component of usability.

Keywords: sketching, parametric drawing, usability of sketching interfaces.

1 Introduction

Despite the great advances in Computer-Aided Design (CAD), available commercial Graphical User Interfaces (GUIs) used by these applications have not evolved from the so-called WIMP (Window, Icon, Menu, Pointing device) interaction paradigm. These CAD tools provide a good and effective way to create the digital geometric representation of the product; however, these systems provide little support for the most creative part of the engineering design process. Usually, this part of the process, known as conceptual design, uses sketches as a powerful tool that helps designers express their creative thinking.

Majority of engineers and designers receive sketching training during their studies. A recent survey performed by the Engineering Design Graphics Division of the American Society for Engineering Education concluded that the "ability to create 3-D solid computer models" and the "ability to sketch engineering objects in the freehand mode" were the two most important graphical communication outcomes for engineering students [1,2].

J. Jacko (Ed.): Human-Computer Interaction, Part II, HCII 2007, LNCS 4551, pp. 115–124, 2007.

If sketching is considered an important skill in engineering design; if engineers and designers usually can create sketches, as they get specific training for it, why sketching is not integrated in the digital design process? In this paper we will try to provide some reasons for the disconnection of sketching from the digital design tools, and show some of our own developments to support sketching with computers, ending with a usability study of one of these tools.

2 Sketch-Based Interfaces and Modeling (SBIM)

We think that SBIM can provide the computer tools required to shift [3] to a new paradigm where sketches could be used as input to create preliminary digital engineering models in the conceptual design stage.

We are speaking about sketches, but have all the sketches the same characteristics? Have they the same purpose? Do they provide the same kind of information? We have followed the classification proposed by Ferguson [4] that distinguishes among "*thinking sketches*" used to focus and guide non verbal thinking, "*talking sketches*" employed to support discussion on the design with colleagues and "*prescriptive sketches*" applied to give instructions to the draftsman who is in charge of making the finished drawing.

Previous researches of our group REGEO (see *www.regeo.uji.es*) explored and developed some applications [5,6] running on Tablet-PCs that were found to be valid to replace *thinking sketches* on paper.

Currently our research group is launching a new investigation line whose objective is to use prescriptive sketches as an alternative input method for geometry modeling in CAD systems. In the Ferguson's definition, *prescriptive sketches* are used to give instructions (see figure 1 for an example) to the draftsman who is in charge of making the drawings. We propose an update for this concept: a virtual draftsman that interprets sketches to construct 3D models instead of drawings.

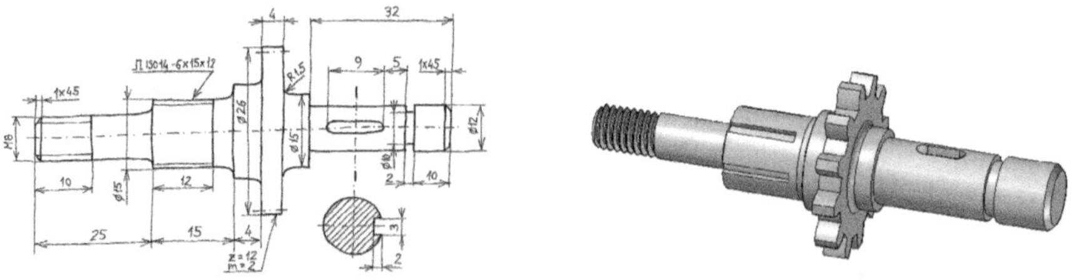

Fig. 1. Prescriptive sketch example and its associated 3D model

A first step in this approach is to build a software prototype to evaluate the feasibility of using a sketching interface to define 2D parametric sections. The design goal of this tool is to create 2D parametric sections in a very simple way, using the conventions of technical drawing to define the shape of the section. With that aim we have developed the ParSketch application that combines a sketching interface with a commercial 2D parametric engine (UGS D-Cubed 2DCM). From the functionality point of view, ParSketch offers many of the features provided by current commercial parametric CAD applications as it is built on top of the most common parametric engine of the market.

3 The ParSketch Application: System Overview

Currently, ParSketch interprets strokes which can be recognized as geometry (line, arc, circle, ellipse, or composed entities that are automatically segmented into those basic entities), or symbols representing constraints (fig. 3 includes current supported constraints). Furthermore, drawing entities can be removed using a scratching gesture. This not only allows errors to be corrected, but also enables more complex shapes to be drawn incrementally, by refining simpler forms (see figure 2 for a sketching example). Besides, new gestures can be added to the system as the gesture recognizer can be trained by providing new gesture samples.

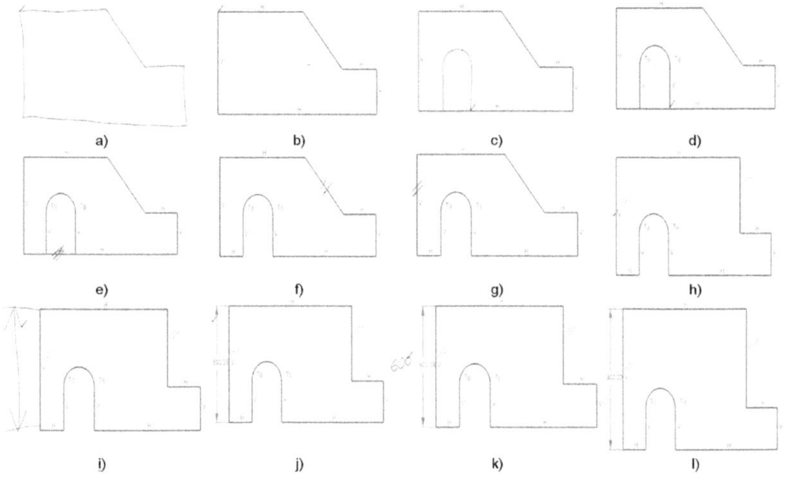

Fig. 2. Sketching sequence in ParSketch (video can be downloaded from [7])

At present the system uses pen pressure to decide whether input corresponds to geometry or to gesture strokes. The criterion is that drawing applying high pressure means a geometry stroke; otherwise stroke is analyzed as a gesture. Both geometry and gesture analyzers make use of two geometric signatures to perform recognition: the direction and curvature graphs of each stroke,.

The application uses the geometric kernel ACIS to store the recognized geometric entities, and the 2D DCM constraint manager from the UGS D-Cubed firm to manage the geometric and dimensional constraints of the drawings.

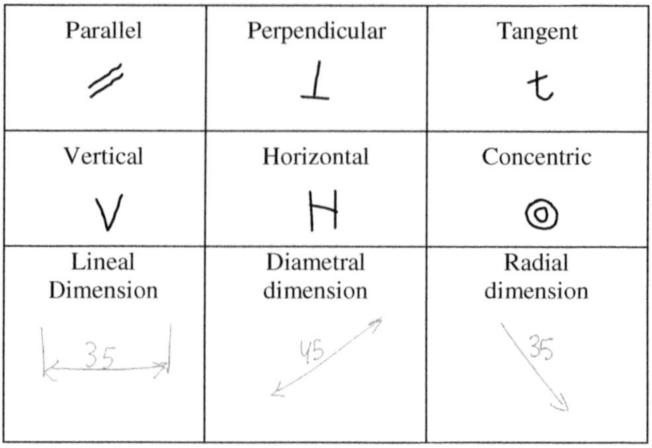

Fig. 3. Gesture alphabet

The user introduces the geometry creating a freehand sketch directly on the Tablet-PC screen. The recognition engine cleans up input data and adjusts edges to make sure they meet precisely at common endpoints in order to obtain geometrically consistent figures by filtering all defects and errors of the initial sketches that are inherent to their inaccurate and incomplete nature.

The user can reconfigure the set of constraints that the system will automatically use to control the sketch. Users can also manage the beautification action by modifying the threshold values used to decide whether a geometric constraint is verified (see Fig. 5 for details).

An example of interaction with the ParSketch application is provided in figure 2. In this example the user draws the whole contour in 2.a. One single stroke is accepted as input, and it is later decomposed by the application into six rectilinear and connected strokes. When the application shows the beautified version (figure 2.b), the user adds another complex stroke composed by two segments and one arc. The geometry is then beautified (figure 2.d). In figure 2.e we can see the use of the scratching gesture to refine the geometry. Drawing this gesture is interpreted by the application as an order to delete those geometric entities intersecting the smallest quadrilateral that encloses the gesture.

Then a parallel constraint is applied by simply sketching its associated gesture over the two segments we want to make parallel (see 2.f, 2.g, 2.h). Once the desired shape has been obtained, we can proceed with dimensional control. A first action is to draw a dimension without the dimension text (see figure 2.i). This is interpreted by the application as a measure command, and the current value of that dimension is shown, as seen in figure 2.j. If the user wants to change the current dimension value, he or she writes the new value next to the current one. Then the system regenerates and displays the new geometry (figures 2.k and 2.l).

Handwritten number recognition is provided by the Windows XP Tablet PC Edition operative system. In this way, we provide a very natural form of imposing the desired dimensions over the sketch.

4 Sketching-Based vs. WIMP Interfaces for Parametric Drawing

From a theoretical point of view we can show that if the sketching application supports complex strokes, i.e. strokes composed by several basic primitives as line segments and arcs (see figure 4 as an example) this means a potential advantage over WIMP interaction. For instance, analyzing sections composed exclusively by arcs and line segments, we can make an approximated calculation of the number of interactions required by a WIMP application to complete the drawing task.

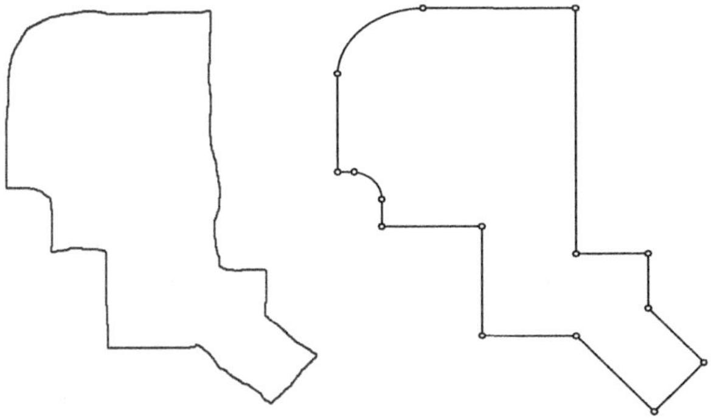

Fig. 4. Automatic segmentation vs. explicit drawing

Usually one interaction is required to initiate the drawing process (one mouse click) and another one for finishing (a double click or pressing the enter key, for example). For drawing the line segments and tangent arcs in figure 4 two more interactions per elements are required. One is for defining the connecting vertex and the other for the selection of the proper geometric constraint as the horizontal, vertical, perpendicular or tangent conditions in this example. We count for this second interaction although, in modern parametric sketchers, geometric constraints are dynamically added as the user moves the drawing cursor. Only after the user detects the proper constraint is when he/she introduces the next entity vertex. This requires user attention, so we add it to the global number of interactions.

The last term in the calculation of total number of interactions is related to primitive switching operation. When the user wants to link for example a tangent arc to a previous polyline, he/she must spend one interaction, providing this information to the system (using for example a contextual menu or icon selection), and then spend a second interaction to come back to polyline mode.

In sum, if n_l and n_a represents the number of line segments and arcs respectively, the total number of interactions N spent by the user is:

$$N = 2 + 2(n_l + n_a) + 2n_a \tag{1}$$

Even for not too complex figures (N= 36 in figure 4) the last equation shows that although a user could employ several strokes to complete the shape and require some corrections to overcome recognition errors by the sketching application, there is a wide margin to compete with WIMP-based interaction in terms of efficiency. So it is feasible to implement a robust geometric segmentation and recognition to keep advantage over WIMP interaction. We think that this is one of the keys for success in providing a real alternative or at least a complement to a WIMP interface. But as Igarashi and Zeleznik noted [8], we must adapt the design of our applications to exploit the pen input's intrinsic capacity for rapid, direct, modeless 2D expression.

To improve segmentation results, our system can be adapted to each user way of sketching by means of a tolerance control panel (see Fig. 5) that defines some key parameters for improving recognition. As explained before, the mode detection has been solved using the electronic pen pressure information, since ParSketch is intended to be used by persons with basic engineering drawing skills. It can be said that line width is the mode-change feature, when reading an engineering drawing. In the usual practice, thick lines are associated to geometry and thin lines to dimensions and other types of annotations. As line width is related to increasing pressure with the pencil while drawing, we have used this information to discriminate among geometry or gesture.

In relation with other typical operations in a parametric 2D application, as imposing geometric constraints or performing dimensional control, the number of interactions required by both systems is similar. So we can conclude that from the efficiency point of view the sketch based approach is a viable option.

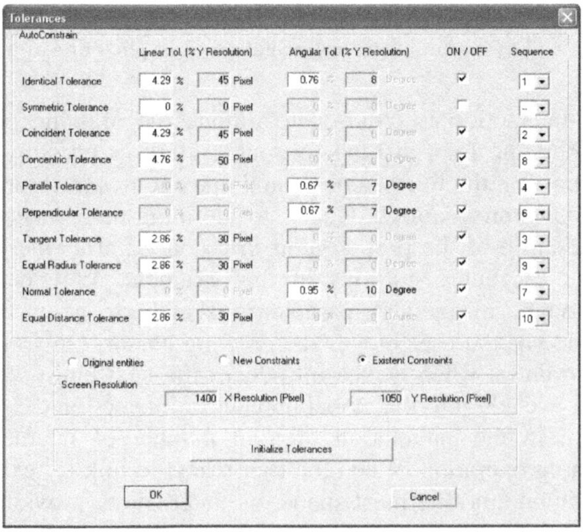

Fig. 5. Tolerance settings for controlling parametric behavior

4.1 Usability Study

The usability of digital thinking sketches as opposed to traditional paper-and-pencil sketches was measured elsewhere [9]. In this work, we have centered our study in the user satisfaction component of usability, following the usability definition provided by ISO 9241-11, where it stands for "*extent to which a product can be used by specified users to achieve specified goals with effectiveness, efficiency and satisfaction in a specified context of use*". At its current development status, we are more interested in the user satisfaction response in order to decide investing more resources in the improvement of effectiveness and efficiency of the tool, although we have selected metrics for each usability component [10].

As noted previously, the main design goals of the ParSketch application are:

- Expeditious creation of shapes composed by polylines, arcs, and circles.
- Dimensional and geometric shape-control though the use of technical drawing conventions.

The evaluation involved six CAD instructors and six students with parametric CAD experience. All but one of the CAD instructors were male with an average age of 55. All students were male with an average age of 24.

We allowed 30 minutes for the evaluation, which had four parts: an overview of the system where some short videos showed the system operation, an instruction stage with a modified version of ParSketch that explicitly informs the user about the recognized entities or gestures (typically 10 minutes were employed in this training), a drawing task, and a final discussion with participants. After the discussion, users filled a questionnaire to evaluate ParSketch and express their comments about it.

Each participant used a Toshiba Tecra M4. This Tablet PC has a 14,1" screen, with a resolution of 1400x1050 dots, and employs Ms Window XP Tablet-PC Edition.

We asked users to accomplish three drawing tasks. Shapes presented in Fig. 6 where used to propose several drawing exercises. The first exercise was to create a parametric section similar to the left shape of Fig. 5. The other two exercises employed the other shapes, and the users had to create the shape and impose some dimensional and geometric constraints.

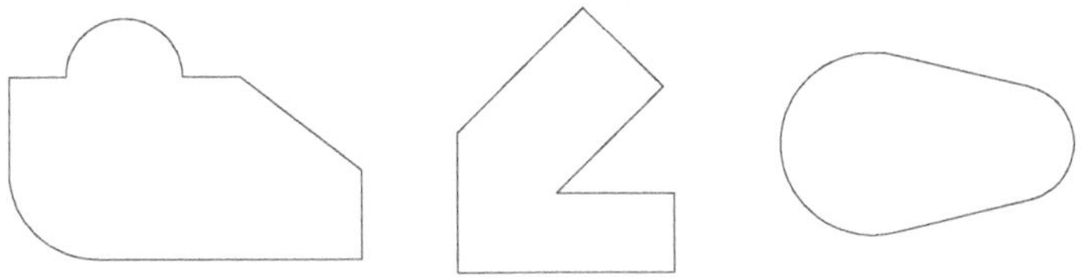

Fig. 6. Shapes for usability study

In relation with the evaluation of effectiveness, we have measured the accuracy and completeness with which users achieved the goals presented previously, using experts' assessment of the produced sketches. This assessment is based on the accuracy of the generated shapes. All the participants completed the requested drawing tasks satisfying all the conditions imposed to the generated shapes.

Efficiency has been measured taking into account the resources expended in relation to the accuracy and completeness with which users completed the drawing tasks. In our study we have used the task completion time and the number of events logged by a modified macro recording application. The most interesting result in this measure was the comparison between the best results obtained with ParSketch and the minimum number of interactions required by PTC's Pro/Engineer Wildfire 3 to complete the drawing tasks (this data are presented in Table 1). For all the participants in the study, this was their first contact with a Tablet-PC, and some of them had problems to control the pressure threshold that changes input mode.

Table 1. Efficiency comparison

Exercise	ParSketch (# of strokes)	Pro/E (# mouse click + # menu selection)
#1 (left)	3	12+4
#2 (middle)	1	8+1
#3 (right)	4	10+4

From Table 1 we can extract a first topic of discussion. Is it comparable the mental effort to generate a stroke on the Tablet-PC with the equivalent mouse operations to define the same geometry? We think that for users with previous experience in sketching on plain paper, drawing is practically an automatic task, which requires less concentration and effort than the mouse operation. Perhaps this justifies that 100% of participants evaluated as easier, the use of ParSketch with respect to the CAD tools known by them.

Finally, user satisfaction has been measured using an adapted version of the QUIS. Questionnaire [9] using a 10 point scale from 0 to 9. A selection of the questions is presented in Table 2. In general, all participants expressed a very positive attitude towards the application, and all of them learnt in a few minutes to use it. Majority of comments about the system came from the pressure-based mode selection and about recognition errors. With respect to the pressure, none of participants had had previous experience with pressure sensible application and this had a distracting effect, requiring some concentration effort to change from the geometry input mode to the gesture one. We think that with more time of use, this mode change would not require so much effort. Also we are thinking about the convenience of providing some kind of online indicator (feedback) of what kind of input is receiving the system. Now, the application uses a paradigm similar to drawing on plain paper. Thickness of the rendered stroke in screen is related to the pressure done by the user while it is drawing. We are thinking on a color-based indication system, that will represent geometry strokes in one color, and gesture strokes in another different one. This color assignment should be done dynamically, because in this way, if the user inadvertently begins to draw the stroke in the wrong mode he/she can correct it on the fly.

The other part of the comments about the system came from mistakes in the recognition process. This creates some kind of frustration in the user, when he/she draws a stroke or a gesture and a wrong interpretation is provided. The recognition rate for gesture recognition was 90 percent. Rates for geometry recognition were very variable, depending on the complexity of the generated stroke and the ability of the user creating the sketch.

In order to improve recognition results, we are studying the creation of a training mode in the application to adapt and tune recognition process to each user procedure of sketching.

Table 2. User satisfaction measures

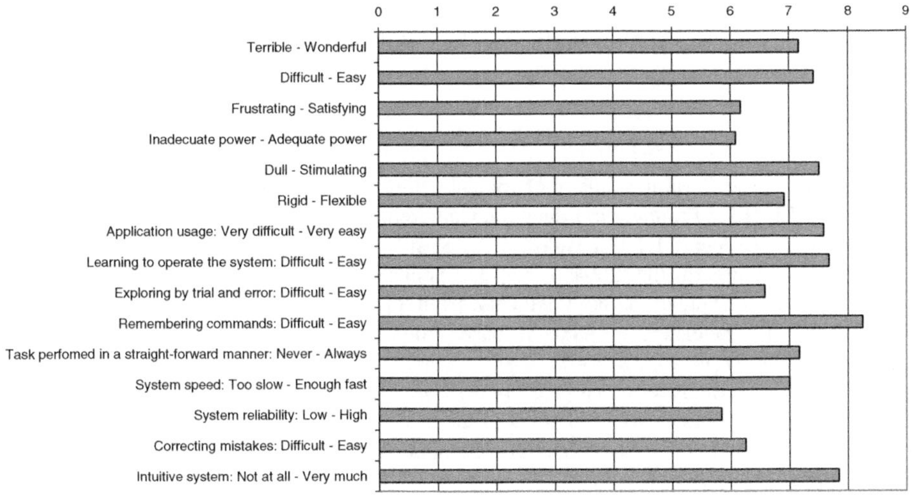

5 Conclusions

ParSketch offers in many cases higher *efficiency* than a comparable WIMP application. This is much related to supporting complex strokes, i.e. strokes composed by mixed basic primitives as line segments and arcs, for defining the shape's geometry.

However a high efficiency in terms of complex stroke support can have an undesired side effect: worse system effectiveness because of the increasing difficulty of the recognition and segmentation tasks. So we can conclude, than the best alternative for getting the best results is the combination of several medium complex strokes, instead of trying to define the whole geometry in one only stroke. Besides, the user can take advantage of the edition strokes (erase and the like) to follow another good strategy: recursive refinement of a first rough version of the stroke. It has some advantages. First, reduces the fail rate of the system. Second, forces the user to sketch in a more convenient way: concentrating in the major shapes, and letting the details for subsequent refinements.

User satisfaction has been very high during the usability study. Users enjoy the simplicity of the system and its powerful control of geometry. However, improvements are needed to give a clearer feedback of pressure mode selection.

Learnability of ParSketch has proven to be very high. Actually, users only have required ten minutes of introduction and demonstration before using the system. This in part is justified by the engineering background of participants. But ParSketch has been specifically designed for this kind of users, trying to exploit their knowledge of technical drawing conventions and their sketching abilities. Perhaps this is one of the reasons of this positive reaction. Users feel that this tool adapts to them, not requiring a special effort for learning to use.

Acknowledgments. The Spanish Ministry of Science and Education and the European Union (Project DPI2004-01373) supported this work. It was also partially supported by Fundació Caixa Castelló-Bancaixa under the Universitat Jaume I program for Research Promotion (Project P1-1B2004-02).

References

1. Barr, R.E.: The Current Status of Graphical Communication in Engineering Education. In: 34th ASEE/IEEE Frontiers in Education Conference, Savannah, GA, pp. S1D8–13 (2004)
2. Barr, R.E., Krueger, T.J., Aanstoos, T.A.: Results of an EDG Student Outcomes Survey. In: Proceedings of the 2004 American Society For Engineering Education Annual Conference & Exposition, Salt Lake City, Utah, pp. 8–13 (2004)
3. Igarashi, T., Zeleznik, B.: Sketch based interaction. IEEE Computer Graphics and Applications 27(1), 26–27 (2007)
4. Ferguson, E.S: Engineering and the Mind's Eye. MIT Press, Cambridge, MA (1992)
5. Company, P., Contero, M., Conesa, J., Piquer, A.: An Optimisation-based Reconstruction Engine for 3D Modelling by Sketching. Computers & Graphics 28(6), 955–979 (2004)
6. Contero, M., Naya, F., Jorge, J., Conesa, J., CIGRO,: a Minimal Instruction Set Calligraphic Interface for Sketch-Based Modeling. In: Kumar, V., Gavrilova, M., Tan, C.J.K., L'Ecuyer, P. (eds.) ICCSA 2003. LNCS, vol. 2669, pp. 549–558. Springer, Heidelberg (2003)
7. http://www.regeo.uji.es/videos/parsketch_01.avi
8. Landay, J.A., Myers, B.A.: Sketching Interfaces: Toward More Human Interface Design. Computer 34(3), 56–64 (2001)
9. Company, P., Contero, M., Naya, F., Aleixos, N.: A Study of Usability of Sketching Tools Aimed at Supporting Prescriptive Sketches. In: Proceedings of the 4th Eurographics Workshop on Sketch-Based Interfaces and Modeling, pp. 139–146 (2006)
10. Hornbæk, K.: Current Practice in Measuring Usability: Challenges to Usability Studies and Research. International Journal of Human-Computer Studies 64(2), 79–102 (2006)
11. Chin, J.P., Diehl, V.A., Norman, K.L.: Development of an Instrument Measuring User Satisfaction of the Human-Computer Interface. In: Proceedings of the SIGCHI Conference on Human Factors in Computing Systems, pp. 213–218 (1988)

The Effects of Various Visual Enhancements During Continuous Pursuit Tracking Tasks

Jaekyu Park[1] and Sung Ha Park[2]

[1] Instrumentation and Control and Human Factors Division, Korea Atomic Energy Research Institute, 150 Deokjin-dong, Yuseong-gu, Daejeon, Korea
{jkpark,KAERI}@kaeri.re.kr
[2] Department of Industrial & Management Engineering, Hannam University, 133 Ojeong-dong, Daedeok-gu, Daejeon, Korea
{shpark,Hannam University}@hannam.ac.kr

Abstract. The present study investigated the effects of visual enhancements in a continuous pursuit tracking task. Participants performed simulated tracking tasks and were instructed to maintain a pointer on a moving horizontal bar of an indicator display using a computer mouse. Within-subject factorial design was implemented with three levels of visual enhancement and three levels of task difficulty. Subjective ratings of workload (using modified Cooper-Harper rating scale) and tracking errors were obtained as performance measures. ANOVA results showed that the tracking error and subjective workload were significantly affected by each of the independent variables (i.e., the types of visual enhancement and task difficulties). The result implies that visual enhancement cues can provide additional visual information of target location during tracking tasks.

Keywords: Tracking Task, Visual Display, Visual Enhancement.

1 Introduction

Tracking and a continuous manual control are normally a critical part of human-vehicle interaction. Also, because aircrafts and ground vehicles are often moving at high speeds, the safety implications of transportation systems are very important [1].

In the case of transportation systems which are typical of tracking tasks, more than a million people are killed on the world's roads each year. For example, more than 40,000 people are killed on the roads of the United States each year. Traffic crashes also damage property, especially vehicles. By converting all these losses to monetary values, it is estimated that US traffic crashes in 2000 cost $231 billion, an amount grater than the Gross Domestic Product of all but a few countries [2]. According to a report by the Ministry of Construction and Transportation and the Korea Transport Institute, there were 222,158 accidents in 2004, resulting in 7,013 deaths and 347,661 injured, including all traffic modes, in Korea. As a result, total accident costs added up to 14.5 trillion won which amounted to about 1.86% of Korea's 2004 GDP [3], [4].

The types of systems and mechanisms people control in their jobs and every day lives vary considerably from simple light switches to complex power plants and

J. Jacko (Ed.): Human-Computer Interaction, Part II, HCII 2007, LNCS 4551, pp. 125–132, 2007.

aircraft systems. Whatever the nature of a system, the basic human functions involved in its control remain the same. Human operators receive information, process it, select an action, and execute the action. The action taken then serves as a control input to a system. In most systems, there typically is some form of feedback to a person regarding the effects of an action taken. In particular, because tracking tasks which are present in all aspects of a vehicle's control, including driving an automobile, piloting a plane, or steering and maintaining a balance on a bicycle require a continuous control of something, they are tasks that often involve complex information processing and decision-making activities to determine a proper control of a system, and these tasks are greatly influenced by the displays and dynamics of the system being controlled. In this regard, effective interfaces in various visual displays can be important factors to reduce the cognitive workload of human beings in a tracking task [5].

This study was performed to investigate the effects of visual enhancements on performance of continuous pursuit tracking tasks. Indicator displays with varying visual enhancements were presented on a CRT monitor. Human operators performed manual tracking tasks by controlling the cursor position with a mouse to pursue the motion of a horizontal bar on the indicator display. Quantitative assessments of different display conditions are made by using tracking errors and a modified Cooper-Harper rating as performance measures [6].

2 Methods

2.1 Subjects

Ten healthy male undergraduate and graduate students (age 28.2±4.2 years) participated in the study. They were required to fill out a personal data form and all were right handed with a normal or corrected-to-normal vision and hearing. All the subjects read and signed a consent form before the experiment. They were paid for their participation.

2.2 Apparatus

The equipment used for this experiment included a desktop computer, a 17" monitor and an optical mouse. The desktop computer was equipped with a Pentium-4 processor with a frequency of 2.66GHz. The sampling rate for data acquisition was 10Hz. The indicator display for the tracking task was simulated using Visual C++ 6.0 computer program language, as shown in Fig. 1. The experimental task was to control the cursor position with a mouse to pursue the motion of a horizontal bar on the indicator display.

2.3 Experimental Design

We used a within-subject factorial design with three levels of visual enhancement and three levels of task difficulty as independent measures. Three visual enhancements were none visual enhancement (None), a shaded reference bar (Shade), and a

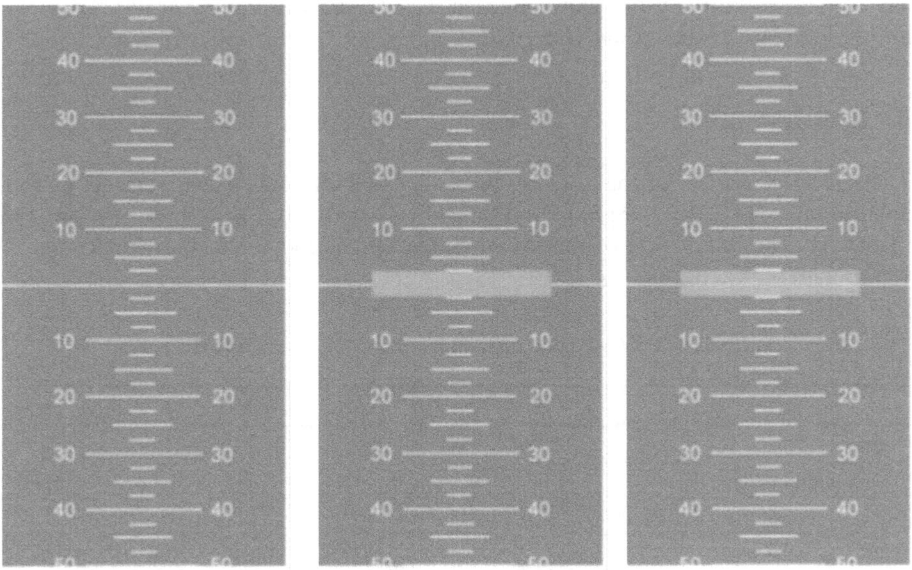

Fig. 1. Indicator displays and visual enhancement cues used in the experiment - From left, none visual enhancement(*None*), a shaded reference bar(*Shade*), and a translucent reference bar(*Shade with line*)

translucent reference bar (Shade with line). The shaded reference bar and translucent reference bar were virtual cues overlaid on the horizontal bar of the indicator display, as shown in Fig. 1. Three levels of the task difficulty were manipulated by changing the speed of the target (i.e., the horizontal bar on the indicator display). The difficulty of the task was adjusted by means of varying the subjects' workload. A preliminary study was conducted in order to tune the difficulty of the task. It was found that reliable changes in the difficulty level could be achieved by varying the speed of the target. As a result, three difficulty levels that were controlled by the speed of the horizontal bar were selected. The average speeds of the target for the low (Low), medium (Medium), and high difficulty (High) levels were 80, 100 and 120pixels/second, respectively.

Dependent measures included tracking errors and subjective ratings of workload. The tracking error was defined as the total number of pixels between the target and the cursor during the task. The order of the task condition within the blocks was counter-balanced across the subjects, in order to minimize the effect of learning.

2.4 Experimental Procedure

Upon arrival for the experiment, participants were instructed to practice the tracking task with all display configurations. Following initial practicing, participants completed the experimental tasks for the data collection. Participant's tracking data was measured for 60 second/condition. After completing each task, they rated their subjective workload using the modified Cooper-Harper rating scale. They were allowed to rest between trials, if necessary.

3 Results

The ANOVA results for the tracking errors showed significant main effects of visual enhancement, F(2, 9)=13.663, p=0.0002 and task difficulty, F(2, 9)=8.619, p=0.0024 (Table 1). The interaction of the visual enhancement and the task difficulty was not significant, p=0.1161.

Table 1. ANOVA results for visual enhancement and task difficulty

Source	DF	SS	MS	F-Value	Pr>F
Subject	9	851.571	94.619		
Visual enhancement	2	78.742	39.371	13.663	0.0002*
Visual enhancement ×Subject	18	51.869	2.882		
Task difficulties	2	72.219	36.110	8.619	0.0024*
Task difficulties ×Subject	18	75.416	4.190		
Visual enhancement × Task difficulties	4	9.930	2.483	1.995	0.1161
Residual	36	44.799	1.244		

*: significant at α=0.05.

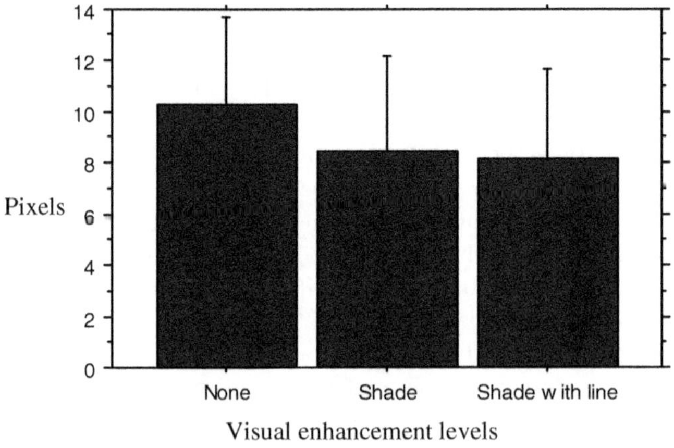

Fig. 2. The means of tracking error for three visual enhancement conditions (*Unit: pixel*)

Student-Newman-Keuls comparisons of the means indicated that the none visual enhancement condition (None) resulted in the largest tracking errors and was significantly different from the shaded reference bar (Shade) and translucent reference bar (Shade with line). The difference between shaded reference bar (Shade) and translucent reference bar (Shade with line) was not significant. The results imply that the shaded reference bar (Shade) and translucent reference bar (Shade with line) were significant in improving tracking performance. The tracking task employed in our study requires frequent use of focused attention. We believe that the visual enhancement cues play an important role in augmenting visual information on target location. Fig. 2 shows mean tracking errors across visual enhancement conditions.

Results of mean comparisons also revealed that the largest tracking errors was committed in high difficult condition (High), followed, in order, medium difficulty (Medium), and low difficulty condition (Low). Fig. 3 shows mean tracking errors across task difficulty conditions.

The ANOVA results for the subjective ratings of workload also showed significant main effects of visual enhancement, F(2, 9)=4.622, p=0.024 and task difficulty, F(2, 9)=11.278, p=0.0007 (Table 2). The interaction of the visual enhancement and the task difficulty was not significant, p=0.2148. Student-Newman-Keuls comparisons of the means indicated that the translucent reference bar (Shade with line) was superior

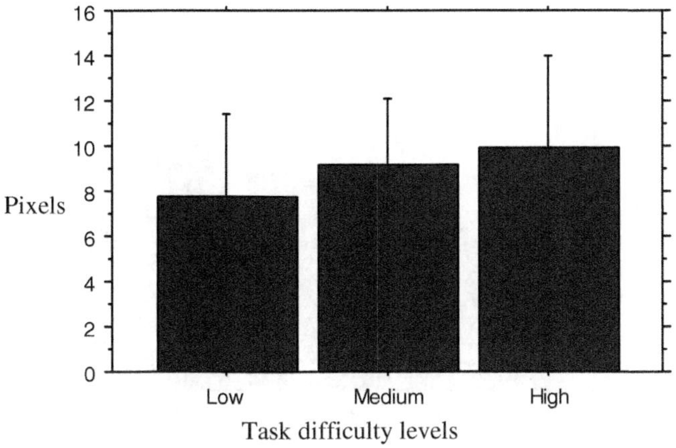

Fig. 3. The means of tracking error for three task difficulty levels (*Unit: pixel*)

Table 2. ANOVA results for subjective workload

Source	DF	SS	MS	F-Value	Pr>F
Subject	9	71.883	7.981		
Visual enhancement	2	38.756	19.378	4.622	0.0240*
Visual enhancement ×Subject	18	75.467	4.193		
Task difficulties	2	42.022	21.011	11.278	0.0007*
Task difficulties ×Subject	18	33.533	1.863		
Visual enhancement × Task difficulties	4	3.644	0.911	1.528	0.2148
Residual	36	21.467	0.596		

*: significant at α=0.05.

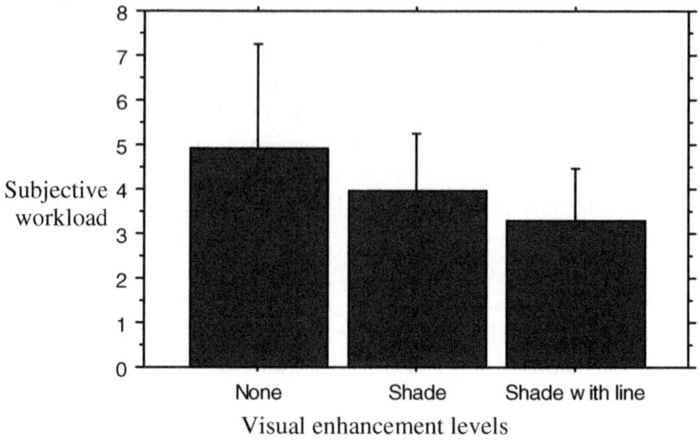

Fig. 4. The means of the subjective workload for the visual enhancement levels

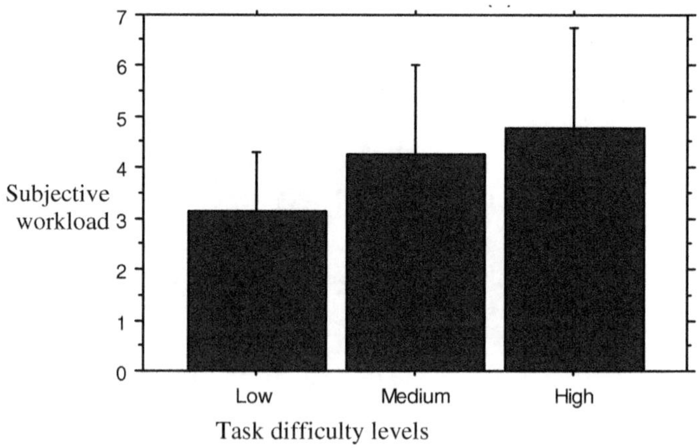

Fig. 5. The means of the subjective workload for the task difficulty levels

to the none visual enhancement (None). However, the difference between shaded reference bar (Shade) and the none visual enhancement (None) was not significant. For the task difficulty, performing the task with high difficulty condition (High) was judged to be more difficult than performing the task with medium (Medium) and low difficulty conditions (Low). Fig. 4 and 5 show means of subjective ratings of workload.

4 Discussion

This study was intended to identify and quantify the effects of visual enhancement cues on the performance of tracking tasks. Present study considered the independent representation of movement of both the target and cursor, such as pursuit tracking displays. In contrast to pursuit tracking displays, compensatory tracking displays present only the movement of an error relative to a fixed reference. Thus, the compensatory tracking display was not considered in this study since this display provides no indication of whether this error arose from a change in system's output or command input.

The results of ANOVA showed that performance and subjective workload were significantly affected by the types of visual enhancements and task difficulties. Also, the results of a pair-wise analysis showed that the amount of deviation between the mouse pointer and the horizontal bar moving on indicator were reduced by tendering visual enhancement cues. Particularly, the performance and subjective ratings were significantly improved in case of providing a shaded reference bar (Shade) and a translucent reference bar (Shade with line). From the results of comparing the means for each level of the task difficulty, as the task difficulty increased, the degree of a deviation between the mouse pointer and the moving horizontal bar of the indicator were gradually increased. The low velocity (LOW) of task difficulty was significantly different from the medium velocity (Medium) and high velocity (High). This results support previous findings that virtual cues can be utilized to provide additional visual information for the tasks requiring considerable attention such as a tracking task [7], [8].

The findings of this study are applicable to the design of a head-mounted display (HUD) in the context of virtual environments. The findings can also be used as guidelines for designing visual displays for tracking tasks accompanied with high speed manipulation such as those found in automobile and aircraft systems. Especially, the results of this study could be applied to design the guidance for the information representation in an information system based HUD such as Smart car [9] which is IVIS (In Vehicle Information System) developed by GM motors and Carnegie Mellon University.

In this study, when the tracking tasks were performed through visual enhancements, it was assumed that participants received visual cues from the same point of view. However, it didn't consider factors such as depth perception and pattern recognition of the subjects who were the main recipients of the visual information. Further studies are needed with considerations on cognitive properties.

References

1. Wickens, C.D., Lee, J.D., Liu, Y., Gordon, S.E.: An Introduction to Human Factors Engineering 2nd edn. Newark, NJ: Prentice Hall (2003)
2. Evans, L.: A crash course in traffic safety, 1997 Medical and Health Annual Chicago: Encyclopaedia Britannica (1996)
3. Ministry of Construction & Transportation.: 2005 Transportation safety enforcement plan (2005)
4. Korea Transport Institute.: 2003 Traffic Accident Estimate Costs in Korea (2006)
5. Sanders, M.M., McCormick, E.J.: Human Factors in Engineering & Design, 7th edn. McGraw-Hill, NY (1993)
6. Wierwille, W.W., Casali, J.G.: A Validated Rating Scale for Global Mental Workload Measurement Applications. In: Proceedings of the Human Factors Society 27th Annual Meeting Santa Monica, CA: Human Factors and Ergonomics Society, pp. 129–133 (1983)

7. Park, S.H., Koo, J.M: Effects of Tele-Robotic Task Characteristics on the Choice of Visual Display Dimensionality. Journal of the Ergonomics Society of Korea 23(2), 2535 (2004)
8. Hardy, G.H., Lewis, E. K.: Cockpit Display of Traffic and Wake Information for Closely Spaced Parallel Approaches. In: Proceedings of AIAA Guidance, Navigation and Control Conference, Providence, RI (2004)
9. GM Collaborative Research Lab.: Carnegie Mellon University [http://gm.web.cmu.edu/]

Stylus Enhancement to Enrich Interaction with Computers

Yu Suzuki, Kazuo Misue, and Jiro Tanaka

Department of Computer Science, University of Tsukuba
1-1-1 Tennodai, Tsukuba, Ibaraki 305-8573, Japan
{suzuki,misue,jiro}@iplab.cs.tsukuba.ac.jp

Abstract. We introduce a technique to enrich user interaction with a computer through a stylus. This technique allows a stylus to be manipulated in the air to operate applications in new ways. To translate the stylus manipulation into application behavior, we take an approach that we attach an accelerometer to the stylus. Such a stylus allows control through new operations like rolling and shaking, as well as through conventional operations like tapping or making strokes. An application can use these operations to switch modes or change parameters. We have implemented a number of applications, called the "Oh! Stylus Series," that can be used with our proposed technique.

Keywords: Stylus Enhancement, Interaction, Accelerometer, Behavior.

1 Introduction

Computer operations based on a stylus, compared to those with a mouse, have the advantage of being direct and easy to understand. In terms of the interaction style, though, most stylus operations simply replace mouse operations, so these operations do not take advantage of all the ways a pen-shaped device can be handled. Potential interface techniques have not been realized because computers cannot detect stylus positions and movements when a conventional stylus is not touching the display.

Our goal is to make pen-based applications more useful by enabling a computer to detect such manipulations of a stylus and use them to govern applications run on the computer. Our approach is to attach an accelerometer to a stylus so that it can obtain context information regarding the stylus; i.e., its positions and movements. Analysis of the obtained context information allows a computer to respond to user commands input through the stylus movements. In this paper, we describe an interaction technique based on this approach, the creation of a context sensitive stylus, applications which use the stylus, and our evaluation of the interaction technique.

2 Proposed Technique

2.1 Primary Idea

Our proposed interaction technique takes advantage of how a user naturally handles a pen-shaped device; that is, it is based on the various ways users manipulate a stylus as

J. Jacko (Ed.): Human-Computer Interaction, Part II, HCII 2007, LNCS 4551, pp. 133–142, 2007.

they use it, and makes use of these behaviors for interaction with a computer. These behaviors include the following:

(a) driving a quill
(b) dotting a point
(c) pressing a point
(d) tapping the head or grip of a pen
(e) shaking a pen up and down
(f) rolling a pen between the fingers

Of these behaviors, (a) – (d) can be done through the same behavior when people use a stylus. In other words, as stylus operations these behaviors are “drag”, “tap”, ”press”, “point”, “push of a barrel button” and combinations of these operations. On the other hand, (e) and (f) are behaviors which cannot be used with a conventional stylus because they cannot be detected when a conventional stylus is used; i.e., the positions and movements of a stylus in the air cannot be detected. However, we enable computers to detect such stylus behaviors by attaching an accelerometer to the stylus, and this makes it possible to use such movements for interaction between the user and the computer.

2.2 Behavior Assignment

We have to assign various behaviors of a stylus, detected from context information regarding the stylus, to particular computer operations. To realize a comfortable, easy to understand interface based on our interaction technique, it is important to assign appropriate behaviors to these operations. We divided this assignment into two parts:

(i) assigning typical behaviors when people use a pen
(ii) assigning another actions

The first type of behaviors allows the user of a stylus with an attached accelerometer to get feedback from an application by operating the stylus as he would use a pen. This enables easy and intuitive operation. However, the variety of such behaviors is not rich.

The second type allows us to increase the variety of behaviors almost infinitely. In this case, though, intuitive computer operation is more difficult to achieve.

We have to discuss another way of behavior assignment.

3 Implementation

3.1 Hardware

Our system consists of a tablet PC (HP Compaq tc 1100), an accelerometer (Cookie (Nokia Research Center Tokyo)), and a Bluetooth USB adapter (Microsoft). Cookie is a coin-shaped, battery-operated complex sensor (Fig. 1, upper-left), and its Bluetooth v1.1 Serial Port Profile enables wireless communication with computers. Attaching Cookie to a stylus thus allowed us to create a smart stylus.

We call this stylus a context sensitive stylus. It was difficult to attach Cookie to a stylus directly, so we created a holder from a marker pen cap and a plastic bottle cap.

While this stylus was a rather crude prototype, we plan to create a more refined version in the future.

Because our Tablet PC was not equipped with a Bluetooth module, we attached a Microsoft Bluetooth USB adapter to the tablet PC so that it could communicate with Cookie.

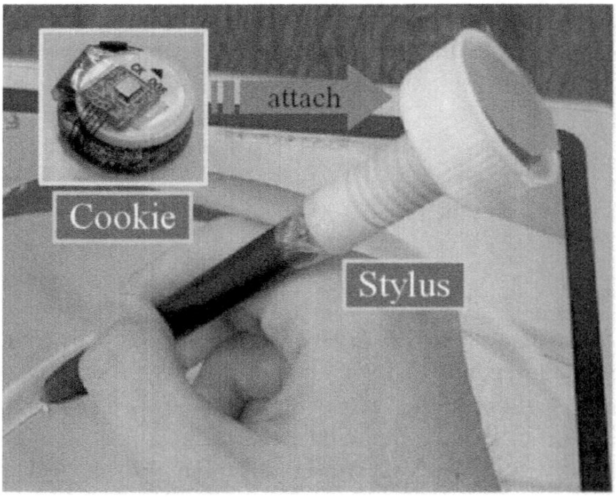

Fig. 1. Stylus with an attached Cookie

3.2 Converting Raw Accelerometer Data into Semantic Data

In this research, we sought to enable interaction with a computer through a "rolling" operation, meaning that the stylus was rotated around the pen axis, and a "shaking" operation, where the stylus was shaken up and down along the pen axis.

We had to convert low level data (acceleration data) from the accelerometer into semantic data to control applications through the rolling and shaking motions. First, three-axis acceleration data (roll, pitch, and yaw) was obtained from Cookie (Fig. 2). Cookie communicated with the computer every 100 ms. The range of acceleration for each direction was -3G to +3G. The rolling motion was detected from the roll and pitch accelerations, and the shaking motion was obtained from the yaw acceleration.

For rolling, we calculate the stylus angle of rotation from the accelerations on two axes (roll and pitch) and the system recognizes rolling from a change in the rotation

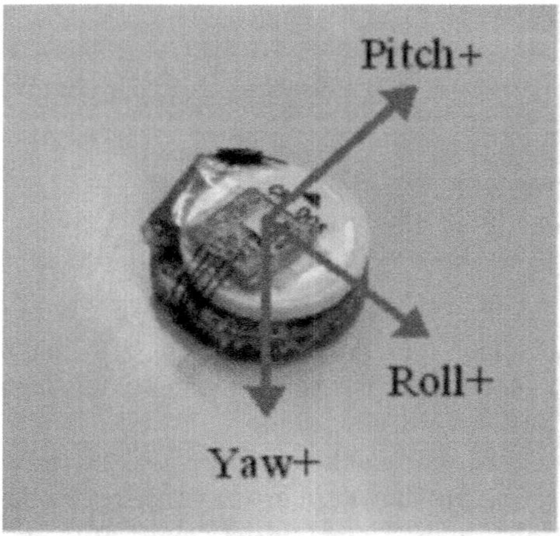

Fig. 2. 3-axis of Cookie

angle from the state 100 ms earlier. We calculate the angle of rotation from the arctangent. If the current roll acceleration is r_t and the current pitch acceleration is p_t, the current angle θ_t can be represented by the following expression.

$$\theta_t = \tan^{-1} p_t / r_t .$$

Likewise, the angle 100 ms earlier, θ_{t-1}, can be represented as

$$\theta_{t-1} = \tan^{-1} p_{t-1} / r_{t-1} .$$

By using θ_t and θ_{t-1}, we can calculate the stylus angle of rotation θ. The way that θ is used depends on each application. (We describe a detailed example of usage in the next section.) Other ways could also be used to recognize the rolling operation.

For shaking, we calculate the stylus angle of rotation from the acceleration on one axis (yaw). When the user raises the stylus, the yaw acceleration decreases, and when the user brings the stylus down, the yaw acceleration increases. If the yaw acceleration 100 ms earlier is y_{t-1} and the current yaw acceleration is y_t, the range for which the system will recognize shaking can be represented by

$$|y_{t-1} - y_t| >= 2G .$$

3.3 Application

We have created a group of applications, called the "Oh! Stylus Series," which are compatible with a context sensitive stylus. We used the following APIs and toolkits.

- Java 2 Platform Standard Edition Development Kit 5.0
- Java Communications API
- Blue Cove (Java Bluetooth API)
- SWT (Standard Widget Toolkit)

3.3.1 Oh! Stylus Draw

Oh! Stylus Draw is a paint tool that allows us to use a context sensitive stylus. Oh! Stylus Draw makes it possible to

(1) change a drawing color by rolling
(2) switch a color palette by shaking
(3) switch a drawing mode by holding down a barrel button + press + rolling.

A screenshot of Oh! Stylus Draw is shown in Fig. 3. There are five panels on the left of Fig. 3, and the upper four panels represent drawing modes (freehand line, straight line, rectangle, and ellipse). The user can switch between these modes by holding down a barrel button + press + rolling.

If the user rolls the stylus in a clockwise direction, the drawing mode switches to the mode one panel downwards (if the current drawing mode is that of the lowest panel, the next mode is the mode of the highest panel). If the user rolls the stylus in a counterclockwise direction, the drawing mode switches to the mode one panel upwards (if the current drawing mode is that of the highest panel, the next mode is the

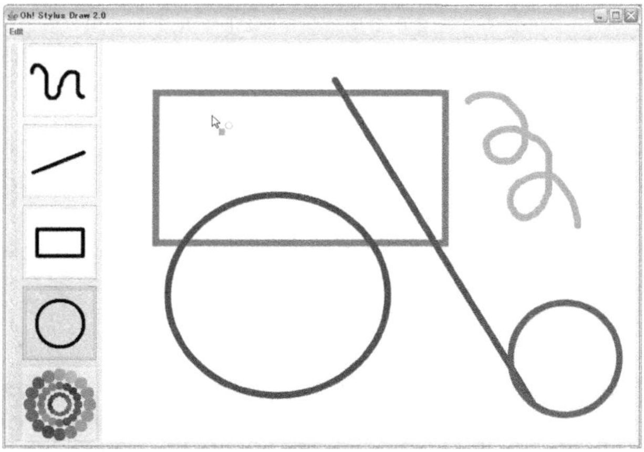

Fig. 3. Oh! Stylus Draw

mode of the lowest panel). This application recognizes clockwise rolling when the difference in the rotation angle from 100 ms earlier exceeds 50° and counterclockwise rolling action when the difference is under -50°. The user receives sound feedback from the application when he switches the drawing mode.

The lowest panel is the color palette panel, which has three zones called the first, second, and third zones (Fig. 4). There are five palettes, and when the user shakes the stylus, these palettes move through the zones. That is, the palette in the first zone is active and the user can choose a drawing color from this palette. When the user shakes the stylus, the palette from the second zone moves to the first zone and becomes active. At the same time, the palette in the third zone moves to the second one and the next palette in the rotation is displayed in the third zone. The motion of the palette switching is animated so that the user can easily see that the palette has changed. When the palette changes, the application also provides sound feedback.

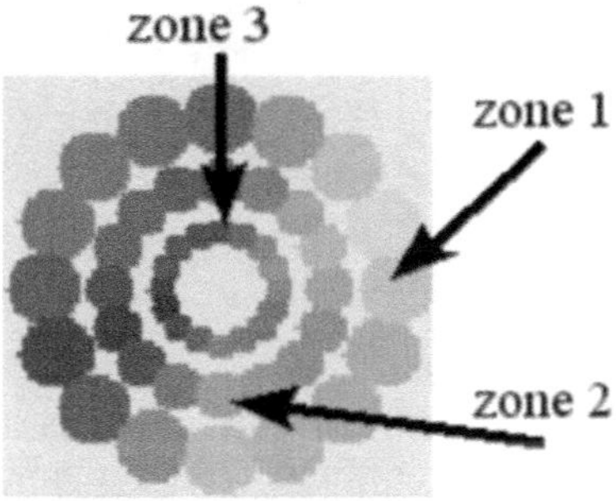

Fig. 4. Zones of the color palette panel

One color palette consists of 16 small circles, each representing one drawing color. Because there are five palettes, the total number of colors is 80. If the user's preferred color does not exist in any of the palettes, he can change one color into his preferred color by tapping one small circle. The drawing color is the color at the top of the current color palette, and the user can choose a drawing color from the current color palette by rolling. If the difference in the rotation angle from 100 ms earlier is over 50° when he rotates the stylus in the clockwise direction, the palette also rotates in the clockwise direction and the drawing color changes to the next color on the left. If the difference in the rotation angle is under -50° when he rotates the stylus in the counterclockwise direction, the palette rotates in that direction and the drawing color changes the next color on the right. The palette rotation is animated, so the user can easily tell when the drawing color is changed. When the palette rotates, the application also provides sound feedback.

3.3.2 Oh! Stylus Scroll

Oh! Stylus Scroll is a scroll support tool that makes it easy for the user to scroll up or down (left or right) on a screen by rolling the stylus. Oh! Stylus Scroll can be used for most applications that have a scroll bar.

A screenshot of Oh! Stylus Draw is shown in Fig. 5. If the user rolls the stylus in a clockwise direction, the screen scrolls down (right), or vice versa. In this application, we provide a mouse wheel event as a target application.

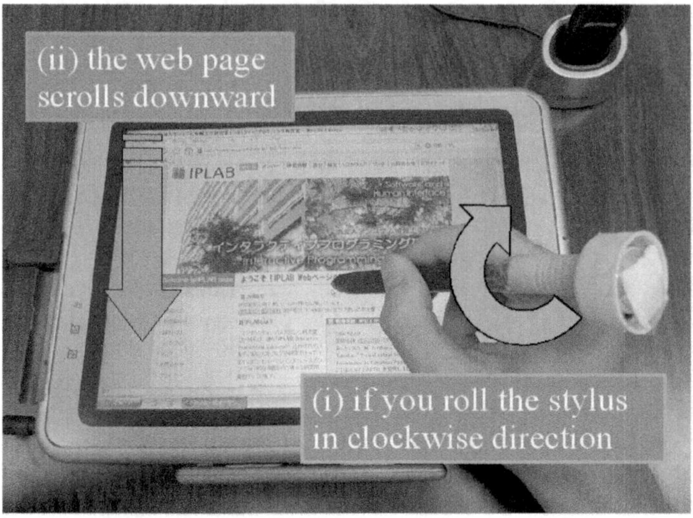

Fig. 5. Oh! Stylus Scroll

The amount of scrolling depends on the difference in the rotation angle from 100 ms earlier. If the difference is under 10°, no scrolling occurs. This prevents unintended scrolling. If the rotation angle difference, dif, is 10° to 100° degrees, the amount of scrolling, s, is calculated as

$$s = dif / 10 \text{ (rounded off to the nearest 10)} .$$

For example, when the change in the rotation angle is 73°, the amount of scrolling is seven lines. If the change exceeds 180°, though, no scrolling occurs; this is to prevent misrecognition of rotation in the opposite direction.

4 Evaluation

4.1 Purpose and Evaluation Method

We did an experiment to evaluate the usability of our proposed technique. The participants were nine students majoring in computer science. Each used Oh! Stylus

Draw and Oh! Stylus Scroll as they like, and then they completed a questionnaire about the usability.

4.2 Result

4.2.1 Oh! Stylus Draw

Typical comments obtained from the completed questionnaires included the following:

- shaking is easy to use
- the sound feedback is easy to understand
- it is easy to draw a gradation picture
- when the participants brought their stylus close to the screen, the drawing color which they had chosen by rolling changed without their intention
- it took a long time to choose a color on the opposite side of palette from the current color

We obtained many other comments, but all participants said that shaking was easy to use.

4.2.2 Oh! Stylus Scroll

Typical comments included the following:

- scrolling by rolling is convenient
- the participants took a long time to figure out the relationship between the difference in the rotation angle and the amount of scrolling
- when the participants tried clicking a hyperlink, the web page tended to scroll without their intention

5 Discussion

The evaluation showed that shaking is easy to use as an operation of a context sensitive stylus. Shaking seems to be a natural action for the user, because it is similar to a typical action when using a mechanical pencil. While some participants commented that rolling is convenient in Oh! Stylus Scroll, others commented that rolling is not an effective way to choose the drawing color in Oh! Stylus Draw. Rolling might not be a common action when we use a pen and the participants did not get used to this action. Because the evaluation results regarding rolling differed between Oh! Stylus Draw and Oh! Stylus Scroll, we think that assigning rolling to effective applications and operations will make it a more easily used interface.

We received many comments from the participants, some positive and others negative. However, most of the negative comments did not indicate that our interface was ineffective in concept; rather they indicated that there were problems in the implementation.

In the future, we plan to test how the display size affects the results of such an evaluation.

6 Related Work

Our goal is to improve computer interaction through stylus use. To achieve this, we want to use the various ways a user can manipulate a stylus by attaching an accelerometer to a stylus so that a computer can detect these manipulations and react to them. For this reason, we describe related work from two fields of research:

(1) research to improve computer operability with a stylus
(2) research on interface devices with an attached accelerometer.

6.1 Research to Improve Computer Operability with a Stylus

Miura et al. proposed RodDirect [1], which is an interaction technique where a stylus is used to resemble non-pen objects. RodDirect associates a stylus with physical metaphors. The user operates a stylus which is in a stylus holder. The amount of stylus rotation and parallel movement in the stylus holder is used as input to a computer. Dual Touch [2], proposed by Matsushita et al., detects multiple pointing points. The user interacts with a PDA by using a stylus and his thumb. In RodDirect and Dual Touch, because the user holds a PDA in one hand and operates the PDA with the other hand, both hands are needed for operation. In contrast, our proposed technique allows the user to operate a PDA with only one hand.

Smith et al. proposed the radial scroll tools [3]. In this system, when the user lays a stylus on a display, a guide appears at the pointing point. The user can then use gestures, like drawing a circle at the pointing point, to scroll a screen. While this system utilizes the advantage of a pen by gesturing, it uses only stroke information. In contrast, our technique uses additional information that cannot be obtained through a conventional stylus.

Siio et al. [4] proposed an interaction technique which uses Paperweight Metaphor. They attach a touch sensor electrode to the bottom or a corner of a PDA and use these sensors to provide seamless and intuitive switching between the scrolling mode and the editing mode. In this system, although the user can operate a PDA with one hand, the usage scenes are limited. In contrast, our technique has a wide variety of usage scenes.

6.2 Research on Interface Devices with an Attached Accelerometer

Rekimoto [5] described the effectiveness of using an accelerometer to operate computers. Since then, much research on this use of accelerometers has been done.

Harrison et al. proposed Squeeze Me, Hold Me, Tilt Me! [6]. They attached an accelerometer to a handheld PC and detected the tilt of the PC. They also developed some applications which can use the tilt information; for example, by tilting a handheld PC, the user can turn pages displayed on the PC. Hinckley et al. [7] attached an accelerometer to a PDA so that a user could scroll a screen by tilting the PDA. Rekimoto proposed Gesture Wrist and Gesture Pad [8], which use gestures for input to a wearable computer. These systems recognize hand gestures through sensors such as an accelerometer. Andrew et al. developed XWand [9], which enables the operation of electronic devices, such as a desk lamp, by gestures. By twisting or shaking the XWand, the user can control an electronic device towards which the XWand is pointed. This system uses various sensors, such as an accelerometer.

As above, accelerometers are frequency used for perceptive user interface (PUI) research. Recent improvements in semiconductor technologies have allowed more compact accelerometers with greater performance. This has made it feasible to create small computer devices that incorporate an accelerometer.

7 Conclusion and Future Work

We have proposed a new interaction technique to enrich stylus-based interaction with computers. To apply various types of stylus manipulation, we attached an accelerometer to a stylus to create a context sensitive stylus. Through this stylus, our computer could recognize a rolling operation, where the stylus is rotated around the pen axis, and a shaking operation, where the stylus is shaken up and down along the pen axis. As applications which utilize a context sensitive stylus, we implemented the Oh! Stylus Series (i.e., Oh! Stylus Draw and Oh! Stylus Scroll). To control these applications, we found we could use rolling and shaking of the stylus. We then evaluated the usability of our proposal technique with respect to the Oh! Stylus Series.

In an evaluation experiment, we learned that shaking is easy for users to use as an operation of a context sensitive stylus. In contrast, the usability of rolling depended on how it was assigned to application operations. Because rolling and shaking are new interaction techniques, further work is needed to determine what kinds of application can best utilize rolling and shaking.

As our future work, we also plan to implement applications to improve the productivity of our proposed technique. In addition, we are developing and will soon implement the following additions to the Oh! Stylus Series:

- Oh! Stylus Map (map viewer)
- Oh! Stylus Popie (character input system by using Popie [10])
- Oh! Stylus Desktop Tools (to improve the desktop environment)

Acknowledgments. We thank Nokia Research Center Tokyo for lending Cookie sensors to us.

References

1. Miura, M., Kunifuji, S.: RodDirect: Two-Dimensional Input with Stylus Knob. In: Proceedings of the 8th International Conference on Human Computer Interaction with Mobile Devices and Services (MobileHCI 2006), pp. 113–120 (2006)
2. Matsushita, N., Ayatsuka, N., Rekimoto, J.: Dual Touch: a two-handed interface for pen-based PDAs. In: Proceedings of the 13th Annual ACM Symposium on User Interface Software and Technology (UIST'00), pp. 211–212 (2000)
3. Smith, G.M.: schraefel, m.c.: The radial scroll tool: scrolling support for stylus or touch-based document navigation. In: Proceedings of the 17th annual ACM Symposium on User Interface Software and Technology (UIST'04), pp. 53–56 (2004)

4. Siio, I., Tsujita, H.: Mobile Interaction Using Paperweight Metaphor. In: Proceedings of the 19th Annual ACM Symposium on User Interface Software and Technology (UIST'06), pp. 111–114 (2006)
5. Rekimoto, J.: Tilting operations for small screen interfaces. In: Proceedings of the 9th Annual ACM Symposium on User Interface Software and Technology (UIST'96), pp. 203–204 (1996)
6. Harrison, B.L., Fishkin, K.P., Gujar, A., Mochon, C., Want, R.: Squeeze Me, Hold Me, Tilt Me! An Exploration of Manipulative User Interfaces. In: Proceedings of the SIGCHI Conference on Human Factors in Computing Systems (CHI'98), pp. 17–24 (1998)
7. Hinckley, K., Pierce, J., Sinclair, M., Horvitz, E.: Sensing Techniques for Mobile Interaction. In: Proceedings of the 13th Annual ACM Symposium on User Interface Software and Technology (UIST'00), pp. 91–100 (2000)
8. Rekimoto, J.: GestureWrist and GesturePad: Unobtrusive Wearable Interaction Devices. In: Proceedings of the Fifth International Symposium on Wearable Computers (ISWC'01), p. 21 (2001)
9. Wilson, A., Shafer, S.: XWand: UI for intelligent spaces. In: Proceedings of the SIGCHI Conference on Human Factors in Computing Systems (CHI 2003), pp. 545–552 (2003)
10. Sato, D., Shizuki, B., Miura, M., Tanaka, J.: Menu-Selection-Based Japanese Input Method with Consonants for Pen-Based Computers. In: Proceedings of 6th Asia-Pacific Conference on Computer-Human Interaction (APCHI 2004), pp. 399–408 (2004)

An Experimental Evaluation of Information Visualization Techniques and Decision Style

WanAdilah Wan Adnan, NorLaila MdNoor, and Rasimah Aripin

Faculty of Information Technology & Quantitative Sciences, Universiti Teknologi MARA, Malaysia

Abstract. This study aims to investigate the extent to which information visualization (IV) techniques and decision style affect decision performance and user preferences in a decision support environment. The study adopted an experimental method. Findings from this study provide theoretical, empirical and practical contributions. The results showed that there were significant differences in decision performance and user preference across IV techniques and decision style. The findings have important implications for the decision support system (DSS) designers, and provide important research issues for future work.

Keywords: information visualization techniques, decision style, human computer interaction, decision support system.

1 Introduction

Information visualization (IV) is an emerging technology that relies on the human's perception and cognitive abilities to visualize data. Incorporating IV techniques to a decision support system is the potential solution to improve system's effectiveness and to provide decision makers with better insights about the data that they are analyzing. Many innovative IV techniques have been developed. However, empirical evaluation on IV techniques is still in early stage and lacking in numbers [2], particularly in the area of business decision-support applications [10]. Besides, the adoption of IV techniques as reported in the literature, is still minimal. More evidence of measurable benefits supporting the use of IV is needed. In addition, attention to individual cognitive differences is recommended, to realize IV's potential advantage. In the human-computer-interaction (HCI) and IV literature, the importance of individual differences has been emphasized. However, decision style, which is recognized as one of the key individual cognitive differences that affects system success, has received little attention in these areas. Decision style reflects the way a person visualizes and thinks about a situation. In decision support system (DSS) literature, decision style has been acknowledged to affect decision-making performance and one's preferences for human-machine-interface [12]. Unfortunately, it has frequently been overlooked and rarely been given priority in the DSS design [3]. Hence, this study aims to bridge these gaps.

J. Jacko (Ed.): Human-Computer Interaction, Part II, HCII 2007, LNCS 4551, pp. 143–150, 2007.

The purpose of this paper is to determine the extent to which IV techniques and decision style affect decision performance and user preferences. The main objective is to explore and reports the potential of main and interaction effects of decision style on decision performance in using IV techniques thru experimental study. The paper begins with theoretical background. Then, the research method and hypotheses are explained. This is followed by the description of the experimental design, procedures and variables. The subsequent section discusses the results and ends with conclusions.

2 Theoretical Background

Te'eni et al.[11] have claimed that the lack of attention to the user interface issues to be the main reason for the poor acceptance of an information system. Based on Vessay's Cognitive Fit theory [13], a solution to a problem is "an outcome of the relationship between the problem representation and problem solving tasks." In the DSS literature, the importance of the cognitive fit has been highlighted. Prior studies showed that the fit between representation of information and task has a positive impact on performance [1].

Current research also continues to address the need to consider cognitive differences among decision makers and determine ways in which these differences can be best supported [9]. A DSS that is designed to support a decision makers' preferred style could enhance one's satisfaction [7].

2.1 Information Visualization Techniques

Many innovative IV techniques have been developed to improve decision performance. However, empirical evaluation of IV is still in its early stage and still lacking, particularly in the area of business decision support environment [10]. Studies on IV have shown conflicting of findings. A study done by Ghosh & Shneiderman [4] shows that overview+detail (*O+D*) techniques provides significant faster completion time over zoom+pan (*Z+P*), due to the presence of overview. However, no difference in user satisfaction was found. In contrast, Hornbaek et al [5] reported different results. They argue that the presence of overview supports for further explorations and thus leads to poorer results in performance.

2.2 Decision Style

Literature recognises decision style as a critical element in DSS design. Te'eni [11] among others, argues that a DSS would be more widely used, more accepted and produce better decision making if it matches individuals' cognitive styles in particular decision styles. In addition, Mintzberg [6] attributes poor decision making to the way in which one processes information. He suggests that methods of representing data should be compatible with an individual's information processing preferences and style of decision-making. According to Rowe and Mason [8], decision style is primarily a cognitive process that combines the mental activities of perception, information processing, making a judgment, and problem solving. It reflects the way that a person visualizes and thinks about situation. They argue that decision style affects the decision behaviour and decision behaviour has an impact on the outcome or the action taken. Further research on the interaction effect of decision style is required for exploring its importance in DSS design.

3 Research Method

This study adopts an experimental method, based on within-subject design approach. IV techniques and task complexity are within-subject variables and decision style is between subject variable. Participants were tested with three conditions of IV techniques: 1) zoom+pan (*Z+P*), 2) overview+detail with tree structure (*O+D Tree*), and 3) overview+detail with Window-Explorer structure (*O+D WinExp*). These techniques differ concerning the organization and representation of the information space. The tasks used in this study are categorized as extraction and exploration. The complexity of these tasks differs in terms of three main criteria: the search criteria, the scope of search and the solution. The decision making style of participants were judged using Decision-Style Inventory (DSI). This instrument identifies four distinct categories of decision styles: *directive*, *analytical*, *conceptual*, and *behavioral.* Meanwhile, the decision performance was measured based on the time taken to complete a task. The differences across the IV techniques are also investigated based on user-preferences.

3.1 Hypothesis

List of hypothesis is presented below:

H1. *O+D* techniques will lead to better performance than *Z+P* technique.
H2. *O+D* technique will have higher ranking in user preference than *Z+P*.
H3. Exploration tasks will require longer completion time than extraction task.
H4. There is significant difference in performance across decision styles.
H5. There is a significant interaction effect between IV and decision style on completion time.

3.2 Experimental Design

An experimental study was conducted to test the hypotheses presented above. This study adopts a within subject approach, where each participant performs an experiment under each condition. An academic workload planning application is used in this study to simulate real workload decisions. This study was conducted with 16 participants who were members of the administration staff of Universiti Teknologi MARA (9 females and 7 males).

3.3 Experimental Variables

There are three independent variables in this experiment: IV techniques, task complexity and decision styles. IV and task complexity are within-subject variables and decision style is between subject variable. Meanwhile, the dependent variables are task completion time and user preferences.

- *Independent Variable: Information visualization techniques*

This study examined three types of IV techniques: *O+D WinExp*, *O+D Tree* and *Z+P*. Interface with *O+D* techniques display the selected details of information space together with an overview of the entire information space. It allows users to maintain a global overview and simultaneously examine details. There are differences between the *O+D Tree* and *WinExp* techniques. In the *Tree-based* technique, the overview structure is presented from the beginning of the application. However, for the *WinExp*, only the root of the structure is displayed at the start point. It can be exploded by a click at its parent node, which is similar to the window explorer file organization. On the other hand, the *Z+P* technique only allows having either a detailed view or the global overview of the information space at a time. Its overview structure is similar to the tree-based structure. This technique requires frequent change between the detailed and the overview. This may result in a greater cognitive load, and may have a negative impact on user performance.

- *Independent Variable: Decision style*

The decision making style of participants are judged using a 20-item questionnaire called Decision style Inventory (DSI), a test instrument by Rowe and Mason [8]. The allocation of the style is based on the highest intensity level of DSI scores. This instrument identifies four distinct categories of decision styles: *directive*, *analytical*, *conceptual*, and *behavioral.* These decision styles are different in regards to their methods of perceive and evaluate information [8].

- *Independent Variable: Task*

The tasks used in this study are categorized as extraction task and exploration task. These tasks require participants to search and explore the information space structure and extract the correct answers. The complexity of these tasks differs in terms of three main criteria: the search criteria, the scope of search and the solution. For extraction task, the search criterion is specified. The exploration task requires participants to explore a larger search area with a greater number of solutions required.

- *Dependent Variable: Decision performance - task completion time*

The decision performance was measured based on the time taken to complete a task using a given IV technique. All participants' interactions with the interfaces were automatically logged by the system and the task completion times were derived from the logged data.

- *Dependent Variable: User preference*

The differences across the IV techniques are also investigated based on user preferences. After having used all three IV techniques, participants filled in the user-preferences questionnaire, which required ranking, indicating which techniques they preferred.

3.4 Experimental Procedures

The participants took approximately two and a half hours to complete the experiment including the training session. All participants started with a set of the extraction task, followed by the exploration task. The order of IV techniques was counter balance to avoid learning effects and bias in results.

4 Analysis and Results

The analysis conducted in this study includes both inferential and descriptive statistics. This study follows standard conventions for significance levels, where p-value <= 0.05 are significant.

The data was examined by employing a repeated measure analysis of variance (RM ANOVA) to detect statistically significant differences in decision performance. A comparable non-parametric test was used, when the data differed extensively form RM ANOVA assumptions. Meanwhile, the Wilcoxon test was used to evaluate the significant of participants' preferences across the three IV techniques. The SPSS version 13.0 was used to analyze the results.

4.1 Decision Performance: Task Completion Time

Decision performance was measured based on the time to complete a task. The results from the RM ANOVA showed that there was a significant main effect of IV on completion time ($F (2, 16) = 8.146$, $p< .05$). A significant difference was detected across the IV techniques. This finding is similar to prior studies [5] and supports H1. The overview+detail techniques significantly outperformed zoom+pan technique in completion time.

It was also found that there was a significant main effect of task complexity on completion time with $p < 0.01$. The test results showed that exploration tasks had longer completion time in all the three IV techniques compared to the extraction task. This is similar to prior studies [10] and supports research hypothesis H3.

The Wilcoxon test was conducted to analyze the effect of IV for each task complexity. No obvious difference was shown across the IV techniques for extraction task. For exploration task, results showed that there was a significant difference in completion time between the *O+D* and *Z+P* ($p < .05$). No difference between the *O+D* techniques ($p>.1$) was recorded. This suggested that for a complex task, the presence of overview provided significantly better performance compared to the *Z+P* with no overview.

The key purpose of this study is to examine decision style effects. It was found that there were significant main effects of decision style ($p<0.05$) on performance (H4). A Post test based on the Bonferrani suggested that the significant difference across decision style was between *analytical* and *behavioral* styles. *Analytical* had the shortest and *behavioral* had the longest completion time.

Further investigation on the interaction effect between IV techniques and individual differences was conducted. The results showed that there were significant differences in completion time across IV for different decision style ($p<0.05$; H5). This indicates that decision style affects the relationship between IV and completion time. This finding provides an important contribution to the HCI and DSS disciplines.

4.2 User Preference

A Wilcoxon test was conducted to evaluate the significant of participant's preferences across the three techniques (H2). The results showed that there was a significant difference in user-preferences for IV techniques, with majority preferred overview+detail. Both *O+D* techniques were equally preferred with 43.8% voted as their first preference. The results showed a significant difference between the *O+D* and *Z+P* techniques (*Tree*: z=1.866, p=0.06 and *WinExp* z=2.623, p<0.01). There was no significant difference between the two *O+D* techniques.

The *Z+P* interface, by comparison performed poorly, with 81.3% ranking it as the least preferred. Several of the participants explained that they disliked *Z+P* because it, "requires more effort", "distracts my attention" and "needs more physical movements". Despite the negative comments, 12.5% (2 out of 16 participants) ranked *Z+P* as the most preferred because of their familiarity with the technique. Their comments include, "I preferred something that I am familiar with".

The Kruska Wallis test was conducted to identify the effects of decision styles on preferences for IV techniques. Though participants provided higher rank for overview+detail compared to zoom+pan, there is no obvious difference between preferences and decision style. In other words, the user preference of IV technique is independent of individual decision styles.

4.3 Discussion

Participants were tested with three conditions of IV techniques: *Z+P, O+D WinExp* and *O+*D Tree. Decision performance was measured based on the task completion time. The results showed that there were significant differences in decision performance across IV techniques (p<.05), decision style (p<.05) and task (p<.01). Participants' comments demonstrate that one's efforts to perform a task vary for different types of IV techniques used. The *O+D* recorded better performance than *Z+P*. User preferences for the IV techniques were strongly in favor of *O+D* techniques. From the participants comments, it can be concluded that location reference were easier to establish in both *O+D* techniques compared to *Z+P*. This study also found that there was a significant main effect of decision style on completion time. Post hoc test for exploration task indicated that there was significant difference between *analytical* and *behavioral. Analytical* took the shortest time and *behavioral* the longest time. This result supports Rowe's argument that high analytical person performed better in a complex task and interface.

In summary, the results strongly support the arguments that decision styles affect decision performance. More significantly, the finding that indicates decision style moderates the relationship between the IV techniques and decision performance provide important issues for further research. These results confirm the argument that states decision style is critical in the DSS design. The summary of the results is shown in Table 1.

Table 1. Summary of Hypothesis testing

Dependent Variable	Independent Variable	Result
Decision Performance (completion time)	H1 :IV techniques	Supported **
	H3:Task	Supported **
	H4:Decision style	Supported **
	H5: IV * decision style	Supported **
User preference	H2: *O+D* is more preferred than *Z+P*	Supported **

NOTE: ** p<0.05.

5 Conclusion

Findings from this experimental study provide theoretical, empirical and practical contributions. This study provides theoretical contribution by introducing decision style into the framework of HCI/IV studies. This paper explores and reports the potential of main and interaction effects of decision style on decision performance in using different IV techniques. The results provide empirical contributions, which supports the importance of matching the interface technology with individuals' task requirements and individuals cognitive and perceptual needs. In terms of practical contribution, these finding have important implications for the DSS designers, and provide important research issues for future work. These empirical findings support the construction of intelligent interfaces that adapt to the individual cognitive and perceptual needs. It suggests that building a DSS that meets the need of decision makers' task and cognitive requirements, is essential and beneficial.

References

1. Benbasat, I,, Dexter, A.S., Todd, P.: An Experimental Program Investigating Color-Enhanced and Graphical Information Presentation: An Integration of The Findings. Communications of the ACM 29(11), 1094–1105 (1986)
2. Chen, C., Yu, Y.: Empirical Studies of Information Visualization a Meta-Analysis. International Journal Human-computer Studies 53, 851–866 (2000)
3. Dehaemer, M.J.: Vulcans, Klingons and humans: the relevance of individual differences for information system. In: Proceedings of the 1991 conference on SIGCPR, pp. 156 –163 (1991)
4. Ghosh, Shneiderman: Zoom-only vs. overview-detail pair. A study in browsing techniques as applied to patient histories. University of Maryland Technical Report CS-TR-4028. (1999) Retrieved from http://hcil.cs.umd.edu/trs/ 99-12/99-12.html
5. Hornbaek, K., Bederson, B.B., Plaisant, C.: Navigation Patterns and Usability of Zoomable User Interfaces with and without an overview. ACM Transactions on Computer-Human Interaction 9(4), 362–389 (2002)
6. Mintzberg, H.: Planning on the left side and managing on the right. Harvard Business Review 4, 49–58 (1976)
7. Robey, D.: Cognitive style and DSS Design: A comment on Huber's Paper. Management Science 29(5), 580–582 (1983)

8. Mason, R.R.O.: Managing with Style: A Guide to Understanding, Assessing, and Improving Decision Making. Jossey-Bass, San Francisco (1987)
9. So, S., Smith, M.: The impact of presentation format and individual differences on the communication of information for management decision making. Managerial Auditing Journal 18(1), 59–67 (2003)
10. Speier, C., Morris, M.G.: The Influence of query interface design on decision making performance. MIS Quarterly 27(3), 397–423 (2003)
11. Te'eni, D., Carey, J., Zhang, P.: Human Computer Interaction Developing Effective Organizational Information Systems, Wiley (2007)
12. Turban, E., Aronson, J.E.: Decision Support Systems and Intelligent Systems, 6th edn. Prentice Hall pp.73–77 (2001)
13. Vessey, I.: Cognitive Fit: A Theory-Based Analysis of the Graphs versus Tables Literature. Decision Sciences 22(2), 219–241 (1991)

Enhancing the Map Usage for Indoor Location-Aware Systems

Hui Wang[1,2], Henning Lenz[1], Andrei Szabo[1], Joachim Bamberger[1], and Uwe D. Hanebeck[2]

[1] Siemens AG, Corporate Technology, Information and Communications, CT IC4, Otto-Hahn-Ring 6, 81739, Munich, Germany
{Hui.Wang.ext,Henning.Lenz,Andrei.Szabo, Joachim.Bamberger}@siemens.com
[2] Intelligent Sensor-Actuator-Systems Laboratory, Institute of Computer Science and Engineering, Universität Karlsruhe (TH), Germany
Uwe.Hanebeck@ieee.org

Abstract. Location-aware systems are receiving more and more interest in both academia and industry due to their promising prospective in a broad category of so-called Location-Based-Services (LBS). The map interface plays a crucial role in the location-aware systems, especially for indoor scenarios. This paper addresses the usage of map information in a Wireless LAN (WLAN)-based indoor navigation system. We describe the benefit of using map information in multiple algorithms of the system, including radio-map generation, tracking, semantic positioning and navigation. Then we discuss how to represent or model the indoor map to fulfill the requirements of intelligent algorithms. We believe that a vector-based multi-layer representation is the best choice for indoor location-aware system.

Keyword: Location-Aware Systems, WLAN Positioning, Map Representation.

1 Introduction

Location-aware systems are receiving more and more interest in both academia and industry due to their promising prospective in a broad category of so-called location-based services (LBS)[1-4], such as people and asset tracking, security applications, navigation and location-based multimedia services. Generally, current location-aware systems can be separated into three groups: satellite based systems, sensor based systems, and local network-based systems. Satellite systems, such as the well-known GPS or Galileo systems, focus on outdoor positioning using satellite signals. However, these systems suffer from the attenuation, reflection, and refraction of buildings and walls when used indoors. To solve this problem, two other kinds of systems use various sensors (e.g. infrared sensor, ultrasonic sensor or inertial sensor) and a local communication network interface (e.g. WLAN, Bluetooth, etc.) to collect indoor location information [5, 6].

In all location-aware systems, the map interface plays an important role, especially for indoor scenarios. This paper addresses the map information for indoor location-aware

J. Jacko (Ed.): Human-Computer Interaction, Part II, HCII 2007, LNCS 4551, pp. 151–160, 2007.

systems. We discuss two problems: 1) How indoor positioning systems can benefit maximally from the map information; 2) How to better model or represent the building maps in order to facilitate the whole positioning system.

In the GPS system, map matching methods are often used to evaluate the trajectories and project them onto streets [7, 8]. In indoor systems, researchers also proposed dozens of map-assisted algorithms. For example, to generate the radio map, [6][9] used multi-wall and dominant path models and [10] used parametric ray-tracing. They all need to know the room and the wall information. For tracking algorithms, [11, 12] both use the map to delete impossible movements. Besides, [13, 14] used the Voronoi map to further restrict a possible trajectory. Other algorithms including [15-17] use maps to assist the sensor fusion.

The indoor positioning system in this paper is based on the emerging WLAN positioning techniques. Its basic structure consists of four layers, including the interface layer, the localization layer, the tracking and fusion layer, and the application layer, as shown in Fig. 1. In contrast to other systems, which typically only use the map in the application layer, we integrate map information into all layers of the system. In the interface layer, map information is used to generate a more accurate radio map. In the localization layer, we are able to estimate not only the user's geometrical location but also semantic location by using the map, e.g., the located floor and room. We also integrate the map information in the tracking level using particle filter, which can reduce the estimation variance by deleting some unrealistic cases like crossing the walls. Finally, map information is used in the application layer to support intelligent room detection, routing or other location/context aware services.

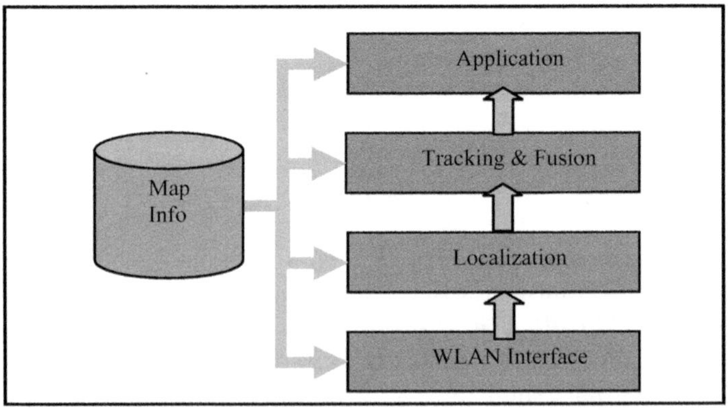

Fig. 1. Structure of a WLAN-based Location-aware System

To facilitate the above mentioned map-related algorithm, the map information has to be well organized. To the best of our knowledge, there is still no standard for modeling and representing indoor map information. AutoCAD provides his own file format DWF (Design Web Format) for representing map information [18]. But since DWF aims at the general product design with a lot of redundant information, it is not suitable for localization systems. Other attempts from industry include SLoP (Spatial

Location Protocol) by the Internet Engineer Task Force (IETF) [19]. It is a purely descriptive model, aiming at unambiguously expressing location information in an interoperable form in the Internet. Some researchers, such as [20-22], presented symbolic or semi-symbolic models to represent the location, which is similar to the model used in this paper.

In this paper, we use a vector-based multi-layer model to represent the indoor digital map. This model organizes the map based on three different aspects. The first is called geometric level, which includes points, lines or polygons. The second is symbolic level, including walls, doors, rooms or floors. The last is semantic level, including the semantic information, such as the name of employee inside the room, the room number, etc. In the symbolic level, the elements are organized using a hybrid tree and graph structure according to their geospatial relationships. The advantage of using this map representation is as follows. The wall or room information required by the localization and tracking algorithm can be easily extracted. In addition, the semantic information can fastly be outputted. Furthermore, the routing algorithm can be easily implemented by the hybrid tree and graph structure in symbolic level. Also, this model can be easily built by analyzing raster or CAD formatted files. Last but not the least, this model also facilitates the information exchange with web service, i.e. the model can also be easily represented by XML or SVG format.

The remainder of the paper is organized as follows. In Section 2, we introduce briefly the principle of WALN based localization system. Subsequently the advantages of using map information for assisting the whole system are discussed in detail. In Section 3, we describe the map representation used in our system and its advantages. Finally, Section 4 concludes the paper.

2 Information Extraction from Maps for WLAN Localization

2.1 Principle of WLAN Localization Systems

As described in Section 1, the WLAN localization systems can be separated into four layers: interface layer, localization layer, tracking & fusion layer and application layer. In the following, we briefly describe the principle and the functionality of each layer. More details can be found in the literature [5, 6, 23, 24, 25].

- *Interface Layer.* In the interface layer, the system measures the WLAN signals and extracts the location-related information. The received signal strength (RSS) is typically used to infer the user's location because it is much easier to be obtained than the other information such as time of arrival (TOA), time difference of arrival (TDOA) or angle of arrival (AOA). The value of RSS is related to the distance between the access point (AP) and the user's mobile terminal. The longer the distance, the lower RSS will be measured. The distribution of RSS at numerous reference points can be measured or calculated before the system runs and is usually stored in a database named radio map.
- *Localization Layer.* In this layer, the mobile terminal compares the measurements with the RSS distributions in radio map. The reference point that has the most

similar RSS distribution to the online measurement is finally chosen as the estimated position. This is the so called nearest neighbor method [5] [6]. Since the wireless channel is noisy, the accuracy of location estimation is limited. The output of this layer is usually a 2-D or 3-D local geometric coordinate. But with the help of map information, symbolic or semantic information (e.g. room number) is also obtainable.

- *Tracking and Fusion Layer.* If the mobile terminal is moving, the filtering algorithms can be used to smooth the moving trajectory. In addition, other information sources, such as extra sensors, building map and other location-related information, can also be fused with the assistance of some sophisticated but flexible filtering techniques like particle filters.
- *Application Layer.* The application layer interacts with the users directly. It applies the location information to support various location-based applications or services, such as asset monitoring, guidance, routing, map-services, location-dependant multimedia services or games, and etc. The way of operating the location information varies depending on different applications. But the basic operation is either to inform the user of location-related semantic information or to guide users to their target places.

2.2 Map-Assisted Radio Map Generation

Theoretically, the received signal power P_r follows the radial propagation model, as described in Equation (1),

$$P_r[dBm] = P_r(d_0)[dBm] - 10n\log(\frac{d}{d_0}) \tag{1}$$

where d is the distance between the mobile terminal and access point. d_0 is the reference distance, normally equal to 1 meter. n is the attenuation parameter, which is equal to $n=2$ in free space and $n=1.5\sim6$ in indoor scenarios.

However, due to the complexity of indoor environments, the radial model is unrealistic for real radio propagation. Since the walls are the major obstacles attenuating the signal, a multi-wall model [26] as in Equation (2) can better model the radio propagation, where WAF means the wall attenuation factor, which is the loss of signal power after crossing a wall.

$$P_r[dBm] = P_r(d_0)[dBm] - 10n\log(\frac{d}{d_0}) - \begin{cases} \sum WAF & l < k \\ C & l \geq k \end{cases} \tag{2}$$

Although the multi-wall model takes the environments into account, it only uses the direct ray between transmitter and receiver. This will lead to an underestimation in many cases. For instance, in Figure 2, the transmitter emits many possible rays to the receiver. The direct path penetrates three walls but there is also another indirect path penetrating only one wall. Since the signal on the direct path is attenuated a lot when crossing the walls, the signal on the indirect path contributes to most of the received power. So if we only consider the direct path, the predicted signal power at the receiver will be much lower than the real measurement. The dominant path model

[6, 9] aims to find the signal propagation path, which dominates the received power. So the idea of the dominant path model is to find the path which has the smallest power loss. The calculation of the dominant path can be found in [6], which is similar to finding the shortest path between AP and mobile terminal.

Figure 3 and Table 1 show the generated radio maps and the positioning results using different channel models [6]. It is obvious that these site-specific models perform much better. For employing the multi-wall model or the dominant path model, the site-specific information, such as the position of the walls and rooms, should be extracted from the map. In addition, the map model should be well organized to facilitate the extraction of wall and room information.

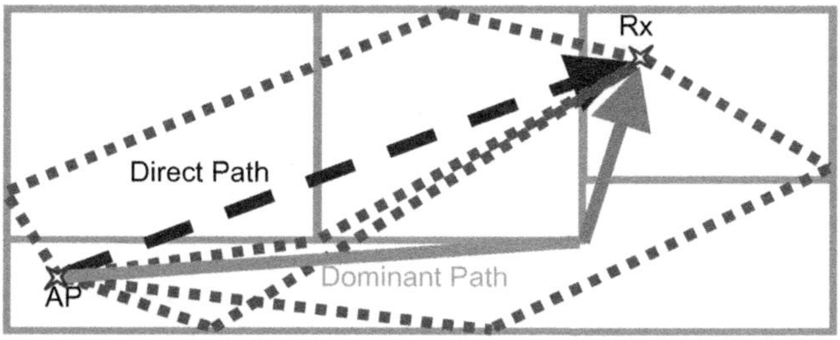

Fig. 2. Illustration of the Dominant Path Model

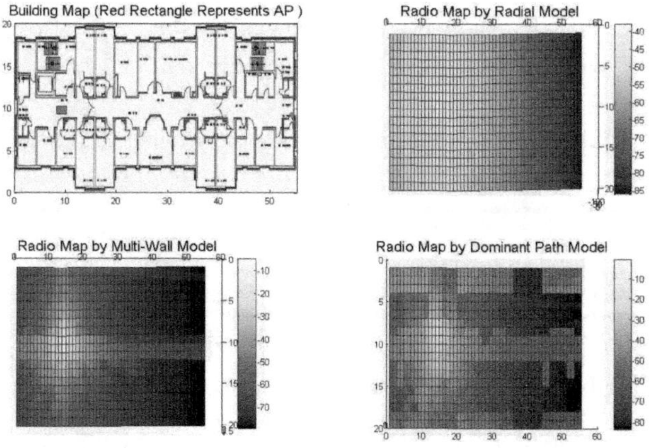

Fig. 3. Example of Radio Maps Using Different Channel Models

Table 1. Mean of Location Errors in a Testbed Using Different Channel Models

Channel Models	Mean (m)
Linear Model	7.11
Mulit-Wall Model	6.73
Dominant Path Model	5.70

2.3 Map-Assisted Tracking and Fusion

Map information also improves the tracking and fusion process. The key idea is that the user cannot pass the walls while moving. In [11], we proposed a map-aided particle filter, which can incorporate the map information efficiently. The basic idea of this particle filter is as follows:

1. Use an amount of particles to represent the probabilistic distribution of user's position.
2. When the filter predicts the user's next step for each particle, the particles which crossed a wall are deleted.

Figure 4 illustrates the filtering process and Table 2 gives the tracking result with and without using map information in one of our testbeds.

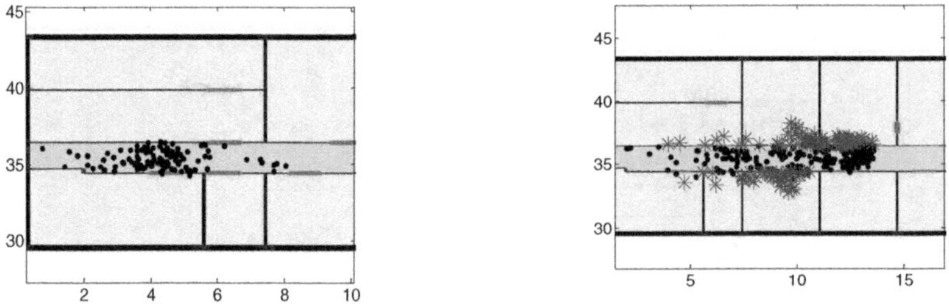

Fig. 4. Example of Two Succeeding Steps in Map-Aided Particle Filters. The red stars in right figure represent the deleted particles because they crossed a wall.

Table 2. Mean and Variance of Location Errors With and Without Using Map Information in a Testbed

	Mean(m)	Variance (m)
Particle Filter without Map	5.57	3.9
Particle Filter with Map	4.5	3.5

2.4 Map's Contribution to Semantic Localization and Navigation

With the help of the map, location-based applications and services can automatically transform the geometric coordinate to high level semantic information. The topologic structure like a room connection matrix as depicted in Table 3 can facilitate the routing algorithm by simply using a Dijkstra or A* algorithm [6].

Table 3. Example of Room Connection Matrix

	Room 1	Room 2	Corridor 1
Room 1	-	No Connection	Door 1
Room 2	No Connection	-	Door 2
Corridor 1	Door 1	Door 2	-

3 A Vector-Based Multi-level Map Representation

For achieving the benefits described in Section 2, the representation of map information should satisfy the following requirements: 1) Site-specific information, such as wall, room and floor information should be easy to extract. 2) The topologic structure should be easy to extract in order to assist intelligent routing. 3) The map representation should be easy to generate.

Typically, map information is organized in vector, raster, or a combined format. But to the best of our knowledge, there is still no standard map format for indoor location-aware systems. Most of the current systems simply plot the estimated position on the JPEG or BMP formatted building map. For this kind of map interface, the semantic information of indoor environment, e.g. room number, is actually identified by the user instead of location-aware systems. It makes advanced semantic based operation impossible, and thus does not fulfil our requirements.

In the paper, we use a vector representation of the indoor digital map. This model organizes the map based on three different aspects. The first is called geometric level, which includes points, lines, or polygons. The second is the symbolic level, including walls, doors, rooms, or floors. The last is the semantic level, including the semantic information, such as the room number, the access right, etc. This structure has the following characteristics.

1. Symbols are the core entities in our model. We define a *symbol* as having both geometric and semantic properties. For example, a symbol *room1* has several geometric properties such as the position of the centre or the shape, and it has semantic properties such as the room number or the owner's name.
2. The symbols are organized hierarchically. In the example in Figure 5, the symbols are organized by a hybrid tree-graph structure according to their spatial relationship. In this structure, *Floor* is superset of *room, elevator,* or *corridor*. *Room* is a superset of *door, wall,* or other symbols inside a room.
3. Spatially, high level symbols *include* the low level symbols. In Figure 1, the symbol *Elevator at Floor 1, Room1, Room2, and Corridor1* are spatially inside the symbol *Floor.*
4. The symbols in the same level are connected in a graph structure according to their spatial connection relationship. Like in Figure 5, *Room1,* and *Room2* are connected with the *Corridor1* and *Corridor1* connects the *Elevator on Floor1*.
5. The high level and low level symbols are connected by the entrance/exit symbols, like *Elevator on Floor 1* in Figure 5.

Using this map representation, the wall or room information required by the localization and tracking algorithm can be easily extracted. They are modelled during the generation of the map structure. In addition, the semantic information can be fastly obtained. People can access the semantic information by simply checking the properties of the symbols. Also, routing algorithm can be efficiently implemented by the hybrid tree and graph structure. For example, if we want to walk from *Room2* to *Room3*, we can find the route: *Room2* $\rightarrow$ *Corridor1* $\rightarrow$ *Elevator on Floor 1* $\rightarrow$ *Elevator on Floor 2* $\rightarrow$ *Room3*. Last but not the least, this model also facilitates the information exchange with web service, i.e. the model can also be easily represented by XML or SVG format.

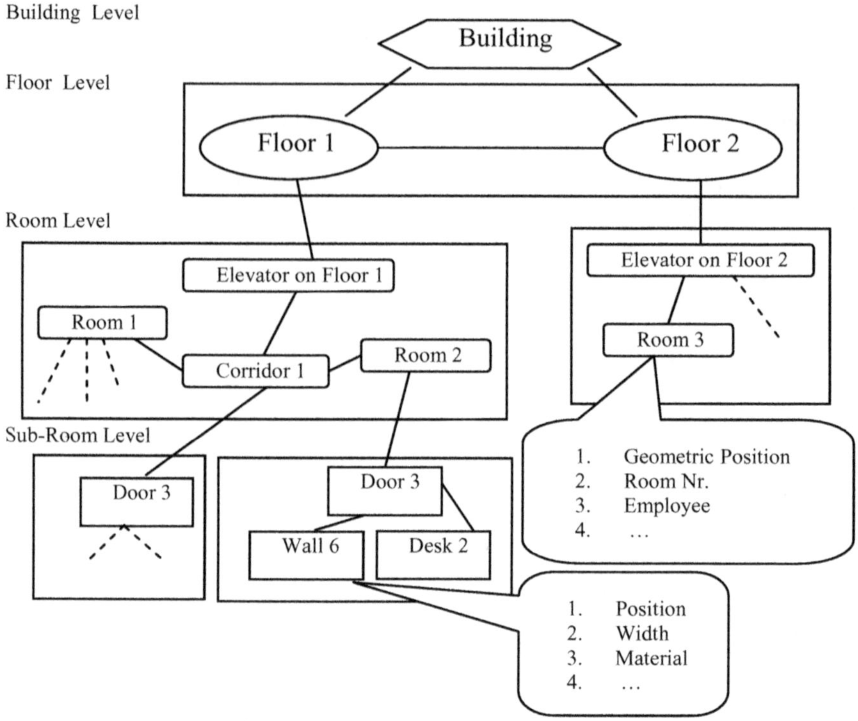

Fig. 5. Example of the Vector-Based Multi-Layer Map Structure

It is also not difficult to generate this model from another map format. For example, we can use the following procedures to generate the above mentioned map model from the raster JPEG or BMG images.

Step 1: Identify the basic symbols, like walls or rooms. Since the symbols have a specific geometric shape, we can use the sophisticated image processing algorithms to identify the symbols. For complex building plans, manual efforts might also be needed.

Step 2: Incorporate the Semantic Information. For each symbol, the semantic information can be inputted as its property.

Step 3: Construct the symbol topology hierarchy. After recognizing the symbols, the topological structure can be conveniently extracted. For example, we can build the room level connection matrix by checking whether two rooms share the some wall or door.

Step 4: Store the structured location information in a database or XML file.

4 Conclusions

This paper comprehensively analyzes the role of map information in modern indoor localization systems. We present the basic principles of our previous work, which integrates map information into multiple layers of a WLAN localization system, from radio map generation, tracking, and fusion to semantic navigation. We also introduce a vector-based hybrid structured map mode, which represents the location information with the symbols layered according to their spatial relationship. We believe that this model can fulfill the requirements of the map-related algorithms, and hence maximize the contribution of the map information to the whole indoor location-aware systems.

Acknowledgements. The authors would like to thank Andreas Igel for his comments and suggestions to this paper.

References

1. Patterson, C.A., Muntz, R.R., Pancake, C.M.: Challenges in location-aware Computing. Pervasive Computing 2, 80–89 (2003)
2. Weiser, M.: Hot Topics: Ubiquitous Computing. IEEE Computer (1993)
3. Hightower, J., Borriello, G.: Location System for Ubiquitous Computing. IEEE computer (2001)
4. Koshima, H., Hoshen, J.: Personal Locator Services Emerge. IEEE Spectrum (2000)
5. Bahl, P., Padmanabhan, V.N.: RADAR: An in-building RF-based User Location and Tracking system. In: proceedings of IEEE INFOCOM 2000 2(3), 775–784 (2000)
6. Wang, H.: Fusion of Information Sources for Indoor Positioning with Field Strength Measurements. Master thesis, Department of Electrical Engineering and Information Technology, TU-München (2005)
7. Obradovic, D., Lenz, H., Schupfner, M.: Sensor Fusion in Siemens Car Navigation System. In: proceedings of IEEE Conference on Machine Learning and Signal Processing, São Luis, Brazil (2004)
8. Obradovic, D., Lenz, H., Schupfner, M.: Fusion of Map and Sensor Data in a Modern Car Navigation System. Journal of VLSI Signal Processing 45, 111–122 (2006)
9. Wölfle, G., Wahl, R., Wertz, P., Wildbolz, P., Landstorfer, F.: Dominant Path Prediction Model for Indoor Scenarios. German Microwave Conference (GeMIC), Ulm, Germany (2005)
10. Zarubo, G.V., Huber, M., Kamanger, F.A., Chlamtac, I.: Monte Carlo Sampling Based In-home Location Tracking With Minimal RF Infrastructure Requirements. In: proceedings of GLOBECOM (2004)
11. Wang, H., Lenz, H., Szabo, A., Bamberger, J., Hanebeck, U.D.: WLAN-Based Pedestrian Tracking Using Particle Filters and Low-Cost MEMS Sensors. In: proceedings of 4th Workshop on Positioning, Navigation and Communication 2007 (WPNC'07), Hannover, Germany (2007)
12. Evennou, F., Marx, F.: Advanced Integration of WiFi and Inertial Navigation Systems for Indoor Mobile Positioning. EURASIP Journal on Applied Signal Processing 2006, Article ID 86706, 1–11 (2006)
13. Liao, L., Fox, D., Hightower, J., Kautz, H., Schulz, D.: Voronoi Tracking: Location Estimation Using Sparse and Noisy Sensor Data. In: Proceedings of IROS-03 (2003)
14. Evennou, F., et al.: Map-aided Indoor Mobile Positioning System using Particle Filter. In: proceedings of WCNC (2005)
15. Wang, H., Lenz, H., Szabo, A., Hanebeck, U.D., Bamberger, J.: Fusion of Barometric Sensors, WLAN Signals and Building Information for 3-D Indoor/Campus Localization. In: proceedings of International Conference on Multisensor Fusion and Integration for Intelligent Systems (MFI 2006), S. 426–432, Heidelberg, Germany (2006)

16. Retscher, G.: Location Determination in Indoor Environments for Pedestrian Navigation. In: proceedings of IEEE/ION PLANS 2006, San Diego, USA (2006)
17. Bohn, J., Vogt, H.: Robust Probabilistic Positioning based on High-Level Sensor-Fusion and Map Knowledge. Technical Report, ETH, Zurich, Switzerland (2003)
18. http://usa.autodesk.com/adsk/servlet/index?siteID=123112&id=6101753
19. Activity, S.: Spatial Location BOF of IETF (2000) http://www-nrc.nokia.com/ietf-spatial
20. Leonhardt, U.: Supporting Location-awareness in Open Distributed Systems. PhD thesis, Department of Computing, Imperial College, London (1998)
21. Narayanan, A.K.: Realms of States: a Framework for Location Aware Mobile Computing. In: proceedings of the first international workshop on mobile commerce (2001)
22. Hu, H., Lee, D.-L.: Semantic Location Modeling for Location Navigation in Mobile Environment. In: proceedings of the 2004 IEEE international conference on mobile data management (MDM'04) (2004)
23. Parodi, B.B., Lenz, H., Szabo, A., Wang, H., Horn, J., Bamberger, J., Obradovic, J.: Initialization and Online-Learning of RSS Maps for Indoor/Campus Localization. In: proceedings of IEEE/ION PLANS 2006, San Diego, USA (2006)
24. Parodi, B.B., Lenz, H., Szabo, A., Bamberger, J., Horn, J.: SLL: Statistical Conditions and Algebraic Properties. In: proceedings of 4th Workshop on Positioning, Navigation and Communication 2007 (WPNC'07), Hannover, Germany (2007)
25. Parodi, B.B., Lenz, H., Szabo, A., Bamberger, J., Horn, J.: Algebraic and Statistical Conditions for Use of SLL. In: proceedings of European Control Conference 2007, Greece (2007)
26. Lott, M., Forkel, I.: A Multi-Wall-and Floor Model for Indoor Radio Propagation. Vehicular Technology Conference (2001)

Freehand Sketching Interfaces: Early Processing for Sketch Recognition

Shu-xia Wang, Man-tun Gao, and Le-hua Qi

Northwestern Polytechnical University, Xi'an, China, 710072
wangshuxia@nwpu.edu.cn

Abstract. Freehand sketching interfaces allow the user to directly interact with tasks without worrying about low-level commands. The paper presents a method for interpreting on-line freehand sketch and describes a human-computer interface prototype system of freehand sketch recognition (FSR) that is designed to infer designers' intention and interprets the input sketch into more exact 2D geometric primitives: straight lines, polylines, circles, circular arcs, ellipses, elliptical arcs, hyperbolas and parabolas. According to whether the stroke needs to be segmented or not, it is divided into single primitives and composite primitives correspondingly. Based on open/closed characteristic and semi-invariant, conic type and category of freehand sketch were defined for subdividing conic curve. Recognition approach for composite-primitive consists of three stages. The effectiveness of the algorithm is demonstrated preliminarily by experiments.

Keywords: Freehand sketching interface, Recognition, Segmentation, Stroke.

1 Introduction

Conceptual design is an early stage of the design process, in which designers use various sketches with vague and imprecise geometry to rapidly express their creative ideas. However, conceptual designers still tend to prefer paper and pencil to a computer aided design (CAD) system, for expression, communication and record of their ideas. The reason often given is that the user interfaces is not suitable for sketching design. Freehand sketching is a natural and powerful means of interpersonal communication. On-line freehand recognition is useful as a human-computer interface in situations where a human would draw sketches and the computer would interpret them. The goal of perceptual processing is to allow the user to perform complicated tasks with a minimum amount of explicit control. In traditional command-based interfaces, the user must decompose a task into a sequence of machine-understandable, fine command operations, and then input the commands one by one. Freehand sketching interfaces try to avoid this process and allow the user to directly interact with tasks without worrying about low-level commands.

Landay [1] described a sketch-based approach for the early stages of user interface design. His work allowed designers to quickly record design ideas in a tangible form. His electronic sketches possessed the advantages normally associated with computer-based tools, making them well suited to user interface design. Eggli [2] proposed a

J. Jacko (Ed.): Human-Computer Interaction, Part II, HCII 2007, LNCS 4551, pp. 161–170, 2007.

solid modeler incorporating a sketching tool; their system is three dimensional but the sketching itself is always constrained to some plane, thereby avoiding the problematic inverse-projection reconstruction phase. A similar system for designing solid objects using interactive sketch interpretation is described [3-5]. Several systems for modeling by sketching already exist. System Sketch [7] allowed the user to create simple geometrical scenes using a set of predefined gestures. There are also systems for sketching of CAD drawings [8]. These systems were a valuable help in creating models consisting of geometrical primitives, but they cannot be used to model free-form shapes, on which this work concentrates. Reference [9] was aimed especially on modeling of simple free-form objects. The system was able to inflate 2D closed curves into 3D objects, which can be consequently edited using simple gestures. During the whole modeling process the system maintained a polygon mesh of the model, displayed in a non-photo realistic way. Reference [10] presented a novel method for interpreting overtracing freehand sketch. The overtracing strokes were interpreted as sketch content and were used to generate 2D geometric primitives. The approach consisted of four stages: stroke classification, strokes grouping and fitting, 2D tidy-up with endpoint clustering and parallelism correction, and in-context interpretation. Strokes were first classified into lines and curves by a linearity test.

All of above methods intending to obtain new user interfaces, however, sketch recognition is important for a novel interface appearing. In this paper, we focus on the early processing for sketch recognition. In the section 2 we present an algorithm for stroke preprocessing by an adaptive threshold. Section 3 presents several classifiers for classification of single-primitives. If the stroke is composite primitive, the recognition approach is depicted in the section 4. Experimental results and conclusions are respective in the section 5 and 6.

2 Stroke Preprocessing

We adopt on the split and merge algorithm of polygonal approximation by [6]. This algorithm is composed of two steps. The split step consists in the subdivision of the stroke into line segments whose endpoints coincide with those of the original. When the maximum approximation error in terms of distance (ε_{max}) is no longer superior to a given threshold (ε_{12}) the subdivision process stops. The merge step consists in the fusion of two line consecutive segments, when the error inherent to the resulting line segment (ε_{max}) is not superior to the maximum admissible error (ε_{12}).

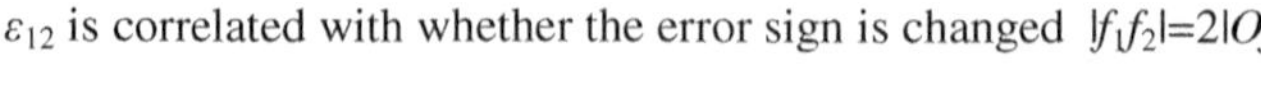

Fig. 1. ε_{12} is correlated with whether the error sign is changed $|f_1 f_2|=2|Of_1|=L_1/3$

This algorithm depends on the given threshold ε_{12}. In fact, if the threshold value ε_{12} is constant can arose some problems in the recognition process [11]. We constructs a measure function for threshold value ε_{12} , which is related with the distance between first point and last point of stroke (L_1), length of stroke (L), pen width (D), and whether the error sign is changed in scope[f_1, f_2] (See Fig.1). It is defined as

$$\varepsilon_{12} = C \cdot (L_1/L + n) \cdot D, \tag{1}$$

where n is a coefficient (=0.5). In the first step, if the error sign is changed in the scope, let C=2.0, otherwise let C=1.0. In the second step, let C=2.0.

3 Single Primitive Recognition

To preserve the original information of sketch, our methods extend ployline to primitive shapes. Primitive shapes are divided into polyline curve (straight line and polyline) and conic curve (circle, circular arc, ellipse, elliptical arc, hyperbola and parabola). We design several classifiers for classification of single-primitives in this section. Polyline classifier can recognize whether a stroke is polyline curve or conic section. If a stroke is conic, the recognition processes consist of three classifiers: open/closed classifier, residual error-based classifier, type and category classifier.

3.1 Polyline Curve Classifier

Given a stroke which contains sequences of sampling points $\{p_i;\ i=0, 1, 2, \ldots, k\}$ and preprocessing points $\{s_i;\ i=0, 1, 2, \ldots, u\}$ $(u \le k)$, where $p_i=(x_i, y_i) \in \{p_i\}$. Let $d(q_{i,j})$ denote a perpendicular distances from the point $q_{i,j}(X_{ij}, Y_{ij})=p_{v(ij)} \in \{p_i\}$ to the line segment that connects the points s_{i-1} and s_i $(1 \le i \le u)$, where $q_{i,j}=(X_{ij}, Y_{ij})=p_{v(ij)} \in \{p_i\}$ and let $v(ij)$ denote a serial number that is expressed by Eq.(3). According to the distance definition for a point to a line, we have

$$d(q_{ij}) = \frac{|A_i X_{ij} + B_i Y_{ij} + C_i|}{\sqrt{A_i^2 + B_i^2}}. \tag{2}$$

$$v(ij) = \sum_{z=0}^{i-1} (N_z - 1) + j,\quad 1 \le i \le u,\quad 0 \le j \le N_i - 1, \tag{3}$$

where N_i is the number of sampling points from s_{i-1} to s_i and let N_0=1. A measurement function of fitting error of polyline curve (ε_z) is obtained as

$$\varepsilon_z = \frac{1}{L} \cdot \sum_{i=1}^{u} \left(\frac{\sum_{j=0}^{N_i-1} d(q_{ij})}{N_i} \right), \tag{4}$$

where L is the length of stroke.

If fitting error of polyline curve ε_z is not superior to a maximum admissible error (ε_{zl}), the stroke is recognized as polyline curve, otherwise can be conic curve or composite primitives. Let u=1; we will interpret the polyline curve as a straight line. Otherwise the stroke is a polyline.

3.2 Conic Curve Classifier

If a stroke can be conic section, the recognition processes consist of three classifiers: open/closed classifier, residual error-based classifier, type and category classifier.

Open/closed classifier

Open/closed classifier is designed for detecting whether a stroke is conic section and whether is open or closed if the stroke is conic section. A closed conic can be circle or ellipses, otherwise can be circular arcs, elliptical arcs, hyperbolas and parabolas. The open/closed detecting method can cope with over-tracing sketching.

Let the central point be denoted as O, which is an average of the coordinates of sampling points of freehand conic curve. Given a preprocessing point s_i, a *radius* is the line segment that connects O and s_i. Constructing all radii that connect O to its consequent points s_0, s_1, s_2,…,s_u in turn, we have a sequence of radii, named as $O–s_0$, $O–s_1$, $O–s_2$, …, $O–s_u$. Let the symbol "<<" stands for the geometrical relation "left-of" and ">>" stands for "right-of" between any two continuous radii viewed in clockwise. We see that these radii form either one of two patterns:

1) in clockwise direction: $O–s_0 << O–s_1 << O–s_2 << \ldots << O–s_u$,
2) in counterclockwise direction: $O–s_0 >> O–s_1 >> O–s_2 >> \ldots >> O–s_u$.

They are illustrated in Fig. 2.

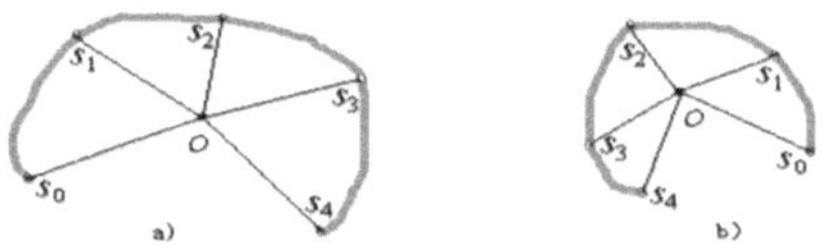

Fig. 2. Examples of the radii on a freehand conic curve: a) in the clockwise direction and b) in the counterclockwise direction

Through the above radii test, we can classify whether the stroke is not conic section, then we proceed the possible conic section by the following method. Let the angle value from the point s to the point p in the stroke be denoted as $O_{s,p}$ in Fig.3.a). We construct the open/closed algorithm for the possible curve section.

1) Let $O_{s0,su} < 1.85\pi$; the stroke is open curve and go to step 4.
2) Let $1.85\pi < O_{s0,su} < 2.15\pi$; Firstly, calculate the distance from the first point s_0 to last point s_u. If the distance is small enough (determined by an adaptive threshold) the stroke is closed curve and go to step 4). Otherwise, if the stroke angle value $O_{s0,su}$ is less than 2π, the stroke is open curve and go to step 4.
3) Let $O_{s0,su} > 2\pi$; search two points p_s and p_e which makes $O_{s0,ps}$ and $O_{su,pe}$ to approximate 2πin the sampling points $P=\{p_1, p_2, \ldots p_k\}$ (See Fig.3.b)). According to the distance definition for two points, we have Eq.(5). If $D(s_0, p_s)$ and $D(s_u, p_e)$ satisfy Eq.(4), the stroke is closed curve and go to step 4.
4) Stop.

$$D(s,z) = \frac{d(s,z)}{d(o,s)} < \frac{1}{4\pi} \cdot o_{s0,su} \quad . \tag{5}$$

$$d(s,z) = \sqrt{(x_s - x_z)^2 + (y_s - y_z)^2} . \tag{6}$$

Fig. 3. Examples for a angle value $O_{s,p}$ *in a)*and open/closed test for conic$|O_{s0,su}|$>2πin b)

Residual error-based classifier
A general conic section in the x-y plane is given by:

$$q(x, y) = ax^2 + bxy + cy^2 + dx + ey + f = 0, \quad (7)$$

where real constant coefficients a, *b*, *c*, *d*, *e*, and *f* are not all zero. In practice, it can be assumed that f≠0 because we can easily program to avoid strokes passing exactly through the origin. The equation can therefore be normalized with *f*=1.

The strokes can be recognized as imaginary curves that have not path by the least-squares fitting. To avoid imaginary curves, this paper adopts Least Median Squares (LMS) algorithm that constraint conditions consider not only residual error square but also recognition result is not imaginary curve. The method effectively avoids vibration influence and enables the algorithm to robust. The least median square fitting conic curve model is represented as

$$\hat{q}_i = \hat{a}_i x_i^2 + \hat{b}_i x_i y_i + \hat{c}_i y_i^2 + \hat{d}_i x_i + \hat{e}_i y_i + f, \quad (8)$$

where $\hat{q}_i$, $\hat{a}_i$, $\hat{b}_i$, $\hat{c}_i$, $\hat{d}_i$, $\hat{e}_i$ are estimated values of q_i, a_i, b_i, c_i, d_i, e_i respectively. Using LMS obtain linear equations defined as

$$\begin{bmatrix} \sum_{j=1}^{m} x_{ij}^4 & \sum_{j=1}^{m} x_{ij}^3 y_{ij} & \sum_{j=1}^{m} x_{ij}^2 y_{ij}^2 & \sum_{j=1}^{m} x_{ij}^3 & \sum_{j=1}^{m} x_{ij}^3 y_{ij} \\ \sum_{j=1}^{m} x_{ij}^3 y_{ij} & \sum_{j=1}^{m} x_{ij}^2 y_{ij}^2 & \sum_{j=1}^{m} x_{ij} y_{ij}^3 & \sum_{j=1}^{m} x_{ij}^2 y_{ij} & \sum_{j=1}^{m} x_{ij} y_{ij}^2 \\ \sum_{j=1}^{m} x_{ij}^2 y_{ij}^2 & \sum_{j=1}^{m} x_{ij} y_{ij}^3 & \sum_{j=1}^{m} y_{ij}^4 & \sum_{j=1}^{m} x_{ij} y_{ij}^2 & \sum_{j=1}^{m} y_{ij}^3 \\ \sum_{j=1}^{m} x_{ij}^3 & \sum_{j=1}^{m} x_{ij}^2 y_{ij} & \sum_{j=1}^{m} x_{ij} y_{ij}^2 & \sum_{j=1}^{m} x_{ij}^2 & \sum_{j=1}^{m} x_{ij} y_{ij} \\ \sum_{j=1}^{m} x_{ij}^2 y_{ij} & \sum_{j=1}^{m} x_{ij} y_{ij}^2 & \sum_{j=1}^{m} y_{ij}^3 & \sum_{j=1}^{m} x_{ij} y_{ij} & \sum_{j=1}^{m} y_{ij}^2 \end{bmatrix} \begin{bmatrix} a_i \\ b_i \\ c_i \\ d_i \\ e_i \end{bmatrix} = -f \begin{bmatrix} \sum_{j=1}^{m} x_{ij}^2 \\ \sum_{j=1}^{m} x_{ij} y_{ij} \\ \sum_{j=1}^{m} y_{ij}^2 \\ \sum_{j=1}^{m} x_{ij} \\ \sum_{j=1}^{m} y_{ij} \end{bmatrix}. \quad (9)$$

$$\min_{\hat{X}s} \underset{i}{med} (q_i - \hat{q}_i)^2. \quad (10)$$

Once the coefficients *a*, *b*...*f* have been solved by minimizing residual error square median value using Eq.(13), we can construct a measurement function of conic fitting error (ε_e) , which is calculated as follow:

$$\varepsilon_e = \frac{1}{L} \cdot \frac{1}{k+1} \cdot \sum_{i=0}^{k} |q_i|. \quad (11)$$

where *L* is the length of stroke. If conic fitting error ε_e is not superior to a maximum admissible error (ε_{el}), the stroke can be conic, otherwise is composite primitive.

Type and category classifier

Once these coefficients have been solved in Eq. (7), some conclusions regarding the conic curve may be derived using the following definition. Denote:

$$I_1 = a + c\,,\qquad I_2 = \begin{vmatrix} a & \frac{b}{2} \\ \frac{b}{2} & c \end{vmatrix},\qquad I_3 = \begin{vmatrix} a & \frac{b}{2} & \frac{d}{2} \\ \frac{b}{2} & c & \frac{e}{2} \\ \frac{d}{2} & \frac{e}{2} & f \end{vmatrix}, \tag{12}$$

where I_1, I_2 and I_3 are conic curve invariants. This paper presents conic type and category of freehand sketch based on open/closed characteristics and invariants (See Table 1). In this table, ε_x is a type threshold, and ε_y is a circle threshold. If the stroke is closed through the open/closed classifier, $\alpha=0$, otherwise $\alpha=1$.

Table 1. Types and categories of freehand conic classified

Type	Category	Condition
Elliptic $(I_2 > \varepsilon_x)$	Ellipses	$I_1 \cdot I_3 < 0;\ I_1^2 - 4I_2 \geq \varepsilon_y;\ \alpha = 0$
	Elliptical arcs	$I_1 \cdot I_3 < 0;\ I_1^2 - 4I_2 \geq \varepsilon_y;\ \alpha = 1$
	Circles	$I_1 \cdot I_3 < 0;\ I_1^2 - 4I_2 < \varepsilon_y;\ \alpha = 0$
	Circular arcs	$I_1 \cdot I_3 < 0;\ I_1^2 - 4I_2 < \varepsilon_y;\ \alpha = 1$
Hyperbolic $(I_2 < -\varepsilon_x)$	Hyperbolas	$I_3 \neq 0$
Parabolic $(\lvert I_2 \rvert < \varepsilon_x)$	Parabolas	$I_3 \neq 0$

4 Segmenting Composite Primitive

If a stroke is not single primitive through the above method, enters into the processing of composite primitives. Recognition approaches consist of three stages: stroke classification, stroke segmentation and single primitive recognition.

4.1 Classification of Composite Primitive

While freehand sketching, a stroke is a single primitive commonly, and numbers of segment is not too much despite it is a composite primitive. This paper classifies composite primitive into non-ultra composite primitive or ultra-composite primitive based on convex-concave characteristic of freehand sketch such as Fig. 4. Non-ultra composite primitive is composed of single primitives. Ultra-composite primitive is composed of single primitives and non-ultra composite primitive. Classification of composite primitives effectively reduces the stroke complication and overcomes the question that stroke segmentation need long time.

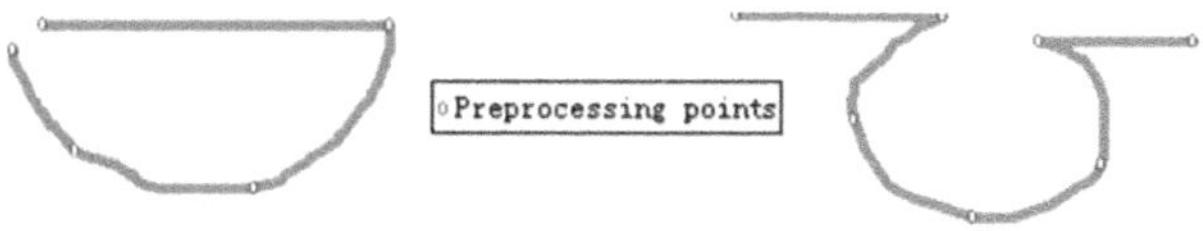

Fig. 4. Examples of non-ultra composite primitive at left and ultra-composite primitive at right

4.2 Segmentation of Ultra-Composite Primitive

Ultra-composite primitive is composed of single primitives and non-ultra composite primitive. So the aim of segmentation is that ultra-composite primitive is segmented as single primitives and non-ultra composite primitives. The algorithm of segmentation for ultra-composite primitive is followed.

1) Defined a sequence of vectors $\{v_i; i=1, 2, \dots, u\}$, where $v_i = \overline{s_{i-1}s_i} \in \{v_i\}$.
2) A sequence of signs $\{r_i; i=1, 2, \dots, u\text{-}1\}$, where r_i is the sign of $v_i \times v_{i+1}$.
3) Divide R into some groups where there are consecutive same sign. In Fig. 5$\{\{s_2\}\{s_3, s_4, s_5, s_6\}\{s_7\}\{s_8\}\{s_9, s_{10}, s_{11}, s_{12}, s_{13}\}\{s_{14}\}\}$.
4) Recognize segmenting points based on the numbers of preprocessing points is most in a unit length. In Fig. 4, the segmenting points:s_2, s_7, s_8, s_{14}.
5) Obtain the sub-strokes from the segmentation points. In Fig. 5, the sub-strokes are$\{\{s_1, s_2\}\{s_2, s_3, s_4, s_5, s_6, s_7\}\{s_7, s_8\}\{s_8, s_9, s_{10}, s_{11}, s_{12}, s_{13}, s_{14}\}\{s_{14}, s_{15}\}\}$.
6) Stop.

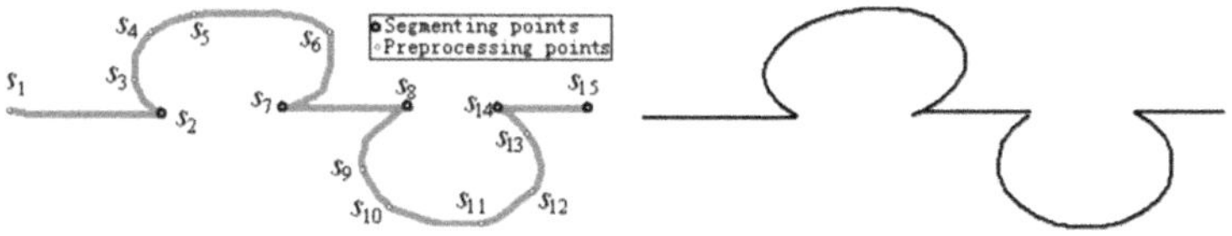

Fig. 5. Example of segmentation of ultra composite primitive: the recognition result at right

4.3 Segmentation of Non-ultra Composite Primitive

The aim of segmentation is that non-ultra composite primitive is segmented as several single primitives. The segmentation algorithm for ultra-composite primitive is expatiated by Fig. 6.

1) Defined a sequence of corresponding single span sub-stroke $L_0=\{l_1, l_2, \dots l_u\}$ where l_i represents a sub-stroke from preprocessing points s_{i-1} and s_i. And an empty sequence of single spans L_1.
2) Pop the first onę from L_0 and push it into L_1until L_0 can be recognized as a single primitive using the methods in the section 3.
3) Obtain the segmentation point s_i that is the communal points of L_0 and L_1.
4) If L_1 can be recognized as a single primitive using residual error-based classifier in the section 4, go to step 6.
5) If not, L_1 is processed as a new stroke and go to step 1.
6) Stop.

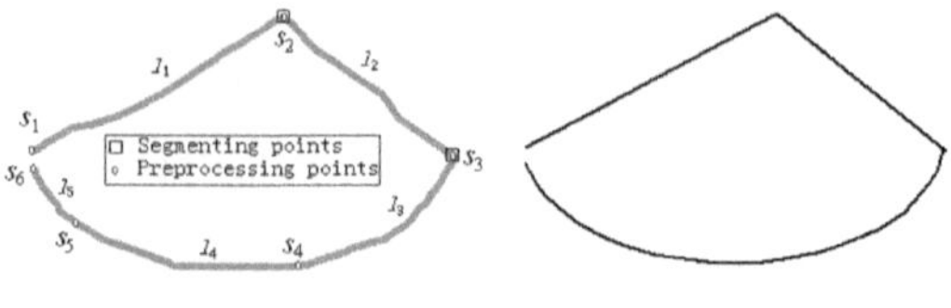

Fig. 6. At left the sequences of preprocessing points and corresponding single span sub-strokes are marked in original sketch and the result of segmentation at right

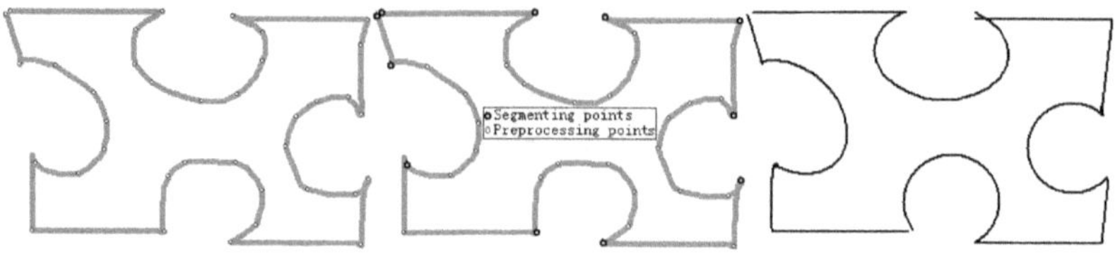

a) Stroke preprocessing b) Stroke segmenting c) Sub-strokes recognizing

Fig. 7. The process of composite primitive recognition

Through classification and segmentation of the composite primitives, it is segmented as several single primitives. Using the recognition of single primitives in the section 4, we can recognize the composite primitives (See Fig. 7).

5 Experimental Results

The freehand sketch recognition system FSR developed in the above method uses the mouse to sketch on the screen. While sketching, data input is received as a sequence of mouse positions from pressing, moving the mouse button to releasing it. These data represent a freehand curve consisting of several single primitive. Fig. 8 shows examples of recognizing single primitive and composite primitive. A recognition result of a freehand sketch doll is shown in Fig. 9.

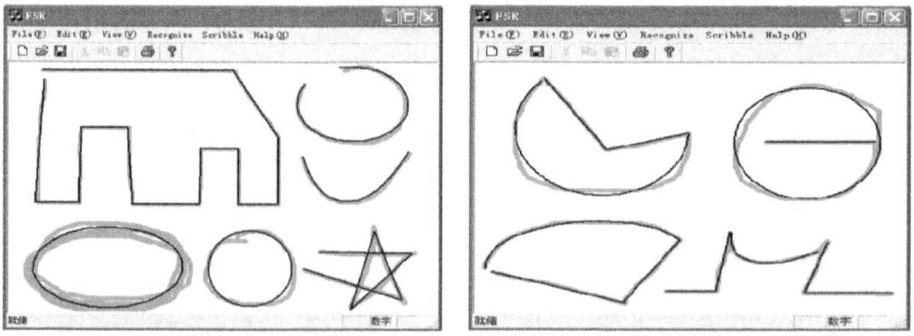

a) Single primitives recognition b) Composite primitives recognition

Fig. 8. Examples of recognizing single primitives and composite primitives

a) Sketch input b) Recognition process c) Recognition result

Fig. 9. Example of recognition result of a freehand sketch doll

6 Conclusion

The paper presents a novel method for interpreting on-line freehand sketch, and develops a human-computer interface prototype system (FSR) for assisting designers during conceptual design stages, which make system interface easy and friendly to use. According to whether the stroke needs to be segmented or not, it is divided into single primitives and composite primitives correspondingly. We design several classifiers for classification of single primitives. If a stroke can not be recognized as single primitives through the above method, it enters into the processing of composite primitives. Recognition approach consists of three stages: stroke classification, stroke segmentation and single primitive recognition. The system (FSR) has been tested with a number of sketched inputs of 2D geometry. The effectiveness of the algorithm is demonstrated preliminarily by experiments. Our recognition approach is based on stroke geometry characteristic and not non-geometry characteristic (speed, acceleration). Therefore it can make the user to sketch freely and easily and can be extended to the off-line recognition. Our method that tolerates high degrees of uncertainty and vague ideas does not rely on any domain-specific knowledge, and therefore it can be easily integrated with other high-level applications.

Acknowledgments. This work was supported by the grants from the Natural Science Foundations of Provinces of Shaanxi and Jiangxi (Project No.2002E$_2$24 and 0311018).

References

1. Landay, J.A., Myers, B.A.: Sketching interfaces: Toward more human interface design. IEEE Computer 34(2), 56–64 (2001)
2. Eggli L., Brüderlin B. P., Elber G.: Sketching as a solid modeler tool, Third Symposium on Solid Modeling and Applications, ACM SIGGRAPH, pp. 313–321 (1995)
3. Pugh, D.: Designing solid objects using interactive sketch interpretation. Computer Graphics Symposium on Interactive 3D Graphics 25(2), 117–126 (1992)
4. Hu, H.-q.: Freehand Sketch-based Three-dimensional CAD System, Zhejiang University (2004)

5. C.-x. Ma.: Research on Gesture Description and Sketch Design System in Conceptual Design PhD thesis, Chinese Academy of Sciences (2003)
6. Pereira, J.: Ambiguous calligraphic interaction for modeling environments, PhD thesis, FEUP (April 2004)
7. Zeleznik, R.C., Herndon, K.P., Hughes, J.F.: Sketch: An Interface for Sketching 3D Scenes. In: SIGGRAPH '96 Conference Proceedings, ACM, 30(4) 163–170 (1996)
8. Shpitalni, M., Lipson, H.: Classification of sketch strokes and corner detection using conic sections and adaptive clustering. Journal of Mechanical Design, Trans ASME 119, 131–135 (1997)
9. Igarashi, T., Matsuoka, S., Tanaka, H., Teddy: A sketching interface for 3D freeform design. In: Proceedings of SIGGRAPH 99 pp. 409–416 (1999)
10. Ku., D.C., Qin, S.-F., Wright, D.K.: Interpretation of Overtracing Freehand Sketching for Geometric Shapes, WSCG' (2006), Plzen, Czech Republic, 2 (2006)
11. Wang, S.-x., Gao, M.-t., Qi, L.-h.: Online Recognition of Freehand Sketching Using Conic Curves, Transaction of Northwestern Polytechnical University, 2 (2007)

Bilingual Mapping Visualizations as Tools for Chinese Language Acquisition

Jens Wissmann[1] and G. Susanne Bahr[2]

[1] City University London, School of Informatics, United Kingdom
[2] Florida Institute of Technology, Melbourne, Florida, U.S.A.
wissmann@soi.city.ac.uk, gbahr@fit.edu

Abstract. We present the approach and prototype of a system that supports the acquisition of bilingual knowledge. In this paper we focus on the domain of vocabulary acquisition for Chinese. Mapping visualizations, especially Bilingual Knowledge Maps [1], can be used to foster acquisition of word knowledge, dictionary navigation, and testing. We developed style sheets that map between knowledge representation and visualization tailored for Chinese-English bilingual data. This is on the one hand used to generate maps that visualize knowledge in a pedagogically reasonable way. On the other hand, user input and knowledge base can be queried. This more sophisticated functionality is enabled by using Semantic Web techniques. These techniques further allow us to integrate different (possibly distributed) data sources that contain relevant relationships.

1 Introduction

The acquisition of vocabulary and the understanding of word meaning are central aspects of language learning. The acquisition process is often long and tedious, especially if the language to be learned belongs to a different language family than the already acquired languages. Difficulties occur regarding depth knowledge, e.g. meaning differences of words, as well as regarding breadth knowledge through the lack of new words that must be acquired. Written Chinese requires familiarity with a large number of commonly used characters and the tonality of the language.

In our approach a user is supported in his acquisition process through mapping components. These components address different aspects of interaction with lexical knowledge (see fig. 1). The first aspect uses maps as presentation format. It has been shown that learning of words is easier if the organization of the visualization reflects the way word knowledge is organized in the human brain. To design pedagogically useful components, we draw on research in the field of knowledge visualization which has its roots in pedagogical-psychological research on pen & paper techniques such as Concept-Mapping [3], Mind-Mapping [4] and Knowledge Mapping [5]. Numerous investigations of these mapping approaches indicate that they enhance the acquisition of words and concepts at the monolingual and bilingual levels [1]. Investigation has been done on the influence of spatial layout and structural elements of the map as well as on the influence of different kinds of relationships that are

J. Jacko (Ed.): Human-Computer Interaction, Part II, HCII 2007, LNCS 4551, pp. 171–180, 2007.

depicted in the map. Though knowledge visualization approaches suggest ways of how to depict knowledge, the layout itself is normally created by a human user or domain expert. For a large lexical knowledge base it is not feasible to manually create maps for each word. To address this problem we use graph layout techniques to automatically create maps. The challenge here is to use the knowledge the layout. Our approach is to use style sheets to map relationships to the semantically to visual structures and layout.

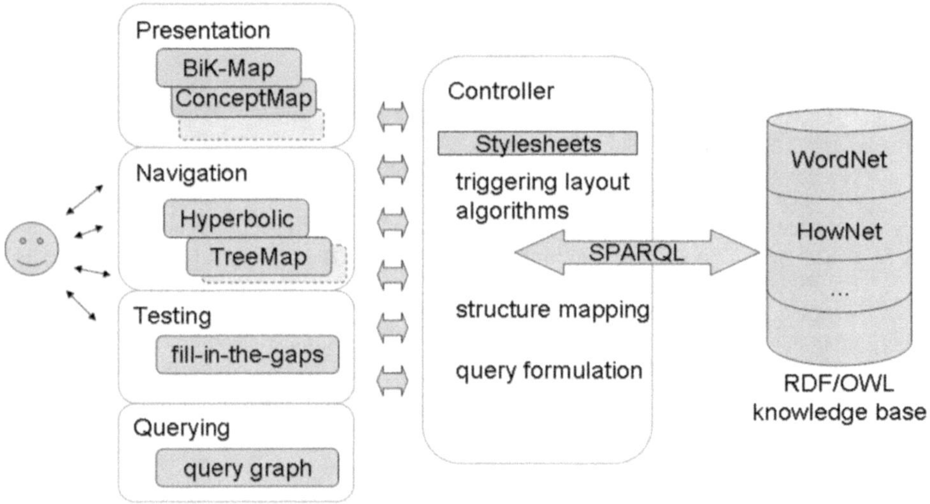

Fig. 1. User interaction with a lexical knowledge base using mapping components

Knowledge visualization focuses on depicting a few words and their relationships. As a second aspect of the interaction, mapping components can be used to explore the overall lexical space. Several techniques have been developed in the field of information visualization. As an example, we implemented a hyperbolic tree view. Relations are depicted in a simple node-edge fashion, but continuous browsing is possible through the use of hyperbolic geometry.

The choice of optimal knowledge representation is important for our interaction concept. The knowledge representation should use graph data structure in order to enable easier matching to the mapping components. As it is important for the pedagogical concept to be able to depict a variety of relationships between words, the representation should be able to integrate different lexical resources. The Semantic Web [4] techniques RDF/OWL meet these requirements. They further offer means of machine processing that we use to design testing and querying components. To test users knowledge, in a fill-in-the-gap maps are generated that are than validated by comparing it with knowledge base. A user can create a graph with blanks to querying the knowledge base to find words that match the relational description. A user can formulate queries as graphs.

2 Aspects of Graph Visualizations and Language Acquisition

Knowledge Visualizations have in common that a central concept is elaborated by visualizing its relationships to other concepts. They differ in the possibilities of *spatial configurations* and *linking concepts*. Empirical research indicates that these techniques in general foster the learning process [1]. The effects are likely to be influenced by different map parameters as well as the kind of student involvement such as active construction or reception of a presented map. Research results do not put forward a final recommendation but suggest context depend use of different configurations. For example, hierarchical layout seems to be preferable if hierarchical relationships like subsumption relationships dominate the organization of the depicted knowledge. A fixed set of knowledge can guide in elaborating knowledge aspects. One the other hand, free labeling of edges is desirable in some unbiased elaboration scenarios. In our approach, we therefore not to bind knowledge representation and visualization, but allow flexible mappings between them. Style sheets can be used to describe this mapping.

Bilingual knowledge maps (BiK-maps) are an extension of knowledge maps to that use bilingual nodes [1,17,16]. They have been used as a tool for foreign vocabulary acquisition. German-English word pairs were used for the studies, connected by a set of link-labels such as 'part of', 'leads to' or 'analogous to'. BiK-maps appear to enhance the recall of foreign vocabulary words and BiK-map learners outperform list learners. These findings are in line with the dual coding hypothesis of vocabulary acquisition. The application of dual coding theory to bilingual memory suggests that learners do not only remember words and their meaning, but also the form in which the vocabulary was presented [19]. According to Paivio, foreign language learners are able to store visual images in conjunction with foreign language vocabulary.

The functionality of current computational mapping tools closely follows the original pen & paper techniques by restricting maps to a limited workspace and thus a limited amount of visualized concepts. Information Visualization techniques that have been developed to make information in graph-structured data accessible for a user can be used. As the data normally do not contain layout information, *automatic layout* algorithms have been developed. These can for example be used to generate radial or hierarchical layouts. Empirical research has been conducted on the benefits of observing Gestalt principles [19].

As the graph structured data that are used in Information Visualization are not necessarily conceptual or semantic information, but could also be numeric or pure structures, research has focused the effects of visual features such as color guidance, geometric distortion or edge routing. Edge continuity and avoidance edge crossing are main factors that influence the quality of a layout [21]. Since the data graph is in usually large, means for *navigation*, *focus&context* and *filtering&clustering* have been developed.

Information Visualization technologies have mainly been used to access lexical knowledge. In most cases the knowledge representation is already a graph that is

[1] See for [1] and [17] for comprehensive surveys.

directly visualized. The Visual Thesaurus [2] for example displays the synonymy relationships of WordNet.

In tools like the Visual Thesaurus[3] and Kirrkirr [11], first a word and its neighbors are visualized. Acquisition of *depth* knowledge through explication of various relationships of a word and *exploration* of a vocabulary stock are thus the two main supported CALL functions of the presented mapping techniques. With the exception of a few research efforts, like BiK-Maps [1], research and application of mapping as a tool for foreign language learning has received little attention As a result, there are many unexplored possibilities to combine features of the different mapping techniques to create new or enhanced CALL techniques. An obvious step would be to generate maps directly from lexical data. In addition, test modi such as fill-in-the-blank maps could be designed.

3 Chinese Specific Aspects

Among CFL-learners there is a widespread and pedagogically reinforced belief that it is an insurmountable task to learn a writing system that is typologically "strange" and that the amount of characters necessary for acquiring a reasonable degree of reading competence is forbidding [12]. A pedagogical practice that explicitly addresses the cognitive motivations underlying the linguistic knowledge, that is, the conceptual meta-knowledge, will help Western students improve their character acquisition and reading ability [12]. We therefore propose to use the mapping techniques to depict these relationships. In the following we refer to a conceptual classification of characters in [14] to identify relevant relationships.

Pictographs (~4%) are characters that represent real-life objects by drawings. For example, 目 resembles an 'eye'. Ideographs (~1%) are a more abstract kind of characters that represent positional and numeral concepts by indication, e.g.上, 下 for up and down. As the style of the characters has changed over time, the direct reference might not be obvious in every case. In such cases, relationships to even more direct depictions such as images or symbols that are familiar to learners can be used in maps.

Though the quantity of Chinese characters is large, most of the characters are made up of a limited number of components. How a word relates to its component is a major [12]. In the case of logical aggregates (~13%) new meaning is formed by combining the meanings of two or more characters, e.g. the character for 'bright' derives from the characters 'sun' 日 and 'moon' 月. The largest class of characters (~82%) consists of semantic-phonetic complexes that are formed by combing the meaning of one character and another character which links to the same sound. One example is character for 'mother' (妈 ma3) formed by combining the character for 'horse' (马 ma3) with another for 'female' (女). Meaning and phonetics of the combined character are in many cases not as obviously connected as in this example, e.g. the phonetic component might be more of a rhyme than the same sound and the meaning transfer might be related on a metaphorical level. Associative

[2] www.visualthesaurus.com
[3] www.visualthesaurus.com

transformations extend the meaning of a character by adding more part(s) to the existing one, e.g. 庭(emperor's court) was transformed from 廷 (emperors court, courtyard) by adding 广(shelter, home/house).

For the integration of these relationships in maps, it is important to note, that *decomposition* can either be done in *plain* way, where character is divided into its smallest components, or in *hierarchical* way, which recognizes components that can themselves contain sub-components (see Figure 2). Meaningful *hierarchical* decomposition is thus key aspect for tools that aim at supporting this learning process.

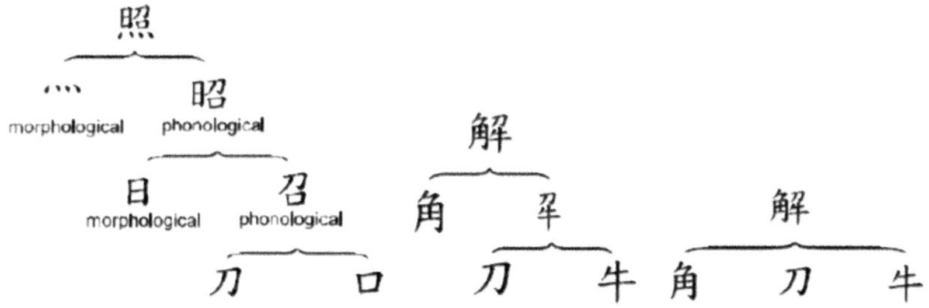

Fig. 2. Decomposition: proper hierarchical (left), improper hierarchical (middle), plain (right)

Three strategies to teach meta-knowledge are proposed in [12]:

1. Reconstruction: Characters should be taught in the larger context of human conceptual patterns on one hand and against the background of unique cultural experience on the other. Learner should be supported in reconstructing the imagic origins of the pictograms and reconstructing the metaphorical link between the compounds and the pictographic radicals. The act of reconstructing the relevant source will provide the learner with a conceptual rationale that explains to the learner that the relationship between the written sign and its meaning is not arbitrary. This is important for students who are used to an alphabetic writing system.
2. Teaching semantic categories: Characters should be taught as integral members of semantic categories by contrasting characters sharing the same radicals e.g. 打 (hit) vs. 揍 (whack) vs. 拧 (wring) as well as phonologically related characters with contrastive radicals e.g. 错 (mistake) vs. 措 (arrange). This engages associative learning and draws on contextual cues such that individual characters are not learned in isolation but always in contrast to related signs within the same semantic category or across semantic categories.
3. Mnemonic associations should be developed to reinforce memory. This draws on the interactional properties of the semantic categories marked by the components. The creation of mnemonic information is a process of forming subjective and interactional connections to the entity to be learned. It requires the individual learner's unique personal experience with images and meanings. Though it may seem to lack 'scientific rigor', the creativity inherent in this kind of interaction based on imagination gives rise to long-term memory.

4 Prototype

We implemented two mapping components, a hyperbolic view and a MultiMap to demonstrate different aspects of interaction with a lexical knowledge base.

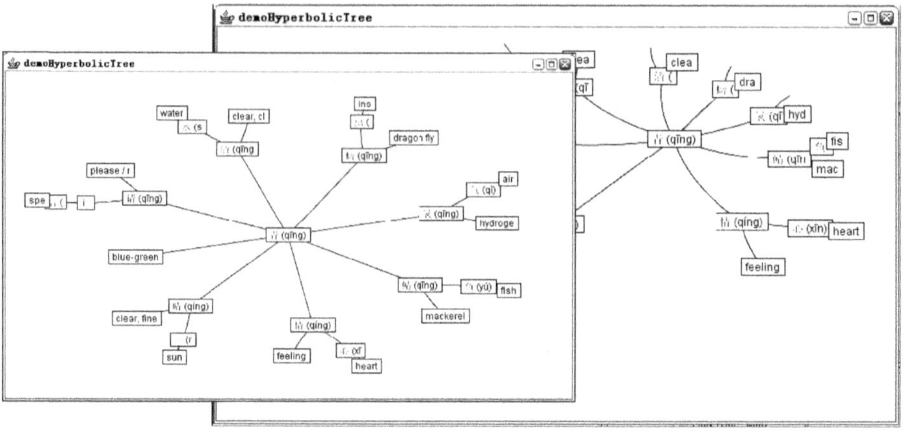

Fig. 3. Dictionary Navigation using a hyperbolic views

Hyperbolic tree visualizations have been used to realize the idea of dictionary navigation and exploration, because they enable fast browsing through a huge lexical graph. The relations between words, characters and component are used as pathways in the data for exploration of the vocabulary space. Because their visual representation at the detail level is rather sparse, a component would normally be used as entry point to other components that offers more sophisticated visualization at the detail level.

Figure 3 shows how dictionary data can be browsed in a hyperbolic view. All words/relations are projected onto an apparent sphere. Words at the border become small or fade out completely. By clicking a node, it is centered and becomes the new focus of the graph. Large graphs can be navigated quickly.

The MultiMap is the main visualization component of our prototype that is used as *detailed view* of a word and its relations has been developed. The intension was to be able to use features of multiple mapping paradigms together in a flexible way. MultiMaps are eature rich by capturing different types of relations (bi-, unidirectional links) and nodes (multimedia nodes, BiK nodes). Further they are flexible to generate a number of appropriate spatial configurations, like radial layout (Mind Map) and hierarchal layout (Concept Map). In addition, split-nodes that have been investigates as in bilingual knowledge maps (BiK-maps) are supported. BiK-maps have been proven valid for foreign language learning, but have not yet been implemented and used in connection with computer dictionaries and linguistic knowledge bases.

A modified spring layout algorithm is used to automatically generate maps from lexical data. Different spatial configurations like radial and hierarchical alignment can be visualized. Additional to text nodes and directed edges that can be used to depict knowledge in a similar way as Concept Map and Mind Map, different extensions have been realized. The underlying hypergraph model allows that edges can point to edges and representation of sets. Multi-dimensional nodes can be used to create BiK-map and list structures. Further media elements like images and audio can be used, e.g. to include authentic material.

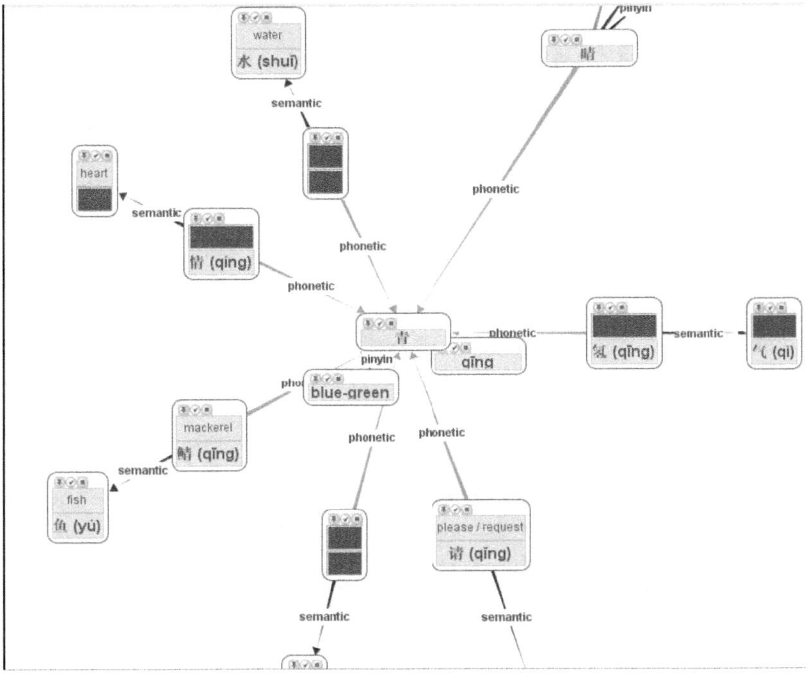

Fig. 4. Radial MultiMap used for fill-in the blank test

4.1 Knowledge Base

We use WordNet for paradigmatic relationships such as synonymy and hyponymy. We use HowNet to depict conceptual relationships.

We included relationships that describe the spatial aspect of character-component relationships. The Unicode standard [15] contains 12 special characters (2FF0-2FFB: ⿰⿱⿲⿳⿴⿵⿶⿷⿸⿹⿺⿻) that can be used to describe the spatial aspect of a composition. So for example the character 明 can be describe by an ideographic description sequence (IDS) "⿰日月". This information could be used to preferred layout algorithm spatial direction of the edges between character and components.

We added further information and relationships for demonstration purposes. For example we added relations for visual similarity of characters, e.g. 天夭矢夫末未失 While maps themselves represent generalized knowledge, authentic could be realized through the inclusion of language usage examples and multimedia elements. As an example, we added images that show the pictographic origin of some characters and audio files of word pronunciation.

4.2 Style Sheets

We use style sheets expressed in the SPARQL to define mappings between the lexical knowledge (RDF/OWL graph) and the visual graph model. The mappings are used to control the automatic layout.

Structural Mapping maps lexical statements to edge and node structures. Translation relations can be mapped to BiK-nodes. By default an RDF Statement S-P-O will be interpreted as two nodes S and O linked by a directed labeled edge P. The style sheet might override this default by defining new mapping either directly for certain predicates or based on properties of the predicates. For example, symmetric properties can be depicted by undirected edges.

Mappings are used to influence the behavior of the force directed layout. For example hierarchical relations like subsumption can trigger an overall top-down hierarchical layout in order to emphasize this property visually. Another example is the assignment of partitions in a radial layout. For example antonyms and synonyms could for example be shown on opposite parts of the graph as means of contrast.

4.3 Query and Testing

The mapping between knowledge and visual graph is bidirectional. The mapping from visual graph to RDF can on the one hand use for storing data.

More interesting, the visualization can directly been used as query the knowledge base. For example, a user can draw a map and leave one or more nodes empty. This user input is than transformed into a SPARQL[4] query with the empty nodes being the variables that are searched for.

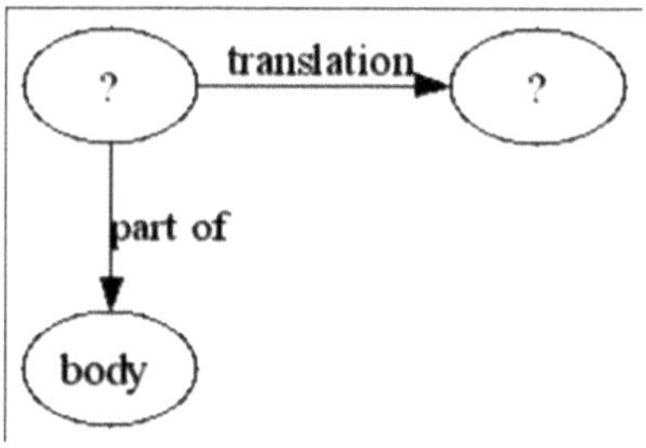


```
SELECT ?x ?y
WHERE {
      ?x :partOf "body" .
      ?x :trans ?y
}
```

A *fill-in-the-gap* test mode has been implemented to test a learner's knowledge. Technically, testing knowledge can be seen as special case of querying. The answer of a user to a fill-in-the-blanks task is correct if it's in the knowledge base. It is necessary to integrate similarity metrics in the query in order to be able to have a measure of correctness. Edit distance metrics can be used to evaluate typing variants and errors, phonetic similarity measures for phonetic variants. One step further a

[4] http://www.w3.org/TR/rdf-sparql-query/

semantic aspects can also be evaluated, e.g. if a user has entered a more a concept that is subsumed by the expected concept, his answer still is correct.

5 Conclusion

We described a framework that uses different mapping visualizations to interact with a lexical database in ways that foster learning. The mechanism that mediates between visual interface and lexical knowledge base is highly flexible. Style sheet make it easy to map features of the knowledge representation to a pedagogically appropriate visualization. Layout of common pen & paper mapping techniques can be reproduced. However, the quality of automatic layout depends heavily on the used layout algorithms and their constraints. The MultiMap we developed was therefore tailored for the specific requirements of BiK-Mapping.

References

1. Bahr, G.S., Dansereau, D.F.: Bilingual Knowledge Maps (BiK-Maps) in second-language vocabulary learning. The Journal of Experimental Education 70(1), 5–24 (2001)
2. Tergan, S.-O., Keller, T. (eds.): Knowledge and Information Visualization. LNCS, vol. 3426. Springer, Heidelberg (2005)
3. Novak, J.D., Gowin, D.B.: Learning how to learn. Cambridge University Press, Cambridge (1984)
4. Buzan, T., Buzan, B.: The Mind Map book. BBC Books, London (1993)
5. Dansereau, D.: The development of a learning strategy curriculum. In: O'Neill, H. (ed.) Learning Strategies, pp. 1–29. Academic Press, New York (1978)
6. Geroimenko, V., Chen, C.: Visualizing the semantic Web. Springer, London (2002)
7. Novak, J.D., Canas, A.J.C.: The origins of the concept mapping tool and the continuing evolution of the tool. vol. 5, pp. 175–184 (2006)
8. Aliprand, J., Consortium, U.: Unicode4 The Unicode standard: version 4.0, Addison-Wesley (2003)
9. Berners-Lee, T., Hendler, J., Lassila, O.: The semanticweb. Scientific American 284, 34–43 (2001)
10. Fellbaum, C.: WordNet: an electronic lexical database. Language, speech, and communication. MIT Press, Cambridge, Mass (1998)
11. Manning, C.D., Jansz, K., Indurkhya, N.: Kirrkirr: Software for browsing and visual exploration of a structured warlpiri dictionary. Literary and Linguistic Computing 16(1), 123–139 (2001)
12. Jing-Schmidt, Z. (2005). Cognitive foundations of the Chinese writing system and their pedagogical implications. In: Poerner, M. (ed.) 汉字认知 Hanzı renzhi - How Western Learners Discover the World of Written Chinese, Germersheim. Fachbereich Angewandte Sprach- und Kulturwissenschaft der Universität Mainz.
13. Dong, Z., Dong, Q.: Hownet And the Computation of Meaning. World Scientific Publishing Co. Inc. River Edge, NJ, USA (2006)
14. DeFrancis, J.: Visible speech: the diverse oneness of writing systems. University of Hawaii Press, Honolulu (1989)
15. Aliprand, J.: the Unicode Consortium, eds.: The Unicode standard: version 4.0. Addison-Wesley, Boston (2003)

16. Bahr, G.S., Dansereau, D.F.: Bilingual Knowledge (BiK-) Maps: Study strategy effects. In: Cañas, A.J., Novak, J.D., González, F.M. (eds.) Proceedings of the First International Conference on Concept Mapping (CMC 2004). Pamplona, Spain, NovaText vol. 1, pp. 59–66 (2004)
17. Bahr, G.S., Dansereau, D.F.: Bilingual knowledge maps (bik maps) as a presentation format: Delayed recall and training effects. The Journal of Experimental Education 73(2), 101–118 (2005)
18. Cañas, A.J., Coffey, J.W., Carnot, M.J., Feltovich, P., Hoffman, R.R., Feltovich, J., Novak, J.D.: A summary of literature pertaining to the use of concept mapping techniques and technologies for education and performance support. Technical report, Institute for Human and Machine Cognition (2003)
19. Paivio, A., Desrochers, A.: A dual-coding approach to bilingual memory. Canadian Journal of Psychology 34, 388–399 (1980)
20. Wallace, D.S., West, S.W.C., Ware, A., Dansereau, D.F.: The effect of knowledge maps that incorporate gestalt principles on learning. Journal of Experimental Education 67, 5–16 (1998)
21. Ware, C., Purchase, H., Colpoys, L., McGill, M.: Cognitive measurements of graph aesthetics. Information Visualization 1(2), 103–110 (2002)

The Perceptual Eye View: A User-Defined Method for Information Visualization

Liang-Hong Wu[1] and Ping-Yu Hsu[2]

[1] Department of Business Administration, National Central University, Chung-Li, Taiwan 320, R.O.C.
93441022@cc.ncu.edu.tw
[2] Department of Business Administration, National Central University, Chung-Li, Taiwan 320, R.O.C.
pyhsu@mgt.ncu.edu.tw

Abstract. With the growing volumes of data, exploring the relationships within the huge amounts of data is difficult. Information visualization uses the human perception system to assist users in analyzing complex relationships and graphical hierarchy trees used commonly to present the relationship among the data. Conventional information visualization approaches fail to consider human factors, they only provide fixed degree of detail to different users. However, different users have different perceptions. A well-known information visualization called 'Magic Eye View' uses a three-dimensional interaction to allow the user to control the degree of detail he would like. However, it fails to consider some important focus + context features such as the smooth transition of the focus region and the global context. In this paper, we propose a novel information visualization method, called the 'Perceptual Eye View,' by which users may control the focus points three-dimensionally enabling different users to view their user-defined degree of detail of information space and to perceive based on their own knowledge and perception. The results demonstrate that our proposed method improve the 'Magic Eye View' by providing smooth transition of the focus region and the global context, which are important focus+context features that the 'Magic Eye View' fails to consider.

Keywords: Human-Computer Interaction, Information Visualization, Human Perception.

1 Introduction

With the growing volumes of data that is captured in digital form, the exploration and analysis of these huge amounts of data has become increasingly difficult. Therefore, information visualization has been developed to tackle this problem [8].

Visualization represents the graphical representation of data or concepts. It reflects the internal construct of human minds [17]. Therefore, information visualization uses the human perceptual system to visually explore the relationships within information, to extract meaning from the data, to uncover the hidden characteristics, to focus attention, to reveal structure, and to find the hidden and valuable patterns in the complex information space [4, 12, 18]. When a user knows little about data

J. Jacko (Ed.): Human-Computer Interaction, Part II, HCII 2007, LNCS 4551, pp. 181–190, 2007.

relationships and does not know what he is exploring for specifically, visual exploring of the information space is quite useful [8]. Visual exploration assists users analyzing the data and making decisions [17].

In many areas, the information space that researchers are interested in is represented graphically using a hierarchy tree. Hierarchical tree visualization is commonly used to model relations visually. Examples for this include Web sites, the clustered hierarchy tree, the classified hierarchy tree, CASE tools, and knowledge representation.

However, the amount of information in these graphical hierarchy trees tends to be immense and complex. Users cannot perceive all elements at once and they prefer to view parts or all of the trees in varying levels of detail [16].

Researchers have proposed several information visualization approaches. However, most of these studies focus on designing the algorithms, rather than combining the human elements within the approaches [17]. The degree of freedom of users to manipulate a focus point is not enough (constrained interactivity in two-dimensional plane); the magnifying ability provided by these approaches is limited [5] and is therefore unable to provide different detailed information spaces for different people; users are forced to view their information space from a single, fixed position. Therefore, the degree of detail provided by these information visualization approaches is limited and different users obtain the same degree of detail.

Research on human perceptual system has shown that, image perceived differently by different users [7]. Because different users have different perceptions, ideal information visualization techniques must not only integrate human perception into the process of visualization, but also provide flexibility in the visualization process [2, 8]. The challenge of creating a human-based information visualization technique is to create flexible user interfaces, navigation tools, and search methods that will be appropriate for each of the existing types of users [6].

In this paper, we propose a novel information visualization method, called the 'Perceptual Eye View', by which users may control focus points three dimensionally. This enables different users to view their user-defined perceivable degree of detail in their information spaces and to perceive the detail of the information spaces based on their own knowledge and perceptual system.

2 Literature Review

Several approaches have been proposed for information visualization. The traditional zoom approach enables users to navigate through structures by zooming into a specific part. However, such viewing, by zooming into the local details of the information space, provides little information about the global context [3, 14, 16].

Therefore, other approaches were proposed to provide local details and global information. One of these approaches is the 'Map View' approach [1], which provides users with a combination of one global view and several detailed views. However, the approach suffers due to the extra space required for the overview and because it forces the viewer to integrate detail and context mentally. Integrate these views must be tediously performed by the user [3, 16].

The focus + context studies of information visualization, which integrates local detail and global contextual information, were proposed to overcome the drawbacks of the above two approaches. One of the focus + context studies is the 'Fisheye View' approach. It allows local detail with a global context in a single view of the information space [5]. Sarkar et al. [14, 15] proposed a two-dimensional graphical approach to fisheye views. When analysts focused in on the focal point in the browser of a two-dimensional layout plane, the focal region, with detail and the surrounding regions, displayed in successively less detail was shown. Another focus + context approach was the 'Hyperbolic Browser' approach [10, 11], in which the hierarchy tree structures are laid out on a hyperbolic plane, and then mapped to a view plane. It provides interaction by enabling both a moving focus and a moving hierarchy tree structure to view the detail in a focus region. However, this motion is limited to two-dimensional space. The 'H3' approach [13] is similar to the 'Hyperbolic Browser' approach except that it draws the tree structure in three-dimensional hyperbolic space to show the detail of a focus region. It allows interaction with a 3D-like view. However, like the 'Hyperbolic Browser' approach, it only permits limited two-dimensional space interaction.

Because the focus point in the above approach may only be moved within a two-dimensional plane (thus, a limited degree of freedom), users are forced to view the information space from the fixed, single perspective. Furthermore, the magnifying powers of these approaches are limited [5] and therefore are unable to provide detail, which is different from user to user.

Based on the ecological argument that, because we have evolved in a three-dimensional world, information presented in three-dimensional space will be processed more easily by the visual system [19]. A focus + context approach called the 'Magic Eye View' approach [9] provides three-dimensional interaction with a focus point to overcome the above limitations. Fig.1 shows the 'Magic Eye View' approach mapped onto a hierarchy tree on a hemisphere by the ray of a fixed direction. Because the direction of the ray is fixed, the detail of the focus region is magnified when the focus is moved.

The 'Magic Eye View' works as follows: "Our approach maps a hierarchy graph onto the surface of a hemisphere. We then apply a projection in order to change the focus area interactively by moving the center of projection" [9]. Therefore, the 'Magic Eye View' computes a ray, S_i, from the 'Center of projection,' $P_0 = (0; 0; 0)$, which is initially located at the center of the hemisphere. Through each node, P_i (in Fig.1 left), of the graphical hierarchy tree, the directions of S_i are determined by the initial positions of node P_i on the hemisphere [9].

The 'Magic Eye View' can arbitrarily move the 'Center of projection' P_0 within the hemisphere, to provide three-dimensional navigation whereby the directions of the rays, S_i, are retained (in Fig.1 middle and right). The 'Magic Eye View' can also rotate, translate and zoom the hemisphere.

In this paper, we propose a novel information visualization method called the 'Perceptual Eye View.' It focuses on visualizing the information space which is formed by hierarchy trees. The 'Perceptual Eye View' provides three-dimensional interaction with which users can control the focus point three-dimensionally. This enables customized view for different users, and users can choose the degree of detail of information space for them to perceive based on their own knowledge and perceptual system.

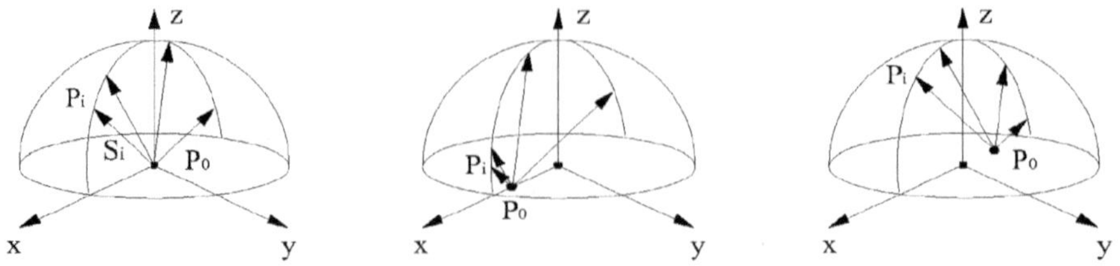

Fig. 1. Moving of the focus point in the 'Magic Eye View' [9]

Compared with the 'Magic Eye View' approach, our method allows users better control magnifying the focused zone, and incorporates important focus + context features that the 'Magic Eye View' fails to consider. The results show that our method improves the 'Magic Eye View' in several ways. Firstly, the proposed method provides users with more detail in the information space for them to perceive. Secondly, the proposed method achieves smooth transition for the focus region and the global context.

3 The 'Perceptual Eye View'

This paper focus on providing information visualization which considers flexible human computer interaction [6] so that user can choose the best perceivable degree of detail to fit their own perceptual system [17].

We will briefly describe the 'Perceptual Eye View' below. Firstly, we must lay out the hierarchy tree. In Fig. 2(a), a hierarchy tree with four layers is laid out on the x-y plane inside a unit sphere. Fig. 2(b) demonstrates the view of the unit sphere and the four-layers hierarchy tree laid out on an x-y plane that is observed from the z-axis.

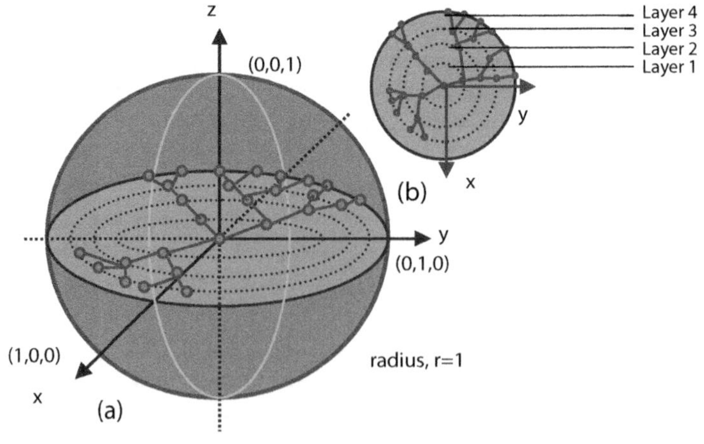

Fig. 2. Lay out the hierarchy tree in a unit sphere

The initial state of the 'Perceptual Eye View' is shown in Fig. 3(a) with the sphere being observed from the x-axis. In the 'Perceptual Eye View' we consider the focus point as a light and denote it by term 'Light.' The directed lines denote rays from the 'Light' through the edge of each layer and intersecting the sphere. The intersection of the sphere and each ray is denoted by P_i. The vertical dotted line denotes the edge of each of the layers of the hierarchy tree. R1 denotes the original height of the layer 1 of the 4-layers hierarchy tree. R2 denotes the original height of the remaining layers. R1' denotes the height of layer 1 that were observed on the sphere from the z-axis after activating the 'Light.' R2' denotes the height of the remaining layers that were observed on the sphere from the z-axis after the 'Light' was activated.

Then user would manipulate the 'Light' to magnify the height of the target layer while de-magnifying the remaining layers. By manipulating the Light directly, different users could get the greatest perceivable degree of detail to fit their own respective perceptual systems. Users can move the 'Light' arbitrarily within the space below the x-y plane but it is not limited to inside the sphere. When we observe the sphere from the x-axis, the shortest vertical distance between the 'Light' and the x-y plane is denoted by K'', where $0 \leqq K'' \leqq \infty$. The shortest horizontal distance between the 'Light' and the z-axis is denoted by K, where $0 \leqq K \leqq \infty$. Fig. 3(b) demonstrates the coordinate system of the 'Perceptual Eye View.'

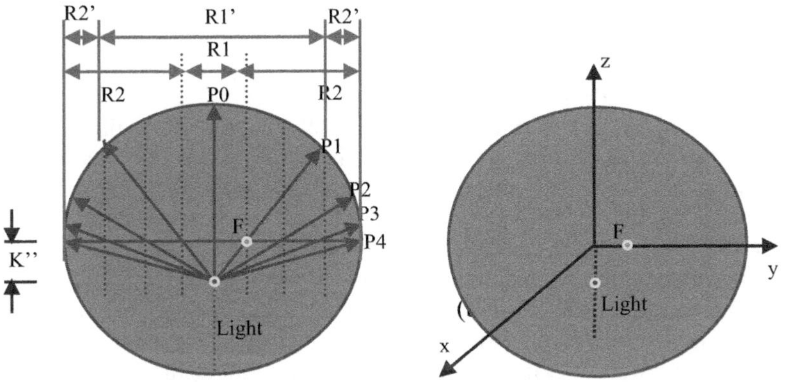

Fig. 3. Initial state of the 'Perceptual Eye View'

Now, we can directly move the 'Light' to get the most perceivable degree of detail in the region of interest, i.e., change the value of K and K''. In Fig. 4(a), R1 denotes the original height of the layer 1 and layer 2 of the 4-layers hierarchy tree. R2 denotes the original height of the remaining layers. R1' denotes the height of the layer 1 and layer 2 that observed on the sphere from the z-axis after we activate the 'Light.' R2' denotes the height of the remaining layers that are observed on the sphere from the z-axis after we activate the 'Light.' When we maintain the value of K'' and move the 'Light' horizontally to the right below the point F (see Fig. 3 and Fig. 4), we can see that we obtain appropriate detail for R1 but less detail for R2. Fig. 4(b) shows that if we wish to control the degree of detail for R1, we can maintain the value of K and move the 'Light'

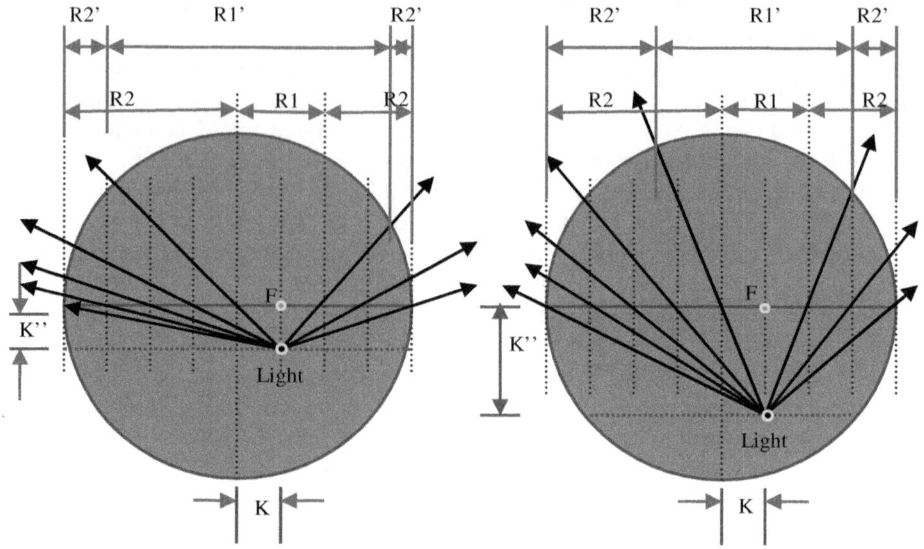

(a) (b)

Fig. 4. Moving the Light arbitrarily

vertically. The 'Light' will still be below the point F. However, we get more detail for R1 than in Fig. 4(a) as the value of K'' increases.

The user should be able to control the 'Light' directly. This allows the user to magnify and de-magnify the focus region until the required degree of detail is obtained. Now, we can obtain the perceivable degree of detail by changing K and K'' i.e., directly controlling the 'Light.' This direct control the 'Light' can achieve the goal of smooth transition of the focus region and the global context.

An ideal information visualization approach should allow for flexible human computer interaction to enable users to choose the most perceivable degree of detail by themselves. Compared with the conventional approaches that provide the same limited degree of detail for all users, the 'Perceptual Eye View' attains its goal of visualization that not only is useful to human perception but also helps users to make full use of their perception by offering different degrees of detail to different users.

4 Evaluation

In this section, we will study whether the 'Perceptual Eye View' and 'Magic Eye View' enable a smooth transition of the focus region and the global context. The objective is to move the focus point to enlarge the part in or near the focus point. It is also to display the part in great detail while the remaining part is relatively less detailed. Finally, the degree of detail should be a smooth function of the distance from the focus [5, 9, 15, 16].

Moving on, we look at the case of visualizing the graphical hierarchy tree. A smooth transition of the focus region and the global context will enlarge the height of the layers that are in or near the focus point. It will further display those layers in greater detail while the height of the remaining layers is reduced and also display them in relatively less detail. The height and degree of detail of each layer of the graphical hierarchy tree should be a smooth function of distance from the focus point. This provides for smooth integration of the focus and its context. Sufficient height would provide a greater degree of detail for target layer of the graphical hierarchy tree.

Firstly, we lay out a 10-layer graphical hierarchy tree on the x-y plane inside the unit sphere. In Fig. 5, we can observe all layers of the graphical hierarchy tree from the z-axis. Then, we activate the 'Perceptual Eye View' and 'Magic Eye View.' The focus point is denoted as 'Light' and 'Center of projection', respectively. We then move the 'Light' and 'Center of projection' along the y-axis. The range for the 'Light' and 'Center of projection' is point (0, 0) to point (0, 1) and point (0, 0) to point (0, -1), respectively. We will study the situation when the 'Light' is moving on the plane {z=-0.5} i.e. K''=0.5 and the 'Center of projection' is moving on the x-y plane, respectively. The targets are layer 1 to layer 10 along the y-axis from (0,0) to (0,1) in Fig. 5. The unit length of moving the focus point is set to 0.05. After moving the focus point step by step, we want to evaluate the heights along the y-axis from point (0,0) to point (0,1) for layer 1 to layer 10, respectively.

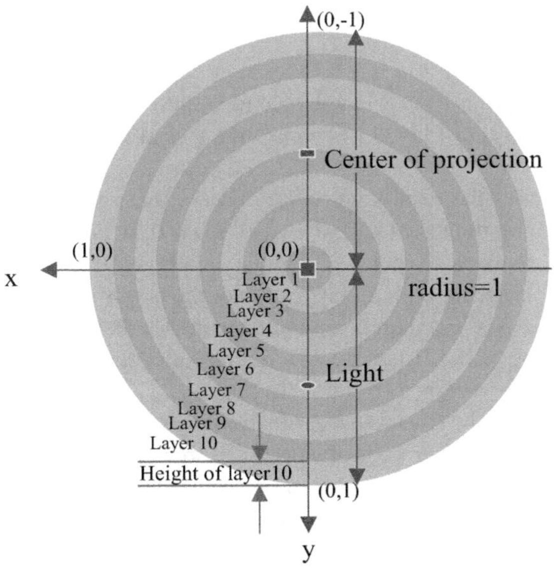

Fig. 5. The 'Perceptual Eye View' vs. the 'Magic Eye View'

Fig. 6 displays the results when we observe the x-y plane from the z-axis and move the 'Center of projection' along the axis {x=0, -1≦y≦0, z=0}. When the 'Center of projection' stays at point (0,0), the height of each layer is equal to 0.1. When we move the 'Center of projection,' the height of each layer changes. After we moved the 'Center

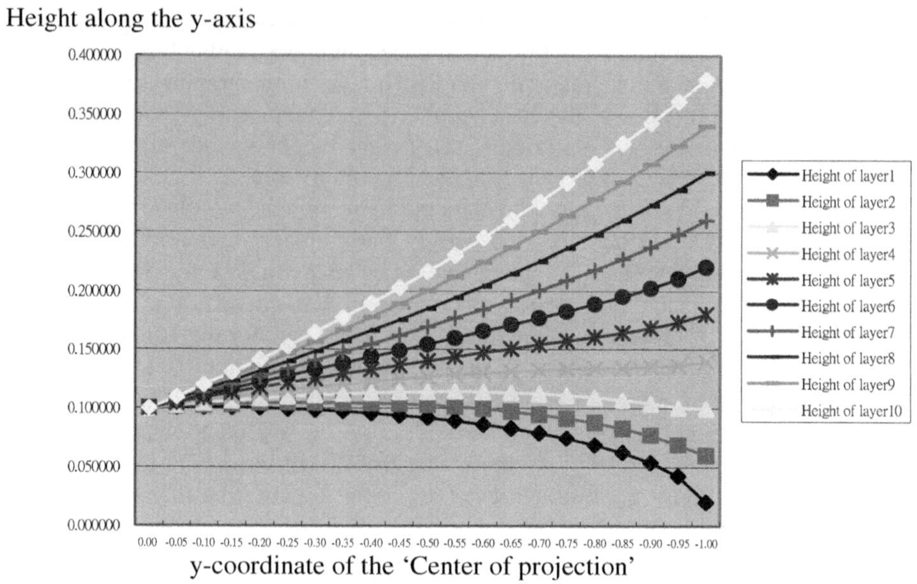

Fig. 6. Smooth transition of the focus region and the global context not achieved ('Magic Eye View')

of projection' to the point (0,-1) on sphere, the height of layer 10 becomes the global maximum and the height of layer 1 becomes the global minimum when comparing all layers.

Fig. 7 demonstrates the results when we observe the x-y plane from the z-axis and move the 'Light' along the axis $\{x=0, 0 \leqq y \leqq 1.1, z=-0.5\}$ i.e. $K''=0.5$ and $0 \leqq K \leqq 1.1$. When the 'Light' remains at point (0,0), the height of the layer 1 was the global maximum when comparing with all layers. Also, the height of layer 2 is less than layer 1, the height of layer 3 is less than layer 2 and so on. The height of layer 10 is the global minimum comparing with all layers. The degree of detail (height) of each layer is a smooth function of the distance from the 'Light.'

However, wherever the 'Center of projection' was moved between point (0,0) and point (0,-1), the height of layer 10 is always the global maximum and the height of layer 1 is always the global minimum compared with other layers. In other words, the 'Magic Eye View' cannot allow all the layers to reach the global maximum when users focus on. For example, the height of layer 8 is never the global maximum when we focus on layer 8. And the height of layer 9 and layer 10 is always longer than the height of layer 8 but it is not the region we are focusing on.

Compared with the 'Magic Eye View,' when we move the 'Light' to each layer along y-axis, the height of this layer will become the global maximum compared with the other layers. The height of the other layers is de-magnified in our proposed method. Therefore, our proposed approach achieves a smooth transition between the focus and context region.

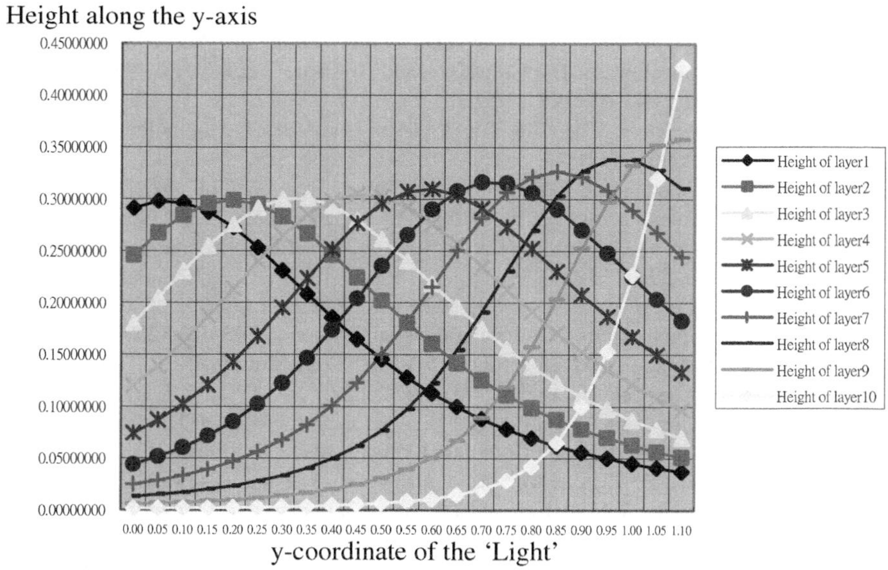

Fig. 7. Smooth transition of the focus region and the global context achieved ('Perceptual Eye View')

5 Conclusion

We propose a novel focus + context information visualization method, called 'Perceptual Eye View,' which overcomes the limitations of the conventional visualization approaches by providing flexible three-dimensional interaction. Moreover, our proposed method improves on the 'Magic Eye View' approach in allowing a smooth transition of the focus region and the global context.

When users move the focus point the smooth transition of the focus region and the global context aims to enlarge the part in or near the focus point. It displays the focus region in greater detail while the remaining part is successively less detail and the degree of detail would be a smooth function of distance from the focus point. Well-designed human-computer interaction must provide this feature to allow users to understand where their focus point is and what is magnified by the focus point. From this point, users can then go on to magnify the next target by controlling the focus point directly. Users will get confused in the process of human-computer interaction lacking this feature due to the fact that users cannot identify what target is focused on and what was magnified by the focus point.

References

1. Beard, D.V., Walker, J.Q.: Navigational Techniques to Improve the Display of Large 2-D Spaces. Behaviour and Information Technology 9(6), 451–466 (1990)
2. Card, S., Mackinlay, J., Shneiderman, B.: Readings in Information Visualization: Using Vision to Think. Morgan Kaufmann Publishers Inc. San Francisco (1999)

3. Carpendale, M.S.T., Cowperthwaite, D.J., Fracchia, F.D.: Three-Dimensional Pliable Surfaces: For Effective Presentation of Visual Information. In: Proceedings of the 8th annual ACM Symposium on User Interface and Software Technology, 1995th edn. pp. 217–226 ACM Press, New York (1995)
4. Foley, J.: Getting There: The Ten Top Problems Left. IEEE Computer Graphics and Applications 20(1), 66–68 (2000)
5. Furnas, G.W.: Generalized Fisheye Views. In: Proceedings of the ACM SIGCHI Conference on Human Factors in Computing Systems, pp. 16–23. ACM, New York (1986)
6. Gershon, N., Eick, S.G.: Information visualization. IEEE Computer Graphics and Applications 17(4), 29–31 (1997)
7. Han, J., Hu, X., Cercone, N.: A visualization model of interactive knowledge discovery systems and its implementations. Information Visualization 2, 105–125 (2003)
8. Keim, D.A.: Information Visualizattion and Visual Data Mining. IEEE Transactions on Visualization and Computer Graphics 8(1), 1–8 (2002)
9. Kreuseler, M., Schumann, H.: A Flexible Approach for Visual Data Mining. IEEE Transactions on Visualization and Computer Graphics 8(1), 39–51 (2002)
10. Lamping, J., Rao, R.: The Hyperbolic Browser: A Focus+Context Technique for Visualizing Large Hierarchies. Journal of Visual Languages and Computing 7(1), 33–55 (1996)
11. Lamping, J., Rao, R., Pirolli, P.: A Focus + Context Technique Based on Hyperbolic Geometry for Visualizing Large Hierarchies. In: Proceedings of the SIGCHI Conference on Human Factors in Computing Systems, Denver, Colorado, United States. pp. 401–408 (1995)
12. McCormick, B.H., DeFanti, T.A., Brown, M.D.: Visualization in Scientific Computing. Computer Graphics 21(6), 1345–1366 (1987)
13. Munzner, T.: Exploring Large Graphs in 3D Hyperbolic Space. IEEE Computer Graphics and Applications 18(4), 18–23 (1998)
14. Sarkar, M., Brown, M.H.: Graphical Fisheye Views. Communications of the ACM 37(12), 73–84 (1994)
15. Sarkar, M., Snibbe, S.S., Tversky, O.J., Reiss, S.P.: Stretching the Rubber Sheet: A Metaphor for Viewing Large Layouts on Small Screens. In: Proceedings of the 6th Annual ACM Symposium on User Interface Software and Technology. pp. 81–91(1993)
16. Schaffer, D., Zuo, Z., Greenberg, S., Bartram, L., Dill, J., Dubs, S., Roseman, M.: Navigating Hierarchically Clustered Networks through Fisheye and Full-Zoom Methods. ACM Transactions on Computer Human Interaction 3(2), 162–188 (1996)
17. Tory, M., Moller, T.: Human Factors In Visualization Research. IEEE Transactions on Visualization and Computer Graphics 10(1), 1–13 (2004)
18. Ward, M.O.: A taxonomy of glyph placement strategies for multidimensional data visualization. Information Visualization 1, 194–210 (2002)
19. Ware, C., Franck, G.: Evaluating Stereo and Motion Cues for Visualizing Information Nets in Three Dimensions. ACM Transactions on Graphics 15, 121–139 (1996)

A Discriminative Color Quantization Depending on the Degree of Focus*

Hong-Taek Yang and Doowon Paik**

School of Media, Soongsil University
Sangdo 5-dong, Dongjak-ku, Seoul, Korea
{seabird845,dpaik}@ssu.ac.kr

Abstract. In this paper, we propose a discriminative color quantization algorithm depending on the degree of focus of the regions. When we take pictures, we usually focus the object that we want to emphasize. This means that focused area on the photograph contains important information. If the focused area is displayed with more colors, we can express the important information in more detail. This paper proposes a color quantization method that determines the focused area and assigns more colors for the area.

Keywords: Color quantization, focus measure, focused area detection.

1 Introduction

Color quantization is a process that reduces the number of colors used in an image, usually with the intention that the new image should be as visually similar as possible to the original image[1]. The objective of the quantization problem is to select a fixed number of colors to represent the original image as close as possible. Many algorithms were proposed and Octree[1][2], Median-cut[3], K-Means[4] and Local K-Means[5] are examples of them. They formulate the quantization problem as a clustering problem and find centers of clusters. To select the proper colors to represent the original image, properties of human color perception are exploited. One of the human color perception properties is that human eyes are sensitive on the area with less change of colors and an algorithm to exploit this property was proposed in [8]. In this paper, we propose a discriminative color quantization algorithm depending on the degree of focus of the regions. When we take pictures, we usually focus the object that we want to emphasize. This means that focused area on the photograph contains important information. If the focused area is displayed with more colors, we can express the important information in more detail. This paper proposes a color quantization method that determines the focused area and assigns more colors for the area.

2 Color Quantization Method Depending on the Degree of Focus

In this paper, we propose a discriminative color quantization algorithm depending on the degree of focus of the regions. For the well focused area, more number of colors

* This work was supported by the Soongsil University Research Fund.
** Corresponding author.

J. Jacko (Ed.): Human-Computer Interaction, Part II, HCII 2007, LNCS 4551, pp. 191–196, 2007.

will be assigned to represent the area, and for the unfocused area, less number of colors will be assigned. This chapter explains the procedure of our color quantization algorithm. Fig. 1 is overall process of our proposed method. Our method is consists of two parts, detection of the focused area and the color quantization.

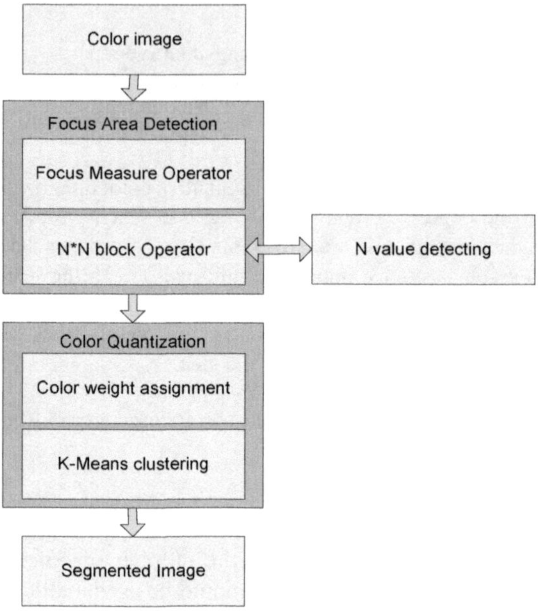

Fig. 1. Proposed method

2.1 Focused Area Detection

To determine if a pixel is focused, Nayer proposed a focus measure operator[9]. The focus measure operator is a modified Laplacian filter and ideally it supposes to have large value when the pixel is well focused. However, if the focused area is composed of pixels with similar colors, the value of the focus measure operator will be small, and those pixels will be classified to be out of focused. To overcome this problem we propose a block based algorithm to find a focused area. Our method divides the image into many blocks and determines whether each block is focused or not. The detailed procedure of our algorithm is described step by step in the followings:

Step 1. For each pixel, calculate focus measure
Step 2. Divide the image into m by n blocks.
Step 3. For each block, calculate the average of focus measures for the pixels inside the block.
Step 4. For each block (i, j), if the average value in Step 3 is greater than the average of focus measures for all the pixels, set b(i, j) = 1. Otherwise, set b(i, j) =0.
Step 5. For each block (x, y), calculate $B(x, y)$, sum of 8 b(i, j)'s for the neighboring blocks of (x, y)

Step 6. For each block (x, y), if $B(x, y)$ is grater than a threshold, determine the block (x, y) is focused.

We implemented the above algorithm and for the discussion of each step, we produced some intermediate images (Fig. 2). Fig. 2 (a) is the source image and as may be noticed, a man with a dog is focused and the surrounding is unfocused. Fig. 2 (b) is the image produced in Step 1. If the focus measure for a pixel is larger, we draw the pixel in brighter color. We can realize that the focus measure in Step 1 is not the appropriate way to determine the focused area since we can notice that focused area in Fig. 2 (a) does not always have brighter colors, and larger focus measure. Fig. 2 (c) is the image produced in Step 4. If b(i, j) = 1, we draw the block in white color. Fig. 2 (d) is the image produced in Step 6. If a block is focused, we draw the block in white color. Comparing Fig. 2 (c) and Fig. 2 (d), we can see that some focused blocks in Fig. 2 (c) are not detected, while in Fig. 2 (d), most of focused blocks are determined to be focused.

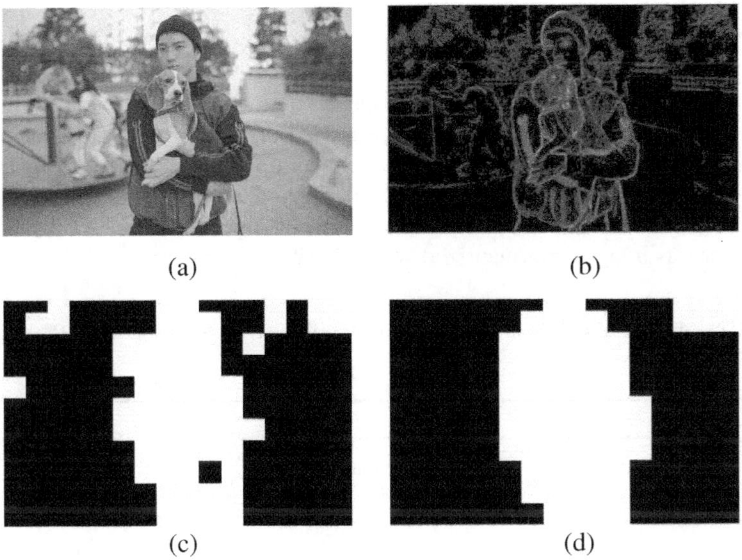

Fig. 2. (a) Source Image, (b) Image applied with focus measure, (c) Result with Step 4 and (d) Result with Step 6

2.2 Modified K-Means Clustering Algorithm for Color Quantization

Our color quantization method is a modified K-means clustering algorithm with weights assigned to each pixel. If a pixel is in the focused area, more weight is assigned to the pixel. And the weight assigned to a pixel is used to count the frequency of the color representing the pixel. This procedure assigns more weights to the colors used in the focused area for color quantization, and finally, colors used in the focused area are quantized more finely. The detailed procedure of our algorithm is described step by step in the followings:

Step 1. For each color c used in the image, calculate *wfreq(c)*, weighted frequency of the color. Weighted frequency of a color c is defined to be the number of occurrences of the color c in the image and the occurrence is counted more than one when the color c is used in the focused block.

Step 2. Construct initial set of centers.
Select colors with the highest weighted frequency in Step 1.

Step 3. Construct clusters.
For each color used in the image, find the nearest center. The set of colors having the same nearest center constitute a cluster with the center.

Step 4. Re compute the new centers of clusters using equation 2.

$$\overline{c_j} = (\sum_{c \in CL_j} wfreq(c) \times c) / \sum_{c \in CL_j} wfreq(c) \qquad (2)$$

where c_j is the new center of the cluster.

Step 5. Repeat the Step 3 and Step 4 until some convergence criterion is met.

3 Experiments

We quantize various images by using proposed algorithm and K-Means algorithm to identify that focused area quantized by proposed algorithm with a larger number of colors than K-Means algorithm. We compare the number of colors used on real focused area of color quantized image by proposed method with the numbers used on real focused area of color quantized image by K-means algorithm. The Table 3 shows the result of various images are quantized with 64, 128, 256 colors.

Table 3. The number of colors in real focused area of the quantized image by the proposed and K-Means method

Image	64		128		256	
	K-Means	Proposed method	K-Means	Proposed method	K-Means	Proposed method
A	64	64	128	128	255	256
B	64	64	127	128	251	256
C	63	64	124	127	246	250
D	64	64	128	128	255	256
E	61	64	110	128	212	252
F	63	64	125	127	242	253
G	59	62	111	127	216	249
H	64	64	128	128	244	254

As a result of the comparison, the number of colors that are used on the focused area of the proposed color quantization has used more colors compares to the number of color used on the focused area of K-means color quantization. Some images such as A, B and D have similar number of colors in real focused area of the quantized by proposed method with number colors in real focused area of the quantized by K-means. But the focused area of image quantized by proposed method is better expressed than the focused area of image quantized by K-means. Because focused area is weighted by proposed method. For an example Fig. 4(b) and (c) which are made by 64 colors has the same number of colors in real focused area, but the flower and the bee on the focused area of Fig. 4(c) are better expressed than of Fig. 4(b). Because the flower, bee and a part of the leaves located around the flower on focused area are weighted by proposed method.

Fig. 4. (a) Experiment Image B, (b) The result of the quantized image B by K-Means method and (c) The result of the quantized image B by proposed method

4 Conclusion

We presented a method that find the focused area of the photographs and display with many colors on determines the focused area. And we proved its utility through an experiment. As a result, it is the high level of accuracy on the focused area detection and it expressed with more color on the focused area.

To make a higher level of accuracy on the focused area detection method needs additionally various suggestions. Also, the image based on 3D reconstruction part should be applied and approved its utility and expects the development of the focused area detection with it.

References

1. Clark, D.: Color quantization using octrees. Dr. Dobb's Journal, pp. 54–57 and 102–104 (January 1996)
2. Gervautz, M., Purgathofer, W.: A simple method for color quantization: octree quantization. In: Glassner, A. (ed.) Graphics Gems I, Acad. Press, pp. 287–293 (1990)
3. Kruger, A.: Median-cut color quantization. Dr. Dobb's Journal, pp. 46–54 and 91–92 (September 1994)
4. Krishna, K., Ramakrishnan, K.R., Thathachar, M.A.L.: Vector Quantization using Genetic K-Means Algorithm for Image Compression. In: Proceedings 1997 International Conference on Information, Communications and Signal Processing. ICICS, vol. 3, pp. 1585–1587 (1997)
5. Verevka, O.: Color image quantization in windows systems with local K-means algorithm. In: Proceedings of VI Western Computer Graphics Symposium, pp. 74–79 (March 1995)
6. Kim, K.M., Lee, C.S., Lee, E,J., Ha, Y.H.: Color Image Quantization using Weighted Distortion Measure of HVS Color Activity. In: Proc. of International Conference on Image Processing, vol. 3, pp. 1035–1039 (1996)
7. Deng, Y., Manjunath, B.S., Shin, H.: Color Image Segmentation. In: Proc. of IEEE Computer Society Conference on Computer Vision and Pattern Recognition, vol. 2, 278 P r o c. S P IE vol. 4572 (1999)
8. Yoon, K.-J., Kweon, I.-S.: Color image segmentation considering of human sensitivity for color pattern variations. In: SPIE proceedings series, pp. 269–278 (2001)
9. Nayar, S.K.: Shape from Focus System. In: Proc. Of CVPR, pp. 302–308 (1992)

Getting Lost? Touch and You Will Find! The User–Centered Design Process of a Touch Screen

Bieke Zaman and Rogier Vermaut

CUO/IBBT - K.U.Leuven, E. Van Evenstraat 2A, 3000 Leuven, Belgium
Phone (+32) 16 32 32 51, (+32) 16 32 36 53
Bieke.Zaman@soc.kuleuven.be, Rogier.vermaut@soc.kuleuven.be

Abstract. Recent reforms in office concepts have led to new intensification strategies that aim at more flexibility and efficiency. Hot desking is one of these new working practices that reduces office space per worker. These new office concepts however, pose new challenges and problems to solve. This paper describes the development phase of an innovative touch screen application for location based services to overcome the problematic edge effects of hot desking such as missing workspace awareness and poor communication. We followed a user-centered design (UCD) process to develop and test the interface so that it could be gradually modified and tailored to the demands and expectations of the end users. First, a methodological overview of the different phases of the UCD-process is given. Then, the results of each phase are discussed, focusing on several interface elements. Finally, the most important and striking results are summarized.

Keywords: Touch screen interface, hot desking, user-centered design process, usability testing, contextual inquiry, conceptual model, paper prototyping.

1 Introduction

Recent developments in office environments can be classified into two major trends. On the one hand, team work becomes more and more important as an orga-nizational condition. On the other hand, more attention is being paid to the reorganization of office concepts to focus on higher personal mobility [1]. In this last trend towards more personal mobility and together with the business' strive for more flexibility and efficiency, new office concepts arose.

Hot desking is one of the more recent office intensification strategies aiming to reduce office space per worker [2]. Hot desking is a new working practice that offers a compensation for space needs in companies that focus on the job activities rather than on the individuals themselves. People then work together based on their job responsibilities without the prerequisite of a shared office environment. In practice, employees can choose an available place instead of going to the same desk every morning [2,3].

Although hot desking has many advantages in terms of flexibility and efficiency, problems such as missing workspace awareness, lacking group cohesion and poor communication must be dealt with [1]. That is why computer supported cooperative work (CSCW) becomes very important [3]. In this paper, however, we focus on the

J. Jacko (Ed.): Human-Computer Interaction, Part II, HCII 2007, LNCS 4551, pp. 197–206, 2007.

consequences and edge effects of hot desking apart from the conditions for CSCW. When employees do not have a place of their own, some uncertainties turn up. For example, how does one know whether someone is at his office, on holiday, on the road or working at home? How to find someone's exact working place when face-to-face contact is necessary? How to locate someone if one cannot reach him on his mobile? As a result of these and similar questions, the go-ahead was given for the this project. The Belgian telecom company Alcatel-Lucent recently chose to switch to hot desking. Alcatel-Lucent is part of the worldwide Alcatel group and focuses on the development of broadband technologies and related applications. To overcome hot desking problems, Alcatel-Lucent decided to invest in a new technological solution that should allow people to easily locate others. The aim of this paper is to describe the user-centered design process rather than the technological development phases.

From the beginning, the project aimed at developing both a touch screen as well as a PC-based solution to overcome workspace awareness related problems in Alcatel-Lucent's hot desking environment. This objective poses a double challenge. Since a PC graphical user interface (GUI) cannot simply be turned into a touch screen GUI, we had to find the right balance between consistency and platform specific requirements. Contrary to a desktop computer GUI, touch screens are mostly used in public environments and characterized with hurried (and often novice) users, easy (and often wizard-like) interfaces and intuitive interaction forms [4].

This paper will focus on the user-centered design process of the touch screen application. The paper begins with a description of the methodology of the UCD process. Then, we discuss the main results according to the different phases of the design process. In particular, we focus on the results of respectively the contextual inquiry, the conceptual model, the paper prototyping and the iterative usability testing. Finally, the paper concludes with a summary of the most important and striking results.

2 Methodology

To develop a user friendly touch screen application, we followed a user-centered design process. This process involves the user in each phase of the design chain. This way, the end-product is geared as much as possible to the wishes and characteristics of the users, resulting in a high level costumer satisfaction [5].

The first phase of the UCD process consisted of a contextual inquiry. In this phase, we not only tried to comprehend who the main users of the final application are, but also how these users perform their present as well as their future tasks [6].

The next phase entailed the drawing of a conceptual model. The conceptual model is the basis of the user interface. It is a first abstract design in which the information gathered during the contextual inquiry has been processed. This way, the conceptual model leans as much as possible on the way users think about the application [7]. Decisions concerning navigation and interaction are made without concentrating too much on details. In other words, this phase focuses not on design, but on general structure, organization and navigation [8].

The conceptual design takes further shape in a number of paper prototypes. Paper prototyping or low-fi prototyping is an excellent way of getting feedback in an early phase of the design process. Putting through adjustments in a later phase of the project would be a more time- and money-consuming matter. On top, paper prototyping gives developers the opportunity to test alternative design ideas before investing in advanced prototypes [8,9].

The next phase comprised the technical development of the interface. As soon as a significant part of the application was developed, we set up a series of usability tests. These tests, rather short and straightforward, goaled the improvement of the development and design process. Finally, a final series of tests took place. In this test, the interface was evaluated thoroughly and in great detail.

3 Results

In this section, we amplify on the results of each phase of the UCD process. From the paper prototype phase onwards, we will not describe every little aspect of the interface. In contrast, we examine the origin and evolution of four crucial interface elements: the auto completion window, the soft keyboard, the status of the contact persons and the possibility to ask for information about the colleagues of a contact person.

3.1 Contextual Inquiry

During our contextual inquiry, we focused on the end users of the system as well as on the tasks they perform in their natural environment. With the contextual inquiry, we wanted to identify all possible requirements end-users need when using the touch screen application. The target group consisted of four types of users: employees, porters, external visitors and secretaries. In this paper however we only focus on the employees since they make the main target group. More particularly, 16 employees were interviewed, concentrating on the following research questions:

- What information do employees need when looking for a colleague in the Alcatel-Lucent building?
- What difficulties do they encounter when locating and contacting their colleagues?
- What information do they expect to find on the touch screen application?

As we expected, our research findings show the importance of surname as a search term. In second place comes searching on first name. Furthermore, we identified department, name of the colleagues' main project and nickname as possibly important search criteria. During our observations, we found that the employees needed the following information when searching a colleague: information about the presence of the colleagues, detailed information about the colleagues' location, the mobile and fixed telephone number, the email address as well as information about team members. The latter becomes particularly important when the person cannot be found or contacted.

Next, we asked the respondents how they would represent the location of a colleague on a touch screen. A great majority thinks a map is appropriate to visualize the location. Suggested representation icons were: a dot, a picture, an arrow or a small person indicating the status of the person, similar to Msn Messenger. These findings confirm the finding of Weilenmann and Leuchovius: *"location based services make use of a map metaphor, presenting geographical location in the form of [...] a dot on the map"* [10].

3.2 Conceptual Model

The actual design process of the touch screen application started with the phase of the conceptual model. A conceptual model describes or shows the reasoning of the user based on the information gained during the contextual inquiry.

However, before we could start with the design, we needed to take several considerations into account:

- Touch screens can be manipulated directly while they do not ask for much user experience. No extra input device is necessary for interaction. To a certain degree, this fosters a fast navigation [4,11].
- Sears [12] reports consistent differences between the location users want to touch and where they actually touch. Fingers which are being used instead of the mouse cursor, have a certain size. Therefore, screen elements have to be designed large enough [11]. More specifically, buttons should have a minimum size of 2*2 cm (or ¾ by ¾ inch). They should be at least 3mm (or 1/8 inch) apart for finger-operated touch screens [13].
- Input is sequential because just one finger is being used. This slows input down compared to normal keyboard input [13]. On top, badly designed interfaces with respect to hand movement can make arm fatigue a major problem [4]. This is why the amount of information to be put in should be limited.

With these and other design considerations kept in mind, we started with the development of the basic application screens. In the following paragraphs, we give a short description of the three main parts of the application: title, search and results page.

The title screen offers two main options: search for a person and search for a room. Although our main target group consists of Dutch speaking employees, we opted for English as the application's default language since all communication is done in English at Alcatel-Lucent. Yet, users can choose the Dutch or French language on the title page.

Users can search a person by name, department, function, name of the project and nickname. At this stage of the project, we could only lean on the lessons learned from our contextual inquiry. Users can give in text with a soft keyboard. As soon as the user enters the first characters of a name, the application shows all possible matches in an auto completion window. It is crucial that the application recognizes all combinations of surname and first name.

The conceptual model for the results page consists of five different building blocks:

- Personal details such as picture, name, phone number, mobile number, email, function and department.
- The status of the person: a person's status can be 'available', 'busy' or 'not present'. Each status is linked with a color code. Green code means available, grey code means not present, red code means busy.

- A textual description of the location of the person: where can this person be found in the building (building, floor and room)?
- A map of the floor which indicates the route to the location of the contact person starting from the user's position. The person is represented by a small dot that corresponds with its status. The map also indicates some reference points such as restrooms, kitchen, elevators, etc.
- Reachability of the contact person: a textual description of the route to the contact person, information concerning the reachability by phone and a link that loads a list of colleagues.

3.3 Paper Prototyping

The conceptual model took shape in a few paper prototypes, made up in Microsoft Visio. Paper prototyping makes it possible to experiment with different ideas, thus promoting rapid iterative development. By testing the paper prototypes, we tried to answer the following questions:

- Is the functionality of the interface sufficiently clear, complete and intuitive for the user?
- Are navigation and interaction sufficiently clear?

To answer the questions, we drafted seven tasks. Ten subjects were told to imagine they were entering a large building where they had to meet a project partner. Tasks were formulated as follows: *"You are looking for the Director Marketing & Communication. How would you find him?"* or *"John Johnson is on his annual holiday. You do not want to disturb him and therefore decide to make an appointment with his secretary. Where can you find her?"*.

While completing these tasks, we asked each subject to say out loud what they were thinking. Using this think-aloud method, the participants communicated what they did, thought and felt while using the application. This made it possible to evaluate the interface thoroughly and in great detail. Pioneering work with the think-aloud protocol shows it to be an effective usability method, capable of identifying serious usability problems with only a few participants [14]. The protocol is very useful in gathering qualitative data about users' mental models, as well as their general impressions and feelings about navigation and design [15].

In the following sections, we discuss our major findings concerning four crucial interface elements.

3.3.1 Auto Completion

We already formulated the expectation that the system should be able to recognize all searches that combine first name and surname. This assumption was confirmed by the user tests. Subjects entered all different combinations: mostly first name + surname, but also surname + first name and even only surname or first name (see figure 1).

3.3.2 Keyboard

A study of Mackenzie, Zhang and Soukoreff [16] suggests that a Qwerty keyboard is convenient in situations where users must get started fast and easy. Since the application will be most often used by novices, we chose to offer a Qwerty keyboard by default.

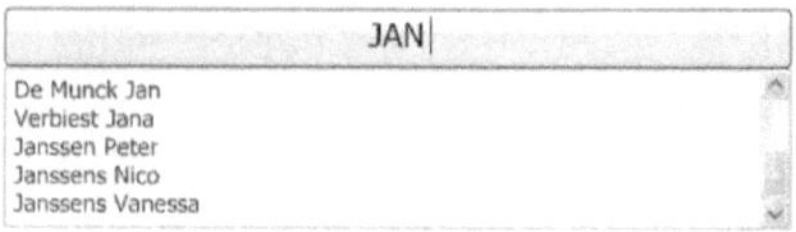

Fig. 1. Auto completion: while typing, the system suggests all possible matches

Participants did not seem to have significant difficulties using the Qwerty keyboard. However, most users did notice making use of a Qwerty keyboard. This because in Flanders, an Azerty keyboard is more widespread than a Qwerty keyboard. One out of 16 subjects explicitly said he preferred an Azerty-keyboard. Based on the users' remarks, we replaced the default Qwerty keyboard with an Azerty keyboard. Nevertheless, we decided to offer the possibility to switch from the default Azerty keyboard to a Qwerty or alphabetical keyboard. In the previous version (see figure 2, left), the keys were also too close to each other and too small to select. That is why we enlarged and separated the keys significantly in the improved version (see figure 2, right). Finally, we removed the 'done button', which caused too much confusion in combination with the search button.

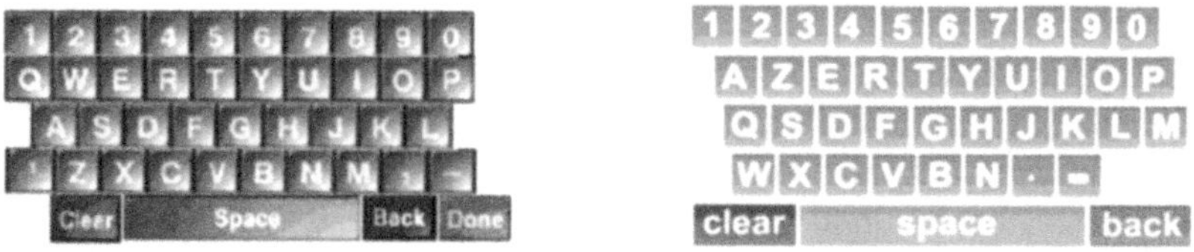

Fig. 2. The keyboard on the left-hand side caused problems and was therefore replaced by a more user friendly keyboard, here placed at the right-hand side of the above figure

3.3.3 Status

Most participants showed an intuitive understanding of the meaning of the status 'available' and 'not present'. However, subjects showed a various understanding of the status 'busy'. Whereas some subjects preferred not to contact a busy colleague, others still tried to call this person. Their reasoning was as follows: *"I would contact this person anyway. After all, I have an appointment and need to speak to him urgently"*. The different interpretations made us decide to elaborate two different types of 'busy' colleagues:

- A status 'do not disturb' which indicates that the person cannot be disturbed (because he is in meeting for example).
- A status 'busy' where a person prefers not to be contacted but it is allowed by exception.

3.3.4 Contact Colleagues

During the tests, we realized that users could only consult the list of colleagues when they clicked on 'show map' (see figure 3, left). However, users already needed this option as soon as they noticed that a person was not present or busy. Thus, we

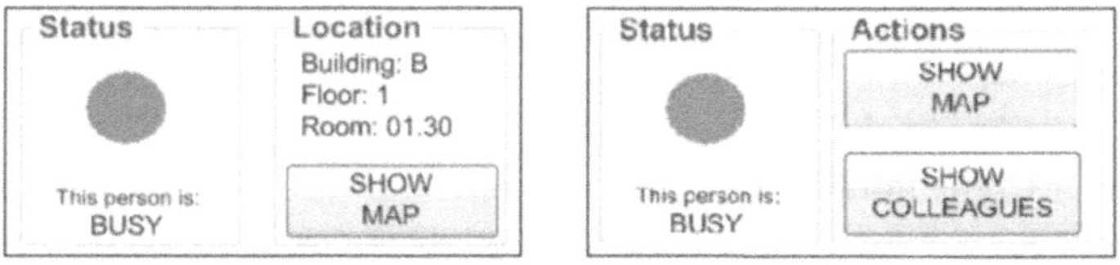

Fig. 3. The interface on the left-hand side did not have a direct link to the action 'show colleagues'; this was improved as shown on the right-hand side of the above figure

improved the interface by offering the button 'show colleagues' already at this screen (see figure 3, right). The location related information was offered in a separate window.

3.4 Second Series of Usability Tests

In contrast to the first usability test sessions that made us develop and test different low-fi paper prototypes, the second and third series of usability tests were performed using a working hi-fi prototype. The second series of tests targeted extra guidelines for developing the touch screen application.

We drew up five tasks for ten participants. Each test took about half an hour. We held these test on location and used a portable usability lab. The portable usability lab is suitable for field research, where the usability of the application in question can be researched in the natural (work) environment of the user. In the following section, the main findings of the second series of usability tests are discussed.

3.4.1 Auto Completion

The positioning of the auto completion window was problematic. The auto completion window partly covered the keyboard. As a consequence, all users got frustrated because they could not strike some of the keyboard characters. Also, participants suggested capitalising the first letter of the names in the auto completion list. As a consequence the window was repositioned and the first letters were capitalised.

3.4.2 Keyboard

Our modifications concerning the keyboard were tested in the second series of usability tests. The buttons to change the type of keyboard proved not user friendly. Buttons were in the left bottom corner whereas the keyboard is situated in the right corner. Also, three options were offered while only two are needed. If, for example, the Azerty keyboard is selected, one should only have a choice between the 'Qwerty' and 'alphabetic' keyboard.

3.4.3 Status

The difference between the busy status and the do not disturb status was immediately clear to our participants. Yet, the majority of our participants would first call an available contact person before visiting him/her. This made us conclude that a call option would be of great value for the application. Therefore, we changed the status icons and integrated a call button (see figure 4). When pressing this button, the fixed number of the contact person is dialled automatically via Voice over IP. This call button was repeatedly suggested and highly appreciated by the majority of our test users during all test sessions.

3.4.4 Contact Colleagues

The repositioning of the 'show colleagues' button proved very successful. However, the findings of both usability tests show that users distinguish between secretary and other colleagues. The majority of test users suggested adding a new button 'show secretary'. As a consequence, we added the button show secretary at the page with the map (see figure 4).

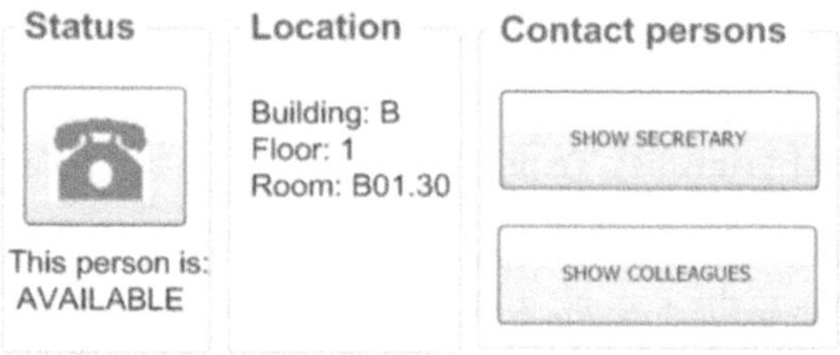

Fig. 4. The buttons 'show secretary' and 'show colleagues' were added at the individual page

3.5 Third Series of Usability Tests

In our final usability test session, we concentrated on the modifications that were implemented following the second series of tests. Of course, we also paid attention to any other usability problems that persisted.

3.5.1 Auto Completion

The problems with the positioning of the auto completion window were corrected. However, few participants noticed that the names in the auto completion list were ordered randomly whereas they expected an alphabetic list. As a result, we took this consideration into account.

3.5.2 Keyboard

The problems with the keyboard selection were solved completely. Users who wanted to change the type of keyboard did so easily. Our test participants also expected a clear-button next to the search input box. We followed this recommendation. This way we also avoided arm fatigue [4] by limiting the distance between the clear button and the search input box.

3.5.3 Status

In this final test, a new problem with the status 'not present' surfaced. When a person is not present, users can still press the button 'show map'. To our test persons, this was rather strange since "a person that is not present, can't be shown on a map". Consequently, in this case we decided to replace the button 'show map' with 'show secretary'. Users whose contact person turns out to be absent, can now address very easily to the secretary or one of the colleagues.

3.5.4 Contact Colleagues

Since we moved the button 'show colleagues' after the first tests, the functionality of the part 'How to reach?' was outstripped. Because this building block only shows information that already can be found at the top of the page, namely the phone numbers, the email address and the link to the colleagues, we decided to drop this building block altogether.

4 Conclusion

The present study examined the user-centred design (UCD) process of a touch screen interface directed at locating colleagues or contact persons in a hot desking environment. Modifications to all designs were based on the feedback of these users.

During the UCD process, some important improvements were made with regard to the developed touch screen. Summarizing, it may be stated that there are six major elements that guarantee a user friendly and successful touch screen application for location based services. First, status information is crucial for an application that locates persons. People with a certain level of computer experience are familiar with different representations of someone's status (like e.g. use of colours or icons). The results of our study show that a single status 'busy' is too ambiguous. That is why one should make the distinction between 'busy' -which means that someone can still be disturbed- and 'do not disturb' –which means that someone is really busy and therefore cannot be interrupted. Secondly, a map is the most obvious way to represent a person's location. This map should be presented from the users' point of view and show the most important reference points such as the elevator, the stairs, the toilets and the restaurant. Our results prove that a function 'show colleagues' is needed when a person cannot be found or contacted. In that case, a distinction between secretary and colleagues should be made. As for the touch screen keyboard, one should make sure buttons are very large (minimum 2*2 cm) and well separated. The type of keyboard (Azerty, qwerty or alphabetic) is of a lower priority. Further, our results prove that auto completion is a handy and efficient feature that facilitates search queries. Last but not least, the results make clear that a phone service integrated in the application via VOIP is *the* killer application that guarantees a successful functionality.

Acknowledgements. This paper is the result of research carried out as part of the T-case project, funded by the Interdisciplinary institute for Broad Band Technology (IBBT). IBBT is a research institute founded by the Flemish Government, that brings together commercial companies (like in this project Alcatel-Lucent) with academic research groups of different backgrounds (i.c. CUO for user-centered design and IBCN for broadband communication networks).

References

1. Röcker, C., Prante, T., Streitz, N.A., van Alphen, D.: Using Ambient Displays and Smart Artefacts to Support Community Interaction in Distributed Teams. In: Proceedings of the OZCHI Conference, University of Wollongong, Australia (2004)

2. Lizieri, C.M.: Occupier Requirements in Commercial Real Estate Markets. Urban Studies 40(5/6), 1151–1169 (2003)
3. Luff, P., Health, C.: Mobility in collaboration. In: Proceedings of the 1998 ACM conference on Computer supported cooperative work, pp. 305–314. ACM Press, New York (1998)
4. Sjöberg, S.: A Touch Screen Interface for Point-Of-Sale Applications in Retail Stores. Master's Thesis in Computing Science, Umea University, Sweden (2006)
5. Vredenburg, K., Isensee, S., Righi, C.: User Centered Design. An integrated approach. PTR Prentice Hall, Indianapolis (2002)
6. Beyer, H., Holtzblatt, K.: Contextual design: Defining customer-centered systems. Morgan Kaufmann Publishers, San Francisco (1998)
7. Benyon, D., Turner, P., Turner, S.: Designing interactive systems: People, Activities, Contexts, Technologies. Addison Wesley, Boston (2004)
8. Stone, D., Jarrett, C., Woodroffe, M., Minocha, S.: User Interface Design and Evaluation. Morgan Kauffman Publishers, San Francisco (2005)
9. Snyder, C.: Paper prototyping. The fast and easy way to design and refine user interfaces. Morgan Kaufmann Publishers, San Francisco (2003)
10. Weilenmann, A., Leuchovius, P.: I'm waiting where we met last time: exploring everyday positioning practices to inform design. In: Proceedings of the third Nordic conference on Human-computer interaction, pp. 33–42. ACM Press, New York (2004)
11. Albinsson, P.A., Zhai, S.: High precision touch screen interaction. In: Proceedings of the SIGCHI conference on Human factors in computing systems, pp. 105–112. ACM Press, New York (2003)
12. Sears, A.: Improving Touch Screen Keyboards: design issues and a comparison with other devices. In: Interacting with computers, vol. 3, pp. 253–269. Elsevier, New York (1991)
13. Waloszek, G.: Interaction Design Guide for Touch screen Applications, SAP Design Guild (2000). Found on: http://www.sapdesignguild.org/resources/TSDesignGL/INDEX.HTM
14. Nielsen, J.: Evaluating the Thinking Aloud Technique for Use by Computer Scientists. In: Advances in Human-Computer Interaction, vol. 3, pp. 69–82. Ablex Publishing Corp, Norwood (1993)
15. Reeves, T.C., Apedoe, X., Hee Woo, Y.H.: Evaluating Digital Libraries: A User-Friendly Guide, National Science Digital Library, University Corporation for Atmospheric Research, 2003. Found on: http://dlist.sir.arizona.edu/398
16. MacKenzie, I.S., Zhang, S.X., Soukoreff, R.W.: Text entry using soft keyboards. Behaviour & Information Technology, Taylor & Francis, Oxfordshire vol. 18 pp. 235–244 (1999)

CoConceptMap: A System for Collaborative Concept Mapping

Mingjun Zhou, Xiang Ao, Lishuang Xu, Feng Tian, and Guozhong Dai

Intelligence Engineering Lab,
Institute of Software,
Chinese Academy of Sciences,
100080 Beijing, P.R. China
{zmj,ax,tf,xls,dgz}@iel.iscas.ac.cn

Abstract. Concept mapping is a technique for visualizing the relationships between different concepts, and collaborative concept mapping is used to model knowledge and transfer expert knowledge. Because of lacking some features, existing systems can't support collaborative concept mapping effectively. In this paper, we analysis the collaborative concept mapping process according to the theory of distributed cognition, and argue the functions effective systems ought to include. A collaborative concept mapping system should have the following features: visualization of concept map, flexible collaboration style, supporting natural interaction, knowledge management and history management. Furthermore, we describe every feature in details. Finally, a prototype system has been built to fully explore the above technologies.

Keywords: collaborative concept mapping, distributed cognition, pen-based user interface.

1 Introduction

CoConceptMap is a pen-based collaborative concept mapping tool for idea capturing, by which a user can sketch concepts, draw their relations and share the map with other users.

A concept map is a visual representation of knowledge, in which concepts are represented by nodes and their relationships are represented by links. Concept maps can help people externalize and organize their internal knowledge and facilitate the exchange of information among the participants. Therefore, Concept maps can be used to stimulate the generation of ideas, and are believed to aid creativity. For example, concept mapping is sometimes used for brain-storming. Although they are often personalized and idiosyncratic, concept maps can be used to communicate complex ideas.

Currently, several computer applications [1] have been developed to support concept mapping which makes the modification of concepts and links easier. In addition, several networked concept mapping applications have the capacity to facilitate geographically separated participants share or construct maps together. For instance, CmapTools [2] is a client-server based software kit developed that is designed to support the construction of concept maps by users of all ages, and to enable collaboration and sharing during that process.

J. Jacko (Ed.): Human-Computer Interaction, Part II, HCII 2007, LNCS 4551, pp. 207–213, 2007.

Although the current tools which are introduced above can support collaborative concept mapping, they lack functions such as natural interaction, history management, etc., which we believe are valuable. In this paper, we focused on the function framework for collaborative concept mapping and the implementation of the prototype system.

The rest of this paper is organized as follows. In section 2, we review the related work. Section 3 presents the function framework. Section 4 describes CoConceptMap in details. Finally, we make some concluding remarks in section 5.

2 Analysis the Functions of Concept Mapping Tool

In this paper, we analyze collaborative concept mapping, argue the fuctions effective systems ought to include, and describe our system CoConceptmap. Collaborative concept mapping is a cognition phenomenon across individuals, artifacts, internal and external representations. We should take these factors into account. The theory of distributed cognition dissolves the traditional divisions between the inside/outside boundary of the individual and the culture/cognition. Furthermore, it emphasizes the distributed nature of cognitive phenomena [3], and has been used to explain HCI phenomena successfully [4]. According to the theory of distributed cognition, an collaborative concept mapping system should have the following features:

- Visualization of concept map
- Flexible collaboration style
- Supporting natural interaction
- Knowledge management
- History management

The relationships between these features are shown in Fig. 1:

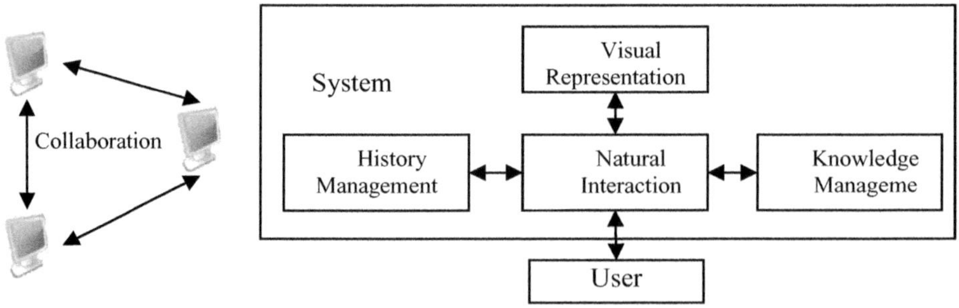

Fig. 1. The structure of CoCreativePen in client sites

3 The CoConceptMap Prototype

CoConceptMap is a pen-based collaborative concept mapping tool for idea capturing (Fig.2), by which a user can sketch concepts, draw their relations and share the map with other users.

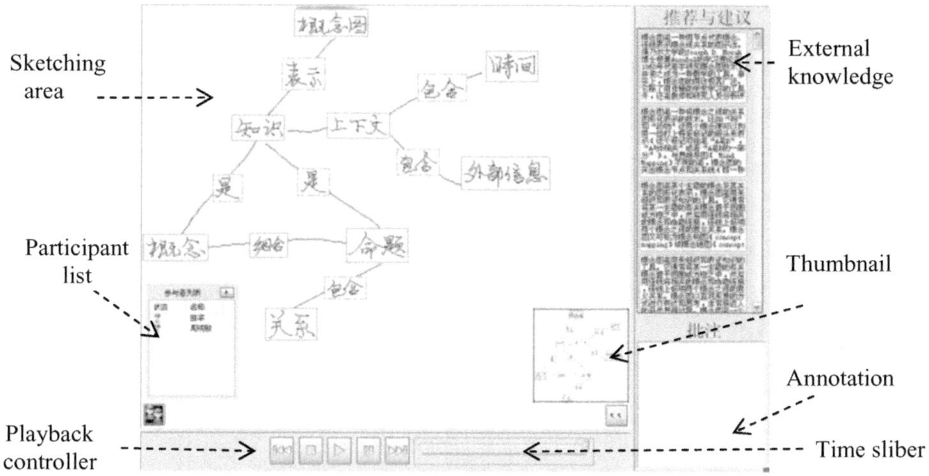

Fig. 2. CoConceptMap system interface

We will describe each part of the system as follows.

3.1 Sketching

Sketching is more suitable for idea capture than mouse and keyboard [5]. During concept mapping, the participants keep thinking while they input information, and using mouse and keyboard may obstruct thinking. On the contrary, pen-based interaction style is much faster and more naturally, and that is why CoConceptMap has a pen-based user interface.

In CoConceptMap, the user can sketch concepts and relationships by strokes, and manipulate them by pen gestures. Based on the features of the strokes and their spatial relationships, the short stroke is automatically grouped into an existing segment or forms a new segment, and the long stroke which connects two segments will be recognized as links. The segment will be treated as a relationship if it is at the middle of a link, or be treated as a concept if it is at the end of a link. Each segment is shown by a bounding box of its strokes, and the user can move a segement by the control bar on the bounding box. To ensure visibility, collision detection is used to keep the segments from overlapping. Besides, the user can combine, split or delete the concepts by pen gestures (Fig.3).

In CoCeptMap, each segment can be viewed as a text line, each segment is separated into words by word segmentation algorithms [6], and then each word will be recognized as Chinese characters (Fig.4). Then the system can provide suggestions according to its meaning.

3.2 Knowledge Management

During collaborative concept mapping, the participants may search concept related to the current concept map and look up explanation of the concepts in the concept map,

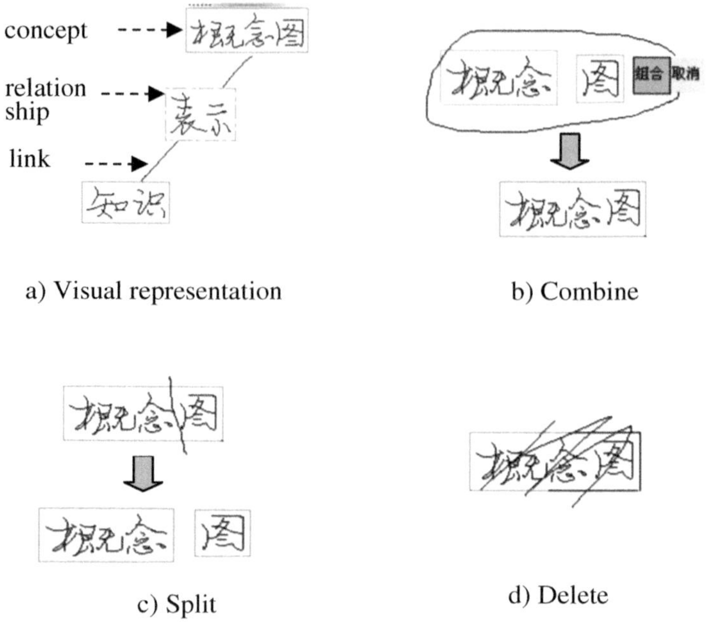

Fig. 3. Pen-based concept mapping

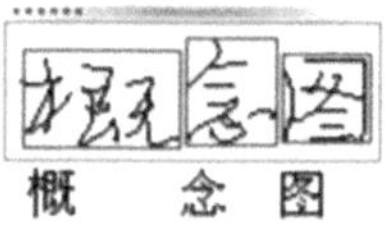

Fig. 4. Words extraction and recognition

so they need to acquire knowledge from a number of different sources. Therefore, providing a knowledge management can help the participants be more effective. Knowledge is typically distributed across individuals, groups and environment, and a knowledge management tool should acquire knowledge from difference sources. Besides, it should also share knowledge between individuals, make recommendations, and aid thinking.

In CoCoceptMap, we represent individuals' knowledge bases as a semantic network by RDF [7], and design a unified interface to extract knowledge from various knowledge sources. The tool can retrieve relevant information from local user's knowledge base, other users' knowledge bases and the WWW. When the user selects a concept, information relevant to the concept will be displayed.

3.3 History Management

Cognitive processes may be distributed through time in a way that the end results of earlier events can change the nature of events that come later [4]. Interaction history is used to trace back the process of concept mapping, and help us find more clues that can't be seen in the concept map. The session initiator and earlier participants may understand the current concept map without difficulty, but new participants or others not at the earlier meetings may be confused because of lacking context. The interaction history enables going back to the time when a visual change was made so it can be interpreted within the original context.

CoConceptMap provides a history management tool for the user to navigate the process of the collaborative concept mapping. In CoConceptMap, participants' operations are recorded. The user can specify the time point directly to observe the specific history point via time slider or playback the operation history to view the dynamic process.

3.4 Collaboration

CoConceptMap supports collaboration. A user can use CoConceptMap individually. However, the user can also invite others into the shared workspace. All participants have the same copies of the concept map. When one manipulates the concept map, the operations will be broadcasted to the others. In order to ensure all participants' maps are identical, a consistency maintenance algorithm is used to guarantee concurrent operations will be executed in the same order at all sites.

Fig. 5. The distributed system architecture of CoconceptMap

The distributed system architecture is shown in Fig. 5, and the underlying communication protocol is based on XMPP(Extensible Messaging and Presence Protocol). XMPP is an open, XML-based protocol for near-real-time, extensible instant messaging and presence information [8]. The interaction information and data are presented as XML stanza, and these information can be broadcast to other participants by XMPP. During the interaction process, the XMPP server only need to dispatches the information to other participants, and the client will serialize all participants' operations in the same order to maintain consistency. In doing so, the current XMPP server-side application can be used as the communication infrastructure to support CoConceptMap without any modification.

Besides communication, maintaining awareness of others is an important part of collaborative activity, and support for awareness in groupware interfaces has been shown to improve groupware usability [9]. In CoConceptMap, we mainly support awareness by feedthrough. Pen-based interaction is not a kind of accurate command-based styles used in traditional WIMP interface, and user's interaction behavior should be analyzed and integrated into interaction task by context or user mediation.

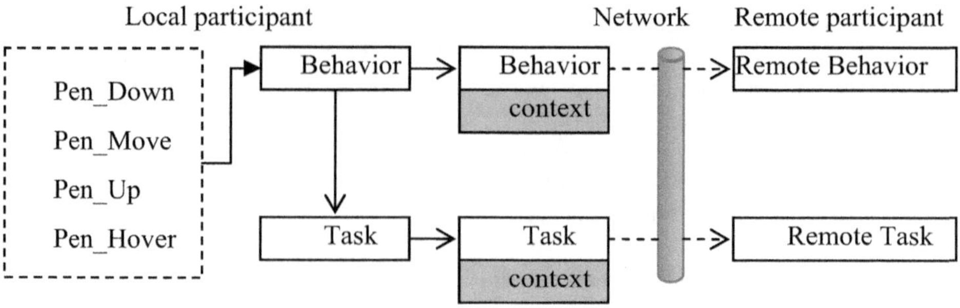

Fig. 6. The processing of feedthough

Fig. 6 shows the feedthrough handling in CoConceptMap. Local participant's interaction behavior is comprised of disperse events, interaction behavior can generated corresponding interaction task according to the local client's context. Because the participants' context are different from each other, interaction behaviors and interaction tasks will be broadcasted to others separately with context atteched on it. In doing so, remote sites can presented these interaction information correctly.

4 Conclusion

In this paper we present our work on a collaborative concept mapping tool: CoConceptMap. Collaborative concept mapping is a kind of cognition process, which concern with many factors such as individuals, artifacts, representation styles etc. We argue the functions that a collaborative concept mapping system should provide, and propose a function framework. Based on the framework, we implement the prototype system.

ConConceptMap has been deployed in our laboratory for a few days, and experimental studies show that the system can support collaborative concept mapping well. Our future work includes enhancement of the existing functionalities, addition of more collaborative facilities such as audio/video conferencing, etc.

Acknowledgments

This paper is supported by the National Fundamental Research Program of China (973 Program) (Grant No. 2002CB312103), the National High Tech Development 863 Program of China (Grant No. 2003AA411330).

References

1. Kim, B., Yang, C., Tsai, I.: Review of computer-mediated collaborative concept mapping: implication for future research. In: Proceedings of the 2005 Conference on Computer Support for Collaborative Learning: Learning 2005: the Next 10 Years Taipei, Taiwan, May 30 - June 04, 2005. Computer Support for Collaborative Learning. International Society of the Learning Sciences, pp. 291–295 (2005)

2. Cañas, A. J., Hill, G., Carff, R., Suri, N., Lott, J., Eskridge, T., Gómez, G., Arroyo, M.,Carvajal, R.: CmapTools: A knowledge modeling and sharing environment. In: Cañas, A. J., Novak, J. D., González F.M. (eds.) Concept maps: Theory, methodology, technology. Proceedings of the first international conference on concept mapping vol. I pp. 125–133 (2004b)
3. Carroll, J. M.: HCI models, theories, and frameworks, towards a multidisciplinary science. Morgan Kaufmann Publishers, San Francisco (2003)
4. Hollan, J., Hutchins, E., Kirsh, D.: Distributed cognition: toward a new foundation for human-computer interaction research. ACM Trans. Comput.-Hum. Interact. 7, 2 (June 2000), pp. 174–196 (2000) DOI= http://doi.acm.org/10.1145/353485.353487
5. Forbus, K. D., Usher, J.: Sketching for knowledge capture: a progress report. In: Proceedings of the 7th international Conference on intelligent User interfaces (San Francisco, California, USA, January 13 - 16, 2002 IUI '02. ACM Press, New York, pp. 71–77 (2002) DOI= http://doi.acm.org/10.1145/502716.502730
6. Ao, X., Li, J., Wang, X., Dai, G.: Structuralizing digital ink for efficient selection. In: Proceedings of the 11th international Conference on intelligent User interfaces Sydney, Australia, January 29 - February 01, 2006 IUI '06. ACM Press, New York, pp. 148–154 (2006) DOI= http://doi.acm.org/10.1145/1111449.1111484
7. Resource Description Framework. http://www.w3.org/RDF/
8. Jabber Software Foundation. Extensible Messaging and Presence Protocol (XMPP). http://www.xmpp.org/
9. Gutwin, C., Greenberg, S.: A Descriptive Framework of Workspace Awareness for Real-Time Groupware. Comput. Supported Coop. Work 11, 3 (November 2002) pp. 411–446 (2002) DOI=http://dx.doi.org/10.1023/A1021271517844

Part II

Mobile Devices and Mobile Interaction

User Expectations from Dictation on Mobile Devices

Santosh Basapur[1], Shuang Xu[1], Mark Ahlenius[1], and Young Seok Lee[2]

[1] Human Interaction Research Center of Excellence,
Motorola Labs, Schaumburg, IL 60196, USA
{sbasapur,shuangxu,mark.ahlenius}@motorola.com
[2] The Grado Department of Industrial and Systems Engineering,
Virginia Tech, Blacksburg, Virginia 24061 USA
yolee10@vt.edu

Abstract. Mobile phones, with their increasing processing power and memory, are enabling a diversity of tasks. The traditional text entry method using keypad is falling short in numerous ways. Some solutions to this problem include: QWERTY keypads on phone, external keypads, virtual keypads on table tops (Seimens at CeBIT '05) and last but not the least, automatic speech recognition (ASR) technology. Speech recognition allows for dictation which facilitates text input via voice. Despite the progress, ASR systems still do not perform satisfactorily in mobile environments. This is mainly due to the complexity of capturing large vocabulary spoken by diverse speakers in various acoustic conditions. Therefore, dictation has its advantages but also comes with its own set of usability problems. The objective of this research is to uncover the various uses and benefits of using dictation on a mobile phone. This study focused on the users' needs, expectations, and their concerns regarding the new input medium. Focus groups were conducted to investigate and discuss current data entry methods, potential use and usefulness of dictation feature, users' reaction to errors from ASR during dictation, and possible error correction methods. Our findings indicate a strong requirement for dictation. All participants perceived dictation to be very useful, as long as it is easily accessible and usable. Potential applications for dictation were found in two distinct areas namely communication and personal use.

1 Introduction

Mobile phones, with their increasing processing power and memory, are enabling a diversity of tasks which demand extensive user interaction. Text input using a small keypad becomes one of the most critical usability issues for mobile interaction design. For instance, the number of text messages sent has continuously increased around the world since its introduction in the late nineties. North American users sent out approximately 12.5 billion text messages in the month of June 2006 [2]. In UK all records were shattered when 4.4 billion messages were sent in the month of December 2006 [14]. It has been shown that teenagers prefer to send text messages to their friends rather than calling them [7].

To solve the problem of text input, research has focused on many methods of interaction which include Speech, Gestures, Handwriting, and Camera-Based such as

J. Jacko (Ed.): Human-Computer Interaction, Part II, HCII 2007, LNCS 4551, pp. 217–225, 2007.

Face Tracking [24]. Some promising solutions currently in the market include: QWERTY keypads on phone, external keypads, virtual keypads on table tops (Seimens at CeBIT '05) and last but not the least, automatic speech recognition (ASR) technology. 'Dictation' using ASR allows users to dictate text to a mobile phone. Users' voice input is converted into text via a speech recognition engine, embedded in the cell phones. Despite their progress, ASR systems do not perform satisfactorily in mobile environments. The complexity of capturing large vocabulary spoken by diverse speakers in various acoustic conditions is the major issue that hinders the successful deployment of ASR.

This research intended to uncover the various uses that a customer could benefit from by using dictation on a mobile phone. This paper focuses on the users' present day requirements and expectations from dictation as a text input medium. Another goal of this study was to seek the users' reactions to common errors found in dictation and also their preferences for error correction techniques. Lastly, design guidelines need to be developed for user-centric applications that optimally use dictation as an input medium.

2 Related Work

Text input in mobile devices has been a known usability problem for some time now. Some of the solutions available in today's handheld device market are described here. Palm utilizes Graffiti [18] that requires users to learn and memorize the predefined letter strokes. Also, it requires a touch screen for the text entry. Similarly, Motorola's WisdomPen [12] supports natural handwriting recognition of Chinese and Japanese characters. Another solution is the Thumbwheel [11]. Thumbwheel is used to scroll and highlight a character in a list of characters shown on a display. The select key inputs the high-lighted character. However, Thumbwheel has been shown to be too slow for text input on a cell phone [23]. Multi-tap and predictive methods of text entry have been proposed as an alterative approach to the mobile text input problem. There have been various estimations of text typing speeds: 14.9~20.8 words per minute (wpm) has been expected for multi-tap and 17.6~40.6 wpm has been expected for predictive text on average [5, 21]. These speed rates are good but they pale when compared to the average speed of typing on a QWERTY keyboard which is 80 wpm [1]. Therefore the devices which advertise high productivity (e.g., RIM's BlackBerry series, Motorola's Q series and the Samsung's BlackJack series phones) tout the QWERTY keypads. But with the limited space available on the mobile devices, the keys remain small thus limiting the text entry speed. All the above issues indicate an inefficient human computer interaction. All these hard-to-use solutions contribute to a dismal user experience which inhibits adoption of technology.

Compared to the above typing speeds, the normal speech of humans which reaches 125-150 wpm [6] makes a compelling argument for high efficiency and utility if used for text entry. Speech based user interfaces can provide an interaction experience that is similar to human-to-human communication. The interaction is more natural and efficient for transfer of information between the human and the machine [10]. Also, manual text entry methods are not conducive to hands-free and eyes-free usage. They demand high cognitive attention by keeping the user involved with the UI both manually as well as perceptually. Hence, the speech recognition systems have been proposed as a better alternative to existing text entry methods [24].

Rudnicky et al in their survey of speech technologies [19] have indicated a wide variety of applications for which ASR has been utilized. From voice-based personal computer control [13] to large vocabulary dictation systems on personal computers such as Dragon Naturally Speaking [4] and from automated call routing to customer service applications such as automated flight status inquiry, there are a number of implementations of speech recognition and speech synthesis technologies [19]. So far, the implementation of ASR in the mobile phone industry (Motorola, Nokia, Samsung phones etc…) has been limited so far to simple voice command features such as name dialing, number dialing and application shortcuts. This is mainly due to the low processing power and memory of mobile phones. With the advancement of technology, ASR is expected to perform better and support features such as text input via voice. Therefore, dictation using ASR is the next frontier for text entry in the mobile phones. Samsung A900 model phone has already brought to market a limited vocabulary dictation feature which enables word-by-word text input.

Despite the progress in ASR technologies and their applications, the complexity of mobile environments hinders the performance in terms of speech recognition accuracy and error handling. Also there are the traditional ASR system problems such as turn-taking (between human and machine) and errors that occur with the opening and closing of the speech recognition window. The challenge for dictation based text input is to capture large vocabulary spoken by diverse speakers in various acoustic conditions. Without an extensive vocabulary it is hard to reach satisfactory recognition accuracy. Since speech-based text input is error prone, three kinds of interactions are needed with users to complete tasks: dictating, navigating to errors and error correction. It has been reported that users spend only 25-33% of the time on dictation of a document and the rest is spent in error detection, navigation to error and error correction [9, 20]. Research by Munteanu et al, [15] shows that state-of-the-art ASR systems trained by an individual can achieve about 3% of Word Error Rate (WER). However, as acoustic conditions degrade, WER can increase to 40-45%. Therefore it is imperative that the dictation feature should also have a robust error correction method that is easy and efficient.

Prior research thus shows us the advantages and problems associated with ASR. It has been shown that users have different expectations and needs based on their previous interaction experience with ASR based systems. Novice users need good instructions to make a task easier, while the experts want efficiency in task completion [8]. Despite the abundant studies about the ASR technology itself, little has been known or explored about users' needs and expectations. For examples, for what applications will the ASR technology be useful? why? How tolerable are dictation errors? Will users tolerate errors at all? How will they prefer to correct recognition errors on mobile devices? This research is therefore motivated to explore and find users' needs, expectations, preferences, and potential concerns from different population segments.

3 Methodology

Four (4) focus groups were conducted in this study, followed by a data analysis workshop. The two independent variables in this study are: (1) users' experience with SMS; and (2) users' experience with ASR. Participants were screened carefully for a controlled balance, which resulted in the four group classifications as shown in Table 1.

Table 1. Focus group classifications

		Text Messaging (SMS) experience	
		Yes	No
Automatic Speech Recognition (ASR/VR) Experience	Yes	Focus Group 1	Focus Group 3
	No	Focus Group 4	Focus Group 4

A dictation based SMS application was prototyped and used to gather data (see Figure 1). This prototype allows the user to dictate a text message. It simulates users' interaction experience with dictation on a cell phone. During the study, participants were shown demonstration of two tasks and later were asked to discuss the ideas with respect to their own needs and lifestyles. The experiment moderator followed a pre-defined script to ensure that the discussion was carried out consistent questions across the four groups. Each group discussion lasted for about two (2) hours. All data was video taped for later review.

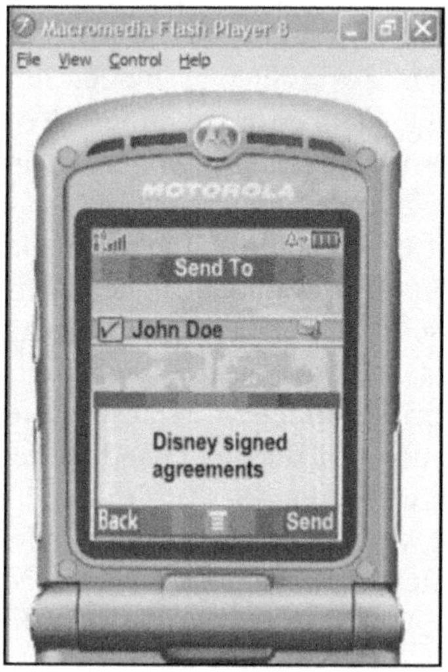

Fig. 1. Screenshot of the prototype

Participants. A total of twenty (20) participants were recruited for this study, five (5) in each focus group. All participants were randomly selected by a marketing research company based on pre-defined criteria. Among the nineteen (19) people who attended the focus groups, there were 11 males and 8 females with a mean age of 35.1 (SD = 10.1). They were all cell phone users and were homogeneous regarding their experience with SMS and ASR within each group. Their cell phone usage varied from minimal use (calling and phonebook only) to extensive use (calling, phonebook, instant messaging, emails, SMS, voice dialing, etc.). Their experience levels were collected via a set of questions during the recruitment screening. Remuneration was paid to each participant for their time.

Task Scenarios. Two tasks were demonstrated to the users using the low-fidelity prototype of a Motorola RAZR phone as described in Table 2. The first scenario was sending of a text message to John Doe and no ASR errors were introduced in this scenario. The second scenario was again sending of a text message to John Doe but now two pre-defined ASR errors occurred back to back in this scenario. Both demos were canned interaction experiences with the moderator performing the tasks in front of the participant group.

Table 2. Use Cases used in focus groups

Use Case 1: Dictation feature with no errors 1) Moderator presses a voice command key 2) Phone speaks: "Say a command" 3) Moderator speaks: "Send a message to John Doe." 4) Phone speaks: "Say the message" 5) Moderator speaks: "I will be there in 15 minutes." 6) Phone displays texts and speaks: "I will be there in fifteen minutes."
Use Case 2: Dictation feature with errors 1 - 4) Same as the use case 1 5) Moderator speaks: "Did he sign the agreement?" 6) Phone displays texts and speaks: "Disney signed agreements" 7) Moderator presses 'back soft key' 8) Phone speaks: "Repeat the message" 9) Moderator speaks: "Did he sign the agreement?" 10) Phone displays texts and speaks: "Did she sign the agreement"

Participants were encouraged to discuss their initial reactions to the demonstrated task experiences. They were also asked to discuss the usefulness of mobile dictation in relation to their lifestyles. The second demonstration was split into two stages to gather participants' reaction to ASR errors. First an error was shown in the dictated text and then was followed-up by an error correction attempt. Users' reactions to errors were discussed along with different error correction options.

4 Data Analysis

The video-taped sessions were reviewed and analyzed by each of the four researchers individually. Each member identified critical incidents, transcribed the relevant verbal data into text, and summarized it using a template as shown in Figure 2. Upon the completion of the individual review, an affinity diagram was completed by the four researchers to cluster the qualitative findings. Labels were assigned to each cluster that represented a common perspective, followed by development of summary statements for each cluster.

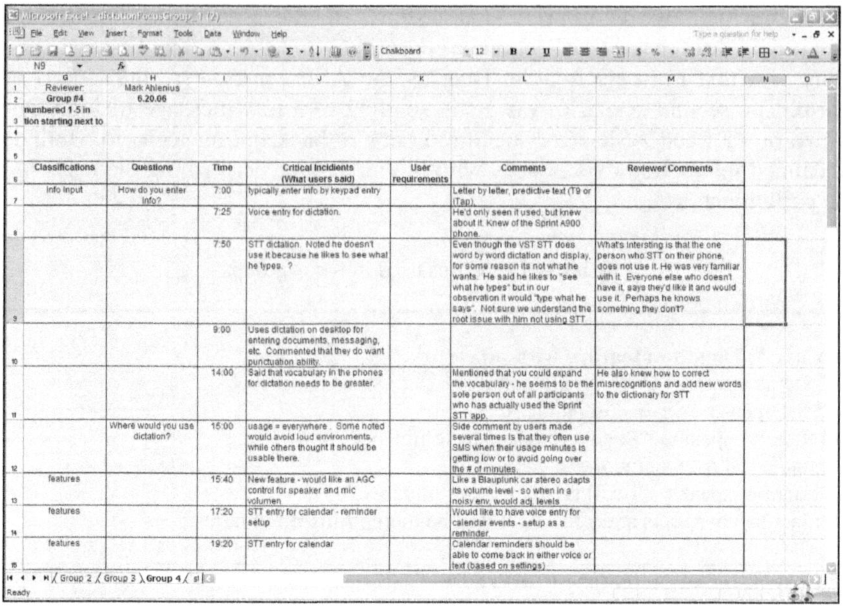

Classifications	Questions	Time	Critical Incidients (What users said)	User requirements	Comments	Reviewer Comments
Info Input	How do you enter Info?	7:00	typically enter info by keypad entry		Letter by letter, predictive text (T9 or (Tap).	
		7:25	Voice entry for dictation.		He'd only seen it used, but knew about it. Knew of the Sprint A900 phone.	
		7:50	STT dictation. Noted he doesn't use it because he likes to see what he types. ?		Even though the VST STT does word by word dictation and display, for some reason its not what he wants. He said he likes to "see what he types" but in our observation it would "type what he says". Not sure we understand the root issue with him not using STT	What's intersting is that the one person who STT on their phone, does not use it. He was very familiar with it. Everyone else who doesn't have it, says they'd like it and would use it. Perhaps he knows something they don't?
		9:00	Uses dictation on desktop for entering documents, messaging, etc. Commented that they do want punctuation ability.			
		14:00	Said that vocabulary in the phones for dictation needs to be greater.		Mentioned that you could expand the vocabulary - he seems to be the sole person out of all participants who has actually used the Sprint STT app.	He also knew how to correct misrecognitions and add new words to the dictionary for STT
	Where would you use dictation?	15:00	usage = everywhere . Some noted would avoid loud environments, while others thought it should be usable there.		Side comment by users made several times is that they often use SMS when their usage minutes is getting low or to avoid going over the # of minutes.	
features		15:40	New feature - would like an AGC control for speaker and mic volumen		Like a Blauplunk car stereo adapts its volume level - so when in a noisy env. would adj. levels	
features		17:20	STT entry for calendar - reminder setup		Would like to have voice entry for calendar events - setup as a reminder.	
features		19:20	STT entry for calendar		Calendar reminders should be able to come back in either voice or text (based on settings)	

Fig. 2. Screenshot of the template used to identify critical incident clusters

5 Results and Discussion

Some of the interesting findings are reported in this section. Regardless of users' experience level with SMS or ASR, the use of key pad for data entry is reported to be time-consuming. Data entry on mobile devices seems to be more difficult for the participants in the first group, who had no ASR and SMS experience, as compared to the other three groups. Participants expected the dictation feature be very accessible and intuitive to use. Some requested that the dictation feature be accessible via a single click. Although the dictation feature was desired for the convenience and safety (e.g., driving), most participants were concerned about the current performance of the speech recognition. Based on their subjective responses in the discussion, a minimum accuracy of 90% was expected by most of the participants to adopt ASR as a text entry method. Users with previous experience (desktop based dictation and/or phone based voice dialing) were more skeptical about the recognition accuracy but were willing to tolerate the errors if the error correction was easy and efficient.

On being asked to name some applications where dictation will be useful, participants listed a variety of daily tasks which were mundane but difficult to accomplish on cell phones due to the slow text input mechanisms. Analysis of data for potential applications found two distinctive trends namely ***communications*** use and ***personal*** use as shown in Table 3. Errors were deemed to matter most when communicating with other people. However, participants indicated higher acceptance, if errors occurred in information that was meant for personal use.

Table 3. User needs for dictation on mobile phones

Communication use	Personal use
• SMS/ Text Messaging • Email • Instant Message • Timed outgoing message • Fax an order • Shared calendar event	• Reminders/ Alarms • To-do list/ Grocery List/ Shopping lists • Calendar • Data entry to phonebook • Recording personal journal • Games • Internet • Quick note • Tracking travel expenses

When potential dictation errors were demonstrated, participants mentioned that they would try to correct the errors by using voice commands. This finding was a bit surprising as the researchers had expected the keypad to be the first resort for error correction. Only a few participants said that they would try and correct errors manually, which again reflects a higher performance expectation.

Other results included the perceived high usefulness of the message read back function using a text-to-speech (TTS) engine after the user is done dictating the text. The mechanical nature of the voice of the TTS engine was not favored by some participants. Lack of punctuation and inflexion in the feedback voice was pointed out as being annoying. The ASR was expected to correctly recognize different accents of non-native English speakers and was also expected to perform in noisy conditions such as on public transportation and in personal automobiles.

6 Design Recommendations and Conclusion

Based on the findings from this study, we recommend the following guidelines to improve the design of applications using dictation on mobile devices:

(1) users are more tolerant to speech recognition errors if the dictated information is for personal use rather than for communication use;
(2) high recognition accuracy is required for dictation feature to be adopted as a text input medium for communication use;
(3) to facilitate the adoption of dictation feature, introduce dictation on mobile phones for personal use prior to communications use; and
(4) participants liked the audible feedback (Text-To-Speech) of recognized text since it enables use of mobile phone in hands-free and eyes-free situations (e.g., driving).

Additionally, the following guidelines are recommended to improve the ease of use and efficiency of error correction methods on mobile devices:

(a) provide "re-speak the entire phrase' technique, as it was the initial reaction for error correction from all users;
(b) provide multi-modal interaction where users are allowed to select a mistaken word manually and speak a target word to replace the error; and
(c) allow users to type individual letters to correct errors when methods (a) and (b) do not work.

The error correction related findings are supported by literatures in this area, which further indicates that speech as an input medium is most effective when combined with other modalities [17, 20]. This was also confirmed by participants' comments on error correction techniques in this study.

In conclusion, the use of key pad for data entry is still time-consuming to most mobile phone users despite technologies like iTAP or T9 [16]. A strong need for dictation feature was identified in this study. All participants perceived the dictation feature to be very useful, but it has to be easily accessible. Potential applications of the dictation feature were found in two areas: communication use and personal use. Despite the potential usefulness, participants were concerned about the speech recognition performance and expected a high accuracy for them to adopt this technology.

References

1. Card, S.K., Moran, T.P., Newell, A.: The Psychology of Human-Computer Interaction, pp. 259–297. Lawrence Erlbaum Associates, New Jersey (1983)
2. CTIA Website: http://ctia.org/research_statistics/statistics/index.cfm/AID/10202
3. Cox, A., Walton, A.: Evaluating the viability of speech recognition for mobile text entry. In: Proceedings of HCI 2004: Design for Life. pp. 25–28 (2004)
4. Dragon Naturally Speaking Software website: http://www.nuance.com/naturallyspeaking/
5. Dunlop, M.D., Crossan, A.: Predictive text entry methods for mobile phones. Personal Technologies, vol. 4, pp. 134–143. Springer, London (2000)
6. Feng, J., Karat, C.-M., Sears, A.: How productivity improves in hands-free continuous dictation tasks: lessons learned from a longitudinal study. Interacting with Computers 17, 265–289 (2005)
7. Grinter, R., Eldridge, M.: y do tngrs luv 2 txt msg. In: Prinz, W., et al.: (eds.)Proceedings of the Seventh European Conference on Computer-Supported Cooperative Work ECSCW '01, Dordecht, Netherlands: Kluwer, pp. 219–238 (2001)
8. Kamm, C.: User interfaces for voice applications. Paper presented in Colloquim: Human-Machine Communication by Voice at National Academy of Sciences at the Arnold and Mabel Beckman Center, Irvine, CA, February 8-9 (1993)
9. Karat, C.-M., Halverson, C., Karat, J., Horn, D.: Patterns of entry and correction in large vocabulary continuous speech recognition systems. In: Proceedings of CHI'99, pp. 568–575 (1999)
10. Leiser, R.G.: Improving natural language and speech interfaces by the use of metalinguistic phenomena. Applied Ergonomics 20, 168–173 (1989)

11. MacKenzie, I.S., Soukoreff, R.W.: Text entry for mobile computing: Models and methods, theory and practice. Human-Computer Interaction 17, 147–198 (2002)
12. Marturano, L., Wheatley, D.: User centered research and design at Motorola. In: Proceedings of CHI'2000, pp. 221–222 (2000)
13. Microsoft Vista: http://www.microsoft.com/enable/products/windowsvista/
14. Mobile Data Association Website: http://www.mda-mobiledata.org
15. Munteanu, C., Baecker, R., Penn, G., Toms, E., James, D.: The Effect of Speech Recognition Accuracy Rates on the Usefulness and Usability of Webcast Archives. In: Proceedings of Computer Human Interaction Conference, Montreal, Canada, pp. 493–502. ACM Press, New York (2006)
16. Oniszczak, A., MacKenzie, S.I.: A Comparison of Two Input Methods for Keypads on Mobile Devices. In: Proceedings of the third Nordic conference on Human-computer interaction, Tampere Finland, pp. 101–104. ACM Press, New York (2004)
17. Oviatt, S.L., Cohen, P.R., Wu, L., Vergo, J., Duncan, L., Suhm, B., Bers, J., Holzman, T., Winogard, T., Landay, J., Larson, J., Ferro, D.: Designing the user interface for multimodal speech and gesture applications: state-of-the-art systems and research directions. Human-Computer Interaction 15(4), 263–322 (2000)
18. Palm Handheld Products website: http://www.palm.com/us/products/input/
19. Rudnicky, A.I., Lee, K-F., Hauptmann, A.G.: Survey of current speech technology. Communications of the ACM 37(3), 52–57 (1994)
20. Sears, A., Karat, C.-M., Oseitutu, K., Karimullah, A., Feng, J.: Productivity, satisfaction, and interaction strategies of individual with spinal cord injuries and traditional users interacting with speech recognition software. Universal Access in the information Society, vol. 1, pp. 4–15 (2001)
21. Silfverberg, M., MacKenzie, I.S., Korhonen, P.: Perdicting text entry speed on mobile phones. In: Proceedings of CHI 2000. Amsterdam: ACM Press, pp. 9–16 (2000)
22. Suhm, B., Myers, B., Waibel, A.: Multimodal error correction for speech user interfaces. ACM Transactions on Computer-Human Interaction 8(1), 60–98 (2001)
23. Tarasewich, P.: Evaluation of thumbwheel text entry methods. Extended Abstracts of the CHI 2003 Conference, pp. 756–757 (2003)
24. Waibel, A., Suhm, B., Vo, M.T., Yang, J.: Multimodal Interfaces For Multimedia Information Agents. In: International Conference on Acoustics, Speech, and Signal Processing 1997, ICASSP 1997, Munich, Germany, 04 (1997)

Design Guidelines for PDA User Interfaces in the Context of Retail Sales Support

Rainer Blum and Karim Khakzar

Fulda University of Applied Sciences, Department of Applied Computer Sciences, Marquardstr. 35, 36039 Fulda, Germany
{Rainer.Blum,Karim.Khakzar}@informatik.hs-fulda.de

Abstract. The development of an in-store sales support system that focuses on the "virtual try-on" of clothing is the main goal of the research project "IntExMa". Within this scope we investigate to what extent mobile devices can support the tasks of the retail sales staff in their daily personal sales activities. In doing so, usability is regarded as the central quality criteria. This paper addresses the resulting question, how a user-friendly design of, in our case, a PDA is characterized. We introduce a compilation of seventeen design principles and detail each with a range of exemplary rules to facilitate practical applicability.

Keywords: PDA, handheld, mobile, guidelines, interface, design.

1 Introduction

Mobile technology is an inherent part of today's private and professional life in the developed nations, with mobile telephony at the forefront. Optimization of business processes with mobile technology presents a topic of interest for enterprises for several years focusing primarily on the sales force and logistics [1].

Employing mobile devices for the retail sales support at the point of sale is a current subject in the research project IntExMa, "Interactive Expert System for Made-to-measure Clothing" at Fulda University of Applied Sciences. In doing so, usability is regarded as a fundamental quality criteria.

Many standards, guidelines and scientific papers document the existing usability knowledge in the field of HCI. While this expertise has predominantly evolved in the desktop computer domain over a period of several decades, interface design for mobile services is still regarded to be 'in its infancy' [2]. Yet, only a few scientific and hardly any generally accepted guides for mobile interface design exist. These are naturally not based on such a broad basis of experiences than in the desktop domain.

Gong & Tarasewich propose a range of usability guidelines for the mobile devices domain [3]. They start from Shneidermans & Plaisants eight "Golden Rules", implicitly termed desktop-oriented, and base them on their own and other research findings. Many other studies concentrate exclusively on the optimized display of web pages on handheld devices, e.g. [4]. The two major companies offering operating systems for handhelds, Palm Source and Microsoft, have each published their own more or less product specific guidelines (see below).

J. Jacko (Ed.): Human-Computer Interaction, Part II, HCII 2007, LNCS 4551, pp. 226–235, 2007.

1.1 Objectives and Significance

Facing the heap of well-established desktop-descending guidelines, standards and recommendations, like e.g. the outstanding ISO 9241, one objective of this work is to answer the question if theses resources are also relevant and applicable for the mobile context. In addition, existing mobile guidelines are also taken into account.

Putting it all together, a compilation of design principles is proposed, each rationally explained and detailed with a range of exemplary, more concrete rules and clarifying examples.

All recommendations are specifically shaped for the context of use at hand: support of personnel selling activities at the point of sale with handheld technology in the hands of the sales persons.

In the IntExMa project, this guidelines collection serves as a central source of information and, if required, starting point for more detailed knowledge gathering in the referenced resources.

We aim to contribute to the state-of-the-art by interpreting existing, mostly desktop-oriented guidelines under a new point of view. In doing so, the lack in the mobile interface design domain shall be attenuated.

1.2 The IntExMa Project

The project's basic concept is to effectively support in-store, "real world" sales processes with e-commerce technology ("virtual shopping"), thus, generating added value for customers, sales staff and shop owners. Made-to-measure shirts constitute the particular sales context to which the system is adapted. According to the customers' body measures, a 3D figure is automatically generated and dressed in the desired shirt applying a highly realistic physical simulation.

Via a PDA, the salesperson has mobile access to the entire functionality of the system: electronic product catalogue with capacious ordering functions, customer data, and 3D scene interaction. This includes interaction with the stationary display showing the "virtual try-on" via the PDA. Within this scope we investigate to what extent mobile devices can support the duties and responsibilities of the retail sales staff in their daily personal selling activities.

Customers are able to use a subset of the system's interactive features via a simple custom-made knob and buttons interface.

2 Method

Several distinct steps were taken in order to gather the necessary theoretical basis to be able to compile the desired specific collection of design guidelines. They were chosen following ISO 13407 [5].

First, the specific characteristics of handheld computing and the PDA device class were analyzed and compared with the desktop computing domain. Thereby, the manifold possibilities concerning interaction techniques and forms became apparent but also the limitations to be considered were diagnosed.

Then, a detailed context of use analysis was conducted and accordant requirements were formulated.

Some of the most important and accepted usability standards, guidelines and scientific papers were analyzed in order to assess which insights are also valid for the mobile domain and can be transferred into the present context.

Taking these results as a theoretical basis, finally, the desired compilation of design principles, concrete rules and clarifying examples is developed.

This project specific standard is currently applied for the development of mobile applications in the IntExMa project. Usability evaluation of these implementations will imply also the indispensable evaluation of the developed guidelines.

3 Context of Use and Requirements

The context of use analyses was conducted in-depth following ISO 13407 [5]. Some major points are reproduced in the following.

Sales support as a central activity is characterized by a broad spectrum of tasks aiming to enhance sales. This study focuses on the domains of the retail business not dominated by self-service but where consultation-intensive products are sold and the customers are served by well-trained personnel. This personal selling is primarily characterized by a direct communication between customer and sales person.

Up to now, sales persons at the point of sale are rarely equipped with handhelds for personal selling enhancement. Individual innovative companies still test these techniques, for example the METRO Group with its "Future Store Initiative".

3.1 User Characteristics, Tasks, Environment

Sales process support in the retail business is characterized by a high heterogeneity concerning users' respectively salespersons' characteristics – gender, age, education, experiences, knowledge, etc.

Skills and knowledge about the business processes and methods to be supported can be estimated as comprehensive. Furthermore, experiences with PDA usage are expected to be very low, but to substantially rise with the usage period. Previous knowledge concerning interaction techniques and modes may exist but can't be assumed for all users. Using a portable touch screen of this size is certainly novel for most of them. A short, e.g. one-day training on the application is expected.

Tasks groups to be supported by the mobile application are informing and giving advice, utilizing and administering customer data, processing payments, providing service and sales preparation and follow-up. The present context of use is characterized by a "hierarchy of tasks" like described in [6]: During interaction, the tasks external to the device are in the center of interest while system-internal tasks, e.g. entering a search keyword, accrue additionally. Also, the social environment only provides minimum freedom for interaction with the mobile device, as, mostly, the customer is in the focus of the attention of the personnel.

3.2 Resulting Requirements

Following the results of the context of use analysis, an important requirement is to design the system for users with diverse experiences, skills and knowledge concerning information technology and to cater for novices as well as for "power users". In order to reduce the acceptance threshold users must be enabled to acquire basic functionality by themselves.

Seamless integration into the existing environment supports the flexible functionality changeover of sales persons during work.

The customer must be taken into account as "indirect user" constantly present during service and with needs taking the center stage of personnel selling. Therefore, the demand of resources, e.g. of attention or time, of the application should be as small as possible. One-hand or, even better, hands-free operation of the device is desirable in order to keep interacting with real objects as much as possible.

The users should - only to a small extent - have to „make place" for the device operation. Their imposed mental workload should be kept low, while simultaneously staying informed about the current process status, despite frequent interruptions.

Also, the sales person should have the possibility to present output information visually to the customer, e.g. if the "spoken word" is not sufficient due to product complexity or lack of the completed product (e.g. mass customization).

The mobile interactive system must provide required information on the spot and in the desired level of detail with flexible search and meaningful comparison options. In addition, a methodic and controlled proceeding of the sales person must be supported and ensured.

Where possible, interaction with physical objects, e.g. via product bar codes, as "information bearers" should be possible, in order to avoid unnecessary searching in electronic resources and to further enhance integration with the real environment.

4 Existing Guidelines

A selection of the most important representatives of desktop-related standards and guidelines was analyzed concerning their relevance and their transferability for the handheld/PDA domain.

The most well-known user interface design standard is probably ISO 9241 [7]. Parts 2, 10 and 11 can be fully applied. In part 12 only the addressed window technique is subject to severe limitations on the handheld platform. User guidance in part 13 is absolutely relevant, with reservations concerning the extent and design of online help due to limited display space. Part 14 has relevance, though only small-sized menu dialogues make sense on PDAs. Command dialogues in part 15 are hardly relevant, unless it comes to speech control. Many recommendations for the direct manipulation concept in part 16 are applicable though the graphical representation and the manipulation features of objects and their states should be much less comprehensive than on the desktop. Furthermore, direct manipulation beyond basic interaction (e.g. dragging objects) demands to much concentration from the user to be reasonably applied in the mobile context [8]. Part 17 is again mostly of high relevance for the handheld domain. Some of the recommendations imply a cursor. Though existent for form fields and text documents, mouse pointers are not standard. They may be activated in certain operating systems or simulated by applications.

ISO 14915 [9] is basically relevant for handheld design, due to similarity to ISO 9241 though it must be considered that the multimedia capabilities of these devices do not approximate those of multimedia desktop computers.

The analyzed "Ten Usability Heuristics" by Nielsen [10] and eight „Golden Rules" by Shneiderman & Plaisant [11] are valid for handheld design, as they are independent of specific technologies and device form factors. They must be individually interpreted in order to apply them practically in a specific context of use.

The basic principles for user interface design and many of the more concrete guidelines and rules presented in the "desktop-descending" IBM Common User Access (CUA) Guidelines as presented in [12], the Microsoft Official Guidelines for User Interface Developers and Designers [13] and the Apple Human Interface Guidelines [14] are applicable for the present setting.

The Windows Mobile Guidelines [15] and the Palm OS User Interface Guidelines [16] are the only available more comprehensive mobile guidelines. Here, Microsoft does not provide basic design principles but some more general guidelines which are converted into very practical Windows Mobile specific recommendations. The Palm starts with basic principles, moves on to concrete design guidelines and ends with detailed technical layout guidelines. Main focus from the point of view of functionality is the PIM-domain. So, practical applicability is ensured in both cases. Both compilations contain relevant information also for the context of use at hand.

5 Specific Design Guidelines Compilation

Based on the insights and recommendations in the previous chapters, seventeen design guidelines is presented in the following.

Every principle consists of a short title, followed by a more detailed wording as a complete sentence in the first paragraph. As interpreting and applying these principles first requires to fully understand their logical foundation, the second paragraph contains accordant explanations. Then, for lack of space, one exemplary of several rules is listed, that focus specific design questions. The reproduction of concrete design examples and the listing of references to existing standards and guidelines is abandoned here. In the full report this serves the underpinning of the scientific significance of each principle and its corresponding rules as well as pointer to further resources.

Choose "Low-absorbing" Interaction Techniques
Design the system in such way, that its use occupies the user's manual resources and sensory functions (vision, hearing, perception in general) as little as possible.

Interaction with an application draws upon the sense of the user and requires manual activity: The system's output has to be perceived visually, acoustically, potentially also tactilely, processed in the brain and subsequently converted into motor reactions. Resources tied up in this process are at the same time required for the primary tasks of the sales person in the sales process support. Due to the importance of non-verbal communication for the personnel selling, the visual senses are highly significant.

An exemplary rule is to make the operation of the system possible without the usually obligatory pen and, even better, with only one hand.

Design on the Basis of the Real Tasks
When designing the user interface, refer primarily to the requirements of the tasks to be completed in the real environment and the requirements of the context of use.

Thereby, the components of the user interface shall "take a back seat" in the perception of the user. An additional charge of the sales person with system-internal tasks during the customer dialogue should be preferably avoided. Also, frustration by reason of inability to tackle tasks adequately is counteracted.

To choose terminology, symbols and metaphors according to the real tasks and, as such, to build on existing knowledge of the user, is one concrete rule.

Design for Short, Frequently Interrupted Tasks
Map tasks in such a way that the separate steps may be processed in a flexible order and action sequences may be interrupted and resumed later.

The hardly to plan course of a customer dialogue demands for a variable but thorough completion of the separate work tasks (task sequence) and a spontaneous and flexible response to the remarks and requests of the customer. The interactive system needs to show the same degree of flexibility while ensuring a well-structured advancement and an exhaustive task processing.

One exemplary corresponding rule is to provide the processing status of a task "at a glance", concretely by presenting all necessary information in one screen form and indicating data fields that are already treated.

Strive for Consistency
Question all user interface components whether they can be designed consistent to the experience of the sales personnel, other employed applications and among each other.

Consistency enables the users to apply existing knowledge and to quickly build a mental model of the application's functional concept. They come across familiar objects and training period can be reduced. Thereby, the user interface should furthermore be operated intuitively and without surplus mental load and additional concentration effort. Consistent positioning of controls enables the salesperson, to operate the application "blindly" (without concentrating on the display).

An exemplary rule is to rarely make exceptions but in situations that justify their use - and to design them coherently.

Cater for Easy and Intuitive Interaction
Give interactive elements a design as simple as possible and make sure, that the user intuitively detects how to interact with them.

Controls, who's operation is apparent should result in a faster learnability and a lower mental workload for the user. If, in addition, the interaction techniques are straightforward, the application should demand less attention from the user.

Exemplary rule: For text fields, make clear which kind of input is expected.

Offer Instantaneous, Informative Feedback
Provide a feedback for every interaction, that, with its "magnitude", reflects appropriately the significance and frequency of occurrence of the particular action and that considers the context of use.

Prompt reaction to the user's interaction supports a sense of controllability. On the one hand, users are informed, that their input was recognized, on the other hand the "new" system state is communicated. Panic, that may occur due to too long response times when pressure to perform is high, can be avoided. A suitable degree of clarity and demand of attention must be ascertained.

A rule is to acknowledge every interaction with a prompt feedback.

Provide Simple and Unambiguous Navigation
Design navigation means in such a way, that the user can ever answer the questions "Where am I, how did I get here?", "What can I do here?", "Where can I go next?".

Due to frequent interruptions, the salespersons must be enabled to recognize at a glance, at which position in the task sequence they are currently. Also, it must be transparent, how they got there (or what the previous steps were) and which options to proceed are offered, i.e. which elements are available for follow up interaction.

For example, an option for navigating back- and, if applicable, forward in a list of lastly visited dialogue pages should be provided.

Cater for Effective, Usable Content
Prepare content (product data, customer data etc.) and structure the design in such a way, that an effective handling by the salespersons is ensured and that, at the same time, their limited attention is considered.

Parts of the information taken from the PDA is passed on to the customer, partly it is needed for processing the more formal steps of the sales process. Preparation and reproduction of information must be oriented along this process and has to consider that the salespersons have to pay the bigger part of their attention to the customer.

One corresponding rule is to make it possible to output content otherwise than via the PDA display (e.g. graphically, as product comparison chart), in order to communicate it to the customer not only verbally.

Design Well-defined Dialogues
Structure tasks in small action groups with obvious start and end; inform the user explicitly about their successful completion.

In a working environment characterized by lots of disruption and distraction, the explicit confirmation about a successfully completed (even small) working process creates a feeling of release and satisfaction by the user. The user can tick off one item on his mental task list and focus on the remaining steps.

An exemplary rule is to structure tasks such that they can be "displayed" on a single screen page.

Reduce Functionality to its Minimum
Reduce the variety of the application's functions to the minimum mainly required by the salesperson during the mobile conducted customer dialogue.

The fewer functions need to be accommodated in the application, the higher are the chances to achieve a good usability. This can lead to a clearer structure and the possibility to dimension control elements more generously. These facts should in turn reduce the practical training for the salesperson, as well as the cognitive load and the demand for concentration. Too many details can obfuscate the structure, complicate the conceptual model on the user's part and produce confusion - especially if the users cannot pay most of their attention to the application.

One corresponding rule is to not try to port a desktop application - in the sense of transforming it with only minimal adjustments.

Consider Different User Characteristics

Try to cover a wide spectrum of user characteristics by providing alternative possibilities of interaction.

Even in a small shop you will find different kinds of characteristics amongst the salespersons, e.g. regarding perception-related abilities, motor coordination skills and cognitive capacity or education, knowledge, abilities and experiences. These differences can be considered with a thoroughly designed device.

Exemplary rule: Alternative interaction paths and short cuts should be offered.

Ensure Easy and Permanent Access to Important Options

The availability of important and frequently used options should vary only little and access to these options should be eased explicitly.

Learnability decreases and cognitive load increases if certain command options are available in some, but not in all situations. Such variations can cause discontent and concern, and potentially complicate the user's mental model of the application.

An exemplary rule is to avoid operation modes, particularly as their marking requires additional status messages.

Minimize the Quantity of Required Interaction and Input

Demand as little interaction from the user as possible and take advantage of already available information.

A low quantity of required elementary interactions, which in addition require only little concentration, should keep the salesperson's stress low. The intensive usage of data that is already available in the system and respectively in the shop, reduces the necessity to reproduce information from memory.

For example, meaningful standard values should always be provided, that constitute a basis for further processing.

Prevent Errors

Analyze which errors can occur. Indicate which error situations can arise or better, eliminate those from the very beginning.

The present context of use with frequent disruptions of the work process is susceptible to operator errors. The salespersons should have the impression that the handling of the PDA is "foolproof" and that they can hardly make a mistake if at all. This feeling should reduce their mental stress.

A corresponding rule is to explicitly indicate unsaved data in order to avoid accidental discarding.

Offer Straightforward Error Recovery

Indicate errors to users and support them during the recovery process.

The possibility to easily recover from errors is a precondition for a self-confident operation of an application by the user. This leads to less mental workload for the salesperson as well as a lower demand of attention during a potentially error-prone stress situation. Being able to cancel a previous action in case of an unexpected reaction of the application can avoid frustration.

Corresponding rule: Canceling of actions should be offered with different granularities, from elementary interaction steps (e.g. not releasing a pressed button) to complete task sequences.

Offer Concise, Context-sensitive Help

Offer an online help corresponding clearly and briefly to the current dialogue context.

The leading principle should be that the system is usable without documentation. Nevertheless, the users should be able to recall help, which refers to the current dialogue situation. This enables them to self-help even during the customer dialogue. Comprehensive help should be offered via the manual or separate learning software.

To specify concrete actions in the help information is a corresponding rule.

Design Easily Perceivable, Readable, Rich in contrast and Aesthetic Dialogues

During the design process, aspire after clearness, simplicity, visual attractiveness and a harmonic overall picture.

One the one hand, the goal is to facilitate the perception and handling of the available information by the salesperson. Variable environmental characteristics (e.g. changing lighting conditions) should not have a negative influence. On the other hand, the visual design should appeal to the users and animate them to use the device.

Example rule: Icons should be simple and rich in contrast and have clear contours.

6 Conclusions

The aim of this paper was to contribute to the development of guidelines for handheld respectively PDA design, a domain not yet sufficiently covered especially when it comes to business process support. A rather complete set of principles and exemplary rules is presented, based on analysis, interpretation and amendment of established guidelines for desktop user interfaces and some of the rare mobile design guides.

The guidelines compilation is adapted to the specific context of use at hand: handheld support for the sales person at the point of sale being involved in personnel selling. Though this setting restricts some of the variable factors to be considered, its heterogeneity is still so high, that applying these guidelines requires a thorough consideration of the specific situation. Therefore, this work should be generally useful to practitioners and HCI researchers.

It proved to be challenging to find a balance between complete coverage of all relevant aspects and treatment of each in sufficient level of detail. Starting from basic principles, explaining their rationale, providing several exemplary, more concrete rules and giving concrete examples is the proposed way to ensure practical applicability but to also allow to asses and integrate new developments.

Evaluation by application and analysis in concrete implementations and the consideration of further related quality aspects, e.g. accessibility or joy of use, are options for next steps.

Acknowledgments. This research was financially supported by the German Federal Ministry of Education and Research. within the framework of the program "Angewandte Forschung an Fachhochschulen im Verbund mit der Wirtschaft" (FH^3).

References

1. Wichmann, T., Stiehler, A.: Prozesse optimieren mit Mobile Solutions, Berlecon Research GmbH, Berlin (2004)
2. USE-ME.GOV: Review of State of the Art in User Interface Design for Mobile Applications. Deliverable D4.1 (2004)
3. Gong, J., Tarasewich, P.: Guidelines for Handheld Mobile Device Interface Design. In: Proceedings of DSI (Decision Sciences Institute) 2004 Annual Meeting (2004)
4. Kärkkäinen, L., Laarni, J.: Designing for Small Display Screens. In: Proceedings of the second Nordic conference on Human-computer interaction, pp. 227–230. ACM Press, New York (2002)
5. ISO 13407, Human-centred design processes for interactive systems (1999)
6. Gorlenko, L., Merrick, R.: No wires attached: Usability challenges in the connected mobile world. IBM Systems Journal, IBM Corporation 42(4), 639–651 (2003)
7. ISO 9241, Ergonomic requirements for office work with visual display terminals (VDTs). Parts 2, 10 to 17 (1993–2002)
8. Kristoffersen, S., Ljungberg, F.: Making Place to Make IT Work: Empirical Explorations of HCI for Mobile CSCW. In: Proceedings of the International ACM SIGGROUP Conference on Supporting Group Work, pp. 276–285. ACM Press, New York (1999)
9. ISO 14915, Software ergonomics for multimedia user interfaces. Parts 1–3 (2002-2003)
10. Nielson, J.: Heuristic evaluation. In: Nielson, J., Mack, R.L (eds.) Usability Inspection Methods, John Wiley & Sons (1994)
11. Shneiderman, Plaisant, C.: Designing the User Interface - Strategies for Effective Human-Computer Interaction 4th edn. Addison Wesley (2004)
12. IBM Corporation: Design basics, Design Principles. http://www-03.ibm.com/easy/page/6 Last retrieved 02/03/07
13. Microsoft Corp.: Official Guidelines for User Interface Developers and Designers https://msdn.microsoft.com/library/en-us/dnwue/html/welcome.asp (1999), retrieved 02/03/07
14. Apple Computer, Inc.: Apple Human Interface Guidelines. http://developer.apple.com/documentation/UserExperience/Conceptual/OSXHIGuidelines/index.html (2005) Last retrieved 02/03/07
15. Microsoft Corp. Design Guidelines, Windows Mobile Version 5.0 SDK. http://msdn.microsoft.com/library/default.asp?url=/library/en-us/mobilesdk5/html/mob5oriDesignGuidelines.asp (2005) Last retrieved 02/03/07
16. PalmSource, Inc.: Palm OS User Interface Guidelines. http://www.access-company.com/developers/documents/docs/ui/UIGuidelinesTOC.html (2003) Last retrieved 02/03/07

Influence of Culture on Attitude Towards Instant Messaging: Balance Between Awareness and Privacy

Jinwei Cao and Andrea Everard

Department of Accounting and MIS, Alfred Lerner College of Business and Economics, University of Delaware, Newark, DE 19711
{jcao,everarda}@lerner.udel.edu

Abstract. This research-in-progress paper investigates how attitudes towards privacy and awareness mediate the relationship between culture and attitude towards Instant Messaging (IM). A conceptual model is proposed to explain the relationships between culture and attitude towards privacy and between culture and attitude towards awareness. Attitudes towards privacy and awareness are then hypothesized to affect attitude towards IM. Related research about IM, user attitudes, and cultural dimensions are reviewed and a proposed survey study is described.

1 Introduction

Instant Messaging (IM) has notably increased in usage, at home as well as in the workplace [1]. Different from email systems, IM enables short message exchanges between online users in real time, with the ability of indicating a user's presence and availability (presence awareness) [2]. Such unique features have helped IM quickly gain popularity as a communication method and socialization tool.

Several recent research studies have investigated why many people are drawn to this specific computer mediated communication technology and how they use it [3]. However, the findings from these studies are mainly based on Western (e.g., America) samples. The research presented in this paper, therefore, aims to investigate the cultural influence on attitude towards IM taking into consideration the findings from Western samples. Particularly, we propose that the impact of culture on attitude towards IM use is mediated by the users' attitude towards privacy and awareness.

2 Theoretical Background

Following Hofstede's research on culture [4], we argue that multiple dimensions of culture impact users' attitudes towards privacy and awareness, which finally affect users' attitude towards IM (According to Fishbein & Ajzen [5], attitude towards using a technology is a firm indication of the actual usage of that technology.) The individual relationships among these factors are described below.

J. Jacko (Ed.): Human-Computer Interaction, Part II, HCII 2007, LNCS 4551, pp. 236–240, 2007.

2.1 IM and Privacy

Research has indicated that IM use may be related to different types of privacy concerns [3]. Grinter and Palen [3] found that IM users are worried about being accessed by strangers or particular peers, or being interrupted while engaging in other tasks. The desire for personal space and privacy asks for access regulation, and therefore might also prevent the use of IM.

Such concerns about access control in IM are related to people's personal privacy concerns described in [6]. In this study, we propose the following hypothesis:

H1: Individuals who are more concerned with *Personal Privacy* will have a more negative attitude towards IM than individuals who are less concerned with *Personal Privacy.*

Grinter and Palen [3] also found that IM users were sensitive to information privacy issues such as protection of communication content. Such concerns about information privacy could also significantly reduce the use of IM. From this perspective, we have the following hypothesis:

H2: Individuals who are more concerned with *Information Privacy* will have a more negative attitude towards IM than individuals who are less concerned with *Information Privacy.*

2.2 IM and Awareness

Similar to privacy, another relevant factor that may affect users' attitude towards IM is their attitude towards awareness. Most IM systems focus on providing two types of awareness information: who and what. They allow people to indicate their presence (online/offline) to others who are on their list of contacts. Most IM systems can also indicate one's current status or activity through various predefined "status messages" [7]. Such information encourages informal spontaneous communications [8]. Therefore, it is reasonable to assume that if individuals are open to awareness, they will also have a positive attitude towards IM. .

H3: Individuals who are open to *Awareness* will have a more positive attitude towards IM than individuals who are not open to *Awareness.*

2.3 IM and Culture

Recent studies show that Eastern and Western cultures differ in IM use [9, 10]. In this paper we argue that users' attitudes towards personal privacy, information privacy, and awareness mediate the relationship between culture and attitude toward IM. Hofstede [4] derived four cultural dimensions: uncertainty avoidance, power distance, individualism, and masculinity. The four dimensions and how they may affect users' attitudes towards privacy and awareness are now discussed in more detail.

Power Distance (PD). Power distance refers to the extent to which a sense of hierarchy or inequality among individuals is considered a way of life. Because individuals who rank high on PD come to expect a greater level of inequality between societal levels and are accustomed to those in positions of authority having access to their personal life, they are less concerned about restricting access to themselves.

H4a: Individuals who rank high on PD will be less concerned with *Personal Privacy* than individuals who rank low on PD.

Similarly, we argue that individuals' concerns about information privacy will be affected by PD. High PD individuals have come to expect that their information may be accessed by those in positions of authority, often without their consent. Unlike low PD individuals, they accept as a way of life that their private information may be disclosed to other parties. Thus,

H4b: Individuals who rank high on PD will be less concerned about *Information Privacy* than individuals who rank low on PD.

In high PD cultures, formality is encouraged while spontaneity is not. The awareness feature of IM supports informal and spontaneous communication and hence individuals who rank high on the PD dimension will be less open to awareness.

H4c: Individuals who rank high on PD will be less open to *Awareness* than individuals who rank low on PD.

Uncertainty Avoidance (UA). Uncertainty avoidance is the extent to which individuals feel a need for formal rules and regulations and lack tolerance for ill-defined situations. Individuals who rank high on UA may not welcome unauthorized access to their personal space as this may lead to uncertainty.

H5a: Individuals who rank high on UA will be more concerned about *Personal Privacy* than individuals who rank low on UA.

Using IM introduces a certain level of uncertainty as shared information could be copied or leaked to unauthorized parties. High UA individuals are more likely to take extra precautions to protect their personal data and information from being accessed by anyone to whom they do not give explicit authorization. Hence,

H5b: Individuals who rank high on UA will be more concerned about *Information Privacy* than individuals who rank low on UA.

High UA individuals may use the awareness feature in IM to mitigate the extent of uncertainty. Even though, as argued above, high UA individuals strive to protect both their personal information privacy, they are likely to enjoy the benefits derived from being able to know what is going on.

H5c: Individuals who rank high on UA will be more open to *Awareness* than individuals who rank low on UA.

Individualism (IND). Individualism is the extent to which individuals are more concerned with issues as they relate to the individuals themselves rather than to the priorities and rules of the group to which they belong. In high IND cultures, individuals' decisions are encouraged, bonds with others are expected to be weak and personal privacy is important. Therefore,

H6a: Individuals who rank high on IND will be more concerned with *Personal Privacy* than individuals who rank low on IND.

Similarly, high IND individuals will take extra precautions to ensure that their personal data is protected.

H6b: Individuals who rank high on IND will be more concerned with *Information Privacy* than individuals who rank low on IND.

Individuals who rank high on this dimension will be less inclined to foster close, committed and strong member groups, whether they are family, extended family or extended relationships. The awareness feature of IM can be seen as an ideal technology to create and maintain such relationships. Hence,

H6c: Individuals who rank high on IND will be less open to *Awareness* than individuals who rank low on IND.

Masculinity (MAS). Masculinity is the extent to which people place emphasis on work goals and assertiveness rather than on personal goals, good working relationships and cooperation. We argue that this dimension will not influence users' attitudes toward personal privacy or information privacy nor their attitude toward awareness.

3 Research Methodology

An online survey has been developed to test the above hypotheses. The three dimensions of *culture* are measured using three multiple-item scales taken from [13]. Users' attitude towards *personal privacy* is measured by five multiple-item scales adopted from [6], and attitude towards *information privacy* is measured by three multiple-item scales from [11]. Users' attitude towards awareness was measured by a four-item scale adapted from [12]. Users' general attitude towards IM is assessed by four items adapted from [14]. All the above mentioned items are ranked on a seven-point Likert type scale ranging from strongly disagree (1) through neutral (4) to strongly agree (7). The survey instrument also collected demographic data.

College students will be selected as the subjects for this survey because they constitute a major part of IM users. The online survey will be distributed to undergraduate college students in China and the US.

4 Conclusion and Implications

This research is important for understanding communication alternatives in ever-increasing multicultural environments due to economic globalization. We expect to find that cultural differences affect users' attitude toward IM, mediated by users' attitudes towards privacy and awareness. If these expectations are supported by our study results, it would be advisable for IT practitioners to manage the use of IM differently depending on the country. For example, when people from a country with low UA but high IND work with people from a country with high UA but low IND, they may find the latter are generally more open to awareness, less concerned about privacy issues, and have a more positive attitude towards IM as a communication tool. To manage such collaboration across countries, therefore, it is important for the former to have an open mind towards IM. Instead of simply prohibiting IM use because of possible privacy and awareness concerns they can solve the problem by setting up clear IM privacy control policies. To summarize, when working on cross-cultural projects, people from different cultures need to understand the impacts of culture and actively work to find the best combination of computer mediated communication methods to support their collaboration and communication.

References

1. Patil, S., Kobsa, A.: Uncovering Privacy Attitudes in Instant Messaging. In: Proceedings of Group'05, 5th ACM Conference on Supporting Group Work, Sanibel Island, FL, pp. 101–104 (2005)
2. Chatterjee, S., Abhichandani, T., Li, H., Tulu, B., Byun, J.: Instant Messaging and Presence Technologies for College Campuses. IEEE Network 19, 4–13 (2005)
3. Grinter, R.E., Palen, L.: Instant Messaging in Teen Life. In: Proceedings of the 2002 ACM conference on Computer supported cooperative work pp. 21–30 (2002)
4. Hofstede, G.H.: Culture's Consequences: International Differences in Work-related Values. Sage Publications, Beverly Hills, CA (1980)
5. Fishbein, M., Ajzen, I.: Belief, Attitude, Intention and Behavior: An Introduction to Theory and Research. Addison-Wesley, Reading, MA (1975)
6. Marshall, N.J.: Dimensions of Privacy Preferences. Multivariate Behavioral Research 9, 255–272 (1974)
7. Patil, S., Kobsa, A.: Privacy in Collaboration: Managing Impression. In: Proceedings of the First International Conference on Online Communities and Social Computing, Las Vegas, NV (2005)
8. Schlichter, J.H., Koch, M., Xu, C.: Awareness - The Common Link Between Groupware and Community Support Systems. In: Ishida, T. (ed.) Community Computing and Support Systems, pp. 77–93 (1998)
9. Heales, J., McCoy, S., Xu, D.: Instant Messaging: A Cross-Country Comparison of Factors Affecting Adoption. In: The 11th Americas Conference on Information Systems, Omaha pp. 1264–1268 (2005)
10. Kayan, S., Fussell, S.R., Setlock, L.D.: Cultural Differences in the Use of Instant Messaging in Asia and North America. In: Proceedings of the 2006 20th anniversary conference on Computer supported cooperative work pp. 525–528 (2006)
11. Smith, H.J., Milberg, S.J., Burke, S.J.: Information Privacy: Measuring Individuals' Concerns about Organizational Practices. MIS Quarterly 20, 167–196 (1996)
12. Gutwin, C., Greenberg, S.: A Descriptive Framework of Workspace Awareness for Real-Time Groupware. Computer Supported Cooperative Work. 11, 411–446 (2002)
13. Dorfman, P.W., Howell, J.P.: Dimensions of National Culture & Effective Leadership Patterns: Hofstede revisited. In: McGoun, E.G. (ed.) Advances in International Comparative Management, vol. 3, pp. 127–149. JAI Press, Greenwich, CT (1988)
14. Taylor, S., Todd, P.: Understanding Information Technology Usage: A Test of Competing Models. Information Systems Research 6, 144–176 (1995)

Usability Evaluation of Designed Image Code Interface for Mobile Computing Environment

Cheolho Cheong, Dong-Chul Kim, and Tack-Don Han

Dept. of Computer Science, Yonsei University,
134, Seodaemun-Gu, Seoul, 120-749, Republic of Korea
{balgeum,dong}@yonsei.ac.kr, hantack@kurene.yonsei.ac.kr

Abstract. Recently, image code interfaces and designed image codes, which can present visual information such as shapes, colors, text, images, and textures within the image code, have attracted increasing interest for use in mobile computing environments. In this paper, we introduce designed image codes and their basic decoding techniques; furthermore, we compare and analyze user preferences by performing a user study. We also implement a high-fidelity prototype of an image code interface based on a mobile computing environment and evaluate its usability by performing a user evaluation. From the evaluation, it is observed that the participants prefer a color-based image code, and this image code has a better merit rating.

Keywords: Image code, designed code, barcode, 2D code, color-based image code.

1 Introduction

With the popularization of the camera phone, the image code interface is being generalized [1], [2] so as to provide information to the user by means of a recognized image code such as a 1D barcode [3], 2D image code [4], and color-based image code [5]. The 1D barcode represents an identity (identifier) and is composed of serial black-and-white bar patterns. Examples of this code include the Universal Product Code (UPC) and the European Article Number (EAN) [6]. In 2D image codes such as PDF-417 [7], Quick Response (QR) [8], and Data Matrix [9], a vast amount of data can be represented because these codes have a higher density than the 1D barcode. In a color-based image code such as ColorCode [5], data is represented by using colors.

By using the image code interface with these image codes and the built-in camera in mobile devices [10], users can easily access various services such as web services, e-commerce, advertising, personal information exchange, and audio and video downloads. In addition to specially designed image codes, visual tags such as ARToolKit tag [11] and AR tag [12] have been used in augmented reality (AR) and mixed reality (MR) services.

These image codes are configured for easy machine readability; however, the users cannot understand the services that are provided for them. Thus, designed codes are developed to present visual information of the code services. Figure 1 shows examples of the original image codes such as the 1D barcode, 2D code, and color-based codes and their corresponding designed image codes.

J. Jacko (Ed.): Human-Computer Interaction, Part II, HCII 2007, LNCS 4551, pp. 241–251, 2007.

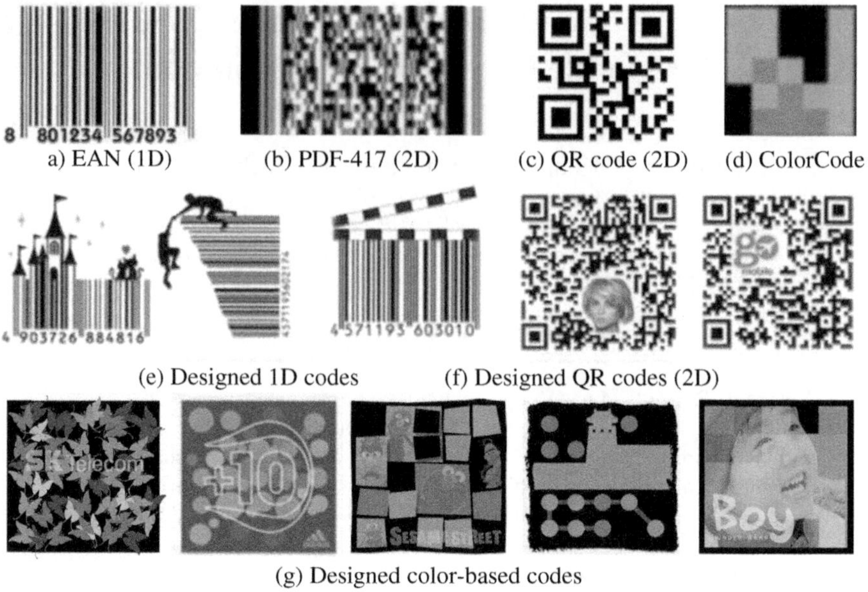

Fig. 1. Examples of various image codes: (top) common image codes, (center) black-and-white-based designed codes (1D codes [13], [14] and QR codes [15]), (bottom) designed color-based codes [5]

Since the interest in the image code interfaces used in camera phones is increasing, there are several researches [16], [17], [18] studying the implementation and usability of a common black-and-white image code interface. However, very little study has been carried out on the usability evaluation of the designed image codes and the color-based image code interface. In this study, we have two major goals. First, we analyze the users' needs and preferences with regard to the designed image codes by performing a user study. Second, we implement a high-fidelity prototype of an interface by using color-based image codes, and we evaluate its usability.

2 Analysis

The goal of this phase was to analyze the technical approaches used for recognizing image codes and the needs and preferences of the users regarding the image codes on the basis of the types of code and printed media.

2.1 Technical Analysis

The designed image code represents visual information of the code by using design elements such as texts, images, and symbols on the original image and by transforming the shape of the code. Occasionally, the design elements and the transformed code shape decrease the performance of the decoding algorithm. Hence, the placement of the design elements and the transformed shape of the code must be considered for facilitating easy recognition of the code.

1D barcode. Ever since the UPC code was proposed by George J. Laurer in 1973 [19], various 1D barcodes have been developed and used for distribution purposes in fields such as industry and the military. Most popular codes such as UPC and EAN are composed of patterns such as guard bars that indicate the initial, final, and central positions of the image code and data patterns that encode the numeric data and the check-sum digit [3]. These patterns are expressed in terms of the relative thickness ratio of black and white bars located parallel to each other. Thus, by sampling the pixels on a scan line that is placed across the patterns, the decoder can recognize the code if there is at least one scan line [4] that covers all the patterns. After reading all the patterns, the decoder verifies the result by using the check-sum digit in the data patterns, but it cannot correct any errors. Figure 2 shows the possibility of decoding the scan line in a 1D barcode. If there is no scan line that is placed across all the patterns of the image code, a data reconstruction technique (DRX) can merge partial patterns obtained from fragments of the code by using several scan lines [20], [21]. While DRX is useful for decoding the fragments of a designed 1D barcode, it cannot read the code even if a single pattern is not covered by the scan lines.

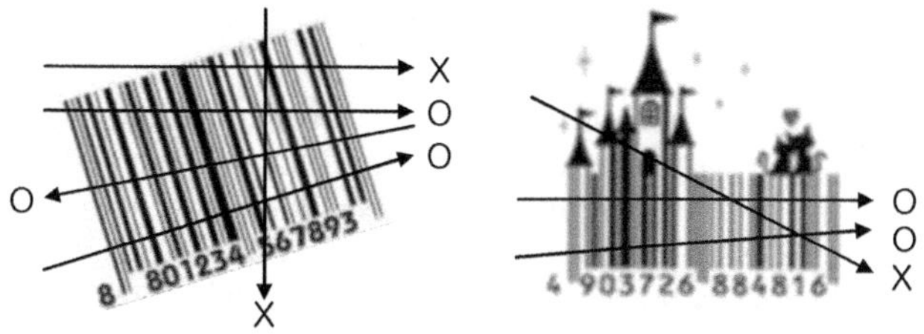

(a) EAN code (b) Designed 1D barcode

Fig. 2. Result of 1D barcode recognition by scan line: "O" and "×" represent success and failure of recognition, respectively

2D code. In comparison with 1D barcodes, most 2D codes encode high-density data for representing a larger amount of data within a smaller size; however, 2D codes must be decoded fast and easily. Therefore, 2D codes have more complex code structures than 1D barcodes. The QR code possesses three finder patterns for finding the code area, two format information patterns for indicating the mask processing method used and error correction level information, two version information patterns for informing the numbers of row and column patterns of the code, two timing patterns and alignment patterns for aligning the code patterns, data codeword patterns for encoding the code value, and error correction codeword patterns for correcting errors in the decoded data [8]. Different 2D codes have different code structures; however, they have identical error correction and data codeword patterns to obtain reliable code values. ISO standard 2D image codes such as QR code, DataMatrix, and PDF-417 commonly use the Reed–Solomon code technique as an error correction algorithm [7], [8], [9].

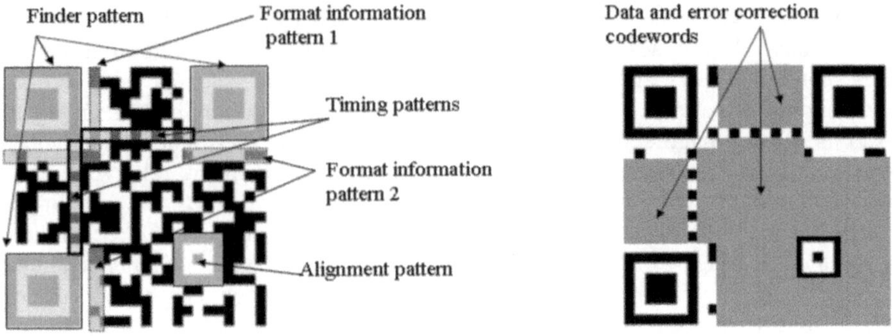

(a) Function patterns and format information patterns [8] (b) Design-enabled area

Fig. 3. QR code structure (version 2): the design elements can be located in the area containing codewords for data and error correction. All versions of the QR code above version 7 (45 × 45 modules) additionally contain version information patterns.

Based on the error correction algorithm, the designed 2D code can be recognized. In Figure 1 (f), the design elements such as the game character image and the logo image are located in the areas containing codeword patterns for data and error correction. In this case, the decoder obtains an erroneous code value because the design elements generate wrong patterns, but the decoder can rectify the value by using the error correction algorithm. However, there are two limitations. One limitation is that the design-enabled area of the code is restricted to the areas containing codeword patterns for data and error correction because other pattern areas have little or no error correction information. For example, if the design elements transform the finder pattern, the decoder cannot find the code area; therefore, it cannot decode the code. The other limitation is regarding the sizes of the design elements on the code. The error correction capacity is predefined by the number of data and error correction patterns of the code and the error correction level. For this reason, the number of damaged codeword patterns generated by the design elements has to be limited to the error correction capacity. Figure 3 describes the QR code structure.

Color-based code. The color-based code is based on the ColorCode shown in Figure 1(d). The ColorCode is a matrix-type image code and consists of a set of N × M cells with four colors. For recognizing the ColorCode, the image code is extracted from the

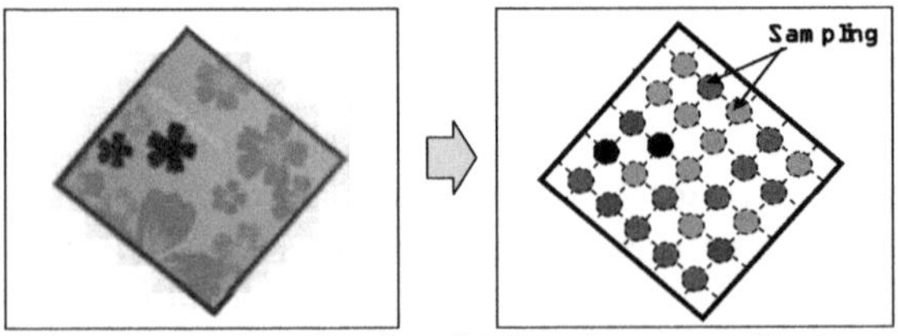

(a) Designed color-based code (b) Sampling areas for decoding

Fig. 4. Sampling areas of designed color-based code

acquired image and color pixels are sampled from the centroid areas of each cell; then, the colors of the cells are determined by classifying the colors of the sampled pixels into predefined color groups. Finally, the cell colors are converted to the corresponding bit-streams, and each bit-stream is verified by an error detection algorithm [22]. The color-based image code is essentially sensitive to variations in color, but if the colors of the centroid areas in each cell are well preserved, the design elements can be applied freely to the other areas of the image code. Figure 4 [23] shows the color-based code and the centroid areas for the sampling pixels.

2.2 Preliminary Survey

Thirteen undergraduate students majoring in computer science participated in the preliminary survey. All the participants were aged twenty and possessed camera phones. Among them, 11 users used the camera phone for still photography and one used it for video mail; however, not all of them had the experience of using an image code interface.

At the beginning of the questionnaire, we explained the concepts of image code interface, common image code, and designed image code for fifteen minutes in a classroom. In addition, through demonstrations and photographs, we showed the participants designed codes based on 1D codes, 2D codes (such as QR codes), and color-based codes printed on papers, magazines, electronic billboards, clothes, and business cards. Subsequently, we surveyed what the participants felt about the 1D code, 2D code (QR code), and color-based code. Table 1 and Figure 5 show the results of the survey.

The participants in the experiment answered that the color-based code provided more emotional and visual information. Moreover, they felt that this code was suitable for various print materials and less objectionable from the viewpoint of culture, psychology, and religion. However, it was perceived to be difficult to recognize as an image code since it looked like an icon or an image and could not be distinguished from the various other images. In the case of the 1D and 2D codes, the participants felt that there was no emotional or aesthetic appeal, even though these codes had a lower cognitive load than the color-based code for distinguishing them from the other images.

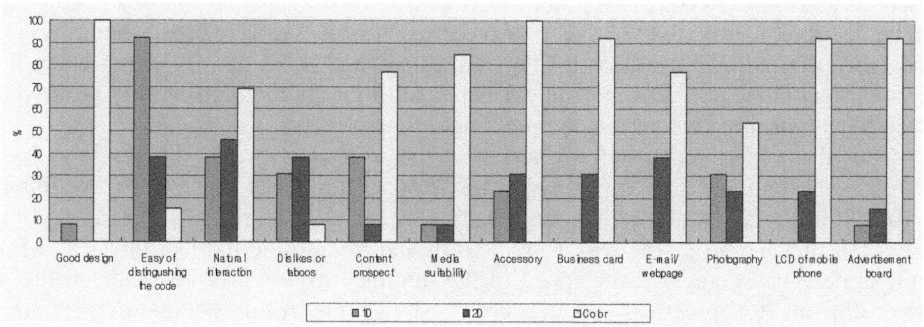

Fig. 5. Comparison of the properties of the image codes

Table 1. Comparison of the properties of the designed image codes(Bad/Low: 0–33.3%, Average/Medium: 33.4–66.6%, Good: 66.7–100%)

Properties		Designed image code		
		1D	2D	Color-based
Good design/aesthetic and emotional aspects of the code		Bad	Bad	Good
Ease of distinguishing the code from other images (Cognitive load for finding the code)		Good	Average	Bad
Natural interaction		Average	Average	Good
Cultural or psychological dislikes or religious taboos		Low	Medium	Low
Prospects regarding service and contents		Average	Bad	Good
Media suitability		Bad	Bad	Good
Media/material	Accessory	Bad	Bad	Good
	Business card	Bad	Bad	Good
	Webpage, e-mail	Bad	Average	Good
	Photography	Bad	Bad	Average
	LCD of mobile phone	Bad	Bad	Good
	Advertisement board	Bad	Bad	Good

3 High-Fidelity Prototyping and Experimental Evaluation

We implemented a high-fidelity prototype and evaluated its usability, which involved recognizing the color-based image code on a PDA. The PDA (HP iPAQ RW-6100) is equipped with an Intel Bulverde PXA270 520 MHz processor, a 1.1 mega-pixel CCD camera, a 128 MB flash ROM, and a 64 MB 133 MHz Mobile SDRAM. The decoding program was developed in Microsoft Embedded Visual C++ 4.0; this is an enhanced version of the program used in our previous study [22].

For the experiment, we provided PDAs and samples of the color-based image code to the users; they were allowed five minutes to experiment. In the experiment, if a user executed the decoder program, the PDA showed real-time previews from the camera; subsequently, the PDA recognized the color-based image code when it was in the field of view. Moreover, it displayed the relevant video or web pages when the decoder recognized the image code correctly. In Figure 6, the high-fidelity prototype, decoding algorithm, and system architecture are described.

After the experimentation, we surveyed the user response by employing seven Likert scale items—1 for "very low," 2 for "low," 3 for "little low," 4 for "medium," 5 for "little high," 6 for "high," and 7 for "very high." According to the survey, the users felt that the prototype was easy to learn and that it required less physical effort to operate. They perceived the speed of the interface to be fairly fast and felt that it was efficient for practical use. Figure 7 shows the result of the experimental evaluation.

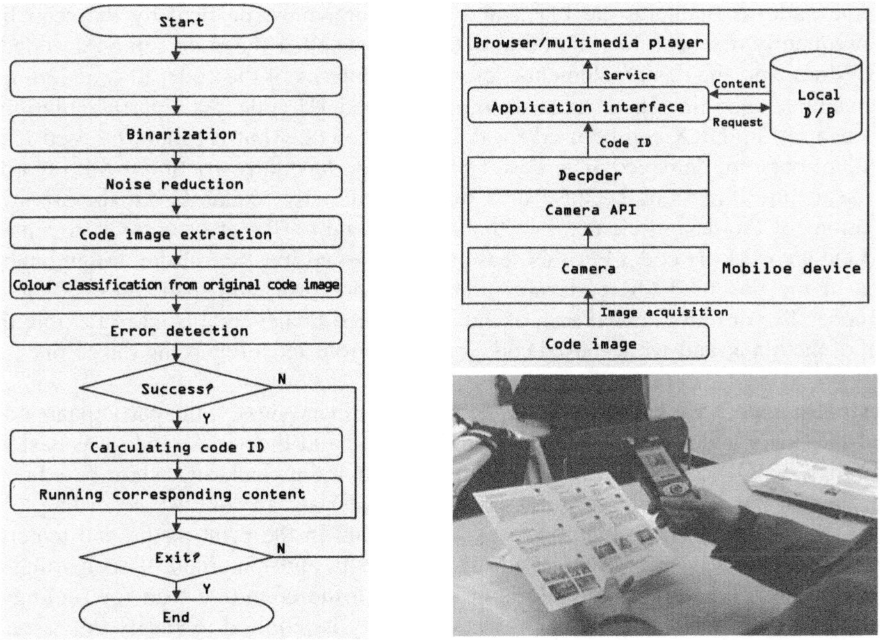

Fig. 6. High-fidelity prototype: (left) flowchart of decoder, (top right) structure of the system, (bottom right) user evaluation of the prototype

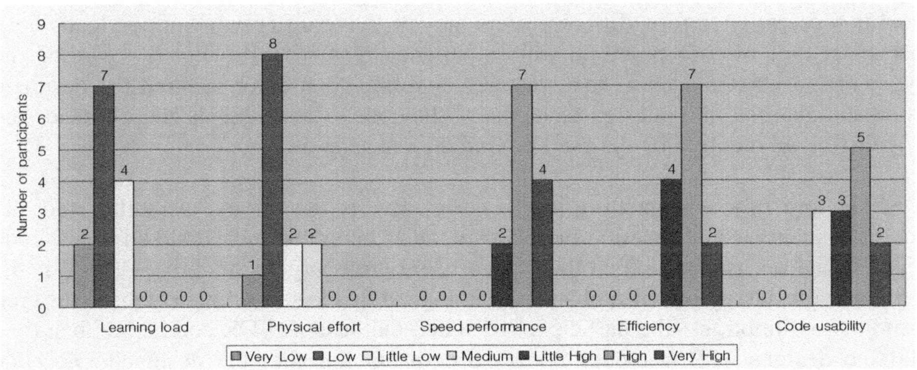

Fig. 7. Result of the survey

4 Discussion

Physical restrictions. The designed image codes effectively present various types of visual information to the users, but the decoding abilities are decreased by the transformation of the original image codes and the design elements on the designed image code. These design factors are more detrimental to the black-and-white-based image code because they consist of fine patterns. In case of the designed 1D barcode, all the patterns, namely, the black and white bars, must be read by the scan line. Consequently, the scan line direction determines whether the code can be decoded or not. Moreover, the design elements deform the patterns of the code; thus, the number of available scan lines is decreased in the designed 1D code. As a partial solution to this restriction, DRX can be used for decoding the code, but it cannot be used if one or more bars are damaged. The designed QR code has no restrictions with regard to the scan line directions because it is omnidirectionally readable, but the sizes and locations of the design elements in the code depend on the error correction capacity and the areas of the code. For this reason, the size and location of the design-enabled area of the designed QR code are relatively more restricted than those of the 1D barcode. The design-enabled area of the color-based image code is more flexible than that of the black-and-white-based code, but limitations exist regarding the colors.

Aesthetic aspect vs. cognitive load. In the preliminary survey, the participants could find the black-and-white-based image code easily, and the 1D barcode was easier to find than the QR code. However, they answered that the black-and-white-based codes were out of harmony with the print media and materials. In contrast, according to the users, the color-based image code was hard to find in the print media and materials even though it was in harmony with diverse media and materials. It seems that the aesthetic design level of the code is at odds with the cognitive load for finding the code. However, more detailed and extensive study is required to clarify this issue on the basis of two factors. The first factor is the user's experience level for different types of codes. The 1D barcode is very familiar to common users. Moreover, the QR code is popular among mobile computing services in Japan [1], but it is unfamiliar to some users in other countries. Color-based image codes are not well known to common users. Therefore, different users may perceive different cognitive loads for a particular type of code based on their experience. The second factor is regarding the types of the objects such as text, pictures, symbols, and colors around the designed code and also the inner design elements of the code. These objects can influence the cognitive load required by the users to find the image code.

Dislikes and taboos regarding image codes. Before the survey, we anticipated that the participants would mention the 1D barcode as being the most disliked image code since it had occasionally been the source of religious arguments [19]. However, the results of the survey on cultural and psychological dislikes or religious taboos differed from our assumption—the participants disliked the designed QR code more than they did the designed 1D barcode. Some participants felt that the designed QR code burdened their eyes with its fine patterns, and they felt giddy when viewing its labyrinth-like patterns. For a more detailed understanding of this issue, it is necessary to conduct a user study of the users' code preferences based on their background, that is, their culture, religion, and code experience.

Prospects regarding service and contents. When we asked the users whether they could estimate the service and contents of the image codes based on the visual information offered in them, they replied that they could estimate the service and contents more easily from the designed color-based image code easier than from the other codes. The visual information depicted by the design elements can be classified into characters, logos, pictures, images, signs, and colors; furthermore, the type of the design element affects the ease of estimation of the code's service and contents. For a more detailed understanding, the influence of the types of design element on the prospects regarding user service must be studied.

User interface. In the experiment on the high-fidelity prototype of the color-based image code interface, most participants were of the opinion that the recognition time was faster than expected. In the prototype, the recognition process worked after program execution, and it repeated the processes of image acquisition and image decoding continuously until any image code was decoded correctly. We refer to this method as the continuous decoding method, and it is generally suitable for common mobile computing services and particularly for AR and MR services. However, a few users proposed that the program could be modified by incorporating a "capture button" for executing the decoding algorithm after displaying the preview images; this was proposed because if there were several codes on the print material, occasionally the non-intended code was captured and recognized accidentally.

5 Conclusions and Future work

In this paper, we have presented an analysis of designed image codes by a user study; we have also implemented a color-based image code recognition interface and evaluated its usability by experimental evaluation. From the evaluation, the image code is found to be better than the black-and-white-based code with regard to the use of design, suitability of materials, and representation of information; however, there is a difficulty in recognizing it as a code. The black-and-white-based code is considered more recognizable. On the other hand, the materials used in the code are less suitable and inconvenient for the user. With regard to the usability evaluation of the high-fidelity prototype for the color-based image code, the users responded that it was a useful and practical interface.

This research constitutes an initial study for the designed image codes. In future work, we plan to conduct a more detailed investigation based on the users' background, that is, their culture, religion, and code experience; in addition, we plan to study the effects of the print materials and the types of design elements used in the codes.

Acknowledgments. Parts of this work were supported by the Korea Science and Engineering Foundation (KOSEF) grant (No. R01-2005-000-10898-0) and by the Small and Medium Business Administration (SMBA) grant funded by the Korea government. We would like to thank Sang-Jin Jeon and Keechoon Lee for their technical supports.

References

1. Info Plant Conducts Survey on QR Code (September 21, 2005). DigInfo (February 2007) http://www.diginfo.tv/archives/2005/09/21/info_plant_conducts_survey_on_2.html
2. Barcodes, ISO Standards: (February 2007) http://www.iso.org/iso/en/CombinedQuery Result.Combined QueryResult?queryString=bar+code/

3. Pavlidis, T., Swartz, J., Wang, Y.P.: Fundamentals of Bar Code Information Theory. IEEE Computer, IEEE Computer Society, vol. 23(4) pp. 74–86 (April 1990)
4. Pavlidis, T., Swartz, J., Wang, Y.P.: Information Encoding with Two-Dimensional Bar Codes. IEEE Computer, IEEE Computer Society vol. 25(6), pp. 18–28 (June 1992)
5. ColorCode. ColorZip Media Inc. (February 2007) http://www.colozip.com
6. General EAN.UCC Specification v.6.0. (February 2007) http://www.ean.se/GSV6.0/HTML_Files/Document_Library/Bar_Code/00103/index.html
7. International Organization for Standardization: Information technology - Automatic identification and data capture techniques - Bar code symbology - PDF-417. ISO/IEC 15438 (2001)
8. International Organization for Standardization: Information Technology – Automatic Identification and Data Capture Techniques – Bar Code Symbology – QR Code. ISO/IEC 18004 (2000)
9. International Organization for Standardization: Information technology - Automatic identification and data capture techniques - Bar code symbology - Data Matrix, ISO/IEC 16022 (2000)
10. Ohbuch, E., Hanaizumi, H., Hock, L.A.: Barcode Readers using the Camera Device in Mobile Phones. In: Nakajima, M., Hatori, Y., Sourin, A. (eds.) Proceedings of the 2004 International Conference on Cyberworlds (CW 2004), pp. 260–265. IEEE Computer Society Press, Los Alamitos, CA (November 2004)
11. ARToolKit. HITLab (February 2007) http://www.hitl.washington.edu/artoolkit
12. Fiala, M.: ARTag, A Fiducial Marker System using Digital Techniques. In: Schmid, C., Soatto, S., Tomasi, C. (eds.) Proceedings of IEEE Computer Vision and Pattern Recognition, vol. 2, pp. 590–596. IEEE Computer Society Press, Los Alamitos, CA (June 2005)
13. Barcode design. Designboom (February 2007) http://www.designboom.com/weblog/read.php?CATEGORY_PK=&TOPIC_PK=774
14. Barcode Revolution (February 2007) http://www.barcoderevolution.com/gallery/index.php?c=all
15. Design QR code. IT Design. (February 2007) http://www.d-qr.net/
16. Toye, E., Sharp, R., Madhavapeddy, A., Scott, D., Upton E., Blackwell, A.: Interacting with Mobile Services: An Evaluation of Camera-Phones and Visual Tags. Personal and Ubiquitous Computing Journal. SpringerLink (February 2006) (February 2007) http://www.springerlink.com/content/f59441g12035q644/fulltext.pdf
17. Leichtenstern, K., Luca, A. D., Rukzio, E.: Analysis of Built-in Mobile Phone Sensors for Supporting Interactions with the Real World. In: Rukzio, E., Hakkila, J., Spasojevic, M., Mäntyjärvi, J., Ravi, N. (eds.) Proceedings of the Workshop on Pervasive Mobile Interaction Devices (PERMID 2005) (May 2005) pp. 31–34 (February 2007) http://www.medien.ifi.lmu.de/permid2005/pdf/Proceedings_Permid2005.pdf
18. Kato, H., Tan, K. T.: 2D barcodes for mobile phones. In: Proceedings of the Second International Conference on Mobile Technology, Applications and Systems (Nov 2005) (February 2007) http://ieeexplore.ieee.org/iel5/11013/34698/01656706.pdf?tp=&arnumber=1656706&isnumber=34698
19. Laurer, G. J.: Consulting - Uniform Product Code & Other Optical Bar Codes (January 2007) http://www.laurerupc.com/
20. Lapinski, C., Eckert, C., Skokowski, R., Cox, J., Scott, W., Chaleff, E., Wagh, M. D.: Scanner for Reconstructing Optical Codes from a Plurality of Code Fragments. US5548107, United States Patent and Trademark Office (August 1996)

21. Sharpe, J. G., Wurz, D. A.: Scanner for and method of repetitively scanning a coded symbology. US6669091, United States Patent and Trademark Office (August 2003)
22. Cheong, C., Han, T. –D., Lee, N. –K.: Apparatus and method for recognizing code. US6981644, United States Patent and Trademark Office (January 2006)
23. Cheong, C., et al.: Pictorial Image Code: A Color Vision-based Automatic Identification Interface for Mobile Computing Environments. In: Proceedings of the Eighth IEEE Workshop on Mobile Computing Systems and Applications, WMCSA 2007 (to appear, February 2007)

The Effects of Gender Culture on Mobile Phone Icon Recognition

Shunan Chung, Chiyi Chau, Xufan Hsu, and Jim Jiunde Lee

Institute of Communication Studies, National Chiao-Tung University, Taiwan

1 Background

Mobile phones have rapidly become the most important communication device in our daily life. According to a recent survey of The Directorate of Telecommunications, Ministry of Transportation and Communications in 2005, the penetration rate of telecom service subscribers in the Taiwan area is 97.37%. That is, on average, almost every Taiwanese citizen owns a mobile phone. This has resulted in extremely keen competition among mobile phone vendors. When compared with others, teenagers have long been viewed as the primary users in the Taiwanese mobile phone market. Regardless of vendors' various kinds of promotion strategies such as special price discounts or newly-added fancy functions, what really matters is whether this daily communication device has been designed according to the true needs and experience of this special age group. The small screen interface design is one of the newest research focuses of the Human-Computer Interaction domain. Due to the limited screen space, icons have been deemed as the dominant mode in the operational process of a mobile phone. The present study is dedicated to exploring the icon design of the mobile phone, especially for the teenage user group in Taiwan.

2 Theoretical Framework

As a well-known proverb says, "A picture is worth a thousand words". Using images as forms of communication requires the least effort to explain the process of problem solving and can represent abstract concepts (Wang & Liu, 1993). According to Yeng, Kao & Hwang (1997), images are visualizations of objects. People use specific images like icons to convey meaning to the group they belong to. Icons are signs standing for objects, representing them in terms of replication or analogy. Icons have been part of the user's experience for decades, and people tend to take them for granted as a part of graphical user interfaces.

In interface design, icons are applied largely to signify commands or functions. In order to avoid memory overload and to help construct the system's images, icons should be carefully designed based on being highly recognizable (Chen, 2003). In Lodding's (1983) study, he divided icons into three categories: concrete, abstract, and arbitrary. A concrete icon replicates the specific characteristics of one object. Users are assumed to be able to understand a concrete icon immediately, since it is a replication of a real object. An abstract icon visualizes the concept of the object. Although users might have to use their imagination to interpret it, the meaning of such an icon will not be easily forgotten once it is understood. An arbitrary icon is

J. Jacko (Ed.): Human-Computer Interaction, Part II, HCII 2007, LNCS 4551, pp. 252–259, 2007.

unrelated to the original object. It often occurs as a result of a particular cultural background. Therefore arbitrary icons demand users to learn repeatedly until they completely adopt them and retain them in their memory.

According to a review of the literature, culture is one of the most important issues affecting icon recognition. People from different cultural backgrounds demonstrate diverse perceptions, cognition, and thinking styles (Hofstede, 1997). For instance, in Kim and Lee's (2005) investigation of western / eastern culture and icon recognition at the abstract level, people in the western world significantly identified abstract icons better, while people in the eastern world possessed better ability in the recognition of concrete icons. In the present study, the cultural issue is examined in terms of age and gender. In particular, in the mobile phone industry, these are the two most fundamental issues to be considered during the process of product development (Meyers-Levy and Sternthal, 1991).

Previous research has shown that gender diversity has an important influence on visual performance. For instance, in space-related visual experiments, males perform better than females. On the other hand, in language-related or communication-related experiments, females perform better (Deaux and Kite, 1987). In McGiven et al's (1998) investigation of visual recognition, adult females could better recognize the forms of abstract and concrete objects. Therefore the study concluded that adult females could perceive more visual stimulation in the environment. Hence, they subconsciously memorized more objects than males.

Based on this discussion, the research questions of the present study are as follows:

- Q1. Will gender differences affect recognition of different types of icons? Why?
- Q2. Which types of icons (concrete, abstract, arbitrary) are Taiwanese teenagers' favorites? Why?

3 Method

According to the market survey in Taiwan, the present study collected icon sets from best-selling brands of mobile phones. After selecting the most often used functions and corresponding icons, the researchers held a focus group meeting to select icon sets which best fit Taiwanese teenage culture. According to the discussion, the present study used the content analysis method to sort these icon sets into three categories: concrete, abstract and arbitrary. The study then developed two questionnaires including 5 concrete icons, 5 abstract icons and 5 arbitrary icons. The questionnaires were designed to examine icon recognition and teenagers' favorite icons.

These 15 icons individually represent 5 basic functions of the mobile phone: "Multimedia", "Call Records", "Settings", "Phonebook" and "Messages". The research divides icons into three categories: 1) abstract icons: the images which visualize objects or notions. Users have to use their imagination to understand their meanings; 2) concrete icons: the images which refer to real objects or visualize the objects' characteristics; 3) arbitrary icons: the images which are established by usage and lack of reference materials. To users, they are often unrelated to the real objects.

The first questionnaire focuses on the degree of icon recognition. The researchers want to understand if the three categories of icon sets could correspond to the meanings of the functions. The second questionnaire utilizes preference ratings. It asks participants to give scores to 5 kinds of icon sets. Before asking participants to complete the questionnaire, the researchers explained the entire process of the experiment and made sure they understood it.

The study used the Internet to recruit subjects from Taiwan Chiao Tung University and National Chengchi University. There were 60 subjects whose ages ranged from 16 to 24. The average age was 21. Of the 60 participants, 27 were male and 33 female. All the participants have used mobile phones for over two years. The analysis focuses on the interrelationship among the users' preferences for different types of icons, icon recognition, and gender culture issues.

4 Results

The first questionnaire tests the recognition rate of these 15 icons. If the answer is correct, 1 point is given. If the answer is wrong, no point is given. According to the statistics, the present study found that both males and females gained higher points for the abstract icons. The average score for males was 4.3 (standard deviation 0.14) and for females, 4.6 (standard deviation 0.11). The second highest score was for the concrete icons. The average score for males was 3.7 (standard deviation 0.1) and for females, 3.9 (standard deviation 0.1). The lowest performance was for the arbitrary icons: males averaged 3.7 (standard deviation 0.2) and females averaged 3.5 (standard deviation 0.17). ANOVA analysis was then conducted to identify whether there was a gender difference in recognition rates. The p values of gender difference for the recognition rate of abstract icons, concrete icons and arbitrary icons were 0.096, 0.353 and 0.470 respectively. Hence the results cannot reject the null hypothesis. It seems therefore that the gender difference for recognition of abstract icons, concrete icons and arbitrary icons is not significant.

While the present study utilized One-way ANOVA to discover if different styles of icon design for the same function are perceived differently according to gender, it was found that there is a significant gender difference in the recognition of the abstract icon for "Call Records" ($p=.019<.05$). The females' average score (0.91) was higher than the males' (0.67). This result infers that the recognition ability of females is better than males for the abstract icons for the "Call Records" function.

The second questionnaire uses preference ratings. The participants need to score different categories of icons within the same function according to their subjective preference. The most preferred icon gets 1 point, while the least preferred is given -1 point. After the statistical analysis, the researchers found that both males and females have a preference for concrete icons. Males' average points were 2.41 (standard deviation 1.25) and females' were 2.52 (standard deviation 0.97). The second highest points were for the arbitrary icons. Males' average points were -0.78 (standard deviation 1.37) and females' were -1.33 (standard deviation 1.53). The lowest score was for the abstract icons: males' average points were -1.74 (standard deviation 1.61) while females' average value was -1.18 (standard deviation 1.4).

When ANOVA analysis was performed, the p values of gender preferences for abstract, concrete and arbitrary icons were 0.16, 0.71 and 0.15 respectively. These results do not reject the null hypothesis. Therefore it seems that there is no significant gender difference in terms of preference for abstract, concrete and arbitrary icons.

5 Discussion

According to the results of this research, Taiwanese female teenagers tend to perform better than male teenagers in the recognition of abstract icons. However there is no gender difference in the recognition of concrete icons or arbitrary icons. According to the participants' comments about these three types of icons, it seems that Taiwanese female teenagers prefer abstract icons because of their richer concepts, while male teenagers prefer concrete icons because of the ease of learning them.

The results of this study are expected to provide a deeper understanding of Taiwanese teenagers' usage of mobile phones, and especially icons. The study hopes to contribute to the icon design of relevant research and the mobile device industry.

References

1. Blankenberger, S., Hahnt, K.: Effects of icon design on human-computer interaction. Man.-Machine Studies 35, 363–377 (1991)
2. Chen, T.: Research On The Functional Requirement And Icon Distinguish Of Mobile Phone For Users. Master dissertation of National Yunlin University of science and technology (1993)
3. Deaux, K., Kite, M.E.: Thinking about Gender. In: Hess, B.B., Ferree, M.M. (eds.) Analyzing Gender: A Handbook of Social Science Research, pp. 92–117. Sage Publications, Newbury Park, CA (1987)
4. Kim, J.H., Lee, K.P.: Cultural difference and mobile phone interface design: Icon recognition according to level of abstraction (2005)
5. Lodding, K.: Iconic Interfacing. IEEE Computer Graphics and Applications 3(2), 11–20 March/April (1983)
6. McGivern, R.F., Mutter, K.L., Anderson, J., Wideman, G., Bodnar, M., Huston, P.J.: Gender differences in incidental learning and visual recognition memory: support for a sex difference in unconscious environmental awareness. Personality and Individual Differences, vol. 25(2), pp. 223–232 (1998)
7. Meyers-Levy, J., Maheswaran, D.: Exploring Differences in Males and Females Processing Strategy. Journal of Consumer Research 18, 63–70 June(1991)
8. Simon, S.J.: The impact of culture and gender on web sites: an empirical study. ACM SIGMIS Database 32(1), 18–37 (2001)
9. The Directorate of Telecommunications, Ministry of Transportation and Communications, Penetration rate of telecom service subscribers in Taiwan 2005. Taipei, Taiwan R.O.C (2006)
10. Wang, J., Liu, S.: Design and understanding of icons for visual communication. Intelligence in Education 83, 402–409 (1993)
11. Yeng, D., Kao, S., et Hwang, Y.: The discussion of significance and recognition of icons in public environment. In: The 12th nation-wide conference of technology and education (1997)

Appendix 1: 15 Questions Of Icon Recognition

A. Basic Information

Name:

Age:

Gender:

Date:

B. Introduction

Please answer the following 15 questions. Each question is independent and requires a single answer. Please indicate the most likely meaning of the given icon based on your intuition.

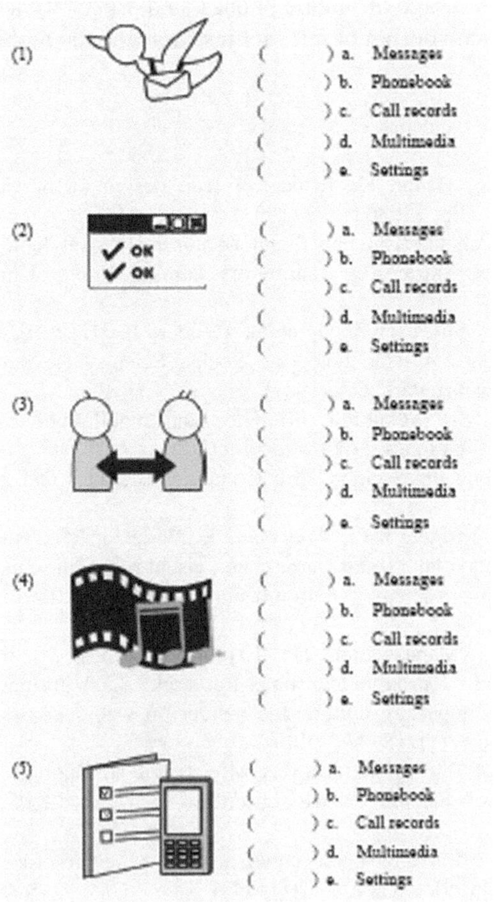

(1)
( ) a. Messages
( ) b. Phonebook
( ) c. Call records
( ) d. Multimedia
( ) e. Settings

(2)
( ) a. Messages
( ) b. Phonebook
( ) c. Call records
( ) d. Multimedia
( ) e. Settings

(3)
( ) a. Messages
( ) b. Phonebook
( ) c. Call records
( ) d. Multimedia
( ) e. Settings

(4)
( ) a. Messages
( ) b. Phonebook
( ) c. Call records
( ) d. Multimedia
( ) e. Settings

(5)
( ) a. Messages
( ) b. Phonebook
( ) c. Call records
( ) d. Multimedia
( ) e. Settings

(6)

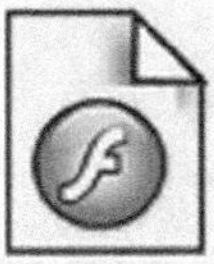

( ) a. Messages
( ) b. Phonebook
( ) c. Call records
( ) d. Multimedia
( ) e. Settings

(7)

( ) a. Messages
( ) b. Phonebook
( ) c. Call records
( ) d. Multimedia
( ) e. Settings

(8)

( ) a. Messages
( ) b. Phonebook
( ) c. Call records
( ) d. Multimedia
( ) e. Settings

(9)

( ) a. Messages
( ) b. Phonebook
( ) c. Call records
( ) d. Multimedia
( ) e. Settings

(10)

( ) a. Messages
( ) b. Phonebook
( ) c. Call records
( ) d. Multimedia
( ) e. Settings

(11)

( ) a. Messages
( ) b. Phonebook
( ) c. Call records
( ) d. Multimedia
( ) e. Settings

(12)

( ) a. Messages
( ) b. Phonebook
( ) c. Call records
( ) d. Multimedia
( ) e. Settings

(13)

( ) a. Messages
( ) b. Phonebook
( ) c. Call records
( ) d. Multimedia
( ) e. Settings

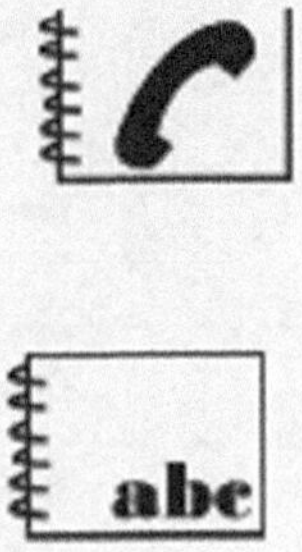
(14)
( ) a. Messages
( ) b. Phonebook
( ) c. Call records
( ) d. Multimedia
( ) e. Settings

(15)

( ) a. Messages
( ) b. Phonebook
( ) c. Call records
( ) d. Multimedia
( ) e. Settings

***Thank you for your help ***

Appendix 2: 5 Question Sets of Icon Preference

Introduction

There are five questions in this questionnaire. For each question you are given a mobile phone function and three possible icons. Please indicate your favorite icon and the one you most dislike, and give the reason for your opinion.

Example:

Set 1	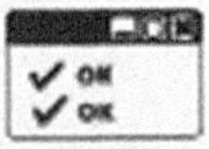		
Reasons for Preference/ Dislike	X I cannot imagine directly.		○ beautiful and easy to understand

A.

Multimedia			
Reasons for Preference/ Dislike			

B.

Call Records		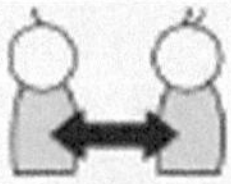	
Reasons for Preference/ Dislike			

C.

Settings	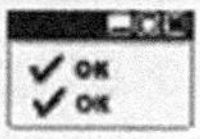		
Reasons for Preference/ Dislike	×		

D.

Phonebook	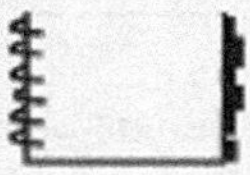		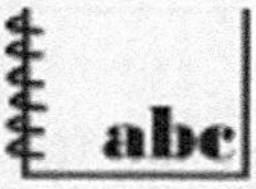
Reasons for Preference/ Dislike			

E.

Messages			
Reasons for Preference/ Dislike			

***Thank you for your help ***

Designing for Mobile Devices: Requirements, Low-Fi Prototyping and Evaluation

Marco de Sá and Luís Carriço

LaSIGE & Department of Informatics, University of Lisbon,
Edifício C6, Campo Grande, 1749-016, Lisboa, Portugal
{marcosa,lmc}@di.fc.ul.pt

Abstract. This paper describes the design process of a set of ubiquitous applications for critical scenarios (e.g., psychotherapy and education). Accordingly, we address the problems that occurred on the various design stages, particularly those that pertain to the mobility and ubiquity of the devices. Regarding these, we detail the various solutions that were adopted along the way, particularly on the data gathering and requirements' assessment, prototyping and evaluation stages. We introduce a set of dimensions to the concept of context and how it is utilized on the design of mobile applications. We describe new prototyping techniques and explain how they improve usability evaluation. Overall, we aim to share the learnt lessons and how they can be used in mobile application's design.

Keywords: low-fidelity prototyping, ubiquitous computing, mobile devices, usability evaluation.

1 Introduction

Mobile devices possess outstanding capabilities that set them apart from common fixed technologies. Their size, weight and corresponding portability, interaction modalities and even multimedia features allow them to be used ubiquitously on several situations and contexts for a wide and diverse set of purposes [8],[12]. They have propelled the surfacing of concepts such as ambient intelligent and context aware applications and defined new usage paradigms on various levels. However, these same potentialities, together with inherent hardware limitations (e.g. small screens, battery life, input capabilities) introduce greater challenges when designing specific applications that target these devices. Consequentially, new requirements and usability guidelines are paramount in order to provide users with applications that enhance their tasks and offer support to pervasive computing, but still maintaining the same usability levels that users are now accustomed to.

While attempting to overcome such difficulties, designers often choose to port existing applications, available for larger platforms, to mobile devices, adjusting the necessary details. However, such approach generally leads to cumbersome and unusable applications that, even if containing brilliant content, quickly become obsolete and avoided by users [3],[11]. A major factor for designers to adopt such strategies is the absence of specific methodologies for mobile, handheld and

J. Jacko (Ed.): Human-Computer Interaction, Part II, HCII 2007, LNCS 4551, pp. 260–269, 2007.

ubiquitous devices [14]. Although some guidelines, available in current user centered design (UCD) methodologies, might apply to this specific design process, the unique features and constraints that ubiquity and pervasiveness, require new or, at least, deeply refined approaches.

Three design stages are particularly sensitive and present a wider set of difficulties [15]. Gathering requirements is the essential bootstrap for every development and design process. For this purpose, current design methodologies include methods such as ethnography, task analysis, inquiries amongst others. However, constantly using a mobile device and application through several tasks and settings introduces details that are hardly detectable with the simple use of such methods. The influence of the context on a specific scenario might be acceptably assessed. Still, the implications that changing from one context to another, and how this might influence the user and his requirements towards the applications fail to be understood.

On the sketching process and evaluation of low-fidelity prototypes, several problems that retract from the process are also evident. Low-fidelity prototypes are, as currently used, poorly suited to the peculiarities of mobile devices and their usage scenarios [15]. Using paper sheets and a set of detachable cards to simulate a UI while a designer uses a Wizard of Oz technique is an acceptable way to test a future desktop application. However, it his likely that such technique fails to provide a clear perspective on usage problems for a mobile device used on a multitude of locations [15]. Furthermore, the technique per se seems difficult to apply on such conditions.

These problems extend themselves to later stages of evaluation as well. Overall, the difficulties inherent to the design process of applications for such devices urge for different approaches and extensions on current user centered design processes.

This paper describes the design process of two different, proactive, mobile applications and how common user centered design approaches were applied. The problems faced throughout the process are stressed highlighting the specific challenges that mobile platforms imposed; how current methodologies fail to properly support it; and how these facts motivated the proposed solution. We start by enumerating the problems that motivated our work and explaining how existing work was insufficient to solve them or, when adequate, facilitated the process. Afterwards we detail our experiences and the contributions that emerged. Finally, we discuss future work and draw some conclusions.

2 Design Problems

The main motivation behind the work hereby presented resulted from the difficulties felt during the design process of two different mobile applications. The first application is directed to psychotherapy (e.g., Cognitive Behavioral Therapies for depression and anxiety) [17] while the second supports educational activities [16]. Both systems target mobile devices with particular focus on PDAs and were designed using a user centered design methodology [2]. These two choices resulted from the need to support the highly pervasive and ubiquitous activities that compose the whole of these problems, and the need to understand the critical requirements that users have.

Data Gathering: Difficulties emerged immediately with the initial requirement assessment and data gathering stages on both projects. UCD methodologies [2],[13] encourage data gathering and analysis of requirements from a user centered perspective. Accordingly, they suggest the use of ethnographic sessions and interviews to gather the necessary information. These two techniques usually bring designers the possibility to understand the work flow on various activities and detect problems that might be solved by introducing a technological system. However, on pervasive and mobile activities as those involved in psychotherapy and education, these methodologies fail to provide sufficient detail and guidelines on how to achieve such results and on how to apply the techniques [15].

On the psychotherapy project [17], ethical issues prevented us from conducting ethnographic sessions and analyzing in-therapy procedures. In order to understand common practices and activities we were required to review videos [5] and interview therapists. Therapy sessions were necessarily simulated and conducted within controlled environments with the participation of therapists and simulated patients. No direct communication with real patients was allowed.

For Test-IT [16], the second project, which supports a wide role of educational activities on different settings, the same techniques were adopted. Ethnographic sessions were conducted within school classes and interviews were made to teachers and students.

These processes introduced multiple problems. Firstly, we were not able to accompany any of the users (e.g., therapists, teachers or students) on their outdoors tasks. Secondly, as we tried to introduce some scenario-based simulations [8], covering a set of activities and contexts (e.g. complete specific tasks on various locations), we noticed that these were frequently incomplete and too artificial, failing to cover important details. Thirdly, since scenarios were mostly self-contained and specific, no context changes were assessed or even noticed. For instance, on simulated sessions, as patients continued their work outdoors and at home, no information could be retrieved, creating a large gap on the workflow and gathered data. Although this scenario-based exercise provided insight on some problems that could occur on several activities, it still falls short to cover most of the possible scenarios and situations.

Prototyping: Once the gathered information was modeled and analyzed, we started to design and prototype possible solutions. Various examples on building low-fidelity prototypes were reviewed, some particularly applied to mobile devices [1],[8],[19]. However, these few examples of low-fidelity prototyping for mobile devices that were found, used classic prototyping approaches, with simple cards or paper, and low accuracy regarding the screen measurements and available components (e.g. drop boxes, text fields, etc) [18],[19].

This introduced a set of problems on the usage of these prototypes. Components and their size confounded users and resulted in unrealistic and unviable prototypes. Since screen measurements were disregarded, the information that each card started to include was excessive and impossible to include on actual devices.

Moreover, together with the design fidelity details (e.g., size, components), more realistic tools than post-its or cards, as exemplified in [2],[18],[19] were needed. These materials started to mislead users regarding weight, size or the interaction with the devices. Furthermore, the cards started to deteriorate during outside evaluation sessions, especially each time a user tried to put a paper PDA prototype in his/her pocket.

This affected the experimentation and evaluation of the sketches that were available and confused the UI design problems with those that depended on the device and used materials. These problems retracted from contextual evaluation sessions, requiring the construction of new prototypes each time new ideas emerged. Once again, alternatives had to be introduced so that the process could provide useful information.

Usability Evaluation: Usability evaluation out of the lab, especially on early design stages, which proved to be essential, is not yet a common procedure [10]. Accordingly, the used methodology provided no insight on how to conduct any type of multiple context/setting evaluation.

Although some recent work addresses this subject [7],[8],[10], stressing the need to evaluate the prototypes on the real situations where they will most likely be used when completed, these practices are rarely applied [10]. On the majority of cases, applications are tested within labs, generally taking advantage of simulation and role playing [10],[18]. Furthermore, despite the existing literature, no substantial advice on this topic was found. For instance, the use of Wizard of Oz techniques [9] with mobile prototypes was extremely demanding. Following a user while he/she tests a prototype on every imagined scenario might be impossible to achieve. The procedure itself might cause ethical and social problems.

This problem was further aggravated when trying to evaluate the software applications. Here users required privacy and long periods of time using the applications. Thus, no observation and detection of usability flaws could be made. Once again, the used methodology provided no guidance on such procedures and solutions had to be arranged.

3 A Design Methodology for Mobile Devices

In order to overcome the stated difficulties, we were required to use alternative techniques on all these design stages. Furthermore, this process propelled the development of new methods which coped with the user centered design of the two user interfaces. The following sections detail how and which techniques were used and some findings that emerged along the way.

3.1 Pervasive Data Gathering

For designers to understand currently faced problems and define more suited solutions, they must work together with future users and understand their needs so that created alternatives are innovative and usable.

As mentioned before, existing techniques provide designers with some directions to gather this information and analyze it. However, these techniques focus mainly on a specific setting and scenario. Even if they are repeated for every imagined scenario and setting, none of these methods provides means to relate the gathered requirements when settings are changed. Furthermore, the requirements and their causes are commonly lost during these transitions. This problem is generally non existent on fixed solutions since scenarios are usually immutable or usage restrictions, and their influence on the user's behavior, are constant.

With mobile technology the case is hardly the same. Due to its pervasive and ubiquitous nature, the context, settings and usage scenarios are constantly changing, such as the requirements and needs that these imply. Therefore, it is crucial to understand the changes between settings and scenarios, which is possibly attainable with current methodologies, but it is also paramount to understand why and how these changes occurred. For example, using ethnographic observations, one can notice that during meetings, only two or three tasks are accomplished by a user on a certain setting and with a particular sequence. On the other hand, while at home only one of these tasks is done and arranged on a different sequence, within a set of other specific tasks. Furthermore, even within one of these settings, depending on privacy or social settings, the sequence may be changed once again. However, there is no explanation on why and how these changes on usage behavior happened and how this should be modeled into a future solution. Moreover, when modeling an application, the UI's changes and triggers are also difficult to picture.

To tackle these problems, we tried to use alternative methods to evaluate and assess requirements on mobile settings. Particular care was directed to understand how usage and user's behaviors are affected by the surrounding environment, emphasizing not only the changes but also their causes and effects. Firstly, we established a high level conceptual framework, which pointed specific directions and highlighted crucial concerns that had to be taken into consideration.

We started by selecting some scenarios which included a set of details that needed be taken into account while designing our applications, each including various contexts. Initially, we used dimensions of context that had been previously defined [6],[14]. Nevertheless, we extended the notion of context and included two other dimensions that seemed important to our study and which focused more the users and their behavior on the real settings and not only the system. First, to assess the influence of personal, social, cultural, and cooperation issues on each context, we tried to establish the notion of user-context. Mainly, this dimension focuses details that affect the user directly or that depend on his/her activities. This allowed us to categorize details such as: (1) the users' positions while working (e.g., walking, standing, seating, etc); (2) different social/cultural events and distractions (e.g., conversation, school, work, meetings, on the bus).

Secondly, we also wanted to detect influences that were directly related to the location in which the user was. Among others we included loud and quiet locations with and without constant distractions, lightened and dark locations, etc., to understand how these affected the usage of the applications.

The aim was to provide guidance on the requirements analysis' first steps focusing our efforts to scenarios and designs that were particularly relevant for each of the case studies. Still, the amount of scenarios was not extensive. However, the selected ones contained the majority of aspects that we wanted to assess.

Afterwards, we relied on actual users to gather information and requirements on realistic scenarios. To achieve so, we provided users with adequate questionnaires, containing contextual questions and that needed to be filled-in on specific situations.

This allowed us to gather contextual data without following users to analyze their work on realistic settings.

A similar technique, called the Experience Sampling Method, has been used to evaluate ubiquitous applications and systems by Consolvo [4] with positive results. Our approach was similar but focusing on data gathering instead of evaluation. Furthermore, we used fewer resources (e.g., paper and pen instead of PDAs). These methods allowed us to detect activities that extended through several settings and acknowledge those that were specific to certain locations. Moreover, we were able to detect how the users' needs changed according to their surroundings (e.g., social and physical).

3.2 Early Stage Design and Prototyping

Since common prototyping techniques started to mislead users and hinder the overall design and evaluation process, we tried some new techniques. These resulted in a set of guidelines which can help application and UI developers to create suitable low-fidelity prototypes for mobile devices.

While prototyping our applications we created a frame using a light wooden material with about the same weight and size of a Palm Tungsten T3 (Figure 1). The frame had a small opening on the top, which allowed the cards (screens) to be switched very easily. It took about forty minutes to build. Even so, this allowed the future users to have an accurate notion on the device and interaction techniques that they would use. Furthermore, it was quickly noticeable that this procedure allowed us to solve a list of UI problems that would not have been found using just cards. For instance, buttons on the bottom of the screen had to be moved to the top for easier access and so that they would not move or disappear if the screen was extended (screen extension is a T3 feature).

Also, we detected that buttons and lists that extended to, or were placed near, the borders of the screen were difficult to read and interact with. This rigid frame and the realistic prototyping techniques also provided additional benefits. Using it, users were able test the applications while walking from one place to another, switching screens at will. This showed that the size of the buttons that were used needed to be larger when the user was walking, which was a common situation in some tasks. Moreover, users that were involved on the initial tests, with traditional techniques, clearly noticed the difference. They all preferred the frame we created since it gave them a realistic feeling regarding interaction and problems while using the devices.

The experience showed that low-fi prototypes can be effectively used for mobile devices. However, the following findings and suggestions should be taken into consideration:

- Common techniques and material do not apply directly for most mobile devices/applications.
- A careful distinction between the device prototypes and the application/UI prototype has to be made.
- The device prototype should be created using rigid materials in order to be used in real-life settings and it should have approximately the same dimensions of an actual device.

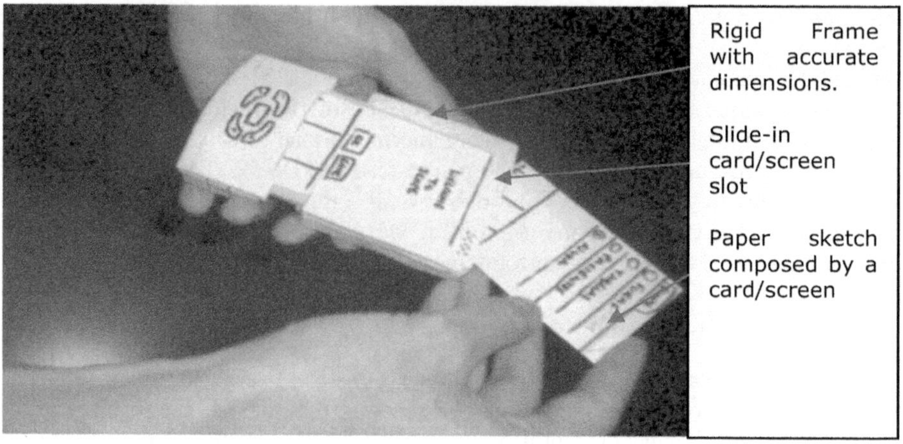

Fig. 1. Low-fi prototype of a PDA with a slot that allows users to easily exchange screens

- A slot where cards can be easily and quickly inserted and removed needs to be available. When this option is unavailable, alternatives that facilitate screen substitution should be provided.
- Sketches must be drawn with the same size of the device's screen using similar components and fonts to those available for a real device.
- The interaction type of the actual device should also be emulated (e.g. stylus/pen, joystick/small colored drawing pin or a thumb tack).
- Although these hints might imply more effort from the designer, they are compensated with more accurate results.

3.3 Mobile Evaluation

Evaluation with low-fidelity prototypes: Complementing the aforementioned procedures to create low-fidelity prototypes, the corresponding evaluation procedures were also updated in order to take advantage of these. Particularly, it was essential to emphasize the importance of context and location while evaluating mobile applications. In fact, as already concluded, these are usually tested on controlled settings and fictitious scenarios retracting from the evaluations sessions and preventing the detection of some usage errors.

During the early evaluation of the two previously mentioned applications the context and settings of use proved to be of extreme importance. With the developed frame and prototypes, users carried the sketches and simulated applications from one place to another. Besides evidencing some design problems that could occur, the ubiquitous evaluation sessions promoted participatory design, allowing users to engage actively on the process. In fact, most of the innovations appeared when testing the prototypes on real situations and scenarios.

On the sessions that occurred several findings were made. For instance, using different colored pencils to interact with the UI, allowed us to easily trace the users' behaviors. Furthermore, even the number of clicks or taps the user had done, as well as the user's accuracy on different settings (e.g. seated, walking, etc) could be verified. Besides, users engaged on the sketching process by themselves, providing input for every feature that they needed according to the situations that appeared. Some of the users even requested the frames that were used so they could use the prototypes at home; and since each user followed the color scheme that was provided, (one color for each task) their performance was also evaluated afterwards and without their presence. This detail is particular interesting for mobile applications where the user can not be followed the entire day.

On this stage some of the main conclusions were:

- Using rigid materials on the prototypes allows users to carry them, keep them in their pockets, take them home and participate on the sketches' design directly on the device, conducting evaluation on relevant locations.
- Context of use is essential for effective usability testing and evaluation should be done in several possible scenarios.
- When using adequate material, users are allowed to participate on the sketching process during contextual sessions, further promoting innovation and adequate ideas that cope with the contextual requirements.
- Tasks should be defined previously (e.g. using scripts), but the possibility of creating new features and test them on the spot should be provided.
- Color schemes can be used to trace users' activities after the evaluation sessions.
- Questionnaires can also be given to users together with the prototypes, so that they can complete them during out of the lab sessions (e.g., ESM).

4 Discussion and Future Work

So far, our work allowed us to detect several shortcomings on existing design methodologies when applied to the design of mobile applications and corresponding user interfaces. These findings, and the "on-the-fly" solutions that were used to cope with them, motivated us to develop an entire methodology with techniques that apply specifically to mobile devices and ubiquitous applications. Globally, these problems led us to believe it was necessary to introduce solid guidelines on the various stages of design focusing on the mobility factor and on the users' varying context.

Although this paper focuses the initial stages of the design process, we are currently working on new notations that tackle the constant behavior and context change during the specification and even evaluation stages. Furthermore, besides the prototyping and early evaluation techniques that were described, we are developing simple and low-cost methods for ubiquitous usability evaluation on later stages. These techniques take advantage of common equipment (e.g., laptops and webcams) and provide rich and useful insight on users' behavior without direct observation.

Also, with the experience gained and ideas that resulted from this process, we started to develop a prototyping framework for mobile devices. Overall, the tool aims at supporting prototyping and evaluation of applications with the peculiarity of creating the prototypes on actual devices. Some of its contributions are (1) the support for prototypes with various fidelities; (2) an automatic mechanism to gather contextual data; (3) the inclusion of ESM and probing techniques; (4) the support of on-the-spot participatory design and (5) the use of pre-established design guidelines.

5 Conclusions

Current design approaches, although providing extensive detail on various stages of the design process, fail to support most of the related activities and tasks when mobility of the system is paramount. Existing techniques, particularly for initial stages of development and evaluation, are rarely applied, especially taking into account the volatile settings in which the applications are likely to be used. Furthermore, these techniques aren't always applicable and, when ill-used, hinder the overall process.

In this paper, we described the problems that emerged while using a common user centered design methodology on the development of two ubiquitous systems. Throughout this process, mobility, pervasiveness and ubiquity required the adoption of new techniques and the adjustment of existing ones in order to cope with the challenges that derived from the constant change of context and multitude of settings that could be envisioned for a specific system.

Overall, these techniques and resulting findings allowed us to gather data on relevant locations and settings. Moreover, they propelled the detection of user interface problems on both low-fidelity and high-fidelity prototypes during the various evaluations sessions that we conducted. In comparison with existing techniques, which were used on initial stages of this process, these provided insight to problems which would not have been detected otherwise.

Finally, the definition of a high level conceptual framework which enclosed criteria and scenarios for data gathering and analysis also improved the design process, on its various stages, and allowed us to focus on significant details.

Acknowledgments. This work was supported by FCT through project JoinTS and LaSIGE.

References

1. Ballagas, R. et al.: iStuff Mobile: prototyping interactions for mobile phones in interactive spaces. In: PERMID 2006, Workshop at Pervasive 2006. Dublin, Ireland (2006)
2. Beyer, H., Holtzblatt, K.: Contextual Design: Customer Centered Approach to Systems Design. Academic Press, San Francisco, CA, USA (1998)
3. Brewster, S.: Overcoming the lack of screen space on mobile computers. Personal and Ubiquitous Computing 6, 188–205 (2002)
4. Consolvo, S., Walker, M.: Using the Experience Sampling Method to Evaluate Ubicomp Applications. IEEE Pervasive Computing 2(2), 24–31 (2003)
5. Davidson, J., Persons, J.B., Tompkins, M.A.: Cognitive-behavior therapy for depression (2000)
6. Dix, A., et al.: Exploiting space and location as a design framework for interactive mobile systems. ACM Transactions on Computer-Human Interaction 7, 285–321 (2000)

7. Duh, H.B.-L., Tan, G.C.B., Chen, V.H.-h.: Usability Evaluation for Mobile Device: A Comparison of Laboratory and Field Tests. Mobile HCI'06, Helsinki, Finland: ACM (2006)
8. Jones, M., Marsden, G.: Mobile Interaction Design, West Sussex, England: John Wiley & Sons Ltd. 377 (2006)
9. Kelley, J.: An iterative design methodology for user-friendly natural language office information applications. Transactions on Office Information Systems 2, 26–41 (1984)
10. Kjeldskov, J., Graham, C.: A Review of Mobile HCI Research Methods. In: Chittaro, L. (ed.) Mobile HCI 2003. LNCS, vol. 2795, pp. 317–335. Springer, Heidelberg (2003)
11. Lee, Young, E: Interface Design for Mobile Commerce. Communications of the ACM 46(12), 49–52 (December 2003)
12. Luchini, K., Quintana, C., Soloway, E.: Design guidelines for learner-centered handheld tools. In: Proceedings of the CHI2004, ACM, Vienna, Austria (2004)
13. Mayhew, D.J.: The Usability Engineering Lifecycle. Morgan Kaufmann, San Francisco, CA, USA (1999)
14. Raptis, D., Tselios, N., Avouris, N.: Context-based Design of Mobile Applications forMuseums: A Survey of Existing Practices. MobileHCI'05, Salzburg, Austria, ACM (2005)
15. Sá, M., Carriço, L., Low-Fi Prototyping for Mobile Devices. In: Proceedings of CHI'06 (extended abstracts), Montréal, Canada, pp. 694–699, ACM.
16. Sá, M., Carriço, L.: Handheld Devices for cooperative Educational Activities. In: Proceedings of SAC'06, ACM Symposium on Applied Computing, Mobile Computing and Applications Track, Dijon, France, pp. 1145–1149, ACM Press (April 2006)
17. Sá, M., Carriço, L., Antunes, P.: Ubiquitous Psychotherapy. IEEE Pervasive Computing, Special Issue on Healthcare, IEEE Press (2007)
18. Svanaes, D., Seland, G.: Putting the users center stage: role playing and low-fi prototyping enable end users to design mobile systems. In: CHI'04, SIGCHI conference on Human factors in computing systems, Vienna, Austria ACM Press (2004)
19. Weiss, S.: Handheld Usability. John Wiley and Sons, England (2002)

Playback of Rich Digital Books on Mobile Devices

Carlos Duarte, Luís Carriço, and Fernando Morgado

LaSIGE – Faculty of Sciences of the University of Lisbon
Edifício C6, Piso 3, Campo Grande
1749-016 Lisboa, Portugal
{cad,lmc,fmorgado}@di.fc.ul.pt

Abstract. This paper presents the mobile version of Rich Book Player, a Digital Talking Book player for mobile devices. The mobile version is based on a desktop version with multimodal and adaptive features. The development of the mobile version tried to retain the look and feel of the desktop version and as much as possible of the features required for an advanced Digital Talking Book player. We describe how the intrinsic characteristics of mobile devices impacted the performance and interaction aspects of the application.

Keywords: Mobile devices, Digital Talking Books, Speech output, Evaluation.

1 Introduction

This paper presents the development of a Rich Book Player for mobile devices. The mobile player is the follow-up to a PC-based version of the Rich Book Player [1]. That version, in addition to complying with the requirements elicited in the Digital Talking Book standard, supports multimedia outputs (presentation of text, audio and images) and adaptation capabilities. Those features combine to offer a personal platform for Rich Digital Books reading, aiming to promote active reading of digital books, by making available a player that departs from the features that make e-books attractive and extends them: simultaneous presentation of audio and text, powerful searching capabilities, compliance with accessibility recommendations for Digital Talking Books, and the possibilities offered by adaptive interfaces. These combine to produce a player capable of changing its presentation and behavior in accordance to usage conditions.

The mobile version of the Rich Book Player, aims to promote anytime, anywhere reading, while trying to retain as most as possible of the features present in the PC-based version. It was also a goal to have a similar look and feel in both applications, and to keep a high degree of coherence between applications, to try to make the transition from one to the other as easy as possible.

Nevertheless, the porting of the PC-based version to a mobile platform introduces great challenges on both technical and interaction design levels. The intrinsic limitations of mobile devices on performance, storage, and interaction aspects enforce restrictions result in changes to the interface, and the redesign of available tasks, which have to be dealt with in combination with the specific characteristics of interaction design for mobile devices [2].

J. Jacko (Ed.): Human-Computer Interaction, Part II, HCII 2007, LNCS 4551, pp. 270–279, 2007.

Even though mobile platform resources are limited, it was a requirement to maintain the capability to present the book in visual and audio formats simultaneously. This is the main feature distinguishing the Rich Book Player from an e-book player, and is also responsible for introducing one the concept of page, which was absent from the desktop version of the Rich Book Player.

The next section introduces in more detail the concept of Digital Talking Book and briefly describes the desktop version of the application. The following section describes in detail the several aspects of the mobile version of the application, drawing attention to the features that had to be redesigned or introduced in comparison to the desktop version. The subsequent section presents the results of a preliminary evaluation tests conducted with the mobile version of the player. The final section presents conclusions and future work.

2 Digital Talking Books

Digital Talking Books (DTBs) are the digital counterpart of talking books, which have been available for many years to print-disabled readers. Talking books have been offered on analogue media, such as audiocassettes, providing human speech recordings of a wide array of print material. The DTB goes beyond the limits imposed on analogue books, because it can include not just the audio recording of the work, but the full text content and images as well. Because the text is synchronized with the audio, a DTB offers multiple sensory inputs to readers. This can be beneficial to learning-disabled readers and to other target audiences such as blind, visually impaired, physically handicapped and otherwise print-disabled readers [3]. For these audiences the DTB offers a significantly enhanced reading experience. For other audiences, balancing DTB modes and media can be explored to overcome the cognitive limitations of human perception and attention [4].

DTB developments over the last years lead to the appearance of several different specifications, with the Daisy Consortium1 being responsible for the major work done in the area, and the publication of several standards. In 2005, the Daisy Consortium selected by the National Information Standards Organization (NISO) published the current DAISY/NISO standard [5]. The standard focuses on the files, their structure and content, needed to produce DTBs. However, specifications for playback devices are absent from the standard. An auxiliary document, the Playback Device Feature List [6], created during the standard's development, describes the main features that playback devices should possess, but it is not normative and does not present specific implementation solutions.

According to the Playback Device Feature List mentioned earlier, the NISO DTB committee recommends that three types of playback devices be developed: first, a basic DTB player, defined as a portable unit capable of playing digital audio recordings, for use mostly by less sophisticated talking book readers who wish to read primarily in a linear fashion. Second, an advanced DTB player, also portable, but designed for use by students, professionals and others who wish to access documents randomly, set bookmarks, etc. Finally, a computer based DTB player, consisting only of software and being the most complete and sophisticated of the three.

With this project we aim to develop a player standing in between the second and third types of playback devices: a player that is portable, and, at the same time, able to retain a comprehensive set of features of the most advanced type of players.

2.1 The Desktop Rich Book Player

By combining the possibilities offered by multimodal interaction and interface adaptability we have already developed the Rich Book Player, an adaptive multimodal Digital Talking Book player [1] for desktop PCs. This player can present book content visually and audibly, in an independent or synchronized fashion. The audio presentation can be based on previously recorded narrations or on synthesized speech. The player also supports user annotations, and the presentation of accompanying media, like other sounds and images. In addition to keyboard and mouse inputs, speech recognition is also supported. Due to the adaptive nature of the player, the use of each modality can be enabled or disabled during the reading experience.

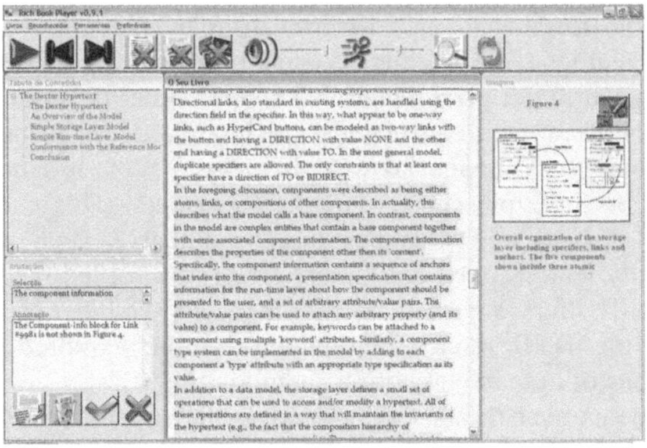

Fig. 1. The Rich Book Player's interface. The center window presents the book's main content. On the top left is the table of contents. On the bottom left is the annotations panel. On the right is the figures panel. The content being presented in the player is the article "The Dexter Hypermedia Reference Model", by Halasz and Schwartz.

Figure 1 shows the visual interface of Rich Book Player. All the main presentation components are visible in the figure: the book's main content, the table of contents, the figures panel and the annotations panel. Their arrangement (size and position) can be changed by the reader, or as a result of the player's adaptation. The other visual component, not present in figure 1, is the search panel. Highlights are used in the main content to indicate the presence of annotated text and of text referencing images. The table of contents, figures and the annotations panels can be shown or hidden. This decision can be taken by the user and by the system, with the system behavior adapting to the user behavior through its adaptation mechanisms. Whenever there is a figure or an annotation to present and the corresponding panel is hidden, the system may choose to present it immediately or may choose to warn the user to its presence. The warnings are done in both visual and audio modalities.

All the visual interaction components have a corresponding audio interaction element, with one exception. Since the speech recognizer currently used in the player does not support free speech recognition, annotations have to be entered by means of a keyboard. All the other commands can be given using either the visual elements or vocal commands.

3 The Mobile Rich Book Player

The mobile version of the Rich Book Player was developed with three main goals in mind: 1) Allow for an anytime, anywhere entertaining and pleasant reading experience; 2) Retain as most as possible of the features available in the desktop version; 3) Support a similar look and feel and foster coherence between both applications.

To achieve these goals, architectural and interaction changes had to be made. The two major limitations of the mobile platform are the limited screen size and processing power.

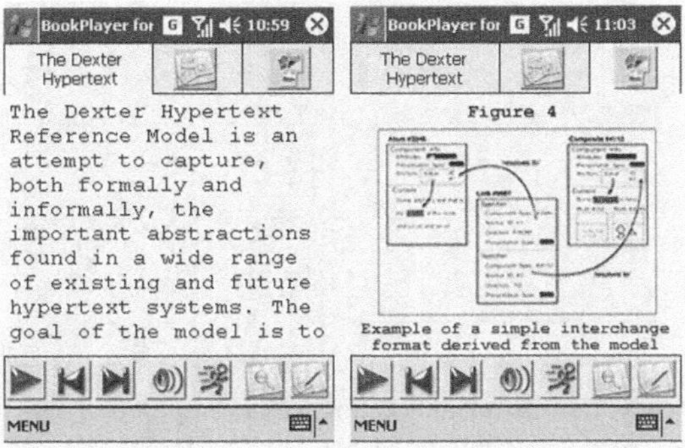

Fig. 2. The mobile Rich Book Player. Main content view on the left and images view on the right.

3.1 Main Components Display

Figure 1 displays the main components of the Rich Book Player: main content, table of contents, annotations and images windows. On the desktop version it is possible to display all the components simultaneously and users can find the arrangement that best suits them. Due to the much smaller screen size of the mobile device it is impossible to follow the same approach.

Figure 2 presents the main content view of the mobile version of the Rich Book Player. The four main areas of interaction can be seen in the figure. On the top, three tabs allow for the selection of the current view. The left tab opens the content view (figure 2 left). The tab is used to display the current chapter number, which, in this way, is quickly available to the user. The middle tab displays the annotations view. This is the view used to read previously entered annotations and write new ones. The right tab is the images view (figure 2 right). In this tab users can see the images that are part of the book, together with their title and caption. All these contents, book text, annotations and images are displayed in the biggest of the interaction areas. Bellow this area is a toolbar which displays the commands to control book playback, navigation, and other features. The final interaction area is the menu bar located at the bottom of the screen. Besides being used to present the menu, the menu bar is also used to display command buttons whenever necessary.

Of the four main components of the desktop version, three of them were already mentioned and although they cannot be displayed simultaneously as in the desktop version, they all can be displayed on their own view. The component not yet mentioned is the table of contents. This component has been downgraded to a menu entry and retained just one of its functions. In the desktop version, the table of contents was used to display the current chapter being read, by highlighting its entry, and as a navigation mechanism, allowing users to jump to a particular chapter by selecting its entry. In the mobile version, only the navigation function was retained. The current chapter feedback is now provided has the header of the main content tab.

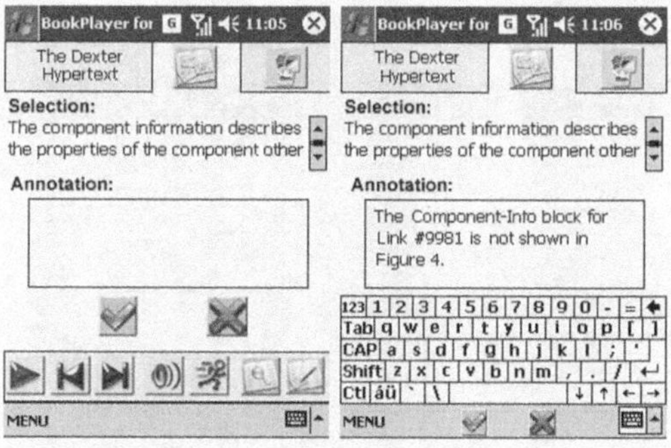

Fig. 3. Annotations view during an annotation creation process. On the right, buttons are reallocated to the menu bar when using the virtual keyboard.

3.2 Annotation Creation and Display

Creating annotations is a two stage process. The user must first select the text to be annotated and only after that enter the annotation. The text selection process is done by selecting the text in the main content view with the stylus and then pressing the create annotation button (the rightmost button in the toolbar). This takes the user to the annotations view in create annotation mode (figure 3, left).

In the annotations view, the user is still able to see the selected text while entering the annotation. When the text box is selected, the virtual keyboard is displayed, and the *confirm* and *cancel* buttons are reallocated to the menu bar (figure 3, right).

Figure 4 presents the annotations view in annotation display mode. When the user changes to the annotations tab, the annotations menu (figure 4, left) displays all the existing annotations in a tree view. By selecting one of the annotations the user is taken to the annotations detail view (figure 4, right). In this view the user can read the current annotation, edit the annotation (which means going to annotation creation mode), delete the annotation, and navigate to the text that has been annotated. The

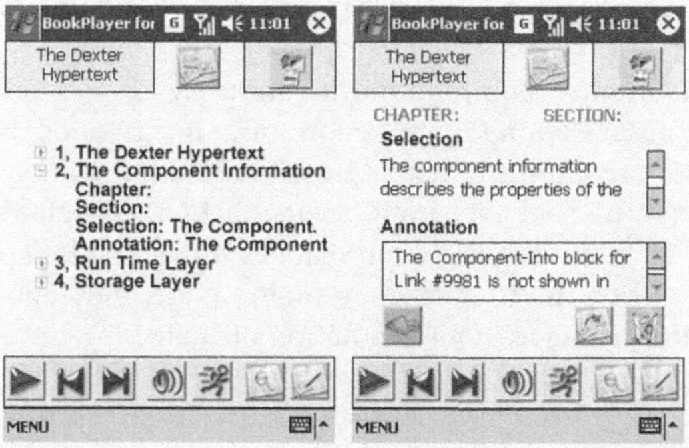

Fig. 4. Annotations view in annotation creation mode. Annotations menu on the left, and details of an annotation on the right.

navigation buttons in the toolbar, which in the content view navigate to the next and previous pages, in this view navigate to the next and previous annotations.

3.3 Speech Recordings and Synchronization

The main feature distinguishing a Digital Book Player from an e-book player is the possibility to present the book's content using speech, either recorded or synthesized. The desktop version of the Rich Book Player supports both modes of speech presentation. The mobile version currently supports the presentation of recorded speech, using the Windows Media Player for Pocket PC for playback.

Speech presentation opens up interaction possibilities that are not available with a visual only interface. With speech, users can change tabs and view images or read annotations while listening to the narration, thus avoiding the forced pause in reading if speech had not been available. Speech also allows users to access the book content without having to look at the device, allowing usage scenarios that, up until now, were available only with portable music devices, but without the limitations of those. For example, performing a search in such a device is extremely cumbersome. In comparison, with the mobile Rich Book Player, search is extremely simple due to the presence of a digital version of the book.

With the benefits of incorporating speech into the interface new challenges are uncovered. With speech comes the need for synchronization mechanisms. The application needs these to be able to know when and what images and annotations to present. We were able to port the synchronization mechanism of the desktop version to the mobile version without loosing synchronization granularity, meaning the mobile version also supports word synchronization. The synchronization mechanism only had to be adapted to the page concept, introduced in the mobile version, which was absent from the desktop version. The synchronization mechanism allows the application to turn to the next page when the narration reaches the end of the current one. It is also used to visually highlight the word currently being spoken, in order to make the narration easier to follow when the user chooses to both read and listen to the book.

3.4 Awareness Raising Mechanisms

Images and annotations require a notification system to alert the user to their presence. Users just listening to the narration need to be alerted through sound signals, while users reading the text need to be alerted through visual signals. Both mechanisms coexist also in the mobile version of the Rich Book Player. Auditory icons [7] are played when the narration reaches a page with annotations or associated images. Visually, when the user reaches such a page, the annotations or images tabs flash to indicate the presence of an annotation or image.

3.5 Pagination

One of the main presentation and interaction differences between the desktop and mobile versions of the Rich Book Player is the introduction of the page concept in the mobile version. The main motivation behind this decision was the desire to avoid the use of scroll bars to read the book. With moderate to large books even small scroll bar movements might give origin to large displacements of the text being displayed, which would quickly turn into a usability problem. Loading a text control with the books full content could also raise performance issues.

To support changing font and font sizes while reading the book, the pagination runs in real-time. Whenever a book is loaded, or the font settings are altered, a new pagination is started. This implies storing the current reading point (when speech playback is active) or current page (when speech playback is inactive), repaginate, and present the page of the current reading point. Several choices are possible for the pagination starting point. Starting the pagination algorithm from the book's first page would mean the user would have to wait a variable period for the display to refresh. This period would vary depending on the current reading point. Reading points near the end of book would mean substantially longer waiting periods, due to the lack of processing power of most mobile devices. Starting the pagination from the current reading point, would mean pages with different contents would result from runs of the algorithm with different starting points, even with the same font settings. This might confuse users used to pages holding the same contents on print books. Both approaches raise usability issues. To overcome these issues we employed the notion of forced page break. A forced page break is a location in the text that is guaranteed to be at the start of page. Employing this notion, the pagination algorithm always produces the same results for the same font settings. The pagination starts from the first forced page break prior to the current reading point and runs to the first forced page break after the current reading point. Since we can control the frequency of forced page breaks, we can guarantee an upper limit on the time that is necessary to paginate until the current reading point, thus assuring the user will not have to wait unacceptably long periods and the pages stay coherent with every run. After this stretch of the book is paginated, the algorithm can run in the background, paginating the rest of the book. Possible choices of forced page breaks, which will be adequate in most situations, are all the entries in the table of contents. This has the added benefit of page breaks being associated with structural book elements, which is something a reader would expect, or, at least, not find confusing.

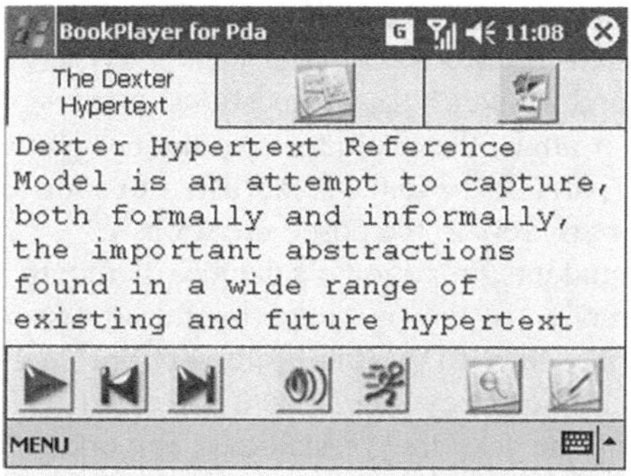

Fig. 5. The Rich Book Player layout is landscape mode

3.6 Adapting the Layout to the Device

Nowadays, mobile devices exist with a multitude of screen resolutions, and even with the possibility of altering the screen orientation. The Rich Book Player visual layout is able to adapt itself to changes in orientation and to different screen resolutions. Figure 5 presents the layout of the Rich Book Player in landscape mode.

Besides changing the layout of the different interface components, a changing in screen orientation also requires a new run of the pagination algorithm, as described in the previous section.

3.7 Performance and Storage

The book's presentation involves parallel processing of three threads: the main interaction thread with audio playback, the synchronization thread and the pagination thread. This might impose some performance constraints on the reproduction platform. We have tested the Rich Book Player on two devices: an HP iPAQ h5500 with a 400 MHz XScale processor, 40 MB ROM and 128 MB RAM running Microsoft's Pocket PC 2003, and a QTEK 9100, with a 200 MHz TI OMAP 850 processor, 128 MB ROM and 64 MB RAM running Microsoft's Windows Mobile 5. We have successfully been able to use the application on both devices to read a book of circa 25000 words (a 279 Kb text file), corresponding to a narration with 2 hours and 15 minutes, recorded in a 158 Mb mp3 file.

Due to the size of the audio files, books will have to be made available in storage cards, since it cannot be expected that internal storage of the mobile devices be able to hold such large amounts of data. The Digital Talking Books can be shared between the two platforms, as well as annotations that have been made in one platform can also be read in the other.

4 Preliminary Evaluation

We have conducted some preliminary evaluation on the mobile player. That assessment was carried out in the sequence of a deeper evaluation of the PC version, reported elsewhere [8]. In that experiment, twenty four students used the Rich Book

Player in a laptop, with a mouse, headphones, microphone and a fixed large monitor. They had to read/listen-to an article ("The Dexter Hypermedia Reference Model"), prepare a summary and answer a set of questions, as part of a Hypermedia Systems' course evaluation. To attain these objectives, students browsed through the article, highlighting specific parts of the text, reread/listen-to some of those parts, took notes, and later searched for answers to the posed questions.

Seven of those students, randomly selected, a month later were requested to perform a reduced version of the first experiment, now using the Mobile Rich Book Player. They were handed a PDA (the aforementioned HP iPAQ h5500), with the application and the article. They were asked to reread it, listen to some parts, take notes on the parts of the text they considered important, and look at the images. During the half-hour of the trial, they were requested to stand up for about 20 minutes. During 10 minutes they could use the stylus and for the other 10 minutes they could use only one hand to hold and operate the device. A researcher accompanied the process, observing, annotation behaviors, and posing opportune pertinent questions (e.g. "what are you doing?", "do you remember what you have done on the PC version?") as part of a contextual inquiring approach. This trial was no longer a part of the course evaluation. At the end the students were encouraged to criticize the mobile application.

Overall, we had a very positive feedback and no major complaints were made relatively to the PC version. Nevertheless, some issues have been identified that require some changes to the interface of the mobile version. The first, concerns the visual appearance of the tabs. The symbols used in the annotations and images tabs resemble a button, thus initially misleading users. Other issue that has been identified becomes relevant in the usage scenario where the user had only one hand available. When operating the device with just one hand, and using the fingers instead of the stylus, reaching for the tabs covers the display, thus causing a slight annoyance. Another related issue concerns the placement of the buttons in the toolbar. The most frequently used buttons, from our experience with the application, are the page forward and backward buttons (when the user reads the book without listening to the narration). These buttons are placed on the left side of the toolbar, which makes one-hand operation more awkward for right-handed people, particularly in landscape mode. A version of the toolbar with the navigation and playback control buttons on the right side of the toolbar will solve this issue.

5 Conclusions

This paper presented the mobile version of Rich Book Player, an application for reading Digital Talking Books in mobile devices. With the Rich Book Player it is possible to read, listen to a book, or have both modalities working in a synchronized fashion.

The introduction of books with speech narration in mobile devices represents a step forward from the traditional text based e-book reader. Besides the narration, the Rich Book Player also supports the presentation of images within the book, and the creation and displaying of annotations. All the different contents are synchronized between themselves, allowing the player to alert the reader to the presence of an annotation or image. This is achieved in both reading scenarios, with or without narration.

The work on the mobile Rich Book Player will carry on with a detailed usability evaluation of the application. More books, with different focus, will be used for evaluation purposes. More devices and more usage scenarios will allow us to have a more precise idea of the performance and the usability problems of the player.

References

1. Duarte, C., Carriço, L.: A conceptual framework for developing adaptive multimodal applications. In: Proceedings of the 11th International Conference on Intelligent User Interfaces, Sydney, Australia, pp. 132–139. ACM Press, New York (2006)
2. Jones, M., Marsden, G.: Mobile Interaction Design. John Wiley and Sons Ltd (2005)
3. Moreno, R., Mayer, R.E.: A coherence effect in multimedia learning: The case for minimizing irrelevant sounds in the design of multimedia instructional messages. Journal of Educational Psychology 97, 117–125 (2000)
4. Gazzaniga, M.S., Ivry, R.B., Mangun, G.R.: Cognitive Neuroscience - the Biology of the Mind. W. W. Norton & Company (1998)
5. National Information Standards Organization: Specifications for the Digital Talking Book. NISO Press (2005)
6. National Information Standards Organization: Playback Device Guidelines (1999) Available at http://www.loc.gov/nls/niso/features.htm
7. Gaver, W.W.: Auditory Icons: Using Sound in Computer Interfaces. Human-Computer Interaction. 2(2), pp. 167–177. Lawrence Erlbaum Associates, Inc. Mahwah, NJ (1986)
8. Duarte, C., Carriço, L., Guimarães, N.: Evaluating Usability Improvements by Combining Visual and Audio Modalities in the Interface. In: Proceedings of the 12th International Conference on Human-Computer Interaction, Beijing, P.R. China, Springer-Verlag, Berlin Heidelberg, New York (2007)

Using Mobile Devices to Improve the Interactive Experience of Visitors in Art Museums*

J. A. Gallud, M. Lozano, R. Tesoriero, and V. M. R. Penichet

LoUISE Research Group – Computer Science Research Institute (I3A),
Castilla-La Mancha University, 02071 Albacete, Spain
[jgallud,mlozano,ricardo,vpenichet]@dsi.uclm.es

Abstract. Many people use a PDA or a smart phone as a daily working tool. These devices allow us to communicate; to organize our life and so on. In this sense, the key question underlying this paper is if this new technology could be used to enrich our experience when we visit museums or other cultural spaces. Museums and art galleries are provided with some electronic guides in order to do more pleasant the visit to the exhibition. It is interesting to know how to use these new devices as a medium to guide and improve the visitors' experience. In this paper we describe a real system deployed in an emblematic museum in Spain, called Cutlery Museum of Albacete. Our approach uses a PDA –offered to visitors– that work jointly with a wireless network to show additional information about old knives, jack-knives and scissors which are showed physically in the museum. The system supports four languages and incorporates special functions for disabled people. The users' satisfaction results collected during the last 18 months demonstrate the validity of our proposal.

1 Using Mobile Devices in Cultural Environments

The application of new technologies in museums is modifying the concept of the traditional cultural environment visit. Users can now experience a modern and enriched way to visit museums and similar cultural spaces, thanks to the use of modern devices and sophisticated software.

This paper describes our proposal based on the use of mobile devices like PDAs to improve the users' experience in art and cultural spaces. Our previous experience in this field has been successfully proved [6, 11].

There are several experiences that work in real cases with success. Technology is used to provide visitors with the ability of interacting with the museum [7]. In a typical scenario, the visitor can use his or her sense of touch (hearing and sight) to learn about the subject of the exhibition. Multimedia devices, 3D sound, DVD and other systems are employed to make people enjoy in the museum. Emerging technologies as virtual reality or augmented reality are also being used in these scenarios [1].

In this project we focused on the use of pocket computers (PDA) as a powerful tool to help visitors in their visit to the museum. The challenge was to find out if our

* This work was partially supported by the Spanish CICYT project TIN2004-08000-C03-01 and the grant PCC05-005-1 from Junta de Comunidades de Castilla-La Mancha.

J. Jacko (Ed.): Human-Computer Interaction, Part II, HCII 2007, LNCS 4551, pp. 280–287, 2007.

system is a new barrier or a helpful tool in the museum, if the PDA technology would be useful to artists and their work of arts or if there are reasons for museums to avoid adopting this new advanced technology. They are not questions easy to answer reading former works, so we decided to define our conclusions building a complete system.

There are several former projects that have tried to use wearable computers in museums. One of the most important references in this subject is the work developed by Ciavarella and Paternò [2, 3] in the Marble Museum of Carrara (Italy). This project is currently working and offers to users a PDA with all the information preloaded by means of memory cards. The PDA is able to detect when the user is entering in a room thanks to infrared devices located at the beginning of each room.

Other Museums have already developed projects based on handled devices [10], as the Field Museum in Chicago, Herbert F. Johnson Museum of Art of New York or Kew Gardens outside London [5, 8]. Most of them use handled devices as a useful tool in the inventory process (see references). These projects are all prototypes and normal visitors do not use any PDA.

The exhibitions are ideal scenarios for applying augmented reality or mixed reality. There are many HCI groups working in this area, as the work of Ciolfi [4] where an interactive museum is designed using PDA; or the work performed by Bernt Schiele [9] where a wearable computer is developed as an alternative to the traditional guides.

The paper is organized in the following sections: section 2 describes the system architecture. In section 3 we describe how the art piece is managed in the system. Section 4 shows some of the results collected with the first implementation of the system. Finally the conclusions and future work are presented in section 5.

2 Description of Our Mobile System Approach for Art Museums

The system we are working in has two different approaches or views. The first one was deployed three years ago and is our test bank because is running in a real museum with real users, the Cutlery Museum of Albacete (Spain).

The first system is described in [6] and was organized in these subsystems:

- A Web application
- A mobile software based on PDA
- A system to manage the database of the Museum and to organize the exhibits

The second approach is being developed in our research laboratory and some new features have been added which are described here.

When new functionality is going to be incorporated in the system, problems like components reuse or system scalability arise. If there are no components reused or if the system can not be easily scaled, one can conclude that the initial system has not been well designed. This is the situation we faced when we decided to incorporate new functionality and it is easy to understand, taking into account the rigorous deadlines.

On the other hand, at the time that the system was released and deployed in the Cutlery Museum, we began to receive users' satisfaction evaluation and a number of improve suggestions.

The functionality desired for the system was almost the same with the addition of the automatic positioning of PDAs and the redefinition of the user interface in order to provide a richer experience. Additionally, we had to integrate our solution with the previous software running in the museum.

Only our experience in mobile software for museums was useful in the design of the new system but we could not reuse any software component..

In summary, we decided to redesign the system in order to support PDA automatic positioning, automatic database synchronization and, the most important fact, redefine the user interface.

We are not going to describe the research aspects devoted to improve the user interface and the experience of visitors (with PDA) in the Museum. We focus on the functional requirements affecting the architecture. So we will focus on the first two main requirements that have been incorporated in the definition of the system: the positioning subsystem and the automatic database synchronization subsystem. Other important requirements we empathized were the following: modularity, technology independence and so on.

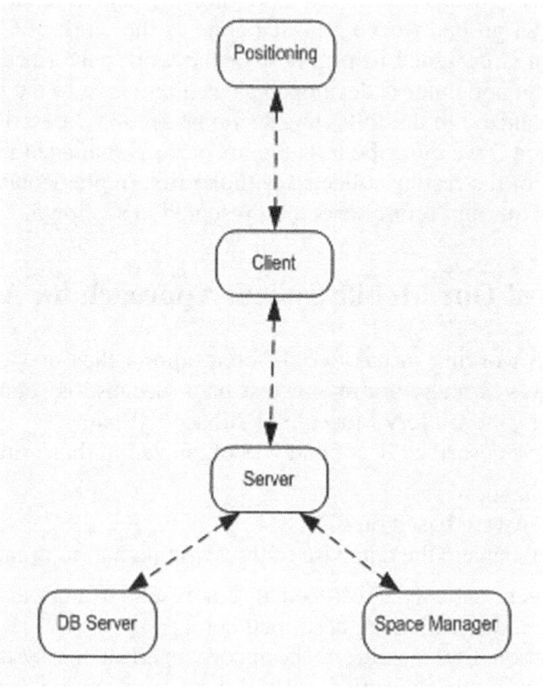

Fig. 1. Main subsystems

The positioning subsystem is responsible of giving the PDA a specific location according to a coordinate system.

The automatic database synchronization subsystem is responsible of maintaining the coherence between both the internal and external databases. As internal database we mean the database eventually installed in the museum. The external database refers to our specific database for supporting the positioning subsystem and the other requirements.

Figure 2 shows a more detailed view of the components of the new system.

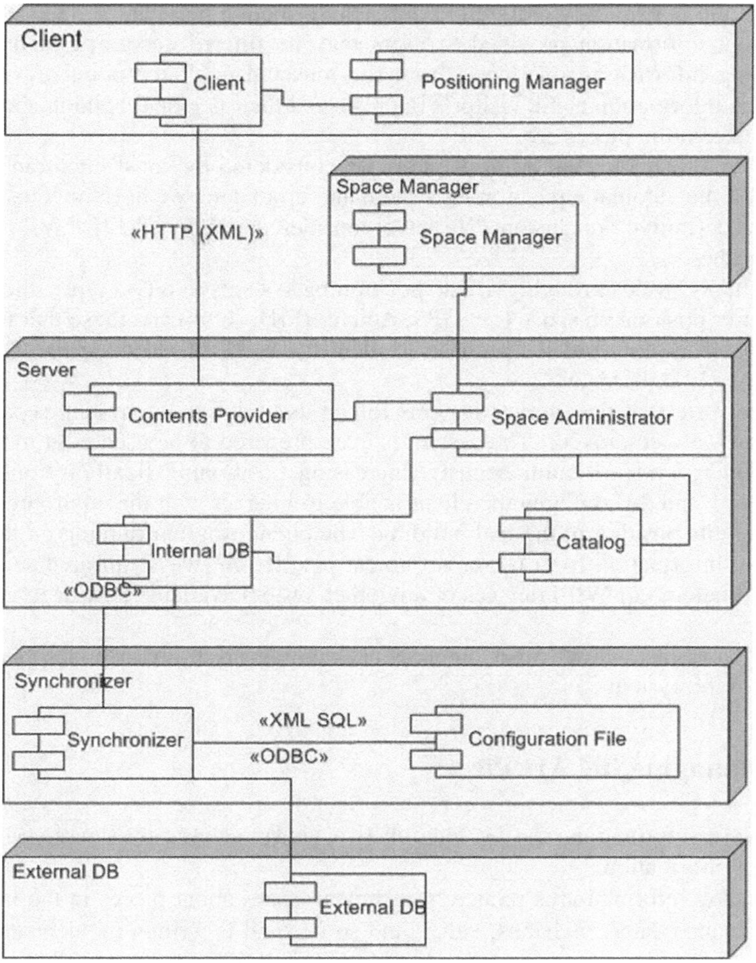

Fig. 2. System's components diagram

In the detailed view depicted in Figure 2 we can see the main components of the system and the specific nodes hosting each component.

Both systems share a common functionality described as follows. A user with a PDA wants to visit a museum; so at the entrance lobby a specific software for museums is provided to the user. In the first approach the user had to locate his or her position in the virtual map showed in the PDA. The new version of the system introduces an improvement by which the PDA is able to detect automatically the position of the user in the museum.

The positioning system allows the system to provide users with an unknown experience when they are visiting an art museum offering location aware information.

From the user point of view, the visitor experiencing this new way of interaction have the following advantages against traditional interaction methods: no specific interaction is explicitly required to access information that can be deduced from user position; information provided to users may be filtered according to user interests avoiding information overload. From the museum exhibitor point of view, it may provide information about visitor's interests and their personal opinion about what the most interesting pieces are.

From a technological point of view, we considered the most important techniques to solve the automatic positioning system and up to date, we have not closed the topic with a definitive conclusion. We have considered infrared, RFID, WIFI and mixed approaches.

Actually, we can roughly divide positioning systems into two types, those that provide user position on space (i.e. GPS, Active RFID, so on) and those that may be used to provide a more precise position to identify an object on the space (i.e. Barcode, passive RFID, IrDA, etc.).

The variety of positioning systems forced us to define the system separately from the hardware employed. The system is even prepared to be used with more than one positioning system simultaneously, increasing positioning flexibility and precision. Figures 1 and 2 show how the client is able to interact with the environment in order to know its position in the real building. The client program running on the PDA can receive information from the environment in different ways: infrared sensors, RFID tags, Bluetooth or WIFI devices or any other system available now or to appear in the future.

Figure 2 also shows other components running on different nodes (a deployment view of the system).

3 Managing the Art Piece

Art piece information may be seen on two views: catalog information and environmental information.

Catalog information is related to technical issues about pieces in the museum (i.e. maintenance dates, revisions, value, and so on) and is written on technical language. On the other hand, environmental information is intended for visitors (i.e. related audios and videos, contextual information, etc) and colloquial language is used in order to improve users' experience and understandability.

Although environmental information is provided to visitors in general; technical information may be extremely useful for users that are related or simply require more information about pieces on the museum.

So, the person responsible for managing the art exhibition uses the Space Manager application to define spaces which will host art objects. The concrete art object is managed by means of a legacy software. This software is supposed to be in the museum before introducing the mobile solution based on PDA.

The existence of legacy software introduces the need of a Synchronizer that will maintain the coherence between the External database and the internal one.

The Catalog component is responsible of managing technical information of an art object with the information provided by the legacy database.

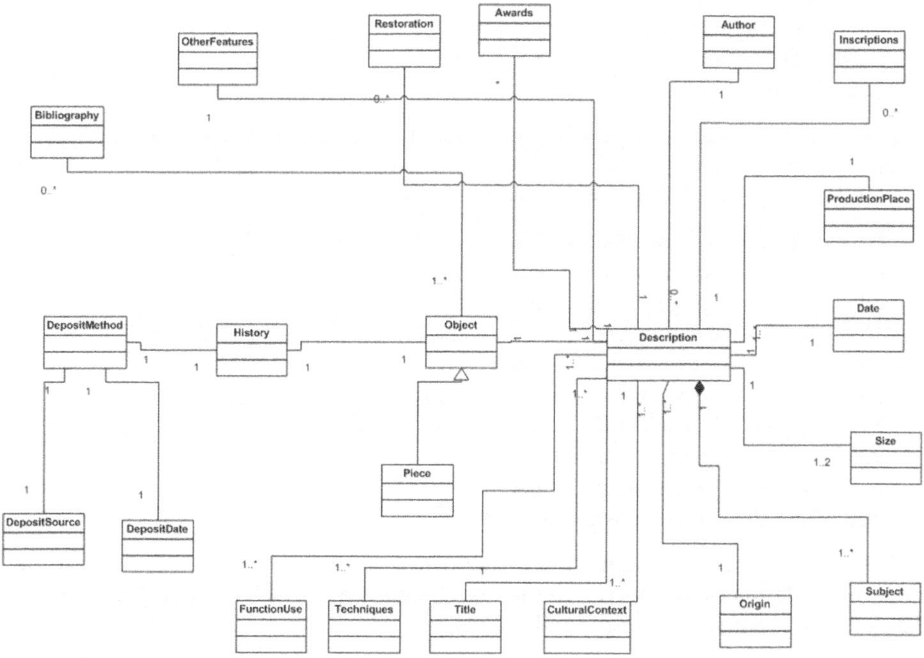

Fig. 3. Class diagram

The Contents Provider provides the Client with the information to be showed and all the information needed to maintain the state.

Figure 3 shows the class diagram of the entities we manage in our system. As we can see, the key entity is the piece, the art piece. This model has been defined according to national and international recommendations [12] [13] allowing us to easily deploy the system in different museums.

4 Summarizing Results

A first version of the system has been running in the Cutlery Museum of Albacete, Spain since September 2004 and during these 3 years, the museum has received over 15.000 visitors and over 3.000 visitors have used the system. An upgraded version of the system will be deployed in summer 2007.

As we describe in detail in [11], the users' satisfaction tests proved the validity of the first approach of our system. A summary of these results is described here. This section does not try to show all the results or their analysis but an overall view of the users' opinion.

We defined a typical usability opinion poll in which the different aspects evaluated were the following:

- Personal opinion about the User Interface
- Aesthetic of the User Interface

- Organization of the interface
- Interpretation: easiness of understanding
- Acquisition: easiness of learning
- Easiness to perform a particular task

One of the most relevant results of the usability test was obtained from an expert group on new technologies, though we did several experiments described in [11]. In this group we collected 75 questionnaires with the next results:

- 60% think the user interface was nice
- 64% like the look and feel of the user interface
- 70% like the graphics used in the system
- 55% think the behavior was easy to understand
- 85% think was nice to use the system
- 85% think was very easy to select a language
- 81% found easy to select a room
- 92% found easy to select a show
- 82% think was easy to select a piece
- 80% think the system was usable

This is the informal presentation of the data collected from the expert group that allow us to demonstrate the validity of the system . A formal and detailed report on the usability evaluation can be found in [11].

5 Conclusions and Future Work

In this paper we describe advanced mobile software based on PDA applied to art museums.

This research is based on the idea that a PDA or pocket computer can be used in art museums to improve the users' experience. We have applied the concepts to a particular museum, the Cutlery Museum of Albacete (Spain).

The evolution of a real system has been described from the initial requirements to the current ones. The most important requirement that will be introduced in a new version of the system is a module for automatic positioning of PDA in the real building by using the available technology (infrared, RFID, etc).

The first version of the system was deployed in the Cutlery Museum of Albacete two years ago and has been visited by over 15.000 people.

The new system is being developed in the LoUISE research group and will be deployed in spring 2007.

References

1. Baber, C., Bristow, H., Cheng, S.-L., Hedley, A., Kuriyama, Y., Lien, M., Pollard, J., Sorrell, P.: Augmenting Museums and Art Galleries (2001) URL http://citeseer.ist.psu.edu/543180.html
2. Ciavarella, C., Paternò, F.: Design Criteria for Location-aware, Indoor, PDA Applications. In: Chittaro, L. (ed.) Mobile HCI 2003. LNCS, vol. 2795, pp. 131–144. Springer, Heidelberg (2003)

3. Ciavarella, C., Paternò, F.: The design of a handheld, location-aware guide for indoor environments. Personal and Ubiquitous Computing. 8(2), pp. 82–91. Springer, Heidelberg (2004)
4. Ciolfi, L., Bannon, L.J.: Designing Interactive Museum Exhibits: Enhancing visitor4curiosity through augmented artifacts. In: Eleventh European Conference on Cognitive Ergonomics (2002)
5. Field Museum in Chicago http://www.fmnh.org/
6. Gallud, J.A., Penichet, V.M.R.: Argandoña, L. González, P., García J.A, Digital Museums: a multi-technological approach. HCI-International Conference 2005. Lawrence Erlbaum Associates (ISBN 0-8058-5807-5) Las Vegas (USA) (2005)
7. Grinter, R.E., Aoki, P.M., Hurst, A., Szymanski, Thorton J.D., Woodruff, A.: Revisiting the Visit: Understanding How Technology Can Shape the Museum Visit. In: Proceedings of CSCW'02, ACM, pp. 16–20. ACM Press, New York (2002)
8. Johnson, H.F.: Museum of Art of New York http://www.museum.cornell.edu/ Kew Gardens outside London http://www.museum.cornell.edu/
9. Schiele, B., Jebara, T., Oliver, N.: Sensory Augmented Computing: Wearing the Museum's Guide. IEEE Micro 21(3) (2001)
10. Steele, B.: Human-Computer Interaction Group tests systems for electronic guides, Computer Science, Cornell University 2002 November 2005. ISBN-10: 0-596-00803-1. ISBN-13: 9780596008031. URL http://designinginterfaces.com/
11. Tesoriero, R., Lozano, M.D., Gallud, J.A., Penichet, V.M.R.: Evaluating the users' experience of PDA-based software applied in art museums. WebIST (2007)
12. ICOM-CIDOC, International Guidelines for Museum Object Information: The CIDOC Information Categories. International Committee for Documentation of the International Council of Museums. ISBN 92-9012-124-6 (1995)URL http://www.willpowerinfo.myby.co.uk/cidoc/guide/guide.htm
13. Carretero, A., Chinchilla, M.: Barraca de Ramos, P., Adellac M. D., Pesquera I., Alquézar E.: Normalización documental de museos: Elementos par auna aplicación informática de gestión museográfica. Ministerio de educación y cultura. Dirección general de Bellas Artes y Bienes Culturales. Spain (1996) ISBN: 84-818-148-3

Model-Based Approaches to Quantifying the Usability of Mobile Phones

Dong-Han Ham[1], Jeongyun Heo[2], Peter Fossick[3], William Wong[1], Sanghyun Park[2], Chiwon Song[2], and Mike Bradley[3]

[1] School of Computing Science, Middlesex University
The Burroughs London NW4 4BT, UK
{d.ham,w.wong}@mdx.ac.uk
[2] MC R&D Centre, LG Electronics
Kasan-Dong Kumchun-Gu Seoul, Korea
{jy_heo,sanghyun,chiwon}@lge.com
[3] Product Design Engineering Department, Middlesex University
Bramley Road N14 4YZ, UK
{p.fossick,m.d.bradley}@mdx.ac.uk

Abstract. Several factors make it difficult to quantify the usability of mobile phones. Nevertheless, a quantified value of the usability could be used for several purposes, such as design innovation and benchmarking. This paper proposes three approaches (task centred, usability indicator-based, and design area-based quantification) to quantifying the usability of mobile phones on the basis of a hierarchical model of usability factors. Each of them provides process and rules for calculating the usability score of a mobile phone by applying weighting value assignment methods. Through two case studies, we could obtain empirical data to be used for determining the weighting value for quantification and confirm the usefulness of the proposed approaches.

1 Introduction

It is well known that usability is a critical attribute affecting the quality-in-use of mobile phones [4]. To assess and manage the usability in a more objective way, there has been an increasing need for usability quantification [3]. However, it is not easy to assign certain score to the usability. The difficulty is due to the fact that usability is a kind of emergent property and could be susceptible to users' subjective preferences [2]. Nonetheless, a quantified value of the usability could be used for several purposes, such as design improvement and benchmarking.

Very few attempts have been made at developing a method for quantifying usability. Rauterberg [6, 7] developed a concept to describe user interfaces on a granularity level and distinguish different types of interaction points. Based on this concept, he developed four measures (functional feedback, interactive directness, application flexibility, and dialog flexibility) and their relevant formula to quantify user interface characteristics. Sauro and Kindlund [10] proposed a method to simplify all the ANSI and ISO aspects of usability into a single, standardized and summated usability metric (SUM). Rubinoff [8] developed a methodology to quantify the user experience in websites. This methodology quantifies the user experience by measuring four

J. Jacko (Ed.): Human-Computer Interaction, Part II, HCII 2007, LNCS 4551, pp. 288–297, 2007.

interdependent, intangible elements: branding, usability, functionality, and content. They are measured with the use of a series of statements or parameters, each of which has a scale of 1 to 20. Lohse and Spiller [5] used a regression model to predict store traffic and dollar sales as a function of cyberstore interface design features, such as image sizes and store navigation features. Although the main purpose of several usability questionnaires like SUMI [11] is not to produce single usability score, many usability engineers have used them as a tool for quantification. Keinonen [3] claimed that quantification of usability should reflect users' preference on specific tasks or interface features with the use of weighting value assignment methods.

While most of earlier studies on quantification have addressed interactive software or websites, little attention has been given to information appliances like mobile phones. The purpose of this study is to propose model-based three approaches to quantifying the usability of mobile phones. Each of them is based on a hierarchical model of usability factors we developed [1]. Additionally, each approach uses various weighting-value assignment methods to reflect the relative importance of variables to be used for quantification. Firstly, we describe the hierarchical model and concepts for quantifying usability. Then each approach is explained in detail in terms of its quantification process and required information, and primary usages. Lastly, two case studies are explained, which were conducted for collecting data to be used for the weighting values and examining the usefulness of the approaches.

2 Hierarchical Model of Usability Factors

Quantification of usability proposed in this study is based on a multi-level hierarchical model that we developed to identify and organize various usability factors in terms of goal-means relations [1]. This model consists of five abstraction levels, each of which represents different aspect of mobile phone usability (Fig. 1).

Usability (Quality in Use)	Emergent feature to be characterized with several context factors
Usability Indicator	Hypothetical, abstract conceptual constructs that are not directly measured
Usability Criteria	Sub indicator that can be directly measured through at least one specific usability property
Usability Property (Metric)	Metrics that can be obtained by observing usability data or using a formula that defines a function
Usability Data	Usability Variable that can be obtained from mobile phones, user manual, user tasks, and so on

Fig. 1. Five abstraction levels of hierarchy model

It is not easy to have the accurate, absolute usability score of mobile phones. However, it can be estimated by combining some usability indicator factors, which measure how human users perceive the usability. Five principal factors we assume include effectiveness, efficiency, learnability, satisfaction, and customization. Usability factors at the level of usability property measure observable features of a particular mobile phone. Usability data below this level provide actual value for usability property. One example of usability property factor is colour and its relevant usability data can be blue, red, and so on. Usability factors related to usability criteria evaluate how well usability property is designed to enhance the usability mobile phone in consideration of task scenarios. Usability criteria link usability property to usability indicator; they provide information to assess how actual, observed features of a mobile phone contribute to usability indicator. For example, we can measure 'minimalism', which can highly influence on 'effectiveness' and 'efficiency', by considering softkey mapping, menu contents, and scrolling method at the level of usability property.

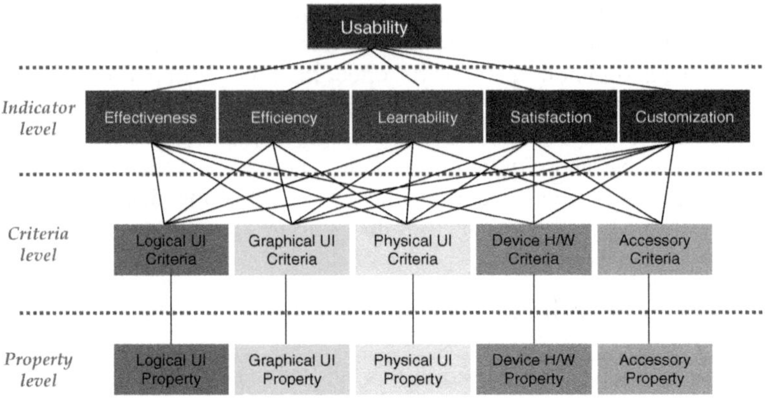

Fig. 2. Hierarchical model of usability factors

Fig. 2 shows hierarchical model consisting of four abstraction levels, excluding usability data level. Main characteristics of this model are many-to-many goal means relations between adjacent levels and distinction of design areas. In general, a mobile phone has six design areas: LUI (Logical User Interface), PUI (Physical User Interface), GUI (Graphical User Interface), device hardware, accessory, and service [1, 4]. LUI is interface concerned with information contents and structure for carrying out tasks. GUI means interface devoted to graphical or visual items presenting information needed for users to conduct a task. PUI is tangible interface supporting physical operation needed for executing a task. The hierarchical model takes account of five areas, without considering service. It can be said that the model seeks to elucidate how the invisible relations between different user interface types or design areas affect the usability of mobile phones.

3 Three Approaches to Quantification

Fig. 3 depicts three quantification approaches and their relationships. It can be regarded that this figure shows a context of use of a mobile phone. To consider the context of use, we can think of two aspects of users' model (cognition or emotion and physiology) and environment surrounding them. User's tasks lie between users' world and mobile phones. Seven arrows reflect meaningful, distinctive paths of user-mobile phone interaction. Although there are other paths influencing the context of use, our stance is that these seven paths are most significant to measure the usability. These paths are related to two aspects of user model and three design areas of mobile phones. For example, a path formed by users' cognition and LUI represent the interaction between logical aspects of user interface like menu contents and structure and users' cognitive aspects like knowledge structure.

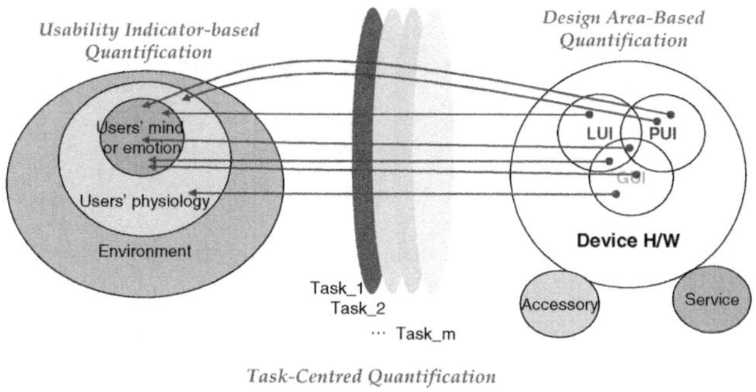

Fig. 3. Three approaches to quantification

3.1 Task-Centred Quantification

Fig. 4 shows the process of task-centred quantification. To use this approach, a set of tasks to be evaluated ($TS = \{T_1, T_2, \ldots T_m\}$) are firstly chosen. Then the usability score of mobile phone is calculated as follows, where $W(T_i)$ is the weighting value of T_i and $U(T_i)$ is the usability score of T_i.

$$Usability\ Score = \sum_{i=1}^{m} (W(T_i) \times U(T_i)) \ . \tag{1}$$

The weighting value of each task can be determined by several methods. In this study we use one of the following seven methods: no weighting value, expert opinion, rank sum weight or rank reciprocal weight based on task usage frequency or task importance, KANO model, entropy model using the usability score of each task, geometric mean of pair-wise comparison result in AHP (Analytic Hierarchy Process), and statistical data from usability problems collected. The usability of each task can be obtained as follows, where $W_L(T_i)$ is the weighting value of LUI when conducting task T_i, $U_L(T_i)$ is the usability score of LUI when conducting task T_i, $W_G(T_i)$ is the weighting value of GUI when conducting task T_i, $U_G(T_i)$ is the usability score of GUI when conducting task T_i, $W_P(T_i)$ is the weighting value of PUI when conducting task T_i, and $U_P(T_i)$ is the usability score of PUI when conducting task T_i

$$U(T_i) = W_L(T_i) \times U_L(T_i) + W_G(T_i) \times U_G(T_i) + W_P(T_i) \times U_P(T_i) \ . \tag{2}$$

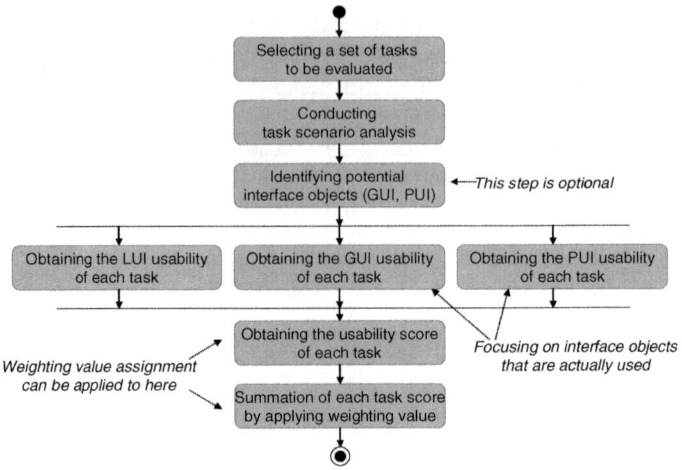

Fig. 4. Process of task-centred quantification

The weighting value of each interface area can be obtained by using the same methods as those used when calculating the weighting value of each task. The usability of each interface area uses the value of usability criteria, which are in the hierarchical model described in section 2, as follows, where $CL_j(T_i)$ is the rated value of the jth criterion related to LUI when conducting task T_i, $CG_j(T_i)$ is the rated value of the jth criterion related to GUI when conducting task T_i, and $CP_j(T_i)$ is the rated value of the jth criterion related to PUI when conducting task T_i.

$$U_L(T_i)=\sum_{j=1}^{n_L} CL_j(T_i),\ U_G(T_i)=\sum_{k=1}^{n_G} CG_k(T_i),\ U_P(T_i)=\sum_{l=1}^{n_P} CP_l(T_i)\ . \tag{3}$$

Fig. 5 shows the usability factors of each design area at the level of usability criteria. In order to make it easier to rate the value of usability criteria factors, we developed a checklist on the basis of the hierarchical model. This checklist associates

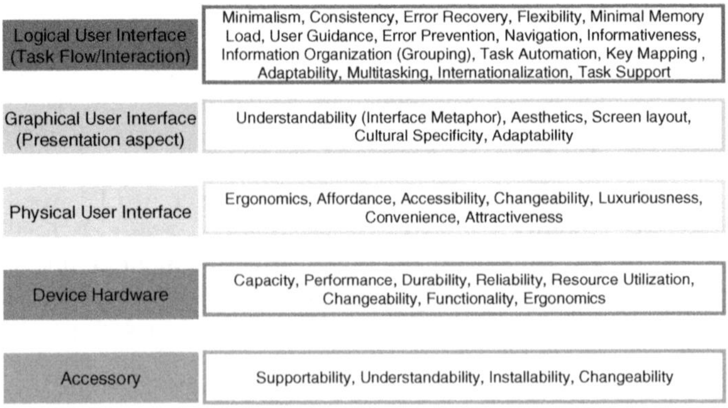

Fig. 5. Usability factors at the level of usability criteria

Criteria Level	Property Level	Metric						Score
Logical User Interface								
1 **Achievement**	Operation Sequence was successful (i.e Call was made)	Yes/No	Yes 2				No -1	
2 **Flow**	Engagement: Time to make call	Time (Secs)	1 ~ 10 4	11 ~20 3	21 ~30 2	31 ~ 40 1	> 40 0	
3 **Error rate**	Input method/ Dedicated key Mapping / Operation Sequence	n (Actions)	0 0	1 ~3 -1	4 ~ 6 -3	7 ~9 -5	>9 -7	
4 **Consistency**	Actions was repeated successfully	Yes/No	Yes 2				No -1	
5 **Navigation**	Menu Sturcture		Excellent 4	V.Good 3	Good 2	Average 1	Poor -1	
6 **Affordance**	Mapping of Soft key with interface		Excellent 4	V.Good 3	Good 2	Average 1	Poor -1	
7 **Multi-tasking (time)** **Multi-tasking (Bench marked)**	User is asked to perform while performing an additional task (e.g. Undertaking a puzzle)	Time (Secs)	1 ~ 10 4	11 ~20 3	21 ~30 2	31 ~ 40 1	> 40 0	
8 **Minimalisation (no. of actions)** description	*Script:*	n (Actions)	1 ~ 3 0	4 ~ 6 -1	7 ~ 9 -3	10 ~12 -5	> 12 -9	
			Note: the inputting of a number does not count.					
9 **Informativess**	Feedback		Excellent 4	V.Good 3	Good 2	Average 1	Poor -1	
10 **Information Grouping**			Excellent 4	V.Good 3	Good 2	Average 1	Poor -1	
11 **Quality of Annotation**			Excellent 4	V.Good 3	Good 2	Average 1	Poor -1	

Fig. 6. Checklist to evaluate LUI

usability criteria with their relevant usability properties and metrics in a systematic way. Fig. 6 shows a part of the checklist, which is concerned with LUI.

3.2 Usability Indicator-Based Quantification

Fig. 7 shows the process of usability indicator-based quantification. This approach assigns weights to the value of usability indicators and combines the weighted value into a single score. Identification of indicators to be measured varies from evaluator to evaluator. Our recommendation is however to use five indicators, as suggested in the hierarchical model of usability factors. The value of each usability indicator can be

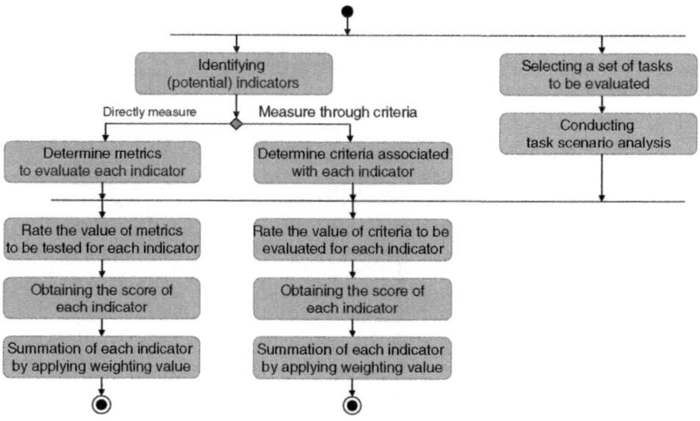

Fig. 7. Process of usability indicator-based quantification

determined in two ways: direct measurement and indirect measurement by using usability criteria. Weighting value assignment can use one of the methods described in section 3.1.

Measurement by using usability criteria can also employ the checklist that is used in task-centred quantification. To use this method, evaluators should identify potential goal-means relations between each usability indicator and its relevant usability criteria, as well as a set of tasks to be used for this measurement. But it is prohibitive to define the relations in terms of time and effort required. Thus a questionnaire survey like SUMI can instead be used [11]. Each indicator can be directly measured by using metrics. For example, effectiveness can be measured by several metrics such as task completion time, error rates, and recall accuracy [2].

3.3 Design Area-Based Quantification

This approach focuses on the usability value of eight design areas (interaction paths) affecting interaction between users and mobile phones. Fig. 8 illustrates the process of design area-based quantification. It calculates the usability of device hardware area and seven areas (seven arrows in Fig. 3) influencing on the context of use and the usability of mobile phones. Although there are other design areas to be concerned, we assume these eight areas are most relevant and sufficient to obtain the usability score. Weighting value assignment can also use one of the methods in section 3.1.

To assess the usability of each design area, evaluators should identify usability factors concerned with the area. Taking into consideration the abstraction level of these factors, most of them pertain to usability criteria or property. In this regard, the hierarchical model can be a useful reference when selecting the factors. For example, one factor of 'PUI↔user's physiology' area is 'comfortable size', and one factor of 'LUI+GUI↔user's mind or emotion' area is 'menu contents and structure'. As Fig. 8 shows, the eight areas are classified into two groups, depending on whether or not they can be evaluated without conducting tasks.

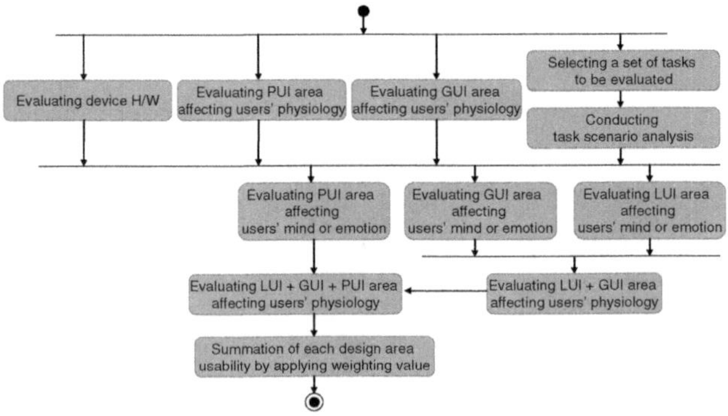

Fig. 8. Process of design area-based quantification

4 Case Studies

We conducted two case studies in order to obtain empirical data to be used for determining weighting values for quantification and examine the practicality of the three quantification approaches. Another purpose of the studies was to verify the usefulness of the hierarchical model of usability factors (this is beyond the scope of this paper).

In the first study in which twenty-one people participated and conducted eleven tasks, we collected the data which were used for examining task usage frequency, classifying tasks by KANO model, and determining the weighting value of usability indicators and the importance of usability criteria. Table 1 shows the rank of tasks by task usage frequency and classification of tasks by Kano model. Kano model is known to be useful for characterizing customers' preferences by dividing product features into five categories (one-dimensional, attractive, one-dimensional, must-be, and reverse) [12]. In this study the eleven tasks were grouped into one of three categories. As space is limited, we don't describe this categorization in detail.

To obtain the weighting value of usability indicators, we applied pair-wise comparison method, which has much been used in AHP (Analytic Hierarchy Process) [9]. The weighting values were calculated by using 'geometric mean' of each pair-wise comparison result, and consistency ratio indicated the obtained values are reasonably reliable. They were: 0.213 for effectiveness, 0.240 for efficiency, 0.190 for learnability, 0.247 for satisfaction, 0.109 for customization.

In the second study, five usability professionals participated and examined the practicality of the three quantification approaches, with particular emphasis on the task-centred quantification method. The conducted three tasks and compared the usability of four mobile phones. The tested tasks include: making a call, sending in text, and adding contact information. Considering that these tasks are mainly concerned with logical aspects of interaction, we focused on usability factors related to LUI

Table 1. Rank by task usage frequency and classification of tasks by Kano model

Task	Rank by task usage frequency	Classification of tasks by Kano model
Call	1	One-dimensional
Message	2	One-dimensional
Telephone book	3	One-dimensional
Setting	4	Attractive
Camera (photo)	5	Attractive
File manager	6	Indifferent
MP3 player	7	Attractive
WAP & Connectivity	8	Attractive
PIM	9	Indifferent
Mobile commerce	10	Indifferent
Mobile TV	11	Indifferent

at the level of usability criteria. Using the set of checklist, we tested the usability of the three tasks at eleven factors: achievement, flow, error rate, consistency, navigation, affordance, multi-tasking, minimalism, informativeness, information grouping, and quality of annotation. To apply task-centred quantification approach, we used five different methods for assigning weights to the task. Fig. 9 shows the task usability of each mobile phone, weighting value of each task by five methods, and the usability

Usability of Task	Task_1	Task_2	Task_3
Phone-A	20	7	16
Phone-B	22	6	16
Phone-C	20	13	13
Phone-D	25	15	15

Weighting values	Rank sum weight	Rank reciprocal	Kano(I)	Kano (II)	Entropy
Task_1	0.500	0.545	1.000	0.400	0.055
Task_2	0.333	0.273	1.000	0.950	0.902
Task_3	0.167	0.182	1.000	0.947	0.043

Usability score of mobile phones by different weighting values

Usability Score	Rank sum weight	Rank reciprocal	Kano(I)	Kano (II)	Entropy
Phone-A	15.00	15.73	43.00	29.81	8.10
Phone-B	15.67	16.55	44.00	29.66	7.31
Phone-C	16.50	16.82	46.00	32.67	13.39
Phone-D	20.00	20.45	55.00	38.46	15.55

Fig. 9. Application of task-centred quantification in the 2nd case study

score of each mobile phone. As expected, the usability score is dependent on the method of determining weighting values.

5 Conclusion

This paper proposed three approaches to quantifying the usability of mobile phones based on a hierarchical model of usability factors. We described the process and rules of each approach to calculate the usability score of a mobile phone. To take account of users' preference on specific mobile phone features or context factors, these approaches employ several methods for assigning weighting value. We could confirm their practicality through case studies. Lastly, what should be noted is that quantified usability score should only be a reference point for design improvement or benchmarking, not an absolute value for judging the quality of mobile phone. It would be more useful when it is used in combination with other usability testing methods.

Acknowledgment. This research was performed under the financial support from LG Electronics.

References

1. Ham, D-H., Heo, J., Fossick, P., Wong, W., Park, S., Song, C., Bradley, M.: Conceptual Framework and Models for Identifying and Organizing Usability Impact Factors of Mobile Phones. In: Proceedings of 2006 Annual Conference of the Australian Computer-Human Interaction Special Interest Group (OZCHI 2006), Sydney, Australia (November 2006)
2. Hornbæk, K.: Current Practice in Measuring Usability: Challenges to Usability Study and Research. Int. J. Human-Computer Studies, 64(2) 79–102 (2006)
3. Keinonen, T.: One-Dimensional Usability-Influence of Usability on Consumers' Product Preference. Unpublished Doctoral Dissertation, University of Art and Design and Helsinki (1998)
4. Ketola, P., Röykkee, M.: The Three Aspects of Usability in Mobile Handsets. Paper Presented at the Workshop of ACM Conference on Human Factors in Computing Systems (ACM CHI 2001), Seattle, USA, March-April (2001)

5. Lohse, G.L., Spiller, P.: Quantifying the Effect of User Interface Design Features on Cyberstore Traffic and Sales. In: Proceedings of ACM Conference on Human Factors in Computing Systems (ACM CHI 1998), Los Angeles, USA, April (1998)
6. Rauterberg, M.: An Empirical Validation of Four Different Measures to Quantify User Interface Characteristics Based on a General Descriptive Concept for Interaction Points. In: Proceedings of IEEE Symposium and Workshop on Engineering of Computer-Based Systems, Friedrichshafen, Germany, March (1996)
7. Rauterberg, M.: How to Measure and to Quantify Usability of User Interfaces. In: Özok, A., Salvendy, G. (eds.) Advances in Applied Ergonomics, West Lafayette, USA Publishing. pp. 429–432 (1996)
8. Rubinoff, R.: How to Quantify the User Experience (2006) Available online via http://www.sitepoint.com/article/quantify-user-experience
9. Saaty, T.L.: How to Make a Decision. The Analytic Hierarchy Process. Interfaces 24(6), 19–43 (1994)
10. Sauro, J., Kindlund, E.: A Method to Standardize Usability Metrics into a Single Score. In: Proceedings of ACM Conference on Human Factors in Computing Systems (ACM CHI 2005), Portland, USA, April (2005)
11. SUMI (2006) Available online via http://sumi.ucc.ie
12. Yang, C-C.: The Refined Kano's Model and Its Application. Total Quality Management 16(10), 1127–1137 (2005)

Accelerated Rendering of Vector Graphics on Mobile Devices

Gaoqi He[1], Baogang Bai[2], Zhigeng Pan[1], and Xi Cheng[1]

[1] State Key Lab. of CAD&CG, Zhejiang University, Hangzhou, 310027, P.R. China
{hegaoqi,zgpan,chengxi}@cad.zju.edu.cn
[2] Dept. of Computer Science and Engineering, Wenzhou University, Wenzhou 325006, P.R. China
bbg@wzu.edu.cn

Abstract. With the great development of mobile communication and devices, graphics on mobile device catches more and more attentions. Compare with static bitmap, vector graphics (VG) is more fit to mobile devices because of small file size and scalability for any display size. Emergence of OpenVG standard motivates the research of VG. This paper focuses on the time-consuming performance of VG rendering and exploits accelerated rendering algorithms. Layered implementation structure and algorithm of drawing one path are introduced firstly. According to the obtained time-consuming data of tiger sample, analysis methodologies are constructed and results are presented. Optimization directions can be concluded into three major aspects: rasterizer, stroke and tessellate. Accelerated rendering methods are discussed with experiments to validate non-uniform subdivision algorithm for Bézier curves. The tiger sample is rendered with improved performance using the proposed algorithm.

Keywords: vector graphics, OpenVG, non-uniform subdivision, rasterizer, tessellate.

1 Introduction

With the rapid growth of mobile communication techniques in the past two decades, it is possible for the transmission of high quality image, large audio & video data and complex 3D geometry model across wireless network. Moreover, the prevalence of mobile devices embedded with augmented-function components produced various mobile applications, such as video, animation, advertising, game and interaction between user and device (or other users). Without loss of generality, mobile devices here refer to the portable devices with considerable computation ability and small display, like Pocket PC, Smart Phone and PDA. However, considering the rather limited resource of current mobile devices like low CPU, small display and battery power, several challenges arises in mobile computing including both the fast transmission of large data across wireless network and high quality rendering on the device.

To meet the rendering purpose mentioned above, increasing attentions are paid on vector graphics against traditionally static bitmap. Main reasons lie at the several

J. Jacko (Ed.): Human-Computer Interaction, Part II, HCII 2007, LNCS 4551, pp. 298–305, 2007.

benefits from vector graphics when used in embedded devices, typically are small file size for extremely high quality graphics, lossless compression without artifacts, scalability for any display size and so on. Vector graphics has already been widely used in the field of portable mapping, file format and game, and will also appear in new applications soon like compelling user interfaces and multimedia messaging. SVG Tiny, SVG Basic and Flash Mobile have been designed for mobile devices. Under the auspices of Khronos Group [2], OpenVG [3] is proposed firstly at SIGGRAPH 2004. OpenVG accelerates the above vector graphics standards by defining a low-level hardware acceleration layer that will enable graphics silicon to provide great performance for these packages at very low power-levels.

Emergence of OpenVG motivates the research of vector graphics on mobile device [4]. Although the ideal pipeline is suggested in the specification of OpenVG with version 1.0, implementations are not required to match the ideal pipeline stage-for-stage. To improve the rendering performance of vector graphics on mobile device, efforts are taken to explore accelerated software algorithms. Software implementation is one feasible solution because graphics accelerator is not equipped in the commonly mobile platform. Moreover, the low-cost software implementation helps to the research and development of hardware accelerator. Without degradation of the visual quality, research purpose of software algorithms is to overcome the performance bottle-neck. Hybrid [5] has proposed the reference implementation of OpenVG and taken the sample of tiger head as example. However, the sample runs on the PC platform and calls several OpenGL functions for rendering purpose, which is not fit to mobile device. Besides, the sample runs much slower. To exploit accelerated software algorithm for vector graphics on mobile device, we use this reference implementation and try to find where the time-consuming performance bottle-necks are and where the optimization directions are. Accordingly, optimized algorithms are presented.

The remainder of this paper is organized as follows. Two methods of OpenVG implementation and algorithm of path drawing are described in section 2. Time-consuming performance analysis methodology and Optimized directions are presented in section 3. The accelerated rendering methods are proposed in section 4. Experiments results are demonstrated in section 5. Finally, conclusions are drawn and future works are described in section 6.

2 Algorithm of Path Drawing

2.1 OpenVG Implementation

According the ideal pipeline introduced in the OpenVG specification, flowchart of reference implementation is illustrated as Figure 1. Path, image and paint are the three basic components. Paths are the heart of OpenVG API, all geometry to be drawn must be defined in terms of one or more paths. Paths are defined by a sequence of segment commands. Each segment command in the standard format may specify a move, a straight line segment, a quadratic or cubic Bézier segment, or an elliptical arc. Paint

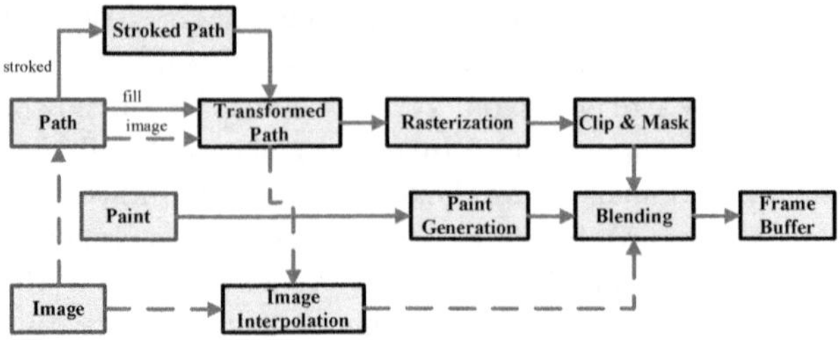

Fig. 1. Implementation flowchart of OpenVG

defines a color and an alpha value for each pixel being drawn, and Images are rectangular collections of pixels. Paint operations are easy and image processing is mature. Vector graphics is high related with path primitives, thus the major attentions are paid on the path drawing.

To realize hardware-accelerated OpenVG APIs, two mechanisms are reasonable. One is inspired by the SVGL toolkit [6], the other is to implement directly. SVGL is a C++ toolkit which works on an SVG tree and displays SVG graphics using OpenGL. The main objective of SVGL is to offload graphical processing complexity of the CPU to the GPU. See Figure 2 for SVGL implementation mechanism. It should be noted that OpenVG is specifically intended to support all drawing features required by a SVG Tiny render. Besides, OpenGL ES is a well-defined subset of OpenGL and used on mobile devices. So it is possible to refer to the implementation of SVGL and implement OpenVG APIs based on OpenGL ES APIs through necessary transformations. However, some difficulties encounter because differences exist between OpenVG and SVG, and OpenGL ES is far not a commonly accepted standard and just possess part functions of OpenGL. Thus we inclined to the direct implementation. Guided by the Hybrid reference implementation, layered structure of the implementation is illustrated as Figure 3. Platform independent OpenVG comprises Math, Path, Paint, Image, Rasterizer and Context modules, while platform dependent layer is made up of context, surface and configure. OpenVG and EGL work together through the contexts between them.

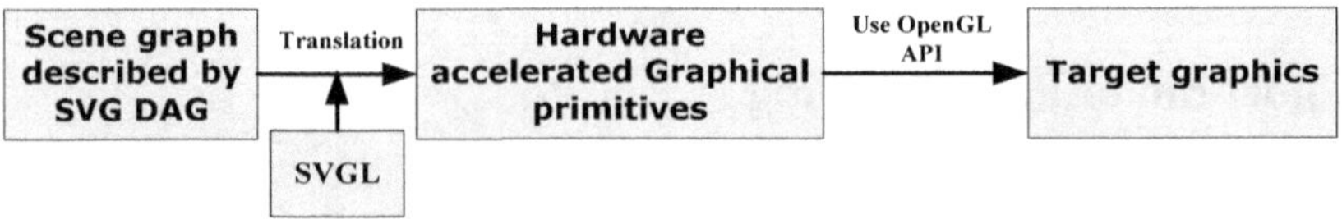

Fig. 2. SVGL implementation mechanism

2.2 Drawing a Path

Vector graphics in OpenVG is mainly embodied by the Path component. The more knowledge of how to draw a path, the more efficient ways found to accelerate rendering. According to the implementation flowchart in Figure 1, an intuitive algorithm of path drawing is illustrated as Figure 4. User can fill or stroke a path. Path segments described in math meaning will be transformed into a series of edges through tessellate operations in step 3.2 and 4.2, respectively. Science finally the vector graphics will be display on raster screen, rasterization processing is necessary to deal with the generated edges.

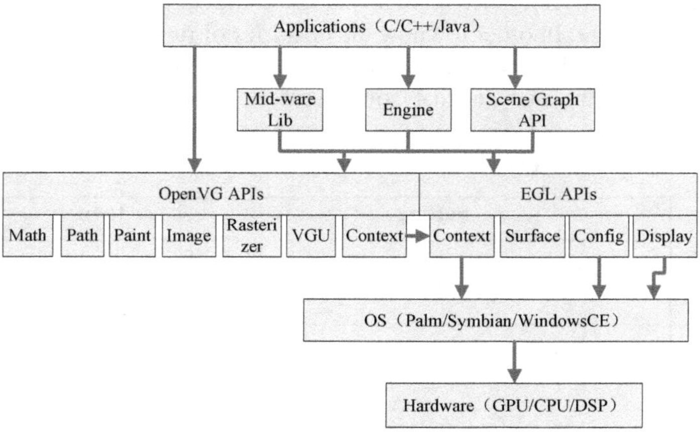

Fig. 3. Layered structure of the implementation

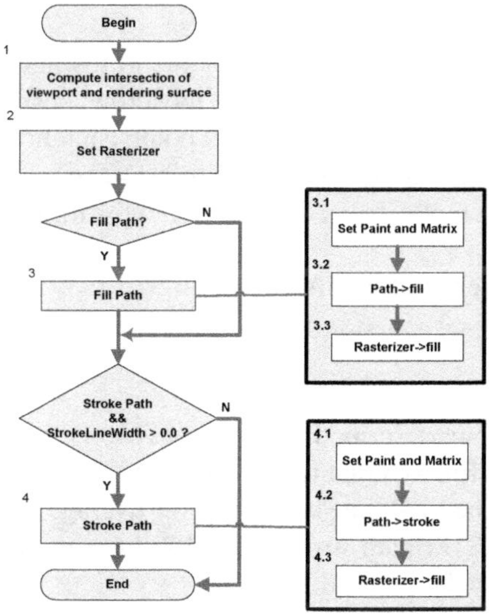

Fig. 4. Flowchart of drawing a path

3 Performance Analysis

3.1 Methodology

The sample of tiger head is made up of 305 different paths with various commands, points and paint modes. When running on the PC with the configuration of 2.2GHz CPU and 1.0GB RAM, reference implementation of the sample need nearly 50 seconds in debug environment. In order to know the obstacles of running much slower and the directions of optimization, we analyse the obtained time-consuming data of each path drawing. Pointed to the analysis goal, some parameters must be set, like Table 1.

Table 1. Some important parameters setting

Item	Setting	Item	Setting
Rendering Quality	VG_RENDERING_QUALITY_BETTER	Image	No image drawing
Paint Modes	VG_FILL_PATH or VG_STROKE_PATH	Use dash	No
capStyle	VG_CAP_BUTT	Use scissor	No
joinStyle	VG_JOIN_MITER	Other settings	default

The item name and its description of the obtained time consuming data are explained in Table 2.

The source time data are analyzed based on the following schemes:

1. Due to each path, to see which stage is the most time costing;
2. Due to two paths with same commands and points, but different paint modes, i.e. fill or stroke, to compare the time costing of similar stages;
3. Under the same paint mode, fill or stroke, to find the most impressive factors of time costing;
4. To evaluate the influence of PathArea.

3.2 Analysis Results

Based on the methodology described above, we get some constructive results.

From scheme 1), we find out that rasterizer (step 3.3 or 4.3) is the most time costing stage, which is 96% of the total time costing on the average no matter which paint mode is. The path fill (step 3.2) or path stroke (step 4.2) take up the second rank, nearly 4%. The rest time costing can be ignored.

From scheme 2), we easily find out stroke path is much more time consuming than fill path. The running time of stroking path is 12 times as much as that of filling path on the average. Time of Path stroke is nearly 5 times as much as that of Path fill, while rasterizer of stroke path is about 15~20 times time costing more than that of fill path. It should be noticed that the edges increase significantly when paint mode varied from fill to stroke.

Table 2. Item and its description of obtained data

Item	Description
No	The No. of path, from 0 to 304
Com	Number of commands of each path
Point	Number of points corresponding to the commands
F_S	Fill(F) or Stroke(S) path
VertNum	Number of vertices after tessellate(in step 3.2 or step 4.2)
FillEdge	The number of edges used to rasterizer
PathArea	The bound area of each path
TessTime	Time used for tessellate a path
PathFill	Time used in stage path→fill(step 3.2)
FillRast	Time used for rasterizer a filling path (step 3.3)
PathStroke	Time used for stage path→stroke(step 4.2)
StrokeRast	Time used for rasterizer a stroking path (step 4.3)
CostTime	Total time used for drawing a path

From scheme 3), we find out the time costing of each stage increases with the same speed as the increasing of FillEdge number. Through insight research, so many edges are produced as a result of segments of curves and arcs.

From scheme 4), we find reducing rasterizer region of each path benefits the whole time consuming, like the usage of path bound box.

Finally conclusions listed below are made from the above discussions.

1. The rasterizer operation should be firstly optimized.
2. Process of path stroke should be concentrated on and number of FillEdge should be reduced without degrading the visual rendering quality.
3. The tessellate stage should be cared for to produce appropriate number of vertices, which will reduce the FillEdge value correspondingly.

4 Accelerated Rendering

Traditionally scan line based rasterization is slow. Technique of Active Edge Table (AET) [7] takes advantages of the relevancy between two neighbor scan lines but more storage is required. The more external data traffic, the more power consumption needed [8]. However, both memory space and power are limited resource on mobile devices

To reach the balance between speed and memory space, AET should be adopted according to the complexity of the path. If the number of FillEdge is smaller than one certain value, AET is used to improve the speed. Otherwise, standard rasterizer algorithm runs. To keep high visual quality, FLIPQUAD [9] and FLIPTRI [10] work as two efficient multi-sample techniques on mobile devices.

With regard to the conclusions drawn in the previous section, well designed tessellated algorithm will benefit both the computation of primitive transfer and rasterization treatment. The majority edges are produced as a result of segments of curves and arcs, so the focus is put on the traditional uniform subdivision algorithm. Traditional method is clear but results in well-proportioned samples no matter what the curve is. Proposed method here is one non-uniform subdivision algorithm according to the curvature radius of the segments like curves and arcs [11]. The curves are typically three order Bézier curve. Under the region with high curvature, more density samples are performed. It is easy to get the parameter t where the slope of curve changes quickly. During the neighbor region of this t, more subdivision edges are got to approximate the original curve. Outside this region, less samples are needed.

5 Experiments

Each curve will be tessellated into constant number of edges, like 64, using uniform subdivision algorithm. Using the proposed algorithm in this paper, flat region is expressed with several edges, and more edges will be prodeced to approximate curve within high curvature region without compromise of visual quality. Figure 5 illustrated the non-uniform subdivision Bézier curve with only 13 edges.

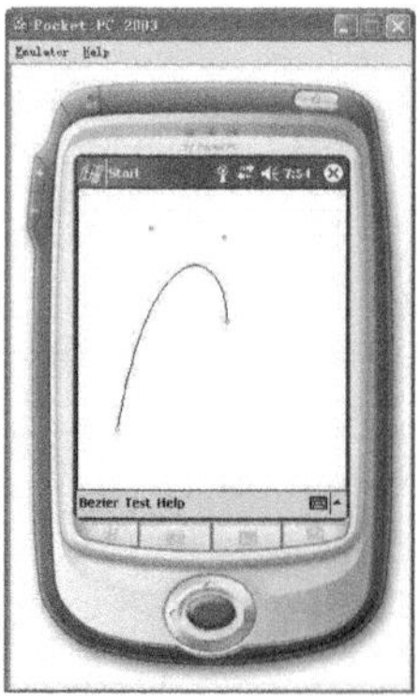

Fig. 5. Three order Bézier curve

Fig. 6. Sample of tiger head

The tiger sample in Figure 6 is again taken as example to demonstrate the power of vector graphics and the proposed methods as well. The whole time costing is reduced nearly 10 percent under the PC environments.

6 Conclusions and Future Work

Research of vector graphics on mobile devices is interesting and promising, especially the newly emerged OpenVG standard. This paper analyses the time costing of path drawing to find where the performance bottle-necks are and where the optimization directions are. According to the analysis results, some accelerated rendering methods are proposed.

Only primary works are introduced in this paper since many contributions to OpenVG are disclosed. The future works include actually running the sample on the Pocket PC, depending on several OpenGL ES APIs at the most. Implementation based on fixed point is also useful since the lack of float point unit on many mobile devices.

Acknowledgements. We would like to thank the members of Advance System Technology Group of STMicroelectronics R&D Co. Ltd. for their great help and close cooperation.

This research was funded by Key NSF Project on Digital Olympic Museum (Grant no: 60533080).

References

1. http://www.ericsson.com/cn/ericsson/publication/viewpoint/01/gsm2_index.shtml
2. http://www.khronos.org/
3. Rice, D.: OpenVG Specification, Version 1.0, Sun Microsystems, Inc.
4. He, G., Pan, Z., et al.: Multi-stroke Freehand Text Entry Method using OpenVG and its Application on Mobile Devices. LNCS, vol. 3942, pp. 791–796. Springer, Heidelberg (2006)
5. http://www.hybrid.fi/
6. Conversy, S., Fekete, J.-D.: The svgl toolkit: enabling fast rendering of rich 2d graphics. Technical Report 02/1/INFO, Ecole des Mines de Nantes (2002)
7. Rogers, D. F.: Procedural Elements of Computer Graphics. McGraw-Hill Science (1998)
8. Antochi, I., Juurlink, B.H.H., et al.: Memory Bandwidth Requirements of Tile-Based Rendering. In: Pimentel, A.D., Vassiliadis, S. (eds.) SAMOS 2004. LNCS, vol. 3133, pp. 323–332. Springer, Heidelberg (2004)
9. Akenine-Möller, T., Ström, J.: Graphics for the Masses: A Hardware Rasterization Architecture for Mobile Phones. In: ACM Transactions of Graphics Proceedings of ACM SIGGRAPH vol. 22(3), pp. 801–808 (2004)
10. Akenine-Möller, T.: An Extremely Inexpensive Multisampling Scheme. Chalmers University of Technology, Technical Report No. 03–14 August (2003)
11. Su, Z., Pei, R.: Geometrical Principle of surface crack processing algorithm based on edge sample. Computer Integrated Manufacturing System 12(4), 621–624 (2006)

Pulling Digital Data from a Smart Object: Implementing the PullMe-Paradigm with a Mobile Phone

Steve Hinske

Institute for Pervasive Computing, ETH Zürich
Clausiusstr. 59, 8092 Zürich, Switzerland
steve.hinske@inf.ethz.ch

Abstract. This paper presents the PullMe paradigm, an interaction technique for easily initializing and confirming the transmission of digital data using a mobile phone. The main idea and benefit is the substitution of less feasible techniques such as manually selecting or confirming a service (e.g., by entering a password) with a simple hand gesture. We describe a prototypical implementation that utilizes an acceleration sensor and radio frequency identification (RFID) technology integrated into a mobile phone. The transmission of data is realized using Bluetooth. We furthermore discuss how near-field communication (NFC) is likely to enable interaction patterns like the PullMe paradigm in the near future.

Keywords: PullMe paradigm, human-computer interaction, HCI, semantic mapping of physical and virtual action, mobile phone, acceleration sensor, radio frequency identification, RFID, near-field communication, NFC.

1 Introduction

This paper presents the concept of the PullMe paradigm and describes a prototype that implements it. The PullMe paradigm is a novel interaction technique for easily downloading digital data using a mobile phone.

The main idea and major benefit is to substitute traditional selection and confirmation techniques, which are often rather intricate and time consuming (e.g., manually selecting services and typing in keys or passwords), for a simple hand gesture. Analogous to the TouchMe and PointMe paradigms [1, 2], where a device is used to touch an object or to point at it, respectively, the PullMe paradigm realizes the idea of triggering an action by pulling the device away from an object.

For a better understanding, visualize the following scenario: you want to see a movie and you are waiting for your friend in front of a cinema. Since your friend is late and you have not yet decided which movie you are going to see, you intend to use the time of waiting to pick a movie already. But before you can actually choose one, you need to have more information about the movies currently running, for example by viewing the trailers of the movies in question.

For this reason, you go to one of the advertising movie posters at the cinema, get your mobile phone out of the pocket, and you hold it close to the poster. After a few

J. Jacko (Ed.): Human-Computer Interaction, Part II, HCII 2007, LNCS 4551, pp. 306–310, 2007.

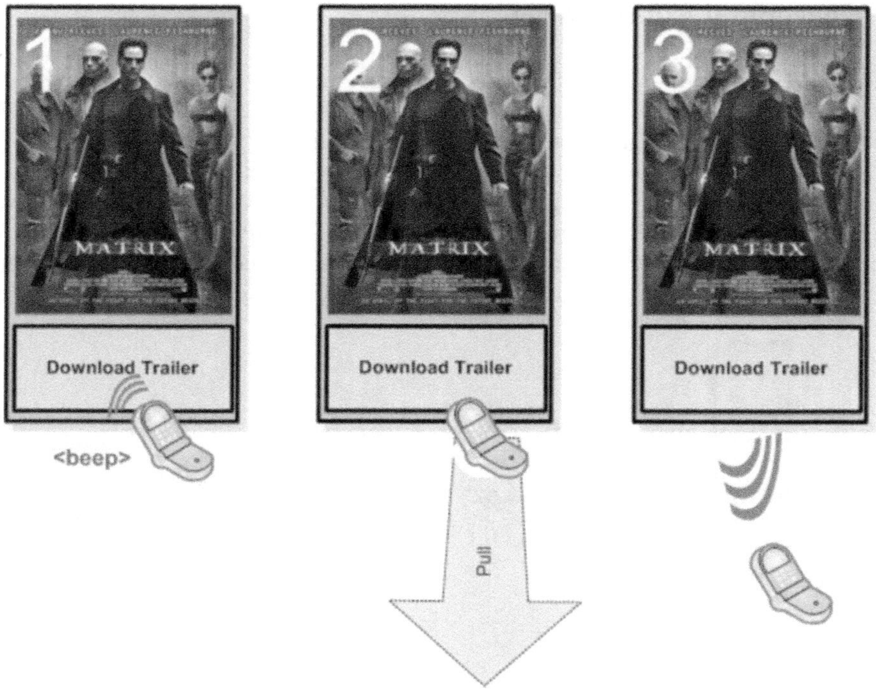

Fig. 1. Downloading a movie trailer from a poster: first, the user holds the mobile phone close to a designated area ('Download Trailer') on the poster. An acoustic 'beep' acknowledges the reciprocal detection of the mobile phone and the device integrated in the poster which offers the download of the trailer (1). The user then physically pulls the device away from the poster, thus confirming that she or he really wants to download the trailer; a virtual connection between the two devices is established subsequently (2). Finally, the trailer is then transmitted to the mobile phone using the already established connection (3).

seconds, your mobile phone gives you a short signal (e.g., an acoustic 'beep'). You then make a swift pull-away move and, subsequently, triggered by this simple gesture, a trailer of this movie is transmitted to your phone (see Fig. 1).

The scenario demonstrates the principle of the PullMe paradigm: by physically pulling away a device (e.g., the mobile phone) from a smart object (e.g. a technically enhanced movie poster or billboard), the user initiates a virtual pull: the transfer of digital data. In the case of the movie trailer, the "pulled" data is information about the actual movie. It would also be possible, however, to provide other digital assets, for example, a coupon for a free drink "pulled" from an advertisement billboard.

The remainder of the paper is structured as follows: first, we introduce the conceptual approach of the PullMe paradigm, including the communication technologies that we use. Second, we discuss the technical realization of a prototype with the focus of this section being on the employed hardware. Third, we conclude this paper with a summary and planned future work.

2 Conceptual Approach

The PullMe paradigm is an interaction pattern that meets two important requirements of human-computer interaction: it is easy-to-use and quite intuitive. By replacing cumbersome menu navigation and manual configuration of services with two simple moves (holding the mobile phone in close proximity to a billboard and then move it away with a swift pull-away gesture, respectively), we can increase the usability significantly. The PullMe paradigm is also quite intuitive due to the semantic mapping of the physical and the virtual action (i.e., the virtual pull of data is triggered by and corresponds to the physical pull of the device (see Fig. 2)).

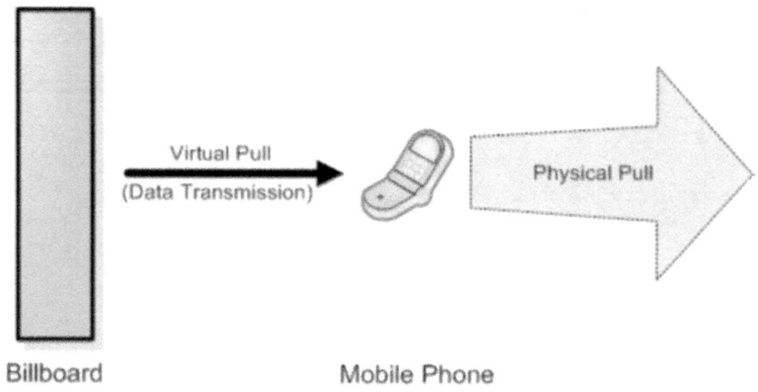

Fig. 2. The semantic mapping between physical and virtual pull action: the virtual pull (i.e., the actual transmission of data from the billboard to the mobile phone) corresponds with and is triggered by the physical pull (i.e., the physical move of the mobile phone away from the billboard)

Thus, we have two main components: on the one hand, we must recognize the pull move which is realized with an acceleration sensor attached to the mobile phone; and, on the other hand, we have to ensure that the devices detect each other beforehand. The principle of bringing two devices closely together in order to initiate a connection is mainly based on the Touch and Connect paradigm, one of the four possible application categories for near-field communication (NFC) presented by Philips [3]. But since currently available mobile phones do not provide full NFC functionality, we have to build our own device that "simulates" this functionality.

We use radio frequency identification (RFID) technology to enable the devices to unambiguously detect each other. To this end, both the mobile phone and the billboard are equipped with an RFID reader and RFID tag(s) which allows reciprocal detection and the subsequent establishment of an initial connection between them. At this moment, however, there is no data transmitted yet.

The transmission must be explicitly authorized by the user doing a swift pull-away move, which is recognized by the aforementioned integrated acceleration sensor. After a successful confirmation, the data is transmitted via Bluetooth (although it is also possible to use other communication technologies such as general packet radio service (GPRS) or universal mobile telecommunications system (UMTS)).

3 Technical Realization

To realize the PullMe paradigm, the mobile phone must be equipped with an RFID tag, an RFID reader module, and an acceleration sensor. We attach a custom-built RFID reader module (a BTnode [4] that operates a Skyetek M1-mini RFID reader [5]; the BTnode is connected via Bluetooth to the mobile phone) to a Nokia 6630. In order to detect the pull-away move, we use a SparkFun WiTilt v2.5 [6], a wireless 2-dimensional accelerometer that also uses Bluetooth to transmit its gathered acceleration data to the mobile phone.

An application aggregates the data from the RFID reader and the acceleration sensors, and implements the protocol of the PullMe paradigm: based on the reciprocal detection, an initial connection is established, and, if a pull-away move has been recognized successfully (meaning the transmission has been confirmed), the data is eventually transmitted from the billboard to the mobile phone (see Fig. 3).

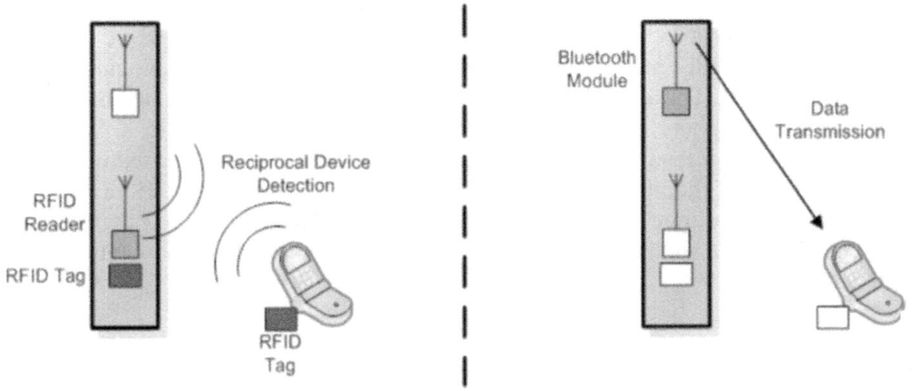

Fig. 3. Reciprocal detection via RFID (left) and the subsequent transmission of data via Bluetooth (right): first, the billboard and the mobile phone detect each other using RFID technology (i.e., both devices are equipped with RFID readers and RFID tags). This leads to the establishment of a Bluetooth connection between the devices. The second step consists of transmitting data from the billboard device to the mobile phone via Bluetooth after the transmission has been confirmed by the user using the PullMe paradigm.

This requires the billboard also to be equipped with a Bluetooth device, an RFID reader, and several RFID tags (this is necessary to cover the complete 'download area'). The tags of the billboard are read by the mobile phone, while the billboard simultaneously detects the mobile phone.

As mentioned before, the reciprocal detection is the initial step of the data transfer, but the consequential action (e.g., downloading the movie trailer) has to be confirmed by the user beforehand using a simple gesture. The main advantage is that the user neither needs to use the keyboard of the mobile phone nor has to navigate through the menu; as a matter of fact, she or he does not even have to pay attention to the mobile phone itself.

4 Conclusion

In this paper we presented the PullMe paradigm, a new interaction paradigm that augments a physical move by coupling it to a "virtual move" (i.e., a transmission). In comparison with navigating through a menu, the pulling-away move is in many cases much more convenient for confirming such a transmission, thus, making the PullMe paradigm an intuitive and easy-to-use addition to human-computer interaction.

We presented a prototypical system that implements this paradigm and demonstrates the general idea based on a real world example. We intend to improve the system, especially from a technological point of view. However, it is very likely that the self-constructed prototype with the externally attached RFID reader and acceleration sensor is to be replaced by mobile phones with integrated near-field communication technology and built-in acceleration sensors in the near future.

In this context we might also extend the prototype to being able to detect visual codes using the built-in camera. This approach would result in an alternative to the RFID/NFC-based detection, but the confirmation of the data transmission, however, remains unaltered. Another point is that, instead of using Bluetooth, it might be desirable and probably more feasible to use other transmission technologies, mainly GPRS and UMTS. The advantage in this case is that the data does not have to be stored in the poster, but can be accessed on the Internet using web links.

We furthermore intend to conduct a user study to evaluate the presented interaction pattern. The aim of the planned study is to evaluate the significance and intuitiveness of the PullMe paradigm compared to other (traditional) means of retrieving digital data. The evaluation should then disclose on how easy to use and on how intuitive our approach really is.

References

1. Pohjanheimo, L., Keränen, H., Ailisto, H.: Implementing touchme paradigm with a mobile phone. In: Proceedings of the joint conference on Smart objects and ambient intelligence: innovative context-aware services: usages and technologies (2005)
2. Rukzio, E., Leichtenstern, K., Callaghan, V., Schmidt, A., Holleis, P., Chin, J.: An Experimental Comparison of Physical Mobile Interaction Techniques: Touching, Pointing and Scanning. In: Dourish, P., Friday, A. (eds.) UbiComp 2006. LNCS, vol. 4206, Springer, Heidelberg (2006)
3. Huang, J.: Access Just a Touch Away, (16.02.2007) Available at: http://www.iss.nus.edu.sg/iss/article_display.jsp?artid=1218
4. BTnode Homepage (16.02.2007) Available at: http://www.btnode.ethz.ch/
5. Skyetek Homepage (16.02.2007) Available at: http://www.skyetek.com
6. SparkFun Homepage (16.02.2007) Available at: http://www.sparkfun.com/commerce/product_info.php?products_id=254

Reading Performance of Chinese Text with Automatic Scrolling

Yao-Hung Hsieh, Chiuhsiang Joe Lin*, Hsiao-Ching Chen, Ting-Ting Huang, and James C. Chen

Department of Industrial Engineering, Chung Yuan Christian University
200, Chung Pei Rd., Chung Li, Taiwan 32023, R.O.C.
hsiang@cycu.edu.tw

Abstract. Auto-scrolling is useful when the reader wishes to move the text continuously to where the reader's eyes are fixated on the visual display without having to press the control button on the scrolling device all the time. In this paper, we conducted an experiment to study the effects of scroll speed in text error search tasks. The study considered three experimental factors, scroll speed, error type, and article length. Reading performance and fatigue were measured with the error search accuracy and subjective evaluation. The result indicates that scrolling at a high speed would cause a decrease in error identification, affecting the quality of reading.

Keywords: Auto-Scrolling, Error Search, Reading Efficiency, Visual Fatigue.

1 Introduction

Electronic visual displays are used almost everywhere today for various information presentation purposes, such as electronic books and electronic periodicals. Today, people read articles and get information in such a different way than before. The major difference is that the content that can be displayed on a page of the A4 paper cannot be completely displayed on a computer screen. This is especially true with mobile computing device in which the display is usually only a few inches. Thus, the scrollbar is invented. Users can use the mouse or any pointing device to move the text for reading. When reading through long text information, scrolling allows the user to turn to different reading points of interest. Auto-scrolling is useful when the reader wishes to move the text continuously to where the reader's eyes are fixated on the visual display without having to press the control button on the scrolling device all the time. The information is updated and scrolled into the reader's useful visual field of view in a continuous way.

There is a need to increase our knowledge on reading activities on the Visual display in such a massive Internet environment. Until today, there is still little known about the efficiency and problems of reading automatic scrolling information. In this study, we explored the different factors of scroll speed, text error types, and article lengths to understand their effects on reading performance.

* Corresponding author.

J. Jacko (Ed.): Human-Computer Interaction, Part II, HCII 2007, LNCS 4551, pp. 311–319, 2007.

2 Literature Review

With the advent of the Internet application, individuals have become able to easily get a huge amount of information on WWW. When reading through the web page information, scrollbar is a useful device which allows the user to read more efficiently in catching various kinds of online publication such as online newspapers, magazines, and so on [3],[5].

A few studies established the effects of scrolling on human reading performances. Past research on the way readers read text on the display has mainly compared scrolling and paging. Piolat et al. [2] conducted a series of experiments to study two types of text presentation (page-by-page vs. scrolling) with reading and revising tasks. They found that the page-by-page presentation could get greater facilitative effects. Nimwegen et al. [7] investigated the influence of structure and reading-manipulation on usability of hypertexts. They studied two kinds of reading manipulation (scrolling or paging) with four types of hypertexts and evaluated the three aspects of usability: efficiency, ease of learning, and user-satisfaction. They obtained that a purely hierarchical structure was often more usable than a hierarchical structure and scrolling appeared to be more useful than paging. The results suggested that a purely hierarchical hypertext with scrolling was most useful. As a matter of fact, scrolling is now commonly used when reading web pages.

Dyson and Haselgrove [6] studied how three presentation factors (reading speed, line length, and the scrolling pattern) affected the comprehension activities. They found that a reduction in overall comprehension when reading fast, but the type of information recalled was not dependent on speed. They also found that the medium line length (55 characters per line) appeared to support effective reading. This produced the highest level of comprehension and was able to read faster than short lines. On the other hand, scrolling patterns (more time in pauses and more individual scrolling movements) were also associated with better comprehension with faster readers showing less time in pauses between scrolling.

Cockburn and Smith [1] introduced the hidden messages concept to program coding presentation, which was implemented with the elision technique. The elision technique allows regions of text to be 'folded' into and out of the display so that programmers can focus on relevant code regions while suppressing the display of irrelevant information. With the elision interface they found that the programmers were able to complete their tasks more rapidly, and the elision decreased the scrolling activities significantly. Huang et al. [4] carried out an experiment to investigate the Chinese dynamic information scrolling. The result showed that the best visual performance and lowest visual fatigue occurred at the scrolling speed of 320 words per minute.

In this study, an experiment was carried out to investigate the effect of scroll speed, different error types, and article lengths on users' visual performance and fatigue. The relationship of scroll speed, error types, and article length was carefully examined.

3 Method

3.1 Subjects

Four females and six male subjects were recruited for participating in the experiment. All subjects were either with normal or corrected-to-normal visual acuity and no one was colorblind. They were 20-25 years old and have been using the personal computer in their daily work.

3.2 Procedure

Before the experiment, subjects were familiarized with the procedure and contents of the experiment. During the experiment, the subject was asked to read the Chinese articles presented on the visual display and respond at the mistakes found by pressing a counter button until the entire article has been read for 30 minutes. The experimental order for the three scrolling speeds with the two article lengths was random. The three types of text error were evenly distributed in each article. Totally there are 3x2 experimental tasks for each subject. The subjects were asked to complete all the 6 tasks on a fixed computer work station environment. In the task, subjects needed to find the errors of the articles at different scroll speeds and press the button if they find an error of any type. After all the tasks were completed, the reading length of the article, the number of words on the screen, and the number of identified errors were recorded. Accuracy was collected as the number of errors found by the subject divided by total number of errors in the text. The subjective questionnaire was given to the participants at the end of each of the 6 tasks. The questionnaire is a visual discomfort questionnaire, containing 4 questions: (1) My eyes feel tired. (2) My eye lids are heavy. (3) My eyes feel dry. (4) I feel dizzy. Response was rated on a 5-point scale with '1' to '5' representing 'not at all' to 'yes, very much'. The entire evaluation lasted approximately 3 hours and was rewarded with $600 new Taiwan dollars.

3.3 Experimental Design

The study considered three experimental factors, scroll speed, error type, and article length. Scroll speed is represented as the time needed to scroll an A4 page. Three levels of scroll speed were used: 90 sec/page, 120 sec/page, and 180 sec/page. Three types of text errors were studied: semantic error (e.g., 閱讀-讀閱), typo (e.g., 閱讀-閱瀆), and repetition (e.g., 閱讀-閱閱讀). Two article lengths were considered: long and short essays. The tasks were selected to meet two criteria. First, they should reflect common long article reading activities. Second, they should reflect the common different kinds of short essays reading activities. A summary of the experimental factors is shown in Table 1.

Table 1. A summary of factors considered in the experiments and their levels

Factor	Level
Scroll speed	90 sec/page, 120 sec /page, 180 sec/page
Text errors	Semantic error, Typo error, Repetition error
Tasks	Long article, Short essays

4 Results

4.1 Error Search Accuracy

The effects of scroll speed, type of errors, and article length on the error search accuracy were tested with ANOVA (see table 2). The results show that the scroll speed, error type, and article length all had significant effects. Note that in Table 3, interaction terms are not included because in the full model they were not significant and were aggregated into error without affecting the result.

Table 2. ANOVA table with F values and significance for accuracy

Source	DF	Seq SS	Adj SS	Adj MS	F	P
Subject	9	5592.8	6216.8	690.7	2.73	0.005
Scroll speed	2	2550.7	2130.3	1065.1	4.21	0.017
Task	1	273.2	195.8	195.8	1.77	0.046
Text error	2	386.3	386.3	193.2	3.76	0.034
Error	165	41792.9	41792.9	253.3		
Total	179	50596				

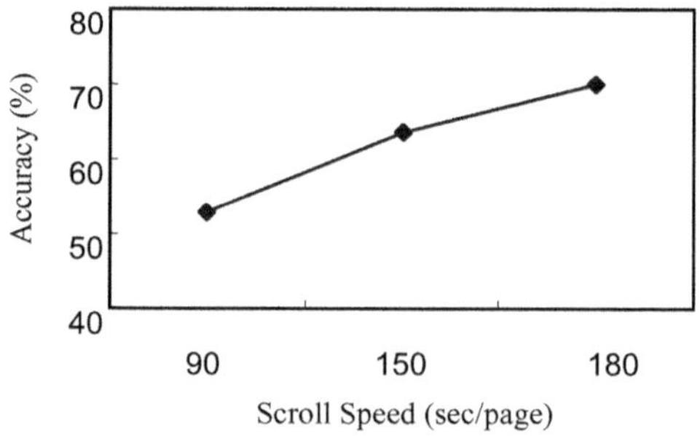

Fig. 1. The main effect plot of scroll speed on accuracy

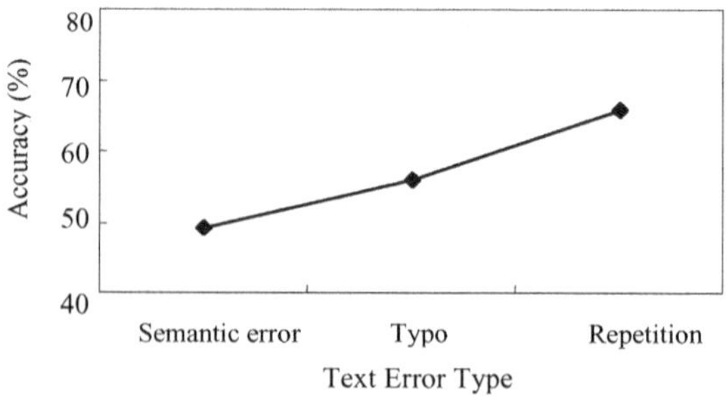

Fig. 2. The main effect plot of text error type on accuracy

The main effect plots of scroll speed, text error type, and article length are shown in Fig.1, 2, and 3, respectively. As shown in the figures, the error search performance was better when reading at 180 sec/page, a lower scroll speed. The users had the worst search performance when reading at the fastest scroll speed of 90 sec/page.

The highest accuracy was found with the repetition error and the subjects got the lowest accuracy with the semantic error. Furthermore, long articles had higher accuracy than short essays.

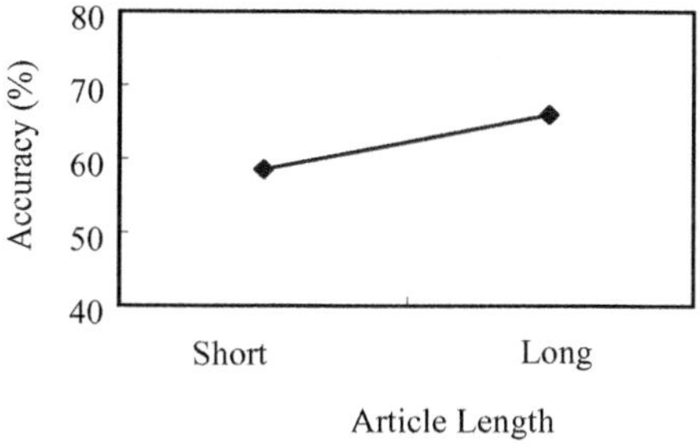

Fig. 3. The main effect plot of article length on accuracy

4.2 Subjective Ratings

In the experiment, reading fatigue was measured by subjective ratings of four questions. Analyses of variance were performed on the mean ratings for each question against the scroll speed and error type. The ANOVA results showed that different scrolling speed had significant effects on subjects' reading fatigue in all four questions, but the article length had no significant effects on subjects' reading fatigue (See Tables 3, 4, 5, and 6). The main effect plots for the four questions (eyes tired, heavy, dry, and feeling dizzy) with respect to scroll speed are shown in Fig.4, 5, 6, and 7, respectively. The subjective ratings showed that the users felt more visual strain at the 90 sec/page scrolling speed in one of the four questions, however, the other three questions showed that fatigue was more apparent at 180 sec/page.

Table 3. ANOVA table with F values and significance for Eye strain

Source	DF	Seq SS	Adj SS	Adj MS	F	P
Subject	9	29.35	29.35	3.2611	10.99	0.000
Task	1	0.4167	0.4167	0.4167	1.4	0.242
Scroll Speed	2	4.4333	4.4333	2.2167	7.47	0.002
Task*Scroll Speed	2	2.6333	2.6333	1.3167	4.44	0.017
Error	45	13.35	13.35	0.2967		
Total	59	50.183				

Table 4. ANOVA table with F values and significance for Eyelids heavy

Source	DF	Seq SS	Adj SS	Adj MS	F	P
Subject	9	29.00	29.00	3.2222	7.71	0.000
Task	1	1.2333	1.2333	0.6167	1.48	0.239
Scroll Speed	2	3.2667	3.2667	3.2667	7.82	0.008
Task*Scroll Speed	2	0.0333	0.0333	0.0167	0.04	0.961
Error	45	18.8	18.8	0.4178		
Total	59	52.3333				

Table 5. ANOVA table with F values and significance for Eye dry

Source	DF	Seq SS	Adj SS	Adj MS	F	P
Subject	9	14.6833	14.6833	1.6315	4.26	0.000
Task	1	0.4167	0.4167	0.4167	1.09	0.302
Scroll Speed	2	5.2333	5.2333	2.6167	6.84	0.003
Task*Scroll Speed	2	0.6333	0.6333	0.3167	0.83	0.444
Error	45	17.2167	17.2167	0.3826		
Total	59	38.1833				

Table 6. ANOVA table with F values and significance for Dizzy

Source	DF	Seq SS	Adj SS	Adj MS	F	P
Subject	9	9.2667	9.2667	1.0296	3.76	0.001
Task	1	0.2667	0.2667	0.2667	0.97	0.329
Scroll Speed	2	2.500	2.500	1.250	2.56	0.046
Task*Scroll Speed	2	0.2333	0.2333	0.1167	0.43	0.656
Error	45	12.3333	12.333	0.2741		
Total	59	24.6				

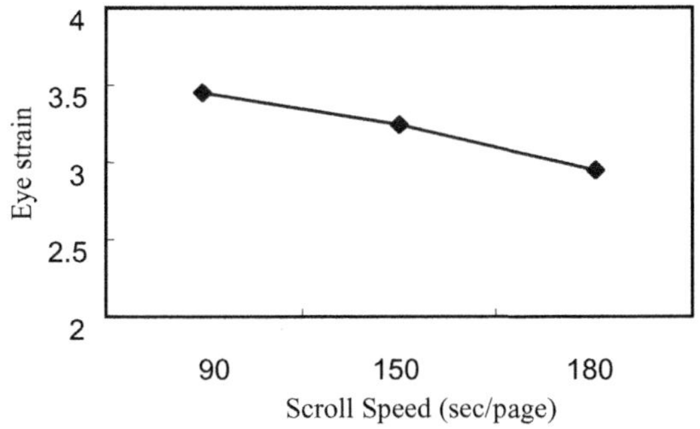

Fig. 4. The main effect plot of scroll speed on eye strain

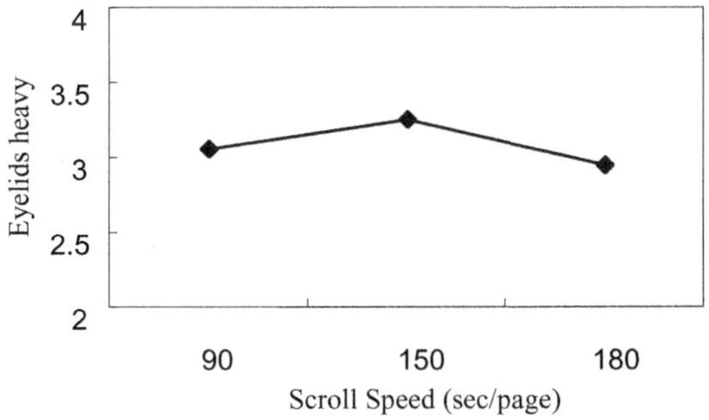

Fig. 5. The main effect plot of scroll speed on eye heavy

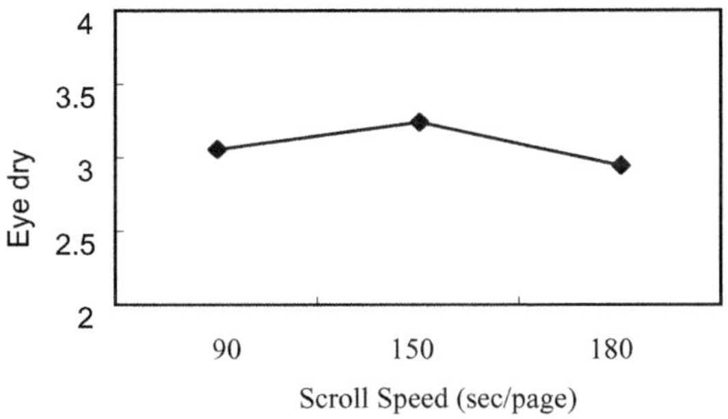

Fig. 6. The main effect plot of scroll speed on eye dry

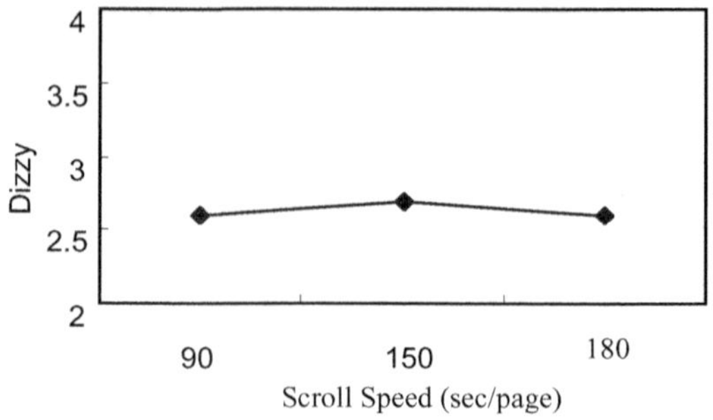

Fig. 7. The main effect plot of scroll speed on dizzy

5 Discussion

The use with the scrolling technique to view documents and text materials on the WWW has never been more common than today. Not only the performance but also the comfort of reading tasks is getting increasingly important in the Internet environment. In this study, we demonstrated that the searching task of Chinese texts in VDT was affected by the scroll speed, text error type, and article length. The searching accuracy decreased as the scrolling speed increased. On the other hand, eye strain was the highest with the high scrolling speed of 90 sec/page. Unfortunately, this fatigue result was not decisive because the other three fatigue questions showed that the participants got the most fatigue at the speed of 150 sec/page. It seemed that the participants tended to avoid staring at the jumpy text on the screen at the fastest scroll speed. This might explain why they obtained the worst accuracy at high scrolling speed but did not felt so fatigued with the searching task at the high speed.

The result found that long articles had a higher accuracy in text error search tasks. The reason for this could be explained by the learning effect of the task. There is more chance to adapt to the error finding context for the human information processor when the article is long enough. The participants might be able to practice more and learn more how to detect the errors in long reading tasks.

Another important question concerns effects of error types on searching performance. The present experiments showed that error types affected the searching ability. The repetition errors were easy to identify, however, the semantic errors were not. This could be attributed to the fact that semantic errors require more cognitive processing than pure repetition of words.

6 Conclusions

In this study, we investigated how scroll speeds, text error types, and article lengths affect the reading performance and visual fatigue in an error search task of Chinese articles which were shown on the visual display terminal (VDT). It was found that, the three factors, scroll speed, error type, and article length all significantly affected the accuracy of the Chinese text error search task. The accuracy decreased with the scroll speed. The fatigue effects were, however, not consistent across the four subjective fatigue questions. The results have implications for the design of automatic scrolling tool that is used to allow reading of long articles in small computing devices.

References

1. Andy, C., Matthew, S.: Hidden messages: evaluating the efficiency of code elision in program navigation. Interacting with Computers 15, 387–407 (2003)
2. Annie, P., Roussey, J.-Y., Thunin, O.: Effects of screen presentation on text reading and revising. Int. J. Human-Computer Studies 47, 563–589 (1997)
3. Sakagami, H., Kamba, T.: Learning personal preferences on online newspaper articles from user behaviors. Computer Networks and ISDN System 29, 1447–1455 (1997)
4. Huang, H.L., Wang, M.Y., Her, C.C.: An experimental study of Chinese information display on VDTs, Human Factor 25, 683–692 (1988)
5. Dyson, M.C., Kipping, G.J.: The Legibility of Screen Formats: are Three Columns Better than One? Computer & Graphics 21(6), 703–712 (1997)
6. Dyson, M.C., Haselgrove, M.: The influence of reading speed and line length on the effectiveness of reading from screen. Int. J. Human-Computer Studies 54, 585–612 (2001)
7. Nimwegen, C.V., Pouw, M., Oostendorp, H.V.: The influence of structure and reading-manipulation on usability of hypertexts, Interacting with Computers 12, 7–21 (1999)

WAP Access Methods on Mobile Phones

Zhang Hua[1] and Cui Yoon Ping[2]

[1] Nanyang Technological University
Singapore
Zhan0083@ntu.edu.sg
[2] School of Mechanical and Aerospace Engineering
Nanyang Technological University
Singapore
MYPChui@ntu.edu.sg

1 Introduction

With the development in telecommunication technology, application on Wireless Application Protocol (WAP) has dramatically increased all over the world. Users can browse the Internet anytime, anywhere, by using small mobile devices. The number of Wireless Application Protocol (WAP) pages grew dramatically on the Internet. In just eight months, the number has grown from almost zero to 4.4 million WAP pages in 2000 [1].

Wireless Application Protocol is a method of global open wireless Internet standards for real-time communication of wireless mobile devices such as Web cellular phones, Personal Digital Assistants (PDAs), and the Internet. WAP is not only a language but also a platform for development and interconnectivity [2]. It is defined as a communication protocol and application environment for the development of information resources, advanced telephony services, and Internet access from mobile devices [3].

Compare with Web Internet, Roche [4] listed several benefits of the mobile Internet as the follow:

- Low fixed costs: Compare with desktop or laptop, WAP enabled mobile device are cheaper. More consumers are able to afford it.
- Immediacy: Users can surf WAP any time, anywhere.
- Personal relevance: Unlike some computers that belong to companies or others mobile device is a personal belonging for individuals
- Location relevance: Mobile phones are more portable than computers. Users can even surf WAP while they are walking or taking bus.

However, WAP is not as popular as we expected. Although many people have WAP enabled mobile phone nowadays, most of them gave up using WAP after several attempts. The limitations of WAP applications in small mobile devices make WAP browsing difficult. The current access methods in WAP applications are designed by following the ways people browse the Internet. It is therefore important to explore the correct design guidelines for quick access for WAP browsing. Moreover, WAP services are charged by connection time or by amount of data transferred. Users have to pay for each step of operation in WAP browsing. It is important to improve access methods which help users to accomplish their tasks in

J. Jacko (Ed.): Human-Computer Interaction, Part II, HCII 2007, LNCS 4551, pp. 320–325, 2007.

minimum number of steps. From the studies of Nielsen Norman Group [5], 70% of the their participants explained that they would not use a WAP phone within one year. And 20% of them would not use WAP within three years.

One of the ways to reduce the operations for WAP users is to improve access methods which facilitate users to reach their goal without unwanted expense. However, because current WAP services are mainly designed by using the Web design principle, the usability of current WAP services is severely reduced [5]. In order to improve access methods and encourage users to use WAP, this project studied methods for quickly accessing WAP, comparing them with Web access methods design guidelines, and finding the guidelines for designing WAP quick access methods. The objective of this research was to find out the guidelines of WAP quick access methods; identify the limitations of WAP quick access methods; study WAP quick access methods and to identify guidelines for WAP access.

2 Literature Review

2.1 WAP Access Limitation

Knowledge transformation from Web sites to WAP sites simplifies users learning. In the WAP Usability Report, Ramsay and Nielsen [5] indicated that WAP navigation aids are generally restricted to *menu options, search engines*, and *bookmarks*, and navigation design on WAP-enable phones is based on the same principles as the Internet. However, compared with normal personal computer, WAP devices have their limitations. Arehart [3] concluded several limitations of WAP devices which encumber WAP surfing:

- Small screen
- Limited input capabilities
- Scrolling
- Limited Processor Power
- Limited Bandwidth
- Limited Graphics and Limited Deck Size

Due to the small screen, limited input keypad, narrow bandwidth and other limitations of mobile devices, WAP surfing is not as convenient as Web sites browsing for the users. Although the technologies are improving to compensate for those disadvantages, for example, screen sizes of the mobile device are becoming larger with color screens; bandwidth increased from 2G, 2.5G to 3G; the keypad was redesigned and pen input was used to overcome input limitations. However, intrinsic short comings still exist, e.g. the smaller screen that desktop system. So WAP sites designers should not directly transfer the Web design knowledge into the WAP sites design. Studies of the WAP users searching and browsing behaviors are important in the improvement of WAP.

One of the barriers to WAP surfing is that users have to pay for each step of the operation. Because WAP services are charged by connection time or by data transfer flux, it discourages users to explore WAP sites. As Ramsay and Nielsen [5] said

"Time on WAP is money - big money - and users will not thank you for wasting theirs".

One of the ways to reduce the operations for WAP users is to improve access methods which facilitate users to reach their goal without unwanted expense. However, because current WAP services are mainly designed by using the Web design principle, the usability of current WAP services is severely reduced [5]. In order to improve access methods and encourage users to use WAP, this project studied methods for quickly accessing WAP, comparing them with Web access methods design guidelines, and finding the guidelines for designing WAP quick access methods.

2.2 WAP Quick Access Methods

Back button: Chan, Fang et al. [6] suggested that the "Back" button should be designed as it has in a regular browser. However, due to the limitation of the WAP bandwidth, the reload of the previous WAP page is time consuming, and dead ends or error messages also blocked the path. [5]
Bookmarks: users need to input text to change the title other than the original URL [7]. due to the limitation of storage on mobile devices, the number of URLs that can be saved is too small to accommodate the number of selections a user is likely to need [5]
History List: Chan et al. [6] suggested mobile devices should provide a history list function that records the order in which hyperlinks have been traversed. But as the limitation of mobile screen and the memory ability, the history list in mobile devices cannot be as powerful as that in PC browser.
Customization: Chan et al. [6] indicated that experts and novice users might expect different interface design and contents. Because different users have different usage patterns, preferences, and skill levels, it is important to allow for variations among different users [8].
Personalization: Roche [4] concluded that the static web cannot offer the services that mobile users are looking for. Generally, people on the move do not have the time to browse, but need personalized information delivered to them in an automatic fashion. However, the static web is not designed to meet this user requirement. Personalization method should be used in WAP surfing in helping users to quickly access their goal without spending time in browsing.

Compare with personalization in Web design, the two important factors in Web personalization [9], language and information arrangement, are also necessary in WAP personalization. Because of the small screen and input limitation in mobile devices, arrange information in order to reduce the page scrolling seems more important for WAP users.

3 Methodology

Thirty participants participated in the survey. Nineteen participants were asked to fill up a questionnaire followed by a short interview. Eleven participants were sent a copy of the questionnaire and emailed back their replies.

The average age of these participants are 22 years old, the youngest is 17 years old and the oldest is 27. All of them had full experience in using computer and mobile phone. They also had experience in WAP surfing and is familiar with using bookmark, history list, and personalization.

4 Results

4.1 Bookmarks

According to the studies in literature review, there were three main limitation of bookmark system in Web browsing. Bookmark arrangement was the major problems for most of users; cognitive workload increased while users making decision to store Web pages; dead link and duplicated links were also the problems for users to arrange bookmarks.

Compare with the result discussion, these three limitations somehow changed in WAP application. Firstly, bookmark arrangement was not the major problem for WAP users because most WAP users save less than 10 bookmarks in their mobile devices. Secondly, cognitive workload did not have much difference while users store WAP pages, but recognizing the saved bookmark may require users to spend more time due to not remembering or recognizing the bookmark titles or URL addresses usually not recognizable enough. Finally, the problem of dead link became more obvious in WAP application. It might due to the change of URL address, or big size of picture in WAP page, or hardware problems.

Because of the limitation of mobile devices, bookmark system design should base on the idea of reducing the operation steps and facilitating users to recognize pages.

4.2 History List

According to the literature review, there were two main problems while using history list in computer. One was that the various navigation models did not match the users' mental model. The other was the URL address was difficult for users to recognize.

In the WAP application, these two disadvantages became more obvious. Firstly, different mobile phones were designed by using different navigation models. Even users were familiar with one navigation model, if they changed their phones. It might take them a long time to be accustomed with the other kind of navigation model. Secondly, not only was history list difficult to recognize, but also the suggestion of integrating picture into history list [10] in Web browsing could not be used in WAP application.

Supposed the users went to the wrong URL address while they traced back through history list. Unfortunately, if they were not familiar with the navigation model, they will most likely to lose their way at the end.

4.3 Personalization

Personalization in WAP application is as necessary as in Web. It helps users feel more in control of the system, and facilitate quick access in WAP browsing. However, according to the survey result, the current WAP personalization is not so popular. It is possibly because users do not use WAP as often as used Web Internet.

5 Discussion

The quick access methods can be classified into three categories: Navigation, Customization, and Personalization. The relationships of the three groups are showed in Figure 2-3:

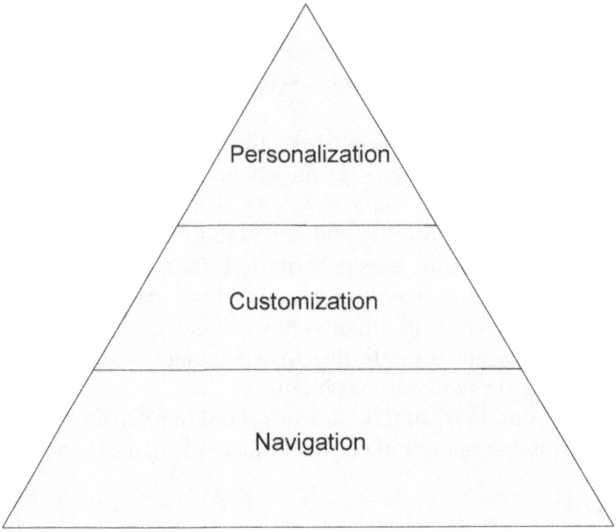

Fig. 1. WAP Quick Access Framework

Navigation is the basic quick access methods which facilitate all users surfing WAP / Web sites without losing their ways, for example: bookmarks, history list, back / forward buttons and so on. The navigation functions are mainly provided either by browsers in personal computer or by mobile devices in wireless application protocol. Some internet services also offer their navigation functions.

Customization used to categorize users and provides different functions for each group of users. It is system initiated, so while Web customization classifies users in computer Internet, WAP customization categorizes users through wireless application protocol service.

Personalization is user initiated. It allows every user to organize their WAP /Web pages account to facilitate quick access. The main difference between Web and WAP personalization is that while Web personalization allows users to finish the personalized operation and then use it in the personal computer, WAP personalization is often performed from a personal computer but used in mobile device platform.

References

1. Funk, J.L.: The future of the mobile phone Internet: an analysis of technological trajectories and lead users in the Japanese market. Technology in Society 27(1), 69–83 (2005)
2. Vujosevic, S., Laberge, R.: WAP Integration: Professional Developer's Guide Series. John Wiley & Sons, Inc, New York (2001)
3. Arehart, C.: Professional WAP. Programmer to programmer, Birmingham, UK Chicago: Wrox Press Ltd. xi, p. 813 (2000)
4. Roche, J.: Web to WAP for a Real Start of the New Millennium, [cited (2000)
5. Ramsay, M., Nielsen, J.: WAP Usability, Nielsen Norman Group (2000) http://www.NNgroup.com/ reports/wap
6. Chan, S.S., et al.: Usability for Mobile Commerce Across Multiple Form Factors. Electronic Commerce Research 3(3), 187–199 (2002)
7. Schmidt, A., Schroder, H., Frick, O.: WAP - Designing for Small User Interfaces. In: Human Factors in Computing Systems, ACM Press, New York (2000)
8. Gong, J., Tarasewich, P.: Guidelines for Handheld Mobile Device Interface Design. pp. 3751–3756 (2004) http://www.ccs.neu.edu/home/tarase/GuidelinesGongTarase.pdf
9. Kumar, R.L., Smith, M.A., Bannerjee, S.: User interface features influencing overall ease of use and personalization. Information & Management 41(3), 289–302 (2004)
10. Kaasten, S., Greenberg, S.: Designing an Integrated Bookmark / History Systme for Web Browsing. In: Proceedings of the Western Computer Graphics Symposium, Panorama Mountain Village, BC, Canada (2000)

Evaluation of Content Handling Methods for Tabletop Interface

Ryoko Ishido[1], Keigo Kitahara[1], Tomoo Inoue[2], and Ken-ichi Okada[1]

[1] Graduate School of Science and Technology, Keio University
{ishido,kitahara,okada}@mos.ics.keio.ac.jp
[2] Graduate School of Library, Information and Media Studies, University of Tsukuba
inoue@slis.tsukuba.ac.jp

Abstract. We focused on face-to-face collaborative learning in a classroom using spatio-temporal contents, which is typically conducted after outdoor class in an elementary school. We have developed a tangible collaborative learning support system that uses physical objects and associating spatio-temporal contents. We have implemented a few methods to handle these contents. Two experiments were conducted to confirm that better information accessibility was provided by the system than conventional pen and paper method.

Keywords: CSCL, TUI, tabletop, physical objects.

1 Introduction

There are researches on tabletop interfaces reflecting the needs of using computer media by multiple people. Much earlier is use of computing in a physical world such as the digital desk. Field trip that aims to get authentic experience has become more common in formal education in Japan recently. Preparation and review of the activity are important for learning, whereas they are not paid enough research attention. Learning resource in the review (content) typically includes physical objects that were picked up and notes that were taken in the activity.

We propose methods to handle these contents on a tabletop display system in this paper. We also describe implementation of the system and experiments for evaluating the methods.

2 Collaborative Outdoor Learning

2.1 Present Outdoor Learning

Outdoor learning is effective to have a social experience under the open sky, and get knowledge about nature. Our goal is supporting in case of getting knowledge.

First of all, learners commonly get the information about plants and animals by using books, illustrated guides or the internet as a preparatory learning. Then, they go outdoors and get involved with observation of the target objects. At the same time, they collect data by taking notes, sketching, taking pictures or gathering the objects.

J. Jacko (Ed.): Human-Computer Interaction, Part II, HCII 2007, LNCS 4551, pp. 326–335, 2007.

After that, they bring the contents back to a classroom to review the outdoor activity. And they do discussion and supplemental learning activity such as investigation. In the investigation, they put and display the contents on a large map or a large white paper for the purpose of visibility in time and space[1]. Through these collaborative learning, they can deepen their understanding of the topic than individual learning[5]. We focus on the reviewing phase of learning that is usually held at the classroom. Importance of experiences such as observation in the outdoors is extremely high. However, it is thought that not only it but also a review in terms of geographical and temporal context after coming back to a classroom is important to deepen understanding.

2.2 Problems of Reviewing Outdoor Learning

In tradition, students put the gathered data or write some information on the paper, and discuss with other students. However, there are some problems on such traditional studies based on the paper. The quantity of the contents they can handle is limited, and it is difficult to store all contents or to relate them. Although some schools use computers for learning, they have problems that it takes long time to get accustomed to use and it must be individual works because it is hard to communicate with other students. An efficient way of review after outdoor class is to share what each individual student has learned. Presentation to each other, discussion among students helps understanding [1]. Therefore, a learning support system in this context should support mutual presentation and discussion among students. Such a system should have an effective method for displaying digital data, and an interface that enables learners to have presentations smoothly.

3 Related Work

3.1 Tabletop Interface

Koike proposed a tabletop system recognizing a hand by difference of temperature of the human body and a desk side with a far infrared rays camera[6]. In addition, Rekimoto proposed a system recognizing hands positions by change of capacitance[7].

In comparison with them, we use a pressure-sensitive display for our system. By using a pressure-sensitive display, it becomes easy to recognize the position and moving of the physical objects on the display. It is accomplished by moving them while pushing to the display lightly.

3.2 Learning Support System with Physical Objects

Sugimoto proposed a Group learning support system that the physical world and the virtual world were combined[8]. In addition, Deguzman proposed a system to display a cross section of the human body with a lay figure[9].

Our system also has physical objects to handle digital data as well as above systems. They mainly uses physical objects to improve learners' understanding, whereas our system has more purpose that learners can study with various information like sight, the sense of smell, the sense of touch by using the physical objects.

4 Design of a Tabletop Display System

In order to solve the above-mentioned problems, we propose a system that multiple learners can review their study collaboratively[10]. Figure1 shows an overview of the proposed system. Pressure-sensitive display laid down on a table allows 2 to 4 learners to surround it and to put something on there as a table. Learners can handle the digital content with their fingers or physical objects on the display when they use the system.

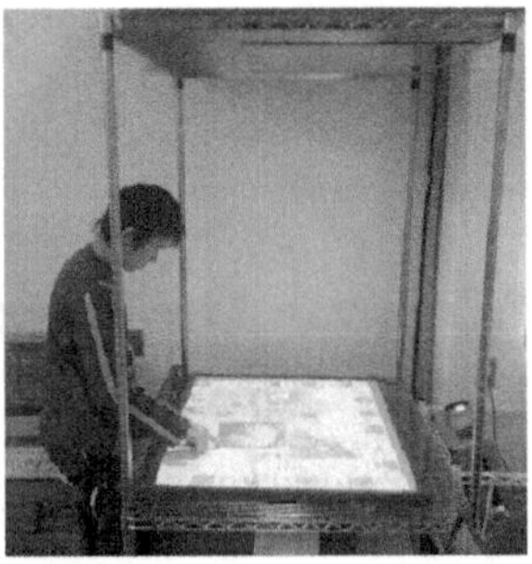

Fig. 1. System overview

4.1 Supporting Collaboration

Learning effects are classified in "improvement of understanding" and "improvement of efficiency", and we can say that a study of an education system aims to achieve one or two of these. In this paper, we aim to improve efficiency of learning from the aspect of human interface.

In collaborative learning that multiple users work together in the same space, it is necessary to support passing digital content between the collaborative working space and the individual working space[11], and they need to share their information[5]. It is also necessary to encourage communication between learners to support learning efficiently. Therefore we implemented 3 types of method for passing and sharing digital data easily, and try to encourage their communication.

4.2 Physical Objects

One of the advanced points of our system is using tabletop interface with physical objects like photos or the models. Collaborative learning using physical objects realizes the effects such as follows; the learners who are inexperienced in a computer can participate in learning easily, it can improve linguistic or non-linguistic communication and support exchanging opinions each other by sharing physical objects with others physically [8], and they can learn in three-dimensional field of view [9]. On the other hand, digital data have advantages that they can treat vast amounts of information (physical object has amount limitation) and they are easy to copy, save, and convert. Because our system can handle both physical data and digital data, it provides high-quality learning effect. The system recognizes physical objects by using barcode symbols and touch-sensitive display. It displays relevant contents around the physical objects. In order to deepen students' understanding, mixing physical objects and digital data makes up for mutual lack of information.

4.3 Related Information

In our proposal system, learners review the learning in the outside by using data gathered by them. The system adds some metadata to collected data, and associate original data to surrounding and past data. The metadata holds following parameters; name of the picture, shooting date and time, shooting area, comments from the photographer.

Accumulating these data like pictures or comments enhances learning about long terms easily. Therefore our proposal clears the problem that only one season or topic can be handled.

5 Implementation

5.1 System Configuration and Implementation Environment

Figure2 shows a system configuration. A screen image is projected by a projector to a pressure-sensitive display (47inches, SMART Board) been laid on the stainless rack. Physical objects are recognized by added barcode symbols and a barcode reader. The system has been implemented on JDK1.4.1.

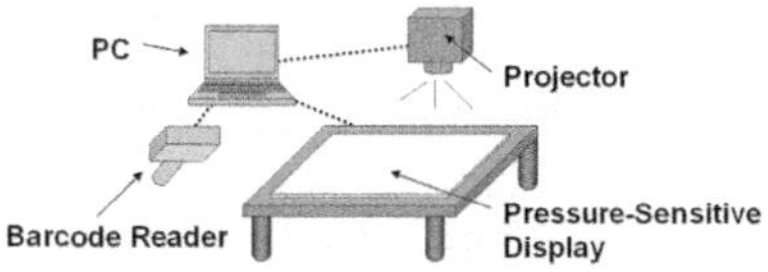

Fig. 2. System configuration

5.2 Function of the Proposed System

We assume that collected data which include pictures and sketches etc. have already been preserved on the server. Learners can handle digital data gotten from the server by using their own fingers or physical objects. Figure3 shows a sample window which has several pictures of plants and insects on the map. Center of the display is map area as shared space. Outside of the center area is delivering and receiving data area. This area also indicates temporal data.

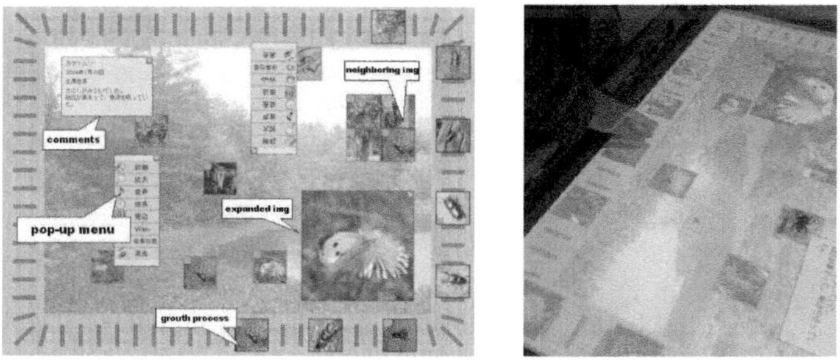

Fig. 3. Sample images

Display Related Information. There are following five types of related information; expanded image, detailed information, surrounding data, temporal data, and web information. Learners can expand the image and compare to other ones, or get the photographer's name, shooting date, and comments from detailed information of the data. Learners need to display the pop-up menu by clicking the digital data that they want to check and display relevant information.

The system displays the surrounding data by checking selected data with the requirement below; shooting point is within some range, and shooting date and time corresponds.It also displays the temporal data by checking selected data with the requirement below; conformity of the shooting place, and conformity of the name of a photo agenda. Temporal data are displayed on the place like railway track out of sharing space in the shooting date order. These requirements apply only about plants, and learners can see the temporal data, growth list of the particular plant. Besides about insects, the system only checks conformity of the name of the photo agenda because they don't grow only in the particular same places, therefore learners can see the growth of a kind of insects (not particular insects).

Web information is the function that displays web search results with a simple browser. Web searching is done with the name of a photo agenda.

Passing the Data. Users can move the digital data by dragging with their fingers or physical objects in our proposed system. However, it is difficult to drag the data far away on a large display. Then we implemented following two delivering methods except dragging.

One of methods is flicking. It is intuitive action because people do the same action in the real world, as well as dragging. Learners can deliver the data which direction they want immediately, and the data automatically turns around the direction that is easy to see for a learner received that. The second method is rubbing right and left on the railway track area. The data on the railway track turn depending on the amount of rubbing on the area. Learners can group the images and deliver them to someone at one time. While turning the track, the order does not change and the surrounding students can see them at the same time. So this method makes the students' works more efficient. One more advantage is that this method does not interrupt the works on the map, sharing space. In both methods, learners can deliver the data which direction they want immediately, and the data automatically rotates in the direction that is easy for them to look at.

These functions provide the users communication with others who stands on the opposite side. This makes their learning more efficient.

6 Evaluation

Our purpose in this study is supporting collaborative learning with advantage of mixing a real world and a digital world. In order to confirm whether the purpose is realized or not, we examined in points of accessing and passing data.

6.1 Experiment1

Purpose. Accessing data in a short time is a point of learning in digital world. We evaluated which can take shorter time to find the required data, the traditional method based on paper or that based on our system. Subjects try to find and read a word that is displayed instead of an image of a insect or a plant, and we measure the time to be found all directed data. This experiment was done about surrounding data and temporal data. Though our system is for elementary school children, we did this experiment for a university student. However we conceive there is not a difference compared with university students in a point of finding.

Experiment Procedure. 18 undergraduate and graduate students participated in this experiment.

Traditional Method based on Paper. We explained to subjects about the traditional method for outdoor learning, and also explained about the situation they were in. That was such as following;

> *You are in the class, and reviewing with white large paper put on data of insects and plants. You have had 15 times of such classes till now, and 15 sheets of white large paper have accumulated. They are prepared piled in time order. There is the latest white large paper with data, separated from them. And now, you are going to learn the growth of insects and the plants living near them.*

We explained the following points for a subject before an experiment.

> *Figure4(a) shows a part of the paper. The data about one insect and two plants, assumed that was collected nearby, are arranged in one area. And such 7 areas are printed on a sheet of paper. Three data of each areas are surrounded with a square frame. 7 areas are printed in same layout with each 15 sheets of paper. The data in a same paper are the data gathered in the same date. In order to evaluate whether subjects can find the data they want, we used a set of data composed with a number and a letter instead of the image of an insect or a plants. The sets of characters are assigned at random in each sheets of paper, even though they're same insects or plants. By measuring the time to find the sets of characters and write down them on the answer sheet, we will evaluate whether subjects can find data printed on paper efficiently.*

We directed subjects to find and write down the sets of characters about two data, also their surrounding data and temporal data. We measured the time to finish writing down them. The process we practically have done is as follows.

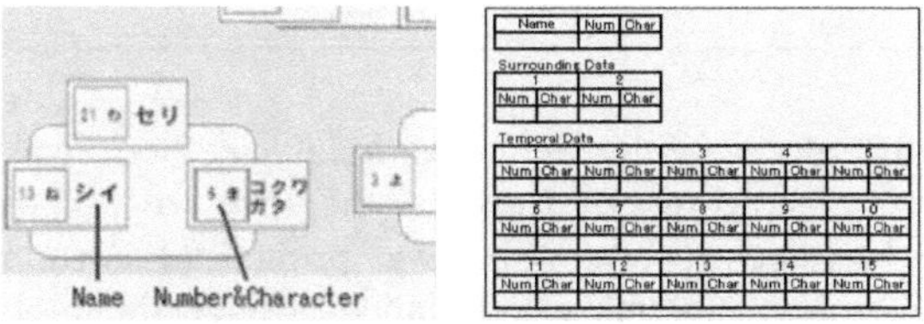

Fig. 4. (a) A paper for traditional method (b) A paper for writing character set

1. An experimenter read out the names, a Miyama stag beetle and a Hirata stag beetle.
2. A subject tried to find two directed data and its surrounding data from a paper printed 7 areas' data, and wrote its set of characters on the answer sheet (Figure4 (b)). An experimenter measured the time till a subject finished writing down.

3. An experimenter directed a subject to find the temporal data and write down the set of characters on the answer sheet by using all accumulated paper put on data. Subject had to fill in the blanks on the answer sheet sequentially from an old data. Same as 2, an experimenter measured the time till a subject finished writing down.

Method based on Our System. *At first, an experimenter gave a demonstration and explained about our system's function. Subjects tried to use our system in 5 minutes with another set of data that wasn't used for an experiment. An experimenter explained following points;*

- How to display the relevant information
- How to move data by dragging, flicking or rubbing a railway track area
- The rule that temporal data is ordered counterclockwise from old one

We directed subjects to find and write down the sets of characters about two data, also their surrounding data and temporal data. We measured the time to finish writing them. The process we practically have done is as follows.

1. An experimenter prepares one insect's data in each 7 areas on the tabletop display.
2. An experimenter read out the names, a common yellow swallowtail and an albocaerulean.
3. A subject tried to find two directed data and its surrounding data, and wrote its set of characters on the answer sheet. An experimenter measured the time till a subject finished writing down.
4. They did about temporal data in the same way as above.

Result and Discussion about Experiment1. Table1 shows the average of the measurement time about all subjects. From this result, it was found that using our proposed system shortened the 42% time that participants find and write about the relevant data in comparison with the traditional method based on paper.

Table 1. Result of experiment1

	based on paper[sec]	*based on our system[sec]*
surrounding data	11.8 (1.4)	13.9 (2.6)
temporal data (growth process data)	258.7 (45.8)	143.7 (34.4)
total	270.5	157.6

Significant difference with the traditional method was recognized about surrounded data by carrying out t-test in the level of significance 5% (t=-3.09, p=4.6E-03). It is because prepared paper was printed all surrounding data on a sheet of paper previously, and subjects could glance through them easier than our system. On the other hand, as surrounding data weren't displayed on our system previously and needed to handle pop-up menu, it took a little more time than the traditional method. However, the difference was less than 2 seconds. Therefore it was able to confirm that needed handling on our system was practical enough to display surrounding data.

Significant difference with the method on our system was recognized about temporal data by carrying out t-test in the level of significance 5% (t=8.51, p=9.9E-10).

It is because data on our system maintained the metadata and it had been implemented to display the temporal data efficiently only by one click. In addition, we consider that subjects could read the temporal data in shorter time as the data gotten from the system was displayed on the railway track area around sharing space in order of time. In comparison with this, there was need to turn over the paper many times to find temporal data in the traditional method, and it took much more time than our system.

From these results, we confirmed that our system enables grasping the relevant data in a shorter time comprehensively. And in comparison with a learning only in a real world, we also confirmed that a learning been added a digital world had more advantages from the point of data access in case that there is comparatively much number of data like our experiments.

6.2 Experiment2

Purpose. In order to confirm the validity about three methods to pass digital data, dragging, flicking, and rubbing the railway track area, we examine which method is used in what kind of situation.

Experiment Procedure. 10 undergraduate and graduate students participated in this experiment. On an experiment, subjects tried to use our system in 5 minutes and an experimenter explained following points;

- A subject is learning about a particular data displayed in the tabletop display in front of her/him, and is going to pass the data to another learner (actually an experimenter).
- How to use three functions to pass the digital data.

Subjects tried to send following amount of data; one data, three data, and seven temporal data. Figure5 shows the position of a subject and an experimenter.

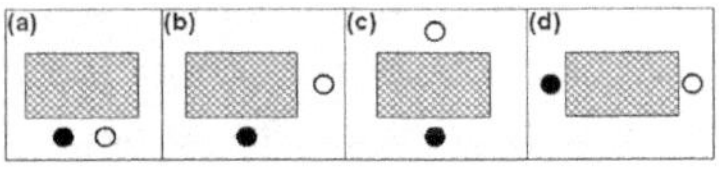

Fig. 5. Positions of subject and experimenter

We examined in the following procedures about each position, (a), (b), (c) and (d) in Figure5.

1. A data was displayed on an edge of a sharing map area in front of a subject, and she/he sent the data to an experimenter.
2. Temporal data was displayed on a railway track area, and a subject sent these data to an experimenter. The choice of passing data function depended on the subjects.
3. We investigated what kind of function was chosen to pass data.

Result and Discussion about Experiment2. It was determined from figure6 that it is different in choosing function to pass the data, by a position of a subject and a kind of data. When a subject sent single data, the function by railway track area was hardly used, and it was observed that dragging was mostly used when the distance of a subject and an experimenter was near each other. And more, flicking was mostly used

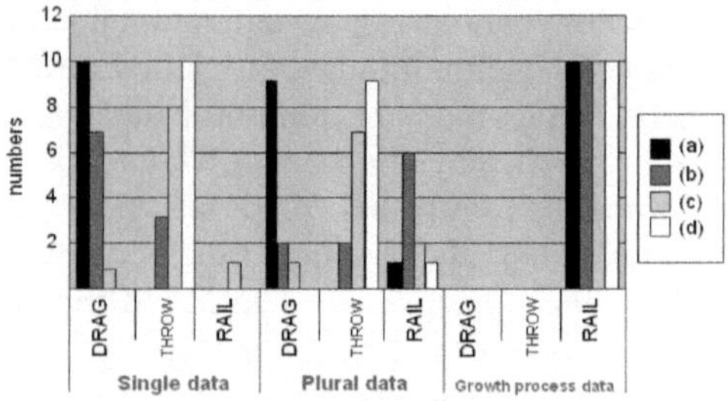

Fig. 6. Result of experiment2

when a subject were distant from the other. The reason why a difference was observed according to their distance might be that the methods except dragging were easier to send single data to distant place. On the other hand, in case that they sent plural data, it was observed that ratios to use dragging and flicking decrease and ratios to use a function rubbing railway track area increases. This result was lead because the function using a railway truck area enabled a subject to send plural data all together. And also all subjects used the method rubbing a railway track area to pass the temporal data. It is because seven data was needed to be passed to the experimenter as keeping their order.

In traditional learning, it is possible to pass many sheets of paper with plural data all together. Since our system can behave same as that with digital data, we can say that our system is effective to learn collaboratively from the point of data passing.

6.3 Discussion

Though we can expect that taking long time to find contents leads learners to be able to get knowledge, it is necessary to be able to find contents in shorter time since we assume that learning time is limited in the elementary school. Since we confirmed that our system enables learners to find contents in shorter time in the experiments, we can say that learners can study much more things in limited time in comparison with the traditional method.

It is desirable that learners have discussions and presentations actively in collaborative learning and it is necessary to support these activities in the point of sharing data each other. Therefore it is necessary to be able to pass the data easily in the case that the system supports sharing digital data on a large tabletop display. From evaluation experiments, we confirmed that our system's methods to pass data are effective.

7 Conclusion

In traditional reviewing outdoor learning, there were some problems such as difficulty of accumulating data or relating each data. Therefore, in this study, we suggested the outdoor learning support system using physical objects and tabletop interface. We implemented the function that enabled displaying relevant data or temporal data using the data including metadata. We also implemented three methods to pass digital data.

In this paper, we minutely described about evaluations. From the results in the evaluation experiments, we confirmed that our proposed system's methods to display the data can grasp needed contents in shorter time than traditional methods, especially in the case of handling a lot of data, and effectiveness of the methods to pass the digital data.

Acknowledgement. This work is supported in part by a project study of Graduate School of Library, Information and Media Studies, University of Tsukuba, 2006.

References

[1] Hatanaka, T.: General Statement of Science Education for Young Science Teachers, Toyokan Pub-lishing Company (2004)
[2] May, T.S.: Elements of Success in Environmental Education through Practitioner Eyes. The. journal of Environmental Education 31(3), 4–11 (2000)
[3] Okada, M., et al.: DigitalEE II: RV-Augmented Interface Design for Networked Collaborative Envi-ronmental Learning. In: Proceedings of the International Conference on Computer Support for Collaborative Learning 2003 (CSCL2003), pp. 265–274 Kluwer Academic Publishers (2003)
[4] Wellner, P.: Interacting with paper on the digital desk. Communications of the ACM 36(7), 86–96 (1993)
[5] Japan Society for Educational Technology, Educational Engineering Dictionary, Jikkyo Publishing Company (2004)
[6] Koike, H., Sato, Y., Kobayashi, Y.: Integrating Paper and Digital Information on EnhancedDesk: A Method for Realtime Finger Tracking on an Augmented Desk System. ACM Transactions on CHI 8(4), 307–322 (2001)
[7] Rekimoto, J.: SmartSkin: An Infrastructure for Freehand Manipulations on Interactive Surfaces. In: Proceedings of CHI'02, pp.113–120 (2002)
[8] Sugimoto, M., Hosoi, K., Hashizume, H.: Caretta: a system for supporting face-to-face collaboration by integrating personal and shared spaces. In: Proceedings of CHI'04, pp.41–48 (2004)
[9] Edward Deguzman, F., Ho-Ching, W.-l., Matthews, T. Rattenbury, T., Back, M., Steve Harrison, S.:EEWWW!: Tangible Instruments for Navigating into the Human Body. In: Extended Abstracts of CHI'03, pp.806–807 (2003)
[10] Kitahara, K., et al.: Development of a tangible collaborative learning support system for spatio-temporal contents. In: The 56th GN group meeting, pp.37–42 (2005)
[11] Rekimoto, J.: A multiple-device approach for supporting whiteboard-based interactions. In: Proceedings of CHI'98, pp.344–351 (1998)

Interacting with a Tabletop Display Using a Camera Equipped Mobile Phone

Seokhee Jeon[1], Gerard J. Kim[2,*], and Mark Billinghurst[3]

[1] VRPM Lab., Dept. Of CSE, POSTECH, Korea
yeager@postech.ac.kr
[2] DXP Lab., Dept. Of CSE, Korea University, Korea
gjkim@korea.ac.kr
[3] HIT Lab NZ , University of Canterbury, New Zealand
mark.billinghurst@hitlabnz.org

Abstract. Today's mobile phones have not only become the most representative device in the new ubiquitous computing era but also dramatically improved in terms of their multi-modal sensing and display capabilities. This advance makes the mobile phone an ideal candidate for a more natural interaction device in ubiquitous computing environment. This paper proposes techniques which use camera-equipped mobile phones for interacting with 2D and 3D applications on a tabletop display environment. The camera acts as the main sensor for a gesture-based interaction. Using the mobile phone with an interactive touch screen allows the use of techniques that move beyond single hand/finger input to improve task performance. The interaction performances of the proposed techniques and design guidelines are also described in this paper.

Keywords: Tabletop, Motion flow, Interaction techniques, Cell/Mobile phones.

1 Introduction

The mobile phone has become one of the most ubiquitous computing devices, with processing power, storage, environment sensing, and display capabilities. Thus, it is very natural to use mobile phones as interaction devices for ubiquitous computing environments. One popular concept in ubiquitous computing environments is the notion of intelligent furniture equipped with a display and interaction interface. In this context, mobile phones could provide a unique "private" information and sensory display (e.g. LCD, sound, vibration). More importantly, the mobile phone's sensing and communication capabilities can be used to provide user input.

A large number of today's mobile phones are equipped with sensing devices such as a movie camera, microphone, and even acceleration sensor. They can also share the computational load with the main server system using communication modules such as Bluetooth, wireless LAN, infra-red communication, and ultra wide band technology.

In this paper, we focus on how to use the mobile phone as a user input device for tabletop display environments for 2D and 3D applications. We focus on interaction

* Corresponding author.

J. Jacko (Ed.): Human-Computer Interaction, Part II, HCII 2007, LNCS 4551, pp. 336–343, 2007.

techniques using the camera from a camera equipped mobile phone, and motion flow tracking. The camera is a natural choice to use for user/cursor tracking, object tracking or gesture recognition depending on the desired interaction mode. The mobile phone can also be used as a second input for touch screen displays for tasks that are not intuitive with a single hand or finger input.

2 Related Work

Possibilities for interaction with smart hand-held devices (e.g. palmtop computers) were first investigated in 1993 by Fitzmaurice et al. [1]. In this paper, the authors suggested several principles for display and interaction using a palmtop computer. Watsen et al. have used a PDA to interact in a virtual environment, but the interaction was mostly button or touch screen based and no tracking was used nor necessary [2]. Kukimoto et al. [3] also developed a similar PDA based interaction device for Virtual Reality (VR), but with a 6DOF tracker attached to it. They were able to demonstrate 3D interaction such as 3D drawing through the PDA by moving it and pressing the button or touch screen..

Several previous researches have tried to use the camera and computer vision techniques for user interactions on handheld devices, especially for 3D interactions [4, 5]. However, robust motion tracking is not easy, particularly since the computational power of mobile phones is often not sufficient for the needed image processing [6]. However, mobile phones are becoming more powerful in terms of their processing and computing efficiency, and so this obstacle might be overcome in the near future. Wagner et al. focused on the application of hand-held devices for augmented reality. He implemented a marker-based augmented reality system using a self-contained hand-held device and applied it to the Signpost project[7]. Paelke et al. developed a hand-held soccer game which uses a camera for detecting a real kick gesture [8]. Hachet et al. used camera-equipped hand-held device as an interaction prop for a virtual environment. In their system, the hand-held camera recognized the movement and poses of a special marker held in the other hand [9, 10]. Rohs et al. [11] combined mobile phones with a large public display. Phone motion tracking was achieved using an optical flow algorithm and software markers on the display. The Spotcode project [12] also focused on the use of a mobile phone for input with a large shared display. They designed context-related markers for the tracking.

3 Interaction Scenario and Requirement

As a starting point, we present a scenario for using a camera phone for interaction with a touch screen operated tabletop display.

(2D Interaction Scenario) Jack and Jill are preparing a joint report. Jack pulls up a couple of files on a shared tabletop display and tries to show one to Jill. He chooses the document with his finger on the touch screen and drags it toward Jill who is sitting at a different side of the table, and at the same time rotates his mobile phone, with the other hand, to rotate the document toward Jill. Jill finds the document to be too small for her viewing pleasure and increases its scale by selecting an anchor point, dragging upward to make space, and gestures her mobile phone, with the other hand, side ways to enlarge the document all at the same time. By a touch of a button, the mobile phone is turned into a magnifying glass allowing Jill to examine the fine details of the figure in the document.

(3D Interaction Scenario) Jill has a 3D model of a product from her company stored in her mobile phone. She wants to discuss the product with Jack. She copies the 3D model file to the tabletop display. She would like to show to Jack a closer look of the bottom part of the model. She rotates the model and zooms into the model using her mobile phone.

These scenarios illustrate the need for two handed simultaneous interaction for object rotation. Without the two handed input, the object rotation must be carried out in sequence. Touch screen systems usually do not allow two handed simultaneous input. Thus, one solution is to use a smart tangible prop, like a sensor equipped mobile phone, as an embodied interface.

4 The Proposed Interaction Techniques

4.1 Gesture-Based Interaction

Based on the scenario and the requirement depicted in Section 3, we propose an approach for object rotation using the mobile phone in a two handed simultaneous interaction. Without the two handed input, object rotation must be carried out in sequence. Touch screen systems usually do not allow simultaneous two handed input. The proposed solution carries out object selection and translation by touch screen input and maps the mobile phone's rotation to the target object's rotation. The mobile phone's rotation is detected by a motion flow technique so the user does not have to aim at anything. Object scaling can be carried out in similar manner.

If the object is a 3D model object, the user can use the mobile phone as a tracking prop. That is, the 3D model just follows motion of the mobile phone. Figures 1 and 3 illustrate the process.

Figure 2 and Figure 3 shows the actual implementation of the proposed interaction for 2D and 3D objects respectively. All proposed interaction techniques were implemented and tested on the Nokia 6630 mobile phone with the Symbian Series 60 Second edition FP2 as its operating system and a NextWindow one finger touch screen on a tabletop display.

Figure 2 illustrates the implementation for 2D rotation (top row). The object pivoted by the finger touch is rotated according to the rotated camera phone. The lower row shows the case for a 2D scaling operation in which the selected object (by finger touch input) is scaled according to the motion of the camera phone.

Similarly, Figure 3 demonstrates two handed manipulation of an object in a 3D environment. An object selected by finger touch (e.g. virtual ray) rotates around its (predefined) local coordinate axes according to the correspondingly rotating camera phone. Thus the phone acts as a physical embodiment of the selected object.

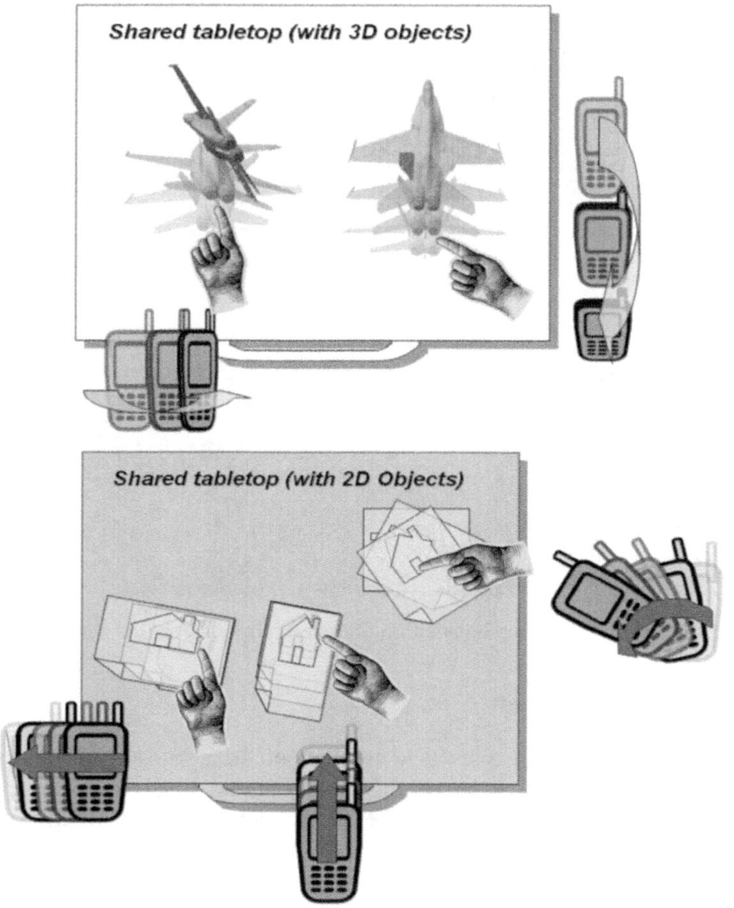

Fig. 1. Object rotation and scaling using a mobile phone and one finger touch. The task is accomplished efficiently in a simultaneous manner: 3D object rotation (above) and 2D object scaling and rotation (below).

Fig. 2. Snapshots from actual implementation of the proposed interaction for 2D object manipulation: object rotation (top row) and scaling (lower row)

Fig. 2. (Continued)

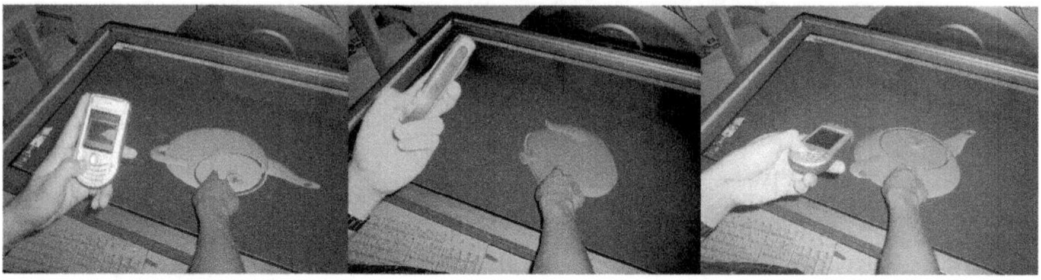

Fig. 3. Snapshots from actual implementation of the proposed interaction for 3D object rotation

4.2 Mobile Phone Tracking

Motion flow based tracking is used to implement the proposed interaction method without special markers. It is based on the pyramidal Lucas-Kanade optical flow algorithm [13]. This algorithm first applies corner detection for finding feature points and then uses image pyramids for tracking those feature points.

Due to the limitation in the processing power of the mobile phone, the tracking accuracy and rate is relatively low. To compensate this limitation, we adjusted the load balance among the frame rate, image resolution of the camera and the number of feature points by trial and error. We finally used 10 feature points, with the camera image resolution of 160 by 120 and obtained about 6~7 frame/sec tracking rate.

The movement vectors, along two adjacent frames, are obtained from the 10 feature points of each frame, and outliers are filtered out. The movement velocity of the camera can be calculated by averaging these movement vectors. This value becomes the velocity of the user's hand. Because it is not possible to distinguish between x-axis/y-axis rotation (roll and pitch) and x-axis/y-axis translation by only using the optical flow, the velocity is regarded as for rotation or translation depending on the interaction mode. The exponential transform is applied to the velocity vector in case of 2D manipulation, while the user's hand velocity is mapped directly to 3D object's rotation in 3D object rotation case. The exponential transform in the 2D case is beneficial both for fine control with small hand movement and in fast control with large hand movement. Also, linear interpolation is employed because of the low tracking rate for smooth cursor movement on the table. The system needs to interpolate at least 6 movement vectors between two adjacent real data to achieve the rendering rate of 40 fps for the tabletop display.

Optical flow only gives two degree of freedom movement data and only has a limited degree of tracking freedom (horizontal and vertical translation or rotation). However, partial information about the z-axis rotation (yaw rotation) can be obtained from analyzing the two degree of freedom information. The z-axis rotation of the phone can be estimated by detecting the differences of moving direction among features. Recognizing the z-axis rotation in this way is somewhat difficult because the rotation always entails translation as well. This means that only the z-axis rotation factor must be extracted from the complex set of feature vectors. Another related problem is that the trajectory data of the feature points is not possible to use for calculating the z-axis rotation because the trajectory of each feature point is too sparse and inaccurate to use due to the slow frame rate. Our simple rotation algorithm is illustrated in Figure 4. First, since the locations of the feature points are known, the quadrant they belong to in the image plane can be decided. Then the means of the movement vectors in each quadrant (big blue arrow in Figure 4) are calculated. Next, the angles of the mean vector of the first quadrant are subtracted from that of the third, and the second from the fourth. If the sum of these two differences is higher than some threshold, it is recognized as a rotation. The direction of the rotation is determined by the sign of the sum and the amount of the rotation is determined by the absolute value of the sum.

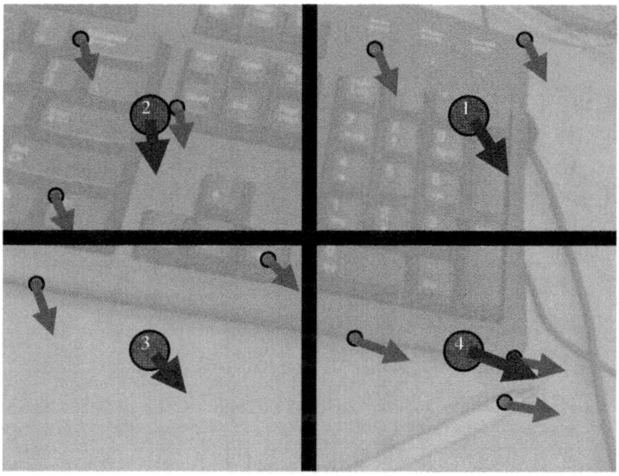

Fig. 4. Finding the rotation factor. The big arrow in each quadrant's centre is the mean of the small red arrows. The algorithm compares means of the quadrant 1 and 3, and 3 and 4 to determine an existence of a rotation.

4.3 Tracking and Interaction Performance

The current implementation is still far short of supporting recognition of "fast" gestures. The camera itself only produces about 10~15 frames of data per second, and the motion flow algorithm about 6~7 frames per second of tracked data. Thus the gesture recognition or tracking performance depends strongly on the speed of the gesture motion, and even more on the speed of rotated motion than that of translated motion. For example, if the mobile phone is rotated faster than 60 degree per second, one third of the area of the frame and corresponding feature candidate disappears from last frame (the field of view of the camera is about 35 degrees). This effect is minimized by finding the features as many as possible and by locating the features evenly distributed around the whole scene.

Another problem is that detecting z axis rotation (yaw) becomes problematic because users tend to rotate the phone around their wrists (instead of around the center of the phone). Rotating around the wrist also causes more feature disappearance. Also, the wrists rotation produces discrepancies in the intended motion and the resulting interaction. These discrepancies can be minimized by introducing an interaction mode which separates the rotation state and the translation state, so that the recognition ambiguity can be reduced.

The system has at most 160ms delay in tracking. Most of the delay is due to the low update rate of the optical flow algorithm, while Bluetooth communication delay is much smaller than the update rate delay.

It is only a matter of time that such hardware (and system software performance) constraints will disappear. Once the system resources become sufficient to support relatively fast gestures also, the proposed interaction should prove to be truly effective.

5 Conclusion

In this paper, we have proposed a two handed interaction method using a mobile phone to interact efficiently with a touch screen equipped display. Mobile phones with cameras have now become a very common platform in our lives and can act as an ideal medium for various interactions in ubiquitous computing environments. Such devices and interaction can further be enhanced with multimodal displays and additional sensing. This work is only the first step in our research to using a multi-purpose handheld device such as a mobile phone as an interaction device. We are currently conducting a formal usability analysis to compare gesture based interactions to more tradition techniques using buttons or one hand/finger touch screen input at a time.

Acknowledgments. Lucas-Kanade feature tracker for Symbian OS was provided by ACID (Australian CRC for Interaction Design). The project was in part supported by the grant from the Korea MIC's ITRC program.

References

1. Fitzmaurice, G.W., Zhai, S., Chignell, M.H.: Virtual Reality for Palmtop Computers. ACM Transactions on Information Systems 11, 197–218 (1993)
2. Watsen, K., Darken, R.P., Capps, M.: A Handheld Computer as an Interaction Device to a Virtual Environment. In: Proceedings of Intern. Projection Technologies Workshop (1999)
3. Kukimoto, N., Furusho, Y., Nonaka, J., Koyamada, K., Kanazawa, M.: PDA-based Visualization Control and Annotation Interface for Virtual Environment. In: Proceeding of 3rd IASTED International Conference Visualization, Image and Image Processing (2003)

4. Bayon, V., Griffiths, G.: Co-located interaction in virtual environments via de-coupled interfaces. HCI International 2003 (2003)
5. Madhavapeddy, A., Scott, D., Sharp, R., Upton, E.: Using camera-phones to enhance human-computer interaction. In: 6th International Conference on Ubiquitous Computing (2004)
6. Lourakis, M.I.A., Argyros, A.A.: Efficient, causal camera tracking in unprepared environments. Computer Vision and Image Understanding 99, 259–290 (2005)
7. Wagner, D., Schmalstieg, D.: First Steps Towards Handheld Augmented Reality. In: Proceedings of the 7th International Conference on Wearable Computers (2003)
8. Paelke, V., Reimann, C., Stichling, D.: Foot-based Mobile Interaction with Games. In: ACM SIGCHI International Conference on Advances in Computer Entertainment Technology (ACE) (2004)
9. Hachet, M., Kitamura, Y.: 3D Interaction With and From Handheld Computers. IEEE VR 2005 Workshop: New Directions in 3D User Interfaces (2005)
10. Hachet, M., Pouderoux, J., Guitton, P.: A camera-based interface for interaction with mobile handheld computers. In: Proceedings of the 2005 symposium on Interactive 3D graphics and games Washington, District of Columbia (2005)
11. Rohs, M., Zweifel, P.: A Conceptual Framework for Camera Phone-based Interaction Techniques. In: Gellersen, H.-W., Want, R., Schmidt, A. (eds.) PERVASIVE 2005. LNCS, vol. 3468, pp. 171–189. Springer, Heidelberg (2005)
12. SpotCode http://www.cl.cam.ac.uk/Research/SRG/netos/uid/spotcode.html
13. Bouguet, J.Y.: Pyramidal Implementation of the Lucas Kanade Feature Tracker Description of the Algorithm (2000)

Mobile Video Editor: Design and Evaluation

Tero Jokela[1], Minna Karukka[2], and Kaj Mäkelä[3]

[1] Nokia Research Center, P.O. Box 100, FI-33721 Tampere, Finland
[2] Nokia Corporation, P.O. Box 50, FI-90571 Oulu, Finland
[3] Nokia Research Center, P.O. Box 407, FI-00045 Nokia Group, Finland
{tero.jokela,minna.karukka,kaj.makela}@nokia.com

Abstract. Mobile phones have evolved from voice-centric communication devices to powerful personal multimedia devices. Among other multimedia features, they enable the users to capture video clips with built-in digital cameras. However, due to the continuous nature of video, it is often difficult to capture a video clip exactly as intended – in many cases the possibility to edit the clip after capture would be useful. We describe the design of a video editor application for mobile devices. We present the main user goals for video editing in the mobile context based on a Contextual Inquiry study and an application design that supports these goals. We demonstrate that video editing on mobile devices is feasible and report a usability evaluation with encouraging results.

Keywords: Mobile devices, video editing, multimedia authoring, user interfaces, user study, contextual inquiry, interaction design, usability.

1 Introduction

Mobile phones have evolved from voice-centric communication devices to powerful personal multimedia devices. Among other multimedia features, they enable the users to capture video clips with built-in digital cameras. But due to the continuous nature of video, it is often difficult to capture a video clip exactly as intended – in many cases the possibility to shorten the clip by removing irrelevant material, to combine several short clips to a single longer clip, or to record a new audio track would be useful. There are numerous PC-based video editors available, which can be used for these kinds of video editing operations – but using a PC for editing requires that the video clips must be transferred from the mobile device to a PC, which is tedious for the user. Editing of the captured clips is also postponed until a suitable PC becomes available.

In this paper, we describe the design and evaluation of the Mobile Video Editor, an application that enables editing of the captured clips instantly on the mobile device and eliminates the need to transfer the video clips to another device for editing. We present the main user goals for video editing in the mobile context based on a Contextual Inquiry study and describe an application design that supports these goals. In addition to cutting, our design enables merging of several video clips to a longer video and enhancing the video with texts, images, music, and special effects. We

J. Jacko (Ed.): Human-Computer Interaction, Part II, HCII 2007, LNCS 4551, pp. 344–353, 2007.

demonstrate that video editing on mobile devices is feasible and present a qualitative usability evaluation with encouraging results.

The rest of this paper is structured as follows. First, we review the relevant related work. Then, we present our approach, including the main user goals and a detailed description of the application design. Finally, we report the results of a usability evaluation, followed by discussion and conclusions.

2 Related Work

There exists a wide variety of commercial video editing applications for PCs. These applications range from professional video editors like Adobe Premiere [1] to simpler editors like Apple iMovie [2], which are primarily intended for consumers. Most of these editors use the timeline metaphor as the primary visualization method.

Several editors have been presented, which aim to simplify video editing by automating various phases of the editing process. For example, Hitchcock [5] uses automatic analysis to find the best quality clips, clusters similar clips into piles, and automatically selects appropriate cut-in and cut-out points for the clips. Silver [4] demonstrates several techniques to utilize metadata, like textual transcripts, to make high quality editing easier. While automating phases of the editing process reduces the required user effort, it typically also reduces the user control over the editing process and may lead to undesired results. Finding the right balance between automation and user control has been a key challenge in automatic video editors [6].

Video editing on mobile devices has received little attention so far. Jokela [10] gives a general overview of multimedia authoring tools for mobile devices but provides no detailed solutions. Wu et.al. [13] present a key-frame based user interface for cutting video but their solution does not support merging of video clips or advanced features like special effects or audio. Hourunranta et.al. [8] describe a video editing system for mobile devices but present no solution for the user interface.

3 Our Approach

The objective of our work was to enable instant editing of captured videos locally in the mobile device and to eliminate the need to transfer the videos to another device for editing. The editing functionality should be easy to learn and use but it should still allow creation of compelling content and support the creativity of the users.

3.1 Design Constraints

The design of the Mobile Video Editor is primarily constrained by the input and output capabilities of mobile devices [11]. PC-based video editing solutions typically assume one or several large high-resolution displays and often special input devices in addition to the standard mouse and QWERTY keyboard. We selected Nokia 7610 (Fig. 1) as our target device. It provides a representative example of the typical characteristics of current mobile devices. Nokia 7610 has a 2.2-inch 65,000-color graphical display with the resolution of 176x208 pixels. The primary input mechanism is the keyboard, consisting of four-way navigation keys with a selection key in the middle, two softkeys, whose functions are context dependent and indicated with textual labels on the display, and an extended alphanumeric ITU-T keypad. The user interface is based on S60 [12]. The device has a built-in one-megapixel camera and it is capable of capturing video clips at QCIF resolution. Equipped with a 64 MB memory card, the device can store approximately two hours of video.

Fig. 1. Nokia 7610, a mobile device with S60 user interface and one-megapixel camera

While desktop video editing solutions typically provide a very broad range of features, due to the user interface constraints a mobile device can support only a much smaller feature set. Therefore, identifying the essential user goals for video editing in the mobile context was one of the key challenges in the Mobile Video Editor design.

3.2 Contextual Inquiry Study

To understand what the user goals are, how they are currently achieved, and what kind of problems the users face related to the application domain, a Contextual Inquiry study focusing on capturing, consuming, editing, and sharing of video was made. Contextual Inquiry [3] is a well-known method for gathering information about the user needs and requirements in the early design phases of interactive systems. It is a part of the Contextual Design methodology and based on ethnographical research.

Our team of designers and usability and technical specialists observed and interviewed nine "active video amateurs" in Germany and Finland. Half of the subjects were teenagers aged 15-18 and living with their parents. The rest of the subjects were 25-44 years old and either had a family or were living in a relationship. Video shooting was an important free-time hobby for all subjects and they captured and edited several videos during a year. The subjects were observed capturing and editing video in their own natural settings, for example at school or at home. Data was collected according to the Contextual Inquiry process and analyzed using the sequence, artifact, and physical data models. At the end of the consolidation, an affinity wall was constructed and the consolidated models were walked through.

The study results showed that the teenagers mostly produced videos working as a group, while the older subjects typically worked alone. The content and style of the videos varied depending on the purpose – for example, work-related videos focused on informative content, while the free-time videos aimed to capture feelings and atmosphere. The subjects had personal principles and styles of editing and this set specific requirements for the editing software. Many subjects were using advanced video editing applications, but used only some of the features as they were still in the learning phase. In addition to video clips, images were commonly used in produced videos. Also music was an important part of the videos and the subjects acquired it from different sources or even produced it themselves. The Internet was commonly used as a source of material and ideas as well as a channel for sharing videos.

To prioritize the user goals and to identify the critical design issues, a Context of Use analysis was made based on the information received from the Contextual Inquiry study. The analysis covered the characteristics of the users, tasks, equipment, and environment within the video editing domain. Frequency of use, potential for mobility, relevancy to the amateur user, and error criticality were used as the main criteria to prioritize the user goals for mobile video editing. Based on the analysis, we identified the following main user goals for video editing in the mobile context:

- Select the clips to be edited from the raw source material
- Combine several separate video clips into one video
- Cut a clip
- Enhance the video with text, images, music, and special effects
- Store the completed video in the device
- Share the created videos with family or with peer group

Additionally, intuitive interaction with the content and the ability to create compelling content were seen as important factors. When doing editing, the user is rarely under time pressure: an entertaining user experience is often as important as the strict task completion time. A level of consistency with the existing video editing applications was also seen beneficial. Finally, the application should adjust for possible interruptions during the editing process and enable the user to continue the editing later.

3.3 Interaction Design

We started the design by creating storyboards of the main steps for achieving the identified user goals. More detailed task flows were then designed and graphical storyboards created. Several iterations were done with informal usability evaluations carried out with hand-drawn paper prototypes. When the design was considered mature enough, user interface layouts with polished graphics were created for formal evaluations and prototyping on real mobile devices. While several alternative designs were considered during the design process, we present here only the resulting final design.

Fig. 2 presents the top-level structure of the Mobile Video Editor user interface. The user interface consists of several full-screen views that together form a complete application. The Gallery View shows all video clips stored in the device. It allows the user to browse the clips and open them for viewing and editing. As our primary focus was on editing videos, we selected a simple list visualization, which is adequate for a small number of videos. For a larger number of videos, more sophisticated solutions (such as those presented in [7]) would be needed. The Play View enables basic video playback. The user can open a video for editing also from the Play View.

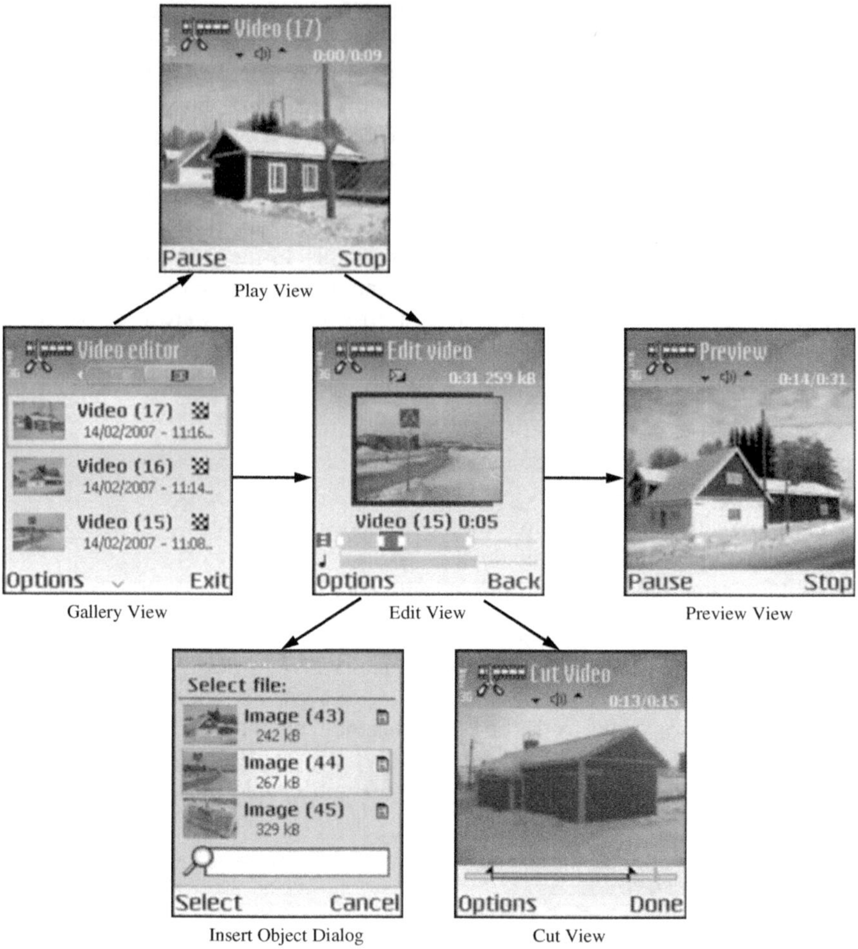

Fig. 2. The top-level structure and navigation of the Mobile Video Editor user interface

The Edit View allows the user to combine several video clips to a single longer clip and enhance the video with text, images, special effects, and music. The Edit View was the primary focus of our work and it is described in more detail in 3.5.

When the user wants to insert a new video clip, image, or audio clip to the video being edited, a dialog for selecting the clip is opened. Also here we used a simple list visualization – for a large number of clips more advanced solutions would be needed. For easy identification, thumbnails of videos and images are provided. It is possible to select and insert several clips with a single operation.

While most editing operations are done in the Edit View, cutting a video clip is done in the separate Cut View. This is because cutting is the most complicated editing operation and it was seen that the Edit View would become too complicated if it included also cutting functionality. In the Cut View, the user can freely seek the video frame-by-frame and mark the cut-in and cut-out points. It is also possible to mark the cut points when the video is playing.

When editing, the user may at any point preview the video in its current form in the Preview View. The Preview View provides similar functionality to the Play View. An important feature is easy seeking of the video with the left and right navigation keys for detailed investigation of the points-of-interest.

It is possible to share the video from the Gallery View, the Play View, and the Edit View. The video can be either sent as an e-mail or multimedia message, or sent to another device in the proximity by using the Bluetooth radio.

3.4 Edit View

A particularly challenging problem in the design of the Mobile Video Editor was how to enable editing of complex videos that consist of several source video clips, images, and audio clips. We investigated several options, but finally adopted an approach based on the timeline metaphor commonly used in desktop video editors. We redesigned and optimized the timeline concept for small displays and keyboard input.

Our timeline consists of two tracks: the upper track shows the visual clips (videos and images) and the lower track the audio clips. The transitions are represented by smaller boxes placed between the visual clips. There is a focus that is indicated by a highlight and always placed on some visual clip, transition, or audio clip. The user can move the focus to the previous or the next clip with the left and right navigation keys and move between the tracks with the up and down navigation keys. The clips on the visual track are always connected, that is, the next clip begins immediately after the previous clip has ended. The clips on the audio track can be freely positioned to begin and end at any time. Synchronization between the start or end times of a visual clip and an audio clip is illustrated by a vertical line connecting the clips.

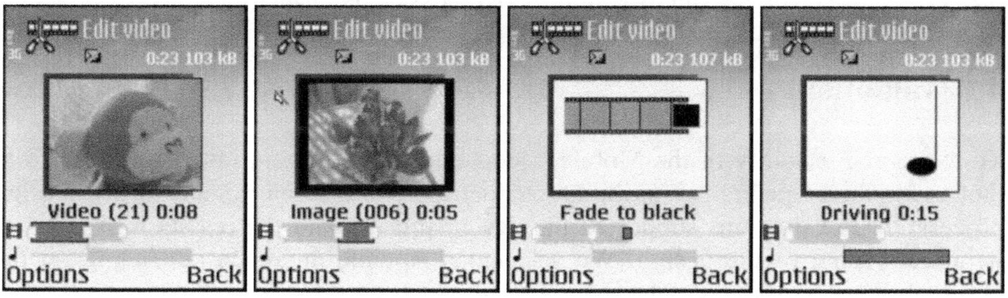

Fig. 3. The Edit View with the focus on different kinds of clips (from left to right): a video clip, an image, a transition, and an audio clip

Detailed information about the clip currently in focus is presented above the timeline. Fig. 3 shows examples of the Edit View with different kinds of clips in focus. For video clips, a video analysis algorithm [9] is used to select a representative frame.

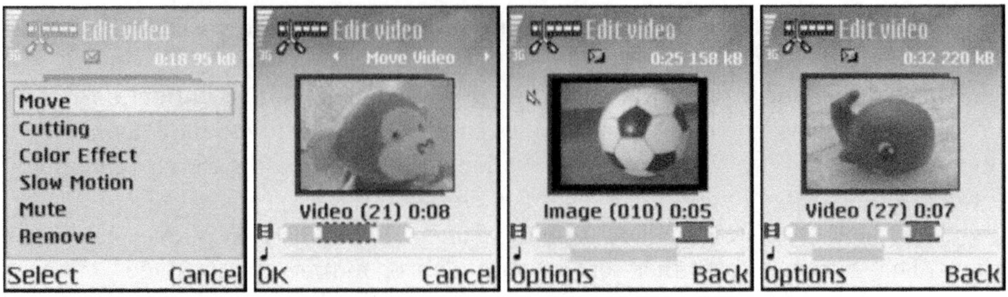

Fig. 4. The Edit View (from left to right): a) Menu showing the editing commands for a video clip. b) Moving a video clip. c) A video that is approaching the current timeline duration of 30 seconds. d) Inserting another clip makes the video duration to exceed the timeline duration, causing the timeline duration to be increased to 45 seconds.

By pressing the selection key, the user can open a menu that shows the available editing commands for the clip currently in focus (Fig. 4 a). For most commands, this initiates a sequence of special editing modes or dialogs for inputting further parameters for the command. Fig. 4 b shows an example of moving a video clip.

Initially, the timeline duration is 30 seconds. If the duration of the video exceeds the duration of the timeline, the timeline is scaled so that the full video duration is always shown. Scaling is done step by step in 15 or 30-second increments. Fig. 4 c and d provide an example of scaling the timeline. Based on our experiments, this design scales well up to 15 clips, which was considered sufficient for our purposes. Scrolling the timeline was considered as an alternative but was rejected as hiding parts of the timeline was found to confuse some users.

The status pane at the top of the display shows the total duration and size of the video in its current form. This is important as the mobile network may have a maximum size limit for the videos that can be sent as multimedia messages. Whether the current video can be sent as a multimedia message is further indicated by an icon.

4 Evaluation

To assess the usability of the Mobile Video Editor and to gain initial response from the users, three qualitative usability evaluations were arranged during the design process. The evaluations supported the design process and the results were used to iteratively improve the design. We selected a suitable approach depending on the phase of the design process: the first evaluation was carried out with paper prototypes whereas in the later two evaluations we used software prototypes running in real mobile devices. In this paper, we describe the third and final usability evaluation and its results.

There were ten participants with various backgrounds, including technical, administrative, marketing, and design. Eight of the participants were male and two female. The ages varied between 30 and 50 years. All participants had experience in capturing videos, but they were not experienced users of video editing software. None of the participants had seen the application prior to the evaluation.

The evaluation was performed on a Nokia 7610 mobile device (see 3.1), which was running a fully functional software prototype of the Mobile Video Editor application with the exception that the seeking functionality was not implemented in the Play View, the Cut View, and the Preview View due to technical restrictions. A miniature camera for monitoring and video recording the device's display and keys and the user's finger movements during the evaluation was attached to the device.

The test consisted of seven pre-defined tasks: an introductory task followed by six tasks based on the identified user goals. The evaluation was carried out in a usability laboratory. There was one participant and the moderator present at a time. First, the moderator explained the test procedure and introduced the Mobile Video Editor application. The participant was encouraged to think aloud while performing the tasks. The participant then independently executed the tasks one at the time. After each task, there was a short post-task questionnaire and discussion about the task. The observers were located in a separate room and collected qualitative data using an observation template. The evaluations were also video recorded for later analysis.

5 Results

The evaluation provided encouraging results. In general, the participants rapidly understood the different elements of the user interface and were able to find and utilize the different functions to accomplish the given tasks.

All participants were able to select and add video clips to the timeline without problems. For several participants, it took a moment to understand how the timeline works, but when they did, they positively commented that the timeline provides a good visualization of the clips, their arrangement, and duration.

Cutting a video clip was found to be the most challenging task. Only seven of the ten participants succeeded in completing the task without assistance. The main problem was that the participants did not notice that in the prototype it was only possible to mark the cut points when the video was playing. Several participants tried to seek the video with the left and right navigation keys instead. Returning from the Cut View to the Edit View after cutting also caused problems.

Nine participants were able to change the order of the clips and all participants were able to add transition and slow motion effects without problems. Overall, these functions appeared easy and straightforward to use. One participant commented that moving is not editing and would have preferred the move command to be separated from the other editing commands. The concept of a transition effect was considered familiar from other applications, for example Microsoft PowerPoint. Some participants would have liked a clearer indication that a slow motion effect has been added to a clip and proposed that the visualization of the clip could change somehow to indicate it.

Nine participants succeeded in inserting music without assistance. While almost all participants succeeded in completing the task, there were some problems in navigating between the visual track and the audio track on the timeline, especially when the audio track was empty. Some participants did not notice the empty audio track. Others were confused of the location of the focus when they navigated to the audio track for the first time.

Overall, the participants indicated that there was a need for this kind of an application for making short video presentations on mobile devices. When the participants were asked what they did not like in the application, one of the participants answered: "The terminology is quite professional." Another commented: "Some functions are too fast, too much happens at once." When the participants were asked what they did like in the application, one participant answered: "It is fun and easy to use." Another said: "The timeline in the Edit View is good and understandable." "You can quickly combine several video clips, for example for sending a multimedia message," commented a third participant.

6 Discussion and Future Work

Our results indicate that video editing on mobile devices is feasible. By careful interaction design, it is possible to overcome the constraints of small displays and limited input devices. The timeline metaphor, commonly used in desktop video editors, can be redesigned to provide a good user interface solution for video editing on mobile devices also.

During the usability evaluation, two clear problem areas were identified and these should be addressed in subsequent versions of the Mobile Video Editor. First, the cutting function, which caused most of the problems detected in the evaluation, should be redesigned. It should be possible to seek the video frames with the left and right navigation keys. It should also be studied if the cutting functionality could be implemented in the Edit View to eliminate the Cut View and the problems in navigating between the two views altogether. Finally, automatic and semi-automatic cutting mechanisms (such as those presented in [5] and [13]) could be explored to reduce the user effort required for cutting.

Second, the visualization of the audio track should be improved to make it easier to notice and to better indicate the location of the focus. For example, small animations could be used to make the audio track and the focus more visible.

Evidence from the Contextual Inquiry and the initial comments of the usability evaluation participants suggest that there is a true need for a video editing application on mobile devices. However, it is difficult to draw reliable conclusions or assess the validity of the identified user goals based on a laboratory usability evaluation only. Therefore, to answer these questions and to better understand the usage patterns of video editing in the mobile context, we plan to arrange a field trial. During the field trial, we plan to observe a number of participants who use the Mobile Video Editor on their personal devices for a period of several weeks.

7 Conclusions

We have described the design of the Mobile Video Editor, an application that enables instant editing of captured video clips locally on the mobile device and eliminates the need to transfer the videos to another device for editing. We have presented the main user goals for video editing in the mobile context based on a Contextual Inquiry study. We have also presented a concrete application design that supports these user goals. Our design is based on the timeline metaphor, commonly utilized in desktop video editors, but we have redesigned the timeline concept for the constrained input and output capabilities of mobile devices. We have implemented a functional prototype on a Nokia 7610 mobile device and conducted a qualitative usability evaluation. The results indicate that video editing on mobile devices is feasible and it is possible to overcome the constraints of mobile devices by careful design. Further studies are needed to better understand the usage patterns of video editing in the mobile context.

Acknowledgements. We would like to thank Mika Mustonen, Sami Vaskuu, Markku Rytivaara, Johanna Säkkinen, Timo Koskinen, and all the other persons, who contributed to the development of the Mobile Video Editor. We would also like to thank Tero Hakala for his assistance in preparing the figures for this paper.

References

1. Adobe. Adobe Premiere [online]. Available: http://www.adobe.com/products/premiere/
2. Apple. iMovie [online]. Available: http://www.apple.com/ilife/imovie/
3. Beyer, H., Holtzblatt, K.: Contextual Design: A Customer-Centered Approach to Systems Designs, p. 496. Morgan Kaufmann, San Francisco (1997)
4. Casares, J., Long, C., Myers, B., Bhatnagar, R., Stevens, S., Dabbish, L., Yocum, D., Corbett, A.: Simplifying Video Editing Using Metadata. In: Proceedings of the Conference on Designing Interactive Systems, pp. 157–166 (2002)
5. Girgensohn, A., Boreczky, J., Chiu, P., Doherty, J., Foote, J., Golovchinsky, G., Uchihashi, S., Wilcox, L.: A Semi-Automatic Approach to Home Video Editing. In: Proceedings of the ACM Symposium on User Interface Software and Technology, pp. 81–89 (2000)
6. Girgensohn, A., Bly, S., Shipman, F., Boreczky, J., Wilcox, L.: Home Video Editing Made Easy – Balancing Automation and User Control. In: Proceedings of 8th International Conference on Human-Computer Interactions (INTERACT2001) pp. 464–471 (2001)
7. Hakala, T., Lehikoinen, J., Korhonen, H., Ahtinen, A.: Mobile Photo Browsing with Pipelines and Spatial Cues. In: Human-Computer Interaction – INTERACT Proceedings, September 2005. pp. 227–239 (2005)
8. Hourunranta, A., Islam, A., Chebil, F.: Video and Audio Editing for Mobile Applications. In: Proceedings of the International Conference on Multimedia and Expo (2006)
9. Islam, A., Chebil, F., Hourunranta, A.: Efficient Algorithms for Editing H.263 and MPEG-4 Videos on Mobile Terminals. In: IEEE International Conference on Image Processing (2006)
10. Jokela, T.: Authoring Tools for Mobile Multimedia Content. In: Proceedings of the International Conference on Multimedia and Expo, vol. 2 pp. 637–640 (2003)
11. Rieck, A.: Aspects of User Interfaces in Mobile Environments. In: Proceedings of the IMC '96 (February 1996)
12. S60 Home [online]. Available: http://www.s60.com/
13. Wu, C., Teng, C., Chen, Y., Lin, T., Chu, H., Hsu, J.: Point-of-Capture Archiving and Editing of Personal Experiences from a Mobile Device. Personal and Ubiquitous Computing [Online] (September 2006)

Perceived Magnitude and Power Consumption of Vibration Feedback in Mobile Devices

Jaehoon Jung and Seungmoon Choi

Virtual Reality and Perceptive Media Laboratory
Department of Computer Science and Engineering
POSTECH
Pohang, Republic of Korea
{uzys,choism}@postech.ac.kr

Abstract. This paper reports a systematic study on the perceived magnitude of vibrations generated from a vibration motor fastened on the user's thenar eminence and its electric power consumption. The vibration motor is widely used in mobile devices for vibration feedback due to its small size and inexpensive price. However, a critical drawback of the vibration motor is that the amplitude and frequency of vibrations generated from it are correlated due to its operating principles that allow only one control variable (applied voltage). Motivated by this fact, we have investigated a relationship between the perceived magnitude of vibrations produced by the motor and its power consumption with the applied voltage as a common parameter. The results showed that using more power does not necessarily increase the sensation magnitude, which indicates vibrations of the same perceived magnitude can be rendered while extending the life span of a mobile device battery.

Keywords: Vibration feedback, vibration motor, perceived magnitude, power consumption, and mobile device.

1 Introduction

In the past decade, vibrotactile feedback has been widely used in a variety of practical applications. Perhaps the most common product providing vibration feedback is the personal mobile device, such as cellular phones, PDA (Personal Digital Assistants) phones, and gaming pads. All of these devices include a vibration actuator to generate vibrotactile signals for certain purposes. For instance, the cellular and PDA phones use vibrations as an alternative for ring tones. Since haptic signals can impart personal sensations directly to a target user [1], the vibration ring tones can be very useful for the environments that require silence. Another application where vibration effects are actively used is gaming. Vibrations can create more exciting and realistic gaming effects, e.g., those for collision or shooting, and this capability is especially valuable to the portable gaming devices that cannot provide rich visual experiences due to their small screens. Recently, Immersion Corp. (USA) released a product named "VibeTonz" [2], which is an authoring tool that enables mobile application designers

J. Jacko (Ed.): Human-Computer Interaction, Part II, HCII 2007, LNCS 4551, pp. 354–363, 2007.

to easily create vibration signals as composing music or by extracting distinguished patterns from music files. VibeTonz has been adopted by many mobile service providers including SK Telecom (the leading service provider in Korea). In addition to these practical applications, the use of vibrotaction has been received much attention in several research areas such as haptics [3], virtual reality (VR) [4, 5], and human-computer interaction (HCI).

Most mobile devices use a *vibration motor* as a vibration actuator. The vibration motor is preferred to other actuators (such as voice-coil type tactors), owing to small size, low cost, and capability to induce relatively "loud" tactile vibrations. However, the vibration motor has two major drawbacks: First, the motor requires high electric power compared to other components in the mobile device. This can significantly shorten the battery life of the mobile device, especially for gaming. Second, vibrations produced by a vibration motor have correlated amplitude and frequency due to its structure. This makes it impossible to render vibrotactile waveforms (see Sec. 3 for details). Despite this problem, little attention has been paid to understanding the perceived intensity of vibrations generated from the vibration motor (although see [6]).

Our research is aimed at developing a systematic method for designing the driving condition of a vibration motor with the goal of maximizing the *perceived magnitude* of resulting vibratory stimulation and minimizing its required *power consumption*. The method is based on the physical characteristics of the vibration motor and the human tactile perception (see [7, 8] for a summary), and can serve for developing mobile devices with longer battery life and richer sensory experiences with vibration feedback. The present study focuses on a case of vibrations applied on the thenar eminence[1] on the palm, because the thenar eminence has rich relevant literature in psychophysics and because most mobile devices are in contact with the thenar eminence during vibration feedback.

The investigation was conducted in the following order:

1. *Measurement of gripping forces:* We measured gripping forces applied on the thenar eminence when a smart phone was held by the user's hand (Sec. 2). The force values served as a reference for determining the pressure with which a vibration motor was fastened on the subjects' thenar eminence in the subsequent experiments.
2. *Physical characteristics of a vibration motor:* We examined the physical characteristics of vibrations produced by a vibration motor while it was fastened onto the thenar eminence (Sec. 3). The vibrations driven with various voltages were measured with an accelerometer and transformed into the frequency domain, and then the amplitudes and frequencies of their principal components were recovered. The power consumption characteristics of the motor were also measured.
3. *Sensation level computation:* We converted the physical vibration amplitudes to sensation levels using the published detection thresholds of vibrotactile stimuli applied on the thenar eminence, and then computed a curve of applied voltage vs.

---

[1] The thenar eminence is the convex part on the palm right below the thumb.

sensation level (Sec. 4). The sensation level is a logarithmic difference between the stimulus intensity and the corresponding absolute detection threshold, and often used as a measure of perceived magnitude in psychophysics.

4. *Absolute magnitude estimation:* We conducted a psychophysical experiment that estimated the perceived magnitudes of vibrations generated from the vibration motor attached on the thenar eminence using the absolute magnitude estimation paradigm (Sec. 5). The results were compared to the sensation levels obtained in the previous step. The comparison exhibited close agreement between the sensation levels and perceived magnitudes, which implies that sensation level can be used as a measure of perceived magnitude. Note that using sensation levels is more convenient since the sensation levels can be acquired with a relatively simple physical experiment (assuming that appropriate detection thresholds are available).
5. *Power consumption vs. sensation level:* Finally, we combined the results of steps 2 and 3 in order to obtain a parametric curve between the power consumption and sensation level (Sec. 6). This curve is extremely useful to understand the trade-off between the electric power requirement for the motor and the perceived magnitude of the resulting vibrations.

The remainder of this article describes the details of each research step in the corresponding section, along with conclusions in Sec. 7.

2 Measurement of Gripping Force

The characteristics of vibrations (e.g., amplitudes and frequencies) generated by a vibration motor depend on its loading condition. Thus, the experiments reported in this article required to regulate the condition under which the vibration motor was fastened on the subjects' thenar eminence. To determine the loading condition, we measured the forces with which the users grasped a mobile device for ordinary use.

2.1 Methods

- *Apparatus:* During the experiment, the subjects held a smart phone (HP; model RW6100) in the hand. The force applied on the thenar eminence was measured using a pressure sensor (Tekscan, Inc.; model Flexiforce A201). The Flexiforce sensor is a thin and flexible film-type pressure sensor, and thus adequate for a curved surface such as the thenar eminence. The outputs of the pressure sensor were sent to a custom-made amplifier board that was in turn connected to a PC using a data acquisition card (National Instruments Corp.; model PCI-6229). The Flexiforce sensor was calibrated using standard masses prior to the experiment.
- *Subjects:* Ten subjects (9 males and 1 female) participated in the experiment. Their ages ranged from 22 to 27 years with the average of 24.9 years. No subjects reported any anomaly with respect to their upper extremities.
- *Procedure:* Before the experiment, the Flexiforce sensor was attached on the thenar eminence of a subject using a pressure sensitive tape. Then, the subject was asked to hold the PDA phone with the non-dominant hand and read texts displayed

on its screen. This task was selected to mimic the ordinary usage of the smart phone. The gripping force of the subject was measured with the Flexiforce sensor (sample rate = 500 Hz). Ten trials were repeated for each subject with each trial lasted for five seconds. The subjects were not informed of the purpose of the experiment.

2.2 Results

An example of measured gripping forces is shown in Fig. 1. The gripping forces were roughly constant, with small fluctuations (< 0.2 N). This tendency was common in the data of all trials and all subjects. The average gripping forces of each subject are plotted in Fig. 2, with the standard deviations in error bars. From the figure, it is clear that the average gripping forces were subject-dependent. Nonetheless, we needed a reference gripping force for the subsequent experiments, and thus computed a grand average across the subjects. This average was 0.66 N with the standard deviation of 0.08 N.

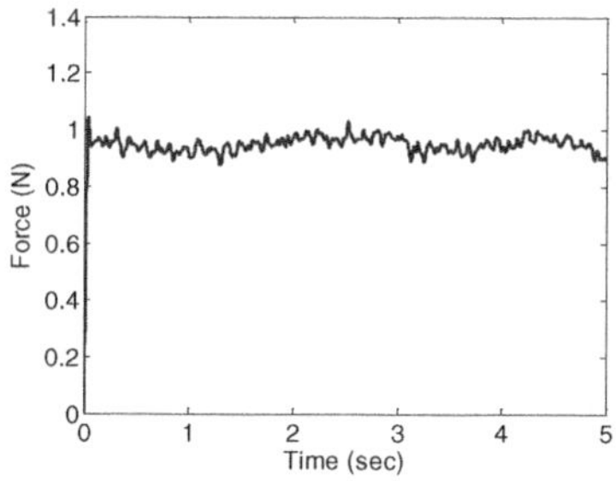

Fig. 1. Example of measured gripping force

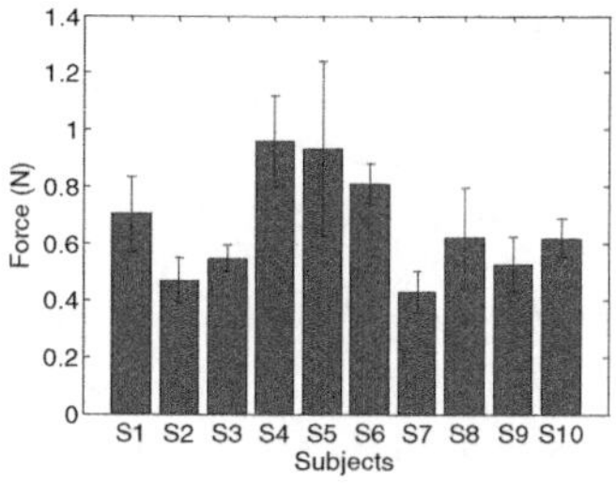

Fig. 2. Average gripping forces

3 Physical Characteristics of a Vibration Motor

The structure of a vibration motor (Jahwa Electronics, Korea; model JHV-12C1-L20) used in our experiment is shown in Fig. 3. Typically, a vibration motor is composed of a common DC motor and a rotor with eccentric mass distribution. To drive the motor, one usually supplies voltage to the motor, which in turn controls the rotation

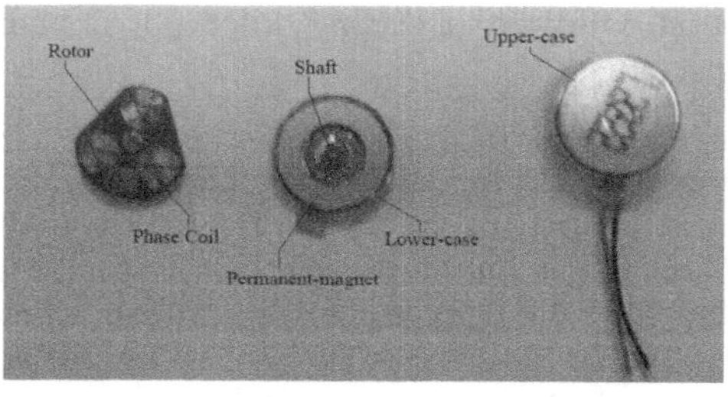

Fig. 3. Structure of the vibration motor used in the experiments

speed of the rotor. Due to the unbalanced mass distribution of the rotor, the rotation induces movements of the whole motor package. These movements are transferred through the surface of the motor enclosure embedded in a mobile device, and finally turned into vibrations that the user feels from the surface of the device. This is a simple yet effective mechanism to create vibrations with large amplitudes.

Despite its effectiveness, the vibration motor allows only one control variable, that is, voltage (v) supplied to the motor. The applied voltage is proportional to motor rotation velocity, and faster rotation generates larger vibration amplitude and frequency. Thus, the magnitude and frequency of a vibration signal from the vibration motor are cannot be varied independently, unlike other vibration actuators.

In order to obtain the physical characteristics of the vibration motor, we measured the vibrations generated from the motor using a high-precision accelerometer (Kistler; model 8765A). During the measurement, the vibration motor was fastened on the thenar eminence of one subject using a pressure sensitive tape with the pressure of 0.7 N (as measured in Sec. 2). The pressure was regulated using the Flexiforce sensor. Vibration measurement was repeated ten times, each of which lasted for one second. The results of ten measurements were averaged for noise reduction.

Fig. 4 shows an example of acceleration data measured when the vibration motor was driven at $v = 1.5\text{V}$. The waveform is almost sinusoidal, with some noises suspected to be resulted from the pressure sensitive tape used for mounting. The power spectrum of the data is also presented in Fig. 5 where a dominant spectral component appears at 120 Hz with the amplitude of 0.76 G. This acceleration amplitude (A_{acc}) is converted to the equivalent amplitude in position (A_{pos}) by $A_{pos} = A_{acc} / 4\pi f^2$, where f is the frequency of the dominant spectral component. This position amplitude is frequently used as a measure of the physical strength of a vibratory signal in the psychophysics literature.

The frequencies, acceleration amplitudes, and position amplitudes of vibrations obtained in this way for various applied voltages (1 V – 6 V in 0.5 V step size) are provided in Fig. 6, Fig. 7, and Fig. 8, respectively. The vibration frequency (Fig. 6) increased with applied voltage almost linearly. On the other hand, the acceleration amplitude characteristics (Fig. 7) were more complicated. The amplitude increased for $v \le 3\text{V}$, then decreased for $3\text{V} \le v \le 4.5\text{V}$, and increased again for $v \ge 4.5\text{V}$. The position amplitudes in position (Fig. 8) increased for $v \le 2.5\text{V}$, then decreased until $v \le 4.5\text{V}$, and slightly increased for $v \ge 4.5\text{V}$. This tendency is due to the fact that the position amplitude is inversely proportional to the square of frequency.

We also estimated the power consumption characteristics of the vibration motor by measuring current values resulted from various applied voltages, as shown in Fig. 9. The power consumption followed a second-order polynomial with respective to applied voltage, as expected.

4 Sensation Levels of Vibration Perception

It is well known that human perception of vibrotactile stimuli is a very complicated process [8]. The baseline physical strength of a signal from which the human starts to recognize the presence of the signal is called an absolute detection threshold (AL). Thus, the AL in the physical dimension corresponds to zero in the perceptual

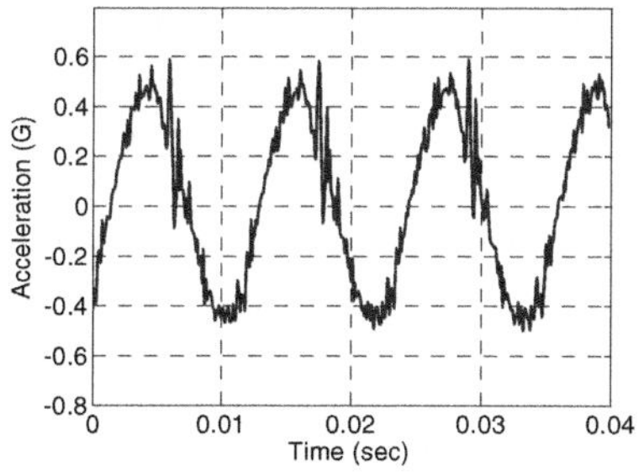

Fig. 4. Measured acceleration at $v = 1.5$ V

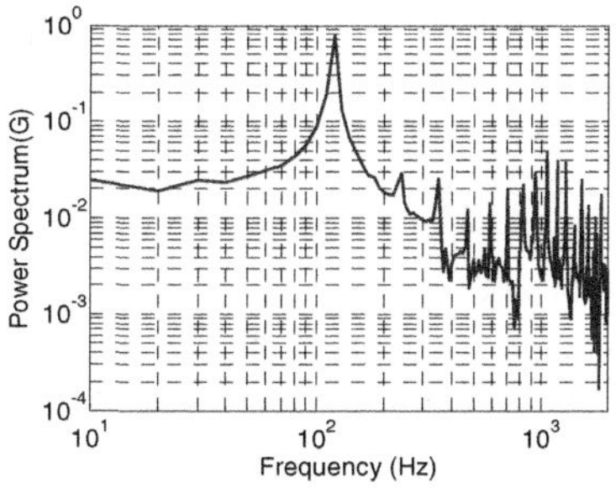

Fig. 5. Power spectrum of the acceleration data shown in Fig. 4

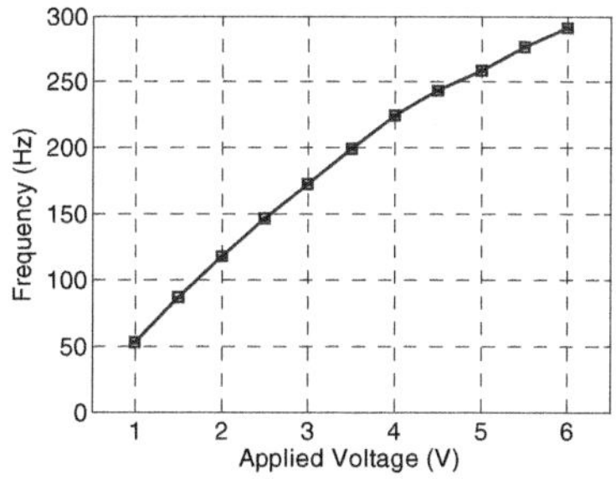

Fig. 6. Applied voltage vs. vibration frequency

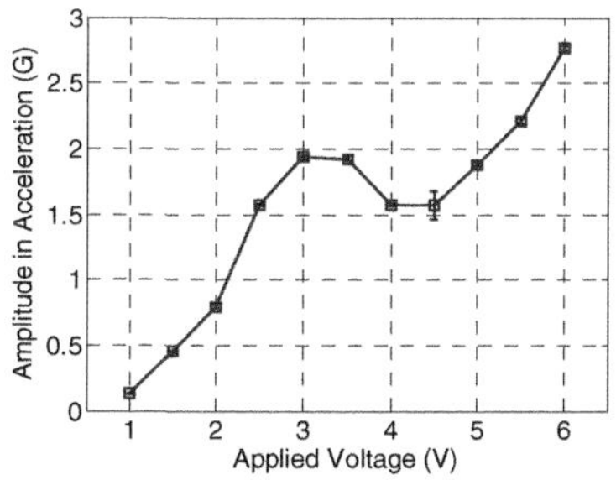

Fig. 7. Applied voltage vs. vibration amplitude in acceleration

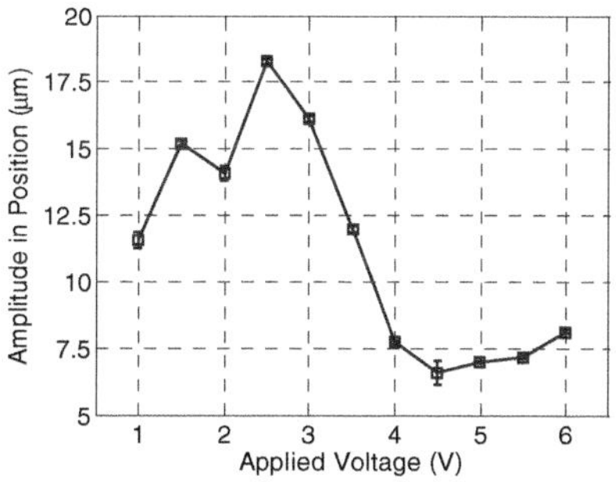

Fig. 8. Applied voltage vs. vibration amplitude in position

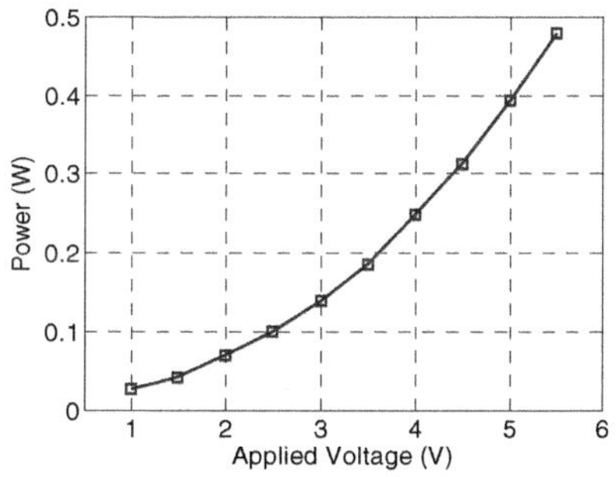

Fig. 9. Applied voltage vs. power consumption

dimension. The detection threshold depends on many factors, such as the frequency of a vibration signal, the size of a contactor on the skin, and the location where a contact is applied [8]. The detection thresholds typically form a U-shaped curve with regards to the frequency of applied sinusoidal vibrations, with its minimum (thus maximum sensitivity) located at 250 – 300 Hz.

Fig. 10 shows a comparison between the position vibration amplitudes (plotted with open squares) rescaled from Fig. 8 and the corresponding detection thresholds (plotted with open circles) of sinusoidal vibrations reproduced from [9], with applied voltage as a common variable. The detection thresholds are those measured using a contactor with the area of 1.2 cm^2 (the area of our vibration motor in Fig. 3 is about 1.1 cm^2) applied on the thenar eminence. Note that the detection thresholds were provided as a function of frequency in [9]. For each applied voltage, we chose the detection threshold of the frequency that is the same to the vibration frequency of the vibration motor driven with the voltage. The measured vibration amplitudes are all much larger than the corresponding detection thresholds, indicating that the vibrations generated from the vibration motor are clearly perceivable to the user.

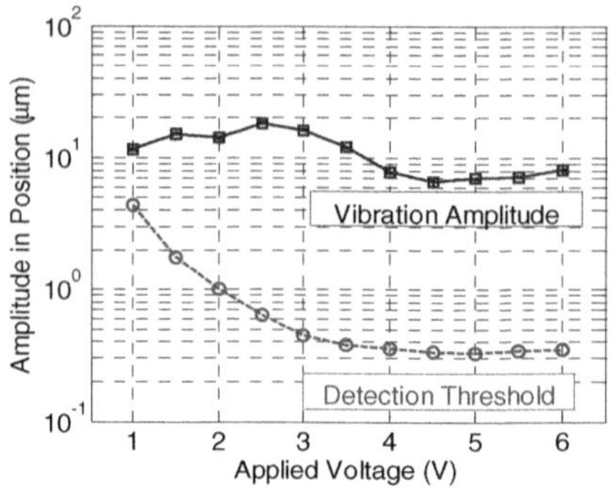

Fig. 10. Vibration amplitudes and the corresponding detection thresholds

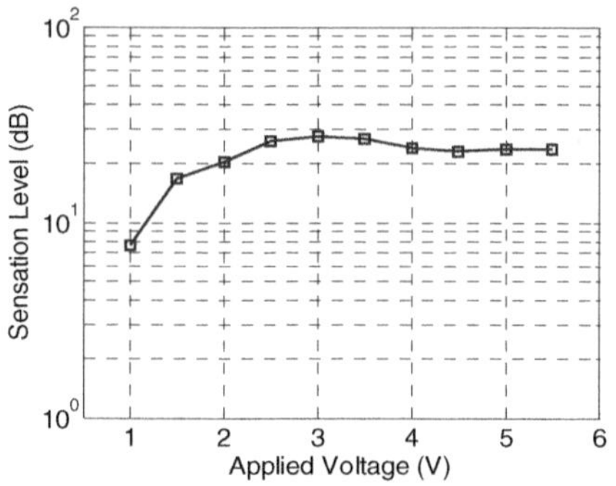

Fig. 11. Applied voltage vs. sensation level

With the difference between the two curves in Fig. 10, we can compute sensation levels by Sensation Level = $20\log\left(S / AL\right)$ (dB), where S is the physical strength of a signal and AL is the corresponding detection threshold. Steven's power law, the well-established empirical law in psychophysics, states that subjective magnitude is proportional to sensation level [10]. It follows that sensation level is a promising candidate for a measure to represent perceived signal strength that the user feels from a physical stimulus. The sensation levels computed from Fig. 10 are shown in Fig. 11. In the figure, the increase of sensation level saturates for $v \geq 2.5\text{V}$, which suggests that using higher voltages does not warrant perceptually stronger vibrations.

It has to be noted that the detection thresholds shown in Fig. 10 were measured with the contactor that has a rigid surround to prevent vibrations from propagating outside the contact region. In general, detection thresholds measured without a surround are lower than those measured with a surround if other conditions are the same. Our experimental setup for the vibration motor did not include any surrounds, considering the ordinary usage of a mobile device. Thus, it is more appropriate to use detection thresholds measured without a surround, but we could not find such data at many frequencies. In spite of that, we believe that our analysis is still valid based on the psychophysical evidence discussed in [11], which showed that detection thresholds measured without a surround at 60 and 250 Hz were lower than the corresponding thresholds measured with the surround by the same amount (9 dB). One may expect that the actual sensation levels are slightly higher than those shown in Fig. 11 by the same amount. However, this does not affect the increase rate of the sensation levels, which is of more importance to determine the driving conditions of a vibration motor.

5 Absolute Magnitude Estimation

To verify whether the sensation levels obtained in Sec. 4 correctly predict the perceived magnitudes of vibrations, we performed another psychophysical experiment where the perceived magnitudes of vibrations produced by the vibration motor were directly measured using the absolute magnitude estimation paradigm.

5.1 Methods

- *Apparatus:* During the experiment, the same vibration motor used in Secs. 3 and 4 was fastened on the subjects' thenar eminence.
- *Subjects:* Ten healthy male subjects participated in the experiment. Their ages ranged from 20 to 33 years with the average of 25.9 years.
- *Procedure:* The method used to attach the vibration motor on the subjects' thenar eminence was the same to that used in Sec. 3. To estimate subjective sensation magnitude, we used the absolute magnitude estimation paradigm [12]. Each subject finished three sessions. The results of first session were discarded, being treated as a training session. In each session, we varied voltage supplied to the motor from 1 to 5.5V by 0.5V step size. Each session was thus consisted of ten conditions. The order of conditions to be presented to a subject was randomized in each session. In each trial, the subject felt vibrations driven at the corresponding applied voltage and was asked to answer its subjective intensity in free scales without a standard stimulus.
- *Data Analysis:* The results of each subject were normalized as follows. We first computed the geometric mean (M_s) of the 20 responses from both sessions and the grand geometric mean (M_g) of the responses of all conditions and all subjects. Then, the normalization constant for each subject was computed by $M_n = M_s / M_g$. This normalization constant was multiplied to the responses of each subject to obtain normalized perceived magnitudes.

5.2 Results

The subjective magnitudes averaged across all the subjects are shown in Fig. 12, along with the standard errors. The average subject magnitude tended to increase as applied voltage increases for $1\,\text{V} \le v \le 3\,\text{V}$, and to be saturated for $3.5\,\text{V} \le v \le 6\,\text{V}$. Indeed, the Tukey's HSD test confirmed that the sensation magnitudes for $3.5\,\text{V} \le v \le 6\,\text{V}$ were not statistically different.

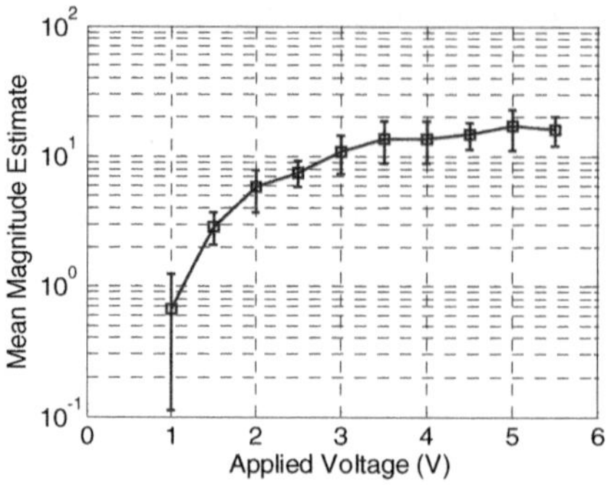

Fig. 12. Applied voltage vs. subjective magnitudes

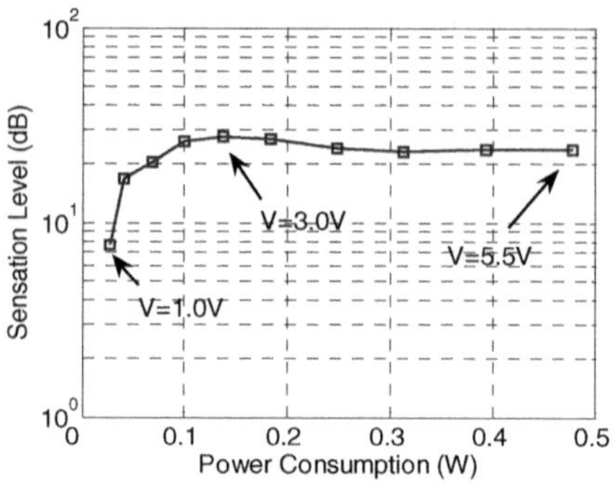

Fig. 13. Power consumption vs. sensation level

6 Power Consumption vs. Sensation Level

Comparing Fig. 11 (sensation levels) and Fig. 12 (perceived magnitude), one can confirm that the sensation levels well predict the actual perceived magnitudes. Moreover, carrying out a physical measurement experiment to estimate sensation levels (assuming adequate detection thresholds are known) is much more convenient for application designers than conducting a psychophysical experiment. Therefore, we use sensation levels to examine the benefits of using higher applied voltage (thus more power) on perceived intensity of the resulting vibratory stimulation.

Finally, the relation between the power consumption of a vibration motor vs. the perceived intensity of resulting vibrations is plotted in Fig. 13 as a parametric curve with supplied voltage as a common parameter. Such a curve is highly informative to systematically determine the driving condition of the vibration motor appropriately to the purposes of an application. For instance, the plot suggests that increasing the driving voltage above 3 V uses more power but does provide stronger sensations to the user. Thus, if a goal of using vibrotactile feedback is to simply deliver the presence of vibrations (e.g., for ring tones), fixing applied voltage to 3 V can be an optimal choice. The curve also indicates that using applied voltages between 1 V and 3 V is suitable for creating vibration effects with varying perceived intensity, which is required for more serious uses of vibrotaction in HCI, VR, and gaming. Although vibrations produced with applied voltages between 3 V and 5.5 V have linearly increasing frequencies (see Fig. 6 again), this is likely to have much limited perceptual effects due to the very low human sensitivity to frequency variation [8].

7 Conclusions

We have presented initial results from our efforts to understand the perceptual characteristics of vibrations generated from a vibration motor in terms of their perceived magnitudes and the power consumption required to induce such vibrations. Our analysis showed that sensations level that can be obtained through a relatively simple measurement experiment is an excellent candidate for predicting the perceived magnitude that requires a time-consuming psychophysical experiment to estimate. Moreover, our results with a coin-type vibration motor indicated that little benefits are gained in terms of perceived intensity once applied voltage is larger than around 3V, whereas wasting more power. To the best of our knowledge, this study is among the few that systemically investigated the perceptual performance of vibration feedback using the vibration motor.

Note that the results of this paper only applicable to a case where the vibration motor itself is placed on the thenar eminence. More general cases for the mobile device are subject to a further in-depth study. At present, we are applying the same sequence of investigation to a cellular phone, which also requires the measurement of appropriate detection thresholds of vibrotactile signals unavailable in the literature.

Acknowledgments. This study was supported by a research grant from Microsoft Research Asia (MSRA) Gaming & Graphics Theme. We thank Sungkil Lee for carefully proof-reading this paper.

References

1. Biggs, S.J., Srinivasan, M.A.: Haptic Interfaces. In: Stanney, K.M. (ed.) Handbook of Virtual Environments. Lawrence Erlbaum Associates, Inc. pp. 93–116 (2001)
2. Immersion Corp.: Mobility Overview http://www.immersion.com/mobility
3. Lindeman, R.W., Yanagida, Y., Noma, H., Hosaka, K.: Wearable Vibrotactile Systems for Virtual Contact and Information Display. Virtual Reality 9, 203–213 (2006)
4. Yang, U., Jang, Y., Kim, G.J.: Designing a Vibro-Tactile Wear for Close Range Interaction for VR-based Motion Training. In: Proceedings of the International Conference on Artificial Reality and Telexistence, pp. 4–9 (2002)
5. Ryu, J., Kim, G.J.: Using a Vibro-tactile Display for Enhanced Collision Perception and Presence. In: Proceedings of the ACM International Conference on Virtual Reality Software and Technology, pp. 89–96 (2004)
6. Linjama, J., Puhakka, M., Kaaresoja, T.: User Studies on Tactile Perception of Vibrating Alert. In: Proceedings of HCI International, pp. 280–284 (2003)
7. Goldstein, E.B.: Sensation and Perception. Wadsworth-Thomson Learning, Pacific Grove, CA, USA (2002)
8. Verrillo, R.T., Gescheider, G.A.: Perception via the Sense of Touch. In: Summers, I.R. (ed.) Tactile Aids for the Hearing Impaired. Whurr Publishers Ltd, 19B Compton Terrace, London N1 2UN, England, pp. 1–36 (1992)
9. Verrillo, R.T.: Effect of Contactor Area on the Vibrotactile Threshold. The Journal of the Acoustical Society of America 35, 1962–1966 (1963)
10. Gescheider, G.A.: Psychophysics: the Fundamentals. Lawrence Erlbaum Associates, Inc, Mahwah, NJ, USA (1997)
11. Verrillo, R.T., Capraro, A.J.: Effect of Stimulus Frequency on Subjective Vibrotactile Magnitude Functions. Perception & Psychophysics 17, 91–96 (1975)
12. Zwislocki, J.J., Goodman, A.: Absolute Scaling of Sensory Magnitude: a Validation. Perception & Psychophysics 28, 28–38 (1980)

Application of a Universal Design Evaluation Index to Mobile Phones

Miyeon Kim[1], Eui S. Jung[1,*], Sungjoon Park[2], Jongyong Nam[1], and Jaeho Choe[3]

[1] Department of Industrial Systems and Information Engineering, Korea University, Anam, Seongbuk, Seoul, 136-701, Korea
ejung@koea.ac.kr
[2] Industrial and Information System Engineering, Namseoul University, 21 Maeju-ri, Seonghwan-eup, Chonan, 330-707, Korea
[3] Department of Industrial System Engineering, Daejin University, 11-1 Sondan-ri, Pochon-eup, Pochon, 487-711, Korea
{my_kim,ejung,jynam2000}@korea.ac.kr, sjpark@nsu.ac.kr, jhchoe@daejin.ac.kr

Abstract. Universal design is considerably analogous to ergonomic design in a way that it takes the capabilities and limitations of users into consideration during the product development process. However, relatively few studies have been devoted to reflect the practical use of ergonomic principles on universal design. This research attempts to develop a universal design evaluation index for mobile phone design to quantify how well a product complies to the principles of universal design. The research also emphasizes on ergonomic principles as a basis of evaluation. A generation of the evaluation lists was done by cross-checking among the personal, activity and product components. Personal components consist of human characteristics including age, physique, perceptual capacity, life style, etc. Activity components were derived from the scenarios of mobile phone use while product components were composed of the parts to which a user interacts. A universal design index was generated systematically from the relationship matrices among the three components. The index was then used to test its suitability by applying it to the evaluation of mobile phones currently on the market. This study demonstrates a development process through which evaluations can be made possible for universal design. The research suggests an improved approach to the appraisal of how well mobile phones are universally designed based on ergonomic principles.

Keywords: Universal design, Mobile phone usability, Evaluation process.

1 Introduction

The concept of universal design has recently emerged as an important aspect of product design. Universal Design Center defines universal design as 'the design of products and environments to be usable by all people, to the greatest extent possible, without the need for adaptation or specialized design' [1, 2]. A group of experts in the

* Corresponding author.

J. Jacko (Ed.): Human-Computer Interaction, Part II, HCII 2007, LNCS 4551, pp. 364–373, 2007.

area of universal design have developed a set of simple principles that designers could use when developing products and environments. As listed in Table 1, the principles actually reiterate ergonomic design principles we use for product design.

Table 1. The seven principles of universal design

Principle	Definition
Equitable use	Make it usable and marketable to people with diverse abilities
Flexibility in use	Accommodate a wide range of individual preference and abilities
Simple and intuitive use	Make it easy to understand, regardless of experience, knowledge, language skills, or current concentration level
Perceptible information	Communicate necessary information effectively to the user, regardless of ambient conditions or sensory abilities
Tolerance for error	Minimize hazards and the adverse consequences of accidental or unintended actions
Low physical effort	Guarantee efficient and comfortable use with a minimum fatigue
Size and space for approach and use	Provide appropriate size and space for approach, reach, manipulation and use, regardless of user's body size, posture or mobility

The concept of universal design can be widely applied to product and environment design, even to all fields of industry. In addition, it may serve as an inevitable design alternative for accommodating diverse values in times of the aged, globalization, and information and communication technology [2]. As the aged or disabled have risen up as a new consumer class, it becomes imperative that the concept of universal design be introduced to everyday products such as mobile phones, automobiles and so on.

Tripod design, a universal design solution company of Japan, has emphasized that a design evaluation index is in need for companies and designers to execute close monitoring with the index to avoid another social discrimination or exclusion of specific people from their users. Only when a company can provide an assurance for design and manufacturing, the products and the company itself win credibility in the market where users become more diverse [3]. In order to continue the success of universal design, Preiser [4] addressed that we need to establish a means to assessing the impact of universally designed products and environments.

However, universal design and evaluation has barely begun. There are few studies on developing of a survey instrument to be used during usability tests that would allow the rating of a product in terms of how well it complies with the principles of universal design. The Universal Design Performance Measures for Products [5] is a representative example intended to provide a systematic way for designers to evaluate their design. However, there is a significant limitation to applying the method to complex or integrated products like mobile phones, home appliances, and cars.

This study attempts to integrate the concept of universal design and ergonomic principles into the development of an evaluation index of universal design. Such an index should answer the following three questions. What criteria should we use to extract the lists for evaluation? Is it possible to develop an effective and quantitative evaluation index for products? If so, how can we organize and structure the evaluation method? Indexed lists for evaluation should be developed to a practical form for field use like questionnaires, survey instrument, etc. In other wards, is the index made easy and accurate for respondents to comprehend and to evaluate the adequacy of design with?

This study demonstrates a development process through which evaluations can be made possible for universal design and suggests an improved method with an example of applying the proposed index to the evaluation of how well mobile phones are universally designed. The case was chosen because over thirteen million people, more than three out of every four Koreans use mobile phones by August, 2006 [6]. In addition, the aged and the disabled rely heavily on the use of mobile phones. For instance, there are about two million disabled people in Korea and 55% of them use mobile phones [7]. Although the rate of mobile phone use of the aged and children is rapidly increasing, there are few efforts for developing and marketing a mobile phone for those who have limited physical and perceptual capabilities.

2 Related Research

Universal design and evaluation has barely begun in the area of product design. Although we may not establish meaningful criteria for future design until we understand the impact of universal design on the usability and quality of products [4], there are several examples that provide a foundation for the development of an index.

Universal Design Performance Measures for Products. The Center for Universal Design at North Carolina State University developed universal design performance measures for products (UDPMP) [5]. This representative example is intended to provide a systematic way for designers to evaluate their design in terms of the principles of universal design. With the measures, evaluators can mark the appropriate boxes to indicate how much they agree or disagree with each statement describing the principles in specific context and they can comment on the statement. It allows them to identify potential areas for improvement for a product and to compare relative strengths of the product to those of similar products.

However, it seems to show limitations when applying the method to complex or integrated products since the lists or statements are too abstract and general to be used for specific products. Since the use of products with complex features involves various activities by a wide range of users, subjective evaluations of each respondent may vary too much. Proper consideration of user needs and task analysis must be essential throughout the development of a universal design evaluation index.

Product Performance Program. Product Performance Program (PPP) includes the seven principles previously mentioned and three sub-principles, which are durability, economical efficiency, product quality and aesthetic appreciation [8]. PPP is very similar to UDPMP. PPP Customize, a method for applying PPP to specific products for evaluation, is worthy of notice. Its purpose is to establish a composite value system for user analysis, market launching, product design and development. However, it is rather conceptual without providing a detailed methodology.

Toyota Universal Design Indices. Toyota Motor Corporation took the initiative on the development of universal design indices for vehicles. The two indices, ergo index (EI) and situational suitability index(SSI), were established at Toyota as a unique criterion and a method for both objectively and subjectively evaluating the level of delight and user-friendliness of a vehicle [9]. EI evaluates and scores 180 items in six areas based on ergonomic principles and SSI quantifies the degree to which each item fulfills user needs for a vehicle.

For this unique method, Toyota had broadly studied user needs and usage situations. However, there are no published details available on the development process or evaluation forms of universal design indices.

Product development process based on universal design. The process of design evaluation is to know if a product conforms to user needs, which is, in fact, a part of the product development process. Thus, developing an evaluation method for universal design can be benefited from the process of concept generation, since concept generation includes research for user needs, user characteristics, diverse design concepts and alternatives [10]. Numerous ideas generated in this process can be the lists for design evaluation.

It was traditionally emphasized in ergonomics area that ergonomic factors must be reflected from the start on the product development process [11,12], In the High-touch process suggested by Lee et al. [13], it was suggested that the hierarchical structures of ergonomic variables and product variables be applied systematically to the product development process. A conceptual cross-checking was done through a matrix between ergonomic variables and product variables. Through the method, potential or latent user needs and ergonomic design ideas were able to be extracted.

In addition, Japanese Ergonomics Society had studied universal design for the product development process [14]. They also used a matrix method for generating the ideas for universal design of a product. The method takes into consideration user grouping and the characteristics and activities of users. The process was known to be easier to understand with diverse examples of the matrix presented.

3 Method and Result

From the concept of product development process, this research developed a universal design evaluation index as shown in Figure 1. Iwarsson's concept of usability [15], involving the personal, environmental and activity components, were used as a foundation for generating the index. The definitions of personal and activity components, used in this study, are similar to those of Iwarsson's suggestion. Environmental component was revised to product component referred to in High-touch process since the application area of interest is mainly mobile phone design. Three components, among which the relationship matrices were formed to generate a potential list of the index, were constructed in the following:

(1) The personal component consists of human characteristics including visual, auditory and tactile sensing, information processing, motor function, anthropometry/biomechanics, and physical work capacity. User groups were

classified according to age, gender, disability and the list of human characteristics was extracted from ergonomics experts.

(2) The activity component was derived from the scenarios of product use through scenario-based activity generation. Each activity has a direct relationship with product components involved in the activity.

(3) The product component was composed of parts to which a user interacts through activities. The newest technologies that may benefit users were surveyed broadly and listed.

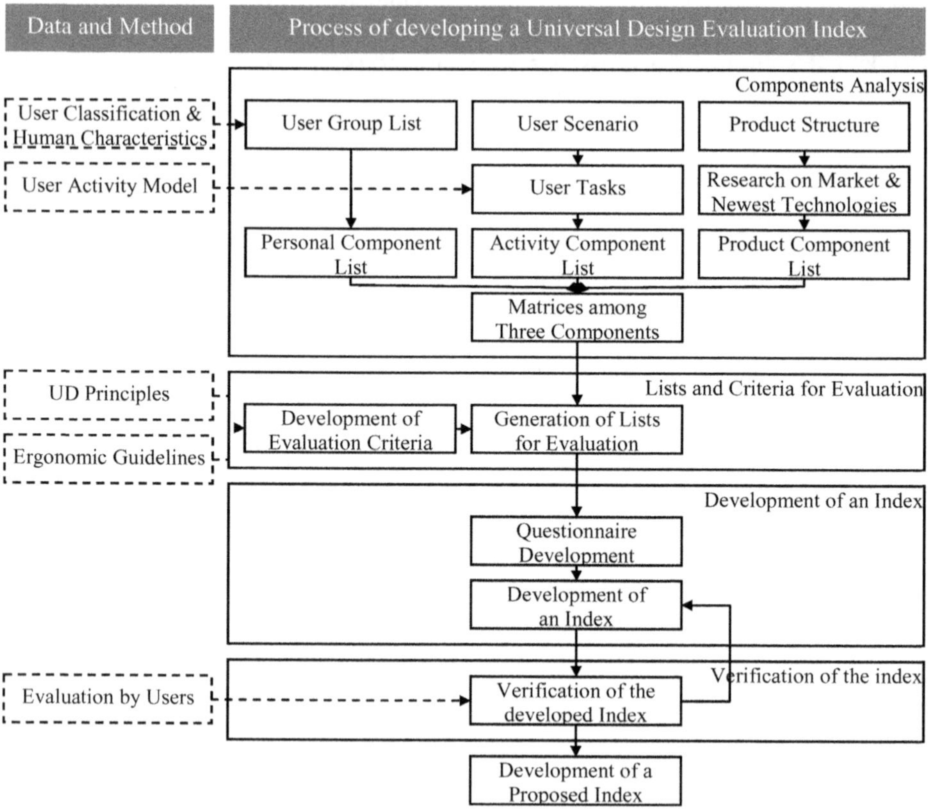

Fig. 1. A process for developing a universal design evaluation index

3.1 Components Analysis

Personal Component Analysis. Personal component analysis is based on demographic and cultural factors and human characteristics of users. Classification of user groups are done by combining demographic variables (gender, age, family life cycle), lifestyle variables (occupation, lifestyle), and human characteristics variables (human characteristics, user type). Tables 2 and 3 show an example of combining demographic variables, lifestyle variables and human characteristics variables. User groups can also be alternately derived according to product characteristics. It is beneficial to draw personas for each user group. Personas generated in this step will be used in the activity component analysis for creating usage scenarios and their activities.

Table 2. An example of combining demographic variables and lifestyle variables

			Occupation								
Sex	Age	Family life cycle	Executive	Expert	Specialty	Office workers	Service/Sales	Laborers	Agriculture and fisheries	Students	Homemaker/Unemployed
Male	Children	Opp.supporter									◎
	Teenagers	Opp.supporter									◎
	Youth	Single			○	◎	◎	△			○
	Middle-aged	Couple with no kids			○	◎	◎	○			
		Couple with kids		○	○	◎	◎	○			
		Middle-aged couple	◎	◎		○	◎	◎	○		
	Old age	Empty nester	○	○				◎	○	○	
		Single								◎	

Lifestyle: Innovators, Thinkers, Believers, Achivers, Strivers, Experiencers, Makers, Survivors

Table 3. An example of combining human characteristics variables

User Type	Human Characteristics											
	Visual		Auditory				Anthropometry			Perception		
	Vision	Color blind	Hearing	Motions	Physical strength	Handedness	Speaking	Size	Weight	Posture	Judgment	Impairment
No care needed												
Care needed with age	A2	B2	C2	D2	E2						K2	
Limitation in specific functionality	A3	B3	C3	D3			G3					L3
Minorities						F4		H4				
With accessories or tools		B5	C5	D5								
Others					E6			H6				

Activity Component Analysis. Activity component analysis is a type of contextual task analysis, by which diverse product usage situations and activities are generated. Critical activities are further decomposed on a basis of ergonomic theories like the seven-stage model of user activities and decision ladder model [16]. Table 4 shows an example of activity component analysis which is, in this case, a contextual task analysis for two different personas. Here, critical activities are 'carrying', 'calling', 'receiving', 'power on/off' and so on.

Product Component Analysis. The purpose of product component analysis is to understand the structural characteristics and functions of the product, the technological advances and other design alternatives in the market.

Table 4. An example of activity component analysis

Persona A (a man in twenties)	General activity	Persona B (spastic person)
Putting in the pocket	Carrying	Hanging on the neck
Putting on the seat in the car		Hanging on the wheelchair
Listening the bell	Receiving the calls	Listening to the bell
Feeling the vibration		Feeling the vibration
Seeing the light of the phone		Seeing the light of the phone
Picking up the phone with the ski glove	Picking up the phone	Slowly and incorrectly
With the ski glove	Flipping the phone	Slowly and incorrectly Accidentally dropped
While driving	Holding the phone	hard to hold it for longer time
With the ski glove	Pushing the button	slowly and incorrectly

3.2 Generation of an Index

Lists for universal design evaluation are generated by a matrix analysis among the three components; personal, activity and product components. As seen in the house of quality used in the area of quality function deployment, each cell of the matrix is cross-checked by importance when the corresponding components potentially satisfy user needs. Table 5 shows an example of the lists for universal design evaluation.

In order to draw an index in the form of questionnaire, each list that was generated should be associated with proper evaluation criteria which were, in this study, extracted from the principles of universal design and ergonomic principles. Although most measures and indices of universal design, such as Beecher's universal design product performance measures, universal design evaluation index of Japanese Ergonomic society and Toyota's PPP, were thought to be made in this way, the index being proposed in this study is much more systematic and extensive.

Figure 2 shows two examples of the index developed. A form for universal design evaluation index consists of the questions, reference materials and 5-point scale for rating. Reference materials have descriptions of the ergonomic principles related to the questionnaire and specific activities of user groups at a disadvantage. Informative descriptions of the newest technologies introduced, useful product drawings and images are also provided to the respondent for proper evaluation on the efficacy of the design.

Table 5. Generation of the lists for universal design evaluation

Activity Components		Personal Components	Product Components											
			Output/Display			Input/Controls			Documentation		Functional allocation			
Activities	Sub-activities	User Group with disadvantages	Visual	Auditory	Tactile	Graphic	Sound	Operation	Graphic	Sound	Hardware	Software	Operation Protocol	General Shape
Carrying	With Hands	Children												◎
	With other stuffs													◎
	In pocket													◎
	In bag													◎
	By hanging or attached to the body	Children, Handicapped									○			◎ A
	In car										○			◎
Being in Motion	Walking													◎
	Running													◎
	Sitting													◎
Percept the calls	Listening the bell	Hearing Impaired		◎						◎				
	Feel the vibration				◎									
	See the light	Visually Handicapped	◎						◎			○		
Operating Buttons	With finger	Olds, Handicapped						◎			○		△	
	With glove							◎	←B→		○		△	△
	With long nails	Women						◎			○		△	

4 User Test

Three typical requirements for the design of mobile phones were chosen to show the validity of the proposed process. These are easy handling, quick information processing, and comfortable control. As a universal design evaluation index, 16 questions – 3 for easy handling, 7 for quick information processing and 6 for comfortable control - were developed and included in the questionnaire. Three types of mobile phones currently on the market; bar-type, folder- type, and sliding-type, were used for a user test. A total of 14 adults including seven healthy persons(3 males, 4 females, 23.3±1.6 years of age) and seven spastic persons with no perceptual impairments(4 males, 3 females, 30.4±5.8 years of age) participated in the user test. All the participants were experienced users of the mobile phone with an average of 4.8 years of experience). Respondents were asked overall level of satisfaction as well as ratings for all the lists.

As shown in Table 6, Pearson correlation coefficients of the evaluation scores of each list of the index with those of overall satisfaction scores were highly positive for most cases. This indicates that the index could be used for other usability tests and effectively reveals the requirements of various user groups. ANOVA showed that the phone type was statistically significant and there were interactions by the disability. The disabled favored bar-type and folder-type over sliding-type phones while normal ones did sliding-type and folder-type over bar type phones.

Example 1. Development of a questionnaire for portability
Evaluation list - A (marked in Table 5) + Evaluation criteria (Low physical effort, Size for use)

Are the size and shape of a phone appropriate for carrying?	▪Evaluation subject: Size, thickness and shape of the phone ▪General principles: The smaller, the thinner, the lighter, the better. ▪It must be comfortable to grip. ▪Related situation: Women carry the phone with another stuffs (wallet, book and so on) in one hand. One can run with the phone in the pocket. One can hang the phone on one's neck or carry at side. 	☐Strongly disagree ☐Disagree ☐Neutral ☐Agree ☐Strongly agree

Example 2. Development of a questionnaire for controllability
Evaluation item – B(marked in Table 5) + Evaluation criteria (Size for use, Reach and access for use)

Are the spacing between controls and the size of controls proper not to cause errors?	▪Evaluation subject: Size of controls, Spacing among controls ▪General principles: The bigger, the better. But not too big. ▪Neighboring controls are not easily operated when you operate a control. ▪Related user group: Older and handicapped users find it hard to exercise precision control, A person with gloves or long nails	☐Strongly disagree ☐Disagree ☐Neutral ☐Agree ☐Strongly agree

Fig. 2. An example of questionnaire developed

Table 6. The result of analysis of variance and correlation

Requirement	UD evaluation list	Pearson Coefficients	ANOVA Phone type	ANOVA Phone type*Disability
Handling	Size/shape	0.827**	<.0001**	0.4746
	Weight	0.801**	<.0001**	0.7858
Info. processing	Info. finding	0.417**	<.0001**	0.4977
	Info. perceiving.	0.567**	0.0202*	0.1385
	Info. understanding	0.462**	0.1387	0.7332
	Menu understanding	0.591**	0.0009**	0.4747
Control	Operating posture	0.665**	<.0001**	0.1640
	Operating protocol	0.628**	<.0001**	0.2250
	Call receiving	0.041	0.4582	0.0032*
	Phone holding posture	0.113	0.3515	0.0013**

5 Conclusion

This study demonstrates a process of developing an evaluation index for universal design. The process suggests an improved approach to the appraisal of how well a product is universally designed based on ergonomic principles. The proposed index was tested by applying to the evaluation of mobile phones. The suggested process and the resulting index are believed to have a potential for practical applications to other products like automobiles and home appliances.

What remains to be explored and extended by future research are the following: how to prioritize the importance among the potential lists of the index, how to determine 'the best design' among the designs of products from the universal design perspective. Further research will be in need to improve the efficacy of the universal design evaluation index.

References

1. Null, R., Cherry, K.: Universal Design: Creative Solution for ADA Compliance, Professional Publications Inc. (1998)
2. UDRC.: Universal Design Principle. Universal Design Research Center, Busan (2004)
3. Tripod Design Co., Business Solution.: Design Assurance, Tokyo (2004)
4. Preiser, W.F.E. et al.: Universal Design Handbook, McGraw-Hill (2001)
5. The Center for Universal Design, N.C. State University.: A Guide to Evaluating the Universal Design Performance of Products, The Center for Universal Design (2003)
6. Ministry of Information and Communication.: Status of Wire and Wireless Communication Service Scriber. Republic of Korea (2006)
7. Ministry of Health and Welfare.: Result report of disabled people's actual condition. Republic of Korea (2006)
8. Nakagawa: Universal Design, Design Rockers (2003)
9. Kenji M., et al.: Toyota's program for universal design in vehicle development. In: Proceedings of the 3rd International conference on Inclusive Design, London (2005)
10. Ulrich, K.T., Eppinger, S.D.: Product Design and Development, 3rd edn. McGraw-Hill (2003)
11. Lund, A.M., Tschirgi, J.E.: Designing for People: Integrating Human Factors into the Product Realization Process, IEEE J. on Selected Areas in Communications 9(4), 496–500 (1991)
12. Broberg, O.: Integrating ergonomics in to the product development process, Int. J. Industrial Ergonomics 19, 317–327 (1997)
13. Lee, M.W., et al.: High Touch – an innovative scheme for new product development: case studies 1994-1998, Int. J. Industrial Ergonomics 27, 271–283 (2001)
14. Japanese Ergonomics Society.: The Universal Design Practical Guidelines, Kyoritsu Publishing Co. (2003)
15. Iwarsson, S., Ståhl, A.: Accessibility, usability and universal design, Disability and Rehabilitation 25(2), 57–66 (2003)
16. Vicente, K.J.: Cognitive work analysis: toward safe, productive, and healthy computer-based work, Lawrence Erlbaum Associates (1999)

Understanding Camera Phone Imaging: Motivations, Behaviors and Meanings

Grace Kim and Wilson Chan

Adobe Systems Incorporated, 345 Park Avenue, San Jose, CA 95110, USA
{gkim,wchan}@adobe.com

Abstract. This paper explores the range and diversity of capture and share practices associated with camera phones and camera phone images. We offer a high level usage model that illustrates some of the key relationships among consumers' behaviors, motivations and meanings and provides an initial framework for building segmentation models as well as recommendations for specific product and marketing strategies.

Keywords: camera phones, mobile phones, mobile imaging, qualitative research, user research, market research.

1 Introduction

Market and technology trends generally speak to an optimistic outlook with regards to camera phones. By the year 2009, it is estimated that worldwide camera phone shipments will reach 900 million, and the number of images captured with camera phones will surpass those taken with digital still cameras and film cameras combined [5]. Advancements in the imaging functionality and capabilities of phones also continue to take place, such as better image sensors, flash, zoom, auto focus, and higher speed wireless bandwidth [3, 5, 6].

Although rapid market penetration and technological improvements represent overall, positive steps for camera phones, the implications of these trends for two key players in the communications and imaging industries—wireless carriers and digital still camera manufacturers—appear far less straightforward.

From the point of view of wireless carriers, enthusiasm around the future of camera phones is tempered by the fact that consumers are not using wireless imaging services to the extent service providers would like. Consumers' lackluster response to imaging and other data services has proven especially disappointing to carriers who need to find new business opportunities and potential revenue streams in the face of steadily declining voice revenue. For very different reasons, digital still camera manufacturers are less than excited about the rising popularity of camera phones. With the quality of camera phone images becoming better and better, the nagging question remains, "Will camera phones ever replace digital still cameras?"

This paper explores some of the issues facing wireless carriers, handset and digital still camera manufacturers, specifically 1) why consumers are not actively adopting a broader range of wireless imaging services and capabilities that support photo sharing

J. Jacko (Ed.): Human-Computer Interaction, Part II, HCII 2007, LNCS 4551, pp. 374–383, 2007.

behaviors and 2) how consumers are positioning camera phone imaging relative to digital still camera imaging. To understand these issues better, we employed a grounded, qualitative research strategy that builds on and extends previous research on how and why people use camera phones and camera phone images [7, 8, 10, 11].

Similar to this previous research, we explore the range and diversity of capture and share practices associated with camera phones and camera phone images. Additionally, we offer a high level usage model that illustrates some of the key relationships among consumers' behaviors, motivations and meanings and provides an initial framework for building segmentation models as well as recommendations for specific product and marketing strategies.

2 Methods

2.1 Participants

Nine camera phone owners—six females and three males, ages 18 to 35—were recruited from the San Francisco Bay Area for this study. Four of these participants represented Young Consumers, defined as 18 to 25 years of age. Given some of the unique generational characteristics of today's youth—e.g., they are the most avid users of camera phones, they have grown up with computers, the Internet and various forms of real-time communication—we felt it was important to include and call out this specific demographic group in the study. All nine participants indicated they were currently taking pictures with their camera phones and sharing these images with others. All but one participant owned a digital still camera in addition to their camera phone.

2.2 Procedures

Similar to the approach taken by Kindberg, Spasojevic, Fleck and Sellen [7], we used a combined method of interviews and grounded discussions around a sample of participants' camera phone images. We spent two hours with each participant and looked at a random sample of 8-10 images. We asked them to recount the story of each image (e.g. why they took the image, who it was shared with and why, as well as other things they had done with the image or thought about doing). This enabled us to explore and document a range of behaviors, motivations, desires and intentions around camera phone imaging.

Throughout this process, we followed up with a series of open-ended questions to understand why participants took certain types of images with their camera phones rather than with other cameras they may have owned, whether one of these capture devices would have been more preferable to another in that particular situation, and why. We also explored the extent to which image quality was an important criteria in participants' overall assessments of an image based on contextual factors such as the type of image captured, relationship proximity to the audience viewing the image, and output destination.

3 Results

3.1 Reasons for Capture

A total of 76 captured images were viewed and discussed with participants. These images were classified using a taxonomy established by Kindberg et al. [7] who offer two key dimensions for understanding variation in intent at the time of capture—Affective vs. Functional and Individual vs. Social. Based on the reasons participants gave for why they captured a particular image, we determined the category to which each of the images belonged. Table 1 indicates the distribution of images across each of these four categories.

Table 1. Distribution of captured images by category

	Individual		**Social**	
Affective	Images were captured primarily for personal reflection and reminiscing	10 (13%)	Images were captured for sentimental or emotional reasons and were shared with other people	51 (67%)
Functional	Images were captured to support a particular task but did not involve sharing	6 (8%)	Images were captured to support a particular task and were shared with others	9 (12%)

We focused our initial analysis on Social Affective images. This category represents the majority of images captured by participants, and by definition, these images were captured for sentimental or emotional reasons and were shared with other people. Our decision to focus on Social Affective images was driven largely by the key questions we were interested in pursuing, as well as time and resource constraints. We assumed that 1) images with a social or shared component would provide the greatest insights into why consumers are not actively adopting wireless services and capabilities that support photo sharing and 2) images with an affective or emotional component would elicit the most interesting reasons for why an alternative capture device may or may not be preferable to the camera phone in that situation.

3.2 Range and Types of Social Affective Images

To understand the diversity and range of Social Affective images, we first identified the reasons, motivations, and intentions participants offered for capturing a specific image and then grouped images with similar stories together. From this process, we identified six distinct types of Social Affective images. When looking across these different types of images, we also determined that some of the motivations and intentions expressed by participants appeared to be a carry-over from their use of digital still or film cameras, while other motivations and intentions appeared to be more specific to their use of camera phones. For this reason, we further organized the range and types of Social Affective images into two broader categories—Traditional Print-Based Images and New Share-Based Images.

Table 2. Types of Social Affective images

Traditional Print-Based Capture is motivated by the desire to preserve memories and document interests. Content is something participants would consider printing if it were high quality.		
1. Accommodate a request to take a photo of a particular event or occasion 	2. Update or reminisce about family, friends, pets, vacations, trips, memorable moments, etc. 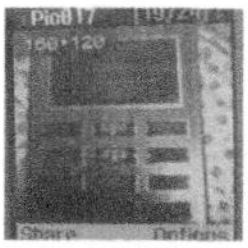	3. Connect around specific, shared interests 

New Shared-Based Capture is motivated by the desire to enhance interactions and communications. Content is something participants are more interested in immediately sharing rather than printing.		
4. Convey spontaneous, everyday moments (e.g. what I'm feeling and doing today, what is happening at this moment) 	5. Make someone laugh, or engage in mischief, pranks or jokes 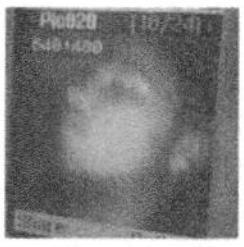	6. Create a memorable experience through the act of sharing itself 

For images in the Traditional Print-Based category, capture was motivated by the desire to preserve memories and document interests, and the content of the image was something participants would have considered printing if the image were of high quality. For images in the New Share-Based category, capture was motivated by the desire to enhance interactions and communication, and the content of the image was something participants were far more interested in immediately sharing rather than printing.

Mapping the types of images captured to our nine participants revealed interesting behavioral and motivational differences (see Fig. 1). The top group of participants captured a broader range of image types. Their capture behaviors spanned across both categories of Traditional Print-based and New Share-based images. In contrast, the bottom group of participants limited their capture behaviors to image types within the Traditional Print-based category. An important motivational difference within the latter group was also evident, with two of the participants expressing a lack of interest in and appreciation of New Share-Based images and the other participant easily and naturally discussing potential scenarios in which such images could be used.

3.3 Sharing Practices

In addition to understanding the types of images participants were capturing with their camera phones, we also wanted to explore how they were sharing these images with

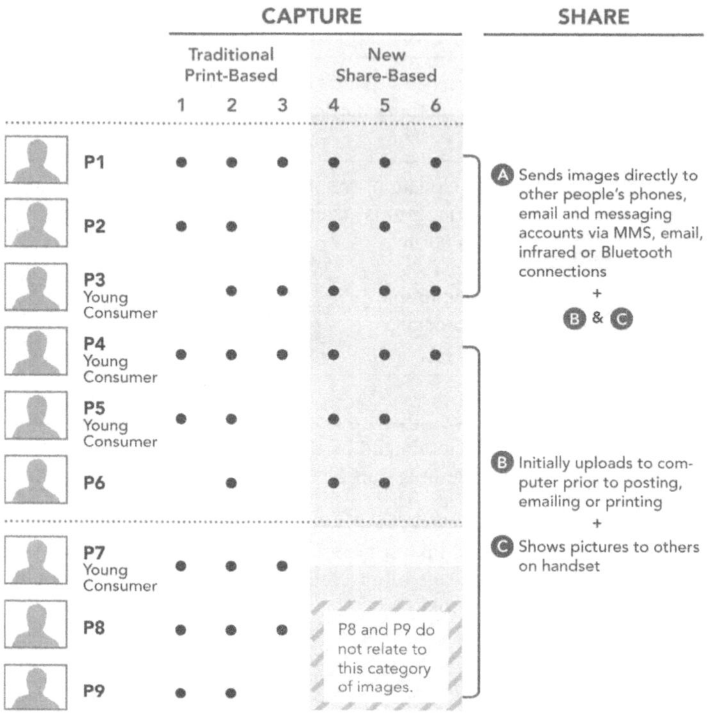

Fig. 1. Capturing and sharing across participants

others and why certain kinds of sharing were not happening more frequently. As noted earlier, although the ability to share photos via camera phones has become more commonplace, the extent to which consumers are taking advantage of these capabilities and services appears less prevalent, especially from the point of view of wireless carriers who have failed to see consumer photo sharing behaviors translate into sustainable revenue streams.

As a whole, participants were engaged in a variety of camera phone sharing behaviors. This included 1) sending images directly to other people's phones, email and messaging accounts via MMS, email, infrared or Bluetooth connections 2) uploading images to the computer in order to post to personal and social networking websites, blogs, and photo-specific sharing sites such as Shutterfly, Kodak, Snapfish and Flickr 3) uploading images to the computer in order to send images to other people's email accounts 4) uploading images to the computer in order to make prints for others and 5) using the camera phone as a "digital wallet" to show other people images directly on the handset.

Despite the range of sharing behaviors we documented, it was not surprising to find that not everyone was engaged in photo sharing to the same extent. We were particularly interested in exploring who was sending images directly from the camera phone, e.g. to other people's phones, email and messaging accounts, because this behavior required the use of services and capabilities that specifically enable communication to take place in a purely mobile environment. While using the camera phone as a digital wallet may also be considered in this same category of sharing, this particular behavior does not encourage getting images off the handset and is limited to face-to-face sharing. For this reason, we decided to treat sharing on the handset separately from direct sending.

All nine participants had tried, at one point or another, to send images directly from their phone, but only three of the participants were currently and actively using this as a photo sharing method (See Fig. 1). Of the three participants who were actively sending images directly from the phone, all were engaged in capturing New Share-Based images. This makes sense given the greater motivation for immediate and spontaneous sharing that goes along with capturing these types of images. While general barriers to camera phone sharing, such as usability, compatibility across handsets and networks, cost, and image quality [1, 7, 9, 11], helped to explain why direct sending was not more common across all participants, we also observed that some participants simply lacked the motivation to engage in this particular form of sharing. For participants limited to capturing Traditional Print-Based images, the motivation to immediately and spontaneously share appeared less urgent and relevant.

3.4 Image Quality

In addition to being a barrier to sharing, the poor image quality of camera phones is often a key point in discussions around the competitive differences between camera phones and digital still cameras. However, as the imaging functionality of camera phones continues to improve, e.g. better image sensors, flash, zoom, and auto focus, digital still camera manufacturers worry that differences in image quality will become negligible from the perspective of consumers who may soon find the quality of camera phone images good enough for all their picture taking needs.

We tend to agree, on this point, with those who observe that advancements in many of the imaging functionalities mentioned above will most likely require greater storage capacity, a different power consumption model, and an increase in overall camera phone bulk [3, 6], potentially threatening the central value consumers place in the small form factor and at-hand convenience of camera phones. Moreover, just as camera phones continue to evolve, so too do digital still cameras, with some models offering features such as ultra thin profiles, WiFi capabilities and GPS technology [2]. Whether or not consumers will ever find a single capture device sufficient for all their picture taking needs remains an open question.

Looking specifically at issues surrounding the poor image quality of camera phones relative to that of digital still cameras, we felt it was important to move beyond a purely technical and functional discussion of image quality and consider contextual factors, such as type of image captured, relationship proximity to the audience viewing the image, and output destination.

We found the type of image captured—whether it fell into the Traditional Print-based or New Share-based category—played an important role in whether or not image quality was an important criteria in participants' overall assessments of an image. When evaluating Traditional Print-based images, the technical aspects of camera phone image quality tended to be evaluated against the digital still camera. When evaluating New Share-based images, the technical aspects of image quality were far less of a concern, with participants focusing on other facets of the camera phone imaging experience, such as convenience, spontaneity and fun.

The issue of camera phone image quality also became more pronounced when participants considered sharing their images on public blogs and social networking sites, with strangers or acquaintances who might easily mistake the intent or meaning behind lower quality photos without the proper context. For instance, one participant was worried her blog readers would fail to understand the image was not a 'badly taken' photo but one taken with her camera phone. Another participant noted how sharing a blurry image of a personally memorable or funny moment would make it doubly difficult for people he did not know to "get what the picture was about."

Finally, depending on whether a participant intended to output a particular image to phone, computer, print, or web, their emphasis on the technical aspects of image quality was more or less pronounced, with output to print representing the greatest need for higher quality images.

3.5 Relative Positioning of Camera Phones

Thus far, we have discussed some behavioral and motivational differences among participants as they relate to camera phone image capturing and sharing. To better understand how these camera phone behaviors and motivations are situated within a broader context of imaging technologies and practices, we looked at how participants were positioning their camera phones in relation to their digital still cameras. Taking into consideration participants' behavioral interactions with these capture devices, as well as the meanings and values that emerge from and guide these interactions, we identified three types of positioning—the camera phone as a Backup, Complementary or Primary capture device relative to the digital still camera.

Participants who positioned their camera phone as a Backup expressed a strong preference for taking photos with a better quality digital still camera. This was in large part due to the traditional content of images they tended to capture—formal events, memorable occasions, portraits, vacations, family moments, etc. When caught in one of these situations without their better still camera, participants resorted to their camera phones, which they regarded as a lower quality option. The value of having a camera phone meant it was always conveniently at hand, but it by no means replaced the quality of imaging offered by the digital still camera. In fact, the language used by participants when describing their camera phones suggested they actually placed a higher value on their digital still cameras.

Participants who regarded their camera phones as Complementary used one or the other capture device depending on the situation. For capturing traditional content, they too expressed a preference for using a better quality digital still camera. But for spontaneous moments and enhancing immediate communication, these participants preferred their camera phones both for the convenience of always having it at hand and the ability to capture and instantly send images to others. For this set of participants, the value of the camera phone extended beyond at-hand convenience to encompass additional capture-and-send behaviors. In spite of a broader definition of camera phone value, these participants still regarded each capture device—camera phones and digital still cameras—as having equal but distinct benefits and purposes.

Finally, the one participant who positioned their camera phone as Primary indicated cost prohibited them from owning an additional digital still camera. For this participant, the value of the camera phone was its low cost and multi-functional capabilities, e.g. the convenience of taking pictures and making voice calls on one low-cost device. Interestingly enough, the same issue around cost that made the camera phone more appealing and accessible to this participant, also prevented them from fully appreciating and exploiting the unique capture-and-send capabilities of the camera phone itself. In spite of their desire to engage in more immediate and instantaneous forms of sharing on the camera phone, the cost of photo sharing services prevented them from translating this interest and desire into actual behavior.

4 Conclusions

The integration of mobile communications and imaging capabilities into one device has created a new product category that has as its central value proposition convenience, connectivity and ubiquity. As we have discussed, however, not all of our participants understood or related to the full value proposition of the camera phone, as evidenced by varying gaps in the motivations, behaviors and meanings surrounding their camera phone practices. By exploring the range and diversity of camera phone practices, we hope to better enable the design of solutions and marketing campaigns that not only support and reinforce existing practices among consumers, but encourage the adoption of new and additional ones as well.

To help in this endeavor, the implications of our research findings are offered here as a high level usage model (see Fig. 2). The top portion of the model provides an initial framework for understanding camera phone capturing and sharing practices, i.e. key relationships among consumers' behaviors, motivations and meanings. The bottom portion of the model generally illustrates how this framework could be leveraged to build potential segmentation models as well as generate recommendations for specific product and marketing strategies. I, II and II represent hypothetical segments, each with a distinct set of capturing and sharing practices. A, B and C represent potential strategies that could support existing practices or encourage the adoption of new practices across segments.

For example, while improving the image quality of camera phone images is important to consumers, it may not always be the primary need. Software and tools that enable consumers to "enhance the message" of a picture may be just as crucial as improving overall image quality, especially for those taking spontaneous photos for use in immediate interactions and communications (See Fig. 2, A). Also, providing easier and more accessible connectivity options to facilitate the seamless transfer of content to other phones, devices and platforms may encourage consumers to adopt and actively engage in a broader range of sharing behaviors (See Fig. 2, B). And finally, consumers using their camera phone as a "digital wallet" may gravitate toward solutions that enable them to quickly access, find, organize and present their pictures on the handset (See Fig. 2, C).

		PRIMARY MOTIVATIONS	BEHAVIORS	MEANINGS, EXPECTATIONS AND VALUE
CAPTURE	1	To preserve memories and document hobbies and interests	Takes pictures of Traditional Print-Based images	Sees the camera phone as a backup; Higher expectations around image quality; Values solutions that help "enhance the photo"
	2	To immediately enhance everyday interactions and communications	Takes pictures of New Share-Based images	Sees the camera phone as complementary; Focus is less on image quality and more on convenience, spontaneity and fun; Values solutions that help "enhance the message"
SHARE	3	To immediately enhance everyday interactions and communications	Sends directly from the camera phone	Understands and appreciates the unique capture-and-send capabilities of the camera phone; Values easy-to-use connectivity options
	4	To share more broadly and provide copies of images to others	Initially uploads to computer prior to posting, emailing or printing	Appreciates the at-hand convenience of the camera phone; Values solutions which enable the easy transfer of content from handset to other devices and platforms
	5	To tell a story about oneself or reminisce	Shows pictures to others on handset	Appreciates the at-hand convenience of the camera phone; Values solutions that help to access, find, organize and present images on the handset

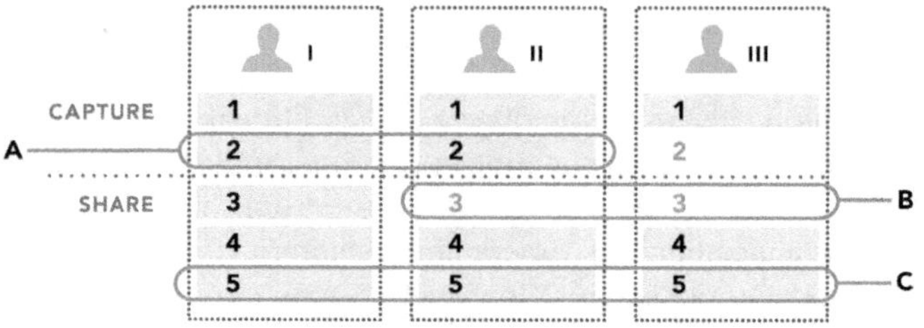

Fig. 2. High-level usage model

Our research suggests, however, that simply offering additional solutions and capabilities to consumers may not be enough. Barriers to use, including usability, compatibility across handsets and networks and prohibitive costs also need to be addressed. Moreover, consumers are not always motivated to take advantage of these solutions and capabilities nor do they have the right set of expectations about how a camera phone may be integrated into their overall imaging practices. Marketing campaigns that help consumers understand the full value proposition of the camera phone and provide them with more compelling scenarios for how camera phones may be used in a complementary rather than substitutive fashion with digital still cameras, also need to accompany the development of new products, capabilities and services in the mobile imaging space.

Acknowledgments. We would like to express our appreciation to Ben Calica and John Lin for their support of this research. Special thanks also to Sheryl Ehrlich and David Welch for reviewing an earlier draft of this paper.

References

1. Buchanan, G., Farrant, S., Jones, M., Thimbley, H., Marsden, G., Pazzani, M.: Improving Mobile Internet Usability. In: Proceedings of the 10th International Conference on World Wide Web, Hong Kong, Hong Kong, pp. 673–680. May 2001 ACM Press, New York (2001)
2. CEA Market Research Report. Digital Imaging Study Update (2006)
3. IDC Opinion. Worldwide Camera Phone and Videophone 2005-2009 Forecast. (2005)
4. Infotrend/CAP Ventures, 2005 Camera Phone End User Survey Analysis (2006)
5. Infotrend/CAP Ventures, Mobile Imaging Study Summary (2005)
6. Jupiter Research. Camera Phones: Assessing the Competitive Threat to the Digital Camera Market (2005)
7. Kindberg, T., Spasojevic, M., Fleck, R., Sellen, A.: How and Why People Use Camera Phones. HP Labs TR No. HPL-2004-216. HP Labs, Bristol, UK (2004)
8. Kurvinen, E.: Only When Miss Universe Snatches Me: Teasing in MMS Messaging. In: Proceedings of the 2003 International Conference on Designing Pleasurable Products and Interfaces, Pittsburgh, PA, pp. 98–102. ACM Press, New York (2003)
9. Nathwani, K., Eason, K.: Perceptions versus Expectations of Multimedia Messaging Service (MMS). Personal Ubiquitous Comput. 9(4), 191–197 (July 2005)
10. Okabe, D.: Emergent Social Practices, Situations and Relations through Everyday Camera Use. 2004 International Conference on Mobile Communication and Social Change, Seoul, Korea, (October 2004) (2004)
11. Van House, N.A., Davis, M.: The Social Life of Camera Phone Images. In: Proceedings of the Pervasive Image Capture and Sharing. New Social Practices and Implications for Technology Workshop (PICS 2005) at the Seventh International Conference on Ubiquitous Computing (UbiComp 2005). UbiComp 2005 (2005)

The Design and Evaluation of a Diagonally Splitted Column to Improve Text Readability on a Small Screen

Yeon-Ji Kim[1] and Woohun Lee[2]

[1] Human Interface Group, Mobile Handset R&D Center, LG Electronics Inc.
P.O. Box 153-801, Gasan-dong, Gumchon-gu, Seoul, Korea
[2] Design Media Laboratory, Dept.of Industrial Design, KAIST(Korea Advanced Institute of Science and Technology)
P.O. Box 305-701, KAIST, 373-1 Kusong-dong, Yusong-gu, Daejeon, Korea
yeonji_kim@lge.com, woohun.lee@kaist.ac.kr

Abstract. Most previous studies comparing paper and computer screen readability show that screens are less readable than paper. There are many factors that could affect the readability of computer screens. However, exactly what factors reduce reading performance on computer screens is not clear. Therefore, this study has tried to find an alternative way to improve the readability of screen displays. A novel suggestion is designed to give readers sense of rhythm by diagonally dividing up screen areas. The diagonal division layout was read significantly faster (24.4%) than a normal layout for 5.5 inches display of e-Book readers. For 3.5 inches display, it was read 13.0% faster. The reason why the total reading time was cut down by the diagonal division layout is that the right-upper part played a decisive role. The number of texts on each line is systematically decreased in the right-upper part. 31.6% of total reading time was shorten by the right-upper part. However, there were no significant differences in subjective satisfaction between the two layout conditions.

1 Introduction

Reading from the screens became a daily routine especially after tiny and handy electronics such as cellular phones, smart phones, PDA, and e-book reader permeated into our everyday lives. The researchers indicate that it is better reading printed materials than reading off of a screen[1]. According to researches related to this, reading from the screens is 20~30% slower. However, it is reported that it's hard to find much relationship between reading from the screens and reading interpretation[2]. It is assumed that the outcome came out this way because people tend to keep their interpretation of sentences at a standard level and adjust time to it[3]. The difference of speed of reading from screens and reading from paper is also related to the efficiency of presenting settings. People like Gould(1987) provided high-resolution display and anti-aliasing texts from a screen to experiment through participants and after

[1] Hansen et al., 1978; Muter et al., 1982; Gould & Grischkowsky, 1984; Weldon et al., 1985.
[2] Muter et al.,1982; Gould & Grischkowsky, 1984.
[3] Mills & Weldon, 1987.

J. Jacko (Ed.): Human-Computer Interaction, Part II, HCII 2007, LNCS 4551, pp. 384–393, 2007.

evaluating the results of their reading performance, it was not much different than reading from paper. The difference of reading performance of the two conditions, as shown in recent researches, will step by step reduce as the display technology progress of showing the latest news makes high-resolution and color appearance more detailed. However, we are faced, now, with a new problem, miniaturization of screens, after technology advancement permeated into our everyday lives. To improve mobility of handy electronics such as cellular phones, PDA, and e-book reader, it is required to miniaturize them and so the screens are also required to become smaller which is interfering our reading performance. As the screens become smaller, the amount of information that can be shown on the screen at once is also reducing and therefore people need to run through many pages in order to enjoy a full content. Therefore solving the problems between mobile facility and readability is a difficult assignment. This experiment came up about in order to compromise these two by analyzing the factors that affect readability of texts shown on screens and to come up with an alternative that can greatly improve readability of texts shown on small screens.

2 Parameters of Text Readability on Screen

The notion of readability not only includes legibility of characters, but even the reader's comprehension of the given text. The legibility of a letter can affect the readability but, on the contrary, the readability does not affect a letter's legibility[4]. Sometimes, the readability means the level of content of a text but in this experiment, it indicates the visual quality that depends on "the rate of how easily a text can be read" such as the form of a letter and it's line's formatting. Therefore, the readability, such as reading speed and interpretation rate, of a text can be evaluated through practice achievement tests[5]. When analyzing the previous studies on readability of sentences shown on screens, it showed that the factors below affected reading performance when looking at it in terms of formatting of texts.

2.1 Characters Per Line and Line's Width

There were a lot of studies already on readability of texts shown on screens. Duchnicky and Kolers(1983) experimented on the difference of readability depending on the presented texts' CPL. According to their experiments, total reading time was 30% shortened with 80CPL than 40CPL. However, there was not a significant difference found in the evaluation on the degree of understanding about the texts. Also, measuring the reading time after providing 3 different types of screens, a full screen(187mm, including seventy eight 'M's), 2/3 width of a full screen(125mm, including fifty two 'M' s) and 1/3 width of a full screen(62mm, twenty six 'M's), it showed that reading from the full screen shortened the reading time by about 28% from reading from the 1/3 width of a full screen. However, there was not a significant difference between reading time from the full screen and 2/3 width of a full screen,

---

[4] Legge et al., 1985.

[5] Mills & Weldon, 1987.

even though reading time from the full screen was faster than from 2/3 width of a full screen. With this evidence, it is claimed that the reading performance improves as the width of a screen increases. Even in Dyson's and Kipping's(1998) experiments, it showed that reading time in 25CPL took the most time and reading time in 100CPL took the shortest when 6 different CPLs, 25, 40, 55, 70, 85 and 100, were given to the experiment participants. On the other hand, in individual satisfaction about reading, people preferred 55 CPL the most. This experiment is similar to Duchnicky and Kolers'(1983) experiment, mentioned above, in that as the CPL increased the reading time decreased. Through these experiments, we learned that when the lines' widths are too short, it affects readability in a negative way and there should be at least 30 characters or more in a line in order to get a satisfactory readability.

2.2 Number of Lines

Duchnicky and Kolers(1983) experimented the difference of readability depending on the number of lines(1line, 2lines, 3 lines, 4 lines, and 20 lines). There was not a significant difference in reading speed between 4 lines and 20 lines and the reading speed was 9% delayed with 1 and 2 lines compared to 20 lines. Being able to achieve similar reading performance with 4 lines and 20 lines of texts in a screen, it can be seen that lines' widths or CPL does not affect reading performance so much.

3 The Concept of the Diagonally-Splitted Column

As shown in other researches, the readability of the text on the screen is influenced by the number of characters in lines, the lines' width, line spacing and the number of the lines. However, there is no research that focused on whether the text justification on the screen or the form of the column affects the readability. There are some experiment trials that examined the relationship between the text justification and the readability using the printed materials. Some researchers compared the fully justified text with the left alignment and they could not find a significant difference in terms of readability and understanding[6]. However, according to the research undertaken by Gregory and Poulton (1970), people with poor reading read worse if the text was set fully justified. Trollip and Sales(1986) said that the college students showed deteriorated readability if the texts were fully justified. These researches indicate that for the printed materials, the fully justified text more or less negatively affected readability.

Texts on small screens need to show in order of pages after dividing it up into a lot more pages than printed materials or big screens. At this time, flow of reading could be easily interrupted because the amount of information coming in at once is not much and need to move around among the pages constantly. Also, reading becomes boring and can easily be stray away from the flow of texts while moving from one line to another with monotonous fully justified rectangular columns. We frequently experience this while reading texts shown from cellular phones, PDA or small windows in computers.

[6] Farbrizio et al., 1967; Hartley & Burnhill, 1971; Hartley & Mills, 1973; Wiggins 1967.

In this experiment, we proposed a new text layout method called diagonally splitted column as a solution to these problems, reading from small screens. Diagonally splitted column is, literally, a method of organizing texts by making up 2 triangular columns by dividing the old traditional rectangular column diagonally in half. As shown in picture 1, diagonally splitted column is made up of a left triangular column and a right triangular column. Different from those common forms with 2 columns, its width of each column gradually increases or decreases. Therefore, it is expected to help readers to understand the flow of texts easily and provide them some fun because its increase in width of lines repeats rhythmically when you read like the arrows shown in Figure 1.

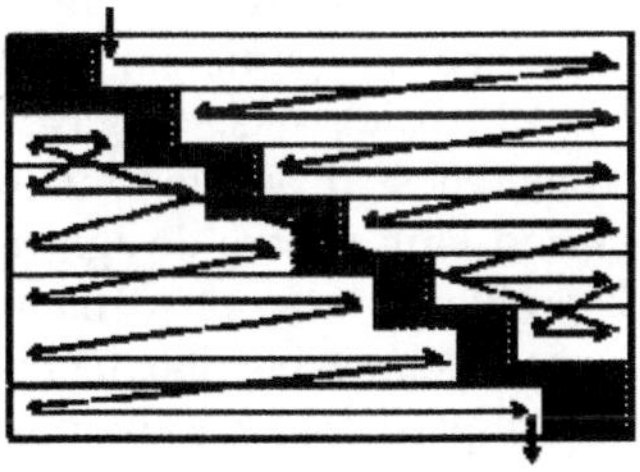

Fig. 1. The Concept of the Diagonally splitted Column (a dotted-arrow line: the Flow of Text)

4 Evaluation of Reading Performance About Diagonally Splitted Column

4.1 Designing the Experiment

In order to verify the utility of a diagonally splitted column suggested as an experimental alternative, we compared it with traditional right-and-left fitted rectangular column. Reading performance is affected by factors such as space, width, and number of lines. Even with same layout, depending on size and proportion of a display area and number of lines of text that can be presented at once also change. Therefore, it is necessary to accurately confirm how a text layout affects reading performance through what kind of reciprocal action with the size and proportion of display. In this experiment, we set up three different screen sizes, $2000mm^2$, $4000mm^2$ and $8000mm^2$, and set up screen proportion of 1:1, 2:1 and 3:1 to evaluate reading performance.

Table 1. Experimental Variables and Levels

Variables	Levels
Text Layout	Rectangular column, Diagonally Splitted Column
Screen Proportion	1:1, 2:1, 3:1
Screen Size	$2000mm^2$, $4000mm^2$, $8000mm^2$

We uniformed the space of lines of texts indicated on screens to 135%. Those three different screen sizes are correspondent to each size of these handy portable electronics, cellular phone, PDA and e-book reader. We measured reading performance subject to eighteen kinds of experimental conditions that combined text layouts(two levels), screen sizes(three levels) and screen proportions(three levels).

4.2 Experimental Instruments and Method

We put up 1050words(±10words), including blanks, in each display(figure 2). We used Batang font with point size10 as the word type in the texts. We used tablet PC(Compaq T1000) to present experimental texts to experiment participants and had them press on displayed buttons on screens to move from one page to another. After installing tablet PC on tables, we had our participants set in a comfortable state and started the experiment. To those 18 participants, we gave them 1 of 18 different types of display and 1 of 18 different types of articles randomly. In order to minimize carryover effect, we used balanced latin square design in presenting order. Then we had each participants solve 2 problems relating to their articles after they finished reading them. Through this experiment using the method of text presentation, we measured the total reading time the participants took to read the article, the time they took to solve problems, percentage of wrong answers to the problems and individual satisfaction about the reading. Dividing the number of characters in presented articles by the total reading time(minutes), we calculated the WPM(words per minute). We set up a 7 point scale, 7 being most comfortable, for rating the individual satisfaction about reading to find out "how easy was it to read" following the method of presenting texts rather than learning the difficulty of the article itself.

(a) 8000mm^2, 1:1 (b) 8000mm^2, 2:1 (c) 8000mm^2, 3:1

Fig. 2. Diagonally Splitted Column

4.3 The Experimental Results

In order to minimize the variation of both individual reading and understanding ability, we had 18 male and female college students(average age of 21.5) who share similar intellectual level to participate in the experiment. After analyzing the results of the experiment, we found out that experimental variables affected reading speed and individual satisfaction of reading but did not affect the time participants took to solve a problem or the percentage of wrong answers to problems. It showed that text layouts($F(1,17)=7.339$, $p=0.0149$), screen sizes($F(2,34)=15.247$, $p=0.0000$) and screen proportions($F(2,34)= 4.008$, $p=0.0274$) uniformly affected reading speed through breakup analysis of participants of experiment results. Rectangular column averaged 607.3WPM(avg. variation:169.3) and diagonally splitted column averaged 685.2WPM(avg. variation:210.6), shown in figure 3a, and therefore we could see that diagonally splitted column was 12.8% better, reading speed wise. Looking at the records of 580.6WPM(avg. variation:227.6) in 2000mm^2, 605.5WPM(avg. variation: 133.6) in 4000mm^2 and 752.7WPM(avg. variation: 208.4) in 8000mm^2, we learned that reading speed improved when surface of screens increased, in screen sizes. Even though there was not a significant difference found between 2000mm^2 and 4000mm^2, reading speed was improved by as many as 29.6% in 8000mm^2 comparing with 2000mm^2(shown in figure 3a). After analyzing the reciprocal effects of three types of experimental variables, we found similar reciprocal effects between screen sizes and text layouts, as shown in figure 3d. After analyzing the data of individual satisfaction, it showed that screen proportions and text layouts did not affect individual satisfaction very much, although screen sizes($F_{(2,34)}$=25.283, p=0.0000) did uniformly affect it. Looking at the ratings recorded, 3.2/7.0(avg. variation:1.2), 4.3/7.0(avg. variation:1.3) and 4.4/7.0(avg. variation:1.3) in screen sizes of 2000mm^2, 4000mm^2 and 8000mm^2, respectively, it can be seen that individual satisfaction is not so great in the case of small screens of 2000mm^2(shown in figure 3e). There were similar reciprocal effects($F_{(4,68)}$=2.807, p=0.0322) between screen sizes and proportions. Individual satisfaction was excellent with 2:1 and 3:1 proportions in small screens and 1:1 proportions in big screens(shown in figure 3f). We analyzed the effects of text layouts

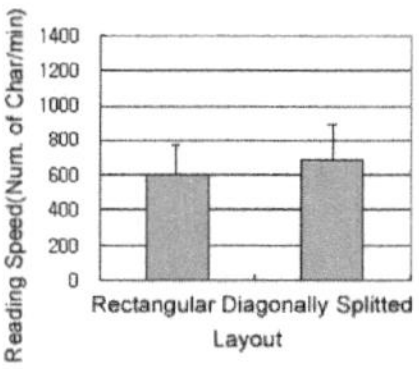

(a) Reading Speed by Layout

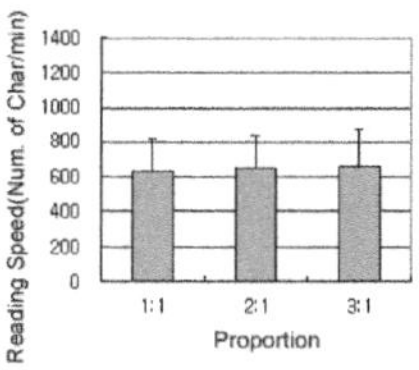

(b) Reading Speed by Screen Proportion

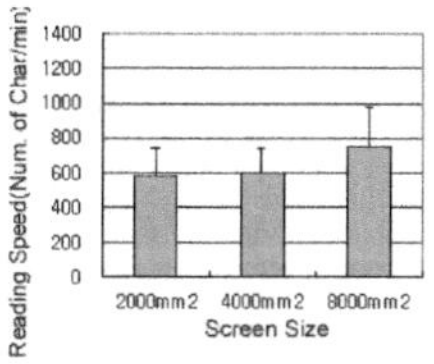

(c) Reading Speed by Screen Size

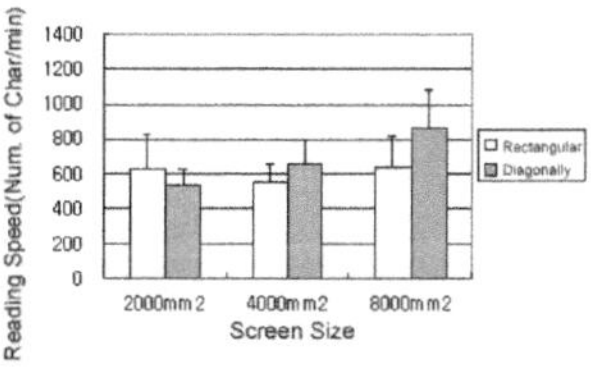

(d) Reading Speed by Interaction between Screen Size and Layout

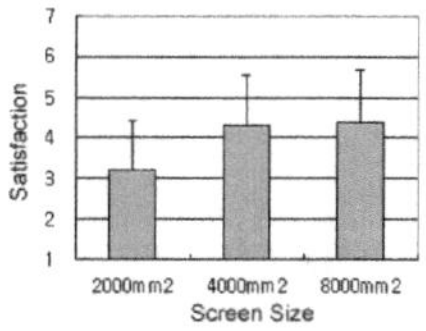

(e) Satisfaction by Screen Size

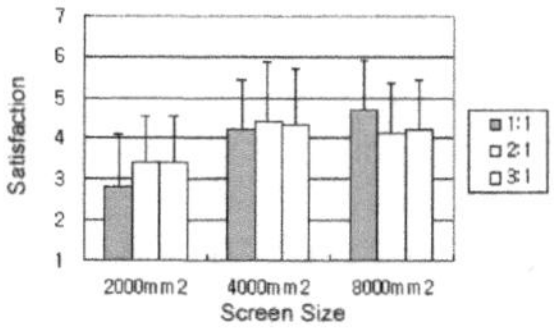

(f) Satisfaction by Interaction between Screen Size and Proportion

Fig. 3. Reading Speed & Satisfaction by Layout, Screen Size and Proportion

on reading speed classified by screen sizes and proportions in order to understand, with more detail, reciprocal effects of screen sizes and proportions on reading speed, shown in figure 4. First, in the case of 2000mm^2, we were able to find significant differences in reading speed depending on text layouts with 1:1(df=17, t=2.706, p=0.0150) proportions and 2:1(df=17, t=2.418, p=0.0271) proportions. With 1:1, 2:1 and 3:1 proportions, rectangular columns were all faster by 9.3%, 16.2% and 17.0%, respectively. We found out that there were a significant difference in reading speed because of text layouts in 1:1 proportion(df=17, t=3.784, p=0.0148) and 3:1 proportion(df=17, t=3.026, p=0.0076). In case of proportion of 1:1, 2:1 and 3:1, all of diagonally splitted columns' reading speed was faster than rectangular columns' reading speed by 39.8%, 29.5% and 33.1%, respectively. It is surprising to learn that diagonally splitted columns' reading speed was about 40% faster comparing with traditional rectangular columns' in the case of 1:1 proportion of 8000mm^2 screens. Looking at the case of 4000mm^2 and 8000mm^2 screen sizes, the effects of diagonally splitted columns were observable in 1:1 and 3:1 proportions.

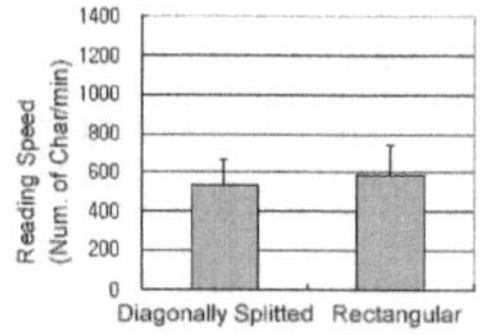

(a) 2000mm^2 / 1:1

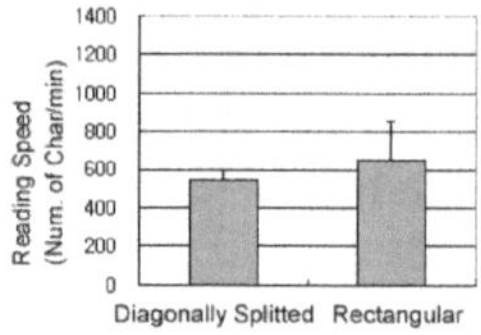

(b) 2000mm^2 / 2:1

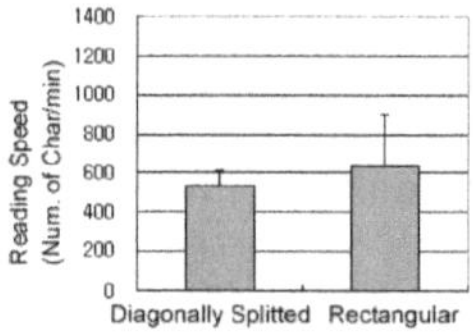

(c) 2000mm^2 / 3:1

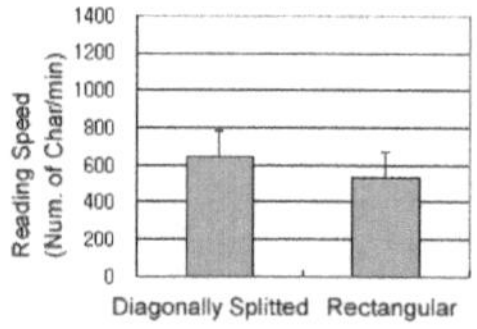

(d) 4000mm^2 / 1:1

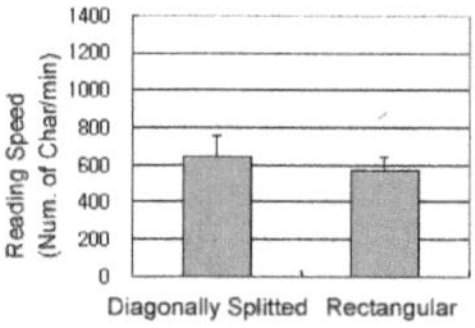

(e) 4000mm^2 / 2:1

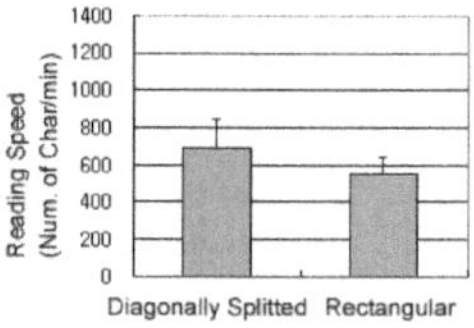

(f) 4000mm^2 / 3:1

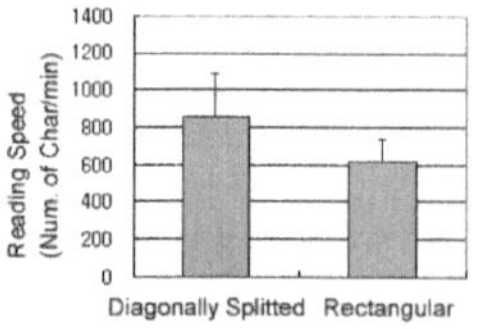

(g) 8000mm^2 / 1:1

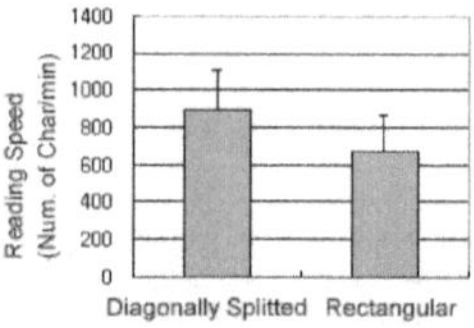

(h) 8000mm^2 / 2:1

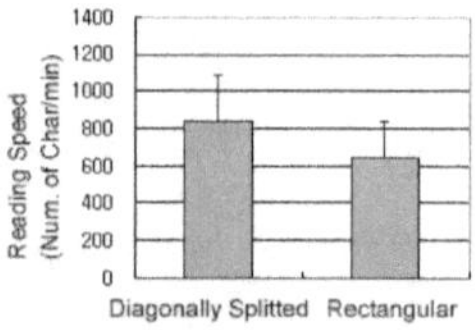

(i) 8000mm^2 / 3:1

Fig. 4. Reading Speed by Layout, Screen Size and Proportion

5 Examination About Increasing Readability

5.1 The Experiment Design

The experiment undertaken under the condition of 4000mm^2 and 8000mm^2 sized screens respectively proved the diagonally-splitted column performed prominently better readability than the rectangular column. The diagonally-splitted layout, which is comprised by two triangles, seems confusing however it is so remarkable that this layout dramatically makes a leap in readability. To examine the causes of such an unexpected result we took the secondary experiment varying dimensions of the diagonally-splitted column. We tried to figure out the causes of improvement in readability through presenting only one triangle area of the diagonally-splitted column. Referring to figure 5, the new layout that fits each triangular column was designed. Comparing readabilities for the three types of the text-layouts would make it known which one would contribute a leap to the readability. This research selected $4000mm^2$ for the screen size; 3:1 for the width x length ratio; 135% for the line spacing, respectively. The experiment 1 shows that the diagonally-splitted column reads 24.8% better than the rectangular one under the condition described.

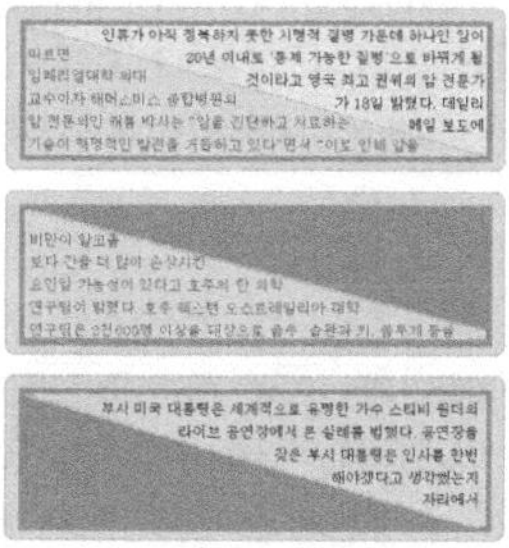

Fig. 5. Diagonally Splitted Column, Right Triangular, Left Triangular

5.2 The Experiment Results

The experiment result reveals significant differences in terms of readability between the three layouts ($f_{(2,34)}$=14.208, p=0.000). On average in terms of readability(WPM: Words Per Minute), the diagonally splitted layout recorded 694.7WPM (s.d.=153.3) ;the left-triangular column 667.0 WPM(s.d.=120.8); the right-triangular column 922.9WPM(s.d.=253.8). The difference between the diagonally splitted column and the left-triangular column was not significant, however, there was an on standing difference between the two triangular columns (df=17, t=3.425, p=0.0032/df=17, t=5.053, p=0.0000). The left-triangular column reads 4.0% slower than the diagonally splitted column; however, this difference is trivial (figure 6). From the first

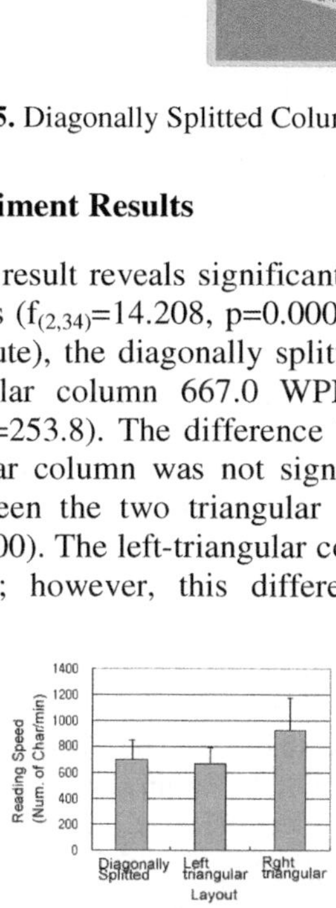

(a) Reading Speed by Layout

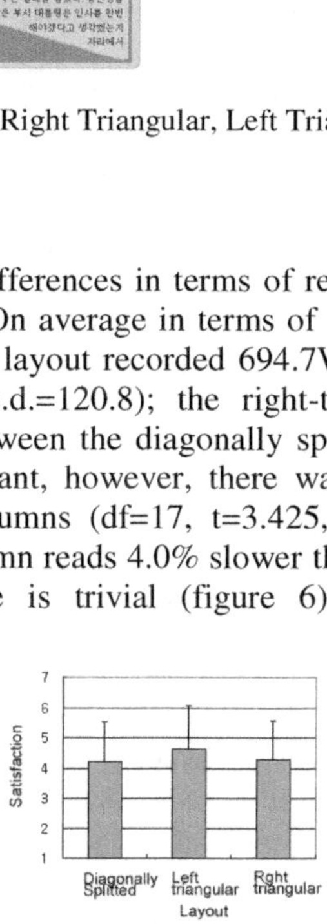

(b) Satisfaction by Layout

Fig. 6. Differences of Reading Speed and Satisfaction by Text Layout

experiment result, the rectangular column screen (4000mm^2 area, width x length 3:1) recorded 550.8 WPM. To compare the first and the second experiment results, the diagonally splitted column indicates improvement in readability by 26.1%; the left-triangular column 21.1%, 'the right-triangular column 67.6% respectively. The diagonally splitted column indicates 4.2/7.0(s.d.=1.3); the left-triangular column 4.6(s.d.=1.5); the right-triangular column 4.3/7.0 (s.d.=1.3). Taking account of the fact that the previous experiment represents 4.4/7.0(s.d.=1.4) for the individual satisfaction of the diagonally splitted column, a significant difference is not observable.

The diagonally splitted column recorded 4.2/7.0(s.d.=1.3); the left-triangular column 4.6/7.0(s.d.=1.5); the right-triangular column 4.3/7.0 (s.d.=1.3). Taking account of the result of the previous experiment that the individual satisfaction rating was 4.4./7.0(s.d.=1.4) for the diagonally-splitted column, this experiment didn't produce a significant difference. The experiment results prove that the right-triangular column is the main factor for the leap in readability of the diagonally-splitted column and that the text-layout does not substantially affect the reading satisfaction.

6 Summary

The results of the two experiments prove that the diagonally-splitted column layout improves readability under the condition of the small-screen size. However, in terms of the satisfaction and the understanding, the change in the experiment conditions did not act as a significant factor. This result can be attributed the point that Mills and Weldon(1987) pointed out, therefore, it is more relevant to compare readabilities, varying the experiment conditions. To compare the experiment results in terms of readability only the diagonally-splitted column produces an interesting effect. The rectangular column recorded 14.3% better readability on the small-screen size, 2000mm^2. However, when the screen-size was altered to 4000mm^2, 8000mm^2 respectively, the diagonally-splitted column showed 18.9%, 34.% superior respectively. It is concluded that as the screen size increases so does the readability of the diagonally-splitted column. This contrasts the existent research[7] that the increase in the width improves readability.

From the experiment result, it is suggested that the rhythmical change in the width, and the regular intent are the main causes of the betterment in reading performance. Moreover, following suggestions are offered in terms of the application of the research. The large-screen size is recommended for the readability if possible. If the screen size is the same, the text layout which is horizontally long is desirable. The small-screen size can adopt the diagonally-splitted column to enhance readability, but it is desirable for the screens larger than 4000mm^2 or 8000mm^2. The small-screen size, 2000mm^2, can deteriorate the text readability. The right-triangular column, which is the altered form of the diagonally-splitted column can be recommended.

It can be a handy way if the informative electronics selects either the diagonally-splitted column or the right-triangular one. Especially, if both the text and the table are presented on the screen, this research can be applied in a way that the table is fixed on the left-triangular column and that the right-triangular column presents the text.

---

[7] Duchnikcy & Kolers, 1983; Dyson & Kipping, 1998.

References

1. Muter, P., Latremouille, S.A., Treurniet, W.C., Beam, P.: Extended reading of continuous text on television screens. Human Factors 24, 501–508 (1982)
2. Gould, J.D., Grischkowsky, N.: Doing the same work with hard copy and with cathode ray tube(CRT) computer terminals. Human Factors 26, 323–337 (1984)
3. Duchnicky, J.L., Kolers, P.A.: Readability of text scrolled on visual display terminals as a function of window size. Human Factors 25, 683–692 (1983)
4. Weldon, L.J., Mills, C.B., Koved, L., Schneiderman, B.: The structure of information in online and paper technical manuals. In: proceedings of Human Factors Society-29th Annual Conference, Santa Monica, CA, pp. 1110–1113 (1985)
5. Mills, C.B., Weldon, L.J.: Reading text from computer screens. ACM Computing Surveys 4, 329–358 (1987)
6. Dyson, M.C., Kipping, G.J: The effects of line length and method of movement on patterns of reading from screen. Visible Language 32, 150–181 (1998)
7. Horton, W.: Designing and writing online documentation: Help files to hypertext, John Wiley & Sons New York (1989)
8. Youngman, M., Scharff, L.: Text length and margin length influences on readability of GUIs. Southwest Psychological Association (1998)
9. Trollip, S.R., Sales, G.: Readability of computer generated fill-justified text. Human Factors 28(2), 159–163 (1986)

Development of Interactive Logger for Understanding User's Interaction with Mobile Phone

Daeeop Kim and Kun-pyo Lee

Human Centered Interaction Design Lab,
Industrial Design, Korea Advanced Institute of Science and Technology
YusungGu, Daejeon, Korea
Up4201@kaist.co.kr

Abstract. User's mobility while using mobile devices requires new types of usability testing methods different from conventional testing methods which are static, verbal, quantitative, indoor, virtual and unnatural. Software, IMOLO (interactive mobile logger) was developed for more practical usability testing for mobile devices. IMOLO allows designers to easily convert their visual interface design of display of mobile devices into a prototype. Conversion is made interactively by simply dragging and dropping. Users can join usability testing with real products in real context. All log data is automatically transmitted to the researcher's server and is replayed exactly the same way the user interacted with mobile devices. IMOLO was found to be useful especially in the stage of validation test1 before product release.

Keywords: Mobile phone prototyping, Mobile usability.

1 Introduction

The concept of usability has become highly valued in the area of mobile devices and software where users' works are mainly mental for its advantages such as 'reduced customer support, service and training costs', 'avoidance of costly delay in schedule', 'simpler-to-prepare product documentation' and 'accurate, ready-to-use marketing claims based on tests'.2 This introduction of the concept of usability to mobile devices has led to the wide application of 'usability testing' for ensuring the quality of usability before releasing a product to the market. Typical methods for usability test range from low fidelity like paper prototyping 3 to high fidelity like online testing4 and real prototype. Usually this kind of testing is done in a closed laboratory equipped

[1] Rubin, Jeffry.(1994). Handbook of Usability Testing. New York: John Wiley and Sons Inc.

[2] Wiklund, Michael E. (1994). Introduction in Usability in Practice edited by Michael E. Wiklund. Boston: AP Professional.

[3] Weiss, Scott. (2002). Handheld Usability. Chichester: John Wiley and Sons, LTD.

[4] Lee, Kun-Pyo. (2002). Remote Usability Testing for Information Appliances through WWW – With the Emphasis on Development of Tool. In Proceedings of Common Ground Conference (Egham, United Kingdom, September 5-7, 2002) Staffordshire. : Staffordshire University Press p. 631-639.

J. Jacko (Ed.): Human-Computer Interaction, Part II, HCII 2007, LNCS 4551, pp. 394–400, 2007.

with a one-way mirror for uninterrupted observation, video recording facilities, and data logging computers. However, despite of the advantages of usability testing, usability testing in the environment of closed laboratory has been known to cause some significant problems: high cost, unnatural environment and limited focus only on measurement. Particularly, mobility in mobile devices makes lab-based low fidelity methods difficult to be effectively applied. To verify user interface design before product release, usability test should be conducted in the real environment with a real product as much as possible.

The software, IMOLO (Interactive Mobile Logger) was developed as a usability testing tool for tackling difficulties mentioned above with objectives as follows:

To generate a working prototype of interface design from simple graphic image of display as easily as possible.

To generate the coded interface software embeddable to mobile device as readily as possible.

To collect log data from various user's interactions with mobile device as automatically as possible.

To provide the software with various analysis methods of log data as realistically as possible.

2 IMOLO (Interactive Mobile Logger)

2.1 Structure and Process

IMOLO is structuralized with roughly three stages of process which includes 'generating', 'testing', and 'analyzing' as shown in Figure 1.

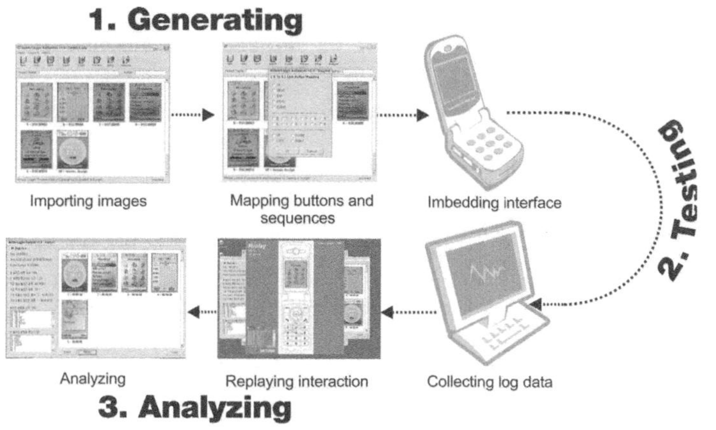

Fig. 1. The process of IMOLO

In the stage of generation, a working prototype of interface design is generated from graphic image files of displays of a mobile device and is embedded into the mobile device. Then, in the stage of testing, usability testing of interface design of mobile device is conducted while a user is carrying his mobile device, and log data from his interaction with mobile device is automatically transmitted to the researcher's server. Finally, in the stage of analysis, various quantitative and qualitative analyses are carried out. This process can be iteratively repeated until satisfactory interface design is found.

2.2 Generation of an Interface Design Prototype

In order to use IMOLO, the designer should be ready to have the so called 'flip book' with all the possible graphic pages of display of mobile device and scenario of interaction. Designer's effectiveness of building the prototype is heavily depending on how easily they can use raw graphic data as they are. For this purpose, IMOLO takes advantage of PNG type of the graphic image files. With graphic image files ready, the designer runs IMOLO and imports all graphic image files (Figure 2). With the imported display images, the designer defines and maps what button of mobile device will invoke a specific display image and what the interaction flow will be by simple drag and drop of display images as shown in Figure3. Then IMOLO immediately generates the simulation of interface design he just created (see Figure 4).

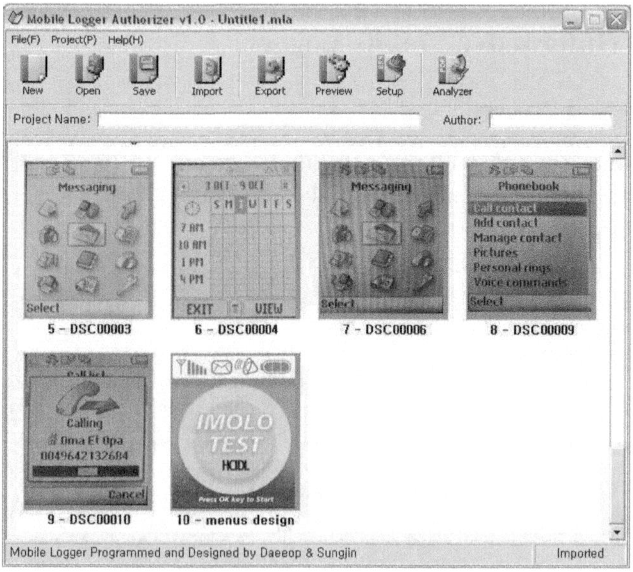

Fig. 2. Imported Images of Display Screens

With the simulated interface design, the designer can preview and check whether the interface design is created as he intended and if he is not satisfied with his design, he can go back to the previous step to revise and create a new one. This interactive way of designing interface design is simple and easy like sketching with pencil and eraser. The designer can repeat the cycle of 'creation' and 'revision' as many times until he is satisfied. After generating a satisfactory interface design, he executes the

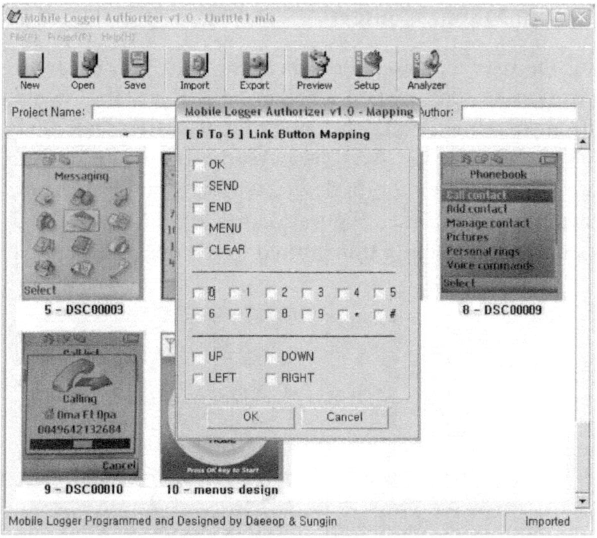

Fig. 3. Mapping Display Pages with Buttons

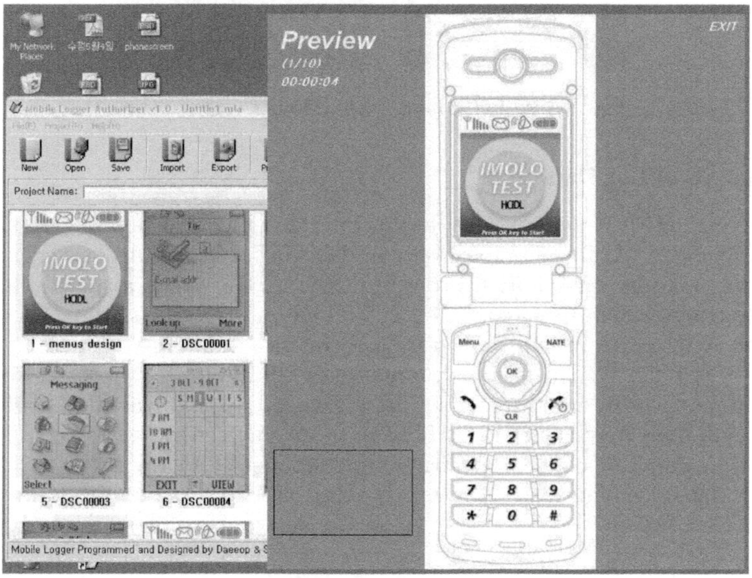

Fig. 4. Previewing Simulated Interface Design

command 'export' to create JAVA Class files and saves them in a designated folder. Then those files are uploaded on the server, and the designer registers the address of the server. The server can be of any type as long as it can be accessed by mobile device.

2.3 Usability Test in Mobile Context

For usability test, the user accesses the server through internet by his mobile device. After accessing the server, he is asked whether he is ready to download the file or not. After confirmation of download, the downloaded files become actual interface contents of user's mobile device. Now he is ready to engage in usability testing with his mobile device. He can use mobile device as usual and perform tasks given by the designer while moving around (see Figure 5). All log data generated while the user is performing tasks are automatically transmitted to the designer's server in real time.

Fig. 5. User Performing Task in Real Context of Use

2.4 Analysis of Log Data

After having finished the usability testing, the designer can now carry out diverse types of analyses. At first, he retrieves log data files saved in the server by clicking the button 'analysis' in IMOLO. From log files, he can select a specific log file he wishes to analyze. On the screen, all graphic images of displays with which the user interacted with are shown in sequence as he interacted along with various usability statistics. Usability statistics include time taken, the number of presses of buttons, average time spent in one display, specification of most and least frequently pressed buttons with their frequencies, specification of display screens exposed in longest or shortest time duration and the sequence of interaction (see Figure 6).

These statistical data can be exported into an EXCEL file for further various analyses. (See Figure 7). With rich log data, the designers can effectively examine the usability of prototype.[5] The designer can also replay user's log data with visualization of user's interaction path on the mobile device. While replaying, relevant usability log data is also shown together so that the designer can analyze both quantitatively and qualitatively. It has interface like VCR so that designer can play and pause at any time for in-depth analysis at specific moments and he can restart as shown in Figure 8. Replaying image with interaction trace at any moment can be saved in a graphic image file for further analyses and documentation.

[5] David M Hilvert et al. (2000). Extracting Usability Information from User Interface Events pp.384-421.

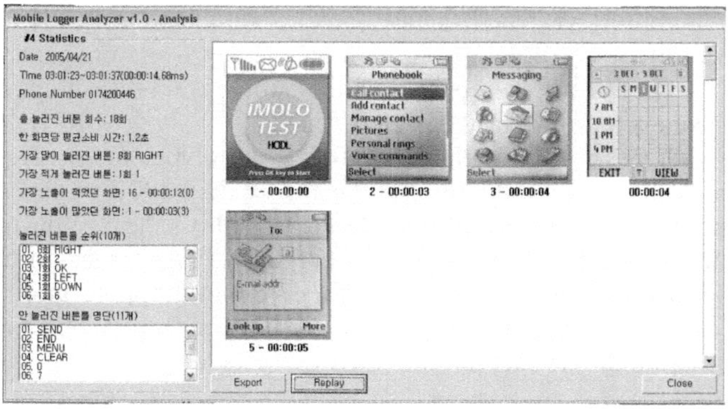

Fig. 6. Screen of Analysis with Usability Statistics

Num	Phone Num	LCD Size	Date	Start Time	Exit Time	Total Time	Button Logged
1	,01048795658	128145	2006/03/18	14:41:42	14:42:04	00:00:22,41	6960•146@8090•148@8820•145@9231•145@10095•146@
2	,01048795658	128145	2006/03/18	14:46:23	14:47:05	00:00:42,79	7227•148@16425•145@18593•145@20114•146@25345•35
3	,0113878448	240320	2006/03/18	16:39:13	16:39:32	00:00:19,46	1730•148@2654•145@3154•145@3751•146@5734•35@17
4	,0113878448	240320	2006/03/18	16:39:53	16:40:11	00:00:18,25	1173•148@2045•146@2545•145@2928•145@3970•35@15
5	,0113878448	240320	2006/03/18	16:41:13	16:41:42	00:00:29,98	1369•148@3096•53@3518•50@3889•49@4185•51@4903•
6	,0113878448	240320	2006/03/19	17:14:56	17:15:07	00:00:11,02	1599•148@2802•145@3019•145@3462•146@4263•35@92
7	,0113878448	240320	2006/03/20	18:33:49	18:34:31	00:00:42,92	5298•148@13202•145@14575•145@15019•145@15400•14
8	,01048795658	128145	2006/03/27	16:14:14	16:14:45	00:00:31,11	4973•148@7109•145@7430•145@7923•145@8846•145@9

Fig. 7. Screen of Exported Logdata of User's Interaction accessed in an EXCEL program

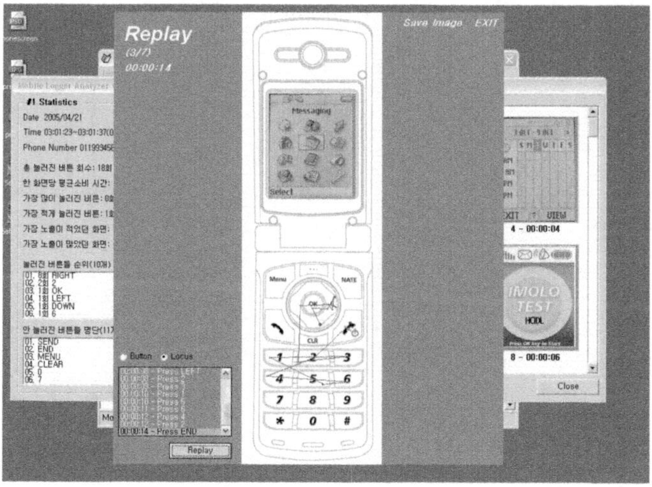

Fig. 8. Screen of Replay of User's Interaction

3 Conclusions and Further Work

A case study of usability test of mobile phone using IMOLO was carried out. It was found that IMOLO was very effective and useful with several distinct advantages: easy and fast generation of prototype of interface design with simple drag and drop; handy way of previewing and revising interface design; direct and natural usability test with real mobile device and actual context; automatic collection of log data; provision of various ways of analyzing log data. This process of 'generation', 'test', and 'analysis' can be iteratively repeated with continuous modifications and revisions until the most satisfactory interface design is found.

However IMOLO is still in the stage of a prototype and it requires further improvements. At first, due to the limit in the size of data (90K in general) users can download from the server in his mobile phone, complex interface design with large size of graphic images cannot be tested. Secondly, IMOLO needs a better way of generating interface design. Although the dragging and dropping graphic images of displays is easy to manipulate, it prevents designers from envisioning complex hierarchical structure of interface.

References

1. Rubin, J.: Handbook of Usability Testing. John Wiley and Sons Inc, New York (1994)
2. Wiklund, M.E.: Introduction in Usability in Practice edited by Michael E. AP Professional, Wiklund. Boston (1994)
3. Weiss, S.: Handheld Usability. John Wiley and Sons, LTD, Chichester (2002)
4. Lee, K.-P.: Remote Usability Testing for Information Appliances through WWW – With the Emphasis on Development of Tool. In: Proceedings of Common Ground Conference, Egham, United Kingdom, September 5-7, 2002, pp. 631–639. Staffordshire University Press, Staffordshire (2002)
5. Hilvert, D.M, et al.: Extracting Usability Information from User Interface Events, pp. 384–421 (2000)

An Improved Model to Evaluate Menu Hierarchies for Mobile Phones

Jeesu Lee and Doowon Paik

School of Media, Soongsil University
Sangdo 5-dong, Dongjak-ku, Seoul, Korea
zsrunrun@gmail.com, dpaik@ssu.ac.kr

Abstract. This study presents a GOMS based model that can predict the performance time of hierarchical menu interface. In the existing GOMS based models, to predict the performance time of hierarchical menu interface, the prediction models are structured under the assumption that all tasks of selecting an item on the menu are experienced tasks. This study presents a model that can predict the performance time of experienced tasks and that of inexperienced tasks separately. When this model is applied, more accurate prediction of the performance time of hierarchical menu interface of mobile phone that include both the experienced and inexperienced tasks will be possible.

This model is designed by measuring the performance time of actual users and the accuracy of prediction is evaluated through an experiment

Keywords: GOMS, mobile phone, interface evaluation.

1 Introduction

Modern day mobile phones are core devices of ubiquitous computing that have numerous functions in addition to making calls. At first, they have only communication functions such as making calls and sending text messages. But today, they contain many other functions, such as electronic dictionary, MP3 player, DMB, games, and Web browsers.

As discussed above, more functions are added to the mobile phones. However, as mobile phones need to be portable, there are input/output device limitations that are hard to overcome. They do not have a keyboard or a mouse like the computer. In addition, as the screen is small, the amount of information displayed on the screen at a time is limited. Therefore, hierarchical menu interface that allows easy selection of a function among numerous functions is generally provided.

To design more effective menu hierarchy, it is possible to predict performance time by utilizing user behavior modeling technique such as GOMS or ACT-R in the stage of mobile phone interface design without having to develop an actual phone.

This means that using the modeling technique allows saving of money and time in the development of mobile phone interface. GOMS(Goals, Operators, Methods, and Selection rules), the modeling technique used in this study is a modeling technique that analyzes user behaviors and interaction system. Several models that used GOMS were very successful [3], and GOMS is considered one of the most influential user

J. Jacko (Ed.): Human-Computer Interaction, Part II, HCII 2007, LNCS 4551, pp. 401–407, 2007.

behavior modeling techniques for HCI. A model that predicted the performance time of hierarchical menus through GOMS was introduced by Robert et al. This model considered a task as reaching a terminal from the initial screen and predicted time assuming that all tasks are experienced tasks. However, users get used to the task of selecting a frequently used terminal (e.g., view text message, and telephone directory), but users do not get used to the task of selecting an infrequently used terminal (e.g., setting international call mode, and view my number). When above model is used to analyze the performance time of hierarchical menus, it is difficult to predict performance time accurately since inexperienced tasks are taken as experienced tasks. Therefore, to predict the use of menu hierarchy accurately, it should be able to predict the performance time of experienced tasks and that of inexperienced tasks separately.

This study presents a prediction model that allows prediction of the performance time of experienced tasks and that of inexperienced tasks separately. In addition, the prediction accuracy of the model is evaluated through an experiment.

2 Procedure

A task in the menu hierarchy interface can be expressed as follows.

Entertainment >> Image box >>> Incoming call screen

(Here, '>' means scroll.)

The prediction of the performance time of menu hierarchy interface of mobile phone is possible by totaling the performance time of all tasks in the menu hierarchy interface. In our model, the performance time of each task is predicted by defining each task as a method, finding out the sequence of operator, the minimum unit that constitute the method, and assigning time for each operator. [1]

A task consists of a sequence of selections. For example, the task of selecting an incoming call screen above can be expressed as a process of selecting in the order of Entertainment, Image box, and Incoming call screen. The selection process can be expressed as follows [1].

```
Select-X
S1  (M1) Look at location for X.
S2  If ((M2)found-X and not on-OK-button),
      (P)move-to OK-button; (K)select-item; goto S4.
      If ((M2)found-X and on-OK-button),
      (K)select-item; goto S4.
      If ((M3)not found-X and on-scroll-button),
      (K)scroll.
      If ((M3)not found-X and not on-scroll-button),
      (P)move-to scroll-button; (K)scroll.
      S3 Goto S2.
S3  Go to S2.
S4  Return with goal accomplished.
```

Here, K, M1, M2, and P in the parenthesis are operators. K is button press time, P is the time of moving a finger to the button, and M1, M2, and M3 are mental preparation time. Mental preparation time differs according to the characteristics shown in Figure 1.

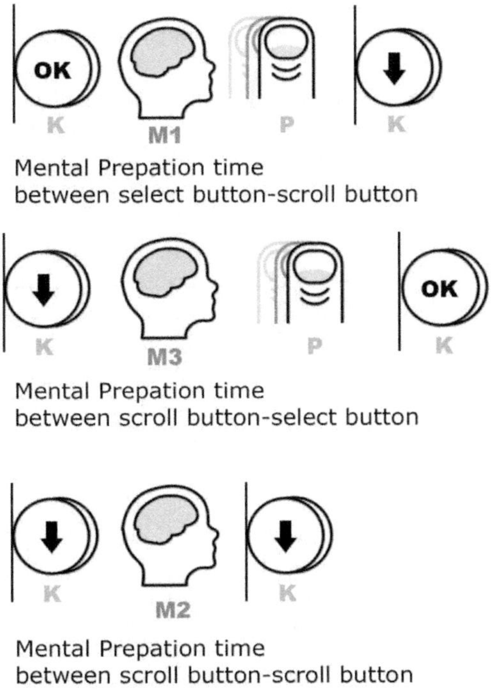

Fig. 1. Three different kind of mental operators

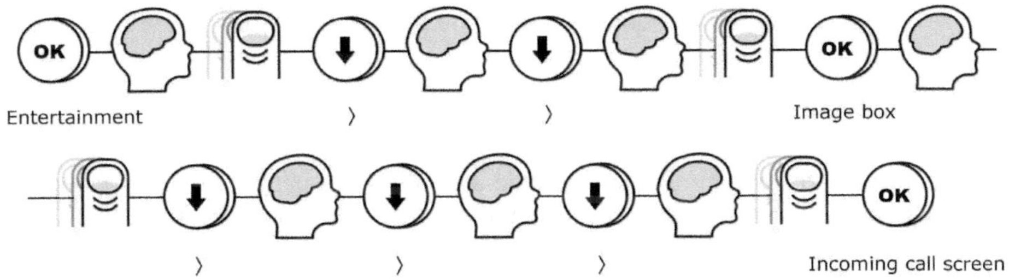

Fig. 2. The task of selecting an 'Incoming call screen'

To complete the model for the prediction of performance time of mobile phone menu hierarchy, it is necessary to define the value of each operator that comprises the procedure.

3 Deciding the Value of Operator

The button press time(K), finger moving time(P), and mental preparation time(M) consist the procedure for menu item selection task. When the value of each of these operators is decided, the model for predicting the performance time can be completed.

In this model, the button press time(K) is the time from a finger placed on a button presses the button and gets ready to press again by recognizing the action through the sense of touch.

The finger moving time(P) is the time from a finger placed on a button moves to another button and gets ready to press the button. In this model, the finger moving time is the time a finger moves between the select button and the scroll button.

The mental preparation time(M) is the time taken to decide whether to press a button or move a finger.

In this study, the value of each operator is determined based on an experiment.

The button press time is obtained by measuring the time between two consecutive presses on a button. The finger moving time is obtained by subtracting button press time from the time between button presses that contain finger moving time.

The mental preparation time(M) is obtained by subtracting button press time and finger moving time from the time of performing a task. Figure 3 shows how the finger moving time and mental preparation time are calculated in diagrams.

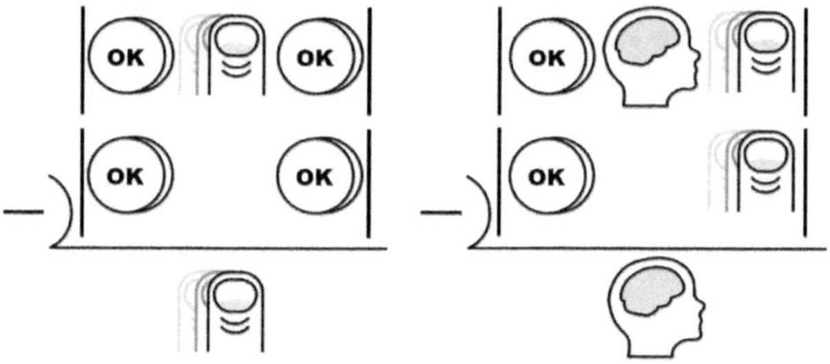

Fig. 3. Calculation of finger moving time and mental preparation time

4 Experiment

The purpose of this experiment is to decide the values of operators that comprise performance prediction model by measuring the user's task performance time.

32 subjects in total, 28 males and 3 females in their mid to late 20s participated in the experiment. All the subjects were right handed.

The mobile phone used for the experiment was Samsung Anycall SCH-S350. (Figure 4)

To measure button press time accurately, application software was loaded in the mobile phone.

Experiment 1: Deciding the values of operators K and P

The time of executing a sequence consisting of random combination of scroll button and select button was measured.

Ex) Select >>> Select > Select >> Select >>>>> Select, Select >> Select

The subjects were requested to press the buttons as fast as they can using only their thumbs. The button press time was obtained by measuring 100 presses per subject.

Fig. 4. Samsung Anycall SCH-S350

Results of experiment 1

The button press time of continuous button press sequence is classified into the following four categories.

Time between scroll button - scroll button:	189ms
Time between select button - select button:	187ms
Time between select button - scroll button:	277ms
Time between scroll button - select button:	265ms

The average time between scroll button - scroll button and the average time between select button– select button are continuous button press time. They do not include finger moving time and these values are very similar. These can be defined as button press time(K). Therefore, the button press time(K) was defined as 188ms, the average of these two values.

The average time between select button-scroll button and the average time between scroll button–select button include button press time and finger moving time. Finger moving time differs according to the size of the button to which to move the finger. In this experiment, the size of scroll button and the size of select button are different. Therefore, the average time between select button – scroll button and the average time between scroll button – select button are different.

The difference between the average time between select button – scroll button and the average time between scroll button –select button is 12ms, which is negligible. Therefore, the finger moving time(P) is obtained by subtracting button press time(P) from the average of these two values.

Button press time(K): 188ms
Finger moving time(P): 83ms

Experiment 2: Deciding the value of M for the inexperienced tasks

The performance time of selecting a certain item from the hierarchical menus was measured. Each subject performed each of 4 tasks 5 times and each task consisted of selecting an item from the list of 6 menu items. Subjects were not experienced with all the tasks and each subject was asked to perform the tasks as soon as possible using only the scroll button and select button.

It was assumed that each subject knows the name of the item to select when he or she performs the task. If we make the subjects to memorize the names of the items, it would take long until they could remember them automatically. So, we used the lyrics of Korean national anthem as menu items since everyone would know it by heart.

(e.g. First task consisted of 5 selection processes)
Donghaemulgwa >> Baekdusani >>> Mareugo > Daltorok >>>>> Haneunimi

Results of experiment 2
The task performance time was broken down into button press time and classified into the following three categories.

Time between select button-scroll button:	963 ms
Time between scroll button-scroll button:	222 ms
Time between scroll button-select button:	409 ms

As M1 is located between the select button and the scroll button, M1 can be obtained by subtracting button press time and finger moving time once from the performance time of select button-scroll button. Similarly, M2 can be obtained by subtracting button press time and finger moving time from the performance time of scroll button-select button. And M3 can be obtained by subtracting button press time and finger moving time from the performance time of scroll button-scroll button.

M1: 678 ms
M2: 148 ms
M3: 34 ms

Experiment 3: Determining the value of M for experienced tasks
The subjects were asked to repeat experiment 2 twelve times. And the last 2 performances were used as experienced performances.

Results of experiment 3

Time between select button-scroll button:	458 ms
Time between scroll button-scroll button :	184 ms
Time between scroll button-select button:	303 ms

Using the method used in experiment 2, the mental preparation times were obtained as follows.

M1: 187 ms
M2: 32 ms
M3: 0 ms

5 Evaluation of the Suggested Model

To evaluate the suggested model, hierarchical menus that contain one experienced task and one inexperienced task were produced. The performance time was predicted using this model and Robert's model. The results were compared with the actual user performance. The results are shown in Table 1.

Table 1. Font sizes of headings. Table captions should always be positioned *above* the tables.

Task	Prediction by this study's model	Prediction by Robert's model	Actual performance time
Task 1 (Experienced)	4,320 ms	7,630 ms	4,265 ms
Task 2 (Inexperienced	6,820 ms	-	6,644 ms

From Table 1, we can see that this study's model predicts both the performance time of experienced task and that of inexperienced task accurately.

6 Conclusion

The model suggested in this study did not use theoretical values for the operators. But the actual performance time of users was measured and applied. This study made it possible to predict performance time more accurately.

When this model for the prediction of performance time of menu hierarchy interface for mobile phones is used, it is possible to predict performance time of experienced tasks and that of inexperienced tasks separately. As mobile phones have inexperienced tasks as well as experienced tasks in general, this model can predict performance time of menu hierarchy interface more accurately.

References

1. St. Amant, R., Horton, T., Ritter, F.: Model-based evaluation of cell phone menu interaction. In: Proceedings of the Conference on Human Factors in Computing Systems, pp. 343–350 (2004)
2. Silfverberg, M., MacKenzie, I.S., Korhonen, P.: Predicting text entry speed on mobile phones. In: Proceedings of CHI, pp. 9–16. ACM, New York (2000)
3. Gray, W.D., John, B.E., Atwood, M.E.: Project Ernestine: Validating a GOMS analysis for predicting and explaining real-world task performance (1993)

Support Zooming Tools for Mobile Devices*

Kwang B. Lee

Computer Science Department, University of Northern Virginia,
10021 Balls Ford Road, Manassas, VA 20109
rensselaer03@gmail.com

Abstract. Mobile devices are quickly becoming powerful devices enough to run personal computers. However to control large visual information is still the critical issue for them. This paper introduces several zooming tools such as a focus zoom, a file zoom and a search zoom which are based on geometric and semantic zooming methods as new viewing methods. These zooming tools are developed to devise an efficient method for handling the viewing issue, displaying large visual information on a small size screen. In addition, the paper introduces usability testing method on mobile devices to find hidden issues in the tool, and mentions further progress to improve the usability of working on devices.

Keywords: Mobile Devices, Personal Digital Assistants (PDAs), Zoomable User Interfaces (ZUIs), Popup and Shadow Zooming, Distorted View and Non-distorted View, Geometric and Semantic Zooming.

1 Introduction

Although mobile devices, cellular phones, Personal Digital Assistants (PDAs) and other handheld devices have hardware constraints such as small screen, small storage, low CPU speed, and low resolution, their popularity has been enormously increasing. This is enhancing the opportunities for researchers to overcome those open problems caused of small size hardware constraints. However, still the biggest difficulty is that these devices are too difficult to load today's visual information because most current information is based on a large visual documentation. How do we present information effectively on mobile devices? This is a main challenge for mobile interface developers since viewing is becoming more and more crucial point in our daily lives.

One of the methods is to build a Zoomable User Interfaces (ZUIs) by using several zooming tools so that the amount of information, which needs to be handled by users, can be shown on a small screen unlimitedly. Smooth zooming technology helps users to interact with their sense of the focus-and-context by shifting the cognitive load to the human visual system, and it can provide a possible solution that satisfies the above demands by means of increasing the effectiveness for using the small screen. Thus supporting zooming tools on mobile devices is a necessary item with enabling users to effectively control the zooming methods.

---

* The short paper has been presented on IPCC 2003.

J. Jacko (Ed.): Human-Computer Interaction, Part II, HCII 2007, LNCS 4551, pp. 408–417, 2007.

The goal of this paper is to increase the performance of user interfaces by developing zooming tools on mobile devices. Three zooming approaches will be introduced in this paper. First, focus zooming tools, which consists of the magnifying glass that was introduced from a "Bifocal Display [7]," the gray scaling and blurring lens that was introduced from a "Focus+Context Visualization [8]," will be proposed. Second, file zooming tools including zoom-in and zoom-out functions to enlarge or reduce data and images based on the geometric zooming technology will be proposed. Finally, search zooming tools, which have two functions support a popup zooming and a shadow zooming functions to assist user easy to control for seeing many files on the device, will be introduced. Furthermore, the paper addresses a new usability testing method which combines heuristic, scenarios, and questionnaire approaches in order to effectively take experimental results from users. Its testing methods and procedures will be introduced by conducting usability test with user.

In this paper, we first describe the basic zooming technique and prototype on a PDA in section 2. In section 3, we introduce a new mobile usability testing method, and conduct usability testing and show the results in section 4. Finally, we conclude by describing some of our experiences in building the system and outlining future work.

2 Basic Zooming Structure

In this section, we discuss the theoretical background for basic zooming techniques on mobile devices, and mention the necessary concept needed to support our approaches.

2.1 Magnifying Process

The magnifying processes transfer pixels from a specified source pan to a specified destination pan, which is the magnifying glass, altering the pixels according to the selected raster operation code. To magnify data, a source pan containing source data on the original screen is smaller than the magnifying glass pan, as seen in Figure 1 (a). Thus, the ratio to magnify data will be decided by comparing the size of two pans, a source pan and a magnifying glass pan.

A degree of interest (DOI) function map which was introduced by Furnas [1] indicates the level of interest in the item and it can be used to control how available space is allocated amongst items. The DOI concept has been changed over time according to the change of user interaction such as searching process and the moving focus. So, instead of using DOI, we suggest another approach to calculate how much data is magnified and how much data is lost.

In the magnifying glass, the technique allows user to determine the glass size and magnifying ratio based on the varying interest levels of parts. To calculate the magnifying ratio, we can use three factors: the source pan (D_1) that is based on the original source data; the data loss (L_1+L_2) that is an obscured region due to the big magnifying glass; and finally, the destination pan (D_2) that is the target window for copied the source data. Thus, the magnifying ratio depends on the size of each pan and data loss.

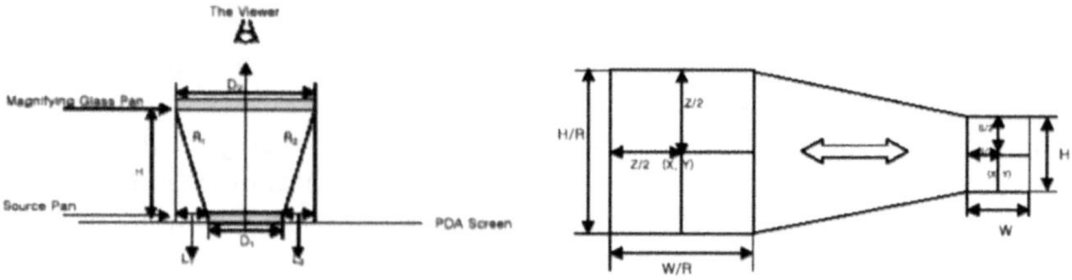

D_1: The size of source pan, $(x_1 \times y_1)$
D_2: The size of the magnifying glass pan, $(x_2 \times y_2)$
R_1, R_2: Magnifying ratio
L_1, L_2: Data loss area
H: Height

a) Magnifying process b) Zoom-in and zoom-out process

Fig. 1. Zooming processes on a PDA screen

2.2 Zooming Process

Zooming processes are copying bitmaps from the source rectangle and transferring them into a destination rectangle by stretching or compressing the size of bitmaps to fit the dimensions of the destination rectangle, if necessary. By the zooming size, *S*, and the zooming ratio, $R=\{0<\ldots\leq 1\}$, defined by the user, we are able to reduce the size by transforming a bitmap image into the zooming size. The PDA screen address, $P=(X, Y, Z)$, has both a location and a scale defined by the rectangle size, $Z=(S/R)$, is defined by the linear transformation, T_p: $(X-(Z/2), Y-(Z/2)) \leftrightarrow (X-(S/2), Y-(S/2))$. A zooming region, $A=[P, W, H]$, is a rectangle defined by an address together with a pixel width and height (W, H), as seen in Figure 1 (b).

The other level of zooming applications is to visibly display windows to the users as a popup or shadow zooming style. Every display window in the popup or shadow zooming applications has a region, $[P_i, W_i, H_i]$ where *i* is window number, which is the portion of the PDA screen, and these windows are located behind the original window by the fingernail-viewing file or the icon-viewing file. In particular, the shadow zooming has another window area, $[P_{i+1}, W_{i+1}, H_{i+1}]$, which is the small magnifying glass to magnify the hidden data instead of showing all data. Here we summarize the properties of zooming methods as follows:

- Visibility window: The visibility range of objects for user.
- Background window: The range of popup or shadow viewing objects which include the source image copied.
- Magnifying window: The glass to magnify data should have a certain range of magnification that allows users to see a small part in which they are interested.

2.3 Basic Structure and Prototype of Zooming Tools

In this part, we design and implement various zooming tools we mentioned with focusing on their usefulness and extensionality on a PDA, as seen Figures 2 - 5. Those tools were written in embedded Visual C++ supported by Microsoft® and developed on common Pocket PC.

2.3.1 Focus Zooming Tools

We introduce the focus zoom mechanism for increasing users' focusing ability in term of two facts. One is that the human transition is based on focusing on a magnified moving object according to the human perceptual system. The other is that the human eye is used to ignoring blurred objects because the eye also has a limited depth of filed by blurring currently irrelevant objects [8]. When these tools are moving on the screen, their movements are represented with interactive magnification or the amount of blur, so that the user easily focuses on what is being displayed. These focus zooming tools give users more detail of certain parts of the screen, which is particularly helpful when lots of data is showing on the device.

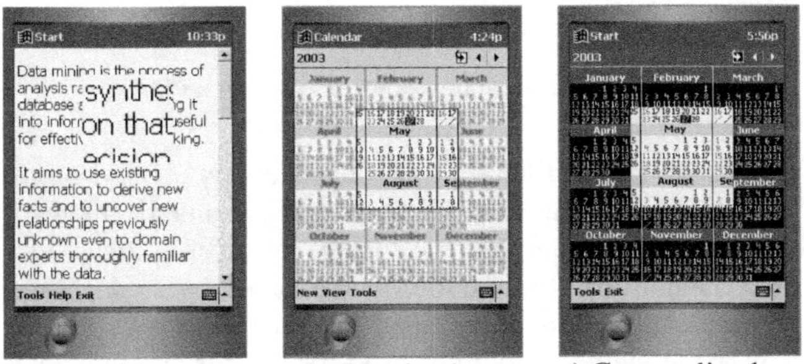

a) Magnifying glass b) Blurring lens c) Gray scaling lens

Fig. 2. Focus zooming tool processes on a PDA

As seen Figure 2, the focusing glass, (x_n, y_n) rectangle, shows a detailed view as a 2D form, and the other regions remain de-magnified or blurring areas according to the physical position. Cutting, pasting, and blurring various sections of bitmaps in real time will generate this focusing area. Even though the focusing glass does not provide good spatial continuity between regions, it is relatively simple in terms of using and implementation, and also it does not need much of the computational power of system memory. Therefore, focus zooming tools will be a good viewing technique for relatively low memory and mobile devices.

2.3.2 File Zooming Tools

Zooming methods can be categorized by the following presentation techniques: distorted and non-distorted zooming, geometric zooming, and semantic zooming methods [2], [9]. While the semantic zooming changes the shape or context in which the information is being presented, the geometric zooming has a scale operator to perform a geometric transformation, which can be used to shrink or magnify the size of an image. Each method will be adapted for making an efficient view for a user by considering the characteristics of hardware, software, and necessary environment.

In Figure 3, the file zoom has zoom-in and zoom-out methods in mobile devices based on this geometric method, which allows the user to specify the scale of magnification to increase or decrease the image or display screen. This shrunken file can be saved on the mobile device without changing the original content of the file. To expand its contents, the user touches the icon or the small image. These two viewing methods represent how to save files into a database, and also efficiently retrieve files from the database in mobile devices.

a) Zoom-out process b) Fingernail viewing files c) Icon viewing files

Fig. 3. File zooming tool processes on a PDA

The first method is to save a file as a fingernail view by using a geometric zooming method. The second method, an icon view, uses the semantic method, so a certain icon can cover the small zoom-out file. Both are useful ideas for making user interaction with a database on the mobile device easier by saving screen space, and also providing visual abstractions to the user for what kinds of files are saved on the database. Moreover, the method should be used for memory buttons that are needed in graphic interaction in the small screen interface where the current file and its status can be saved as a small image or an iconic representation [4]. Thus, if users desire to access the previous file state or browser, just handling the graphical memory button will bring up the previous file or browser status.

2.3.3 Search Zooming Tools

This section introduces the search zoom implementation using a popup and a shadow zooming methods to make another viewing tool of the above zoom-out files. These two viewing tools will be used for searching and retrieving files in a database of mobile devices according to users' preferences.

As seen in Figure 4 (a), the first method is a popup viewing tool which allows for the touching of the area of the original zoom-out files, and then a bigger zooming window is shown as a popup style. The popup zooming window promptly fades away when the user's attraction is moved to another place. So, the user easily knows what file or data included in the zoom-out file. In Figure 4 (b) and (c), the other method is a shadow viewing tool. When a user has located the point of interest with a small magnifying glass, which is embedded, the magnifying glass reveals the content of the file as a background, like a shadow. If the user touches the area of the file with the magnifying glass, then the embedded background of the zoom-out file will be shown. The more the magnifying glass moves on the area, the more background image appears. When the user's attention moves to another place, then the zooming promptly fades away.

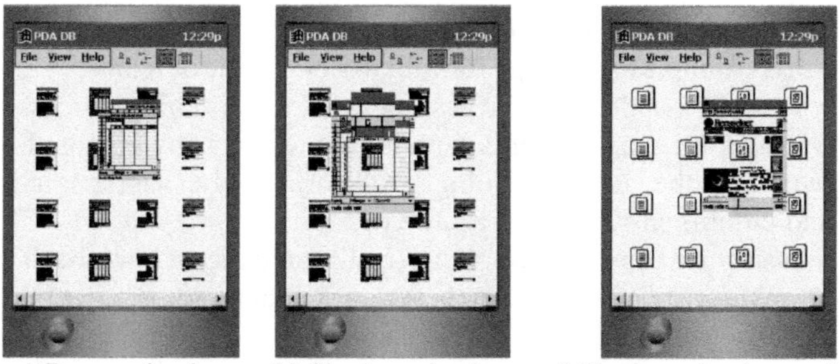

a) Popup viewing b) Shadow viewing c) Shadow viewing on icons

Fig. 4. Search zooming tool processes on a PDA

In this way, the user easily knows what files or data are saved in the original file. Here, we summarized two types of methods as follows:

- Popup Style: This shows the overview file information as a thumbnail image size like a popup menu when a user points to the file location.
- Shadow Style: This shows the overview file information with the magnifying glass, where the magnifying caption views the content of a file.

Both techniques will be potentially powerful tools by saving the searching time to see a full text or image in the mobile device database. We expect that great research efforts should be focused on exploring the application for searching methods and building databases with these applications on mobile devices.

3 Key Components for Usability Test on Mobile Devices

In this section, we discuss a usability testing method we designed, and discuss how to build the testing plan for mobile devices.

1. Preparing Guidelines: In doing mobile application evaluation, well-defined guidelines enable the developers to easily assist participants for operating tools when they have problems caused by unstable prototypes and limited domain expertise.
2. Developing Prototype: To build final tools much faster and much more cheaply in mobile devices, we use a prototype on a PDA. In many cases, using the prototype reduces the likelihood that people have erroneous communications about the product, and increases better understanding of the user interface designed.
3. Making Scenario-Based Tasks: Scenarios describe tasks in a way that takes some of the artificially out of the test such as explaining situations and environments, and also they can have an encapsulated description of an individual user or group using a specific set of computer facilities to achieve a specific outcome under specified circumstances over a certain time interval. Thus, the scenario-based task is a necessary approach for building mobility tasks to simulate certain mobile environments
4. Preparing Presentation: We prepare enough presentation time for introducing each developing function or interface which includes a step-by-step description of how

to manipulate functions and complete given tasks. By using a checklist, we prepare detailed examples and steps for inexperienced participants.

5. Conducting Test: In conducting the testing itself on mobile devices, we have a time to interact with the participants without expressing any personal opinions or indicating whether the user is doing well or poorly. Users are interacting physically and emotionally with the prototype.
6. Debriefing Session and Post Testing: After all evaluations have been completed, we should prepare a meeting in which all participants come together to discuss their impressions from the test. This session is conducted primarily in a brainstorming mode and focused on discussions of the major usability problems and general problematic aspects of the design on mobile devices.

Table 1. Given tasks to participants for usability test

Function Level	Given Tasks
Focus Zoom	• Task 1 – Use magnifying lens to see the interesting content of a file • Task 2 – Use blurring lens to see the interesting content of a file
File Zoom	• Task 3 – Use zooming operation on a file • Task 4 – Save a file as Fingernail view by zooming out function • Task 5 – Save a file as Icon view by zooming out function
Search Zoom	• Task 7 – Search a file by using popup viewing on Icon based PDA database • Task 6 – Search a file by using popup viewing on Fingernail based PDA database • Task 8 – Search a file by using shadow viewing on Fingernail based PDA database • Task 9 – Search a file by using shadow viewing on Icon based on PDA database

4 Experimental Results

4.1 Conduct Usability Test

To achieve usability test under mobile environments, we design a combination method prescribed in the previous section, and then conduct usability test for zooming tools using this method [5], [10], [11]. This combined testing method include heuristic evaluation, questionnaires and scenario-based tasks, and it consists of six attributes such as overall impression, success and timing, satisfaction and preferences, feature use and understanding, compatibility and interoperability and functionality.

To conduct the test, we recruited 17 students who were students, and then classified them into two groups based on pre-screening testing results:

- Expert Group: The group members have substantive knowledge regarding mobile devices, and they are familiar with both HCI and usability. Also, they have fundamental knowledge of mobile devices and personal computers. We choose four students from all participants who have a history of operating mobile devices.

- Novice Group: The group members lack substantive knowledge regarding mobile devices, but they are reasonably familiar with HCI and usability. We recruited 13 students who do not have any experience with mobile devices; however they can manipulate personal computers

All testing was conducted in the class lab, and individual users were asked to inspect the prototype alone. After each user tested the prototype and completed given tasks at least two times, the user started to answer questions, which were based on dialogue elements based on heuristic categories. There were nine tasks that included a proper scenario to help users to evaluate the prototype well, as seen Table 1.

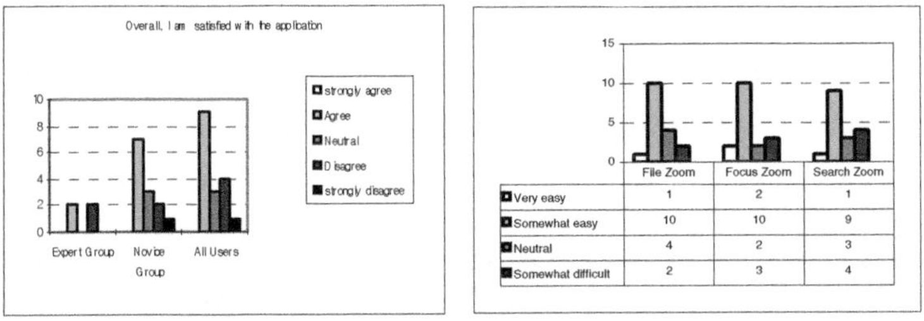

a) Overall satisfaction b) Post-test evaluation

Fig. 6. Usability testing result

We evaluated the users' satisfaction and preference for how the prototype solves physical limitations, provides an easy way to use zooming tools, and supports feedback for increasing users' interaction. Usually we focus on job completion time: rapid, accurate and completeness of task processing for each main task because it is important that the application is working rapidly and accurately as the user request. Generally, all users agree that the application allows for rapid, accurate and complete task processing.

As seen Figure 6 (a), in testing users' overall satisfaction with the zooming tools, we find that the expert group has split opinions, both agreeing and disagreeing. One reason is based on the expert group's experience, because they may have expected a desktop quality application on a mobile device. However, the actual zooming functions on mobile devices are of much lower quality. A second reason is the choice of sample files, graphics and figures in the test may have highlighted the low quality more than the text files, so we chose non-suitable files for the test. The novice group however is satisfied with this application.

In Figure 6 (b), even though some users disagree with each approach, typically more than 65% of the users are satisfied with each function, the focus zoom, the file zoom, and the search zoom. The preference rates of the focus zoom and the file zoom is bigger than the search zoom method. However, many users answered "neutral" and "somewhat difficult" because of unclear terminology and non-suitable tasks. Therefore, to increase usability, we have to find proper terminology and modify the application according to the results when we redesign the product.

4.2 Preference and Recommendations

In order to ameliorate the most pressing usability problems with the zooming tool by considering the global problems, we describes each group's preference and recommend future changes for developers as follows:

- Expert User Preferences: Usually, expert users want fast and accurate functions to complete tasks, and they need good feedback from the tool. Also, they want to modify the tools to be more compatible with other tools, and feel the difficulty of handling several functions. Finally, expert users need clearly defined instruction to properly use them.
- Novice User Preferences: Many novice users are satisfied with the tool more than expert users. They think this approach is a very useful tool for solving small devices' problems, however they have great difficulty with the tools' feedback, and they want to easily access and exit each function. They think the tool needs more compatibility working with other programs and exchanging information

Here, we summarize user recommendations for redesigning the product.

1. Reducing many clicking steps: The tools ask users to click the pen several times to operate the menu. This procedure might be awkward for users.
2. Making well-organized menu interfaces and more functions: Preparing useful functions and constructing well-organized menus are critical points to increase usability.
3. Trying to develop other uses of the zooming function: Developers should try to develop other uses of the zooming function and to find kinds of tasks/areas to which it would be useful.
4. Drawing borderline when zooming functions are working on the screen: All zooming windows should have a borderline because users cannot easily recognize which parts are zoomed.

5 Conclusion

This paper has described specialized zooming tools on mobile devices with designing and developing basic geometric and semantic zooming methods in order to increase the usability of the device. Based on three zooming methods, we created new zooming tools for the device by describing the detail prototype and implementation of these applications were introduced in this paper.

However, we have problems because the tools were designed for the PDA simulation program in a desktop computer. So, we do not know how many different results exist between the application program and the real physical device. Especially, in terms of hardware, the current PDA does not have enough pixels, so users could potentially encounter broken characters when the magnifying glass is used.

Although these zooming tools are not substantially implemented in commercial PDAs, it will be used for new interfaces in mobile devices by supporting various zooming functions. We look forward to continuing the research and development of this tool according to the future development of the PDA's hardware performance and elements. Therefore, the biggest contribution of this paper is the creation of zooming tools on PDAs by encouraging the development of practical zooming methods over theoretical methods.

References

1. Furnas, G.W.: Generalized Fisheye Views. In: Proceedings of ACM SIGCHI '86, pp. 12–16. ACM Press, New York (1986)
2. Furnas, G.W., Bederson, B.B.: Space-Scale Diagrams: Understanding Multiscale Interfaces. In: Proceedings of the SIGCHI conference on Human Factors in Computing Systems CHI '95, pp. 234–241. ACM Press, New York (1995)
3. Gheel, J., Anderson, T.: Data and Metadata for Finding and Reminding. In: Proceeding of the, International Conference on Information Visualization 4th, Washington DC (1999) pp. 446–451(1999)
4. Lee, K.B., Grice, R.: Developing a New Usability Testing Method for Mobile Devices. IPCC 2004, IEEE Professional Communication Society, Minneapolis MN pp. 115–127 (2004)
5. Lee, K.B., Grice, R.: The Embedded Zooming Application for Personal Digital Assistant. IPCC 2003, IEEE Professional Communication Society, Orland FL pp. 109–116 (2003)
6. Apperley, M.D., Tzavaras, I., Spence, R.: A Bifocal Display Technique for Data Presentation. In: Proceedings of Eurographics 82, pp. 27–43 (1982)
7. Giller, V., Tscheligim, M., Schrammel, J., Fröhlich, P., Rabl, B.: Experimental Evaluation of Semantic Depth of Field, a Preattentive Method for Focus+Context Visualization. Technical Paper TR-2001-3, Vienna University of Technology (2001)
8. Leung, Y.K., Apperley, M.D.: Readings in Information Visualization Using Vision to Think. A Review and Taxonomy of Distortion-Oriented Presentation Techniques, Morgan Kaufman Publishers, Inc. pp. 350–367 (1999)
9. Johnson, P.: Usability and Mobility; Interactions on the move. In: Proceedings of the First Workshop on Human Computer Interaction with Mobile Devices (1998)
10. Lindroth, T., Nilsson, S.: Context Usability, Rigour meets relevance when usability goes mobile. ECIS Doctoral Consortium, pp. 24–26 (2001)
11. Khella, A., Bederson, B.B.: Pocket PhotoMesa: A Zoomable Image Browser for PDAs. MUM 2004, College Park MD pp. 19–24 (2004)
12. Bartram, L., Ho, A., Dill, J., Henigman, F.: The Continuous Zoom: A Constrained Fisheye Technique for Viewing and Navigating Large Information Spaces. In: Proceedings of the 8th annual ACM symposium on User Interface and Software Technology, Pittsburgh PA, pp. 207–215 (1995)

Design of a Pen-Based Electric Diagram Editor Based on Context-Driven Constraint Multiset Grammars

Sébastien Macé and Eric Anquetil

IRISA – INSA
Campus Universitaire de Beaulieu, 35042 Rennes Cedex, France
{sebastien.mace,eric.anquetil}@irisa.fr

Abstract. This paper deals with the computer-aided design of pen-based interfaces for structured document composition. In order to take advantage of the interaction with the user, the goal is to interpret the user hand-drawn strokes incrementally, i.e. directly as the document is being drawn. We present a generic approach for such purpose: it is based on a new formalism, Context-Driven Constraint Multiset Grammars (CDCMG), and its associated incremental parser. CDCMG model how documents of a given nature are composed; they can be applied on various natures of documents. We demonstrate how it has been exploited to develop, in collaboration with a society that spreads out industrial pen-based solutions, a prototype for electric diagram composition and editing. We also present an evaluation of the system. Experimental results first emphasize the gain of time in comparison with more classical user interfaces. They also demonstrate its user-friendliness and its usability.

Keywords: Pen-based interfaces, on-line interpretation, structured document analysis, visual languages, incremental parsing, software assessing.

1 Introduction

Pen interaction permits to dialog with computer systems thanks to a pen: users draw gestures, interpreted by the system, on a sensitive screen. The use of systems such as tablet PCs is very user-friendly, because it reproduces the *pen-paper metaphor*. Thus, whereas people often make a draft of a document and then copy it neatly thanks to software classically based on mouse and buttons, tablet PCs offer a merged solution: people directly design, compose and edit documents on the computer system. Fig. 1 presents such a tablet PC: the user composes electric diagrams by drawing the symbols on the sensitive screen. This software is an example of interface that has been designed thanks to the methodology we present in this paper.

There is a lack of software taking advantage of this user-friendly way to compose and edit *structured documents*, i.e. documents with a predefined structural arrangement, such as electric diagrams, plans, musical scores, tables, etc. Indeed, *on-line interpretation*, which is the interpretation of *strokes* (the sequences of points captured by the sensitive screen between a pen-down and a pen-up), is difficult due to the diversity of handwriting styles. This recognition process is even more complex in the context of structured document analysis, because these documents are constituted of

J. Jacko (Ed.): Human-Computer Interaction, Part II, HCII 2007, LNCS 4551, pp. 418–428, 2007.

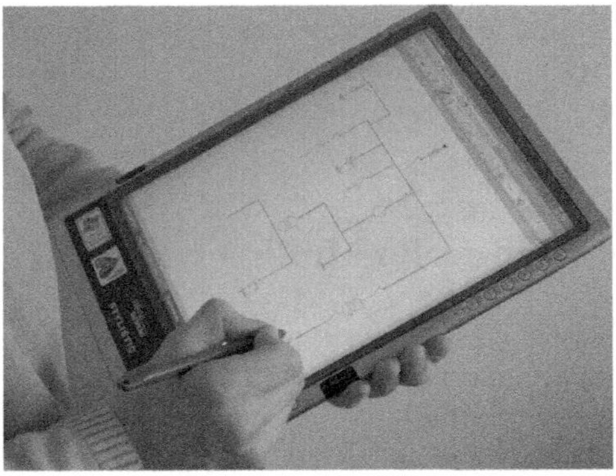

Fig. 1. A tablet PC with the presented pen-based electric diagram editor

many elements of various natures. Moreover, a same stroke can have different meanings according to the context in which it has been drawn.

In this paper, we present a generic method for the design of pen-based interfaces for structured document composition. Our goal is to take advantage of the interaction with the user and thus enable him to incrementally compose his documents: each time he draws a stroke, it is replaced by the corresponding neatly transcribed symbol. Therefore, there is systematically a visual feedback to the user who can therefore implicitly validate it or explicitly correct it if necessary; he can then enrich the document that has already been understood. We believe that integrating the user in the analysis process is a pertinent and more user-friendly alternative than letting him correct the interpretation errors at the end of the composition: it is reassuring for him because he is sure the system has well understood what he has drawn. Nevertheless, this requires dealing with incomplete documents and making a decision as quickly as possible.

We have presented in [1-3] the first version of a generic system based on an architecture with well-separated components. The most original one was a context-sensitive visual formalism that made it possible to model the way structured documents are composed and, therefore, must be interpreted. This offered the advantage of facilitating the exploitation of the system to various natures of structured documents. This method has already proved itself in domains such as several musical notations and UML class diagrams. In this paper, we do not focus on the general architecture of the system and its other components. Interested readers can refer to [1].

The goal of this paper is triple. Firstly, it aims at improving the proposed formalism in order to be able to deal with more complex documents. We propose a new dedicated formalism, Context-Driven Constraint Multiset Grammars (CDCMG), for that purpose: they are an extension of an existing formalism (Constraint Multiset Grammars). Secondly, we explain how they are used in the domain of electric diagram editing. This already functional prototype has been designed in collaboration with a society that spreads out industrial pen-based solutions (Evodia [5]). Thirdly, this paper also aims at assessing the systems that are based on the presented method.

The following section introduces the new grammatical formalism (CDCMG) we have designed to deal with on-line structured document analysis. Then section 3 presents the corresponding incremental parser that makes it possible to design interactive systems. Section 4 introduces the prototype for electric diagram composition, and presents experimental results; they highlight its performances in terms of gain of time in comparison with more classical button-based systems and its recognition rates.

2 Context-Driven Constraint Multiset Grammars

As mentioned previously, the generic method we propose is based on a formalism for rich pen-based input that models the way structured documents are composed (*composition conventions*), and thus the way they have to be interpreted. It can be applied to different notation domains and composition conventions in order to model how to interpret a very large panel of hand-drawn structured documents. This knowledge is externalized from the system, which facilitates its modification and its finalization.

The new formalism is the merging of *Constraint Multiset Grammars* (*CMG*) [6,7] with our previous works [1-3]. A CMG G is a quadruplet $G=(V_N,V_T,P,S)$ where V_N, V_T, P are sets of *non-terminals*, *terminals*, and *productions* respectively, and S is the *starting symbol*. A production in P has the form:

$$\alpha \rightarrow \beta \text{ where } \{C\} \text{ and } (D)$$

where α and β are multisets in $(V_N \cup V_T)^+$, C are constraints to satisfy in order to reduce the production, and D are the definitions of the attributes of the elements in α. C makes it possible to model both semantic constraints and structural arrangement of the elements in β (i.e. their *structural recognition*, to ensure they are correctly relatively positioned). The main originality of CMG is that they allow using existential and negative constraints in C, which makes them context-sensitive.

Unfortunately, CMG as presented in [6,7] are not sufficient to deal with on-line structured document composition, and this for several reasons. Firstly, CMG are based on the segmentation of strokes into pre-defined primitives, such as lines or arcs, which we believe is not well suited for hand-drawn data (see for instance `stroke2` in Fig. 2(b) for an example of a stroke difficult to segment into such primitives). Secondly, CMG do not take into account the context of a stroke in order to interpret (or even segment) it, which can turn out to be insufficient (as indicated previously, a same stroke can have different interpretations depending on its context). Thirdly, CMG are only based on the structural recognition of the elements in β and do not take advantage of *morphological hand-drawn shape recognition systems* (based for instance on hidden Markov models, neural networks or support vector machines) which have already proved themselves in the context of handwriting recognition.

As a consequence, we propose a new formalism, *Context-Driven Constraint Multiset Grammars (CDCMG)*, to deal with this inadequacy: it is the merging of CMG with our previous work. The first originality of CDCMG is the choice of the domain-independent primitive: instead of segmenting the strokes into pre-defined primitives, we define our only primitives as the stroke; formally, it means that V_T={stroke}. We then avoid the recurrent segmentation problem. On the opposite, V_N is domain dependent and is the set of all the possible visual elements in the document. The definition of CDCMG is the same as the definition of CMG, except that this time, C is dedicated to context-driven parsing. A production in P now has the following form:

```
α → β where {
     document context verification (DCV) block
     constraint verification (CV) block
     shape recognition (SR) block
     document context creation (DCC) block
} and (C)
```

These blocks model the coupling of a global vision of the document (DCV and DCC blocks) with a local vision of the analyzed elements, i.e. of β (CV and SR blocks). This block organization allows both natural constraint encoding and efficient parsing. Before presenting these four blocks more in detail, we present an example of production in order to explicit the notations used in CDCMG. This CDCMG production, illustrated by Fig. 2, is dedicated to the interpretation of the switch electric component; according to this specific production, the switch has to be drawn with two strokes:

```
Switch:switch → Stroke:stroke1,Stroke:stroke2 where {
     DCV:  Connection:c exists where
                c[below,all]stroke1 && c[below,all]stroke2.
     CV:   stroke1[belowNear,all]stroke2.
     SR:   componentRecognizer({stroke1,stroke2} , Switch).
     DCC:  switch[below,any]Connection¹.
} and (
     switch.connection = c.
)
```

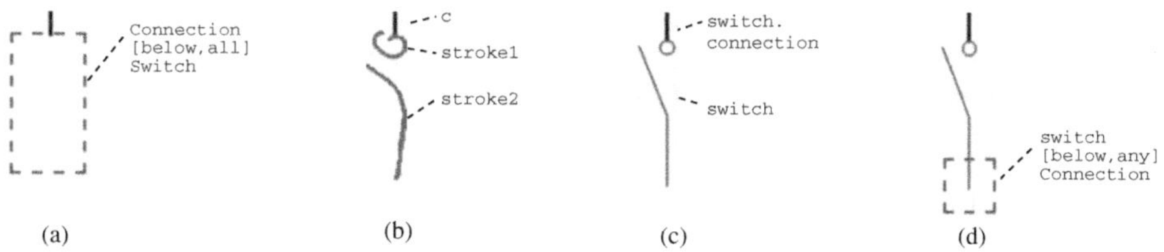

Fig. 2. The precondition of the `switch` production *(a)*, a hand-drawn switch *(b)*, the corresponding recognized symbol *(c)* and the postcondition of the production *(d)*

2.1 DCV and DCC Blocks

The coupling of the DCV and DCC blocks model a global vision of the document. They also offer the advantage of driving the interpretation process by the context analysis, which allows filtering possible interpretations depending on the context of the analyzed elements. These blocks are based on the definition of *document structural contexts*, which are specific locations in the document in which some particular elements can or must exist: a DCV block is a precondition that specifies the structural contexts that have to be verified by a production to try it (i.e. how the analyzed elements must be positioned relatively to the other document elements), whereas a DCC block is a postcondition that indicates the structural contexts that are created due to the production reduction (i.e. which new elements can now exist and where). This document global vision is the second major originality of our approach.

In the presented `Switch` production, the DCV block specifies that for this reduction to be considered, the two analyzed strokes `stroke1` and `stroke2` must have all their points in a document structural context located below a same connection `c` (c.f.

Fig. 2(a) and (b)). As to the DCC block, it indicates that if the production is reduced, i.e. if a switch is interpreted, then one document structural context has to be created below this new switch: it models that one connection can now exist there, and more specifically that the `Connection` production will be considered on the forthcoming elements that will have any of their points located below this new switch (c.f. Fig. 2(d)).

2.2 CV and SR Blocks

The coupling of the CV and SR blocks model a local vision of the analyzed elements, mainly in order to recognize the shape of the elements in β. They offer the advantage of exploiting at the same time semantic information, structural recognition and morphological recognition. On the one hand, a CV block models semantic constraints and structural arrangement that have to be satisfied by the elements in β; this block corresponds to `c` in classical CMG. On the other hand, this structural recognition can be strengthened by a SR block which makes it possible to use morphological hand-drawn shape recognition systems. This is the third major originality of our approach.

In the presented `Switch` production, the CV block models how the two analyzed strokes (`stroke1` and `stroke2`) must be relatively positioned: `stroke2` must be below and near `stroke1`. This assures that the strokes are consistency positioned to be a switch. Nevertheless, this is not enough to deduce that the strokes morphologically look like a switch. It is the function of the SR block that exploits a morphological hand-drawn shape recognizer that is able to recognize hand-drawn electric components: this one must more specifically interpret the strokes as a switch.

3 Parsing CDCMG

Interactive document composition requires efficient real-time incremental parsing. This allows integrating the user in the interpretation and error correction processes, because he is aware of how his strokes are understood by the system: he can then implicitly validate an interpretation by going on with the document composition, or explicitly reject it, either by deleting the new symbol or by replacing it by the right one.

Thus, we have defined an incremental parser associated to CDCMG: it is able to progressively analyze the user strokes. It is based on the parser dedicated to CMG presented in [6,7]. The CMG incremental parser performs in a bottom-up fashion; it consists in repeatedly trying to reduce multisets of document elements into other multisets. It lies in particular on the deterministic principle: once a production has been reduced, in can not be re-considered later except in very specific situations (related for instance to the existential and negative constraints in `c`). In the context of document incremental analysis, this deterministic principle is consistent, because it may not be pertinent to change an interpretation that has sooner been validated by the user.

Some adaptations of the CMG incremental parser have been done to deal with CDCMG: we present two of them. The first one is due to the DCV and DCC blocks that make it possible to drive the analysis process by the context analysis. In fact, document structural contexts act as triggers: when looking for productions to apply on an analyzed element, the principle consists in determining in which of these contexts (created in some DCC blocks) it is located and thus activating the associated productions. Then, all the contexts listed in the DCV block of a production must be satisfied in order to really test it. This gives predictive capabilities to the parser: depending on the context of an element, only relevant rules are tested. The advantages go from a substantial gain of time to the fact that only context-relevant stroke recognition systems are used, which increases the robustness of the decision-making process.

The second originality of the CDCMG parser is its exploitation of *reject options*. The principle is based on the idea that if the system is not able to understand a stroke (or a set of strokes, as in the presented `Switch` production) or hesitates between two different interpretations, then it is more user-friendly to not display an answer (and thus to *reject* the stroke) than to display an answer that has a high probability of being wrong. Indeed, in the first case, the user only has to draw it again, whereas in the second one, he has to delete the misunderstood symbol and then to draw it again. This also offers the advantage of less intruding in the user creative process. For that purpose, we exploit fuzzy logic in various steps of the analysis process in order to take the imprecision of hand-drawing into account. For instance, document structural contexts are represented on a qualitative way: for such a context to be satisfied, the strokes do not have to be exactly located in it. Fig. 3 represents an instance of the document structural context that is exploited in the `Switch` production. It models the correct positioning of a switch relatively to a connection: the more a point if far from `below` a connection and the less the structural context is satisfied. This permits to coherently evaluate the degree to which a context is satisfied. Thanks to such information, it is possible to compare several possible reductions and make a decision.

Finally, we would like to note that the convergence of the analysis mechanism is assured by the use of coherent productions; some needed requirements for the parsing of CMG are expressed in [6,7]; they are also valid for the parsing of CDCMG.

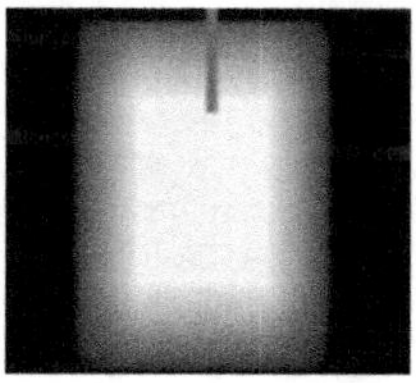

Fig. 3. A fuzzy document structural context modeling qualitatively how a switch must be positioned relatively to a connection (brighter colors represent higher membership values)

4 Design and Evaluation of a Pen-Based Electric Diagram Editor

Thanks to CDCMG, we have already been able to design several pen-based systems, for instance for several musical notation editing [3] or UML diagram editing [1,2]. In this section, we demonstrate the capacities of the proposed method within the context of electric diagram editing and evaluate the corresponding system.

4.1 Presentation of the Developed Software

Using CDCMG enables developers to easily integrate the user in the interface design process with an iterative *implementation-evaluation cycle*; it facilitates and speeds up the modification and the finalization of the software. This is a major advantage to optimize user interfaces in order to allow an optimal use of the software and to favour its acceptance. We have designed the prototype for electric diagram editing in collaboration with a society that spreads out industrial pen-based solutions (Evodia) [5].

Typically, workers need to draw electric diagrams while they are on building sites, often standing in front of electric installations. The use of tablet PCs is well adapted to such working constraints, because it avoids people to have to scribble diagrams on paper and to recopy them once back in their office. Nevertheless, such working conditions are not comfortable, even when using tablet PCs. That is why we facilitate and speed up the composition process by using *graphical completion*: when users draw the first stroke of a multi-stroke symbol, if this stroke is enough to deduce the complete symbol without ambiguity, then the system directly displays it (c.f. Fig. 4(a)). Furthermore, we enable users to replace a symbol by another one just by drawing the new symbol on the old one (c.f. Fig. 4(b)). Pen-based editing possibilities, such as copy and paste, also increase the user-friendliness of the system. As presented in Fig. 5, in order to copy a visual symbol, the user has to select it and draw a copy gesture (e.g. the character "c"); then, the copied elements are automatically associated to the pen tip, and the user can paste them by tipping on the desired location.

Fig. 4. Graphical completion *(a)* and replacement of a symbol by another *(b)*

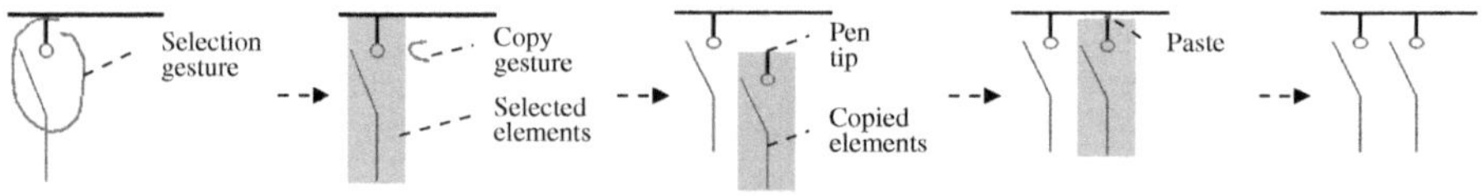

Fig. 5. Copy and paste gestures available in the pen-based electric diagram editor

Fig. 6 presents two screenshots of the pen-based interface. It highlights in particular the graphical completion that speeds up the composition process. It is also interesting to note that in the presented diagram, several shapes look like a circle but are interpreted differently depending on their context. Although it is not visible on the figure, the hand-drawn strokes are interpreted incrementally.

4.2 Evaluation of the Developed Software

The goal of the first experiment is to compare two composition and editing paradigms. The first one, based on button, offers the advantage of being accurate but

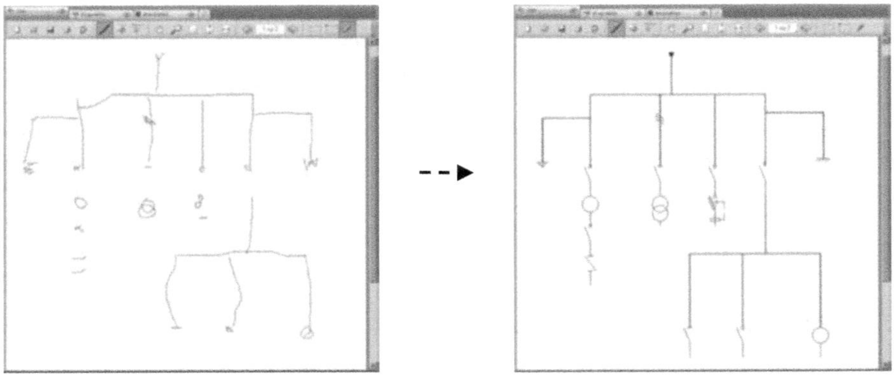

Fig. 6. Two screenshots of the developed system: on the left the hand-drawn strokes; on the right the corresponding neatly transcribed symbols

requires focusing on both the diagram and a button bar, which breaks the creative process. The second one, based on hand-drawing, is more natural and enables users to only focus on the edited diagram, but is dependent on recognition performances.

For the purpose of the experiment, we have designed the complementary button-based prototype of the pen-based electric diagram editor: users have to select each electric component on a button bar (c.f. Fig. 7(a)) and then put it at the appropriate place in the document. Only connections can be drawn the same way as in the pen-based software. We then compared the use of each of these interfaces.

Six writers were asked to compose twice on a tablet PC four predefined electric diagrams (c.f. Fig. 7(b-e)) with both of the software, beginning alternatively by one or another. Writers were asked to take all the time they needed to get used to the interfaces before taking part in the experiments; these training phases lasted from 10 to 30 minutes, which proves the software ease of getting used to. Table 1(a) presents for each user the average time needed to complete an electric diagram with each of the prototypes without using editing possibilities such as copying and pasting elements. These results emphasize a significant contribution from an ergonomic point of view, because the pen-based interface enables users to save about 36.1% of time in comparison with the button-based one. The minimum gain of time was of 22.4%, but one user managed to save more than 50% (50.9%). This phenomenon is of course due to the fact that when using the pen, the user can directly draw the electric components where he wants without the intermediary of a button bar. This also implies that he only has two *focuses of attention* (a sheet of paper with the diagram to reproduce and the diagram in the process of creation) against three in the button-based interface (the two same diagrams plus the button bar), which increases its user friendliness [8].

We also evaluated the impact of using editing functions, such as copying and pasting elements. For that purpose, we asked writers to draw several times the diagram presented Fig. 7(e); it has the particularity to contain an electric component (a circuit breaker) that is repeated several (23) times. This time, using copy and paste functions was encouraged. Results are presented in Table 1 (b): even when the interaction with buttons is decreased thanks to such editing functions, it is still faster to draw diagrams

Table 1. Diagram drawing time for each user depending on the used system

Writer	(a): drawing all diagrams without editing			(b): drawing one diagram with editing		
	Button-based (s)	Pen-based (s)	Gain (%)	Button-based (s)	Pen-based (s)	Gain (%)
#1	117	83	29.4	120	70	41.7
#2	91	55	39.3	100	60	40.0
#3	109	68	37.4	80	55	31.3
#4	118	73	37.2	115	95	17.4
#5	143	111	22.4	170	115	32.4
#6	133	65	50.9	100	50	50.0
Average	118	76	36.1	114	74	35.1

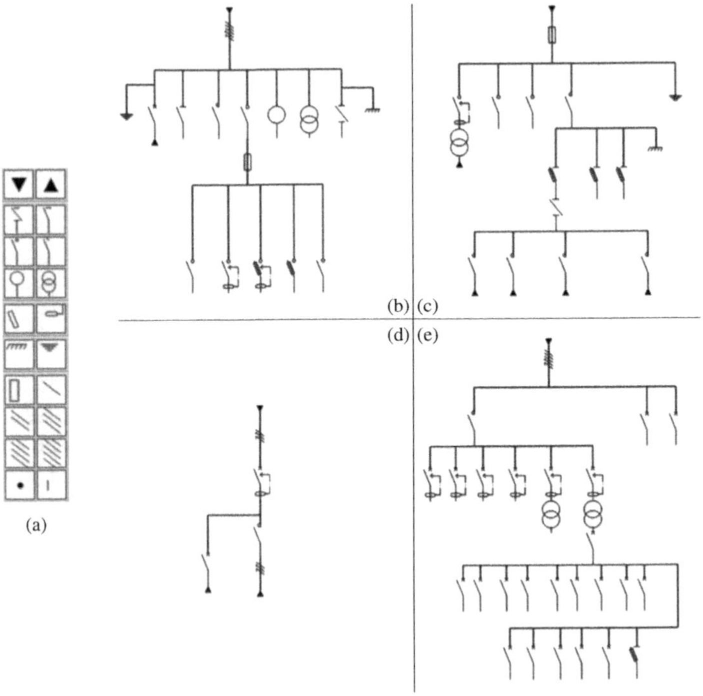

Fig. 7. Button bar developed for the button-based system *(a)* and the four electric diagrams that have been drawn for the evaluation of the pen-based system *(b-e)*

with the pen. Moreover it is interesting to note that for four of the six users, it took less time to draw a diagram with pen without editing than with buttons with editing.

We then focused more specifically on the pen-based electric diagram editor in order to evaluate more specifically its performances. For that purpose, we analyzed the error rates (i.e. when a stroke is misunderstood by the system and has to be deleted and re-drawn) and the reject rates (i.e. when a stroke is deleted by the system and only has to be re-drawn) during its use in the first experiment. The results, based on a total of 2442 strokes from 22 classes of symbols, are presented in Table 2. The average error rate is 2.5%; this is very low, which implies that the software is usable. The average reject rate is 9%, which is a little bit higher. Nevertheless, as explained before, reject is less constraining because the user just has to re-draw the symbol. Actually, we give advantage to the reject in order to limit the errors, which we believe is better from an ergonomic point of view: it less intrudes in the user creative process.

Table 2. Reject and error rates using the pen-based electric diagram editor

Writer	Reject rate (%)	Error rate (%)
#1	14.1	1.5
#2	4.6	2.9
#3	3.5	1.2
#4	10.6	2.6
#5	12.2	4.8
#6	10.2	1.8
Average	9.0	2.5

5 Conclusion

In this paper, we have presented a new approach for designing pen-based software for interactive structured document composition. It is based on Context-Driven Constraint Multiset Grammars, which is a context-sensitive grammatical formalism modeling how the elements of a given document nature are drawn. In order to design pen-based systems that are as user-friendly as possible, we incrementally interpret the hand-drawn strokes and thus integrate the user in the analysis process: he can validate or reject an answer of the system. We have focused more specifically on a pen-based electric diagram editor that has been designed thanks to the presented methodology in collaboration with an industrial society. The evaluation of this system emphasizes, on the one hand, its usability, and, on the other hand, its benefits in terms of gain of time in comparison with button-based systems.

Future works will aim at applying the approach on new structured document domains in order to evaluate its genericity. Assessing the pen-based electric diagram editor at a larger scale is also an interesting perspective.

Acknowledgments. The authors would like to thank Guy Lorette, Professor at the University of Rennes 1, and all the people who took part in the experiments for their contribution to this work. This project partially benefits from the financial support of the Brittany Region.

References

1. Macé, S., Anquetil, E.: A Generic Approach for Pen-Based User Interface Development. In: Pribeanu, C., Santucci, G., Vanderdonckt, J., Calvary, G. (eds.) Computer-Aided Design of User Interfaces V, Proceedings of the Sixth International Conference on Computer-Aided Design of User Interfaces (CADUI'06), pp. 57–70. Springer-Verlag, Heidelberg (2006)

2. Macé, S., Anquetil, E.: A Generic Approach for Eager Interpretation of On-line Handwritten Structured Documents. In: Proceedings of the Eighteenth International Conference on Pattern Recognition (ICPR'06), pp. 1106–1109 (2006)
3. Macé, S., Anquetil, E., Bossis, B.: Pen-based Interaction for Intuitive Music Composition and Editing. In: Shen, J., Shepherd, J., Cui, B., Liu, L. (eds.) Intelligent Music Information Systems: Tools and Methodologies (2007)
4. Bouteruche, F., Macé, S., Anquetil, E.: Fuzzy Relative Positioning for On-Line Handwritten Stroke Analysis. In: Proceedings of the Tenth International Workshop on Frontier in Handwriting Recognition (IWFHR'06) (2006)
5. http://www.evodia.fr
6. Marriott, K.: Constraint Multiset Grammars. In: Proceedings of the IEEE Symposium on Visual Languages vol. 94, pp. 118–125 (1999)
7. Chok, S., Marriott, K.: Automatic Generation of Intelligent Diagram Editors. In: ACM Transaction on Computer-Human Interaction, vol. 3(10), pp. 244–276 (2003)
8. MacKenzie, I., Soukoreff, R.: Text Entry for Mobile Computing: Models and Methods, Theory and Practice. In: Human-Computer Interaction, vol. 17, pp. 147–198 (2002)

To Effective Multi-modal Design for Ringtones, Ringback Tones and Vibration of Cell Phones

Taezoon Park[1], Wonil Hwang[2,*], and Gavriel Salvendy[1,3]

[1] School of Industrial Engineering, Purdue University
315 N. Grant St. West Lafayette, IN 47906, USA
[2] School of Industrial & Information System Engineering, Soongsil University
511 Sangdo-Dong, Dongjak-Gu, Seoul, 156-743, South Korea
wonil.hwang@gmail.com
[3] Department of Industrial Engineering, Tsinghua University
Beijing 100084, P.R. China
{tzpark,salvendy}@purdue.edu

Abstract. Multimedia content downloading service is one of the primary sources of revenue for the wireless service provider other than basic voice call. In this paper, the attitude of the consumers to the existing and newly suggested customizable ringtones, ringback tones, and vibration is explored from the result of the survey. Among the existing services, the inexperienced user showed the highest willingness to use of customizable ringtones although the experienced users are most satisfied by the personalized ringtones. The attitude to vibration services and push-type advertisement ringtones appeared to be negative. Since the attitude to new technology does not always connects to the willingness to use new services, it is needed to find the motivation which can bridge the gap between the attitude and willingness.

1 Introduction

The primary purpose of wireless service is to provide reliable cell phone connection to the consumer. However, the current wireless service includes various types of added services, such as, SMS (simple messaging service), MMS (multimedia messaging service), music and movie download service, and other value-added information. Among those services, customizable ringtones and ringback tones are one of the most successful services which return non-voice revenue for wireless service providers. In the United State, the market of downloading ringtones reached up to $300 million in 2004, and 2005. In worldwide, it is expected to be a more than $4 billion market [3].

Although the original function of ringtone is notifying the incoming call to the customer, contemporary cell phone has a capability of customizing a personalized ringtone. Several different types of sound are currently used as a ringtone, like natural sounds of birds, single-voice melodies, and full harmonic compositions. Also, MIDI format file and MP3 files are actively used as a customized ringtones. Personalized

* Corresponding author.

J. Jacko (Ed.): Human-Computer Interaction, Part II, HCII 2007, LNCS 4551, pp. 429–437, 2007.

ringback tone also known as "caller ring" is one of the successful applications that entice wide range of users by providing novel experience of using ring tones. When a caller makes a phone call using caller ring services, a customized sound, which the receiver has chosen, rings instead of the typical connecting sound.

However, when the sound of cell phones is deactivated, the customized ringtone cannot make any difference. In this sense, it is expected that providing cell phone users with customizable vibration in combination with ringtone increases not only reliability of notifying incoming calls by broadening the path of information transfer, but also user's satisfaction by perceiving multi-modal signals. Vibration of cell phone is currently used as a secondary method for notifying incoming calls or messages to cell phone users when the sound alarm is not available. Even though vibration has potentials as a passage for delivering more information, other than just as a warning signal, the use of vibration is still limited in many areas, including cell phones.

Since there exist vast chances of extending the functionality of ringtones, ringback tones, and vibrations, this study tries to capture the attitude of wireless service customers about personalized ringtone and ringback tones. In this study, a survey is conducted with participants who have used cell phones in the US in order to find users' needs for multi-modal design with ringtones/ringback tones and vibrations. Also, this paper investigates the possibility of embodying personalized vibration, and suggests guidelines for practitioners derived from the responses of cell phone users.

2 Related Literatures

Research about ringtone and ringback tone is quite limited until recently. Kallinen [5] conducted an experiment to measure the emotional responses to single-voice ringtones, and found out that major mode and fast music is preferred by the consumers. However, the context of using cell phone is not included in the experiment.

In this paper, operational definitions of different types of ringtones and ringback tones are clarified. Also, people's perception about multi-modal stimulus and characteristics of vibration are covered as a theoretical background.

2.1 Operational Definitions of Ringtones and Ringback Tones

When making a phone call there are two parties related; calling party who send a phone call and a called party who receives a phone call. The calling party will hear ringback tones through the telephone line which indicates the status of the phone call currently being made. On the called party's side, if s/he received a phone call a ringtone sounds to indicate that the calling party tries to connect to the called party. The operational definitions of ringtones and ringback tone are as follows:

- A **ringback tone** is the audible ringing that is heard on the telephone line by the *calling party* after dialing and prior to the call being answered at the distant end.
- A **ring tone** is the sound made by a telephone to indicate an incoming call on the *called party's* side.

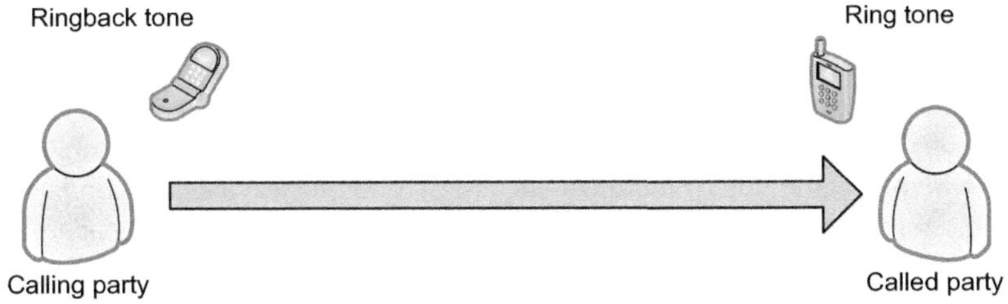

Fig. 1. Ringtones and ringback tones while making a phone call

2.1.1 Ringtones

The wireless service providers and cell phone manufacturers are continuously enhancing their service and product to meet the request of the user. The ringtones of cell phone can be customizable in several different ways. First, the receiver can select either pre-loaded or downloaded ring tones to differentiate caller or caller groups. In this paper, ring tones customized by the called party are classified into two different groups according to whether it has the capability of differentiating the caller or not. However, the ringtones are not available if the called party disables the sound of the cell phone in case they are in a public place. Therefore, the customizable vibration which can differentiate calling party is suggested by the authors.

- **Customizable ringtones** enable *called party* to hear an audio selection that has been previously determined by *called party* regardless of the *calling party*. Audio selections can include music, messages, and special effects.
- **Personalized ringtones** enable *called party* to hear an audio selection that has been previously determined by *called party* to differentiate the *calling party*.
- **Personalized vibrations** enable *called party* to feel vibration that has been previously determined by *called party* to differentiate the *calling party*. Vibrations can vary its frequency, amplitude, and duration.

Push type of ringtones and vibrations are expected to open a new chance of using cell phone although the technology that supports to push ringtones is not available yet. Providing push type service means that the calling party can specify the type of ring tone and vibration on the called party's cell phone at their preference. In order to implement this service, the wireless service provider and cell phone manufacturer should agree on the method for transferring ring tone and vibrations. In the user's perspective, several supporting functionalities, such as choosing whether the incoming ring tone can override the existing one or not, need to be implemented.

- **Personalized push ringtones** enable the *called party* to hear an audio selection that has been selected by the *calling party* when making a phone call.
- **Personalized push vibrations** enable the *called party* to receive vibrations that has been determined by *called party* to differentiate the *caller*.

2.1.2 Ringback Tones

Whereas the service regarding ring tone is actively provided and used, the customization of ringback tone is somewhat limited until recently. However, several wireless service providers in worldwide have started personalized ringback tone service, which became one of the most successful content services in mobile network. The fundamental purpose of ringback tone is to notify the status of connection to the calling party, but the personalized ringback tone makes it possible to identify the called party. This concept of personalized ringback tones is extended in this paper by specifying who determines ringback tones when making a phone call. For the rihg backtones personalized by the calling party, different ringback tones are specified by the calling party according to the person he or she makes a phone call to.

- **Personalized ringback tones by called party** enables *calling party* to hear an audio selection applied to the telephone line that has been previously determined by the *called party.*
- **Personalized ringback tones by calling party** enables *calling party* to hear an audio selection applied to the telephone line that has been previously determined by the *calling party.*

2.2 Multimodal Interaction

The growing interest in multimodal interface is inspired by the purpose of developing more transparent, efficient, and flexible means of interaction. Multimodal systems process two or more combined input mode, like pen, speech, and vision, and generates multimedia outputs as a feedback to the user. The multimodal interfaces are thought to be efficient and easier to learn and use than unimodal systems which uses only a single recognition technology. One of the representative applications using multimodal system is immersive type virtual reality systems for simulation and training [1, 8].

From the perspective of performance, the cognitive load theory provides a theoretical foundation, which claims that learning can be impaired if excessive information is presented within a single modality, for instance, visual display resulting in a split-attention effect. In order to avoid the overburdening of the limited capacity, it is generally recommended to employ different modalities rather than single modality [6]. Vitense et al. [10] examined the performance of multimodal feedback by comparing uni- bi- and trimodal feedbacks which employ auditory, haptic and visual feed back in a direct manipulation task. They pointed out that bimodal feedback can offer better performance without the increase of workload if it is designed appropriately to the task.

2.3 Haptic Interface in Mobile Device

Multi modality in cell phone can be achieved by employing auditory, visual, and haptic senses as the communication channel for information transfer. Cell phone can play multimedia contents, like music, movie, animation clip, and game sometimes in combination with vibrations. From the early history of cell phone, vibration is used to notify incoming calls and alarms, but recently the application area of vibration keep growing, including mobile game. As an example, Chang and O'Sullivan [2] propose a method of creating and optimizing audio-haptics, which increased the satisfaction of the users as a result. They suggested an algorithm to automatically generate haptic stimulus based on the sound profile, and applied the technology to incorporate user interfaces.

2.4 Characteristics of Vibration

Variables influencing human responses to oscillatory motion are categorized as extrinsic and intrinsic variables. Extrinsic variables are related with vibration itself, such as, magnitude, frequency, direction, input positions, and duration, whereas intrinsic variables are the body configuration, age, gender and experiences, all of which is related with human who experience the vibrations [4]. In terms of human perception, the threshold, just noticeable differences (JND), and perceived subjective equality are investigated by several studies. Weinstein [11] measured the two-point discrimination threshold on the whole body, and found out the sensitive spot is lips and fingertips. Verillo [9] found that the frequency and contact area influences the sensitivity to vibratory stimulus if the contact area is larger than 0.02 cm2. From his experiment, the absolute sensitivity to vibration is found to have U-shaped curve, which has maximum value around the frequency of 250 Hz. From the exploratory research, it is claimed that vibration itself can invoke good or bad feelings without combination with other visual or auditory stimulus, and two hedonic dimensions of vibration are reported [7].

3 Methods

A survey was designed, which asked the attitude of the wireless customers to customizable and personalized ringtones, ringback tones and vibrations. It included questions asking demographic information, the experience of using wireless services, satisfaction of the current service, current cell phone features, and the willingness to use new technology. As for the existing services, such as customized ringtones, personalized ringtones, and personalized ringback tones by called party, the questionnaire asked perceived existence (categorical) and satisfaction based on the experience (7-point scale). As for the non-existing services that we proposed in this study, such as personalized vibrations, personalized push ringtones, personalized push vibrations and personalized ringback tones by calling party, the willingness to use (7-point scale) was questioned. Twenty seven participants, who have experiences of using cell phone, responded the questionnaire regarding the use of their current cell phone.

Since the experiment in this study is for pilot tests, the number of participant is relatively small. In this study, a couple of descriptive statistics, such as frequencies of categorical variables, and mean and standard deviation of interval scaled variables were reported. In addition, the correlation analyses were conducted to find the relationship between the attitude to new technology and non-existing proposed new services, and between satisfaction of current cell phone services and proposed new services.

4 Result

4.1 Demographic Information of Participants

Nineteen male and eight female participated in this study, who were mostly graduate students of engineering school aged between 23 and 42 (mean = 32.8; stdev =4.13).

Table 1. Demographic Information

Classification		Frequency	Percentage
Gender	Male	19	70.37
	Female	8	29.63
Major	Engineering	20	74.07
	Science	1	3.70
	Consumer & family sciences	1	3.70
	Management	2	7.41
	Pharmacy	1	3.70
	Liberal arts	1	3.70
	Other	1	3.70
Cell phone experience	1 – 2 years	1	3.70
	2 – 3 years	4	14.81
	More than 4 years	22	81.48
Cell phone manufacturer	Samsung	7	25.93
	LG	7	25.93
	Motorola	6	22.22
	Nokia	4	14.81
	Sony Ericsson	2	7.41
	Other	1	3.70
Wireless service provider	Cingular	13	50.00
	Verizon	7	26.92
	T-mobile	2	7.69
	Sprint	1	3.85
	Other	3	11.54

Most of the participant has over 4 years of experience of using cell phone, and is familiar with cell phone services. The survey covered major cell phone manufacturer, such as Samsung, LG, Motorola, Nokia, and Sony Ericsson, and famous wireless service providers, such as Cingular, Verizion, T-mobile, and Sprint (see Table 1).

4.2 Survey Results of Existing and Proposed Services

Among the existing services, the customizable ringtones is most popular to the customers (74% of participant recognized), whereas personalized ringtones (52% of participants recognized) and personalized ringbaek tones by called party (15% of the participants recognized) are not well-known to the customer. (see Table 2) Personalized ringtones seem to be more satisfying to the customers when compared to other two services, but inexperienced customers showed the highest willingness to use of customizable ringtones among three existing services.

The results indicate that the attitude to vibration and push-type ringtone advertisement are negative, whereas sending and receiving personalized push ringtones and personalized ringback tones by calling party showed positive willingness to use.

Table 2. Descriptive statistics for ringtone and vibration services

Classification	Perceived existence (%)	Satisfaction based on experience* (mean (stdev.))	Willingness to use if no experience* (mean (stdev.))
Customizable ringtones	74.07	4.71 (1.85)	5.17 (1.33)
Personalized ringtones	51.85	5.30 (1.70)	4.76 (1.60)
Personalized vibration	-	-	3.59 (1.67)
Personalized push ringtones	-	-	Sending: 4.44 (1.95) Receiving: 4.67 (1.86) Receiving ads. ringtones: 3.15 (1.63)
Personalized push vibration	-	-	Sending: 3.93 (1.52) Receiving: 3.56 (1.65)
Personalized ringback tones by called party	14.81	4.70 (0.82)	4.41 (1.73)
Personalized ringback tones by calling party	-	-	4.04 (1.65)

*Notes: 1= Strongly Negative,..., 4 = Neutral, ..., 7 = Strongly Positive.

4.3 Correlation Analyses for Proposed Services

The attitude to new technology and the willingness to use of the proposed services appeared to be positively correlated as shown in Table 3, but only two correlation coefficients are moderately significant: the willingness to use personalized push ringtone ($r=0.3370$, $p=0.0857$), and the willingness to use personalized ringback tones by calling party ($r=0.3363$, $p=0.0863$).. The satisfaction of current cell phone seems to be negatively correlated with the willingness to use the proposed services, but no statistically significant effects are found.

Table 3. Correlation Analyses

Classification		Attitude to new technology	Satisfaction of current cell phone & service
Personalized vibration		*r*=0.1504, *p*=0.4539	*r*=-0.1233, *p*=0.5400
Personalized push ringtones	Sending	*r*=0.3370, *p*=0.0857	*r*=-0.1551, *p*=0.4399
	Receiving	*r*=0.3123, *p*=0.1128	*r*=-0.1107, *p*=0.5825
	Receiving ads. ringtones	*r*=-0.1219, *p*=0.5449	*r*=-0.1429, *p*=0.4772
Personalized push vibration	Sending	*r*=0.2071, *p*=0.3000	*r*=-0.2715, *p*=0.1707
	Receiving	*r*=-0.0961, *p*=0.6336	*r*=-0.2082, *p*=0.2973
Personalized ringback tones by calling party		*r*=0.3363, *p*=0.0863	*r*=-0.0249, *p*=0.9018

5 Conclusion

In this study, the currently available services related with ringtones and ringback tones were evaluated in terms of the perceived existence and the satisfaction of the users. In addition, this study proposed possible services, such as personalized vibration, personalized push ringtones, personalized push vibration, and personalized ringback tones by calling party, and investigated the willingness to use the proposed services by current cell phone users.

Customized ringtones, the most famous existing services, showed the highest willingness to use for inexperienced consumers, which indicates that the customer wants to try functions that has been already used by others, in other words, conservative. This is also supported by the low willingness to use of new proposed services. Meanwhile, the willingness to user new proposed services is not significantly correlated with the attitude to new technology and the users' satisfaction of their current cell phone, albeit they were expected to have significantly positive correlation and negative correlation, respectively. It implies that there exist gaps between the attitude to adopt new technology and the willingness to use new services. Thus, the motivation which can fill the gaps explained above is necessary, such as showing the better performance and satisfaction of cell phones users when using the newly proposed services.

There is limitation in this study because the number of collected samples is not enough to generalize the findings, though this study has characteristics of pilot survey. Future direction of the follow-up study will be based on the predictive models with sufficient number of participants.

References

1. Chandler, P., Sweller, J.: The split-attention effect as a factor in the design of instruction. British Journal of Educational Psychology 62, 233–246 (1992)
2. Chang, A., O'Sullivan, C.: Audio-Haptic Feedback in Mobile Phones CHI2005 April 2-7, 2005 Portland, Oregon, USA (2005)

3. Ewalt, D.M.: What Does Your Ringtone Say About You, accessed, at (December 2006) http://www.forbes.com/digitalentertainment/2005/06/01/cx_de_0601ringtone.html
4. Griffin, M.J.: Vibration and motion. In: Salvendy, G. (ed.) Handbook of Human Factors and Ergonomics, 2nd edn. pp. 828–857. John Wiley & Sons, Inc. New York (1997)
5. Kallinen, K.: Emotional Responses to Single-Voice Melodies: Implications for Mobile Ringtones, unpublished paper (2003)
6. Mousavi, S.Y., Low, R., Sweller, J.: Maximizing constructivist learning from multimedia communications by minimizing cognitive load. Journal of Educational Psychology 91(4), 638–643 (1995)
7. Park, T., Hwang, W.: Derivation and validation of optimal vibration characteristics for pleasure and attention: implication for cell phone design. In: Proc. of HCI International 2005, Las Vegas (July 2005)
8. Sweller, J., van Merrienboer, J.J.G., Pass, F.G.W.C.: Cognitive Architecture and Instructional Design. Educational Psychology Review 10(3), 251–296 (1998)
9. Verrillo, R.T.: Effect of contactor area on the vibrotactile threshold. Journal of the Acoustical Society of America 35, 1962–1966 (1963)
10. Vitense, H.S., Jacko, J.A., Emery, V.K.: Multimodal feedback: an assessment of performance and mental workload. Ergonomics 46(1-3), 68–87 (2003)
11. Weinstein, S.: Intensive and extensive aspects of tactile sensitivity as a function of body part, sex, and lterality. In: Kenshalo, D.R (eds.) The skin senses, Springfield, IL: Thomas (1968)
12. Personalized Ringback Tones Ring with Revenue Potential http://www.sun.com/solutions/documents/articles/te_alcatelprbt_aa.xml accessed at (December 2006)

Automatic Word Detection System for Document Image Using Mobile Devices

Anjin Park and Keechul Jung

HCI Lab., School of Media, College of Information Science, Soongsil University
156-743, Seoul, S. Korea
{anjin,kcjung}@ssu.ac.kr

Abstract. In the current age of ubiquitous computing age that uses high bandwidth network, wearable and hand-held mobile devices with small cameras and wireless communication will be widespread in the near future. Thus, computer vision and image processing for mobile devices have recently attracted a lot of attention. Especially, many approaches to detect image texts containing useful information for automatic annotation, indexing, and structuring of image are important for a prerequisite stage of recognition in dictionary application using mobile devices equipped with a camera. To detect image texts on the mobile devices that have limited computational resources, recent works are based on two methodologies; the image texts are detected not by automatically but by manually using stylus pen to reduce the computational resources, and the server is used to detect image texts requiring many floating-computations. The main disadvantage of the manual method is that users directly select tentative text regions, and recall and precision rates are determined by the selected regions. The second method to automatically detect the image texts is difficult to perform it in real-time, due to transmission time between the mobile device and the server. Accordingly, this paper proposes a real-time automatic word detection system without support of the server. To minimize the computational time, one word in the central region of the image is considered as a target of the system. The word region is tentatively extracted by using edge density and window transition, and the tentatively extracted region is then verified by measuring uniform distribution among sub-windows of the extracted region. In the experiments, the proposed method showed high precision rates for one word in the central region of the image, and showed fast computational time on the mobile devices.

1 Introduction

In the ubiquitous computing age that uses a high bandwidth network, mobile devices such as a Personal Digital Assistant(PDA) with a small camera and wireless communication will be widely used in the near future. The camera attached to mobile or portable devices is getting into smaller and lighter, and an image acquisition module is becoming more easily integrated with various networks. Based on these advantages, computer vision and image processing for mobile devices have recently attracted a lot of attention, and many approaches to detect image texts containing useful information for automatic annotation, indexing, and structuring of image[1] are especially

J. Jacko (Ed.): Human-Computer Interaction, Part II, HCII 2007, LNCS 4551, pp. 438–444, 2007.

important for a prerequisite stage of recognition in dictionary application using mobile devices equipped with a camera.

When computer vision techniques with high computational times, such as text extraction, are implemented on the mobile devices, the major problems are encountered[2]; the mobile devices have limited computational resources. Almost all CPUs for mobile devices are integer CPUs, which have no floating-computation component. It results in slow computation because a complier uses a float emulation library to implement the floating-computation.

To reduce the computational resources, recent works used not an entire image, but manually selected regions of the images. Watanabe et al.[3] reported a mobile application that translates Japanese text into English. The text regions are detected not by automatically but by manually using a stylus pen, and are extracted by a binarization process with Otsu method. Haritaoglu[4] described computer vision techniques for text extraction using a camera attached to a PDA, and implemented an automatic sign/text language translation for foreign travelers who want to see text or signs in their own language. After text regions are manually selected by a user, the system enhances the selected text region using a SNF filter, separates the characters from background using a hierarchical connected component(CC), and performs wavelet transformation to verify the text region. Here, text detection is the process of determining the location of text in the image and generating boxes around the text, and text extraction is the stage where the detect text components are separated from the background[1]. The main disadvantage of the above mentioned papers is that users directly select text regions, and recall and precision rates are determined by the selected regions. To detect image texts in an entire image without a user's manual selection, text detection and extract requiring many floating-computations are performed on the server, and the system utilized to make best use of the computational resources of the mobile devices and the server is proposed for faster and efficient text extraction[2]. However, it is difficult to perform text detection and extraction in real-time, due to transmission time between the mobile devices and the server.

Accordingly, this paper proposes a real-time automatic word detection system the on document images without support of the server. To minimize the computational time on the mobile devices, one word in the central region of the image is considered as a target of the system. The tentative word region is first detected by using edge density[1] within window translated based on the boundary information of the window. The tentatively detected word region is then verified by measuring uniform distribution among sub-window of the detected region, based on an assumption that the text pixels are distributed throughout the window. In the experiments, the proposed method shows high precision rates for one word in the central region of the document image, and shows fast computational time on the mobile devices.

The remainder of this paper is organized as follows. The proposed method for word detection is proposed in Section 2, and the experimental results are presented in Section 3. Finally, section 4 summarizes the paper.

---

1 The edge density is the number of edge pixels in NXN window, and is appropriate for the mobile devices due to the simple computation.

2 Word Detection Using Edge Information

Document images consist of words, tables, and figures, and the words are a target of the proposed method. The words of document images have distinctive characteristics that have gaps between words and higher edge density in a minimum boundary rectangle(MBR) of words compared with figures and tables. Fig. 1(a) shows examples of words, tables, and figures on the document images, and Fig. 1(b) shows an MBR of the word located at the central region on an edge image extracted from Fig. 1(a). As shown in Fig. 1, words within the MBR(left and center of Fig. 1(b)) have higher edge density than figure(right of Fig. 1(b)). Using this point, the word is extracted based on edge density.

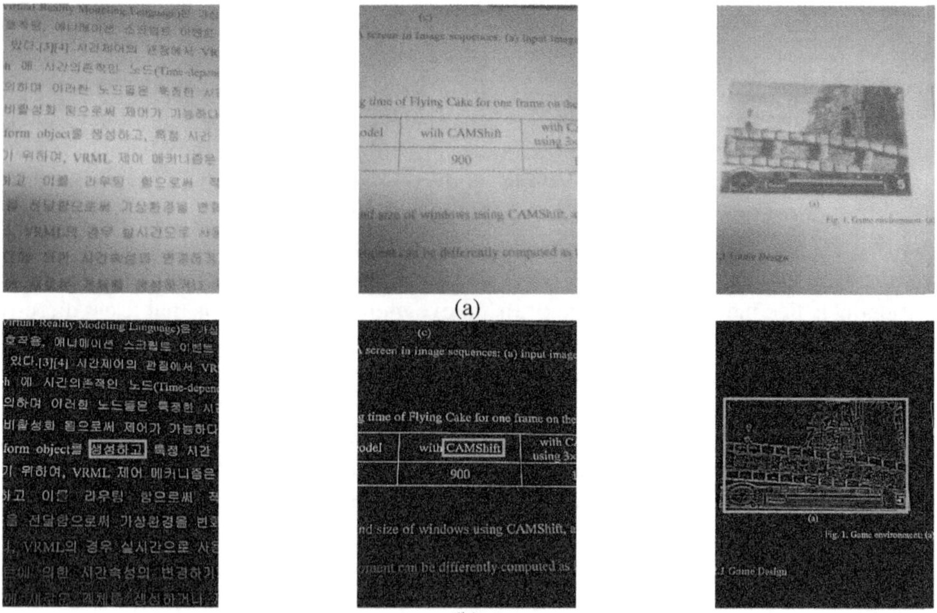

(a)

(b)

Fig. 1. Document images: (a) words(left), table(center), and figure(right) of document image, and (b) MBRs based on gap information on edge image

Fig. 2 shows a flow chart of the proposed method, and the method consists of two steps: tentative word detection and then verification of the tentative word region. The tentative word detection is performed by using edge density and window translation, and then verification based on uniform distribution is used to determine whether the window has the word or not.

2.1 Tentative Word Detection

The outer of text is composed of an edge, and the words of document images have a distinctive characteristic that gaps between words are longer than gaps between

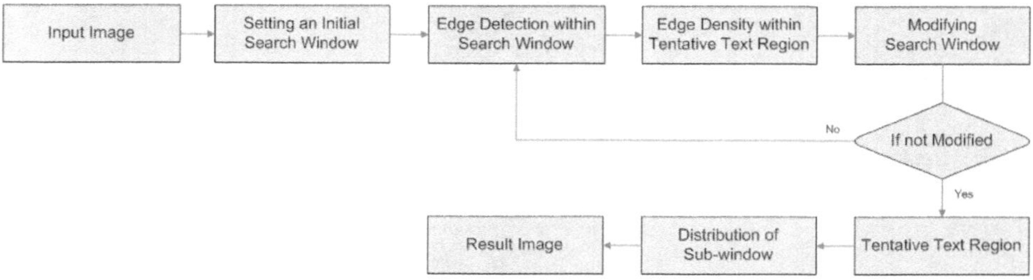

Fig. 2. Flow chart of proposed method

letters. In this paper, one word in the central region of the input image is considered as a target of the system. Window transition from initial window located at the central regions to final window that satisfies the predefined conditions is used for faster computation.

An initial stage for the tentative word detection determines whether the initial window contains edge information or not and edge density has a higher value than given threshold or not. If two conditions are satisfied, the consecutive iterations estimate the size and position of the window, based on information whether each boundary that is left, right, above, and below of the window has edge information or not. The goal of the proposed method is not letter detection but word detection, but an above mentioned method can not extract word. To concisely solve this problem, an expanding operator is used to connect adjacent edge information, based on the assumption that the length of gaps between the words is longer than the length of gaps between letters. Fig. 3 shows the window translation on input images.

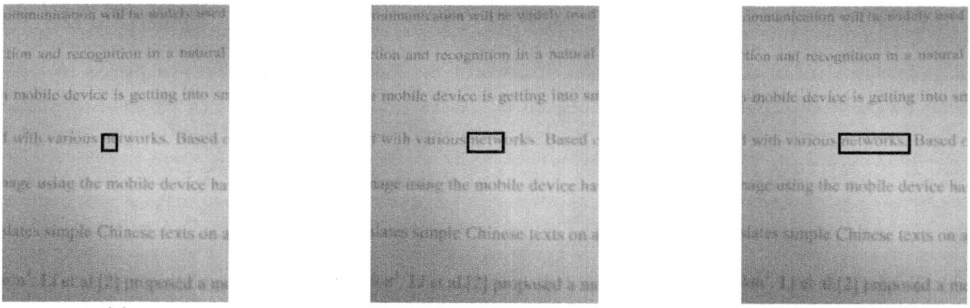

(a) (b) (c)

Fig. 3. Window translation on input images: from (a) to (c)

Fig. 4 shows result images using gaps between words and window translation, and internal rectangles indicate initial search windows, and external rectangles indicate results. If the initial window is not located at the word regions, the system generates wrong results. To tackle this problem, the edge density is used when the window is translated.

The edge density is the number of edge pixels in each NXN window. The search window is translated if and only if the edge density has a larger value than a given

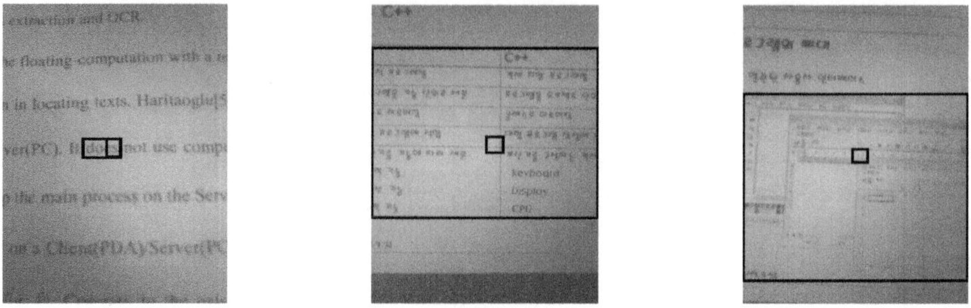

(a) (b) (c)

Fig. 4. Result images using gap between two words and window translation: (a) when the initial window is on the word, (b) line of table, and (c) figure

threshold value in the search window. In the case of Fig. 2 that the initial search window is on the line of the table, the search window is not translated more and more from the initial stage, as the edge density of the initial search window has smaller than the given threshold. In the present experiments, the threshold is 60 percents of the search window.

2.2 Verification

Since complex figure regions are also extracted in case of using only edge density to extract the word region, a verification step is needed for definitive word detection. In the experiments, edge of word regions within windows shows uniform distribution, compared with figure regions. Based on this assumption, the window is separated several sub-windows, and then the dissimilarity between sub-windows are used to approximately measure the uniform distribution, as number of edges of each sub-window is similar to each other, but the number of edges of each sub-window in figures has not uniform distribution.

To simply measure uniform distributions, we use variations of each sub-window, and if the average of the variations is less than given thresholds, we consider that the windows have text regions.

3 Experimental Results

In the present results, an HP iPAQ h5450 model equipped with a camera as mobile devices were used, and the h5450 model was a Pocket PC 2002-based system and had a 64MB SDRAM. The camera had 320K pixels, and the size of input images use in the experiments is 240X320.

We considered the one word for evaluation of the proposed system, the extraction rates were evaluated on a pixel level using two metrics (precision and recall rates). The extraction rates were evaluated with 50 document images, and the recall rates 92.5% and the precision rates were 78.8%.

$$precision(\%) = \frac{\#\text{of } \textit{correctly} \text{ detected text pixels}}{\#of\ \det ectedtextpixels} \times 100$$

$$recall(\%) = \frac{\#ofcorrectly\det ectedtextpixels}{\#oftextpixels} \times 100$$

Table 1 showed average computational times, and we compared the proposed system with methods using client/server architecutres[2]. As shown in Table 1 and recall and precision rates, the proposed method showed better performance compared with methods using client/server architectures, as the proposed method made the most of the characteristics of the words that has gap between each word and uniform distribution between each sub-window. Moreover, the proposed method can help the dictionary application to perform in real-time.

Table 1. Average Computational Time

	Proposed Method	Method using Server[2]
Computational Times(ms)	100	499

4 Conclusions

Computer vision and image processing for mobile devices have recently attracted a lot of attention, as wearable and hand-held mobile devices with small cameras will be widespread in the current age of ubiquitous computing age. Especially, many approaches to detect image texts containing useful information for a prerequisite stage of recognition in dictionary application using mobile devices equipped with a camera. The main disadvantage of the mobile devices to perform detecting image texts is that it has limited computational resources. Accordingly, recent work tried to quickly and precisely perform detecting image texts on the mobile devices, and was based on two methodologies: a manual method and a method using server. The main disadvantage of the manual method is that users directly select tentative text regions, and recall and precision rates are determined by the selected regions. The second method is difficult to perform it in real-time, due to transmission time between the mobile devices and the server.

In this page, we proposed a real-time automatic word detection system without support of the server. To minimize the computational time, one word in the central region of the image is considered as a target of the system. The word region is tentatively extracted by using edge density and window transition, and tentatively extracted region is then verified by measuring uniform distribution among sub-windows of the regions. In the exponents, the proposed method shows high precision rates for one word in the central region of the image, and showed fast computational time on the mobile devices.

The main drawback of the proposed method is that the method can not extract words in skewed document images. Therefore, we will solve this problem using 2D moments used in CAMShift algorithm.

Acknowledgements. This work was supported by the Soongsil University Research Fund.

References

[1] Jung, K., Kim, K.I., Jain, A.K.: Text Information Extraction in Images and Video: a Survey. Pattern Recognition 37(5), 977–997 (2004)

[2] Park, A., Jung, K.: PDA-based Text Localization System using Clien/Server Architecture. Lecture Notes in Artificial Intelligence vol. 3157, pp. 833–842 (2004)

[3] Watanabe, Y., Sono, K., Yokomizo, K., Okada, Y.: Translation Camera on Mobile Phone. In: Proceedings of IEEE International Conference on Multimedia and Expo, vol. 2, pp. 6–9 (2003)

[4] Haritaoglu, I.: Scene Text Extraction and Translation for Handheld Devices. In: Proceedings of IEEE Conference on Computer Vision and Pattern Recognition, pp. 408–413 (2001)

[5] Aoki, H., Schiele, B., Pentland, A.: Realtime Personal Positioning System for a Wearable Computers. pp. 37–43 (October 1999)

[6] Torralba, A., Murphy, K.P., Freeman, W.T., Rubin, M.A.: Context-based Vision System for Place and Object Recognition. In: Proceedings of International Conference on Computer Vision, pp. 273–280 (October 2003)

User Customization Methods Based on Mental Models: Modular UI Optimized for Customizing in Handheld Device

Boeun Park, Scott Song, Joonhwan Kim, Wanje Park, and Hyunkook Jang

Samsung Electronics Co.,Ltd 416 Maetan3, Yeongtong, Suwon, Gyeonggi 443-742
Republic of Korea
{be.park,sangkon.song,joonhwan.kim,wanje.park,
yunk.jang}@samsung.com

Abstract. The ongoing conflict designers face between the Universal User Interface, focusing on general predispositions, and the Customized User Interface, adjusted to individualistic characteristics, is more prevalent than ever. One reason for this enduring conflict is that mobile devices require that user interfaces (UI) be optimized for each individual user across a global marketplace. This issue inspired us to build a conceptual model of a UI, which supports the maximization of customization and optimization by reflecting personal characteristics. This Modular (each application is defined as its own modular and can be assembled and disassembled) UI was based on four premises: what is reflected, how it was grouped, how it was provided, its affect. Usability testing of the UI was performed in three countries with 8 user groups from each country. Web surveys and FGI (Focus Group Interview) for with 8 user groups from the three countries showed that this type of modular UI can effectively optimize interactions for largely diverse groups of users. This research on customization for user experience is significant because it can generate its users with an optimum interface that aligns with their unique set of biological and cultural characteristics. This study also shows a need for additional research analyzing cultural elements of optimized UI in order to deepen our level of understanding of the influence of cultural factors on the usability of handheld device UIs.

Keywords: User Customization, Handheld Devices, Modular UI, Optimization, HCI.

1 Introduction

Handheld devices are ubiquitous; used around the world by highly diverse groups of people. In terms of efficiency of production and manufacturing costs, handheld devices are highly uniform not only in exterior design, but also in interface design as UI. In designing theses standard mobile technologies, the designers and engineers need to formulate UI's and devices that are usable to as largely of an inclusive as possible, or follow the rules of Universal Design.

J. Jacko (Ed.): Human-Computer Interaction, Part II, HCII 2007, LNCS 4551, pp. 445–451, 2007.

However a challenge arises in the universal design of mobile devices for a global market, as there are countless cultures around the world, demonstrating as many differences in their behavioral patterns. It can therefore be is impossible to satisfy all users' needs, unless you are targeting a very small user group.

In this research, we identified cultural factors that affect customization and when taken into account can maximize device usability. Finally, we identified efficient ways to apply theses factors into practical UI design. This paper will introduce how designing UIs for Global products can maximize user satisfaction. In addition, we will demonstrate how implementing individual-oriented UI for mobile devices can provide user optimization, more so than in other devices, such as home appliances.

2 Approach

The conflict designers face between the Universal User Interface, focusing on general propensity, and the Customized User Interface, adjusted to individual characteristics is ongoing. This has been a basic, necessary and sufficient condition for recent UI, regardless of its forms or design attributes, complementing each other on a certain level. Universal UI design finds standardization by searching for the common denominator amongst people with varied recognition and behavior patterns. However, there should be consideration of individual user experience that stems from users' psychological, cultural and historical makeup through customization of the UI. It is necessary to build a concept of the interface, which maximizes customization and optimization in order reflecting individualistic interaction requirements.

In the context of this research, customizing refers to something the user can change in appearance or function to suit their own usage requirements and/or preferences.

The following questions were directed the goals of maximizing the customization of UIs:

1. What demographic factors that needs to be reflected through UI customization?
2. How should customizable options be grouped?
3. How should customization be provided to users?
4. How do individual differences affect how a user customizes their interfaces?

The following further describes the premises of these questions, with the overarching goal to develop a UI based on the answers to the questions.

1. What demographic factors need to be reflected through UI customization?
Demographic factors affect psychological tendencies and ways of thinking, and there are biological factors to consider as well. If a way of thinking is a factor that the user decides to customize, significant factors can be applied on customized UI. User groups are categorized by country (cultural zone), gender, and age. [1]

2. How should customizable options be grouped?
Users should be able to group/ungroup or divide/combine UI components for customization. We set 'Structure', 'Interaction', 'Layout', 'Design' for UI components, and 'Arranging', 'Combining', 'Categorizing', 'Changing Setting' for customizing functions. [2]

3. How should customization be provided to users?
Our proposed interface will customize UIs through modules. The concept of customizing originated from nature, and factors that affect and are affected by customization are considered.

One module is considered an individual unit that a user can modify at their will. Furthermore, when the user moves, aligns, and groups the modules, intrusion of consistency between modules should be minimized. If the frequency and degree of modification is proportional to user satisfaction, the module is defined to sustain overall UI structure. As a representative tool for customization, our interface, Modular UI, was designed. The fundamental concept behind Modular UI is that each application is defined as its own module concept and can be assembled and disassembled. [3]

4. How do individual differences affect how a user customizes their interfaces?
Individual mental models are affected by an array of social factors (e.g., .individualism, problem solving, uncertainty avoidance) and there are links between the factors that implicate customization. For example, users with logical thought have a tendency to systematize modules according to properties, while others compose modules by accessibility or frequency or by self-consciousness. [4]

3 Research Method

A usability test was performed to design specific modular concepts on the basis of the 4 assumptions. The test was implemented in three phases. The 1st phase was an Internet-Based Question & Answer for, and the 2nd phase was an FGI (Focus Group Interview). An Expert test about customization was done in the 3rd phase.

Customization preference and provision methods were reviewed using FGIs and the 1:1 usability tests. Participants were mobile device users aged 10 to 40. The investigation was replicated with users in Korea, China, England and the US. In each country 32 people were tested, 4 people in each FGI. Gender was equally balanced within and across all the groups. Recruited participants were representative of users from each country in terms of race, vocation and education. After the FGI, participant individually participated in 1:1 usability assessments of the UI.

Separate from the FGI and 1:1 assessment, a web survey was used for questions that needed large data samples. In the web survey, 500 Britons, 500 Americans, and 500 Koreans were included and the collection of subjective opinion went as well.

For a sampling of task about verification modular UI, a customization method is concretized. The functionality to facilitate users to assemble their preferred options and optimum customizability was tested via three methods below:

Menu Customizing- Create Menu Structure Corresponding to User Characteristics
This is a method for designating frequently accessed menus according to individual usage patterns. It increases the ease of access of these menus by performing Short Cuts by registering frequently used menus as a Quick Menu. In addition, this function may change how functions are grouped or classified, by function (Video, Music…) and by movement (Playing, Recording…) to best match each user's mental models for the device.

Button Customizing- Establishing combination of buttons
This sets up different functions in each mode so that it provides execution of various groups functions via one single button or control. In addition, it is a way to enable changing button mode from its existing mode (using LED or Color).

Interaction Customizing- Automation of frequently performed interactions
This is a setting that enables frequently and continuously operated interactions to be performed automatically.

The test of Menu Customizing is significant in the following aspects. The number of menus provided in devices is increasing as a result of functionally rich devices. Users want to have intuitively easy access to them without additional learning; they are not willing to look through a thick manual to learn these menus and functions. In addition, some tasks that are shown, hidden, deleted, grouped, or related are considered. Above all, the access to each preferred menu section becomes varied according to individual propensities.

4 Research Result

The 1st (Q&A) and 2nd (FGI) usability test targets Normal user preference of customizing tasks by using modular UI, the 3rd (Expert test) verifies the usability for

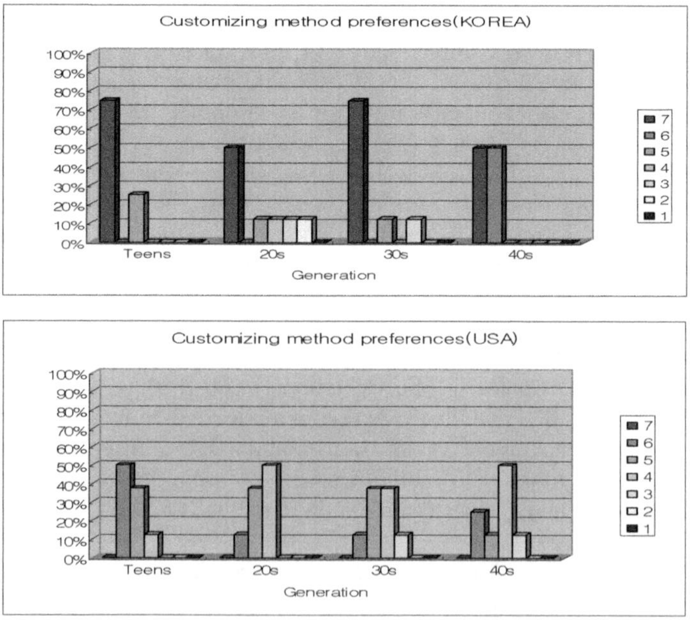

Fig. 1. Preferences for customization by age group. It shows that teenagers prefer customizing more than any other age group. This data also shows that the preference of Korea is stronger than that of USA.

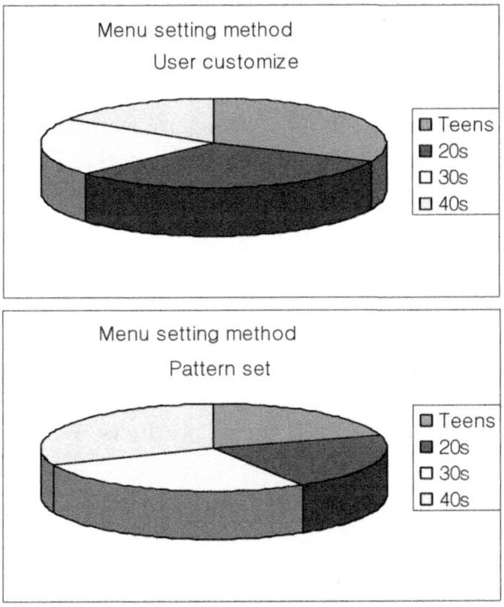

Fig. 2. This data shows the preference of menu setting methods in pattern selection & user customization

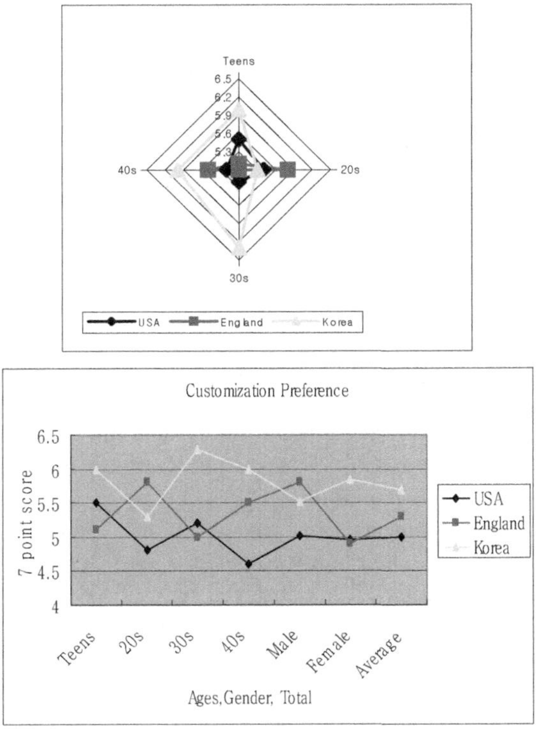

Fig. 3. A drawing of figure 1 and 2 which is combined by three countries

modular UI. The significant results of the 1st and 2nd test are below, categorized by country (cultural zone), gender, and age of the participants.

- Preferences for arranging menus were measured by checking preferences between using a menu pattern provided and arranging menus by direct manipulation. Young generations and male users tend to want 'User customization'
- Preference of recombining menus based on the function of editing arrangement or application by user's desire was measured. The preference was high overall for Americans, Britons and Koreans, and was very appealing to the American and Korean young generations. In particular, the advantage of possible optimization was preferred to a great extent in the USA or in countries where people have been exposed to advanced products. However, elderly users were not willing to use such functions.
- Preference categorizing menus was measured. A device which has many functions with various applications, categorizing is very important. There were two methods: one method, in which menus need to be categorized by function in China and Korea, and another method based on action in western countries. Americans preferred action-based categorizing methods such as "Playing", "Creating", "Searching" and "Settings", while Koreans preferred function-oriented categorizing methods such as Music, Photo and Movie. Britons, however, did not place their preference significantly on either one.
- Preference of Design manipulation was high. Teenage students and students in their twenties wanted to put pictures of their preferred celebrities or themselves on their devices, and people in their thirties and forties wanted images of their family members or natural scenes.

Furthermore, professional opinions of additional verification tests supported the claim that customization enables more optimized usability.

5 Conclusion

A UI that accounts for social factors was developed and its usability is demonstrated in this work. As a result, preferences for modular UI customization were observed to be generally high. This result verifies the utility of customizable modular UI design.

Moreover, the impact of social factors was observed in the application of UI development. There were substantial differences between groups classified by culture, gender and age. This suggests that meaning that individualism, logicalism, psychologism-Dynamic and uncertainty avoidance is different from specific social circumstances. When a modular UI is optimized on user psychological factors, a very detailed segmentation of customers needs could be applied. [5]

This research on customizing for the provision of user experiences demonstrated successful methods to provide users with optimum interfaces in accordance with biological and cultural characteristics of device users.

6 Discussion and Future Work

It was necessary to provide a balanced optimum interface between Universal UI for existing manufacturers and Customized UI for users, and preference varied in accordance with cultural and individual predisposition. To this end, this research leveraged a modular UI, which applies socio- factors to usability, devised and verified through a three phases. Results demonstrated that these types of modular UIs appeal to a large number of users effectively while serving individualistic needs.

In further research, we can attempt to verify the relationship between elements using a usability test to configure a mental model based on the elements that effect Customization. Building on our current findings, we would build mental models that distinguished key factors and adjust UI for each target segment. Mental elements, which are presumed to have a relationship with customization, can be collected and organized according to their attributes.

We propose continued research in the area of optimized UIs through the analysis of key cultural elements that contribute to individual predisposition as well as applying the more general factors shown vary due to differences in gender, generation and culture. Furthermore, research is necessary to understand deeper levels of cultural factors and the impact on a networking between mobile devices. With future work for the concretization and development of the mental model, we could find an impetus to the development of optimized UI for hardware of all shapes and sizes.

References

1. Preece, J., Preece, J., Sharp, H.: INTERACTION DESIGN beyond human computer interaction, pp. 453–469 (2002)
2. Halfhill, T.R.: Network-centric user interfaces are coming to PCs as well as to network computers (1997)
3. Patalano, A., Wengrovitz, S.: Cross-cultural exploration of the indecisiveness scale (2003)
4. Nisbett, R., Miyamoto, Y.: The influence of culture Trends in Cognitive Science (2005)
5. Http://www.adobe.com/products/acrobat/

Fisheye Keyboard: Whole Keyboard Displayed on PDA

Mathieu Raynal and Philippe Truillet

DIAMANT Team
IRIT CNRS
Université Paul Sabatier
31062 Toulouse Cedex 9, France
{raynal,truillet}@irit.fr

Abstract. In this article, we propose a soft keyboard with interaction inspired by research on visualisation information. Our objective is to find a compromise between readability and usability on a whole character layout for a PDA soft keyboard. The proposed interactions allow displaying all keys on a small screen while making pointing easier for the user by expanding any given key as a function of its distance from the stylus.

Keywords: soft keyboard, personal digital assistant (PDA), fisheye view.

1 Introduction

With the widespread use of mobile devices, text input technique has become an active research area and new constraints have appeared: restricted display, devices intended for single hand use, etc. As yet, these systems lack a dominant technique for text input [5]. There are two principal research directions: on the one hand, systems based on gestures recognition close to the handwriting process; on the other hand, the virtual (also called soft) keyboard for touch screens, a promising method. For soft keyboard, stylus interaction consists of either typing on the keys like the Metropolis [11] or OPTI soft keyboard [4], or producing gestures like Quikwriting [7].

Either gesture recognition or soft keyboard presents disadvantages. For recognition systems, handwriting requires learning a gesture alphabet, which can be a huge limit for novices. For soft keyboards, novice users have difficulties finding and/or tapping characters (especially for non alphabetic character) on the device. When all characters are displayed, reduced space in the screen of a PDA (3.5 inches of diagonal), make pointing difficult. One solution is to display the entire keyboard on different pages accessible by tapping on a special key. With this method, keys are bigger but novice users waste time to find characters on the different pages.

In order to avoid this drawback, we propose different new interactions on soft keyboard based on expanding targets. Our goal is to display the whole keyboard on the screen while making pointing easier for the user. In spite of studies [3] showing that the use of a technique like expanding targets does not entail faster pointing movements, studies [6,10] show that we can reduce pointing time. Two techniques use expanding targets for text entry [2,13] but the character layouts used are not the classic AZERTY or QWERTY.

J. Jacko (Ed.): Human-Computer Interaction, Part II, HCII 2007, LNCS 4551, pp. 452–459, 2007.

Our hypothesis rests on the fact that a user might well prefer to enter text on a known character layout rather than on a minimal soft keyboard where he must sometimes search for a character or press several keys to enter one given character.

2 Fisheye Keyboard

2.1 Principles

We reproduced a whole soft keyboard (see Figure 1) while keeping the same characters layout as Windows soft keyboard. Each "classic" key measure 10 x 10 pixels: the width of our whole keyboard is 240 pixels.

Fig. 1. Character layout of our soft keyboard

In the passive state, characters are too small to be legible for the user. Nevertheless, the characters layout on the keyboard being known, an expert user is able to locate a character approximately. When the stylus is in contact with the screen, keys expand as a function of their distance from the stylus: the closer the stylus, the larger the key (see Figure 2).

Characters combination is possible: for example, an upper-case letter is obtained by tapping consecutively the 'Shift' key and the letter. When a key that is a "modifier", such as 'Shift', is pressed, the results of all possible combinations of 'Shift' with others keys are displayed accordingly on each appropriate key (see the difference between the two instances of the keyboard on Figure 1).

We suggest two animation types for expanding keys:

The first one is based on the principle of the expanding targets suggested by Mc Guffin and Balakrishnan [6]. The first proposition (see Figure 2) is to expand each key according to the distance between its center and the stylus. The biggest keys are

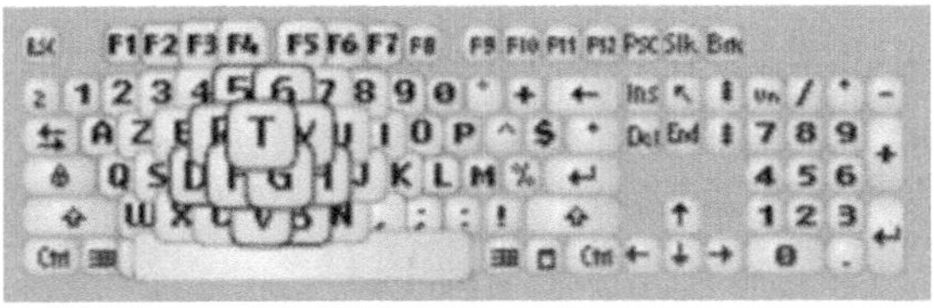

Fig. 2. First animation applied on soft keyboard when stylus is closest to the key 'T'

displayed in the foreground. In order to prevent the biggest keys from covering up others keys, the latter are lightly moved aside. Thus, users can easily read characters that are close to the stylus.

The second animation is based upon researches on visualization information, most notably on fisheye view [1]. We do not handle keys straight but we translate each vertex and main points of the soft keyboard. The translation is bounded by 0 and the distance between the stylus and the point under consideration. We calculate the coefficients according to a Gaussian function (see Figure 3 and 4 for an illustration).

Fig. 3. Second animation applied on soft keyboard when stylus is closest to the key 'K'

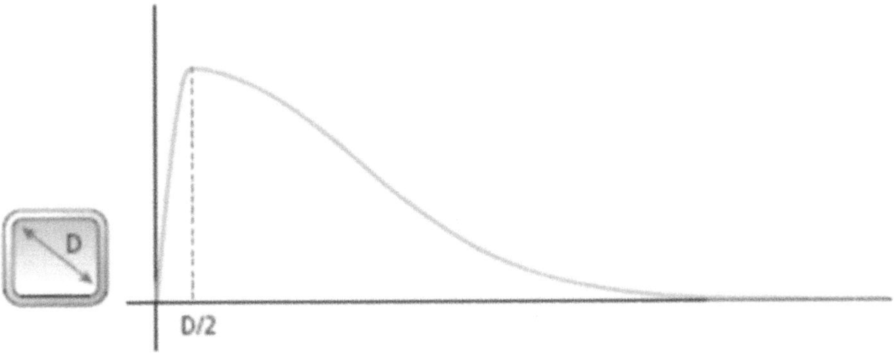

Fig. 4. Gaussian function used to calculated the deformation

2.2 Character Selection

We study different strategies to enter a character:

- The user lifts up the stylus when it is on the key;
- He presses a PDA hard button when the chosen key is under the stylus.
- We could also use the shark system [12]: i.e.

2.3 Retained Choices

We finally chose a technique for expanding the keys at the intersection of the two techniques presented above. Each one presented a major disadvantage:

- With the first technique, the keys which are farther from the pointer are partly covered by the largest keys ;
- The second are not cover up by the other keys, but, certain keys could be tilted and then the characters on these keys are not readable.

Thus, we chose to keep the principle of the first: i.e. the keys are expanded according to the distance which separates the center of this one and the stylus. On the other hand, the spacing of the keys is calculated by using the Gaussian function of the second technique. Thus, the keys are always flat and outspread for a better legibility (see Figure 5).

Fig. 5. Soft keyboard used for experiment

3 Experiment

3.1 Participants

Six people, three female and three male, participated in the experiment. They ranged in age from 20 to 38. There were five right-handed and five computer specialists.

3.2 Hypothesis

Our hypothesis is that the deformation of the keys when the stylus is close does not reduce users' performances. We define performances of the user by his text input speed and by his accuracy.

3.3 Apparatus

We chose for this first experimentation to restrict us to a soft keyboard which contained only the 26 characters of the Latin alphabet and the space bar (cf. Figure 5). Each key measures 15 pixels on side.

The soft keyboard was developed with Java. The experiment software was the E-assist platform [8].

The experiment was conduct on a OptiPlex GX620 DELL PC running Microsoft Windows XP. A tablet Wacom was attached to the system and was the only device used by participants. Users used a stylus to interact with the soft keyboard.

3.4 Procedure and Design

The experiment began with a training step during which the subjects had to type 12 words with fisheye system. Then, they realized two exercises of word copy out: one exercise was made with the AZERTY keyboard without fisheye animation, and the other with Fisheye.

For each exercise, the subject had to copy out 30 words, which were the same for the two exercises. The words which form the test corpus belong to the words most usually used by the French language. We chose them so as to represent a maximum of different co occurrences.

The source word is presented on a line, and the result of the user keyboarding appears on the lower line. The text entry errors are not displayed on the result line and there is a visual and audio feedback. The strip does not move while the subject enters an erroneous character. At the end of each word, participants must type on the space character.

The six subjects had been divided in two groups in order to balance the order of the exercises.

4 Results and Discussion

Firstly, the order in which were realized the exercises had no impact on the results.

The twenty words of an exercise correspond to 230 characters on the whole by hoping the space character to be seized at the end of each word.

4.1 Text Entry Speed

On average for the 6 subjects, participants keyboards the twenty words on 225 seconds (that is to say 1.02 cps[1]) with the soft keyboard without animation, whereas it takes only 153 seconds (1.5 cps) with the Fisheye keyboard. Thus they gain on average 25% of time the keyboard fisheye than with the traditional keyboard.

Moreover, we can see on the figure 6 that 5 subjects out of 6 have better performances with the keyboard fisheye.

4.2 Error Rates

An error was recorded when the user entered character differed from the given character. On the mean (see Figure 7), participants made 15.67 errors for soft keyboard without animation (that is to say an error rate of 6.81%) and 11.67 errors (5.07 %) with fisheye keyboard.

[1] cps = characters per seconds [9].

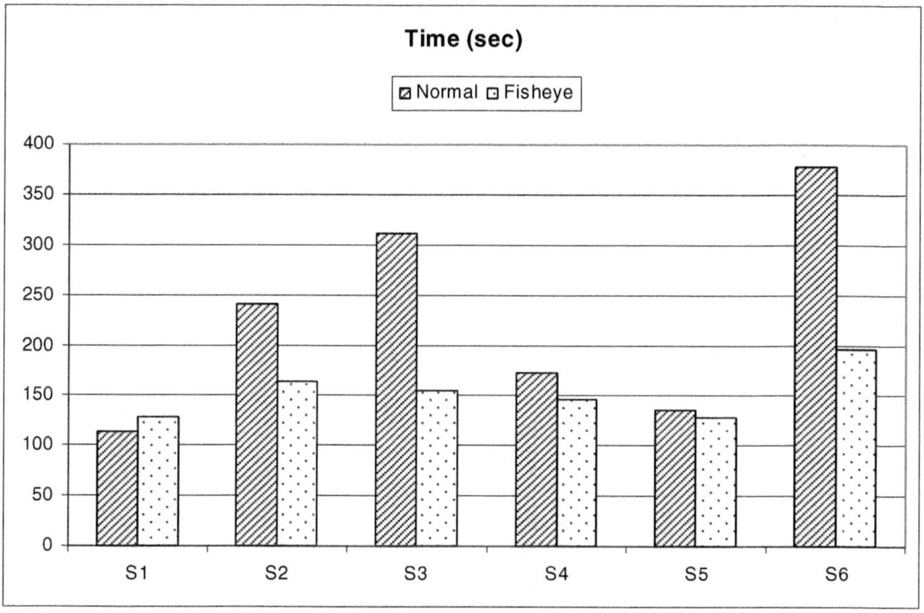

Fig. 6. Tapping time of each participant

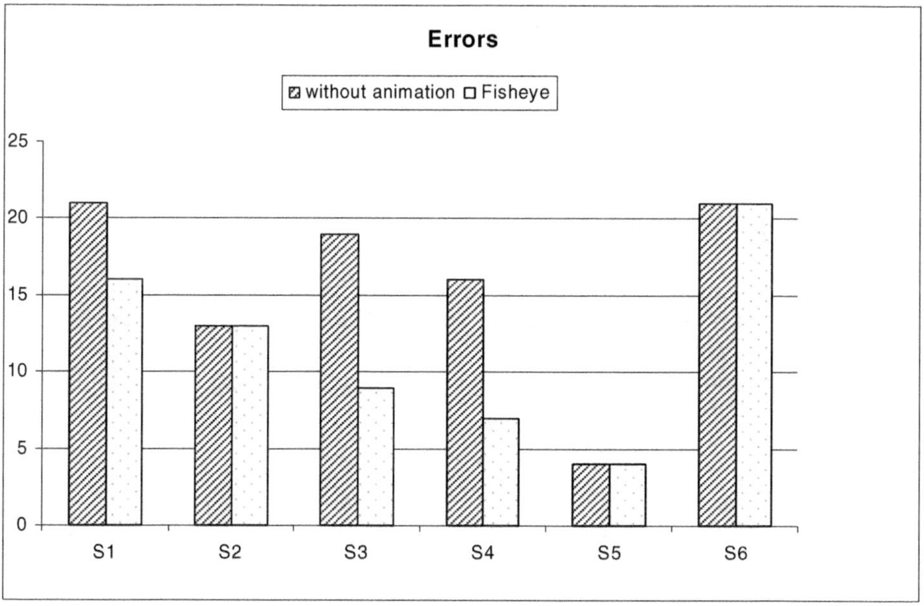

Fig. 7. Number of error for each participant

4.3 Distance

Distance was also computed for every situation. On the mean (see Figure 8), distance was 14.85% less with fisheye keyboard than standard keyboard (11256 pixels versus 13219). More precisely, for each participant, distance was minimized with fisheye keyboard.

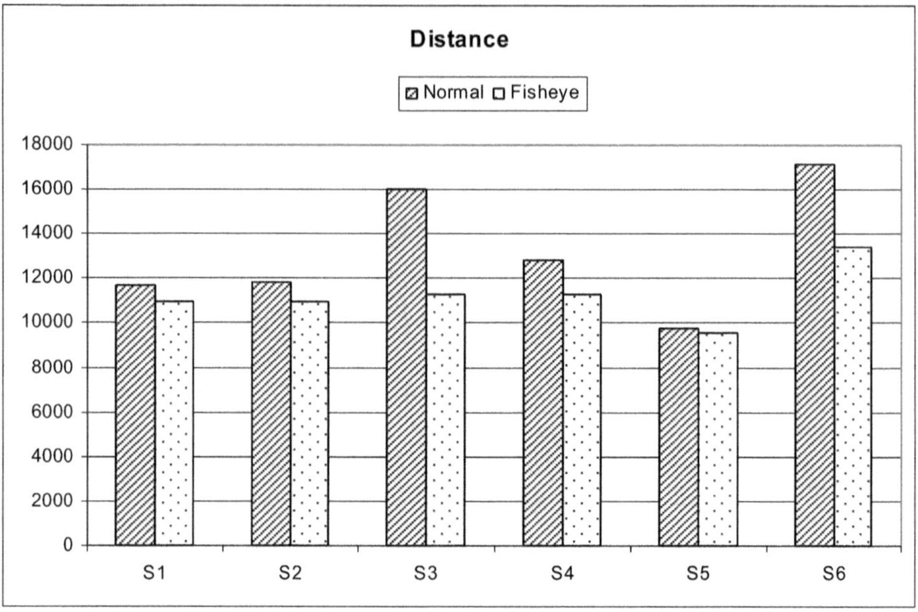

Fig. 8. Distance (in pixels) travelled by the stylus by each participant

5 Implementation and Future Work

These animations are planned for use on hand-held devices. For technical reasons, we implemented the first version of our prototype on a Tablet PC. At the present time, we are working on a PDA version.

Animations proposed in this article will be evaluated in the next months on PDA.

References

1. Carpendale, M.S.T, Montagnese, C.: A Framework for Unifing Presentation Space. In: Proceedings of the ACM Symposium on User Interface Software and Technology: UIST'01, pp. 61–70. ACM Press, New York (November 2001)
2. Cechanowicz, J., Dawson, S., Victor, M., Subramanian, S.: Stylus based text input using expanding CIRRIN. In: Proceedings of the Working Conference on Advanced Visual interfaces AVI '06. pp. 163–166, ACM Press

3. Gutwin, C.: Improving focus targeting in interactive fisheye views. In: Proceedings of the ACM Conference on Human Factors in Computing Systems – CHI'02, pp. 267–274. ACM Press, New York (2002)
4. Mackenzie, I.S., Zhang, S.X.: The design and evaluation of a high-performance soft keyboard. In: Proceedings of the ACM Conference on Human Factors in Computing Systems – CHI'99, pp. 25–31. ACM Press, New York (1999)
5. Mackenzie, I.S., Soukoreff, R.W.: Text entry for mobile computing: Models and methods, theory and practice. Human Computer Interaction 17, 147–198 (2002)
6. McGuffin, M., Balakrishnan, R.: Acquisition of expanding targets. In: Proceedings of the ACM Conference on Human Factors in Computing Systems – CHI'02, pp. 57–64. ACM Press, New York (2002)
7. Perlin, K.: Quikwriting : Continuous stylus-based text entry. In: Proceedings of the 11e annual ACM symposium on User Interface Software and Technology – UIST'98, pp. 215–216. ACM Press, New York (1998)
8. Raynal, M., Maubert, S., Vigouroux, N., Vella, V., Magnien, L.: E-ASSISTE: A Platform Allowing Evaluation of Text Input Systems. In: Proceedings of UAHCI'05, CD ROM (2005)
9. Soukoreff, R.W., Mackenzie, I.S.: Theoretical upper and lower bounds on typing speed using a stylus and soft keyboard. In: Behavior and Information Technology, vol.14(6) pp. 370–379 (1995)
10. Zhai, S.C., Conversy, St., C., Beaudouin-Lafon, M., Guiard, Y.: Human on-line response to target expansion. In: Proceedings of the ACM Human Factors in Computing Systems Conference - CHI, pp. 177–184. ACM Press, New York (2003)
11. Zhai, S., Hunter, M., Smith, B.A.: The metropolis keyboard – an exploration of quantitative techniques for virtual keyboard design. In: Proceedings of the 13th annual ACM symposium on User Interface Software and Technology – UIST'00, pp. 119–128. ACM Press, New York (2000)
12. Zhai, S., Kristensson, P.-O.: Shorthand Writing on Stylus Keyboard. In: Proceedings of the ACM Conference on Human Factors in Computing Systems – CHI'03, CHI Letters vol. 5(1), pp. 97–104, ACM. Baldonado, M., Chang, C.-C.K., Gravano, L., Paepcke, A.: The Stanford Digital Library Metadata Architecture. Int. J. Digit. Libr. vol. 1, 108–121 (1997)
13. Ward, D.J., Blackwell, A.F., MacKay, D.J.: Dasher—a data entry interface using continuous gestures and language models. In: Proceedings of the 13th Annual ACM Symposium on User interface Software and Technology - UIST'00

Mobile Phone Video Camera in Social Context

Erika Reponen, Jaakko Lehikoinen, and Jussi Impiö

Nokia Research Center, Visiokatu 1, FI-33720 Tampere, Finland
{Erika.Reponen,Jaakko.T.Lehikoinen,Jussi.Impio}@nokia.com

Abstract. Video recording is becoming available in various everyday situations, thanks to the quickly spreading video capabilities of modern mobile phones. Recording decision is now often made spontaneous, as the recording devices are constantly available without explicit planning. We discuss the effect of this change in the social environment on the basis of a study where four groups of people used digital video cameras in their everyday life. While this new way of communicating enables new social patterns, it also raises new concerns for privacy and trust. We discuss the relation of context and video recording through a model of primary and secondary contexts. We also analyze acceptability and transparency of video recording as functions of time.

Keywords: Mobile phones, cameras, video, context, privacy.

1 Introduction

Stand-alone video cameras are usually not carried all the time, and their use requires some planning. In contrast, people usually keep their mobile phones on and with them most of the time. As a result, devices with video capabilities are now more frequently available in everyday situations, where video recording has not been explicitly planned. Large numbers of people are participating in the video recording situations in the roles we defined as cameramen (who records), targets (who are recorded) or passers-by (who are unintentionally in the situation). Spontaneous recording of video is enhancing our memories and enriching communication, but also raising new concerns of privacy. People perceive video recording differently from imaging; they approach recording situations even with familiar people differently depending on the intended use of the material; and the attitude of people towards video recording tends to relax over time. This is evident, for instance, in the popular "Big Brother" TV show, where the observed participants gradually become more and more accustomed to the omnipresent cameras and start acting more naturally.

In this paper we discuss the effect of mobile phone video camera in social context with regard to a user study that was carried out among people using video recording as part of their everyday lives. In the remainder of this paper, we first highlight some related research, then propose a way to model recording situations in terms of primary and secondary context, and discuss the issues of awareness and privacy. We then describe the user study and analyze its results. Finally, we summarize the main results.

J. Jacko (Ed.): Human-Computer Interaction, Part II, HCII 2007, LNCS 4551, pp. 460–469, 2007.

2 Related Research

HCI research on digital imaging has largely looked at the perspective of the person doing the recording, focusing on what is recorded and how the sharing of images is done. In this paper, we view the imaging devices and people as part of a communication system.

A user evaluation by Sarvas et al. presents as a result that 89% of taken digital photos are shared at least once and most of the sharing is done within 3 days after taking [12]. While some other studies may offer lower figures for sharing, it is still evident that digital photography has lowered the barrier for sharing.
Kindberg et al. [7] have presented a division of images into affective versus functional and social versus individual categories. They discuss photographing situations and what is considered worth publishing and to whom. Their results suggest that people mostly take affective images. Those images are used for both social and individual needs. Frohlich [4] introduces digital photography, where still images are enhanced by audio. He argues that audiophotos can be better than videos. However, he states that the advantage is dependent on the content being captured: for some situations video may still be the preferred choice. The empirical studies showed that annotations of still images with audio could be used for stories and narrations. Difference between still and video recording is not self-evident anymore. A Sony DSC-M1 camera has a hybrid mode for capturing combined still and video, video being recorded all the time and part of it saved before and after still image capture.

In media science, there is research on how information and communication technologies are used to preserve our cultural knowledge for the future. For example, a French philosopher Jean Baudrillard discusses on notions of time [3]. He observes two indications of human willingness to get rid of the limitations of linear time: Firstly, we want to capture everything and share it almost before it happened to have a feeling of living the situation; secondly, we want to record everything to be archived as a record of our culture. There is relatively little research about how people react to being targets for mobile phone video recording. Huhtamo [6] states as a media-archaeological notion that already in 19th century there were frequent complaints about amateur photographers transgressing existing social rules related to privacy and decency. The threat of anyone being a target of a snapshot was noticed already then and a camera used to have a de-humanizing effect on the person carrying it. Huhtamo compares the situation to the discussions now taking place with the mobile phones and specifically to the emerging use of camera phones.

2.1 Context Approach to Video Recording

We model the situations where mobile video is recorded and consumed in primary and secondary contexts (see Fig. 1) [10 and 11]. We present an overview of the model of primary and secondary contexts and discuss how the mobile phone video camera affects the social context as well as how the situation changes during time. We analyze the conditions that context must fulfill to make video recording getting started and, conversely, what is the effect of the video recording to the context.

Primary context means the immediate physical surroundings where the people can experience each other and the event without technological devices. The physical location and common time are identifiers of the primary context. The situation turns to feel more risky when the camera is present since there are more privacy concerns arisen due to the possibility for capturing and sharing the material. A user study by Koskinen et al. [8] reports that photos taken of strangers were shared to friends. This makes primary context with a camera risky to the persons who are in the photos by accident and/or who are not friends of the shooter. There are attempts to protect privacy and prevent unnoticeable photographing; in Japan and Korea it is mandatory by law to have shutter voice in digital cameras. In the context of this paper, we understand privacy as follows: "Privacy is the claim of individuals to determine for themselves when, how and to what extend information about themselves is communicated to others" [13].

Fig. 1. Primary and Secondary Contexts

The secondary context surfaces when material which was recorded in primary context is published and also sensed by someone. A video camera enabled mobile phone is an example of a device which makes secondary context possible but also less sophisticated devices such as analog cameras and tape recorders make appearing of secondary context possible but slower. People within the primary context may be aware or unaware of the existence of the secondary context. Secondary context has no boundaries; it may occur in any time and any place where it is possible to consume captured material.

Thanks to the camera phones, the possible secondary contexts can now have a greater effect for primary contexts. This can change the way people behave in such situations. The effect is bi-directional. If the existence of the secondary context is seen inevitable and the nature of it is known, the affect to primary context is specified, but even possibility for secondary context affects the primary one. An early example of the real-time sharing was "Hole in Space" media art experiment by Kit and Sherrie [5]. This bi-directional video call between Los Angeles and New York was used for real-time video and audio communication with people in secondary context. In the mobile domain, covering the whole end-to-end chain from creating the content to consuming it is already possible. There is equipment available for each part of the chain (capturing, editing, sharing, and consumption) even within one device such as a mobile phone; and the recorded material is always available. When compared to earlier capturing and publishing possibilities, the video call enabled mobile phone makes the secondary context more probable. This makes rich communication easier than before between two or masses of people who are not in the same primary context. In addition to services like YouTube [14], emerging technologies, such as DVB-H and RSS, make self-made mobile television broadcasts more practical, secondary context may spread to larger audiences.

3 Study

We conducted a user study with 22 participants in Italy, 2003-2004 aiming to examine how people are using video recording as part of their everyday lives. Recording situations and subjects, as well as sharing and preserving were in the scope of interest. A qualitative research method was selected to get rich data on usage behavior related to a phenomenon that was not widely investigated before. It also allowed interpretation of the meanings that the participants attributed to video recording with a mobile phone.

3.1 Participants, Methods and Data

Participants consisted of four groups: two families (Fa1 and Fa2) and two groups of friends (Fr1 and Fr2). The groups were connected; one family member was also a member of another group. Choosing groups with an existing social network was crucial in order to gain realistic understanding of how people use video cameras and share the resulting content in their daily lives. None of the participants had used mobile phone with video recording and sharing capabilities before and they neither studied nor worked in the related field.

Fa1 was a typical Italian family with six members and three generations; grandparents, middle-aged mother and 15, 16 and 18 years old children. The father of the family did not participate in the study. The oldest child belonged also to another friends group. Fa2 consisted of five members and three generations; grand parents, middle-aged father, son and his girlfriend, who were in their twenties. All members of these two families were familiar with information and communication technologies and they had used e.g. e-mail. Fr1 consisted of five members between 15 to 17 and one 24 years old. Fr2 was a coherent group of six socially active young adults who were studying either at a university or a college. They used to spend a lot of time together. Both genders were represented in both friend groups.

Participants were supplied with video camera phones, equipped with video editing software and 128Mb memory cards for the time of usage period. They were able to cut segments of video clips, combine them, and change audio tracks. The participants had software for editing the still images and they were also given a possibility to transfer the multimedia material created on the phone to the computer with a memory card readers. Furthermore, each group was given a video camera for shooting DVD or TV quality video. The video camera was small enough to carry on a constant basis and therefore used to simulate the capabilities of a mobile phone with a good quality video camera. Mobile phone subscriptions were provided for the participants.

The study consisted of an introduction meeting, usage period, final interviews, and data analysis. In the introduction meeting the study and users' tasks as well as the technologies were described to the participants. The participants were asked to use the mobile devices and the additional software as naturally as possible. Further, they were asked to send the material created to those with whom they would communicate in their typical everyday life setting. All the configurations and other settings were made so that starting to use the devices was easy. The participants used the devices and the pre-installed additional software for one month. They also had a possibility to contact a service desk maintained by the subcontractor in case of a problem or a need for technical advice. After the usage period all 22 participants were interviewed either in one-to-one or pair interview. The interviews that took from one and a half to two hours were simultaneously interpreted to the project team, which was observing the interviews in an observation room.

The study produced two kinds of data that was used to construct the understanding on user behavior concerning video recording with a mobile phone. First, the interviews, which were recorded and transcribed, provided qualitative data. Second, all the multimedia material, including videos, still images and messages that the participants produced was another set of qualitative and quantitative data. The participants had a possibility to delete the most private material, if they wished, before they returned the devices. However, they were encouraged to return their devices including as much material as possible.

4 Results

We found out that motivations of video camera usage can be divided into four areas. The first one concerns creating and using multimedia for preserving it for one's own use. We call this behavior (1) *for archiving one's life*. The other areas of recording behavior are related to communicative usage and self-expression; two of them being connected to publishing for others via a communication device (2) *for sharing one's life* and (3) *to enhance social presence* and the fourth meaning to affect the immediate social surroundings (4) *as a facilitator in group dynamics*.

The factors which define the attitude towards filming situation are: (A) *target's relation to the cameraman*, (B) *target's impression of cameraman's intentions* and (C) *the filming context*. We found that acceptability of video recording changes in a process of time. Sharing possibility raised some privacy concerns.

The participants were active in using their camera phones and video cameras during the trial. They took from 50 to over 600 pictures in a month. Videos were shot less with the phone, from 0 to 40 clips in a month, due to bad quality and the 9-second length limitation. Specific video cameras were used more actively. The study brought out that the motivation to use a video camera is highly dependent on personal preferences: some liked photographing more, while others were more interested in filming. Those who found filming awkward said that it requires much more concentration than photographing. Another criticism towards shooting video was that it excludes the cameraman from the social situation longer than photographing. According to this study, male participants were more into filming than female participants. The participants highly appreciated the immediate nature of photographing with a mobile phone. They were able to capture images and videos anytime and anywhere and share them with their friends. Photographing with a mobile phone was much more spontaneous than photographing with other camera devices since it was carried around all the time. However, users complained that the camera phone did not support immediateness well enough. The camera application in that particular model could be opened only by using soft keys and took far too much time. In some contexts a phone was more acceptable than a specific camera device. For instance, photographing during a dinner with colleagues with a traditional camera would have been odd, but taking a couple of pictures and filming a few seconds of video with a phone was acceptable.

4.1 Usage Motivations and Behaviors

Archiving one's life. Participants wanted to save all the pictures and videos created during the test period even if they were bad in quality. One of them put it as follows: *"I want to save every moment of my life and make a media-album of important things of my life."* Especially females thought that image material construct a pictorial diary. The diary was seen as a very personal place for personal pictures and videos, and many participants mentioned a need for a protected and secured folder for their personal material. Another interesting finding was that some people collected things by taking a picture of an item and saving it. For instance, one participant took a large amount of pictures of logos from advertisements, labels on clothes, etc. Another one photographed graffiti made by a famous graffiti painter. Also CD-covers, art, cars, and paintings were photographed in order to collect these items.

Sharing one's life. Several participants expressed wishes to share their lives by the means of photographs and videos. They sent photographs via MMS and e-mail and also showed them in face-to-face occasions on their phone display. They also tried to send videos but due to the quality weakening remarkably in the transfer process, interest towards sending videos via MMS decreased. The shared material presented places, people, or activity that shaped the persons' lives. Sometimes a photograph or a video clarified the message which the sender wanted to convey. Some of the participants said that they did not need to explain so much when the receiver could see what they meant. In addition, pictures in a message strengthened expression of moods. Participants also wanted to share the results of their creative activity. For instance, a middle-aged housewife, who took about 40 video clips during the usage period, stated that *"I found my creativity when filming and editing the films"*. She was amazed how dramatically the atmosphere and mood of the film can be edited by only changing the audio clip. Image-editing software was used for making simple modifications, such as frames, text boxes, or blurring to photographs and also to add a personal touch to the pictures in order to make them more fun or more valuable.

Enhance social presence. Pictures and videos in messages are extremely strong in enhancing feeling of presence and togetherness when communicating with a person or persons not present. This kind of activity took place mostly between couples and close friends. In many occasions these messages were responded to and sometimes they started a dialog. Video captures the surroundings, including audio, and thus conveys social presence. Due to the fact that MMS supported video transmission poorly, the participants who were familiar with PC usage sent videos via email. In their opinion, mobile phones should better support sending email instead of having an MMS format of its own.

Facilitator in group dynamics. Video camera also had a big role in group dynamics both in primary and via the secondary contexts. Sometimes when participants recorded some social situation they discussed and made jokes with people in nearby surroundings. We found out the bi-directional correlation between the camera and the context. The presence of the camera in the social event shaped the way people behaved; the cameramen often interacted with others in order to make them talk to the camera and make the end result more collective while targets behaved the way they thought was wished. On the reverse side, the context and situation formulated the camera use. The study also showed examples of loosely planned, spontaneous short sketches that were made just for fun. Flirting is one example where the role of the video camera facilitates group dynamics. This kind of behavior was common especially in the school environments. Some of the videos shot during the trial show how one cameraman flirted with the targets by making jokes, flattering, and teasing them. In some cases the recording made the target to flirt with the cameraman. Because people are interested in how the others see them, they take photos or videos about themselves by using the camera as a mirror to see how they look like.

A multimedia phone was frequently used as a tool for joking. As an example, a common activity for students was to take a picture of a friend at school, modify the face with image editing tool and send it via Bluetooth to friends in the class. This kind of activity made immediate feedback possible, but in some cases even required an immediate response. Generally, the younger participants appreciated the possibility to share pictures for free via Bluetooth, but they complained about the slow process of searching for available Bluetooth devices. Bluetooth messaging was also used for flirting. One of the participants shared pictures in a bar with unknown recipients. She recognized those who received Bluetooth message by observing how people used and handled their mobile phones. In the interview, she said that Bluetooth messaging made it easier to start a conversation with those who received her picture.

4.2 Acceptance of the Video Recording

Perception of privacy depends on the situation, the emotional closeness between the present people, and the familiarity of the context. The trust between familiar people in primary context makes recording situation more acceptable.

Target's relation to the cameraman. The presence of camera affects the social dynamics between the subjects. Further, the relation to the cameraman affects the target's response to the recording. If the target doesn't feel comfortable with the cameraman, may use of the camera be experienced hostile. When being exited by the presence of a video camera, users tend to perform TV or movie like role plays. Sometimes the camera strengthens the cameraman and puts the target into an interrogation. Emotions are caricaturized and acted out in movie style when a camera is present. With constant exposure to the video camera presence this phase usually fades rapidly.

Target's impression of cameraman's intentions. The target has an assumption about the cameraman's intentions when recording starts. This assumption characterizes the attitude towards the cameraman. As an example of the primary context intentions was the late teenager male participant filming his girlfriend with flirty and cuddly style, and getting the flirty and cuddly response. in another case, when the cameraman was acting as a reporter, the target immediately took the role of an interviewee. When cameraman's intentions are miss-assumed, the response can be unwanted. Possible sharing to secondary context makes the intentions even more interesting for the target.

The filming context. The more familiar the filming context, the more open and natural is the response towards the cameraman; anger, frustration and affection have been noticed. In the public context, the target's response is more acted and joyful.

In general, the attitude towards recording and presence of the camera changed in few weeks from excitement trough annoyance to ignoring (See Fig. 2). We claim that adjusting to the camera makes targets less aware of it and thus feeling more safe. Relation between a cameraman and a target had an impact on the change on the behavior. In the study like this privacy concerns are presumably low since the recorded material is shared only within the group of pre-defined familiar people and trusted researchers.

Fig. 2. The four week period with 3 cameramen and 6 targets visualized in the chart; the faces representing the targets. Sunny smiling face: excitement, joking, making faces, acting and imitating TV and movie stars and interest to the filmed material. Circular face: diminishing excitement and slight embarrassment. Triangle face: anger and frustration. Square face: ignoring the camera.

4.3 Sharing and Themes

Benefits of the possibility to share the captured multimedia content included: *"real time"*, *"immediate"*, *"spontaneous"*, *"message is polite"*, *"it's is like a gift"*, *"feeling of being connected and reachable"*. Having the material created in a mobile phone and thus always available was also considered as a big benefit. Sharing raised concerns such as need to control the spreading to the secondary context. Participants felt that the rich information in MMS sometimes revealed more of their situation than they desired. Editing seemed to be done to prevent that. We noticed that the material which was intended to be shared was edited more often than the private material.

The study suggests that although mobile phone video camera brings up new video recording themes, the old, familiar ones such as: people (e.g. you and me, jokes and social life), pets (e.g. cats, dogs and birds), occasions (e.g. family events, soccer game and events) and holiday (e.g. monuments and landscapes) still remain. New themes that derive from the always-with characteristics of the mobile phone video camera include: daily life (e.g. work, school, places and activities), practical (e.g. notes), object (e.g. CD covers, graffiti and works of art), celebrities (e.g. from TV screen and magazines) and surprises (something noteworthy comes across).

5 Discussion and Concluding Remarks

Camera in the primary context affected the behavior of the present persons. That was recognizable e.g. by the posing acts. Subjects' behavior changed all the time during the study which we presume being an indicator of four weeks being too short time for the participants to develop their own mobile video camera usage habits as cameramen or targets. Time was long enough to get results from the acceptance of the video cameras in social context though.

This study brought up that the participants did not perceive remarkable privacy threats due to the fact that the recorded material was shared mostly with familiar and trusted people [See also 8]. Furthermore, some earlier studies [See e.g. 1, 2 and 9] have shown that people do not tend to pay much attention to possible privacy threats, unless they have personally encountered invasion of privacy with regard to the information or multimedia content they have shared. For instance, after posting some highly personal material e.g. to a personal blog or an on-line community, the material is fairly easy to publish all over the web. Today, it seems that many people do not either know or care about this. One can easily find such material from the web that seems to be recorded spontaneously in a private sphere and express something that has not been meant to be visible for the whole world. As one possible explanation for that, we suggest that the more people get used to the cameras around, the less they pay attention to them and in time become almost unaware of them. That seems to lead to less artificial behavior and lower concerns of publishing and privacy loss.

These observations bring up the two-folded nature of privacy in terms of designing and developing systems allowing capturing and sharing videos and images. On the one hand, designers should take privacy regulation features into account and try to avoid such functionalities that might be harmful for users. On the other hand, users will inevitably apply the given means to their own purposes, and especially in a case of mobile devices enabling recording and sharing videos and images, designers and developers have very limited means to regulate their usage.

The recent technological and behavioral evolution related to capturing and sharing multimedia content have resulted discussion of radical change of privacy. The private sphere has diminished whilst the public sphere has extended due to video recording capability of mobile phones. Many are truly concerned of this development. However, one can also take an alternative viewpoint. The future where everything is recorded and viewable for everyone can be seen as a relief and give an opportunity to live un-stressful life without secrets and hiding. People's openness in publishing extremely private content in the web is one indicator witnessing this trend. In addition, monitoring authorities has become easier for citizens (a phenomenon called sousveillance) and this might have positive implications of rightness of society.

Since the study was made only in one country, we can't claim that the results are valid in every culture. However, the study illustrates that mobile phone video camera affects the social context in various ways such as expanding group dynamics and giving possibility for preserving material for own use or sharing it with others. In other words, the reason for recording is either in the primary or secondary context, sometimes both of them. About half of the videos are taken in some new situations where camera wasn't available before the appearing of mobile phone video cameras. Target's behavior in primary context where the camera is present changes in the course of time; in most cases it starts with joy and turn to ignoring.

References

1. Adams, A.: The Implications of Users' Privacy Perception on Communication and Information Privacy Policies. In: Proc. Telecommunications Policy Research Conference (1999)
2. Adams, A.: Multimedia information changes the whole privacy ballgame. In: Proc. The tenth conference on Computers, freedom and privacy, pp. 25–32 (2000)
3. Baudrillard, J.: Lopun illuusio. Galilée. Gaudeamus Kirja. Helsinki, 25 (1995)
4. Frohlich, D.: Sound, paper and souvenirs: Some resources for an alternative digital photography. International Forum Less is more - Simple Computing in an Age of Complexity, Microsoft Research, Cambridge, UK, pp. 27–28 (April 2005)
5. Galloway, K. and Rabinowitz, S.: Hole in Space (1980) (last visited: February 5th 2007)http://www.ecafe.com/getty/HIS/index.html
6. Huhtamo, E.: Pockets of Plenty: An Archaeology of Mobile Media. In: Proc. ISEA 2004. pp. 24–27 (last visited: February 5th 2007)http://www.isea2004.net/
7. Kindberg, T., Spasojevic, M., Fleck, R., Sellen, A.: I Saw This and Thought of You: Some Social Uses of Camera Phones. In: Proc. CHI 2005, pp. 1545–1548. ACM Press, New York (2005)
8. Koskinen, I., Kurvinen, E., Lehtonen, T-K.: Mobiili kuva, pp. 80–81. Edita/IT Press, Helsinki (2001)
9. Lehikoinen, J.T., Kaikkonen, A.: PePe Field Study: Constructing Meanings for Locations in the Context of Mobile Presence. In: Proc. The 8th conference on Human-computer interaction with mobile devices and services MobileHCI '06, pp. 53–60 (2006)
10. Reponen, E., Huuskonen, P., Mihalic, K.: Mobile Video Recording in Context. ACM Interactions Magazine. Special issue: Gadgets '06 vol. 13(4) (July + August 2006)
11. Reponen, E., Mihalic, K.: Model of primary and secondary context. In: Proc. International workshop in conjunction with AVI 2006 on Context in advanced interfaces, Venice, Italy, pp. 37–38. ACM Press, New York (2006)
12. Sarvas, R., Oulasvirta, A., Jacucci, G.: Building Social Discourse Around Mobile Photos – A System Perspective. In: Proc. Mobile HCI 05, pp. 31–38. ACM Press, New York (2005)
13. Westin, A.: Privacy and Freedom (2nd edn.) Atheneum, New York (1970)
14. YouTube: (last visited: February 5th 2007) http://www.youtube.com/

Developing a Motion-Based Input Model for Mobile Devices

Mark Richards, Tim Dunn, and Binh Pham

Faculty of Information Technology, Queensland University of Technology
Queensland, Australia
{m3.richards,tl.dunn,b.pham}@qut.edu.au

Abstract. This paper discusses a new input model for camera- equipped mobile devices which is more efficient, intuitive and intelligent. This model takes advantage of the motion captured from the camera: the general movement of both device and user. These movements are mapped to a three-dimension space and input methods are devised depending on the current situational context. Such an interface allows users to far more quickly interact with their devices, avoids navigation though nested menus and allows the device to perform natural tasks without the user having to knowingly interact with it.

1 Introduction

The mobile phone has gradually evolved over time to become a multi-functional device that transcends simple voice communications. Mobile phones are commonly used as task schedulers, portable music players, games machines and internet browsing devices.

These devices typically use a 12 to 15 key ISO complaint interface with an additional input device (scroll wheel/joystick) for additional finer-grained input. The phone's interfaces have advanced over time to encompass the additional functionality to these devices, but multiple-level menus. Such are not a user friendly option and only add additional complexity to the experience and additional learning time for the end users of such a device [1].

Hierarchical menus rely on the users' knowledge of the system before-hand so that they can traverse the correct path to find the item they want. This has been found [2] not to perform ideal for learning users since the design is geared towards what the designers believe is the best path to follow.

Predictive input (such as T9 [3] on a phone) can be used to dynamically search for an application/action the user wants to perform. While it is easier for the user to find the correct result by predictive typing, it hinders progress if the user is not entirely sure what functionality they intend, or they are simply browsing options.

This is where a predictive model based on user action comes to the fore-front. A user can learn motions quickly, they can act out what they wish or can express their state of mind (confusion, anger) in ways that aid in understanding what they wish for.

The multi-functionality of these devices can be taken advantage of to open new human-interaction pathways with the devices. The camera embedded in many of the newer devices can be used to track the general movement of the device while being

J. Jacko (Ed.): Human-Computer Interaction, Part II, HCII 2007, LNCS 4551, pp. 470–479, 2007.

held and basic information about the current environment the device is in (light/dark). This information combined with general human motion in response to specific situations allows an entirely new input model to be developed.

The advantages of such a model compared to methods currently available on mobile devices are numerous. First, the attempt to mimic and replicate human motion can ease adaptation to the model and increase learning speeds. Motion prompts require little attention to be paid to the screen/keyboard and allows the user to concentrate more on the world around them with little distraction from the portable device. Natural motion can also be tracked and interpreted so that the user is supplying useful information to the device without their knowledge.

Motion input can be considered analog by nature allowing a lot more subtle controls of directions, speeds and amplitude, something not readily available on most mobile devices. Coupled with intelligent parsing of information around it the model can easily adapt to the users requirements in ways that are simply not possible with methods currently in place.

The work presented here was divided into four design and implementation milestones. There was the need to understand how motion could be applied to a mobile device. This motion was classified into sub-types that could be used to aid in the description of this motion. The design of this model is presented in section 2. After this initial structure and framework was created multiple surveys were conducted to determine the validity of the concept as well as find out how users reacted to situations on a mobile device via motion. This is discussed in section 3.

After the knowledge was gained there was the need to apply it directly to a mobile device. This included finding efficient ways to detect motion given the limited resources of a mobile device as well as developing a prototype capable of showing that motion was indeed being tracked.

2 Design of Model

Previous work, including Hex [4] and TiltText [5], show that motion-based text input models are viable on mobile devices. These approaches utilised orientation data gathered from an external sensor (accelerometer), and therefore have limited applicability. The research presented here aims to further develop this approach by encompassing a larger variety of functionality available to the user at any given time, and create a general model for motion-based user input. Using a variety of stimuli, a user's required outcome can be achieved much faster and definitely does not have to be limited to textual input.

In addition, we use data taken from a mobile device's embedded camera to gain orientation information, and provide an additional form of user input. This data can determine the phone's current situation or the direction along which it is being moved. The image data changing from light to dark could indicate the device has been placed in the owner's pocket. This could be considered an indication to turn on the device's key lock. An intelligent model could also determine if silent mode should be engaged (in a meeting or at the movies.)

Motion can be used to supplement button-based input or in certain circumstances replace it completely [Fig. 1]. If listening to music, moving the device right while pressing a button can indicate an input to skip the currently playing song. Pressing the same button while moving the device up can be an indication to increase the volume.

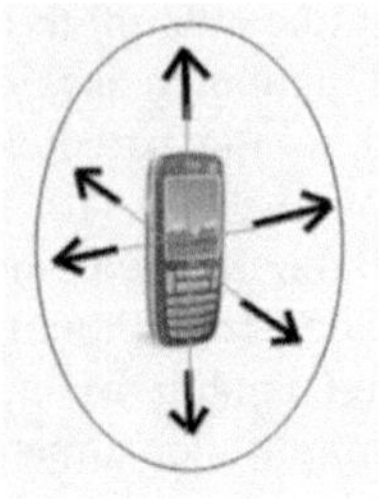

Fig. 1. Linear motion can be tracked via a device's embedded camera. While a lower quality camera makes tracking imprecise, it can be used to track general, simple motions.

Most inputs make sense only in specific circumstances (e.g. next song while listening to music). This fact allows actions to be mapped to multiple inputs depending on the situation. Thus it greatly decreases the complexity of actions needed and the amount needed to be learned by the users. Small buttons on devices typically hinder input and hence replacing a lot of the multiple buttons presses with a combination of one button and a direction should decrease input time similar to web browser mouse gestures (Opera, NetCaptor). A lot of these inputs can be designed to make sense to the user as well by following typical human movement patterns. Moving the device up and down can easily be recognized as the same motions as nodding one's head in agreement. Moving the device to one's ear can be interpreted as answering a call. Such mimicking of normal human motion can dramatically reduce learning time since the knowledge is already used by the users prior to adapting to the model (Table 1).

Table 1. Simple breakdown of possible differences (Note that motion can not be seen in the dark)

Situation	Currently	Input Noticed	Response
Dark	Playing Music	Button Press	Ignore
Light	Playing Music	Button Press	Stop Music
Dark	Playing Music	Button Press and Left Motion	Ignore
Light	Playing Music	Button Press and Left Motion	Next Track

The initial model will be created with multiple users input and insight. Surveyed users will judge appropriate functions to be applied to the model and an initial list will be created. User interaction and experimentation over multiple repetitions will provide further information to build upon this model and certify the appropriate inputs to be set for each of the desired functions. User testing will ensure the motions remain relevant over the iterations, do not overlap and are appropriate for most users.

Users never have identical needs; therefore a provision for user customization will be added in later revisions. These will be in the form of shortcuts for certain functions. They can either take totally new commands inputs → functions or override presets that the users find little use for. The same provisions as before (situation, current action) will be applied. Multiple profiles for different users upon the one device remain a possibility.

The proposed model extends and builds upon current mobile input schemes by adding three significant stimuli for the device's input channels.

2.1 Device Instigated Input

Tracking the motion of the device is useful in predefined situations. Many of these are where the device is expecting specific input because of the current situation. These are commonly considered low-level inputs and include functionality such as: scrolling, selection, confirmation and acknowledgement. Such situations occur when the device initiates the communication path and awaits the users' response.

- Confirm deletion of a SMS - *Move device up and down (nod)*
- Pan down an image - *Move device down*
- Scroll right through options - *Tilt device to the right*

These are all set and obvious motions for the above situations where the device awaits the user's response before continuing.

2.2 Human Instigated Input

Tracking human motion allows for the impersonation of natural activities and the ability to apply them to relevant situations. These actions are typically instigated by the user and should generally mimic an action that is in context with what the user wants if they were to perform that motion naturally.

- Lower Volume - *Move device away from head while in a call*
- Make call - *Move device to ear after entering number*
- Enter *landscape* display mode - *Turn device 90 degrees to left*

The device would constantly check for movements that relate to these actions and act accordingly if they are appropriate for the current situation.

2.3 Scene Input

Information cannot only be retrieved from motion that the device detects, but also information captured and interpreted directly from the imagery stored while looking for motion. Such scene information is the crux of the intelligent input of this model. Retrieving certain data from the images can instigate events automatically (if they are appropriate at the time).

- Turn on key lock and silent -*Detect dark surrounds (pocket)*
- Take picture - *A face is the focus of the camera*
- Attempt Bluetooth discovery - *See another mobile device*
- Find and store name and number in phonebook - *See a business card*

Such functionality is supplementary to the core of this model (which is the motion detection), but is a significant step to true intelligent input and device automation. Therefore the allowance of such a form of input is important to the model's overall design. [Fig. 2] demonstrates a typical image that a camera could collect from a mobile device. Much contextual information gathered from this can open up more advanced types of input because of the situation the device is in [6]. In this image it is daytime, located at an airport with taxis nearby. These fragments of data derived from the image can be used to open up specialized input paths on top of what is already available. Items of interest include the taxi, luggage and the airplane icon upon the sign. From this it could be derived that we might be looking for a way home or possible flight times.

Fig. 2. A sample picture for scene input. Much information can be gathered from this scene.

3 Survey Design

To create a model that users could react naturally to, it was required that these same users with mobile devices had their reactions recorded. Initially, to create an understanding of the users, a simple survey was carried out to gather information about their history and how they thought such a model would work.

After this information was recorded a more advanced survey structure was created that emphasized on particular areas of input (selection, choosing, modification, adjustment, confirmation).

Each of these areas was modeled by an automated survey that was run on a Windows Mobile 5 device. This device simulated tasks that correlated to one of these inputs types. User's reactions and motions were recorded both externally by a video camera and internally by the device. Markers were placed around the environment to easily translate minor movements made by the user to the device.

The tests comprised of:

- Selection - Selecting points of the screen.
- Modification - Changing the hue of video streamed from the camera.
- Adjustment - Modified and rotated video from camera shown to the user.

- Confirmation - Reacting to happy and sad faces.
- Adjustment - Reading scrolling text that gets faster and faster
- Functionality - Phone call emulation

4 Survey Results

Results showed [Fig. 3.] that a significant number of users reacted in a way that closely mimicked real life motions for the situation if there was no device, i.e.

- nodding device = nodding head - confirmation to prompt
- twisting device = rotating head - rotating an image

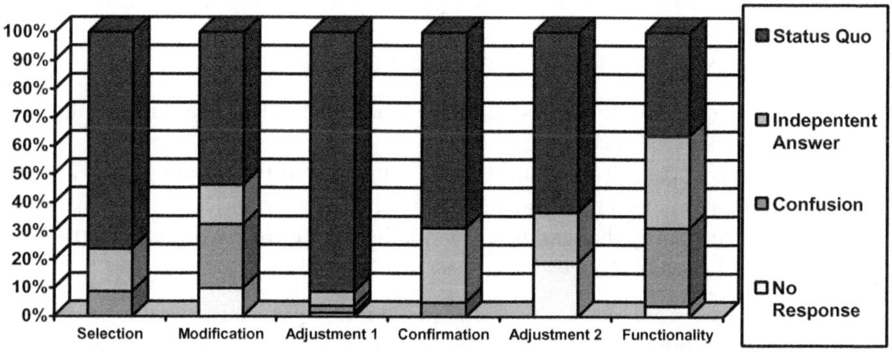

Fig. 3. Automated survey response distribution. Status quo answers were where the participants supplied answers similar. Independent answers are a collection of answers that were complete but different from the most common (status quo) answer.

A finding that was not expected was how confusion was handled in the motion inputting of simple commands. Initially the surveyed participants were generally confused with the entire process of moving the device to correspond to input. What was noted was the almost universal reaction by these people when placed in a situation they would not express their input.

Confusion was recorded as people shaking the device, much like the stereotypical response by people attempting to get a broken device to work. Such an input could easily be detected as a plea for help and therefore added to the model. Prompts could then be given to the user.

The model resulted in being contextual in nature so that certain motions can have different meaning depending of the situation (typically simple motions such as twisting the device to signify simple adjustments such as numbers or images). However, some motions applied well to specific situations are unique to only that instruction. ('help' for example.) Finally some input/motions need the ability to disable other inputs while awaiting an appropriate input (e.g. disabling many actions while awaiting the user to respond to a confirmation dialog.

An attempt was made to further instruct confused users on how the model was to work to determine if general learning of the input method was possible. Users responded positively to this effort, therefore it was determined that such a model was indeed feasible.

5 Detecting Motion

Detecting motion between different frames of video traditionally encompasses finding objects that have moved between the frames and then analyzing these objects to obtain data. This has limited application in this field as instead of tracking what has moved between the frames, we are expecting the entire picture to move and we work backwards to determine how the device has moved. This involves picking certain highlights that are easy to identify in the picture and tracking there location changes between frames.

Many problems have to be tackled when taking this approach:

- Objects in the scene might move independently and therefore give totally wrong data if they were picked to be tracked.
- We need an approach that can at least some way differentiate between rotation movement and lateral movement.
- We also need a way that can use low quality images and work within the limited restraints of mobile devices.

Initially, it was concluded that edge-detection algorithms would be the most appropriate way to approach this problem. Straight edges are commonly attributed to static objects in the environment (tables, buildings, roads) and are relatively easy to track between frames. Problems arose when trying to determine the differences between rotation and movement since the edges had no reference point to compare when determining rotation. This resulted in having to examine edges in order to compare their changes to each and other edge. If an edge grew smaller on one side while one on the other side grew then it was presumed rotation was being performed. This resulted in additional complexity and often unreliable results as reference edges were often inappropriate to compare with. Therefore a simpler method will need to be devised.

The Augmented Reality Toolkit (ARToolkit [7]) allows users to track icons (small black and white images embedded in a black bounding square) inside a scene. It tracks possible icons, their location in the screen and other 2D space information (area, vertices and rotation.) The toolkit makes tracking rotation easier as the edges of a icon now have appropriate references (the opposite edge of the square.) [Fig. 4.]

The main component of the ARToolkit, which is the detecting of the information inside the square, was an unnecessary step for detection motion between frames and was therefore removed from the calculation. This gave us information on black polygons on the frame that could possibly be rotated in a 3D plane to give a square. This give an additional level of 3D rotation detection as not only can we track vertex data on the square, but can also create transformation matrices that would transform our polygon back to a square and track these matrices between frames.

Fig. 4. Detecting black screens of a Nintendo DS within a Direct3D application

Often multiple squares would be detected upon the screen and while tracking multiple squares and averaging the data would be the perfect result mobile device limitations once again came into play so an algorithm was devised to determine the 'most appropriate polygon (MAP).' Each polygon returned by the ARToolkit's detection routines was given a score to grade how appropriate the polygon would be to track [Fig. 5.]. Quick tests are then performed to determine if the MAP of the current frame is the same as the MAP from the frame before (by comparing screen size, centre and vertices.) If so, then changes between frames are calculated. If not, an attempt to find the previous polygon in the current scene occurs and calculations are applied before shifting to the new polygon.

Fig. 5. An image before and after the filter is applied, MAP highlighted

To determine a MAP score, the following factors were include:

- α - Appropriate size of polygon (easier to detect changes on polygons taking up more screen space)
- β - Vertices distance from screen edge (further from edge, higher chance square will still exist in the next frame. If the polygon gets cut off by the screen edge it can no longer be detected.) Determined by adding the distance of the X and Y co-ordinate of each vertex to the closest screen-corner and taking the smallest result from the four vertices.
- γ - Edge Length (easier to track rotation in both directions if the edges are not short.) Result is the addition of (100/edge length) for each edge so that smaller edges will give a larger γ.
- δ - Chance it is a true polygon (0.0-1.0) (ARToolkit returns confidence results. The lower the confidence the less likely this is a square, and the more likely it will not be detected next frame.)

Examination along with trial and error were employed to determine an algorithm that gives the strongest results.

The algorithm currently being using to give a MAP score is:

$$\alpha/10 + \beta/10 - \gamma * \delta .$$

6 Software Development

We have chosen to carry out the initial development of a prototype based upon the model on a Microsoft Smartphone device. Because of further integration of cameras within the SDK, Windows Mobile 5 devices were selected.

The mobile versions of DirectShow and Direct3D are not as advanced as their desktop counterparts but are sufficient for processing this information. Connecting the device's camera to a capture graph allows us to pass a filter over the image stream in an attempt to find what we are looking for (black polygonal objects). Querying the filter allows us to extract information about the object (its corners/vertices) in screen space [Fig. 4.]. This can be translated into a Direct3D world.

The cut down version of ARToolkit that only detects the required information was encapsulated into a DirectShow filter so that the Direct3D libraries could be used to aid in the processing of this information. Creating a filter also allows the detection algorithm to easily be incorporated by other programs because of the COM interfaces it supplies. Such a filter easily allows other programs to start the camera and send all information through the filter before asking for the information found. [Fig. 6]

Fig. 6. Desktop COM detection filter spotting squares through GraphEdit (dots on corners)

Once the MAP is found, it is placed into 3D space with the aid for Direct3D so that information between frames can easily be detected and translations detected. [Fig. 7]

Fig. 7. Mobile application displaying both the video stream and the 3D filtering of the MAP (video is flipped horizontally in example)

The next step to achieving the goal is to hook the underlining framework to the OS of the devices to automate functions when motion is detected. This requires knowledge of the current status of the phone and ways to directly call functions that the OS is expecting at the time (e.g. choosing 'No' at a message box prompt.)

7 Conclusion

We have presented an intuitive input model for mobile devices based on the movements of the device and user. Such a model design opens up a logical pathway to take in human-machine interaction and is developed with a cost-effective and currently available environment in mind. As more learning is developed over time, an increased set of logical functions will be able to increase the autonomous level of the phone tasks. Users' natural motions in situations can be understood and harnessed more effectively to perform these functions with little conscious thought required from the user. In addition, we have developed a working prototype using DirectShow and Direct3D that shows that motion detection using a camera is indeed possible. Overall this method offers a more dynamic, intuitive and automated interface than what is currently available with little or no changes to the hardware requirements of the phones. Real world applications of such a model are highly plausible and become only more relevant as the trend towards all-in-one integrated devices continues.

References

1. Amant, R.S., Horton, T.E., Ritter, F.E.: Model-based evaluation of cell phone menu interaction. In: CHI '04: Proceedings of the SIGCHI conference on Human factors in computing systems, pp. 343–350. ACM Press, New York (2004)
2. Marsden, G., Jones, M.: (Ubiquitous computing and cellular handset interfaces - are menus the best way forward?)
3. Tegic Communications, I.: T9 home page (2006)
4. Williamson, J., Murray-Smith, R.: Hex: Dynamics and probabilistic text entry. In: Switching and Learning in Feedback Systems. vol. 3355/2005, pp. 333–342. Springer, Heidelberg (2005)
5. Wigdor, D., Balakrishnan, R.: TiltText: using tilt for text input to mobile phones. In: Proceedings of the 16th annual ACM symposium on User interface software and technology, pp. 81–90. ACM Press, New York (2003)
6. Canny, J.: The future of human-computer interaction. Queue 4, 24–32 (2006)
7. Human Interface Technology Lab, U.o.W.: ARToolkit home page (2006)

Designing Input Method of Hand-Held Device with International User Studies

Scott Song, Joonhwan Kim, Wanje Park, Boeun Park, and Hyunkook Jang

Samsung Electronics Co.,Ltd 416 Maetan3, Yeongtong, Suwon, Gyeonggi 443-742
Republic of Korea
{sangkon.song,joonhwan.kim,wanje.park,be.park,
hyunk.jang} @samsung.com

Abstract. In a small hand-held device, a common method of interaction design is expressed by metaphors. Additionally, the labeling can help to understand the meaning of metaphors. Two elements are important to express information and functions appropriately within the physically limited range of the device. For global products, the metaphors should be recognized and transmitted by a large number of users in this labeling. This study conducted a user preference test in the USA, the United Kingdom and China to find the optimal form for the arrangement of such input method design and labeling. As a result of the test, the study could figure out the effective labeling metaphor that would express the arrangement of appropriate input-buttons and their functions in the hand-held device. In addition, the metaphor would be applied to actual product.

Keywords: Hand-held Device, Input Method, International User Study, Cultural Differences, User Experience Design, Metaphor, Interface design, Button Label.

1 Introduction

One of the most important issues in user experience design is the interpretation of cultural characteristics in general-purpose content recognized commonly by users in the world. The other is how to reflect the difference the regions and countries where user groups belong. These two important issues have both contradictory and supplementary aspects. In terms of the effectiveness of development and the usability of products, it is also crucial for user interface designers of digital home appliance products released in the worldwide markets to optimize and reflect them appropriately in the outcome of design. As an example of a digital home appliance product, this study will describe the research on input methods among important elements necessary to the user experience design of hand-held devices, which can play multimedia files.

It is crucial for various images used in the external and internal screen of hand-held devices to be transmitted to users intuitively and to enable interaction to occur immediately. However, hand-held devices are limited in physical size and the amount of information expressed. In this regard, it is a generally accepted input method to use metaphors instead of words, transmitting meaning and accepting commands when

J. Jacko (Ed.): Human-Computer Interaction, Part II, HCII 2007, LNCS 4551, pp. 480–485, 2007.

expressing information. Visual thinking manifests itself especially in the use of metaphors. They show the mainly intended characteristics of an object through a parallelism with something else [1].

In this case, the most important thing is whether the metaphors expressed in accurate locations are to be accepted and understood in their original meaning by most of the users. Therefore, this study attempted to find out ways for effective input method design in the external part of the device. Then, it performs a test by dividing them into several parts, verifying them.

2 Method

It is absolutely necessary for users to understand mental models and to excavate and develop universal metaphors when designing the input method of a hand-held device. Therefore, it is always crucial to figure out a user's understanding and degree of universal adaptation. In order to examine these elements, a comprehensive user test was performed in the USA, the United Kingdom and China.

The mentioned countries were selected on the basis of representatives of main product markets and continents. China represents the Asian market, America the North American and the United Kingdom the European. The participants ranged in age from in their late teens to early forties and had previous experiences with using hand-held devices frequently. Meanwhile, the gender of the participants was equally divided. Groups were made up of 4 people each; 32 people in 8 groups participated from each country. Therefore, the number of participants was 96 in total. Data were collected and analyzed out of 96 participants. In terms of a survey method, FGI (Focus Group Interview) was conducted for listening to overall opinions on the hand-held device. Then, preferences for input method design were taken through paper survey, and subsequent additional methods of collection for individual comments were performed. Main data regarding the arrangement preference of metaphors and input buttons were the results collected form the paper survey.

2.1 Elements of Input Design in the Hand-Held Device

When users intend to input certain behaviors in the interaction, they take an action using the corresponding button. In order to provide them with the operation using a method like this button in its optimum state, it is crucial to make an arrangement for the device form. In addition, it is necessary to provide the users with effective labeling for input button function. We performed research using the following tests, while considering these two elements as verification factors of input method design.

1. Effective button arrangement for input method design

For the arrangement of buttons for input method design, the verification was performed based on horizontal- and vertical-type devices. The former was an image display device, such as a PMP (Personal Multimedia Product) and a DMB (Digital Multimedia Broadcast); the latter included devices such as MP3 players and mobile phones.

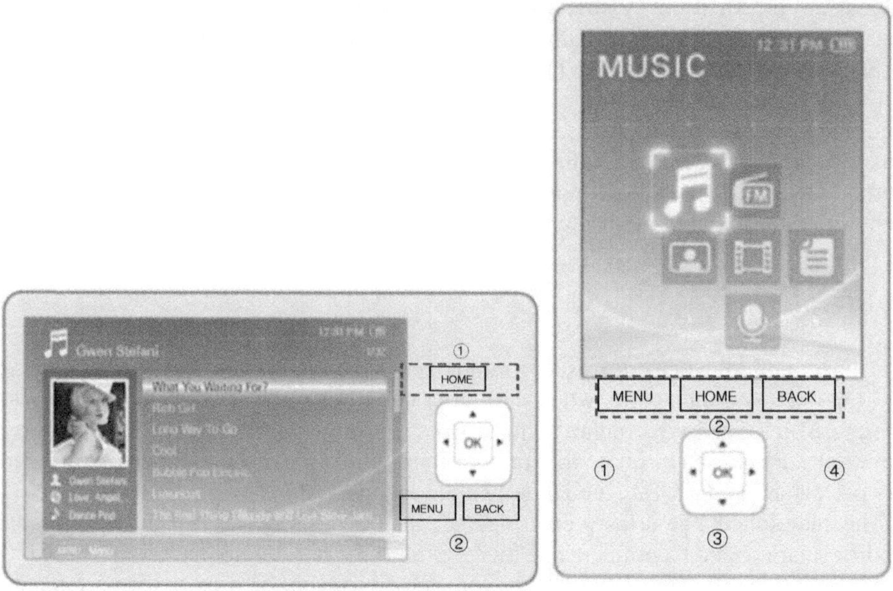

Fig. 1. It is example of preference position of horizontal & vertical screen device. This shows a n approximately position in device space type. Peoples want to control easily stretch their finger and grip in vertical or horizontal situation.

In many cases, those buttons functioning as short cuts are arranged as input buttons for controlling the screen. The button for context function, the button that makes it go back to the previous stage and the button that makes it go back to the initial screen are essential. These three short-cut functions were called MENU, BACK and HOME, respectively. Meanwhile, this study examined the optimal state wherein these three functions were arranged. (The special function button was not applied to all products so that they were excluded. Therefore, OK and upward & downward and left & right buttons were essential and they were arranged in advance).

The responses to the most preferred location and reasons corresponding to arbitrarily marked numbers were collected. The data was analyzed by country, age group and gender.

2. Effective button labeling for input method design

After the selection of the location and arrangement of input buttons, subsequent labeling commenced. In theory, the metaphors for input labeling demonstrate the deducible media through representative images, with the form recognizable by people. The use of metaphors in the existing products could be divided into those in the external and those in the screen part. We have further studied the labeling connected with the external button concerning input instead of screen design. The best icons are very simple representations, usually nouns. Verbs are difficult to convey as icons [2]. When classifying the test items, HOME and MENU corresponded to the noun forms and BACK corresponded to the verb form. The generation methods of such labeling metaphors could be divided largely into three parts. First, there was an iconic symbol that was derived from the original form of objects and was changed into a simple form. Second, it was a symbolic symbol that gathered or drew the parts of words or letters designating objects. Third, it was an indexical symbol designed to enable many people to agree to metaphysical forms derived from thought [1].

While keeping this in mind, the study conducted a test with multinational users for those selected from the examples expressed, as in the above method. The design metaphors corresponding to this example were recognized globally. In addition, they were extracted by the designers from metaphors that are commonly used. Four selected instances for each question were provided. According to the analysis of the results based on data collection, the following elements were found.

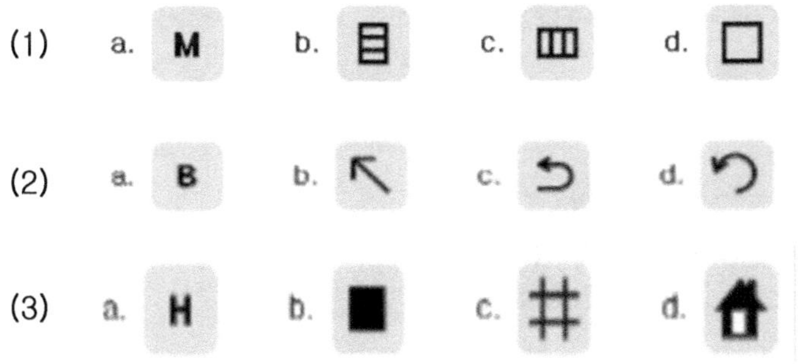

Fig. 2. It is an example of preference several metaphor type. Participants' choose depends on their region, culture, and language. It is important to adopt a metaphor in a global product.

3 Results

1. Results of effective button arrangement for input method design

The statistics of users who wanted ① location for horizontal screen devices and ② location for vertical screen devices was tabulated. There were 20% more respondents for this than the number of users who wanted other locations. However, this preference was mostly due to convenience in accordance with the method of right-hand grip. In the case were it was impossible to arrange three buttons in the horizontal screen, a triangular arrangement with a lower center of gravity was selected. The arrangement order of "HOME", "MENU", "BACK" buttons corresponding to this location slightly varied by country. However, they were not derived from differences in special structural meanings and mental models, but they were within the scope of effective errors. Therefore, satisfaction did not automatically increase by putting the MENU button on the right side or putting the BACK button on the left side. This had something to do with the elements of screen configuration. However, it did not really have a correlation with input method.

2. Results of effective button labeling for input method design

The user survey showed data representing the differences by country for the preference of designed metaphors, and those for the common parts in said three countries were ensured. The following analysis was conducted for the representative labeling test. (1) and (2) items were the test items for the configuration of the mental model whose image did not exist. Meanwhile, (3) was the item that compared the image that was characterized to the image was simplified in the model that had a form.

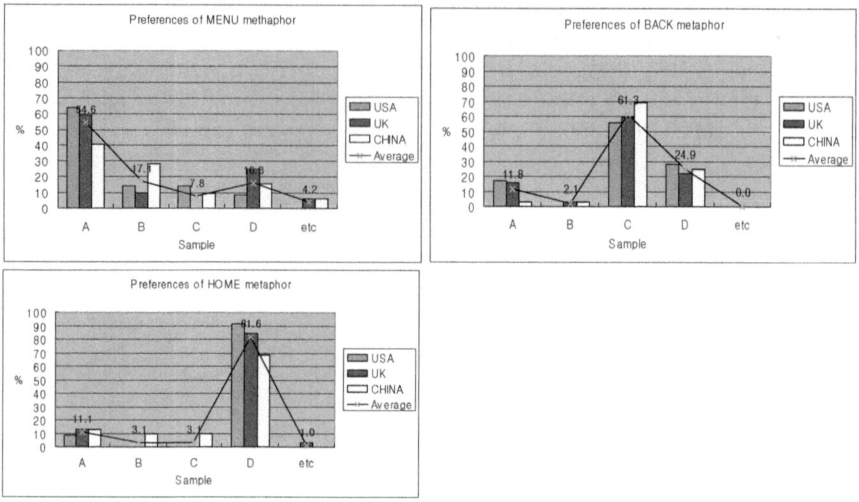

Fig. 3. This graph is showing an preference of "MENU", "BACK", and "HOME" metaphor

Analyzing the graph, the characteristic and global items by country are apparent. It has been believed that the simple configuration items of objects b, c and d would be mostly preferred. However, there were some parts showing different results in accordance with linguistic or cultural aspects of each country. In the items for (1) MENU, the letter 'M' from the word 'MENU' was selected more than the letter 'M' from the word Metaphor, However, 28.1% of people also chose (b) in China due to the influence of Chinese cultural spheres. It has been explained that (b) was selected because it was similarly associated with a certain Chinese letter (the character representing the catalogue). In the case of (2)'s BACK metaphor, the concept of RETURN (reverse movement of time) was well expressed predominantly by demonstrating the rotation of counterclockwise direction' this was selected a lot. In the case of (3) HOME, the participants absolutely preferred the classical metaphor expressing the characteristic chimney and roof of home to the simplification. '#' design used the HOME function in phone button and new forms of metaphors designed by simplifying a house were not chosen by many people because there was no pre-learning effect. It has been assumed that the HOME metaphor effect has been influenced by Internet Explorer (Copyright © Microsoft Corp) or other well-known metaphors. As such, 'Shape' was determined not only by observing an object, but also by something more. The experience of the present moment is never independent from others. It signifies the latest things among numerous sensory experiences that has happened in one's life time. Therefore, new images would enter the traces of memory for shapes sensed in the past. Since the meaning of a sign is entirely determined by the establishment of its rules of use, the meaning of any sign can – at least in principle – be fully established by an objective investigation [3].

When looking at characteristics in the USA, China and the United Kingdom, the items understood as the metaphors of universal design were compatible with the selected items related to each country's characteristic metaphors. Based on these differences, it would be necessary for input method designers to overcome mentioned differences, interpret others and make their optimal design.

4 Conclusion and Future Work

Most users have an ability to recognize and distinguish metaphors by experience and education in operating other devices. However, there were some test items that revealed the differences in users in terms of learning, a country's distinctiveness and the ability to understand symbols in the existing devices. From this fact and the descriptions of respondents' subjective opinions, it has been found that the influence on people by actual standard products in specific devices with high market occupancy rates has an impact on their recognition ability. As such, it should be possible for the metaphors used in hand-held device to be easily accessible and recognizable to users who have never used it before. Meanwhile, product manufacturers should benchmark and apply it to users from various classes and countries [4, 5]. In order to do so, it would be necessary to find out the best possible form. That should be overcome and improved by realizing different recognition methods or differences due to variations in learning effects or mental models for each country, in the case of manufacturing and selling global products [5]. The meaning of symbols shall be determined thoroughly by the establishment of their using principles. For this reason, theoretical meaning can at least be built up completely by this objective survey [1]. It is believed that the findings obtained from this study will be beneficial to the design process and the direction of outcomes in end-user products released in global markets.

References

1. Heinz Kroehl. 2,000 Communication Design. ABC veriag. Zurich (1987)
2. Weiss, S.: Hand-held Usability. John Wiley & Sons, Ltd. Chichester, West Sussex, England (2002)
3. Arnheim. R.: Art and Visual Perception. University of California Press. 1 edn. (2004)
4. Lindhlom, C., Keinonen, T., Kiljander, H.: Mobile Usability. McGraw-Hill, New York, USA (2003)
5. http://msdn.microsoft.com/library/default.asp?url=/library/en-us/dnwue/html/ch02b.asp
http://msdn.microsoft.com/library/default.asp?url=/library/en-us/dnwue/html/ch14f.asp
http://msdn.microsoft.com/library/default.asp?url=/library/en-us/dnwxp/html/winxpicons.asp

Positional Mapping Multi-tap for Myanmar Language

Ye Kyaw Thu and Yoshiyori Urano

Graduate School of Global Information and Telecommunication Studies (GITS),
Waseda University, Tokyo, Japan
ykt@akane.waseda.jp, urano@waseda.jp

Abstract. This paper is an attempt to enable a practical and efficient composing of message text with Myanmar language on a mobile phone. In this paper, we propose a new idea of key mapping (Positional Mapping) for Myanmar language. Positional Mapping is the key mapping idea for mobile phones based on Myanmar language characters writing positions. We compared our new mapping idea with our proposed Multi-tap keypad layout in terms of key strokes and users tapping speed. Although key strokes requirement for typing Myanmar consonants in Positional Mapping is higher, average tapping speed is 22.5% faster than Multi-tap model. And we can also prove that our Positional Mapping idea is simple and easier to memorize for users from the user studies. Our Positional Mapping idea can be applied not only to Myanmar language but also to other similar phonetic based languages such as Khamer, Thai, Hindi and Bangla etc.

Keywords: Text Input, User Interface, Positional Mapping, Human Computer Interface in Mobile, Mobile Phone Keypad Layout, Myanmar Language.

1 Introduction

One of the Developing countries Myanmar (Burma) started Short Message Service (SMS) for local people officially in October 2, 2005. However, the service is provided only for English language, and SMS for Myanmar language is necessary. We proposed Multi-tap keypad layout for Myanmar language mobile phones in October 19, 2005 [1]. But we noticed that our proposed Multi-tap keypad layout has some limitations from the follow-up analyses. They are mapping one button (i.e. Number 3 Button) for the "rarely used Myanmar consonants" and assigning many "vowel symbols, killer stroke, tone marks etc." only on one button (i.e. Number 8 Button). These factors lead to reduce users tapping speed in Myanmar language SMS. We believe that key mapping or keypad layout is very important to get efficient tapping speed for multi-tap input methods. And thus, we continued our research.

In this paper, we propose a new key mapping concept for multi-tap input methods. We named it "Positional Mapping" (PM) because key mapping is logically based on Myanmar language characters writing position. By using PM concept, we can create very user friendly key assignments, which enable novice users to type Myanmar sentences faster than our proposed multi-tap model.

J. Jacko (Ed.): Human-Computer Interaction, Part II, HCII 2007, LNCS 4551, pp. 486–495, 2007.

2 Myanmar Language

Myanmar Script has been a majority language of Myanmar for over 1000 years old. It is the official language in Myanmar. It belongs to the Tibeto-Burman language family and derives from Sino-Tibetan. Myanmar alphabets adapted the Mon script in the 8th century. Myanmar language has various types of characters comparing with English. i.e. consonants, dependent vowels or medials, independent vowels, finals and stack characters or conjunction alphabets etc. And Myanmar language contains many Pali words especially for religious things such as praying. Despite great differences in appearance and detail, the Myanmar script follows the same basic principle as Devanagari. Overall writing direction is from left to right. In a Myanmar sentence, spaces are used to mark phrases, not dividing words.

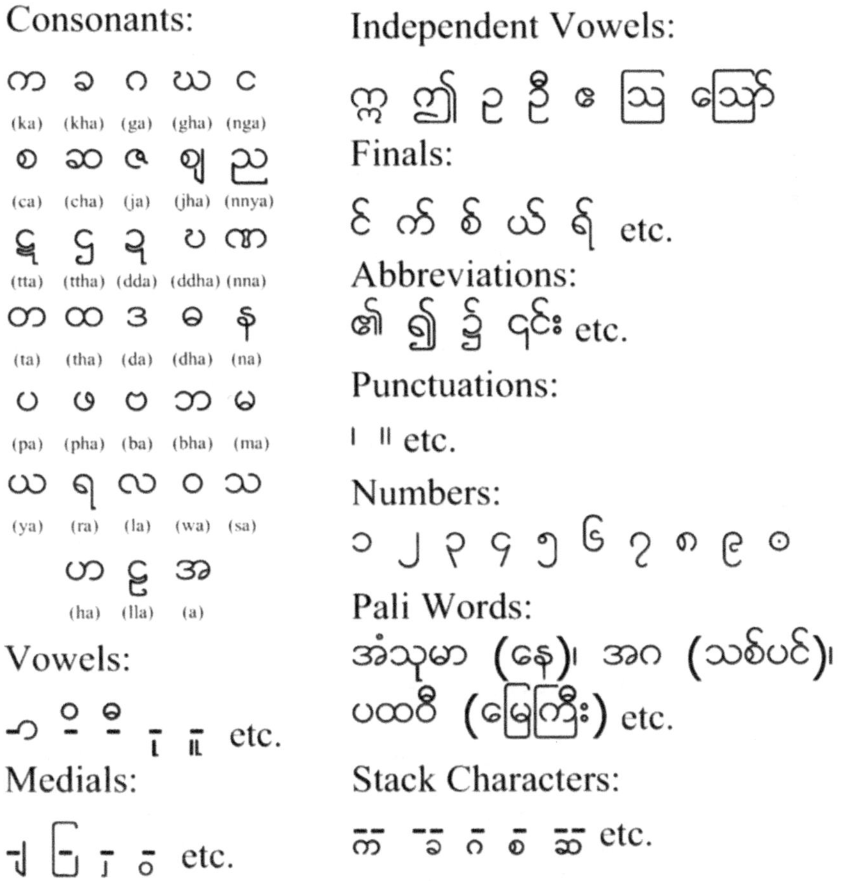

Fig. 1. Myanmar language (Consonants, Vowels, Medials, Independent Vowels, Finals, Abbreviations, Punctuation, Numbers, Pali Words and Stack Characters)

3 Mobile Phone Keypad and Multi-tap Input Method

Mobile phone keypads contain 12 standard keys and these keys are usually laid out in a 3×4 matrix. They are number keys 0-9 and two additional keys (* and #). Text entry on a mobile phone is based on these 12 keys. In English, the letters "a to z" are spread over keys 2-9 in alphabetic order, and "space character" is often assigned to the number 0 key, but this varies depending on the mobile phone.

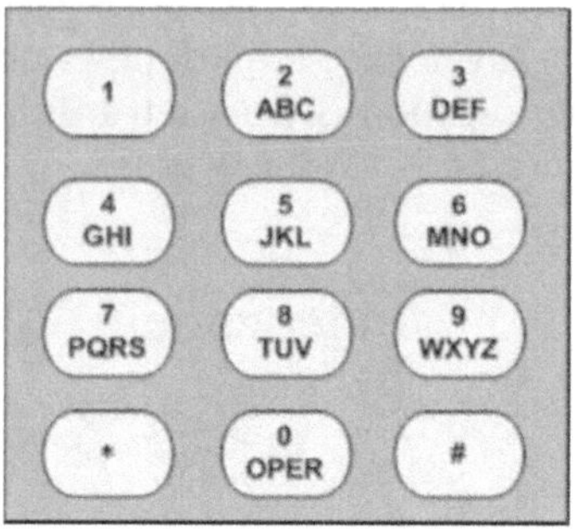

Fig. 2. The standard 12 key mobile phone keypad

With traditional "Multi-tap" input method, users press each key one or more times to get the desired letter. For example, the 3 key is pressed once for the letter'd', twice for 'e' and three times for 'f'. One of the problems arises in Multi-tap when users attempt to enter more than one letter from the same key consecutively. For example, to type the word "moon", we have to break the number 6 rotation sequence because the letters 'm', 'n' and 'o' are on the 6 key. To overcome this, Multi-tap employs "timeout" (usually 1-2 seconds) or "timeout kill button" (usually down arrow or right arrow key). In "timeout" method, users need to wait the timeout, and on the other hand, in the "timeout kill button" method, users can break the key sequence by pressing timeout kill button. Some mobile phones use a combination of the two solutions. Another drawback of Multi-tap is the keystrokes per character (KSPC), which increase based on the number of letters assignment on a key.

4 Proposed Multi-tap Keypad Layout for Myanmar Language

This method works by cycling through letters on a key with each successive press. In our proposed Multi-tap input method, we assigned consonants to key 1 to 7 according to traditional alphabetic order (refer to Fig.1). Here, 1-key is assigned for Myanmar letter Ka, Kha, Ga, Gha, Nga, 2-key is assigned for Myanmar letter Ca, Cha, Ja, Jha, Nnya and so on. Other symbols such as "killer stroke", "vowel symbols", "tone marks" are assigned on 8-key. "Conjunct consonants" or "stack characters" are assigned on 9-key and others are assigned on remains keys on the keypad.

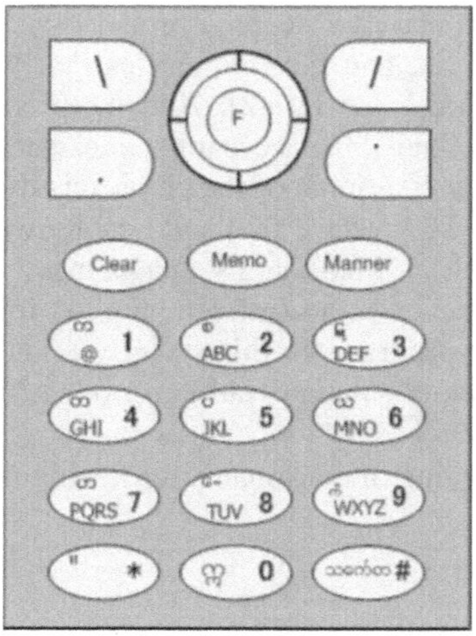

Fig. 3. Our proposed Multi-tap keypad layout for Myanmar language

5 Multi-tap with Consonants Ordered by Usage Frequency (Multi-tap Frequency)

In this model, in order to get higher tapping speed, we change the order of Myanmar consonant letters (key 1 to key 7) based on the usage frequency. Although this idea is well known for English, it is the very first attempt for Myanmar language.

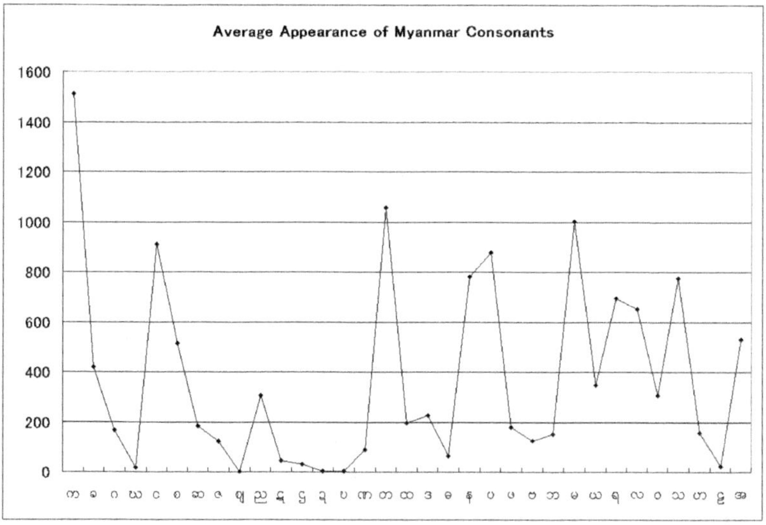

Fig. 4. Average appearance of Myanmar consonants "Ka" to "A" (X axis represents 33 Myanmar consonants, and Y axis represents numbers of characters)

Here the problem is that there has been no proper usage frequency table for either Myanmar letters or words yet, and the frequencies that we use in this paper is the result of our experiments made so far [2]. And there is no encoding standard for Myanmar language either. And thus, we cannot make text processing like sorting, searching and word breaking etc. Some of the characters drop out when we copy from one application to another. To produce frequency table, we have to start from typing many Myanmar books such as dictionaries, magazines and cartoons etc. Then we produced the average frequency table (refer to Fig. 4) for Myanmar consonants by using our developed utility program. In this stage, we can only consider frequencies of consonants due to the lack of standardization for other Myanmar characters such as medials (e.g. in the case of '‑ြ': '‑ာ'+'‑ှ' (or) '‑ါ' + '‑ှ' (or) separate character '‑ြ'). We consider frequency ordering of consonants for Positional Mapping Model also.

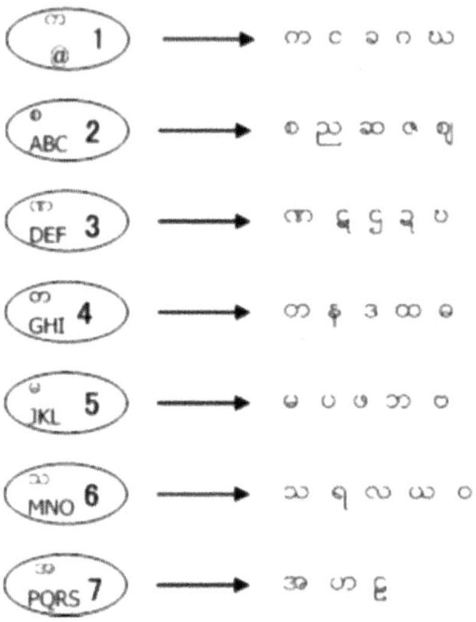

Fig. 5. Key mapping in order of usage frequency

6 Multi-tap with Positional Mapping (Multi-tap PM)

In this model, key assignment is based on Myanmar language writing system. When we make an analysis on Myanmar sentences, basically we can consider that Myanmar characters are written in three levels (up, normal, under) and most of the characters have their defined positions (e.g. T have to be written as front vowel, -T, --T, -T, -T, -T, -T, -T etc. should be written as a lower vowel and -T, -T and -ံ etc. should be written as an upper vowel and '‑ာ' and '‑ျ' etc. should be written right side of the consonants). But there are several exceptional cases, e.g. although consonant T (ka) is usually written in the normal level, when it becomes 'subscripted ka'

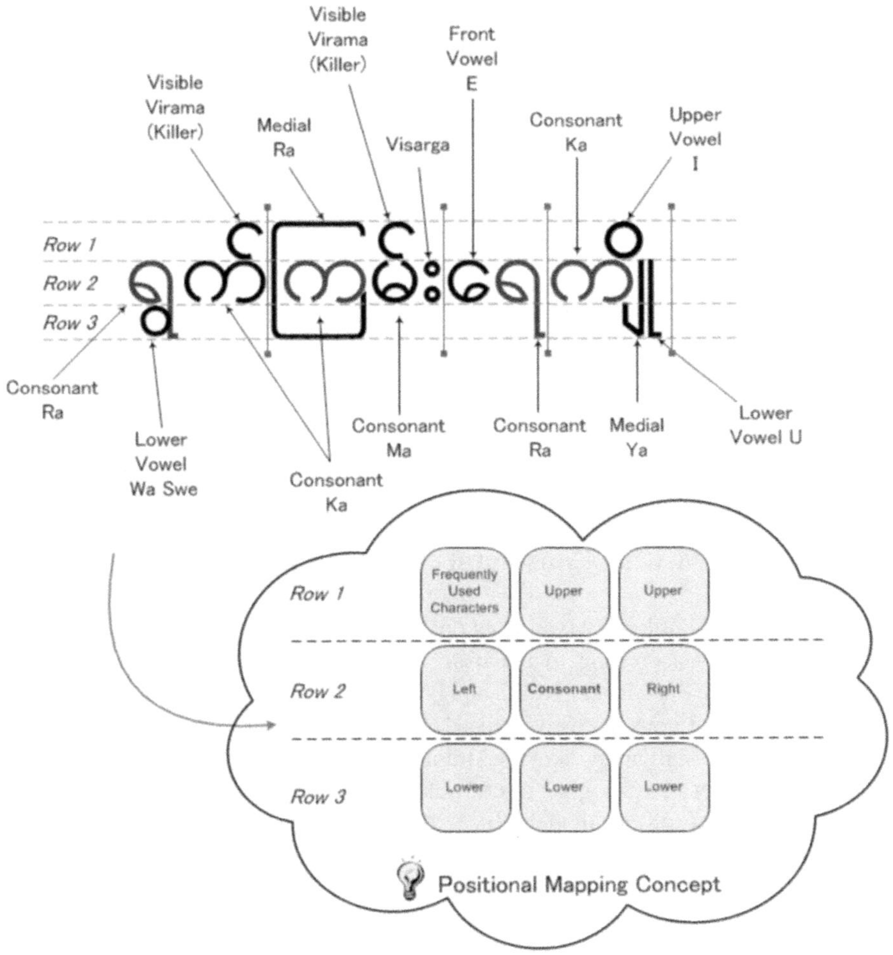

Fig. 6. Concept of Positional Mapping for Myanmar language

or 'stack character' it becomes smaller than normal ka and written in the lower level as '[illegible]' in '[illegible]'.

We divide mobile phone keypad into three levels, e.g. 1, 2 and 3 keys are upper, 4, 5 and 6 keys are normal or center and 7, 8 and 9 keys are under. In the normal level, 4 key is seen as the front part, 5 key as the center position and 6 key as the rear part. According to the Myanmar language writing method, we assigned upper vowels at 2 and 3 keys, front vowels on 4, main consonant on 5 key, rear vowels on 6 keys and lower vowels on 7, 8 and 9 keys. Here, the consonants will be shown as a list. We assigned "frequently used Myanmar characters and words" such as 'ပါ', 'လား', 'ကျော်', 'ထို', 'ဟို', 'ငါ', 'သူ', 'ကျမ' and 'ဒီ' etc. at number 1 key. The detail of the key mapping is as follows:

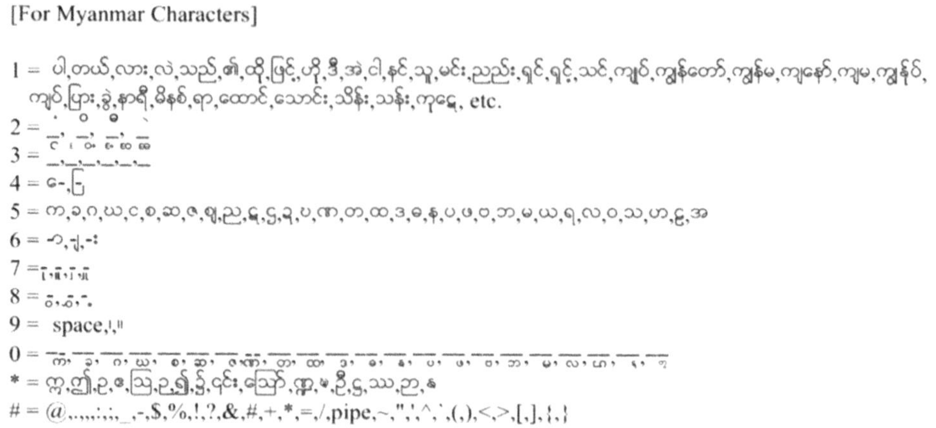

Fig. 7. Myanmar letters assignment for Multi-tap Positional Mapping

7 Multi-tap PM with Consonants Ordered by Usage Frequency

In this model, we reordered Myanmar consonants Ka to A (i.e. key mapping change only on No.5 key) according to the usage frequency. Other key mappings are the same as Multi-tap PM. Both "Multi-tap PM" and "Multi-tap PM with Frequency" display all of the 33 consonants as a list. Users have to specify the desired consonant by using navigational arrow keys. Although this kind of interface can increase required keystrokes, it can give easier selection by navigational arrow keys. And comparing with Multi-tap models (i.e. Multi-tap and Multi-tap Frequency), key assignments for "vowel symbols, killer stroke, tone marks etc." fairly spread over keys 2, 3, 4, 6, 7, 8 and 9 according to Myanmar letters writing positions. We assume that this assignment is better than our proposed Multi-tap because some of the keys only assigned 2 or 3 characters (e.g. key 4, key 6, key 8 and key 9) and it will reduce requirement of keystrokes.

8 User Study and Evaluations

To evaluate the performance, we developed a simulation program for four Multi-tap input interfaces. The simulation program is developed with Microsoft Visual Studio .Net 2003. The program uses configuration files or key mapping files to change four input methods. We made a user study with 5 native participants who are between 23 and 31 years old. We gave 20 minutes practice time for each user to learn four Multi-tap input methods (i.e. 5 minutes for each model). Then, we recorded the total time spent to type 6 sentences Myanmar SMS message (including error correction time) for 10 times. And 7 days longitudinal study was performed for 4 Multi-tap models, with slowest tapping user of 10 times experiments. The tapping

(a)
အအာဣဤဥဦဧအဲဩဪအံအား
အအာအိအီအုအူအေအဲအောအော်အံအား
ကကာကိကီကုကူကေကဲကောကော်ကံကား

(c)
သူငယ်ချင်း၊
မတွေ့ရတာကြာပြီနော်။
နေကောင်းရဲ့လား။
ငါ့ဖုန်းနံပါတ်အသစ်က၅၀၀၇၄၅၉၊
အားတဲ့အခါဖုန်းပြန်ဆက်ကွာ။
ဒါပဲနော်။

(b)
ပါတယ်လားလဲသည်၏ထိုဖြင့်
ဟိုဒီအဲငါနင်သူမင်းညည်းရှင်
ရှင့်သင်ကျုပ်ကျွန်တော်ကျွန်မ
ကျနော်ကျမကျပ်ပြားခွဲနာရီ
မိနစ်ရာထောင်သောင်းသိန်း
သန်းကုဋေ

(d)
တက္ကသိုလ်၊ဝဏ္ဏ၊ဥက္ကာ၊ဥက္ကဋ္ဌ၊ဝိဇ္ဇာ၊
သိပ္ပံ၊ဗြဟ္မာ၊လက္ခဏာ၊ဝေဿန္တရာ၊
ယောက္ခမ။

Fig. 8. Myanmar text for user experiments (a) A, Ar, I, II etc. (b) some frequently used Myanmar words (c) short Myanmar SMS message (d) stack words

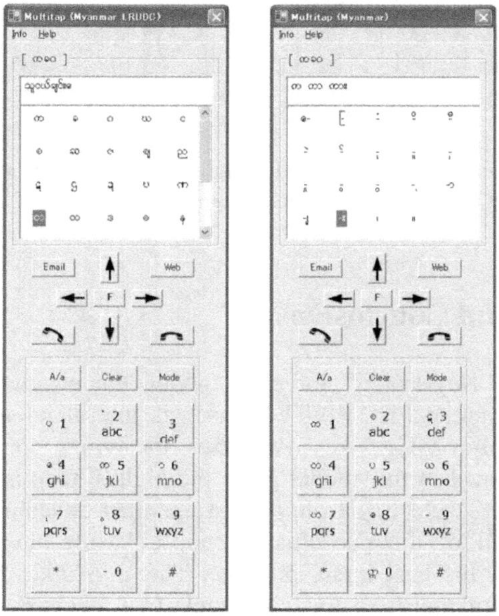

Fig. 9. Simulation program for user study (left: running with Multi-tap PM configuration file, right: running with Proposed Multi-tap configuration file)

speed improvement for each model can be seen in Figure 11. We also made analysis on keystroke requirements of each model for Myanmar consonants "Ka to A", Myanmar vowels "A, Ar, I, II etc", some frequently used Myanmar words, short Myanmar SMS message and some of the selected stack words (PaikSint).

Table 1. The maximum tapping speed (min:sec) for four Multi-tap Models by 5 native users

Input Method	User1	User2	User3	User4	User5
Multi-tap	6:52	9:33	6:15	5:15	4:26
Multi-tap (Frequency)	5:42	6:56	5:58	4:47	5:13
Multi-tap (PM)	4:29	4:43	4:16	4:24	4:20
Multi-tap (PM Frequency)	4:17	4:00	4:18	4:03	4:04

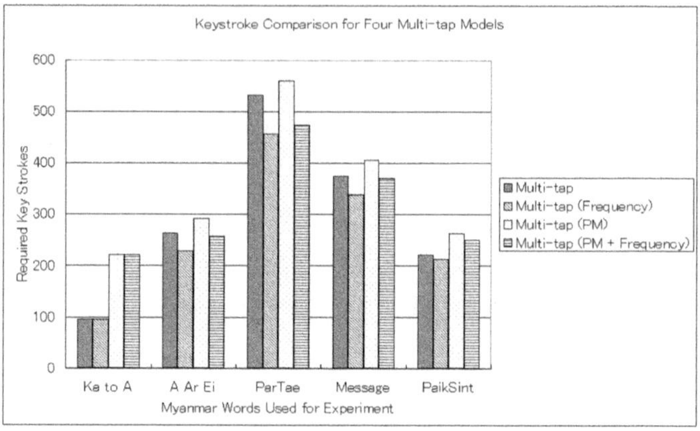

Fig. 10. Keystrokes comparison for four Multi-tap models (Here X axis represents Myanmar characters group, word groups and simple SMS message etc. and Y axis represents required keystrokes)

9 Discussions and Conclusions

When we compare "Keystrokes" for each model, the positional mapping requires more keystrokes. (refer to Fig. 10) The reason is that all of the 33 consonants are assigned as a list only on No.5 key. And thus, the typing consonants require some arrow keys movement. But this model gives the highest tapping speed because users can type consonants by selecting from the list. Another advantage of this model is its user friendliness. All of the participants choose "Multi-tap (PM)" or "Multi-tap (PM+Frequency)" as the best input interface. The keystrokes can be reduced if we assign second layer of multi-tap for consonants (e.g. change to Multi-tap mode for consonants by pressing number 5 key). Another option to increase tapping speed is the combination with predictive text input. We believe that positional mapping idea can be applied not only to Myanmar language but also to other similar phonetic based languages such as Khmer and Bangla etc.

In this paper, we did all of the user experiments using with simulation program and computer mouse. User tapping speed can go up with real mobile phones. We are now preparing to make user study with real mobile phones. From the result of user experiments, it is proved that Positional Mapping is easier to memorize and can give appropriate tapping speed (around 22.5% faster than proposed Multi-tap).

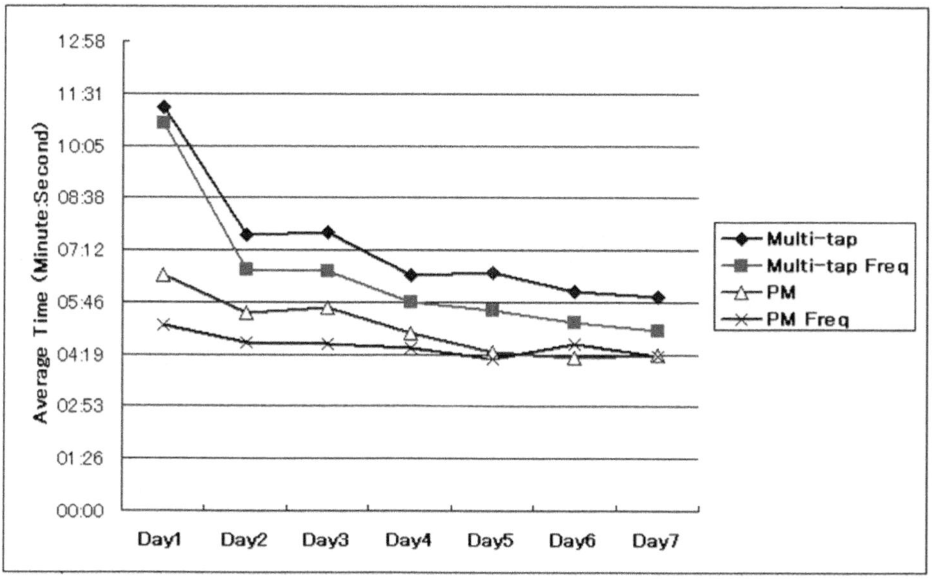

Fig. 11. Tapping speed improvement of slowest users for 4 Multi-tap input methods (lower values are better tapping speed)

Acknowledgments. This research was supported by Prof. URANO Lab., Graduate School of Global Information and Telecommunication Studies, Waseda University, Tokyo, Japan. We would like to give special thanks to 'Mr. Ye Kyaw Thein' (younger brother of Ye Kyaw Thu) who assisted us in information gathering and experiments.

References

1. Thu, Y.K., URANO. Y.: Development of Efficient Input Methods for Myanmar Language SMS. In: Global Information and Telecommunication Open Research Paper Reading, October 19, 2005 Honjo Campus, Graduate School of Global Information and Telecommunication Studies (GITS), Waseda University, Honjo, Japan, pp. 4–5 (2005)
2. Thu, Y.K., URANO, Y.:Text entry for Myanmar language SMS: Proposal of 3 Possible Input Methods, Simulation and Analysis. In: Proceeding of 4th International Conference on Computer Application (ICCA), Yangon, Myanmar, pp. 199–207 (2006)
3. MacKenzie, I.S., Soukoreff, R.W.: Text entry for mobile computing. Models and methods, theory and practice, Human-Computer Interaction 17, 147–198 (2002)
4. MacKenzie, I.S.: KSPC, (keystrokes per character) as a characteristic of text entry techniques. In: Proceedings of the Fourth International Symposium on Human-Computer Interaction with Mobile Devices, pp. 195–210.Springer-Verlag Heidelberg, Germany

Pen-Based User Interface Based on Handwriting Force Information

ZhongCheng Wu[1,2], LiPing Zhang[2,3], and Fei Shen[1,2]

[1] Hefei Hign Magnetic Field Laboratory,PRC, Hefei, 230031 Anhui, China
[2] Institute of Intelligent Machines, CAS, Hefei, 230031 Anhui, China
[3] Department of Automation, University of Science & Technology of China, Hefei, 230026 Anhui, China
zcwu@iim.ac.cn, lpzhang@mail.ustc.edu.cn, shenfei@iim.ac.cn

Abstract. Pen-based computing attracts many researchers recent years. Pen-computer generally uses pen tip position and pen pressure information at present. Actually, the force between the pen tip and writing plate is a three-dimensional vector, which represents more important information in the process of writing. In this paper we firstly describe an innovative force sensitive device (F-Tablet) for pen-based computing, and it can acquire three perpendicular forces and position of the pen-tip simultaneously. The second part deals with problems of Pen-User Interface design based on this tablet. Experimental results show that this pen-user interface considers context awareness and some characteristics of user cognition. Furthermore the pen-user interface can complete most functions of keyboard and mouse.

Keywords: Pen-based computing, Pen-computer, Pen-User Interface, handwriting.

1 Introduction

Handwriting is an input modality that is very familiar to most users since everyone learns to write as he/she begins to study. As one of natural human forms of communication (e.g. handwriting, speech, and gesture), using pen to communicate with computer is becoming commonplace and pen-based computing has held promise for decades. It has a rich history of innovative hardware and software solutions as human computer interface (HCI) [1].

The earliest technology in pen computing can be traced back to 1957, when T. L. Dimond presented a device called "Stylator" which could read handwritten characters. After that, more tablet and stylus devices were developed for handwriting data acquisition on-line. Pen-based data acquisition devices include I-pen (Inductum) [2], Virtual Pen (GOU Lite) [3], E-Pen (InMotion) [4], N-scribe (Digital Ink) [5] and Compupen (Pen2Net) [6] etc. To tablet-based data acquisition device, Wacom tablets [7] and ePad-ink [8] are two commercially popular tablets on the market. Tablet PCs employ Wacom's authorized sensor technology [9]. All these handwriting devices have

J. Jacko (Ed.): Human-Computer Interaction, Part II, HCII 2007, LNCS 4551, pp. 496–503, 2007.

the common ability to acquire pen movement as sequences of pen tip positions in succession. Some of them have sensors for pen pressure and inclination information acquisition additionally. As we know Handwriting is the trajectory of the writing pen's contact movement on the writing surface driven by writing forces, So writing forces are one of the most important information of writing dynamics and many researches have been done on them. Crane and Ostrem developed a three-dimension force-sensitive pen to get the writing forces [10]. Shimizu developed an electrical pen using two-dimensional optical angle sensor to get writing forces [11]. But most devices can only get the writing pressure.

In this paper, we present an F-tablet as pen-computer interface input system. It can acquire kinematics and kinetics handwriting information of pen tip, including strokes of pen-up and pen-down, velocity and acceleration of pen-tip, three dimension forces of pen-plate contacting point and shape of character etc ïï ï ïïïIn the following Pen-User Interface based on F-Tablet is described in detail. The pen user interface is composed of two work mode: pen script mode and pen control mode. The former one mainly handles with pen input and the latter controls pen cursor move and activates pen click events. Thus it can implement most functions of keyboard and mouse.

2 F-Tablet

As handwriting is the process of human hand acting on contacting plate (such as paper) with pen, the writing information includes pen-tip trajectory, contacting force direction and amplitude. Up to now various pen-computing devices cannot acquire all those information simultaneously. In our design a force sensitive tablet named F-Tablet (Fig.1) is capable of capturing three perpendicular forces of the pen-tip to the contacting plane and torques in two directions directly with a multi-dimension force/torque sensor. Furthermore, with the specially designed structure, the static trajectory of the pen-tip on the writing plane and the other dynamic information such as the velocities, accelerations and slants of the pen-tip can be calculated indirectly [12]. The device is connected to computer via USB interface with a maximum sample rate of 120Hz. And there is no special requirement on the writing pen.

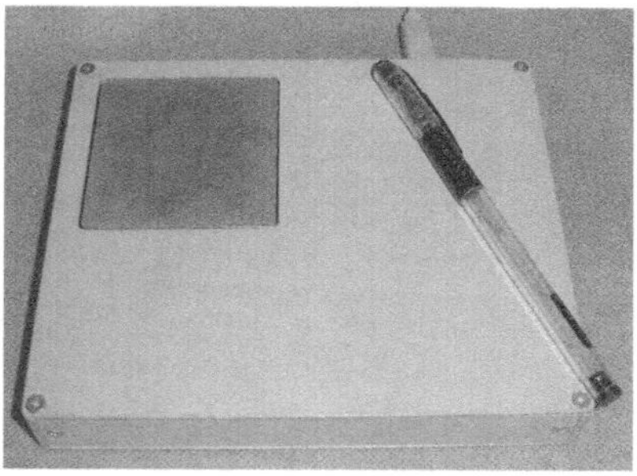

Fig. 1. Photo of the F-Tablet

When a pen writes on the input tablet at point p (Fig.2), force F can be decomposed into forces in three perpendicular directions $F_x(t_i)$ $F_y(t_i)$ $F_z(t_i)$. At the same time, $M_x(t_i)$ and $M_y(t_i)$ are also measured directly by the multi-dimension force/torque sensor. These five elements are all functions of time t_i. The coordinates ($x_p(\mathrm{t_i})$, $y_p(\mathrm{t_i})$) of the point p can be calculated from the equilibrium of moments. They can be expressed as (1):

$$x_p(\mathrm{t_i}) = \frac{M_y(\mathrm{t_i}) - F_x(\mathrm{t_i}) \cdot h}{F_z(\mathrm{t_i})} \quad . \qquad (1)$$
$$y_p(\mathrm{t_i}) = \frac{-M_x(\mathrm{t_i}) - F_y(\mathrm{t_i}) \cdot h}{F_z(\mathrm{t_i})}$$

Where h denotes the distance between the input tablet and the origin of the coordinate.

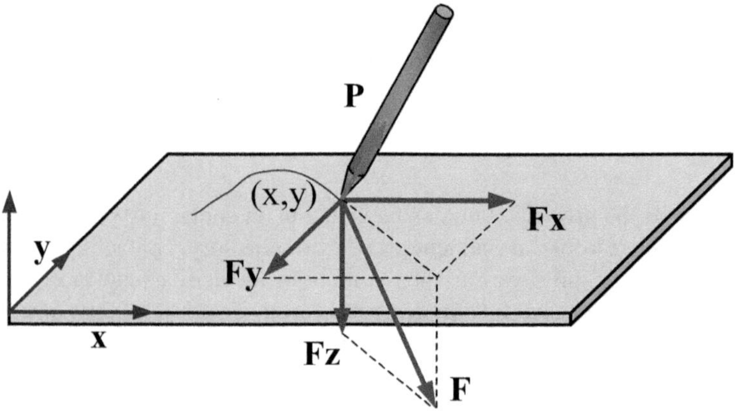

Fig. 2. Schematic Diagram of Force Action

Fig.3 displays the handwriting of Chinese "中" and its forces information acquired by the F-Tablet.

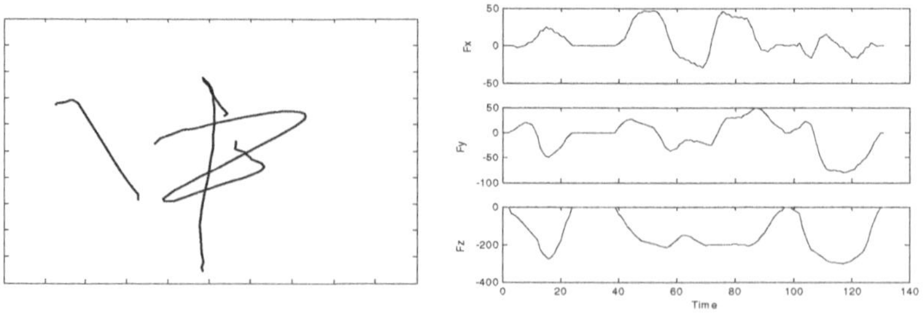

Fig. 3. The Chinese "中" by F-tablet and its force curves

3 Pen-User Interface

While markets or labs have invented various type pen-computing devices, computer users also need a bridge to help them interact with pen computers. This section will introduce the detailed design of our pen user interface. Given the merits and some disadvantages of F-Tablet, this paper would like to split the pen user interface into two parts. The first part mainly concerns on how to write characters naturally by the F-Tablet although the writing area is not big enough as Wacom or Hanwang, while the second one introduces how to implement pen clicks and pen cursor movement called pen control mode in this paper.

3.1 Pen Script Mode

In this mode, pen user interface mainly concerns on handwriting related. Authors divide the writing into five zones in this mode which is described in Fig.4. Each zone manages a specific task and the width of all zones except the largest zone is the $1/15^{th}$ length of writing pad in below.

Zone one mainly enables users switch to pen control mode when users click. It is note that users need to click the zone one for a while at begin in order to filter noise signals or other error motions. Similarly, zone two, three and four need the same operations. The location of zone one has two choices in our pen user interface. The default is on the left side of the writing pad. Because most users are right hand privilege, the left side is rarely touched. Of course, if the user is a left hand privilege, the zone one location could also be set on the left side by users and the zone three will be set on the left side.

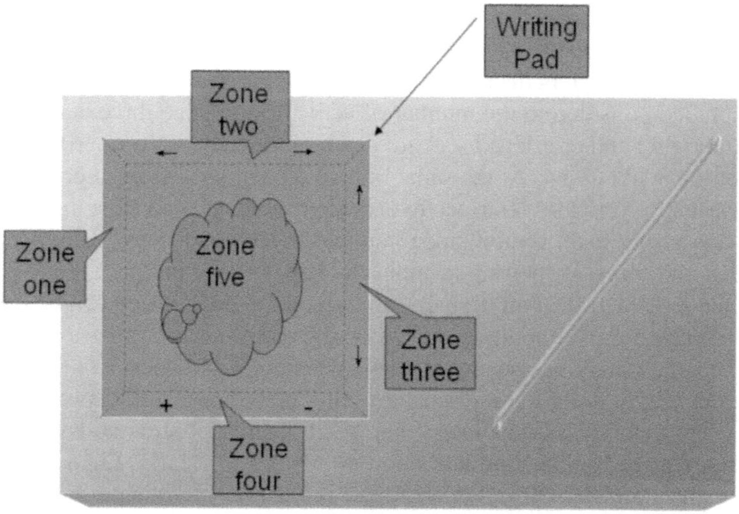

Fig. 4. Schematic Diagram of Zone Division of Pen Script Mode

Zone two takes charge of left or right slide of writing region and the left part of zone two makes writing region slide to left, while if users want the writing region slide to right, they could click the right one. Figure 4 shows the writing region which is a white square on the screen.

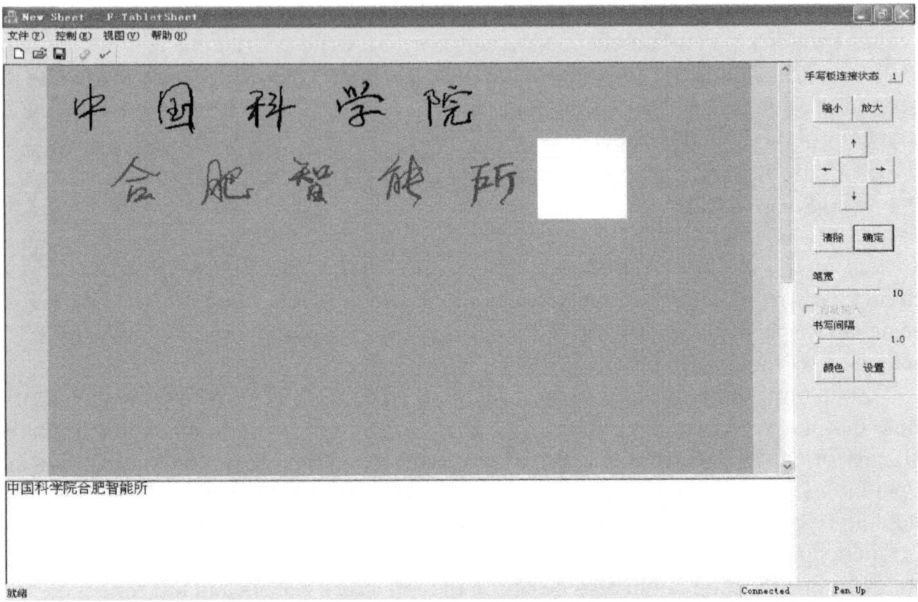

Fig. 5. Writing Region

Zone three is responsible for up or down slide of writing region on the screen shown as Fig.5. Like zone two, the upper part of zone three enable the writing region slide up and the lower region offers the contrary function.

Additionally, considering the number of activation of zone three is more than zone one and the right hand privilege users are much more than left hand privilege people, a default set looks like Fig.4. At the same time, if a user is a left hand privilege, the pen user interface also provides interface to exchange zone one and zone three.

Zone five is the main region since handwriting is input here. This paper utilizes coordinates and forces of pen tip to input the handwriting on the screen. When users write on the F-Tablet, the real time coordinates and forces of pen can be captured, so handwriting can be easily rendered based on the real time coordinates. Unfortunately, this type of handwriting has no any aesthetic perception and does not look like Chinese character. Hence, in order to render handwriting more beautiful, this paper uses z-axis force (F_z) to embody the blackness and width degree of strokes. Users write more powerful, stokes of handwriting will be more black and clearly. Fig.6 shows Chinese characters and corresponding 3-Axis force and 2-dim coordinate curves. From the shape of the character, we can see that not only the trajectory of the pen, but also the writing style of the writer is recorded.

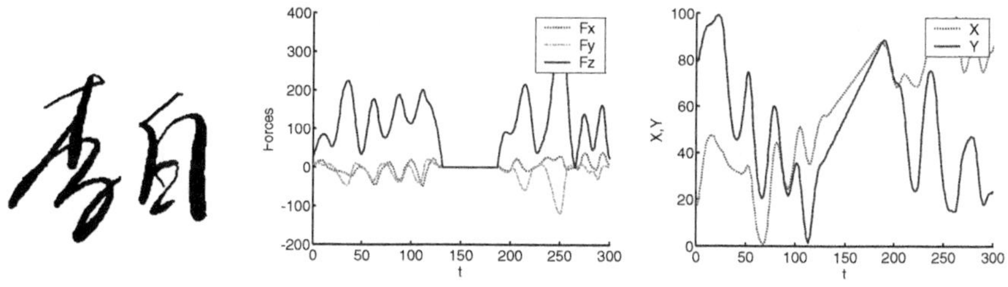

(a) (b) (c)

Fig. 6. 3-Axis force (b) and 2-dim coordinate(c) curves of Chinese Handwriting (a)

3.2 Pen Control Mode

Every graphic user interface user is familiar with mouse or cursors with which users could control computers visually. Considering clicks and cursors are still effective in most selection/check events, this paper on one hand inherits the advantages of clicks and cursors, on the other hand, provides users much usabilities for avoiding so many switches between mouse and keyboard when in the graphic user interaction. Hence, the next work has to complete is to implement the pen clicks (double clicks) and pen cursor movement.

Because all information of F-Tablet has only one communication channel, it is very important to recognize pen click information, pen cursor movement signal or other usable information exactly. This paper proposes the design as below. Firstly, authors divide the script pad into four regions as Fig.7 describes. In that way, according to the pen tip position, pen user interface could reorganize and do what users want exactly.

Like pen script mode, the zone width except zone four is the 1/15th length of writing pad.

Zone one enables users switch to pen script mode as the function of zone one of pen script mode.

The functions of zone two and zone three are similar. As human beings are not good at drawing erect lines, it is difficult when human beings want to control the pen cursors move erectly. In addition, in some fine control situations, noise of F-Tablet can not be neglected. According to that, the pen cursor can only slide left or right direction horizontally with a stable slide rate similar as the ←or→ key on keyboards when users click the left or right part of zone two. Similarly, zone three provides a stable rate, vertical up or down direction slide as ↑ or ↓key works.

Zone four mainly completes pen clicks, namely pen double clicks, and pen cursor movement. The idea of pen clicks is simple. If F-Tablet senses two or more than two clicks in a short given time, double click action will be executed. The event of clicks can be detected when the value of F_z is higher than pre-defined threshold.

It is not difficult to complete pen cursor move. Depending on (2) and the velocities of pen to move the cursor, the pen user interface can control the cursor easily.

$$\begin{aligned} CursorPos.x &= Cursorpos.x + ratio * \Delta x \\ CursorPos.y &= CursorPos.y + ratio * \Delta y \end{aligned} \quad (2)$$

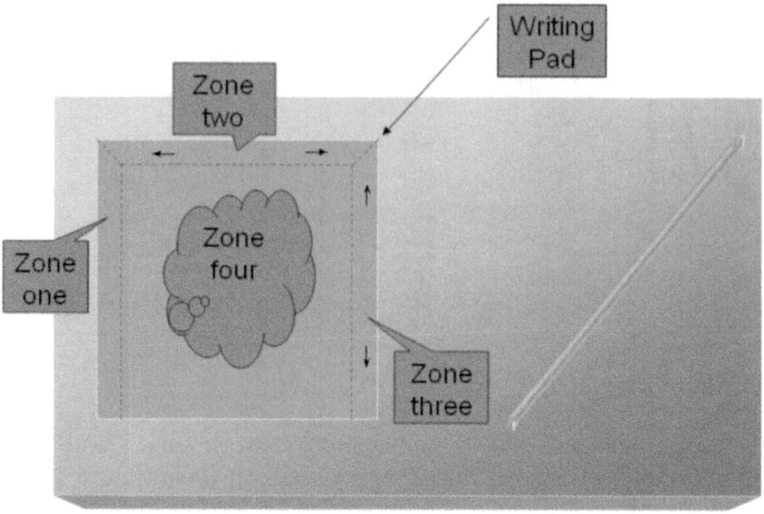

Fig. 7. Schematic Diagram of Zone Division of Pen Control Mode

Where $ratio$ is a given threshold and Δx , Δy are calculated by the distances and velocities of pen.

By the way, the ratio is not fixed because when user moves pen cursor fast, generally speaking, they want the cursor reach the region they expect soon. Therefore, the faster velocity of cursors is, the higher the ratio value is.

However there emerges a problem. The two actions, including pen double clicks and pen cursor controls are coupling, as a result, the pen user interface has to separate the action accurately. Fortunately, pen double clicks and pen cursor control action are easy to be separated since a double click is a low-high-low-high-low signal procedure while pen cursor moves just a low-high-low procedure. The extra low-high-low signal provides pen user interface enough information to discriminate from pen double clicks and pen cursor move.

4 Conclusion

The paper describes the F-Tablet, which can acquire the kinematics and kinetics information of human handwriting, including strokes of pen-up and pen-down, pen nib trajectory and three-axis forces of pen tip directly and simultaneously. Then a new pen user interface has been designed based on the merits and some disadvantages of F-Tablet. With this interface, users not only can control pen clicks and pen cursor movement but also input handwriting naturally. The experimental results show that the interface is effective and natural. Next step in our work, we will pay more attention on the potential advantages of pen computing in relation to applications.

Acknowledgement. The work was supported in part by a grant No.60475005 and No.60575058 from the Nature Science Foundation of China.

References

1. Jarrett, R., Su, P.: Tablet Computing Comes of Age. Building Tablet PC Applications, Microsoft Press (2003)
2. I-Pen Producer Homepage http://www.inductum.com
3. OTM Technology Overview http://www.otmtech.com
4. E-Pen documentation http://www.mediaforte.com.sg/products/graphic/epen/
5. N-Scribe Product documentation http://www.n-scribe.com/
6. MediPen, SciPen and NotePen Documentations http://www.compupen.com
7. Wacom Tablet PC Homepage, http://www.wacom/productinfo/
8. Cyber SIGN Inc. homepage http://www.cybersign.com
9. Microsoft Tablet PC Specification http://www.microsoft.com/tabletpc/
10. Crane, H.-D., Ostrem, J.-S.: Automatic Signature Verification Using a Three-Axis Force-Sensitive Pen. IEEE Transactions on Systems, Man, and Cybernetics 3, 329–333 (1983)
11. Shimizu, H., Kiyono, S., Motoki, T., Gao, W.: An electrical pen for signature verification using a two-dimensional optical angle sensor. Sensors and Actuators 111, 216–221 (2004)
12. Wu, Z.-C., Meng, M., Fang, P., Shen, F.: A Novel Force sensitive Tablet for Handwriting Information Acquisition. In: Li, S.Z., Lai, J.-H., Tan, T., Feng, G.-C., Wang, Y. (eds.) SINOBIOMETRICS 2004. LNCS, vol. 3338, pp. 654–662. Springer, Heidelberg (2004)

BetweenKeys: Looking for Room Between Keys

Youngwoo Yoon and Geehyuk Lee

School of Engineering, Information and Communications University,
119, Munji-ro, Yuseong-gu, Daejeon, Korea
{zeroyy,geehyuk}@icu.ac.kr

Abstract. A conventional keyboard has a large footprint because it should serve numerous functions with independent keys. With demand for smaller keyboards, the present paper analyzes a practical method that leverages overlap of two ordinary keys and may reduce the keyboard size. By analyzing overlap frequencies and key stroke timings in normal use, we investigated whether key overlaps are practically usable. From the results, four pairs are recommended that are practically available and preferred by users. Hangul / English mode transition is described as an application.

Keywords: keyboard, chord keyboard, key overlap, key stroke timing, Hangul / English toggling.

1 Introduction

Smaller computers require smaller keyboards. Except for extremely small computers such as mobile phones, however, the full-sized keyboard with a traditional layout is still the most favored. In order to accommodate such a keyboard in a small device such as a small notebook, omission of a few keys is inevitable. The problem with this approach is that uncommon keys, though not used frequently, are still important and must be supported in some other way. Our approach is to find room between keys. For instance, pressing two adjacent keys such as '1' and '2' together triggers 'F1' while 'j' and 'k' together triggers the Hangul mode key that allows input of Korean characters. In other words, we suggest assigning functions to the overlaps of ordinary keys. In addition to having a reduced number of keys, the resulting keyboard is expected to support more seamless typing, i.e. a reduction in the amount of finger movements to and from special keys.

One of the key questions to be answered before this concept can serve as a practical solution is whether a computer can distinguish intentional overlaps from accidental overlaps, since key overlaps are in fact natural in the normal use of a keyboard. Touch typists, in particular, presses two or more keys together in many cases. We studied and analyzed overlapping statistics of ordinary keys in the normal usage of a conventional keyboard, and attempted to answer whether assigning functions to overlaps of keys is a practical option in the design of a small keyboard. We attempt to identify available pairs of ordinary keys to serve specific functions by analyzing overlap frequencies (section 5) and key stroke timing (section 6) in normal use. A practical application is introduced (section 7).

J. Jacko (Ed.): Human-Computer Interaction, Part II, HCII 2007, LNCS 4551, pp. 504–512, 2007.

2 Pressing Two Keys at Once

Touch typists normally press a key before releasing a previous key in typing, and consequently natural overlaps of keys occur. An unintentional key overlap is called an *implicit overlap* while an *explicit overlap* is an overlap of keys with intention, for which a function can be assigned. Implicit overlaps are frequently observed but explicit overlaps are observed only when a user uses a modifier key - 'Ctrl', 'Alt', and so on. Users are not leveraging explicit overlaps with two ordinary keys including character keys. The present paper focuses on explicit overlaps. While three or more keys may be pressed altogether, we only examine overlapping of two keys in this paper.

2.1 Problem

Except some special cases such as in games, explicit overlaps are not recommended since implicit and explicit overlaps conflict. A primary goal is to find pairs of character keys that do not have conflicts between explicit and implicit overlaps. A way to avoid such conflicts is also considered here.

2.2 Our Approach

First, we attempted to identify pairs of keys that do not have implicit overlaps. These pairs are completely free from conflicts with explicit overlaps. The authors speculate that the sequence of letters in text and positions of keys determine whether implicit overlaps occur. For instance, implicit overlaps of 't' and 'h' occur often since 'th' is one of the most common digrams in English text. 'n' and 'u' also occur frequently in juxtaposition but do not cause overlaps to the degree anticipated by the authors, because most users press the characters using the right index finger, and thus press 'u' after releasing 'n'.

It is difficult to analyze the entire dynamics of the hands and corresponding key strokes. Therefore, we empirically investigated frequencies of implicit overlaps for all pairs of ordinary keys. The pairs of keys that do not have implicit overlaps are available for explicit overlaps; however, only a few pairs are available (experimental results are presented in section 5). Hence, an additional strategy that examines the time gap between two key strokes in an overlap is applied to separate two types of overlaps. We hypothesized that the gap in implicit overlaps is larger than that in explicit overlaps, and experimentally analyze this in section 6.

3 Related Work

Rochester, et al [3] introduced a chord keyboard that offers small size. The chord keyboard permits overlaps of two or more adjacent keys. Through the pressing of several keys, the chord keyboard offers the full functionality of a conventional keyboard with fewer keys. However, the chord keyboard has a unique mechanical structure and method and thus users who are familiar with the conventional keyboard have to learn how to use the new chord keyboard.

Gaines, et al [1] presented preliminary results on key stroke timing. They gathered statistical results for authentication by keystroke timing. Time differences between two consecutive key down events were summarized, and these results provided a useful reference for our experiment design.

4 Preliminarily Study on Preferences for Keys Pairs

Before the experiments to find available pairs for explicit overlaps, we conducted a preliminary study on users' preferences. Through this study, we attempted to filter out unwilling pairs for explicit overlaps. Eleven graduate students responded to a question asking their ten favorite pairs for explicit overlaps. Prior to asking the question, we fully explained the study including the concept of explicit overlap. All subjects were familiar with computers and keyboards. The average age was twenty-four and they were allowed to choose special keys including modifier keys and could press the keys on their keyboards.

Table 1. Frequencies of implicit overlaps of selected pairs (out of 47098 overlaps, QWERTY layout). Additional key errors [4] are sifted for the four highlighted pairs (frequencies before sifting in parentheses). Digram frequencies of the experiment are also present.

Key pair	Hands used to type	Digram frequency	Frequency of an implicit overlap
<A, ;>	L - R	8	3
<A, S>	L - L	415	53
<C, V>	L - L	9	0 (1)
<D, F>	L - L	661	142
<D, K>	L - R	1539	523
<E, R>	L - L	612	337
<F, J>	L - R	528	200
<G, H>	L - R	402	200
<J, K>	R - R	14	0
<K, L>	R - R	87	7 (10)
<S, D>	L - L	917	190
<S, L>	L - R	1043	435

Among one hundred and ten pairs that the eleven participants chose, fifty-two different pairs existed. Twenty-seven pairs consisted of only character keys, not special keys. In addition, there were only two pairs having two keys on different rows of a keyboard. Thirteen pairs laid on the middle row, i.e., the keyboard baseline. Twelve pairs were related to only the left hand, nine pairs to the right hand, and the others were related to both hands. Table 1 shows twelve pairs chosen by more than three subjects along with frequencies of implicit overlap (described in section 5). For the selected pairs, we conducted further experiments.

5 Implicit Overlap Frequency

We performed an experiment to identify overlapping frequencies. A keystroke logger program, which counts key overlapping frequency and records key-down and up time with millisecond precision, was installed on each participant's computer. The logger program ran in the background and we asked the subjects to use their computers as usual with the exception that they could not play games, as these could lead to application-specific overlaps.

Table 2. Total number of strokes and overlaps for eight subjects. Percentages in last column are calculated as: (Number of overlaps * 2) / (Number of strokes) because one overlap takes two strokes.

Subject	Total number of strokes	Total number of overlaps	Percentage of overlaps to strokes
1	151182	8644	11.4 %
2	112618	6192	11.0
3	210416	3519	3.3
4	232354	1624	1.4
5	154361	12594	16.3
6	352722	7905	4.5
7	202888	2410	2.4
8	1289567	4199	0.7
Average	338264	5886	6.4
Standard Deviation	391117	3693	5.8

5.1 Participants

Eight Korean graduate students participated in this experiment; none of them are native English speakers but they reported that they type in English about 45% of the time in normal use. Ages ranged from twenty-two to thirty-two with an average age of twenty-five. Only one participant was female. All were touch typists and had at least seven years' experience in typing with a QWERTY-layout keyboard. One subject used a scissor-switch membrane keyboard (c.f. many laptop computers are equipped with this type of keyboard) and the others used typical membrane keyboards.

Over a period of three days, 218056 strokes and 47098 overlaps were recorded from the participants. Table 2 summarizes the total number of strokes and overlaps. We assumed that all overlaps involving two character keys are implicit overlaps.

5.2 Results

The logger program calculated frequencies of implicit overlaps for all pairs. Complete results are depicted in the appendix and results for selected pairs are given in table 1. Among twelve pairs that the subjects preferred, <A, ;>, <C, V>, <J, K>, and <K, L>

are good candidates for the explicit overlap since the pairs have low frequency of implicit overlap. For these pairs, we manually checked the overlaps to sift additional key errors [4] that occur by mistake. The four pairs have very low frequency of implicit overlap compared to the other pairs, but even a small number of conflicts between explicit and implicit overlaps could prove critical in practical uses. Therefore, on the basis of this experiment, we could only confirm that <C, V> and <J, K> are available pairs for explicit overlaps.

6 Stroke Time Differences in Implicit and Explicit Overlaps

To avoid conflicts between implicit and explicit overlaps, stroke time differences in overlaps were considered. We hypothesized that time differences between key down events of two keys in implicit overlaps would be larger than differences in explicit overlaps. The differences of key down events in implicit overlaps are recorded by the key logger described in section 5 and another experiment was conducted to check differences in explicit overlaps.

6.1 Participants and Procedure

Four subjects who participated in the previous experiment with the key logger took part in this time difference experiment. We explained the concept of explicit overlap and asked the subjects to press two keys at the same time for explicit overlaps. To create a realistic environment, we developed a test program that detects overlaps of certain pairs and triggers the caps lock key. A sentence with upper and lower cases was given and the participants typed with explicit overlaps instead of the caps lock and shift key. Each subject typed five sentences for each key pair. The original sentences were randomly chosen from [2]. The following is an example sentence: 'I do NOT fully AGREE with YOU'

6.2 Results

Figure 1 summarizes the results. Time differences between key down events for implicit overlaps are recorded by the key logger and are shown in figure 1. Two types of overlaps should be separated completely, and thus we compared time differences between consecutive key down events for implicit and explicit overlaps.

As shown in figure 1, implicit overlaps of two pairs, <K, L>, are distinguished from explicit overlaps by leveraging stroke time differences, but <A, ;> is not completely distinguished; the time difference for one explicit overlap is about 106 milliseconds that is very close to implicit overlaps. Subjects reported that A and ; are located far apart and that they consequently experienced some difficulties in pressing these two keys simultaneously. However, overall time differences in explicit overlaps are much lower than the minimum time difference in implicit overlaps. However, it cannot be conclusively stated that the present experimental results verify that implicit and explicit overlaps are separable by using stroke time differences, as only a few cases during short time periods were assessed. Indeed, other pairs that have high frequency of overlap could not be separated on the basis of only stroke time differences. A more sophisticated statistical analysis will be conducted in the future.

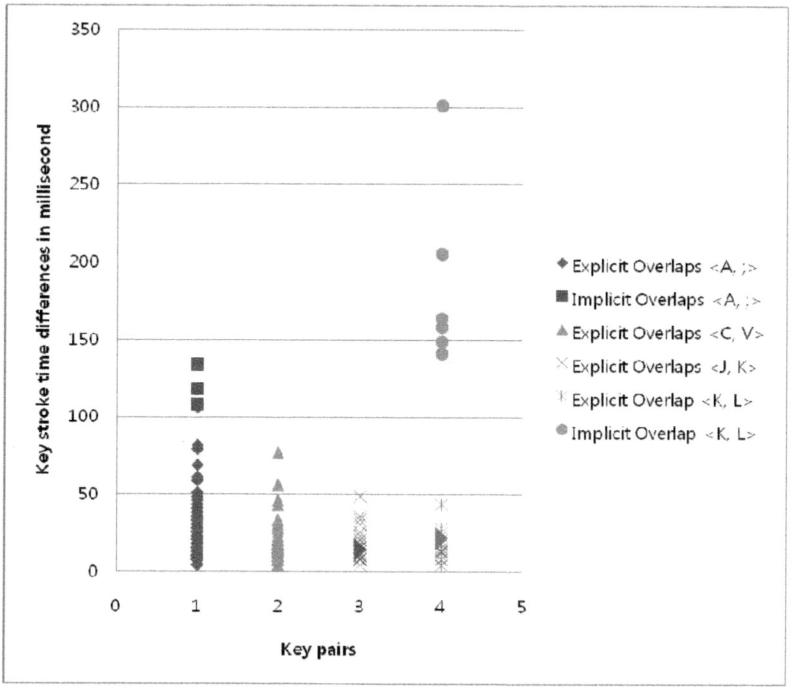

Fig. 1. Time differences between key down event of two overlapping keys in four pairs

7 Applications of Explicit Overlaps

Keyboard users who have to use two different alphabets, such as Koreans, inevitably experience inconvenience in switching modes between two languages. While keyboards have a special key for switching modes, it interrupts seamless typing. In addition, since a single key is used for toggling between two modes, typists are not always sure as to the current mode or which mode they are switching into. If explicit overlapping can be leveraged, two or more pairs of keys may be allocated to functions that change the input mode to a specific language.

Another possible use of an explicit overlap is to use the J-K key combination for activating the numeric keypad mode of a notebook keyboard. Most notebook computers do not have a separate numeric keypad but has a number-lock mode when a part of a notebook keyboard is converted to a numeric keypad. The number-lock mode is usually activated by a special function key but may be activated by pressing the J-K key pair, which is in fact located within the numeric keypad part of a notebook keyboard.

As we pointed out in the introduction, we could seldom observe an overlap between digit keys, which are usually arranged in a row above alphabetic keys, and therefore the function keys (F1, F2, and so on) may be replaced by combinations of adjacent digit keys. For instance, pressing '1' and '2' together may trigger 'F1', and pressing '0' and '-' together may trigger 'F10'. This may be a typical application of explicit overlapping when a device has limited space for a full keyboard. All these ideas of using explicit overlapping may be most effective when key-labels and/or key shapes are re-designed so that they can provide an appropriate visual cue about such uses of explicit overlapping.

8 Conclusion

We analyzed overlaps of character keys to assign functions to the overlaps. Not all pairs of keys were adequate, but some pairs were determined to be sufficiently idle to be overloaded with special functions. By considering user preferences, implicit overlapping frequencies, and stroke timings, we found four pairs that are practically usable. Most subjects who participated in the experiments reported a high rate of satisfaction with the explicit overlaps. However, the results are incomplete, because the experiments were conducted with limited subjects and period. We are planning to carry out the same experiments with more diverse users, including native speakers of English, and obtain more general statistics that can better support the validity of the use of explicit overlaps. Finally, we aim to discover complete statistics of all overlaps not just for a few pairs.

References

1. Gaines, R.S., Lisowski, W., Press, J., Shapiro, N.: Authentication by Keystroke Timing: Some Preliminary Results, Rand, Report R-256-NSF, Rand Corporation (1978)
2. MacKenzie, I.S., Soukoreff, R.W.: Phrase Sets for Evaluating Text Entry Techniques. Ext. abstracts, CHI 2003, ACM Press (2003) 754–755
3. Rochester, N., Bequaert, F.C., Sharp, E.M.: The Chord Keyboard. Computer, Vol. 11 (1978) 57–63
4. Trewin, S.: Extending Keyboard Adaptability: An investigation. Universal Access in the Information Society, Vol. 2. Springer-Verlag, Berlin Heidelberg New York (2002) 44–55

Appendix: Complete Results of the Implicit Overlap Frequency

The following figure shows frequencies of implicit overlaps. Characters in the first column indicate pairs of overlapping keys and numbers in the second column show corresponding implicit overlap frequencies.

A;	3	AJ	92	AS	53	BC	1	BL	19
AB	33	AK	354	AT	84	BD	51	BM	2
AC	63	AL	224	AU	179	BE	5	BN	10
AD	78	AM	154	AV	20	BF	13	BO	8
AE	42	AN	230	AW	39	BG	5	BP	1
AF	39	AO	41	AX	0	BH	0	BQ	0
AG	25	AP	77	AY	4	BI	7	BR	8
AH	133	AQ	0	AZ	0	BJ	0	BS	14
AI	19	AR	126	B;	0	BK	2	BT	3

BU	11
BV	8
BW	4
BX	1
BY	0
BZ	3
C;	1
CD	2
CE	28
CF	0
CG	0
CH	46
CI	32
CJ	19
CK	46
CL	57
CM	7
CN	33
CO	97
CP	16
CQ	0
CR	1
CS	13
CT	0
CU	45
CV	0
CW	0
CX	0
CY	12
CZ	0
D;	2
DE	32
DF	142
DG	37
DH	290
DI	173
DJ	532
DK	523
DL	964
DM	710
DN	343
DO	93
DP	336
DQ	22
DR	17
DS	190
DT	27
DU	220
DV	0
DW	8
DX	7
DY	269
DZ	11
E;	3
EF	30
EG	38
EH	419
EI	20
EJ	91
EK	493
EL	154
EM	181
EN	119
EO	74
EP	192
EQ	12
ER	337
ES	490
ET	166
EU	11
EV	29
EW	31
EX	1
EY	15
EZ	29
F;	1
FG	1
FH	261
FI	28
FJ	200
FK	415
FL	378
FM	430
FN	74
FO	137
FP	15
FQ	2
FR	4
FS	24
FT	0
FU	147
FV	0
FW	14
FX	0
FY	20
FZ	0
G;	3
GH	200
GI	12
GJ	60
GK	448
GL	65
GM	32
GN	58
GO	169
GP	8
GQ	1
GR	11
GS	143
GT	0
GU	41
GV	0
GW	3
GX	0
GY	6
GZ	0
H;	0
HI	35
HJ	2
HK	335
HL	221
HM	0
HN	0
HO	122
HP	5
HQ	198
HR	508
HS	119
HT	140
HU	1
HV	31
HW	187
HX	20
HY	0
HZ	7
I;	0
IJ	4
IK	0
IL	81
IM	41
IN	290
IO	112
IP	8
IQ	1
IR	39
IS	70
IT	101
IU	8
IV	8
IW	12
IX	5
IY	0
IZ	2
J;	0
JK	0
JL	0
JM	0
JN	133
JO	1
JP	1
JQ	161
JR	314
JS	263
JT	410
JU	0
JV	11
JW	273
JX	72
JY	0
JZ	13
K;	9
KL	7
KM	0
KN	4
KO	1
KP	0
KQ	187
KR	682
KS	817
KT	217
KU	3
KV	26
KW	270
KX	76
KY	0
KZ	16
L;	1
LM	192
LN	143
LO	1
LP	3
LQ	115
LR	274
LS	435
LT	288
LU	23
LV	39
LW	394
LX	36
LY	3
LZ	19
M;	1
MN	2
MO	103
MP	6
MQ	43
MR	265
MS	663
MT	149
MU	0
MV	37
MW	16
MX	95
MY	1
MZ	29
N;	0
NO	141
NP	12
NQ	104
NR	140
NS	166
NT	207
NU	2
NV	12
NW	145
NX	7
NY	0
NZ	11
O;	0
OP	41
OQ	22
OR	113
OS	139
OT	98
OU	95

OV	15	PZ	5	RV	0	TV	0	TY	8
OW	33	Q;	0	RW	11	TW	16	TZ	0
OX	16	QR	4	RX	1	TX	6	WX	0
OY	4	QS	16	RY	49	UW	9	WY	19
OZ	2	QT	67	RZ	0	UX	0	WZ	0
P;	0	QU	35	S;	0	UY	3	X;	0
PQ	10	QV	0	SW	0	UZ	6	XY	1
PR	188	QW	6	SX	0	V;	0	XZ	1
PS	144	QX	0	SY	10	VW	0	Y;	0
PT	60	RS	133	SZ	0	UV	14	YZ	0
PU	32	RT	11	SV	1	VX	0	Z;	0
PV	8	RU	71	T;	1	VY	7		
PW	111	QY	0	TU	35	U;	0		
PX	57	QZ	0	SU	199	VZ	0		
PY	4	R;	2	ST	140	W;	0		

Mobile Magic Hand:Camera Phone Based Interaction Using Visual Code and Optical Flow

Yuichi Yoshida, Kento Miyaoku, and Takashi Satou

Nippon Telegraph and Telephone Corporation, NTT Cyber Communications Laboratory
Hikari-no-oka 1-1 Yokosuka, Kanagawa, Japan
{yoshida.yuichi,miyaoku.kento,satou.takashi}@lab.ntt.co.jp

Abstract. We propose the "Mobile Magic Hand" interface; it is an extension of our previous visual code-based interface system. Once the user acquires the visual code of interest, the user can then manipulate the related virtual object/system without having to keep the camera centered on the visual code. Our new interface does this analyzing the optical flow as captured by the camera. For example, consider a visual code that represents a 3D object, such as a dial. After selecting the code, the user can freely rotate and/or move the virtual object without having to keep the camera pointed at the code. This interface is much more user friendly and is more intuitive since the user's hand gestures can be more relaxed, more natural, and more extensive. In this paper, we describe "Mobile Magic Hand" , some applications, and a preliminary user study of a prototype system.

Keywords: mobile, visual code, gestural interface.

1 Introduction

Interaction methods that use a visual code and a camera phone have been proposed[1][2][3]. This approach allows users to control virtual attributes with real world actions that have 6 degrees of freedom(6DOF), see **Fig. 1**. and **Table 1**. The ID of a visual code is detected and the pose and position of the mobile device relative to the code is determined by analyzing the image sequences captured by the built-in camera. The content, which corresponds to its ID, and pose and position are displayed on the mobile device. **Fig. 2** shows the user adjusting a parameter, such as audio volume, by rotating the mobile device as if rotating a control dial.

The existing methods require the user to keep the camera centered on the visual code while manipulating the related virtual object/system. This prevents the use of natural and intuitive gestures. For instance, the gesture of tilting, shown in **Fig. 3**-(a) is intuitive. The user can't keep the camera centered on the visual code if he/she makes the natural gesture of tilting. The user's gesture must be constrained to keep the camera centered on the visual code, see **Fig. 3**-(b).

"Mobile Magic Hand" extracts the code's ID and gets the related virtual object/system which includes pictures, movies or music, according to the ID. "Mobile Magic Hand" measures its pose and position by analyzing the shape of the visual code in the image when detecting the visual code of interest[4] "Mobile Magic Hand" measures

J. Jacko (Ed.): Human-Computer Interaction, Part II, HCII 2007, LNCS 4551, pp. 513–521, 2007.

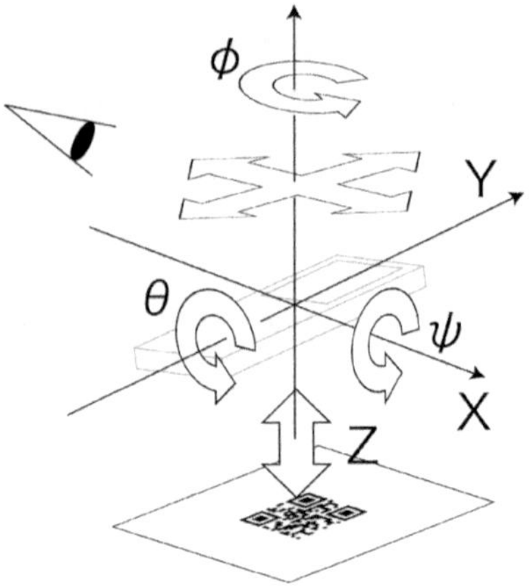

Fig. 1. Concept

Table 1. Primitive operations

Name	Image	Description
pointing	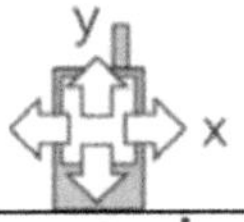	Translation in X or Y axis direction.
distance	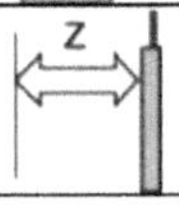	Translation in Z axis direction.
tilting		Rotation around X or Y axis.
rotation	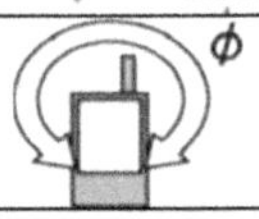	Rotation around Z axis.

Fig. 2. Adjusting volume

its pose and position by analyzing the optical flow and feature points when the code is not detected[5].

In this paper, we describe previous works related to gestural interfaces which use a visual code and camera phone and propose "Mobile Magic Hand". We introduce the results of preliminary user tests and examples of "Mobile Magic hand" applications.

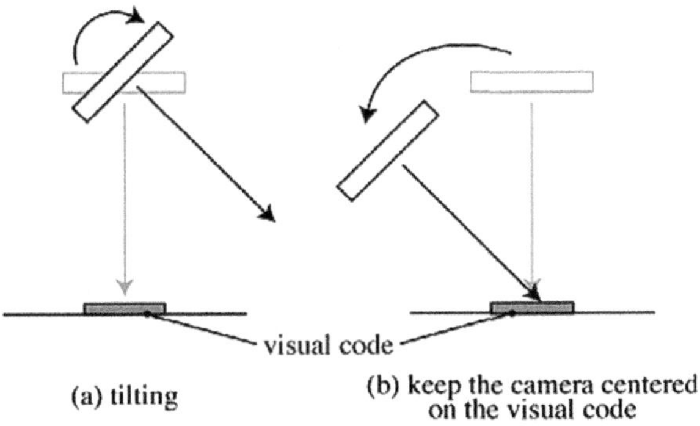

Fig. 3. One weakness of existing methods

2 Related Works

2.1 Interface That Uses the Position and Pose Between the Mobile Phone and a Visual Code

This interface, based on a visual code and a camera phone, uses the distance along X, Y and Z axes and the rotation around the axes as parameters to control a virtual object/system related to the code. We associate the distance along the X and Y axes with *pointing*, the distance along the Z axis with *distance*, the rotation around the X and Y axes with *tilting* and the rotation around the Z axis with *rotation*(Table 1). We call them spatial operations. Spatial operations enable us to design an operation which is a metaphor for a real behavior. For example, the user can adjust sound volume as if rotating a dial knob, can acquire more detail of a map as if using a magnifying glass by zooming.

MIXIS is the interface that permits manipulation of the information related to a circle visual marker[1]. The circle visual maker consists of a circle and a figure inside it. MIXIS acquires the information by recognizing the figure inside the circle and calculates the position and pose of the phone relative to the marker by analyzing the shape of the marker's circle in the captured image. Authors built the application ImageViewZoom; it permits panning and zooming of a map by moving the phone in front of the circle. They tested this application by comparing the proposed MIXIS to the existing button operation. They reported that the examinees prefer MIXIS over the existing interface.

Rohs et al. proposed ***keystroke*** operation which lets users use buttons, and ***stay*** operation which lets users keep a position or pose for a moment in addition to our spatial operations[2] They evaluated its usability. No published work has, however, tackled the problem that the gestural operation is highly restricted because users have to keep the camera centered on the visual code.

2.2 Method of Estimating the Mobile Phone's Position and Pose

There are some methods other than the visual code approach that can be used to estimate the position and pose of a mobile phone.

Acceleration Sensor. We can estimate the position and pose of the mobile phone with an acceleration sensor. Acceleration sensors have already been used as the input device for mobile phones[6].

Rotary Encoder. We can estimate the planar distance (for example on paper) with a rotary encoder. FieldMouse uses a barcode reader[7]. Users can point to any location by capturing the visual code and then tracing paper. But, FieldMouse enables users to operate by making a planar gesture.

Using extract of Feature Quantity. We can estimate position and pose by analyzing the movement of feature quantity which is extracted from the captured image. The optical flow, which is based on the motion vectors of the subject, and block matching, which uses a color histogram every area, have been reported[5][8].

We can't cheaply utilize the methods that use acceleration sensors and rotary encoders because we have to add devices to the mobile phone. It is easier to implement the method that analyzes feature quantity because existing mobile phones already have digital cameras. This method has the problem is that the unit of results is different from the real one. But, we can convert the unit of results into the real one by analyzing the size and shape of a visual code in the captured image.

3 Proposed Method ~ "Mobile Magic Hand"

3.1 Implementation

"Mobile Magic Hand" estimates the pose and position of the mobile phone relative to the visual code by analyzing the shape of the code in the captured image when detecting it. On the other hand, when the visual code can't be detected, it estimates them by analyzing the optical flow of the captured image, see **Fig. 4**. "Mobile Magic Hand" uses QRCode as the visual code[9].

Fig. 5 shows a flowchart of "Mobile Magic Hand" software operation. At first, it captures the desired QRCode, extracts the Code's ID, and gets the related virtual object/system which includes pictures, movies or music. When the QRCode is detected, the position and pose are calculated using the coordinates of the four corners of the QRCode (assuming a square QRCode). "Mobile Magic Hand" measures its pose and position by analyzing the optical flow and feature points if the visual code cannot be detected.

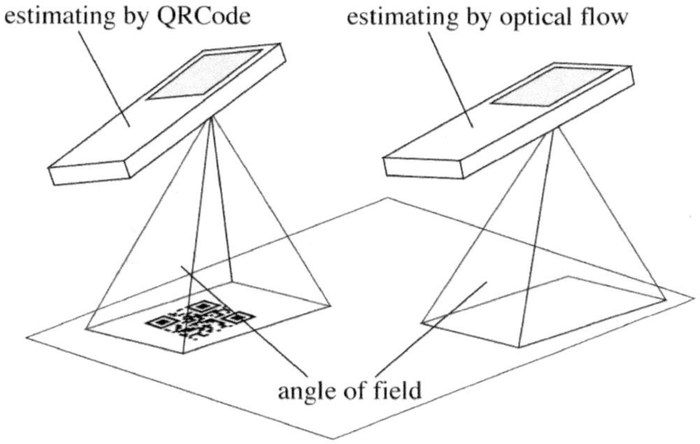

Fig. 4. Switching acquisition mode

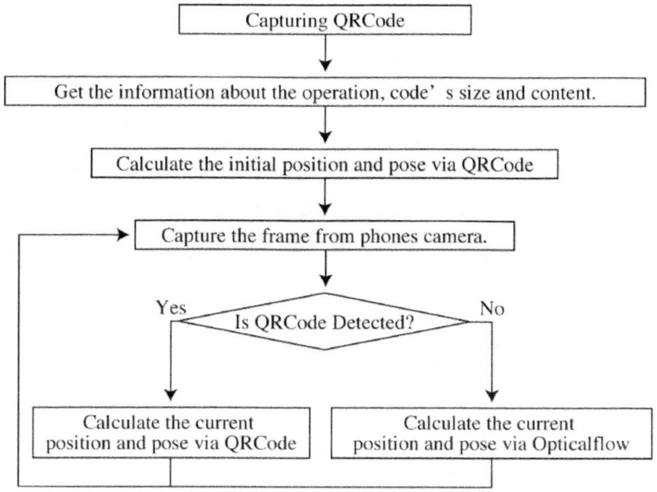

Fig. 5. Flowchart of software operation

3.2 Feature

"Mobile Magic Hand" allows users to manipulate the related virtual object/system by making a gesture even when the terminal's camera can't detect the visual code. Therefore, our proposal has two advantages over the existing methods. First, the user can access a wider range of values because the spatial range is extended. For example, if *pointing* is used for menu selection, the number of items that can be selected is increases, see **Fig. 6**. If *distance* is used for map zooming, greater scale changes are possible.

Second, once the user acquires the visual tag of interest, the user can then manipulate the related virtual object/system without having to keep the camera centered on the visual code. It allows hand gestures to be more intuitive, relaxed, natural, and extensive, see **Fig. 7**. For example, the users can rotate the virtual object on the terminal's screen as if rotating a real world object by rotating the terminal.

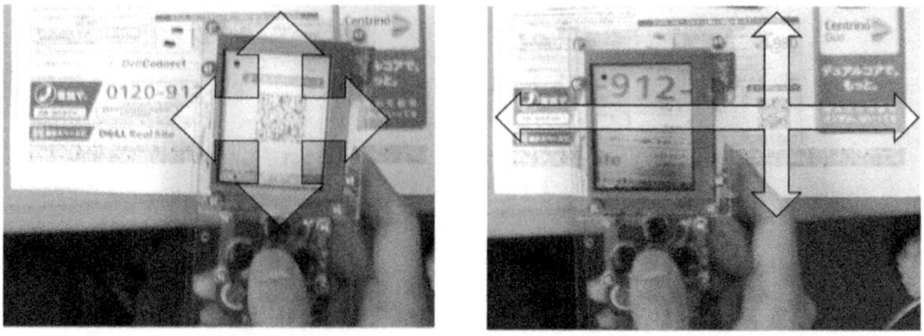

(a) The existing method
4 choices

(b) The proposed method
4 + α choicces

Fig. 6. Advantage of *pointing*

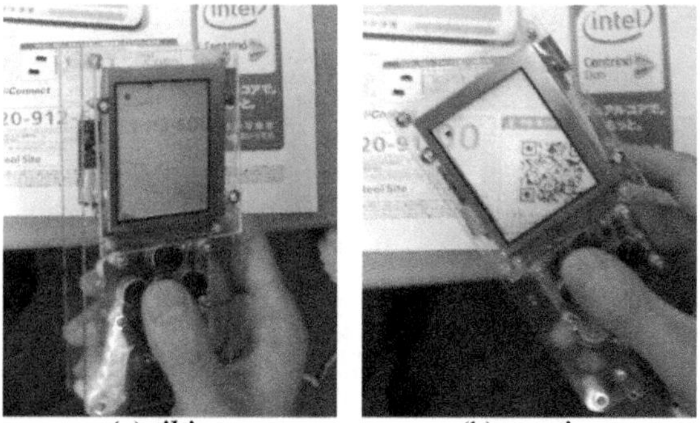

(a) ***tilting***

(b) ***rotation***

Fig. 7. No need to keep the camera centered on the visual code

4 User Test

We constructed a prototype terminal that is as small as current cellular phones and used it to evaluate the performance of "Mobile Magic Hand". The prototype terminal was connected to a PC by a cable in order to run the software, see **Fig. 8**.

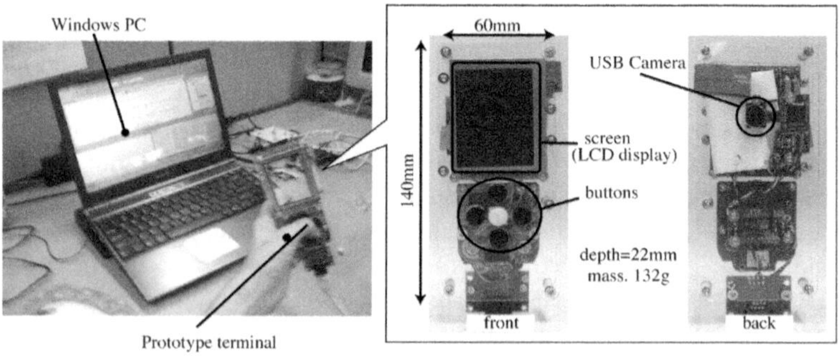

Fig. 8. Prototype system

We asked some subjects with no previous experience of "Mobile Magic Hand" to use the prototype terminal. The tasks for *distance*, *tilting* and *rotation* were to adjust the parameters of the pose and position to the target values. The task for *pointing* was to select the target objects from among the objects surrounding the visual code.

After all subjects were taught how to use the prototype system, all could perform the tasks for *distance*, *tilting* and *rotation*. Some subjects had difficult with *pointing* because the prototype system couldn't calculate the *pointing* parameters within an acceptable degree of error if the prototype terminal was moved too quickly. After being instructed to move the terminal more slowly, they could perform this task.

The results of the preliminary user study show that the advantages of the proposed system make *distance*, *tilting* and *rotation* more useful.

5 Applications

"Mobile Magic Hand" will yield many new applications. We describe two prototypical applications: the interactive map and an adventure game paper.

Interactive Map. The interactive map uses *pointing* and *distance*. *Pointing* enables users to select a region of interest on the map, and *distance* enables users to adjust system parameters. "Mobile Magic Hand" extracts the position and operation of landmarks and content, which includes satellite images, according to the ID.

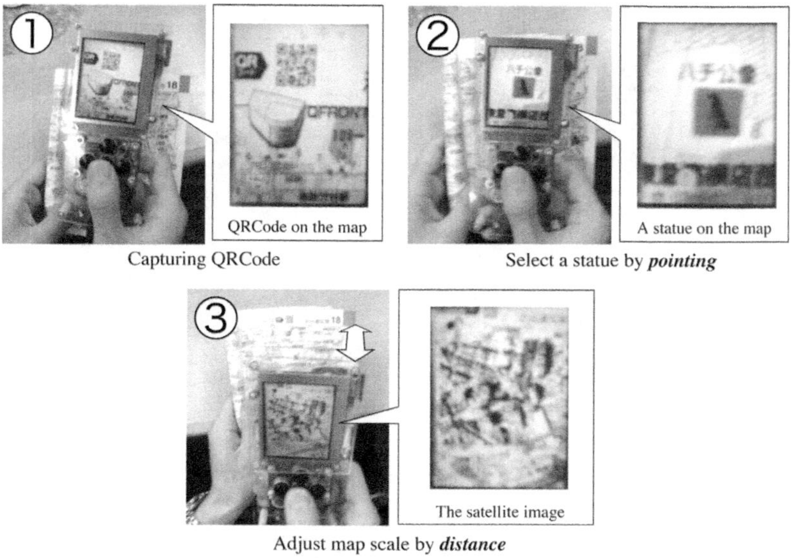

Fig. 9. Interactive map

The user moves the mobile phone to the landmark of interest after capturing the QRCode(*pointing*). As the user scans the terminal, "Mobile Magic Hand" detects the lateral movement and determines the landmark of interest. The user can get a satellite image of the area around the landmark by pushing the select button. Moreover, the user can change the scale of the satellite image by bringing the phone toward or away from the map(*distance*).

Adventure Game Paper. The adventure game requires the user to manipulate virtual objects printed on a piece of paper by making natural gestures. Fig. 10 shows an adventure game paper that contains a door, a cashbox, a chest, and a piece of paper on a table. User can open the door by *tilting*, unlock the cashbox by *rotation*, and open a drawer of the chest by *pointing*. In addition, user can also move the paper and check the table by *pointing*.

We can combine these operations and design complex adventure games. For example, a possible scenario is that the user opens the drawer, finds a paper on which a number is written. The number is used to unlock the cashbox.

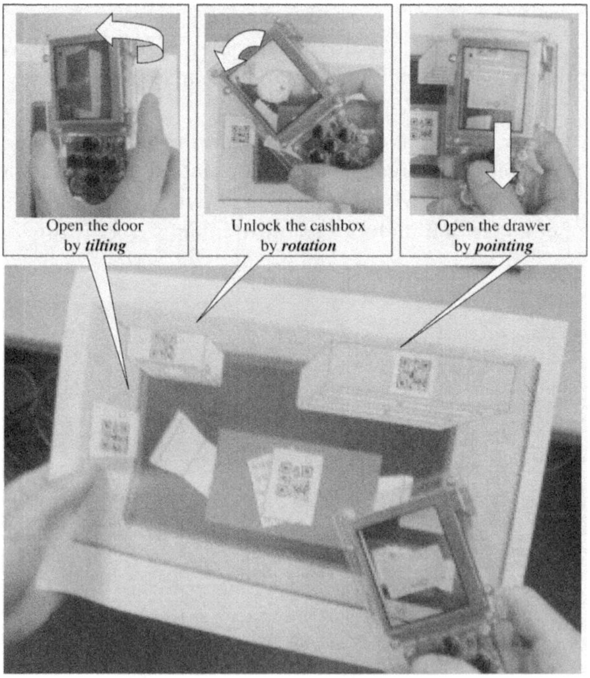

Fig. 10. Adventure game paper

6 Conclusion

Our proposal, "Mobile Magic Hand," calculates the mobile phone's position and pose by analyzing the optical flow if the visual code can't be detected. We described a preliminary evaluation of the performance of its basic operations. The results confirm that "Mobile Magic Hand" well realizes the key functions of *rotation, tilting* and *distance*.

We intend to develop a new method that can more accurately calculate the mobile phone's translation in order to improve the usability of *pointing*, and evaluate the performance of practical applications of "Mobile Magic Hand".

References

1. Hansen, T.R., Eriksson, E., Lykke-Olesen, A.: Mixed Interaction Space - Expanding the Interaction Space with Mobile Devices. In: People and Computers XIX - The Bigger Picture, Proceedings of British HCI, Springer, Heidelberg (2005)
2. Rohs, M., Zweifel, P.A.: Conceptual Framework for Camera Phone-based Interaction Techniques. In: Gellersen, H.-W., Want, R., Schmidt, A. (eds.) PERVASIVE 2005. LNCS, vol. 3468, pp. 171–189. Springer, Heidelberg (2005)
3. Yoshida, Y., Satou, T., Miyaoku, K., Higashino, S.: Reacher Interface for Intuitive Information Navigation. In: Costabile, M.F., Paternó, F. (eds.) INTERACT 2005. LNCS, vol. 3585, pp. 1091–1095. Springer, Heidelberg (2005)
4. Rekimoto, J., Nagao, K.: The world through the computer:Computer augmented interaction with real world environments. In: Proceedings of the 8th annual ACM symposium on User interface software and technology pp. 29–36 (1995)
5. Lucas, B.D., Kanade, T.: An Iterative Image Registration Technique with an Application to Stereo Vision. In: International Joint Conference on Artificial Intelligence, pp. 674–679 (1981)
6. Wigdor, D., Balakrishnan, R.: TiltText: using tilt for text input to mobile phones. In: Proceedings of the 16th annual ACM symposium on User interface software and technology. pp. 81–90 (2003)
7. Siio, I., Masui, T., Fukuchi, K.: Real-world interaction using the FieldMouse. In: Proceedings of the ACM Symposium on User Interface Software and Technology. pp. 113–119 (1999)
8. Wang, J., Canny, J.: TinyMotion: Camera Phone Based Interaction Methods. In: Conference on Human Factors in Computing Systems CHI 2006, extended abstracts on Human factors in computing systems. pp. 339–344 (2006)
9. QRCode http://www.qrcode.com/

Online Chinese Characters Recognition Based on Force Information by HMM

Mozi Zhu[1,2], Fei Shen[1], and ZhongCheng Wu[1,3]

[1] Institute of Intelligent Machines, CAS, Hefei, 230031 Anhui, China
[2] Department of Automation University of Science & Technology of China
[3] Hefei High Magnetic Field Laboratory, CAS, 230031, Hefei, Anhui, China
Hefei, 230026 Anhui, China
zcwu@iim.ac.cn, mozi@mail.ustc.edu.cn

Abstract. Pen computing draws more and more researchers' attention. One of the most important problems is online Chinese Characters Recognition (OCCR). The information of Pen-tip position is widely used for handwritten recognition traditionally. In this paper, a new method using force information is proposed for OCCR, in which the force directions are extracted as the feature of strokes. In our method, every stroke has its own Hidden Markov Model (HMM) and the process of building stroke HMM is described in details. Handwritten Characters are recognized following the stroke tree after every stroke has been recognized as described. Finally experimental results on analysis of five persons' handwriting are presented.

Keywords: Force Information, HMM, OCCR, Stroke Recognition.

1 Introduction

Character recognition is a hotspot in pattern recognition. OCCR is hard work and contains all problems in pattern recognition. [1] Handwritten Chinese Characters are characterized with large vocabulary, complex structure, lots of similar characters and serious irregular variations of shapes [2].Many researchers have tried to find a valid model to express the characters for recognition.

Methods of pattern recognition are generally composed of rule based methods and statistical methods. Most reliable and flexible work on recognition developed is based on statistical methods, including artificial neural networks (ANNs) and HMMs.

ANN has strong discriminating abilities and widely used for classification and recognition. But ANN also has many disadvantages, such as net structure construction is not credible, and algorithm is very slow, etc. Satisfactory work on classification and integration with ANN is scarce [3].

HMM is an effective method established for speech recognition. It can also performs good applied to on-line cursive handwriting recognition. In this paper, we introduce a new method based on HMM. We mix the rule based methods with HMM. We segment characters into strokes. First we extract strokes from the handwriting information from F-tablet. As the 2-D HMMs for characters usually need a large number of samples and long time for learning, 1-D(dimension) features is extracted to

J. Jacko (Ed.): Human-Computer Interaction, Part II, HCII 2007, LNCS 4551, pp. 522–528, 2007.

build 1-D HMMs for every stroke The third step, recognize every stroke. Finally recognize the characters following the character tree. From our F-tablet, we get F_X, F_Y, F_Z, M_X, M_Y. F_X, F_Y, F_Z are defined to denote the force in x, y, z-axis respectively. M_X, M_Y describe the moment in the direction of x, y –axis.

The rest of this paper is organized as follows: Section 2 concisely introduces the principle of HMM. In sections 3 the recognition process is discussed. How to extract the features and how to build HMM are described in detail in this section. Experimental results are analyzed in Section 4. Conclusion is given in Section 5.

2 The Principle of Hidden Markov Model (HMM) [4]

HMM is an important statistical model for processing text and speech. It can be used for observed events and hidden events as causal factors in probabilistic model.

Now we turn to algorithms for computing things with the structure of HMM. An influential tutorial by Rabiner [5], based on tutorials by Jack Ferguson in the 1960s, introduced the idea that HMM should be characterized by three fundamental problems:

Problem 1 (Computing Likelihood): Given an HMM $\lambda = (A, B, \pi)$ and an observation sequence O, determine the likelihood $P(O/I)$.

Problem 2 (Decoding): Given an observation sequence O and an HMM $\lambda = (A, B, \pi)$, discover the best hidden state sequence Q.

Problem 3 (Learning): Given an observation sequence O and the set of states in the HMM, learn the HMM parameters A and B.

The standard algorithm for HMM training is the forward-backward or Baum-Welch algorithm, a special case of the Expectation-Maximization or EM algorithm. The algorithm will let us train both the transition probabilities and the emission probabilities B of the HMM. In this paper, we use HMM for learning. We build different HMMs for every stroke. And we use Baum-Welch algorithm. [6]

Assuming variable $\xi_t(i, j)$:

$$\xi_t(i, j) = P(i_t = s_t, i_{t+1} = s_j \mid O, \lambda) \tag{2.1}$$

It means the probability that transferring from state q_i of time t to q_j of time t+1, and simultaneity model and sequences of observation are confirmed. So we can get:

$$\xi_t(i, j) = \frac{\alpha_t(i) a_{ij} b_j(o_{t+1}) \beta_{t+1}(j)}{P(O \mid \lambda)} \tag{2.2}$$

$$\gamma_t(i) = \sum_{j=1}^{N} \xi_t(i, j) \tag{2.3}$$

$\sum_{t=1}^{T-1}\gamma_t(i)$ is the number of state q_i, and $\sum_{t=1}^{T}\gamma_t(i)$ records the times that the state q_i change to the state q_j. So we can get Baum-Welch formula:

$$\overline{\pi_i} = \gamma_1(i) \tag{2.4}$$

$$\overline{a_{ij}} = \sum_{t=1}^{T-1}\xi_t(i,j) / \sum_{t=1}^{T-1}\gamma_t(i) \tag{2.5}$$

$$\overline{b_j(k)} = \sum_{\substack{t=1 \\ O_t=k}}^{T}\gamma_t(i) / \sum_{t=1}^{T-1}\gamma_t(i) \tag{2.6}$$

3 Recognition Process for Online Handwritten Character

The algorithm of recognition contains five parts: preprocessing, strokes extraction, feature extraction, stroke recognition and character recognition.

3.1 Preprocessing

The goal of preprocessing is to reduce or eliminate some of the variations in handwriting that may exist that are not useful for pattern class discrimination. Strokes captured by a digitizing tablet tend to contain a small amount of noise, most likely introduced by the digitizing device, causing the sampled curves to be somewhat jagged. In order to reduce this noise, fast Fourier transform algorithm (FFT) is used to filtering.

Here, we resample the data so that points are equi-distant in space rather than equi-time. This provides a time normalization, without which slowly written strokes would contain a much larger number of sample points than quickly written strokes of the same shape.

3.2 Strokes Extraction [7]

Strokes extraction in F-Tablet makes use of changing force information in z-axis. Strokes consist of basic strokes and joined-strokes. To basic strokes extraction, a threshold L is defined. If $|F_Z|$ <L, we think that it is an interval between strokes. But to joined-strokes, a threshold r_z ($0< r_z <1$) is defined and $F_Z(n)$ $(n=1\cdots N)$ is also defined to describe the force sequences in z-axis, and $max(F_Z)$ denotes the maximum $F_Z(n)$. Reading $F_Z(n)$ in turn, if $F_Z(i)/\max(F_Z) < rz$, we consider it at the interval between joined-strokes. So joined-strokes are extracted.

3.3 Feature Extraction

We choose the direction of the force F_X, F_Y as feature. It is described in formula 3.1

$$\theta = \tan^{-1}\frac{F_Y}{F_X} \qquad (3.1)$$

θ is a continuous variable($0^\circ \leq \theta \leq 360^\circ$), and has been divided into 16 equal regions(0-15), shown in figure 3.1. For example, the writing direction of stroke "—" is from -60° to 60°, so its θ is in 6 region to 10 region, red part in figure 1.

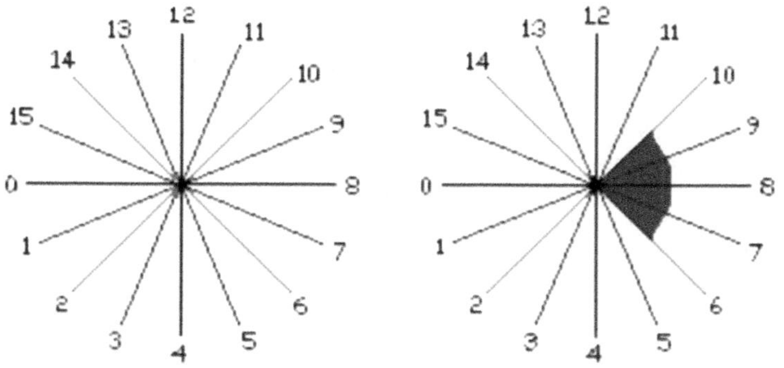

Fig. 1. Sketch map of dispersed θ (red part shows possible area of "—")

3.4 Strokes Recognition

We use left-right HMM for strokes recognition. Supposing each stroke has N-states, the algorithm of strokes recognition by HMM is as follows:

1. Modeling HMM: The parameters of this stroke's HMM are modulated via training samples, in order to maximize the probability that HMM produce these training samples. The algorithm is Baum-Welch formula.
2. Recognizing a stroke: every stroke's HMM is used to compute the probability that HMM produce this stroke. The HMM with maximum probability is the recognized stroke's.

Different stroke has different HMM topology. It is shown in figure 2.

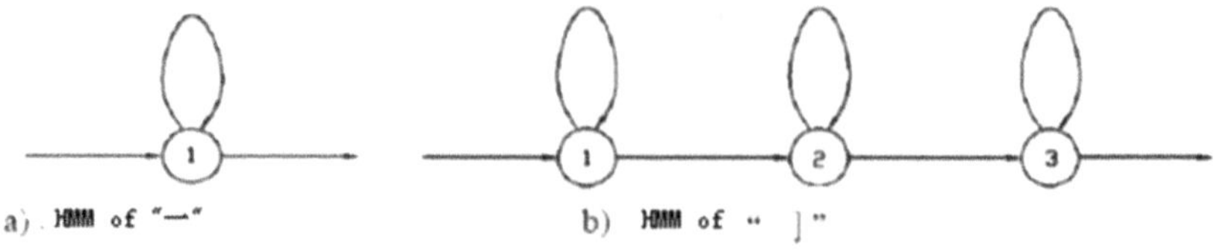

Fig. 2. HMM for different strokes

Usually, to strokes, fixing the regions of the force directions makes HMM more valid. For example, the regions of stroke "—" is in 6-10(as is shown in figure 3.1).

3.5 Character Recognition

Every character has a sequence of strokes, so we construct a stroke tree. When every stroke of a character is extracted and recognized, we recognize the character by the stoke tree.

In actual writing process, there are several problems:

1. The sequences of strokes of the same character are different when different persons write;
2. Some strokes may be lost in writing;
3. Some strokes may not be recognized exactly;
4. Joined-strokes may faze the recognition.

So sometimes wrong sequences of strokes are produced, and no character has been found in the stroke tree. In order to solve these problems, we use Character-Matching (CM) algorithm.

The aim of CM is to find the most suited character sequences of strokes. For example, "一、丨、丿" is not a character recognized in the stroke tree. But if it is "丨" in stead of "亅", we can rectify the sequence to "一、亅、丿", and the corresponding character "才" is found.

Here, DP Matching algorithm is applied. We found the table of strokes' resemblance first, and then using DP Matching to compare the sequences of strokes with those in the stroke tree. The character whose sequence has the maximum resemblance is chosen.

4 Experimental Result Analysis

We have done three experiments. In the first one we compared the results of the training which has finite observational bound with that hasn't. Secondly, we analysis the effect created by the number of regions that θ is divided into. Thirdly, we evaluated our algorithm for character recognition as a whole.

In experiment 1, every stroke samples 4 times. We choose force direction as feature. PS is defined as the logarithm of probability of the same stroke appears in

HMM after training; PO denotes the logarithm of probability of other strokes appears in HMM after training and PR denotes the logarithm of probability of other stroke that is not recognized exactly in HMM after training. (We deem that it is not recognized exactly when probability > PS). So the less the PR is, the better the HMM is. The results are too small, so we change them to logarithm.

Taking character "乙" for example, the HMM with 3 topologies was founded. The training result is shown in table 1.

Table 1. Training Result of Character "乙"

	Infinite Observational Bound	Finite Observational Bound
PS	-75.77	-45.35
PO	-∞	-∞
PR	7.69%	0%

From Table 1, we can see that the result of training with finite observational bound is better than that with infinite observational bound.

In experiment 2, we take 8、16、24、32 as the number of regions for account. The training result is shown in figure 4.1. In the figure, y-axis denotes PR, and x-axis denotes common strokes. Different number has different color of curve (8: red, 16: shamrock, 24: blue, 32: purple).

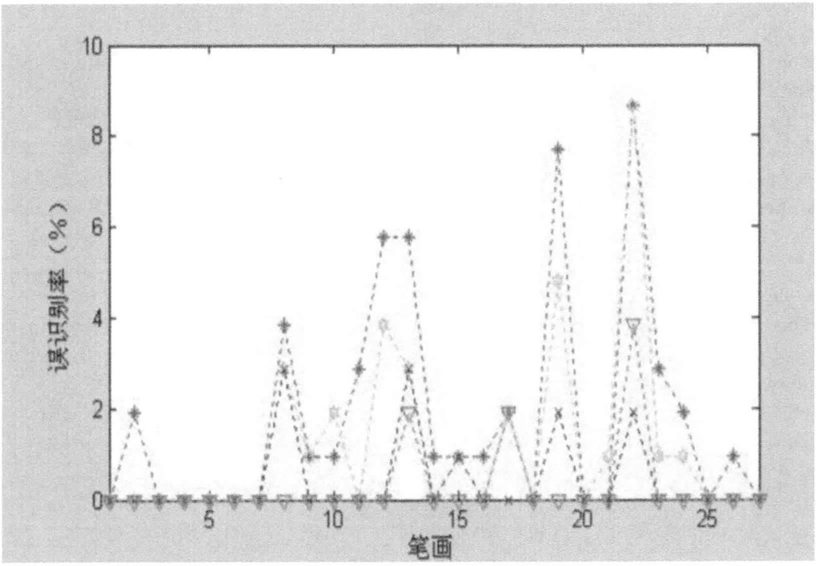

Fig. 3. Probability of fault recognition

In figure 3, we can see that, the greater the number is, the less the PR is. But when it exceeds 24, PR changes slowly. So we choose 24 for training.

In experiment 3, we build a database of common Chinese characters to validate the algorithm. Then 5 persons are requested to write 30 characters each. The result is shown in table 2.

Table 2. The Result of Character Recognition

person	A	B	C	D	E
Probability of recognition	90.0%	96.7%	93.3%	93.3%	96.7%

5 Conclusions

In our paper, HMM of force information for Online Chinese Character Recognition is discussed. We solved the problems such as how to extract joined-strokes, and how to construct HMM topologies to different strokes and so on. Then after every stroke has been recognized, we use character tree to recognize a Chinese character with the help of DP-Matching algorithm. According to the results of experiments, the probability of recognition can reach 90%.

References

[1] Hao, S. Y.: The principle, method and realization of Chinese character recognition. Beijing: Advanced Education Press (1992)

[2] Wang, C. H.: recognition system of Handwriting Chinese character based on ANN. Thesis submitted to Institute of Automatic for Doctor Degree, vol. 7 (1999)

[3] Huang, B.Q., Kechadi, M.T., Campilho, A., Kamel, M.A.: HMM-SNN Method for Online Handwriting Symbol Recognition. In: Campilho, A., Kamel, M. (eds.) ICIAR 2006. LNCS, vol. 4142, pp. 897–905. Springer, Heidelberg (2006)

[4] Rabiner, L. R, Juang, B. H.: An Introduction to Hidden Markov Models, IEEE ASSP, pp. 4–16 (1988)

[5] Rabiner, L.R.: A tutorial on hidden Markov models and selected applications in speech.recognition. In: Proceeding of the IEEE vol. 2(77) (1989)

[6] Baum, L. E, Eagon, J. A.: An inequality with applications to statistical estimation for probabilistic functions of Markov processes and to a model for ecology. Bulletin of the American Mathematical Society 3(73), 360–363 (1967)

[7] Wei, M. X., Wu, Z. C., Ge, Y. J., Yu, Y., Shen, F.: A New Method to Rectify Chinese Character Based on Force Information. In: The 6th World Congress on Intelligent Control and Automation, vol. 6(4) (2006)

GPSR Compliance

The European Union's (EU) General Product Safety Regulation (GPSR) is a set of rules that requires consumer products to be safe and our obligations to ensure this.

If you have any concerns about our products, you can contact us on ProductSafety@springernature.com

In case Publisher is established outside the EU, the EU authorized representative is:

Springer Nature Customer Service Center GmbH
Europaplatz 3
69115 Heidelberg, Germany

Batch number: 10830943

Printed by Printforce, the Netherlands

Lecture Notes in Computer Science 4551

Commenced Publication in 1973
Founding and Former Series Editors:
Gerhard Goos, Juris Hartmanis, and Jan van Leeuwen

Julie A. Jacko (Ed.)

Human-Computer Interaction

Interaction Platforms and Techniques

12th International Conference, HCI International 2007
Beijing, China, July 2007
Proceedings, Part II

Springer

Volume Editor

Julie A. Jacko
Georgia Institute of Technology
and Emory University School of Medicine
901 Atlantic Drive, Suite 4100, Atlanta, GA 30332-0477, USA
E-mail: jacko@hsi.gatech.edu

Library of Congress Control Number: 2007929780

CR Subject Classification (1998): H.5.2, H.5.3, H.3-5, C.2, I.3, D.2, F.3, K.4.2

LNCS Sublibrary: SL 2 – Programming and Software Engineering

ISSN 0302-9743
ISBN-10 3-540-73106-7 Springer Berlin Heidelberg New York
ISBN-13 978-3-540-73106-1 Springer Berlin Heidelberg New York

Springer is a part of Springer Science+Business Media

springer.com

Printed in Germany

Typesetting: Camera-ready by author, data conversion by Scientific Publishing Services, Chennai, India
Printed on acid-free paper SPIN: 12077953 06/3180 5 4 3 2 1 0

Foreword

The 12th International Conference on Human-Computer Interaction, HCI International 2007, was held in Beijing, P.R. China, 22-27 July 2007, jointly with the Symposium on Human Interface (Japan) 2007, the 7th International Conference on Engineering Psychology and Cognitive Ergonomics, the 4th International Conference on Universal Access in Human-Computer Interaction, the 2nd International Conference on Virtual Reality, the 2nd International Conference on Usability and Internationalization, the 2nd International Conference on Online Communities and Social Computing, the 3rd International Conference on Augmented Cognition, and the 1st International Conference on Digital Human Modeling.

A total of 3403 individuals from academia, research institutes, industry and governmental agencies from 76 countries submitted contributions, and 1681 papers, judged to be of high scientific quality, were included in the program. These papers address the latest research and development efforts and highlight the human aspects of design and use of computing systems. The papers accepted for presentation thoroughly cover the entire field of Human-Computer Interaction, addressing major advances in knowledge and effective use of computers in a variety of application areas.

This volume, edited by Julie A. Jacko, contains papers in the thematic area of Human-Computer Interaction, addressing the following major topics:

- Graphical User Interfaces and Visualization
- Mobile Devices and Mobile Interaction
- Virtual Environments and 3D Interaction
- Ubiquitous Interaction
- Emerging Interactive Technologies

The remaining volumes of the HCI International 2007 proceedings are:

- Volume 1, LNCS 4550, Interaction Design and Usability, edited by Julie A. Jacko
- Volume 3, LNCS 4552, HCI Intelligent Multimodal Interaction Environments, edited by Julie A. Jacko
- Volume 4, LNCS 4553, HCI Applications and Services, edited by Julie A. Jacko
- Volume 5, LNCS 4554, Coping with Diversity in Universal Access, edited by Constantine Stephanidis
- Volume 6, LNCS 4555, Universal Access to Ambient Interaction, edited by Constantine Stephanidis
- Volume 7, LNCS 4556, Universal Access to Applications and Services, edited by Constantine Stephanidis
- Volume 8, LNCS 4557, Methods, Techniques and Tools in Information Design, edited by Michael J. Smith and Gavriel Salvendy
- Volume 9, LNCS 4558, Interacting in Information Environments, edited by Michael J. Smith and Gavriel Salvendy
- Volume 10, LNCS 4559, HCI and Culture, edited by Nuray Aykin
- Volume 11, LNCS 4560, Global and Local User Interfaces, edited by Nuray Aykin
- Volume 12, LNCS 4561, Digital Human Modeling, edited by Vincent G. Duffy

- Volume 13, LNAI 4562, Engineering Psychology and Cognitive Ergonomics, edited by Don Harris
- Volume 14, LNCS 4563, Virtual Reality, edited by Randall Shumaker
- Volume 15, LNCS 4564, Online Communities and Social Computing, edited by Douglas Schuler
- Volume 16, LNAI 4565, Foundations of Augmented Cognition 3rd Edition, edited by Dylan D. Schmorrow and Leah M. Reeves
- Volume 17, LNCS 4566, Ergonomics and Health Aspects of Work with Computers, edited by Marvin J. Dainoff

I would like to thank the Program Chairs and the members of the Program Boards of all Thematic Areas, listed below, for their contribution to the highest scientific quality and the overall success of the HCI International 2007 Conference.

Ergonomics and Health Aspects of Work with Computers

Program Chair: Marvin J. Dainoff

Arne Aaras, Norway
Pascale Carayon, USA
Barbara G.F. Cohen, USA
Wolfgang Friesdorf, Germany
Martin Helander, Singapore
Ben-Tzion Karsh, USA
Waldemar Karwowski, USA
Peter Kern, Germany
Danuta Koradecka, Poland
Kari Lindstrom, Finland
Holger Luczak, Germany
Aura C. Matias, Philippines
Kyung (Ken) Park, Korea
Michelle Robertson, USA
Steven L. Sauter, USA
Dominique L. Scapin, France
Michael J. Smith, USA
Naomi Swanson, USA
Peter Vink, The Netherlands
John Wilson, UK

Human Interface and the Management of Information

Program Chair: Michael J. Smith

Lajos Balint, Hungary
Gunilla Bradley, Sweden
Hans-Jörg Bullinger, Germany
Alan H.S. Chan, Hong Kong
Klaus-Peter Fähnrich, Germany
Michitaka Hirose, Japan
Yoshinori Horie, Japan
Richard Koubek, USA
Yasufumi Kume, Japan
Mark Lehto, USA
Jiye Mao, P.R. China
Fiona Nah, USA
Shogo Nishida, Japan
Leszek Pacholski, Poland
Robert Proctor, USA
Youngho Rhee, Korea
Anxo Cereijo Roibás, UK
Francois Sainfort, USA
Katsunori Shimohara, Japan
Tsutomu Tabe, Japan
Alvaro Taveira, USA
Kim-Phuong L. Vu, USA
Tomio Watanabe, Japan
Sakae Yamamoto, Japan
Hidekazu Yoshikawa, Japan
Li Zheng, P.R. China
Bernhard Zimolong, Germany

Human-Computer Interaction

Program Chair: Julie A. Jacko

Sebastiano Bagnara, Italy
Jianming Dong, USA
John Eklund, Australia
Xiaowen Fang, USA
Sheue-Ling Hwang, Taiwan
Yong Gu Ji, Korea
Steven J. Landry, USA
Jonathan Lazar, USA
V. Kathlene Leonard, USA
Chang S. Nam, USA
Anthony F. Norcio, USA
Celestine A. Ntuen, USA
P.L. Patrick Rau, P.R. China
Andrew Sears, USA
Holly Vitense, USA
Wenli Zhu, P.R. China

Engineering Psychology and Cognitive Ergonomics

Program Chair: Don Harris

Kenneth R. Boff, USA
Guy Boy, France
Pietro Carlo Cacciabue, Italy
Judy Edworthy, UK
Erik Hollnagel, Sweden
Kenji Itoh, Japan
Peter G.A.M. Jorna, The Netherlands
Kenneth R. Laughery, USA
Nicolas Marmaras, Greece
David Morrison, Australia
Sundaram Narayanan, USA
Eduardo Salas, USA
Dirk Schaefer, France
Axel Schulte, Germany
Neville A. Stanton, UK
Andrew Thatcher, South Africa

Universal Access in Human-Computer Interaction

Program Chair: Constantine Stephanidis

Julio Abascal, Spain
Ray Adams, UK
Elizabeth Andre, Germany
Margherita Antona, Greece
Chieko Asakawa, Japan
Christian Bühler, Germany
Noelle Carbonell, France
Jerzy Charytonowicz, Poland
Pier Luigi Emiliani, Italy
Michael Fairhurst, UK
Gerhard Fischer, USA
Jon Gunderson, USA
Andreas Holzinger, Austria
Arthur Karshmer, USA
Simeon Keates, USA
Zhengjie Liu, P.R. China
Klaus Miesenberger, Austria
John Mylopoulos, Canada
Michael Pieper, Germany
Angel Puerta, USA
Anthony Savidis, Greece
Andrew Sears, USA
Ben Shneiderman, USA
Christian Stary, Austria
Hirotada Ueda, Japan
Jean Vanderdonckt, Belgium
Gregg Vanderheiden, USA
Gerhard Weber, Germany
Harald Weber, Germany
Toshiki Yamaoka, Japan

George Kouroupetroglou, Greece
Jonathan Lazar, USA
Seongil Lee, Korea
Mary Zajicek, UK
Panayiotis Zaphiris, UK

Virtual Reality

Program Chair: Randall Shumaker

Terry Allard, USA
Pat Banerjee, USA
Robert S. Kennedy, USA
Heidi Kroemker, Germany
Ben Lawson, USA
Ming Lin, USA
Bowen Loftin, USA
Holger Luczak, Germany
Annie Luciani, France
Gordon Mair, UK
Ulrich Neumann, USA
Albert "Skip" Rizzo, USA
Lawrence Rosenblum, USA
Dylan Schmorrow, USA
Kay Stanney, USA
Susumu Tachi, Japan
John Wilson, UK
Wei Zhang, P.R. China
Michael Zyda, USA

Usability and Internationalization

Program Chair: Nuray Aykin

Genevieve Bell, USA
Alan Chan, Hong Kong
Apala Lahiri Chavan, India
Jori Clarke, USA
Pierre-Henri Dejean, France
Susan Dray, USA
Paul Fu, USA
Emilie Gould, Canada
Sung H. Han, South Korea
Veikko Ikonen, Finland
Richard Ishida, UK
Esin Kiris, USA
Tobias Komischke, Germany
Masaaki Kurosu, Japan
James R. Lewis, USA
Rungtai Lin, Taiwan
Aaron Marcus, USA
Allen E. Milewski, USA
Patrick O'Sullivan, Ireland
Girish V. Prabhu, India
Kerstin Röse, Germany
Eunice Ratna Sari, Indonesia
Supriya Singh, Australia
Serengul Smith, UK
Denise Spacinsky, USA
Christian Sturm, Mexico
Adi B. Tedjasaputra, Singapore
Myung Hwan Yun, South Korea
Chen Zhao, P.R. China

Online Communities and Social Computing

Program Chair: Douglas Schuler

Chadia Abras, USA
Lecia Barker, USA
Stefanie Lindstaedt, Austria
Diane Maloney-Krichmar, USA

Amy Bruckman, USA
Peter van den Besselaar, The Netherlands
Peter Day, UK
Fiorella De Cindio, Italy
John Fung, P.R. China
Michael Gurstein, USA
Tom Horan, USA
Piet Kommers, The Netherlands
Jonathan Lazar, USA
Isaac Mao, P.R. China
Hideyuki Nakanishi, Japan
A. Ant Ozok, USA
Jennifer Preece, USA
Partha Pratim Sarker, Bangladesh
Gilson Schwartz, Brazil
Sergei Stafeev, Russia
F.F. Tusubira, Uganda
Cheng-Yen Wang, Taiwan

Augmented Cognition

Program Chair: Dylan D. Schmorrow

Kenneth Boff, USA
Joseph Cohn, USA
Blair Dickson, UK
Henry Girolamo, USA
Gerald Edelman, USA
Eric Horvitz, USA
Wilhelm Kincses, Germany
Amy Kruse, USA
Lee Kollmorgen, USA
Dennis McBride, USA
Jeffrey Morrison, USA
Denise Nicholson, USA
Dennis Proffitt, USA
Harry Shum, P.R. China
Kay Stanney, USA
Roy Stripling, USA
Michael Swetnam, USA
Robert Taylor, UK
John Wagner, USA

Digital Human Modeling

Program Chair: Vincent G. Duffy

Norm Badler, USA
Heiner Bubb, Germany
Don Chaffin, USA
Kathryn Cormican, Ireland
Andris Freivalds, USA
Ravindra Goonetilleke, Hong Kong
Anand Gramopadhye, USA
Sung H. Han, South Korea
Pheng Ann Heng, Hong Kong
Dewen Jin, P.R. China
Kang Li, USA
Zhizhong Li, P.R. China
Lizhuang Ma, P.R. China
Timo Maatta, Finland
J. Mark Porter, UK
Jim Potvin, Canada
Jean-Pierre Verriest, France
Zhaoqi Wang, P.R. China
Xiugan Yuan, P.R. China
Shao-Xiang Zhang, P.R. China
Xudong Zhang, USA

In addition to the members of the Program Boards above, I also wish to thank the following volunteer external reviewers: Kelly Hale, David Kobus, Amy Kruse, Cali Fidopiastis and Karl Van Orden from the USA, Mark Neerincx and Marc Grootjen from the Netherlands, Wilhelm Kincses from Germany, Ganesh Bhutkar and Mathura

Prasad from India, Frederick Li from the UK, and Dimitris Grammenos, Angeliki Kastrinaki, Iosif Klironomos, Alexandros Mourouzis, and Stavroula Ntoa from Greece.

This conference could not have been possible without the continuous support and advise of the Conference Scientific Advisor, Prof. Gavriel Salvendy, as well as the dedicated work and outstanding efforts of the Communications Chair and Editor of HCI International News, Abbas Moallem, and of the members of the Organizational Board from P.R. China, Patrick Rau (Chair), Bo Chen, Xiaolan Fu, Zhibin Jiang, Congdong Li, Zhenjie Liu, Mowei Shen, Yuanchun Shi, Hui Su, Linyang Sun, Ming Po Tham, Ben Tsiang, Jian Wang, Guangyou Xu, Winnie Wanli Yang, Shuping Yi, Kan Zhang, and Wei Zho.

I would also like to thank for their contribution towards the organization of the HCI International 2007 Conference the members of the Human Computer Interaction Laboratory of ICS-FORTH, and in particular Margherita Antona, Maria Pitsoulaki, George Paparoulis, Maria Bouhli, Stavroula Ntoa and George Margetis.

Constantine Stephanidis
General Chair, HCI International 2007

HCI International 2009

The 13th International Conference on Human-Computer Interaction, HCI International 2009, will be held jointly with the affiliated Conferences in San Diego, California, USA, in the Town and Country Resort & Convention Center, 19-24 July 2009. It will cover a broad spectrum of themes related to Human Computer Interaction, including theoretical issues, methods, tools, processes and case studies in HCI design, as well as novel interaction techniques, interfaces and applications. The proceedings will be published by Springer. For more information, please visit the Conference website: http://www.hcii2009.org/

General Chair
Professor Constantine Stephanidis
ICS-FORTH and University of Crete
Heraklion, Crete, Greece
Email: program@hcii2009.org

Table of Contents

Part I: Graphical User Interfaces and Visualization

Part II: Mobile Devices and Mobile Interaction

Part III: Virtual Environments and 3D Interaction

Part IV: Ubiquitous Interaction

Part V: Emerging Interactive Technologies

Part III

Virtual Environments and 3D Interaction

Comparative Characteristics of a Head-Up Display for Computer-Assisted Instruction

Kikuo Asai[1,2] and Hideaki Kobayashi[2]

[1] National Institute of Multimedia Education, Mihama-ku, Chiba 261-0014, Japan
[2] The Graduate University for Advanced Studies, Hayama-cho, Miura 240-0193, Japan
{asai,hidekun}@nime.ac.jp

Abstract. Computer-assisted instruction (CAI) using a head-up display (HUD) is a new way of providing information on operating complicated equipment. A head-mounted display (HMD) with a camera enables head-up interaction, presenting information related to what a user is looking at. We previously examined a practical HUD-based CAI system used to operate a transportable earth station. In our trial, participants using the HUD-based CAI system performed better than those using other media such as printed material and laptop PCs. However, it was not clear which part of the system was responsible for the improved performance. To clarify this, we conducted a laboratory experiment in which participants read articles and answers questions about them. The goals were to evaluate how readable the display of the HMD is, how easy it is to search information using the system, and how the system affects work efficiency. Participants using the HUD system found the articles faster, but took longer to read the articles and to answer the questions than participants using other media.

Keywords: CAI, HUD, HMD, user study.

1 Introduction

Downsized head-mounted displays (HMDs) have been incorporated into various applications that use head-up display (HUD) technology. One promising application is in computer-assisted instruction (CAI) [1] that supports functions such as operation of equipment [2], assembly work [3], and maintenance of machines [4]. HUD-based CAI applications are characterized by real-time presentation of instructional information related to what a user is looking at.

It is commonly thought that HUD-based CAI will increase productivity in instruction tasks and reduce errors by properly presenting task information based on a user's field of view. Compared to conventional printed manuals, HUD-based CAI has the following advantages:

1) Hands-free presentation

HMDs present information with a display mounted on the user's head. Therefore, although cables are attached to supply electric power and data, both hands can be used for a task.

J. Jacko (Ed.): Human-Computer Interaction, Part II, HCII 2007, LNCS 4551, pp. 531–540, 2007.

2) Reduction of head and eye movements

Projecting virtual objects onto real-world views enables users to view both virtual objects and real scenes with less movement of the eyes and the head. Spatial separation of the display beyond 20 deg. involves progressively larger head movements to access of visual information [5], and information access costs (effort required to access information) increase as spatial separation increases [6].

3) Viewpoint-based interaction

Information related to the scenes detected by a camera attached to an HMD is presented to the user. Unlike printed media, there is no need for the user to search for the information needed for a specific task. The user simply looks at an object, and the pertinent information is presented. This triggering effect enables efficient retrieval of information with little effort by the user [7].

We applied a HUD-based CAI to a support system for the operation of a transportable earth station containing many pieces of equipment used in satellite communications [8]. The transportable earth station was designed so that non-technical staff could manage the equipment in cooperation with a technician at a hub station. However, operating unfamiliar equipment was not easy for them, even though a detailed instruction manual was available. One of the basic problems staff has was to understand what part of the instruction manual related to which equipment and then figuring out the sequence of steps to carry out a procedure. Another problem was that the transmission at a session leaves little room for error in operating the equipment because mistakes of the transmission operation may give serious damage to the communication devices of the satellite.

We developed a HUD-based CAI system that enables non-technical staff to operate the transportable earth station [9]. We then observed that staff using the HUD-based CAI system performed only slightly better than staff using conventional PCs and paper manuals [10]. However, it was not clear which factors significantly affected performance in operating the system. We conducted a laboratory experiment in which participants read statements and answered questions. The goals were to evaluate how readable the display of the HMD is, how easy it is to search information using the system, and how it affects work efficiency. We discuss the characteristics of HUD-based CAI and compare the task performance of people using the system with that of people using laptop PCs and paper manuals.

2 Related Work

HUD systems were first developed for aircraft landing simulation to reduce pilots' head and eye movements [11]. However, use of HUDs did not always improve user performance, especially when unexpected events occurred [12]. Measurement of the time required to mentally switch between the superimposed HUD symbology and the moving real-world scene revealed that it took longer to switch when there was differential motion between superimposed symbology in a fixed place on the HUD and movement in the real-world scene behind the symbology caused by motion of the aircraft [13]. As a result, scene-linked symbology that moved as the real objects moved was drawn on the HUD to reduce the time it takes to switch attention [14]. This scene-linked symbology is based on the same concept as spatial registration of virtual and real objects in augmented reality technology.

While many systems have been designed based on implicit assumptions that HUDs improve user performance, little direct empirical evidence concerning their effectiveness has been collected. There have been investigations of how effectively information is accessed in annotated assembly domains. User performance was evaluated in experiments on a Duplo-block assembly [15] and a car door assembly [16] in laboratory conditions. The results showed that the AR systems improved task performance and relieved mental workload on assembly tasks by overlaying and registering information to the workspace in a spatially meaningful way. However, there are not enough empirical studies that show which factors of HUDs improve user performance. A considerable amount of systematic research must be carried out in order for HUD-based CAI to fulfill its potential to use scene augmentation to improve human-computer interaction.

3 System

Our system was originally designed to improve operation of the transportable earth station. Here, the outline of the prototype system assumes that the system will be used to operate the pieces of equipment in the transportable earth station, though the experiment described in the next section was done under laboratory conditions.

3.1 Configuration

Figure 1 shows a schematic configuration of our prototype HUD-based CAI system. A compact camera attached to the user's head captures images from the user's viewpoint. These images are transferred to a PC through a DV format. Markers registered in advance are stuck on the equipment, and each marker is detected in the video images using ARToolkit [17], which is a C/OpenGL-based open-source library that is highly accurate and stably detects and tracks objects using square markers.

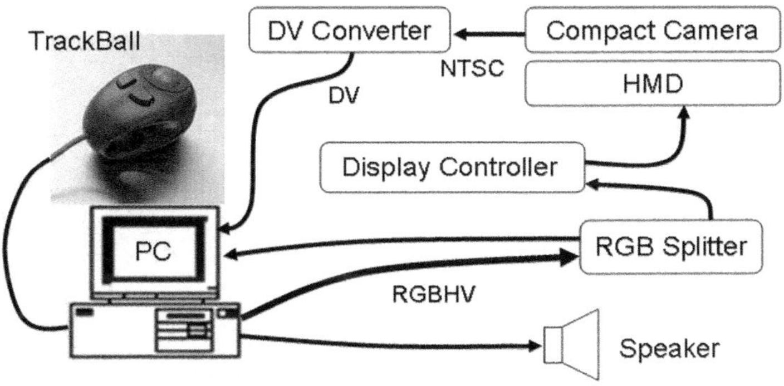

Fig. 1. System configuration

When the marker is found in the registered list, ARToolkit identifies the piece of equipment and the appropriate instructions are presented to the user via an HMD. At the same time, the name of the equipment is stated audibly by a recorded voice to alert the user and make sure he or she works on the right piece of equipment. A square marker centered in or close to the center of the scene is detected, as several markers are present in the same scene. A trackball is used to control pages by, for example, scrolling pages, sticking a page, and turning pages.

3.2 Software Architecture

Figure 2 shows the software architecture of the prototype system. The software consists of two parts that have a server-client relationship: image processing and display application. The server and client exchange data using socket communications with UDP/IP. The server-client architecture enables the load to be distributed to two processors, though the prototype system was implemented on one PC.

It is common for graphical signs or simple icons to be presented with spatial registration to real objects in assembly tasks. In our case, however, using such graphical metaphors is insufficient to represent the amount of information because detailed operating instructions for the equipment should be provided based on conditions. Such documents contain too much information to be spatially registered with a single piece of equipment. Unfortunately, the resolution and field of view of currently commercially available HMDs are limited. Therefore, we displayed the manual documents with large fonts, sacrificing spatial registration for realism. The lack of spatial registration may not be a problem for us because, unlike aircraft landing simulation, there is no differential motion in the manipulation of the equipment and the background scene is stable.

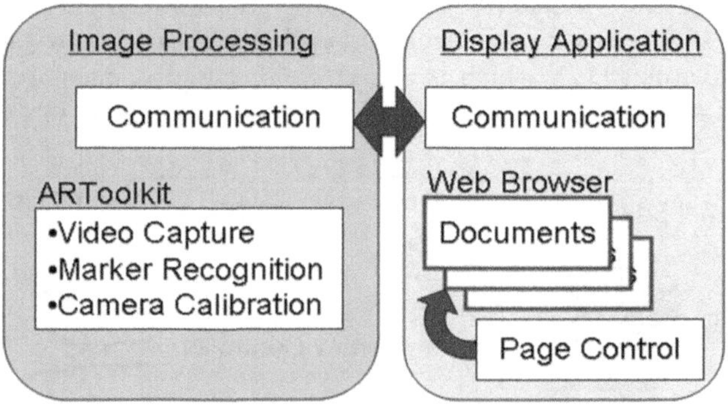

Fig. 2. Software architecture

Pages presented on the HMD are formatted in HTML, which enables a Web browser to be used to display multimedia data and makes instruction writing easier. Writing content for this kind of application, which has usually required programmers and graphics experts, is often costly and time consuming. Instructions must be customized to each piece of equipment and sometimes need to be revised, which may greatly increase the workload. The use of a Web browser enables fast implementation and flexible reconfiguration of the component elements in the instructions.

3.3 Implementation

The prototype system was implemented on a 2.8-GHz Pentium 4 PC with a 512-MB memory. The video frame rate of the image processing was roughly 30 frames per second. A single-sided HMD (SV-6, produced by Micro Optical) was installed as shown in Figure 3, attaching a compact camera. The HMD has a viewing angle of roughly 20 degrees in the diagonal and the pinhole camera has a viewing angle of 43 degrees. The HMD, including the camera, weighs 80 g.

Figure 4 shows a sample ID marker. When the surroundings are too dark, the camera images become less clear, degrading marker detection and recognition accuracy. Although the recognition rate depends on illumination, no recognition error has been observed at a viewing distance within 80 cm when the illumination environment is the same as that in which the markers were registered.

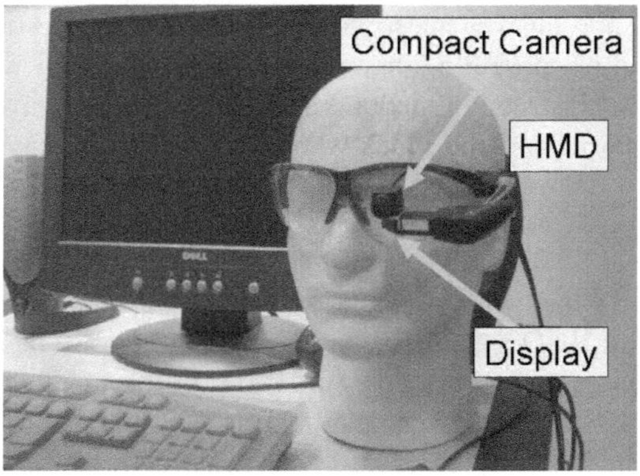

Fig. 3. HMD with a camera

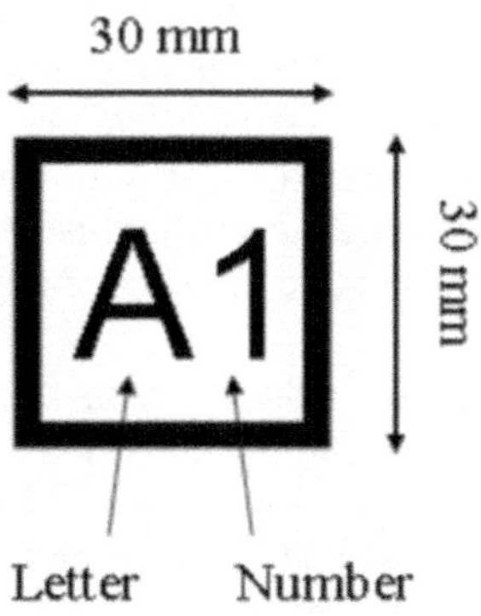

Fig. 4. Sample ID marker

4 User Study

We conducted an experiment that compared the performance of participants using a HUD system, a laptop PC, and a paper manual. We hypothesized that the HUD system would make users receive the HUD profits (hands-free environments, reduction of head and eye movements, and awareness of real objects) and difficulty viewing information on an HMD. We expected that these would affect the time required to perform tasks. Figure 5 shows photo of the experiment being carried out: a) HMD system, b) laptop PC, and c) paper manual.

4.1 Method

Participants. Thirty-five people participated in the experiment. The participants were undergraduate and graduate students who had normal vision and no previous experience of HUD-based CAI.

Fig. 5. Experimental tasks (a: HMD system, b: laptop PC, and c: paper manual)

Task. The task was to read articles and answer questions about them. The questions were multiple choices and had three possible answers each. Participants were instructed to read 20 articles with each instruction media. For each article, participants were required to write down the answer and the times when they found the answer possibilities and when they finished answering the questions. The participants were instructed to complete the task as quickly and accurately as possible.

Stimuli. In the experiment, slips of paper with possible answers were taped to the wall in front of the participant. In the HUD system, each possible answer slip has an ID marker, and articles and questions are presented on the HMD. In the PC and the paper manual, articles and questions are presented on the PC monitor and paper sheets, respectively.

All three media used the same format to present the articles, but there were differences among the media in how the questions and answers were presented. In the HUD system and the PC, the title and marker number were displayed in blue at the top of the page, and the headings of the article were displayed in black below the title. These headings were presented in larger fonts on the HMD (24 pt) than on the PC monitor (12 pt). When the participant centers the marker on the display, the article is identified, and the article's top page is presented on the HMD. While reading an article, a participant presses a button of the trackball to hold the page.

Measurements. The time required to find and complete each article were recorded for all 20 articles. Finding time is defined as the time it took the participant to find the possible answers for a question, and completion time is defined as the time it took the participant to finish answering the question. These times were recorded by the participants themselves using a stopwatch, and participants were asked about which media was best for performing the task. The questions are listed in Table 1.

Table 1. Preference test questions

	Question
1	The instruction medium was easy to use.
2	Practice was not necessary.
3	Looking for possible answers is easy.
4	Identifying the answer to the question is easy.
5	The task was not tiring.
6	The medium is enjoyable.

Procedure. The participants were divided into three groups and each group started performing the task using one of the three different instruction media. There were three trials with each group using each medium once. For example, if a participant began with the HUD system, he or she would use the laptop PC in the second trial and the paper manual in the third trial. The preference test was conducted immediately after participants had finished all three trials.

For the HUD system to work properly, the position of the HMD and the direction of the compact camera needed to be calibrated. Calibration took approximately five minutes. The participants practiced with the HUD system, and any questions were answered at that time. The trials started when the participants reported feeling comfortable using the HUD system.

4.2 Results

Figure 6 shows the results of the experiment. The bars indicate average times required by participants to complete trials. The black, shaded, and unshaded bars represent times for the HUD system, the laptop PC, and the paper manual, respectively. The error bar on each bar represents the standard deviation.

Analysis of Variance (ANOVA) was carried out on the task time data. Presentation media significantly affected finding time ($F[2,102]=62.01$, $p<0.01$). Post hoc analysis for all possible pairs of presentation media showed that the trial with the HUD system was significantly shorter than those with the others. Presentation media also significantly affected work time (the time required to finish the article after the possible answers had been found) ($F[2,102]=12.01$, $p<0.01$). Post hoc analysis showed the trial with the HUD system took significantly longer than those with the other media but no significant difference between the PC system and the paper manual. Presentation media also significantly affected completion time ($F[2,102]=5.48$, $p<0.01$). Post hoc analysis showed that the trial with the PC took significantly longer than those with the other media, but there was no difference in completion time between the HUD system and the paper manual.

Figure 7 shows the results of the preference test. Scores for questions by number, as listed in Table 1, are ranged along the horizontal axis. The bars indicate the average score reported by participants. The black, shaded, and unshaded bars represent scores for the HUD system, the laptop PC, and the paper manual, respectively. The error bar on each bar represents the standard deviation.

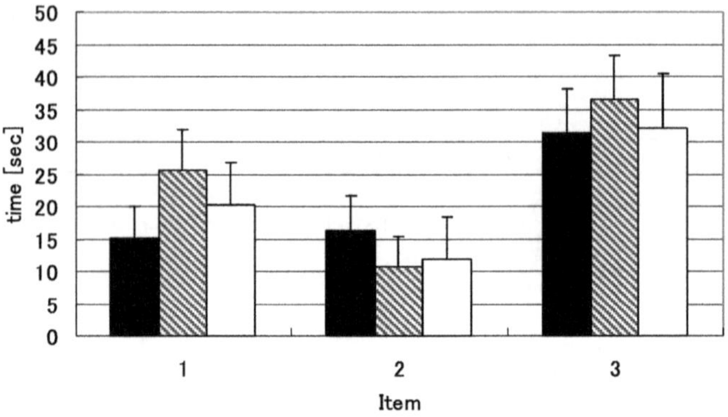

Fig. 6. Experimental results

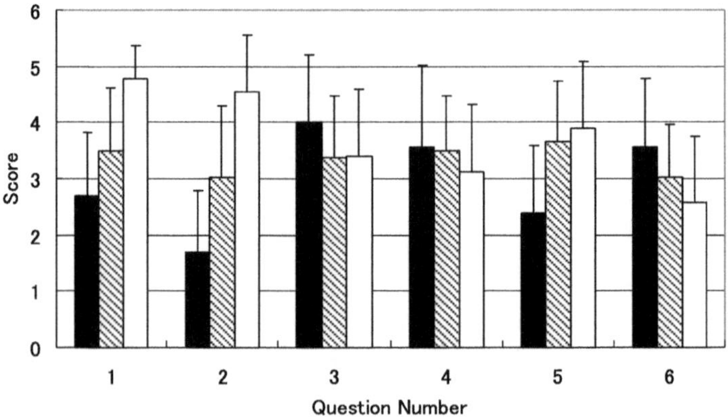

Fig. 7. Preference test results (Black: HUD, Shaded: PC, Unshaded: paper)

In answers to questions 1 and 2, related to ease of use and practice, the same tendency was observed: the paper manual was the preferred instruction medium, the PC was ranked second, and the HUD system was third. In answer to question 5, which asked about how tiring the task was, participants reported that they preferred the PC and the manual to HUD, but neither of these two was clearly preferred over the other. In answers to question 4, about mental switching, all the scores were comparable. In answers to question 6, participants reported that the HUD system was the most enjoyable, the PC was next most enjoyable, and the paper manual was boring. In answers to question 3, the HUD system was reported to be the most helpful in searching articles, and the other media had comparable scores.

4.3 Discussion

Overall, the performance and preference test results did not show that the HUD system was clearly superior to the other media over the whole course of the task. As expected, the participants using the HUD system took less time finding the possible answers and more time reading the articles and the question on the HMD than participants using the other media. We observed that the ID on the answer possibility sheet made it easy to identify the location of the answer on the wall and the article on the HMD. That is, the ID worked as a sign guiding the task procedure, but the HMD required the participants to see small characters with their own eyes, which affected the task time.

We observed that there was a difference between the experimental results and those obtained in the actual operation of the transportable earth station. In the experiment, the task completion time was comparable among the three media. In the actual operation, however, people using the HUD-based CAI system performed better than those using the other two media. This was interpreted as a difference of the task or the experimental condition that worked against the HUD system or in favour of the paper manual in this experiment.

5 Conclusion

We investigated the use of our HUD system, comparing user performance with the HUD system, a laptop PC, and a paper manual. The results showed that the HUD system excelled at finding the answer but seemed to hinder efforts to find the answer by reading the article carefully. This suggests that the HUD-based CAI system is good at indicating which equipment the user needs to use but not at presenting needed instructional information.

Acknowledgements. This research was partially supported by the Ministry of Education, Science, Sports and Culture, Grant-in-Aid for Scientific Research (18500754, 17300283).

References

1. Feiner, S., MacIntyre, B., Seligmann, D.: Knowledge-based augmented reality. Communications of the ACM 36, 52–62 (1993)
2. Caudell, T.P., Mizell, D.W.: Augmented reality: an application of head-up display technology to manual manufacturing processes. In: Proc. International Conference on System Sciences, pp. 659–669 (1992)
3. Sharma, R., Molineros, J.: Computer vision-based augmented reality for guiding manual assembly, Presence. Teleoperators and Virtual Environments 6, 292–317 (1997)
4. Lipson, H., Shpitalni, M., Kimura, F., Goncharenko, I.: Online product maintenance by web-based augmented reality, New Tools and Workflow for Product Development, pp. 131–143 (1998)
5. Previc, F.H.: Neuropsychological guidelines for aircraft control stations, IEEE Engineering in Medicine and Biology, pp. 81–88 (2000)
6. Wickens, C.D.: Computational models of human performance, Technical Report No. ARL-92-4/NASA-A3I-92-1, University of Illinois, Aviation Research Laboratory (1992)

7. Neumann, U., Majoros, A.: Cognitive, performance, and systems issues for augmented reality applications in manufacturing and maintenance. In: Proc. IEEE VRAIS'98, pp. 4–11 (1998)
8. Tanaka, K., Kondo, K.: Configuration of inter-university satellite network Space Collaboration System, IEICE Transactions on Information & System, J82-D-I, pp. 581–588 (1999)
9. Asai, K., Kobayashi, H.: Computer assisted instruction using augmented reality in operating the transportable earth station – Comparison between single-sided and both-sided HMDs-. In: Proc. Human Computer Interaction International (CD-ROM)(2004)
10. Asai, K., Kobayashi, H., Saito, F.: Comparative effectiveness of computer-assisted instruction using a head-up display for operation of the transportable earth station, IEEJ Transactions on Electronics. Information and Systems 126, 465–473 (2006)
11. Haines, R., Fischer, E., Price, T.: Head-up transition behavior of pilots with and without head-up display in simulated low-visibility approaches, Technical Report: NASA Ames Research Center, Moffett Field (1980)
12. Weintraub, D.J., Haines, R.F., Randle, R.J.: Head-up display (HUD) utility, II: Runway to HUD transitions monitoring eye focus and decision times. In: Proc. Human Factors Society 29th Annual Meeting, pp. 615–619 (1985)
13. McCann, R.S., Lynch, J.M., Foyle, D.C., Johnston, J.C.: Modeling attentional effects with head-up displays. In: Proc. 37th Annual meeting of the Human Factors Society pp. 1345–1349 (1993)
14. Foyle, D.C., McCann, R.S., Shelden, S.G.: Attentional issues with superimposed symbology: formats for scene-linked displays. In: Proc. 8th International Symposium on Aviation Psychology, pp. 98–103 (1995)
15. Tang, A., Owen, C., Biocca, F., Mou, W.: Comparative effectiveness of augmented reality in object assembly. In: Proc CHI (2003) pp. 73–80 (2003)
16. Wiedenmaier, S., Oehme, O., Schmidt, L., Luczak, H.: Augmented Reality (AR) for assembly processes design and experimental evaluation. International Journal of Human-Computer Interaction 16(3), 497–514 (2003)
17. Kato, H., Billinghurst, M., Poupyrev, I., Imamoto, K., Tachibana, K.: Virtual object manipulation in a table-top AR environment. In: Proc. ISAR (2000) pp. 111–119 (2000)

Flight Crew Perspective on the Display of 4D Information for En Route and Arrival Merging and Spacing

Vernol Battiste[1], Walter W. Johnson[2], Nancy H. Johnson[1], Stacie Granada[1], and Arik-Quang Dao[1]

[1] San Jose State University Foundation, San Jose, CA 95112
[2] NASA Ames Research Center, Moffett Field, CA 94035

Abstract. This paper introduces and describes a 3D Cockpit Situation Display (CSD) that includes the display of ownship and traffic, flight path intent, terrain and terrain alerting relative to current and proposed flight paths, conflict alerting and 3D weather. The primary function of the 3D CSD is to support the task of flight path management, although it is also designed to promote visual momentum and task awareness across displays. In this paper, we will discuss the approach to the design of the 3D CSD as well as describe the features of the display and their importance to traffic, terrain and general situation awareness. We will also list some of the pilot identified benefits of the 3D display. Finally, we will report on flight crew ratings of the usefulness and usability of the 3D display to support en route and arrival decision making.

Keywords: Primary Flight Display (PFD), NAV Display (ND), 2D Display, 3D display, Cockpit Situation Display (CSD), Cockpit Display Of Traffic Information (CDTI).

1 Introduction

Although the current air traffic management (ATM) system is considered safe, there seems to be very little room for growth, given that controller workload in the current sector-oriented airspace is recognized as one of the limiting factors. In response to this limitation, NASA has developed decision support tools (DSTs) to increase controller productivity. However, even with more advanced DSTs we do not expect controllers to manage 3 times current traffic levels. Thus, there is a need to re-think the role of air and ground assets in the future ATM system and the tasks to be performed by humans and automation.

The current ATM architecture involves ground-based controllers managing traffic flows while eliminating conflicts. In the next generation ATM environment, where three times (3X) the current traffic levels are expected, traffic separation and flow management may be distributed between ATM users, providers, and automation [1]. In such a transformation, information requirements, roles, and responsibilities must evolve. In the discussion of what changes are required in air and ground systems, ATM researchers have paid significant attention to the design and development of the ground system's architecture. In contrast, flight deck architecture and tools have been

J. Jacko (Ed.): Human-Computer Interaction, Part II, HCII 2007, LNCS 4551, pp. 541–550, 2007.

largely left to evolve as they have in the past, based on the users' and developers' differing visions of the future ATM system, and the users' abilities to factor those future visions into their current bottom-line.

1.1 2025 Concepts

Although a well equipped and fully integrated flight deck is central to most, if not all, ATM concepts envisioned to support 3X traffic in the 2025 NAS, airside research is only a small portion of the total ATM research and development effort. While the Intelligent Integrated Flight Deck Technologies element of NASA's Aviation Safety Program is focusing on flight deck safety, the NGATS vision is also focusing on achieving simultaneous significant increases in capacity, safety, efficiency, and security of air transportation operations and improving the bottom-line for all users.

In particular, one of the main thrust areas identified by the JPDO to achieve traffic throughput at crowed hub airports are performance-based services, which require flight decks to be suitably equipped in order to receive enhanced and expedited ATM services during peak traffic periods. For performance-based services to have a positive impact on ATM operations users will be expected to take advantage of network-enabled information access, and to assimilate weather information into flight deck and airline operation center (AOC) decisions. In order to enable operations in super dense airspace, the flight decks of the future will use broad area precision navigation to adhere to 4D trajectories and ATM constraints. Finally, future flight decks will need to perform operations equivalently well in all weather and visibility conditions.

To support the 2025 ATM goals, NASA has studied several operational concepts focused on sharing air/ground decision-making [2], and more recently on an Automated Airspace Concept (AAC) [3] in which the distributed decision-making includes a potentially autonomous automation component. In addition to redistribution of roles between the ground, the flight deck, and automation, these concepts require a significant change in the distribution and availability of information to all parties in the system. Some of the more advanced concepts (e.g., autonomous flight-deck based flight path management – "free flight"), assume advanced real time distribution of traffic position and flight plan intent on all aircraft operating in the system. This information, in turn, supplies a suite of flight deck tools that allow flight crews to maintain separation from traffic while managing to ATC constraints (e.g., required times of arrival). A second similar, but less radical concept allows the flight deck to plan conflict-free routes using all the same information and equipment as that needed for free flight, but requires the flight deck to transmit their new plan to the air traffic controller for concurrence. Finally, both near and far term concepts assume a transition from voice to advanced data link for flight plan clearances and clearance requests [5].

In considering the types of tasks that can be safely performed by flight crews, Battiste in 2000 asked controllers and flight crews about the transfer of separation responsibility from the ground to the flight deck [4]. He reported that both controllers and pilots agreed that separation responsibility should remain with the controllers. In recent investigations, responsibility for autonomous flight operations, trajectory negotiations, and specific clearances for merging and spacing operations was delegated to pilots. The pilots in these studies were provided advanced displays and tools and were able to safely and efficiently conduct autonomous flight operations and to execute specific (limited delegation) clearances. Participating controllers reported that managing unequipped traffic in a mixed traffic environment with autonomous aircraft was workable and that managing arrival traffic while equipped aircraft were conducting arrival merging and spacing did not significantly increase their workload.

1.2 Concept of Flight Path Management

The concept of flight path management is not new. However, potential flight deck displays and tools that support flight path management can now provide a new way of cognitively and intuitively integrating information to support new roles and responsibilities on the flight deck. In the future, the transport pilot's role will continue to be that of supervisor or manager. That task is one of information and system management, thus the need for displays and tools that optimally integrate and present task relevant information.

2 CSD Display Overview

The 4D CSD (see Figure 1)[1], is an example of such a tool that provides the pilots with the ability to view traffic weather and terrain information in a planar or profile view, and to dynamically position the display in some combination between these two choices with a 3D perspective. An earlier paper describes some of the features of our 3D CSD in detail [5].

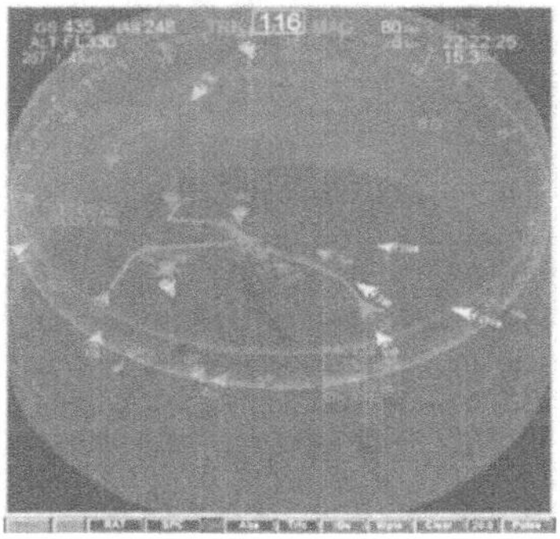

Fig. 1. 3D CSD - footnote 1

Our goal in designing the 4D CSD was to create a seamless integrated graphical flight deck tool for flight path management that interfaced directly to the flight management computer (FMC). An additional goal was to support crew decision making with automation that supports current and future task completion.

CSD - Display Basics. Due to limited space, only the key DSTs within the Ames CSD are described in this paper[1]. The CSD offers two traffic display modes: *Expanded and Full.* In *Expanded mode, planar view,* a compass rose depicts 100 degrees of heading at the top-most portion of the CSD, with ownship at the center of the display. In this *mode*, the user can only view the CSD in a 2D top-down view. In *Full mode,* the user can manipulate the CSD to examine the display as a 3D object. In full mode, two projected views are available: *Orthographic* and *Perspective.* In the orthographic view, the sizes and perspective of elements on the display are discrete and constant - supporting distance and direction judgments. In contrast, the perspective view affords relative judgments regarding the relative distance between objects - aircraft that are farther away diminish in size.

[1] For more information, download the Ames 3D CSD User Guide at http://human-factors arc.nasa.gov/ ihh/cdti/download.html

In addition, the full mode provides a *Central* and *Temporal* view that manipulate the position of ownship on the display. In the *Central* view, ownship is position in the center of one or more range rings, affording detection of aircraft by a distance from ownship. The display can be zoomed in for a detailed look at the airspace around ownship (10nm) or zoomed out as far as 640nm to facilitate viewing or planning far-term trajectories. In the *Temporal* view ownship is positions closer to the bottom edge of the display, maximizing the area in front of Ownship. The depiction of traffic is relative to a time parameter, where for example, any aircraft displayed along the 10-minute arc can reach Ownship within 10 minutes.

Attributes of the display, like the magenta color of ownship and its path, the color-coding of traffic above (blue) and below (green) ownship, provide the visual momentum needed to maintain situational awareness as the display is manipulated by the flight crew. The display can be manipulated into any 3D view using a mouse or touch pad.

CSD - Aircraft Intent. Through access to Automatic Dependent Surveillance Broadcast (ADS-B) or other datalink technologies, CSD-equipped aircraft will have access to flight plan information on equipped aircraft in range (e.g., ADS-B range ~120nm). The CSD allows the crew to view intent information in two ways. First, a user may choose to display the entire flight plan of one or more aircraft by individually selecting their traffic symbol, or by selecting the traffic button on the display which shows intent for all displayed traffic. Flight plan intent, emanating from selected aircraft includes level flight and descent or ascent segments.

The second option to view intent is through the use of the "fast-time predictor." The user again can select *all* or selected individual aircraft. Fast-time predictors are shown as a pulses of light (reflecting current speed) along the flight path of the selected aircraft(s). The users can select the time they would like the intent information "forecasted"; traffic may be displayed with the fast time predictor for from 0 to 20 minutes in the future. Intent information is depicted for the "current" state of each aircraft and updates as the flight state changes.

CSD - Route Assessment Tool (RAT). The RAT provides the user with the ability to create and visualize in-flight route modifications, submit proposed route modifications to ATC, receive route modifications from ATC, and execute the modification by loading the graphical data directly into the flight management system (FMS). The planning and implementation of flight plan modification are subject to provisional alerting and are made available for 1) strategic conflict resolution, 2) RTA requirements, 3) weather avoidance, 4) direct route efficiency, 5) dynamic Special Use Airspace (SUA) avoidance, and eventually 6) terrain avoidance.

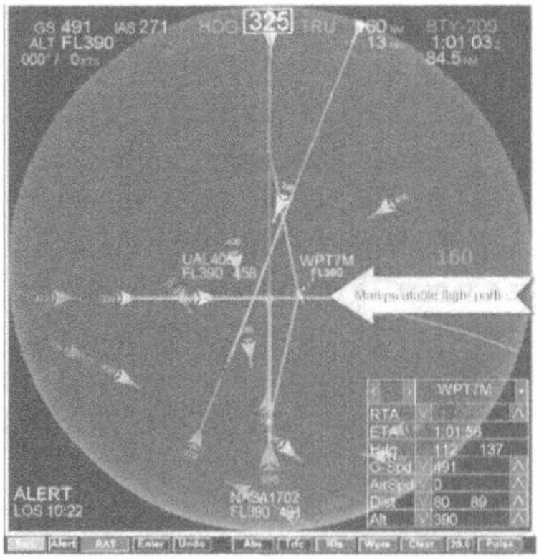

Fig. 2. Route modification with RAT

To perform any of the functions outlined above, the user must first turn the RAT on by clicking the RAT button on the CSD toolbar. This provides the user with access to a waypoint table, a flight path that can be manipulated (see Figure 2), and options for execution or datalink.

Once a waypoint is identified, the user can enter an RTA for the waypoint, enter a new altitude for that waypoint, or move the waypoint to a new lateral position. RAT functions/modifications can be visualized and evaluated before execution, which assures that the new plan reflects the pilot's desired goal.

CSD - Alerting. The 3D CSD alerts are designed to depict strategic conflicts as opposed to tactical conflict. Strategic alerting is designed to encourage less drastic changes to the flight plan by resolving conflicts early to help reduce time, cost, and to increase safety. The alerting logic detects conflicts (or losses of separation) based on an algorithm of temporal proximities, which takes into account the aircraft intent information and aircraft state information (current heading, altitude, speed).

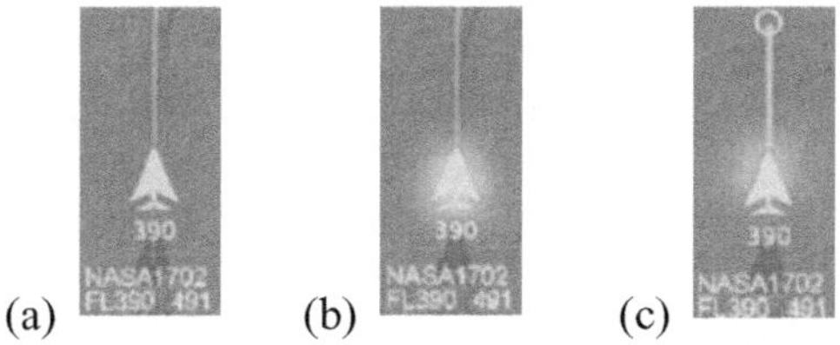

Fig. 3. (a) Level 1 alert, (b) Level 2 alert, (c) Level 3 alert

The CSD depicts 3 levels of alert (See Figure 3a, b, c). Alert level 1 is the lowest level of alert and is depicted on the CSD by ownship and the conflicting aircraft symbol turning yellow or amber. At Alert Level 2, an amber glow is added, and at Alert Level 3, yellow predictor lines with intersecting Loss of Separation (LOS) rings are added to the alert symbology. These depictions provide information regarding how imminent any particular alert may be.

3 Autonomous Flight Operations

In a recent joint study conducted at NASA Ames and Langley Research Centers, pilots with advanced displays developed at Ames were able to manage en route and arrival traffic separation, while conforming to ATM arrival constraints. Significant advancements to ground side controller displays were developed in the NASA Airspace Operations Lab to facilitate autonomous flight and to manage lesser-equipped en route and arrival traffic [6].

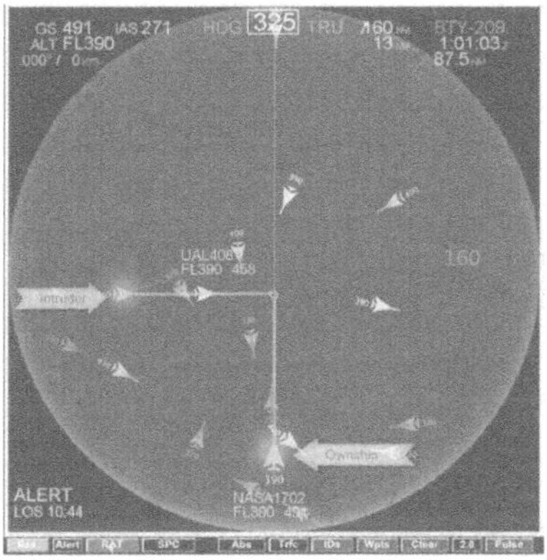

Fig. 4. Level 3 alert with co-altitude Traffic

In the simulation, autonomous arrival traffic into Dallas Forth Worth airport from the west were provided with a required time of arrival (RTA) at the BAMBE corner post (a location about 40 nm northwest of the airport). They were cleared via a standard arrival route, that required the aircraft to cross BAMBE at 11,000 ft. and 250 knots. Participants drawn from commercial flight crews flew 8 PC-based simulators and one high-fidelity

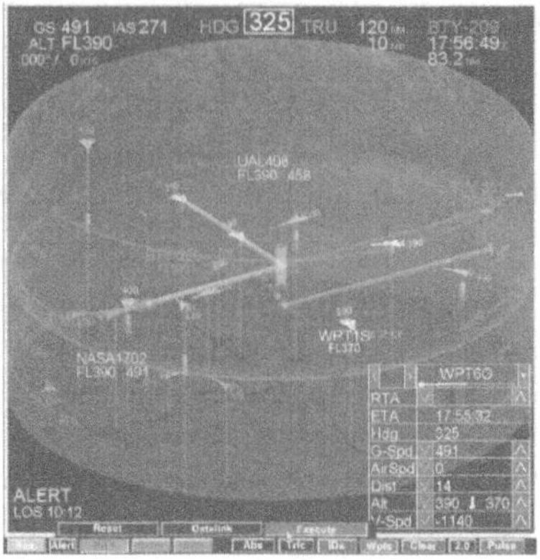

Fig. 5. 3D display with a vertical resolution to conflict with UAL 408

full mission simulator, and were provided with 3D flight displays with advanced conflict detection and resolution logic. They were also provided with a route assessment tool (RAT) as described above that allowed them to graphically design and implement a conflict-free, and RTA-compliant, 4-D flight plan that their FMS would then follow. Figure 4 depicts an initially detected conflict, and Figure 5 shows how the RAT is used to affect a vertical resolution.

While performing a flight plan-based conflict resolution task might seem at first to be very complex and demanding, especially while managing the aircraft during en route and arrival operations, crews were able to successfully accomplish over 100 such conflict resolutions without significant increases in their workload. Additionally, they gave highly favorable ratings to the overall concept, and to the usability of the display and the RAT.

3.1 Flight Crew Performance and Comments

Pilots using the CSD were able to meet their meter fix crossing restrictions while maintaining separation with other aircraft. Pilots reported using the CSD in 3D mode 36% of the time and in 2D mode 64% of the time. Table 1 provides pilots' ratings of features within the Ames CSD in terms of usability and usefulness.

Table 1. Pilot Ratings of CSD Tools

Tool	Usability MSD	Usefulness MSD
Display settings		
Display range	4.90.32	5.00.00
3D view	4.21.14	4.11.29
Route information		
3D flight plans	4.31.34	4.71.00
Path predictors	5.00.00	4.70.67
RAT features		
RAT path	4.50.53	4.60.70
RAT: drag/drop	4.50.85	4.60.84
Alerting system		
Alerting warning	4.50.71	4.50.71
Alert symbology	4.40.52	4.01.05

N = 10; Scale: 1 = not very usable/useful, 5 = very usable/useful

Based on flight crew ratings, the RAT provided an easy method for visualizing, manipulating, and changing the flight path. In addition, the RAT requires little mental effort or calculations. Since the RAT provides immediate visual feedback and provisional alerting, flight crews know immediately whether a proposed flight change will safely meet their desired goal. Pilots were able to use the RAT to strategically solve conflicts when the traffic levels exceeded the capacity of today's airspace. Table 1 also indicates that pilots found the design of the RAT path, and the drag and drop features of the RAT, to be usable and useful.

The data indicates that flight crews using CSDs to fly autonomous arrivals were able to meet their assigned RTA's as well as the speed and altitude restrictions at the meter fix. It is also worth noting that an increase in traffic did not alter the pilots' performance in meeting the ATM requirements.

Finally, all pilots were able to easily use the CSD/RAT capabilities to maintain separation with both the managed and autonomous aircraft, even with the increases in traffic.

4 TOOWiLD Study

In a second simulation that investigated Trajectory Oriented Operations With Limited Delegations (TOOWiLD), we evaluated a concept where separation responsibility remained with the controller. The primary focus of the study was on improving operations at major airports, by delegating responsibility to the flight deck for inter-arrival spacing which could be assigned by the AOC or by the controller. By delegating the spacing to the flight deck the controller would have fewer tasks per arriving aircraft, thus reducing their workload.

In this simulation 8 airline pilots performed a merging and spacing task using the 3D CSD during en route and arrival operations into the UPS Hub at Louisville's Standiford International Airport. En route and terminal ATC was provided by controllers in the AOL.

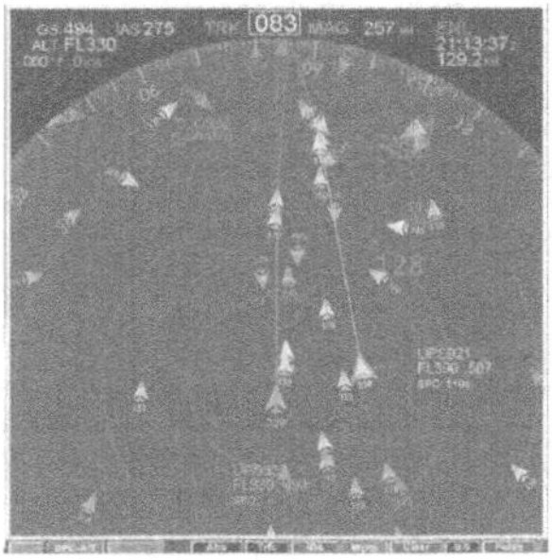

Fig. 6. Ownship and lead on converging path to merge point

At approximately 300nm from the airport an arrival message was sent by the AOC, and the pilots were responsible for determining when to engage, disengage, and re-engage the spacing algorithms based on the information presented on their NAV/CSD display. The NAV display range was from 10 to 640 nm. However, ADS-B targets were only visible out to 120 nm from ownship. As shown in Figure 6, pilots were presented information on surrounding traffic with ballistic intent based on the current heading of the traffic. Pilots used this information to determine if an assigned lead aircraft was proceeding to the merge point and if so to begin spacing on that lead. If the lead aircraft was not proceeding direct to the assigned merge waypoint or if ATC maneuvered the aircraft, the crew was to disengage spacing but continue on the arrival unless instructed otherwise by ATC. To support the merging and spacing task, the CSD provided both relative and absolute information about target speed (Figures 7, 8 and 9) and the crew could manipulate the display to any viewing perspective to support increased SA. In Table 2 below, we present a brief summary of crew comments on the use of the 3D CSD during limited delegation merging and spacing operations.

4.1 Summary of Autonomous and Limited Delegation Studies

The subjective and objective data from the study of autonomous flight operations and crew comments on the acceptability of limited delegation clearances to manage en route and arrival merging and spacing suggest that with properly equipped flight decks, revised procedures, and training, flight crews would be willing to take on additional responsibility for meeting ATM goals. Additionally, flight crew feedbackon the CSD suggest that in properly equipped aircraft a wide range of task, from autonomous flight operation to accepting limited delegation for managing arrivalspacing, could be performed successfully and that flight crews are willing to accept greater responsibility as we move from a ground centric ATM system to the 2025 NGATS vision.

Table 2. TOOWiLD crew comments on en route and arrival merging and spacing

	Rating (1–5)
Concept:	
• With training, I would routinely fly this procedure:	4.9
• It'd be acceptable to modify the term "visual separation" to include use of the CSD:	3.9
• I'd be willing to perform merging and spacing and the CDA procedure using the CSD:	4.3
• I would be willing to accept a spacing assignment using only the CSD for reference:	4.4
Performance:	
• The CSD would be beneficial for acquiring and tracking traffic:	4.6
•The traffic information provided on the CSD was useful:	5.0
Safety of Flight:	
• Confusion with additional call-sign use could be resolved:	4.5
• Using the CSD for merging/spacing will compromise SOF:	1.3
• Use of the CSD would enhance safety of ILS approach ops:	4.4
• Use of the CSD will enhance safety of arrival/approach ops:	4.6
• I am less confident using the CSD compared to out-the-window cues when spacing:	1.4
• The CSD would be useful during arrivals/approaches when loss of visual contact occurs:	4.5
• The benefits of using other a/c callsigns are worthwhile:	4.1
• The increased head-down time is acceptable considering the information gained:	4.6
Display Features:	
• The spacing tool provided enough feedback to do the task:	4.3
• Using the CSD in 3D mode improved my situational awareness:	3.6
• I could easily find the information I needed on the CSD:	4.8

Rating: 1 2 3 4 5

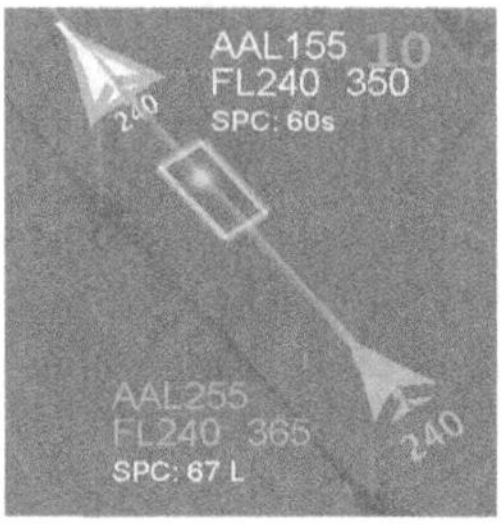

Fig. 7. Ownship 60 Seconds behind the white box - spacing goal

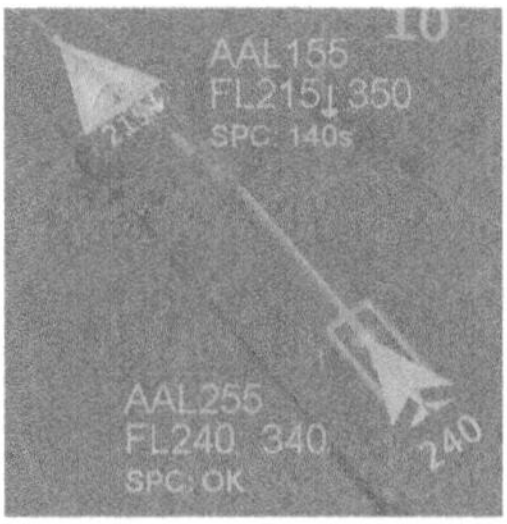

Fig. 8. Ownship in Green box, has achieved spacing goal

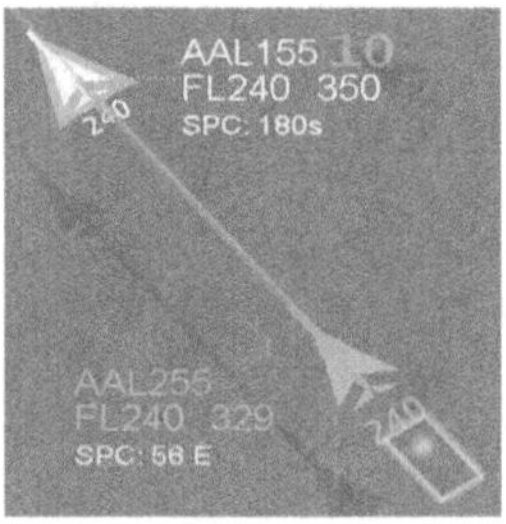

Fig 9. Ownship 56 Seconds ahead of the Yellow box - spacing goal

5 Future Additions to CSD - Terrain and Weather

5.1 Ground Proximity Alerts Linked to Flight path

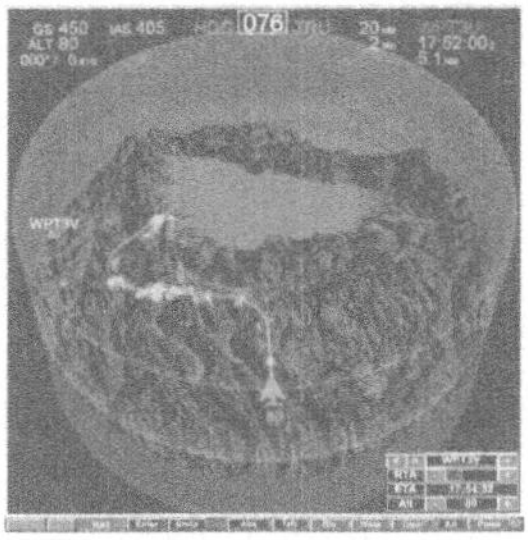

Fig. 9. CSD with alerted current flight path and lateral path modified

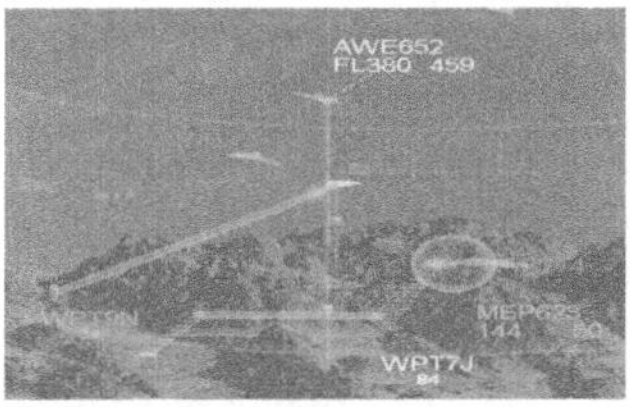

Fig. 10. CSD with Vertical path modification that clears terrain

In Figure 9, the 3D CSD affords a very quick and accurate assessment of the potential ground impact risk relative to current flight path and lateral path modifications. This depiction of the planned flight path allows the crew to determine the location of any potential problem. Additionally, with the route assessment tool the crew can quickly make modifications to the projected path, to eliminate any ground hazard to flight, as in Figure 10. The presentation of ground proximity alerting along the aircraft's current FMS flight path, with an associated aural alert, should allow the flight crew to quickly discern any problems or potential problems during the initial arrival setup or departure setup phases and should allow them to modify the path to meet the minimum safe distances at that time. During times when the aircraft is maneuvering manually or via the heading-bug the system would quickly assess any potential risk based on the heading selected.

5.2 3D Weather

Convective weather has been identified as the most disruptive factor in aviation today. Although flight crews have had access to onboard weather radar for many years, the range and fidelity of these tools have only supported tactical decision relative to flight safety.

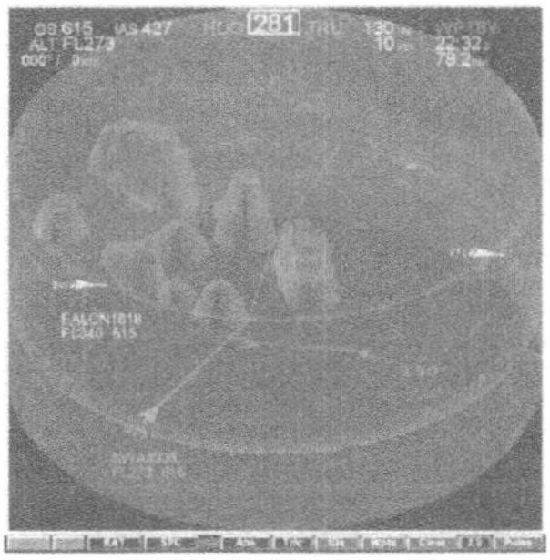

Fig. 11. 3D CSD with weather

Our goal in integrating weather into the CSD is to support improved flight deck decision making and to allow crews to integrate weather considerations into traffic management decision. Currently, crews use onboard weather radar to determine how to maneuver their aircraft to remain clear of convective weather and turbulence. Normally, the request to deviate is conveyed via voice and does not include a precise path and only considers other traffic in terms of their bearing and distance from ownship and whether or not they have found "calmer weather - good air." By integrating 3D weather into the CSD we will aid flight crew in assimilating weather information into flight deck ATM safety and efficiency decisions, Figure 11.

Acknowledgements. We would like to acknowledge NASA's AATT and NGATS - Separation Assurance, and Super Density Operations – programs.

References

1. JPDO, Concept of Operations for the Next Generation Air Transportation System, Draft version 0.2 (July 24, 2006)
2. NASA, Concept Definition for Distributed Air/Ground Traffic Management (DAG-TM) (1999) http://www.asc.nasa.gov/aatt/dagconop.pdf
3. Erzberger, H.: Transforming the NAS: The Next Generation Air Traffic Control System. In: 24th International Congress of the Aeronautical Sciences, Yokohama, Japan, August 2005 (2004)
4. Battiste, V., Johnson, W., Holland-Bochow, S.: Enabling Strategic Flight Deck Route Re-Planning Within A Modified ATC Environment: The Display of 4-D Intent Information on a CSD. In: Proceeding of the 2000 SAE World Aviation Congress and Exposition, San Diego, CA (2000)
5. Granada, S., Dao, A.Q., Wong, D., Johnson, W.W., Battiste, V.: Development and integration of a human-centered volumetric cockpit display for distributed air-ground operations. In: Proceedings of the 12th International Symposium on Aviation Psychology, Oklahoma City, OK (2005)
6. Prevot, T., Battiste, V., Callantine, T., Kopardekar, P., Lee, P., Mercer, J., Palmer, E., Smith, N.: Integrated Air/Ground System: Trajectory-Oriented Air Traffic operations, Data Link Communication, and Airborne Separation Assistance Air Traffic Control Quarterly Special Issue on ASAS, Casaux, F. (ed.) vol. 13(2) pp. 201–229 (2005)

Designing a Direct Manipulation HUD Interface for In-Vehicle Infotainment

Vassilis Charissis[1], Martin Naef[1], Stylianos Papanastasiou[2], and Marianne Patera[1]

[1] University of Glasgow/ Glasgow School of Art, Digital Design Studio,
10 Dumbreck Road, G41 5BW, Glasgow, UK
{v.charissis,m.naef,m.patera}@gsa.ac.uk
[2] University of Glasgow, Department of Computing Science,
17 Lilybank Gardens, Glasgow G12 8QQ, Glasgow, UK
stelios@dcl.gla.ac.uk

Abstract. This paper introduces a novel design approach for an automotive direct manipulation interface. The proposed design, as applied in a full-windshield Head-Up Display system, aims to improve the driver's situational awareness by considering information as it becomes available from various sources such as incoming mobile phone calls, text and email messages. The vehicle's windshield effectively becomes an interactive display area which allows the system to increase the quality as well as throttle the quantity of information distilled to the driver in typical driving situations by utilising the existing mobile phone network. Opting for a simplistic approach of interaction, the interface elements are based on minimalist visual representation of real objects. This paper discusses the challenges involved in the HUD design, introduces the visual components of the interface and presents the outcome of a preliminary evaluation of the system on a group of ten users, as performed using a driving simulator.

Keywords: HCI, direct manipulation, infotainment, HUD.

1 Introduction

The proliferation of mobile communication devices and significant advances in related technologies have placed users at the centre of an information cluster, wherein immediate access to data and instant notification of communication opportunities is required. In particular, mobile phones, PDAs and the promise of urban wireless connectivity have significantly empowered users into a "nomadic" mode of operation, where the need to maintain access to available information remains constant even when "on the move" by means of vehicular transport. Overall, modern drivers have prominent infotainment requirements which need to be met adequately.

Recently, developments in vehicular manufacturing have rendered Head-Up Display (HUD) interfaces as an increasingly viable alternative to traditional Head-Down Displays (HDD) [6]. These interfaces present fresh opportunities for the portrayal of information using symbolic/alphanumeric representation and feature a larger viewing area than was previously possible. Thus far, it has remained an open research question whether these new types of interfaces may portray infotainment

J. Jacko (Ed.): Human-Computer Interaction, Part II, HCII 2007, LNCS 4551, pp. 551–559, 2007.

data in a useful manner, without endangering or inconveniencing the driver. Notably, HUDs present a particularly suitable medium to convey such information as they, in contrast to HDD instrumentation, may situate visual queues in close proximity to the driver's road-seeking gaze; as long as the queues are subtle and non-distracting there is little need for the driver to divert attention away from the driving task [11].

Motivated by the above observations, this paper presents a study on the effects of in-vehicle communication and investigates the design philosophy behind the proposed direct manipulation HUD interface. The rest of the paper is organised as follows. The next section offers a brief overview of a full-windshield HUD oriented design and outlines its main components. The rationale of interrupt strategies and information manipulation of the HUD system are analysed in Section 3. Section 4 discusses the design requirements of each HUD component in the context of infotainment visualization and direct manipulation functionality. Section 5 contains a description of the simulation run performed to evaluate the effectiveness of the HUD system and Section 6 provides the rationale for the experiment. A discussion on the evaluation results is offered in Section 7. Finally, the study further outlines the evolution of the system design as a result of ongoing evaluation and user trials, and offers suggestions for further research and a tentative plan for future work.

2 HUD Visual Feedback

Our previous research with respect to HUD systems has indicated that such interfaces may enhance significantly the driver's spatial and situational awareness resulting in faster responses and successful collision avoidance [2]. Drawing from this past experience, in this work we entertain the possibility of expanding the HUD interface to provide the driver with information on email, mobile calls and text messaging. Significantly, related studies in the field have noted the safety risks involved with the presentation of extraneous information to the driver [9]. Mindful of such observations, we propose an infotainment mode of a HUD interface that attempts to tackle the visual cluttering and cognitive capture effects, evident in contemporary instrumenttation panels. Further, the system has been designed with technological limitations in mind so that it may be implemented in a physical prototype in the near future; essentially we have taken great care to place the work in the context of what is currently technologically feasible and economically viable.

In its final form, the prototype HUD interface design aims to present information in a timely and intuitive manner. Following the design mantra successfully applied in our previous work we have opted for a simplified symbolic representation of the available information [1]. It should also be stressed that the role of our proposed infotainment system is not strictly presentational; there is an interactive element associated with it, whereas the driver is probed to identify pieces of information that are of interest and, thus, to be displayed. This type of interaction requires a sophisticated interface that can process feedback non-intrusively in the in-vehicle environment. In this work, such an interface using a direct manipulation style has been considered and justified in depth [4, 5, 7]. Two screenshots of the driving simulator with and without the interface illustrate the above intentions in Figure 1.

Fig. 1. Simulator screenshots with and without the superimposed HUD interface

3 Interruptability and Information Manipulation

In this study we attempt to touch a raw nerve of the existing regulations regarding in-vehicle mobile communication and provide a possible solution to current issues. It has evidently been proved through multiple experiments that mobile-calls significantly distract the driver from the main task, thus increasing the danger of collisions [10]. Nevertheless, recent studies that recorded drivers using various means revealed that 1/3 of the drivers observed were accepting phone-calls while driving [10]. Extrapolating from these results we hypothesise that SMS and email messaging can be equally distracting activities during driving. However, there is a large sample of drivers who are highly dependant on constant connectivity through mobile systems. Amongst other reasons, medical emergencies can be a strong reliance on in-vehicle mobile communications.

The *interruptability* of the information flow is essential for compliance with existing laws and norms, whereas in the same time can provide the driver with the incoming information utilising various interrupt strategies. *Interruptability* can secure the driver's undisturbed attention by stage-managing human behaviour through controlling the reason that provoked the behaviour/action. Pinker suggests that ordinary *events* have *causes*, but *human behaviour* has *reasons* [8]. Therefore if the *reason* (i.e. phone call) which triggers a human behaviour/action (i.e. responding to a phone call) can be prevented or delayed in a fashionably manner (i.e. blocking the call, recording message from the caller etc.) it is feasible to accommodate in-vehicle mobile communications. The recent legislations for mobile communication on the move attempt to pursue a similar solution. However, devices such as mobile phones and their derivatives do not inflict any impact on the *reason* itself which actually stems from the human need for communication; hence the response to a call is a typical human reaction/behaviour and not a mobile-phone specification.

In this case, if the driver is forced to accept the phone call, his/her attention is trichotomised amongst a) the urge to respond to the call and proceed to a conversation b) the driving task and c) to visually scan the area for law-enforcement systems (i.e. traffic cameras, police vehicles etc. Prohibiting in-vehicle communication by law may produce unwanted results and actually increase the chances of an imminent collision.

However this prohibition can be successfully applied by selectively interrupting or delaying the call and logging the event and a short message which will be accessible once the vehicle is stopped. Contemporary instrumentation panels (HDD) already burdened with various infotainment devices provide an inadequate solution for tackling issues as those described above. Therefore we opted for an interface that can effectively control and suggest different types of communication in a timely manner.

In particular, the proposed interface is designed for specifically conveying mobile communication activities to the driver, utilizing a distilling process depending on the nature of the call (i.e. level of emergency), current driving condition and vehicle's movement. Subsequently, the use of the windshield area reduces substantially the "eyes off the road" time. We assert that when visual cues are superimposed on the periphery of the windshield can effectively convey information and avoid visual cluttering as the driver's field of view remains unconcealed. The suggestion of the phone-call management is a generalised framework that we currently expand in other in-vehicle communication actions such as SMS texting, emailing and web-browsing.

4 Vehicle's Direct Manipulation Interface

The main case-study examines the suitability of the proposed interface in a motorway environment. By employing off-the-self icons we attempted to directly apply publicly accepted interface components to the automotive environment. However, the utility, colour coding and functions of these icons has been partially altered to adhere to our previous research in low visibility navigation HUD interfaces thus expanding the original idea of effectively informing drivers. Through direct manipulation logic we enhanced the icons with interactive attributes that imitate real life objects and actions. The driver could manipulate the icons (moving and clicking) on the simulated vehicle's windscreen, through button combinations positioned on the top of the simulator's steering wheel. An analytical review of these icons and their functionalities follows.

4.1 Iconic Representation

In this phase of the design process we focused our efforts on the representation of five pieces of information that were initially identified as the most typical for causing instant driver distraction, generating a potential collision situation. Considering this information, we defined five icons namely *phone-call, countdown cloud, phone-call message, sms* and *email* notification. These had been superimposed on the side of the windshield utilising the area that produces less distraction as illustrated in previous research [12]. The icons appear in context in Fig. 2 and are described in turn below.

Phone Call. The "phone call" icon is a simple representation of a phone outlined by a square which is colour coded (green or red) depending on the incoming call status. The appearance of the green icon denotes a suitable time gap in which the driver can respond to the phone call by enabling the hands-free or Bluetooth device. In contrast, the red icon signifies that the situation is not appropriate for receiving the call as the vehicle may be approaching or manoeuvring amongst traffic. Additionally, the red phone icon can also serve as an early warning system for traffic congestion as it communicates this information well in advance of the actual congestion point.

Fig. 2. Icons used in the direct manipulation interface. Key: (a) Phone Call (b) Count-down Cloud (c) Phone Call Message (d) SMS and (e) E-mail.

Count-down Cloud. This icon completes the pre-mentioned green phone icon functionality by harbouring countdown information into a conversation cloud-shaped icon. It can be enabled by the sensor and tracking devices of the vehicle when approaching dense traffic. For initial experimentation we had a fixed "time-window" of 20 seconds, entailing two colour states - white and black - denoting the first and the second half of the provided time for conversation respectively. By the completion of this time-period, the cloud disappears and the green phone icon turns to red, interrupting abruptly the phone call. The positioning of the cloud icon points at the phone icon suggesting the activated communication channel.

Phone Call Message. This is effectively a messaging system provider that records the message from the caller. The interruption of the incoming phone call before it reaches the driver necessitated the addition of this icon for transferring the recorded information in a timely manner i.e. motionless car before a red traffic light or during traffic congestion. In such situations, it would be sufficient to rely on the icon messaging system to respond to the caller's message using a number of pre-defined text responses (templates). The symbol used for this purpose is a black rectangular button-like shape that presents the number of missed or interrupted calls and the identity of the caller(s).

The icons representing *SMS* and *E-mail* are briefly introduced in this paper as they have been presented only as visual cues to the users without any established functionality. Mobile communication through SMS and e-mail while driving is highly prohibited for well defined and proved safety reasons. Both icons follow the presentation style of blue square outline which visually reduces the significance of the provided information. As expected, the SMS icon shares the same functionality with the E-mail icon, which can provide further information to the driver by simply clicking the icon when the vehicle is stopped.

5 Simulation Requirements

In order to evaluate the effectiveness of the proposed HUD interface, we built a custom driving simulator (medium to high-definition). For these particular experiments we implemented a further version (Fig. 3) of our driving simulator that was previously used in other HUD elements evaluation. It simulates driving on a straight motorway with a variable traffic density. The other cars are implemented as autonomous agents that try to keep a constant speed and use a basic overtaking and collision avoidance logic. The simulator displays a HUD with control logic that is adapted to each experiment. Various events and driving conditions are stored in a log-file for further analysis.

The driving simulator is implemented based upon a standard virtual reality simulation software toolkit (Multigen VEGA Prime) that runs on a standard PC with high-end graphics hardware. Users control the simulation using a steering wheel and pedals fixed to a comfortable car seat while the system operator has additional control over the experiment using a keyboard. We use a range of projection environments for our experiments; previously we evaluated focusing effects of the HUD using a back-projected stereoscopic environment whereas here we opted for a high-resolution wide-screen monoscopic environment as shown in Fig. 3.

Fig. 3. Driving Simulator set-up

6 Experiment Rationale

The evaluation experiments of the proposed HUD interface have to meet two objectives; first, to determine an effective combination of symbols (and positions) for efficiently communicating information to the driver, without causing distraction and secondly, to determine whether the system could be measurably conductive for improving safety when used as an alternative to obtaining information in a more conventional manner. For instance, the accident propensity of a driver was measured when picking up a mobile phone to respond to a call as opposed to examining the auto-reply messages on the HUD. In particular, four situations have been identified in the driving simulation scenarios presented below.

After a familiarisation run, *Scenario 1* involves a phone-call in low density traffic (20 vehicles per 1.5km on three motorway lanes). The user was told to accept the call if he/she felt comfortable with the driving environment. *Scenario 2* is a repetition of the first event, although the traffic density has risen substantially (20 vehicles per 500m on three motorway lanes). Again the user was prompted to accept or decline the call after judging the driving situation themselves. In *Scenario 3* the driver can accept the phone call through a hands-free device or preferably through a Bluetooth connection as the system identified the situation as safe to accept a call.

In a practical implementation, this can be achieved through an advanced collision avoidance system (ACAS) that scans the area around the vehicle, identifying the average number of vehicles in close proximity through distance sensors, radar and ad-hoc wireless networks [3]. However as the vehicle approaches traffic with higher density, the system presents another icon (countdown cloud icon) that performs a countdown depending on the relevant distance and speed from the leading traffic. By the completion of the countdown, the mobile communication is interrupted abruptly.

Scenario 4 re-enacts a mobile call during high-density traffic where the driver's attention has to be focused on manoeuvring the vehicle and avoiding possible collisions. In this case, the interface follows an interrupt strategy, manipulating the incoming phone calls. A red phone icon appears in the windscreen denoting the blocked phone-call. Additionally a second icon appears to inform that the blocked phone-call has been stored as a memo including caller's number, time and recorded personal message. This information can be accessed as soon as the vehicle is stationary by clicking the superimposed icon.

Participants of varying driving experience, gender and age were invited to perform the trials on a number of traffic scenarios re-enacting mobile call annoyance during driving. The users were called in real-time on their personal mobile phones for enhancing further the reality factor of the experimentation. During those trials the reaction time and correctness of the driver's reaction to a given situation were measured. After the trial each participant was asked to complete a post-test questionnaire.

7 Results and Discussion

During the trials, several metrics have been recorded with particular interest in the response time and error occurrences. Additional data regarding driver's speed, lane position, simulation elapsed time and distance from the leading vehicle were collected every second. Furthermore we used observation notes, pre and post test questionnaires to assess driver performance. By altering the traffic density, we increased the difficulty level for each response. If the driver's failure to take action resulted in a collision (mild or otherwise), a driver's error event was recorded.

While an in-depth evaluation of the results is still ongoing, early analysis suggests that the proposed HUD interface design drastically reduces the chances of an accident. In support of the above observations, the derivable feedback from the questionnaires is illustrated in Figure 4. In essence, users were asked to evaluate the system's features on a 1 to 5 scale, ranging from "Extremely helpful/useful" to "Not helpful/useful at all". Participants' preferences and feedback regarding the visual elements highlights the acceptance of the icon functionalities. The first seven questions addressing the interface components suitability are provided below:

A visual inspection of the figures reveals that deployment of the HUD interface in simulations 3 and 4 altogether resulted in a responsible driving judgement based on the information provided by the system. Almost half of the subjects (43%) indicated that they were tempted to pick up the phone (Q5) in a heavy traffic situation, yet, the red phone icon prevented successfully all the drivers (100%) from accepting the call as depicted in the graph of the question 6 (Q6). In general, the red phone icon has been favoured by the results as for question 4 (Q4) the positive feedback achieved 86%. The green phone icon was highly appreciated by the users with 57% declaring that the icon was extremely useful and 29% very useful, leaving a small percentage to the neutral opinion. The icons which had mixed results were the *cloud countdown* and the *message icon* as questions (Q2) and (Q7) show respectively. An interpretation of this drawback is that both icons involved alphanumeric information that were not instantly legible as opposed to the other more simplistic icons. Reflecting upon the questionnaire suggestions and the user's preferences we shall focus on the design and implementation of new icons.

Overall, the incoming data "interrupt strategy", allows the interface mechanism to be more efficient in coordinating the transmissions from and to the vehicle achieving an undisturbed driving environment for the user.

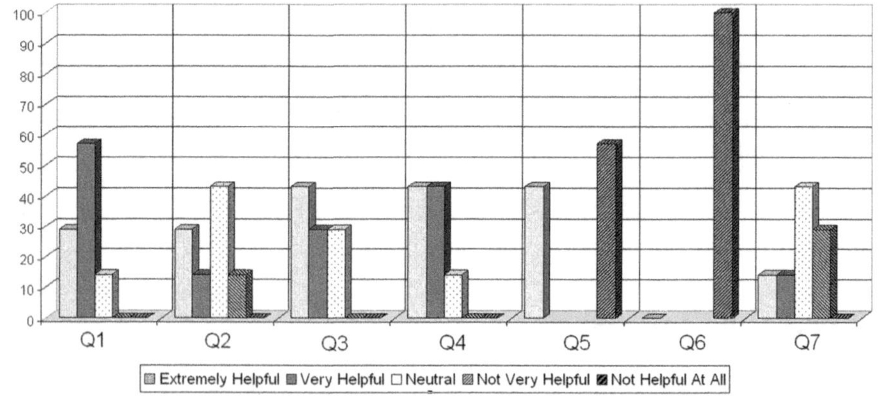

Q1: How helpful was the green icon for indicating accepted incoming phone call?
Q2: How helpful was the time countdown icon colour coding for estimating your remaining phone call time?
Q3: How helpful was the red icon for indicating rejection of the incoming phone call?
Q4: How helpful was the red phone icon for preventing you accepting the call?
Q5: Were you tempted to pick up the phone when the red icon appeared?
Q6: Did you picked up the phone when the red phone icon appeared?
Q7: How useful did you find the message icon for informing you about the blocked call?

Fig. 4. Depicts the percentage of a subjective feedbacks derived from the user preference ranking of the designer's choices of icon designs and functionalities

8 Conclusions

We have presented our initial evaluation of a proposed HUD design, which aids driver awareness during in-vehicle mobile communications. To facilitate an appraisal of the system user trials have been conducted to compare the driver's performance with and without the use of the proposed HUD interface. The experiments have shown that the system delivers on its promise for an efficient, non-distracting information display conduit. Our future research aims are three-fold. First, we aim to examine the behaviour of drivers in scenarios where faulty, or otherwise incomplete, information is available. Secondly we aspire to create a new set of icons which would depict the incoming information without involving any alphanumeric representations. Finally we intend to extrapolate the functions of the system in general by amplifying its artificial intelligence capabilities in order to provide automated responses to the remote caller on behalf of the user. In such case the interface will interact with both ends of the conversation, without distracting the driver or interrupt the incoming call with no prior notice for the remote caller. Concluding, it is our belief that in-vehicle communications can be improved substantially in the future if the interface design incorporates supplementary direct manipulation features and effectively exploit the large and currently unused windshield space for their depiction.

References

1. Charissis, V., Anderson, P.: Enhancing driver's vision with the use of prototype Automotive Head-Up Display Interface. In: 11th International Conference in Vision in Vehicles, VIV'06, Dublin, Ireland (2006)
2. Charissis, V., Arafat, S., Chan, W., Christomanos, C.: Driving Simulator for Head Up Display Evaluation: Driver's Response Time on Accident Simulation Cases, Driving Simulation Conference, DSC'06 Asia/Pacific, Tsukuba/Tokyo, Japan (2006)
3. Charissis, V., Papanastasiou, S.: Exploring the ad-hoc network requirements of an automotive Head-Up Display Interface. In: Proceedings of the 5th International Conference on Communication Systems, Networks and Digital Signal Processing, CSNDSP'06, Patras, Greece pp. 538–542 (2006)
4. Dourish, P.: Where the Action Is: The Foundations of Embodied Interaction. The MIT Press, Cambridge Massachusetts (2001)
5. Guimbretiere, F., Martin, A., Winograd, T.: Benefits of Merging Command Selection and Direct Manipulation. ACM Transactions on Computer-Human Interaction 12(3), 460–476 September 2005 (2005)
6. Karvonen, H., Kujala, T., Saariluoma, P.: In-Car Ubiquitous Computing: Driver Tutoring Messages Presented on a Head-Up Display. In: Proceedings of the 9th IEEE International Intelligent Transportation Systems Conference Toronto, Canada, September 17-20, pp. 560–565 (2006)
7. Lenman, S., Bretzner, L., Thuresson, B.: Using Marking Menus to Develop Command Sets for Computer Vision Based Hand Gesture Interfaces. In: Proceedings of the 2nd Nordic Conference on Human-Computer, Interaction, Aarhus, Denmark, pp. 23–242 (2002)
8. Pinker, S.: The Blank Slate: The Modern Denial of Human Nature, Penguin Books Ltd, London, England (2002)
9. Salvucci, D., Zuber, M., Beregovaia, E., Markley, D.: Distract-R: rapid prototyping and evaluation of in-vehicle interfaces. In: Proceedings of the SIGCHI Conference on Human Factors in Computing Systems, CHI '05, pp. 581–589. ACM Press, New York (2005)
10. Schneider, M., Kiesler, S.: Calling While Driving: Effects of Providing Remote Traffic. In: Vehicle Interfaces, CHI 05, April 2-7, Portland, Oregon, USA (2005)
11. Ward, N.J., Parkes, A.M., Crone, P.: Effect of Background Scene Complexity on the Legibility of Head-Up Displays for Automotive Applications. In: Proceedings of IEEE Vehicle and Navigation and Information Systems International Conference, Yokohama, Japan (1994)
12. Yoo, H., Tsimhoni, O., Watanabe, H., Green, P., Shah, R.: Display of HUD Warnings to Drivers: Determining on Optimal Location, Technical Report, the University of Michigan, Transportation Research Institute (2001)

Using Agent Technology to Study Human Action and Perception Through a Virtual Street Simulator

Chiung-Hui Chen[1] and Mao-Lin Chiu[2]

[1] Department of Information and Design, Asia University
No.500,Lioufeng Road,Wufeng Shiang, Taichung, Taiwan
chchen@asia.edu.tw
[2] Department of Architecture, National Cheng Kung University
No.1, University Road, Tainan, Taiwan
mc2p@mail.ncku.edu.tw

Abstract. Human activities are the foundation of the social processes that drive the urban system. The emergence of information technology provides opportunities to extend the transformation of the physical city into the digital city or virtual city. As navigation in virtual environments is evidently difficult and as many virtual worlds have been designed to be used by untrained users that explore the environment, navigation supports are critically needed. Furthermore, users or participants within the digital cities are often foreign to the environment without navigational aids. Therefore, this paper is aimed to build an agent-based system in a virtual environment to study user behaviors and interactions. The study aims to indirectly collect information about the user's desires in order to build a model of user preference and produce simulative scenarios that more closely match it.

Keywords: agent, behavior, simulation, virtual environment, street design.

1 Introduction

The emergence of the internet and information technologies clearly influences how people live and gradually extend their life and activities from the physical space to the cyberspace. It provides the opportunity to extend the transformation of the physical city into the digital city. Currently, most 3D digital cities are often created by a collection of huge spatial information to represent the real world and less concern about the interactions between the users and the created virtual world. In other words, the creation of a digital city that can accommodate the social interactions between the users and the created virtual world becomes an essential issue. Furthermore, agent-based computing started in the 1970s and recently has become important for internet applications. An agent is a computer program that is situated in some environment, and an agent is capable of autonomous action in the environment to meet its design objectives (Wooldridge, 2002). Therefore, the purpose of this paper is to build an agent-based system for participatory simulation. The methodology undertaken in this research is as follows: (1) literature surveys and analysis, (2) studies of user behaviors and interactions within the agent-based system to develop scenarios for a participatory

J. Jacko (Ed.): Human-Computer Interaction, Part II, HCII 2007, LNCS 4551, pp. 560–568, 2007.

simulation, and (3) To simulate the navigational patterns from observation and agent interface is invented for identify the navigational patterns. The findings, demonstration, and testing results are presented.

2 Agents and Avatars

Agents are autonomous, active computer processes that possess some ability to communicate with people and other agents and to adapt their behaviors. In artificial intelligence, there is a strong view of agents; they have desires, intentions and can learn, adapt and communicate. Much of this work is concerned with activities such as scheduling and controlling computer networks. Recently, an agent system considers issues related to agent communication and collaboration. The research area on multi-agent system usually conceives agents in human-like terms, a number of researchers have proposed to apply the multi-agent approach to the cognitive functions of intelligent behavior (Minsky, 1988; Maes, 1994; Brooks, 1990). A virtual world as a society of agents provides the means for constructing flexible and dynamic worlds that adapt to user needs (Smith, Maher and Gero, 2003).

Our previous studies (Chen and Chiu, 2006) found that a scenario is developed as a script consisting of role, time, scenes, and activity. A user can select an established scenario in the virtual city, and change the scenes or time sequence of the scenario to make his personal experience. Meantime, cross-cultural communication is an advanced challenge for social interaction agent. For this reason, the role of agent in virtual environment is expected to support social interaction among users or participants. Therefore, this study adopts a scenario-based approach by the role-play model in which the particular behavior is called an avatar. Each person in the virtual environment is represented by an avatar agent that is a three-dimensional animated character for navigation. The avatar agents system allows each users participating in a scene under a set of scenarios.

2.1 Definition of the Scenario-Based Agents

Scenarios can help to integrate the variety of experience and skills required in a design project by making it easier for different kinds of experts to communicate and collaborate. Scenarios include agents and actors. Every scenario involves at least one agent, one goal and has a story; they include sequences of actions, events and characteristic elements. Each scenario is described as state transitions, and semantic is depending on cues and actions.

Furthermore, based on the observation of human behaviors in a real street environment, scenarios are developed to define the relationship between people and places. We proposed the agent system which treats with scenario-based within 3D virtual environment based. Thus, two types of agents are proposed for the functional and social purposes: (1) the reactive agent: it re-acts to users' pre-defined behaviors, such as provides street information or stories to supplement the rich visual environment of a digital street about its background; (2) the proactive agent: it pro-acts to undefined behaviors with scene-driven interaction derived from people to people and people to place activities.

2.2 The Architecture of the Participatory Simulation System

The participatory simulation is an agent-based simulation. This paper focuses on the area which humans control some of the avatar agents. The humans observe the virtual space from the view of their avatar agents, and operate their avatars by using controllers such as 3D interfaces. The coexistence in virtual space of agents controlled by humans can realize indirect interactions between agents and humans. In order to clarify the relations between the problem domains in this research, we provide the architecture in terms of four perspectives: avatar agent, user interface, digital street model, and scenario-based model. The relations are shown in Fig 1.

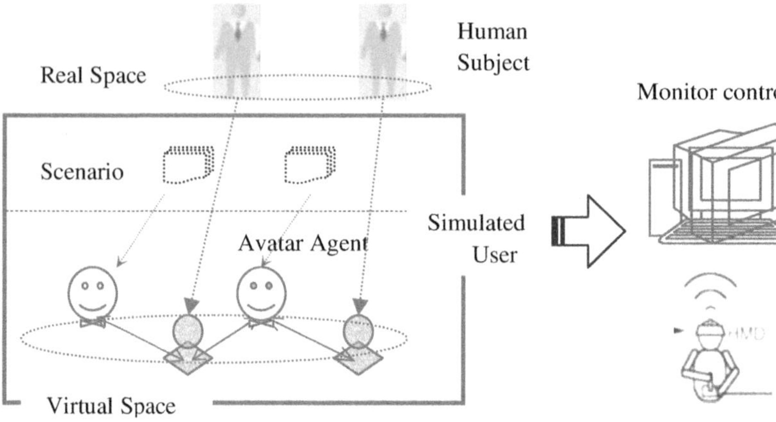

Fig. 1. The architecture of the participatory simulation system

3 Design of the Experiment

An important recent development in the agent techniques was the changes in the mode of presentation: from passive mode to active one. This active mode of visual perception is essential in environmental perception, because active attention is necessary to manipulate from the enormous information in the environment. Imagine a virtual city where people can visit plenty of artifact objects and sightseeing that can be enjoyed only in the city. Thus, the present study attempts to make clear some physical features which are influential for changing atmosphere based on the experiments conducted in existing and simulated spaces.

The methodology proposed in this paper provides a guideline directed to experts but also to non-expert users that wish to model a scenario using the platform as simulation tool. A popular shopping street in Taiwan was chosen as an experimental environment. In order to adopt this approach in the street environment context, the agent must essentially define two phases: the spatial abstraction, in which the simulated entities are situated, the relevant elements of this structure which are able to shape the movement of users, and the behavioral specification of moving entities. We assume that specific active elements of the environment can be perceived as reference points influencing the movement of users. The second phase of the methodology is to define the behavior of the agent. The model allows defining heterogeneous agents thanks to the notion of agent type, which comprises the definition of related state, perceptive capabilities and behavioral specification. Each state represents diverse priorities, and a different attitude of the agent towards movement in the street environment. These two phases define an abstract computational model for a specific situation. The configuration for an experiment in a specific simulation scenario follows these phases, and it requires setting the number, position and initial state of the agent that will populate the simulation.

3.1 A Hierarchy of Individual Behavior

Ethnologist such as Lorenz (1973) and Tinbergen (1951) viewed behaviors as being complex, temporally extended patterns of activity that address a specific biological need. As such, each behavior is viewed as a self-interested goal-directed entity that competes against other behaviors for control of the creature. They compete for expression based on a measure of relevance to the current internal and external situation. Each behavior determines its own degree of relevance by taking into account the creature's internal motivational state and its perceived environment.

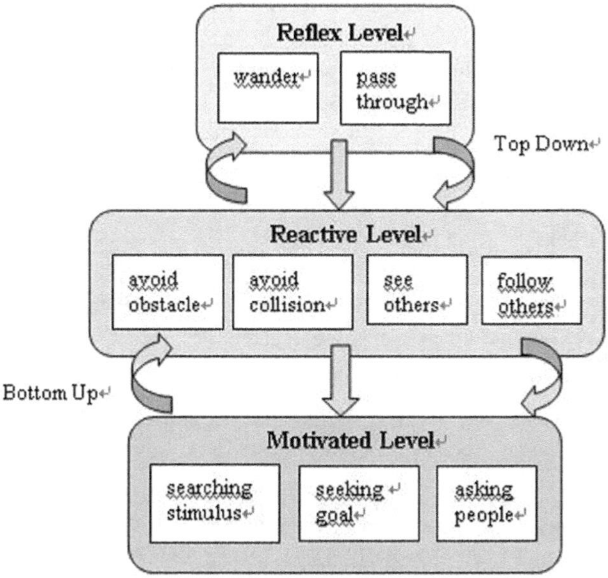

Fig. 2. A hierarchy of individual behavior at each level and levels of behavioral organization

We define a hierarchy of individual behavior that produces behaviors to control the avatar agent. The system implements principles and properties present in user behavior following the bottom-up approach simple to more complex and it is structured so as to allow an experiment to incorporate new behavior over the existing behavioral rules. Therefore, we first build the system to model reflex behavior, which constitutes an initial layer. Then we add a second layer to model reactive behavior on the previous layer. Next, we add another layer dealing with the problem of the motivated behaviors as the third layer over the previous ones. We construct the behavior production system connecting to the external perception and the internal perceptual, as seen in Fig 2.

Table 1. Behavior category

Behavior Level	Behavior Type	External Perceived Environment	Internal Perceptual State
Reflex	Wander	In street sidewalks	Aimless when an undesired stimulus appears
	Pass through	In street sidewalks	Success in achieving goal when an undesired stimulus appears
Reactive	Avoid obstacle	A large tree is planted in middle of a street	Move away from streetlamps or trees
	Avoid collision	Orientation signs for showing information in a street corner	Detect the distance and location when a sudden stimulus and people appear
	See others	In a small greenery space that is connected with a street	Green spaces, especially under trees are also used to do activities due to the tropical climatic conditions in the daytime
	Follow others	Public facilities are located in middle of a street	Fun to play with something and evoke attention when sitting in the arcade
Motivated	Searching stimulus	The artists and musicians used the street space to gather and discuss their performances with each other	Looking for a logo (a coffee shop) in a street
	Seeking goal	Food stalls for resting and chatting	Looking for a rest area or seats
	Asking people	At the crossroad, visitors try to way-finding	The diversity of activities and products sold by vendors along the arcade

3.2 Design of the Virtual Behavior

Avatars in street are a basic element and it is needed to analyze the relationship between characters based on these avatars' behavior category. A qualitative analysis was performed on the Table 1. Each of these behaviors needs both signals from external perception and internal state to drive them to move around and react to their environment. External or internal stimulus conditions pay attention as an inborn exploratory drive. In our study, exploration refers to all activities concerned with gathering information about the street environment. Motivation is defined as the direction and persistence of behavior (Franken, 1994), such as a need, thirst or desire for knowledge.

4 System Implementation

In the agent-based virtual street simulator, a human behavior may be triggered by any change in the data about the environment and the action is determined through the agent's ability to reason about itself in the environment and then modifying the environment. Therefore, in order to find out any differences that may be existed under the system examination section, we experiment to evaluate the virtual street simulator, and how the sscenario-based model functions in a real application.

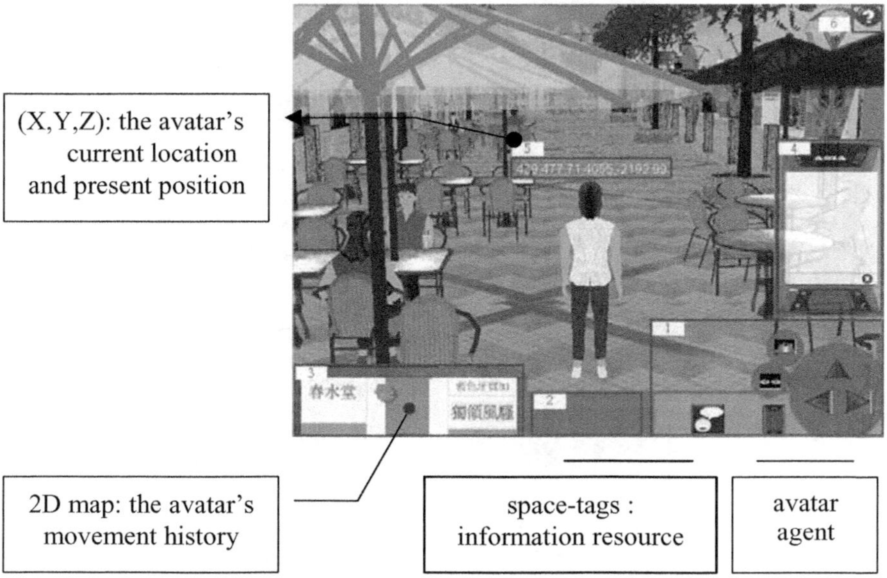

Fig. 3. The 3D interface of the virtual street simulator

4.1 Virtual Street Simulator

As shown in Fig 3, the simulator as a set of the following individual elements: user behaviors, space-tags and environments. We have identified four underlying properties which are described by the quadruplet: (1) where user behaviors are properties of avatar agent, for example, an avatar walks, stops, seats and talks; (2) space-tags are the set of all represented passive entities that do not react to stimulus (e.g., street furniture in urban spaces); (3) environments are the urban street where agents and space-tags are located, where they can move and act, and (4) where signals propagate, such as sounds, smell, etc. The avatar agent perceives these stimuli and act upon them. These properties were derived from empirical studies of observing pedestrians walking in a popular shopping street in Taiwan. The user can change the information displayed by touching the menu on the screen.

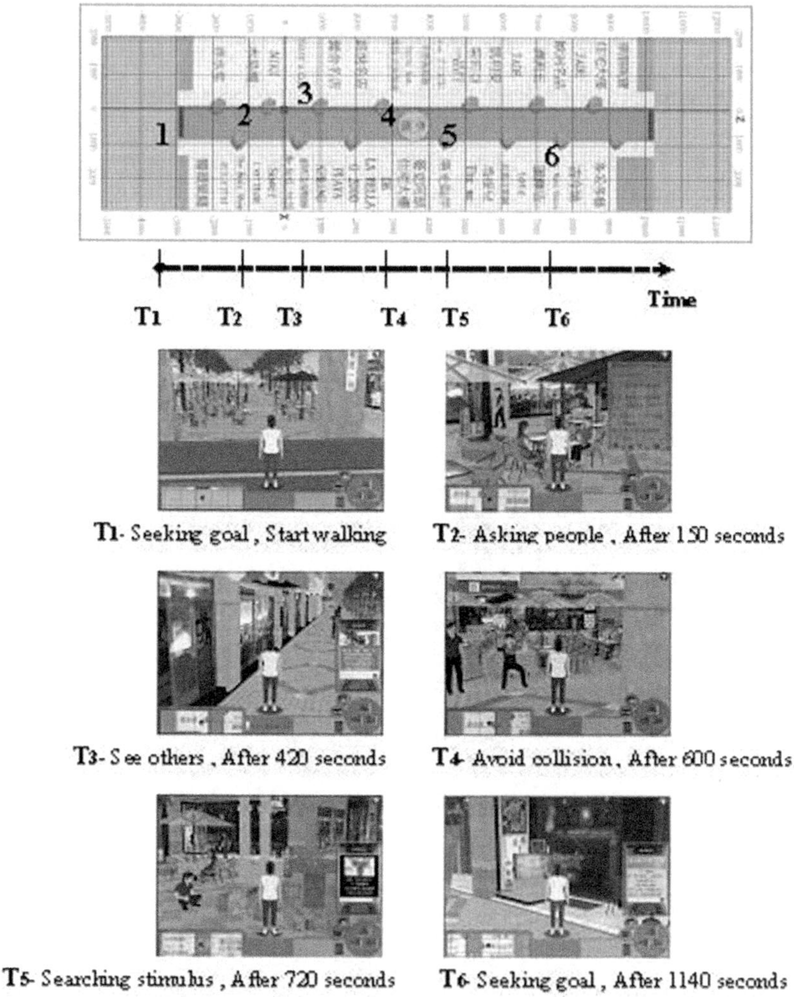

Fig. 4. Sequence of simulation with position and location detection during the walking in a virtual street environment and navigation with the agent interface

4.2 Social Interaction in a Virtual Street Simulator

Forty students participated in the experiment, including twenty males and twenty females. The age of the participants varied between 19 and 25.We made the following observations during walking in the virtual street environment:

1. Asked them to exchange remarks on what they saw and what they thought, just as they would if they were walking in the virtual street environment.
2. The remarks they made during the virtual walk. To record the data on what they saw and what they pay attention during the walking, the recordings were used in later analysis. Fig 4. Illustrates the sequence of images with position and location detection during the virtual walk and navigation with the agent interface.
3. How the agent behaves? For instance, agent explains the shops in which you take an interest.

- Explain or not:
  If you keep watching at a shop, the agent explains the shop.
  If you are not looking at any shop, the agent walks along a guidance route.

- Walk or not:
  If you are far behind the agent, the agent stops walking and waits for you.
  If you are walking close to the agent, the agent continues walking.

The use of participatory simulation in the process brings the following four benefits:

1. It enables user to capture a subject's screen, which is then shown to the subject at the interview stage to acquire user operation rules effectively.
2. It enables user to employ scenario-controlled agents in order to compensate for the lack of participants.
3. A user is shown as an avatar; space-tags are shown with icons around the user.
4. List up all the space-tags that can be accessed and these space-tags are detected by the user behaviors.

5 Conclusions and Future Studies

The study indicates the importance of people to people and people to place interactions in the transformation from the physical into the virtual environment. By observing human behaviors, the interaction in the virtual environment can be enhanced through agent. The navigational patterns generated from this experiment, and the trace of movement pattern is a useful technique for graphically recording the dynamic quality of behavior and environment relationships. In addition, in this study process, we find humans interact in various ways and at many levels. For instance, they observe and model one another, they request and provide information, they negotiate and discuss, they develop shared views of their environments. In other words, if agent can learn to access people's experiences (past, current and potential), and make inferences about what they do, then can make user experience the source of inspiration and ideation for design.

In brief, the above simulation suggests that quality of visual information observed has an important influence in guiding users and the space-tags can be used to provide navigational information and supplemented with additional details about the tags in the environment. In other words, virtual maps are social tags, they are there to give information and help people explore, understand and find their interests. Thus, a virtual environment with multi-purpose space tags and navigational aids such as guide agents will be useful for interesting navigation.

An important further step of this research will concern the degree of changeability that is desirable or acceptable for users. As indicated, agents may become more adaptive, the virtual environment itself tends to become more complex, and consequently multiple agents as needed may be present at same time. As more humans and agents coexist, the need for describing interaction scenarios becomes essential. If we allow agents to be completely autonomous, the whole system becomes hard to control. Thus, it is necessary to give social constraints as scenarios so that the behaviors of agents are reasonable.

Acknowledgments. The author is grateful for the assistance by Ya-Wen Lo and Chun-Jen Wu. This study is supported by the Taiwan National Science Council, grant-NSC 95-2221-E-468-010.

References

1. Chen, C.-H., Chiu, M.-L.: SCALE: A street case library for environmental design with agent interfaces. In: van Leeuwen, J.P., Timmermans, H.J.P. (eds.) Innovations in Design and Decision Support Systems in Architecture and Urban Planning, pp. 137–150. Springer-Verlag, Heidelberg (2006)
2. Breazeal, C.L.: Designing Sociable Robots. The MIT Press, Cambridge, MA (2002)
3. Benyon, D., Turner, P., Turner, S.: Designing Interactive Systems: People, Activities, Contexts, Technologies. Addison Wesley, Reading, MA (2005)
4. Deutsch, J., Deutsch, D.: Attention: Some theoretical considerations. Psychological Review 70, 80–90 (1963)
5. Reynolds, C.W.: Computational Models of Complex, Life-like Behavior http://www.red3d.com/cwr
6. Sullivan, S.P., Churchill, E.(eds.): Embodied Conversational Agents, pp. 95–122. MIT Press, Cambridge, MA (2000)
7. Ishida, T., Isbister, K.(eds): Digital Cities: Experiences, Technologies and Future Perspectives. Springer-Verlag, Heidelberg (2000)
8. Treisman, A., Gelade, G.: The feature-based theory of attention. Cognition Psychology 12, 97–136 (1980)
9. Wooldridge, M.: An Introduction to Multi-Agent System. John Wiley and Sons, Chichester, England (2002)

Visualizing Interaction in Digitally Augmented Spaces: Steps Toward a Formalism for Location-Aware and Token-Based Interactive Systems

Yngve Dahl and Dag Svanæs

Norwegian University of Science and Technology (NTNU),
Department of Computer and Information Science
Sem Sælandsvei 7-9
7491 Trondheim, Norway
{Yngve.Dahl,Dag.Svanes}@idi.ntnu.no

Abstract. Location and token-based methods of interaction form two broad sets of interaction techniques for ubiquitous computing systems. Currently there are few tools available that allow designers to pay attention to the physicality that characterizes human-computer interaction with such systems, and how users experience them. This paper reports on ongoing work that focuses on creating a visual formalism that addresses these limitations. The current approach is inspired by established storyboard techniques, and aims to complement de facto modeling formalisms such as UML.

Keywords: Ubiquitous computing; Modeling formalisms; Interaction design; Embodied interaction; Visual design.

1 Introduction

Human-computer interaction is currently not only about PCs with mouse and keyboard, but involves a number of different devices that can be used in many different environments. Mobile phones, portable computers, and wireless networks are examples of some of the innovations that have helped make computer interaction "beyond the desktop" a reality. The new interactive possibilities that this has opened up for has formed the basis for an interaction paradigm commonly referred to as *ubiquitous computing* (UbiComp) [1]. Investigating methods that support seamless interaction with computer systems in mobile settings has become a major branch of HCI research over the last 10 to 15 years.

While conventional desktop interaction in many ways builds on the assumption that the user is sitting in a chair in front of a table with a PC, with a standard set of input and output devices at his or her disposal, assumptions about the physical and social use situation, or the availability and appropriateness of interaction devices often cannot be made for UbiComp. Generally, interaction with such systems tends to be more physical in nature, and is usually mediated through sensors embedded in the user's surroundings. These sensors are typically sensitive to certain aspects of the environment in which they are embedded (e.g. the physical position of users). The current approach is often referred to as *context-aware computing*.

J. Jacko (Ed.): Human-Computer Interaction, Part II, HCII 2007, LNCS 4551, pp. 569–578, 2007.

Methods of interaction in context-aware environments differ, and can be mediated through e.g. the users physical location, physical objects that are digitally augmented, pointing and gesturing, speech, and tracking of eye-movements. Dourish [2] fittingly use the term *embodied interaction* to denote such methods.

One of the key implications UbiComp has for interaction design is that the usability of the employed interaction techniques becomes much more dependant on the physical and social aspects of the immediate use situation [3, 4]. Conversely, the usability of the keyboard and the mouse in conventional systems is relatively stable, and designers can assume that these devices form appropriate tools of interaction for all desktop applications.

Although computer devices are increasingly used in mobile situations and changing environments, we find few formalisms and notations suitable to guide thinking about accommodating the physical aspects of this kind of human-computer interaction. Conventional computer system modeling formalisms (e.g. UML class and object diagrams) are often inappropriate for this purpose because they are principally intended to describe how computer systems work on the "inside"—their primary concern is how information is represented in, and exchanged between software objects. Even UML use-case diagrams and formal HCI methods like task analysis, although they aim to represent a user-perspective, are to a large extent blind to the physicality that characterizes UbiComp systems. We will in the following refer to this class of models as *system models.*

Our primary objective with the current paper is to describe some of the results of ongoing work on a visual formalism allowing location-aware and token-based interactive systems to be described from the perspective of users in situ, with a focus on the physicality of the use situations. The resulting representations are *physical models* in the sense that they describe the physical reality of the human-computer interaction.

We will account for the background and inspiration for the current work, and describe some selected notational building blocks. To illustrate the added value of having a formal way of describing the physicality of interaction in digitally augmented spaces, we will present a generic use scenario and compare two UML diagrams (use-case and sequence diagrams) that match the example scenario with models created using the presented notation.

Lastly, the paper will discuss some directions for further development of the current approach based on feedback from an expert group evaluation.

2 Background and Inspiration

The formalism discussed in this paper has its origin in Svanæs' phenomenological perspective on context-aware computing described in Ref. [5]. It has subsequently been modified, applied, and evaluated in more recent work [3, 6]. The formalism has also been used as part of internal discussions on design solutions, and in student exercises.

In many ways, the current modeling technique takes its inspiration from the storyboard technique, which was developed by Walt Disney and his staff in the early days of animated films. It allows snapshots or frames of an unfolding event to be captured and sequentially put together. Disney and his designers used storyboarding as a management tool, and to facilitate creative thinking.

Storyboarding was quickly adopted as a modeling technique for graphical user interface design [7]. With the development of electronic sketching and animation tools (e.g. SILK [8] and Flash), visualization of dynamic interactive behavior has also become possible. In recent work, storyboarding has also been recommend as a useful technique for off-the-desktop interaction design [9, 10].

Storyboards are typically used as informal prototyping tools during early phases of a design process to create rough, sketch-based models [11]. The complexity of computer-based systems, however, has raised the need for more formal ways to describe such systems. The advantages of modeling formalisms are well known. Formal descriptions of computer systems can act as a common language for developers and other stakeholders, and a way of creating a common understanding of the system that is built. They can make it easier to compare and detect similarities between alternative design models, and reuse previous solutions when developing new computer systems. In addition, many computerized modeling tools are able to turn formal models into source code.

3 Notation

The employed notation is based around a variety of components that can be used to describe interaction in digitally augmented space. For the current purpose we will only use a selected set of components out of the more extensive collection described in earlier work [6]. Specifically, we will focus on *users*, *tokens*, *virtual zones*, and *computer devices*. The symbols that represent these various components are illustrated in Fig. 1. All of the above components can be associated with, or act as links to particular information objects (e.g. web pages, voice messages, etc.). In Fig. 1 such references are denoted with an "*a*".

Tokens, virtual zones, and computer devices come in fixed and mobile variants. Mobile components can be moved around by users (mobile virtual zones are considered relative to a user's physical position).

Tokens, as typically used in UbiComp, are tangible objects that can contain references to digital information objects, or exclusively identify a particular person (e.g. the user). A token can be either a digital or a non-electronic artifact. Tokens typically act as passive interaction elements in UbiComp solutions, i.e. users must actively scan tokens with appropriate readers to get access to the associated information.

Virtual zones correspond to the detection area of location and presence technologies that can respond to the physical presence of users. Examples of technologies that can facilitate this include GPS, WLAN positioning, Bluetooth, IR, and face recognition. The size, shape, and accuracy of a virtual zone depend on the applied sensor technology. Similar to tokens, virtual zones can contain links to digital information. As apposed to tokens, interaction with location-aware systems typically requires no conscious action from the user. Entering a digitally augmented area is more likely to be a consequential act and part of an ongoing activity [12].

Computer devices correspond to the media that respond to a user's (inter)actions in digitally augmented spaces. They can contain 0..N information object references, and can present the actual information object to users, as a response to events taking place in the digitally augmented spaces in which they are located. A computer device presenting an information object is denoted with a "flashing" device symbol (see Fig.1).

Users initiate events in ubiquitous computing environments, through their interaction with the other interaction components. For location-based solutions user interaction typically occurs through physical presence or proximity. Token-based interaction, on the other hand, typically implies that the user must put the token in physical contact or in immediate proximity of a corresponding reader or device.

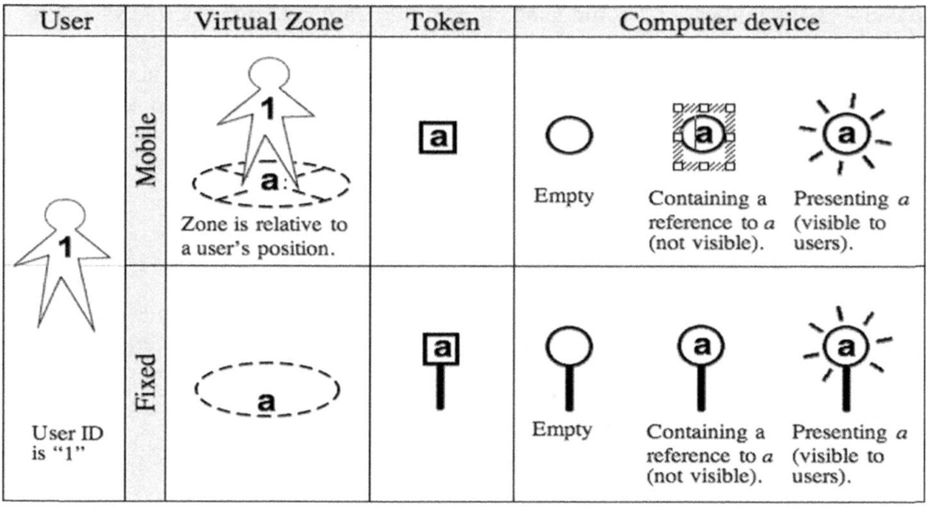

Fig. 1. Notation. Users, virtual zones, tokens, and computer devices are represented with distinct symbols. An "*a*" denotes a contained information object reference.

4 Comparing Conventional System Models and Physical Models

To illustrate the added value of the physical design models that can be created with the described notation, we will address a generic use scenario:

> "A mobile user wants to retrieve electronic information related to his current physical location."

Ubiquitous and context-aware computing in general builds on the premise of changing use situations, and mobility is often the cause of such change. Providing users with the possibility to access digital information at while on the move has motivated research on ubiquitous computing for a number of application areas, such as guiding [13], hospitals [3, 12], entertainment and gaming [14], and m-commerce [15].

4.1 System Models

Fig. 2 shows a possible UML use-case diagram for a location-aware or token-based design solution for the example scenario. It is assumed that all interaction elements (users, tokens, virtual zones, and computer devices) have unique identities that can be registered by the sensors in use.

Initially, a user indicates which information he wants to retrieve by walking into a virtual zone or scanning an appropriate token. The event is detected by the employed sensor technology, which registers the unique identities of the relevant interaction elements. Based on the registered sensor data the correct information object is found, and presented on the user's computer device.

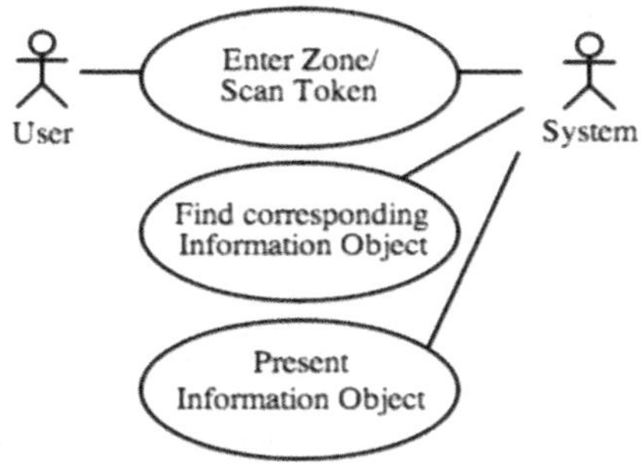

Fig. 2. Use-case diagram for a location-aware or token-based interactive system

A corresponding sequence diagram is illustrated in Fig. 3. In the current setup it is assumed that the information objects that the user can access are web pages, and that the interpreter-object finds the matching URL based on the provided sensor data.

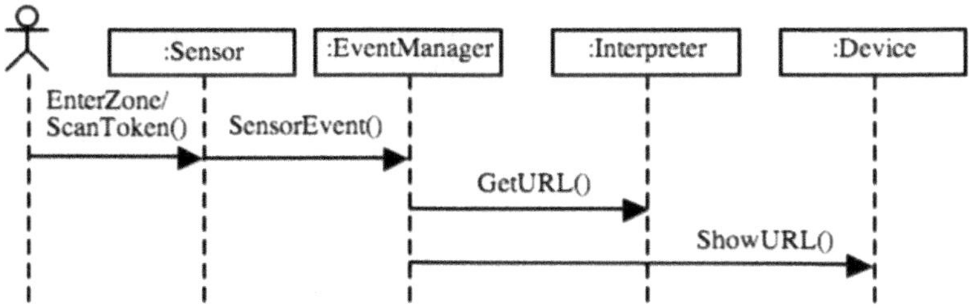

Fig. 3. Sequence diagram for example scenario

4.2 Physical Models

Fig. 2 and Fig. 3 show how information is exchanged between actors and software objects. With regard to the example scenario, the respective diagrams are principally similar for all conventional client-server solutions, independently of the employed sensor technology and interaction tools.

But how, then, can we expect that the same service will look from a user's perspective? Which metaphors are suitable for describing physical interaction with location-aware and token-based interactive systems? The notation described in Sect. 3 allows us to put together a number of alternatives. Some of these have frequently been employed in UbiComp designs.

Fig. 4-6 show different variants of location-based interaction. In Fig. 4 the user carries a mobile computer device, which responds and presents the associated information object as the user enters a virtual zone. Fig. 5 shows an alternative model where the same information object is presented on a fixed device located in the virtual zone that the user enters. The model illustrated in Fig. 6 shows a fixed computer device that initially contains a reference to one specific information object. This is presented as the user (i.e. his associated mobile virtual zone) comes within a given range of the device. In this configuration, the mobile virtual zone identifies the user and work as an access key to the information object.

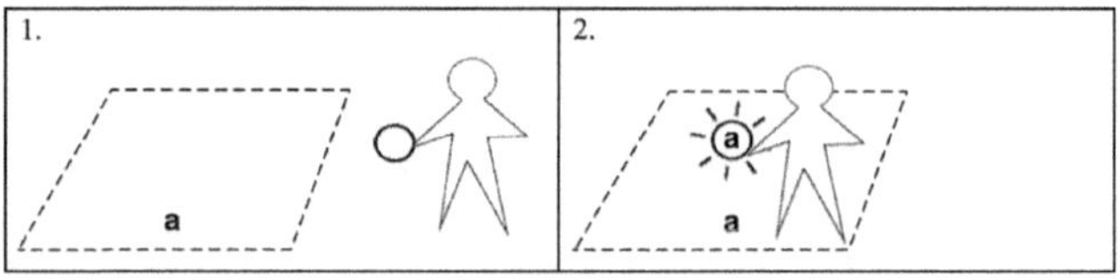

Fig. 4. The user enters a virtual zone, causing his mobile computer device to present the associated information object

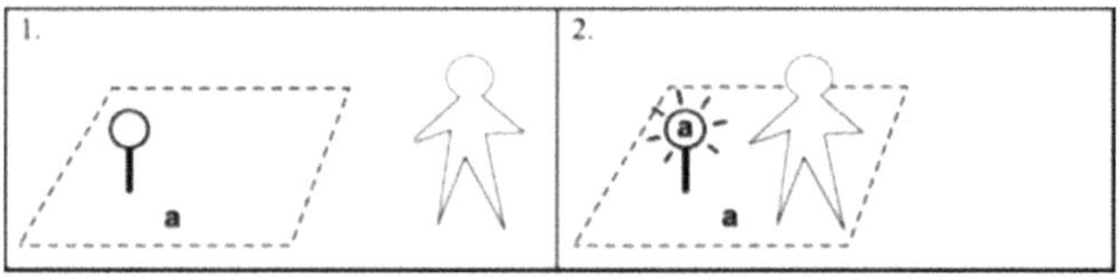

Fig. 5. The user enters a virtual zone containing a fixed computer device. This causes the device to present the information object linked to the virtual zone.

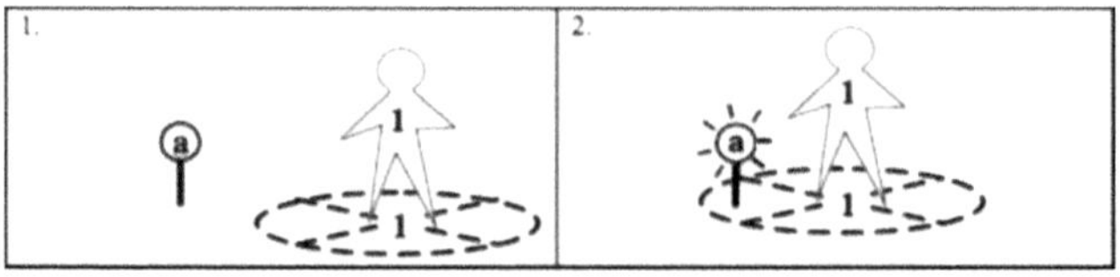

Fig. 6. An information object is presented as the user comes within a given range of fixed device. The device is dedicated to present one particular information object.

Figs. 7-9 show three token-based variants of the same scenario. In Fig. 7 the user's mobile computer device responds as it scans a fixed token with a link to an information object. In Fig. 8 the token and the computer device have switched roles from the model illustrated in Fig. 7—the computer device is now fixed, and presents the information object associated with the particular mobile token that the user scans. The user might carry multiple tokens, each pointing to a different information object.

The model shown in Fig. 9 involves the same components as the model illustrated in Fig. 8, but the reference associated with the token now identifies the user, rather than an information object. Thus, the token is analogue to the mobile zone in Fig. 6.

Fig. 10 illustrates a modified version of the model provided in Fig. 9. Instead of using an external representation in form of a token for user identification, this is now done directly (e.g. through fingerprint recognition) as the user touches the computer device. Similar to the model shown in Fig. 9, the fixed computer device is initially dedicated to present one particular information object.

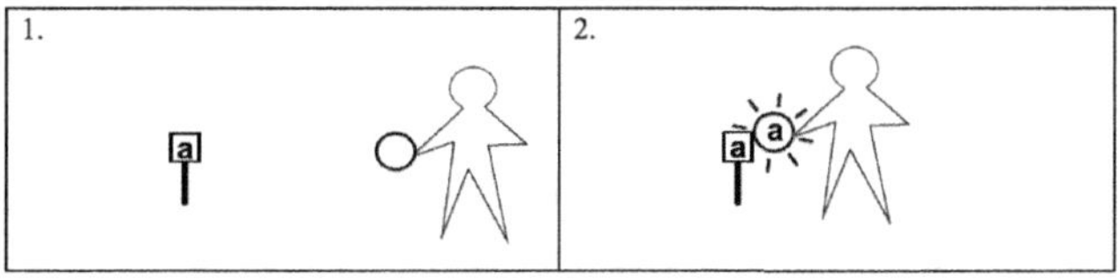

Fig. 7. The user carries a mobile computer device, and scans a fixed token containing a reference to an information object

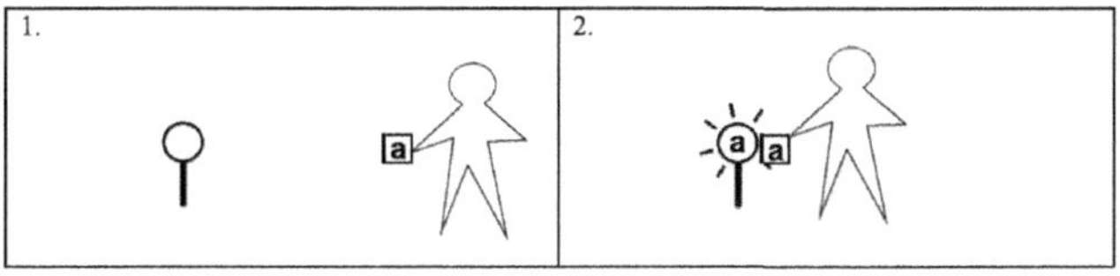

Fig. 8. The user carries one or more mobile tokens. Each token can contain a reference to a specific information object.

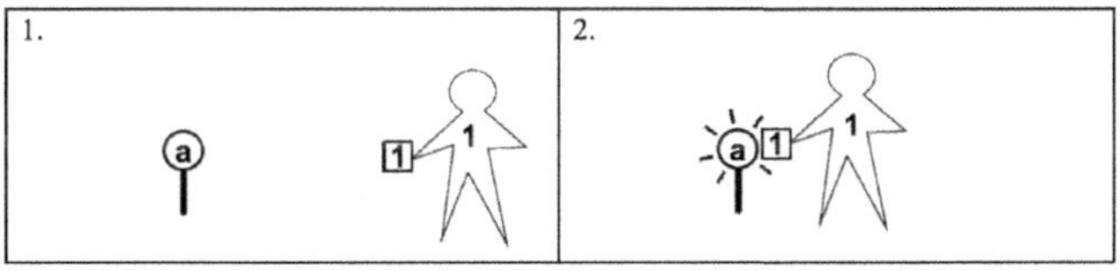

Fig. 9. The mobile token identifies the user, and provides access to the information object associated with the fixed computer device

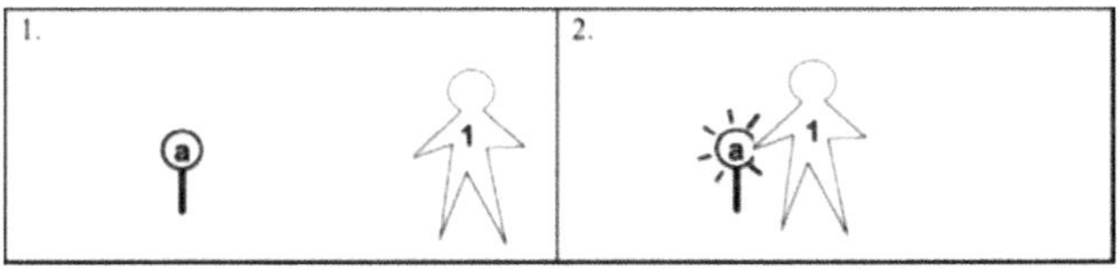

Fig. 10. The user triggers a specific information object associated with the computer device by touching the device

Some of the models described above can be regarded as emerging interaction design patterns for ubiquitous computing. The current formalism, however, also supports modeling of more specific scenarios, which combine various methods of interaction. Models of more extended scenarios can be found in earlier work [6].

5 Suggestions for Further Development

To assess the applicability of the formalism we have previously conducted a preliminary evaluation with a usability expert group, described in detail in Ref. [6]. The evaluation suggested that the formalism was intuitive, and that the expert group quickly managed to combine the notational building blocks into meaningful interaction models. Moreover, it revealed the formalism promotes discussion and reflection on design solutions.

Feedback from the expert group has also inspired investigation of how to further develop the formalism. In particular, we have considered ways to complement the formalism through sublevels, or supplementary representations, of implementation specific aspects of the design. The possibility to construct models of computer systems at various levels of abstraction is a central aspect of de facto modeling formalisms such as UML. For example, a UML sequence diagram may hide details, showing only the interaction between actors and the system, or may provide an in depth view depicting detailed logic at object-level. Flexibility with regard to level of detail is also an essential feature of storyboards [16].

The level of detail supported by formalism in its current form, allows interaction to be described in terms of *presence*, *proximity*, or *touch* (immediate proximity). One feasible way to achieve a more detailed or implementation specific view is to supplement the interaction models with icons or visual hints indicating e.g. the concrete interaction tools that implement the model, and how users can operate them. The graphic language for touch-based interactions described by Arnall [17], can serve as an inspiration for development of a suitable iconography for this purpose. Fig. 11 and Fig. 12 give examples of how such visual representations may supplement models built with the presented notation.

Fig. 11 shows the token-based interaction model illustrated in Fig. 8, with a visual hint indicating the how the computer device response is triggered—a barcode card being inserted the correct way into a terminal slot. Fig. 12 demonstrates the same

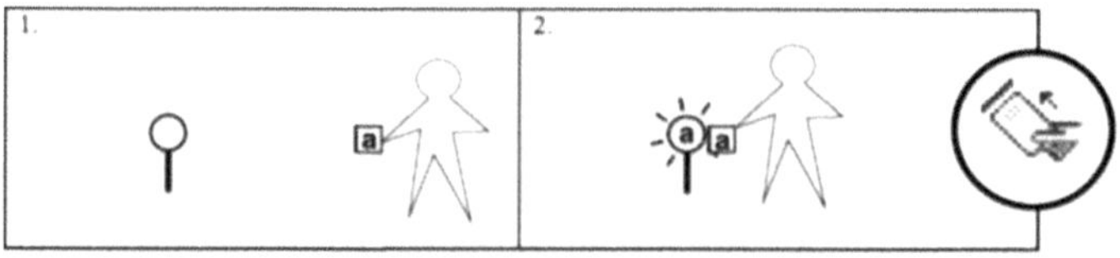

Fig. 11. Token-based interaction. The visual hint to the right suggests how the current interaction technique can be implemented.

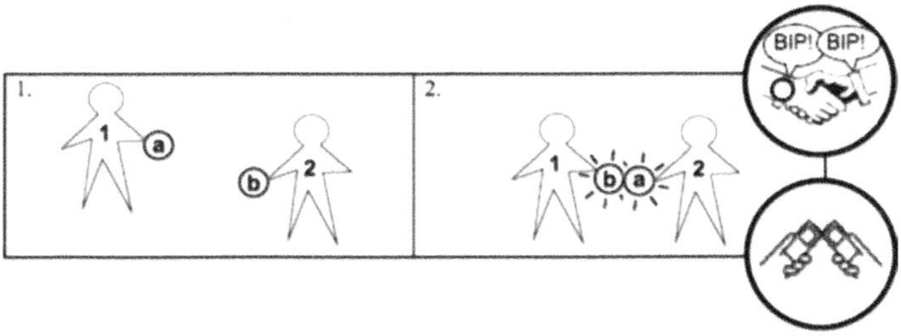

Fig. 12. Two users exchanging digital information as their computer devices are brought physically close to each other. The hints suggest two different ways to achieve this.

principle applied to an interaction model where computer devices as well as information object references are mobile. In this model, information is exchanged between mobile devices that are brought physically close to each other. The associated visual hints show two potential ways to achieve this. The upper hint shows handshake-augmented interpersonal information exchange—a technique employed in the *iBand* system [18]. Alternatively, as shown in the lower hint, the same model can be realized using handheld computer devices that can exchange information over short physical distance (e.g. via IR communication).

6 Summary and Conclusions

The current paper has described some of the results of ongoing work on a visual modeling formalism for describing location and token-based interaction in digitally augmented spaces. We have argued through examples that the physically oriented perspective that the formalism offers, can complement conventional system modeling formalisms such as UML. Finally, we have demonstrated how informal icons or visual hints can supplement the presented formalism by representing more implementation specific aspects of a design model.

Essentially, the paper has shown that what from a software-perspective is seemingly trivial, and basically can be handled through a small number of method calls, opens up for many potential interaction design solutions in a UbiComp environment. Ubiquitous computing has in many ways contributed to expand the design space for interactive systems. The presented modeling formalism can be considered a tool for exploring that design space.

References

1. Weiser, M.: The Computer for the 21th Century. Scientific American 265, 66–75 (1991)
2. Dourish, P.: Seeking a Foundation for Context-Aware Computing. Human-Computer Interaction 16, 229–241 (2001)
3. Dahl, Y., Svanæs, D.: A Comparison of Location and Token-Based Interaction Techniques for Point-of-Care Access to Medical Information. Accepted for publication. Personal and Ubiquitous Computing. To be published

4. Svanæs, D., Alsos, O.A.: Interaction Techniques for Using Handhelds and PCs Together in a Clinical Setting. NordiCHI 2006, Oslo, Norway (2006)
5. Svanæs, D.: Context-Aware Technology: A Phenomenological Perspective. Human-Computer Interaction 16, 379–400 (2001)
6. Dahl, Y.: Toward a Visual Formalism for Modeling Location and Token-Based Interaction in Context-Aware Environments. Accepted for publication. IASTED-HCI 2007 (2007)
7. Verplank, W.L.: Designing Graphical User Interfaces. Tutorial notes. CHI'86 Conference, Boston, MA (1986)
8. Landay, J.A., Myers, B.A.: Sketching Interfaces: Toward More Human Interface Design. Computer 34, 56–64 (2001)
9. Li, Y., Hong, J.I., Landay, J.A.: Using Electronic Tools in the Iterative Design of a Context-Aware Tour Guide: A Case Study. CS Technical Report, University of California, Berkeley (2005)
10. Dow, S., Saponas, T.S., Li, Y., Landay, J.A.: External representations in ubiquitous computing design and the implications for design tools. In: Proc. of the 6th ACM conference on Designing Interactive systems. pp. 241–250 University Park, PA, USA, (2006)
11. Landay, J.A., Myers, B.A.: Interactive sketching for the early stages of user interface design. In: Proceedings of the SIGCHI conference on Human factors in computing systems, ACM Press/Addison-Wesley Publishing Co, Denver, Colorado, United States (1995)
12. Dahl, Y.: You Have a Message Here: Enhancing Interpersonal Communication in a Hospital Ward with Location-Based Virtual Notes. Methods of Information in Medicine 45, 602–609 (2006)
13. Cheverst, K., Davies, N., Mitchell, K., Friday, A.: Experiences of developing and deploying a context-aware tourist guide: the GUIDE project. In: Proceedings of the 6th annual international conference on Mobile computing and networking, pp. 20–31. ACM Press, Boston, Massachusetts, United States (2000)
14. Chalmers, M., Bell, M., Brown, B., Hall, M., Sherwood, S., Tennent, P.: Gaming on the Edge: Using Seams in Ubicomp Games. In: Proc. ACM Advances in Computer Entertainment (ACE) (2005)
15. Rahlff, O.-W.: CybStickers – Simple Shared Ubiquitous Annotations for All. UbiPhysics workshop, UbiComp 2005, Tokyo, Japan (2005)
16. van der Lelie, C.: The value of storyboards in the product design process. Personal Ubiquitous Computing 10, 159–162 (2006)
17. Arnall, T.: A graphic language for touch-based interactions. Mobile Interaction with the Real World (MIRW 2006). In: Workshop held in conjunction with MobileHCI 2006, Espoo, Finland (2006)
18. Kanis, M., Winters, N., Agamanolis, S., Cullinan, C., Gavin, A.: iBand: A Wearable Device for Handshake-Augmented Interpersonal Information Exchange. In: Adjunct Proceedings of the Sixth International Conference on Ubiquitous Computing. Nottingham, U.K (2004)

Assessment of Perception of Visual Warning Signals Generated Using an Augmented Reality System

Marek Dzwiarek, Anna Luczak, Andrzej Najmiec, Cezary Rzymkowski, and Tomasz Strawinski

Central Institute for Labour Protection - National Research Institute
ul. Czerniakowska 16, 00-701 Warsaw, Poland
madzw@ciop.pl

Abstract. One of the important measures to prevent industrial accidents consists in informing a machine operator about the appearance of hazardous situation quickly and effectively enough. The main aim of the paper is to present and discuss a methodology of proving – by means of the perception assessment – that the warning signals generated using the AR approach reveal the same effectiveness as standard visual signals coming from an industrial signalling device that is of common use in machinery. Twenty volunteers constituted a paid subject population for the study. In the course of experimental task execution the warning visual signals were generated using either a standard industrial signalling device or augmented reality glasses. Despite the fact that the experimental procedure has not been completed yet very promising primary results have been obtained has indicating that both the objective and subjective assessment indicators are better for the AR warning signals.

Keywords: safety of machinery, warnings, augmented reality.

1 Introduction

Basing on the results of industrial accidents analysis presented in [8] one can arrive at the conclusion that every year accidents happen because a warning signal is either not heard or not heeded. The same conclusion was drawn in [12]. Therefore, one of the important measures to prevent undesired events consists in informing a machine operator about the appearance of hazardous situation quickly and effectively enough. Standard ISO 12100-2:2003 [11] recommends employing warning signals as an additional means for risk reduction, especially in the cases when other safety measures are not effective enough. This additional means plays an especially important role in the courses of machine regulating, maintaining and repair since in those cases the protective devices are usually disconnected and a direct access to dangerous zones is required. One can deal with such a situation also when maintaining an assembly line, where the operator should work during the line standstill and has to leave the dangerous zone when the line moves on. The warning signals are of crucial importance also in the cases when the operator starting a

J. Jacko (Ed.): Human-Computer Interaction, Part II, HCII 2007, LNCS 4551, pp. 579–586, 2007.

machine has no possibilities of controlling of all access zones. In such a case there arises the necessity for signaling the intention of starting a machine in the way ensuring that all the persons present nearby will be warned against the danger early enough. It is, therefore, obvious that the warning devices are very important elements of the machine equipment and conducting the investigations into new designs to improve their effectiveness and ergonomics is well-grounded. The overall prospective potential benefits of technology for future warning development and research have been indicated in [17], but there is still much experimental work to be done. The promise of more advanced, technology-based warning systems is enticing.

The main aim of the paper is to present and discus of the methodology of proving – by means of the perception assessment – that the warning signals generated using the AR approach reveal the same effectiveness as standard visual signals coming from an industrial signalling device that is of common use in machinery.

1.1 The Augmented Reality (AR) in a Workplace

Some information about the attempts made at application of the augmented reality approach (AR) to workplace in industry has been available from the literature for the last few years. To the best of our knowledge, however, those attempts consisted in employing the AR systems for improving the efficiency of inspection and maintenance as well as for training purposes. A general analysis of the AR systems serviceability when applied to inspection and maintenance was carried out in [13], while the possibilities of the AR system application to trainings for maintenance technicians were given in [2]. A way of AR system application to periodic inspection of machinery was presented in [5] and [16]. In [1] the authors presented some primary results of currently conducted investigations into AR system application to improving the work efficiency in automotive maintenance, while in [7] the possibility of AR system application to manufacturing system design was discussed. All the aforementioned applications were characterised by the following features:

- AR images were directly associated with the executed task;
- AR images were displayed continuously and should have been situated in the vicinity of the devices the operator kept his sight on;
- Operator's attention was concentrated on the images he expected to_appear.

Therefore, the investigations were planned basing on the HTA approach and, where possible, conducted on the real workstations.

1.2 Requirements for the AR Warning Signals

As far as we know, there is a lack of information available in the literature about the investigations into application of the AR systems to generation of visual warning signals used in machinery operation for warning operators. For closer examination of potential serviceability of AR warning signals in machine operation, two industrial enterprises were visited for the case studies. Six different workplaces were analysed for which it was proven that the accidents that happened could have been prevented if the operator had been warned early enough. The analysis results have proved that the AR systems can be applied in the cases where standard warning systems are not effective enough; especially in the cases of: warning about the machine start, when the operator's sight of dangerous zones is limited, warnings in works transport operations – e. g. in the case of overhead cranes and warning signals in semi-automatic manufacturing systems.

Some basic features have been specified to distinguish between the warning and information signals, respectively:

- usually, warning signals are hardly ever connected with the current operations;
- warning signals appear only occasionally in unusual situations and are displayed far enough from the device the operator keeps his sight on;
- warning signals appear unexpectedly, when the operator's attention is focused on other operations.

Due to the aforementioned features of warning signals, as well as the fact that there is a broad variety of workplaces they can be used it is impossible to determine using the HTA approach the operations typical for all users of the warning signals. It is possible, however, to determine special categories of psycho-motoric and cognitive skills as well as other abilities the workers should have that are necessary for safe and efficient operations in workplaces equipped with machinery. After analyzing the results presented in [14] and the characteristics of respective occupational groups and workstations equipped with machinery it was stated that main abilities necessary for efficient machine operation consisted in reaction time and attention.

2 Methods

The AR systems can be applied to generation of visual warning signals provided that perception of such signals is effective enough in the considered case. The main aim of the research consists in examination of the AR signal perception in view of exploring the applicability of AR approach to warning signal generation in case of hazards in workplaces equipped with machinery. To this end we have decided to verify experimentally the following hypotheses:

Hypothesis 1
There is no substantial difference in perception of warning signals generated using the AR and standard (ST) approaches, respectively, in view of both objective and subjective assessment indicators.

Hypothesis 2
The perception of visual warning signals generated using the AR approach varies only slightly - in view of objective assessment indicators – for different types of the AR signals.

2.1 Most Common Methods for Examination of Warning Signal Perception

Basing on the available literature one can conclude that a typical method for examination of perception of industrial warning signals consists in application of the „*criterion task set*" (CTS) defined in [15] (version 2.1 i.e., „*probability monitoring task"*, is most common in the case of machine operation). In the course of experiment presented in [3] throughout the tracking task, a warning against the hazard of system failure was displayed at 30 s intervals and the circular target changed into a square. If the square target then went out of the joystick control and started to drift outside the specified rectangular boundaries, the tracking system had failed. The subjects were required to press the push-button in order to resume tracking. The reaction time was recorded from the instant when the tracking system failed until the push-button response moment. A similar experiment was described in [6], where due to accommodation accompanying warning signals: (a) the icon jumped from side to side, (b) the curved arrow moved circularly, (c) wavy lines marched across from left to right. In the course of the experiment presented in [4] aiming at the perception assessment of visual and acoustic warning signals generated in both the synchronous and asynchronous ways the subjects sat in front of a computer screen wearing stereophonic headphones, through which acoustic signals were emitted. The visual signals had a form of red circles of 20 mm in diameter displayed on the computer screen at a distance of 80 mm to the left or right of a green circle of the same diameter. The subjects were required to keep their sight on the green circle and respond to the visual or acoustic signals appearing in the left or right hand side through pressing of one of the two buttons. The response time was measured. The response correctness was registered as well.

In al the aforementioned experiments the perception indicator of warning signals consisted in the response time and possibly in the number of mistakes made in the course of task execution.

2.2 Subjects

Twenty three male volunteers constituted the paid subject population for the study. Subject ages ranged from 21 to 25 years, with a mean age of 23 years. Those were people having normal sight, with no needs for glasses and no sight defects (e.g. daltonism).

2.3 Test Stand

The tests were performed using a special experimental stand constructed. The stand, presented in Fig.1, was designed to simulate a workstation in machine operation.
The stand comprised:

- a console
- arm of the co-operating robot,
- assembly elements:
  - palettes with holes in different colours
  - boxes with cylinders in the corresponding colours
- signaling devices (light signalization, glasses with diode, glasses with a display),
- push button.

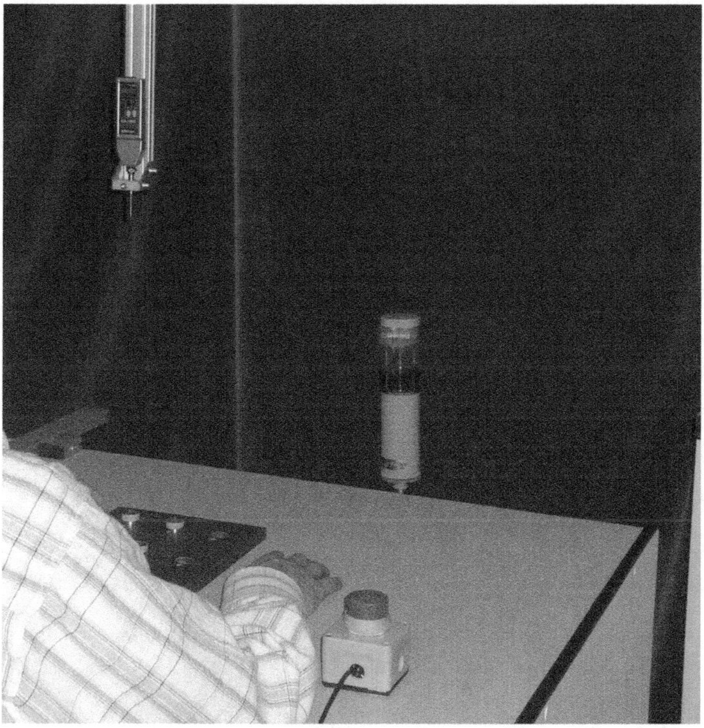

Fig. 1. General view of the experimental stand

For generating the AR warning signals two devices were used; i.e., the AR glasses described in [9] and [10], and designed especially for this purpose at Warsaw University of Technology in cooperation with CIOP-PIB; and AR glasses of the LITEYE type available on the market. The AR signals presented during the experiment had the following three forms applied consecutively in a series of sessions: red circle, flicking red circle and alphanumerical sign "STOP" (see Fig. 2).

2.4 Experiment

After analysing the characteristics of respective occupational groups and workstations equipped with machinery it was stated that main abilities necessary for efficient machine operation were reaction time and attention. The task executed during the experiment by the tested subjects involved the same abilities and consisted in putting the element of one colour into the hole of the same colour made in the palette, e.g. blue-to-blue, green-to-green, etc. After all holes in a palette had been filled a tested subject put it aside in the proper place of console situated within two strips. Then he took the next palette and repeated the whole cycle of putting elements into the proper holes. Each session lasted for 20 minutes. During the whole session time a robot standing in the vicinity was simulating the movements made usually when measuring the element size. The aforementioned sequences were repeated consecutively until the

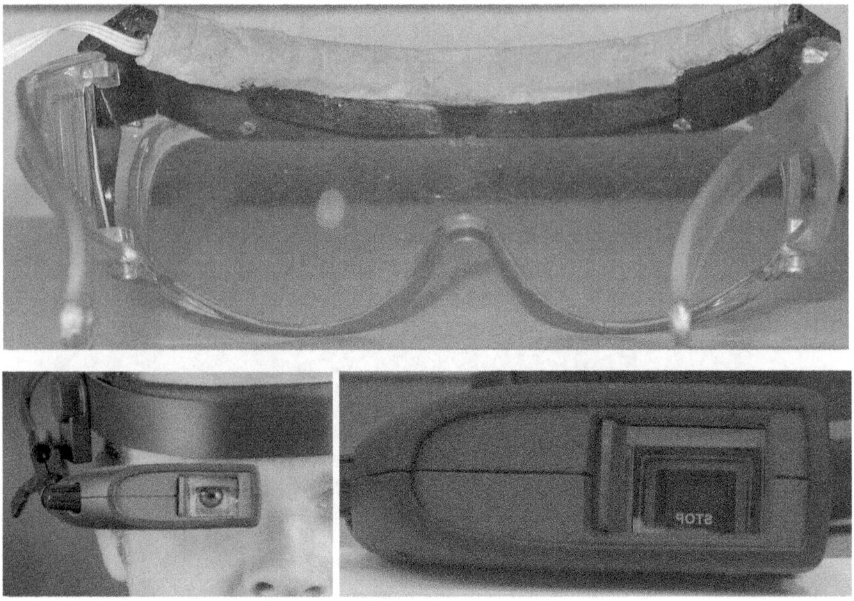

a)

b)

Fig. 2. AR systems used during the experiment **a)** AR glasses designed for the experiment **b)** LITEYE glasses with the alphanumerical sign "STOP"

session ended. In the course of experimental task execution the warning visual signals were generated using either a standard industrial signalling device or augmented reality glasses. The tested subject had to press a push-button as soon as the signal was generated. The warning signals were randomly generated during the test session. Each warning signal lasted for 10 seconds and if during that time the push-button was pressed the signal was cut off and the reaction time was registered. In case the push-button was not pressed within 10 seconds the signal omission was registered. Each tested subject took part in 3 testing sessions. In one session two variants of the experiment were performed each of 20 minutes duration. In the first variant standard warning signals were generated, while in the second variant the AR signals were applied having one of the aforementioned three forms. Between both the experimental sessions at least 20-minute-break was made so that the effect of fatigue could be eliminated.

3 Analysis of the Experimental Results Obtained

We are still in the course of experimental procedure. After it is completed, to assess properly the perception of AR warning signals and standard warning signals both objective and subjective indicators will be used. The following objective indicators were assumed: reaction time, number of signal omissions, number of mistakes made when putting elements into the holes. A subjective indicator has a form of questionnaire including four questions about the assessment of tested subject's reaction time to stimuli of both kinds and about preferences between the kinds of signal. Despite the fact that the experimental procedure has not been completed yet very promising primary results have been obtained indicating that both the objective and subjective assessment indicators are better for the AR warning signals. The shorter reaction times have been registered as compared to the standard warning signals. A much lower number of omissions have been observed as well as the subjects have made much fewer mistakes. According to the questionnaires, the tested subjects consider the AR signals to be better visible than the standard ones. However, it turned out that the design of glasses should be improved in the aspect of their ergonomics. The primary results show that AR systems can be efficiently used as warning signals in industry provided that the glasses design satisfies the requirements of ergonomics.

Acknowledgments

This paper has been prepared on the basis of the results of a task carried out within the scope of the second stage of the National Programme "Adaptation of Working Conditions in Poland to European Union Standards", partly supported - within the scope of research - in 2005 -2007 by the Ministry of Science and Higher Education. The Central Institute for Labour Protection - National Research Institute was the main co-ordinator of the Programme.

References

1. Anastassova, M., Burkhardt, J.M., Mégard, C., Ehanno, P.: Results from a user-centred critical incidents study for guiding future implementation of augmented reality in automotive maintenance. International Journal of Industrial Ergonomics 35(1), 67–77 (2005)
2. Bound, A.C., Haniff, D.J., Baber, Steiner, S.J.: Virtual reality and augmented reality as a training tool for assembly tasks. In: Proceedeings of 1999 IEEE International Conference on Information Visualization. Los Alamitos pp. 32–36 (1999)
3. Burt, J.L., Bartolome, D.S., Burdette, D.W., Comstock, J.R.: A psychological evaluation of the perceived urgency of auditory warning signals. Ergonomics 38(11), 2327–2340 (1995)
4. Chan, A.H.S, Chan, K.W.L.: Synchronous and asynchronous presentations of auditory and visual signals: Implications for control console design. Applied Ergonomics 37, 131–140 (2006)
5. Chung, K.H., Shewchuk, J.P., Williges, R.C.: An application of augmented reality to thickness inspection. Human Factors And Ergonomics In Manufacturing 9(4), 331–342 (1999)
6. Cohn, T.E.: Engineered Visibility Warning Signals: Tests of Time to React, Detectability, Identifiability and Salience. IDEA Program Transportation Research Board, National Research Council May 1, 1996 (1996)
7. Dangelmaier, W., Fischer, M., Gausemeier, J., Grafe, M., Matysczok, C., Mueck, B.: Virtual and augmented reality support for discrete manufacturing system simulation. Computers in Industry 56(4), 371–383 (2005),

8. Dzwiarek, M.: An analysis of Accident Caused by Improper Functioning of Machine Control Systems. International Journal of Occupational Safety and Ergonomics 10(2), 129–136 (2004)
9. Dzwiarek, M., Holejko, K., Nowak, R., Czarnecki, T.: A system for signalling of emergency situation based on the augmented reality concept. In: Human & Organisational Issues in the Digital Enterprise. Fallon, E. F.(ed.) The Department of Industrial Engineering, National University of Irlend, pp. 479–488 (2004) ISBN 0-9538974-1-9
10. Dzwiarek, M., Czarnecki, T., Holejko, K., Nowak, R.: Application of augmented reality to the industrial systems for signalisation of emergency situations. In: Photonics Applications in Astronomy, Communications, Industry, and High-Energy Physics Experiments IV. Romaniuk, R. S. (ed.) Proceedings of SPIE (The International Society for Optical Engeenering), vol. 6159 pp. 1147–1156 (2006)
11. Safety of machinery. Basic concepts, general principles for design - Part 2: Technical principles. (International Standard Organization) ISO 12100-2:2003
12. Haas, E.C, Casali, J.G.: Perceived urgency of response time to multi-tone and frequency-modular warning signals in broadband noise. Ergonomics 38(11), 2313–2326 (1995)
13. Chung, K.H., Shewchuk, J.P., Willinges, R.C.: An analysis Framework for Applying Virtual Environment Technology to Manufacturing Tasks. Human Factors and Ergonomics in Manufacturing 12(4), 335–348 (2002)
14. Luczak, A.: Wymagania psychologiczne w doborze osób do zawodów trudnych i niebezpiecznych (2001) ISBN 83-87354-61-9
15. Shingledecker, C.A.: A task battery for applied human performance assessment research Technical Report AFAMRL-TR-84-071 (Air Force Aerospace Medical Research Laboratory, Wright - Patterson Air Force Base USA) (1984)
16. Weidenhausen, J., Knoepfle, C., Stricker, D.: Lessons learned on the way to industrial augmented reality applications, a retrospective on ARVIKA. Computers & Graphics 27(6), 887–891 (2003)
17. Wogalter, MS., Mayhorn, CB.: Providing cognitive support with technology-based warning systems. Ergonomics 48(5), 522–533 (2005)

Force Field Based Expression for 3D Shape Retrieval

Xi Geng, Wenyu Liu, and Hairong Liu

Department of Electronics and Information Engineering,
Huazhong University of Science and Technology,
Wuhan 430074, P.R. China

Abstract. In this paper, we established an algorithm to obtain 3D shape descriptors based on a novel force field model. Based on this model, 3D models as surface particle sets are assumed and the force interactions between particles are computed to constitute a spherical descriptor. During the force computation, the mass of the particle is defined to maintain local information which improves the discrimination of the spherical descriptor. The experimental results show that this algorithm is valid for 3D shape matching with high efficiency.

Keywords: force field model, 3D shape retrieval, surface flatness.

1 Introduction

Over the last decade, 3D models and tools for acquiring and visualizing 3D models have been widely adopted in a number of disciplines, including medicine, architecture, entertainment and etc. At the same time, a large amount of 3D models sprout out both from the Internet and specific laboratories. To classify and search the models, methods of obtaining comparable 3D shape features with high efficiency are to be found out.

The methods to extract 3D shape features can be sorted into two categories: statistics based and transformation based. Statistics based methods need to find out suitable mathematical measurements first. Ohbuchi[1] constructed a shape histogram by recording the parameterizations along the principal axis of inertia of the model. Osada[2] computed several statistical characteristics of angles, intervals and areas of the sampled points of 3D models. Transformation based methods include Hough transform, Fourier transform and so on. While Statistics based methods are often rotation-depended, Kazhdan[3] presented a general approach based on spherical harmonics to educe rotation independent descriptors. Spherical harmonic representation was proved to be one of the best algorithms of 3D shape retrieval. However, it was proved to have two major kinds of information loss, and it is incapable of distinguishing models with partial rotations.

To solve the problem, three kinds of methods have been proposed:

1) Make changes to preserve local information: radial projection and modified radial projection method[4];

2) Construct spherical functions with global information of the object: radial projection method based on Delta Function and Fourier transform[5];

J. Jacko (Ed.): Human-Computer Interaction, Part II, HCII 2007, LNCS 4551, pp. 587–596, 2007.

3) Project the harmonic functions on a Cartesian coordinates in order to provide additional axis as reference: 3D Zernike descriptor[6].

The first method has a higher executive efficiency, but can not eliminate information loss intrinsically, and faces the multiple intersection points (by the radials and the object surface) problem which occurs constantly when obtaining spherical functions; the second method is novel and effective, but not stable; the third one is optimal among 3D model matching algorithms, however, it is usually complicated and time-consuming, which does not adapt to a large-scale database search engine.

The complexity of 3D models makes 3D feature extraction an unstable, time-consuming procedure. Therefore current methods are hard to satisfy both discernment and efficiency requirement, and new solutions should be found out in extraction of 3D shape descriptors.

In this paper, we propose a novel algorithm, which is based on a Force Field Model, of obtaining the 3D shape descriptors. We regard all 3D models as surface particle sets, and construct spherical functions by computing the forces of particles on the surface and at the center of mass. During the computation of forces, we append local features such as inter-projection areas and etc, and thereby improves the discrimination of the spherical function and reduce the information loss of spherical harmonic representation. Besides, a new way of perceiving 3D models is brought out instead of perceiving them as normal spatial geometric models. Finally, spherical harmonic transform is applied to the spherical function, and the experimental results show the validity and high efficiency of the whole algorithm.

2 Force-Field Based Representation of 3D Models

In this section, we introduce a novel 3D descriptor based on Force Field Model. One significant pivot of the algorithm is how to correspond the definitions in physics to a discrete spherical function mathematically. The main idea of this section is to make a clear definition of each physical measurement in a force field.

2.1 Discrete Force Field Model

To begin with, we assume that each 3D model can be represented as a particle set P whose elements p is distributed on the surface of the 3D model.

In order to construct a particle set P, an equi-longitude and equi-latitude sampling is taken first on the object to obtain a finite particle set P_s. We record intersection points of the object surface and the lines in the following 2B×2B directions as elements in P_s (see figure 1 (a)):

$$(\theta_i,\varphi_i),\theta_i=(i+0.5)\frac{\pi}{2B},\varphi_i=(j+0.5)\frac{\pi}{B},i,j=0,1,...,2B-1\ . \tag{1}$$

We also assume there is a particle O placed at the center of mass of the model, and then each element in particle set P is under the effect of O. We quantify this effect simply by Newton's Law of gravitation that:

$$F = G\frac{m_O m_p}{r^2} . \tag{2}$$

where G is the gravitational constant, r is the distance between particle O and p, m_O and m_p stand for the mass of particle O and p respectively. Let m_O=1, we can obtain a discrete spherical function as follows:

$$F(\theta,\varphi) = G\frac{m_p}{r_p^{\ 2}}, p \in P_s . \tag{3}$$

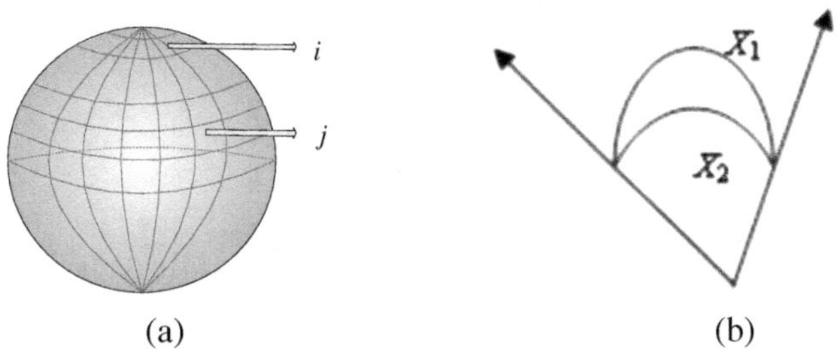

Fig. 1. (a) mesh i is much smaller than mesh j, for the sampling is not uniform; (b) The curvature of surface X_1 is greater than surface X_2. Then the area of X_1 will be greater than X_2, therefore higher curvature results in greater area within the sampling interval of the same size.

2.2 Force Field Modeling

Referring to the physical definition, we have:

$$m = \rho \times V . \tag{4}$$

Where ρ denotes density and V denotes the volume of the particle. We assume the surface of 3D models is equal dense and thin enough to neglect, thus we get:

$$\rho = 1, h = 1 : m = \rho \times S \times h = S . \tag{5}$$

where S stands for the area of each surface section within the scale:

$$\theta \subseteq [\theta_i - \frac{\pi}{2B}, \theta_i + \frac{\pi}{2B}), \varphi \subseteq [\varphi_i - \frac{\pi}{B}, \varphi_i + \frac{\pi}{B}) . \tag{6}$$

As we know, the equi-longitude and equi-latitude sampling is not uniform. In a unit sphere illustrated in figure 1 (b), section i is much smaller than section j at different latitudes, though they are both the sampling intervals. When computing S, the larger sampling interval should have higher weights to compensate the information loss induced by sampling. Thus we assure that:

$$m_p = S_p \propto \text{the size of the sampling interval in the direction of } (\theta_i, \varphi_i) \ . \tag{7}$$

where p is the intersection point in the direction of (θ_i, φ_i). The size of the sampling interval can be evaluated by computing the area of meshes partitioned by lines in all sampling directions (such as mesh i and j in figure 1 (b)).

Besides, within the same sampling interval, the curvature of the surface will also influence the area. Usually a higher curvature results in a greater area within the same sampling interval. Assuming c is the curvature of the sampled surface sections, according to figure 2, we have:

$$m = S \propto c \ . \tag{8}$$

Combining equation (7) and (8), the final representation of the mass at point p is approximated as:

$$m_p = S_p \propto s_i \times c_i, p \in T_i \ . \tag{9}$$

2.2.1 Computation of the Size of the Sampling Interval

To quantify the size of each sampling interval, the areas of the surface sections obtained by sampling a unit sphere are concerned. From figure 3, the surface of the unit sphere is smooth everywhere, thus it is convenient to approximate the area of each surface section, denoted by s, as follows:

$$s(\theta_i, \varphi_i) \approx a \times b = r^2 \frac{\pi^2}{2B^2} \cos\theta_i \ . \tag{10}$$

where r is the radius of the surface section. The approximation is illustrated in figure 3.

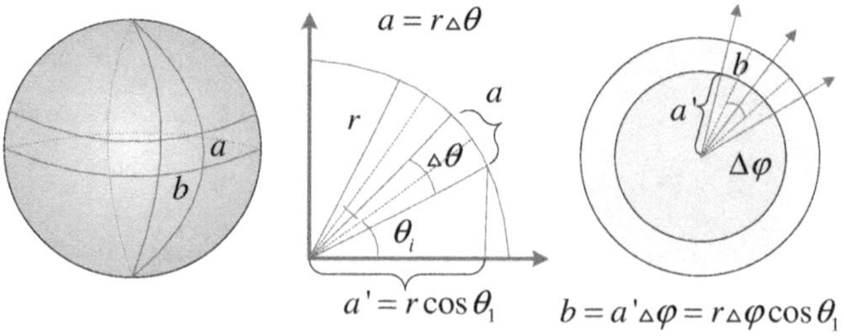

Fig. 2. Detailed calculation to approximate area of surface s

2.2.2 Approximation of Curvature

Lots of methods of calculating the surface curvature have been proposed till now. But many of them are generally vulnerable to noises, and record very local information, usually at only one point, to demonstrate the local evolution trend of the surface. The surface signal[7], or face flatness was brought forward with local area information instead of local point information, and with less algorithm complexity.

For mesh models, assuming T_s is the set of all faces in the given mesh model. ADJ_i is used to denote all adjacent faces of T_i. The surface signal or flatness of a given face T_i is defined by[7]:

$$c_i = \left| \frac{\sum (area_j * (n_i \cdot n_j))}{\sum area_j} \right|, T_j \in ADJ_i \quad . \tag{11}$$

where $area_j$ is the area of faces in T_j , and n_i, n_j denote the unit normal of the corresponding faces. The equation works out a proportion of the sum of projection areas (on T_i) and the original sum of adjacent faces. If the sub-surface is a plane, the value will be 1.0. The more bending the sub-surface is, the smaller the value will be.

To make c direct proportional to S, we define a modified flatness of a given face T_i by:

$$c_i = 1 - \left| \frac{\sum (area_j * (n_i \cdot n_j))}{\sum area_j} \right|, T_j \in ADJ_i \quad . \tag{12}$$

Equation (12) suggests that the computation of the curvature include the interrelations of adjacent meshes in a local area, which is important because the curvature covers information of a local area instead of a local point, and makes the approximation of mass more accurate.

According to equation (3) and (9), we obtain a spherical function F as follows:

$$F(\theta_i, \varphi_i) \propto \frac{m_p}{r_i^2} \propto \frac{s_i \times c_i}{r_i^2} \quad . \tag{13}$$

The intersections of the object surface with the line in the direction of (θ_i, φ_i) may be more than one point. Since forces in the same direction are additive, let K be the number of intersection points along direction (θ_i, φ_i), we get:

$$F(\theta_i, \varphi_i) \propto \sum_K \frac{c_k s_k}{r_{ik}^2} = \sum_K \frac{c_k r_{ik}^2 \frac{\pi^2}{2B^2} \cos\theta_i}{r_{ik}^2} \text{, or}$$

$$= \frac{\pi^2}{2B^2} \cos\theta_i \sum_K c_k, k = 1, 2, ..., K$$

$$F(\theta, \varphi) = W \frac{\pi^2}{2B^2} \cos\theta \sum_K c_k, k = 1, 2, ..., K \quad \cdot \tag{14}$$

where W is a constant, K is the number of intersection points along each direction, $F(\theta, \varphi)$ is the final 3D descriptor based on force field model.

3 Dissimilarity Computation

With the spherical function in equation (14) as the descriptor of 3D models, it is convenient to compute the dissimilarity of two 3D models. The method we adopt here is to obtain a rotation-invariant descriptor using spherical harmonic transform (SHT)[3]. The dissimilarity will be computed by comparing the coefficients obtained by SHT.

The overall procedure of computing the dissimilarity of 3D models is described below:

Step1: Create lines in all directions of sampling, and calculate the sampled points according to the following algorithm:

```
 for(each direction) {
   for(each surface mesh){
     calculate the intersection point p of the direction
line and each mesh;
     if(p is inside the corresponding triangular mesh T_i)
       record p as p_ij (i for mesh index and j for inter-
section index);
     Else
       Delete p;
   }
 }
```

Step2: Go through all meshes to obtain adjacent meshes of mesh T_i, and compute the modified surface signal c_i of mesh T_i according to equation (12);

Step3: For particle set p_{ij}, compute $\sum_j c_{ij}$, and obtain a spherical function according to equation (14), which is recorded as $[F(\theta,\varphi)]$;

Step4: Apply SHT to $F(\theta,\varphi)$ to obtain coefficients of spherical harmonics, and work out the dissimilarity of two 3D models by computing the L2-norm of the SHT results.

Suppose a 3D model has N meshes, the complexity of sampling is $O(N\times B^2)$, complexity of computing m is $O(N^2)$, and complexity of spherical harmonic transform is $O(N\ log^2N)$. Therefore, the complexity of force field based descriptor is $O(N^2)$, and the overall complexity goes to $O(N(B^2+N+\ log^2N\ ))$.

The force field based descriptor represents the interactions of points on the surface and the point at the center of mass. According to the concept of force field, the nearer is the point (to the center of mass), the greater is the force. In this situation, radius r acts as an attenuating factor to the value of force, and produce unstable situations. However, when we get the final result, r no longer exists at the position of denominator with the calculation of m. Besides, the curvature computation retains local information which may be lost when obtaining a rotation invariant descriptor, and therefore improves the discernment of the final descriptor.

4 Experimental Results

4.1 Flatness Computation Experiments

Figure 3 shows some models with their meshes gray according to the modified surface flatness. The greater is the curvature *c*, the darker is the gray. It is clear to identify the areas with high curvature according to figure 3.

Fig. 3. Gray graphs of mesh models according to the surface signal. The higher is the signal, the darker is the gray.

4.2 3D Model Search Experiments

To measure the efficacy of the descriptor based on force field model, we evaluate its performance by applying the method to searching selected models in a database named BenchMark[8] from Princeton University. All models in the database are mesh models.

We computed the spherical representation as 64×64 grids corresponding to regular sampling along the lines of longitude and latitude, and we used SPharmonicKit[9] to obtain the SHT representation. The algorithm is implemented on platform VC 6.0.

Table 1. Searching results with a dog model as the query with B=64

No.97	No.97	No.95	No.98	No.96

Query	1.000000	0.99998	0.99701	0.99665
	No.99	No.107	No.86	No.91

	0.97731	0.97721	0.95064	0.89452

Some of the searching results are shown in Table 1, the 8 most matched searching results are listed after the query. The numbers on top of the models are their indexes in the database, and the numbers under the models are the dissimilarities compared with the query.

In Table 1, the input query is a standing leopard with a long neck. Although the order of some searching results does not accord with human vision (Model No.95 is not more similar with the query than model No.98 in human vision), it searched out all leopard models in the database, and the rest of searching results are all similar animal models. As the results indicate, the descriptor based on force field model is valid in 3D model searching.

Table 2 listed the searching results with a chair model as the query.

Table 2. Searching results with a chair model as the query with B=64

No.823	No.823	No.826	No.803	No.810

Query	1.000000	0.974914	0.945553	0.80436
	No.816	No.815	No.812	No.822

	0.765979	0.722863	0.703815	0.675669

However, dismatches occur in the searching results (Model No.803 is an office chair which is different with the dining chair), for the topology of a chair is very complicated. Besides, any sampling procedure may discard some detailed information, and leads to instability of the searching. But still, it searched out most of the dining chairs in the database.

4.3 Comparison with Other Methods

In table 3, the space requirements of the descriptor mentioned in the introduction are compared by recording the number of floating point numbers used for each descriptor. We can see that the Force Field Based descriptor has the lowest.

Table 3. The number of floating point numbers used to describe each representation.

Representation	Space required
Force Field Based Descriptor	64×64
Radial Distribution	2×64×64
Shape Histogram	4×64×64
Voxels	32×64×64

Table 4 listed the searching results by the classic method of Shape Histogram. Generally, the method of Shape Histogram has a good stability; however it represents a 3D model only by a single curve, which does not contain abundant information. Therefore, two models vary greatly in shape may have same histograms. This situation is listed in Table 4:

Table 4. Searching results with a chair model as the query by the method of Shape Histograms

No.823	No.823	No.820	No.814	No.800

	No.826	No.1	No.810	No.821

From the experimental results, the algorithm proposed in this paper contains more information which provides better compensation to the information loss brought out by Spherical Harmonic Transform, and therefore has better discernment. Besides, the force-field model algorithm is proved to occupy less storage spaces and higher efficiency.

5 Conclusion and Future Work

In this paper we introduced a novel algorithm of representing 3D models based on force field model. The application of the model provides a new sight on 3D model matching and was proved to have good discrimination. The algorithm is preponderant in three aspects: first, it solves the 3D shape matching in the view of physics, and naturally solve multiple intersection points (with the object surface) problem; second, the computation of force retains local area information, which compensates the information loss of spherical harmonic representation; third it is executed with high efficiency.

This paper suggests a new way of 3D feature extraction, and based on force models, more solutions can be worked out as 3D descriptors, such as moments that can be thought about in the future work. Besides, topological information will be considered later to add to the 3D model matching, to recognize the same human model with different motions.

Acknowledgment

This work received support from the Cultivating Fond for Momentous Scientific Innovation Project of Higher Education (Grant no.705038).

References

1. Ohbuchi, R., Minamitani, T., Takei, T.: Shape-similarity search of 3D models by using enhanced shape functions. In: Proceedings of the Theory and Practice of Computer Graphics (TPCG'03), pp. 97–105 (2003)
2. Osada, R., Funkhouser, T., Chazelle, B., Dobkin, D.: Shape distributions. ACM Transactions on Graphics 21(4), 807–832 (2002)
3. Kazhdan, M., Funkhouser, T., Rusinkiewicz, S.: Rotation invariant spherical harmonic representation of 3D shape descriptors. In: Eurographics Symposium on Geometry Processing, pp. 156–164 (2003)
4. Tangelder, J.W., Veltkamp, R.C.: A survey of content based 3D shape retrieval methods. In: Proc. Shape Modeling International, Genoa, Italy, pp. 145–156(June 2004)
5. Liu, Y., Pu, J., Xin, G., Zha, H.: A Robust Method for Content-based 3D Model Retrieval. In: Proc. Pacific Graphics 2004 (PG2004), Seoul, Korea, pp. 3–9 (October 6-8, 2004)
6. Novotni, M., Klein, R.: Shape retrieval using 3D Zernike descriptors. In: Computer-Aided Design vol. 36 pp. 1047–1062 (2004)
7. Pan, X., Ye, X.: 3D Mesh Segmentation Using A Two-stage Merging Strategy. In: Proceedings of the Fourth International Conference on Computer and Information Technology (CIT'04), pp. 730–733 (2004)
8. Shilane, P., Min, P., Kazhdan, M., Funkhouser, T.: The Princeton Shape Benchmark.Shape Modeling International, Genova, Italy (June 2004)
9. SPharmonicKit 2.5 (1998) http://www.cs.dartmouth.edu/ geelong/sphere/

Comparing Two Head-Mounted Displays in Ultrasound Scanning

Juha Havukumpu[1,2], Jukka Häkkinen[2,3], Eija Grönroos[1], Pia Vähäkangas[1], and Göte Nyman[2]

[1] Helsinki Polytechnic Stadia, Specialist Fields in Health Care, P.O. Box 4033, 00099 City of Helsinki, Finland
[2] University of Helsinki, Department of Psychology, P.O. Box 9, 00014 University of Helsinki, Finland
[3] Nokia Research Center, P.O. Box 407, 00045 Nokia Group, Finland
juha.havukumpu@helsinki.fi, jukka.hakkinen@nokia.com, eija.gronroos@stadia.fi, pia.vahakangas@stadia.fi, gote.nyman@helsinki.fi

Abstract. Head-mounted displays have been tested in various medical fields. According to some results, using a head-mounted display makes medical operations faster, more effective and accurate than using a conventional table display. In this study we aimed to examine midwives experiences of using a head-mounted display during an ultrasound scan. Our preliminary results indicate that a head-mounted display in an ultrasound scan could work better than the conventional method which is still in common use. We also noticed that the use of a monocular head-mounted display was more comfortable than a see-through display.

Keywords: Head-mounted displays, monocular display, see-through display, user experience, ultrasound scan.

1 Introduction

The possibilities of head-mounted displays in medicine have been widely studied [1-8] and the results have generally been positive [4]. This can be attributed to several factors, but one of the most important issues is the decreased need to shift attention between two or more displays during an anaesthesiological or other medical operation [5,3 and 9]. In the present study the purpose was to investigate the issue of attention shifting in an ultrasound scan task, where a midwife has to alternately observe the patient and the display showing the scan results. We wanted to determine how midwives with previous experience of conventional ultrasound scanning would experience using an HMD in an ultrasound scan task. We also compared two different head-mounted display types in the scan task.

In Finland, an ultrasound scan is performed on mothers twice during pregnancy, the first in weeks 12+0 to 13+6 and the second after 19+0 to 20+0 weeks. The purpose of the screening is to check that the fetus is developing well and there are no abnormalities. As approximately 60 000 births occur per year, the total annual number of normal/routine fetus screenings is about 120 000.

J. Jacko (Ed.): Human-Computer Interaction, Part II, HCII 2007, LNCS 4551, pp. 597–604, 2007.

Because the midwife must constantly look at either the display or the patient, an ultrasound scan can place strain on the neck and other upper body muscles and can be uncomfortable during a long working day. An HMD would reduce the need to turn the head because the scanning result is constantly visible in the visual field of the midwife.

However, there are a number of possible problems related to the using an HMD in an ultrasound scanning task. Firstly, earlier studies related to head-mounted displays have indicated subjective visual strain symptoms in users, although other studies have suggested that the symptoms are similar to those when using an ordinary display [10, 11 and 12]. Secondly, an HMD might hamper the relationship between the midwife and the patient, as the head-worn display covers part of the visual field. This might reduce eye contact and make the expressions of the midwife more difficult to interpret. Thirdly, an HMD might occlude parts of the visual field and thus make the performance of the scanning task more difficult. In this study we wanted to find out how midwives would react to using an HMD in an ultrasound scanning task. We collected mainly qualitative data related to their preconceptions and reactions related to HMD use.

2 Methods

The participants performed an abdominal ultrasound scan with a see-through Sony Glasstron in experiment 1 and with Micro-Optical SV-6 PC viewer in experiment 2. The participant had to find, mark, identify and measure different abdominal organs. The organs were the uterus or prostate, depending on patients' sex, the both of the kidneys and the bladder. Each organ was measured linearly and crosswise and the volume of the bladder was also determined. Each of the identified organs was documented by printout. The task lasted 20 minutes. During the task the experimenter observed the user from behind. The experimental starting times were randomly distributed in the morning (9 am – 11 am) so that the existing eye strain would not affect the results. The participants did not know the ultrasound machine used in the experiment beforehand but they were able to familiarize themselves with the machine before the experiment.

2.1 Participants

Twenty-four registered midwives (mean age 43.1 years) with normal or corrected-to-normal vision participated in the two experiments: 13 in Experiment 1 (mean age 41.6 years) and 11 in Experiment 2 (mean age 44.8 years). The age of the youngest participant was 33 years and oldest 52 years. All participants were female and already had several years of experience of ultrasound methods in fetus scanning; 42.0% worked in a local hospital, 33.5% in Helsinki University Central Hospital, 17.0% in central hospitals, 4.0% in a healthcare centre and 4.0% of them were returning to working life, so they had no current working place.

In the main experiment the participant first filled in a background questionnaire that contained general questions regarding the health state of the participant. They described their head-mounted display and virtual reality experience, daily near work time, their frequency of computer gaming, motion sickness and headaches, and their handedness. We also asked when was the last time they had eaten and taken any medicines that made them more susceptible to nausea (sedatives or tranquilizers, decongestants, anti-histamines, asthma medication or alcohol). In addition, we measured their technical innovation using the Diffusion of Innovation Questionnaire. Finally, the participants described their preconceptions and opinions about head-mounted displays. After completing the background questionnaire the participants began to carry out the task. Following the task the participants described in a questionnaire their opinion of the head-mounted display as well as the level of sickness symptoms they experienced after its use.

2.2 Apparatus

We used two head-mounted displays: a see-through Sony Glasstron head-mounted virtual display in experiment 1 and a monocular Micro-Optical SV-6 PC viewer in experiment 2. The resolution of both displays was set to 640x480 pixels in both experimental conditions. The virtual image was at a distance of 1.4 meters with both displays. We placed a monocular display in front of the leading eye measured with the target aiming method. We used a Vivid 3 ultra sound machine where we connected displays one at a time.

Fig. 1. The Micro-Optical SV-6 PC viewer in use during the fetus scan

2.3 Procedure

In the main experiment the participant first completed a background questionnaire that contained general questions regarding the health of the participant. They described their head-mounted display and virtual reality experience, daily near-work time, computer-gaming frequency, motion-sickness frequency, headache frequency and handedness. We also asked when was the last time they had eaten and taken any medicines that made them more susceptible to nausea (sedatives or tranquilizers, decongestants, anti-histamines, asthma medicine or alcohol). Furthermore, their technical innovation was assessed using the Diffusion of Innovation Questionnaire [13]. Finally, the participants described their preconceptions and opinions about head-mounted displays. After completing the background questionnaire the participants began to do the task. After the task we gave the participants a questionnaire in which they described their opinions about the head-mounted display as well as the level of sickness symptoms they experienced after the use of the head-mounted display.

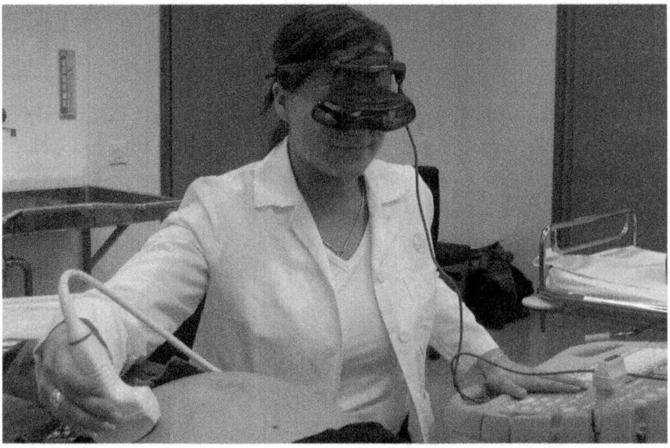

Fig. 2. The Sony Glasstron in use during a fetus scan

3 Results

We categorized the answers given to open questions after the experiments in which they were asked to state their positive and negative opinions about using the HMD. There were 18 positive and 22 negative responses in experiment 1 and 13 positive and 24 negative responses in experiment 2. The responses were diverse, but there were some issues that were brought up more frequently (Table 1). We do not report response categories with a frequency less than three, so there are several empty cells in the left column of Table 1.

The most commonly mentioned issue after the task completion was the better ergonomics of scanning with the HMD (33.3% of positive post-task responses in Table 1). In the responses, the participants indicated that using the HMD allowed them to move more and helped them to find a better working position. This matched their pre-task expectations, as the same number of participants expected better ergonomics before the task (positive pre-task answers in Table 1). The participants expected to have a better working position and less strain in their neck and upper limbs with the HMD.

The image quality was also regarded as important, as 16.6% of the participants mentioned that the image quality was better with the HMD than with the ultrasound

Table 1. The most frequent positive and negative opinions in experiments 1 and 2 before and after the task

Positive pre-task		Negative pre-task	
Ergonomics may be better	8	Adverse symptoms	6
Don't know	6	Decreased contact patient	6
Better display quality	3	Lack of eye contact	6
Positive post-task		**Negative post-task**	
Ergonomics were good	8	Difficult to wear the display	4
Good image	4	Difficult to keep display in the correct position	3
Focus on patient	4	Difficult to communicate with patient	3
Better concentration on task	3	Reduced visibility	3
		Small working area through display	3
		Problems with vision	3

machine (positive post-task answers in Table 1). Interestingly, the participants expected this, as some had already mentioned this before the experiment (positive pre-task answers in Table 1). In task 1, 29.1% of participants liked the opportunity to focus on the patient all the time. Similarly, the ability to concentrate on the task more was mentioned in some answers.

Difficulties in wearing the display were most commonly mentioned negative post-task opinions (Table 1). Also, difficulties in communication with the patient and reduced visibility in the visual field due to the occluded areas were often mentioned. Interestingly, the sickness symptoms that were often mentioned in the pre-task questionnaire were not regarded as problematic in the post-task questionnaire.

If the two displays are compared, there are no clear differences in the post-task opinions (Tables 2 and 3). However, certain display-specific issues were found to be disturbing. With the Glasstron the difficulty in wearing the display, the reduced visibility and difficulties in communicating with the patient were emphasized (Table 2). On the other hand, with the MD-6 the main problems were related to difficulties in

Table 2. The most frequent positive and negative post-task response categories in experiment 1 (Glasstron)

Positive post-task		Negative post-task	
Focus on patient	4	Difficult to wear the display	4
Ergonomics were good	4	Reduced visibility	3
Better concentration on examination	3	Difficult to communicate with patient	3

Table 3. The most frequent positive and negative post-task response categories in experiment 2 (MD-6)

Positive post-task		Negative post-task	
Ergonomics were good	4	Difficult to keep display in correct position	3
Good quality of image	3	Small working area through display	3
Focus on patient	3	Problems with vision	3

Table 4. Change in opinion towards two HMDs

Change in opinion toward HMDs	Glasstron	MD6	Total	%
Clearly more negative	3	0	3	12.5
More negative	3	2	5	21.0
Neutral	1	2	3	12.5
More positive	4	4	8	33.0
Clearly more positive	2	3	5	21.0

keeping the display stationary in the correct position in front of the eye, the small size of the display and perceptual problems related to binocular vision experienced by the participants (Table 3). Positioning the display was especially difficult for the participants who used progressive or bifocal spectacles.

After the experimental task we asked the participants to indicate how their opinion of head-mounted displays had changed during the experiment (Table 4). The answers indicate that slightly over half of the participants (54.0%) felt that their opinion had shifted in either a positive or clearly more positive direction, while 33.5% of the participants reported that their opinion had shifted in either a more negative or clearly more negative direction. The positive shift in opinion was approximately the same with the Glasstron and MD-6. The positive experiences were reflected in the open comments section, where six participants, three in both experiments, reported a willingness to try the HMD with their own ultrasound machine.

There were larger differences in the negative opinions, as 18.0% of users of the MD-6 had an opinion shift towards a more negative direction, but 54.0% of Glasstron had a more negative opinion of the HMDs after use. The fairly small number of observations prevented statistical analysis of the data, but the results suggest that there might have more negative experiences with the Glasstron.

4 Conclusions

Use of a head-mounted display can be more precise than the use of a conventional desktop system. It also allows better accuracy and safety of clinical decisions based on images. However, psychological factors have a strong effect on the acceptance of the new technology. The use of head-mounted displays in medicine is in a preliminary stage and further research is needed to evaluate its long-term clinical impact on patients, nurses, doctors and hospital administrators. The widespread use and the universal transfer of such technology will remain limited until there is a better understanding of user experience issues related to this application.

Our preliminary results indicate that midwives regarded head-mounted displays as acceptable accessories to an ultrasound scanning task. Using the monocular head-mounted displays prompted slightly fewer negative comments than the use of a binocular see-through display. The reason for the differences might be related to the fact that the small monocular display disturbed the users less than the see-though display, which decreases the contrast of the visual scene and occludes peripheral vision. However, a larger study will be needed to validate these results and to evaluate the possible trends in user performance over single sessions and over longer time periods.

There were also complaints about difficulties in wearing the display and keeping the display stationary in front of the eye. In the long term such issues might greatly decrease the satisfaction of users, so attention should be paid to the design of the displays so that wearing the display would be effortless and the display would remain stationary on the head in all work situations.

It is difficult to draw generalized conclusions due to the preliminary nature of these experiments, as there may also be significant variability between users in performance accuracy and fatigue effects. A study with a much larger number of participants would be needed to eliminate these individual variations. Another limitation is the use of unvalidated rating scales for the assessment of image quality and the size of display.

Our results suggest that the use of head-mounted displays is feasible during ultrasound scan. However, improvements in image quality as well as the design of the head-mounted display are necessary before the headset can be recommended for general use during ultrasound scanning.

References

1. Howarth, P.A.: Virtual Reality: an occupational health hazard of the future? RCN Occupational Health Nurses Forum. Working for Health. April 1994 (1994)
2. Letterie, G.S.: How virtual reality may enhance training in obstetrics and gynecology. American Journal of Obstetrics and Gynecology 187, 37–40 (2002)
3. Ross, B., Naluai-Cecchini, A.: Use of a See-Through Head-Worn Display of Patient Monitoring Data to Enhance Anaesthesiologists' Response to Abnormal Clinical Events. Proc. Computer Society. In: Proceedings of the 6th International Symposium on Wearable Computers (ISWC.02) (2002)
4. Rosenthal, M., State, A., Lee, J., Hirota, G., Jeremy Ackerman, J., Keller, K., Etta, D., Pisano, E.D., Jiroutek, M., Muller, K., Fuchs, H.: Augmented reality guidance for needle biopsies: An initial, randomized, controlled trial in phantoms. Medical Image Analysis, pp. 313–320 (2002)
5. Reisman, M., Gray, W.A., Ormerod, D.F., Hyde, J.P.: Use of a Head-Mounted Confluent Display of Fluoroscopic and Echocardiographic Images to Enhance Operator Feedback during Catheter-Deployed Closures of Cardiac Septal Defects. In: Proc. of the 10th Annual Medicine Meets Virtual Reality Conference. Newport Beach, USA (2002)

6. Satava, R.M.: Emerging medical applications of virtual reality: A surgeon's perspective. Artificial Intelligence in Medicine, pp. 281–288 (1994)
7. Satava, R.M., Jones, S.B.: Current and Future Applications of Virtual Reality for Medicine. In: Proc. of the IEEE vol. 86, pp. 484–489 (1998)
8. Shuhaiber, J.H.: Augmented Reality in Surgery. Archives of Surgery 139, 170–174 (2004)
9. Linda, S., Lee, L.S., Carr-Locke, D.L., Ookubo, R., John, R., Saltzman, J.R.: Randomized trial of a video headset vs. a conventional video monitor during colonoscopy. Gastrointestinal Endoscopy 61(2), 301–306 (2005)
10. Häkkinen, J., Takatalo, J., Havukumpu, J., Komulainen, J., Särkelä, H., Nyman, G.: Simulator sickness symptoms caused by a visual search task in a monocular virtual display. In: Proc. the 11th International Display Workshops (IDW '04) December 8-10, Niigata, Japan (2004)
11. Peli, E.: The visual effects of head-mounted display (HMD) are not distinguishable from those of desk-top computer display. Vision Research 38, 2053–2066 (1998)
12. Rushton, S., Mon-Williams, M., Wann, J.P: Binocular vision in a bi-ocular world. New-generation head-mounted displays avoid causing visual deficit. Displays issue 4, pp. 255–260 (1994)
13. Rogers, E.M.: Diffusion of innovations, 4th edn. The Free Press, New York (1995)

Evaluating the Usability of an Auto-stereoscopic Display

Zhao Xia Jin[1], Ya Jun Zhang[1], Xin Wang[1], and Thomas Plocher[2]

[1] Honeywell Technology Solutions Laboratory,
Shanghai, China
[2] Honeywell Automation and Control Solutions Laboratory,
Minneapolis, Minnesota, USA
{zhaoxia.jin,yajun.zhang,xin.wang,plocher.tom}@Honeywell.com

Abstract. A considerable number of different auto-stereoscopic display systems are available on the market. Increased resolution of flat panel displays and greatly reduced cost have made auto-stereoscopic displays practical to use in applications for games, 3D television, the military, and industrial manufacturing. However, the usability and qualitative user experience provided by auto-stereoscopic 3D display has not been widely studied. This study sought to evaluate the qualitative user experiences with auto-stereoscopic 3D displays and their potential shortcomings by testing specific user tasks and comparing the difference between a stereo 3D display and flat 3D display. The results provide a good reference for the product application developer trying to select a display system and for the user interface designer.

Keywords: Autostereoscopic, 3D display, usability, stereo user interface.

1 Introduction

Since the invention of the stereoscopic image's principle in 1838, stereoscopic images have captured extensive interests in the area of scientific, media and mass public. Over the years, many display technologies have been developed Stereoscopic images have captivated a wide scientific, media and public interest in attempt to artificially recreate our experiences of viewing a real 3D object in natural world. Recently, a considerable number of different auto-stereoscopic display systems are available on the market which provides real-time, interactive and natural 3D experiences with significantly enhanced image quality and without any form of viewing aid such as anaglyph glasses, HMD and shuttle-glasses. As Dodgson [1] pointed out, auto-stereoscopic displays would find practical use in applications in which 3D depth perception is vital and where the novelty of stereo parallax is a selling point. The former category includes scientific and medical visualization of complex 3D structures and remote manipulation of robots in dangerous environments. The latter includes computer games and advertising. Today, with increased resolution of flat panel displays and greatly reduced cost, auto-stereoscopic displays have the potential to reach the mass consumer market. The affordable Sharp LL-151-3D display is a prominent example which is price at only several hundred of US dollars that delivers eye-popping 3D images to the naked eye.

J. Jacko (Ed.): Human-Computer Interaction, Part II, HCII 2007, LNCS 4551, pp. 605–614, 2007.

However, auto-stereoscopic 3D displays are still not widely used. Also, we believe there have not enough evaluations exploring the usability and user experience on using auto-stereoscopic 3D displays. Research has focused primarily on displays, with little effort spent on content human factors, as T. Kawai pointed out [2].

This study evaluated the qualitative user experiences with auto-stereoscopic 3D display and their potential shortcomings by testing specific user tasks in stereo 3D mode compared to flat 3D (stereo disabled) mode. Sharp LL-151-3D was selected because it can be easily switched between flat 3D and stereo 3D to avoid any contrast between two displays that will affect the evaluation. Secondly, it has similar technical parameters (e.g. resolution, screen size) to the traditional LCD display when view in a flat 3D mode. Thus it can provide same user experience as traditional LCD display.

Two tests were conducted to achieve the purposes in this paper. Firstly, a preliminary usability test was carried out to investigate the overall user experience of using the auto-stereoscopic 3D display in stereo 3D mode and flat 3D mode. With lessons learned from Test 1, a demo system with stereo user interface was designed and developed. A further usability test was conducted on the demo system to evaluate the usability of auto-stereoscopic display by a set of specific tasks which were performed in both stereo 3D mode and flat 3D mode.

2 Test 1 – Preliminary Usability Test

2.1 Method

Participants: Six participants (4 males and 2 females, aged from 25 to 33 years) from Honeywell (China) Co. Ltd. participated in the Test 1. All had normal or corrected-to-normal visual acuity and reported having no color defects. Three of them had the viewing experience of stereo 3D movies or stereoscopic pictures.

Equipment: A Sharp 15' 3D display (LL 151 3D) was used in our test. It is driven by a 2.8GHz Pentium 4 operating with Windows XP computer and powered by nVidia GeForce 7900GT graphics card with integrated 256MB memory. Brightness for the display is 370cd/m2 (2D mode) / 140cd/m2 (3D mode). View angle is Horizontal 130° / Vertical 115°.

Materials: In this test, we used stereo 3D materials which are commonly available and easily to be executed during the experiments over a short period of time. Two typical types of stereoscopic materials, static stereoscopic images and interactive stereoscopic VR (Virtual Reality) scenario, were used. The interactive 3D scenario, which simulates a commercial center, can be presented as a preset animation or an interactive virtual walking tour using mouse and keyboard.

Tasks & Procedures: Two tasks, Task 1- viewing static stereoscopic images and Task 2 - viewing and interacting with interactive scenario, were tested to investigate the user experience of finding the 'sweet spot', display effect, stereo effect, comfort and overall acceptance. In order to balance the sequence effect, half of the participants conducted Task 1 first and the others counterturn. Both tasks were tested in two different modes, which were stereo 3D mode and flat 3D mode. We didn't counterbalance the order of switching between two display modes, since all participants had experience in using traditional displays, which offer flat 3D viewing. In using stereo mode, all participants were informed that there was a best viewing position called 'sweet spot' and were asked to find it as quickly as possible.

Once the subjects completed the tasks in both display modes, they were asked to complete a questionnaire and answer questions of the after-text interview.

2.2 Results

In this test, the Mean Opinion Score (MOS) was collected. Time of completion for finding 'sweet spot' was collected for each trial. Also, participants' feedbacks were elicited in the after-test interview.

Stereo Effect. Without surprise, MOS of stereo effect, depth perception and immersive feeling in stereo 3D was higher than flat 3D (Figure 1, Figure 2). This indicates that for static images and the interactive scenario, the stereo 3D mode indeed provided superior depth feeling, immersive feeling and stereo effect.

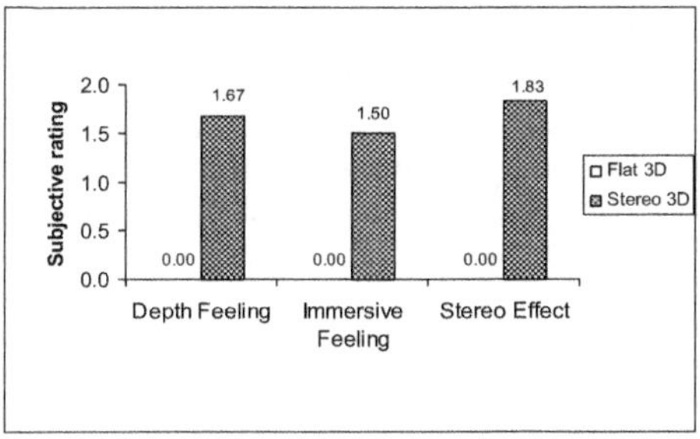

Fig. 1. MOS of depth feeling, immersive feeling and stereo effect for static images

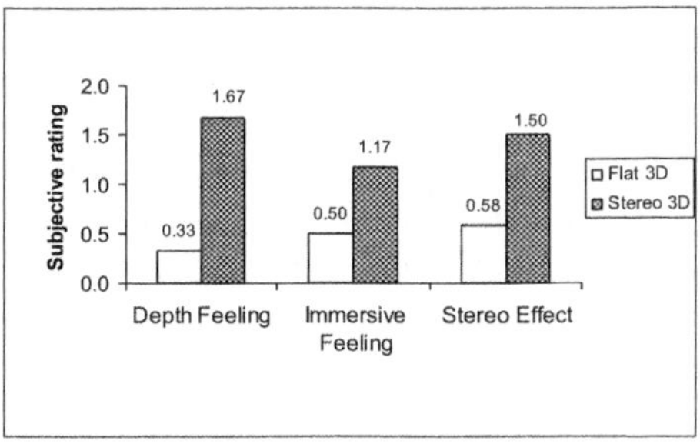

Fig. 2. MOS of depth feeling, immersive feeling and stereo effect for interactive scenario

Display Effect. Parallax barrier technology used in the Sharp 3D display actually reduced brightness and resolution. MOS of brightness and resolution for both static image and interactive scenario (Figure 3, Figure 4) shown that the participants were able to perceive the reduction of the brightness and resolution when switching to stereo mode. Also, MOS of color saturation was lower in stereo mode compared to flat 3D mode, which might be another side effect caused by the reduction of brightness and resolution. Interestingly, MOS of contrast was higher in stereo mode than in flat 3D mode for the static image and the same in both modes for interactive scenario. As reported, participants felt details including contrast effect seem enhanced in stereo mode due to the stereo effect, 3D lighting effect and shadowing effect.

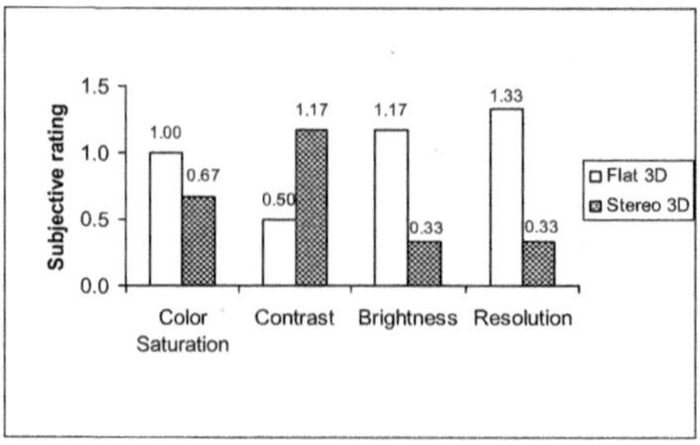

Fig. 3. MOS of color saturation, contrast, brightness and resolution for static images

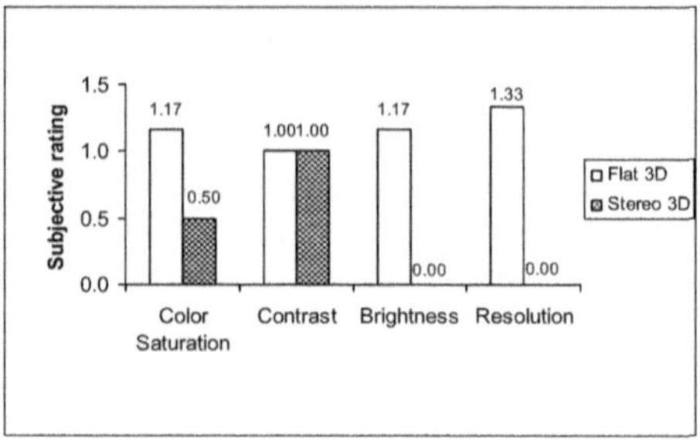

Fig. 4. MOS of color saturation, contrast, brightness and resolution for interactive scenario

Sweet Spot. Figure 5 and Figure 6 showed the time of completion in finding the 'sweet spot' for the first six trials for the static image and first three trials for the interactive scenario. Without guidance, the time spent in finding 'sweet spot' for the first trial varies greatly between different participants. Some participants who found the 'sweet spot' faster always had a good strategy or previous experience. For example, they assumed that the 'sweet spot' position is at the center of the display so they adjusted their head slightly to find the 'sweet spot'. However, participants who did not have a good strategy spent a longer time started searching from a position which was far away from the 'sweet spot' or they moved their head in very large range.

After the first trial, the time spent in finding 'sweet spot' decreased and remained at a certain level. This might indicate that once participants had a successful experience in finding the 'sweet spot', they could find it quickly in the next attempt.

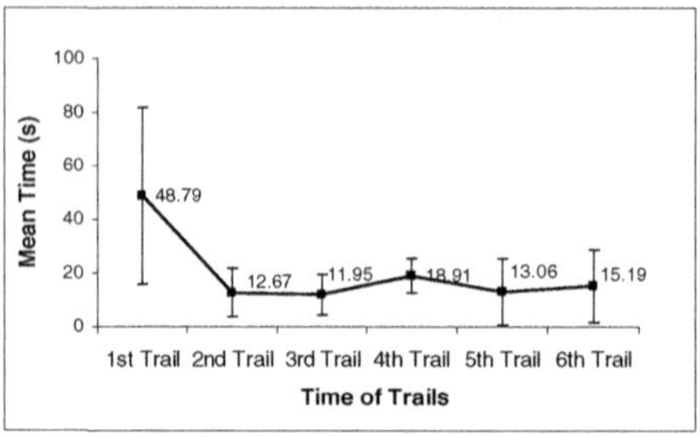

Fig. 5. Mean time spent in finding sweet spot in static images in stereo 3D mode

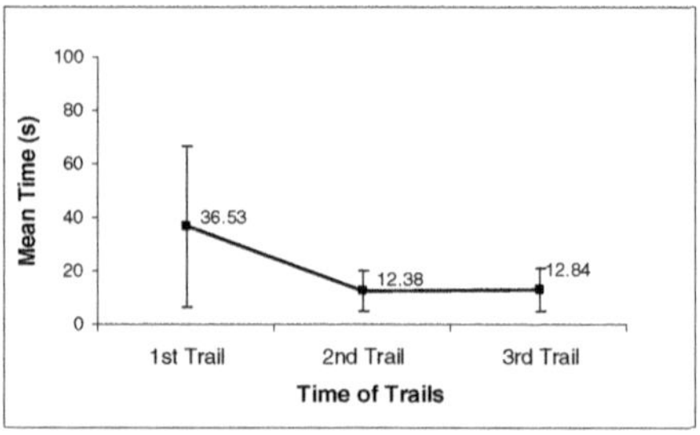

Fig. 6. Mean time spent in finding sweet spot in interactive scenario in stereo 3D mode

Comfort. The MOS of comfort of viewing both materials in stereo 3D is lower than flat 3D (Figure 7). Participants reported that they suffered from eyestrain, dizziness or even feelings of sickness when using the stereo 3D. As soon as the viewer's head moved out of the 'sweet spot', he experienced uncomfortable effects like feeling dizzy and seeing multiple vertical lines or double images.

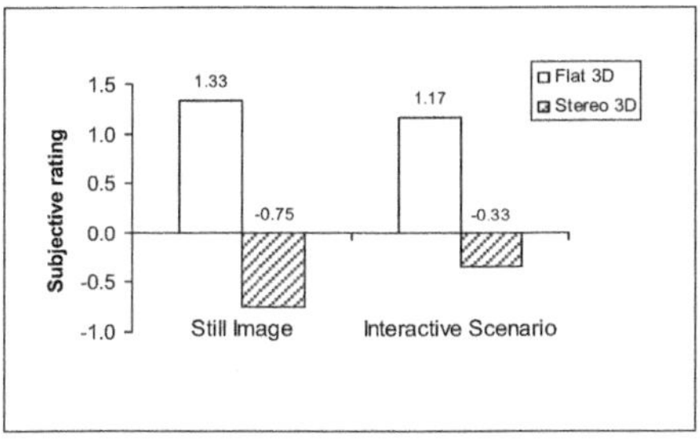

Fig. 7. MOS of comfort of both still image and interactive scenario in stereo 3D mode and flat 3D mode

Acceptance. Only two out of six participants expressed that they could accept the stereoscopic display. One participant reported that he "didn't know" whether or not he could accept the stereoscopic display. The remaining three participants reported that it was difficult for them to accept the auto-stereoscopic display mainly because of the discomfort issues.

3 Test 2 – Usability Test with Stereoscopic User Interface

3.1 Method

Participants: Six participants (3 males and 3 females, aged from 23 to 41 years) from Honeywell (China) Co. Ltd. participated in the Test 2. All had normal or corrected-to-normal visual acuity and reported having no color defects. Among the participants, five of them had viewing experience of stereo 3D movies or stereoscopic pictures.

Materials & Equipment: In Test 2, a demo system developed for a building-related project was tested. The demo driven by nVidia graphics card supported flat 3D mode, stereo 3D mode and 2D mouse interaction. The main view of the user interface was divided into several parts. The center region of the screen was used to display a 3D building model, related objects and widgets. On the top right of the screen, was a context-aware menu. At the bottom of the screen was the navigation panel with button groups to manipulate the view. Based on the Test 1, key design parameters were adjusted in order to achieve optimal effect in stereo mode. For example, the value of diffuse lighting was set to 0.25 (value = 0 ~1) in flat 3D mode while in stereo mode, it was set to 0.5 to increase the brightness of the user interface. The stereo separation was set to 20% for stereo 3D mode. The user interface provided an overall perspective view which didn't allow the user to immerse into it.

Tasks and Procedure: Test 2 consisted of three tasks: Task 1- identifying crossed routes, Task 2 - selecting target floor, and Task 3 - navigating to target location. All tasks needed to be completed in both stereo 3D mode and flat 3D mode. For each task, the participants were given different target object for identification, selection (task 2 and task 3) and navigation. In this way we varied the task content but not task difficulty for two display modes. Also, switching between two display modes was counterbalanced for each task to avoid sequence effect. Here we intended to compare the time of task completion and ease of task completion between stereo 3D mode and flat 3D mode. Again, for stereo mode, all participants were informed for the 'sweet spot'. Also, they were asked to find the 'sweet spot' and complete the tasks as soon as possible.

As in Test 1, once the subjects completed all tasks in both display modes, a questionnaire with subjective rating and an interview was followed.

3.2 Results

In test 2, the MOS and time of completion were collected. Also, participants' feedbacks, preferences and acceptance were elicited.

All participants completed all tasks successfully both in stereo 3D mode and flat 3D mode. Participants spent more time completing each task in stereo 3D mode compared to flat 3D mode (Figure 8). Also, the MOS of ease of task completion for interactive tasks (task 2 and task 3) is lower for stereo 3D than for flat 3D (Figure 9). This indicates that it was more difficult to complete the interactive task in stereo 3D mode. Participants reported that interaction in auto-stereoscopic viewing has a little unnaturalness. First, sometimes, they saw double images when trying to click a target object. Second, there was a distance in the z-axis between the cursor and the target object when using traditional 2D mouse. The cursor was floating on the surface while the target objects existing in the location with different depth.

However, the MOS of ease of task completion for Task 1 indicated a different trend. Participants rated it is easier to complete the task, 'identifying inter-crossed route', in stereo 3D mode. Participants reported that it is easier for them to capture depth cues that appeared between paths in stereo 3D mode compared to flat 3D mode. While in flat 3D, the two paths that are intercrossed as in an 'X' are difficult to identify as '/' shape path of 'X' or as a '>' shape path of 'X'. In stereo 3D, they can be differentiated easily since the two paths are actually layered in depth with a gap in the z axis.

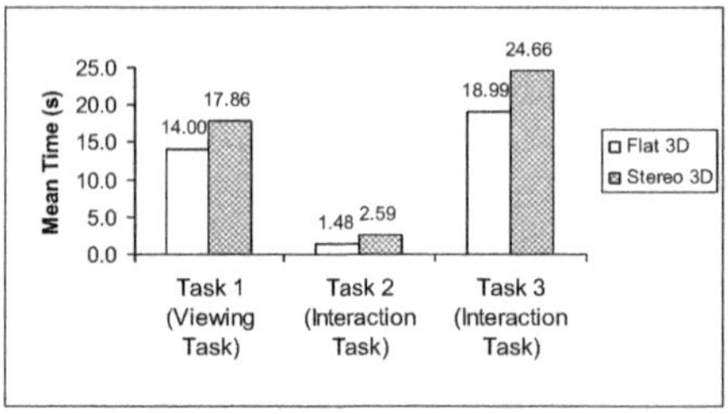

Fig. 8. Time of task completion

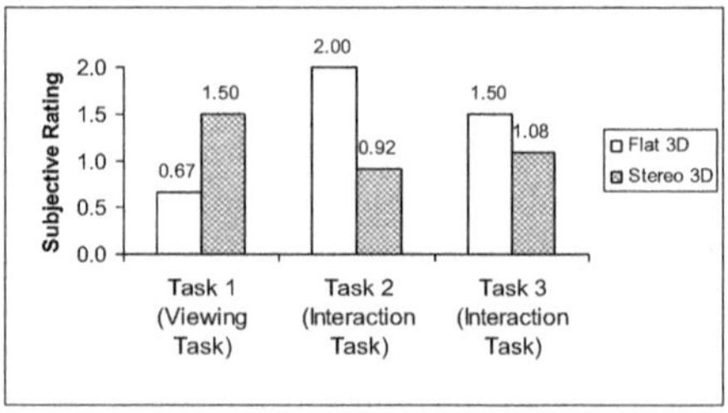

Fig. 9. MOS of ease of task completion

Stereo Effect. MOS of stereo effect, depth perception and immersive feeling in stereo 3D was higher than flat 3D (Figure 10). Not surprisingly, the stereo 3D mode indeed provided strong depth feeling, immersive feeling and stereo effect for the stereoscopic user interface. Also, participants felt that in stereo 3D mode they get wider field of view as they felt immersed in the space.

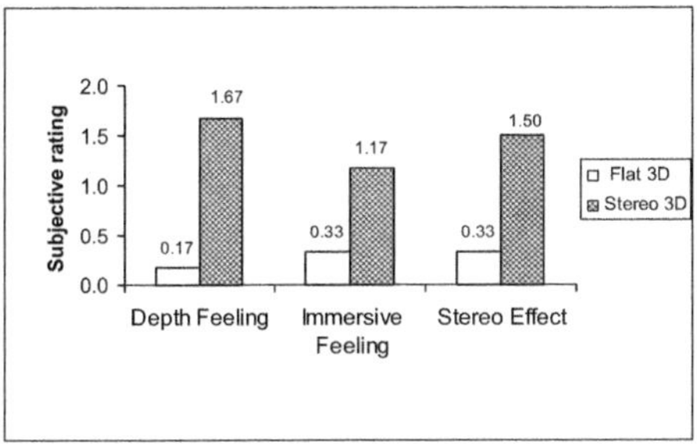

Fig. 10. MOS of depth feeling, immersive feeling and stereo effect for stereoscopic UI in flat 3D mode and stereo 3D mode

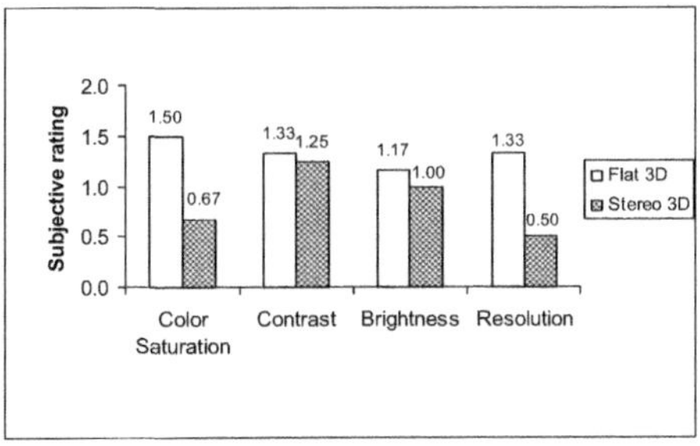

Fig. 11. MOS of color saturation, contrast, brightness and resolution for stereoscopic UI in flat 3D mode and stereo 3D mode

Display effect. Though the brightness and contrast were optimized by adjusting design parameters including lighting effect and color, the MOS of color saturation, brightness and resolution for user interface was still rated lower in stereo 3D mode than in flat 3D mode (Figure 11). The participants reported the User Interface looks much darker in stereo 3D mode. The MOS of contrast of user interface was lower in stereo 3D mode too, which is different from Test 1.

Sweet Spot. Figure 12 shows the time of completion for the first three trials in finding the 'sweet spot' while viewing the stereoscopic User Interface. Same as Test 1, without guidance, the time spent in finding 'sweet spot' for the first trial varied greatly for different participants. After the first trial, the time spent in finding 'sweet spot' saliently decreased and remained at a certain level. Participants used or formed the same strategy in finding sweet spot as summarized in Test 1. The participants also found that the Sharp stereo could not ensure good stereo effect for the whole display. Even though participants maintain their head in a fixed position which achieved good stereo effect of center view of the display, they still saw double images from the UI widgets located in the edge of the display.

Comfort. Test 2 confirmed the results of comfort collected in Test 1. The MOS of comfort was lower for stereo 3D than flat 3D (Figure 13). Similar to Test 1, the participants reported that they suffered from discomfort issues. Also, discomfort is associated with the 'sweet spot' limitation.

Preference and Acceptance. Five of six participants expressed that they could accept the auto-stereoscopic display. Another participant expressed that he "didn't know" whether or not he could accept it. Three participants preferred to use the flat 3D mode over the stereo 3D mode in viewing and operating the demo system. Two participants expressed that they did not have particular preference. Only one participant preferred to use stereo 3D mode. However, when we noted to the participants that new auto-stereoscopic displays have a very wide stereo viewing area, participants showed great interests and thought they would like the stereo display if there's no 'sweet spot' issue.

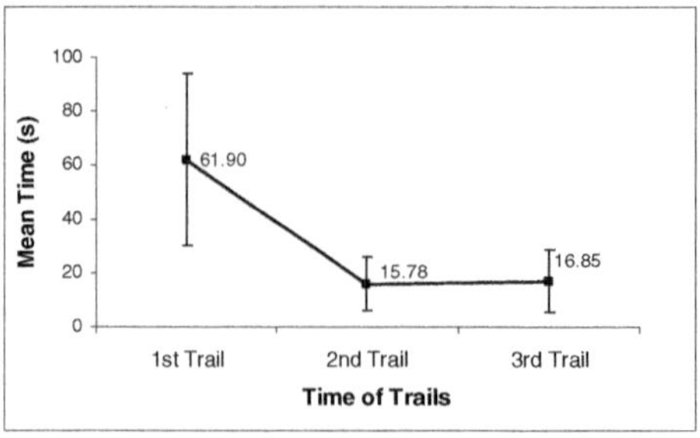

Fig. 12. Mean time spent in finding Sweet Spot in real UI in stereo 3D mode

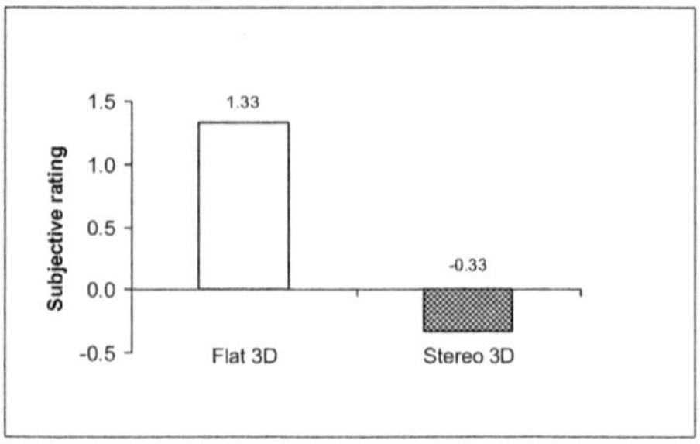

Fig. 13. MOS of comfort in both flat 3D mode and stereo 3D mode

4 Discussion and Recommendations

4.1 Discussion

Stereo Effect, Depth Perception and Immersive Feeling. We found evidence that stereo 3D is superior to flat 3D in presenting complex structures such as two inter-crossed paths in the 3D building model. Also, as W.R.Waltkins [3] and Frank L.Kooi [4] pointed out, the stereoscopic display is able to provide wider field of view, improve perceptual separation of details (e.g., UI widgets) and their background.

Resolution. A characteristic of all 3D displays is the tradeoff between pixel resolution and depth. In a scene viewed in 3D, pixels that in 2D would have contributed to high resolution are used instead to show depth. Most participants noticed the step down of the resolution in the stereo 3D, but the reduction was not very significant.

Brightness, Contrast and Color. Part of the light is blocked when switching to stereo 3D display mode. Most participants noticed the step down of the brightness in stereo 3D as well as the color. The viewers' feeling of contrast was more complex. For a static image or interactive scenario, the participants felt the contrast was improved when switching to stereo 3D display mode. For the user interface, the participants felt the contrast decreased.

Interaction. Results from Test 2 showed that the participants could complete the viewing and interaction test successfully in both stereo mode and flat 3D mode. Interaction with an auto-stereoscopic display can seem a little unnatural owing to the double images of the UI widgets and the distance in z-axis between cursor and the target object when using traditional 2D mouse. However, we observed that the sufficient feedbacks provided by the demo system significantly helped the users to interact with the stereo UI. Users could successfully hit the target objects with hover effect and selecting effect while errors were observed when the participants were trying to select the target objects without hover and selecting effect.

Sweet Spot. One drawback with the Sharp auto-stereoscopic 3D display is the narrow 'sweet spot'. This problem has been overcome by other autostereoscopic displays such as multiview display (e.g., NewSight-40" TFT 3D Display) and tracking display (e.g., ACT3D-21LN). The multiview display provides numerous viewing windows and thus allows observation from various physical locations. The tracking display can dynamically move viewing windows to correspond with a measurement of observer location and thus stereopsis is assured regardless of viewer position. These displays have not been fully accepted by present stereoscopic consumers but could represent the future of the technology [6].

Comfort. Our tests with Stereo 3D raised some discomfort issues. Participants reported discomfort symptoms like eyestrain, other visual fatigue, dizzy headaches, or even nausea and sick when using the stereo 3D. Two major factors contribute to the discomfort. First, as Sullivan [7] pointed out, in stereo 3D mode, users' eyes must remain focused at the depth of the display but must converge, or point, to depths either in front of or behind the display to cause the images from the two eyes to overlap. The mismatch between focus and convergence in stereo mode strains the eyes. Secondly, the Sharp autostereoscopic display used in the tests has a narrow 'sweet spot'. Discomfort results when it is lost.

Acceptance. Some of the participants expressed that they could accept the auto-stereoscopic display. However, most of them still preferred to use the flat 3D display to view our demo system. They reported that this is mainly due to the discomfort issues.

4.2 Recommendations

Achieving Optimal Display Quality. Due to the reduction of resolution and brightness and perceived reduction of display quality, it's important to view the design results in stereo mode so that "what you see is what you get". The parameters like color should be adjusted and tested to achieve the optimal display quality.

Space in Depth – A New Opportunity for Stereoscopic UI Design. In auto-stereoscopic viewing, there is space in depth, which alleviates the occlusion issue in UI components and display content. Auto-stereoscopic displays provide larger space for UI layout and also bring a new opportunity for UI design.

Interaction. It's more difficult to interact with a stereoscopic user interface using a traditional 2D mouse as compare to flat 3D mode due to the distance between cursor and the object in the z axis and the double image issue. Thus, it's very important to provide sufficient feedbacks to the user to ensure selecting a target object accurately. Providing hover effect and selecting effect proved to be effective in improving target object selection in stereoscopic user interface with stereo separation as 20%.

Pay Attention to the 'Sweet Spot' Limitation. If you have to use a display with such a 'sweet spot' limitation, make sure the major information is presented in the area which is within the best observation range. Give users some guidance on how to find the 'sweet spot': 1) Put the chair in the right position; 2) Provide the cues for finding 'sweet spot' to the users, such as centering the head in the middle of the display, do not move their heads in wide range, micro-adjust the head. 3) Confirm to user that when he/she is in the position of 'sweet spot', 4) Focus the eye to a single point.

Comfort Issue. Attention should be paid to how to help users smoothly get through the adjustment period. Also, with the currently available technologies, using auto-stereoscopic displays for tasks that require viewing over an extended period of time should be avoided.

5 Conclusion and Future Work

In this paper, we explored the usability of a Sharp stereo display from both a viewing and an interactive point of view. The results provide a good reference for the product application developer trying to select a display system and for the user interface designer. The results also provide a reference to vendors about improving auto-stereoscopic display technologies. Stereo 3D mode has the advantages of stereo effect, depth feeling, immersive feeling and well presenting complex structure and spatial relationship. But it also has the drawbacks of perceived reduction of resolution, brightness, color saturation, and discomfort. The difficulty of interaction may increase in stereo mode which should be a focus of future work.

References

1. Dodgson, N.A: Autostereoscopic 3D Displays. IEEE Computer 38(8), 31–36 (2005)
2. Kawai, T.: 3D displays and applications. Displays 23, 49–56 (2002)
3. Watkins, W.R., Heath, G.D., Phillips, M.D., Valeton, J.M., Toet, A.: Search and target acquisition: single line of sight versus wide baseline stereo. Optical Engineering 40(9), 1914–1927 (2001)
4. Kooi, F.L, Toet, A.: Visual comfort of binocular and 3D displays. Displays 25, 99–108 (2004)
5. Holliman, N.: 3D display systems. Handbook of optoelectronics. IOP Press (2002)
6. Bradshaw, J.: A business case analysis of auto-stereoscopic technology, in relation to the development of an interactive tourism website. Unpublished technical report University of Durham, UK (2003)
7. Sullivan, A.: 3 Deep. IEEE Spectrum: pp. 22–27 (2005)

Aspiring for a Virtual Life

Hee-Cheol Kim

School of Computer Engineering, Inje University, Gimhae, Obang-dong 607,
621-749 Gyung-Nam, S. Korea
heeki@cs.inje.ac.kr

Abstract. There has been a drastic change in the ways that computers are used. They have evolved from being tools for dealing with reality, e.g., for recording data and calculating complex equations, to being tools for fashioning virtuality, including virtual reality systems, on-line games, and virtual communities. This phenomenon, to some extent, stems from rapid technological development. What is more important, however, is that this phenomenon is also deeply rooted in the human longing for a virtual world. This paper argues for the importance of understanding such a desire, and discusses, in this context, how virtual reality may become a promising realm of the future, by setting out a theoretical foundation to examine it.

Keywords: Human computer interaction, mental representation, virtuality, virtual reality, virtual space.

1 Humans Exist Because They Aspire for a Virtual Life

People seem to live, simply, in reality. However, this is not quite the case. There is much evidence to show that we are actually living in a vast expanse of virtual space. When Martin Luther King said, "I have a dream", one may suppose that he was referring to a virtual world of "dream", where all people would be equal, a dream that had not been realized when he spoke of it. Dreams pertain to a kind of mental process that operates in virtual space. Imagination, belief, planning, and even lying are other forms of this process.

According to Pierre Levy, virtuality and reality are two important modes of human existence [1]. Just as humans cannot live outside reality, we cannot exist without a virtual world either. In fact, the idea of a virtual life can break the monotony of mere physical life, making it seem richer and more meaningful.

The word "virtual" has its origin in the Latin word "virtualis", derived from "virtus" which means force or potency. In this respect, virtual space can be thought of as potential space. Therefore, the virtual is what exists potentially, but not actually. As many philosophers, such as Levy, Deleuze, and Serres have noted [1-3], virtuality is not a notion opposed to the real, but to the actual. Let us go back to Martin Luther King's dream. He imagined a virtual space in which blacks and whites could sing and dance together, hand in hand. This space was not actuated at the time he spoke, but it did exist *in potentia*. Nowadays, of course, King's virtual space is no longer merely potential space, it exists as actuated space.

J. Jacko (Ed.): Human-Computer Interaction, Part II, HCII 2007, LNCS 4551, pp. 615–623, 2007.

Reality can be hard and painful. It is also sometimes dull and monotonous. Reality is a useful word that can symbolize various types of limitation, in that actions, words and plans are limited, in reality, with respect to time and space. There seems to be no way by which we, as humans, can escape reality. However, certain individuals aspire to overcome the limitations imposed by reality, and search for freedom and change. The question is how such aspirations may be realized. One way is to create virtual worlds or spaces. By living in a virtual space, humans can augment monotonous lives, and forget an embattled reality that has become hard and dreary. In a virtual world, we can do whatever we want; we can meet a friend who is far away face to face, get a job that we desire, or travel wherever we want to go without money. The old can be young, and the young can be old. We have a thirst for things that cannot be achieved in our real lives, and people strive to quench that thirst. The truth is that relief from that desire does not come from our real, physical lives; it comes from our virtual lives. This is why virtuality is key to our lives.

Fig. 1. Humans living in a virtual world. Humans cannot live outside of reality. At the same time, we cannot exist without some kind of virtual world, either. (2007. Feb. 14th, From http://indolentdandy.net/fitzroyalty/wp-content/uploads/2006/07/fly.jpg)

Arguing for the importance of understanding the human desire for a virtual life, this paper explores two conditions that underlie this desire: (1) humans think in *mental space* and (2) humans live their individual, secret lives in *private space*. Importantly, both mental and private space denote virtual space.

The human body is limited, but human thought is unlimited. Therefore, human beings seek freedom and ways to overcome the limitations that they face in the real world by means of thought. Virtual space is not simply physical space like 2D or 3D space; it is mental space. Virtual space ensues because human beings think. People also want their own private spaces to be apart from public spaces, where manners, formalities, structures and restraints are in place. Private space plays a role as a shelter, by which we can escape social judgment. It is particularly necessary when it comes to protecting freedom of thought. If all our thoughts were to be disclosed to others, it would be difficult to survive in a social world. Some thoughts must be in secret spaces, that no one has access to. This shows that both private space and mental space can be understood in the same way.

Section 2 presents various forms of evidence for the human aspiration for a virtual life. In sections 3 and 4, I claim that virtual space is mental space, and that it is also private space. It is argued that the human drive for secrecy is also the drive for virtual life. Section 5 concludes with the idea that virtual reality systems offer promise for the future, in that they are associated with intrinsic human drives for some kind of virtual life.

2 Evidence of the Desire for Virtual Life

From ancient times to the present, there has been much evidence supporting the idea that people live virtual lives. Granted that terms related to virtuality, such as virtual reality, virtual life, virtual space and virtual community have come to the fore at present, owing to the rapid development of information technology, it is also true to say that virtual life existed before the age of computers. This section explores evidence for the existence of virtual life before and after the invention of computers. This kind of approach is useful in that it shows that the desire for a virtual life is intrinsic to human thought processes, and that it did not begin with the emergence of computer technology.

2.1 Virtual Life in an Everyday Context

Virtual life is a reality that everyone experiences. No one lives in reality alone. Everyone imagines, plans, dreams and believes. Virtual life existed before the birth of computers and multimedia technology.

When an individual watches a movie, he or she can be moved to tears by a powerful story in which an actor may endure unbearable situations or loves and then forgive an enemy. The actor's story is not the viewer's story. The actor is not the viewer; nor is the actor his or her friend, relative, or child. There is no connection between the viewer and the actor in reality. Furthermore, the actor is not portraying a real person, but a fictitious character. So, why do tears well up in the eyes of the viewer? Can we say that he or she is psychologically problematic, since tears are shed for a fictitious character, who does not exist in reality? Not at all. In fact, most of us have experienced similar emotions. It appears to be an undeniable fact that we all live virtual lives. We may not be movie stars, but we can become a star in virtual life. We are all moved, inspired, and affected by movies, novels, poems, newspapers and magazines.

Suppose that a student scores 80 in a mathematics exam. He or she can then dream of obtaining a perfect grade of 100 in the next exam, imagining that he or she will be at the top of the class. This imaginative act can be realized, depending on personal effort and various, conducive situations. Does such an ambition denote an actual event? No, it does not. He or she lives a virtual life in which he or she is the number one student. In a similar manner, we all imagine, plan and dream about the future, clearly indicating that human beings aspire for, and live, virtual lives.

Virtual life is not concerned with the future only; it may also be focused on the past. Regretting something in the past, we sometimes wish that we had not done certain things. We actually want to go back to the past in our minds, as if we could travel in a time machine. There are other examples regarding this phenomenon. Watching sports games, we can feel vicarious satisfaction through identifying with the sports stars, despite the fact that we may not be players of that sport. Additionally, with respect to religion, people have various beliefs, all of which constitute a form of desire for a virtual life. As we see in the examples described, all of us long for a virtual world, and may spend more time in virtual space than we do in real space.

2.2 Virtual Life with Computers

Which is larger, a computer or the Earth? In a physical sense, this might seem to be a stupid question. However, if we think beyond physical objects, and think about what is within a computer, the nature of the question changes. A computer does not simply consist of chips, discs, and wires. There are post offices within it, for e-mail systems. There are also banks (Internet banking), museums, libraries, musical performances, communities, and a host of other things within a computer. Practically every virtual space is represented within this single machine, a computer.

Computers are not merely data-processing machines. In the beginning, users thought that they were simply using a tool for manipulating data. However, following the development of the user interface technique known as direct manipulation [4], users began to feel that they faced invisible data rather than machines. People have gradually come to regard themselves as inhabitants or visitors, occupying a computer space, generated by a vast amount of data. This constitutes a change of our perception; we are now not simply tool users. We have changed from being tool users to being space visitors. Terms like visitor, visit and inhabit are common to many websites. Hedman claimed that we are visitors as well as users, and advocated visitor-oriented systems design [5]. Importantly, Hedman's point indicates that computers help people to occupy various virtual spaces.

Virtual life by means of computers is very common nowadays. We are already familiar with communication in Internet space. Many people enjoy on-line games that create a kind of virtual world, where different characters appear and engage in activities. A serious case involving participation in such a virtual world occurred when a man died because he indulged in the artificial world of computer games to the extent that he ignored his physical needs for food and rest. People also use blogging as an outlet for their thoughts, opinions and emotions [6]. Because commenting on a blog is possible, interaction between bloggers and readers, interaction that occurs without them meeting face to face, is greatly facilitated in cyber space. With the development of haptic devices, we can even touch and feel the weight of objects using computers. As a result, it has become possible for medical students to practice as surgeons before they actually operate.

Let us go back to the question, “Which is larger, a computer or the Earth?” Here, we may have to answer, “The computer is much larger than the Earth.” A large number of virtual spaces abound in the computer. Until now, media such as books, movies, TV, and so on have been mediators, making connections between human beings and virtual space. From now on, however, a much more powerful mediator, the computer, will change our lives. Computers are not only tools for users but they also constitute a gigantic space, satisfying the human desire for virtual life.

3 Virtual Space Is Mental Space

Virtual space, in a computer-scientific sense, can be, for example, a 3D space that looks real. In a different sense, virtual space can be a mental space or thinking space. A well known text-based virtual world, MUD, was very successful in the 1990s, despite the fact that it had no 2D or 3D visual effects. This shows that human mental space is as important as visual space.

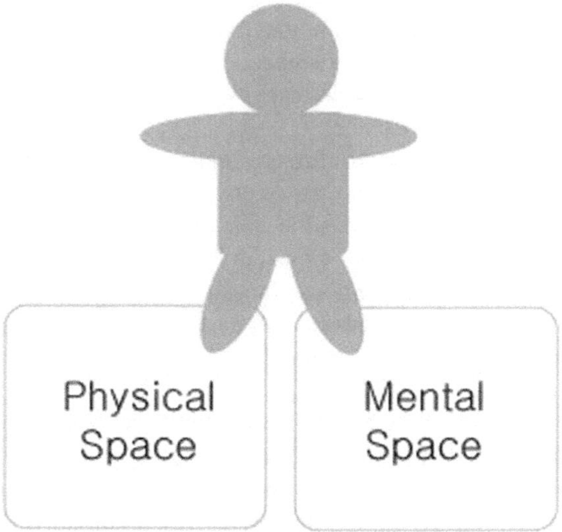

Fig. 2. We humans are both physical and mental beings. Therefore, we live in both physical and mental spaces. In computer science, virtual space has been more about physical space. However, one should remember that humans are thinking creatures and build virtual space by thinking.

There are two kinds of space in this respect: physical and mental. ‘Physical space’ is of the senses and is supported by various physical tools such as computer screens, multimedia systems, and pen and paper. Virtual space in a computer-scientific sense is a physical space. Many systems developers are more concerned with how to make the world visible and touchable. This is why multimedia technology such as 3D graphics and sound are crucial in computer science. Mathematics and engineering govern everything in the creation of physical spaces.

'Mental space' is untouchable and invisible and can be thought of as a mental representation or mental model, in the psychological sense proposed by Craik and Johnson-Laird [7, 8]. Mental space is created because man thinks. What is thought and what is represented in the mind are more important than what can be seen in this space. In this regard, let us examine an excerpt from Hermann Hesse's novel, *Demian*.

> The bird fights its way out of the egg.
> The egg is the world.
> Who would be born first must destroy a world.
> The bird flies to God.
> That God's name is Abraxas.

The "world" that Hesse is referring to here is not a visual space, but a space depicted in the mind. Therefore, to destroy a world does not mean to ruin it by instruments or weapons. It is, rather, to break a world of the mind in order to enter another. Descartes' famous supposition, "I think therefore I am," tells us that in doing the thinking, we are also existing simultaneously. Thus, thinking is a fundamental element in understanding human existence. Virtual space is a space for human thinking. A house is necessary for human physical existence, and virtual space is necessary for human mental existence.

Plato believed that there was an ultimate reality, a reality that we could not see around us. According to him, what we sense physically may not be real. This points to the idea that there is something invisible and unapprehended by the senses that is more important than the real world. Consider the following example. A couple get divorced after they have bought the house that they have dreamed about for ten years. During the course of making the money to buy the house, the husband and the wife were happy and loved each other. A period of ten years is not a simple time interval. It is a period that provides a thinking space for the couple, one in which they can imagine and look forward to their future happiness. However, once they owned the house, they lost the mental space where their happiness and expectation had existed. This example shows us that human happiness does not come from a physical space like a house, but from a mental space constructed in the mind, over time.

Computer scientists tend to be more concerned with virtual space as a physical entity, while philosophers focus on it as a mental entity. While two kinds of virtual space, physical and mental spaces, are required for human existence, this paper emphasizes mental space, in that the desire that leads to life in a virtual world arises from our intrinsic longing for virtuality rather than from having the tools to create a physical space. Humans have long used mental spaces to express virtuality, with or without tools, before computers existed. Humans are thinking creatures, and they build virtual worlds by thinking.

4 Virtual Space Is Private Space

From the perspective of structuralism, human beings are understood in the context of social structure. With the development of the Internet, however, it has also become important to consider how an individual constructs his or her own world. This view is exactly opposite to that posed by structuralism. In the digital age, the agency of individual human beings has become more emphasized, as opposed to social structure. Anonymity is very common on the net to keep individual freedom rather than public order. People create their own worlds using home pages, blogs, games, and the like.

There are two spaces in our lives, which we can call public and private spaces. Public space is a space in which my personal thoughts, feelings, and actions are exposed to others. There, my words and actions are restricted. My own peculiar styles are not always allowed. I cannot express what I think and believe to others freely. I always have to consider people around me. However, my private space is quite different from my public one. There, no one knows or intrudes on my thoughts, emotions, or actions, and I have freedom at all times in terms of my words and actions.

Freedom is a key word by which we better understand the distinction between the two spaces. Private space is needed to protect and guarantee my freedom of thought and action, while public space restricts and intrudes on people's freedom. People can live together by knowing others through public space. That is why intrusion on others' freedom is indispensable. Ironically, we can also live because something important and secret in us is protected within our own private spaces. In the bible, Samson lived with Delilah (Judges: chapter 16). But he soon faced death by telling her the truth about the source of his power; in this manner he moved from his secret private space in which he alone had stayed into a public space that both he and Delilah shared. We humans need public space to live together as social beings. At the same time, however, we also need private space to survive in the wild world of this earth, without breaking human relationships.

Private space has many advantages. In a factor-analysis study, Pedersen identified the privacy functions contemplation, autonomy, rejuvenation, confiding, creativity, disapproved consumption, recovery, catharsis, and concealment [9]. There are likely more factors than these, or similar functions expressed by analogous terms. While all of these functions are meaningful for understanding privacy and private life, this paper focuses on freedom.

Another important reason that people aspire for virtual space is that they are free within their own spaces. People often want to inhabit a space where freedom is total, apart from the spaces that society and reality provide, such as the physical space provided in schools, offices, and meeting places, and the mental space that arises from customs, laws, and duty. They want a virtual space where complete freedom of their thoughts and actions is guaranteed. This is private space.

In particular, freedom of thought should be protected, in relation to virtual space as mental space. If all of our imagination were revealed to others, we would find it impossible to live social lives. We need to live in our own virtual space where no one watches us. The importance of a private life should not be underestimated, and the idea of virtual life is strongly related to this secret and private life. These days, everyone freely expresses his or her thoughts and feelings via the Internet. This is not strange. With computer technology, we have more opportunities to live in private space.

One may argue that virtual space is also public space, because there are a large number of people inhabiting various virtual communities. This is true. I do not deny that it is also a public space. Nevertheless, the relationships between the participants in those communities often differ from the ones we experience in the real world. By Buber's definition, it is an I-and-it relationship rather than an I-and-you relationship [10].

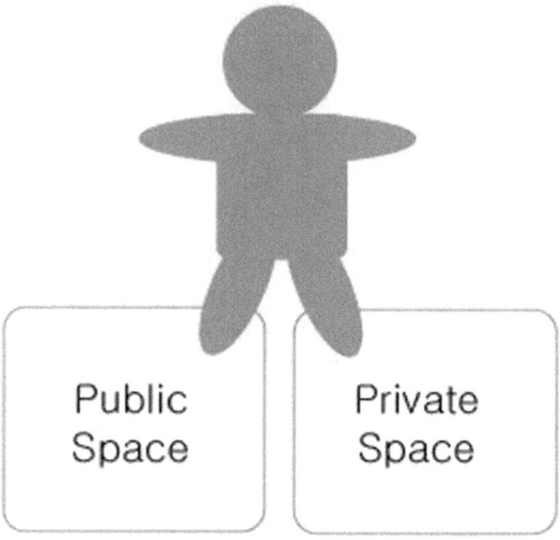

Fig. 3. To live in this world, I expose myself in public space and simultaneously hide myself in private space. Freedom-seeking people want to build virtual private spaces.

5 Conclusion

A fundamental momentum for our virtual lives is the human desire for a virtual world. This paper shows that aspiration for a virtual life comes from two conditions: first, that human beings think in mental space and second, that they search for a secret life in private space. Virtual space is both mental and private space. Computers are powerful tools that enable the creation of virtual space, thus helping to fulfil the two basic human drives noted above. The present achievement of virtual reality systems in a broad sense, including on-line games, virtual communities, and avatars, has not come about by mere chance; it reflects the human longing for a virtual world. This development will continue into the future, as long as the human desire for a virtual life continues.

Acknowledgments. This work was supported by a grant from the 2005 Inje University Research Grant.

References

1. Levy, P.: Becoming Virtual: Reality in the Digital Age. Plenum Publishing Corporation (1998)
2. Deleuze, G.: Difference and Repetition. Columbia University Press (1995)
3. Serres, M.: Atlas. Paris, Juliard (1994)
4. Shneiderman, B.: The Future of Interactive Systems and the emergence of Direct Manipulation. Behaviour and Information Technology 1(3), 237–256 (1982)
5. Hedman, A.: Visitor Orientation in Context. PhD Thesis at the Department of Numerical Analysis and Computer Science (NADA), Stockholm University/The Royal Institute of Technology, Stockholm, Sweden. TRITA-NA-0329 (2004)
6. Nardi, B.A., Schiano, D.J., Gumbrecht, M., Swartz, L.: Why We Blog. Communications of the ACM 47(12), 41–46 (2004)
7. Craik, K.: The Nature of Explanation. Cambridge University Press, Cambridge (1943)
8. Johnson-Laird, P.N.: Mental Models. Harvard University Press, Cambridge (1983)
9. Pedersen, D.M.: Psychological Functions of Privacy. Journal of Environmental Psychology 17, 147–156 (1997)
10. Buber, M.: I and Thou. Free Press, Glencoe (1971)

Immersive Viewer System for 3D User Interface

Dongwuk Kyoung, Yunli Lee, and Keechul Jung

Department of Media, Soongsil University,
Seoul, South Korea
{kiki227,yunli,kcjung}@ssu.ac.kr

Abstract. 3D user interface research is increasing rapidly as development of area in virtual environment, virtual reality and augmented reality. Recently, the 3D user interface is not favorable because it needs high cost and uses cumbersome devices. However, the 3D user interface gives a great impact to the user which motivated us to implement an immersive viewer system (Im-viewer system) to test the 3D user interface. The Im-viewer system uses a tiled display to provide an immersive image to user, and it uses the proposed 3D volume reconstruction and representation for input interface with low computational as advantage. The input interface is used to control the tiled display operation such as on/off, next/previous slide command in Im-viewer system. The experimental results show that the proposed techniques of 3D user interface perform well on the Im-viewer system.

Keywords: 3D User Interface, Tiled Display, 3D Shape Reconstruction, Gesture Recognition, Dimension Reduction.

1 Introduction

As the acceleration of development in digital based information science and technology, the area of technology has expanded to the social and cultural field, such as media, films, games, media art, etc. Study in realistic interactive environment which can be applied to various fields, aims to provide users with realistic image and information input of user's various motions. Tom Cruise, in the film 'Minority report' demonstrated an action of searching for information with his hands on a large sophisticated display using a state-of-art input device. It is becoming a reality to provide realistic images for users by an input device that is capturing the user's gestures.

The three-dimensional (3D) environment or real-world needs a new set of interface components: new devices, new techniques, and new metaphors. Some of these new components may be simple refinements of existing components; others must be designed from scratch. Many researchers study 3D user interface for the 3D interaction in realistic interactive environment or 3D environment. As such, the development of 3D user interface has emerge to technology driven application including 3D graphics technology, augmented reality [1] and virtual environment [2] technology, flight simulator technology and many more. Each of these technologies creates new applications leading to unexplored area in user tasks, new challenges in

J. Jacko (Ed.): Human-Computer Interaction, Part II, HCII 2007, LNCS 4551, pp. 624–633, 2007.

user interface and usability issues. Researches in 3D user interface become a necessity in today's application [3-4].

Recently, the usage of gesture for 3D input interface is widely used [5]. It consists of using tracking device [6] or vision-based gesture recognition which uses one or more cameras to capture images. There are a number of tracking systems which primary used for tracking eye, gaze, hand configuration and overall body position that commercially available and it can be used as input to gesture recognition. In the context of virtual environment, each sensor type has it own strengths and weakness. However, the tracking system is too cumbersome and it is the most significant drawback. The vision-based gesture recognition is the solution for the tracking system drawback. The computer vision techniques have the potential to provide real-time data that is useful for analyzing and recognizing human motion which is passive and non-obtrusive. Therefore there are many researches actively involved computer vision community on detecting and recognizing faces, facial expression, human gesture and etc.

This has provoked us to implement an immersive viewer system to test our proposed techniques for the 3D input and 3D output for 3D user interface. We named the system as Im-Viewer system. The system using the proposed method for 3D shape reconstruction and representation which is use as 3D input interface. The output will be project to the 3D output interface on the tiled display. The basic operation of the Im-viewer system is to recognize the gesture of user command as 3D input, and generated the feedback or output of the commands to the tiled display. The 3D user interface of Im-viewer system give a great impact for the user while interact with the system through the 3D user interface [7-8].

This paper is organized as follows. In section 2, we provide an overview of Im-viewer system. The proposed model of 3D shape reconstruction and representation for input interface is described in section 3. Section 4 presents the output interface of tiled display and experiment results are shown and discussed in the next section. The final section presents the conclusion and future work.

2 Im-viewer System Overview

The Im-viewer system uses a tiled display to provide an immersive image to user, and it uses the proposed 3D volume reconstruction and representation for input interface.

(a) Tiled Display

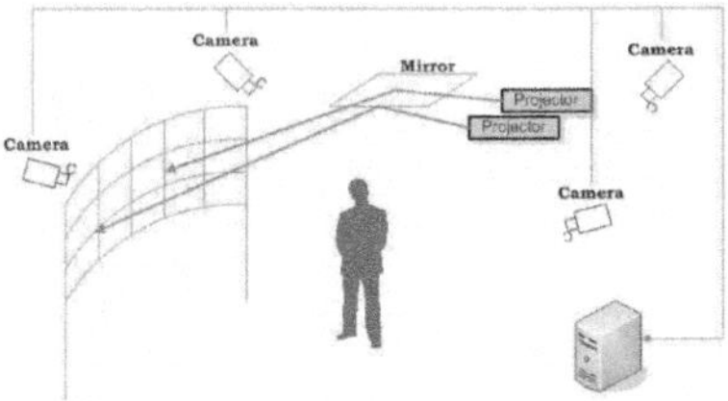

(b) Overall System Environment

Fig. 1. System Environment of Im-viewer System

The input interface is used to control the tiled display in Im-viewer system (i.e., on/off, next slide and previous slide). The overall system environment is shown in Figure 1. The Figure 1 (a) is an image of experiment results, and the overall system environment (Figure 1(b)).

The input interface of Im-viewer has basic 4 poses to control 4 steps of the system, such as system on/off, next slide and previous slide. The user is able to control the system from any angle of the position without any limitation.

Figure 2 is the system architecture of the application. The architecture of 3D user interface consists of input and output interface. The input interface uses a database for gesture recognition and the proposed methods, such as 3D volume reconstruction and representation. Input interface has 3 processes: 1) to choose the poses and store into database, 2) to generate 2D data using proposed methods, 3) matching between generated 2D data and existing 2D data in database.

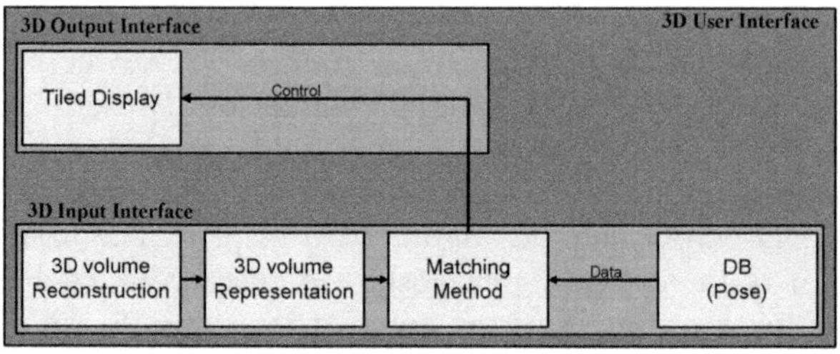

Fig. 2. Im-viewer System Architecture

3 Input Interface

The Im-viewer system uses some poses for interaction between Human and Computer. We use a 3D gesture input interface in Im-viewer system for interaction, and the system consists of 3D shape reconstruction, representation and matching method using a database. In this section, we omit the detail explanation of both the 3D shape reconstruction and 3D shape representation.

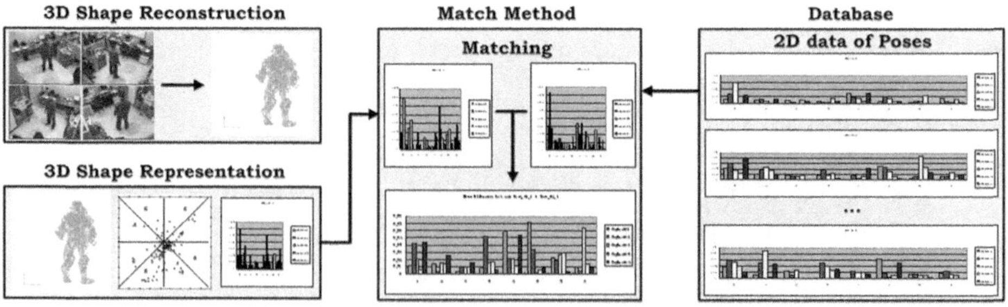

Fig. 3. Overall Process of Input Interface

The input interface consists of 3 processes (Figure 4). First process stores the initial poses which use the gesture model for Human-Computer Interaction. Second process is to generate a 2D data using proposed method in real-time, such as 3D volume reconstruction and representation described [7]. The last process is matching between the 2D data that is generated in real-time and with all existing 2D data in the database. The matching method finds the best pose using error value, and recognizes the best pose using threshold value. The threshold value is used to decide the input pose whether it is correct or otherwise.

3.1 Generated 3D Shape Reconstruction

We use our proposed method for 3D shape reconstruction and representation in real-time. Our environment of 3D shape reconstruction use 4 cameras and DVR board. Although the web camera is useful and cheap, however, it has 2 disadvantages, such as low speed and low accuracy. Therefore, we use CCD Digital Cameras for high speed and DVR board (Digital Video Recorder board) for high accuracy. The DVR board is able to record 16 digital cameras and 30 frames per second in a PC. The environment of capturing human gesture using 4 cameras is shown in Figure 6 (a-d).

Fig. 4. Capture Images from all Cameras

Generally, 3D shape reconstruction system is important for 3D video and gesture recognition. We use the plane-based volume intersection method for the 3D shape reconstruction system. This system consists of 3 steps. The first step is synchronized multi-view image acquisition. The second step is silhouette extraction. And the last step is silhouette volume intersection (Figure 5).

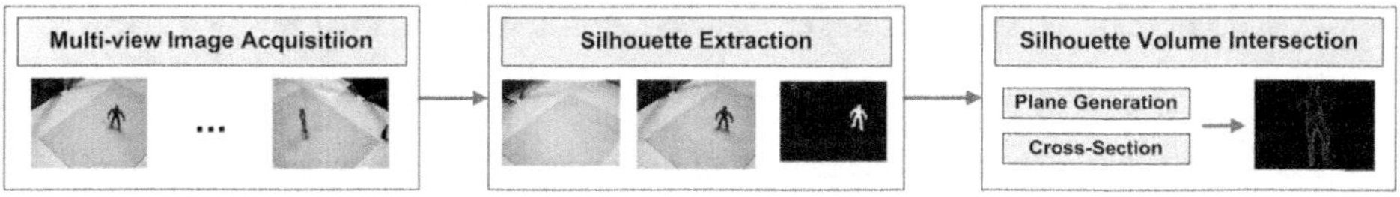

Fig. 5. 3D Shape Reconstruction Process

3.2 Generated 3D Representation

The images shown in Figure 6 are used to generate 3D volume data and 3D dimension reduction is performed using an improvement method of meshless parameterization with cylindrical boundary which described in [8].

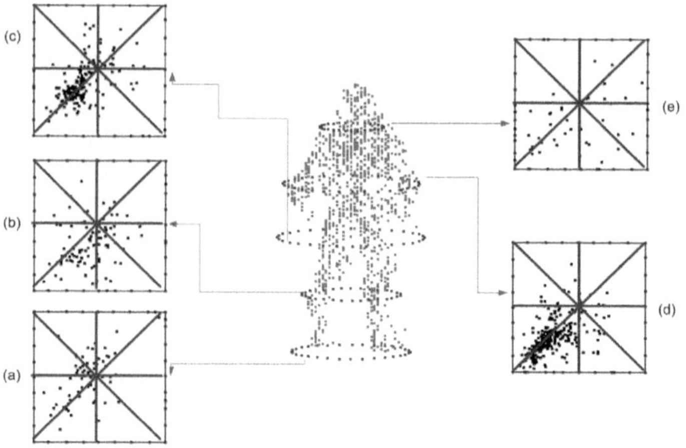

Fig. 6. Result of 3D Shape Reconstruction and Representation; (a-e) shows the multi-layered 2D appearance of 3D voxel data based on each cylindrical boundary layer

Figure 7 shows the graph represents the normalized data in multi-layered 2D appearance of 5 layers segment that are divided into 8 regions. The graph shown in Figure 7 is the representation of multi-layered 2D appearance as a result of 3D mapping. The graph data is based on the normalized data result of the mapping 3D voxels into 2D appearance. The legend shows the 5 layers segment which has an order from bottom to top. Segment 1 represents the most bottom segment of layers follow by the segment 2 until the top layer. Each layered segments are divided into 8 regions. The number of parametric data is counted and plot into the graph. The x-axis is the number of regions in layer segment, while the y-axis is the normalized value of parametric data for each region.

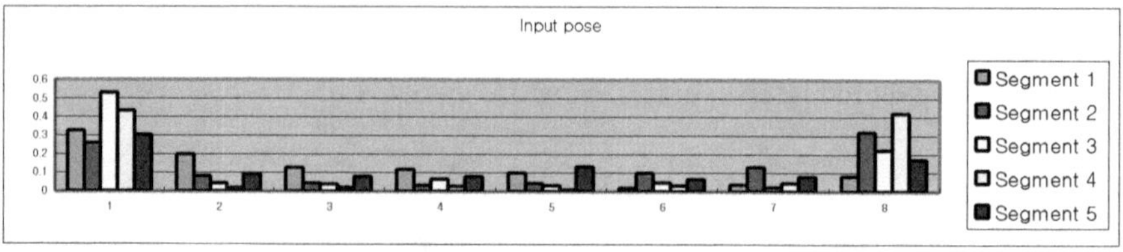

Fig. 7. Graph Representation of Multi-layered 2D Appearance Result

4 Output Interface

A necessary component of any 3D UI is the hardware that presents information to the user. This component called 3D output interface or display, present information to one or more of the user's senses through the human perceptual system.

The proposed tiled display system provide user with large and high resolution using two mirrors. This system has two advantages. The first advantage is it needs a smaller space than front projected display. The second advantage is that the user does not obstruct the projected image. The environment of proposed system consists of two projectors and a cylinder screen of size 3mx2m (width × height) meter (Fig. 7). We solved some problems: calibration, image and projector alignment, luminosity matching, and seam problem.

Fig. 8. Our Tiled Display Environment

(a) Distortion image of curved screen

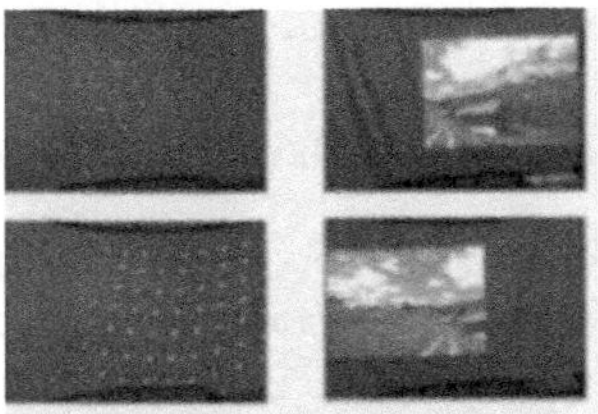

(b) Calibration of distortion image

(c) Image Alignment of Multi-Projector

(d) Intensity Blending of Multi-Projector

Fig. 9. Process of Tiled Display in Curved Screen

4.1 Image Alignment of Multi-projector and Geometric Calibration

The tiled display is important for the image alignment of multi-projector. Although, the projection system using a projector is easily used by calibration method, the projection system using multi-projector is difficult to provide the immersive image which is alignment image using multi-projector. Fig. 10 (a) shows a distortion image of two projectors. The corrected area is determined with the consideration of distortion area. Fig. 10 (b) shows the determined area in distortion area. The white line is the corrected area of each projector, and the block line is shared area of two projectors.

(a) (b)

Fig. 10. Image Alignment Process: (a) Distortion Image, (b) Determined Area

Our tiled display system in geometric calibration solves non-linear distortion using the method of dividing a small rectangular area. This method can be compute as linear distortion because the problem changes non-linear distortion into linear distortion using smaller rectangular area. The proposed system computes warping functions for each small rectangular using keystone correction method [9]. The warping function is computed by using the relation between each area (e.g. 1, 2, 3, …) in Figure 10 (a) and each area (e.g. 1, 2, 3, …) in Figure 10 (b).

4.2 Intensity Blending of Multi-projector

After the projections from multiple projectors are geometrically registered, the regions of display surfaces where projections overlap, the perceived intensity is higher than where the projections do not overlap. This increase is primarily dependent on the number of projectors active in the overlap region (Fig. 12).

(a) (b)

Fig. 11. Brightness Problem of Overlap Region: (a) Brightness Problem Images, (b) Corrected Image using Intensity Blending Method

The image generated by projections from multiple projectors is said to be intensity normalized if the intensity at any pixel in the observing camera is equal to the intensity due to the same image generated by a single projector.

The projection overlap is observed using camera or alignment of Multi-Projector. The intensity normalization method use alpha values in RGBA color space. The RGBA color space stands for Red Green Blue Alpha. The color is RGB as usual, and the brightness is A(alpha). We solved high intensity of the overlap region using alpha values.

The intensity contribution from one projector decreases linearly with an alpha value intensity weight of 1.0 at one end and 0.0 at the other end. For the other projector active in this overlap region, the weight changes linearly from 0.0 to 1.0 in the same direction. Outside the overlap region and where only one projector is active, the intensity weight for all pixels for that projector is 1.0. Thus, the sum of intensity weights of all projectors at any pixel is always 1.0 (Fig. 13).

5 Experimental Results

The Im-viewer system uses the pre-define poses for gesture recognition. The pre-define pose need to compute 2D representation for matching a corrected pose. The 4 pre-define poses is as follow. Fig. 14 (a-b) shows one of all pre-define pose. Fig. 15 (a-d) shows the graph representation of the multi-layered 2D appearance for each gesture poses based on the pixels value distribution of each segment layer that divided into 8 regions [8].

We use the matching method in order to choose a correct pose. The matching method has 2 processes. First, we match between 2D input appearance with all 2D appearance in database and find the best pose in database using error value. Second, we determine the best pose to ensure the pose is correct or not correct using threshold value. Fig. 16 shows a matching process of input appearance between pose 1 of database.

However, the best pose is not a correct pose because the system always has the best pose using a matching method. Therefore, we need a threshold value to evaluate a

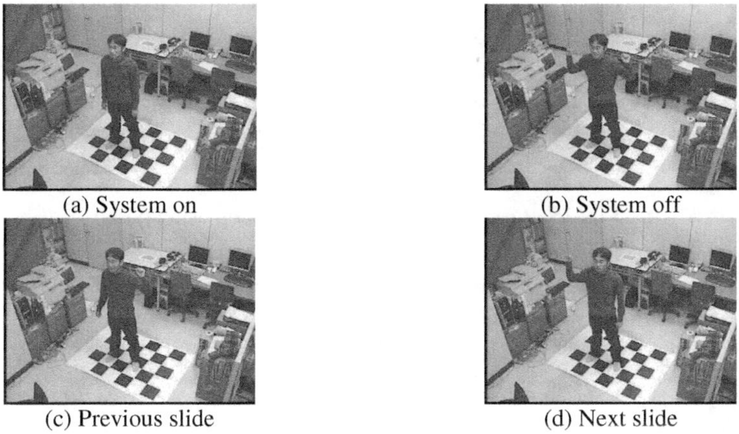

(a) System on (b) System off (c) Previous slide (d) Next slide

Fig. 12. Pose Definition for System Control

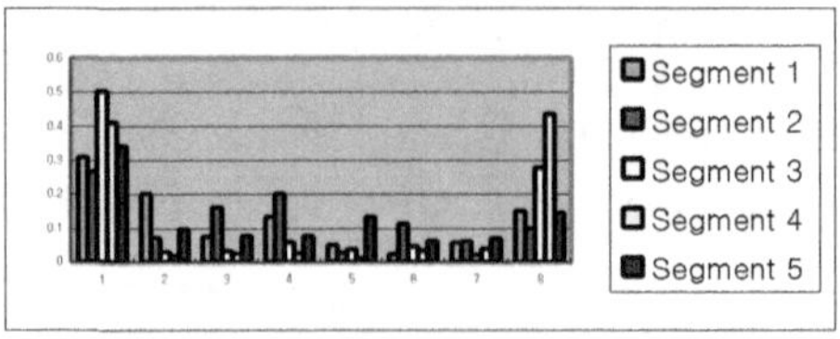

(a) Graph representation of pre-define pose - a

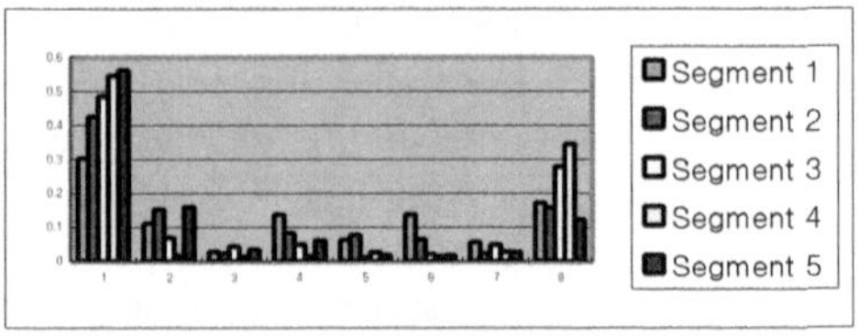

(b) Graph representation of pre-define pose - b

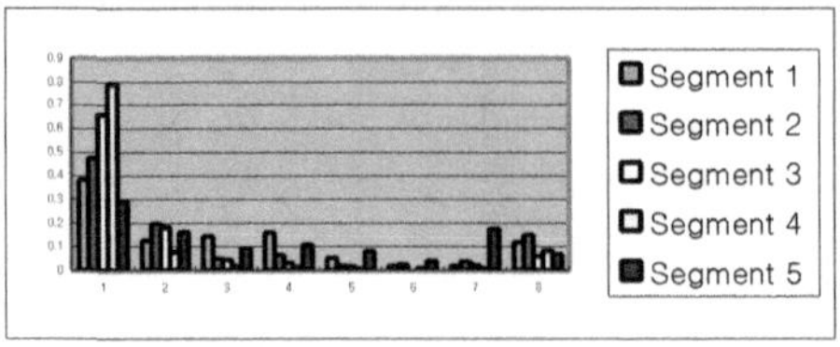

(c) Graph representation of pre-define pose - c

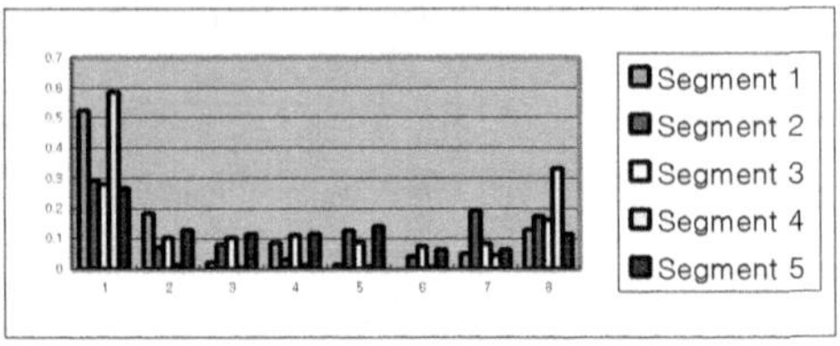

(d) Graph representation of pre-define pose - d

Fig. 13. Posture and Graph Representation of Multi-layered 2D Appearance Result

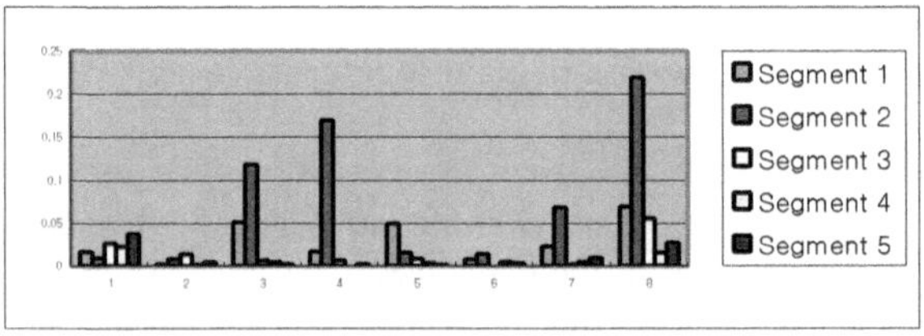

(a) Error different between input data and pose 1

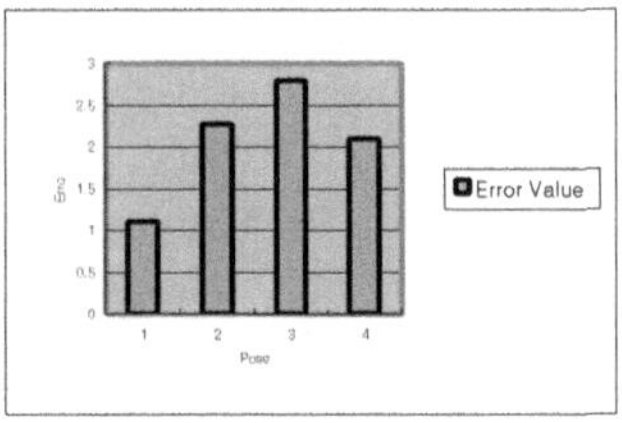

(b) Matching Result

Fig. 14. Result of Matching Between an input data and all pose in database

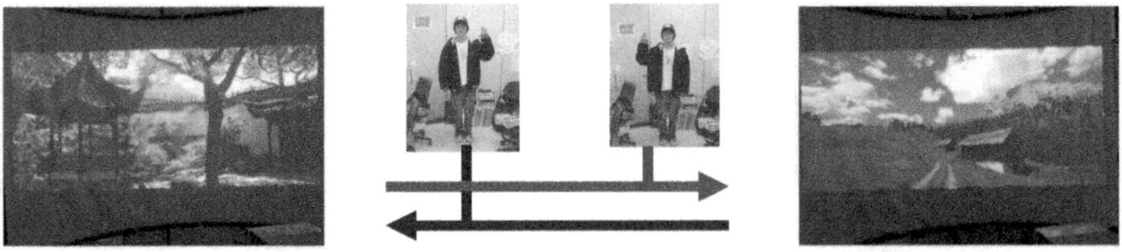

(a) Previous slide (b) Control poses (c) Next slide

Fig. 15. Result image of proposed system using pose

correct pose or not a correct pose. The threshold value is determined from the user training data of the system. This system uses 1.5 as the threshold value. Fig. 5-3 shows the example of the user using the input gesture to control the system.

6 Conclusions

Many users of virtual reality or augmented reality environment application require a suitable and immersive interface, such as 3D user interface. In the paper, we focus a

3D input interface using 3D shape reconstruction and representation. The advantage of 3D input interface is reasonable computational time in order to adapt to application which required wide display. Therefore, we have implemented an Im-viewer system to evaluate the input interface using gesture input and 3D output interface using tiled display.

The Im-viewer system provides a test environment of 3D user interface using our proposed method and tiled display. The proposed method used to control the Im-viewer system using 4 basic poses. The 4 poses are defined as 4 processes which are system on, off, next slide and previous slide. Also, the tiled display able to provides realistic image to multi-user because it has a high resolution and large image on curved screen.

For future work, we are implementing more gestures for control the 3D input interface for multiple users.

Acknowledgments. This work was supported by Korea Research Foundation Grant funded by Korea Government(MOEHRD,Basic Research Promotion Fund)(KRF-2005-003-D00336).

References

1. Wellner, P., Mackay, W., Gold, R.: Back to the Real World. Communications of the ACM 36(7), 87–96 (1993)
2. Foley, J.: Interfaces for Advanced Computing. Scientific American 257(4), 126–135 (1987)
3. Poupyerv, Kruijff, E.: 20th Century 3DUI Bibliography: Annotated Biblegraphy of 3D User Interfaces of the 20th Century. (2000) Available at:: http://www.mic.atr.co.jp/p̃oup/3dui/3duibib.htm
4. Bowman, D., Kruijff, E., LaViola, J., Poupyrev, I.: An Introduction to 3-D User Interface Design. Presence. Teleoperators and Virtual Environments 5(3), 207–211 (2001)
5. Sherman, B., Craig, A.: Understanding Virtual Reality. Morgan Kauffman Publishers, San Francisco (2003)
6. Foxlin, E.: Motion Tracking Requirements and Technologies. Handbook of Virtual Environments. In: Stanney, K. (ed.) Design, Implementation, and Applications, pp. 163–210. Lawrence Erlbaum Associates, Mahwah, NJ (2002)
7. Lee, Y., Kyoung, D., Han, E., Jung, K.: Dimension Reduction in 3D Gesture Recognition using Meshless Parameterization. In: Chang, L.-W., Lie, W.-N. (eds.) PSIVT 2006. LNCS, vol. 4319, Springer, Heidelberg (2006)
8. Kyoung, D., Lee, Y., Beak, W., Han, E., Yang, J., Jung, K.: Efficient 3D Voxel Reconstruction using Precomputing method for Gesture Recognition. In: First Korea-Japan Joint Workshop on Pattern Recognition (2006)
9. Sukthankar, R., et al.: Smarter Presentations: Exploiting Homogra-phy in Camera-Projector Systems. In: Proceedings of International Conference on Computer Vision, pp. 247–253 (2001)

Resolving Occlusion Between Virtual and Real Scenes for Augmented Reality Applications

Lijun Li, Tao Guan, and Bo Ren

Digital Engineering and Simulation Centre,
Huazhong University of Science and Technology,
No.1037 Luoyu Road,430074 Wuhan, China
lilijun@hust.edu.cn,
qd_gt@126.com,
fibin@263.net

Abstract. In this paper, we propose a method to resolve occlusion problem for tabletop AR based city plan system using stereo vision and accurate boundary depth recovery of foreground objects. Firstly, we design a color and brightness based foreground subtraction approach to avoid the negative effect of shadows. Then, we get the depth information for represent correct occlusion between virtual and real objects based on contour matching and depth interpolation. Some experiments have been carried out to demonstrate the validity of the proposed approach.

Keywords: Augmented Reality, Occlusion, Stereo Vision, Epipolar Geometry, Depth Recovery.

1 Introduction

The ultimate goal of augmented reality (AR) is to add information generated by computers to a real object or place. Unlike virtual reality, AR does not create a simulation of reality. Instead, it takes a real scene as the foundation and incorporates technologies that add contextual data to deepen a person's understanding of the subject. Augmented reality has been put to use in a number of fields, including medical imaging [1], where doctors can access data about patients; training [2], in which technology provides students or technicians with necessary data about specific objects they are working with; and in museums [3], where artifacts can be tagged with information such as the artifact's historical context or where it was discovered.

Geometrical consistency is one of the most important problems which limits the augmented reality become more widely used. There are two geometrical consistencies to be coped with in Augmented Reality Systems. The first one is the pose consistency between the real and virtual worlds. It means that the virtual scenes generated by computers must be aligned with the real world seamlessly. The second one is occlusion consistency between virtual and real scenes. While occluding background, the virtual objects should also be occluded by foreground correctly. However, in most AR systems virtual objects are usually superimposed on the video image without

J. Jacko (Ed.): Human-Computer Interaction, Part II, HCII 2007, LNCS 4551, pp. 634–642, 2007.

using depth information from the real scenes, so real objects are always occluded by virtual objects. This problem reduces the impression that the virtual objects are part of the real world scene and affects the user's recognition of the geometrical relationship between real and virtual objects.

A number of efforts have been carried out to cope with the occlusion consistency in AR systems. Lepetit proposed a contour based approach [4]. They obtain the depth information of real objects by estimating their contours. Since the contour of a real object will change in each frame, they manually define the contour of object in key frames and use this to estimate the object contour in the current frame. However, their algorithm is impossible to run in real-time and cannot be applied to deformable objects. Kim et al. used stereo vision to estimate the depth of the real scene [5]. In their system, the depth of boundary of real objects is calculated to find the natural occlusion between real and virtual objects. However, their technique is computationally expensive and difficult to run in real-time.

The main goal of our work is to resolve the case when a user's hands are occluded by virtual objects in a tabletop AR based city plan system. The remainder of this paper is organized as follows. Section 2 presents some background and notations. A primitive overview of proposed method is described in section 3. Section 4 presents the color and brightness based foreground subtraction approach. Section 5 deals with the problem of depth recovery for real objects. Experimental results are shown in Section 6. Final remarks and conclusion are given in the last section.

2 Background

2.1 Camera Model and Homographies

In our research, both 2D and 3D points are represented with homogeneous vectors, so that the relationship between a 3D point $M = [X, Y, Z, 1]^T$ and its image projection $m = [x, y, 1]^T$ is generally given as follows under the pinhole camera model.

$$m = \lambda C T_{cm} M \qquad \text{Where } C = \begin{bmatrix} f_x & 0 & o_x \\ 0 & f_y & o_y \\ 0 & 0 & 1 \end{bmatrix}, T_{cm} = [R \mid T] \cdot \tag{1}$$

Where λ is the homogeneous scale factors unknown a-priori. [R | T] is the extrinsic parameters of the camera, $R = [r_x \ r_y \ r_z]$ is a 3×3 rotation matrix ,and $T = [t]$ is the translation of the camera.

When a 3D point exists on the Z=0 plane of the world coordinate, (1) will be [6]:

$$\begin{bmatrix} x \\ y \\ 1 \end{bmatrix} = \lambda C [r_1 \ r_2 \ t] \begin{bmatrix} X \\ Y \\ 1 \end{bmatrix} \cdot \tag{2}$$

We represent $[X,Y,1]^T$ with M', then (1) can be rewritten as (3).Where the 3×3 matrix H is the planar homography which transforms points on the world plane to the current image. We can get H using SVD and more than four corresponding points.

$$m = HM' \ . \tag{3}$$

2.2 Depth Recovery in Stereo Vision

When two images are acquired by a stereo camera system, every physical point M yields a pair of 2D projections m_1 and m_2 on two images. If we know both the intrinsic and extrinsic parameters of the stereo system, we can reconstruct the 3D location of the point M from m_1 and m_2 [7], [8].

In the simple case of a parallel camera system as shown in Fig. 1, the depth of a point M can be simply calculated by:

$$Z = fB/(x_2 - x_1) \ . \tag{4}$$

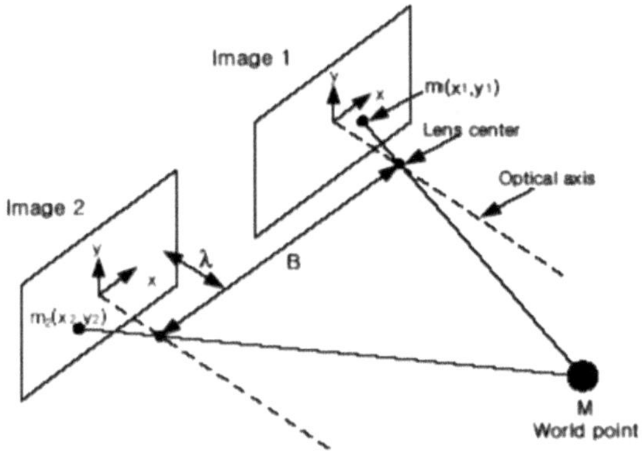

Fig. 1. Parallel stereo camera geometry

Where *B* is the baseline distance between two cameras and *f* is the focal length of the camera. We assume the parallel camera geometry in the following process of this paper for simplicity.

3 Overview of Proposed Method

The main goal of this paper is to resolve the case when a user's hands are occluded by virtual scenes in a tabletop AR based city plan system. Our method can be divided into three stages, namely, foreground segmentation, depth recovery and rendering.

1. Foreground segmentation: We use homography to establish the correspondence of pixels between current and key frame. To overcome the negative effect of shadows, we design a color and brightness based approach to segment foreground objects from background scenes.

2. Depth recovery: We use contour based stereo matching method for finding real object depth. We achieve real time results by performing stereo matching on the boundary of foreground objects and acquire the depth of the inner pixel by interpolating the boundary depth values.
3. Rendering: The recovered depth values of moving objects and Z-Buffer are used to realize the correct occlusion between real and virtual scenes.

4 Foreground Segmentation

To subtract the foreground objects in real environment, we must firstly establish the pixels transform relationship between current and model frames. Fig.2 gives a perspicuous illustration of the proposed method.

From the discussion of section 2.1, we know that the transform relationship between a point X_m of the model image and its projection on the key and current frame can be represented as (5) and (6). Where H_{mc} and H_{mk} are obtained using the correspondences of markers' corners and SVD algorithm.

$$x_c = H_{mc} X_m . \tag{5}$$

$$x_k = H_{mk} X_m . \tag{6}$$

From the above two equations, the following equation can be obtained:

$$x_k = H_{mk} H_{mc}^{-1} x_c = H_{ck} x_c . \tag{7}$$

With (7), we have established the pixels transform relationship between current and key frames, and the following task is how to subtract the moving objects from background using this relationship.

In our experiments, we find that if a simple method such as Sum of Absolute Difference is adopted, shadows of foreground scenes may also be detected as moving objects. To avoid this problem, we design a color and brightness based foreground subtraction approach as follows:

$$P_k' = P_k / \| P_k \| . \tag{8}$$

$$P_c' = (P_c \cdot P_k') P_k' . \tag{9}$$

$$\sigma = \| P_c' \| / \| P_k \| . \tag{10}$$

$$d = \| P_c' - P_c \| . \tag{11}$$

Where, P_c and P_k represent a pixel value of the current and reference image respectively, which consist of R, G, and B channel. P_k' is a normalized vector of P_k and P_c' is a vector formed when P_c is projected into P_k space. The value σ indicates a ratio of brightness, and d indicates a difference of color.

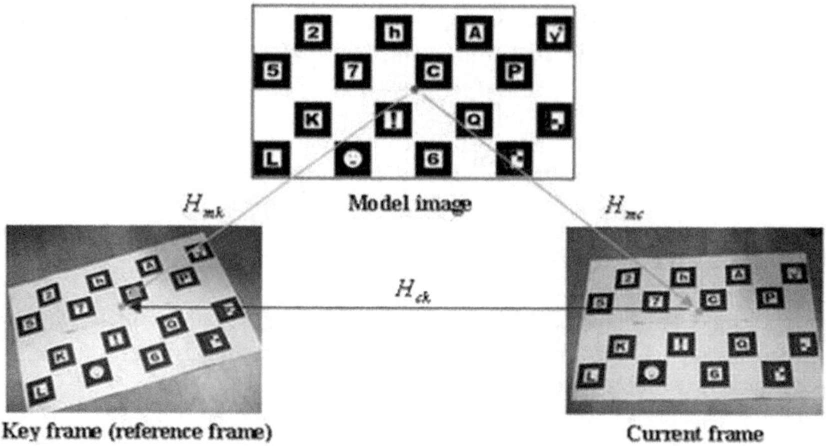

Fig. 2. Pixels matching based on model frame

If a pixel accord with the (5), then we consider it belongs to a foreground object.

$$d > \alpha \ or \ \sigma < \theta_1 \ or \ \sigma > \theta_2 \ . \tag{12}$$

Where α is the predefined threshold of color difference, θ_1 and θ_2 are defined according to experience which are set to 0.2 and 0.6 respectively in our algorithm.

5 Foreground Depth Recovery

To achieve the correct occlusion between virtual and real objects, we should first obtain the depth of foreground objects. We adopt the method proposed in [9] by which we can achieve real time results by performing stereo matching on the boundary of moving objects and acquire the depth value of the inner pixel by interpolating the boundary depth values. The method consists of two steps: region matching and depth calculation.

In order to calculate the depth of the foreground objects, we need to establish the correspondences of the foreground objects' regions between right and left images. The boundaries of the foreground object region in each camera image are traced. Its size, boundary length, and center of mass are recorded. Since stereo cameras used in our systems are placed close to each other, and have almost the same camera parameters, we assume that the region parameters of the corresponding regions are not too different. Therefore, we can determine the corresponding regions by evaluating the ratio of each parameter with a certain threshold. As shown in Fig.3, in order to establish the correspondence of hand contours, we use area and length to get the initial matching result. Then the epipolar line corresponding to the center of mass of the hand contour in the left image is drawn in the right image. The correspondence is identified by searching in the right image for a region whose mass has the smallest distance with the drawn epipolar line.

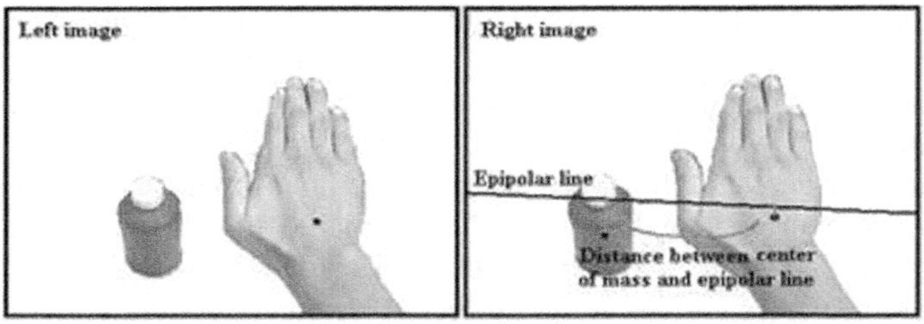

Fig. 3. Region matching based on epipolar constraint

With the corresponding regions between the left and right camera images determined, the next task is to recover the foreground depth using boundary line matching according to following steps:

1. Segment the contour of the foreground object region into segments with equal lengths. Then, extract the points which have the largest curvature in each segment as illustrated in Fig.4 (a). In the case of parallel stereo matching, the depth estimation error tends to be small at the point that has a large curvature.
2. Establish the correspondences of key points between right and left image. As shown in Fig.4 (b), we select a key point X_l in the left image and draw its

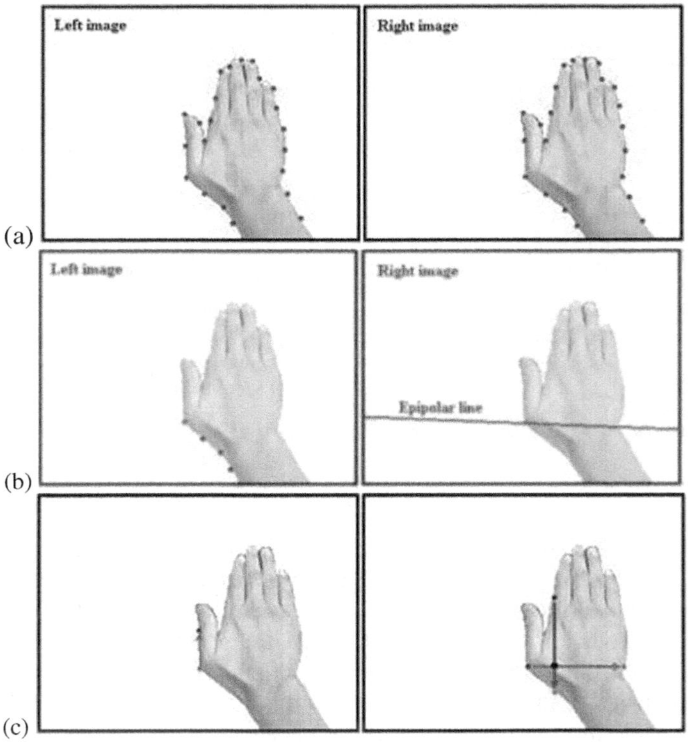

Fig. 4. Foreground objects depth recovery.

corresponding epipolar line in the right image. The correspondence X_r is found from the corresponding contour in the right image, which minimize the distance from the epipolar line of X_l. With the obtained correspondences, we recover their depth using (4).

3. Interpolate the depth of intermediate points on the boundary line by the depth values of neighboring sampled points. Obtain the depth of the inner pixels with the average value of vertical and horizontal interpolation with the boundary depth values as shown in Fig.4 (c).

6 Experiment Results

We implement the algorithm using Open CV and Open GL on a fast graphics workstation (Dell 530, CPU 1.8G×2). ARTOOLKIT is used to calculate the position and pose of the parallel stereo vision system. The frame rate is more than 25fps under the resolution of 320 x 240. Experiment results are shown in Fig.5, in which Fig.5 (a)-(d) are the results without inflicting virtual and real occlusion, Fig.5 (e)-(h) are the results of our method. We can see that our method is more actual than the traditional approaches, and greatly enhance the third dimension of the AR system.

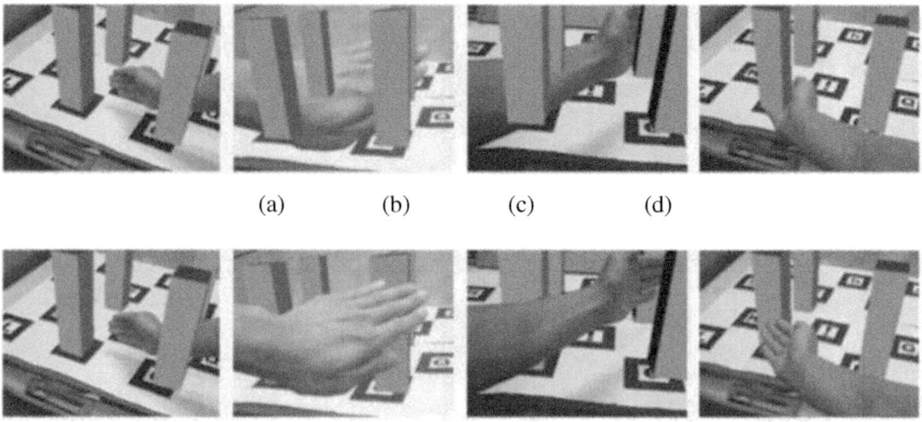

(a) (b) (c) (d)

(e) (f) (g) (h)

Fig. 5. Experiment results

We use the depth obtained by man made fiducial marker as default correct value to evaluate the accuracy of our method. The measurement range is from 250mm to 950mm. The depth is measured 50 times at the same range, we calculate the average depth value and standard deviation. Fig.6 shows the result. The measurement error is less than 6mm within the range 250mm - 700mm. If the distance is more than 700mm, the error became larger. The maximum error in depth is 9mm, found at 880mm . Considering the length of arm and head movement characteristic, we can draw the conclusion that our method can precisely accomplish the depth recovering task in tabletop AR system.

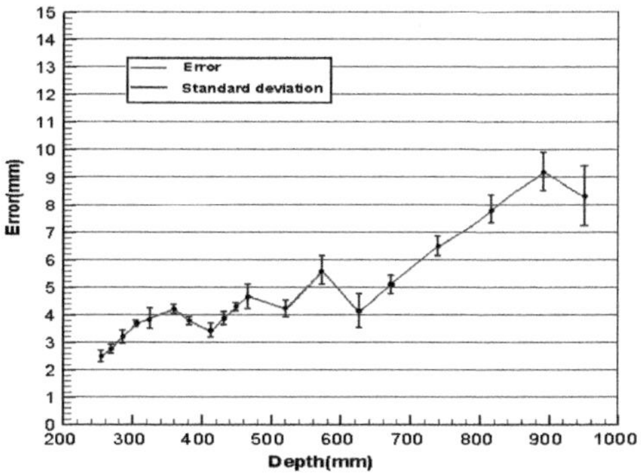

Fig. 6. Accuracy analysis

The method described in this paper is also used to resolve the occlusion problem in a tabletop AR based urban-plan system. In tradition method, the users' hands are always occluded by virtual scenes which cumber the communication between different users to a large degree. By our method, as shown in Fig.7, the users' hand can correctly occlude the virtual objects in the work space which really facilitate the communication between different users.

Fig. 7. Depth recovery in tabletop AR system

7 Conclusion

This paper use stereo vision and contour matching based depth recovering method to resolve the case when a user's hands are occluded by virtual objects in a tabletop AR based city plan system. Experimental results show that our method can effectively resolve occlusion problem and really enhance the third dimension of the tabletop AR system. The future work is to design a real time approach to accurately recover the depth information of the inner pixels of the foreground and this will be the key step to realize collision detection between real and virtual scenes.

References

1. Soler, L., Nicolau, S., Schmid, J., Koehl, C., Marescaux, J., Pennec, X.: Virtual reality and augmented reality in digestive surgery. In: Proc. of the ISMAR, pp. 278–279 (2004)
2. Brown, D.G., Coyne, J.T., Stripling, R.: Augmented Reality for Urban Skills Training. IEEE Virtual Reality, pp. 35–35 (2006)

3. White, M., Mourkoussis, N., Darcy, J., Petridis, P.: ARCO - an architecture for digitization, management and presentation of virtual exhibitions. In: Proc. of the ICG, pp. 622–625 (2004)
4. Lepetit, V., Berger, M.O.: A semi-automatic method for resolving occlusion in augmented reality. In: Proc. of the CVPR, pp. 225–230 (2000)
5. Kim, H., Yang, S., Sohn, K.: 3d reconstruction of stereo images for interaction between real and virtual worlds. In: Proc. of the ISMAR, pp. 167–177 (2003)
6. Hartley, R., Zisserman, A.: Multiple View Geometry in Computer Vision. Cambridge University Press, Cambridge (2000)
7. Faugeras, O.: Three-Dimensional Computer Vision: A Geometric Viewpoint. MIT Press, Cambridge (2001)
8. Trucoo, E., Verri, A.: Introductory Techniques for 3-D Computer Vision. Prentice-Hall, Englewood Cliffs (1998)
9. Hayashi, K., Kato, H., Nishida, S.: Occlusion Detection of Real Objects using Contour Based Stereo Matching. In: Proc. of the ICAT (2005)

Augmented Reality E-Commerce Assistant System: Trying While Shopping

Yuzhu Lu and Shana Smith

Human Computer Interaction Program,
Iowa State University, Ames, IA, USA.
yuzhu@iastate.edu, sssmith@iastate.edu

Abstract. Traditional electronic commerce (e-commerce) is limited, because it cannot provide enough direct information about products to online consumers. The technology presented in this paper shows how Augmented Reality (AR) can be used to help overcome the limitations and enhance e-commerce systems. An e-commerce assistant tool was developed, using user-centered design principles. The tool was developed as an Internet plugin, so it can be used on different kinds of computers and handheld devices. A usability experiment was conducted, to compare the developed AR e-commerce assistant tool with traditional e-commerce and Virtual Reality (VR) e-commerce systems. Results show that an AR e-commerce system can provide more direct information about products than traditional or VR e-commerce systems.

Keywords: Augmented Reality, Electronic Commerce, User Centered Design.

1 Introduction

Standing [1] defined e-commerce as the online exchange of goods, services, and money within firms and between firms and their customers. In the past decade, E-commerce and online shopping have become popular, because they make peoples' lives easier, especially for individuals with disabilities and for others who have difficulty engaging in onsite shopping. In fact, in 2002, Lefebvre [2] showed that e-commerce was growing faster than expected, and that it was likely to have a dominant position in the future economy.

However, e-commerce and online shopping still cannot fully replace onsite shopping, especially for products like clothing, shoes, jewelry, and furniture. For such products, onsite shoppers frequently engage in some sort of interaction with their potential purchase, before buying it, to discover the product's scent, texture, appearance, fit, or sound. Unfortunately, such interaction is often impossible for online purchases. As a result, online shoppers, particularly those shopping for clothing and shoe products, are often unhappy with the products they receive and related customer service, because of the lack of interaction which onsite shopping could otherwise provide [3].

2D pictures or written descriptions used in traditional e-commerce systems often cannot provide enough product information. Is there any technology which could

J. Jacko (Ed.): Human-Computer Interaction, Part II, HCII 2007, LNCS 4551, pp. 643–652, 2007.

provide more sensory information to help online shoppers make better purchasing decisions?

2 Background

2.1 VR in E-Commerce

Virtual reality (VR) is a computer-simulated environment which allows users to manipulate 3D virtual models online. Recently, researchers have been using VR for e-commerce, to provide consumers with a new type of shopping experience [4-10]. Hughes, Brusilovsky, and Lewis [5] presented an adaptive navigation support system for using a virtual environment for online shopping. Sanna, Zunino, and Lamberti [10] presented a VR e-commerce system based on VRML. They used Quick 3D to generate 360-degree image-based immersive backgrounds and an animated virtual human to help online shoppers navigate through their e-commerce environment. Daugherty, Li, and Biocca [4] conducted five experiments to study the usability of VR in e-commerce. Their results showed that users acquired more information about product when using a VR-based e-commerce than when using other tools.

2.2 Moving from VR to AR

Although prior studies show that VR can enhance e-commerce by providing more product information, through enhanced human-computer interaction, current VR methods for e-commerce still only provide scaled virtual product models displayed on traditional computer screens. New methods are needed to provide consumers with more realistic product models, with respect to size, customer experience, and user interaction.

AR is a technology which can mix or overlap computer generated virtual objects with the real world scenes or objects. Unlike VR, which experientially replaces the physical world, AR enhances physical reality by integrating virtual objects into a physical scene. Generated virtual objects become, in a sense, an equal part of the natural environment.

In recent years, much research has focused on developing AR applications. However, there has been little research conducted regarding the use of AR in enhancing e-commerce. In 2001, Azuma, Baillot, and Behringer [11] reviewed new advances in AR, after 1997, including display devices and methods, indoor and outdoor tracking, model rendering, and interaction technologies. They identified several problems, at that time, that still needed to be addressed, such as occlusion, broader sensing, advanced rendering, and user perception issues.

Among a limited number of prior research studies, Zhang, Navab, and Liou [12] proposed and developed a prototype direct marketing system that used AR technology. Salespeople could use the system to show the main features of a product, by manually holding a plate with specially designed markers. With their marker-based system, they could mix a 3D virtual product with a real scene, video tape the resulting scene, and then send the video tape to interested customers by email. In their study, they designed the new marker system and tested and proved the real-time performance of their system. However their method of combining AR into e-commerce did not make full use of the advantages of AR. With their method, online shoppers had no direct interaction with either physical products or virtual product models. With only video recordings of AR scenes, customers still might not know whether products were suitable for them, in their real physical environments.

In this paper, a new AR e-commerce system is presented, which integrates a realistically-sized virtual product model into an online shopper's physical environment and provides the customer methods for "realistically" interacting with the virtual product. This paper presents both the design of the AR e-commerce assistant system and a usability study. Study results show that the AR e-commerce assistant system provides more direct information and experiences to online customers, by combining physical environment information with virtual products, which can help customers make better purchasing decisions. Several key issues related to using AR to enhance e-commerce are also discussed and analyzed.

3 Marker-Based Augmented Reality

Visual markers are widely used in existing AR applications. Marker-based AR systems commonly use live video as input. As a result, the performance of a marker-based AR system strongly depends on the tracking system used for marker detection and pose estimation. The tracking process is described as follows.

Step 1. Capture video: capture live video, with a camera, and send the result to a computer, frame by frame in real time.

Step 2. Detect marker: detect marker, with the image-processing algorithm, frame by frame in real time.

Step 3. Calculate transformation matrices: calculate the position of the camera, relative to the marker.

Step 4. Render virtual objects: render and integrate 3D virtual objects into the live video stream.

As shown in Fig. 1, the relationship between an actual marker point (X_m, Y_m, Z_m) and its corresponding point (x_c, y_c) on the image screen can be expressed by equation (1) [13].

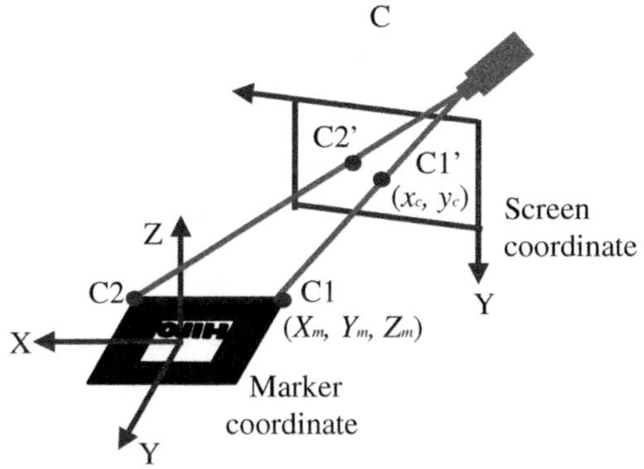

Fig. 1. Relationship between a real marker point and its corresponding screen image

$$h\begin{bmatrix} x_c \\ y_c \\ 1 \\ 1/h \end{bmatrix} = \mathbf{P}\begin{bmatrix} X_c \\ Y_c \\ Z_c \\ 1 \end{bmatrix} = \mathbf{P}\begin{bmatrix} V_{11} & V_{12} & V_{13} & W_x \\ V_{21} & V_{22} & V_{23} & W_y \\ V_{31} & V_{32} & V_{33} & W_z \\ 0 & 0 & 0 & 1 \end{bmatrix}\begin{bmatrix} X_m \\ Y_m \\ Z_m \\ 1 \end{bmatrix} \quad (1)$$

In equation (1), **P** is the camera intrinsic matrix, which can be obtained by camera calibration, (X_c, Y_c, Z_c) is the point in camera coordinates, and V and W are the rotation and translation transformation matrices between the real world coordinate system and the camera coordinate system. Since we use standard markers, the marker coordinate (X_m, Y_m, Z_m) is already known, and its image on the screen (x_c, y_c) is also known. Thus, the transformation matrices between the real world coordinate system and the camera coordinate system can be calculated using four detected marker corners. The transformation matrices can then be used to render and integrate virtual objects into the live video stream.

Although marker-based AR is quite powerful and relatively easy to implement, marker-based AR has some limitations related to using computer vision and image processing technologies [14]. For example, with marker-based AR, actual physical markers must be visible in the live video scene, for tracking purposes, which limits the size and location of markers, as well as the types and extent of human interaction which users can have with the virtual objects. If part of a marker is covered, the marker will not be detected. At the same time, the accuracy and stability of detecting markers and calculating transformation matrices also greatly depends on the size of the markers used, marker pattern complexity, and lighting conditions.

4 System Design

As mentioned earlier, traditional e-commerce systems often cannot provide enough direct information to or product interaction for consumers. However, sufficient direct information and product interaction are very important for helping consumers make inclusive decisions. VR technology alone cannot completely solve the problem. In this study, an AR e-commerce assistant system was designed to provide consumers with more realistic product experiences and interactions. With the developed AR e-commerce assistant, online consumers can bring a product into their homes and even try or visualize the product in their physical environments, while shopping.

Primary users of the system were expected to be common computer users, with minimal computer experience. As a result, the user interface of the system was made as simple and user-friendly as possible. In our study, we determined that consumer shopping typically includes three main tasks:

1. Searching for products.
2. Interacting with products.
3. Acquiring product information.

As a result, the user interface was designed to facilitate the three primary shopping tasks. The three tasks were combined into a two-level menu system within the AR assistant window. Several capabilities were also developed, to make product searching efficient, such as searching by keywords, sorting by properties, image viewing, listing operations, and price displays.

With the new tool, users can recursively search for and switch product models in an AR display, to compare products and thus gain enough direct information to make purchasing decisions. For tracking purposes, different types of products correspond to different markers. Online shoppers can also combine different types of products together when shopping. For example, a shopper can combine a table with different chairs or sofas to check the appearance of different combinations in their home.

4.1 Structure

Like traditional e-commerce systems, our AR e-commerce system uses the Internet as the primary user interaction platform. However, with our assistant system, a camera is needed to capture the consumer's physical environment and then integrate it with virtual objects. The current system uses a head-mounted display (HMD) to provide a greater sense of immersion, when compared to using a traditional computer monitor.

Our system was developed as an Active X plugin for an e-commerce web page, as shown in Fig. 2. Online users can search and view pictures and product related information, as they would on a traditional e-commerce website. However, online shoppers can also use the assistant plugin to bring virtual product models into their physical environment and then interact with the products to determine if the products are suitable.

The plugin was made using the MFC and OpenGL libraries. The plugin works between clients and an e-commerce assistant server through an Internet Explorer interface. ARToolkit is used for tracking, and Open VRML is used for rendering models. The complete structure of the system is shown in Fig. 3.

Fig. 2. E-commerce web page and the assistant system plugin

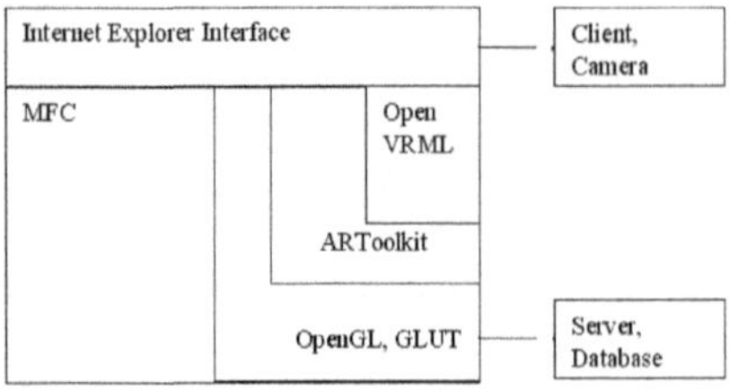

Fig. 3. The structure of our AR e-commerce assistant system

4.2 Hardware Devices

In general, there are two types of AR systems, video-based AR systems and optical see-through-based AR systems. In our current prototype system, we use video-based AR, because optical see-through devices are currently too expensive for common users. In our study, we made a simple video see-through device by combining a camera with a normal HMD. ARToolkit library is used for marker-based tracking in real scenes [13][14]. Large markers are used for large virtual objects, such as furniture. With large markers, online consumers can bring virtual furniture or other large virtual products into their homes and then consider the impact, appearance, and layout of their homes. Large markers are needed for large virtual objects, because virtual object size depends upon marker size; if we used small markers, virtual objects would have become very small and unrecognizable. Fig. 4 shows a virtual sofa in a consumer's physical home, as rendered using our AR e-commerce assistant system.

Fig. 4. A product model in a real scene

5 Usability Experiment

5.1 Experiment Design

A client user test was designed to test usability of the prototype AR assistant system. The test compared usability of the developed AR enhanced e-commerce assistant system with a traditional e-commerce system, which used 2D pictures, and a VR-enhanced e-commerce system. The traditional e-commerce system (Fig. 5 (a)) was designed to present a series of 2D product images from different perspectives, along with some product information, such as price, product features, a product description, and customer reviews. The VR-enhanced e-commerce system (Fig. 5 (b)) was designed to include a VR application with which users could conveniently manipulate (rotate, translate, and zoom) virtual 3D product models, using a mouse. The VR-enhanced e-commerce system (web page) contained the same product information as the traditional web page. The AR enhanced e-commerce web page (Fig. 5 (c)) contained a product picture, the previously described AR application, and the same product information as the traditional web page.

The main goal of the usability test was to determine which of the three designed e-commerce web pages best helped study participants decide if they would like to buy a sofa for an existing living room. Study participants were asked to make their decisions based upon information gained from the three web pages, without considering budget. They were also asked to give reasons for their decisions.

In the experiment, participants used the three different e-commerce systems, in random order, when shopping for new furniture. Operation times, malfunctions, and complaints were recorded for later analysis. The "consumers" were also asked to fill out a questionnaire, after they completed the comparison experiment in which they were asked to make buying decisions about the product and to provide reasons for their decisions. The main research questions of the designed usability experiment include:

- Did the user gain more information about the product, to help him/her make a better purchasing decision, when using the AR e-commerce system than when using the other two e-commerce systems?
- Did the user feel uncomfortable when using the AR e-commerce system?
- Did the user experience any social or cognitive problems that could prevent acceptance of the AR system for e-commerce?

(a)Traditional e-commerce (b) VR enhanced e-commerce (c) AR enhanced e-commerce

Fig. 5. Three e-commerce web pages designed for usability experiment

5.2 Pilot Test

The pilot usability test was conducted, in a living room setting, with 14 participants. The 14 participants were given an opportunity to gain information about a sofa from three designed furniture e-commerce web pages (see Fig. 5), while shopping from a living room setting. After participants used the three e-commerce web pages, they were asked to complete a questionnaire.

All 14 study participants agreed that the AR-enhanced e-commerce web page provided more product information than the other two web pages. In addition, 86% of the participants preferred the AR enhanced e-commerce web page, while 7% of the participants preferred the traditional web page. The other 7% of the participants preferred the VR-enhanced web page, because they felt the VR enhanced web page was easier to use than the AR enhanced web page. Comparison results for all participants are shown in Fig. 6. The overall higher rating of the AR enhanced e-commerce system, when compared to the other two systems, is statically significant ($\alpha = 0.05$), as shown in Fig. 6 (a). The AR enhanced e-commerce system also shows a statistically significant higher rating for ability to provide more product information to online shoppers, as shown in Fig. 6 (b). However, the current AR e-commerce system shows a lower rating for the ease of use, as shown in Fig. 6 (c).

93% of participants mentioned that the VR enhanced e-commerce system provided more "freedom" than the traditional e-commerce web page and that, as online shoppers, they could "freely check the product model from different perspectives and gain more information", or something equivalent. At the same time, all participants mentioned that the AR enhanced e-commerce system provided more information about "how the sofa looked in the room and how it fit in the room", or something equivalent. 79% of participants agreed that AR enhanced e-commerce is more socially acceptable, while others took a neutral position. However, 21% of the participants still mentioned that "They would not buy furniture using e-commerce", because they want to "sit on it" and "touch and feel it" before they buy it, especially when it is a new product rather than a used product.

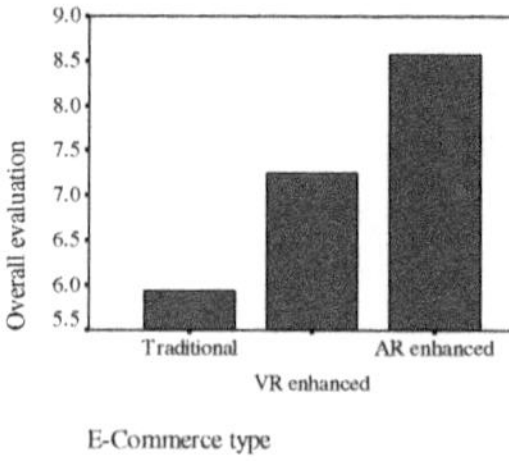

(a) Overall evaluation

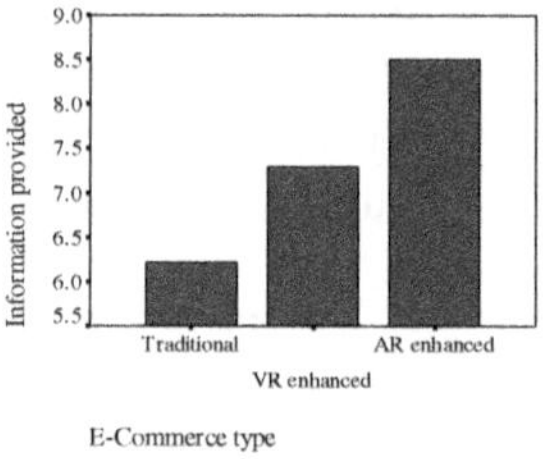

(b) Information provided

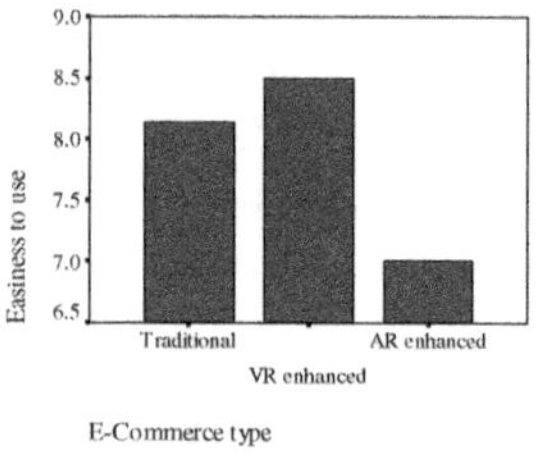

(c) Easy to use

Fig. 6. Comparisons between the three e-commerce web pages

Most participants thought that AR e-commerce is a good idea and has potential in the future. However, 79% participants felt that the current AR e-commerce system is not as easy to use as the traditional web page or the VR enhanced web page, including operations such working on the laptop computer and setting up and moving the markers. As a result, some participants suggested using prerecorded video for virtual product input, rather than laptop computer computations based upon camera images, and using smaller standard markers.

57% of participants also mentioned that AR e-commerce will not replace onsite shopping, because AR e-commerce still can not provide some experiences that onsite shopping can provide, such as touching and sitting. 36% of participants felt that the AR scene was not very real, and that the current AR rendering technology further improvement.

In addition, 21% of participants pointed out that the Internet access speed is another limitation of the current AR e-commerce system. Some participants mentioned that making high quality models might increase overall AR system acceptance. Some participants also suggested that it might be possible to increase e-commerce usability by combining VR e-commerce together with AR e-commerce, and even with onsite shopping.

6 Conclusion and Discussion

The development of e-commerce tools has reached a limitation that needs to be overcome, because it does not provide enough direct information for online shoppers, especially for products like furniture, clothing, shoes, and jewelry. In this paper, we studied the possibility of using AR to enhance e-commerce and provide more direct information to online shoppers.

Contributions of the study include the development of a working AR e-commerce assistant system, based upon user-centered design principles, and the realistic application of AR in e-commerce. In particular, key tasks, which were completed, include creating an AR e-commerce user interface, model normalization, real-time rendering, and merging models into real-world scenes. A usability experiment was also designed and conducted. Usability test results verified that the developed AR e-commerce assistant system could be used to provide more direct product information to online shoppers and, thereby, to help them make better purchasing decisions.

Although AR e-commerce provides more information and interaction than other e-commerce tools, from the study results, some limitations still exist in the proposed approach. The biggest limitation of using AR in e-commerce is that, according to study participants, it is currently not as easy to use as traditional or VR-based e-commerce systems. AR system rendering also needs to be improved to make merging virtual models and real scenes more seamless. Realistic product models can be very expensive to make. In addition, currently, the Internet is still not fast enough to transfer and render high-resolution product models in real time.

References

1. Standing, C.: Internet Commerce Development, Artech House, Hardcover, (February 2000)
2. Lefebvre, L.A., Lefebvre, E.: E-commerce and Virtual Enterprises: Issues and Challenges for Transition Economies. Technovation 22(5), 313–323 (2002)
3. Cho, Y., Im, I., Hiltz, R., Fjermestad, J.: An Analysis of Online Customer Complaints: Implications for Web Complaint Management. In: 35th Hawaii International Conference on System Sciences, Hawaii (2002)
4. Daugherty, T., Li, H., Biocca, F.: Experiential commerce: A summary of research investigating the impact of virtual experience on consumer learning, Society of Consumer Psychology. In: Online Advertising, Lawrence Erlbaum Associates, Mahwah, NJ (2005)
5. Hughes, S., Brusilovsky, P., Lewis, M.: Adaptive navigation support in 3D e-commerce activities, May 28, 2002 AH'2002, Malaga, Spain, pp. 132–139 (2002)
6. Santos, C.T., Osorio, F.S.: AdapTIVE: An Intelligent Virtual Environment and Its Application in E-Commerce, COMPSAC (2004). pp. 468–473 (2004)

7. De Troyer, O., Kleinermann, F., Mansouri, H., Pellens, B., Bille, W., Fomenko, V.: Developing semantic VR-shops for e-Commerce. In: Special Issue of VIRTUAL REALITY: Virtual Reality in the e-Society, London, Springer, Heidelberg (2006)
8. Fomenko, V.: Generating Virtual Reality Shops for E-commerce, Dissertation, Vrije Universiteit Brussel (2006)
9. Bogdanovych, A., Berger, H., Simoff, S., Sierra, C.: 3D Electronic Institutions: Social Interfaces for E-Commerce. In: 2nd European Workshop on Multi-Agent Systems, Barcelona, Spain (December 16-17 2004)
10. Sanna, A., Zunino, C., Lamberti, F.: HAVS: a human animated VRML-based virtual shop for e-commerce. In: SCI'02 Proc, vol. XII, pp. 24–29 (2002)
11. Azuma, R., Baillot, Y., Behringer, R., Feiner, S., Julier, S., MacIntyre, B.: Recent Advances in Augmented Reality, IEEE Comp. Graph. & App. 21(6), 34–47 (2001)
12. Zhang, X., Navab, N., Liou, S.P.: E-Commerce Direct Marketing using Augmented Reality, IEEE International Conference on Multimedia and Expo (I), pp. 88–91 (2000)
13. Kato, H., Billinghurst, M.: Marker tracking and. hmd calibration for a video-based augmented reality conferencing system. In: Proc. of IWAR, San Francisco, CA, USA, (October 1999)
14. ARToolkit document: http://www.hitl.washington.edu/artoolkit/documentation/

RealSound Interaction: A Novel Interaction Method with Mixed Reality Space by Localizing Sound Events in Real World

Mai Otsuki, Asako Kimura, Takanobu Nishiura, Fumihisa Shibata, and Hideyuki Tamura

Graduate School of Science and Engineering, Ritsumeikan University
1-1-1 Noji-Higashi, Kusatsu, 525-8577, Shiga, Japan

Abstract. We developed a mixed reality (MR) system which merges the real and the virtual worlds in both audio and visual senses. Our new approach "RealSound Interaction" is based on the idea that the sound events in the real world can work as interaction devices with an MR space. Firstly, we developed a sound detection system which localizes a sound source. The system consisted of two types of microphone arrays, fixed type and wearable type. Secondly, we evaluated the accuracy of the system, and proposed three practical usages of the sound events as interactive devices for MR attractions.

Keywords: Mixed Reality, Sound Input, Microphone Array, Sound Source Localization, and Interactive Device.

1 Introduction and Objectives

In this paper, we present a very unique and novel method for interacting with a mixed reality (MR) space that merges the real and the virtual worlds. Our approach "RealSound Interaction" is based on the idea that the sound events occur in the real world can work as input or interaction devices into/with an MR space.

Until now, the various devices like sensors, keyboard and mouse have mainly been used for input into virtual reality (VR) or MR space, and these devices needed to change their shape to keep proper mental model of users. It means that we had to prepare many differently shaped sensors with different functions.

On the other hand, it is not difficult to prepare some sound sources when we use a sound for the input. In addition, it would be simple and easy to customize sounds for each user. Our approaches to use the sound event as interaction device for MR systems were able to realize the intuitive interface. Though, the use of this function is not necessarily limited to MR, it could be expected to be used in a general system as new interaction device.

This paper describes the method of detecting sound events in the real world and its actual implementations as inputs to the virtual or mixed world.

J. Jacko (Ed.): Human-Computer Interaction, Part II, HCII 2007, LNCS 4551, pp. 653–662, 2007.

2 Related Work

There are some studies on sound inputs into the VR space with one microphone 1. An ON/OFF switching function could be easily implemented only by detecting input sounds. Mihara et al. 2 developed "the migratory cursor" system which operates a cursor by a certain nonverbal vocalization as well as voice commands. However, some of the testers felt unnatural to use the nonverbal vocalization as commands.

On the other hand, as a study example using microphone array, Nagai et al. proposed an accurate speech recognition method in noisy environments, which estimates sound source direction and enhances only sounds of this direction 3.

Our method can detect not only ON/OFF but also the direction and location of sound events occurred in the real world by using microphone arrays. Compared to the studies described above, we aim at a real world oriented and intuitive interactive device used in MR space.

3 Key Component and Its Function

3.1 Wearable Microphone Array

Fixed type of linear microphone arrays have been investigated in the field of acoustics. One of its drawbacks is that it can work well only in a limited range of the front direction because of the low angular resolution in the crosswise direction. In this research, we newly use a microphone array in a wearable fashion by attaching it onto a head mounted display. Since the user moves freely, the array can capture sound constantly in his/her front direction and near the sound source in an effective range of magnetic sensor. Consequently it can estimate angular resolution with higher accuracy. Fig 1 shows both fixed and wearable microphone arrays used in this research.

3.2 Direction Estimation of Sound Events

A sound source direction can be estimated by one microphone array. CSP (Cross-power Spectrum Phase analysis) method is used for sound source direction estimation algorithm 4. This method gives a direction of sound source in a horizontal plane. It is assumed that the environment using this system includes background noise, so that additional estimation errors are expected. Therefore, using Nishiura's method adding CSP coefficient of several microphone pairs 5, we implement the noise robust system.

3.3 Localizing Sound Events

Two or more microphone arrays can localize a sound source. In this research, the position and the orientation of the fixed type microphone array are measured beforehand. On the other hand, the position and the orientation of the wearable type microphone array are determined by a magnetic sensor. Besides, this system using two microphone arrays can estimate the location only on the horizontal plane. Estimable area and accuracy depend on the interval of microphones, the number of

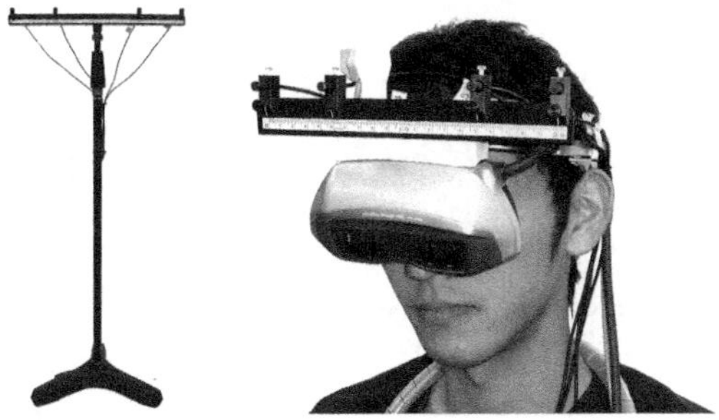

Fig. 1. Microphone arrays (Left: fixed type, Right: wearable type)

microphones, the sampling frequency, the positions of two microphone arrays, and the angle between two microphone array's lines.

4 System Overview

shows the system configuration detecting sound events in the real environment and reflecting it into the MR space. We use Canon MR Platform system for managing and displaying the MR space. Users watch the MR space through HMD (Canon VH-2002). Magnetic sensor 3SPACE FASTRAK (Polhemus) detects position and orientation of the HMD.

We use microphone arrays Fig. 3) for detecting sound events in the real environment. Signal from microphone array is amplified to a line level by Microphone Amplifier (PAVEC MA-2016C 16ch Microphone Amplifier). After going through AD converter (Thinknet DF-2X16-2) with a sampling frequency of 32kHz, the signal is input into PC for detecting the direction and location of sound events.

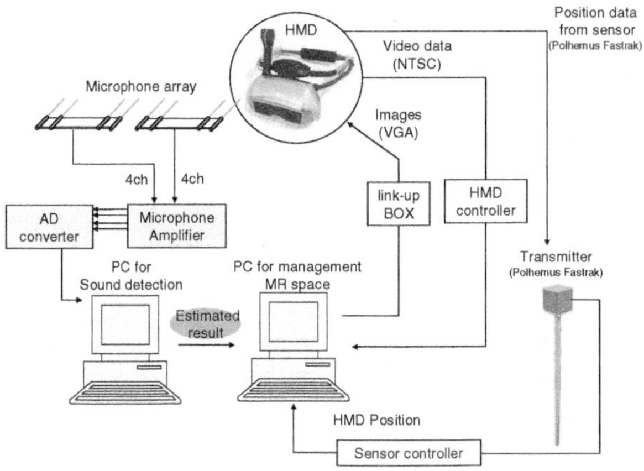

Fig. 2. System configuration

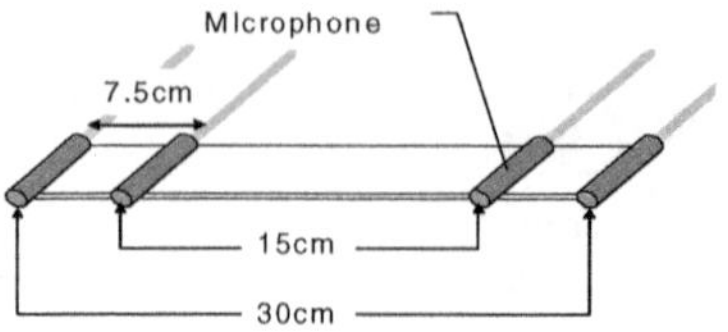

Fig. 3. Microphone array configuration

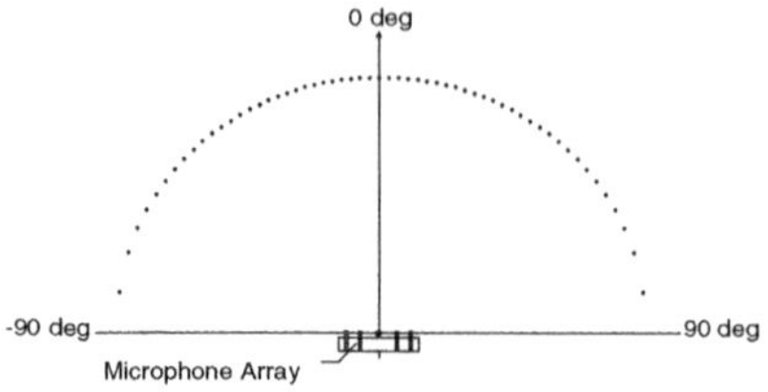

Fig. 4. Angle resolution of fixed type microphone array (sampling frequency: 32 kHz)

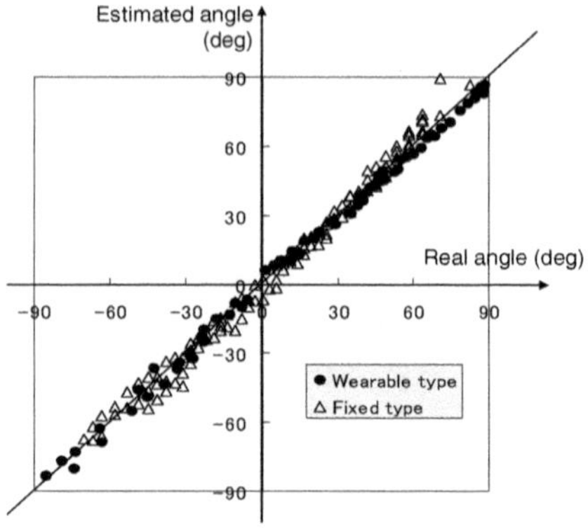

Fig. 5. Results of direction estimation for fixed type and wearable type microphone array

5 Evaluation

5.1 Accuracy of Direction Estimation

Fig. 4 shows the angle resolution of the fixed type microphone array on the horizontal plane. It can detect the direction in the range between -90 to 90 degrees with 58 points. The resolution becomes lower near the -90 and 90 degree (crosswise) directions. In contrast, since the wearable type microphone array can constantly track the sound source in front of the array, the accuracy becomes higher.

Fig. 5 shows the relation between the estimated angle (vertical axis) and the real angle (horizontal axis) of the fixed type and the wearable type microphone array. The 45 degree slope line in this graph indicates an ideal case that the estimated angle is the same as the real angle. The results of the wearable type are overlapped on the ideal line much better than the results of the fixed type. Especially, when looking at the results of estimation in the crosswise direction, the wearable type microphone array shows a better accuracy than the fixed type's.

5.2 Accuracy of Localization

We evaluated the localization accuracy depending upon the layout of two microphone arrays in the cases of 90, 120, 180 degrees of the angle between the two arrays.

Fig 6 shows the error map for the layout of 180degrees, 120 degrees and 90 degrees respectively. Each bubble size shows the error size. The dotted lines show the front regions of the microphone arrays. In this paper, the front region of a microphone array is defined as the range (from - 34.5 to +34.5 degrees) where the angle resolution of each microphone array is smaller than 2.5 degrees from Fig. 4. According to this figure, localization accuracy is higher in the intersection region of the microphone array's front regions, and the error becomes larger for the sound source being further away from the microphone array, even though it is in the intersection region.

Fig 7 shows the error average of localization for three cases of the layout of two fixed microphone layout. From this figure, the error average of the 120 degrees case is found to be smallest.

We also tried the case where one of the fixed type microphone arrays was replaced by a wearable type for the best array layout of 120 degree angle as is also shown in Fig 7. The result of the latter case is shown in Fig **8** where A is the wearable microphone array's position in the real environment, and B is the position detected by magnetic sensor on the HMD.

The tendency of the result from one fixed and one wearable type microphone array (Fig **8**) seems to be almost the same as the former result. However, in the case of using wearable microphone array, the location and direction error of the magnetic sensor causes the sound localization errors becoming larger. If the magnetic sensor on the HMD is far from the transmitter, its error becomes also larger. Consequently, in figure 7, the error average seems to become larger for a combination of wearable type and fixed type, than those using two fixed types.

However, there are some advantages for wearable type microphone array. Firstly, sound source would be always taken in front of the microphone array because the user

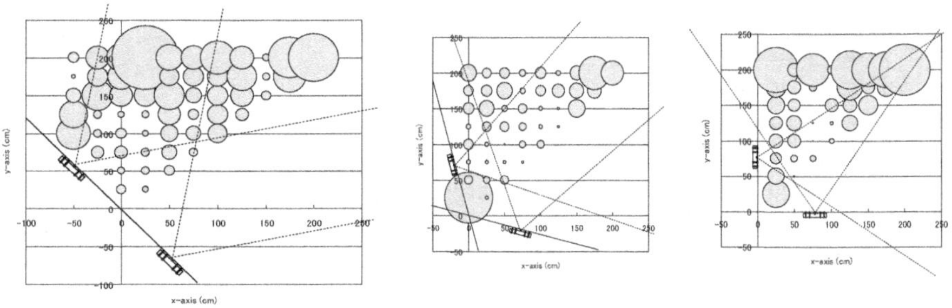

Fig. 6. Error maps (Left: 180deg, Center: 120deg, Right: 90deg)

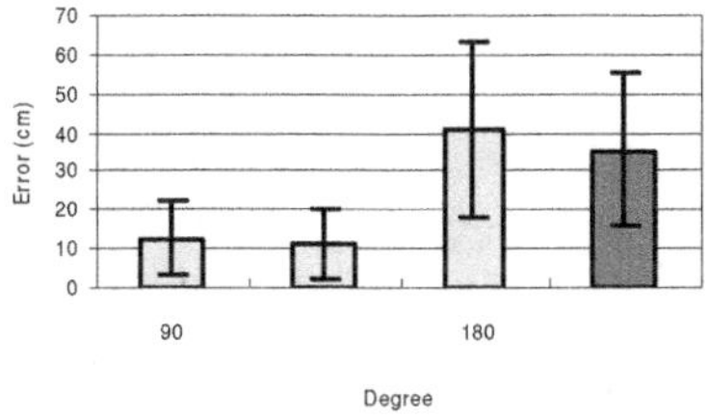

Fig. 7. Error averages of localization

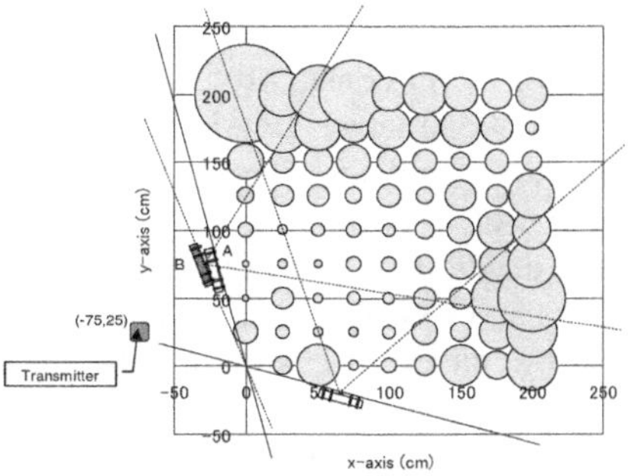

Fig. 8. Error map (Combination of fixed type and wearable type microphone array)

can turn to a sound source in the effective area of magnetic sensor. Secondly, the distance between the microphone array and the sound source would be shorter because user can get closer to the sound source.

6 Implementation of New Interaction Devices

6.1 Discrete Menu Selection Interface

As one example of the new interaction device using sound source direction, we tried to implement a menu selection interface using one wearable type microphone array. Some CG menu items aligned cylindrically are superimposed onto the real scene around the user. Upon recognizing the menu items, the user generated a sound signal in front of the item which he/she wants to select. In other words, the sound source direction detected by the wearable type microphone array is used as "pointing," and occurrence of the sound signal is used as "input".

The menu items are aligned with a radius of 60cm from the user within a semicircle of front 180 degrees (Fig 9). When the direction of sound source is recognized, the menu item which is located in the estimated direction is "Selected," (Fig 10) and the colour of the menu item is changed from green to pink (Fig 11).

In this system, a handclap is chosen as a sound source, since it is simple and intuitive for people. Other sound sources satisfying the following conditions could also be available, for example a buzzer and a castanet.

- Point sound source
- Easy to grasp
- Easy to generate a sound
- Able to make a sound only when users need

An assessment experiment with 10 subjects was made in order to evaluate the utility of this interface. In the experiment, almost all subjects directed their wearable type microphone array on the HMD toward the target menu item and generated a sound in front of the menu item. At the beginning of the experiment, some selecting error has occurred when the sound is small or pointed to the boundary area. Finally, all subjects could select menu items reliably with all devices (hands clap, a buzzer, and a castanet) in a few trials. Fig 12 shows the rate of successful input into each menu item by the castanet in the case of two, four, and six items. This result means that our system constantly estimated sound source direction in a high accuracy range of microphone array. In addition, the sound generated by themselves seemed natural as auditory feedback of input confirmation. Consequently, all these feedbacks seemed to help user's learning.

We developed, after all, a general-purpose interface like menu selection. If sound sources and CG objects are changed, a sound event can be used for a command input in various cases, and extendible for various applications.

6.2 Non-step Direction Selection Interface

In the previous section, we achieved the discrete menu selection interface. As the novel step, we developed the non-step (in other words, non-discrete) direction

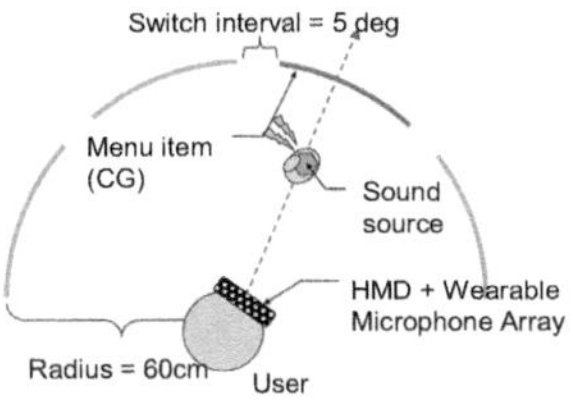

Fig. 9. Layout of menu items (in case of four menu items)

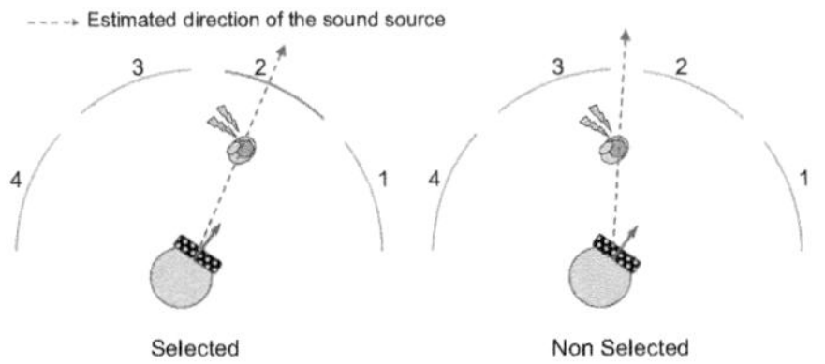

Fig. 10. Menu selection method

Fig. 11. A scene selecting a menu item using a sound device

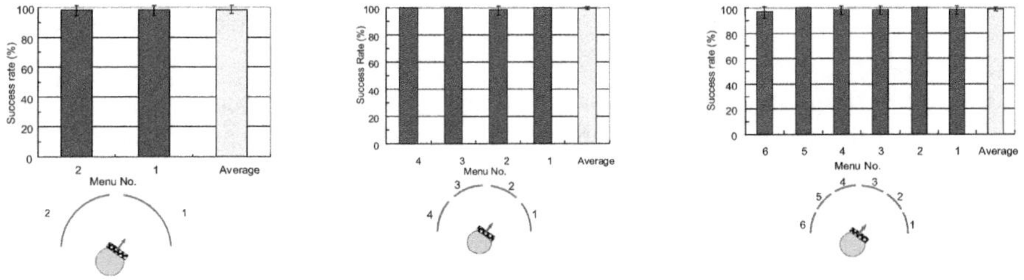

(a) Two items (b) Four items (c) Six items

Fig. 12. Success rate of menu item selection (by the castanet)

selection interface. Firstly, we implemented the system which estimates a sound source direction, and superimposes a CG object in the direction as shown in Fig 13. This interface seems to be enough to be used as interactive device

This function was implemented in the MR attraction named "Watch the Birdie!" which is demonstrated in VRSJ 11th conference in Sendai, Japan in September, 2006 as technical exhibit. In this attraction, users can watch many birds (CG) flying in the air (Fig 14). The birds fly from the direction indicated by a sound source "birdcall[1]" (Fig 15). The result means that a very intuitive sound device can be used as an interaction device in the MR space.

However, unlike in fundamental experiment in adjusted environment, estimation error would be expected to occur more often by user and audience voice, and ambient noise in the exhibition hall. Therefore, we gave a weight in high frequency range

[1] Birdcall is a device imitating the sound of a bird. It is used for bird watching.

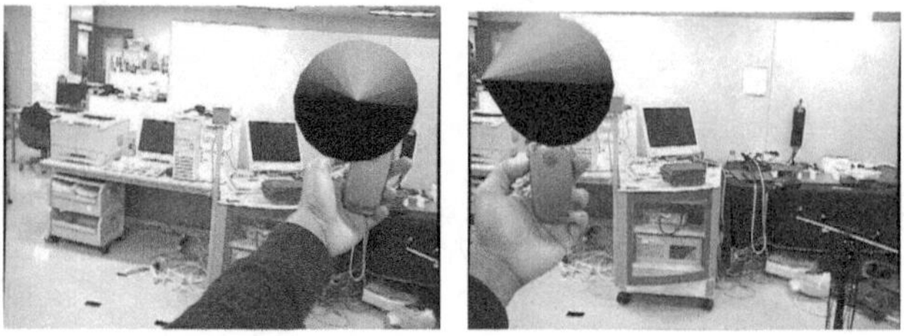

Fig. 13. Superimposing a cone-shaped CG object to the direction of sound source (A mobile phone speaker) at a distance of 50cm from the user

Fig. 14. User's view of "Watch the birdie!"

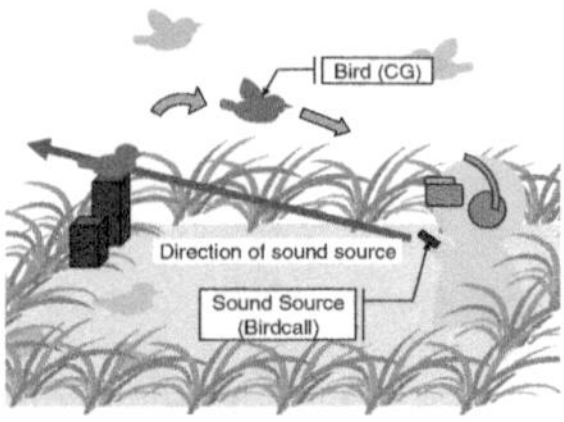

Fig. 15. In "Watch the Birdie!," user can select a CG bird using the sound device

because the frequency of the birdcall sound is higher than noise, and also discriminated the input sound from noise by "weighted CSP analysis" method which Denda et al. proposed 6. The visitors of this exhibition commented that this device was intuitive and easy to understand.

6.3 Localization of a Sound Event and Its Response

Localization of a sound event could be used to superimpose a CG object at the sound source position. Fig. 16 shows that an octahedral crystal (CG) is superimposed at "the location" of sound source (handclap) estimated by one fixed type and one wearable type microphone array in horizontal plane at a height of user's eyes (note that in Fig 13, the CG object was superimposed just onto "the direction" looked from the user).

This function was also applied to "Watch the Birdie!" This system determines the location of a mother duck which is a real toy with a speaker squawking, and then many ducklings (CG) move toward their mother (Fig. 17). In addition, a user can call

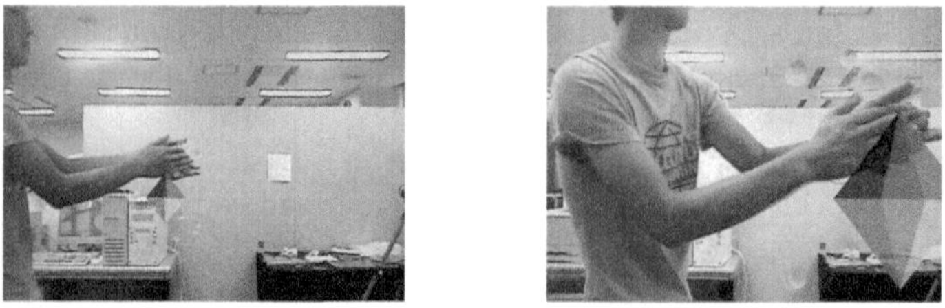

Fig. 16. Superimposed CG object in the location of a sound source (handclap)

Fig. 17. Ducklings (CG) gather toward mother duck (real toy object with speaker) by using sound source localization in "Watch the Birdie!

the ducklings around him/her using the birdcall. This is the designation of gathering spot by localization of sound source, so that it is different from indicating direction by a sound source described in the preceding section.

By tracking the estimated location of a sound generated continuously, it is possible to guide a CG object. It could also be used as a novel representation method such as a paint tool which draws a trajectory of a sound in the air.

7 Conclusion

We have developed novel interfaces to reflect sound events in the real environment into the MR space, and these are unique and useful interactive interface.

In these interfaces, we implemented not a single microphone customarily utilized in the field of VR, but the microphone arrays which are remarkable in the field of acoustics. Accordingly, we can use them not only for ON/OFF of sound events but also for direction and location of sound events as inputs into the MR space. We have also proposed a new usage of microphone arrays by implementing both traditional fixed type and a new wearable type microphone array attached onto a HMD.

The intuitive interface that was not provided by other methods became available by implementing our proposed approaches to the MR system. This function does not necessarily be used only in MR, but is expected to be widely used in a general system.

Acknowledgements. This research is supported by the Japan Society for the Promotion of Science through Grants-in-aid for Scientific Research (A), "A Mixed Reality system that merges real and virtual worlds with three senses."

References

1. Irawati, S., Calderon, D., Ko, H.: Spatial ontology for semantic integration in 3D multimodal interaction framework. In: Proc. of VRCIA 2006, pp. 129–135 (2006)
2. Mihara, Y., Shibayama, E., Takahashi, S.: The Migratory Cursor: Accurate Speech Based Cursor Movement by moving Multiple Ghost Cursors using Non-Verbal Vocalization. In: Proc. of ASSETS 2005, pp. 76–83 (2005)
3. Nagai, T., Kondo, K., Kaneko, M., Kurematsu, A.: Estimation of Source Location Based on 2-D MUSIC and Its Application to Speech Recognition in Cars. In: IEEE Proc of ICASSP 2001, vol. 5, pp. 3041–3044 (2001)

4. Omologo, M., Svaizer, P.: Acoustic Event Location Using a Crosspower -Spectrum Phase Based Technique. In: IEEE Proc. of ICASSP 94, Adelaide vol. 2, pp. 273–276 (1994)
5. Nishiura, T., Yamada, T., Nakamura, S., Shikano, K.: Localization of multiple sound sources based on a CSP analysis with a microphone array. In: IEEE Proc. of ICASSP 2000, vol. 2, pp. 1053–1056 (2000)
6. Denda, Y., Nishiura, T., Yamasita, Y.: A Study of Weighted CSP Analysis with Average Speech Spectrum for Noise Robust Talker Localization. In: Proc. of 9th EUROSPEECH 2005, Lisbon pp. 2321–2324 (2005)

A New Model of Collaborative 3D Interaction in Shared Virtual Environment

Nassima Ouramdane-Djerrah, Samir Otmane, and Malik Mallem

Laboratoire IBISC – Université d'Evry 40, rue du Pelvoux - 91000 Evry – France
{ouramdane,otmane,mallem}@ibisc.univ-evry.fr

Abstract. Recent advances in both Virtual Reality (VR) systems and Computer-Supported Cooperative Work (CSCW) technologies have resulted in the appearance of the Collaborative Virtual Environments (CVEs) systems supporting different forms of collaboration and interaction between users. The collaboration in these systems refers to the simultaneous interaction (collaborative interaction) of multiple users on a virtual object in an immersive or semi-immersive Virtual Environment (VE). However, in some cases, the collaborative interaction is reduced to a simple communication between users. In this paper, we propose a new model of collaborative interaction that supports group interaction in CVEs. Our model defines the functional role and the functional clover of the 3D interaction. This Model is based on group awareness concepts (focus, nimbus and degree of interaction) combined with 3D interaction paradigms (navigation, selection and manipulation). The aim of our model is to manage and control the simultaneous user actions.

Keywords: 3D interaction, collaborative interaction, collaborative virtual environment, virtual reality.

1 Introduction

The Collaborative Virtual Environments (CVEs) technology is the result of the convergence of research interests within Virtual Reality (VR) and Computer-Supported Cooperative Work (CSCW) communities [2].

Currently, collaborative interaction is one of the main issues related to the majority of applications in the field of CVEs. There are various existing CVE systems, which attempt to create virtual worlds where, in one hand the users interact naturally and easily between them and, in another hand, the systems may be able to solve the problem of simultaneous interaction on the virtual objects [1], [7], [8], [9], [12]. In general, these systems concern particular application domains and they are not able to combine simultaneous user actions. We think that it may be possible to define a generic formal model for the collaborative interaction for a variety of applications.

In this paper, we propose a formal model of collaborative interaction in the CVE. Our model provides generic technique for managing interaction, in one hand, between different users and in another hand, between users and virtual objects.

Our model defines the functional role and the functional clover of the 3D interaction. This model is based on group awareness concepts (focus, nimbus and

J. Jacko (Ed.): Human-Computer Interaction, Part II, HCII 2007, LNCS 4551, pp. 663–672, 2007.

degree of interaction) combined with 3D interaction paradigms (navigation, selection and manipulation).

This paper is organized as follows: in section 2, we will present a short related work in this area. In section 3, we will present the collaborative 3D interaction model. In section 4, we will finish with a conclusion.

2 Related Work

Currently, the main issue of the majority of applications in the area of CVEs is to obtain a user simultaneous interaction (Collaborative interaction) on the virtual objects [13]. There are various existing CVE systems, which are devoted to the development of the support tools and the minimisation of the network traffic [2], [6]. As an example of these CVEs systems, we may refer to the DIVE system [5], the MASSIVE system [11], [10] and the NPSNET system [4].

DIVE (Distributed Interactive Virtual Environment) is among the first CVE systems developed at the beginning of 1990. This system is a software platform for multi-users Virtual Environments that has served as a framework for many distributed VE applications [12]. The MASSIVE system, also called inhabited television, has been used to support an extended series of experimental trials of teleconferencing over wide area networks [10]. The NPSNET system, also called simulating battles, is a 3D networked virtual environment system developed to support large-scale military training and simulation exercises.

Although some CVE systems exist nowadays, in most of them, dynamic collaborative interaction is not possible. There are few models and formalisms that can control the group interaction in the CVEs. The Spatial Model of Interaction [1] is one of the first models developed for supporting group interaction in large-scale VEs. This model uses the properties of space as the basic for mediating interaction. It is defined by some key words: Medium, Aura, Awareness, Focus, Nimbus and Adapters. The Spatial Model of Interaction has been applied in the DIVE system. Ding and Zhu proposed a model of Dynamic Interest Management [7] which is dedicated to manage the awareness in multi-user shared environment. This work is devoted to simulate the dynamic interaction of the users in spatial populated environments. It describes the semantic of the behaviours of the users and the changes of the interest focus of users. Another example of model is the conceptual model of CVE [9]. This work presents a framework for the design and evaluation of distributed and collaborative 3D interaction systems.

3 The Collaborative 3D Interaction Model

Collaboration in VE consists to realize a collective work by several users that compose the shared virtual space. CVE is a Virtual Environment in which several users interact, in one hand between them and in another hand with the virtual objects which can be selected and/or manipulated.

In our case, the CVE can be represented by a set of virtual objects and a set of users that can manipulate these objects. It is represented as follows:

$$CVE = < U, O >$$

With

$$U = \{u_1, u_2, u_3, \dots u_n\} = \{u_i / i = 1..n\}$$
$$O = \{o_1, o_2, o_3, \dots o_m\} = \{o_j / j = 1..m\}$$

A user u_i is represented by the couple $\left(IDu_i, Ru_i^{Head/Hand}\right)$, such as IDu_i is the identifier of the user u_i and $Ru_i^{Head/Hand}$ is the referential of the head or the hand of the user u_i.

An object o_j can be also represented by the couple (IDo_j, Ro_j), such as IDo_j is the identifier of the object o_j and Ro_j is his referential.

3.1 The Functional Decomposition of the 3D Interaction

We define the functional role of 3D interaction as the function that a user is performing at a given time in the VE. There are four basic 3D interaction tasks [3]: the Navigation task, the Selection task, the manipulation task and the System Control task. Therefore, the user may have as function in the virtual environment, the Navigation, the Selection and/or the Manipulation. The System Control task is a task system which is present at each stage of the 3D interaction. In this paper, we propose a functional representation of the 3D interaction by using the functional clover of the 3D interaction which is composed of tree functional spaces: the navigation space, the selection space and the manipulation space (see Figure 1).

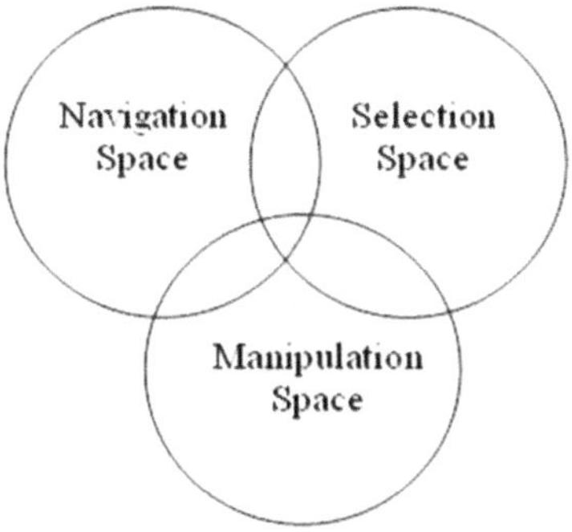

Fig. 1. The Functional clover of the 3D interaction

The Navigation space. This space corresponds to the functionalities allowing the user to change his position and/or orientation (navigation) in the virtual environment. These functionalities also allow taking into account the navigation of other users in the VE (awareness of navigation). In our case, we consider the Navigation Space (*Navigation_Space*) as the set of users who navigate to approach a given object in the

VE. Then, this space can contain the set of the couples (IDu_i, IDo_j), such as the user u_i navigates in the direction of the object o_j in virtual space:

$$Navigation\_Space = \{(IDu_i, IDo_j) / u_i \in U, o_j \in O\}$$

The Selection space. The selection space corresponds to the functionalities dedicated to the specification (selection) of an object or a set of objects in the VE. These functionalities allow also for each user to have a global view on the selections that are done by other users in the virtual world *(awareness of selection)*.
In the case of our study, the Selection Space (*Selection_Space*) can be represented by the set of the couples (IDu_i, IDo_j), such as the user u_i selects the object o_j :

$$Selection\_Space = \{(IDu_i, IDo_j) / u_i \in U, o_j \in O\}$$

The Manipulation space. This space corresponds to the functionalities allowing the changes of the properties of an object (manipulation) or a set of objects (in general position and/or orientation) by the users in the virtual world. These functionalities consider also the manipulations of other users in the VE *(awareness of manipulation)*.
In our case, the Manipulation Space (*Manipulation_Space*) will be composed from the set of triplets $(IDu_i, IDo_j, Action_k)$, such as the user u_i performs the action $Action_k$ on the object o_j :

$$Manipulation\_Space = \left\{ \begin{matrix} (IDu_i, IDo_j, Action_k) \\ / u_i \in U, o_j \in O, Action_k : elementary\ action \end{matrix} \right\}$$

3.2 The Conceptual Model of the Collaborative 3D Interaction

The CVEs are virtual spaces lived by objects that may be persons, informations and/or virtual objects. In these world, the users interact between them and act on the virtual objects in order to realize a common goal.

Most problems in the field of CVEs are related to the 3D interaction. To remedy to these problems, we use in our model some concepts of Benford's Spatial Model of Interaction [1]. In the following, we present the concepts which are necessary to understand our conceptual model.

The Awareness of Interaction. The Awareness of Interaction "AI" measures the degree, the nature or the quality of an interaction between two objects [1]. The measure of the AI between two objects is not mutually symmetrical (the Awareness of the object A compared to the object B is not equals to the Awareness of the object B compared to the object A). The AI between objects for a given support is measured by the Focus and the Nimbus of interaction.

The Focus of Interaction. The focus of interaction corresponds to a set of virtual objects with which a user may interact; these objects form a zone of the virtual space in which the presence of the user can be perceived by the objects.

The focus of interaction are geometrical forms which are carried by the users when they navigate in the VE. When two focus (or more) overlap (collision of focus), even partially, the interaction between the users, which correspond to these focus, becomes possible. The focus can have various sizes and forms.

In our work, we consider the focus as an infinite cylinder emanating from the head or the hand of the user and that is in the same direction of the look of this user. The figure 2 shows an example of focus associated to the head of the user.

The focus of interaction can be seen as a tool to direct the attention. It filters the information according to the borders delimited by the focus geometrical form (in our case the volume of the cylinder *C*).

The focus defines for each user u_i the set of objects which belong to the cylinder C_i emanating from the head or the hand of the user. It is represented by the following function:

$$Focus : U \rightarrow O$$
$$Focus(u_i) = \{o_j / o_j \in O \ \ and \ \ o_j \in C_i\}$$

The Nimbus of Interaction. The nimbus of interaction corresponds to a subset of the set of the users in which users see themselves mutually. In this set, the user renders some of his aspects available to other users. These aspects can be his presence, his identity, his activity or a combination of these last.

The nimbus function returns for each object the set of users that work in common to realize a specific mission. It is defined as follows:

$$Numbus : O \rightarrow U$$
$$Numbus(o_j) = \{u_i / o_j \in Focus(u_i)\}$$

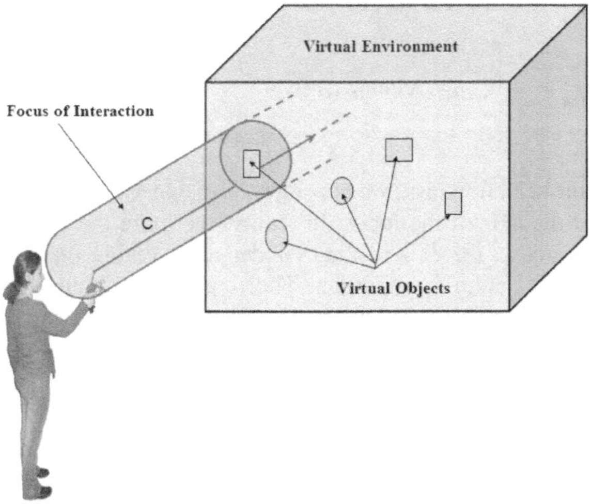

Fig. 2. Example of focus associated to the head of the user

When the intersection of the focus of several users is equal to only one object, this one is potentially a shareable object between these users.

The Degrees of Interaction. The function degree of interaction of a user u_i on an object o_j ($DI_{ui/oj}$) is defined by the both functions focus and nimbus. This function takes into account the users interested by the same object (see function 1):

$$DI_{ui/oj} : U \times O \rightarrow [0,1]$$

$$DI_{ui/oj} = \begin{cases} \frac{1}{Card(Nimbus(o_j))} \times k_i & if \quad o_j \in Focus(u_i) \\ 0 & otherwise \end{cases} \tag{1}$$

The function $Card(Nimbus(o_j))$ returns the number of users who are able to share the object o_j. k_i is a real coefficient which depends on the states of user's interaction (navigation, selection or manipulation state).

In the following, we will present how this coefficient is calculated compared to the three functional spaces: the navigation space, the selection space and the manipulation space.

The degree of interaction compared to the navigation space of a user u_i on the object o_j ($DI^N_{ui/oj}$) can be defined as the probability that a user u_i navigates to the object o_j. This probability is the same for all users that are located in the nimbus of the object o_j. We obtain in that case the following equation with the coefficient k_i fixed at 1.

$$DI^N_{ui/oj} : U \times O \rightarrow [0,1]$$

$$DI^N_{ui/oj} = \begin{cases} \frac{1}{Card(Nimbus(o_j))_i} & if \quad o_j \in Focus(u_i) \\ 0 & otherwise \end{cases} \tag{2}$$

In the case of the selection task, we consider the distances between the center of gravity of the objects and the axis of the focus. In reality, the more the object is near of the axis of the focus (in our case, the axis of the cylinder representing the field of the focus) the more the degree of selection is important. The figure 3 illustrates the distances between the center of gravity of an object and each axis of the focus of three users.

The degree of interaction compared to the selection space of a user u_i on the virtual object o_j ($DI^S_{ui/oj}$) can be defined as follows:

$$DI^S_{ui/oj} : U \times O \rightarrow [0,1]$$

$$DI^S_{ui/oj} = \begin{cases} \frac{1}{Card(Nimbus(o_j))_i} \times \frac{r - d_{oj/\Delta i}}{r} & if \quad o_j \in Focus(u_i) \\ 0 & otherwise \end{cases} \tag{3}$$

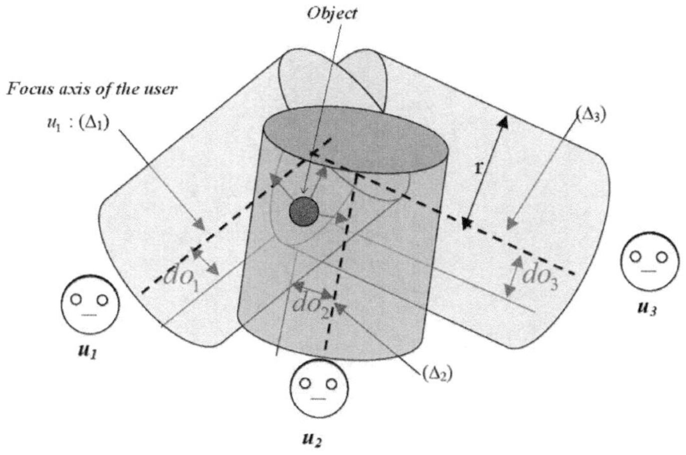

Fig. 3. Example of the distances between the gravity center of a virtual object and the axis of the focus of the users

With r is the ray of the cylinder C representing the field of the focus. $d_{oj/\Delta i}$ represents the distance between the gravity center of the object o_j and the focus axis Δ_i of the user u_i.

The degree of 3D interaction compared to the manipulation space of a user u_i on the object o_j ($DI^M_{ui/oj}$) can be defined using the relationship given by the distance of the user u_i to the center of the gravity of the object o_j. In this case we consider that more the user is near to the object, more the degree of manipulation is important. Figure 4 illustrates the distances between the center of gravity of an object and 3 users represented by virtual avatars.

The degree of interaction compared to the manipulation space of a user u_i on the virtual object o_j $\left(DI^M_{u_i/o_j}\right)$ is calculated as follows:

$$DI^M_{ui/oj} : U \times O \rightarrow [0,1]$$

$$DI^M_{ui/oj} = \begin{cases} \dfrac{1}{Card(Nimbus(o_j))_i} \times \dfrac{d_{oj/ui}}{\sum_{i=1}^{n} d_{oj/ui}} & if \ o_j \in Focus(u_i) \\ 0 & otherwise \end{cases} \quad (4)$$

With d_{o_j/u_i} is the distance between the gravity center of the object o_j and the avatar of the user u_i.

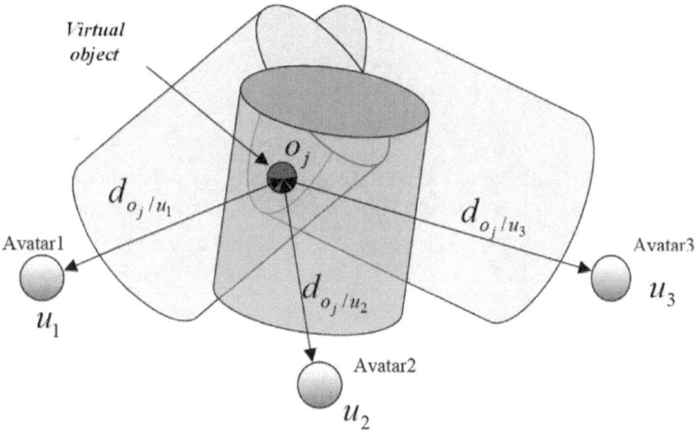

Fig. 4. Example of the distances between the gravity center of a virtual object and the users

We define the degree of interaction matrix compared to the different interaction tasks (navigation task, selection task and manipulation task) as analysis tools of interaction between, on the one hand the different users, and on the other hand the users and the virtual objects. The different degree of interaction matrix associated to the different 3D interaction tasks (navigation, selection and manipulation) are represented respectively by I^N, I^S and I^M, such as:

$$I^N = \begin{array}{c} \\ u_1 \\ u_2 \\ u_3 \\ . \\ . \\ u_n \end{array} \begin{array}{c} \begin{array}{cccccc} o_1 & o_2 & o_3 & . & . & o_m \end{array} \\ \begin{pmatrix} n_{11} & n_{12} & n_{13} & . & . & n_{1m} \\ n_{21} & n_{22} & n_{23} & . & . & n_{2m} \\ n_{31} & n_{32} & n_{33} & . & . & n_{3m} \\ . & . & . & . & . & . \\ . & . & . & . & . & . \\ n_{n1} & n_{n2} & n_{n3} & . & . & n_{nm} \end{pmatrix} \end{array} \quad I^S = \begin{array}{c} \\ u_1 \\ u_2 \\ u_3 \\ . \\ . \\ u_n \end{array} \begin{array}{c} \begin{array}{cccccc} o_1 & o_2 & o_3 & . & . & o_m \end{array} \\ \begin{pmatrix} s_{11} & s_{12} & s_{13} & . & . & s_{1m} \\ s_{21} & s_{22} & s_{23} & . & . & s_{2m} \\ s_{31} & s_{32} & s_{33} & . & . & s_{3m} \\ . & . & . & . & . & . \\ . & . & . & . & . & . \\ s_{n1} & s_{n2} & s_{n3} & . & . & s_{nm} \end{pmatrix} \end{array}$$

$$I^M = \begin{array}{c} \\ u_1 \\ u_2 \\ u_3 \\ . \\ . \\ u_n \end{array} \begin{array}{c} \begin{array}{cccccc} o_1 & o_2 & o_3 & . & . & o_m \end{array} \\ \begin{pmatrix} m_{11} & m_{12} & m_{13} & . & . & m_{1m} \\ m_{21} & m_{22} & m_{23} & . & . & m_{2m} \\ m_{31} & m_{32} & m_{33} & . & . & m_{3m} \\ . & . & . & . & . & . \\ . & . & . & . & . & . \\ m_{n1} & m_{n2} & m_{n3} & . & . & m_{nm} \end{pmatrix} \end{array}$$

With $n_{ij} = DI^N_{ui/oj}$, $\sum_{i=1}^{n}(n_{ij}) = 1$, $s_{ij} = DI^S_{ui/oj}$ and $m_{ij} = DI^M_{ui/oj}$.

These degrees of 3D interaction matrix are dynamic; they change in function of the number of users and objects in the virtual environment.

The created matrices contain information about degrees of interaction of the different users compared to the different 3D interaction tasks. This information is needed to provide an adaptive workflow for coordination of collaborative 3D interactions in order to assist and help users in their collaborative tasks.

4 Conclusion

In spite of the technological advances in both Virtual Reality and Human-Computer-Interface fields, there are little chance to find models and formalisms for the collaborative interaction, even if this last represent the main base for all CVEs applications. In this paper, we have discussed the problem of the 3D interaction through two stages of modeling by taking account the group interaction. First, we have proposed a functional decomposition of the 3D interaction on three functional spaces: the navigation space, the selection space and the manipulation space. Each space corresponds to a set of functionalities which allowed achieving the required task. We have also proposed a conceptual model for the 3D interaction. This model takes into account some concepts such as focus, nimbus and degree of interaction. The aim of our formalism is to control the flow of information exchanged in the virtual space so that the system can inform each user about the presence of other users and to coordinate their interactions. Our model must allow an easier and more effective group interaction.

In the future work, we will design an adaptive workflow for coordination of collaborative 3D interactions based on the proposed model followed by implementations. Experimentations and evaluations are envisaged in multi-users with single virtual reality platform and also in multi-users with multiple remote virtual reality platforms.

References

1. Benford, S., Fahlen, L.: A spatial model of interaction in large virtual environments. In: Third European Conference on CSCW (ECSCW93), pp. 80–88 (1993)
2. Benford, S., Greenhalgh, C., Rodden, T., Pycock, J.: Collaborative virtual environments. COMMUNICATIONS OF THE ACM 44(7), 99–108 (2001)
3. Bowman, D., Kruijff, E., Laviola, J., Poupyrev, I.: 3D user interfaces: Theory and Practice. Wesley, addison-wesley edn. (2005)
4. Capps, M., McGregor, D., Brutzman, D., Zyda, M.: Npsnet-v: A new beginning for dynamically extensible virtual environments. IEEE Computer Graphics and Applications 20(5), 12–15 (2000)
5. Carlsson, C., Hagsand, O.: Dive - a multi-user virtual reality system. IEEE Virtual Reality Annual International Symposium (VRAIS), pp. 394–400 (1993)
6. Damer, M.: Demonstration and guided tours of virtual worlds on the internet. In: CHI'97 Supplementary Proceedings, pp. 83–91 (1997)
7. Dawei, D., Miaoliang, Z.: A model of dynamic interest management: Interaction analysis in collaborative virtual environment. In: ACM VRST'03, pp. 1–6 (2003)

8. Dumas, C., Degrande, S., Chaillou, C., Saugis, G., Plnacoste, P., Viaud, M.: Spin: A 3-d interface for cooperative work. Virtual Reality Journal 17(4), 15–25 (1999)
9. Goebbels, G., Lalioti, V., Gobel, M.: Design and evaluation of team work in distributed collaborative virtual environments. In: ACM VRST'03, pp. 83–91 (2003)
10. Greenhalgh, C.: Large scale collaborative virtual environments. In: van Rijsbergen, (ed.) Distinguished Dissertation series, Springer, Heidelberg (1999)
11. Greenhalgh, C., Benford, S., Taylor, I., Bowers, J., Walk, G., Wyver, J.: reating a live broadcast from a virtual environment. In: SIGGRAPH'99 (1999)
12. Rodden, T.: Populating the application: A model of awareness for cooperative applications. In: Computer Supported Cooperative Work '96, pp. 83–91 (1996)
13. Tisseau, J., Ndlec, A.: Realite virtuelle: un contexte historique interdisciplinaire. Revue internationale de CFAO et d'infographie. 17(3), 263–278 (2003)

Multi-finger Haptic Interface for Collaborative Tasks in Virtual Environments

Maria Oyarzabal, Manuel Ferre, Salvador Cobos, Mary Monroy, Jordi Barrio, and Javier Ortego

Universidad Politécnica de Madrid. Dpto. Automática, Ing. Electrónica e Inf. Industrial, C/. José Gutierrez Abascal, 2. 28006 Madrid (Spain)
{moyarzabal,mferre,cobosalvador,mmonroy,jbarrio, jortego}@etsii.upm.es

Abstract. Haptic devices allow a high level of immersion in virtual environments by providing the sense of touch. We present a two-finger device that allows the performance of power and precision tasks in virtual environments. We have also developed a mathematical model of the human hand and a statistical procedure to identify different hand gestures. Both have been implemented in the virtual environment in order to have a mathematical model of haptic interactions, which runs in real time so as to provide contact forces and object movements depending on the manipulation commands received from the haptic device.

Keywords: haptic interface, multi-finger, collaborative task, manipulation.

1 Introduction

Haptic interaction is a term increasingly gaining interest within the HCI community. There has been a remarkable progress in the fields of visual and auditory devices for recreating virtual environments. Nevertheless, it requires further research in order to achieve a higher level of immersion. Haptic interfaces are devices that provide users with force information while they are interacting with virtual objects, allowing them to perform manipulation tasks and cooperate among users.

Human hand dexterity is based on using several fingers during object manipulation. Multi-finger haptic interfaces take advantage of such properties, thereby processing a large number of degrees of freedom to improve interaction with virtual environments.

There are two types of grasp: power grasp and precision grasp. Power grasp usually involves all fingers, therefore obtaining high power and low precision. On the other hand, precision grasp involves only two or three fingers that usually perform delicate tasks with low power [1]. We chose a multi-finger interface because it allows such types of hand configurations. Our objective is to perform cooperative tasks, where it is important that people interact directly with their fingers instead of using a tool.

Current multi-finger interfaces are mostly glove [2] and exoesqueleton structures [3] in which users withstand the weight of the device and actuators, and have limited degrees of freedom. This paper presents an alternative two-finger haptic interface, the

J. Jacko (Ed.): Human-Computer Interaction, Part II, HCII 2007, LNCS 4551, pp. 673–680, 2007.

Masterfinger, which attempts to improve haptic perception and cooperative object manipulation in virtual environments. In the following sections, we describe the device and the thimble, and we present a mathematical model of the human hand applied to identify hand gestures.

2 Haptic Device

The two-finger device is composed of a serial-parallel structure with six degrees of freedom (DOF) for each finger (fig. 1). The first one represents the movement of the wrist and the other five characterize the movement of the finger. Users insert each finger in a thimble and are free to move them in a natural way.

All DOF are measured in order to determine the user's finger configuration and the first three DOF are actuated by DC motors to provide the user with force information during interaction in the virtual environment.

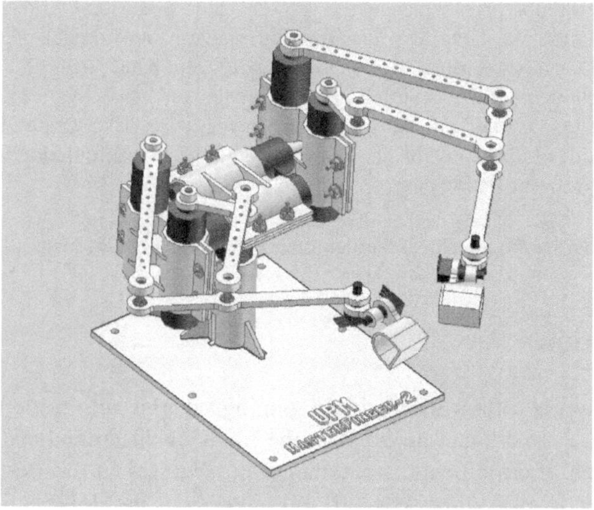

Fig. 1. Prototype of the Haptic Device

In this section we present the mechanical structure and a device to control the ensemble. The thimble is discussed in section 3.

2.1 Mechanical Structure

The structure of the parallel part is shown in figure 2. Point P is the place where the 3 DOF joint is located. Motors are placed in points A and B. They move point P in a plane through the movement of bars 1, 2, 3 and 4. Coordinates of point P are:

$$\begin{cases} x = l_1 \cos(\varphi) + l \cos(\varphi + \psi) \\ y = l_1 \sin(\varphi) + l \sin(\varphi + \psi) \end{cases} . \quad (1)$$

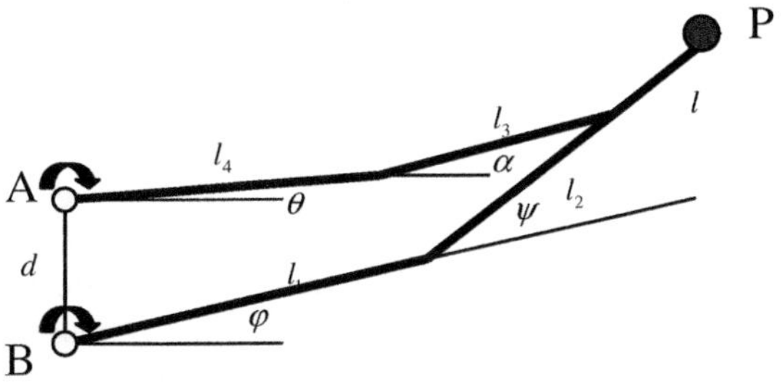

Fig. 2. Parallel structure for the first DOF of one finger

The angles labelled as φ and θ are measured by the motor encoders. The parallel structure has 2 DOF and, from the four parameters used to define the position of links (φ, θ, α and Ψ), only two of them are independent, since there are 2 constraints, which are described by equations (2) and (3).

$$l_1 \cos(\varphi) + l_2 \cos(\varphi + \psi) = l_3 \cos(\alpha) + l_4 \cos(\theta) \ . \tag{2}$$

$$l_1 \sin(\varphi) + l_2 \sin(\varphi + \psi) = d + l_3 \sin(\alpha) + l_4 \sin(\theta) \ . \tag{3}$$

Eliminating α from equations (2) and (3), a new equation is achieved:

$$\begin{gathered} l_1^2 + l_2^2 - l_3^2 + l_4^2 + d^2 + 2l_1 l_2 \cos(\psi) - 2l_1 l_4 \cos(\varphi - \theta) \\ -2l_2 l_4 \cos(\varphi + \psi - \theta) - 2l_1 d \sin(\varphi) - 2l_2 d \sin(\varphi + \psi) \\ +2l_4 d \sin(\theta) = 0 \end{gathered} \ . \tag{4}$$

From (4) it is possible to get any of the three parameters as a function of the other two. Following equations are used in the calculus of direct and inverse kinematics.

$$\theta = -\tan^{-1}\left(\frac{B}{A}\right) - \sin^{-1}\left(\frac{b}{2l_2\sqrt{b - l_2^2 + l_3^2}}\right) .$$

$$B = -2l_1 l_4 \cos(\varphi) - 2l_2 l_4 \cos(\varphi + \psi) \ .$$

$$A = 2l_4 d - 2l_2 l_4 \sin(\varphi + \psi) - 2l_1 l_4 \sin(\varphi) \ .$$

$$b = a + 2l_1 l_2 \cos(\psi) - 2l_1 d \sin(\varphi) - 2l_2 d \sin(\varphi + \psi) \ .$$

and

$$\psi = \tan^{-1}\left(\frac{B}{A}\right) - \sin^{-1}\left(\frac{b}{2l_2\sqrt{b - l_2^2 + l_3^2}}\right) .$$

$$B = -2 \cdot l_1 \cdot l_2 + 2 \cdot l_2 \cdot l_4 \cdot \cos(\varphi - \theta) + 2 \cdot d \cdot l_2 \cdot \sin(\varphi) \ .$$

$$A = 2 \cdot l_2 \cdot l_4 \cdot \sin(\varphi - \theta) - 2 \cdot d \cdot l_2 \cdot \cos(\varphi) \ .$$
$$b = a - 2 \cdot l_1 \cdot l_4 \cdot \cos(\varphi - \theta) - 2 \cdot d \cdot l_1 \cdot \sin(\varphi) + 2 \cdot d \cdot l_4 \cdot \sin(\theta) \ .$$

2.2 Controller

The controller manages all the information transmitted to and from this multi-finger haptic interface; it can process all data required by both finger devices. Sensors included in the haptic interface are: 3 motor encoders that provide the angle position of each actuated joint, 3 potentiometers that provide the angle position of the last non-actuated DOF, measurement of current that goes through each motor to estimate the torque generated by the actuator and 4 force sensors embedded in each thimble.

The controller is basically made up of two main parts. One part is a control card by Xilinx, the ML-403 model which includes a FPGA Virtex4 and provides a strong process capacity (400MHz PowerPC) and flexibility (up to 78 configurable inputs). The other part is an instrumentation card that adapts all input and output signals.

3 Thimble

We use a close-fitting design for the thimble. It completely encloses the user's finger, ensuring that the interface always follows the operator's movements. Four Flexiforce sensors (Tekscan Inc., Boston, MA) are embedded in the design in order to obtain an estimation of normal and dragging forces exerted by the user. Normal force is obtained by a sensor placed in the fingertip and dragging forces are estimated from sensors placed on the side and upper fingertip. Figure 3 shows the prototype of the thimble with four force sensors.

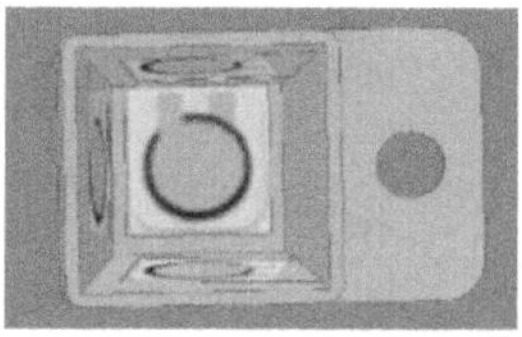

Fig. 3. Prototype of a thimble with four Flexiforce sensors

4 Gesture Identification

We have developed a mathematical model of the human hand, to be used in hand movement simulations and in calculating force feedback reflections. Based on this model, we have made an identification of hand gestures in order to differentiate the proper hand configuration during manipulation.

4.1 Hand Model

The human hand model is based on a skeletal model with 24 DOF and 20 bones. It satisfies all active movements of the five fingers. All "normal and natural" constraints were taken into account thanks to the physiological and anatomical study of the hand [4], [5], [6], [7], [8].

The kinematics model is done by means of the Denavit–Hartenberg convention used in robotics. Hand model kinematics can be simplified into two finger model kinematics. One model shows the kinematics of the index, middle, ring and little fingers with five DOF each. The other model represents the kinematics of the thumb, with four DOF.

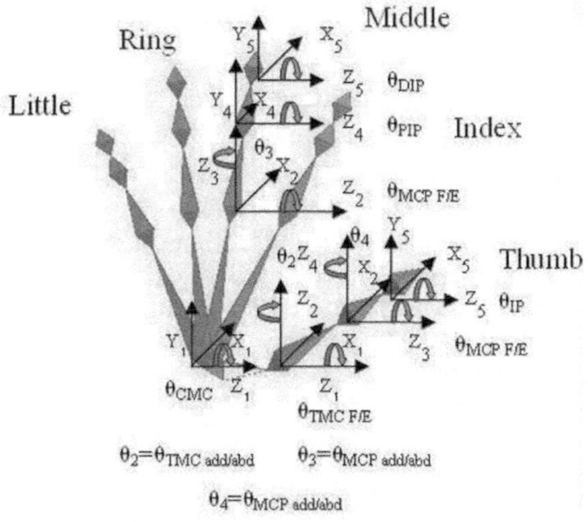

Fig. 4. Kinematics model of the hand

General finger model. The four fingers have four types of bones: metacarpal, proximal, middle, and distal. The joints corresponding to these fingers are: Carpometacarpal (CMC) joint, metacarpophalangeal (MCP) joint, proximal Interphalangeal (PIP) joint and distal interphalangeal (DIP) joint (see fig. 4).

There are two types of movements, the first one is flexion/extension (F/E) and refers to close-packed or open-packed positions. The second one is adduction/abduction (Add/Abd) and refers to movements that make fingers approach or move away with other fingers.

Table 1 shows the Denavit-Hartenberg parameters for the fist model

Table 1. Denavit-Hartenberg parameters for the first model

Joint	θ_i	d_i	a_i	α_i
1	θ_{CMC}	0	L1	0
2	$\theta_{MCP\ F/E}$	0	0	$\pi/2$
3	$\theta_{MCP\ Add/Abd}$	0	L2	$-\pi/2$
4	θ_{PIP}	0	L3	0
5	θ_{DIP}	0	L4	0

Thumb model. The thumb has four main bones: trapezium, metacarpal, proximal and distal. The joints of this finger are: Trapeziometacarpal (TMC) joint, Metacarpophalangeal (MCP) joint and Interphalangeal (IP) joint. The TMC joint can have up to three degrees of freedom although only two have been considered in this model.

Table 2 shows the Denavit-Hartenberg parameters for this model.

Table 2. Denavit-Hartenberg parameters for the second model

Joint	θ_i	d_i	a_i	α_i
1	$\theta_{TMC\ F/E}$	*0*	*0*	$\pi/2$
2	$\theta_{TMC\ Add/Abd}$	*0*	*L1*	$-\pi/2$
3	$\theta_{MCP\ F/E}$	*0*	*L2*	*0*
4	θ_{IP}	*0*	*L3*	*0*

The thumb represents by itself almost all functions of the hand, thanks to its ability of opposition in relation to other fingers; the index and the middle with the thumb form precision grip; the ring and the little, with rest of the hand are important for the palm grip. Hand grip in all fingers is the most important factor in manipulating objects in diverse situations in order to get stable hold.

4.2 Gesture Identification

Gesture identification is done with statistical methods that are based on Principal Component Analysis (PCA) [9]. It has been successfully applied in order to identify the main factors that classify power grasp and precision grasp.

The 24 variables or DOF of the hand model are linearly dependent. PCA is applied so as to make a linear transformation to keep a subspace with five principal components. Discriminate function analysis is applied in order to determine which group membership belong to a set of predictors among the five principal components. Canonical analysis is applied to determine some optimal combination of variables so that the derived functions provide the maximum overall discrimination among groups. This procedure is designed to develop a discriminate function series that can help predict the grasps based on the values of other quantitative variables. 17 cases were considered in developing a model that classifies 5 kinds of grasp. 24 forecast variables were taken into account. 4 discriminate functions with p-values lower than 0.05 have shown 95% reliability rate.

We carried out a cluster analysis to obtain the amount of association between the strong and the weak members and/or clusters. Figure 5 shows the dendrogram of the cluster analysis and explains the classification of grasps that has been done while getting a book, holding an iron bar, holding a ball, manipulating with dexterity a coin and manipulating with dexterity a pen.

It is important to take into account the relation of forces to discriminate gestures that have similar movements. Force generation inside the virtual environment has to be considered for this purpose.

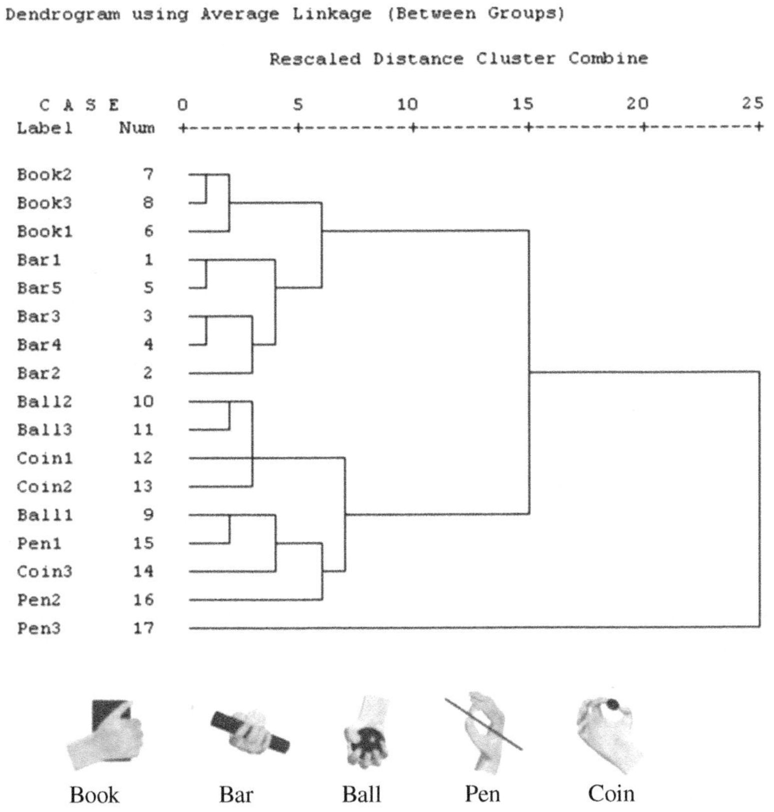

Fig. 5. Hierarchical cluster analysis

5 Conclusions and Future Work

We have presented a two-finger haptic device with serial-parallel structure and a controller device to manage all the signals of the interface. We have also achieved a mathematical model of haptic interactions, which runs in real time in order to provide contact forces and object movements according to the manipulation commands received from haptic devices.

Figure 6 shows a general view of the system. Commands are being continuously received by the Haptic-Server, which processes this information in order to calculate forces exerted by the user during manipulation. These forces have two consequences; first, movements can be done in manipulated objects, and second, the corresponding manipulation forces in the operator hand are reflected by the haptic device.

Current hardware allows two-finger manipulation. Moreover, the interface has been designed so as to be easily configured with three fingers. Future work is also focused on the implementation of a second interface that can accomplish collaborative tasks with the one we have already developed.

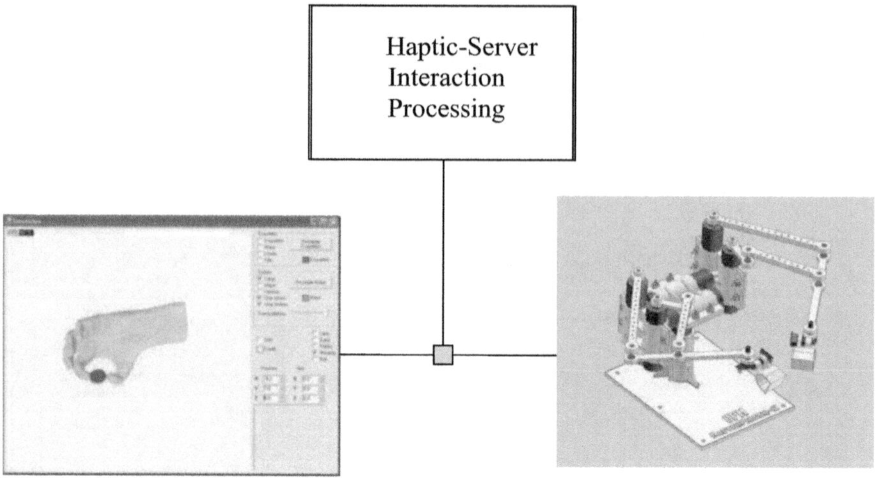

Fig. 6. Architecture of a haptic interaction using the haptic-server and the haptic device

Acknowledgments. This work is fundedd by the European Commission under the IMMERSENCE Integrated Project of the Sixth Frame Program (IST-4-027141-IP).

References

1. Jones, L.A., Lederman, S.J.: Human hand function. Oxford University Press, New York (2006)
2. Cybergrasp User Guide. Inmersion Co
3. Bouzit, M., Burdea, G., Popescu, G., Boian, R.: The Rutger Master II – New Design Force-Feedback Glove.IEEE Transactions on Mechatronics, vol. 7(2), (June 2002)
4. Kapandji, A.: The Physiology of the Joints, E&S Livingstone, Edinburgh and London, 2 edn. vol. 1 (1970)
5. Casas, A. P., Bengoechea, M.E.: Functional Anatomy of the Locomotive Apparatus, Paz Montalvo (In Spanish) (1978)
6. Worthinghanm, D.: Functional and Muscular Tests. McGraw-Hill, New York (In Spanish) (1991)
7. Gray, F.R.S.H.: Grays Anatomy: The Illustrated Running Press Edition of the American Classic. Running Press, Philadelphia, PA (1974)
8. Rouviére, H., Delmas, A.: Descriptive Human Anatomy, Topographical and Functional. Masson, pp (30–40, 79–89, 267–276, 294–312) (In Spanish) (2005)
9. Jobson, J.D.: Applied Multivariable Data Analysis. Volume II: Categorical and Multivariate Methods. Springer, Heidelberg (1992)

Measuring Presence in Mobile 3D

Hyun Jong Ryu, Rohae Myung, and Byongjun Lee

Korea University, 1, 5-ga Annam-dong, Sungbuk-gu,
Seoul, 136-701, Korea
{Hyun Jong Ryu,Rohae Myung,Byongjun Lee,rayan}@korea.ac.kr

Abstract. In this paper, we developed valid mobile presence measurements, and proposed the factor structure of the resulting scale. The measurements of items came from previously published questionnaires in the area of VR and from the experience of mobile 3D developers. We also added our concept factors. The 60 subjects experienced the mobile 3D game for about 40 mins. After finishing the mobile 3D game, they completed the questionnaire immediately. Factor analysis was performed on the data. The factors of mobile 3D presence were divided into 4 super-factors; condition factor, interface factor, attention factor, and feedback, and were further divided into 20 sub-factors.

Keywords: mobile 3D game, presence, measurement, presence factors.

1 Introduction

A major trend in mobile applications is the rapid move towards 3D graphics. An important differentiating characteristic of mobile 3D compared with other human-computer interfaces are their ability to create a sense of 'being there' in the environment. Presence is the subjective experience of being located in one place or environment, even if physically existing in another (Witmer & Singer, 1998). Following from psychological features, presence is relevant in attempting to evaluate human experience in Virtual Environments (IJsselsteijn et al., 2000). In addition to VEs, presence is also used globally to explain the human experience in a variety of other media (Freeman, Avons, Meddis, Pearson and IJsselsteijn, 1999).

Mobile 3D may be used to provide information about the user's context, including location, and to further deliver some or all of the images, sounds or data streams that support a particular presence. Mobile presence is considered as emerging from the sequence of actions the user performs, integrating the physical and psychological dimension of the user's presence, including what happens outside the 3D mobile setting. In contrast, mobile 3D with VR exposes the user environments. It can be maintained that advanced forms of virtual reality only differ from previous media in quantity and quality of presence (Biocca, 1992).

When understood under broad interpretation, augmented reality (e.g., mobile 3D) belongs in the virtual reality domain, but several differences exist. Augmented reality is where 3D displays are used to overlay a synthesized world on top of a real world, and Virtual reality, is a technology that allows a user to interact with a

J. Jacko (Ed.): Human-Computer Interaction, Part II, HCII 2007, LNCS 4551, pp. 681–688, 2007.

computer-simulated environment. Virtual reality makes possible a wide range of applications. A major factor that determines the quality of an implementation of a virtual environment is the extent at which the simulation is able to induce a feeling of physically existing in the virtual reality (Draper, Kaber, & Usher, 1998).

In so far, previous research has touched on the subject of measuring presence in virtual environments (Sheridan, 1996; Barfield et al., 1995; Slater et al., 1993). Mobile 3D is a different media mechanism to a virtual environment, which provides the same sense of presence, but with a different degree and type of virtual presence. However, to date, few efforts have focused on measuring presence in mobile 3D environments; user-centered design and user interface evaluation in mobile augmented reality as a practice still lags far behind what is needed by UI designers. As a result, new measurements are needed to create mobile 3D games. Since Mobile 3D is generally considered as relatively insignificant, few efforts have been reported in actually making mobile 3D measurements to date.

In this study, we developed that selected measurement was needed to create mobile 3D. First, we identified the factors that influence mobile presence. Then we developed suitable measurement for presence in mobile 3D environments. Finally, the measurement verified whether new 3D mobile presence measurement evaluates well the presence of mobile 3D.

1.1 Presence

Presence can be defined as the subjective experience of being located in one place or environment, even if physically existing in another (Witmer & Singer, 1998). It is defined as the user's feeling of "being there" in a mediated environment (e.g., IJsselsteijn, deRidder, Freeman and Avons, 2000). Lombard and Ditton (1997) defined it as the illusion of non-mediation in which the user no longer perceives the display medium. The synonym of the term presence are synthetic presence, virtual presence, ego presence and telepresence, which all refer to the same phenomenon of being in a mediated environment (Draper, Kaber & Usher, 1998). The sense of presence can be thought of as the sense of being that one receives from the perception of one's physical environment through automatic and controlled mental processes (Barfield, Sheridan, Zeltzer, & Slater, 1995; Barfield & Weghorst, 1995; Steuer, 1992).

3D mobile may be used to provide information about the user's context, including location, and to deliver some or all of the images, sounds or data streams that support a particular form of presence. The sense of "physical reality" is "a consequence of internal processing rather then being something that is developed only from the immediate sensory information we receive" (Ellis, 1991, P.874). Only by taking these processes into account it is possible to understand how 3D games play on a monitor without direct mapping between body movements and corresponding movements in a virtual world, and even text-only VEs can elicit high degrees of presence (Schiano, 1999; Towell & Towell, 1997). In conclusion, it can be maintained that advanced forms of virtual reality only differ from previous media in quantity and quality of presence (Biocca, 1992). The difference between virtual reality and other media is defined as the difference in the level of presence (e.g., Steuer, 1995).

1.2 Presence Is a User Interface Goal

Over the past 15 years, there have been many studies performed to evaluate various aspects of human experience using virtual environment technology. One major factor that determines the quality of an implementation of a virtual environment is the extent at which the simulation is able to induce a feeling of being in a virtual reality (Draper, Kaber, & Usher, 1998). Due to its psychological nature, presence is relevant in attempting to evaluate human experience in VEs (IJsselsteijn et al., 2000). Besides VEs, presence is also used as a global measure to explain the human experience in many other media (Freeman, Avons, Meddis, Pearson and IJsselsteijn, 2000). Compared to more traditional media such as television, radio and telephone, VR technology such as high definition television, home theatre and video conferencing provides a stronger sense of presence (Lombard and Ditton, 1997; Steuer, 1992).

The mobile 3D interface is highly interactive and promotes a degree of presence in the mobile 3D environment. Mobile 3D is very different to mobile 2D in terms of visual, sound, and tactile feedback. By being able to take full advantage of these functions, mobile 3D will help attract and hold users' attention for a variety of applications. The users present in a mobile 3D environment experience being there and focus their attention on the mobile 3D environment, experiencing it as something real.

The goal of the user interface in the existing mobile game takes into account usability, efficiency, legibility and allocation; everything but presence. However, the main goal of mobile 3D games is the sense of presence. The purpose of the mobile 3D interface is the feeling of being there. This trend of human-computer interface design is changing from existing performance-based and work-related design and evaluation (e.g. effectiveness, efficiency and user satisfaction (ISO 1996)) to a more non-work-related emphasis. Today, researchers are interested in user` s mental satisfaction, such as, presence, fun, enjoyment, fantasy and curiosity, etc.

2 Factors Contribute to Presence

We identified the factors that influence the feeling of presence in mobile 3D. These factors came from previously published questionnaires in the area of VR and the experience of mobile 3D developers. We also added our concept factors. The factors from which our items were derived are conceptually based and have not been verified. The factors interact with one another in presence. Factor analysis was performed on the data. The factors of mobile 3D presence were divided into 4 super-factors; condition factor, interface factor, attention factor, and feedback, resulting in 20 sub-factors; degree of control, immediacy of control, anticipation of events, mode of control, motion, connectedness & continuity, consistency with the objective world, meaning of icons, view of field, resolution, visual display quality, control of event, interface awareness, intuitive mapping, being there, response delay, selective attention, speed, sound, tactile.

Table 1. The factors assumed to contribute to presence

Condition Factors	Interface factors	Attention factors	Feedback Factors
Degree of control	Control of event	Response delay	Sound
Immediacy of control	Interface awareness	Selective attention	Tactile
Anticipation of events	Intuitive mapping	Speed	
Mode of control	Being there		
Motion			
Connectedness & continuity			
Consistency with the objective world			
Meaning of icons			
View of field			
Resolution			
Visual display quality			

With the result, we developed a valid 3D mobile presence measurement method. In this study, both 7-point rating scales and open-ended questionnaires were used. 7-point rating scale items were correlated with the sense of presence, and consisted of 20 items, 1 item represented 1 factor, using ‘not at all’ and ‘very much’ at the ends of the scale. The format of the 7-point rating scale was based on the semantic differential principle (Dayer, Matthews, Stulac, Wright, Yudowitch, 1976).

3 Measuring Presence

Presence is a mental state; it is no wonder that subjective reports are the most common measurement method (Nash, Edwards, Thompson, & Barfield, 2000). And because of the cognitive nature (such as attention factor et al.,) of presence, the act of presenting a questionnaire while performing a virtual task not only distracts from the task, but also most likely changes the individual's location of presence from the virtual world to the real world. In addition, finding ways to provide an alternative and indirect way to assess presence is a key concept in the evaluation and design of mobile 3D. The most common approach to measure the sense of presence is the method of post-test questionnaires. Measuring presence should be post tested for the psychological features of presence, such as attention and concentration.

3.1 Experiment

We tested in an experimental setting consisting of 60 subjects. The mean age was 25.1 years, SD=2.09, the range was 21 to 32 years. The subjects interacted with the mobile 3D game for about 40 mins. After finishing the mobile 3D game, they completed the questionnaire immediately. They entered the -3D realm with Fortune Golf-, and experienced stunningly detailed 3D graphics, including 3D-rendered characters and a plethora of backgrounds.

Fig. 1. A 3D mobile game example

3.2 Measurement

The items came from previously published questionnaires in the area of VR and from the experience of mobile 3D developers. We also added our concept factors.

In this study, both the 7-point rating scale and open-ended questionnaire were used. 7-point rating scale items were correlated with the sense of presence, and consisted of 20 items (Fig. 2), anchored with 'not at all' and 'very much'. The format of the 7-point rating scale was based on the semantic differential principle (Dayer, Matthews, Stulac, Wright, Yudowitch, 1976).

> Did you enjoy the game?
>
> Thinking back to the game, please answer the questions by 7-point rating scale
>
> (1= Not at all, 7= Very much)
>
> 1. In the LCD. Do you know the meaning of icons?

Fig. 2. An example of the questionnaire

4 Results

Since presence is a mental state, it is no wonder that subjective reports are the most common measurement method in studies to identify its reliability and validity. Reliability is related with the quality of measurement. The internal consistency measure of reliability (Cronbach`s Alpha) of the mobile 3D presence questionnaire yielded 0.8312. The mean score was 5.035, with a standard deviation of 1.47. Factor analysis was performed on the data. The data were factorized using Principal Analysis and rotated using oblique Direct Oblimin rotation. Missing values were excluded pairwise. These values were replaced with the mean. The scree plot suggested that 4 factors should be extracted, and these 4 factors explained 51.87% of the total variance.

Table 2. Factor analysis

Component	Name	Label	Number of items	Eigen value	% of variance explained
1	Condition Factor	CF	11	5.054	25.271
2	Interface Factors	IF	4	1.929	9.646
3	Attention Factors	AF	3	1.444	7.222
4	Feedback Factors	FF	2	1.104	5.518

5 Conclusion and Further Study

We performed factor analysis on the data, the factors of mobile 3D presence were divided into 4 super-factors; condition factor, interface factor, attention factor, feedback factor, and from factor analysis, found 20 sub-factors. These factors are not limited to mobile presence only. The cluster of possible factors can be applied to other display forms, regardless of wether it is VR, it will act to describe a feeling of presence.

Presence frequently becomes an issue because it is thought to correlate with improved task performance in virtual environments (Hendrix, 1994). We have planned to try to identify the potential relationship between mobile presence and performance. Within the general area of performance, the topic of presence has been expanded, and is seen as an important aspect of tasks performed within mobile 3D, drawing much attention from researchers and developers.

6 Lecture Notes in Computer Science in the ISI SCI Expanded

The Lecture Notes in Computer Science volumes are sent to ISI for inclusion in their Science Citation Index Expanded.

Acknowledgments. This work was supported by the Brain Korea 21 Project in 2006.

References

1. Barfield, W., Sheridan, T., Zeltzer, D., Slater, M.: Presence and performance within virtual environments. In: Barfield, W., Furness, I.T. (eds.) Virtual Environments and Advanced Interface Design, Oxford University Press, UK (1995)
2. Biocca, F., Delany, B.: Immersive virtual technology. In: Biocca, F., Levy, M.R. (eds.) Communication in the age of virtual reality, Hillsdale, NJ, USA, Lawrence Erlbaum Associates, Mahwah, NJ (1995)
3. Biocca, F., Levy, M.R.: Communications applications of virtual reality. 4. In: Biocca, F., Levy, M.R. (eds.) Communications applications of virtual reality, Hillsdale, NJ, USA, Lawrence Erlbaum Associates, Mahwah, NJ (1995)
4. Draper, J.V., Kaber, D.B., Usher, J.M.: Telepresence. Human Factors 49(3), 354–375 (1998)
5. Dyer, R., Matthews, J.J., Stulac, J.F., Wright, C.E., Yudowitch, K.: Questionnaire construction manual, annex literature survey and bibliography. Palo 20. Alto, CA: Operations Research Associates (1976)
6. Freeman, J., Avons, S.E., Pearson, D., IJsselsteijn, W.A.: Effects of sensory information and prior experience on direct subjective ratings of presence. Teleoperators and Virtual Environments 8(1), 1–13 (1999)
7. Ellis, G.: Compiled hierarchical retrieval. In: Proceedings of the 6th Annual Workshop on Conceptual Graphs, Binghamton pp. 187–207 (1991)
8. Hendrix, C.M.: Exploratory Studies on the Sense of Presence in Virtual Environments as a Function of Visual and Auditory Display Parameters. Master's Thesis. Human Interface Technology Laboratory of the Washington Technology Center at the University of Washington (1994)
9. IJsselsteijn, W.A., de Ridder, H., Freeman, J., Avons, S.E.: Presence: Concept, determinants and measurement. In: Proceedings of the SPIE, 3959. Presented at Human Vision and Electronic Imaging V 24-27 January 2000, San Jose, USA (2000)
10. Lombard, M., Ditton, T.: At the heart of all: the concept of presence. Journal of Computer-Mediated Communication, vol. 3(2) (1997) Available: http://www.ascusc.org/jcmc/vol3/issue2/lombard.html
11. Nash, E.B., Edwards, G.W., Thompson, J.A., Barfield, W.: A review of Presence and performance in Virtual Environments. Journal of human-computer interaction 12(1), 1–41 (2000)
12. Schiano, D.: Lessons from LambdaMOO: A social, text-based virtual environment. Presence: Teleoperators and Virtual Environments 8(2), 127–139 (1999)

13. Sheridan, T.B.: Further Musings on the Psychophysics of Presence. Presence: Teleoperators and Virtual Environments 5(2), 241–246 (1996)
14. Slater, M., Usoh, M.: Representations systems, perceptual position, and presence in immersive virtual environments. Presence 2(3), 221–233 (1993)
15. Steuer, J.: Defining virtual reality: dimensions determining telepresence. Journal of Communication 42(4), 73–93 (1992)
16. Steuer, J.: Defining virtual reality: Dimensions determining telepresence. In: Biocca, F., Levy, M. (eds.) Communication in the age of virtual reality, Hillsdale, NJ, pp. 33–56. Lawrence Erlbaum, Mahwah, NJ (1995)
17. Towell, J., Towell, E.: Presence in text-based network virtual environments or MUDs. Teleoperators and Virtual Environments 6(5), 590–595 (1997)
18. Witmer, B.G., Singer, M.J.: Measuring presence in virtual environments: A presence questionnaire. Presence: Teleoperators and Virtual Environments 7(3), 225–240 (1998)

IMPROVE: Designing Effective Interaction for Virtual and Mixed Reality Environments

Pedro Santos[1], André Stork[1], Thomas Gierlinger[2], Alain Pagani[2], Bruno Araújo[3], Ricardo Jota[3], Luis Bruno[3], Joaquim Jorge[3], Joao Madeiras Pereira[3], Martin Witzel[4], Giuseppe Conti[4], Raffaele de Amicis[4], Iñigo Barandarian[5], Céline Paloc[5], Maylu Hafner[6], and Don McIntyre[7]

[1] Fraunhofer-IGD, A2
{Pedro.Santos,Andre.Stork}@igd.fhg.de
[2] TU-Darmstadt, FB21,GRIS
{Thomas.Gierlinger,Alain.Pagani}@igd.fhg.de
[3] INESC-ID
{brar,jota.costa,bruno,jaj,jap}@inesc-id.pt
[4] GraphiTech
{martin.witzel,giuseppe.conti,raffaele.de.amicis}@graphitech.it
[5] VICOMTech
{Inigo.Barandarian,Celine.Paloc}@vicomtech.es
[6] UNIMEP
MayluHafner@yahoo.com.br
[7] Lighthouse
don.mcintyre@urbanlearningspace.com

Abstract. In this paper we present evaluation results of an innovative application designed to make collaborative design review in the architectural and automotive domain more effective. Within IMPROVE, a European research project in the area of advanced displays, we are combining high resolution multi-tile displays, TabletPCs and head-mounted displays with innovative 2D and 3D Interaction Paradigms to better support collaborative mobile mixed reality design reviews. Our research and development is motivated by application scenarios in the automotive domain involving FIAT Elasis from Naples, Italy and in the architectural domain involving Page/Park architects from Glasgow, Scotland. User evaluation took place at Glasgow (UK), Naples (ITA) and Darmstadt (GER), where we tested the integrated IMPROVE prototype application. The tests were conducted based on several heuristics such as ergonomics and psychomotorial factors and they were conducted based on guidelines recommended by ISO 9241 to verify whether the developed interfaces were suitable for the applications scenarios. Evaluation results show that there is a strong demand for more interactive design review systems, allowing users greater flexibility and greater choice of input and visualization modalities as well as their combination.

1 Introduction

Design Review is one of the most prominent areas benefiting from Virtual Reality and Immersive Projection Technologies. Today Virtual Reality is used to present design

J. Jacko (Ed.): Human-Computer Interaction, Part II, HCII 2007, LNCS 4551, pp. 689–699, 2007.

alternatives, but fully interactive commercial VR or AR design review applications are still being developed or not available. Use cases generally comprise many observers in front of a back projection wall discussing a design decision on a virtual model. This is why in IMPROVE we include support for large single- or multi-tile displays as well as support for TabletPCs. In the above mentioned scenarios we can have users controlling what is visualized on the power-wall from their TabletPCs and vice versa. In addition we also aim at supporting mobile mixed reality using optical see-through HMDs which allow architects to go on site or meet around a table to look at the virtual model of a new building inserted into the real environment featuring the same lighting and reflections as the surroundings.

Components of the IMPROVE system tested by users and performance aims:

- 2D Interaction techniques as well as 3D Interaction techniques for 3D environments were assessed, as is the case when users use a TabletPC to alter the design of a model or proceed to attach annotations or choose material properties or when they use a stereo optical see-through HMD or stand in front of a Power-wall. In any case both performance and learnability were assessed.
- For the combination of display technology and rendering techniques the image quality was assessed, e.g. a comparison between standard OpenGL Lighting and GPU-based pre-computed radiance transfer.
- For the HMD ergonomic issues have been addressed such as brightness, weight, display resolution and power consumption.
- Marker-less tracking for mobile mixed reality environments has been paid special attention during the tests with respect to tracking accuracy, tracking speed, tracking area and final cost of the system.
- The mobile video transmission component has been tested to analyse whether image quality and latency times are enough for the target scenarios. Stereo video stream transmission is used to transmit high quality rendered images to a mobile user receiving the compressed 3D stereo video stream and decompressing it onto the optical stereo-see-through HMD.

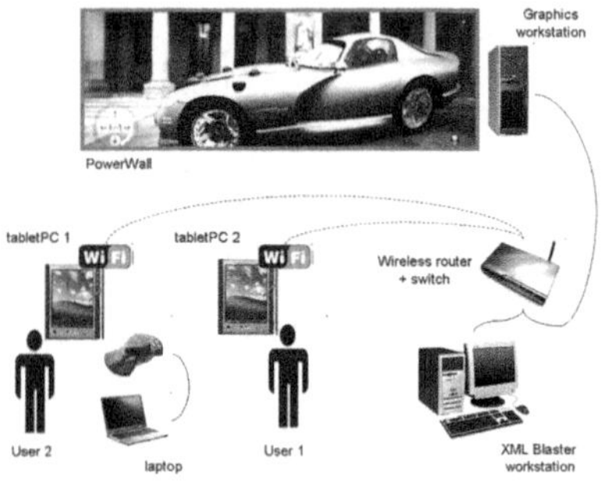

Fig. 1. A possible IMPROVE Setup

For the first user evaluation in IMPROVE (Figure 1) we set up the following scenarios at the following locations:

Glasgow (UK): We tested collaborative Design Review between TabletPCs for the architectural domain.

- Darmstadt (GER): We tested the mobile video transmission component and 3D interaction in a 3D virtual environment.
- Naples (ITA): We tested the collaborative Power-wall scenario for the automotive domain, where multiple users have a TabletPC of their own and can control and interact with the design of a vehicle.

The usability tests main goal was to assess the functionalities and performances of the interfaces as well as the level of usability of the interaction paradigms developed.

We have prepared two questionnaires with specific goals, heuristic testing and isometric testing according to ISO 9241.

Among the heuristic goals were: Ergonomic factors; Hardware and Setup; Scenario and Tests; Human factors; Psychomotorial factors.

Further tests, followed the guidelines defined by the International Standard ISO 9241 recommendations, aimed at validating whether the interface developed could be considered suitable to the application scenario chosen. Here the assessment has been done on the basis of the following categories: Suitability for the task; Self descriptiveness; Controllability; Conformity with user expectations; Error tolerance; Suitability for individualization; Suitability for learning. Each of these categories was accompanied by a questionnaire. For each question the user was asked to answer through a scale from 1 to 5 (from strong disagreement to agreement). Additionally the tests were supported by recording of video and audio during the session for further analysis.

2 User Tests of the Architectural Scenario

This usability tests took place at Lighthouse, the Scottish Centre for Architecture, from the 24th to the 27th of April, with the participation of six users with different experience and tasks in architecture:

- Two users were undergraduate students, working at Page & Park, Architects, Glasgow. They were younger than average age and more willing to experiment new approaches;
- The remaining four users were graduate architects with experience in user review scenario, working at Page & Park. They also have experience with common 3D drawing tools such as ArchiCAD. Furthermore, only one user had minimal experience with GIDeS.

Each test had the duration of approximately 1 hour and 10 minutes.

*Initial Questionnaire:*The initial questionnaire is divided into 3 groups of questions: The first group explains the review collaborative scenarios definition used in the questionnaire and presents generic questions regarding Tablet PC usage and professional experience in both scenarios. The second and third groups present specific questions regarding each scenario. The second gathers information about annotation and its importance in a review scenario. The third gathers information about collaborative work and what type of collaborative work was executed by the user.

Our objective was to interpret user expectations regarding our software and review collaborative scenarios. The Usability test consisted in three modelling tasks of different complexity. At the beginning of the Usability tests the users were briefed about the required tasks. A task description document was provided so the users would not lose track of the tasks workflow. This document can be found in the appendix. Once the briefing was concluded and the users were given the task descriptions, the actual test execution began. The initial questionnaire was composed of 23 questions from which we present an excerpt and the conclusion:

Concerning the project design, I classify computers as helpful
I often use CAD systems in my work
The annotations taken during design review with clients are relevant to interpret their requests
The annotations taken during the design review session with clients are enough to track and solve their requests
I often use software to take annotations during design review sessions with clients
I am satisfied with the way annotations are taken during design review sessions with others designers
I am satisfied with the software already used in design review.
I perceive computer software as a good aid on taking annotations on collaborative work
I often use software to take annotations during collaborative work
I am satisfied with the way annotations are taken during collaborative work
I am satisfied with the software already used in collaborative work

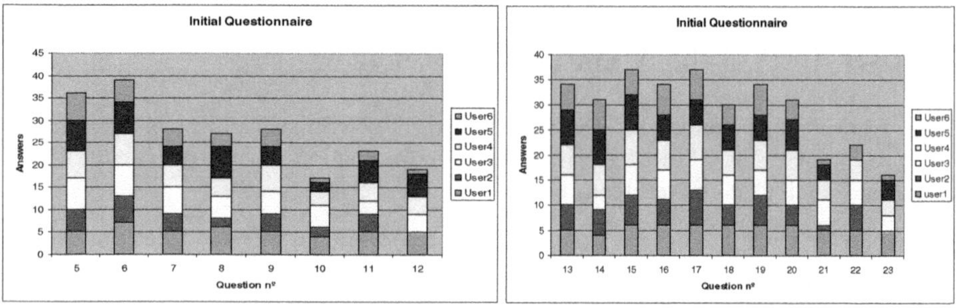

Fig. 2. Initial Questionnaire Results

Conclusion: Every user often uses CAD systems in their work and reviews collaborative sessions with other team members. All of them have the need to make annotations during design review sessions with clients and they consider these notes to be very important to interpret their requests.

However, only two out of six users use software to take annotations during design review sessions with clients. We have verified that only two users are clearly satisfied with the way annotations are taken during design review sessions with other designers and with the software they already use.

In the collaborative section, we have verified that only two users often use software to take annotations in collaborative work sessions and the majority is not satisfied with the software already used by them in collaborative work.

So, based on the most representative questions we could conclude that the participants recognized the importance of the annotations as a method to record information from clients and other team members during review sessions but most users don't often use software to take annotations in collaborative or non-collaborative work and are not clearly satisfied with the software already used in these contexts.

Usability: The Usability test was divided into three modelling tasks of different complexity. Each task increased the last task difficulty. The first task had an easy difficulty. We asked the user to create simple shapes and create an annotation on the back face of the shape. The main aim of this task was to assess the annotation creation in a non-collaborative environment. We'd also tried to assess if the annotation system integrated well with the rest of GIDeS. Finally, we asked the user to execute this task three times, so that we could evaluate the tools learning curve regarding simple operations such as annotations.

The second task also focused on annotations. It involved the user being presented to an already loaded scene in order to find and execute three annotations. The annotations were inserted into the scene. The users needed only to track and execute their instructions. This allowed us to evaluate the impact of annotations, open and closed, and whenever the users could easily identify existing annotations.

The final task required two users to execute a collaborative task. In order to simulate a real collaborative environment, the session users had different tasks assigned to them. The user using the 12'' Tablet PC was given the User-A assignments while the 15'' Tablet PC user was given the User-B assignments. The collaborative task involved both users connecting to the OSGA Server and create simple shapes and annotations. It also involved the execution of instructions included in annotations created by the other user. Even though users had different assignments, the experience was the same for each user. The difference relied on the assignment order. User-A would first create shapes and annotation and then respond to the annotations created by User-B. User-B would first respond to User-A's annotations and then create his own shapes and annotations. The task allowed us to recognize problems presented in collaborative work, to evaluate the users notion of collaboration and to test annotations and its uses on a collaborative environment. Users were given specific instructions on how to transmit information regarding instructions; we are looking forward to evaluate the feedback created by users when completing an instruction.

Based on users' tasks observations, user comments and video analysis, it was possible to notice that users enjoyed the annotations over objects 3D and the collaboration features of the system, such as shown for the next user sentences:

Table 1. Positive user statements on architecture collaborative scenario

The software is quite easy to operate and add annotations;
Open and close (annotations) is very easy. Editing needs improving;
As a tool for reviews this could be very helpful. Especially remote working - dynamic update of information is content to success.

The users have clearly manifested some pertinent comments about the system. The most common was on how to write on annotations using pen / tablet PC. It has produced by user statements like the following:

Table 2. User suggestions on architecture collaborative scenario

Hard to annotate with handwrites on screen;
Takes a few tries to get used to write on the screen;
I found it quite difficult to write (probably my lack of experience with tablet PC). Difficult to zoom while writing;
It's easy to create but not write to in it;
I found it difficult to write in general;
It is difficult to find space to write and not always obvious how to erase the writing.

These comments were due to different aspects, such as: the limited rendering speed which made writing of annotations not very interactive, the limited amount of screen space available for notes and difficulties to zoom in the annotation areas.

Another important comment manifested by users were about the difficulty in finding annotations on 3D scene space. The anchors of annotations are attached to the objects surfaces and if the view point of the user is not synchronized with anchor view, he is not able to see it. This matter produced statements like the following:

Table 3. User comments about the to find annotations on 3D scene space

It is sometimes difficult to find the annotations again;
It was often hard to find them (annotations);
Not always easy to find the annotation.

One user has made a suggestion to this issue:

Table 4. User suggestion about to find annotations on 3D scene space

I find it a little hard to imagine how this would work a simple list would be the generally this takes too long perhaps.

Some miscellaneous comments about annotations were produced, like the following:

Table 5. Some miscellaneous comments about annotations

More amounts of info - and quicker creation;
It is difficult to delete things from annotations box;
Audio notes may be quicker.

Other pertinent issue was the navigation process (camera operations). Some users found it difficult and produced some comments, like the following:

Table 6. User comments about navigation process

Finding a "plain" view is not very obvious;
Rotation of the camera is difficult to control;
It should has more control over movement needs;
Difficult to navigate to the right position (zooming);
Sometimes zoomed in close rotating object makes harder to understand its position.

Some users have made the following suggestions about navigation:

About the difficult to rotation the camera: “Maybe would be easier if you could control the viewpoint graphically (pointed represented in plan?)”;

About more control over movement needs: “such as ArtLantis/Sketchup - move control over individual axes”.

Another issue was related to the use of the contextual popup menu. Some users have considered difficult to select a menu option after they taped with pen. Some comments were produced about this issue, like the following:

Table 7. User comments about difficulties to select menu options

Difficulties in working out the pen. How to touch and switch? A move in the menu?
Takes a few tries to work out tools;
The tablet PC can be difficult to use.

About the collaborative issues the users had some problems about the sharing of the annotations and the objects between the two GIDeS++ system instances. So, when a user create one of this resources, it is sent to the other user GIDeS++ system. But if the receiving user's scene viewpoint is not appropriate, he doesn't see it. Some comments were produced about this issue, like the following:

Table 8. User comments about collaborative issues

Sometimes I can't see in my view perhaps. A small notification could tell me that userB has made an annotation - and show me this;
It was not always obvious who had done it;
It is not always obvious which users are online.

So, it is important to notify the users when resources are created on this scene, as well as when the resources created by them are sent to the other users. In this collaborative issue it's important to know which are the users online in that project review.

Final Questionnaire: At the end of the experience, we gave the users another questionnaire to obtain more feedback from the users experience. The final questionnaire was organized according the ISO-9241 – part 10, thus we grouped the questions according the following groups: Suitability for the Task; Self Descriptiveness; Controllability; Conformity with User Expectations; Error Tolerance; Suitability for Individualization; Suitability for Learning.

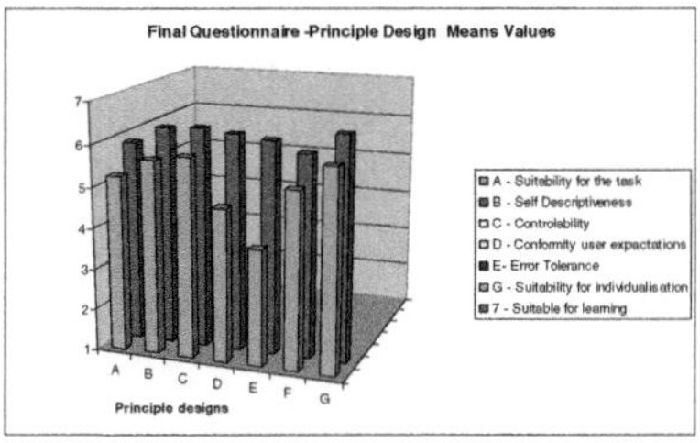

Fig. 3. Means values of the ISONORM principles

We allowed the users to comment and measure the level of importance of each question for their work. Our questions focused mainly on annotation and collaborative tasks, as the other features were previously tested. Finally, during verbal debriefing, we asked for general suggestions and criticism from the users, getting additional user input that users felt wasn't covered by the questionnaire. Overall our system got the lower rates on Error Tolerance and Conformity with user expectations (see the next Figure). The prototype wasn't very error tolerant mainly because annotations could not be undone or deleted. Arguably on could imply that the low question number - Just two - brought the group average down, nevertheless the problems encountered are relevant to future work. Users were expecting a lot more from Annotations. Our idea was to make annotations work just like real post-it notes, with free-sketch. But the resulting implementation was not what users were expecting. They wanted to be able to use sound and typing to define their annotations. This doesn't not mean that annotations are not useful as they are, the suitability for the task was high, it just says that there is room for improvement.

2.1 Future Changes for 2nd Prototype Version

Accordingly to the tests executed and users interviewed the following changes are suggested:

Annotations

- Improve annotations with handwriting on screen, maybe complemented with typing (faster and more legible);
- The speed to handwrite an annotation should be improved;
- Tighten the switch between graphic edition mode and annotation edition mode
- Eliminate the use of keyboard (type 'A') to create annotations;
- The list of annotations should be provided to users and allow them to select and open one of them, because the user only sees the annotations on his view;
- Allow users to delete annotation and erase information from it;
- Provide ways to add audio and text file attachments to annotations;
- All annotations should stay attached to object, independently of the user view (Implementation error.);
- The colours of anchors should be evaluated;
- The annotations should support attributes like ID author, timestamp creation, timestamp, solved, etc;
- The process to zoom in/out the annotations should be improved;
- The size of annotations should be improved;
- Implement a undo/redo system over annotation edition;
- Annotation should have a comment history.

Collaborative review scenario issues

- The connection mechanism to OSGA should eliminate the IP input by user;
- The user should be notified when other user creates some annotation;
- The user should be notified when other user solves some annotation;
- When an annotation is being edited by one user the system should inform other users;
- The user should be notified when other user create an object on the scene;
- The system should show the users list that are online.

General issues

- The navigation process should be improved in order to allow camera rotation and find locate the annotation creation view;
- The brightness of tablet PC's screen must be calibrated suited to environment light conditions;
- The access to the popup menu should be improved to users;
- The system should provide some kind of parameter calibration system to the user, like pen sensitivity, screen brightness, etc;
- The system should have an help system.

Conclusions of the Architectural Scenario: The first prototype focuses on annotation operations and collaborative scenario. Using this first prototype we conclude that the second prototype requirements need to be reviewed.

The first prototype was implemented on a Tabletop workstation, however we feel that the second prototype must take into account other technical scenarios defined be IMPROVE – IMPROVE also defines a Powerwall and a see-through glasses scenarios. Regarding the tasks defined, the second prototype should also take into account navigation tasks and some object edition tasks. In conclusion, the second prototype requirements should take into account the following guidelines:

- The prototype should be implemented into two or more improve user scenarios;
- The prototype should apply new interaction techniques whenever possible;
- The prototype should implement not only Annotation tasks but also Navigation and Object edition tasks.

3 User Tests of the Automotive Scenario

The user test took place at Fiat, Elasis premises close to Naples on Friday 5th 2006. Graphitech, with the support of Technical University of Darmstadt, was responsible for the technical set-up and coordination of the activity (Fig.3).

Fig. 4. Pictures of the preparation of the test

The test results were similar to the ones in the architectural scenario. We will summarize the conclusions as follows.

From the test it has emerged that a number of changes have to be done on future implementations besides those already planned. These include:

- Possibility to delete and move notes.
- Improve the selection of already defined note by changing the picking mechanism.
- Improvement of the interface's level of feedback.
- Approval/disapproval of annotation should be better implemented.
- Annotation quality should be improved by increasing the efficiency of the rendering system and ultimately the refresh rate at which annotations are drawn.
- Some form of "help" (e.g. help, wizard etc.)function must be provided.
- Some form of shortcut available to the user for frequently used functionalities.
- Support of "abort" function to interrupt an action at any time.
- Support for some sort of calibration of the sensitivity of the pen's speed etc should be provided to the user.

- Error tolerance must be improved. More information should be also provided in case an error situation arise.
- Support for "undo" should be provided.

As far as the use of the TabletPC is concerned, given the current hardware performance, it is not possible to avoid strain and discomfort caused by overheating of the pc. Therefore the requirements related to degree of ergonomics after prolonged use of the system must be lowered, being aware that future more efficient CPUs/GPUs might lead to lower working temperature.

4 Results

The general feedback about the IMPROVE software was positive, although several unexpected comments have been made about the physical usability of the system like heavy weight of the TabletPCs, and their increasing heat levels. The use of pen and TabletPC has been considered fairly intuitive. A clear indication of the good performance is the perceived short latency time between users during the test sessions, which together with a generally good sense of collaboration and rendering quality, proved to be a good success of the collaborative feeling delivered by the system. Our system showed good results in particular regarding controllability and suitability for learning, however error tolerance and user conformity were lower that expected. This might reflect the fact that users are expecting modeling systems to be more robust and effective. The evaluation process based on ISO9241 norm shown several benefits since user recommendations were clearly identified as valid.

We consider the presented results as a good motivation to the future research to be handled in the next iteration of our collaborative system.

Acknowledgements. This work was partially funded by European Commission Research Grant IMPROVE IST-2003-004785.

References

1. Regenbrecht, H., Wagner, M.: Interaction in a Collaborative Augmented Reality Environment. In: Proc. Of CHI 2002, Minneapolis, Minnesota, USA, pp. 504–505. ACM Press, New York (April 20-25, 2002)
2. Schmalstieg, D.: Designing Immersive Virtual Reality for Geometry Education, IEEE Virtual Reality, Alexandria, VA, USA, March 27, IEEE, Virtual Concept 2006 Short Article Title Paper Number -11- Copyright Virtual Concept (2006)
3. Klinker, G., Dutoit, A.H., Bauer, M., Bayer, J., Novak, V., Matzke, D., Morgana, F.: –A Presentation System for Product Design, Intl. Symposium on Augmented and Mixed Reality, Darmstadt, ISMAR (2002)
4. Bern, M., Eppstein, D.: Optimized color gamuts for tiled displays, SCG '03. In: Proceedings of the nineteenth annual symposium on Computational geometry, San Diego, California, USA, pp. 274–281. ACM Press, New York (2003)

5. Brown, M., Majumder, A., Yang, R.: Camera-Based Calibration Techniques for Seamless Multi-Projector Displays, IEEE Transactions on Visualization and Computer Graphics, vol. 11(2) (2005)
6. Debevec, P.E., Malik, J.: Recovering High Dynamic Range Radiance Maps from Photographs. Computer Graphics, SIGGRAPH 31, 369–378 (1997)
7. Debevec, P.: Rendering synthetic objects into real scenes: Bridging traditional and image-based graphics with global illumination and high dynamic range photography. In: SIGGRAPH 98 (July 1998)
8. Drummond, T., Cipolla, R.: Real-Time visual tracking of complex structures, IEEE Transaction on Pattern Analysis and Machine Intelligence 27, 932–946 (July 2002)
9. Fiorentino, M., de Amicis, R., Monno, G., Stork, A.: SpaceDesign: A Mixed Reality Workspace for Aesthetic Industrial Design, Intl. Symposium on Augmented and Mixed Reality, Darmstadt, ISMAR (2002)
10. Fröhlich, B., Hoffmann, J., Klüger, K., Hochstrate, J.: Implementing Multi-Viewer Time-Sequential Stereo Displays Based on Shuttered LCD Projectors. In: 4th Immersive Projection Technology Workshop, Ames, Iowa, (May 2004)

Evaluation of Wayfinding Aids Interface in Virtual Environment

Anna Wu[1], Wei Zhang[1], Bo Hu[1], and Xiaolong Zhang[2]

[1] Lab of Virtual Reality & Human Interface Technology,
Department of Industrial Engineering, Tsinghua University, 100084, Beijing, China
wanclubs@gmail.com, zhangwei@tsinghua.edu.cn,
bo-hu05@mails.tsinghua.edu.cn

[2] College of Information Sciences and Technology,
Pennsylvania State University, University Park, 16802, PA, USA
lzhang@ist.spu.edu

Abstract. It is difficult for a navigator to find a way to a given target location in an unfamiliar environment. Often, wayfinding guidance such as an overview map is provided to assist the navigator. However, overview maps can only show survey knowledge at one particular scale, and cannot provide other kinds of spaital knowledge (e.g. procedure knowledge) or survey knowledge at different scales. In this study, we compared effectiveness, efficiency and satisfaction of three wayfinding aids, View-in-View Map (VVM), Animation Guide (AG) and Human-System Collaboration (HSC) in support of navigation in virtual reality. Our experiment results show that while an overview still outperforms AG and HSC, AG serves better for most people with ordinary spatial ability and people with superior spatial ability tends to perform better using HSC.

Keywords: Wayfinding, Virtual environments, Interactive techniques, Spatial cognition.

1 Introduction

Research on wayfinding in virtual environment is numerous and with highly diversified purposes. When a navigation destination is known, tools often focus on how to get a navigator to the destination quickly and accurately. For example, some tools, like logarithmic movement [1], let systems execute viewpoint movement after the destination is specified. While these tools are efficient in movement, they deprive the navigator's opportunities to actively explore virtual environments.

Exploration is critical to some navigation. In situations, such as training spatial knowledge of places that are rare, remote or dangerous [2], as well as geographical information visualization (GIS) and scientific data visualization [3][4], a navigator often needs to explore the space during wayfinding to understand spatial relationship among objects in virtual environments. Such exploration can help constructing of a comprehensive cognitive map about the space, which is important to other spatial activities, such as choosing an alternative route when the planned is unavailable.

J. Jacko (Ed.): Human-Computer Interaction, Part II, HCII 2007, LNCS 4551, pp. 700–709, 2007.

This paper presents an experimental study to compare three wayfinding aids to support exploration-oriented navigation with a known destination. The paper first reviews relevant research in Section 2, and proceeds to the brief introduction of wayfinding aids of our interest in Section 3. Then, Section 4 describes the experimental study and presents the results in Section 5. After discussion in Section 6, we conclude the paper with future work.

2 Related Work

Most designs to support virtual environment navigation are based on human navigation behaviors in the real world. Three levels of spatial knowledge in navigation have been identified [5] [6]: landmark, procedure, and survey knowledge. It has been found that spatial knowledge in virtual world is similar to that in real world [7] [8] [9] [10].

Massive research has been done to support wayfinding. Different wayfinding aids have been proposed for different activities. A tool that is effective and efficient in one situation may not be helpful in another. There is a need to understand what kinds of navigation activities that different wayfinding aids may support. Here, we classify these aids based on where a navigator wants to go and how to reach there. Thus, we can identify four kinds of navigation activities: reaching a known destination by exploration, reaching a known destination with a system tool, reaching an unknown destination with exploration, and reaching an unknown destination with a system tool. The last case is not meaningful, because without knowing the exact location of destination, systems tools would not work.

Often a navigator wants to get a known place quickly and does not need self-exploration. In such situations, system tools, like teleportation, can simply take the navigator from one place to another, which are preferable when efficiency is a concern. Nevertheless, the navigator is very passive in obtaining knowledge about the space between the origin and destination. However, in many situations, to have route knowledge and survey knowledge is indispensable.

If the destination is unknown and the navigator needs to explore the space to find the target, navigation aids usually focus on providing visual information about the environments. Visual information could be the overview of environments or significant landmarks [10]. An overview can be in 2D or 3D maps and both have been tested to be useful in assisting wayfinding activities in virtual world [11][12]. Map-based aids can also be used to show the user's real-time position. A You-Are-Here map [13] dynamically updates position and orientation which help to keep the users' spatial awareness. If a separated overview is not preferred when screen estate is limited, zooming techniques can be applied [14]. Google earth is an application of using zooming to provide users with different levels of bird-views. However, it still requires people to establish a connection between 2D satellite images with 3D real architectures and such transition is impossible for users to replicate.

Sometimes, even the system knows the target location, it is still necessary for a navigator to get the destination in person. For example, in spatial knowledge training, firefighters and military soldiers need to transfer their spatial knowledge into the real world and thus exploration becomes important to building a cognitive map about the space so that trainees can deal with unexpected events, such as changing to a new route. Moreover, large-scale collaboration asks [15][16] each user to explore the space within her own action domain in order to work with partners. Such exploration is often not naive search, because destination is usually known.

3 The Considered Wayfinding Aids

Because exploration-based navigation with a known target still possesses values, our research focuses on evaluating three tools that support such navigation activities. In this section, we introduce these tools briefly.

3.1 Human-System Collaboration (HSC)

Our HSC tool provides movement direction guidance to the navigator. Direction information is calculated automatically by the system based on the location of the target and the user. The system only presents direction information when necessary, such as at decision-making points like intersections. By following ‘simple interaction’ design criteria to limit the caused visual obstruction and extended application of query-based designs [17][18], our design is aimed at creating a collaborative relationship between human users and system tools.

Fig. 1 shows the interface design of the HSC aids. Direction information is presented at the window label. By guiding the user’s movement direction, such directional information may play an important role in helping the user mentally building a route.

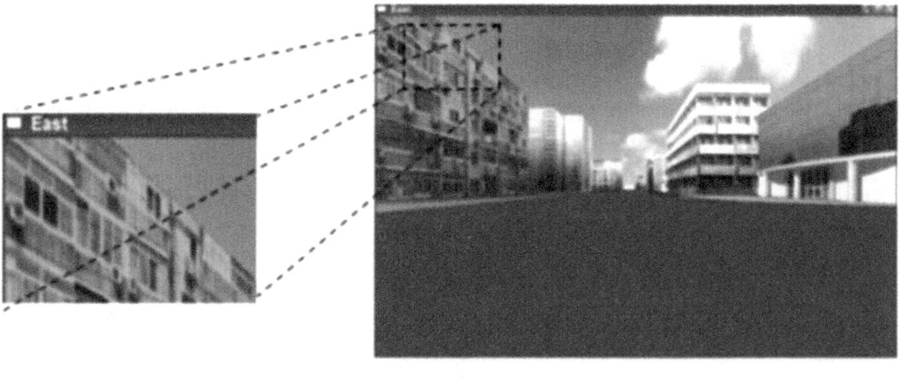

Fig. 1. HSC aid interface (Perspective lines added to show direction information, which tells the user that the target is on the east at that moment)

3.2 Animation Guide (AG)

An AG tool provides the user a dynamic view of a region through animation. Unlike an overview tool, which is static and is fixed at a particular scale, the AG tool shows how the user’s starting point and the destination are connected with a series of views at different scales. Inspired by the space-scale animation approach [16], our design of the AG tool first lifts the user’s viewpoint from the starting point and then lowers it

(a) Front view of animation guide trajectory (b) 3D view of AG trajectory

Fig. 2. AG aid interface

on the way towards the target (Fig. 2). This AG tool not only allows the user to acquire landmark knowledge, also provides survey knowledge at different scales.

3.3 View-in-View Map (VVM)

A VVM tool shows the target location and a user's current location, as seen in Fig 3. In the VVM, the target is represented as a dot, and the user as a triangle. This VVM tool can be regarded as an overview map without detailed information, like buildings and streets. Such information is omitted because we focus on the guidance of the relative direction to the target, rather than survey knowledge.

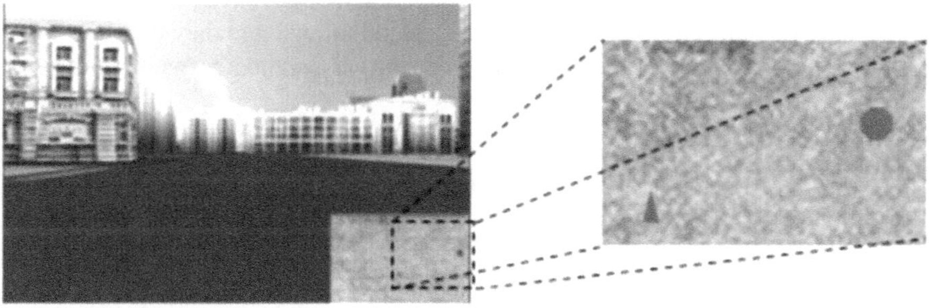

Fig. 3. VVM aid interface (Perspective lines added to show relative direction to the target)

4 Experimental Study

Our experimental study compared the effectiveness, efficiency and satisfaction of the above three tools in support of wayfinding.

4.1 Experiment Design and Hypotheses

The experiment had four treatments: the HSC tool, the AG tool, the VVM tool, and an environment without any wayfinding aid where only self-navigation (SN) is allowed to serve as a baseline condition.

Wayfinding task used in the experiment had three difficulty levels: easy, medium, and difficult. The difficulty of the task was measured by the minimum traveling distance and the number of turns. By 'minimum', we mean the least necessary travel distance along street to get the target. For example, Fig. 4 shows a wayfinding task, which starts from the *triangle* and ends at the *dot*. The line illustrates the shortest path, and the length of this path is the minimum travel distance to complete this task. Only one turn is involved in this task. The minimum travel distances of tasks at three levels are 200m, 400m, and 800m, respectively. The minimum turns are 0, 1, and 2, respectively.

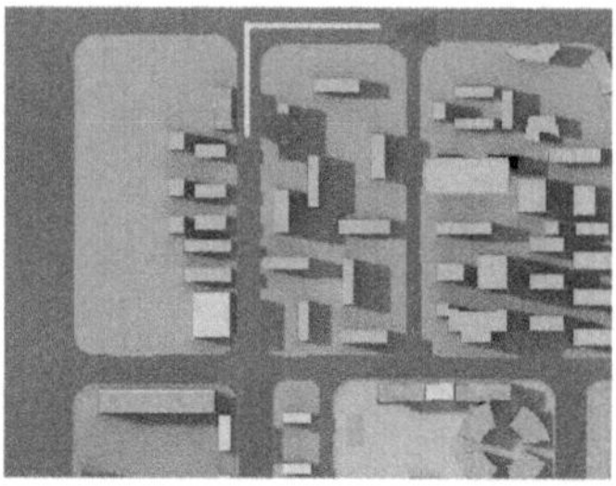

Fig. 4. Wayfinding tasks difficulty

The hypotheses of this research are:

- Wayfinding aids can improve subjects' performance in navigation, in terms of task completion time and error rate;
- The effectiveness, efficiency and satisfaction of different wayfinding aids vary because the different kinds of spatial knowledge they provide;
- The preference of these aids may depend on a subject's spatial ability.

4.2 Subjects

Twenty four (12 male and 12 female) college students participated in the study. Their ages were between 21 and 27, and the average was 23.

4.3 Apparatus

The experiment was performed on a workstation (Pentium 4 CPU 2.8GHz, 2.0 GB RAM). The machine had a NVIDIA Quadro FX1100 graphs card and a 19" ViewSonic Professional Series P95f monitor with a 1024 X 768 resolution. Subjects interacted with the virtual environment through a 3-button mouse and a standard keyboard. Keys needed in the experiment were labeled by tapes with action names.

4.4 Test Scenes

Four high fidelity different virtual city models were created. Each was used to test an aid interface or the non-aids situation, Self-Navigation (SN). The size of each model was 1500 X 1000 m^2. All models shared the common street layout and most of the background buildings. The only difference of four models was the target building type: one with three restaurants, one with three student association buildings, one with three banks and one with three bookstores. The target buildings in one city model did not appear in the others so that subjects would not meet the same target building in different models.

4.5 Procedure

Subjects were required to fill a background survey with detailed instructions upon arrival and then did two standard spatial ability tests, paperfolding test [19] and Purdue Visualization of Rotations Test (ROT) [20]. We allowed as much time as possible for subjects in the training practice so that they could get familiar with the virtual environment and also were able to act freely using each interface. Subjects entered to perform formal tasks until two pretests were successively passed. For each task in the formal experiment, subjects were asked to find a named target building in the virtual city by using one of the interfaces. Each subject had 5 minutes maximum to perform a task and were asked to stop if they cannot find the target when time is up. Each subject took all the twelve tasks and success rate and performance time for each task were recorded. The order of all four treatments was counter-balanced to reduce the carry-over effect. After the test, subjects were asked to fill in a satisfaction questionnaire to evaluate their perception of different wayfinding aids.

5 Results

Fig. 5 presents aggregate task completion performance across different interfaces in terms of success rate (SR) and performance time (PT). For every task, a failure is recorded when the subject could not find the target in a maximal time of 5 minutes and 5 minutes is recorded as performance time for this task in our analysis.

Chi-Square test shows the SR of non-aids situation (SN) is approximated to 50% ($\chi^2_{1,24} = 2.667$, $p = 0.102$). Chi-Square test found SRs of the three aids interfaces

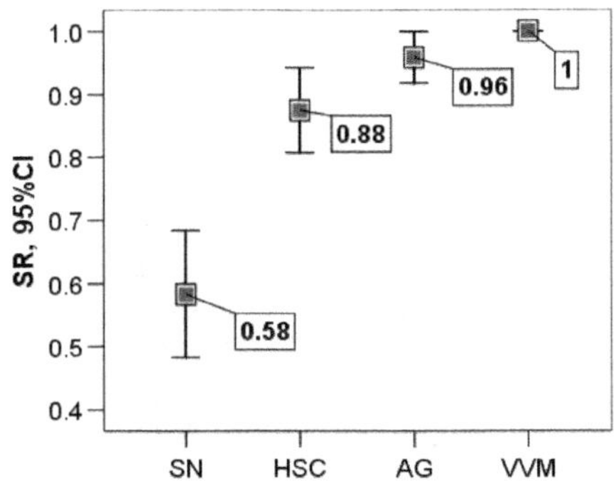

Fig. 5. Task Success Rate comparison

had better subject performance than SN (HSC: 88%, $\chi^2_{1,24} = 54.000$, $p < 0.001$; AG: 96%, $\chi^2_{1,24} = 80.667$, p = 0.001; and VVM: 100%). Cochran's Q tests shows significant difference among the three aids interfaces ($Q_{2,\ 72} = 16.17$, $p < 0.001$). However, McNemar Test shows no statistical differences of SR between AG and VVM.

A two-way within-subject ANOVA testing performance time (PT) suggests significant main effect of aids interface type ($F_{2,193} = 52.412$, $p < 0.001$) and task difficulty levels ($F_{2,19} = 53.524$, $p < 0.001$) as shown in Fig. 6. A significant interaction effect between aids interface type and task difficulty is found as well ($F_{4,193} = 14.256$, $p < 0.001$).

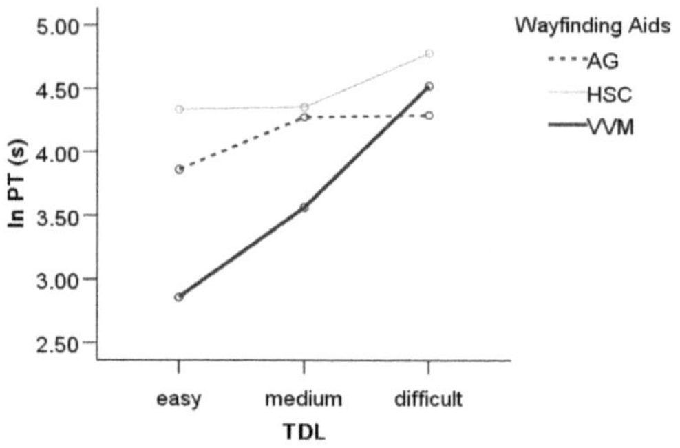

Fig. 6. Task completion comparison: Mean Performance Time in searching target (in logarithm) for different Task Difficuly Levels (TDL)

Fig. 7 illustrates the overall preference of the four interfaces. Frieman's test and Wilcoxon sign rank test showed significant overall satisfaction difference among the three interfaces ($\chi^2_2 = 35.03$, $p < 0.001$; for HSC and AG: $Z = -2.711$, $p = 0.017$).

In addition to these three primary measurements, other effects were also observed. Pearson tests show that performance time has a negative correlation with score in spatial ability tests ($r = -0.53$, $p = 0.008$). Among the three aids interfaces, a strong correlation between subjects' performance using HSC aids interface and spatial ability exists ($r = -0.80$, $p < 0.001$).

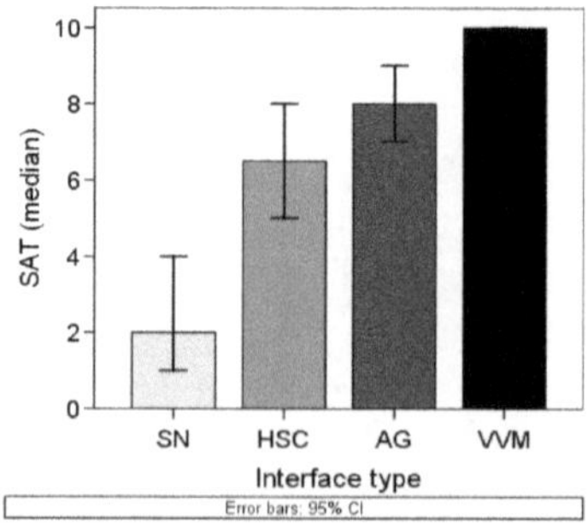

Fig. 7. Satisfaction ratings comparison

Fig. 8 shows the distribution of different spatial ability subjects' performance time using AG and HSC. Most subjects with normal spatial ability spent significant less time finding the target with the AG tool than with the HSC tool (58.3% of all 24 subjects), though subjects with low scores in spatial test still had to spend much time in both aids (25% of all 24 subjects). For those who had superior spatial ability watching animation was a time burden; they could search more efficiently by using the HSC aid interface (16.7% of all 24 subjects).

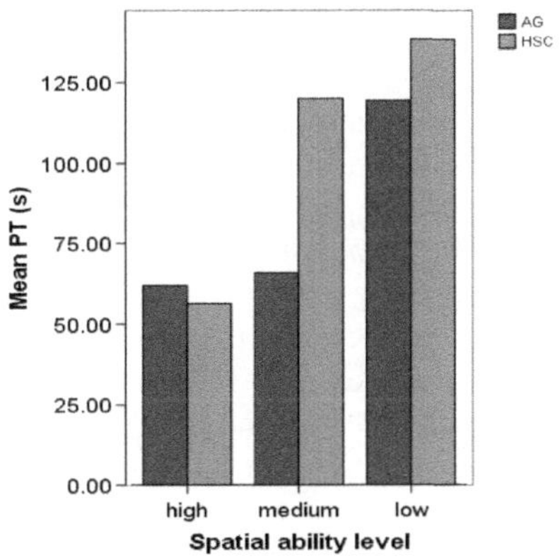

Fig. 8. Performance comparison between HSC and AG grouped by spatial ability

6 Discussion

Experiment results seem to indicate that wayfinding aids can greatly help users in exploration-based wayfinding in a virtual city. For the self-navigation condition, though 5 minutes is enough to navigate the whole city once without repeated route, subjects wandered aimlessly in the virtual city and could not relocate the buildings they have just visited. Without any wayfinding aid, the average success rate of finding the target is only approximate 50%, where possibility is almost like get head after throwing a coin. As Witmer et. al [7] has pointed out that spatial knowledge was developed more difficult in VE than real world.

Although different comments were addressed for the three aids, they all gained success rate above 85%. By providing additional information about the relationship between the navigator and target position, wayfinding aids help users to form their cognitive map and thus facilitate their decision making and executing process in wayfinding. As shown in Fig. 6, the performance time with the VVM tool was almost linear to the necessary travel distance which may indicate that subjects seldom wasted time in extra wandering. Animation provides guidance for users to know where the target is and how to get there before searching by themselves, but users still possess risk to forget what they have seen in the animation and such risk made subjects nervous in later searching. Using the HSC tool, users need spatial ability to translate exo-centric direction information into ego-centric movement direction. Most subjects found it difficult to use the HSC tool. This might be due to the mental burden to do the translation.

7 Conclusion and Future Work

This paper presented a study to evaluate three wayfinding aids in support of exploration-based navigation in virtual environments. The results of our subject study are encouraging. We found that the three aids are effective and usable. We also found that these tools may benefit people with different spatial capabilities in different ways. The View-in-View Map aid is favorable in general; the Human-System-Collaboration tool suits people with high spatial ability better; and the Animation Guided aid is a beneficial alternative to people with normal or low spatial capabilities.

Future research efforts should be extended into two directions. First, we like to deepen our study by looking at wayfinding processes, such as how these tools may affect the assessment of wayfinding activities and how people translate exo-centric wayfinding guidance into ego-centric movement action. Second, we are interested in studying the individual preferences of wayfinding aids, especially in spatial capability. This paper has shown that wayfinding aids could have different impacts on people with different spatial capabilities, but it is still unclear why this happened.

References

1. Mackinlay, J.D., Card, S.K., Robertson, G.G.: Rapid Controlled Movement through a Virtual 3D Workspace. Computer Graphics 24(4), 171–176 (1990)
2. Bliss, J.P.: The Effectiveness of Virtual Reality for Administering Spatial Navigation Traning to Firefighters. Presence: Teleoperators and Virtual Environments 6, 73–86 (1997)
3. Bartram, L.: Perceptual and Interpretative Properties of Motion for Information Visualization. In: The 1997 Workshop on New Paradigms in Information Visualization and Manipulation, Las Vegas, NV, USA (1997)
4. Bjork, S.: Hierarchical Flip Zooming: Enabling Parallel Exploration of Hierarchical Visualizations. In: Proceedings of the Workshop on Advanced Visual Interfaces, Palermo, Italy (2000)
5. Downs, R.M., Stea, D.: Image and Environment: Cognitive Mapping and Spatial Behavior. Aldine Publishing, Chicago (1973)
6. Siegel, A.W., Herman, J.F: The Development of Spatial Representations of Large-scale Environments. In: Reese, H.W. (ed.) Advances in Child Development and Behavior, vol. 10, pp. 9–55. Academic Publisher, New York (1975)
7. Witmer, B.G., Bailey, J.H., Knerr, B.W., Parsons, K.: Virtual spaces and real world places: transfer of route knowledge. International Journal of Human-Computer Studies 45(4), 413–428 (1996)
8. Ruddle, R.A., Payne, S.J., Jones, D.M.: Navigating Buildings in Desk-Top Virtual Environments: Experimental Investigations Using Extended Navigational Experience. Journal of Experimental Psychology 3(2), 143–159 (1997)
9. Goerger, S.R., Darken, R.P., Boyd, M.A., Gagnon, T.A.: Spatial Knowledge Acquisition from Maps and Virtual Environments in Complex Architectural Spaces. In: Proceedings of the 16th Applied Behavioral Sciences, Colorado Springs, CO, USA (1998)

10. May, M., Peruch, P., Savoyant, A.: Navigating in a Virtual Environment With Map-Acquired Knowledge: Encoding and Alignment Effects. Ecological Psychology 7(1), 21–36 (1995)
11. Darken, R.P., Sibert, J.L.: A Toolset for Navigation in Virtual Environments. In: Proceedings of ACM User Interface Software & Technology, New York, NY, USA (1993)
12. Chittaro, L., Venkataraman, S.: Navigation Aids for Multi-floor Virtual Buildings: a Comparative Evaluation of Two Approaches. In: the ACM Symposium on Virtual Reality Software and Technology, Limassol, Cyprus (2006)
13. Levinew, M., Marchon, I., Hanley, G.: The Placement and Mispalcement of you-are-here Maps. Environment and Behavior 16(2), 139–157 (1984)
14. Buering, T., Gerken, J., Reiterer, H.: Usability of Overview Supported Zooming on Small Screens with Regard to Individual Differences in Spatial. In: the working conference on Advanced visual interfaces, Venezia, Italy (2006)
15. Zhang, X., Furnas, G.W.: mCVEs:Using Cross-Scale Collaboration to Support User Interaction with Multiscale Structures. Presence: Teleoperators and Virtual Environments 14(1), 31–46 (2005)
16. Zhang, X.: Space-Scale Animation: Enhancing Cross-Scale Understanding of Multiscale Structures in Multiple Views. In: Proceedings of Coordinated and Multiple Views in Exploratory Visualization, London, UK (2005)
17. Ballegooij, A. v., Eliens, A.: Navigation by Query in Virtual Worlds. In: Proceedings of the sixth international conference on 3D Web technology, Paderbon, Germany (2001)
18. Chittaro, L., Burigat, S.: 3D Location-pointing as a Navigation Aid in Virtual Environments. In: Proceedings of AVI 2004: 7th International Conference on Advanced Visual Interfaces, Gallipoli, Italy (2004)
19. Ekstrom, R.B., French, J.W., Prince, L.A.: Kit of Reference Tests for Cognitive Factors. Educational Testing Services Princeton, NJ (1963)
20. Bodner, G.M., Guay, R.B.: The Purdue Visualization of Rotation (ROT) Test. The Chemical Educator 2(4), 1–17 (1997)

A 3D Sketching Interacting Tool for Physical Simulation Based on Web

Ziyi Zheng, Lingyun Sun, and Shouqian Sun

College of Computer Science, Zhejiang University,
Hangzhou 310027, PR China
{magicyang,sunly,ssq}@zju.edu.cn

Abstract. Sketching interface, as a user-friendly means for expression and communication, is not only an important medium for inputting 3D objects, but also a significant step of visualizing user's conceptual ideas. To bring early sketching interface to network utilities, the paper defines several rules that can create and edit 3D models. These gesture schemes support both regular and freeform modeling, and can be embedded in multi-user interface through network. A brief introduction about sketch-based collaboration in client-server architecture is proposed. A tool with this sketch interface and physical simulation functionalities is presented. The experimental results show that it can explore users' ideas in aiding 3D collaboration in network environment.

Keywords: Computer aided sketching, pen-based gesture interaction, sketch-based 3D modeling, physical simulation, 3D collaboration.

1 Introduction

Pen-based human-computer interaction is a natural way to express user's ideas. It is natural, easy, creative and efficient. It would be very helpful if such method can be used in 3D application. Unfortunately, most of current 3D application interfaces are based on WIMP structure, which offer little assistance to the visualization of user's conceptual ideas. Further more, a large variety of activities, such as gaming and teaching, need computer's aid in conceptual input and collaboration. Then current input interface becomes a serious bottle-neck.

Therefore, it is highly desirable to develop a tool that can interpret user's gestures into 3D commands. This tool should allow users to sketch freely, without modifying their drawing style, yet still be able to interpret users' drawings and allow them to interact with it in a friendly manner. Several pen-based sketch modeling methods have been achieved in some researches, such as [1] and [2]. Based on these achievements, we did some exploring work in collaboration field.

This paper proposes schemes for 3D model communication through gestures. The method is built upon freeform sketch and 2-stroke sketch, which are integrated into one system by intersection detection. To illustrate this method, first, a set of strokes, together with algorithms to process them are defined for natural input. Then a lock-based administrating method in client-server model is presented to eliminate

J. Jacko (Ed.): Human-Computer Interaction, Part II, HCII 2007, LNCS 4551, pp. 710–719, 2007.

multi-user's confliction. The 3D models' optimizations required for physical simulation are also proposed.

As a practical example, we developed a 3D sketching tool, named WebSketch, with web collaboration and physical simulation features. It interprets the sketch as users draw and can simulate the scene at any time during the layout designing process. This paper describes the tool, discusses the experimental result, and indicates its development trend.

2 Related Works

Other sketch-based design tools include the Electronic Cocktail Napkin [3] and SILK (Sketching Interfaces Like Krazy) [4]. The ASSIST [5] is with physical simulation functions. But all of these tools are 2-dimensional and can not deal with 3D model interaction.

Related works on creation of 3D object from 2D strokes may be divided into 2 areas: freeform creation and regular wire frame construction. Papers related to freeform sketch focus on directly using user's original natural strokes for modeling and deformation [6], [7]. Papers in the second group try to regulate the whole input into a standard form, and then reconstruction a model based on machine recognition [8], [9]. Our work explores some similar issues as theirs, but brings a platform which supports both regular modeling and freeform modeling. Since our system can deal with both curves and straight lines, it can handle gestures previous method can handle, as well as they can not.

Another paper [10] presented a method for representing the ambiguity and then applied a series of "mediators" to the possible recognitions. Our approach is different. In the first level, the two-step method avoids the ambiguities in advance. Then our system uses a fuzzy logic algorithm to reduce ambiguity in gesture regulation, which is first presented in [11].

3 User Interface in WebSketch

Users can draw with mouse and see their strokes appearing under their cursors as they draw them. They interact with the system through network which allows them to view other client's successful input results.

We describe a scene in which two users draw a ball falling from a hill. User "A" begins by drawing a crossed triangle in one stroke that constitutes the hill. As A is drawing, A sees stroke appearing on the screen under the pen in red. As A lifts the pen, the system waits for another dimension because the stroke is self-crossed.

A draws another line connected to the triangle. After that, the system replaces these two strokes with a 3D object to indicate its recognition (1st line in Fig. 1). A has created a hill with planar faces which closely match the strokes. A can change his view position in this 3D space. After finishing drawing the hill, A anchors it to the background by clicking it and drawing a line which stands for the horizontal plane. The first object is automatically placed on it, as seen by the other user "B".

Then B draws a cylinder. Using a circle to indicate the planar face, B draws the second straight line to indicate the other dimension. A cylinder with the same length appears under the pen (2nd line in Fig. 1). A draws a ball in the similar manner by clicking inside a circle (1st line in Fig. 1).

After these operations, A wants to try something different. A describes an object by drawing an uncrossed line with arbitrary shape. The system constructs a 3D model according to the outline, which looks like a dumbbell (Fig. 2).

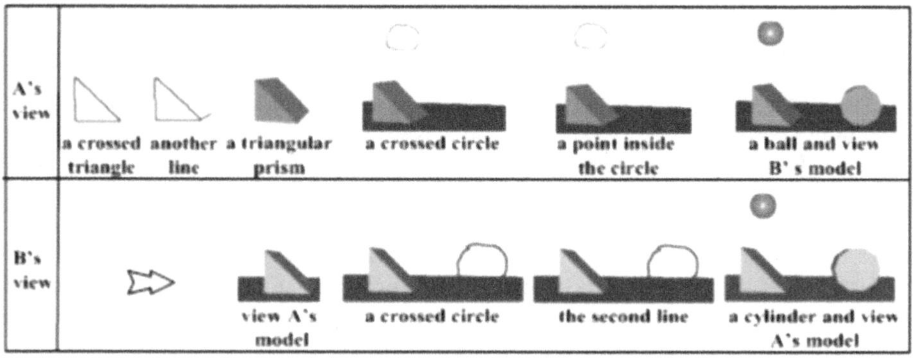

Fig. 1. The multi-user interface for creating model

At this time the ball is not floating vertically above the hill. To move it, one of users left-clicks it with his mouse; the ball turns high-bright to indicate it has been selected. The user moves it by dragging it until it rests above the hill. As the user drags his mouse, the whole object moves with it.

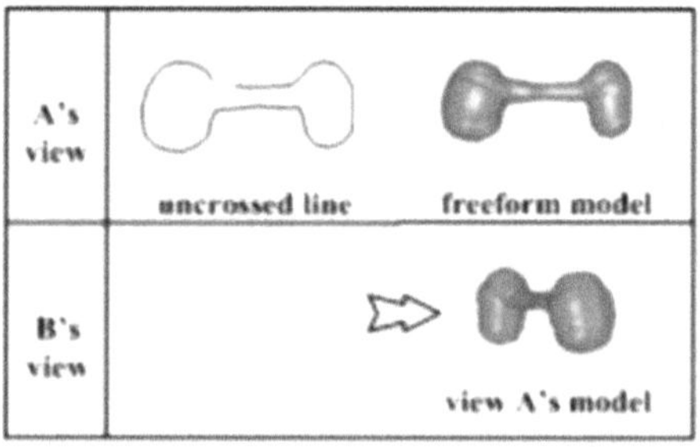

Fig. 2. Uncrossed stroke creates freeform object, which looks like a dumbbell

They continue to draw other pieces of the drawing. A draws a freeform object which looks like a capsicum. Then A wants to have another same object. To copy it, A first left-clicks it then draws a "C"-shaped line to notify the system for copying. Then A drags a new identical object from the original object. Unfortunately, B doesn't like such capsicum-shaped object and wants to delete it. B left-clicks it, and the model turns high-bright. Then B draws a crossed line. It has been deleted. A and B can not successfully select the object which is under modification by the other user (Fig. 3).

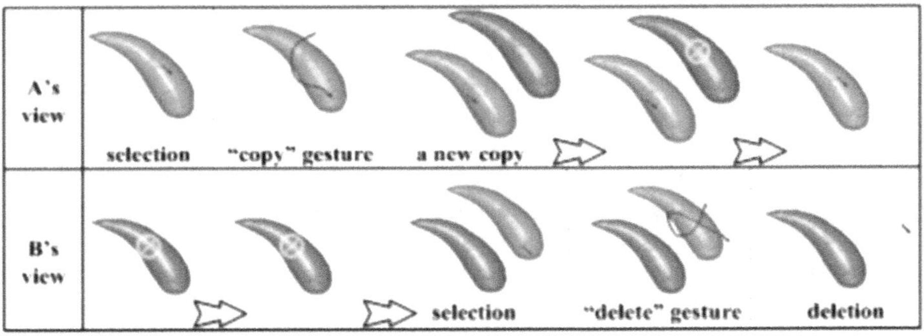

Fig. 3. The multi-user interface for editing model

Finally, when finishing designing of the scene (or at any time during the designing process), one of the user taps the "Run" button to observe a physical simulation of these objects: A new window appears, showing the ball falls to the hill and then rolls down the hill, collides with the cylinder, and the cylinder rolls and collides with the dumbbell-shaped object (Fig. 4). The original drawing remains unchanged, allowing for a convenient sketch-modify-simulate loop.

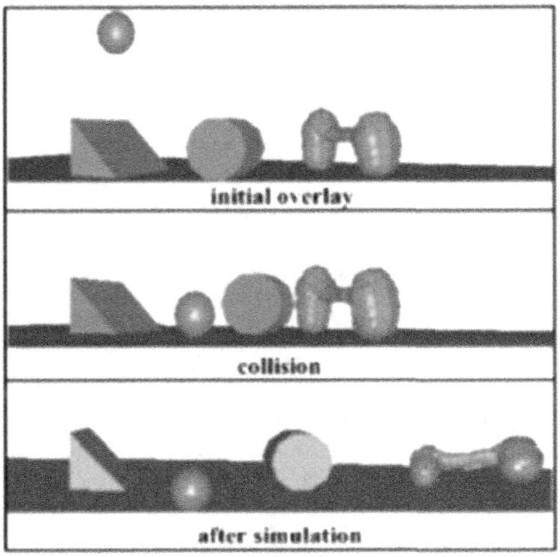

Fig. 4. Physics simulation effect

4 Approach

4.1 Gesture Definition and Recognition Process

The first step to recognize a user's sketch is identifying the meaning of his "pen's gesture". To identify these patterns without forcing the user to significantly change his drawing style, WebSketch is based on the viewpoint that simple rule is the best.

In this pen-based sketching process, a stroke may represent a part of an object as well as an editing command. There is a great deal of confliction between modeling and editing. For example, considering a C-shape line, is it a freeform sketch for a small ball or a gesture of "copy"? The recognition process should choose the right representation from several similar strokes.

Furthermore, although objects with regular shape perform well in both physical and in graphic computing, only ideal models limit the simulation to a large extent. To express complex model according to the user's will, the system has freeform modeling function. Thus, another work is to define a rule that can eliminate the ambiguity while the two types of modeling are being integrated. In consideration of these requirements, the overall gesture definition is illustrated below (Fig. 5).

Fig. 5. Gesture definition and recognition flow

To avoid ambiguity, WebSketch uses a two-step method to construct new models. The first step is the selecting detection. If the user points to one of the object, the system will enter into editing mode. Two main editing gestures are "copy" and "delete".

Similar to early recognition efforts like [3], our scheme looks at pen path through a 3x3 grid according to gesture size. The coordination sequence can be converted to matrix's position sequence. Finally, the position sequence can be matched with defined gesture. For example, the copy sequence is 3214789. One gesture can have more than one position sequences, such as "delete".

If no object is selected in the first step, then system will enter into the construction state. WebSketch then recognizes the inputs according to the existence of crossing point. So it can create object of regular or arbitrary shape respectively.

One category is the uncrossed line. Based on this 2D Silhouette, the system constructs a 3D object automatically. The constructing algorithm is referred as freeform sketch, illustrated in [7]. The other category is the crossed input. If there is a crossing point in the input line, system requires an additional line to create an object with regular shape and planar faces. Fig. 6 illustrates the 2-stroke construction gestures. The original circle is refined according to fuzzy logic algorithm. The system performs hull calculation, characteristic value computation and fuzzy decision. The method to refine the input stroke is presented by Manueal J Fonseca [11].

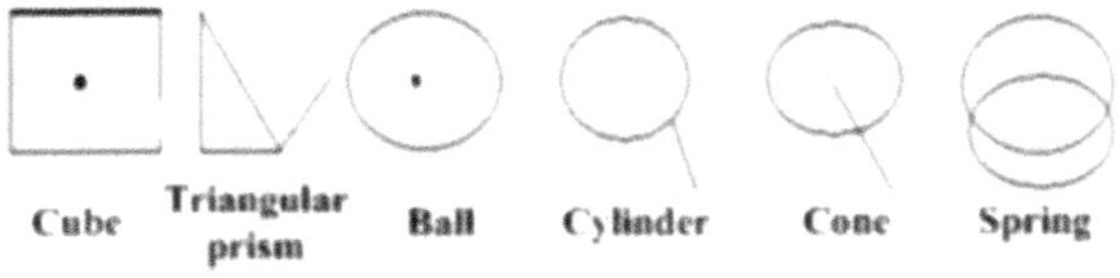

Fig. 6. Predefined two-stroke gestures

4.2 3D Modeling

As defined above, the system divides its construction into two classes. Regular modeling (using 2-stroke construction gestures) is relative simple. First, the system constructs a refined silhouette, and then extends the object according to the second stroke. The system recognizes the input as user's view by default.

Freeform modeling is much more complicated than regular modeling. The basic algorithm for freeform sketch is presented in reference [7]. In that paper, Takeo Igarashi created this algorithm and developed a system called Teddy. Teddy can interpret the user's uncrossed stoke, and finally create a 3D solid model. Our system performs constrained Delaunay triangulation, pruning insignificant branches, subdividing the sleeve triangles and junction as Teddy.

However, the objects created by Teddy [7] algorithm are not always convex and smooth, even not qualified for physical simulation. As a result, WebSketch uses optimized method which is more robust and more effective than the original one.

While calculating the spine's height, the system traverses the spine, and then uses the average value to make it smoother. While calculating the height of the spine, it uses the current height and two neighbor points' height to create the local average value. The physical simulation will be more robust after this additional optimization. This optimization is useful to some extent. More powerful modification is the use of subdivision. This algorithm can convert uneven surface to a relative smooth one.

Furthermore, the original implement of Teddy is a prototype without surface, which has no information of the inner or outer side of the model. But physical collision detection needs to know the specific information of the surface direction. WebSketch calculates the surface normally while constructing the mesh. Every surface triangle has a normal vector pointing away from the spine, so that the system can compute the volume of the object and implement collision detection.

4.3 3D Collaboration

The system adopts the thin-sever-strong-client structure. This architecture can effectively fulfill the requirement of real-time interactive operations since most of the geometric computing for modeling and modification is carried out in the clients locally.

A significant problem for the 3D collaboration systems is that communication efficiencies are still quite far from satisfactory when large-size models are designed collaboratively. To accelerate communication, different from using progressive mesh method, the system chooses the smallest information unit in collaboration. The smallest information unit is the user's viewpoint and stroke input. Thus, its communication cost is much less than mesh coordinates and still complete for reconstruction. Since other clients share the same method to interpret strokes, they can make an identical copy in their local system.

WebSketch is designed to support fine-function collaboration. To handle the multi-user's editing confliction, it assigns every object a unique lock. The method is illustrated in Fig. 7. First, a client notifies the server after successfully creating a model. Then the server registers an instance in lock pool, return a new ID to the client who creates it, and broadcasts the ID and reconstruction information to other users.

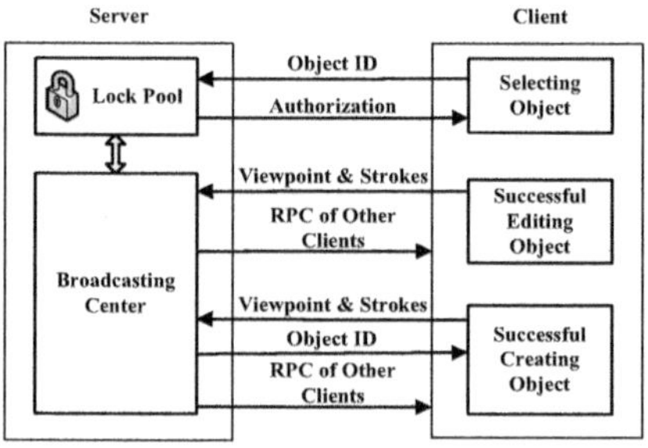

Fig. 7. Communications between a server and a group of clients

Clients must use object ID to reference the model in selection. If the object is currently under modification of one client, the server will reject selection requests from others. For example, in Fig. 3, while A is copying a model, B can not select it successfully. The same situation occurs to A when B deletes a model.

4.4 Physical Optimization

The physics engine contains some basic environment parameters such as gravity, restitution, which are necessary to simulate the real world. These parameters are predetermined to all the objects, except spring, which has a different set of properties.

After the setting of environmental parameters, physics engine rebuilds a model for every 3D graphic object. Then, the system makes a careful decision about the level of optimization. Physics engine can use several rigid models to dynamically detect the collisions between two objects. Sphere, Box and Capsule are three basic models to construct objects. However, they are unable to represent more complex object models as we see in the real world. But mesh structure is too complex for real-time collision-detection. Furthermore, it requires tremendous time to calculate the torque and rotation properties.

An excellent solution is PMap[12]. In WebSketch, mesh-mesh collision is detected by PMap, which voxelizes meshes so that inside-outside queries become faster and more efficient. Though still time-consuming in the initialization before start, PMap performs well after 3D real-time simulation begins.

4.5 System Frameworks

The system is divided into 4 layers. They are input layer, recognition layer, geometry layer and physical layer respectively. The physical layer directly interacts with render system. In a predefined time interval, the render system flushes the new information from the physics engine. The overall structure is illustrated in Fig. 8.

5 Result and User Evaluation

In the following experiment, there are 800 MHz Pentium III PCs with 16M Graphic Card running on a 100Mbps LAN. 9 volunteers took part in the experiment. 5 of the subjects had a background in computer science; 4 were major in industrial design. Sessions with the volunteers lasted 30 minutes. We first showed them the diagrams in Fig. 1&2&3 and told them they would be asked to draw a scene together, once on 3D system they like to use and once using our system. They were told not to worry about replicating the details exactly. After they drew the figures on other system, we gave them a 5 minute introduction to WebSktech that included drawing simple parts. We also told them how to select, move and delete objects. We then asked them to use WebSketch simultaneously to draw the same systems they had drawn before. Then every user is required to modify one of other users' models according to his suggestion. After they were done sketching we asked them a series of questions. The first two questions measure the perceived number of mistakes the system made and how tolerant users were of these mistakes; the last three are open ended.

1. How often did you feel the system got the correct interpretation for your strokes?
2. When the system misinterpreted your stroke and how reasonable was its misinterpretation?
3. How easy was it to modify the drawing?
4. How often did you feel that you knew other user's idea?
5. Compare using this system to using a WIMP 3D collaborative interface.

The first observation was that learning the system was easy. All volunteers were able to successfully draw all of the systems in Fig. 1&2&6. While they had to pay attention to the intersection rule, for the most part they were either able to use their natural drawing styles or quickly learn the small changes required to work successfully. The three examples in Fig. 1&2&6 took the volunteers about 9 minutes total to sketch on the system. And they interacted with each other about 20 minutes.

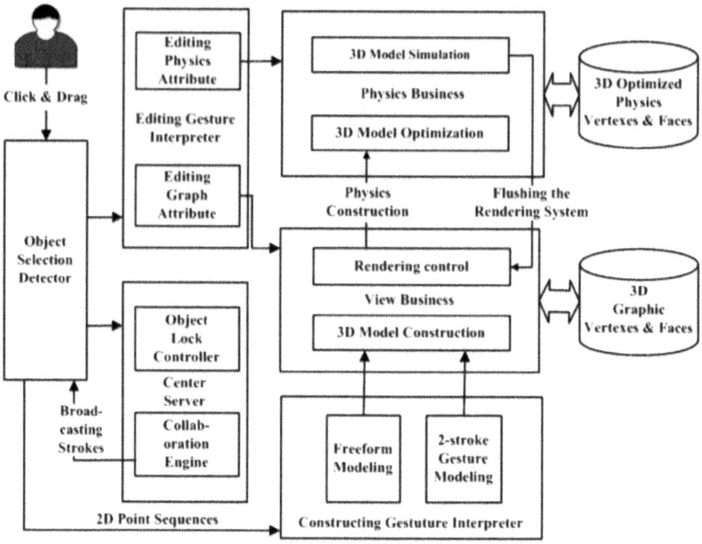

Fig. 8. Overall structure of the WebSktech

In response to question 1, almost all subjects reported that the system got the correct interpretation of their strokes between 75 and 85 percent of the time. Most recognition errors were intersection errors. It is necessary to inform subjects that the system can not handle designs with precision data. Even though the icon is fitted to user's stroke as closely as possible, the match is never exact, so the stroke appears to "jump" a little when it is replaced. This behavior bothered some people because they felt that they no longer had total control of the strokes they were drawing.

As for question 5, most subjects said that this tool could express the 3D part needed for conceptual-level communication. While some of them met problems in creating complex and fine object, they general agreed that this real-time collaboration was a fast tool to convey conceptual ideas.

People were quite pleased with the power that the system brought to the drawing process in the realm of industrial engineering. Although 3 subjects thought that the mesh-mesh collision requested a long preprocessing time before simulation, all subjects found the effect of real-time simulation was quite appealing.

6 Conclusion and Future Work

This system is an attempt to integrate the 3D sketch and remote collaboration. We have been working to improve low-level recognition algorithms to remove ambiguity.

We are exploring sketch interface further in two levels. In sketch level, more effort is need to integrate simple gestures for complex models, colors and textures. In application level, with physical engine, the platform can be used to support future CAD, computer animation, remote-education, digital conference and so on.

References

1. Varley, P.: Automatic Creation of Boundary-Representation Models from Single Line Drawings. Ph.D. Thesis, Cardiff University (2003)
2. Igarashi, T.: 3D Graphics for Everyday Communication. In: Proceedings of SICE Annual Conference 2004, Sapporo, pp. 1702–1704 (2004)
3. Gross, M.D.: The Electronic Cocktail Napkin-A Computational Environment for Working with Design Diagrams. Design Studies, vol. 17, pp. 53–69
4. Landay, J.A, Myers, B.A.: Sketching Interfaces: Toward More Human Interface Design. IEEE Computer 34(3), 56–64 (2001)
5. Christine, A.J., Randall, D.: Preserving the freedom of paper in a computer-based sketch tool. In: Proceedings of Human Computer Interaction International, New Orleans, Louisiana, pp. 687–691 (2001)
6. Igarashi, T.: Freeform User Interfaces for Graphical Computing. In: Proceedings of 3rd International Symposium on Smart Graphics, pp. 39–48 (2003)
7. Igarashi, T., Matsuoka, S., Tanaka, H., Teddy: A Sketching Interface for 3D Freeform Design. In: Proceedings of ACM SIGGRAPH Los Angels pp. 409–416 (1999)
8. Cao, L., Liu, J., Tang, X.: 3D Object Reconstruction from a Single 2D Line Drawing without Hidden Lines. In: Proceedings of ICCV, vol. 1, pp. 272–277 (2005)
9. Liu, J., Lee, Y.T, Cham, W.K.: Identifying faces in a 2D line drawing representing a manifold object. IEEE Transactions on Pattern Analysis and Machine Intelligence, vol. 24(12) pp. 1579–1593 (2002)
10. Mankoff, J., Hudson, S E, Abowd, G D.: Providing integrated toolkit-level support for ambiguity in recognition-based interfaces. In: Proc. CHI'00 Human Factors in Computing Systems, Hague, Netherlands, pp. 368–375. ACM, New York (April 1-6, 2000)
11. Fonseca, M.J, Pimentel, C., Jorge, J.A: Cali-an online scribble recognizer for calligraphic interfaces. In: AAAI Spring Symposium on Sketch Understanding, AAAI Technical Report SS-02-08, Stanford University, pp. 51–58. AAAI Press, Stanford, California, USA (2002)
12. NovodeX, A., NovodeX Physics, S.D.K.: Documentation (August 2004) http://mickyoun.free.fr/ ogre/ novodex/sdk%20traduit/PhysicsSdK.pdf

Visual and Auditory Information Specifying an Impending Collision of an Approaching Object

Liu Zhou[1], Jingjiang Yan[1], Qiang Liu[1], Hong Li[1], Chaoxiang Xie[1], Yinghua Wang[1], Jennifer L. Campos[2], and Hong-jin Sun[2]

[1] School of Psychology, Southwest University, China
[2] Department of Psychology, McMaster University, Canada

Abstract. Information about the impending collision of an approaching object can be specified by visual and auditory means. We examined the discrimination thresholds for vision, audition, and vision/audition combined, in the processing of time-to-collision (TTC) of an approaching object. The stimulus consisted of a computer simulated car approaching on a flat ground towards the participants which disappeared at a certain point before collision. After the presentation of two approaching movements in succession, participants pressed a button to indicate which of the two movements would result in the car colliding with the viewpoint sooner from the moment it disappeared. The results demonstrated that most participants were sensitive to TTC information provided by a visual source, but not when provided by an auditory source. That said, auditory information provided effective static distance information. When both sources of information were combined, participants used the most accurate source of information to make their judgments.

Keywords: visual, auditory, multisensory integration, time-to-collision, motion-in-depth, looming.

1 Introduction

Humans constantly experience and react to movements in their environment. When an object looms towards an observer, the object movement typically elicits an escape or avoidance response. The sensory information specifying such an impending collision can come from both visual and auditory sources via several cues in each sensory modality.

Visually, as an object looms towards an observer, the retinal image of the object expands almost exponentially as the object approaches the eye. Using an ecological framework, Lee [1] proposed that the timing of behavioural responses to approaching objects could be controlled by the optical variable τ, which is equal to the inverse of the relative rate of expansion of the object's retinal image θ (Equation 1, where t is the time). It was demonstrated mathematically that the optical variable τ could specify time-to-collision (TTC); that is the time that will elapse before the object will collide with the observer's eye.

$$\tau = \theta/(d\theta/dt) \ . \qquad (1)$$

The strongest support for the use of the optical variable τ comes from work describing the neural mechanisms by which the brain processes information about

J. Jacko (Ed.): Human-Computer Interaction, Part II, HCII 2007, LNCS 4551, pp. 720–729, 2007.

impending collisions. We have previously reported a group of neurons in the brain that selectively respond to looming objects approaching on a collision course towards the eye [2, 3, 4]. More importantly we identified a type of looming-sensitive neuron that signals the inverse of the *relative* rate of expansion (τ).

There has been great interest in behavioural studies examining scenarios involving potential collisions between a participant and objects in their environment [5]. If τ is indeed used, then information about neither distance nor speed is required. The probable use of the τ strategy for computing TTC information has received both support and criticism [5, 6]. With the exception of a few attempts [7, 8], TTC information has not been manipulated independently of other movement variables such as distance. Whether humans use a dynamic variable such as τ or static distance cues for controlling collision avoidance remains to be tested empirically. In fact, some studies have demonstrated alternative results in that an observer actually used information about the distance of approaching objects to guide their responses [9, 10].

Apart from visual information, auditory information can also inform the observer about an impending collision. It has been proposed that auditory information from a sound-emitting object can provide information about distance and TTC [11, 12, 13, 14]. Changes in loudness caused by changes in distance from a sound source may provide important information about TTC in a similar fashion that the changes in retinal image size provide information about τ in the visual modality [14].

While the integration of visual and auditory spatial information related to static objects has been well investigated, very few studies have directly compared the processing of movement information from these two sources or specifically assessed how they are integrated. In the current study, we examined humans' perceptual ability to process information about an impending collision by comparing relative TTC judgments (discrimination) of an approaching object that is represented by visual, auditory, and audiovisual combined modalities. Although the task required relative TTC judgments, the possibility of participants using distance information to perform the task was also examined. Moreover, which of the sensory input from both visual and auditory modalities (such as retinal image size, sound intensity, etc.) is more heavily relied on for performing the task was also investigated.

2 Methods

Nine paid undergraduate students (4 females and 5 males) from Southwest University of China participated in this experiment. All participants had normal or corrected-to-normal vision and normal hearing, and were naive to the purposes of the experiment.

The stimulus was created using Virtools 3.0, an authoring software used to develop interactive 3D content. Through this software participants were provided with realistic simulations of visual and auditory information associated with a real, approaching object. The visual scene consisted of an approaching car (2m in width and 1.5m in height) moving at a constant speed on a flat ground surface covered with random texture. The visual information was presented on an LCD projection screen (1.38m x 1.02m) and was viewed binocularly (but not in stereo) by the participants who sat in a fixed position 3m away. The projection screen subtended a visual angle of 26 degrees. The auditory information about the approaching car was provided to both ears through stereo headphones. The sound of a running vehicle engine, which increased in intensity as the car approached, was controlled and presented through software. This auditory information was presented in isolation or in synchrony with the visual information.

The approaching car was visible/audible for a period of time then disappeared (and/or became silent) well before the point of collision. The onset of disappearance marked the point when participants were asked to note the TTC of the car assuming that it continued to move towards the viewpoint at a constant speed. The manipulation of TTC was achieved through the duration of the second part (invisible) of the movement. The duration of the first part and thus the total duration of the car's movement were also varied (1500–2500 ms) and participants were informed of such variation, to avoid their using movement history as a way to judge the TTC. One second before the onset of the disappearance, an auditory tone was presented briefly to prepare the participants to anticipate the moment of the disappearance. After experiencing two approaching movements of the same car in succession, participants used a button press to indicate which movement (the first or second) would result in the car arriving sooner.

The two approaching movements were comprised of a reference movement and a comparison movement, with the order of the two randomized. The TTC and the approaching speed of the reference stimulus were held constant at 2500ms and 20m/s respectively. The TTC of the comparison stimuli was varied according to the method of constant stimuli and consisted of 7 levels (700ms, 1300ms, 1900ms, 2500ms, 3100ms, 3700ms and 4300ms). The movement speed of the comparison stimuli consisted of 5 levels (8.9m/s, 13.3m/s, 20m/s, 30m/s and 45m/s). The sensory information about the impending collision was presented in three conditions: visual only, auditory only and audiovisual combined, with the reference and comparison stimuli always presented in the same sensory modality. All possible combinations of different levels of TTC, speed, and modality were tested in a within-subject, completely randomized factorial design. Each of the 35 stimulus configurations (7 TTCs and 5 speeds) was presented via each of the 3 sensory conditions with 10 repetitions each. All 1050 trials were presented to each participant (N=9) in a random order.

3 Results

We obtained a series of psychometric functions (plotted based on a cumulative normal distribution) which illustrates the relation between the proportion of responses for "comparison stimulus arrives later" (i.e., TTC longer) against the TTC values for the comparison stimulus. Figure 1A illustrates the psychometric function for a typical participant. When evaluating participants' ability to discriminate between two TTCs, the Just Noticeable Difference (JND), was calculated by subtracting the TTC required to achieve 75% accuracy, from that required to achieve 25% accuracy (as determined by the best-fit function) and dividing this value by two. The JND represents the degree to which the comparison TTC must differ from the reference TTC in order for a participant to correctly discriminate the two. In addition, the Point of Subjective Equivalence (PSE) is defined as the point at which the comparison TTC was judged to be longer 50% of the time.

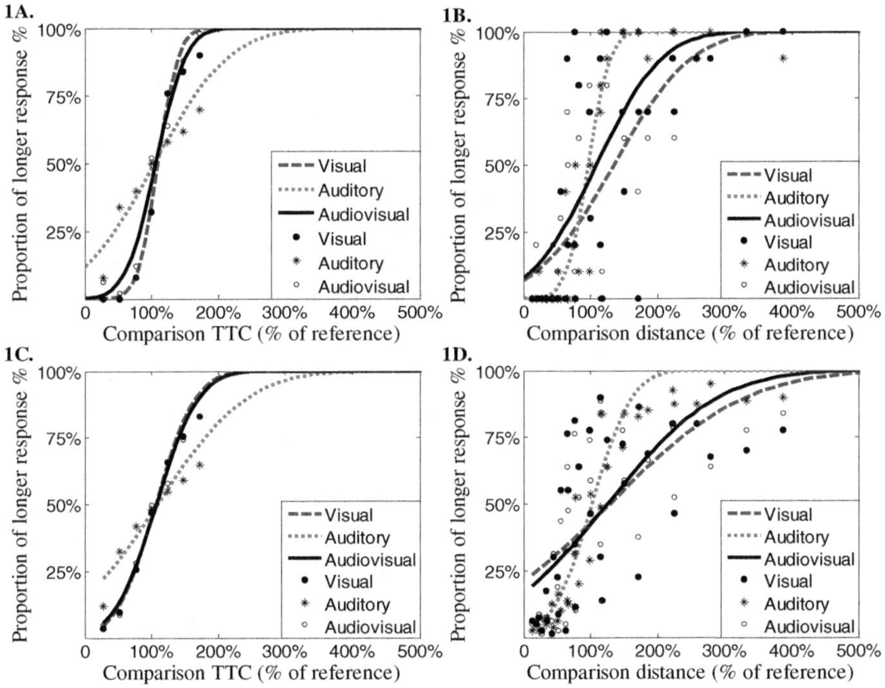

Fig. 1. Psychometric functions for one typical participant (1A and 1B) and a combined function for 8 out of 9 participants (1C and 1D), when plotting the probability of responses for "comparison stimulus arrives later" against the TTC value for the typical participant (1A) and the group (1C) and against the distance value for the typical participant (1B) and the group (1D). Note that for the sake of comparison, both TTC and distance in the horizontal axis are expressed in relative terms as a percentage of the reference stimulus.

It is evident from Figure 1A that when either visual cues or audiovisual cues were presented, the participant was better at judging the difference in TTC than when auditory cues were presented alone. This result demonstrates a clear visual advantage in the TTC judgment.

In order to explore the possibility of participants using distance information to perform the task, we also plotted another series of psychometric functions using the same variable on the vertical axis ("comparison stimulus arrives later"), but plotting *distance* on the horizontal access (rather than TTC). This distance measure specifically refers to the distance of the car at the moment when the stimulus disappeared. The purpose of such an analysis was to explore the possibility that participants used other variables available from the stimulus to make their judgments, even though the instructions explicitly stated that participants were to judge TTC. As shown in Figure 1B, the same participant shown in Figure 1A was more sensitive to the distance information in the auditory condition than that in the visual condition, suggesting that the participant was likely using a distance variable (any variables directly proportional to distance)_to perform the TTC task in the auditory condition.

Eight out of 9 participants showed a similar pattern of responding. The response functions of their combined performance are plotted in Figure 1C and 1D for TTC and distance respectively. The results show that these 8 participants were sensitive to the differences in TTC provided by vision, with a discrimination threshold of 794ms (32% of the TTC for the reference stimulus), however the TTC provided by auditory cues was not as effective, with a discrimination threshold of 1780ms (71%). Moreover, for these 8 of the 9 participants, when plotting TTC on the horizontal axis, the performance for the audiovisual condition (with a discrimination threshold of 846ms or 34%) was almost identical to the visual only condition. It is possible that when both sources of information were combined, participants used the most accurate source of information to make the judgment.

When we examined the possibility of participants using distance information, a reversed pattern was observed. These 8 participants were sensitive to the distance information, with a threshold of only 15.7m (31% of the distance in reference stimulus) when auditory information was presented alone, but with a much higher threshold (54 m, or 108% of distance in reference stimulus) for the visual condition.

Although all 9 participants had normal or corrected-to-normal vision and good hearing, 8 of them showed a visual dominance for TTC judgments and likely used distance information to perform the auditory TTC task. Interestingly, the remaining participant (1/9) showed a differential pattern of performance between visual and auditory processing, in that the auditory TTC judgment (and also the TTC through combined sources) was better than the visual TTC judgment (see Figure 2). This was evident when the psychometric functions are plotted both against TTC and against distance as shown in Figure 2A and 2B.

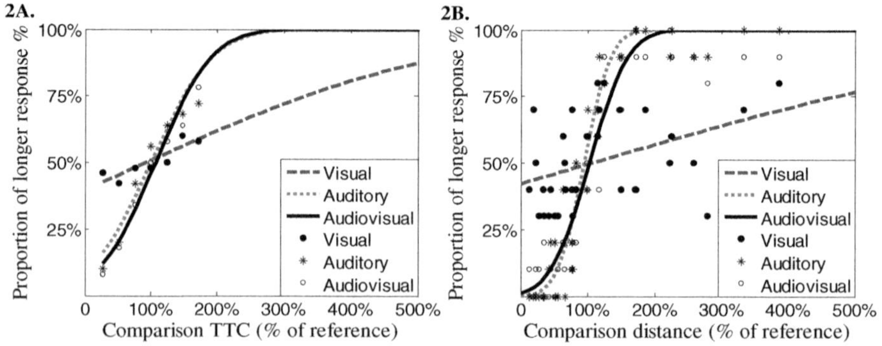

Fig. 2. The psychometric functions for Participant 4 who showed a differential pattern of sensory advantage from the other 8 participants when plotting the probability of responses for "comparison stimulus arrives later" against TTC (2A) and against distance (2B)

Tables 1 and 2 illustrate the threshold values for all participants when plotting the probability of responses for "comparison stimulus arrives later" against the TTC values and distance values respectively. Note that for Participant 4, the sensitivity for auditory and audio-visual conditions were better than for the visual alone condition.

Table 1. PSE and JND for all participants when plotting the probability of responses for "comparison stimulus arrives later" against the TTC value

Participant No.	Visual PSE	Visual JND	Auditory PSE	Auditory JND	Audiovisual PSE	Audiovisual JND
1	1.03	0.61	0.91	0.82	1.14	1.50
2	1.07	0.15	1.09	0.54	1.07	0.18
3	1.04	0.28	1.26	0.74	1.09	0.31
4	0.87	2.54	1.00	0.50	1.07	0.45
5	1.10	0.17	1.04	0.60	1.07	0.24
6	1.15	0.28	1.58	1.36	1.20	0.31
7	1.14	0.47	1.00	0.75	1.12	0.48
8	1.00	0.25	1.08	0.58	1.00	0.28
9	1.02	0.42	0.99	0.66	1.07	0.52

Table 2. PSE and JND for all the participants when plotting the probability of responses for "comparison stimulus arrives later" against the distance value

Participant No.	Visual PSE	Visual JND	Auditory PSE	Auditory JND	Audiovisual PSE	Audiovisual JND
1	0.93	4.58	0.96	0.49	0.50	3.18
2	1.18	0.47	1.00	0.14	1.03	0.32
3	1.33	1.80	1.23	0.50	1.48	1.72
4	1.06	3.65	0.94	0.21	1.03	0.30
5	1.35	0.61	1.00	0.17	1.09	0.52
6	1.64	1.44	1.71	1.49	1.64	1.33
7	2.26	4.80	1.00	0.25	1.36	1.01
8	1.02	0.45	1.03	0.17	0.96	0.28
9	0.92	0.15	0.94	0.30	0.99	0.25

Table 3. Sensitivity to different sensory inputs revealed in the TTC task (N=8)

Information related to impending collision	Visual PSE	Visual JND	Auditory PSE	Auditory JND	Audiovisual PSE	Audiovisual JND
TTC	1.06	0.32	1.09	0.71	1.07	0.34
Distance	1.29	1.08	1.02	0.31	1.26	0.87
Vis Angle θ	1.02	0.88	–	–	1.00	0.77
$d\theta/dt$	1.13	0.93	–	–	1.07	0.80
Intensity I	–	–	1.13	0.60	1.29	1.88
dI/dt	–	–	1.18	0.87	1.45	1.82

As a way of assessing the contributions of individual sensory inputs to participants' judgments, we plotted the probability of responses for "comparison stimulus arrives later" against four variables in addition to TTC and distance, including: visual angle

(θ), the time-dependent derivative of the rate of the image's expansion ($d\theta/dt$), sound intensity (I) and the time-dependent derivative of the change in sound intensity over time (dI/dt). For each source of information the PSE and JND value from the combined psychometrical function of the 8 participants' data showing similar response patterns are listed in Table 3. As in Figures 1 and 2, in order to compare the contributions of different sensory inputs, the value of the comparison stimuli were expressed in relative terms (all divided by the corresponding value of the reference stimulus).

The results confirm that participants were more sensitive to TTC than to any other component in the visual condition, while participants were more sensitive to distance than any other component in the auditory condition. Note that the instructions to the participants were to discriminate between the TTC of the two stimuli, yet for the auditory condition participants were apparently using distance (or anything directly proportional to distance) to perform the discrimination task. This meant that the participants were thus ignoring the instruction and the stimulus manipulation that the car was moving at different speeds in different trials and consequently the TTCs would be different, even for the same distance. It is thus reasonable to infer that the poor performance for the auditory TTC judgments to large extent is not because of the inherent noise in the system, rather it reflects a reliance on the wrong type of information (distance or distance related sensory inputs).

To analyze the cost of using distance information for the TTC task, we examine how the movement speed affected the sensitivity of TTC judgments for different sensory modalities. Table 4 illustrates that for the different levels of movement speed, the combined PSE and JND values for the 8 participants show a similar response pattern. The results indicate that the PSE and JND values for TTC discrimination in visual and audiovisual conditions were not affected by speed variation, however the PSE and JND values in the auditory only condition were greatly affected by speed variation. In particular, when looming information was presented through an auditory source, the discrimination sensitivity was better for high movement speeds, such that the faster the movement speed, the more accurate the TTC discrimination became.

Table 4. PSE and JND in different speed levels (N=8)

Speed	Visual		Auditory		Audiovisual	
	PSE	JND	PSE	JND	PSE	JND
8.9m/s	1.18	0.34	3.36	1.04	1.30	0.40
13.3m/s	1.04	0.29	1.09	0.57	1.15	0.34
20m/s	1.02	0.31	1.01	0.37	1.03	0.28
30m/s	1.01	0.31	0.53	0.20	0.99	0.35
45m/s	1.09	0.35	0.32	0.26	1.00	0.35

4 Discussion

Traditional constructivist views of the perceptual process emphasize the inferential and constructive nature of perception [10]. Based on this view, in order to estimate TTC, both the distance and speed of an approaching movement would have to be used simultaneously to derive the ratio of the two which equals to the TTC. Whether this mathematical solution reflects the processes humans actually use to compute TTC is still debated [10]. Alternatively, Gibson's ecological approach emphasizes information that is directly accessible in the form of extended spatial and temporal patterns in the optic array. According to this view, TTC can be directly specified by the optical variable τ (see Equation 1) with neither distance nor speed being necessary [1]. Empirical evidence suggests that observers are indeed sensitive to τ [5]. The results of the current study both verify and expand upon these findings by demonstrating that, when vision is available, most participants are more sensitive to τ than to either, the visual angle (θ), the time-dependent derivative of the rate of the image's expansion ($d\theta/dt$), or most importantly, the distance. Moreover, the PSE and JND in the visual condition were not affected by the variation of approaching speed. Thus the results suggest that the participants most likely depended on the optical variable τ.

The optical variable τ has also been shown to have several possible auditory analogues [14,12], the most notable of which is the rate of intensity change over time (see Equation 2). However the similarity to visual τ and the use of acoustic τ to guide human behaviour are doubted [15]. Taking a more general and inclusive view, Gordon and Rosenblum [11] have argued that τ can be defined as an informational variable that specifies the amount of time before an object reaches an observer, as derived by the inverse rate of change of a sensory dimension (visual or auditory). However, in the current study, our results demonstrate that TTC tasks were most likely performed using a distance related strategy and not an auditory "τ" variable. Although our results show that distance could be the variable which participants performance seems to be best correlated with, it is more likely that it is the primary sensory input which directly proportional to distance that was being used. In fact, intensity of a sound is directly related to the inverse of the square of distance (Equation 3, where *d* refers to the instantaneous distance between the object and the observer and *k* is a constant), therefore participants would likely be sensitive to the inverse of square root of absolute sound intensity. Our results also showed that encoding sound intensity, thus distance, would create a greater cost in the accuracy of TTC estimation if the movement speed of the approaching object is slower.

$$\tau = 2I/(dI/dt) \ . \tag{2}$$

$$I = k/d^2 \ . \tag{3}$$

Although much is known about within-modality visual and auditory TTC [5,16], very little research has addressed multi-modal detection or assessed independent visual and auditory performance measures on a directly comparable task. In a study by Schiff and Oldak [17], participants viewed and/or heard an approaching vehicle presented through a film clip then pressed a button when they thought the car reached their position. In their absolute TTC judgment task, visual information was found to be processed more efficiently than audiovisual and auditory information. Our results, using a relative TTC judgment task, were similar to Schiff and Oldak's finding in that visual performance was much better than auditory performance, but the visual performance was not much different from that in audiovisual condition. Gordon and Rosenblum [11] described a "modality-neutral strategy" which specifies that when the information from one sensory modality is interrupted, information from other sensory modalities is used, consequently the accuracy of TTC estimation was not affected. According to their findings, observers can use the most flexible and useful strategy to estimate TTC. The results of the current study are consistent with such contentions. When both visual and auditory sources were combined, our results suggested that participants most likely used the most accurate source of information to formulate their judgment.

It is important to note that in the real world, information specifying the distance of an object from the observer is provided by multiple visual cues, such as physiological cues (accommodation and convergence), binocular disparity, pictorial cues (linear perspective, texture gradient, familiar image size) etc. Our visual display limited distance information to pictorial cues. Although it is possible that in a real environment, participants may perform differently (such as computing TTC values based on distance and speed information), our results demonstrated that human observers *are capable of* estimating TTC information and that such processing is likely achieved through the optical variable τ.

A similar issue applies when discussing the implications of our results to auditory processing under natural, real world conditions. Our analysis of auditory performance is concentrated on sound intensity level, which we believe is the major contributor of auditory processing of object motion-in-depth. Additional auditory cues that are present in the real world are more difficult to reproduce in a virtual environment. Such natural auditory cues include: the selective amplification of high frequency components, the proportion of direct versus reflective sound, the Doppler shift, and dynamic binaural structure [13].

Our research on human processing of object motion-in-depth has important implications in the design of smart sensing devices and in the field of simulation. The simple algorithm in the calculation of visual TTC from a function of retinal image size (Equation 1) could be implemented in the sensors that control next generation autonomous vehicles and such implementation requires little computational resources. Since τ can be generated from monocular information alone there is also no need to require two cameras/sensors which are often needed for robotic devices to generate stereoscopic depth information. Moreover, the differential performance of different sensory modalities would guide us in creating realistic and at the same time cost-effective simulation. For example controlling the right level of absolute sound intensity might be much easier than accurately recreating the motion of a sound source in a three dimensional space, however both approaches may have the similar effect of creating the sensation of an object moving in depth.

References

1. Lee, D.N.: A theory of visual control of braking based on information about time-to-collision. Perception 5, 437–459 (1976)
2. Sun, H.J., Frost, B.J.: Computation of different optical variable of looming objects in pigeon nucleus rotundus neurons. Nature Neuroscience 1, 296–303 (1998)

3. Frost, B.J., Sun, H.J.: The biological basis of time to collision computation. In: Hecht, H., Savelsbergh, G.J.P. (eds.) Time-to-contact, Advances in Psychology Series, pp. 13–37. Elsevier, North Holland, Amsterdam (2004)
4. Frost, B.J., Sun, H.J.: Visual motion processing for figure/ground segregation, collision avoidance, and optic flow analysis in the pigeon. In: Srinivasan, M.V., Venkatesh, S. (eds.) From living eyes to seeing machines, London, pp. 80–103. Oxford University Press, Oxford, UK (1997)
5. Hecht, H., Savelsbergh, G.J.P. (eds.): Time-to-contact, Advances in Psychology Series. Elsevier, North Holland, Amsterdam (2004)
6. Wann, J.P: Anticipating arrival: Is the tau margin a specious theory? Journal of Experimental Psychology: Human Perception & Performance 22, 1031–1048 (1996)
7. Regan, D., Hamstra, S.J.: Dissociation of discrimination thresholds for time to contact and for rate of angular expansion. Vision Research 33, 447–462 (1993)
8. Sun, H.J., Carey, D.P., Goodale, M.A.: A mammalian model of optic-flow utilization in the control of locomotion. Experimental Brain Research 91, 171–175 (1992)
9. Delucia, P.R., Kaiser, M.K., Bush, J.M., Meyer, L.E., Sweet, B.T.: Information Integration in Judgments of Time to Contact. The. Quarterly Journal of Experimental Psychology 56, 1165–1189 (2003)
10. Norman, J.: Two visual systems and two theories of perception: an attempt to reconcile the constructivist and ecological approaches. Behavioral and Brain Sciences 25, 73–144 (2002)
11. Gordon, M.S., Rosenblum, L.D.: Effects of intrastimulus modality change on audiovisual time-to-arrival judgments. Perception & Psychophysics 6, 580–594 (2005)
12. Neuhoff, J.G.: An adaptive bias in the perception of looming auditory motion. Ecological Psychology 13, 87–110 (2001)
13. Rosenblum, L.D.: Acoustical information for controlled collisions. In: Schick, A. (eds.) Contributions to Psychological Acoustics. Bibliotheks Oldenburg Germany, pp. 303–322 (1993)
14. Shaw, B.K., McGowan, R.S., Turvey, M.T.: An acoustic variable specifying time-to-contact. Ecological Psychology 3, 253–261 (1991)
15. Guski, R.: Acoustic tau: an easy analogue to visual tau? Ecological Psychology 4, 187–189 (1992)
16. Rosenblum, L.D., Carello, C., Pastore, R.E.: Relative effectiveness of three stimulus variables for locating a moving sound source. Perception 16, 175–186 (1987)
17. Schiff, W., Oldak, R.: Accuracy of judging time to arrival: effects of modality, trajectory, and gender. Journal of Experimental Psychology: Human Perception & Performance 16, 303–316 (1990)

Part IV

Ubiquitous Interaction

Coin Size Wireless Sensor Interface for Interaction with Remote Displays

Atia Ayman, Shin Takahashi, and Jiro Tanaka

Department of Computer Science, Graduate school of systems and information engineering, University of Tsukuba, Japan
{ayman,shin,jiro}@iplab.cs.tsukuba.ac.jp

Abstract. Human gestures are typical examples of non-verbal communication, and help people communicate smoothly [1]. However, using camera to recognizing gesture needs high processing power and suffer from delays in recognition [2]. Sometimes distance between large screen and user is a problem as for example in pen based interaction user must be attached to screen. So our main motivation is how we should design a user interface that use cookie wireless sensor [3] as an input device. In this paper we describe the interface setting, method of extracting motion and direction from 3D accelometer, using the tilting gesture. Then we proposed a method that allows users to define their own tilting positions and refer it to certain directions. Then we describe a menu selection interface that is based on pie menu for interaction with remote displays. An evaluation of the proposed interface in terms of accuracy, time and attached objects has been conducted.

Keywords: Wireless sensor, interaction with large screen display, Human computer interaction.

1 Introduction

The fast development of wireless sensor devices leads to new trends in wearable devices. Gesture interface is a promising interface for ubiquitous computing environments. Human gestures are typical examples of non-verbal communication, and help people communicate smoothly [1]. Interaction with computers can be done by traditional keyboards, mouse and remote controls designed mainly for stationary interaction. Mobile devices such as PDAs, mobile phones provide new possibilities for interaction with various applications, but introduce new problems of small displays and small input devices [4]. Another way to interact with remote screen displays is by using a camera for hand recognition or LED light tracking. The camera captures an image then transfers it to some application that will do the analysis for the image and extract cursor motion. The main disadvantage of this method is that it needs a large processing power and that might cause delays between the real gesture movement and the analyzed gesture movement. Sensors have been used previously for example in [6]. Blue wand was used to control devices like TV-set, mp3 player. In this paper, we propose a technique that allows users to interact with remote graphical

J. Jacko (Ed.): Human-Computer Interaction, Part II, HCII 2007, LNCS 4551, pp. 733–742, 2007.

user interface items through the use of a 3D accelerometer sensor and tilting gesture. To enhance the accuracy of detecting tilting gesture, we propose a method by which users can define their own tilting positions. We call this method "*customized directions*". We have conducted experiments to find the relation between different objects and recognition methods. In this paper we show how to use the recognition methods and evaluate interaction with graphical user interface items like pie menus.

The rest of this paper is divided as follows: System overview, extraction of motion with 3D accelerometer, Interface evaluation.

2 System Overview

In this paper we build a system that can receive wireless sensor data, recognize and translate it into commands. The system is composed of plasma screen, Nokia sensor, Bluetooth connector and a server. The architecture of the system is shown in Fig. 1. The sensor is attached to some object like pen, sphere and cellular phone. If the sensor is turned ON it will send data to the Bluetooth connected device. The Bluetooth connected device can then send this data to manager server and hence it will execute the appropriate commands according to the user's gesture. The user is able to interact with the remote display within the range of Bluetooth distance.

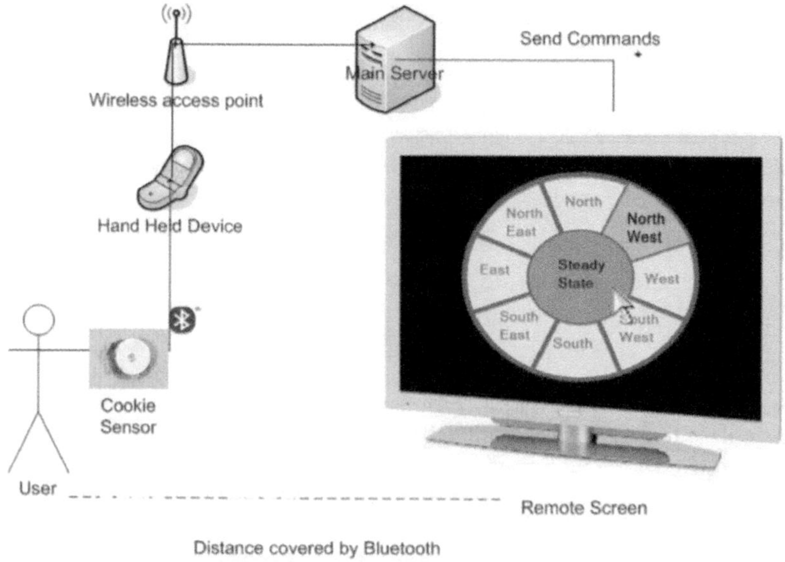

Fig. 1. Proposed system overview

The system has been used to interact with pie menus. Another kind of application that can be used with our system can be a presentation viewer that controls presentation navigation remotely. The user can flip slides forward/backward by moving hand up or down, right or left.

2.1 Nokia Sensors

Nokia cookie is an experimental device developed to test ubiquitous context aware applications. The chassis contains 6 sensors and sends data using Bluetooth. The device is about the size of 5 stacked quarter coins [3].

The sensor is composed of 2-axis linear accelerometer, Compass 3-axis sensor, Ambient light sensor, Galvanic skin response sensor, Heart rate sensor and Skin temperature sensor (see Fig.2 and Fig. 3). There are some other extension sensors that can be attached to give more flexibility to the sensor, for example, 3-axis linear accelerometer, ambient light sensor extension board (RGB color, UV), force vibration motor. The sensor has two communication interfaces, Bluetooth and UART wired connection [3].

Fig. 2. Nokia Sensor with 3D accelerometer

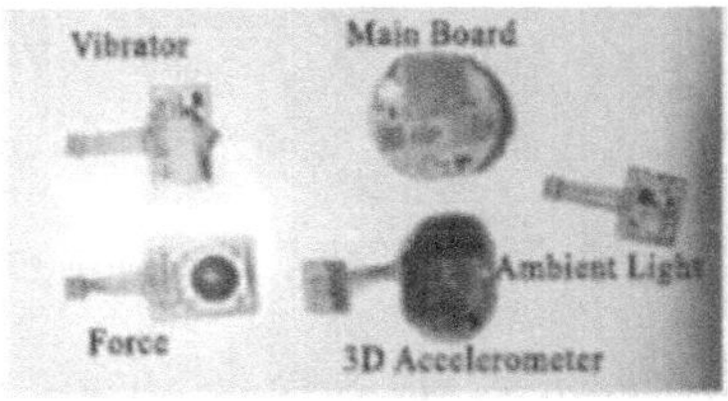

Fig. 3. Nokia Sensor Extension boards

3 Extraction of Motion with 3D Accelerometer

We propose three methods to convert 3D accelerometer data into an orientation of tilting gesture: predefined directions, customized directions and free direction movement. It is important to understand how cookie-3D-Accelometer calculates acceleration.

$$\mathbf{G}_i = 2.8 / 0.333 * (d_i / 1023 - 1 / 2). \textit{ where } i \textit{ is } x,y, \textit{ or } z. \qquad (1)$$
$$\mathbf{G} = (Gx, Gy, Gz)$$

G is the acceleration applied to each axis and d is the voltage input to the cookie processor [3]. The sensor sends accelerometer captured data every 50 millisecond. G is calculated inside the cookie and then sent to the Bluetooth device.

3.1 Predefined Directions

By tilting the sensor in different directions the gravity value is added over the x, y, and z axis respectively. We have to define three threshold values Tx, Ty, and Tz. We pre-measure these threshold values for each of the basic 8 directions (North, North West, North east, east and west, south, south east, and south west). Also we measure the threshold values for the position of no tilting, we call this *steady state*. These positions must have no conflicts between each other. If the user tilts the sensor in some direction the system will match the value of G with the defined threshold values. Table 1 shows each direction and the axis used for comparing threshold values. We start comparing with directions that use 3 axes: northwest, northeast, southwest, southeast then steady state. After that we compare directions that use 2 axes north, south, west and east. We call this method *predefined directions*. Fig. 4 shows the direction of gravity over the x axis while tilting the sensor in the east and west (left and right) directions.

Fig. 4. Hand gesture tilting and gravity directions

Fig. 5 shows the threshold values of tilting the sensor over the x axis. The spots represent the threshold values for one tilt to east/west then returning back to steady state.

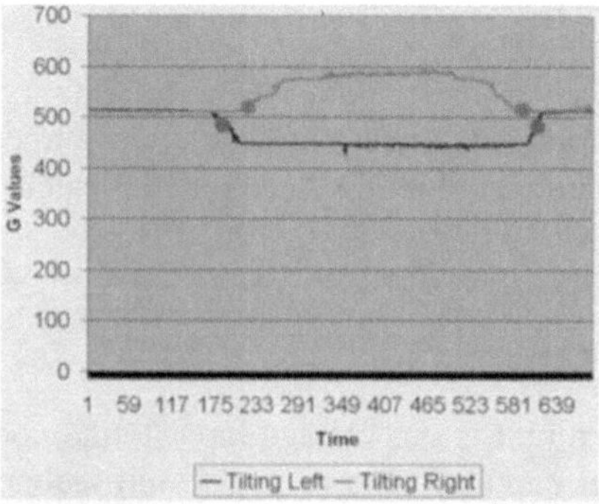

Fig. 5. Threshold values for left / right tilting

Table 1. Directions and axis used

Direction	X	Y	Z
North East	⊗	⊗	⊗
North West	⊗	⊗	⊗
South East	⊗	⊗	⊗
South West	⊗	⊗	⊗
Steady State	⊗	⊗	⊗
North		⊗	⊗
South		⊗	⊗
East	⊗		⊗
West	⊗		⊗

3.2 Customized Directions

The main idea of customized directions is to have a more flexible interface that doesn't depend on predefined threshold values. Users can assign their own gesture tilting to eight preferred directions. In the beginning the user is requested to pose his hand in any position. The system will record this position as steady state position. The user is then requested to tilt the sensor in the basic 8 directions. The user has a freedom in choosing his tilting positions.

The number 8 sphere in Fig. 6 shows the assignment of the steady state position, and the other spheres represent the positions of the eight directions. During the assigning of positions any point must satisfy two conditions to be marked as a customized user position:

First, the distance between the new point and *all* the old points must be greater than the virtual border value (Fig. 6 -dashed circle surrounding the points). The distance is calculated by this equation:

$$\text{distance}=\sqrt{difx^2+dify^2+difz^2} \tag{2}$$

where difx, dify and difz are the absolute difference between two successive $G_{x,y,z}$ over the x , y and z axis successively. This distance will represent a virtual border between the adjacent points to resolve any conflict that might arise while users assign positions.

Second, the user must settle hand in a certain position for at least two successive 50 milliseconds, i.e. the distance between two successive points less than or equal to 1.

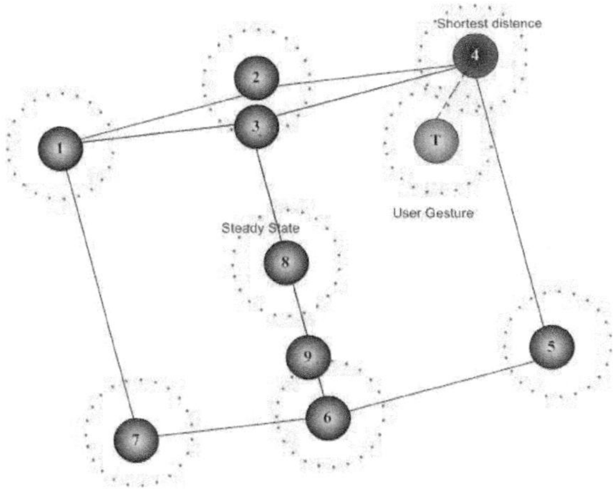

Fig. 6. Shortest distance between user gesture and customized thresholds

After defining a customized position for each direction, the user can tilt the sensor in any new position. This position will be compared to all the values in terms of distance. We get the minimum distance from all the points.

Fig. 6 shows the situation of point (T) being located near point 4. The shortest distance between the (T) point and all other points is calculated. A decision is made that orientation is in the direction of point 4.

In order to test how this method can be used, we attached the sensor to some type of cone shape. User holds the cone horizontally; we record this position as steady state (see Fig. 7). Then by holding the sensor vertically and rotating it 360 degrees. The user can assign each 45 degree tilt for one of the eight directions. Fig. 8 shows a sample of the customized gesture.

Fig. 7. horizontal position steady state

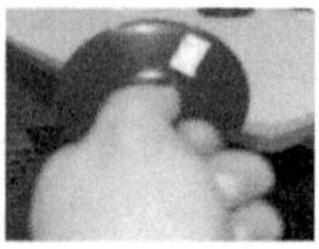

Fig. 8. vertical position up and right

3.3 Free Direction Movement of a Cursor

Using predefined directions, we extract motion while interacting with remote display screen. The algorithm depends on calculating a displacement value according to the captured acceleration $\mathbf{G}_i$ then translates it into remote screen display positions. The center point of remote display screen is the initial starting point for cursor movement. We calculate a displacement value that depends on the value of the tilt of the sensor and screen resolution factor. This displacement value was used to set the new position on the remote display screen. We call this *free direction movement.* This technique was tested to control a ready made flight simulator game.

4 Interface Evaluation

The main purpose of the evaluation is to test the usability of the interface while interacting with graphical user interface items like pie menu items. First experiment concerns measuring accuracy and time to select items. The second experiment compares different type of objects that can be attached to the sensor, so that we can find the effect of the attached object to the proposed methods. Then we evaluate the usability of customized directions method.

Subjects are 7 users between the age of 22 and 27 take part in the first experiment. We evaluate usage of Cone, Shop sticks, Sphere (ball) objects and projector mouse device. Each subject has to finish three sessions per each object. Each session is composed of 12 target selections. The first two targets are for training only. Targets are appearing on the pie menu randomly with marked color, and the user must tilt the sensor until hitting the target. Fig. 9 shows steady state, eight directions, current and next targets. The motion is composed of two gestures: selecting direction and, moving towards then returning back to steady state in order to execute another command. If the user hits unmarked pie items then this case will be counted as an error.

The primary results in Fig. 10 show that most of the users can hit targets using wireless mouse within 1~1.5 seconds. Wireless mouse takes more trials to select an item. This is because using the thumb to control mouse makes user gesture very fast without giving eye focus on next targets. This makes the cursor frequently pass by error pie menu items. This was also similar to free direction movement except it takes much time to hit targets because the motion orientation is hard to figure by users. The results show that predefined directions method can select menu items within 1.5~2 seconds. It records high frequency of selecting items from the first time. This means that predefined directions method can achieve more accurate menu selection items compared to other techniques. This is because the predefined directions method depends on moving to target directly so this means a reduced number of errors.

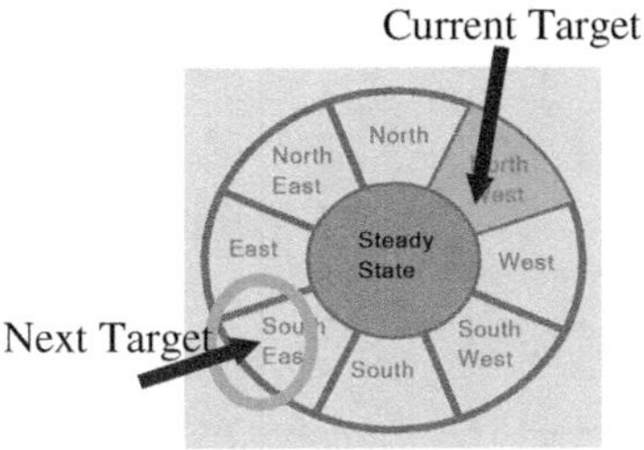

Fig. 9. Pie menu interface showing 9 directions and targets

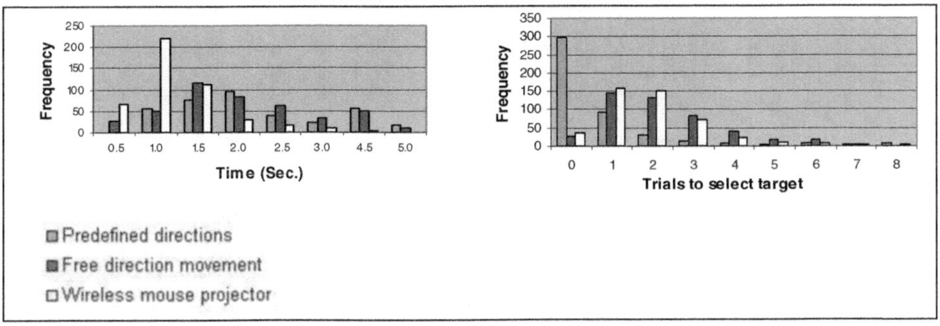

Fig. 10. Comparing proposed technique to wireless projector mouse in means of time/trials to select target

We then evaluated the usage of different type of objects that can be attached with the sensor. In this experiment the subjects are 3 users. We attached Nokia sensor to cone, shop sticks and ball objects, as can be seen in Fig. 11. For each object we have compared three methods: predefined directions, free direction movement and customized directions.

Fig. 12 (a) and (b) shows that using ball object can achieve good results for the eight directions and customized gestures methods and can also lead to a reduced number of errors. When we use the shop sticks as a controller, we observed a semi-normal distribution in the time to hit the targets, in contradiction to error rate, and this means that sensor takes time to return back to steady state. Then thin object might not be so appropriate to reach steady state fast (see Fig. 12 (c) and (d)). When we use the cone object (Fig. 12 (e) and (f)), we get good results at 1.5 seconds to hit the targets using predefined directions method and also a reduced number of errors.

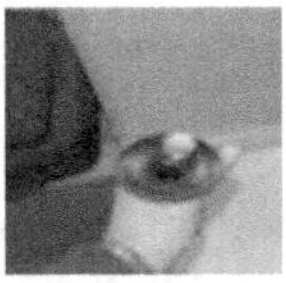
Cone

Shop Sticks

Ball

Fig. 11. Attaching sensor to different objects

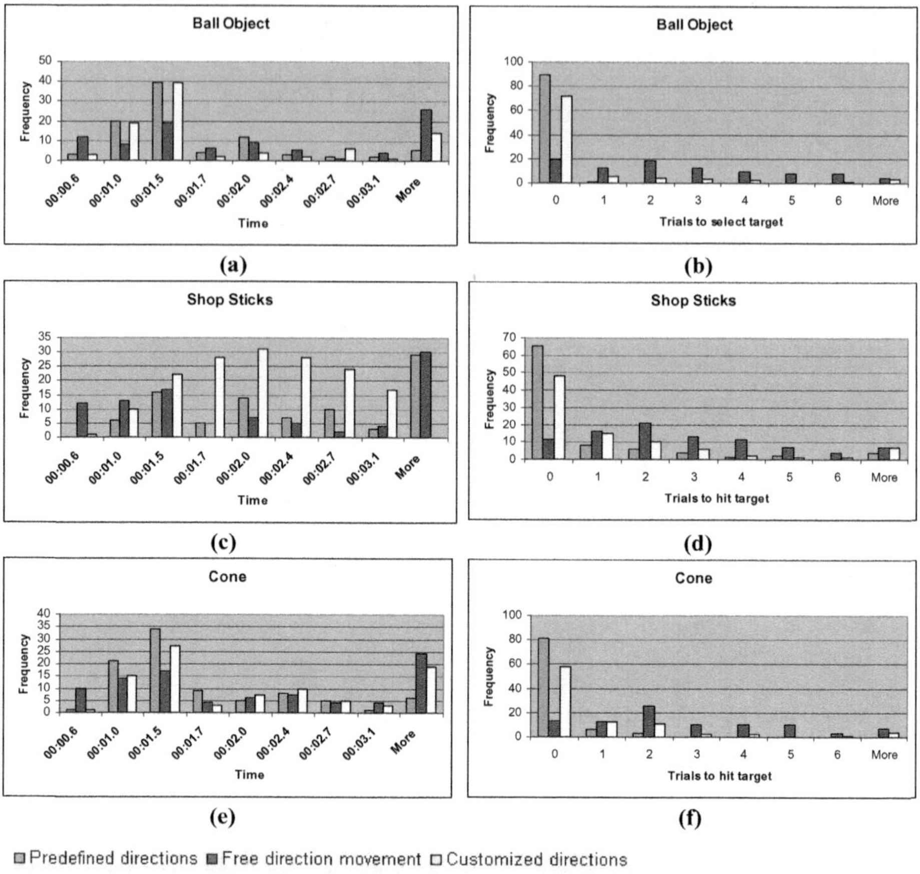

Fig. 12. Objects effect on predefined directions, free direction movement and customized directions

To know which object is suitable to which interface we compare each method and the corresponding objects. Fig. 13 shows that the sphere object is most suitable with predefined directions method and shows low error rates. Also we can observe that all the objects perform almost the same rates to hit targets. The sphere objects show low error rates. For the customized directions method it can be observed that it is very similar to predefined directions method, which means that it can achieve the same low error rate with sphere object.

Users have some comments while using the proposed methods: sometimes in free direction movement method the movements of mouse were very fast compared to real gesture. This case happened when user tilted the sensor suddenly and very fast so the displacement value calculated is very large, which makes movement be interpreted as jumps. Moving in south west and south east is difficult gesture. When an average person tilts the wrist of the hand towards the northwest and northeast direction the elbow assist the motion, while moving backwards (south) and tilting the elbow is fixed which makes the motion very difficult. When using the customized directions interface, the users have some problems in understanding how the calibration of positions is performed. Whenever the calibration of positions is wrong, the movements are difficult to achieve. This happens when the users forget the points they mark, and this situation leads to false gesture tilting detection. Using the shop sticks with predefined directions method and moving to north and south direction is confusing. This situation can be resolved by using the customized directions interface.

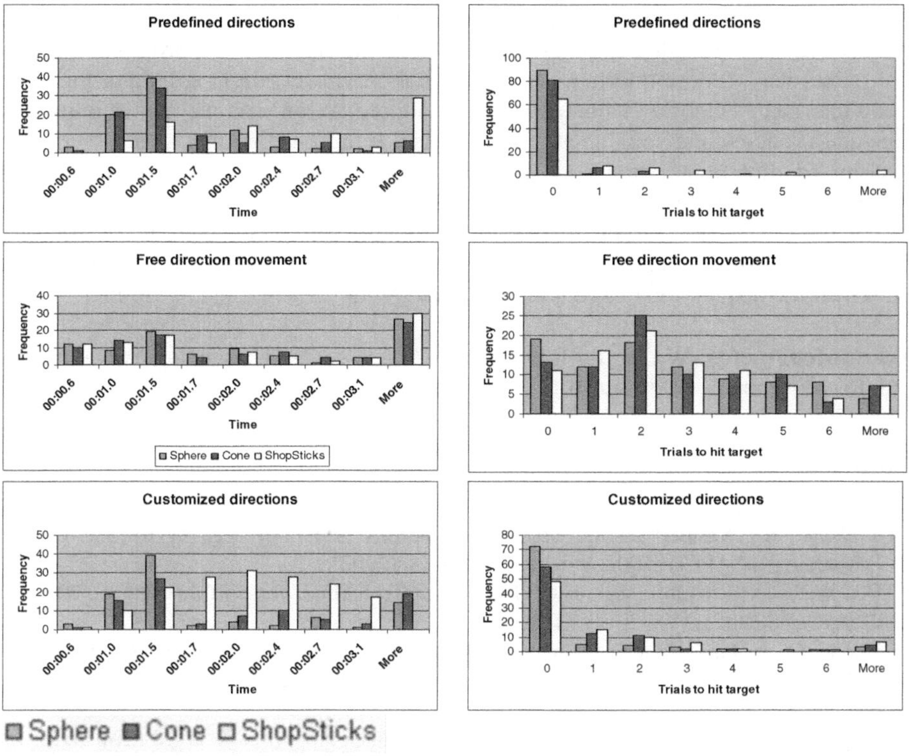

Fig. 13. Each method and appropriate object

5 Related Work

J.Kela et. al [4] use the accelerometer to extract commands from natural hand gesture movements to control external device. The proposed system in their work depends on using HMM to analyze a gesture which means that the system needs to be trained first by the users. At the beginning of recognizing gesture, an accuracy error appears which sometimes make users abandon the usage of such system. They do not propose continuous full hand gesture recognition. In our research we provide a method of continues recognition of tilting gesture only, without the need of providing training from the users except when we use customized directions method. H.Kimura, et. al [5] define three motions rotating, tilting, and knocking as gestures, then they use these gestures for map viewer application. Users observed less motion accuracy and time delay between gesture and system action. This paper does not define personalized gestures.

6 Conclusion

In this paper we propose a gesture interface that can work using sensors and can support the interaction with remote displays. Then we define a customized gesture interface that can be adapted to user's gesture positions. We have proposed a system that makes use of these interfaces like presentation viewer, flight simulator game, pie menu interface. Then we evaluate the system in interaction with pie menus in terms of time and accuracy and suitable attached objects. It has been noticed that the proposed customized directions can be an initial good step for further enhancement of the method of detecting thresholds.

We need to conduct more experiments on evaluating different kinds of tilting positions with more users. The usage of more than one sensor must also be studied. Moreover the acquisition of full hand free gesture movement must be studied.

Acknowledgments. We would like to thank Nokia research center .Nokia Japan Co. Ltd. for using their cookie sensor.

References

1. Tsukada, K., Yasumura, M.: Ubi-Finger: Gesture Input Device for Mobile Use. In: Proceedings of APCHI 2002, vol. 1, pp. 388–400 (2002)
2. Badillo, et al.: Literature Survey on Interaction Techniques for Large Displays. TR-06-21, Computer Science, Virginia Tech (2006)
3. Hideki, O.: Nokia Cookie users manual, Nokia research center. Nokia Japan Co. Ltd (2005)
4. Kela, J., et,: Accelerometer-based gesture control for design environmen. ubiquitous computing 10, 285–299 (2006)
5. Kimura, H., et al.: CookieFalvors: Easy Building Blocks for wireless tangible input. In: CHI 2006, Montreal, Canada. work-in-progress (2006)
6. Fuhrmann, T., Klein, M., Odendahl, M.: The BlueWand as Interface for Ubiquitous and Wearable Computing Environments, EPMCC'03 (2003)

Hit Me Baby One More Time: A Haptic Rating Interface

Christoph Bartneck[1], Philomena Athanasiadou[1], and Takayuki Kanda[2]

[1] Department of Industrial Design
Eindhoven University of Technology
Den Dolech 2, 5600 MB Eindhoven, The Netherlands
christoph@bartneck.de, p.athanasiadou@student.tue.nl
[2] ATR Intelligent Robotics and Communications Labs
2-2-2 Hikaridai Seikacho Sorakugun, Kyoto, Japan
kanda@atr.jp

Abstract. As the importance of recommender systems increases, in combination with the explosion in data available over the internet and in our own digital libraries, we suggest an alternative method of providing explicit user feedback. We create a tangible interface, which will not only facilitate multitasking but provide an enjoyable way of completing an otherwise frustrating and perhaps tiresome task.

Keywords: explicit feedback, recommender system, tangible interface.

1 Introduction

Recommender systems play a key role in academia and industry. One of the best - known recommender sytems is the, "Customers who bought this item also bought..." application from Amazon. The research area of Ambient Intelligence is based on user adaptation and anticipation [1]. The success of the algorithms responsible for the recommendations and adaptations depend on information they gather from the user. They may either do this implicitly through observation, such as logging users' buying behavior, or explicitly by recording direct ratings from the users. Explicit feedback can be very laborious for the users [2, 3] and hence implicit feedback is often preferred. However, not all desirable knowledge about the users' state manifests itself in observable behavior. The decision of which music a certain person likes in a specific situation may depend on factors that are not detectable through current sensor technology. A certain lighting condition may, for example, evoke a particular sentimental memory, which causes the user to pick a piece of music from that period. Explicit feedback may help to overcome limitations of implicit feedback-based recommendation systems.

One way to overcome problems associated with gathering data from users is to turn the task into a fun activity, as was presented convincingly by Ahn [4-6]. We developed a haptic interface to turn the process of giving feedback into a fun activity (see Figure 1). We took inspiration from a game often found in Sega World arcades called, "Hammer the Gopher". In this game, the player has to hit gophers with a

J. Jacko (Ed.): Human-Computer Interaction, Part II, HCII 2007, LNCS 4551, pp. 743–747, 2007.

Fig. 1. The Haptic Interface

hammer as soon as they emerge from their holes. Hitting a cute character is a fun activity and the strength of the hit can easily be mapped to a negative rating. A second inspiration came from Nintendo's "Dogs", and "Aibo". In both cases the user can encourage a certain behavior of the creature by petting it. The number of strokes can then easily be mapped onto a positive rating. Our haptic interface is embedded into a flat teddy bear and incorporates a touch sensor and a force sensor. The touch sensor is located in the forehead and responds to even the slightest strokes. The force sensor is embedded into the teddy's nose, since the nose is the teddy's highest point. Through a series of test we were able to develop an algorithm that reliably distinguished between strokes and hits based on the sensor readings.

2 Need for Effortless, Fast Rating

Over the past few years we have observed an explosion in the amount of data and media available over the internet. Not only have online resources increased but our digital libraries at home have also grown exponentially. The tiny iPod Nano, with its slim design allows for storage of up to 8 GB, which translates to approximately 2000 songs. With the regular iPod providing up to 80GB of storage, which translates to 20.000 songs or 100 hours of movies, we can assume that 8 GB is only a fraction of what people have stored on their PCs. It is evident that not only "mobile" media players (iPods etc.) but also the media we have safely secured on our PCs has increased dramatically. A quick review of several forums [7, 8] that discuss the number of songs in the members' music libraries reveals that on an average people have about 5400 songs. To navigate through this bulk of information, recommender systems can prove invaluable. As the thought of rating 5400 songs in one go could seem overwhelming or even be branded, "mission impossible", it seems essential to have a fast, simple, effortless way of rating music. To that end, the development of an interface that permits the users to rate the music while listening to it, without distracting them from their daily PC activities, sounds ideal.

3 Tangible Interfaces Facilitate Multitasking

By using a simple tangible interface for rating music, the task of rating becomes simple and fast without taking the users' attention away from other activities. Imagine the following scenario: Someone is busy searching for information on the internet and reading documents while listening to music. The interface we created is located next to his PC. While listening to some music, the user realizes he really likes it and wishes to provide/record a rating. There is no need for the user to change application and go through a set of menus in order to rate the music; all he needs to do is simply reach out and pet the teddy bear without taking his eyes off the screen, thus making the process seamless. The existence of peripheral devices can increase the user's ability to multitask as indicated by the creation of Kimura, on office environment that uses peripheral displays in order to facilitate common multitasking practices. The success of Kimura and its advantages compared to other similar projects like Rooms [9], lies in the fact that it does not rely on displaying even more information in the already overloaded desktop, but instead distributing it in the environment [10]. In the same way, by distributing activity to the environment via a peripheral tangible interface, multitasking is facilitated. "Moreover, constraining the interaction to the desktop is a poor match for common human behaviors such as using large amounts of physical space to simultaneously organize, monitor and manage multiple activities" [10, 11].

4 Need for Explicit Feedback

The need for explicit feedback has been made evident through extensive research in the field of recommender systems. Quiroga and Mostafa [12], compared 3 different methods for user profiling using a) only explicit feedback, b) only implicit feedback and c) a combination of the two. The results showed that the method using explicit feedback initially proved superior but at a certain stage reached a plateau, which surpassed only by the combined method. Combining implicit with explicit feedback is also supported by Zigoris and Zhang [13], who point out the necessity of explicit feedback at the early stages where recommender systems are still getting to know the user. Therefore it makes sense to concentrate efforts on creating an interface that will provide an easy, fast and pleasurable way of giving feedback. By creating this interface, we have attempted to satisfy/fulfill this need. By highlighting the possibility and benefits of using a tangible interface, we hope to inspire future research in this direction.

5 Evaluation

In a pilot study, we asked the participants to rate music using either our haptic interface (See Figure 1) or a standard graphical user interface (GUI). The experiment was set up with the type of interface as the only within participant condition. The participants were allowed to rate as many or as few songs as they wished. The following measurements were automatically logged by the software: the number of songs rated, the total duration the participant spends on rating the songs, the average duration the participant spends on rating each song, the number of positive and negative ratings, and the total intensity of positive ratings. It did not make sense to compare the intensities of negative ratings, since the GUI provided very different data (scale) compared to the haptic interface (force sensor data). Two female and sixteen male participants, between the ages 21 and 42 years (mean 27.1), partook in the experiment. They were all associated with ATR, Japan. An analysis of variance (ANOVA) revealed that there were not significant differences between the measurements across the two conditions. Table 1 shows the mean and standard errors of the mean (SEMs) for all measurements in both conditions.

Table 1. Means and standard errors of all measurements in both conditions

Measurement	Haptic	Std. error	GUI	Std. error
Number of Songs	43.61	10.04	45.83	13.92
Number of Positive Ratings	22.06	3.77	22.06	3.67
Intensity of Positive Ratings	34.00	5.01	50.61	7.95
Total Duration of Ratings (sec)	982233.50	112273.46	997538.33	117572.21
Average Duration per Song (sec)	28803.60	3077.73	33407.38	4467.52
Number of Negative Ratings	21.56	6.78	23.78	11.08

6 Conclusion

The participants were given the specific task of rating music, which naturally favors efficient rather than enjoyable interaction. Even with such a focused task, the haptic interface did perform as well as the GUI. It can be expected that the haptic interface may perform better than the GUI if it is integrated into the daily activities of the users. Next, we intend to perform a long-term study, in which the haptic interface will be available to the users during their daily computer–based work.

As other studies also suggest [14, 15], there seems to be a preference towards tangible interfaces when compared to GUIs. The haptic interfaces appear to score higher on 'hedonic quality' [16]. Furthermore, by integrating this interface into the users' daily activities we will be able to study whether this interface facilitates multitasking as expected. The interface is of course not limited to rating music, but can be used for any kind of explicit feedback.

By answering the call for explicit feedback with the creation of a fun and easy–to–use tangible interface that is expected to support multitasking, we have opened a new way for the improvement of recommender systems. Most research in recommender systems, as discussed in the introduction, merely refers to recommender system types and algorithms. This paper indicates the potential benefits in using a tangible interface for supporting recommender systems and thus points out the importance of studying and exploring not only the recommender types and algorithms, but also the interface, in order to improve recommender systems.

Acknowledgements. This research was in part supported by the Japan Society for the Promotion of Science, Grants-in-Aid for Scientific Research No. 18500024. We would like to thank Aoife Currid for proofreading.

References

[1] Aarts, E., Harwig, R., Schuurmans, M.: Ambient Intelligence. In: Denning, P. (ed.) The Invisible Future, pp. 235–250. McGraw Hill, New York (2001)

[2] Adomavicius, G., Tuzhilin, A.: Toward the next generation of recommender systems: a survey of the state-of-the-art and possible extensions. Knowledge and Data. Engineering, IEEE Transactions on 17, 734–749 (2005)

[3] Nichols, D.M.: Implicit Rating and Filtering.In: presented at 5th Delos Workshop on Filtering and Collaborative Filtering, Budapest, Hungary (1997)

[4] Ahn, L. v., Liu, R., Blum, M.: Peekaboom: a game for locating objects in images. In: Presented at Proceedings of the SIGCHI conference on Human Factors in computing systems, Montreal, Quebec, Canada (2006)

[5] Ahn,L.v., Kedia, M., Blum, M.: Verbosity: a game for collecting common-sense facts. In: presented at Proceedings of the SIGCHI conference on Human Factors in computing systems, Montreal, Quebec, Canada (2006)

[6] Ahn, L.v., Ginosar, S., Kedia, M., Liu, R., Blum, M.: Improving accessibility of the web with a computer game. In: presented at Proceedings of the SIGCHI conference on Human Factors in computing systems, Montreal, Quebec, Canada (2006)

[7] Mac OS X Hints, How much music do you have? (2005) Retrieved February 2007, from http://forums.macosxhints.com/archive/index.php/t-44861.html

[8] My ADSL, How much music do you have? (2006) Retrieved February 2007, from http://mybroadband.co.za/vb/showthread.php?t=63616

[9] Henderson, D.A., Card, S.: Rooms: the use of multiple virtual workspaces to reduce space contention in a window-based graphical user interface. ACM Transactions on Graphics 5, 211–243 (1986)

[10] MacIntyre, B., Mynatt, E.D., Voida, S., Hansen, K.M., Tullio, J., Corso, G.M.: Support for multitasking and background awareness using interactive peripheral displays. In: 14th annual ACM symposium on User interface software and technology, Orlando, Florida, ACM Press, New York (2001)

[11] Mynatt, E.D.: Writing on the Wall, presented at Interact, Edinburgh (1999)

[12] Quiroga, L.M., Mostafa, J.: Empirical evaluation of explicit versus implicit acquisition of user profiles in information filtering systems. In: Proceedings of the fourth ACM conference on Digital libraries, Berkeley, California, United States, ACM Press, New York (1999)

[13] Zigoris, P., Zhang, Y.: Bayesian adaptive user profiling with explicit & implicit feedback. In: Proceedings of the 15th ACM international conference on Information and knowledge management, Arlington, Virginia, USA, ACM Press, New York (2006)

[14] Jacob, R.J.K., Ishii, H., Pangaro, G., Patten, J.: A tangible interface for organizing information using a grid. In: Proceedings of the SIGCHI conference on Human factors in computing systems: Changing our world, changing ourselves, Minneapolis, Minnesota, USA, ACM Press, New York (2002)

[15] Waldner, M., Hauber, J., Zauner, J., Haller, M., Billinghurst, M.: Tangible Tiles: Design and Evaluation of a Tangible User Interface in a Collaborative Tabletop Setup,presented at OzChi2006, Sydney (2006)

[16] Vastenburg, M.H., Ross, P.R., Keyson, D.V.: A user experience-based approach to home atmosphere control, Universal Access in the Information Society (2007)

Minimising Pedestrian Navigational Ambiguities Through Geoannotation and Temporal Tagging

Ashweeni Beeharee and Anthony Steed

Department of Computer Science, University College London, Gower Street, London WC1E 6BT, United Kingdom
A.Beeharee@cs.ucl.ac.uk

Abstract. The increasing power and ubiquity of smart devices such as mobile phones and PDAs means that a visitor to a city now carries with them a device capable of giving location-specific guiding and routing information. Whilst there have been a number of studies on the use of photographs to supplement text and map-based guiding applications for mobile devices, in this paper we want to propose and give an initial exploratory study of a guiding system that utilises *geoannotation* to mark photographs. In geoannotation, each photograph is selected from a repository of photographs based on the content and its relevance to the route. The photograph itself is then geoannotated with arrows and other markers on the fly so as to give routing information. Because the photograph in the database will not be taken from the location of the visitor who needs routing information, we need to take care and design cues that are unambiguous. The main contribution of this paper is the discussion of the geoannotation technique, and some informal results from pilot trials on how it helps in addressing certain navigational ambiguities arising in the use of photographs in pedestrian navigation systems.

Keywords: Pedestrian Navigation, Design, Human Factors, Ambiguities, Geoannotation.

1 Introduction

Over the last few years, with the proliferation of smart devices and increased accessibility to global positioning technologies through cheaper GPS receivers, there has been a growing interest in navigation aids for pedestrians. The latest generation of these aids saw the usage of real life photographs of landmarks to better assist in the navigation task [7]. However this gives rise to certain ambiguities, since pedestrians may be confused with conflicting information in the photographs and the instructions given in text. Such problems may be addressed by providing additional information on the photographs.

There is currently no system that annotates photographs themselves on the fly to point out the navigation information. In this paper, we present a system which geoannotates photographs on the fly with navigation information, giving directions and minimizing ambiguities arising through differences between pedestrian's viewpoint, camera viewpoint in photographs and text instructions.

J. Jacko (Ed.): Human-Computer Interaction, Part II, HCII 2007, LNCS 4551, pp. 748–757, 2007.

The paper is structured as follows. In the following section we present a more detailed conceptual overview of the potential of geoannotating photographs in guiding and routing systems. This includes a discussion about the new challenges arising from the use of photographs not specifically taken for use as navigation aid. In the following section we then discuss related work in photo based pedestrian guiding and routing systems. In the System Overview section we present a prototype system for retrieving, geoannotating and displaying photographs. Finally we conclude and give an outline of our future work in further evaluation of the concept and further development of supporting infrastructure.

2 Conceptual Overview

The use of photographs in pedestrian navigation systems is not novel. Such photographs are taken for the specific purpose of providing routing information, giving compelling results as they prove to be very effective visual aids. If photo-assisted pedestrian navigation systems are to be widely adopted in everyday life, a large number of photographs will have to be taken along every possible routes – a very expensive and Herculean venture, even if applied to only one city like London.

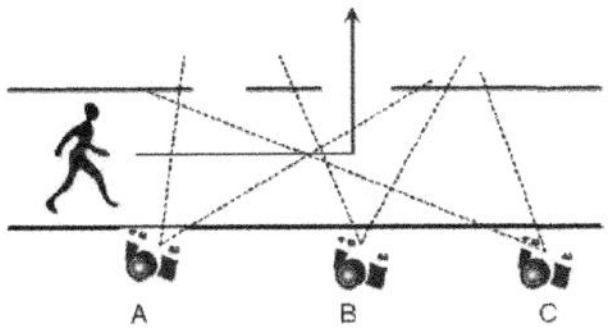

Fig. 1. Augmenting with routing information – the challenge

However, if these photographs could be sampled from a repository of randomly collected photographs, it would eliminate the need to specifically collect photos for navigational purposes. With the increased availability of digital cameras at affordable prices and in mobile phones, more photos are taken nowadays than ever before. In addition, recent years have seen a proliferation of online photo repositories to address problems related to the management of the growing number of photos that individuals have. Such repositories could be exploited to feed into photo-assisted pedestrian navigation system.

This novel approach poses new challenges. Firstly, the selection of the photographs from the repository requires an algorithm to evaluate the appropriateness of the photos in giving routing information using criteria such as visibility. We tackled this in [2].

Secondly, once the photos are chosen, augmenting them with routing information in both textual and graphic form presents an interesting challenge. Consider figure 1, where the pedestrian is moving towards the point where a left turn is required along the route. Three camera positions (A, B, C) are considered, representing the actual photos shown in Figure 2 from left to right respectively. The dotted lines in figure 1 represent the field of view from each camera position. One of the photos will be presented to the pedestrian along with navigation instructions.

(a) Photo from camera position A (b) Photo from camera position B

(c) Photo from camera position C

Fig. 2. Photos taken from three different camera positions

The textual instruction could be 'Turn through the gate on your left after 10 metres'. This would have minimal ambiguity if photo from position A or even B is shown, because the instruction to left in the photo is the same directional sense as the visitors' current motion. However, if the third photo is shown, the instruction would seem ambiguous, as on the photo the turn is to the right relative to the camera position. This is similar to the concept in film "do not cross the eye line". On the other hand, if the photos are augmented with direction arrows, these could equally be ambiguous. The solution proposed in this paper aims at minimising the effect of such ambiguities.

The photo selection can also be improved by considering the timestamps of the photos. We identified in our previous study that climatic conditions can have remarkable impact on the appearance of certain buildings in real life, thereby increasing the ambiguity in the photographs presented. Thus, if the photographs are selected by considering temporal attributes, the ambiguities are reduced right from the start.

Another problem is related to positioning errors in two instances – one during the capture of the photograph and the other during presentation of the photograph to the pedestrian. The recording of position and orientation of the camera is crucial, since this information would be used in the selection of photos and the presentation of navigation instructions. Current technical and legislative trends suggest that most mobile phones and cameras in the future will have a GPS receiver, thus the recording of position does not seem to be such a big issue. However, errors in positions during capture would lead to ambiguities in instructions. During presentation, photographs may be augmented with directional information. Direction arrows would be drawn relative to current pedestrian position (determined through GPS or self positioning) to augment the photographs presented. Needless to say that positioning errors in this case would generate misleading arrows. Hence, we propose an alternative way to automatically augment photographs on the fly, such that small positioning errors do not hinder the navigation.

3 Related Work

Nowadays, navigation systems generally comprise of a map, in either 2d or 3d, and make use of text and speech to give routing information. This is not only confined to motorists who use applications such as TomTom [12], but also pedestrians [11]. In the case of pedestrian navigation, the use of landmarks has proven to be very effective in directing pedestrians to their destination [10]. It has also been noted that different people may have different preferences in terms of modalities used [6]. However, the general effect seems to be that photos make navigation more effective.

Photos, used in navigation applications, can be augmented in a number of ways to provide direction and distance cues. As suggested in [13], photos can be augmented with symbols which convey information about distance. However, augmenting photographs with such symbols on the fly, using an unassisted algorithm is not trivial. One of the major problems is the detection of the ground plane, which can be achieved very neatly through simple human intervention [5]. Other problems are related to the detection of geometry from a single photograph. For photographs of building, detection of horizontal and vertical lines is relatively easy. This task becomes almost impossible to automate, if features such as irregular and discontinuous curb on the road have to be used in establishing 3d lines.

Geo-tagging photographs has received a lot of attention recently. As the precision of geo-tagging increases, interesting application will certainly emerge. For instance, A9 [1] is devoting a lot of effort in scanning cities with an aim to present a novel view of city maps augmented with photos. Another recent demonstration [9] by Microsoft showed the ability to navigate around parts of the city in car or as a pedestrian and visualising the environment through photos.

A few sophisticated pedestrian navigation systems have also been developed. In [4], the pedestrian's view is augmented with 3d computer graphics through the use of a head mounted display. Information about the real world, such as building names, is presented to the user. This requires quite a complex equipment and setup, making it difficult to scale across a large number of users.

4 System Overview

The system presented in this paper differs from the ones discussed in the previous section in several ways. Firstly, the photographs used are not specifically taken along the route to aid navigation, as would be the case in most landmark based navigation aids. Secondly, the photos are geoannotated with information to improve navigation and address ambiguities arising from the use of photos. Thirdly, the system runs on cheap and readily available hardware – making it a good candidate for large scale adoption and usage.

The pedestrian navigation system comprises of three main software components – the Navigation Application, the Map Server and the Photo Server.

4.1 Navigation Application

The application is designed for use on PDAs, and has been implemented in C# for the .NET Compact Framework, specially targeted to run on PDAs with Pocket PC 2003. Several iterations of the interface were tested. We integrated features modelled on those in commercial applications and included the lessons learnt from previous applications that we developed on the PDA [2]. We did several informal usability tests to make sure icons and annotations were legible. The navigation application is capable of presenting routing information in different modalities to the user. The application has four tabs - viewer, map, route and help.

In the map tab, a map of the area is presented to the user, as shown in Figure 3(a). The user is able to pan the map to look at other areas. Preliminary trials revealed that the zooming function was not found useful and confused most users. The map is retrieved from a map server, described in the following section. The route to be followed is drawn on the map in red, and as the user progresses along the route, the completed segment is displayed in blue.

An icon representing the position of the user is displayed and updated as the user moves across the map. Since this application was to be tested in an area with a high density of high rise buildings, contributing to the poor GPS coverage, self reporting was the preferred method for recording the user's position.

Once a route is loaded into the application, routing instructions relevant to the current position of the user are presented below the map, whereas the route tab is populated with the complete route to be followed (Figure 3(b)). The user can explore instructions in advance or review the previous ones by using the navigation arrows on the map in any of the tabs. As the user moves along the path, picture icons appear on the map at locations where real photographs of landmarks and buildings were taken. The user can choose to view the photograph by clicking on the picture icon, which acts as a hyperlink to the resource. Focus is transferred to the viewer tab, which has an embedded browser, loading the requested photograph from a web server.

(a) Map tab - Showing the map, the route and some instructions (b) Route tab - showing the complete list of instructions (c) Photo tab - showing the photograph taken at a given location

Fig. 3. Navigation Application

4.2 The Servers

The map server generates maps of the area on the fly based on the user's position, by reading from a spatial database storing Ordnance Survey Mastermap data. This is the same map server used in [2]. At the moment, the collected photos around the area for experimentation are stored on a web server which serves them on demand. It is envisaged that further extension to the system would tap into online photo repositories. Previous versions of the system described so far did not support marking up of photographs. The next section describes the concept and the implementation of this novel component of the system.

4.3 Geomarking Photographs

Routing information in text or audio which are used to complement the information provided through photographs, may not suffice in giving accurate instructions to the user. This is specially true when the photograph shown is not taken from the current viewpoint of the user. In such cases, geoannotating the actual photographs with additional information may help in removing certain ambiguities. In figure 4(a), the unmarked photo of a gate is shown where the pedestrian is instructed to take a left turn. Depending on where the pedestrian is actually positioned, the gate may look different in perspective and the instruction may be interpreted either relative to current user location where the photo is shown or relative to the camera position from which the photo is taken. Augmenting the photo with a simple arrow as shown in figure 4(b) eliminates this type of uncertainly.

(a) Unmarked photo of the gate with text instructions (b) Augmented photo with simple arrow (c) Showing both the 'to' (blue arrow head) and the 'from' (grey arrow tail) information on the photo

Fig. 4. Removing ambiguities by augmenting the photo

The direction of the arrow is determined based on information about the photograph itself (camera position and view direction) and the route to be followed. The arrow is then drawn based on the angle subtended by the direction of travel along the route relative to the view direction of the camera where the photograph was taken. However, test runs revealed that though augmenting with these arrows were beneficial, some confusion still existed when the photos were not taken in the direction of travel along the route.

To address this problem, we decided to not only indicate the 'to' direction as in the previous case, but also to present information about the 'from' in the photograph. Consider Figure 5, the route already completed ('from' direction) is represented by vector *f*, and the direction of turn ('to' direction) by vector *t*. The photograph presented was shot in the direction *p*. Angles a and b are computed to determine the 'to' and the 'from' direction of the arrows relative to the viewpoint of the photograph. This enables us to geoannotate the photograph with arrows having the correct orientation.

Thus, the user will have clear indications about the next move *relative* to the route completed so far. In order to achieve this, we made use of an elongated two-colour 3d arrow as shown in figure 4(c). The grey part of the arrow showing the direction of the completed route and the blue part indicating the direction to follow. The grey part helps because an instruction to turn left, might be given with a narrow pointing right, for instance if the photo shown is taken from location C in Figure 1.

We favoured this approach to the 'dot and arrow' representation where the dot would represent the current user position and the arrow the direction to follow. This is because there will always be uncertainty about the current user position therefore representing this position in the photo may lead to further confusion.

Normally, in order to augment the photos with virtual objects (such as arrows in this case), it is required to extract the ground plane to correctly position the objects in the coordinate system of the photograph. This is even more crucial if the arrow has to be placed on the bottom of the photograph. Since we have assumed that the real horizon is horizontal in the photograph and roughly midway up, it is visually more consistent to put the arrow at the top. It has been noted that doing so increases the tolerance to misalignments of the arrows relative to the true ground plane in the photograph.

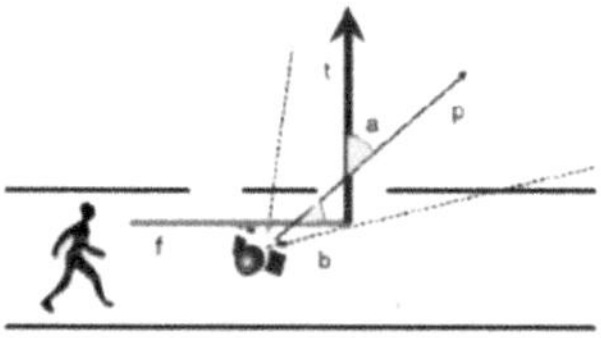

Fig. 5. Projecting the route directions of the arrows onto the photograph

4.4 On the Fly Augmentation and Benefits

The photos augmentation takes place on the fly and is unassisted. In typical augmentation scenarios, if geometry is extracted from a scene which contains easily identifiable straight lines, such as in buildings, the augmentation process can be automatic. In other cases, such as most of the photos in real life, human intervention is required to correct the extraction tool. Since in this application we are only interested in providing approximate but highly meaningful geoannotations in the photos, precise geometric extraction is not required. This removes the need to register the camera to the scene in the photographs [8] using authoring softwares.

As a result, the photos used on a particular route can be reused on several different routes, indicating various turning arrows as required. The photos can also be updated or completely replaced as more useful photos are found in the repository and not so useful ones are eliminated.

4.5 Minimising Wrong Turns

The increased degree of freedom and mobility of a pedestrian, compared to motorist who is confined to the road, raises the risks of taking wrong routes. For instance, multiple pathways may exist at a given junction (Figure 7(a)), and solely giving directions along the route not be sufficient. To remove ambiguities, wrong alternatives can be ruled out by marking an appropriate symbol, such as a cross or a red dot on the photographs shown. Using traffic lights like symbol is Another alternative which is easily understandable by everyone. This is specially relevant to pedestrian navigation where very often paths and alleyways do not have names, and therefore cannot be referred to in text or otherwise as being a wrong, increasing ambiguity in navigation.

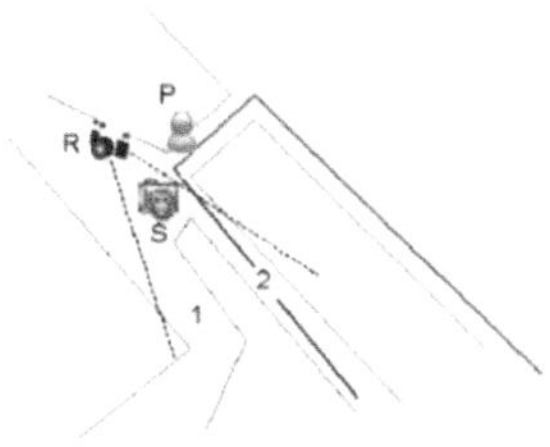

Fig. 6. Photograph S (shot from R) is presented when user reaches position P. Instruction to turn left leaves ambiguity whether to take Route labeled 1 or 2

(a) Photo showing two options for moving ahead (b) Using traffic light symbols to mark out one of the alternatives

Fig. 7. Disambiguation using traffic lights

Consider figure 6. The instruction to turn left is given to the pedestrian when he reaches the point P, together with the photograph taken from location R, though the icon presented on the map will appear at point S along the navigation route. The corresponding photograph presented (figure 7(a)) has two possible paths for navigation along the same direction on the route. The ambiguity as to which path is to be followed can be removed by placing virtual traffic lights symbols 'roughly' in the relevant areas on the photo as shown in Figure 7(b). The location of the symbols is computed from the information about the geometry of buildings in this area stored on the map server, and the view volume of the camera. This enables the pedestrian to proceed along the correct route, by making, perhaps the non-obvious decision to take the minor pathway. As the positioning of these symbols within the photos need not be precise, errors in pedestrian tracking and geo-tagging of the photos can be accommodated.

5 Evaluation

In evaluating the effectiveness of the geoannotation technique on pedestrian navigation, we planned to use the following quantitative metrics.

- Number of wrong turns at decision points on the path where photograph is shown
- Time taken at decision points before proceeding
- Time taken to go back onto designated route when lost

The recorded data will be compared with data from previous experiments [3]. In addition, questionnaire will be used to evaluate the effectiveness of the approach from usability perspective.

We have carried out a pilot study involving on ten subjects. The pilot has not only given some positive indication about the potential of geoannotation, but also highlighted certain aspects that would need to be accounted for.

For the simple arrows, users found it useful when the photograph was aligned to their viewpoint while walking down the route. When not aligned, it created confusion as the arrows conflicted with the reality. However, with 3d arrows, users could relate to the 'from' and 'to' concept and therefore were more forgiving to misalignment of both the photograph and the arrows themselves.

Preliminary trials suggest that in general geoannotation is very useful when text instruction and photograph alignment do not have a close relationship with the reality of the user both in terms of space and time.

6 Conclusion

In this paper, we presented a novel approach which enables both greater scalability of photo-based navigation system and their increased usability by concentrating on the reduction of ambiguities. By geoannotating the photos using colour coded arrows, pedestrians can be given a better sense of navigation direction relative to the photo presented. Other augmentations using virtual traffic lights eliminate confusion arising from multiple pathways presented in one photo. We have planned to conduct extensive user trials to evaluate the effectiveness of the approaches presented on the paper and to extend geoannotation of photographs with other useful cues, leveraging on the increasing availability and precision of geo-tagged photographs from online resources.

Acknowledgements. This work was supported by the UK projects, EQUATOR Interdisciplinary Research Collaboration (EPSRC Grant GR/ N15986/01) and Advanced Grid Interfaces for Environmental e-science in the Lab and in the Field (EPSRC Grant GR/ R81985/01). The vector data used was supplied by the UK Ordnance Survey.

References

1. A9. A9.com – scanning and mapping cities.accessed on (April 04, 2006) http://maps.a9.com
2. Beeharee, A., Steed, A.: Filtering location-based information using visibility. Lecture Notes in Computer Science 3479, 306–315 (April 2005)
3. Beeharee, A.K., Steed, A.: A natural wayfinding exploiting photos in pedestrian navigation systems. In: Mobile HCI, pp. 81–88 (2006)
4. Feiner, S., MacIntyre, B., Höllerer, T., Webster, A.: A touring machine: Prototyping 3d mobile augmented reality systems for exploring the urban environment. In: ISWC, pp. 74–81 (1997)
5. Freeman, R., Steed, A., Zhou, B.: Rapid scene modelling, registration and specification for mixed reality systems. In: Proceedings of ACM Virtual Reality Software and Technology, pp. 147–150 (November 2005)

6. Goodman, J., Brewster, S., Gray, P.: How can we best use landmarks to support older people in navigation? Behaviour and Information Technology 24(1), 3–20 (2005)
7. Goodman, J., Gray, P., Khammampad, K., Brewster, S.: Using landmarks to support older people in navigation. In: Brewster, S., Dunlop, M.D. (eds.) Mobile Human-Computer Interaction – MobileHCI 2004. LNCS, vol. 3160, pp. 38–48. Springer, Heidelberg (2004)
8. Hartley, R., Zisserman, A.: Multiple View Geometry in Computer Vision. Cambridge University Press, (2000) ISBN: 0521623049
9. Microsoft. Microsoft live local. accessed on (April 04, 2006) http://local.live.com
10. Millonig, A., Schechtner, K.: Developing landmark-based pedestrian navigation systems. In: 8th International IEEE Conference on Intelligent Transport Systems (September 2005)
11. Miyazaki, Y., Kamiya, T.: Pedestrian navigation system for mobile phones using panoramic landscape images. In: SAINT 06: Proceedings of the International Symposium on Applications on Internet. Washington, DC, USA, IEEE Computer Society, pp. 102–108 (2006)
12. TomTom. Tomtom, –.: portable gps navigation for cars. accessed on (September 15, 2005) http://www.tomtom.com
13. Verbree, E., Van Anrooij, A.: Interactive navigation through distance added valued panoramic images. In: Maas, H. G., Schneider, D. (eds.) Panoramic Photogrammetry Workshop, Institute of Photogrammetry and Remote Sensing, Dresden, Germany, vol. 34(16) pp. +4 (February 2004)

Paper Metaphor for Tabletop Interaction Design

Guillaume Besacier[1], Gaétan Rey[1], Marianne Najm[2], Stéphanie Buisine[2], and Frédéric Vernier[1]

[1] Limsi-cnrs, bp 133, 91403 Orsay Cedex, France
[2] Ensam-lcpi, 151 boulevard de l'hôpital, 75013 Paris, France
guillaume.besacier@limsi.fr

Abstract. The aim of this paper is to explore new metaphors for interaction design on tabletop system. Tabletop systems are shared horizontal surface for co-located collaboration, which leads to original problems when designing interactions. We propose two metaphors based on the paper: the peeling metaphor, and the slot metaphor, and then suggest a way of using them to design new interactions for solving some of the problems of tabletop systems: documents organization, documents transmission and documents duplication.

Keyword: Tabletop, interaction design, paper metaphor.

1 Introduction

Nowadays revolution to mobile and miniaturized devices hides another creeping evolution toward very large surfaces usable simultaneously by more than one user, called Tabletops. Tabletop is a new form of computer, complementary to the usual desktop and laptop. It is especially efficient for performing co-located collaborative tasks. Indeed, we observe that classical computers can tend to get in the way of having the work done. In the setting of a staff meeting aiming to agree on the wording of a given document and collectively approve it, the usual solution involves a laptop per participant, each one with its own digital copy of the document. People have to handle the document versioning and updates themselves, and each modification has to be applied individually on each copy of the document. This work could be done by the computer in natural and easy-to-understand way by having a single digital copy of the document physically shared by the participants. With tabletop computers, the participants can gather around a digitally-augmented table. The table is at the same time an input device and an output device, allowing for direct manipulation of the data (using one's finger or an augmented pen). Our experiments [5] with creativity meeting show that tabletop systems increased the collaboration among users and give them a feeling of improved efficiency.

Tabletop systems introduce new challenges in user interaction design. The main challenges include:

Multiple users have to share the same surface and interact seamlessly together or in parallel.

J. Jacko (Ed.): Human-Computer Interaction, Part II, HCII 2007, LNCS 4551, pp. 758–767, 2007.

They are located all around the table, leading to different points of view on the documents.

Direct finger or pen interaction limits one's possibilities of interaction to one's physically reachable table space. This space can be divided according to the effort needed to access it (i.e. right in front of the user, need to get up and lean on the table, need to move across the room, etc.)

These challenges lead us to rethink the traditional desktop metaphor. To explore the new possibilities we are developing DiamondSpin [14], a toolkit to build user interfaces for tabletop systems. We invented new interactions and experienced the need for new mechanisms in graphical toolkit. Features we already implemented include color coded frames for distinction of window ownership, automatic window rotation within a polar coordinate system, relocatable and non-modal pop-up menus, push-up menubars sliding along the table edge, and free-hand annotation mechanisms.

1.1 Paper Metaphor

We reckon that, while the technologies like videoconferencing, digital paperboard, and the like are being introduced in the users' workplace, face-to-face pencils and paper meetings are still extremely common. Participants to such meeting intuitively perceive the interactions they can perform with a sheet of paper, a file, or a filing cabinet. In order to facilitate the transition to tabletop systems we have to offer the same intuitiveness.

At the same time we observed other new user interaction techniques based on paper metaphor [1, 2, 8]. In that context, the correspondence between sheet of paper and windows is fundamental. We think this metaphor must be extended to the way users interact with the system. Indeed, even if rotated windows look similar to real paper, the current interaction techniques to rotate them may be difficult to understand. Most of them are barely metaphoric (i.e. adding corners to the windows, and have the user touch the corners to rotate it), or can be difficult to perceive at first glance because of a lack of on screen indications or feedback (i.e. two fingers rotation).

1.2 New Interactions

In this paper, we present two new metaphors based on the paper: peeling and slots, and how we suggest using them to design new interaction techniques.

The peeling metaphor allows users to peel a document in a permanent way (as opposed to the temporary peeling used to see underneath the peeled document). Like with real paper, users can use this technique to reduce the space used by a window. They can also use it to access the verso of the window, where we placed a fully functional graphical user interface, and to make folders of documents in an informal way, by sliding documents between the two sides of a peeled container-document.

The slot metaphor allows the use of slots in tabletop applications. Slots are an affording place to insert paper document, like the slot of a letterbox, but are also commonly accepted as a processing place, like a CD slot where the disk is played. We use a set of slots to move documents to unreachable places on a very large tabletop system, and a special copy slot to duplicate a document.

2 Related Works

Tabletop system first raised hardware challenges and different technologies were developed for tabletop hardware (vision-based [4], electric contact [7], with more than two states [9], etc.) and output system (video-projector, individual head mounted displays [3], screen sensitive to the user's position around the table [11], etc.). While finding standard application don't fit well on tabletop systems, the need for new interaction technique bring us to build the DiamondSpin[14] toolkit to allow WIMP applications to work in a tabletop world. DiamondSpin allows concurrent work on the table but barely support collaboration without specific development for document sharing. Many research works claim the WIMP approach isn't rich enough and should be extended to new interaction styles ([2], [8]) called post-WIMP or rich desktop.

Studies on tabletop interface have been numerous with the first *IEEE International Workshop on Horizontal Interactive Human-Computer Systems* and the special issue of Computer Graphics and Applications on Tabletop systems [10] although they tend to exemplify their interaction techniques only on static documents, with tasks like organizing pictures, or use abstract icons to figure documents [1]. In our work, indeed, we think tabletop documents can be constructed like desktop windows, by mixing standard interactors with original interactions for manipulating whole document or group of documents. Our approach is toolkit-based, with purposes similar to those of Metisse [6] for the desktop computer.

3 Peeling

The possibility to peel (or to fold) digital windows has been proposed as a temporary state of the window, with the purpose of seeing other windows stacked below [2], or facilitating inter-documents interactions between overlapping windows [8]. When the user releases the document or finishes the interaction which prompted for peeling, the document springs back to its unpeeled initial state.

We, on the contrary, would like to explore the possibility to peel documents definitely. It would allow the users to further interact with the peeled document, and unpeel it manually later.

Peeling interaction needs to be both obvious and natural. It needs to be obvious because it's a new interaction. If it's triggered by some obscure sub-sub-option or by a complicated movement of the finger, users will not search for it, and thus will not find it. It also needs to be natural because it's a high level interaction that can be performed on any document. It must not annoy the user while s/he is working on her/his documents.

We propose three ways to activate peeling:

- With a dedicated interactor in the document frame, for example a corner of the document, which can be dragged. This is the most obvious way: when they see an interactor they don't know yet, users may try it. On the cons side, it is not very metaphoric, and does not allow for an arbitrary peeling. The peeling corner has to be on the peeled side, while the opposite corner has to be static.

- With a quick drag gesture from a border of the document to the inside of it. The document can be peeled in any shape the user wants. S/he could also peel a document more than once.
- Automatically, when the document hits an obstacle (the border of the table, another document, etc.). With a physic-like reaction, the document peels itself to avoid the collision with the obstacle. This technique has the advantage of not introducing a new interaction: it uses the standard interaction for moving document, thus probably reducing the learning time for the user.

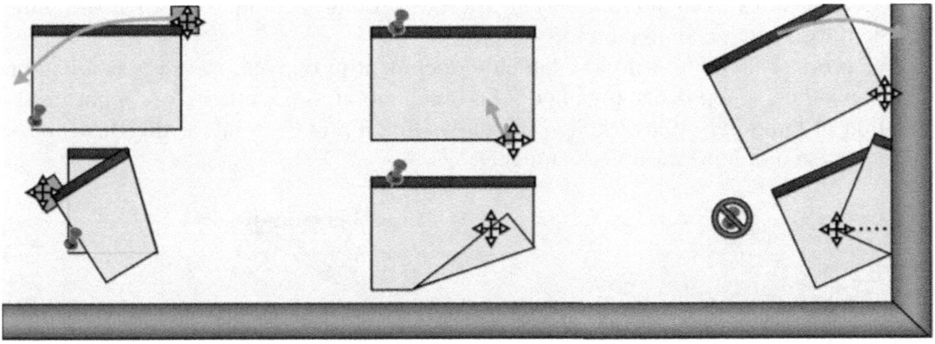

Fig. 1. Three ways for peeling documents. For each technique, the gray line indicates the user gesture, the four arrows indicate the location of the moving point on the peeled side, and the pinpoint indicate the location of the static point on the front side.

3.1 Recto Verso Documents

The first consequence after peeling a document is to make visible a new artifact: the back side of the document. It is empty for temporary peeling (see for example, [6] and [8]), because the user can not interact with it. S/he is already interacting with the component that caused the peeling, and if s/he stops this interaction, the document will stop being peeled. In our case, the user could interact with the peeled side. We think it would be interesting to use this space as the verso of the document. Like the verso of a sheet of paper, the verso of the document should have the same properties than the recto. As our documents are composed of GUI components, the verso of a document can also hold a fully functional graphical user interface. The user can interact with it as if it was a normal document, within the limits, of course, of the visible part of the peeled side.

We think the verso of the document is especially adapted to put the control interfaces associated with the content of the recto. Indeed, tabletop systems are not adapted to the usual pop-up dialog boxes. The link between the dialog box and the document is not visually obvious. While this is not a problem with desktop computer, where a single user works on a single foreground window, it is a problem on tabletop, where multiple users work, together or in parallel, on multiple documents. Putting the dialog boxes contents on the back of the associated document creates a strong link between them.

We envision a translucent texture for the peeled side. The user could see a part of the document content through the peeled side, and thus see the result of his/her modifications.

3.2 Peeling for Piling

Grouping and classifying documents is an important task on computer systems. Many solutions have been studied, but we think they lack of freedom to improvise. In real world, we noticed piles of documents surrounded by a folded piece of paper on many desks. It leads us to imagine a way to use the peeling technique to solve the piling problem we were faced on tabletop systems.

We propose a way to fold any tabletop document in two and to use it as a handler to keep others documents together. Our main point is to allow for opportunistic creation of temporary piles. Study [12] shows that a pile is an interesting structure to support casual organization of documents.

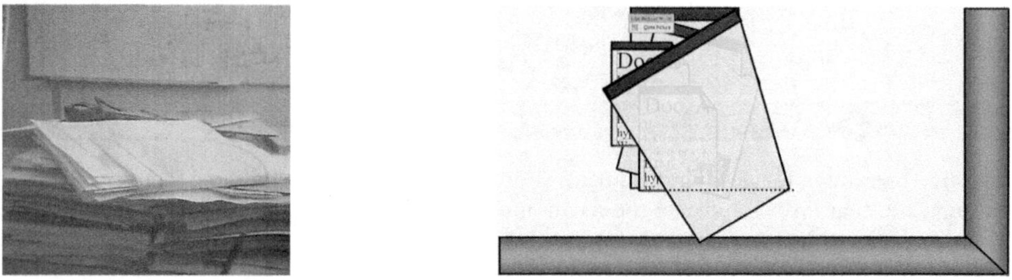

Fig. 2. On the left, a pile of papers in a folded piece of paper, used as inspiration for our metaphoric interaction technique. On the right, a design prototype with three tabletop documents held by a fourth document peeled in two.

The life cycle of a pile can be divided in two phases: the creation of the pile as a set of documents, and the manipulation of the resulting pile and of its documents. For the creation, we envision two ways of building a pile: the pile handler precedes the grouping of the documents, or the documents are grouped and then a handler is put around them. Both ways have pros and cons and will need to be experimented.

In the first case, the user first peels a document, and then slides other documents in between the two sides of it. We have to determine at what time a potential handler grabs a document. Users might want to move a document close to or over a pile without putting it in the pile. Modifying the behavior of a basic interaction (moving documents around the surface) might disturb them.

In the second case, the user first regroups his//her documents on a user-chosen spot on the table, and then peels a document that is underneath the stack. Problems of occlusion and z-order can arise. If the documents to be piled are covering the handler, the user will have difficulties to interact with the latter, especially to peel it. This technique also implies a change to the z-order management. Usually, when a user touches a document, the document moves to the top of the z-order. Here, it would need to stay at its position for the metaphor to work. Only the peeled face should be drawn top-most.

For the second phase, manipulation of the pile, we foresee further than just keeping documents together. Indeed, for our technique to be a contribution to the user effectiveness when manipulating collection of data, we need to break the metaphor and take advantage of the digital information documents carry (document type, metadata, document content). This information could be used to quickly perform tiresome tasks on the pile. For example, all piles could be sorted by document creation or modification date, document title, type, or author. Piles containing a single type of documents could expose document-defined behavior:

- A pile of pictures could launch a slideshow or display thumbnail view of all the contained pictures.
- A pile of graded homework could compute the mean and standard deviation of the grades, display a repartition graph or sort the works by grade or student's group.
- A pile of business cards could expose advanced search functionality, allow sending a mailing to all the people is the pile, or update existing older business cards when user puts in new ones.

The pile handler being peeled in two, the verso of the pile handler is visible. Usually, we would put an interface to manipulate the document recto (that is, the pile handler). The latter having been "recycled" as a pile handler, we can reuse its verso to display the interface to manipulate the pile.

4 Slots

One main challenge of tabletop system is document management. As tabletop systems don't have a preferred orientation managing document doesn't only imply moving and organizing them but also orienting them. As tabletop system remain small in size and resolution much poorer than real paper a tabletop system aiming to manage large numbers of documents must allow zooming in and out of documents. With all these constraints in mind when we explored the paper metaphor we found the idea of slot very useful for document management.

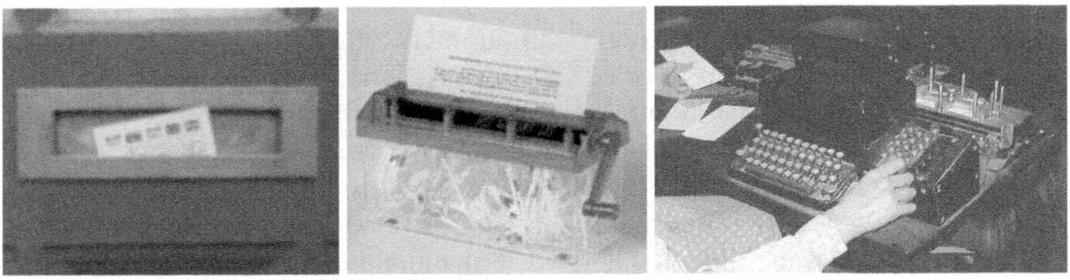

Fig. 3. A letter slot, a paper shredder and a punch card computer (IBM Type 31) used as inspirations for the slot metaphor on tabletop

4.1 Moving Documents with Slots

In real life, slots can be used to hide partially document while showing their presence (See Figure 3), to destroy document (Paper shredder), transmit document (fax copier), etc.

Among all these possible facets of the slot metaphor, transmission looked very promising for tabletop systems for two reasons. First, transmitting document across two tabletop systems raise the spatial problem of addressing the document to the right person on the remote tabletop system. The second interesting problem slot can address occurs when transmitting a document locally to someone on the other side of the table. In this very common scenario we don't have a good solution when the table is very large, and even when the table is small enough orientation of the content never satisfies fully both users. As illustrated in Figure 4 we propose to use a slot to transmit a document from one side of the table to another. If the tabletop system addresses multi-touch technology, a second finger could be used in order to activate the functionality (illustrated as a finger pressing a green button), making the slot armless when a document is just moved over it. In some sense the slot acts as a Transfolder as defined by Sire [15] with a more explicit feedback.

As illustrated on the right part of Figure 4, reception can also act only on demand. What is really specific to tabletop in this technique is the ability to control how the document is received since the target is on the same display and the possibility to rotate the document on the reception side. As shown on the top right part of the figure, the document can flip at the end of transmission or even during transmission (not shown on the illustration).

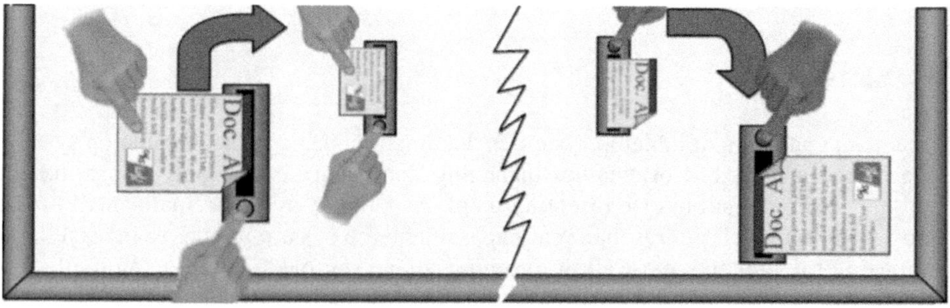

Fig. 4. Document transmission across the table with a slot

The other part of the slot metaphor we find interesting is the affordance to process document (like shredder, laminator or CD slot). An important task we could improve on tabletop system are the free-hand annotation mechanisms (as well known for TabletPC). The slot metaphor could be used to erase annotations, change their color, recall old ones, reveal colleague's annotations and so on.

In the same way an important problem with tabletop system is document sharing policies arising when multiple people start to manipulate document at the same time. A possible resolution of concurrent action is to prevent action from a second user when another user already touched the document. This approach works fine for concurrent work but need to define an explicit way to exchange document in order to also allow group work and processing a document through a slot afford an owner's change (like for letter's slot).

At last the slot metaphor may help to resolve a key challenge of tabletop systems: grouping of documents. If a slot is not fixed on the table but moveable it may serve as a convenient container like the piling technique suggested in the previous section.

4.2 Duplication of Documents

Document duplication is a major element in a collaborative workspace. To facilitate duplication of document we suggest the following interaction techniques based on the paper metaphor.

Copy slot. This technique illustrated in Figure 5 is based on a copier-like slot. When inserted in the slot, a number of copies of the document come out of it. Another version of this slot may be understood as a fax metaphor when only the original document get out of the slot and copies get out of another slot.

Fig. 5. Copy slot metaphor

Tearing-regeneration. Tearing regeneration differs from the previous technique because it doesn't need a dedicated slot. This metaphor uses direct manipulation to create a copy of the document. We suggest two different ways to activate the technique, by stretching and by folding, both needing two fingers.

In pulling activation, when document is pulled in two opposite directions, it first grows until a given size limit if zoomable and when a size limit is reached a crack appears. The crack acts like a generic slot with two half document out of it and notifies users the ongoing possibility to duplicate the document. If user pursues her/his action the crack totally splits the document in two and each parts finally regenerates its missing half. The same technique performed by two users could explicitly solve a conflict (two users trying to move the same document, like [13]).

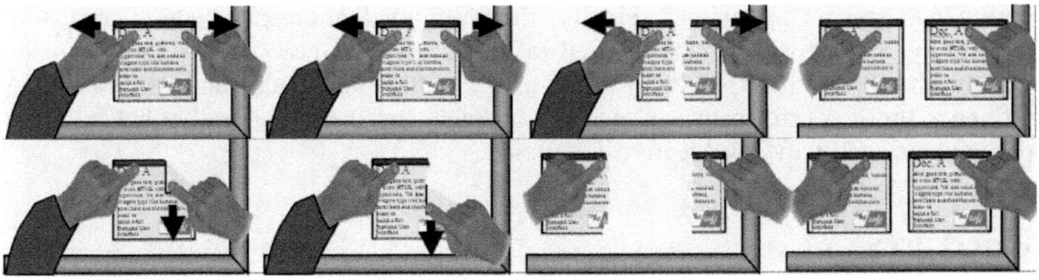

Fig. 6. Tearing-regeneration metaphor by stretching (top) and by folding (above)

Our second two-hand method is based on the folding technique presented previously. The technique occurs when a pivot point is set with a first finger while the document is folded with a second finger like illustrated in the Figure 6. When the folding line reaches the pivot point, a crack appears like in the stretching method. If the second finger takes the torn far enough to split the document in two, it regenerates missing parts again. The choice of sizes of the two parts may indicate an original and a copy. At Last, comparing to the previous activation mode, the feedback duration will give more opportunities to cancel the duplication.

5 Conclusion

In this article we investigated metaphors related to paper in order to solve tabletop centric problems like document sharing and document grouping. As tabletop systems are far more complicated than traditional desktop systems (with more than one user, more than one control point per user, multiple valid orientations around the table, unreachable part of the table, etc.), it seamed important to us to find new sources of inspiration to design metaphoric solutions compatible with the existing user experiences. Our study highlighted two specific rich metaphors we could use to design interactive techniques meeting tabletop needs: slot and peeling.

We are now going to implement these interaction techniques in our DiamondSpin toolkit[14]. These new techniques will be provided as generic tools reachable in the default menu so existing tabletop applications using DiamondSpin will take advantage of them.

Finally we will have to conduct the evaluation phase, which gives rise in itself to new research challenges. Indeed the choice of a protocol is not straightforward to catch the specificities of an interaction metaphor, to test its power, its relevance and usefulness. For example we could set up a three-step evaluation process: in the first step users would have to achieve some pretext task and would be exposed to the metaphor with no instruction on what its purpose is and how to use it. In this phase we would just observe users' behavior and collect their spontaneous comments. In the second evaluation step we would instruct the users to try and discover the target widgets: here we could study the affordance of our design elements (how do the graphical features of the widgets suggest the way to use them) by recording users' behavior and performance. We could also investigate the extent to which this affordance matches the intended metaphor by collecting users' feelings about the design and the metaphor, etc. Finally, the third evaluation step would consist in making the metaphors available to well-informed users in the context of a given task. In this phase we could study the free usage of the metaphors and examine their influence on the performance in task achievement, on the collaborative behaviors of participants and on their subjective experience.

References

1. Agarawala, A., Balakrishnan, R.: Keepin' it real: pushing the desktop metaphor with physics, piles and the pen. In: Proc. CHI 2006 pp. 1283–1292 (2006)
2. Beaudouin-Lafon, M.: Novel Interaction Techniques for Overlapping Windows. In: Proc. UIST 2001 pp. 153–154 (2001)
3. Benko, H., Ishak, E., Feiner, S.: Cross-Dimensional Gestural Interaction Techniques for Hybrid Immersive Environments. In: Proc. IEEE Virtuel Reality (VR'05) (2005)
4. Bérard, F.: The Magic Table: Computer-Vision Based Augmentation of a Whiteboard for Creative Meetings. In: Proc. PROCAMS'03 (2003)

5. Buisine, S., Besacier, G., Najm, N., Aoussat, A., Vernier, F.: Computer-supported creativity: Evaluation of a tabletop mind-map application. HCII 2007 (2007)
6. Chapuis, O., Roussel, N.: Metisse is not a 3D desktop! In: Proc. UIST'05, pp.13–22 (2005)
7. Dietz, P., Leigh, D.: DiamondTouch: A Multi-User Touch Technology. In: Proc. UIST 2001, pp. 219–226 (2001)
8. Dragicevic, P.: Combining crossing-based and paper-based interaction paradigms for dragging and dropping between overlapping windows. In: Proc. UIST 2004, pp. 193–196 (2004)
9. Forlines, C., Shen, C., Buxton, B.: Glimpse: a novel input model for multi-level devices. Ext. Abstracts CHI 2005 pp. 1375–1378 (2005)
10. IEEE Computer Graphics and Application. Interacting with Digital Tabletops. vol. 26(5) (September/October 2006)
11. Kakehi, Y., Iida, M., Naemura, T., Shirai, Y., Matsushita, M., Ohguro, T.: Lumisight Table: Interactive View-Dependent Tabletop Display Surrounded by Mutiple Users. IEEE Computer Graphics and Applications 25(1), 48–53 (2005)
12. Mander, R., Salomon, G., Wong, YY: A Pile. Metaphor for Supporting Casual Organization of Information. In: Proc. CHI'92, pp. 627–634 (1992)
13. Ringel, M., Ryall, K., Shen, C., Forlines, C., Vernier, F.: Release, Relocate, Reorient, Resize: Fluid Techniques for Document Sharing on Multi-User Interactive Tables. In: Proc CHI 2004 pp. 1441–1444 (2004)
14. Shen, C., Vernier, F., Forlines, C., Ringel, M.: DiamondSpin: An Extensible Toolkit for Around-the-Table Interaction. In: Proc. CHI 2004, pp. 167–174 (2004)
15. Sire, S., Chatty, S., Gaspard-Boulinc, H., Colin, F.R.: How can groupware preserve our coordination skills? Designing for direct collaboration, Interact 99 (1999)

Advanced Drivers Assistant Systems in Automation

Caterina Caleefato[1], Roberto Montanari[2], and Fabio Tango[3]

[1] University of Turin, Department of Computer Sciences, Corso Svizzera 185 - 10149 Torino (Italy)
calefato@di.unito.it
[2] University of Modena and Reggio Emilia, Department of Science and Methods of Engineering, Via Amendola 2, Padiglione Tamburini, 42100 Reggio Emilia, Italy
montanari.roberto@unimore.it
[3] Centro Ricerche Fiat, Department of Advanced Safety, Strada Torino 50, 10043 Orbassano, Italy
fabio.tango@crf.it

Abstract. One of the current research areas in automotive field is aimed at improving driving safety with regards to the development of preventive support systems, also called ADAS (Advanced Driver Assistance Systems). These systems are able to detect a critical situation and to inform timely the driver, so that a repairing maneuver can be performed. From the human factors point of view, driving is considered as a complex cognitive task that can be summarized by four main sub-processes: perception, analysis, decision and action . To be performed, each phase presumes the achievement of the previous one, An exception occurs when humans overcome planning / decision phase and go directly from analysis / interpretation to action / execution (almost in automatic way). This paper intends to propose, following the main literature on human-centered automation, how the ADAS intervention can be designed without negative impact on driving safety. In particular, a forward collision warning has been studied. For this study, the Levels Of Automation (LOA) classified by Parasuramam and Sheridan (2000) has been used as well as the studies in the domain of the so-called Adaptive Automation (AA) (Kaber Riley, Endsley 2001; Scerbo 1996), that allow to adapt the information to the driver's workload and to the context level of dangerousness.

1 Introduction

The ergonomic studies about the driving safety are a wide and well-known field (Campbell et al. 1998; Carrea et al. 2000; Mariani, Bagnara, Montanari 2001; Bekiaris et al. 2003; Green 2003). Particularly, the systems that foresee the integration of automation elements into the driving task[1], like in-vehicle information systems[2], integrated

[1] For instance the ACC (adaptive cruise control).

[2] Today also the nomadic devices like pocket pc and mobile phones are part of IVIS (In-Vehicle Information System).

J. Jacko (Ed.): Human-Computer Interaction, Part II, HCII 2007, LNCS 4551, pp. 768–777, 2007.

dashboards[3], innovative commands[4], are studied by the information ergonomics (Marcolin et al. 2002: 59), a field that deal with the improvement of signalling and command devices whose efficient information is often crucial. ADAS (Advanced Driver Assistance Systems), thanks to their sensors, allow monitoring the external environment and in case the presence of a critical situation is assessed, to alert the driver about a possible danger (Berghout et al. 2003; Montanari et al. 2001), supporting him/her in several driving tasks. It is known that preventive information can improve the road-safety: the driver needs to be supported with scenario and task information especially when some dangerous events can occur all-around the vehicle[5]. A typical situation is the detection of dangerous obstacles ahead. Other situations that can be supported by ADAS are low visibility[6] or correct driving behaviour handling[7].

ADAS, both the prototype and the devices already available on the market, alert the driver by visual, acoustic and tactile alarms that a critical situation has been detected, but they also modify the driver behaviour: the driver is earlier warned about dangers, but the same warnings may interfere with the driving task (Wickens 1984; 1989), augmenting the driver's mental workload, often already high (De Waard 1996) and favouring the failure of the whole human-machine system (Montanari 2004).

2 ADAS and Adaptive Automation

Automation does not simply supplant human activity but rather changes it, often in ways unintended and unanticipated by the designers of automation and so poses new coordination demands on the human operator. Designers have to consider some hard choices regarding what has to be automated and to what extent, given that there is little that cannot be automated. It is clear that automation is not all or none, but it can be applied across a *continuum* of levels[8] from low to high, i.e., from fully manual to fully automatic. Any system can involve automation of all types at different levels (Parasuraman, Sheridan 2000: 286-287): the automatic systems can work at a specific level of this *continuum*: a function can be assigned in part to the machine or only in some circumstances (Di Nocera 2004: 78-80). Even if it is technically possible to totally substitute the human with the machine, this substitution is never done, because the operator's role is fundamental, especially if some information is not present

[3] The new dashboards show, apart from traditionally information (such as speedometer, odometer, rev counter, etc.), other information about the trip (instantaneous consumption, fuel autonomy, covered distance, direction to follow, etc.).

[4] Like haptic devices or vocal commands.

[5] It is the case of the collision avoidance system and of blind spot systems.

[6] Like the night vision systems.

[7] It is the case of lane keeping or lane warning.

[8] One of the most relevant automation model is the Parasuraman and Sheridan model (2000: 286-287), made of ten levels: 1) the computer offers no assistance: human must take all decisions and actions; 2) the computer offers a complete set of decision/action alternatives, or 3) narrows the selection down to a few, or 4) suggests one alternative, 5) executes that suggestion if the human approves, or 6) allows the human a restricted time to veto before automatic execution, or 7) executes automatically, then necessarily informs the human, and 8) informs the human only if asked, or 9) informs the human only if it, the computer, decides to 10) the computer decides everything, acts autonomously, ignoring the human.

(Sheridan 1992). ADAS represent the use of intelligence into the vehicles: machines in general can lead an increasing number of tasks, thanks the implementation of rules, decision making and problem solving strategies. The development of adaptive and customised solutions able to lead the driver towards a correct driving performance, should be the basis of the IVIS (In-Vehicle Information System) design, following the must of the "joint cognitive system" model. This model has a real realization in the Driver, Vehicle and Environment model (DVE model) (Hollnagel, 2004).

The driver's tasks are often reduced to the supervisory and detection of the changes in the system status: this shift from performing tasks to monitoring automated systems can inhibit human's ability to detect critical situations (emergencies, false alarms and system faults). So an operator's manual skills can begin to deteriorate in the presence of long periods of automation (Wickens, 1992). Unfortunately, into the automatic systems, problems may propagate more quickly and they may be more difficult to isolate (Scerbo 1996). The human must deal with not "designed" emergencies: designers cannot foresee all the possible scenarios or faults and provide solutions: the human is the guarantee for the system functioning during faults (Di Nocera 2004: 82). This context of action and the complex driving scenario pose new difficulties for the design of the human-machine interaction, that has to be more flexible, as shown in the adaptive automation (AA) researches (Kaber, Riley, Endsley 2001: 37-57). In AA, the level of automation or the number of systems operating under automation can be modified in real time: changes in the state of automation can be initiated by either the human or the system Consequently, AA enables the level or modes of automation to be tied more closely to operator needs or to the context at any given moment (Hancock, Chignell, 1987; Parasuraman et al. 1992; Rouse, 1976; Scerbo, 1996)

Adaptive systems improve the human's and system safety, but because of their dynamism and partial unpredictability, they may cause the operator's disorientation. Automation has to face with the out-of-the-loop performance and the loss of situation awareness, problems to which AA try to give a solution, maintaining the human in loop. Well-designed information can modify the mental workload until lead it to an adequate level to work out the task. If the human is out-of-the-loop, when s/he detects an error, s/he needs an often critical additional time to verify the system status, to understand what has happened and to proceed appropriately. The possible outcomes can vary from a little delay about the return to normality to a catastrophic failure (Endsley 1996; 1997; Kaber, Riley, Endsley 2001; Parasuraman e Sheridan 2000).

When situations arise that the automation cannot handle, humans are expected to step in and resolve the situation, but their ability is impaired by the high levels of automation that have been introduced. (Harrison, Johnson, Wright, 2001). The solution offered by AA can be applied not only to the automatic functions but also to the user interface that manage them. Several studies are developing interesting solutions of dynamic adaptation of interface to the external context and to the user psychophysical condition. More sophisticated mechanisms provide proper information at proper time. For example, a current research field is the introduction of dynamic displays into adaptive system interfaces. Dynamic displays allow *ad hoc* configurations of informative needs and of interaction styles. For instance, dynamic in-vehicle displays can show specific interface features on the basis of the time of the day, like the night modality of navigator displays, which invert their colours. Thanks to the presence of a flexible display configuration in order to satisfy driver's information needs, the situation awareness is enhanced and the driving performance improves. The interface dynamic adaptation may be performed also by the personalisation of content and layout. A practical example is given by the "Information Manager" proposed by Geddes and Hammer (Kaber, Riley, Endsley 2001): the system allow to intelligently set commands and displays into a plane cockpit, in order to provide pilots relevant information related to their task and to the automatic subsystems. Nowadays, an interesting research about the adaptation of interface and information in the automotive domain is the AIDE (Adpative In-vehicle Driver interfacE) European project (www.aide-eu.org).

3 A Proposal of Adaptive Frontal Collision Warning System

The Forward Collision Warning (FCW) systems are able to detect object(s) ahead and in case they are (dangerous) obstacles[9], to warn the drivers, so that a corrective action can be taken. These obstacles can be moving or fixed. Once the system detects such an object, it sends warnings to the driver. There can be different levels of system intervention: from the simple warning (by means of different HMI channels), through a cooperative automation (the car is slowing down or breaking only after the driver has started an action), until a fully automated action (the car is able to perform a total automatic intervention (e.g. complete braking). This is the case of systems that are more involved in the "collision mitigation" or pre-safe area: in this situation, the car is able to brake down even if the crash is unavoidable, in order to reduce at least the consequences of it. In some other case, it is possible to suggest the properly manoeuvre (as described in some project and prototype vehicles, for more details, see PReVENT Integration Project, www.prevent-eu, org). The action (to send a warning or to slow down) depends on which phase of information processing has been automated: sensory processing and perception or decision making and selection (Parasuraman, Sheridan 2000: 287). Some ADAS applications are already available on the automotive market, but this market is still young and not wholly explored yet. Today FCW systems are available on some USA trucks and buses and they are produced by Eaton-Vorad, while in Europe they are implemented on prototype vehicles (Saroldi 2002; 2003). These FCW systems are very useful when the environment conditions are critical, for example when it is foggy or – generally speaking – when the driver's judgement is limited or even wrong. These systems have some technical limits, because they detect high-positioned objects as road obstacles: roads signals, bridges, three branches, etc. Anyway these are all examples of static automation: once the level of automation (LoA) has been established during design development, it will no more vary. To really support the driver, the system has to understand its own limits and to work with them. The new generation of FCW

[9] An obstacle is an object regarded as inside the *host-vehicle* trajectory, where "host-vehicle" is meant to be the vehicle on which the system is installed.

systems has to join the system needs with the user centred design principles (Brusilovsky 1996; Hoedemacker 2003; Rothrock et al. 2002). The perception and analysis of in- and out-vehicle environment (internal and external scenarios) have to be improved, in order to develop an advanced adaptive user interface (like in the AIDE project, www.aide-eu.org) and to integrate cooperative systems able to exchange crucial information with the vehicles and the road infrastructures (in the SAFESPOT project, www.safespot-eu.org).

The user interface of the FCW system prototype presented in this paper has been developed[10] starting from this technological scenario. The figure 1 shows the prototype interface, similar to common FCW system interfaces: there are command buttons on the steering wheel and a little display in the instrument cluster, between the speedometer and the odometer, that provides short and critical information. Another display in the middle of the dashboard provides not crucial information.

The aim of this prototype is to study, with an adequate range of approximation, the user's reaction about the introduction of different levels of automation. In other words: should the driver accept on his/her vehicle an automated adaptive system that may vary its autonomy level into the automation *continuum*, switching between fully manual and automated situations? This prototype increments its automation level directly proportionally to the risk, inferred from the "time-to-collision" and it returns to the manual process managing when the critical situation disappears[11].

Fig. 1. User interface of the FCW system virtual prototype

4 Function Allocation

To develop an adaptive FCW system it is needed a task analysis and function allocation preliminary study. Task analysis and function allocation both aim to match the human abilities with the system ones, in order to automate the tasks best suited to

[10] The user interface prototype of the FCW system has been developed with the rapid prototyping tool "Altia", distributed in Italy from Teoresi s.r.l, Turin. (Calefato 2005).

[11] For some years the automotive research has been studying adaptive ADAS, today available as prototype (www.aide-eu.org, www.prevent-ip.org).

machines and to maintain as manual the functions best suited to human (Harrison, Johnson, Wright, 2001). The task analysis is a graphic representation (as flow chart) of tasks and sub tasks that the operators may accomplish with the system. Once the basilar functions have been founded, they will be allocated, in order to consider the consequences of the match of functions[12] with roles [13] and scenarios.

The York Method (developed at the Department of Computer Science, University of York) provides theoretical instruments to define functions, rules and scenarios, and then represents them by some specific grids. The aim is to decide which functions are suitable to which rules, considering different scenarios. "A function may be separable from all roles, and technically feasible and cost effective to automate, in which case the function may be totally automated. Alternatively it is possible that the function maps entirely to one of the roles, and is infeasible to automate, in which case the function is totally performed within that role. In most cases however functions fit into neither category. In this situation the function is to be partially automated" (Harrison, Johnson, Wright, 2001). Functions and roles have to be set into one or more scenarios. The scenario development process involves several steps (Wide Allen 2004): 1) identification of goals and objectives; 2) scenario definition, including specifications and development of needed model elements and performance measures; 3) preparation of specific component models; 4) program specific performance measures; 5) scenario programming; 6) testing, upgrading and validating of the system on the chosen scenarios. In taking into account the driving scenario, it has to be measured the driver's competences in tasks critical to performance and safety.

5 The FCW System Automation Levels Related to the User Interface

As it has been described above, the FCW system can increment its LOA (Level Of Automation) when the potential danger increases. Under this viewpoint, when the frontal obstacle becomes closer and the driver has not started a repairing manoeuvre yet, the system enhance possibly its automatic intervention and tries to solve the situation "alone".

With reference to the Sheridan model, the LoAs for an FCW system are illustrated in the following table, where the type automation and support are associated to different HMI status, where it has been done the hypothesis that it is constituted by a display in the instrument cluster (Parasuraman, Sheridan 2000: 287). This table can be considered for the design of the FCW system interface[14].

---

12 "Work systems perform functions or units of work. A function is an activity that the man-machine system is required to be capable of performing in order to achieve some result in the domain under consideration" (Harrison, Johnson, Wright, 2001).

13 Role is difficult to define. It makes sense to consider it as an activity that can be performed either by human or machine (Harrison, Johnson, Wright, 2001).

14 The LoA 8, 9, 10 are not adequate to the automotive field, because the driver has always to be in loop, partially at least.

Table 1. The table shows FCW system automation levels related to the user interface behavior. Every interface message is reinforced by acoustic or vocal warnings.

Level of Automation	User Interface behaviour
1. the system offers no assistance: human must take all decisions and actions	The instrument cluster display gives no information.
2. the system offers a complete set of decision/action alternatives	The system recommends to maintain a safe driving behaviour, for example with a cautionary alert message[15].
3. the system narrows the selection down to a few	The system provides a warning level for an imminent danger: driver has to take an action. Moreover, the system can filter the incoming calls and the pre-navigator manoeuvres.
4. the system suggests one alternative	The system can suggest the optimal manoeuvre to take, depending on the scenario and on the external conditions. The indication is provided by the instrument cluster display.
5. the system executes that suggestion if the human approves	The system can take automatically an action, for example it can start braking. In this case, driver has to approve, pressing the braking pedal, then the control is shifted to the system until the action is ended.
6. the system allows the human a restricted time to veto before automatic execution	The system is able to perform a more "sophisticated" action, for example a complete avoiding manoeuvre (such as controlling the steering wheel), based on the situation and on the external condition. In this case, however, the instrument cluster display inform the driver about what's happening; he/she can stop the repairing manoeuvre at any time.
7. the system executes automatically, then necessarily informs the human	Now the system is able to perform a completed automatic manoeuvre. It is the case, after providing warnings, if the driver continues to take no actions, the system start, for example, an emergency braking. It can occur that the crash is not avoidable anymore and in this case at least a collision mitigation is carried out, to reduce the consequences of an impact. This fact depends on when the system intervention is set up; in other words, it is a matter of system design. The instrument cluster display inform anyway the driver of the incoming repairing manoeuvre.

[15] Thinking of a warning system with 3-levels of alert, the first point is equivalent to a level 1 (or "Green" level), the point 2 to a level 2 (or "Yellow" level) and eventually point 3 to a level 3 (or "Red" level)

It is worth to note that the previous table offers several level of automation, referred to FCW application, which are based on the Sheridan's model. In particular, the last point deals with collision mitigation aspect, joined with the frontal collision function. The studies about the development of an adaptive FCW system are open. The results of a preliminary test with thirty users, in order to measure the perception of utility and acceptability of such a system are positive. The system is useless for the for the 3,3% of the sample, useful for the 53.3% and very useful for the 43,3%. The system is unacceptable for the 3,3% of the sample, neutral for the 23,3%, acceptable for the 63,3% and very acceptable for the 10%.

6 Conclusions

Driving scenario and manoeuvres have been broken down into functions and sub-functions in order to outline which functions have to be performed manually, automatically or both. System and driver's role have been combined with functions in order to outline which functions suite best to which roles, considering the given scenarios. The scenarios have been selected in order to measure the driver workload and situation awareness. The FCW system presented has to perform two tasks: to inform the driver of the presence of a frontal obstacle and to take part in the repairing manoeuvre, if the driver doesn't realize it. Consequentially the selected scenario shows the whole behaviour of The FCW system, along the seven LoA implemented. The repairing manoeuvre (i.e. to slow down, to brake, etc.) have been broken down into the four building blocks of a function: information, decision, action, supervision on ongoing execution (Harrison, Johnson, Wright, 2001), in order to match functions with roles. These analyses lead to a FCW system concept that foresees two modules:

1. The warning and recommendation module that alerts the driver of the obstacle presence: the adaptive automation is applied to the user interface and is based on the human driving behaviour.
2. The intervention module: the adaptive automation is applied to the driving task performance and the system can physically support the driver, suggesting how to lead the vehicle[16] (or to cooperate with the driver, by different levels of automatic support/intervention in most advanced functions).

The virtual prototype of the FCW system user interface allows studying acceptability and utility of the system perceived by the user, so it is a powerful mean to correct the system behaviour in the early steps of design.

References

1. Bekiaris, E., Amditis, A., Panou, M.: DRIVABILITY: a new concept for modelling driving performance, Cognition Technology and Work, June 2003 (2003)
2. Berghout, L., Versteegt, E., van Arem, B.: Advanced driver assistance systems; Results of the State of the Art of ADASE-II (2003) available on http://www.adase2.net

---

[16] E.g. to slow down or to apply a light strength to the steering wheel, in order to suggest the properly manoeuvre.

3. Brusilovsky, P.: Methods and Techniques of Adaptive Hypermedia, In: Journal of user modeling and user-adapted interaction. vol 6(2-3) 1996, pp. 87–129 (1996)
4. Cacciabue, P.C.: Guide to Applying Human Factors Methods—Reference odel of Cognition Chapter. Springer, Berlin (2004)
5. Calefato, C.: 2005, HMI e Adaptive automation. In: info@teoresi - news&notes, periodico di Information Technology, N 3/4 (December 2005)
6. Campbell, J.L., Carney, C., Kantowitz, T.H.: Human Factors Design Guidelines for Advanced Traveller Information Systems (ATIS) and Commercial Vehicle Operations (CVO). Georgetown Pike, VA: Office of Safety and Traffic Operations R&D Federal Highway Administration FHWA-RD-98-057 (1998)
7. Carrea, P., Deregibus, E., Montanari, R.: The Invisible Hand: How to design the best interaction between Advanced Driver Assistance Systems and Car Users, SAE 2000-01-CO34 (2000)
8. De Waard, D.: The measurement of drivers' mental workload, Dissertation Rijksuniversiteit Groningen (1996)
9. Di Nocera, F.: Che cos'è l'ergonomia cognitiva, Carocci editore, Roma (2004)
10. Endsley, M.R., Endsley, M.R.: Automation and situation awareness. In: Parasuraman, R.e, Mouloua, M. (eds.) Automation and human performance: Theory and applications, pp. 163–181. Lawrence Erlbaum, Mahwah, NJ (1996)
11. Endsley, M.R.: Situation Awareness, Automation and Free Flight, presentato al FAA/Eurocontrol Air Traffic Management R&D Seminary, Saclay, France – June 1997 (1997)
12. Fitts, P.M.: Human Engineering for an Effective Air Navigation and Traffic Control System. Washington, DC: National Research Council (1951)
13. Green, P.: Alliance of Automobile Manufacturers Statement of Principles, Criteria and Verification Procedures on Driver Interactions with Advanced In Vehicle Information and Communication Systems (draft version 3.0), Alliance of Automobile Manufacturers Washington, D.C (2003)
14. Hancock, P.A., Chignell, M.H.: Adaptive control in human-machine systems. In: Hancock, P.A. (ed.) Human factors psychology, pp. 305–345. Elsevier Science Publishers, North Holland (1987)
15. Harrison, M.D., Johnson, P.D., Wright, P.C.: Automating Function in multi agent control systems: supporting the decision process. In: Proceedings of the Tenth Safety-critical Systems Symposium (2002)
16. Hollnagel, E.: Driver Distraction, Telematics Design, and Workload Managers: Safety Issues and Solutions, SAE Paper Number 2004-21-0022 (2004)
17. Kaber, D.B., Riley, J.M., Tan, K., Endsley, M.R: On the Design of Adaptive Automation for Complex Systems. In: International Journal of Cognitive Ergonomics, vol. 5(1), Lawrence Erlbaum Associates, Mahwah, NJ (2001)
18. Francesco, M., Gianna, M., Adriano, O., Fernando, L., Sergio, P., Liza, V.B.: a cura di, Glossario di Ergonomia, Inail, Sovrintendenza Medica Generale (2002) available at http://www.inail.it
19. Mariani, M., Bagnara, S., Montanari, R.: Fasi iniziali della progettazione centrata sull'utente per sistemi multimediali d'auto, Convegno nazionale della SIE (Società Italiana di Ergonomia), Firenze 2001 (2001)
20. Montanari, R.: Safety and driver's information: designing adaptive in-vehicle user interface, PhD. Thesis, University of Florence 2004 (2004)

21. Parasuraman, R., Bahri, T., Deaton, J.E., Morrison, J.G., Barnes, M.: Theory and design of adaptive automation in aviation systems (Technical Report No. NAWCADWAR-92033-60). Naval Air Warfare Center, Aircraft Division, Warminster, PA (1992)
22. Parasuraman, R., Sheridan, T.B.: A Model for Types and Levels of Human Interaction with Automation, Fellow, in Transactions on systems, man, and cybernetics – Part A: Systems and humans, IEEE vol. 30(3), May 2000,(2000)
23. Prinzel, L.J.: Team-Centerede perspective for Adaptive Automation Design, Langley Research Center, Hampton, Virginia, available from NASA Center for Areospace Information (CASI) (2003)
24. Ling, R., Richard, K., Frederic, F., Michael, H., Gavriel, S.: Review and reappraisal of adaptive interfaces: toward biologically-inspired paradigms, publication: Theoretical Issues in Ergonomic Science (2002)
25. Rouse, W.B.: Adaptive allocation of decision making responsibility between supervisor and computer. In: Sheridan, T.B., Johannsen, G. (eds.) Monitoring behavior and supervisory control, pp. 295–306. Plenum Press, New York (1976)
26. Saroldi, A.: Traffic Scenario Sensors: needs and perspectives – Presentation at ATAEL Conference on ADAS – Siena (2002)
27. Saroldi, A., Bianco, E.: ADASE II Project Deliverable: Status of Practise (2003)
28. Scerbo, M.W.: Theoretical perspectives on adaptive automation. In: Parasuraman, R., Mouloua, M. (eds.) Human performance in automated systems: Theory and applications, Lawrence Erlbaum Associates, Mahwah, NJ (1996)
29. Sheridan, T.B.: Telerobotics, Automation, and Human Supervisory Control. MIT Press, Cambridge, MA (1992)
30. Wickens, C.D.: Processing resources in attention. In: Parasuraman, R., Davies, D.R. (eds.) Varieties of Attention, pp. 63–102. Academic Press, London (1984)
31. Wickens, C.D.: Attention and skilled performance. In: Holding, D.H. (ed.) Human Skills, Chichester, UK, pp. 71–105. John Wiley & Sons, New York, NY (1989)
32. Wickens, C.D.: Engineering psychology and human performance, 2nd edn. New York: Harper Collins (1992)
33. http://www.aide-eu.org
34. http://www.safespot-eu.org

Implementing an Interactive Collage Table System with Design Puzzle Exploration

Teng-Wen Chang and Yuan-Bang Cheng

Graduate School of Computational Design,
National Yunlin University of Science and Technology, 123 University Road, Section 3, Douliou, Yunlin 64002, Taiwan
{tengwen,g9434716}@yuntech.edu.tw

Abstract. By combining puzzles as the metaphor as well as the mechanism, design puzzles provide an interesting computational method to both design exploration and representing the design ideas via collage images. By using multi-touch technology such as FTIR, this research implements a physical controlling device called Collage Tables (CoTa) for directly manipulating the design collages, which using the mechanism developed over the years from design puzzles. By focusing on the interactive behaviours of design collage, the exploration rules as well as puzzle rules are further developed and elaborated in this paper. The exploration search mechanism and the system (CoTa) in both hardware and software part of CoTa is also evaluated and computed for the purpose of reification. A set of possible interaction is also documented in this paper.

Keywords: interactive collage table, design collage, multi-touch and sketch, design puzzle, design exploration.

1 Introduction

Inspired by design-as-puzzle-making process [1], [2] propose an inspiring design games called design puzzles using puzzles as both metaphor and gaming process mechanism. Design puzzle is comprised of hints, rules and goals. With exploration of design iteration, design puzzles provide both representation and the exploration methods over a specific representation, particular puzzle servers and puzzle rules [2], [3], [4]. Among those design puzzles, design collage that is the main focus of this paper indicates the visual manipulation and feedbacks under the control of design puzzle mechanisms.

Additionally, tangible user interface [5] provides a lot of implication over the design as well as the interface itself. With intuitive input devices (such as hand or fingers), tangible user interfaces offer the mostly needed functionality: direct manipulation. With direct manipulation, tangible user interaction can make users focus on what they want to do not how they are doing.

J. Jacko (Ed.): Human-Computer Interaction, Part II, HCII 2007, LNCS 4551, pp. 778–787, 2007.

Furthermore, inspired by the low-cost multi-touch sensing interface implementation [6], we use the technology of FTIR (Frustrated Total Internal Reflection) for implementing the 2D sketch drawing and collaged images required for collage games.

Based on the technology developed in [7], [8], the first experiment on implementing tangible interface (collage table) for design collage has been conducted and reported in [9]. Furthermore, the project called *Collage Tables* (CoTa) has been established, and the details of the system operations and mechanisms are described in this paper. The rules for the mechanism of CoTa have further elaborated as 1) *Exploration Rules*, and 2) *Puzzle Rules*.

The user studies over the user interactions and feedbacks via physical interaction interface with the design collage game have also conducted and described in the paper.

2 Collage Table (CoTa) - with a Visual Interaction Game to Explore the Design Concepts

Design puzzle is comprised of three main elements: *hints*, *rules*, and *goals*. Designer's abstract ideas are presented by visual information (images) to form the hints that stimulate the exploration by an intuitive and direct visual manipulation. The designer can adjust these images to change their representation via visual manipulation with intuitive interface. Once all images have already arranged and collaged on the *Collage Area*, such collaged images will then become another new hint to bring to next new exploring process. This is an iterative process for exploring the possible alternatives that can inspire or represent the glance of complex design concepts (or the design itself). Under this iterative process, a *collage* (the outcome of one exploration process) will be generated once one exploration process is completed. A new exploration with different hint will then be started. A design goal will be determined while the satisfaction signals have been received from users for one exploration session to complete the game (as shown in Fig. 1).

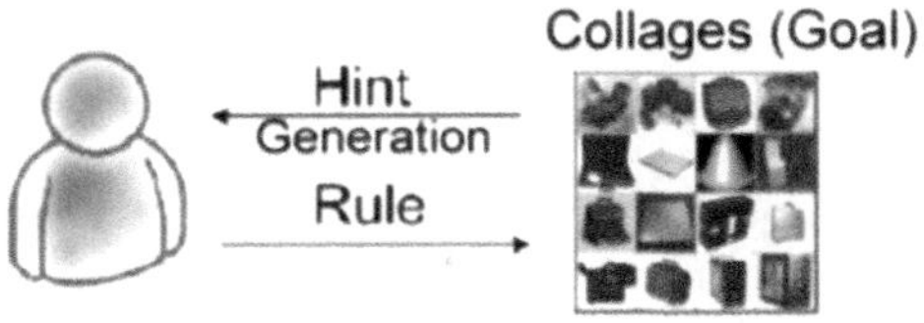

Fig. 1. Design collage game exploratory concepts

2.1 Collage Table System Mechanism Diagram

In this paper, we propose a refined the mechanism diagram of four Units (Concept Input Units, Interpreter Units, Representation Units and Exploration Units) of CoTa is shown in (Fig. 2). First, in the Concept Input Unit, the user sketches the design concepts using the *Sketch interface*, and then with simple *Keyword Tag & Logic interface,* the users convert the sketched elements using keywords and logic relation between the two keywords. In the Interpreter Unit, the CoTa will interpret the Concept Input Unit into a computable representation. Through these computational representations, CoTa will then search out these relevant images via a search engine (such as Google image search engine) in the Representation Unit. The outcome will be a hint for the design puzzle.

Further, in the Exploration Unit, the user can play the design collage game using the *Design Collage Game interface* according to the Exploration Rules. And then the user might generate a new hint according to the Puzzle Rules. This is an iterative process until Collages is satisfying the user to turn into a goal, and then the exploration process is done.

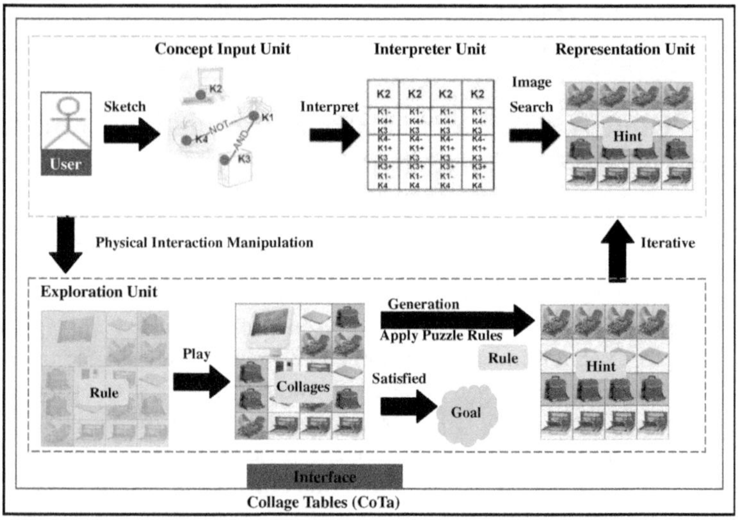

Fig. 2. Collage Table (CoTa) mechanism diagram

2.2 System Mechanism

The system details about the four units described above will be elaborated under the following sections.

Concept Input Unit. The purpose of this unit is providing an input interface to lead the designer to express their abstract concepts, and then getting their design knowledge structures. One example is shown in Fig. 3. After users have done the sketches, then a simple keyword-relation graph can be produced via pattern recognition. At the same time, based on our scope (building up the interface) and for simplifying the search operations, it can only generate one path in the Concept Input Unit, and it should not have cycles in the path.

Interpreter Unit. The purpose of this Interpreter unit is explaining the design knowledge structures from Concept Input Unit to become a computable representation, and this unit is further mapped to a related Representation Unit. Through the design

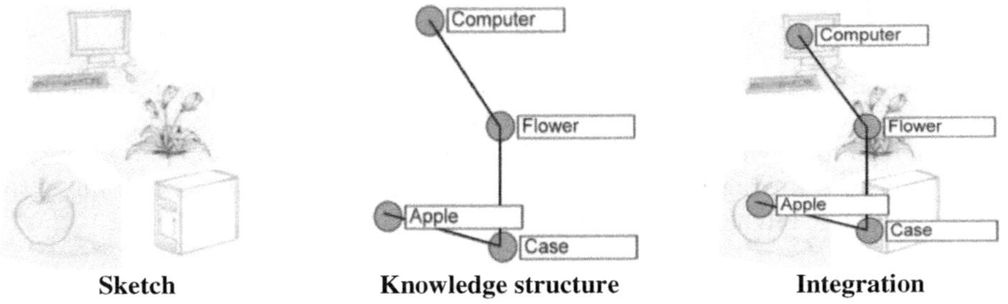

Fig. 3. Concept Input Unit

knowledge structures, this unit is getting three variables. They are: 1) keywords (drawings), 2) logic relations of keywords (And or Not), and 3) location orders (top-down and front-rear). The interpretive result is a series of "keywords and simple logic", and storing into the two-dimension array for sending to Representation Unit to use.

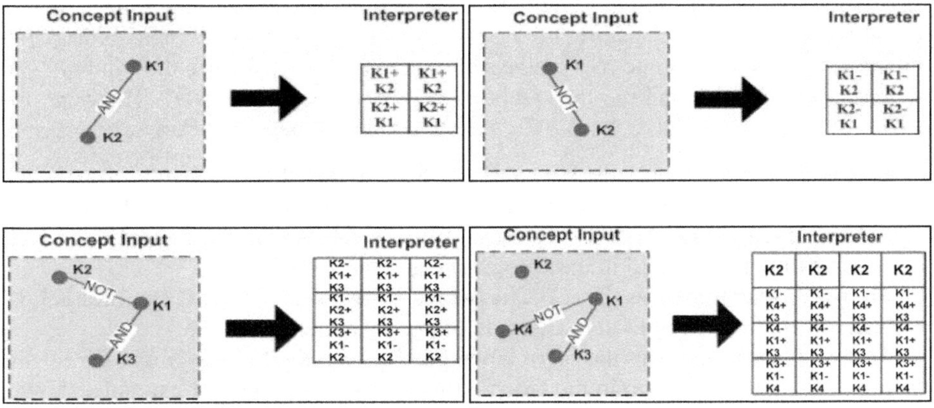

Fig. 4. The transformations in the Interpreter Unit (from left to right and up to down): 1) Two keywords have the AND logical relation. 2) Two keywords have the NOT logical relation. 3) Three keywords have the AND & NOT logical relations. 4) Four keywords have the AND & NOT & no logical relations.

The keywords have the effects on the size of two-dimension array and the amount of collage images in the Representation Unit. The logic relation of keywords is used for feeding the searching engine such as Google image search engine. The location orders are including: order of keywords and order of linked-lists. This is for the orientation of the knowledge structure. First, the order of keywords is the location of top to down. Second, the order of linked-list is the order of front node to rear node. Front node has an upper location than rear node in a linked-list. In the Interpreter Unit, only one linked-list (as limited by the search engine) will be generated and this list is processed along the path of the linked-list. The location orders are mapped to the arrangement of the collage images in the Representation Unit. The following figures (Fig. 4) illustrate the transformations from Concept Input Unit to Interpreter Unit.

Representation Unit. The purpose of this unit is to provide a representation interface to execute interpretive result. Executing process is to integrate search engine to search images, then to download the image information in order according to the array, and finally to paste the images on the interface to finish the initial *Registered Collage Image* for forming a hint to be explored (Fig. 5).

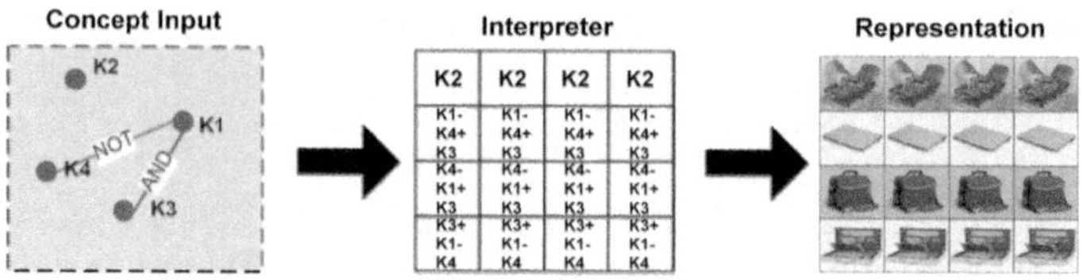

Fig. 5. The representation of design collage

In the above the figure, the CoTa interpreted the Concept Input to form a 4×4 square size. They have four different sets of the keywords to execute the search from Google image search engine, such as row 1 to row 4. It will paste the next alternative image into the next column in the same row by the same searching way. We use the symbol "-" to represent the "NOT", and use the symbol "+" to represent the "AND". This is no any logic relation, which is like the "OR". We explain about them as following:

1) Row 1: searching uses the keyword K2. Such as, input K2 to search from the text field in the Google image search engine. For example, show in the right of Fig. 6.
2) Row 2: searching uses the set of keywords K1-K4+K3. Such as, input K1 K3 -K4 to search from the text field in the Google image search engine.
3) Row 3: searching uses the set of keywords K4-K1+K3. Such as, input K4 K3 -K1 to search from the text field in the Google image search engine.
4) Row 4: searching uses the set of keywords K3+K1-K4. Such as, input K3 K1 -K4 to search from the text field in the Google image search engine. For example, show in the left of Fig. 6.

Exploration Unit. The purpose of this unit is to add the exploring actions (manipulations) for playing design collage game in the collage interface for design exploration. User can use selection and movement to pick the interesting images from Registered Collage Image in the Hint Zone. When the image is moved and the user puts the image into the Collage Area or Buffer Area, the blank space shown on the gird of the Registered Collage Image will show the other images in the same place instead through the original image's keywords searching. When the user drags the image(s) to move and puts the image(s) into the Collage Area, the image(s) will return to its/their original size. Within the Collage Area, user can do the adjustments of scale and rotation for the Collage Image, and also do the arrangements and collages on the Collage Table physical interface. Exploration process needs the rules that decide the next explorative hint. We will explain more its details in the next sections.

Fig. 6. The searching way example (from left to right): 1) Searching uses the keyword K2. 2) Searching uses the sets of keywords K3+K1-K4.

3 User Behaviors and System Rules

The CoTa has two main rules operations, and they are *Exploration Rules* and *Puzzle Rules*. They are both also operating under the Exploration Unit. Exploration Rules are for playing the design collage game, and Puzzle Rules are for generating a new hint.

Table 1. User behaviors, game operations, and Exploration Rules

User behaviors	Game operations	Exploration Rules
1. Touch some image(s) through the finger(s), and then leave right away.	Selection	1. IF "generate some point(s) on the image(s), and then disappear right away." THEN "select the image(s)."
2. Touch some image(s) through the finger(s), and then move the finger(s) to drag some image(s) on the panel.	Movement	2. IF "generate some point(s) on the image(s), and then move some point(s) to change its/their current location(s)." THEN "move the image(s)."
3. Touch some image through using two fingers, and then increase/decrease the distance from one finger to the other finger.	Scale	3. IF "generate two points on the image, and then increase/decrease the distance from one point to the other point." THEN "scale the image." Long distance is to become bigger, and short distance is to become smaller.
4. Touch some image through using two fingers, and then fix one finger and move the other finger to anticlockwise or clockwise.	Rotation	4. IF "generate two points on the image, and then fix one point and move the other point to anticlockwise or clockwise." THEN "rotate the image." The image can be anticlockwise rotation, or clockwise rotation.
5. Drag some image(s) inside of the Collage Area.	Collage	5. IF "generate some point(s) on the image(s), and then move some point(s) inside of the Collage Area." THEN "collage the image(s)."
6. Drag some image(s) outside of the Collage area	Buffer	6. IF "generate some point(s) on the image(s), and then move some point(s) outside of the Collage Area." THEN "put the image(s) into the Buffer Area."

Exploration Rules control the user's manipulations for playing the game. Because the game is based on the multi-touch tangible interface, user operates the game through the user's hand(s) (or more precisely the figures). We list the user behaviors (actions) and the game operations with Exploration Rules, such as the Table 1.

In the Exploration Unit, the user can make the CoTa generate a new Registered Collage Image as a new hint for the user. According to the computational mechanism of the CoTa, it takes the result of the Collage Image(s) as called Collages from the Collage Area, and generates the new hint through the Puzzle Rules to search again from Google. The Puzzle Rules are including the following parameters:

1) Location: the locations of every image on the Collage Area.
2) Size: the sizes of every image on the Collage Area.
3) Amount: the amount of the images on the Collage Area.
4) Keyword: every image has the attached keywords from Google image search engine.
5) Keywords and simple logic: every image has the set of keywords and simple logic from Interpreter Unit.

The images can be arranged and collaged through the visual weight or difference. In the location parameter, we divide the Collage Area (blue base frame) into night zones to represent the priority about the location, and the Fig. 7 as an example. These zones have an order in the priority, and showing these numbers represents the priority in the following figure. The order is number 1 to 4, and the number 1 is the prior order. Furthermore, the image is bigger size, and it has a prior order. When two images have the same priority in the location, the order of the two images will be according to the size. In contrast, when they have the same priority in the size, they will be according to the location. If they have the same priority in the location and the size, they will be re-set the order via the integrations of the keywords and logic.

4	3	4
2	1	2
4	3	4

Fig. 7. The order of priority in the night zones

4 Implementing a Physical Design Collage - Collage Tables

4.1 System Hardware

The physical system (Collage Tables) conceptual diagram for CoTa is shown in Fig. 8. The components are: 1) User interface, 2) Google image database and Internet, 3) Computer, 4) Projector, 5) Mirror, and 6) Webcam.

In the Collage Table, the user interface is made a multi-touch panel using the FTIR technology. The designer can sketch out drawings of own design concepts on the

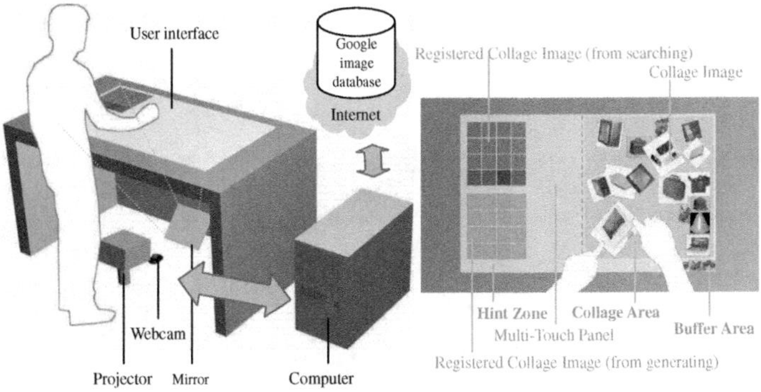

Fig. 8. The components in the Collage Table (from left to right): 1) The component units. 2) User interface.

multi-touch interactive interface. The user interface is divided into left, right, and bottom area and they are Hint Zone, Collage Area, and Buffer Area. Hint Zone is showing Registered Collage Image from searching or generating. The user can also take these needless images to drag them outside of the Collage Area, and then these images will stay at this Buffer Area. Collage Area (blue base frame) is a game area for playing the design collage game, and user can also put many Collage Images on this area.

4.2 System Software

The system comprises the three main functions (interfaces). It is including: 1) *Sketch Interface*, 2) *Keyword Tag & Logic Interface*, and 3) *Design Collage Game Interface*. The CoTa Software Operation Framework such as the following figure (Fig. 9).

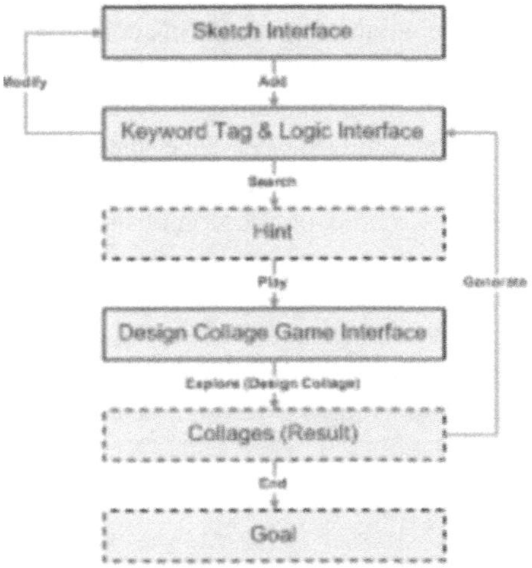

Fig. 9. The CoTa Software Operation Framework

Finally, by combing both software and hardware, the physical CoTa user interface is shown as the following figure (Fig. 10).

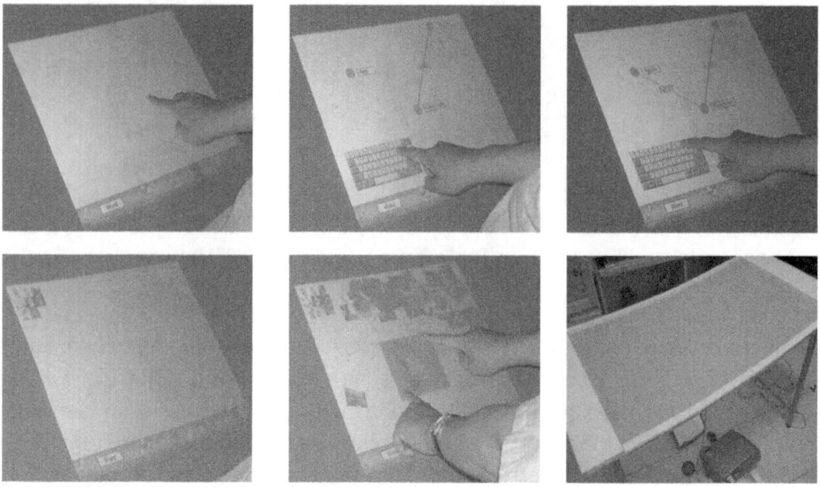

Fig. 10. The CoTa's user interfaces (from left to right and up to down): 1) Sketch Interface. 2) Keyword Tag & Logic Interface 1. 3) Keyword Tag & Logic Interface 2. 4) Design Collage Game Interface 1. 5) Design Collage Game Interface 2. 6) The Collage Tables hardware, etc.

5 Conclusion

A physical table with design collage built-in has been implemented and tested for understanding the possible interaction of manipulating collaged images (hints). We use the design collage game model to implement a physical interactive interface in this paper. The mechanism for guessing how the manipulation over collaged images has been elaborated based on previous works done by [8], [9]. The nature of games and multi-touch environment has brought the playful experience to the users of Collage Table. For the first implementation, the gaming environment has accomplished and need further development in the content related to design. Further research, how such interaction can be mapped to design context and what kind of design context is suitable using design collage will be the next step towards developing a useful tool for exploring design puzzles. Furthermore, by testing more game-like design puzzles using the same interface, we hope to establish a playful design environment for assisting the design process.

References

1. Archea, J.: Puzzle-Making: What Architects Do When No One Is Looking. Computability of Design, New York, Wiley-Interscience, pp. 37–52 (1987)
2. Chang, T.W.: Supporting Design Learning with Design Puzzles - Some Observations of on-Line Learning with Design Puzzles. DDSS' 04, Kluwer Academic (2004)

3. Lin, C.J., Chang, T.W., Yang, L.C., Chen, H.C.: E-Learning with Puzzle Collages. In: The 5th European Conference on Product and Process Modeling in the Building and Construction Industry, Turkey, ECPPM2004 (2004)
4. Yang, L.C., Chang, T.W., Lin, C.J., Chen, H.C.: Exploring Visual Information with Puzzle Rule–a Design Collage Approach. ISARC2004, Korea (2004)
5. Rekimoto, J., Ullmer, B., Oba, H.: Datatiles: A Modular Platform for Mixed Physical and Graphical Interactions. In: SIGCHI' 01, Seattle, WA, USA, ACM Press, New York (2001)
6. Han, J.Y.: Low-Cost Multi-Touch Sensing through Frustrated Total Internal Reflection. In: UIST' 05, Seattle, Washington, USA, ACM Press, New York (2005)
7. Lin, C.C.: Puzzle Server - a Framework for Record, Share, Organization in Design Process. National Yunlin University of Science & Technology (2004)
8. Yang, L.C.: Exploring Visual Information with Puzzle Rules-a Design Collage Approach. National Yunlin University of Science & Technology (2004)
9. Cheng, Y.B., Chang, T.W.: Solving Design Puzzle with Physical Interaction - a Collage Table Implementation. CAADRIA 2007, Nanjing, China, CAADRIA Proceeding (2007)

Designing Smart Living Objects – Enhancing vs. Distracting Traditional Human–Object Interaction

Pei-yu (Peggy) Chi[1], Jen-hao Chen[2], Shih-yen Liu[3], and Hao-hua Chu[2]

[1] Graduate Institute of Networking and Multimedia
[2] Department of Computer Science and Information Engineering
[3] Department of Information Management
National Taiwan University
peggychi@csie.org, {r95922023, b90701219}@ntu.edu.tw,
hchu@csie.ntu.edu.tw

Abstract. To realize Weiser's vision of ubiquitous computing, a popular approach has been to create so-called *smart living objects*, which are everyday objects in our living environment augmented with digital technology. In this paper, we survey different smart living objects and classify their design choices into different types of digital enhancement. These design choices are about choosing the relation between the object's digital enhancement and its traditional use – (1) whether the object's digital function *enhances* or *distracts* its original function, and (2) whether the object's digital interaction *matches* or *conflicts* with its original interaction. Finally, we formulate design heuristics that new digital enhancement should consider the object's traditional function and interaction method, and avoid conflict between the digital enhancement and the traditional use.

Keywords: smart object, smart living object, smart living space, human-computer interaction, context-aware computing, ubiquitous computing.

1 Introduction

Recently, many researchers are working toward the vision of ubiquitous computing put forward by Weiser [1], with the goal of distributing computing into our everyday environments. A popular approach to realize this vision has been to create so-called *smart living objects*. They are traditional objects (which commonly exist in our living environment and whose functions and uses are familiar to us) augmented with a variety of digital technology to bring about novel functions, interaction, and user experience with computing. When Ubicomp researchers experiment with new smart living objects, they are often faced with a challenging design question as to how/what to digitally augment traditional objects in a way that the *enhanced functions* are *sensible* and the *enhanced interaction* is *natural* to human. Are there any general design heuristics for digital enhancement of smart living objects? What design heuristics have Ubicomp researchers tried in the past?

In this paper, we survey and analyze different smart living objects, and classify their design choices into different types of digital enhancement. Based on our

J. Jacko (Ed.): Human-Computer Interaction, Part II, HCII 2007, LNCS 4551, pp. 788–797, 2007.

observations, we identify two important design choices resolving the relation between the object's digital enhancement and its traditional use – (1) whether the object's digital function *enhances* or *distracts* its original function, and (2) whether the object's digital interaction *matches* or *conflicts* with its original interaction. Based on our own past experience in designing smart living objects and studies done by other researchers [17], we believe that these two design choices affect usability of smart living objects. After analyzing these design choices, we come up with the following design heuristics: *the digital enhancement should respect the object's traditional function and interaction, and avoid any conflicts between its digital and the traditional function and interaction.* In other words, the new digital capabilities should enhance or complement (and never reduce or distract) an object's original use. Our design heuristics are consistent with Nielsen's usability heuristics [2]. For example, one of his usability heuristics states "Match between the system and real world", which means that digital systems should follow conventions in real world and make information appear in a natural and logical order to human.

Below we define these two design choices that resolve the functional and the interaction relation between the object's digital enhancement and its traditional use.

- *Relation between digital and traditional functions*: Adding new digital features and functions is common to enrich user experience with everyday objects. We define three types of possible relation between digital and traditional functions: (1) *enhancement,* (2) *complement*, and (3) *unrelated.*
  - For the enhancement type, the new digital function does not only match with the object's original function, but also enhances its original function. An example is the Adidas bionic running shoes [12]. Its digital enhancement incorporates sensors to detect different walking/running surfaces, and then dynamically adjust shoes' cushions for better human comfort and performance. This digital function matches the shoes' traditional function to provide comfort and support for human feet.
  - For the complement type, the new digital function complements the object's original function, or offers a new possibility that extends its original function. An example is the Dietary-aware Dining Table in our previous work [8]. Its digital function incorporates weight and RFID sensors to track what and how much a table participant eats from the table. Then it provides awareness feedbacks about his/her dietary intakes. This digital function complements the dining table's traditional function in helping users with sensible eating.
  - For the unrelated type, the new digital function is unrelated to the object's original function. An example is the Internet Refrigerator from LG Electronics [7]. It embeds a computer with a LCD display mounted on the fridge door for Internet and multimedia access. Although its digital enhancement provides a rich set of features such as Internet browsing, a digital photo album, DVD playback, etc., these features have loose relationship to a fridge's traditional function of food preservation.
- *Relation between digital and traditional interaction*: To access the object's new digital function, an interaction method needs to be designed into the object's interface. We again define three types of possible relation between the object's digital interaction and its traditional interaction: (1) *natural*, (2) *intuitive*, and (3) *unrelated.*

- For the natural type, the interaction to access the object's digital function is the same as its original interaction. Since a user is already familiar with the original interaction, accessing its digital function requires almost no new learning. An example is the I/O Brush from MIT Media Lab [3]. Its digital interaction method of using the I/O Brush to pick up digital paints from the physical environment is designed to be the same as using a traditional paintbrush to pick up color paints from a palette.
- For the intuitive type, although the digital interaction is not exactly the same as the object's original interaction, it is intuitive and has high relevance to its original interaction. An example is Topobo from MIT Media Lab [14]. Although assembling Topobo components is similar to assembling LEGO blocks, a child still needs to learn a new control interface to operate the motion record and playback buttons. This new control interface is intuitive because a child animates Topobo components in the same way as he/she animates LEGO blocks.
- For the unrelated type, the digital interaction bares no resemblance to the object's original interaction. An example is the Color Camera Wrist Watch [11] from Casio, which integrates a color camera into a wrist watch. Since camera features require operating a different set of buttons and interaction sequence than in the traditional clock features, a user needs to learn a new different picture-taking and picture-viewing interface.

Since an everyday object often has multiple functions and interaction methods, there exists *ambiguity* in determining the functional and interaction relation between digital and traditional. For example, a cup can serve multiple functions other than drinking, such as holding pens, social toasting in a party, etc. Furthermore, each function often comes with a different interaction method – if a cup is used as a pen holder, the interaction is dropping or grabbing a pen to/from the cup; whereas if the cup is used for toasting, the interaction is to raise the cup toward the person of honor. Therefore, the functional and interaction relation depends on how users perceive an object's traditional function and interaction. For example, an object's digital enhancement may be regarded as complementary or natural to a traditional function or interaction, but as unrelated to its other traditional functions and interaction. In this paper, we acknowledge this ambiguity and leave the decision of an object's possible functions and interaction to its designer and end-users. Since our classification method is about design choices, it is independent of different perception about an object's original function and interaction.

The remainder of this paper is organized as follows. Section 2 surveys different smart living objects and analyzes their design choices on the functional and interaction relation between the digital and traditional. Section 3 discusses these design choices, formulates our design heuristics on how to choose the functional and interaction relation, and provides rationale to support our design heuristics. Section 4 describes the related work. And Section 5 draws our conclusion.

2 Smart Living Objects

We survey 13 smart living objects from research works and commercial products. For each smart living object, we provide a general description of its digital enhancement, followed by its design choices on the functional and interaction relation between the digital and traditional. A smart object's functional (interaction) relation is determined by comparing its original function (interaction) and its digital function (interaction).

Project name: I/O Brush [3]
Affiliation: MIT Media Lab, 2005
Description: The I/O Brush augments a regular paint brush with a new digital capability to pick up color, texture, and movement from any surfaces in our physical environment. This is done by hiding a digital camera with a touch sensor and LEDs inside the I/O Brush.
Functional relation: enhancement. The I/O Brush's digital function matches exactly with the function of a traditional paintbrush, which is to paint pictures. Its functional enhancement comes from enabling a traditional paintbrush to pick up digital paints, which are any physical surfaces that can be captured by a hidden camera in the brush.
Interaction relation: natural. Using the I/O brush to pick up digital paints from physical surfaces is designed to be the same as using a traditional paintbrush to pick up color paints from a palette. In addition, the I/O brush stroke is also designed to be the same as a traditional paint brush stroke.

Project name: Pick-A-Drawer [4]
Affiliation: Georgia Institute of Technology, 2002
Description: The Pick-A-Drawer interconnects two remote drawers through the concept of a virtual shared drawer. The goal is for distant family members to connect and share parts of their physically disjoint living spaces. In a chest of drawers, one drawer contains a digital camera to capture images of the drawer's content, which is then transmitted and shown on a LCD display of its remote drawer pair.
Functional relation: enhancement. A traditional drawer serves the function as space for family members to store and share living things, e.g. schoolwork, treasures, etc. The Pick-A-Drawer enhances this sharing function by breaking its physical boundary and by enabling remote family members to enjoy this space sharing experience.
Interaction relation: natural. The Pick-A-Drawer retains the same interaction as a traditional drawer – pulling out a drawer, seeing contents inside, putting objects in it, and pushing to close. From children to grandparents can use its digital function naturally and experience this warm feeling of sharing interesting living things.

Project name: Lover's Cups [5]
Affiliation: MIT Media Lab, 2006
Description: The Lover's Cups are based on the idea of sharing feelings of drinking between two people located in distance places. Two cups are connected to each other wirelessly and embedded with sip, liquid, and pizeo sensors to detect drinking actions. LED illumination is used to show the drinking status of the other Lover's cup. For example, when two lovers are drinking at the same time, both Lover's Cups glow.
Functional relation: enhancement. In a social setting, traditional cups are not only used for drinking but also for toasting to reinforce social ties between people. The Lover's Cups enhance a traditional cup's social function by enabling far-away people to engage in this social experience of sharing a drink together at the same time.
Interaction relation: natural. The Lover's Cups do not change the cups' traditional drinking interaction, which is to pick up and drink with them.

Project name: Nutrition-Aware Kitchen [6]
Affiliation: National Taiwan University, 2007
Description: It provides digital awareness of nutrition facts in food ingredients that go into a meal preparation. To recognize cooking activities and food ingredients used, weighing sensors are embedded underneath the kitchen surfaces. The goal is to promote healthy cooking to family cooks. They can cook naturally while receiving nutritional information during the cooking process.
Functional relation: complement. A kitchen's traditional function is meal preparation. This digital nutritional awareness complements a kitchen's traditional function through a passive, ambient display to bring nutritional awareness of food ingredients to family cooks.
Interaction relation: natural. It is natural because nutritional monitoring and awareness display are recognized by sensors without any explicit human input. A family cook simply cooks naturally in the kitchen while he/she can choose to read or ignore the nutritional information.

Project name: Internet Fridge [7]
Affiliation: LG, 2002
Description: LG's Internet fridge embeds a computer with a LCD display mounted on the fridge door for Internet and multimedia access. Through the LCD display, it offers a rich set of digital features and interaction such as Internet browsing, a digital photo album, DVD playback, etc. This smart fridge can also be used as a server for remote controlling other home appliances, such as a microwave, a washing machine, and an air conditioner.
Functional relation: unrelated. A fridge's traditional function is to store and preserve the freshness of foods. However, the Internet browsing, multimedia access, and appliance remote control features have little relationship to a fridge's traditional function.
Interaction relation: unrelated. The digital interaction for Internet browsing, multimedia access, and appliance remote control differs from a fridge's traditional interaction of storing and retrieving foods.

Project name: Diet-aware Dining Table [8]
Affiliation: National Taiwan University, 2006
Description: It augments a traditional dining table by embedding weighing and RFID sensors to recognize what and how much a table participant eats from the table. Then it provides awareness feedbacks to the users about their dietary consumption. The goal is to help users with sensible eating.
Functional relation: complement. The dietary tracking and awareness function complements a dining table's traditional function by not only presenting available foods on a tabletop surface but also bringing awareness of actual amount of food intake.
Interaction relation: natural. It is natural because nutritional monitoring and awareness feedback are automated without any explicit human input – a user simply eats naturally from the table while he/she can choose to read or ignore his/her dietary information.

Project name: The History Tablecloth [9]
Affiliation: Goldsmiths College, U. of East Anglia, and Lancaster U., 2006
Description: It augments a traditional tablecloth by recording and displaying how long an object has been left on a table. Its goals are to bring awareness about the flow of things over a surface at home, and to provide an aesthetical looking home décor with rich information for people to interpret.
Functional relation: enhancement. One of tablecloth's traditional functions is decoration. This digital function enhances this decorative function by dynamically changing the artistic patterns on the tablecloth according to how long things have been left on it.
Interaction relation: natural. It is natural because users can simply put things on the tablecloth as on any traditional tablecloth.

Project name: Digital Family Portrait [10]
Affiliation: Georgia Institute of Technology, 2001
Description: It augments a traditional family portrait by providing qualitative visualizations of a family elder's daily life using iconic imagery on the picture frame. The displayed information includes the elder's health, environment, social interaction level, activity level, etc., over the past few weeks. The goal of this digital awareness is to communicate the elder's well-being and to bring peace of mind to his/her concerned family members.
Functional relation: complement. A family portrait's traditional function is to bring back the memory of a loved family member, and also to serve as a reminder to care for him/her. The digital awareness provides additional, complementary information to the caregivers about recent health condition of the elder.
Interaction relation: natural. It is natural because a caregiver simply needs to glance at the iconic frame to interpret the elder's health condition.

Project name: Color Wrist Camera Watch [11]
Affiliation: Casio, 2006
Description: It integrates a color camera into a traditional digital watch. It combines two unrelated features, showing time and taking picture, into a watch-sized device.
Functional relation: unrelated. A watch's traditional function is to track and show the time of day. The new digital camera functions, such as taking and browsing pictures, have little relationship to a watch's traditional function.
Interaction relation: unrelated. Since camera features require operating a different set of buttons and interaction sequence than in the traditional clock features, a user needs to learn a new different picture-taking and picture-viewing interface.

Project name: Bionic Running Shoes: Adidas_1 [12]
Affiliation: Adidas Group, 2006
Description: Adidas_1 incorporates sensors and a microprocessor to detect different walking and running surfaces, and then dynamically adapts shoes' cushions for better human comfort and performance. The goals are to provide users with better running experience and to protect their feet when striking ground.
Functional relation: enhancement. The shoes' traditional function is to provide comfort, support, and protection for human feet while running or walking. Adidas_1

improves this traditional function through intelligent adaptation to different physical walking or running environment.
Interaction relation: natural. It is natural because intelligent adaptation to the environment is automated. Users simply wear the Adidas_1 shoes, and they can run and walk naturally in the environment as any other traditional shoes.

Project name: ComSlipper [13]
Affiliation: Carnegie Mellon University, 2006
Description: ComSlipper augments traditional slippers, enabling two people in an intimate relationship to communicate and maintain their emotional connection over long distance. To express emotions such as anxiety, happiness, and sadness, users perform different tactile manipulations on the slippers (e.g. press, tap at a specific rhythm, touch the sensor at the side of slippers, etc.) which ComSlipper recognizes. The remote slipper pair then displays these emotions through changing LED signals, warmth, or vibration.
Functional relation: complement. Slippers' traditional function does not only protect our feet, but also brings an intimate feeling of comfort and warmth [13]. Thus, ComSlipper complements this traditional function by communicating intimate messages between two people.
Interaction relation: unrelated. The interaction of ComSlipper is unrelated to its traditional interaction, which is to simply wear them. That is, users need to learn different tactile manipulations of slippers and mapping to different emotions, which may not be natural or intuitive for most people. In addition, users need to learn how to interpret messages through LED lights, warmth, or vibration.

Project name: Topobo [14]
Affiliation: MIT Media Lab, 2004
Description: Topobo is a LEGO-like constructive assembly toy enhanced with so-called kinetic memory, or the ability to record and playback physical motion. After a child manipulates toys with a certain motion, Topobo can record and replay this motion again.
Functional relation: enhancement. One of the traditional functions of a constructive assembly toy, such as LEGO, is to stimulate a child's creativity through playing and making. This digital animation function brings out a child's creativity while enhancing the toy's enjoyment.
Interaction relation: intuitive. Although assembling Topobo components is similar to assembling LEGO blocks, a child still needs to learn a new control interface to operate the motion record and playback buttons. This new control interface is intuitive because a child animates Topobo components in the same way as he/she animates LEGO blocks (e.g., compose blocks into a vehicle and make it move), except that Topobo motion can repeat itself.

Project name: Shopping Buddy [15]
Affiliation: IBM for Retail, 2004
Description: It augments a traditional supermarket shopping cart with a RFID reader to scan all RFID-tagged items placed into the cart. Through a LCD display mounted

on it, a consumer can see pricing information on each item, as well as calculating the total amount in the cart. It helps budget-conscious consumers with sensible shopping.
Functional relation: complement. A shopping cart's traditional function is to hold to-buy items for users. This new digital function complements a shopping cart's traditional function by helping users shop appropriate amount of items according to his/her planned budget.
Interaction relation: intuitive. It is intuitive because after a user places items into the smart shopping cart, they will see price information on the LCD monitor. This is similar to the experience on the point-of-sale machine.

3 Discussion

The design choices made by the surveyed smart living objects are categorized in a classification matrix shown in Table 1. Most smart living objects fall into the lower left four cells. Their design choices are in agreement with our design heuristics that functional relation between the digital and the traditional should be enhancement or complementary, and the interaction relation should be natural or intuitive.

Table 1. Classification matrix

Interaction relation \ Functional Relation	*Enhancement*	*Complement*	*Unrelated*
Unrelated		- ComSlipper	- Internet Fridge - Color Camera Wrist Watch
Intuitive	- Topobo	- Shopping Buddy	
Natural	- I/O Brush - Adidas_1 - Pick-A-Drawer - History Tablecloth - Lover's Cups	- Diet-aware Dining Table - Nutrition-Aware Kitchen - Digital Family Portrait	

We would like to further give rationale to support our design heuristics. Note that these design heuristics should be considered as good general design practice applicable to many of smart living objects, but not universal design principles for all of them. The rationale can be explained from *functional sensibility* and *ease of interaction*. Functional sensibility means how well users perceive the value of a new digital function added to these everyday objects – are they acceptable, sensible, and fitting? Ease of interaction means the amount of user efforts to learn to interact with the digital functions. Since many everyday objects have been in existence for years, their practical and sensible functions and usability have been proven with extensive testing and refinement. Applying digital technology to radically alter these functions or interaction styles without considering these objects' traditional functions and interactions, is likely to run a risk of defying their well-established convention, which may lead to potential confusion and poor acceptance. Adapting our design heuristics in everyday living objects harmonizes the relation between their digital enhancements and traditional uses, making them simple, intuitive, and natural.

4 Related Works

Several studies have addressed related issues on smart living objects. Bohn *et al.* [16] classified the social, economic, and ethical implications about developing smart every objects. Kranz *et al.* [19] focused on implementation issues related to prototyping smart objects, covering the hardware, software, and device aspects. Bouchard *et al.* [17] identified both conceptual and practical issues related to augmentation of everyday items, e.g., physical embodiment vs. external augmentation. Our paper shares their viewpoint that the distribution of computing power into our physical environment is through "enriching ordinary, commonly used objects with extraordinary capabilities". Rogers [18] criticized the current Ubicomp work in ambient and ubiquitous intelligence, and pointed out the difficulties in building calm computing systems with them. Rocker *et al.* [20] employed a scenario-driven approach and adopted quantitative and qualitative methods to elicit user requirements for intelligent home environments. Rather than discussing and listing social or general issues of smart objects, we propose design heuristics based on the functional and interaction relation between the object's digital enhancement and traditional use.

5 Conclusion

We survey different smart living objects and classify their design choices into different types of digital enhancement. Based on our observations, we identify two important design choices resolving the relation between the object's digital enhancement and its traditional use – (1) whether the object's digital function *enhances* or *distracts* its original function, and (2) whether the object's digital interaction *matches* or *conflicts* with its original interaction. Finally, we formulate design heuristics that the digital enhancement should consider the object's traditional function and interaction, and avoid any conflicts between its digital enhancement and traditional use.

References

1. Weiser, M., Brown, J.S.: The Coming Age of Calm Technology. In: Beyond calculation: the next fifty years (1995)
2. Nielsen, J.: Ten Usability Heuristics (2005) http://www.useit.com/papers/heuristic/heuristic_list.html
3. Ryokai, K., Marti, S., Ishii, H.: Designing the World as Your Palette. In: Proceeding of Computer Human Interaction (ACM CHI 2005) on Conference Extended Abstracts on Human Factors in Computing Systems (2005)

4. Siio, I., Rawan, J., Mynatt, E.: Peek-a-drawer: Communication by Furniture. In: Proceeding of Computer Human Interaction (ACM CHI 2002) on Conference Extended Abstracts on Human Factors in Computing Systems (2002)
5. Chung, H., Lee, C.H., Selker, T.: Lover's Cups: Drinking Interfaces as New Communication Channels. Alt.CHI Paper in the Extended Abstracts of Computer Human Interaction (ACM CHI 2006) (2006)
6. Chi, P.-Y, Chen, J.-H., Chu, H.-H.: Enabling Nutrition-Aware Cooking in a Smart Kitchen. Work-in-Progress Paper in Extended Abstracts of Computer Human Interaction (ACM CHI 2007) (2007)
7. LG Internet Family. GRD-267DTU Digital Multimedia Side-By-Side Fridge Freezer with LCD Display (2002) http://www.lginternetfamily.co.uk/fridge.asp
8. Chang, K.-H., Liu, S.-Y., Chu, H.-H., Hsu, J., Chen, C., Lin, T.-Y., Huang, P.: Dietary-Aware Dining Table: Observing dietary behaviors over tabletop surface. In: Proceedings of the 4th International Conference on Pervasive Computing (Pervasive 2006) (2006)
9. Gaver, W., Bowers, J., Boucher, A., Law, A., Pennington, S., Villar, N.: The History Tablecloth: Illuminating Domestic Activity. In: Proceedings of the 6th ACM conference on Designing Interactive systems, Symposium on Designing Interactive Systems (2006)
10. Mynatt, E.D, Rowan, J., Craighill, S., Jacobs, A.: Digital Family Portraits: Providing Peace of Mind for Extended Family Members. In: Proceeding of Computer Human Interaction (ACM CHI 2001) on Conference Extended Abstracts on Human Factors in Computing Systems (2001)
11. Casio Inc. Color Wrist Camera Watch (2006) http://www.casio.com/
12. Adidas Group. adidas_1 Intelligent Level 1.1 (2006) http://www.adidas.com/campaigns/hatsnext/content/microsites/adidas_1
13. Chen, C.-Y., Forlizzi, J., Jennings, P.: ComSlipper: An Expressive Design to Support Awareness and Availability. Alt.CHI Paper in Extended Abstracts of Computer Human Interaction (ACM CHI 2006) (2006)
14. Raffle, H.S., Parkes, A.J., Ishii, H.: Topobo: A Constructive Assembly System with Kinetic Memory. In: Proceeding of Computer Human Interaction (ACM CHI 2001) on Conference Extended Abstracts on Human Factors in Computing Systems (2001)
15. IBM Retail. Stop & Shop Grocery Drives Sales and Boosts Customer Loyalty with IBM Personal Shopping Assistant (2004) http://www-03.ibm.com/industries/retail
16. Bohn, J., Coroama, V., Langheinrich, M., Mattern, F., Rohs, M.: Living in a World of Smart Everyday Objects – Social, Economic, and Ethical Implications. In: Journal of Human and Ecological Risk Assessment (2004)
17. Bouchard, D., Costanza, E., Merrill, D., Sadi, S., Maes, P., Pinhanez, C., Susani, M.: Making Ubicomp Approachable: Interaction Design for Augmented Objects. In: Workshop proposal for 8th International Conference on Ubiquitous Computing (Ubicomp 2006) (2006)
18. Rogers, Y.: Moving on from Weiser's Visions of Calm Computing: Engaging UbiComp Experiences. In: Dourish, P., Friday, A. (eds.) UbiComp 2006. LNCS, vol. 4206, pp. 404–421 Springer, Heidelberg (2006)
19. Kranz, M., Schmidt, A.: Prototyping Smart Objects for Ubiquitous Computing. In: Workshop on Smart Object Systems, 7th International Conference on Ubiquitous Computing (Ubicomp 2005) (2005)
20. Rocker, C., Jnase, M.D., Portolan, N., Streitz, N.: User Requirements for Intelligent Home Environments: a Scenario-driven Approach and Empirical Cross-cultural Study. In: Proceedings of the 2005 joint conference on Smart objects and ambient intelligence: innovative context-aware services: usages and technologies (ACM sOc-EUSAI 05) (2005)

Drawing Type Tactile Presentation for Tactile Letter Recognition

Ju-Hui Cho and Minsoo Hahn

ICU Digital Media Lab, 517-10 Dogok-dong, Gangnam-gu,
Seoul 135-854, Korea
{aquaevil,mshahn}@icu.ac.kr

Abstract. Tactile displays don't disturb other people and transfer the information secretly by directly contacting with person's body. Tactile letter recognition means that the users recognize the ordinary language conveyed on the skin surface. We propose stimulus presentation of drawing type for tactile letter recognition. It is the type that is drawing the line directly to the skin with a pen instead of dot stimulus of array type. We built the prototype of drawing type device. The tracing mode was a good at recognition rate of the letters averagely than static mode in tactile letter recognition. But it was still hard to recognize special letters having same number of stroke or similar stroke style, because touch sensory is dull of localization and perception of stimulus. To improve recognition rate of confused letters, we redesigns stroke patterns to a new sequence pattern having less stroke number and unique pattern.

Keywords: Tactile letter recognition.

1 Introduction

The tactile displays convey the information by directly contacting with person's body. To convey the information using tactile display has some advantages. The tactile displays don't disturb other people and transfer the information secretly. And tactile channel can be complement or substitution of audiovisual sensory in special situations or for people disable or impaired in either hearing or vision.

Tactile letter recognition means that the users recognize the ordinary language conveyed on the skin surface using tactile displays. Existing tactile display for tactile letter recognition consist of a number of tactile stimulators(ex. pin or vibrator) that form two-dimensional array to present spatial information by varying the stimulation from each stimulator. And a tracing mode is mainly used for presenting letter. In tracing mode, tactile displays present tactile patterns by sequentially activating the tactile stimulators [1]. That is, people trace the letter stroke in the same order as hand writing. This is most effective for transmission of complex letters [2].

But tactile presentation of array type has some problems to recognize the letter through tactile sensory. The stimulus presentation of array type has spatial gaps between stimulators and time intervals between stimuli and between strokes. In order to present the letter using array type, duration of stimulus (Dos) for recognizing each stimulus, inter-stimulus onset interval (ISOI) which is the time interval until next

J. Jacko (Ed.): Human-Computer Interaction, Part II, HCII 2007, LNCS 4551, pp. 798–807, 2007.

stimulator, and inter-stroke interval which is the time interval between strokes are needed. These factors obstruct the users to feel continuous flow of the stimuli composing a stroke. And the more complicated the letter shapes are, the more stimulator, Dos, ISOI, and inter-stroke intervals are needed. This fact results in burdening the user's memory and reduction of recognition rate of the letter through tactile sensory.

People are all familiar with "finger writing" on the back as a way of communication patterns. Moving a single continuous point in time and space permits high recognition accuracy. And one research about vibrotactile display shows accuracy of the letter recognition was improved by providing flow feeling [3]. Getting inspiration from this, this paper proposes drawing type tactile presentation for presenting the letter on skin surface. Drawing type means to draw the letter directly on skin surface with a pen. The stimulus drawing on skin surface is continuous line. That is, it provides a line stimulus in stead of a point stimulus. This type can reduce the burden of user's memory and improve the accuracy of recognition by giving a natural feeling of a line. And drawing type doesn't increase the complexity of a device according to the complexity of presenting pattern however the complexity of array type device is increased for complex pattern. In this paper, the prototype of drawing type, hardware mechanism to control, and program to use were built and it was showed that drawing type is more suitable for presenting the letter by giving a natural feeling of a line.

Existing studies of tactile letter recognition using tracing mode shows that the accuracy of recognition is various according to a character. Tactile sensory is not sensitive to the position of stimulus, unlike visual sensory. For this reason, people recognize the letter shape through pattern of strokes rather than absolute position. Therefore, similar pattern of strokes between characters or the same number of strokes can make people confuse.

As a font means the style of characters in printing, this paper defines "tactile font" as style of characters in touching, namely pattern of strokes presenting a character. However former studies only use the writing order, this paper proposes easier fonts by analyzing characters that people confuse and prove the proposed fonts improve the accuracy of recognizing the letter.

2 Related Works

Bach-y-Rita [4] and Collins [2] constructed a tactilevision substitution system (TVSS) with 20×20 pin array covering an area of 22.8×22.8 cm^2 on the back. Because this system was developed to provide haptic substitution for television systems, initially letters were displayed as-is, i.e., vibrating pins were activated simultaneously to compose a dot array pattern of the letter as it is displayed on a visual display, that is, they use static mode. Loomis [5] used the same TVSS system and introduced a method to control the vibration stimuli such that the letters are "scanned" through a slit. He proposed two scanning techniques: a stationary letter scanned by a moving slit (moving-slit mode) and a moving letter scanned through a stationary slit (moving-letter mode). The experiments show that accuracy of letter recognition of static, moving-slit and moving-letter mode is each 34%, 51%, and 47%. In both moving-slit and moving-letter mode, the performance of letter recognition was improved over that of static mode.

Saida et al. [6] constructed a small-sized 10×10 TVSS system and introduced tracing mode, a temporally sequential pattern of vibrotactile stimuli: tracing the letter stroke in the same order as hand writing. It achieved significant improvement in the accuracy of vibrotactile letter reading. They obtained 95% correct letter recognition among the 46 letters of katakana (Japanese phonetic character set) on the abdomen in tracing mode, while the static or moving-letter mode yielded less than 50% accuracy. And Shimizu et al. [7] obtained more than 90% correct recognition among 46 letters of katakana using a 7×9 dot pin array on the palm.

Yanagida et al. [8] focused to reduce the number of stimulators as much as possible while still maintaining an acceptable level of expressive performance. They examined the ability to distinguish letters of the alphabet and numbers through vibrotactile stimuli provided by 3x3 stimulator array on the back of a chair. The stimulators are driven sequentially in the same sequence as if someone were tracing the letter on the back. The result showed 87% successful letter recognition in some cases.

Hayashi et al. [9] explored the possibility of letter presentation at the fingertip. Nine subjects participated in alphabet presentation through a tactile-by-eletrocutaneous-stimulation display. The average rate of correct answer was 57%, the maximum rate was 90%, and minimum rate was 22%. Seo et al. [3] constructed 5x5 vibrotactile display on the top of the foot in tracing mode and new tracing mode. New tracing mode provides flow of vibration by activating two continuous stimulators simultaneously. New type of tracing mode improved the average rate of correct answer from 60.3% to 86.7%.

3 Drawing Type Tactile Presentation

Drawing type means to draw the letter directly on skin surface with a pen. The stimulus drawing on skin surface is continuous line, not point.

3.1 Device

In order to draw the letter, three-dimensional movements are needed. Two-dimensional motions draw the letter shape and one-dimensional motions move the pen up and down. The prototype of drawing tactile display was made using 3 stepping motors, 2 rods, 6 pulleys, 4 gears, 3 bands, aluminum pieces for frame, and acetal pieces for structures moving on x-axis and y-axis. This prototype consists of device part for moving the pen and case part for supporting skin surface.

This prototype can move the pen in 100×140 mm area and consists of four major subassemblies: a frame, x-translation assembly, y-translation assembly, and z-translation assembly.

A frame. The frame consists of a 0.6mm thick aluminum which gave envelope dimensions of 300×300×130 mm, as shown in Fig.1.(a). Its main functions were to support the other subassemblies.

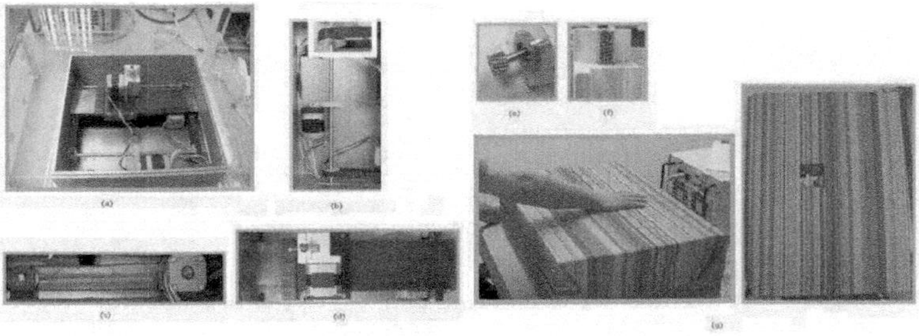

Fig. 1. Prototype of Drawing Tactile Display

X-translation Assembly. This assembly is what provides the x directional motion, namely x-axis. A motor drive a gear on one the shafts which in turn drive the pulleys and belt, and then the belts provide the linear motion, as shown in Fig.1.(b). Since the belts are joined to a carrier including y- and z-translation assembly, this x-axis carrier also has linear motion on x-axis.

Y-translation Assembly. This assembly holds a motor mounted to x-axis carrier, as shown in Fig.1.(c). The pulley is attached on the axis of rotation of a motor. A motor drive a pulley on one the shafts which drive the belt joined to a carrier having z-translation assembly. Fig.1.(d) shows a small carrier loaded with z-translation assembly and this carrier move on y-axis by the movement of belt.

Z-translation Assembly. A motor drive the gear mounted on motor's axis of rotation (Fig.1.(e)), and then the rack gear engaged with the gear (Fig.1.(f)) moves up and down. This movement makes the motion on z-axis.

Case. This device can be used on user's palm or back, etc. Among them, we tried to draw the letter on the palm. The standard of Koreans' palm size was investigated in order to decide the size of the area in which the letter is drawn. The width of drawing area has to be smaller than 75.21mm, palm length perpendicular of women. And a palm is not perfectly flat. The bottom part of palm is usually plumper than the other part of palm. Therefore, we present the letter besides the bottom part of palm. Based on these facts, it was decided that the size of drawing area is 60×60mm. And to overcome a delicate difference of palm's height in drawing area, this prototype uses the pen with a spring. However when drawing the letter, this pen still bring about a delicate difference of pressure, the user can feel good enough to recognize the stroke.

3.2 Hardware Mechanism to Control the Device

Figure 2 shows overall flow for drawing the letter by converting the coordinate of the letter into movements of each axis. The drawing program conveys the motions and its coordinates for drawing the selected letter to the motion controller. The motion divides line and circle. The motion controller translates these data into the pulse data of each axis for driving the motor and delivery them to motor driver of each axis. And motor drivers amplify the received pulse data with considering the specification of step motors. The amplified signals drive the step motors, and then a carrier with the pen moves. 5V and 24V source of electricity are supplied each for the motion controller and for motor drivers.

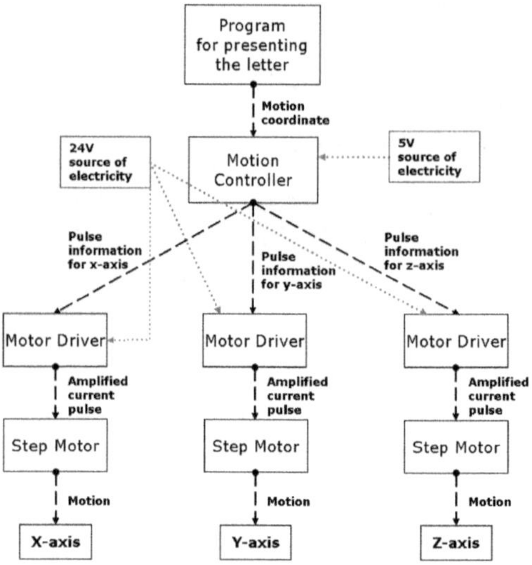

Fig. 2. The flow of converting the coordinate of the letter into movements of each axis

3.3 Software Mechanism to Control the Device

The program for drawing the letter was made using LabVIEW 8.2 which is a programming development tool with graphical development environment for signal acquisition, measurement analysis, data presentation, and motion control. The program consists of Front Panel that constructs user interface and Block Diagram that draws source codes presenting the structure of program.

Figure 3 shows the Front Panel of Program. Board ID is the identification number of motion controller and X, Y, Z Axis are axes constructing a space. Velocity and Acceleration are the velocity and acceleration of motors. Three ring menus on left bottom are for choosing a character. X-Y Position History and Z-position show the presenting process.

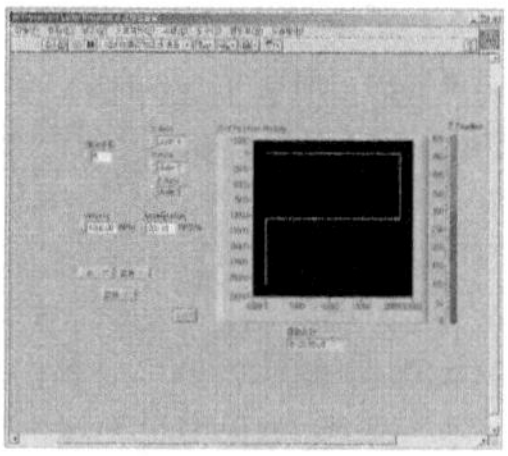

Fig. 3. Front panel of the program for presenting the letter

Figure 4 shows the algorithm of program. First, program sets up the motion contoller that outputs siginal and axes used in motion controller, and then creates the vector space by using given three axes. Created vector space is initialzied with velocity, accerlation.

Next, the position and motion of selected character in Front Panel is created by combining the position and motion of each phoneme. Created elements of the postion and mottion are processed one-by-one.

This program has two motion mode, one is “Line”, another is “Circle”. Required position according to motion mode is roaded into the vector space. And then, the program calls start motion vi that create needful pulse by comparing the current position with the position of vector space.

After motion strarts by start motion vi, the program observes and draws progress of the motion until the motion completes. The program repeats this process until the last motion is entered. Lastly, the time elapsed is presented.

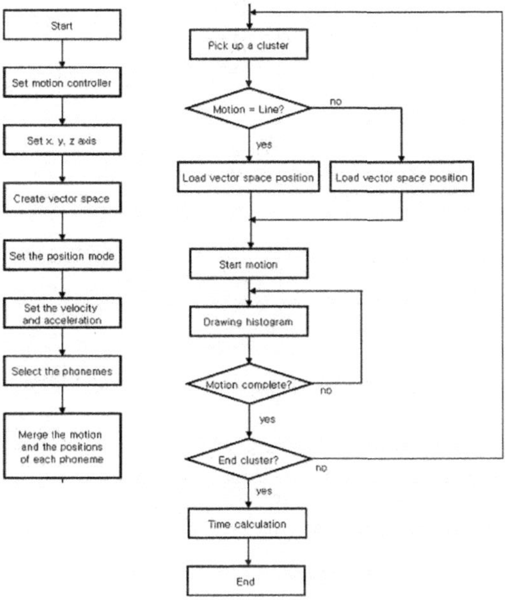

Fig. 4. Program Algorithm

3.4 Experiment

Experiment Design. The first experiment examined the effect of drawing type on tactile letter recognition of sequentially tracing a stimulus in the order of making the necessary strokes by comparing with the point stimulus of array type. The array type tactile presentation was constructed in order to present the letter as the point stimulus and the new tracing mode was used. The characters of drawing type have exactly the same size and the order of lines with the letters of array type. The letters are 14 single consonants and 10 single vowels of Hangeul (Korean alphabet). The order of strokes is the order as hand writing. Fig.5. illustrates digitized consonants and vowels and those writing procedures are used in the experiment. A total of 12 subjects were run in the experiment. They were natives of Korean and familiar with the visualized letters. All subjects were naïve of device for tactile letter recognition. The experience consisted of twice of each letter of 14 single consonants and 10 single vowels under each of the 2 stimulus types. Each character was presented once. Subjects were asked to respond verbally to each letter as soon as possible. And another experiment examined the recognition accuracy of drawing type tactile presentation after learning. The experiment conditions were the exactly same with first experiment.

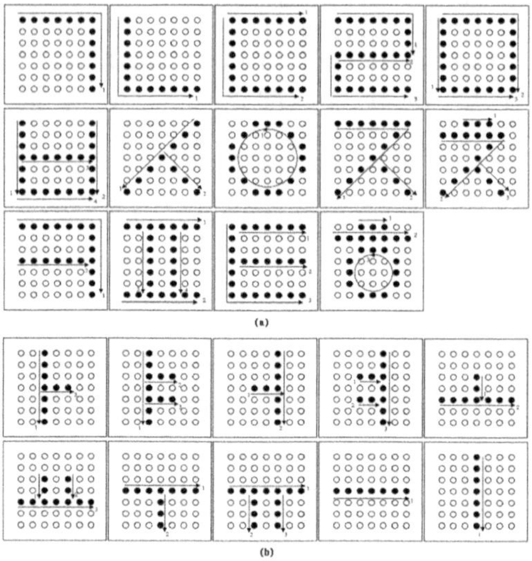

Fig. 5. Illustration of letter pattern and the order of strokes (a) 14 consonants (b) 10 vowels

Results. The average recognition accuracy was each 75% and 88.889% in array type and drawing type. The analysis result shows the letter recognition in drawing type was improved ($p<0.05$, $t=-5.518$). And the average recognition accuracy after learning was 97.917%. This is the improved result as comparing with 88.889% of drawing type without learning in first experiment. The analysis result shows the letter recognition after learning was improved ($p<0.05$, $t=-5.543$).

4 Tactile Font

In this chapter, recognition experiments of the Korean alphabet were implemented. The Korean alphabet, Hangeul, makes a letter by arranging the consonant and vowel unlike English letter. Therefore, to distinguish between the consonant and vowel in a letter is very important issue. First, we examines the letter recognition in point of arrangement of consonant and vowel, Next we analyzes the result obtained in first experiment and assumes the factors that effect recognition accuracy, and proposes and evaluates a new tactile font.

4.1 Experiment of Arrangement of Phenomenon

We compare two kinds of arrangement, overlap mode and division mode. The overlap mode presents the consonant, and then presents again the vowel in same space as if

English alphabet is presented. The division mode presents the consonant leaning to the left, and then presents the vowel leaning to the right. The experiment examined the effect of position difference to distinguish the consonant and the vowel. The letters were presented as tracing mode and drawing type, and the pattern is the stroke order in hand writing. Stimuli are the letters that consist of random compound of 14 single consonants and 10 single vowels of Hangeul, therefore total 140 letters were presented. A total of 12 subjects were run in the experiment. The experiment consisted of 30 presentations in overlap mode and 30 presentations in division mode.

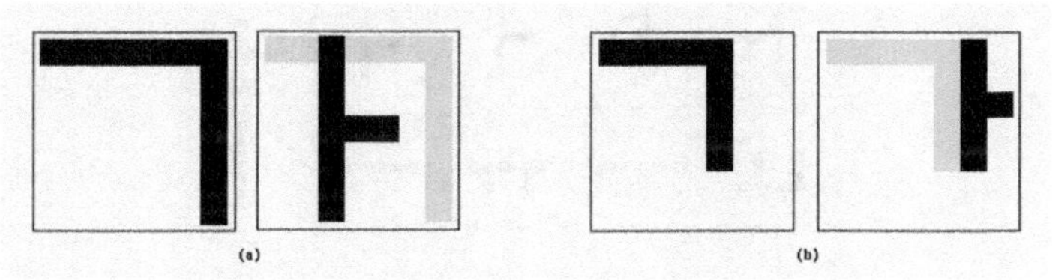

Fig. 6. Arrangement of phenomenon (a) Overlap mode (b) Division mode

Results. The average recognition accuracy was each 66.111% and 77.5% in overlap mode and division mode. Subjects responded that distinguishing between consonant and vowel in overlap mode was very difficult, but that in division was relatively easy. The analysis result shows that the letter recognition in division mode was more easy ($p<0.05$, $t=-2.259$). That is, a relative difference of space helps distinguishing between the consonant and the vowel. And the recognition errors in each mode show some characters of complicate strokes especially have many recognition errors. We analyzed the number of errors and the respond of subjects. Some characters such as "ㅍ", "ㄹ" were confused because the number of their strokes is many and the pattern is complex, turning horizontal line and vertical line. However character "ㅂ" has many strokes, the recognition error was low because of the unique pattern, two consecutive horizontal line. Therefore, we assumes that the number of strokes and originality of pattern effect the recognition.

4.2 Experiment of New Tactile Font

We design a new tactile font to prove our assumption. The design direction is to reduce the number of strokes and to make unique pattern of strokes. We designed several patterns of each character, tested each pattern, and decided the final pattern. Fig.7. shows the final design of tactile font. The experiment examined the effect of new tactile font. The letters were presented as tracing mode and drawing type. Total 140 letters were presented the same as arrangement experiment was. The same subjects with arrangement experiment run the experiment.

Results. The average recognition accuracy improved from 77.5% to 93.333%. The analysis result shows that the letter recognition in new tactile font was more easy ($p<0.05$, $t=-4.394$).

Fig. 7. New tactile font

4.3 Overall Experiment

We compare three method of character presentation; array type-writing order font, drawing type-writing order font, drawing type-new designed font. Stimuli are the letters that consist of random 10 characters having a final consonant: 답, 뱜, 플, 듶, 셜, 픔, 클, 켯, 큼, 듭. The experience consisted of 60 presentations, twice of each 10 letter of under each of the 3 stimulus methods.

Results. The average recognition accuracy is each 52.5%, 75.417% and 90% in array type-writing order font, drawing type-writing order font, drawing type-new designed font. Subjects responded that drawing type-new designed font was the most easy. The analysis result shows that the letter recognition in new tactile font of drawing type was the most easy ($p<0.05$, $F=44.954$).

5 Conclusion

We built the prototype for drawing type tactile presentation. And the experiment showed that stimulus presentation of drawing type can improve the accuracy of the tactile letter recognition. And new tactile font proved that reduction of the number of strokes and originality of pattern can improve the accuracy of recognition.

- Propose drawing type tactile presentation
- Tactile letter recognition for Korean Character
- Propose new tactile font
- Drawing type tactile presentation improved recognition accuracy comparing with array type tactile presentation on tactile letter recognition.
- The number of strokes and the originality of patterns effect the recognition accuracy
- Newly proposed tactile font improved recognition accuracy comparing with writing order font.

References

1. Wada, C., Shoji, H., Ifukube, T.: Development and evaluation of tactile display for a tactile vocoder. Technology and Disability 11, 151–159 (1999)
2. Collins, C.C.: Tactile television – mechanical and electrical image projection. IEEE Transactions on Man.-Machine Systems MMS-11, 58–70 (1970)
3. Seo, C.H., Kim, H.H., Lee, J.H., Lee, B.C., Ryu, J.H.: Development of Wearable Vibrotactile Display Device, HCI Korea (2006)
4. Bach-y-Rita, P.: A tactile vision substitution system based on sensory plasticity. In: Sterling, T.D., Bering, J.E.A., Pollack, S.V., Vaughan, J.H.G. (eds.) Visual Prosthesis: The Interdisciplinary Dialogue, New York, pp. 281–293. Academic Press, San Diego (1971)
5. Loomis, J.: Tactile letter recognition under different modes of stimulus presentation, Perception & Psychophysics. Perception & Psychophysics 16(2), 401–408 (1974)
6. Saida, S., Shimizu, Y., Wakke, T.: Contruction of Small TVSS and Optimal Mode of Stimulus Presentation. In: 4th symposium on Sensory Substitution, Ibaraki, Japan, pp. 68–73 (1978)
7. Shimizu, Y.: Temporal Effect on Tactile Letter Recognition by a Tracing Mode. Perceptual and Motor Skills 55, 343–349 (1982)
8. Yanagida, Y., Kakita, M., Lindeman, R.W., Kume, Y., Tetsutani, N.: Vibrotactile Letter Reading Using a Low-Resolution Tactor Array. In: proceedings of the 12th International Symposium on Haptic Interfaces for Virtual Environment and Teleeoperator Systtems, pp. 400–406 (2004)
9. Shimizu, Y., Saida, S., Wake, T., Nakamura, A., Ohzu, H.: Optimal design of tactile display for a reading aid, Confrerence on use of computers in aiding the disabled, Amsterdam: North-Holland, in press

MKPS: A Multi-level Key Pre-distribution Scheme for Secure Wireless Sensor Networks*

Sung Jin Choi and Hee Yong Youn

School of Information and Communications Engineering
Sungkyunkwan University, Suwon Korea
{choisj,youn}@ece.skku.ac.kr

Abstract. Key distribution is one of the most challenging issues for secure communication in wireless sensor networks. Even though the random key pre-distribution approach is suitable for sensor nodes of low power and resource, a shared key between a pair of nodes is not guaranteed to be found and thus they cannot communicate with each other. This paper proposes a new robust key pre-distribution scheme solving this problem while security is not compromised even though the data exchanged between the nodes are tapped by an adversary. This is achieved by using the keys assigned through LDU decomposition of the symmetric matrix of a pool of keys. A general form solution of L, D, and U matrix is also developed to minimize the time overhead of LDU decomposition. Computer simulation reveals that the proposed scheme also significantly improves the energy efficiency compared with the existing random key pre-distribution scheme.

Keywords: Energy efficiency, key pre-distribution, LDU decomposition, security, wireless sensor network.

1 Introduction

Wireless sensor networks (WSNs) consist of a large number of small sensor nodes which have limited computation capacity, restricted memory space, limited power resource, and short-range radio communication device. In addition to various commercial applications, the sensor nodes may also be deployed in a hostile environment such as battlefield. Security and privacy are challenging issues for WSNs since an adversary can easily access mission critical or private information by monitoring the communications between sensor nodes. Therefore, it is important to encrypt the data transferred between sensor nodes to maintain confidentiality [1-3]. The main problem is how to set up the key among them to secure the communication among sensor nodes.

This is a kind of key agreement problem which has been extensively studied for general network environments. There are three types of key agreement schemes:

* This research was supported by the Ubiquitous Autonomic Computing and Network Project, 21st Century Frontier R&D Program in Korea and the Brain Korea 21 Project in 2007. Corresponding author: Hee Yong Youn.

J. Jacko (Ed.): Human-Computer Interaction, Part II, HCII 2007, LNCS 4551, pp. 808–817, 2007.

trusted-server scheme, self-enforcing scheme, and key pre-distribution scheme. The trusted-server scheme depends on a trusted server for key agreement between the nodes, e.g., Kerberos [4]. This approach is, however, not suitable for WSNs since there is usually no trusted infrastructure. The self-enforcing scheme depends on asymmetric cryptography such as key agreement using public key certificates. However, limited computation and energy resource of sensor nodes often make it undesirable to use a public key algorithm such as Diffie-Hellman key agreement [5] or RSA [6]. With the key pre-distribution scheme [7], keys are distributed among the sensor nodes prior to deployment. This scheme may work if the nodes located in the same neighborhood can be decided before deployment. However, because of the randomness of the deployment, the assumption of knowing the neighboring nodes deterministically might not be feasible. In case of the random key pre-distribution scheme a common key between two nodes wanting to communicate is not guaranteed to be found.

A new key pre-distribution scheme solving this problem was recently proposed by [15]. It is achieved by key assignment with LU decomposition of the symmetric matrix of the keys. One pitfall of this scheme is, however, that some data need to be exchanged between the nodes for key authentication. This may compromise the security if the exchanged data are tapped by an adversary. In this paper, thus, we further enhance the security of the approach by employing LDU decomposition, which still allows high security even when the exchanged data are tapped. A general form solution for constructing the L, D, and U matrix is developed in order to minimize the time overhead of LDU decomposition in the key pre-distribution step. Also, computer simulation reveals that the proposed scheme significantly improves the energy efficiency compared with the existing random key pre-distribution scheme, while it allows high security even in quite hostile environment.

The rest of the paper is organized as follows. Section 2 discusses the existing key distribution approaches proposed for wireless sensor network, and Section 3 presents the proposed scheme. Section 4 evaluates and compares the energy efficiency of the proposed scheme with the earlier scheme, and finally concluding remark is given in Section 5.

2 Related Works

There exist a number of key pre-distribution schemes. One solution is to let all the nodes carry a master secret key. Any pair of nodes can use this global master key to achieve key agreement and obtain a new pairwise key. This scheme does not exhibit desirable network resilience; if one node is compromised, the security of the entire sensor network is compromised. Some existing studies suggest storing the master key in tamper-resistant hardware to reduce the risk [8], but this increases the cost and energy consumption of each sensor node. Furthermore, tamper-resistant hardware might not always be safe. Du et al. [9] proposed another key pre-distribution scheme which substantially improves the resilience of the network compared to other schemes. This scheme exhibits a threshold property; when the number of compromised nodes is smaller than the threshold, the probability that any node other than the compromised nodes is affected is close to zero. This desirable property lowers initial payoff of small scale network breaches to an adversary, and makes it necessary for the adversary to attack a significant portion of the network.

Blundo et al. [10] proposed several schemes which allow any group of some parties to compute a common key while being secure against collusion between some members of them. These schemes focus on saving communication cost while memory constraints are not placed on the group members. Perrig et al. [11] proposed SPINS, a security architecture specifically designed for sensor networks. In SPINS, each sensor node shares a secret key with the base station. Two sensor nodes cannot directly establish a secret key. However, they can use the base station as a trusted third party to set up a secret key.

Recently, Eschenauer and Gligor [7] proposed a random key pre-distribution scheme. Here a pool of random keys is selected from a key space. Each sensor node receives a subset of random keys from the pool before deployment. Any two nodes able to find one common key within their respective subsets can use it as their shared secret to initiate communication. Based on this scheme, Chan, Perrig, and Song [12] proposed a q-composite random key pre-distribution scheme, which increases the security in key distibution such that an attacker has to compromise a large number of nodes to achieve a high probability of compromising communication. The difference between the q-composite scheme and the scheme in [7] is that q common keys ($q \geq 1$), instead of just a single one, are needed to establish secure communication between a pair of nodes. It was shown that network resilience against node capture is improved by increasing the value of q. The main issues in the random key pre-distribution approach are that a common key may not be found between a pair of nodes and node-to-node mutual authentication is not allowed. We next present the proposed scheme solving these problems.

3 The Proposed Scheme

In this section we present the basic features of the proposed scheme, deferring the analysis of energy efficiency to the next section. First, we briefly describe how the proposed key pre-distribution scheme works. The proposed scheme uses a random graph like the Eschenauer's method [7]. It, however, guarantees that any pair of nodes can find a secret key between them while allowing mutual authentication.

3.1 Preliminaries

We capitalize some important properties of matrix in developing the proposed key pre-distribution scheme.

Definition 1. If a square matrix K has the property $K^T = K$, where transpose of matrix K is denoted by K^T, we say that K is a symmetric matrix. A symmetric matrix means that $K_{ij} = K_{ji}$, where K_{ij} is the element in the ith row and jth column of matrix K.

Definition 2. LU decomposition of an $m \times m$ matrix K decomposes it into two matrices such that K = LU, where L is an $m \times m$ lower triangular and U is an $m \times m$ upper triangular matrix, respectively, i.e., product of the lower triangular matrix L and upper triangular matrix U gives rise to K.

Definition 3. Now suppose that K is a square matrix with K=LU, and the pivots on the diagonal of U are all nonzero. By dividing ith $(1 \le i \le m)$ row of U by the nonzero pivot d_i, the matrix U is decomposed into a diagonal matrix D whose diagonals are just the pivots $d_1, d_2, \ldots, d_n$ and a new upper triangular matrix, denoted by U', whose diagonals are all 1's. Then $K=LDU'$.

3.2 The Proposed Key Distribution Scheme

We now explain the proposed key pre-distribution scheme. The key pre-distribution scheme consists of four off-line steps, namely generation of a large pool of keys; generation of an L and U matrix whose product results in a symmetric matrix; applying decomposition to the U matrix; and key pre-distribution to each sensor node.

Step 1 (Generation of a large pool of keys (e.g., $2^{17} \sim 2^{20}$ keys)). We propose a key pre-distribution scheme employing the random key approach. Here each sensor node is assigned a subset of random keys before deployment. Therefore, we first need to generate a large pool of keys.

Step 2 (Forming an L and U matrix using the pool of keys). The second step is the formation of an L matrix using the pool of keys generated in the first step. Then, a U matrix is obtained such that product of them yields a symmetric matrix.

We present the computation step using a case of 4×4 matrix as an example.

$$\begin{bmatrix} l_{11} & 0 & 0 & 0 \\ l_{21} & l_{22} & 0 & 0 \\ l_{31} & l_{32} & l_{33} & 0 \\ l_{41} & l_{42} & l_{43} & l_{44} \end{bmatrix} \cdot \begin{bmatrix} u_{11} & u_{12} & u_{13} & u_{14} \\ 0 & u_{22} & u_{23} & u_{24} \\ 0 & 0 & u_{33} & u_{34} \\ 0 & 0 & 0 & u_{44} \end{bmatrix} = \begin{bmatrix} k_{11} & k_{12} & k_{13} & k_{14} \\ k_{21} & k_{22} & k_{23} & k_{24} \\ k_{31} & k_{32} & k_{33} & k_{34} \\ k_{41} & k_{42} & k_{43} & k_{44} \end{bmatrix} \tag{1}$$

$$\begin{aligned} & l_{11} \cdot u_{12} = l_{21} \cdot u_{11} = k_{12},\ l_{11} \cdot u_{13} = l_{31} \cdot u_{11} = k_{13},\ l_{11} \cdot u_{14} = l_{41} \cdot u_{11} = k_{14} \\ & l_{21} \cdot u_{13} + l_{22} \cdot u_{23} = l_{31} \cdot u_{12} + l_{32} \cdot u_{22} = k_{23} \\ & l_{21} \cdot u_{14} + l_{22} \cdot u_{24} = l_{41} \cdot u_{12} + l_{42} \cdot u_{22} = k_{24} \\ & l_{31} \cdot u_{14} + l_{32} \cdot u_{24} + l_{33} \cdot u_{34} = l_{41} \cdot u_{13} + l_{42} \cdot u_{23} + l_{43} \cdot u_{33} = k_{34} \end{aligned} \tag{2}$$

In Equation (1), the k and l values are arbitrarily decided and thus the equations required to be solved becomes as follows.

$$\begin{aligned} & u_{12} = \frac{l_{21}}{l_{11}} \cdot u_{11},\ u_{13} = \frac{l_{31}}{l_{11}} \cdot u_{11},\ u_{14} = \frac{l_{41}}{l_{11}} \cdot u_{11} \\ & u_{23} = \frac{l_{31} \cdot u_{12} + l_{32} \cdot u_{22} - l_{21} \cdot u_{13}}{l_{22}},\ u_{24} = \frac{l_{41} \cdot u_{12} + l_{42} \cdot u_{22} - l_{21} \cdot u_{14}}{l_{22}} \\ & u_{34} = \frac{l_{41} \cdot u_{13} + l_{42} \cdot u_{23} + l_{43} \cdot u_{33} - l_{31} \cdot u_{14} - l_{32} \cdot u_{24}}{l_{33}} \end{aligned} \tag{3}$$

Note here that there exist six equations with ten unknown variables (the U elements). Therefore, there exist many solutions for the linear system, and we randomly decide four u elements (here u_{11}, u_{22}, u_{33}, and u_{44}, the diagonal elements) and the remaining variables are decided using Equation (3).

The general form solution can be derived from Equation (3) as follows.

$$u_{ij} = \frac{l_{j1}}{l_{11}} u_{11} \text{ where } i=1, j=1,...,m \tag{4}$$

Equation (4) presents the elements of the first row of the U matrix. The values of other elements is obtained as follows.

$$u_{ij} = \frac{\sum_{a=1}^{j-1} l_{ja} u_{ai} - \sum_{a=1}^{i-1} l_{ia} u_{aj}}{l_{ii}}, \quad where\ 1 < i < j \leq m \tag{5}$$

Step 3 (Applying decomposition to the U matrix). After U matrix is obtained in Step 2, it is decomposed into D and U' matrix such that $U=DU'$. Note here that all elements of D matrix except the diagonal elements are zero, and U' matrix is as follows.

$$D = \begin{bmatrix} d_1 & 0 & \cdots & 0 \\ 0 & d_2 & \cdots & 0 \\ \vdots & & \ddots & \vdots \\ 0 & 0 & \cdots & d_m \end{bmatrix}, \quad U' = \begin{bmatrix} u_{11}/d_1 & u_{12}/d_1 & \cdots & u_{1m}/d_1 \\ 0 & u_{22}/d_2 & \cdots & u_{2m}/d_2 \\ \vdots & & \ddots & \vdots \\ 0 & 0 & \cdots & u_{mm}/d_m \end{bmatrix} \tag{6}$$

Step 4 (Key pre-distribution). In this step one row from L, one column from U, and the diagonal elements from D are assigned to every node. One and only one requirement here is that the same row and column position such as L_{r_i} and U_{c_i} are assigned to a node.

(Finding a common key). Assume that node_x and node_y contains (L_{r_i}, U'_{c_i}, and D) and (L_{r_j}, U'_{c_j}, and D), respectively. When node_x and node_y need to communicate, they first exchange the columns, and then obtain the common key. In node_x, $L_{r\_i} \times (D \times U'_{c\_j}) = L_{r\_i} \times U_{c\_j} = K_{ij}$ is obtained, while $L_{r\_j} \times (D \times U'_{c\_i}) = L_{r\_j} \times U_{c\_i} = K_{ji}$ is obtained in node_y. Recall that K is a symmetric matrix, and thus $K_{ij} = K_{ji}$. node_x and node_y can then confirm that they have a common key. Note that the proposed scheme allows any pair of nodes to find a common secret key between them. By exchanging the columns and computing the key value, the sensor nodes can also mutually authenticate each other. The following is an example of the operation steps of the proposed scheme.

Step 1. Generation of a large pool of keys using a random graph. Assume here that a pool of keys is generated in the range of S (−3~3).

Step 2. After selecting (−1, 1, 2, 3) from the pool of keys, randomly construct an L matrix using the selected keys.

$$\mathrm{L}=\begin{bmatrix}1&0&0&0\\2&3&0&0\\-1&1&2&0\\3&1&2&-1\end{bmatrix}$$

Assume that u_{11}=1, u_{22}=2, u_{33}=3, and u_{44}=−1.

$$u_{12}=\frac{l_{21}}{l_{11}}\cdot u_{11}=\frac{2}{1}\cdot 1=2,\ u_{13}=\frac{l_{31}}{l_{11}}\cdot u_{11}=\frac{-1}{1}\cdot 1=-1,\ u_{14}=\frac{l_{41}}{l_{11}}\cdot u_{11}=\frac{3}{1}\cdot 1=3$$

$$u_{23}=\frac{l_{31}\cdot u_{12}+l_{32}\cdot u_{22}-l_{21}\cdot u_{13}}{l_{22}}=\frac{-1\cdot 2+1\cdot 2-2\cdot -1}{3}=\frac{2}{3}$$

$$u_{24}=\frac{l_{41}\cdot u_{12}+l_{42}\cdot u_{22}-l_{21}\cdot u_{14}}{l_{22}}=\frac{3\cdot 2+1\cdot 2-2\cdot 3}{3}=\frac{2}{3}$$

$$u_{34}=\frac{l_{41}\cdot u_{13}+l_{42}\cdot u_{23}+l_{43}\cdot u_{33}-l_{31}\cdot u_{14}-l_{32}\cdot u_{24}}{l_{33}}=\frac{3\cdot -1+1\cdot 2/3+2\cdot 3+1\cdot 3-1\cdot (2/3)}{2}=\frac{6}{2}=3$$

$$\mathrm{U}=\begin{bmatrix}1&2&-1&3\\0&2&2/3&2/3\\0&0&3&3\\0&0&0&-1\end{bmatrix}$$

Step 3. After deciding the U matrix, decompose it into D and U' matrix.

$$\mathrm{D}=\begin{bmatrix}1&0&0&0\\0&2&0&0\\0&0&3&0\\0&0&0&-1\end{bmatrix},\ \mathrm{U}'=\begin{bmatrix}1&2&-1&3\\0&1&1/3&1/3\\0&0&1&1\\0&0&0&1\end{bmatrix}$$

$$\mathrm{LDU}'=\begin{bmatrix}1&0&0&0\\2&3&0&0\\-1&1&2&0\\3&1&2&-1\end{bmatrix}\cdot\begin{bmatrix}1&0&0&0\\0&2&0&0\\0&0&3&0\\0&0&0&-1\end{bmatrix}\cdot\begin{bmatrix}1&2&-1&3\\0&1&1/3&1/3\\0&0&1&1\\0&0&0&1\end{bmatrix}=\begin{bmatrix}1&2&-1&3\\2&10&0&8\\-1&0&23/3&11/3\\3&8&11/3&50/3\end{bmatrix}$$

Observe that LDU' above results in a symmetric matrix as we expected.

Step 4. Assume that $\mathrm{L}_{\mathrm{r\_2}}$, $\mathrm{U}'_{\mathrm{c\_2}}$ and D are assigned to node_x. Similarly, $\mathrm{L}_{\mathrm{r\_4}}$, $\mathrm{U}'_{\mathrm{c\_4}}$ and D are assigned to node_y. The process of key authentication between node_x and node_y is summarized in Table 1. Notice that they find a common key of the value of 8.

Table 1. The process of key authentication

Operation	node_x	node_y
Key pre-distribution	L_{r_2} (2, 3, 0, 0) U'_{c_2} (2, 1, 0, 0) D (1, 2, 3, −1)	L_{r_4} (3, 1, 2, −1) U'_{c_4} (3, 1/3, 1, 1) D (1, 2, 3, −1)
Column-exchange	L_{r_2} (2, 3, 0, 0) U'_{c_4} (3, 1/3, 1, 1)	L_{r_4} (3, 1, 2, −1) U'_{c_2} (2, 1, 0, 0)
Key-computation	$U_{c\_4} = D \times U'_{c\_4}$ = (3, 2/3, 3, −1) $L_{r\_2} \times U_{c\_4} = 8$ (=K_{24})	$U_{c\_2} = D \times U'_{c\_2}$ = (2, 2, 0, 0) $L_{r\_4} \times U_{c\_2} = 8$ (=K_{42})

As in the previous scheme [15] where the nodes keep L and U matrix components and the U matrix components are exchanged for key authentication, the security can be severely degraded if an adversary taps the exchanged data. Note, however, that D matrix is reserved in each sensor node in the proposed scheme, and it is not exposed to outside. As a result, even though the exchanged data are tapped, the adversary cannot authenticate the key with another sensor node since it does not have D matrix. This is an important property when the WSNs are deployed in a very hostile environment such as battlefield.

4 Energy Efficiency

We evaluate the energy efficiency of the proposed scheme through computer simulation by applying it to the LEACH protocol [13], which is one of the representative routing protocols for WSNs. The number of cluster-heads in the simulation is about 5% of the total number of nodes. We consider a sensor network of 100 sensor nodes randomly arranged in a 100 × 100 region. A base station is located at (50, 50). In order to identity relative efficiency of the proposed scheme, we also consider the earlier random key-distribution scheme [7]. In the simulation we set E_{elec} to run the transmitter or receiver circuitry and ε_{amp} for the transmitter amplifier to 50nJ/bit and 100 pJ/bit/m^2 [13, 14], respectively and initial residual energy of a sensor node is 0.25J. The size of one sensor data is 3000 bits, the number of key ring of [7] is 100, and key length is 32 bits. The energy consumption model [14] is described as follows. For transmission, when a node transmits k-bit data to another node with distance d between them, the energy it consumes is:

$$E_{Tx}(k,d) = E_{elec} \times k + \varepsilon_{amp} \times k \times d^2 \quad (7)$$

For receiving, when a node receives k-bit data, the energy it consumes is:

$$E_{Rx}(k) = E_{elec} \times k \quad (8)$$

The parameters used in the simulation are summarized Table 2.

Table 2. The parameters used in the simulation

Parameters	Value
Network size	100 × 100
Base station location	(50, 50)
Number of nodes	100
Initial energy of node	0.25 J
E_{elec} : Transmit and Receive energy	50 nJ/bit
ε_{amp} : Amplifier energy	100 pJ/bit/m^2
Data size	3000 bits
Number of key ring	100
Key length	32, 64, 256 bits

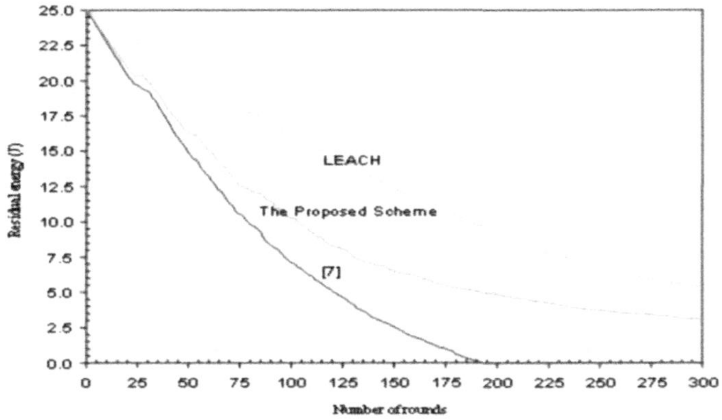

Fig. 1. Comparison of the residual energy of the schemes as communication round proceeds

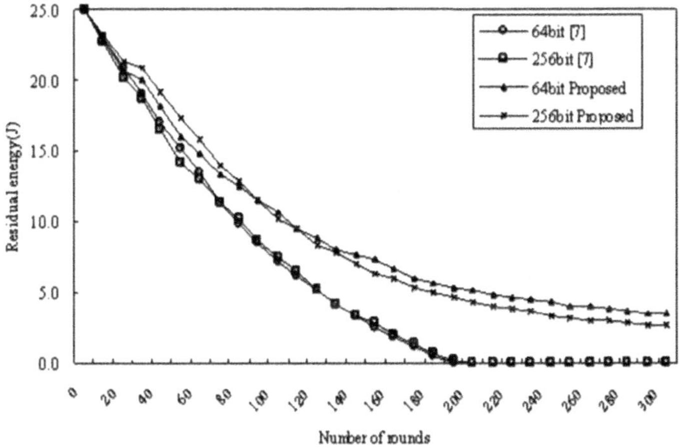

Fig. 2. Comparison of the residual energy of the schemes as the key length varies

Figure 1 compares residual energy of the two schemes as communication round proceeds. Here we also show the case when no key authentication scheme is applied to the LEACH protocol as a reference. Notice that the proposed scheme and [7] show smaller residual energy for each node due to key authentication process at each round compared to the case of no authentication. The proposed scheme, however, allows significantly higher energy efficiency than the existing scheme.

Figure 2 compares residual energy of the proposed scheme with that of the existing scheme when the key length is 64 and 256 bits. Observe from the figure that the residual energy decreases as the key length increases, while the proposed scheme still displays much better results than [7] regardless of the key length.

5 Conclusion and Future Works

Most earlier schemes proposed for the security of sensor network adopt asymmetric cryptography such as Deffie-Hellman key agreement or RSA. However, the schemes are often not suitable for distributed sensor network due to limited computation and energy resource of sensor nodes. The existing random key pre-distribution scheme proposed to address this issue has a drawback of unguaranteed shared key between two nodes wanting to communicate. In this paper we have proposed a new key pre-distribution scheme guaranteeing that any pair of nodes can find a common key between them using the keys assigned by LDU decomposition of a symmetric matrix. A general form solution constructing the L, D, and U matrix has also been developed to minimize the time overhead of LDU decomposition required in the key pre-distribution step. The energy efficiency was evaluated through computer simulation by applying the key pre-distribution scheme to the LEACH protocol. It reveals that the proposed scheme significantly improves the energy efficiency compared with the existing random key pre-distribution scheme. A new model considering security in a more formal way will be developed in the future.

References

[1] Akyildiz, I.F., Su, W., Sankarasubramaniam, Y., Cayirci, E.: A survey on sensor networks: IEEE Communications Magazine 40(8), 102–114 (2002)

[2] Stajano, F.: Security for Ubiquitous Computing: John Wiley and Sons (2002) ISBN 0-470-84493-0

[3] Carman, D.W., Kruus, P.S., Matt, B.J.: Constraints and approaches for distributed sensor network security: NAI Labs Technical Report #00-010 (2000)

[4] Neuman, B.C., Tso, T.: Kerberos: An authentication service for computer networks. IEEE Communications 32(9), 33–38 (1994)

[5] Diffie, W., Hellman, M.E.: New directions in cryptography. IEEE Transactions on Information Theory 22, 644–654 (1976)

[6] Rivest, R.L., Shamir, A., Adleman, L.M.: A method for obtaining digital signatures and public-key cryptosystems. Communications of the ACM 21(2), 120–126 (1978)

[7] Eschenauer, L., Gligor, V.D.: A key-management scheme for distributed sensor networks. In: Proceeding of the 9th ACM Conference on Computer and Communication security, pp. 41–47 (2002)

[8] Anderson, R., Kuhn, M.: Tamper resistance – a cautionary note. In: Proceeding of the Second Usenix Workshop On Electronic Commerce, pp. 1–11 (1996)
[9] Liu, D., Ning, P.: Establishing pairwise keys in distributed sensor networks. In: Proceedings of the 10th ACM Conference on Computer and Communications Security, pp. 52–61 (2003)
[10] Blundo, C., Santix, A.D., Herzberg, A., Kutten, S., Vaccaro, U., Yung, M.: Perfectly-secure key distribution for dynamic conferences. In: Brickell, E.F. (ed.) CRYPTO 1992. LNCS, vol. 740, pp. 471–486. Springer, Heidelberg (1993)
[11] Perrig, A., Szewczyk, R., Wen, V., Cullar, D., Tygar, J.D.: Spins (Security protocols for sensor networks). In: Proceeding of the 7th Annual ACM/IEEE International Conference on Mobile Computing and Networking(MobiCom), pp. 189–199 (2001)
[12] Chan, H., Perrig, A., Song, D.: Random key pre-distribution schemes for sensor networks: IEEE Symposium on Security and Privacy, pp. 197–213 (2003)
[13] Heinzelman, W.R., Chandrakasan, A., Balakrishnan, H.: Energy-Efficient Communication Protocol for Wireless Micro-sensor Networks. In: Proceedings of the Hawaii International Conference on System Science, Maui, Hawaii, pp. 323–327 (2000)
[14] Kim, K.T., Youn, H.Y.: Energy-Driven Adaptive Clustering Hierarchy (EDACH) for Wireless Sensor Networks. LNCS, vol. 3823, pp. 1098–1107 (December 2005)
[15] Choi, S.J., Youn, H.Y.: An Efficient Key Pre-distribution Scheme for Secure Distributed Sensor Networks. LNCS 3823, pp. 1088–1097 (December 2005)

AGV Simulator and Implementer Design

Qiang Huang[1], TianHao Pan[2], and WenHuan Xu[1]

[1] College of Information, Shenzhen University P.R. China 518060
[2] Imperial College of London
jameshq@szu.edu.cn

Abstract. Vision navigation [1] has been a significant research area in recent year for robotic industrial. Various algorithms for obstacle detection and avoidance have been developed. Successfully testing of these algorithms require implementation in a realistic robot vehicle, which demands extra effort for researcher. The developed integrated autonomous guided vehicle [2] simulator and implementer (AGV-SI) emulates the realistic robot vehicle operating environment. Researchers can develop the algorithms based on the commonly used language - Matlab. Then simply input the algorithm and testing environment settings into the AGV-SI, an evaluation result is obtained. With the AGV-SI user can also choose to practically implement the algorithm by downloading the algorithm into a robot vehicle connected to the PC. With the support of the AGV-SI a novel algorithm was developed with the integration of adaptive median filter [3], inverse perspective map [4] and edge detection techniques. Both simulation and practical implementation validate the feasibility of the algorithm.

Keywords: AGV, computer vision, simulator, implementer, human robot interaction.

1 Introduction

Computer vision navigation has been a common research focus for robotics for recent years. Obstacle detection [5] is one of the most fundamental programs for Autonomous Guided Vehicle (AGV) system. Conventional testing of the AGV algorithms requires practical implementation, which will be time consuming. An integrated graphical-based AGV algorithm simulator and implementer is developed together with a novel algorithm. It acts as middleware for human robot interaction. The AGV-SI provides development support for AGV developer with more efficiency.

2 AGV-SI Structure

The vehicle is simulated by the AGV-SI program that has exactly the same interface with realistic vehicle, the simulation process is based on physical parameters such as time, vehicle speed and vehicle size. Thus, the simulation result is stable for various hardware implementations. The simulation structure consists of robot vehicle model and camera-based environment [6] simulation as shown in Fig. 1.

J. Jacko (Ed.): Human-Computer Interaction, Part II, HCII 2007, LNCS 4551, pp. 818–826, 2007.

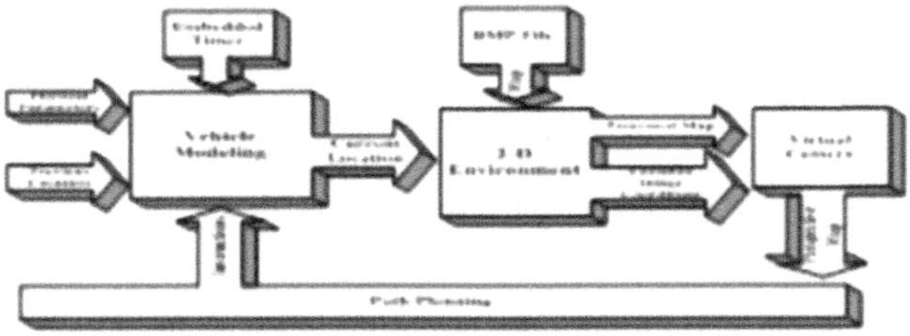

Fig. 1. AGV-SI structure

2.1 Vehicle Simulation

Simulating an ideal vehicle encounters two situations [7]. First is to simulate the vehicle's straight movement and second is to simulate maneuvers. These behaviors can be simulated by the turning angle and the distance. For straight movement, the distance (denoted as L) is equal to $L = v \times t$, which v and t are speed and time respectively. When the vehicle is turning, the turning angle, denoted as α is equal to $\alpha = \frac{v \times t}{r} \approx \frac{v \times t}{w}$, where r is the length between two wheels. It is approximated with the width of the vehicle, denoted as w. A timer is embedded into the program for keeping time track.

2.2 Representation of Vehicle Location

Location [8] is recorded for simulation of vehicle movement. The location information contains vehicle heading direction, runtime and velocity. The original location from the calculation in Cartesian coordinate is then transferred into image coordinate system for getting the perceptive view.

AGV-SI employs 'Path & Compass' panel to illustrate the vehicle track and direction. The program calculates vehicle's direction and transfer into an angle, which denote the starting direction as 0 degree and corresponding to it. Then AGV-SI calculates the path using embedded timer and the vehicle's angle.

2.3 Camera Simulation

The AGV-SI locates the 'area' of the real camera. All parameters determine the inverse perspective's scope [9], which is shown in Fig. 2.

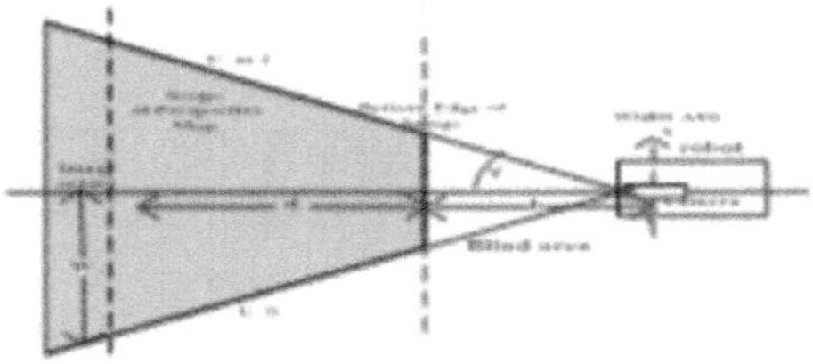

Fig. 2. Inverse Perspective's scope

The simulated camera employs those parameters to determine the available scope with (1).

$$y = h\tan\left(\beta + \frac{2\alpha(n-1-v)}{(n-1)}\right)$$
$$x = y\tan\left(\frac{\gamma(2u-m+1)}{(m-1)}\right) \quad (1)$$

Where, x and y is set as the four corners of the image. A mask is then made that the simulator can get the same scope form an entire map. The mask of the simulated camera provides the same inverse perspective scope with the real camera to represent the environment. However, catching a correct Inverse Perspective map has to depend on the vehicle's direction. The AGV-SI utilizes an image to represent the environment, which is the data source for the simulated camera. The camera picks up the correct Inverse Perspective area with a rotation which depends on the current direction of the vehicle. The method of getting the right inverse perspective map (IPM) with an angle is shown on Fig. 3.

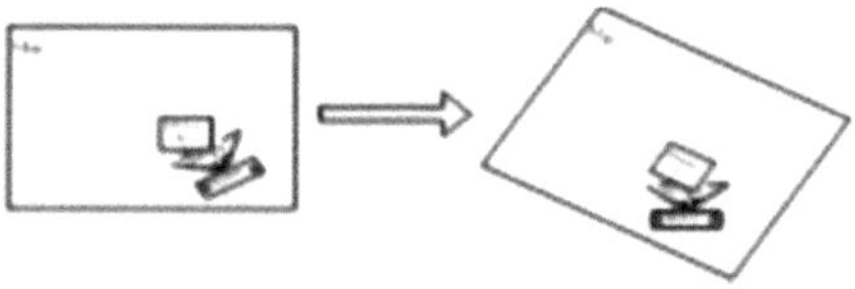

Fig. 3. Image rotation for correct IPM

Image rotation is based on the nearest interpolation method [10]. The nearest neighbor interpolation, also called zeros-order interpolation, is a forward interpolation and uses the nearest pixel for the assignment of the values.

The entire image is rotated to ensure that the simulated camera picks up a correct inverse perspective area. After the image rotation, the program will calculate the new location of the robot. An image rotation is based on the centre point. Thus, the robot's location will be transferred from image coordinate into Cartesian coordinate by (2).

$$n_y = \frac{s_y}{2} - y$$
$$n_x = x - \frac{s_x}{2} \quad (2)$$

s_y and s_x represent an image with $s_y \bullet s_x$ pixels. The rotation matrix is given as $\begin{bmatrix} \cos\theta & -\sin\theta \\ \sin\theta & \cos\theta \end{bmatrix}$, the new location, denoted as $\begin{bmatrix} x_o \\ y_o \end{bmatrix}$, can be calculated by (3).

$$\begin{bmatrix} x_o \\ y_o \end{bmatrix} = \begin{bmatrix} \cos\theta & -\sin\theta \\ \sin\theta & \cos\theta \end{bmatrix} \begin{bmatrix} x_i \\ y_i \end{bmatrix} \quad (3)$$

$\begin{bmatrix} x_i \\ y_i \end{bmatrix}$ is the location before the rotation. After the image rotation, the coordinate will be transferred into image coordinate, which is given by (4).

$$r_y = \frac{n_y}{2} - y$$
$$r_x = x + \frac{n_x}{2} \quad (4)$$

Where n_y and n_x is the size of the image after rotation and (x, y) is the robot's new location. Fig 4 illustrates the result of the simulated camera.

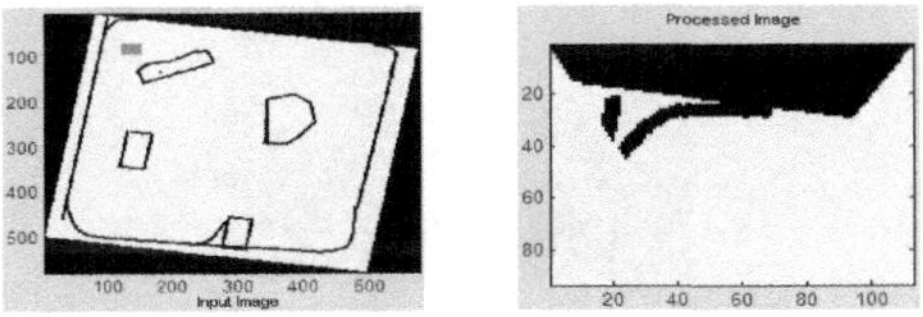

Fig. 4. Result of the simulated camera

2.4 Environment Representations

The simulation environment is 2-D based, using a binary BMP file. The AGV-SI applies inverse perspective map to represent the environment. The movement of vehicle is determined by the path planning program which receives IPM as its input. Thus, the simulated camera and the environment can be simplified into 2-D. The simulator is able to load the map file anytime, i.e. using GUI to enable user to load the map file directly instead of changing the specified program code.

3 AGV Implementer

The AGV implementer consists of real-time image processing [11] and robot design.

3.1 Real-Time Image Processing

Getting a frame in right time sequence is the first important step for AGV [12]. The navigation process is designed as an infinite loop. The implementer will send out instructions to the mobile robot after receiving an image from the onboard camera. The framework consists of data acquisition, image conversion, noise reduction and distance recovery.

3.2 Data Acquisition

A standard USB camera is applied to create a video input object and be recognized as the tag of 'winvideo'. The implementer then creates the video stream and acquires the single frame. A single frame is loaded into the framework; it checks the status of the video data stream before acquiring the image. The video source is released afterward.

3.3 Mobile Robot Design

The mobile robot has been developed with two driving wheels by stepper motor and one free running wheel. A communication link is designed between the mobile robot driving component and the commanding PC via parallel communication port. The commanding message is sent by the PC implementer then received and interpreted by the mobile robot controller. Fig. 5 shows the mobile robot implementation.

Fig. 5. Mobile robot design

4 A Novel AGV Algorithm Design

A novel AGV algorithm is developed with the support of AGV-SI. The algorithm exhibits good perform result over the implementation solely with edge detection [13].

Fig. 6. A novel AGV algorithm

4.1 Edge Detection

Color images acquired are converted into gray level to detect the obstacle with edge detection. It provides real-time image processing solution with better performance in execution time. A simple convolution kernel of Sobel edge detector [14] is used to create vectors of gradient magnitude.

4.2 Noise Reduction with Filtering

Wiener filter and Median filter are used normally to remove noise from the original image. The algorithm applies the filters to reduce noise yielded by the sensitive Sobel edge detection.

Fig. 7 shows the results of the image pre-processing. Images on the left side are the original images captured from the camera. The ground of the top image has no pattern or texture and the ground of the bottom image contains a small size texture. The ground is eliminated on both of the images and edge is detected completely. Therefore, the image pre-processing provides a reasonable and stable binary map to the post-processing program.

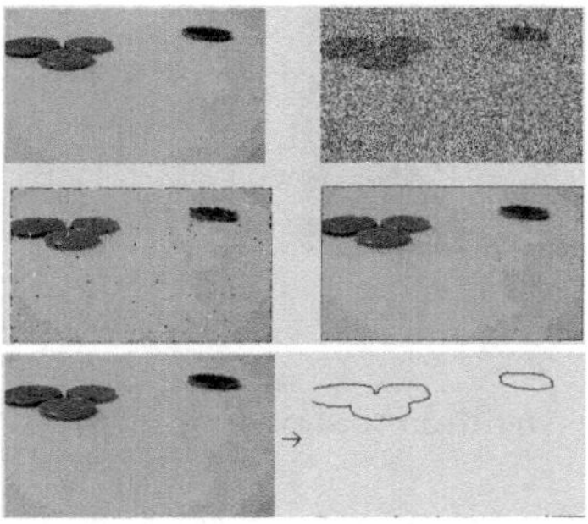

Fig. 7. Noise reduction with filtering

4.3 Distance Recovery

Field Of View (FOV) [15] is used to recover the inverse perspective map. The FOV also called angle of view, is the amount of a given scene shown on the image sensor. There are two parameters of angle of view which are horizontal and vertical angle. Fig. 8 illustrates FOV.

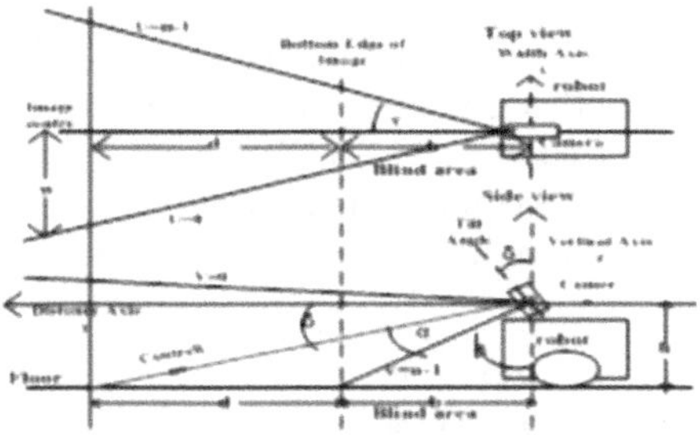

Fig. 8. Field of view

As the horizontal and vertical FOV for the mobile robot, D is the distance between the mobile robot and any point (u,v) on the image's ground is calculated by (5).

$$D = \sqrt{x^2 + y^2} \tag{5}$$

Where, the parameters are calculated as (6).

$$\begin{aligned} y &= h\tan\left(\beta + \frac{2\alpha(n-1-v)}{(n-1)}\right) \\ x &= y\tan\left(\frac{\gamma(2u-m+1)}{(m-1)}\right) \\ \tan(\beta) &= \frac{b}{h} \\ \tan(\alpha+\beta) &= \frac{(b+d)}{h\tan(\gamma)} = \frac{w}{(b+d)} \\ \alpha+\beta+\gamma &= 90^\circ \end{aligned} \tag{6}$$

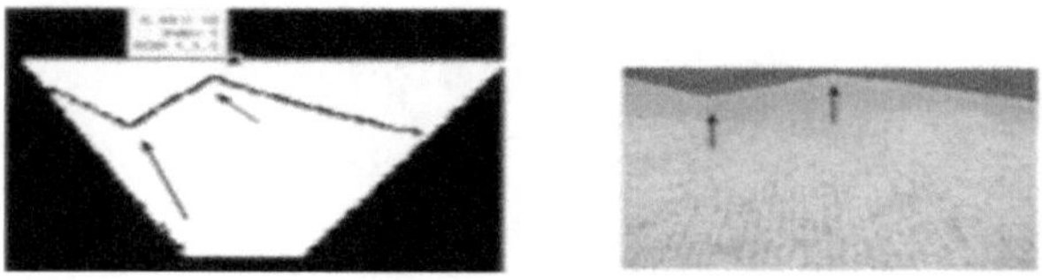

Fig. 9. Distance recovery testing

The result of the testing condition is shown on Table 1.

Table 1. Distance recovery testing result

Experiment parameters	Example	Experiment results
Blinding Area	20cm	13.2%
Height of the camera	21cm	8.7%
Horizontal FOV	0.4420	20cm – 82cm
Vertical FOV	0.2812	24cm – 98cm
Image size	240*320	20cm

4.4 Path Planning

The path planning [16] strategy is based on local path planning, which makes decision based on current position and surrounding environment as shown in Fig. 10. The first step of the algorithm is to find the accessible region. The algorithm tries to make the vehicle's locomotion in the accessible area. Then sort out a path that enables the vehicle to move in the current Inverse Perspective Map. The whole process is described as followings.

- Set a detection area. The detection area is the area for triggering the path planning program. When there is obstacle appear on the detection area.
- Analyzing the dangerous area. The dangerous area is the area where collision will occur for the robot when turning. The dangerous area set in this program is half of the vehicle's width.
- Find the safety area. The safety area will be found in particular range where the y axis is the same with the dangerous area. This will be more efficient than searching the whole image because the area without obstacle is always safe for robot.
- Choose the suitable safety area for path planning. The safety area found by program is a 2*n array which has to be analyzed for discriminating the different area. If there is more than one safety area divided, the program will find the area with the biggest size.
- Find the center of the area. The center of the biggest area is found and referred as the target location for the robot. The turning angle will be calculated by tangent.

Fig. 11 shows the process and result of the path planning for this algorithm. The targeting area is the white space within the image, while the circus on the right side of the image indicates a calculated accessible area. This area is marked as safety area while others are marked as dangerous area for mobile robot.

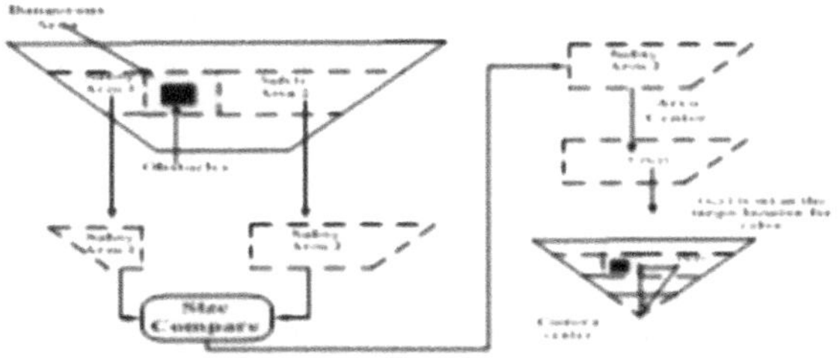

Fig. 10. Process of choosing accessible area

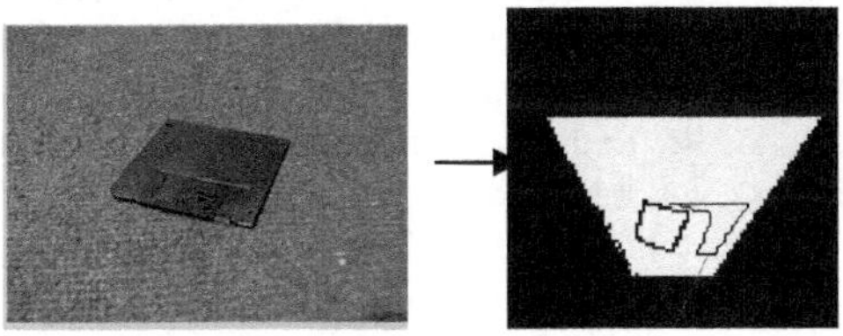

Fig. 11. Result of path planning

5 Simulation and Implementation Result

AGV-SI incorporates a graphical-based user interface; it integrates the simulation program and the mobile robot control program. The robot simulator contains three control panels and four display windows for test map, the perspective map displaying panel, 'path & compass' panel, 'Load Map' panel, 'Simulation Parameters' panel and robot simulation panel. Fig. 12 shows the AGV-SI in simulation mode and implementation mode.

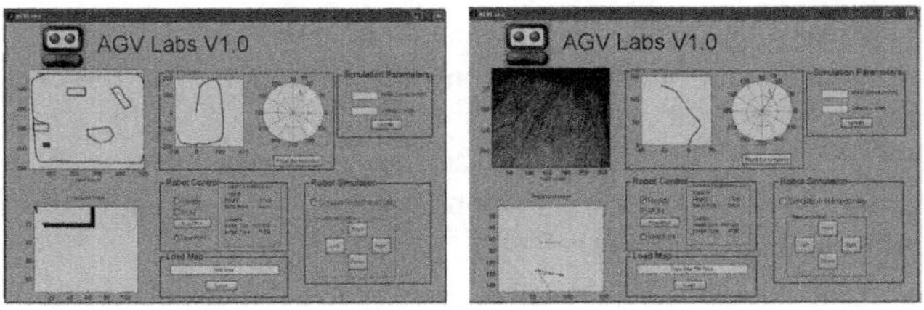

Fig. 12. AGV-SI in simulation and implementation modes

6 Conclusion

AGV is being applied in both academic research and industrial area. The lack of an integrated simulator and implementer could lead to extra workload. The developed AGV-SI is focus on providing support for AGV design. Further more it provides practical implementation for rapid industrial application development. The proposed AGV algorithm is designed with integration of Sobel edge detection and filtering techniques. The algorithm is then simulated and implemented by the AGV-SI with feasible result.

Acknowledgments. This work was supported by Natural Science Foundation of China (60501026), Research and Teaching Foundation of ShenZhen University (200513, A20050311).

References

1. Das, A K, Fierro, R., Kumar, V., Southall, B., Spletzer, J., Taylor, C J: Real-time vision based control of a nonholonomic mobile robot. IEEE International Conference on Robotics and Automation, Seoul, Korea (2001)
2. Jüngel, M., Hoffmann, J., Lötzsch, M.: A real-time auto-adjusting vision system for robotic soccer. In: Polani, D., Browning, B., Bonarini, A., Yoshida, K. (eds.) RoboCup 2003. LNCS (LNAI), vol. 3020, Springer, Heidelberg (2004)
3. Burns, J. B., Hanson, A. R.: Extracting Straight Lines, IEEE Trans. on Pattern Analysis and Machine Intelligence vol.8(4) (1986)
4. Duda, R.O., Hart, P.E.: Use of the Hough Transformation To Detect Lines and Curves in Pictures, Graphics and Image Processing vol. 15(1) (1972)
5. Ulrich, I., Nourbakhsh, I.: Appearance-Based Obstacle Detection with Monocular Color Vision. In: 17th National Conference on Artificial Intelligence, Austin, Texas (2000)
6. Lim, J.S: Two-dimensional signal and image processing, pp. 476–487. Prentice Hall, Englewood Cliffs (1990)
7. Howard, A., Kitchen, L.: Fast Visual Mapping for Mobile Robot Navigation. IEEE International Conference on Intelligent Processing Systems, Beijing, China (1997)
8. Ulrich, I., Nourbakhsh, I.: Appearance-Based Place Recognition for Topological Localization. In: Proceedings of the IEEE International Conference on Robotics and Automation (2000)
9. Taylor1, T., Geva, S., Boles, W W: Monocular Vision as a Range Sensor. In: Proceedings of CIMCA 2004, Gold Coast Australia (2004)
10. Bertozzi, M., Broggi, A., Fascioli, A.: Stereo inverse projection mapping: theory and applications. Image and Vision Computing 16, 585–590 (1998)
11. Cheng, G., Zelinsky, A.: Real-Time Visual Behaviors for Navigating a Mobile Robot. IEEE/RSJ International Conference on Intelligent Robots and Systems, Osaka, Japan (1996)
12. Papanikolopoulos, N. P., Khosla, P. K., Kanade, T.: Visual Tracking of a Moving Target by a Camera Mounted on a Robot: A combination of Control and Vision. IEEE Trans. on Robotics and Automation vol. 9(1) (1993)
13. Canny, J A.: Computational Approach to Edge Detection, IEEE Trans. Pattern Analysis and Machine Intelligence 8, 679–714 (1986)
14. Maar, D., Hildreth, E.: Theory of edge detection. In: Proceedings of Royal Soc. London vol. 207, pp. 187–217 (1980)
15. Saptharishi, S.A., Ollennu, M.T: Cyber-ATVs: Dynamic and Distributed Reconnaissance and Surveillance Using All Terrain UGVs. In: Proceedings of the International Conference on Field and Service Robotics, pp. 329–334 (1999)
16. Latombe, J.C: Robot Motion Planning. Kluwer Academic Publishers, Boston (1991)

Interactive Browsing of Large Images on Multi-projector Display Wall System

Zhongding Jiang, Xuan Luo, Yandong Mao, Binyu Zang, Hai Lin, and Hujun Bao

Computer Graphics Lab, Software School, Fudan University, Shanghai, China
State Key Lab. of CAD&CG, Zhejiang University, Hangzhou, China
{zdjiang|byzang}@fudan.edu.cn, {lin|bao}@cad.zju.edu.cn

Abstract. With the precision of data acquisition increases, large images that may occupy terabytes, become common in research and industry fields. Since multi-projector display wall systems can provide higher resolution, they becomes paramount to display the large images. In this paper, we present one large image viewing system designed for display wall system. Our system need not totally downloading the whole image data to each rendering node. It enables users to browse the out-of-core images in real time using data streaming techniques. In the system, the original out-of-core raw image is compressed and represented using one hierarchical structure in multi-resolution manner. We design one proxy architecture that interactive streams data from remote data server to all rendering nodes. Our system allows users to interactively pan, and zoom the large images with versatile graphical user interface.

1 Introduction

With the precision of data acquisition increases, large images are common from medical imaging, satellites and Arial photography. One large image may occupy terabytes, which is out-of-core of main memory of desktop PC [3]. When examining large images, users should be able to interactively teleport to different areas, pan and zoom at fine resolutions for investigating the image details. Since the resolution of PC monitor is limited, multi-projector display wall system, providing higher display resolution, becomes paramount to display the large images [7,4].

Enabling users to browse out-of-core images on multi-projector display wall system with limited memory is a challenging task. Since the large images are usually created and owned by special organizations, it is prohibitive for users to download the entire dataset from the remote server before browsing the image. It is more attractable for users to stream the image data from remote server in on demand manner. This scheme need not totally downloading the whole image data to each rendering node [3].

This paper presents one large images viewing system designed for display wall system, which enables interactive browsing large images that are stored on remote data server. In our system, the original out-of-core raw image is compressed and represented using one hierarchical structure in multi-resolution manner. We design one proxy architecture that interactive streams data from the remote data server to the

J. Jacko (Ed.): Human-Computer Interaction, Part II, HCII 2007, LNCS 4551, pp. 827–836, 2007.

rendering nodes. Our system allows users to pan, and zoom the large images with Graphical User Interface (GUI) running on the console node. As to our best knowledge, the system is the first one that enables users to remotely browse large images on multi-projector display wall system at real time frame rate. It allows users to interactively examine any important portion of the large images at full resolution without losing fine details.

The remainder of the paper is organized as follows. Section 2 describes the related work. The architecture of the system is described in Section 3. The details of our system are presented in Section 4. The experimental results are shown in Section 5. Finally, we draw conclusions and point out the future work.

2 Related Work

The *Clipmap* representation [5] can efficiently cache the out-of-core texture in limited memory for real time graphics applications. It achieves this goal by combination of low-level hardware and high-level system software. Since it is originally designed for single graphics workstation, the Clipmap representation does not address issues relating to image rendering on multi-projector display wall system, such as user interaction, and efficient access to remote data.

By duplicating the whole image data on each rendering node, Binns et al. propose one cluster-based image viewing system [1]. In this system, every rendering node reads raw image data from disk on demand during the browsing process. It does not address remote access to image data, thus limiting its application scenario to local area network.

JuxtaView [3] is the first large image viewing system for PC cluster using data streaming techniques. It employs one cluster memory pool to address out-of-core image rendering. At startup, it statically pre-partitions the whole image data set for distributing data in memory pool of remote data server cluster. When a user interaction event occurs, the application running on each rendering node acquires the data from its local cache or from remote data servers. The drawback of such a system is that the entire image data must fit into the collective memory of the data server cluster. Furthermore, JuxtaView does not achieve image browsing at real-time frame rate due to its complexities of distributed shared memory protocols. Our proxy-based architecture is simpler, leading to better system performance.

The previous large image browsing systems designed for display wall [1,3] represent the raw image data in RGBA format with single resolution. This raw data format provides good support for fast data extraction, preventing decoding overhead. Compared with a compressed representation, the raw format is inefficient for storage and network transmission, leading to a severe performance penalty. Another practice issue is that the single resolution representation does not allow users to select appropriate image resolution according to the zoom factor [2]. Since the representation is un-tiled, it can not support large images occupying terabytes. Our compressed and hierarchical image representation attempts to solve these issues.

3 System Architecture

Our system has been implemented with the multi-projector display wall installed at our laboratory, the hardware setup is shown in Figure 1(a). The display wall system is driven by six PCs, each connecting to one projector. The projectors are arranged in 2x3 layout, and each one displays a portion of the whole display content. Figure 1(b) illustrates its architecture.

(a) Hardware setup

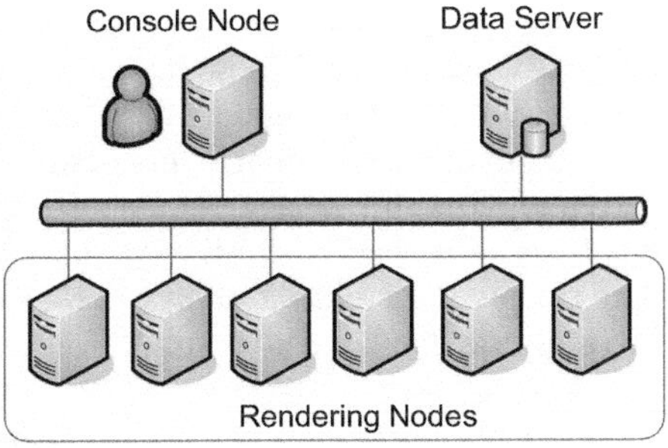

(b) System architecture

Fig. 1. The architecture of large image browsing

In the system, the original out-of-core raw image is compressed and represented using one hierarchical structure in multi-resolution manner. The compressed data is stored on the remote data server. Since the compressed data may occupy much storage space, downloading the whole data to each render node before displaying it, requires long time to wait. Thus, streaming data to each render node on demand will improve the performance of our system, achieving real-time frame rate.

Each rendering node renders its corresponding portion of the whole image on display wall into the framebuffer of graphics card. Then, the content of the framebuffer at each rendering node is geometric warped and photometric corrected before being sent to the projector connected to the rendering node. Finally, the swap-buffer events of all rendering nodes are synchronized. After passing through the imaging system of projectors, the modified images appear seamless on the display wall.

The Graphical User Interface (GUI) is running on the console node. With the GUI, users can perform panning and zooming operations to navigate the images using keyboard and mouse. When the interaction events occur on the console node, these events will be converted into commands to be sent to the rendering nodes. The rendering nodes compute the required image portions using the geometric parameters of the projector array arrangement and user navigation events.

During image browsing, the data reference history exhibits good spatial and temporal localities. The recent-visited data on the render node will usually be reused in the near future. Therefore, we design one three-level cache hierarchy that stores the image data at each rendering node. When data missing occurs during users' navigation, the console node first sends data requests to the data server, caches the received data locally, and transfers them to the corresponding rendering node. The console node also records the cache structure of each rendering node, acting as the proxy between the rendering nodes and data server.

4 The Large Image Browsing System for Display Wall

4.1 Graphical User Interface

With the GUI on the console node, users freely navigate the large image using keyboard and mouse. When the interaction event occurs, both the display wall and the console GUI will be updated for keeping consistency with the currently viewable portion of the large image. For example, when user pans left with 50 pixels, the currently viewable image region of each rendering node will also pan left with 50 pixels as response. Accordingly, the image region of the display wall will pan left with 50 pixels. Figure 2 shows one snapshot of the console node and one captured image of the display wall result.

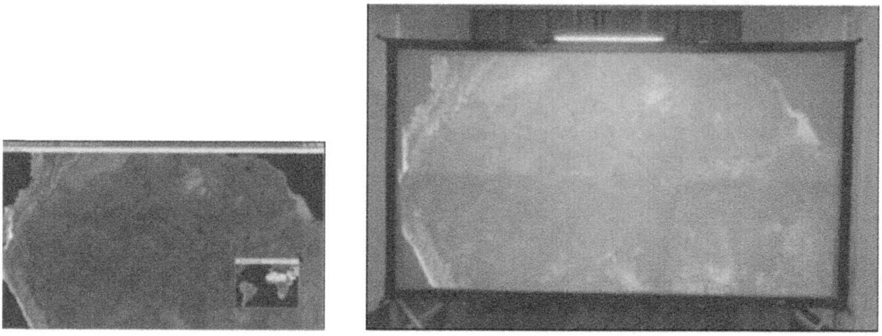

(a) GUI on the console node (b) Result on the display wall

Fig. 2. Graphical user interface

The GUI on the console node consists of two components: the *view-canvas* and the *overview-window* floating on the view-canvas. The view-canvas shows one small version of the image region that is currently rendered on the display wall. The overview-window shows one thumbnail of the large image. One blue transparent region inside of the overview-window, overlays exactly on the portion that is being displayed in the view-canvas. The overview-window provides visual context to help users determine position and region of the display region relative to the whole image.

Our GUI supports mouse and keyboard devices for fluid navigation of large images. With three-button mouse, users can drag the canvas to pan around, or scroll the middle button of mouse to zoom the view-canvas. Users can conveniently jump to one desired portion of the large image by drag-and-drop the blue region in the overview-window. Users can change the viewable region of the large image by scrolling/moving around the content of the overview-window.

4.2 Image Representation

For easy data management and flexible transmission over network, we design one hierarchically compressed data structure to represent the large out-of-core raw image (Figure 3(a)). It first partitions the original image into multiple tiles when the image is extremely large that occupies terabytes. Second, each tile is organized as a collection of correlated images of increasingly reduced resolution arranged as an inverted resolution-pyramid. Starting with the finest level, each lower level resolution-image is constructed by per-filtering the superior level one with the half pixel size in each dimension. Third, each resolution-image is segmented into fixed sized image blocks. Each individual image block is compressed with standard JPEG by choosing appropriate quality parameters. In this representation, the lowest resolution-image only contains one image block.

The set of required image blocks must be determined before rendering can be carried out on each rendering node. This process consists of three steps. First, each render node figures out the set of image tiles that are visible in its currently viewable image region. Second, the resolution-images are determined obeying that the ratio between the screen-resolution and the resolution-image is closest to one to one. Third, image blocks in these chosen resolution-images will be put into the set of required image blocks if they are not occluded.

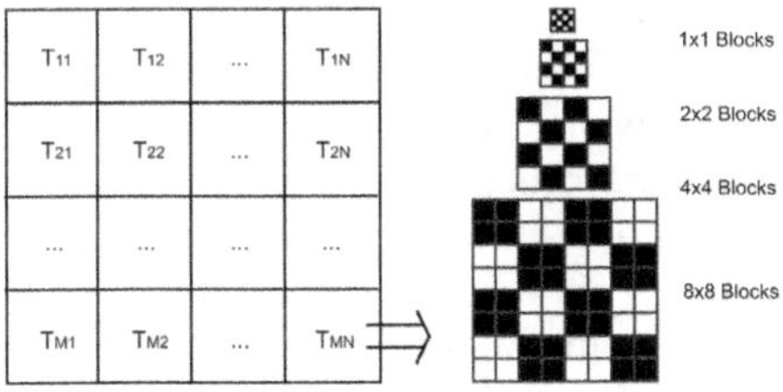

(a) Tiling-based resolution pyramids

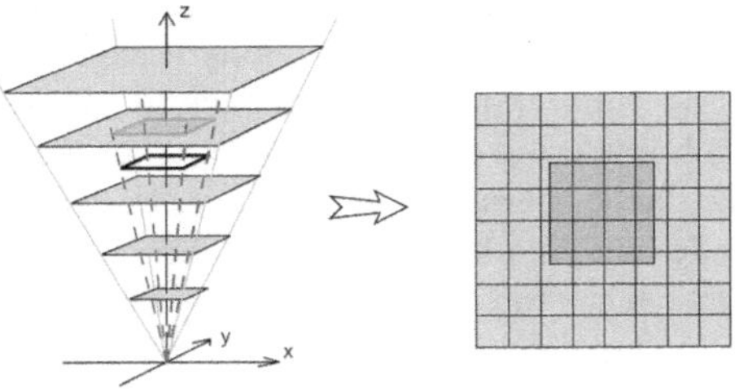

(b) The required image blocks

Fig. 3. Image representation

Without loss of generality, we use one image tile represented with one resolution pyramid to illustrate how to choose image blocks on one rendering node (Figure 3(b)). The horizontal axes represent the two dimensions of image, while the vertical axis represents the image scale. We define a fixed-size viewing window which moves through the 3D space during the browsing process. For example, when a zoom in interaction event occurs, the viewing window is shifted up for a certain distance. When rendering, the viewing window is projected to the nearest and higher resolution-image with the projection region corresponding to the currently viewable image portion. In this example, the viewing window is projected to the fourth resolution level, which has 64 image blocks. The image blocks in blue color are covered by the projection region, and will be transmitted from the data server for rendering.

Our representation provides many features suitable for browsing large images on display wall system. The tiling scheme can handle extremely large images from remote sense and satellite, especially useful for large scale visualization applications. It relaxes the constraints of single tile representation [2]. Organizing data in multi-resolution manner, rendering nodes adaptively select the required image blocks according to the zooming factor, avoiding transferring and re-sampling the large, finest detail image portion if single resolution representation is used [3]. Since the raw image is compressed and cut into blocks, it allows easy extraction data from the compressed bitstream, and enables to efficiently transfer them over network with small bandwidth.

4.3 Interactive Data Streaming

During image browsing, the required image blocks exhibit spatial and temporal localities. For panning operation, most of the image blocks that are visible in the currently viewable image region, will still be visible in the next frame. In most cases, only the image blocks around the region will be streamed from the data server, passing through the console node. The received data will be decoded into raw (RGBA format) image blocks stored in the main memory. As rendering, the raw image blocks are loaded into the video memory of graphics card. For zooming operation, users control the level-of-detail of the currently viewable image region by switching from several adjacent resolution-images back and forth. In this case, the recently referenced resolution-image is much likely to be revisited again.

To fully exploit the reference locality, we present a three-level cache hierarchy on each rendering node to speed up the interactive browsing process. Figure 4 illustrates the cache hierarchy and the whole data transmission process between the rendering node and data server. The bottom level cache is in blue. It is one main memory pool that caches the compressed image blocks streamed from the data server. It is used for reducing data retransmission over network. The memory pool of the middle level cache stores the decoded raw image blocks in red. Since decoding one JPEG image block need much CPU cycles, this cache makes trade off between decoding time and memory consumption. The top level cache is one memory pool in graphics card. It stores the image blocks using RGBA textures to reduce the download time from main memory to video memory. In the three-level cache hierarchy, each cache is organized as an array of several resolution-level set. It is implemented using hash table and the least-recently-used (LRU) replacement policy.

Most of the display wall systems have limited number of internet connections. The PCs driving the display system usually access the internet service by using proxy. In the same spirit, our system treats the console node as the proxy between the rendering nodes and data server. The console node is responsible for sending data requests to the data server and distributing the received data to the corresponding rendering nodes. For reducing data retransmission between the rendering nodes and data server, the console node maintains one local cache that stored the received compressed image blocks from the data server.

In addition to the local cache, the console node maintains one simulating cache for each rendering node. We refer the three-level cache hierarchy on each rendering node as rendering cache. A simulating cache is the counterpart of a rendering cache. It does not hold the content of its corresponding rendering cache resident on the rendering node. Instead, it only records which image blocks are still available on the rendering node. The simulating cache simulates the behavior of the corresponding rendering cache to keep consistence with it.

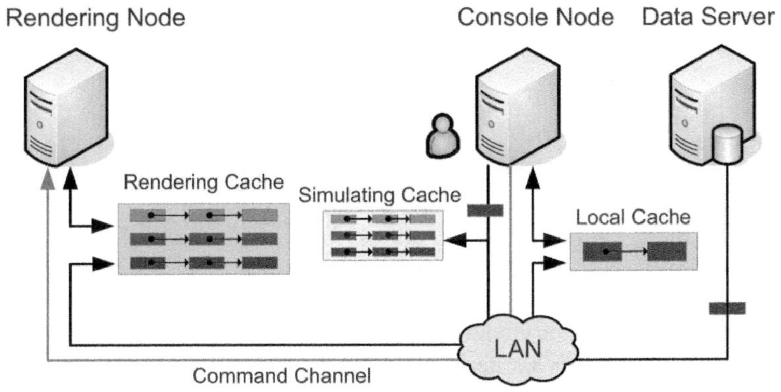

Fig. 4. Interactive data transmission

Besides the local and simulating caches, the console node records the currently viewable region of each rendering node. When the user interaction event occurs, the console node is in charge of determining the image blocks needed by each rendering node, but not resident in the rendering cache or its local cache, according to the updated parameters. These image blocks are referred as the required image blocks. Once the required image blocks are computed, the console node retrieves them from the data server in on demand manner. After receiving, it caches them in the local cache, and delivers them to the corresponding rendering nodes. Meanwhile, the simulating caches corresponding to the rendering nodes are updated.

During image browsing, each rendering node receives the interaction commands sent by the console node and waits for the required image blocks. Once the required image blocks are arrived, the rendering node caches them in the rendering cache, and carries out rendering immediately. Since the required data is determined and distributed by the console note, all rendering nodes receive the required image blocks in asynchronous manner, which leads to higher frame rate.

5 Experimental Results

Our system has been implemented with the multi-projector display wall system shown in Figure 1(a). Each rendering node is equipped with one Intel 3.0GHz CPU, one NVIDIA GeForce 6800GT graphics card, and 1GB DDRII memory. The console node is equipped with one Intel E6700 Core2 Duo CPU, one NVIDIA GeForce 8800GTX graphics card and 2GB DDRII memory. The data server, console node, and rendering nodes are connected in the same LAN with a bandwidth of 1 Gbps. The dataset used for our experiments is acquired from NASA blue marble dataset with a resolution of 43,200 x 21,600 pixels. The raw data of the large image occupies up to

2.6 GB disk space. The image data is organized into one five-level resolution pyramid. The resolution-image of each level is cut into blocks with fixed size 512 x 512 pixels. Each image block is compressed individually using JPEG standard with the quality setting of 85. The final data representation occupies 118 MB on disk.

Two navigation manners, panning and zooming, are used to test the performance of our system. In the diagonal panning test, we pan the image from the left-bottom corner of the display wall to the right-top at the resolution-level of 10,800 x 5,400 pixels with 250 steps. Each operation pans along the diagonal of the image with an offset of 40 pixels. For the zooming in test, the initial state is chosen to be that the image is rendered as a small portion at the center of the display wall, using image blocks from the resolution-level of 2,700 x 1,350 pixels. 120 zooming in operations are performed, yielding a continuous magnification of the image.

The latency in the experimental results refers to the time taken to complete an operation. Figure 5 depicts the latency time during the panning and zooming processes. The marked points are obtained by calculating the average latency of every 5 panning operations or every 3 zooming operations. As shown in Figure 5(a), the latency time of panning repeats periodically in regular pattern. The reason is that the cache missing on each rendering node is similar during the panning process. In Figure 5(b), the latencies of 4 marked points are much larger than others. The reason is that the required image blocks change dramatically when users switch to one new resolution-image as zooming in, which increases the latency time. Figure 5 shows that our system can achieve an average latency time of 16 ms for panning and 12 ms for zooming, achieving interactive frame rate.

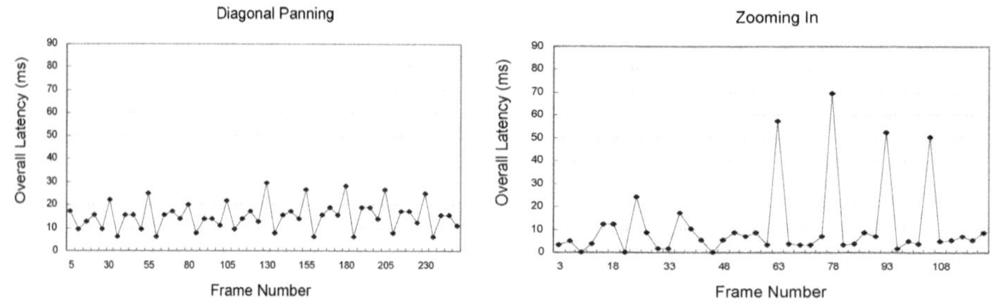

(a) Latency as panning (b) Latency as zooming

Fig. 5. Latency between frames when performing panning and zooming

The bandwidth requirements of the panning test are illustrated in Figure 6. The number of the required blocks (Figure 6(b)) is varied over time, showing patterns similar to that of latency time. Figure 6(a) shows the actual bandwidth requirements, which also exhibits the regular pattern in Figure 6(b). The local peak values are varied since the image blocks are compressed using JPEG without constant bit-rate control mechanism. Figure 7 shows the number of the required image blocks on each rendering node during the panning process. Figure 8 and Figure 9 show the bandwidth requirements and the required image blocks of each rendering node as users perform zooming in operations. Both figures show similar pattern of the latency time in Figure 5(b).

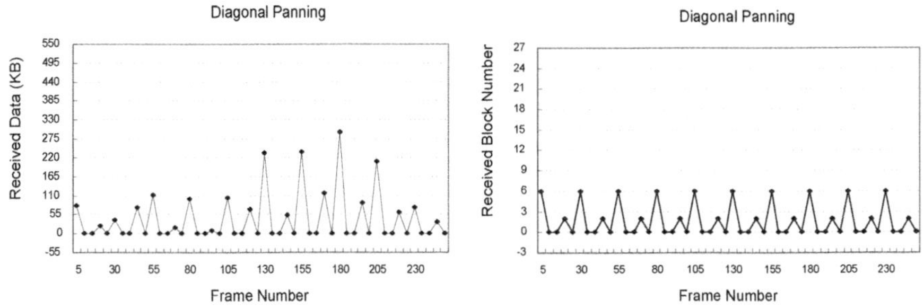

(a) Received data size (b) Received block number

Fig. 6. Bandwidth requirement as panning

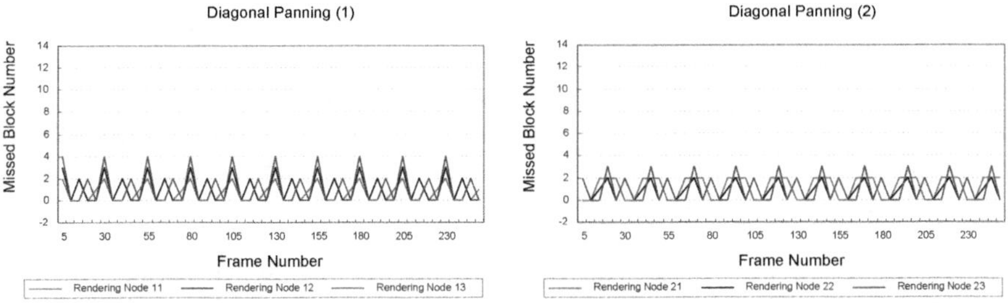

(a) Received block number of top row (b) Received block number of bottom row

Fig. 7. Required block number when panning operations are carried out

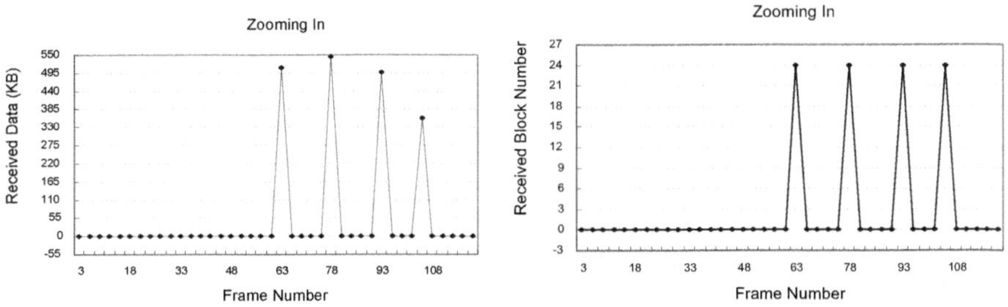

(a) Received data size (b) Received block number

Fig. 8. Bandwidth requirement as zooming in

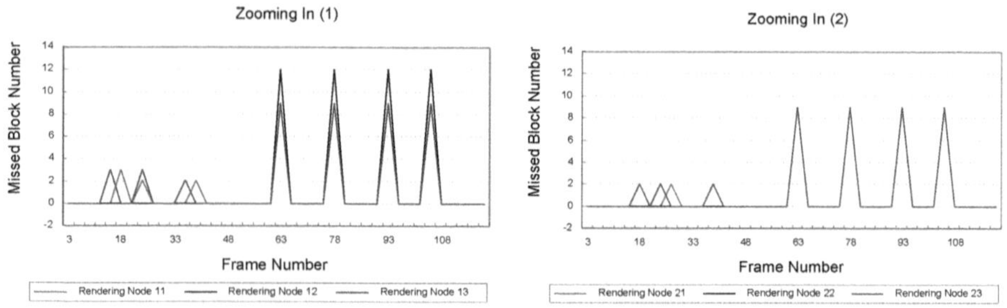

(a) Received block number of top row (b) Received block number of bottom row

Fig. 9. Required block number when zooming in operations are carried out

6 Conclusions and Future Work

This paper presents one large images browsing system designed for multi-projector display wall system. Our system enables users to browse the out-of-core images in real time using data streaming techniques. The original out-of-core raw image is compressed and represented using one hierarchical structure in multi-resolution manner. We design one proxy architecture that interactive streams data from the data server to the rendering nodes. In the future work, we will improve the current system to support large images encoding using JPEG2000[6].

Acknowledgments. This work is supported in part by the 863 Program (Grant No. 2006AA01Z325), 973 Program (Grant No.2002CB312104) of China, and gift from Microsoft Research Asia.

References

[1] Binns, J., Papka, M.E., Stevens, R.: Development of Cluster-based Image Viewer. http://www.fusiongrid.org/research/papers/hpdc02-viewer.pdf
[2] Jao, C.S., Hier, D.B., Brint, S.U.: IEEE: Transactions on Information Techonology in Biomedicine, vol. 3(1) pp. 70–73 (1999)
[3] Krishnaprasad, N., Vishwanath, V., Venkataraman, S., Rao, A., Renambot, L., Leigh, J., Johnson, A.: JuxtaView - a Tool for Interactive Visualization of Large Imagery on Scalable Tiled Displays. In: Proceedings of IEEE Cluster 2004, pp. 411–420 (2004)
[4] Ni, T., Schmidt, G., Staadt, O., Livingston, M., Ball, R., May, R.: A Survey of Large High Resolution Display Technologies, Techniques, and Applications. In: Proccedings of IEEE conference on Virtual Reality (2006)
[5] Tanner, C.C., Migdal, C.J., Jones, M.T.: The Clipmap: A Virtual Mipmap. In: Proceedings of SIGGRAPH 98, pp. 151–158 (1998)
[6] Taubman, D., Marcellin, M.: JPEG2000: Image Compression Fundamentals, Standards and Practice. Kluwer Academic Publishers, Boston (2002)
[7] Wallace, G., Anshus, O.J., Bi, P., Chen, H., Chen, Y., Clark, D., Cook, P., Finkelstein, A., Funkhouser, T., Anoop, G., Hibbs, M., Li, K., Liu, Z., Samanta, R., Sukthankar, R., Troyanskaya, O.: Tools and applications for large-scale display walls. IEEE Computer Graphics and Applications 25(4), 24–33 (July-August 2005)

Wearable Healthcare Gadget for Life-Log Service Based on WPAN

Sang-Hyun Kim[1], Dong-Wan Ryoo[2], and Changseok Bae[2]

[1] Department of Computer Software & Engineering
Korea University of Science and Technology (UST), Daejeon, South Korea
[2] Post PC Research Group,Electronics and Telecommunications Research Institute,
161 Gajeong-Dong, Yuseong-Gu, Daejeon, Korea
{ksh41,dwryoo,csbae}@etri.re.kr

Abstract. The advent of ubiquitousness has been changing the uses as well as the paradigm of services, and emphasizing the importance of services being personalization. In this paper, we propose Wearable Healthcare Gadget based on Wireless Personal Area Network (WPAN) to gather health information of user and a new approach to life-log service using the Wearable Healthcare Gadget. It can be wearable and gather physiological information and environmental information which can provide life-log service. Also it has the processing and networking capability.

Keywords: healthcare, gadget, ECG, accelerometer, GPS.

1 Introduction

As advancing of the technology of Information and Communications and coming of an old-aged society, the concern about the health has been gradually increasing. In this current, much research has been studied to get the useful information such as the (user) the status and health of user from a physiological signal.

Recently, research related the logging personal information has been getting much attention with the name of the life log. The life log implies the digitalized user information stored and maintained. The stored information, that can be users' experience or health related information, for example can be retrieved later for various kinds of purposes. By storing and maintaining diverse kinds of user specific information, it allows many possibilities to provide personalized services that are specific to certain users.

The U-Health environment makes it possible for users to be able to receive a medical service and a medical treatment in anytime and anywhere through using various portable devices that are connected through the network. Under this kind of environment, the needs of individualized healthcare services are growing more and more. This leads the necessity of systems with convenient interfaces to extract user's health status, and well-defined network functions to deliver gathered information to others [1],[2].

J. Jacko (Ed.): Human-Computer Interaction, Part II, HCII 2007, LNCS 4551, pp. 837–844, 2007.

For healthcare services based on the life log server, the information stored on the life log server should include person's physiological information. These kinds of information should be easily obtained and measured the physiological signals. Furthermore, it should be convenient enough to be worn by users, and this leads the necessity of the portability.

In this paper, we propose a Wearable Healthcare Gadget that can be worn by the user and that can gather wearer's health information. Wearable Healthcare Gadgets communicate and cooperate each other by establishing wireless personal area network (WPAN). With the network enabled feature of the Wearable Healthcare Gadgets, the gathered or processed information can be delivered to life log servers. Similarly, the stored information can be retrieved by the Wearable Healthcare Gadgets to provide personal Healthcare services.

Wearable Healthcare Gadgets consist of the physiological signal measurement part, the environment signal measurement part, the wireless network part and processing unit. Currently, the physiological signal measurement part of the Wearable Healthcare Gadget measures the Electrocardiogram (ECG) signal from the heart using electrodes attached on the body.

The environment signal measurement part consists of an acceleration sensor and a global positioning system (GPS) sensor to get the movement and location information of users, respectively. Sensing movement information with an accelerometer allows the abstraction of the motion artifact of the ECG signals [3]. GPS sensors sense the position and time information. The usability of data can be increased by merging and associating with time, ECG, and acceleration information.

We adapt ZigBee as the wireless network part of Wearable Healthcare Gadget which provides a low powered wireless data transmission and inherently provides WPAN. Through the ZigBee network, the sensed information can be exchanged among the Wearable Healthcare Gadgets [4].

The rest of this paper is organized as follows. In section 2, we explain the physiological signals that can be adapted for the life log service. We then describe the design and implementation of Wearable Healthcare Gadgets in section 3. Section 4, we present a life log service that can be applicable to personalized services using Wearable Healthcare Gadgets, followed by our conclusion in section 5.

2 Signals for Life-Log Service

2.1 Physiological-Signals for Life-Log

In this section, physiological signal and the extracted features from physiological signal are described.

HRV. The electrocardiogram is electrical signals, detected on the surface human body. That has been used in the medical. The ECG is one of the most vital signals, and is used to extract the heart rate. Heart Rate Variability(HRV) is a periodic variation of heart rate. It is related to the interaction between a sympathetic nerve and parasympathetic nerve that affect sinus node. Therefore HRV is used for measuring the status of user. The HRV of healthy people is irregular and complex. Otherwise the people who have diseases have monotonous change of HRV. That means the ability to adapt to changing environments inside body decreases. Temperature, blood pressure and SPo2 of healthy people rapidly adapt to environment. Therefore the body goes to the physiological balanced status and control homeostasis. Also stress can be inferred by using HRV analysis of the ratio LF component, HF component or sympathetic and parasympathetic activity. Analysis of HRV provides an effective way to investigate the different activities of the autonomic nervous system [5].

Figure 1 shows the signal processing flow chart to find HRV, SDRR and Stress Level.

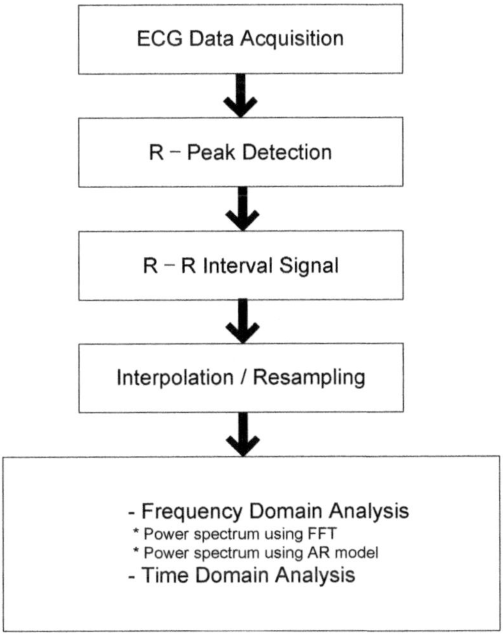

Fig. 1. Signal processing flow chart to find HRV, SDRR and Stress Level

Mean HR. Mean Heart Rate (HR) is the average of heart rate during unit time and is the index of health status of user. Mean HR of healthy people is 60~90. Over 90 Mean HR, it is tachycardia and below 60 Mean HR, it is bradycardia. A sudden exercise make tachycardia, also stress or unbalance of the autonomic nervous system causes tachycardia. If high Mean HR over 160 is maintained, that can make a heart attack. Bradycardia is appeared by stress or acute myocardial infarction. If abnormal bradycardia is sustained for a long time, it can also make a heart attack. Therefore monitoring of Mean HR is important in the view of prevented medicine [5].

SDRR. Standard Deviation of the RR-interval (SDRR) is standard deviation of an interval between R peak and R peak of ECG. It is index of variation of heart rate. High SDRR means that HRV is irregular and complex. That means high SDRR indicates healthy state. As decrease of SDRR, mechanism of homeostasis maintenance of autonomic nervous system is weakened. A counter and repelling power against stress is lost. The patients are weakened. Continuous low SDRR causes myocardial infarction, arrhythmia and angina pectoris [5].

Stress Level. Very Low Frequency (VLF) is distributed in 0.0033Hz ~ 0.04Hz frequency bandwidth of ECG. It represents additional information of sympathetic activity. Fatigue and arrhythmia make power spectrum of VLF low.

Low Frequency (LF) is 0.04Hz ~ 0.15Hz frequency width of ECG, so-called Mayer wave. LF reflects sympathetic and parasympathetic activities (especially sympathetic activity) and blood pressure control. It is related with spiritual stress.

High Frequency (HF) ranges 0.15Hz ~ 0.4Hz frequency width of ECG. It is index of parasympathetic nervous activity and related with respiration activity. In healthy people, HF does not decrease. But HF of the people suffered from continuous stress and fear or patients who has a cardiac disorder is low.

These frequency ratio of ECG can infer the stress level [6], [7]. of Wearable Healthcare Gadget

Table 1. Sensing Signal, Data Feature and Communication

.Sensing Signal	Data/Feature	Communication
ECG (or PPG)	ECG raw data Mean HR Heart Rate Variability SDRR LF/HF(Stress Level)	Wireless LR-WPAN (ZigBee)
GPS	Time(UTC) Position (Latitude, Longitude)	
Accelerometer	Posture(walking) Activity	

2.2 Environmental Signals for Life Log

In this section, environmental signals and feature of environmental for life log is stated.

Accelerometer. The accelerometers have been used to monitor human movements or postures in a variety of circumstance. It is able to extract useful human information.

Some recent studies researched that determining activity using accelerometers. Also the falling detection using accelerometer has been researched. And it can remove motion-artifact noise of ECG sensor.

Time and Position. GPS module in the wearable gadget provides time information and position information. GPS module gets UTC(Universal Time Coordinated) from the satellite and uses the NMEA0813 standard. Also, GPS module provides coordinate of longitude, latitude and altitude. If these information are merged with other signals, those are more useful information such as synchronized data with time and location.

Table 1 represents sensing signals, data, features and communication of Wearable Healthcare Gadget based on WPAN.

3 Wearable Healthcare Gadget Based on WPAN

Wearable Healthcare Gadget has physiological data acquisition module, accelerometer data acquisition module and GPS module. And Wearable Healthcare Gadget sends sensing data to the Basic Module such as PDA or UMPC through ZigBee Communication. Rechargeable battery and charging circuit make Wearable Healthcare Gadget operate outside.

Figure 2 is a block diagram of data mining using time information and position information from GPS in Wearable Healthcare Gadget.

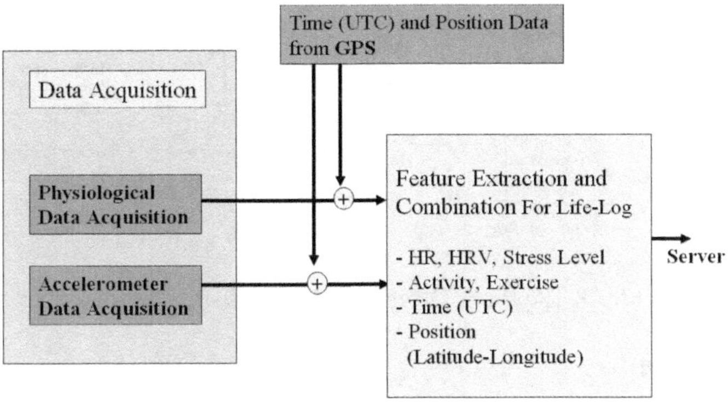

Fig. 2. Block diagram of data mining using time information and position information from GPS

3.1 Component of Wearable Healthcare Gadget

Wearable Healthcare Gadget has physiological data acquisition module. 3 electronodes are attached on the body to get ECG signal. ECG signal is amplified and noises are removed by filter. From ECG signal we can get the physiological information through signal processing such as Fig. 1. In Fig.1, HRV, SDRR and Mean HR can be inferred by time domain analysis and Stress Level can be analyzed by frequency domain analysis.

By the signal from the acceleration sensor of Wearable Healthcare Gadget, we can estimate the number of step. Also, we can estimate the quantity of user's movement by this. And we can infer the user's status such as running and walking using an inference engine.

If we know the accurately measured time and position information of these continuously measured signals, we can get the more available information. For this purpose, the GPS sensors provide position and time information. The measured physiological signals and environment signals in a daily life can be merged with the synchronized time and position information. If these informations are sent to the server or the Basic gadget through the ZigBee network and saved, it can be easy to retrieve and provide the useful information.

Figure 3 shows the block diagram of Wearable Healthcare Gadget including physiological data acquisition module and environmental data acquisition module.

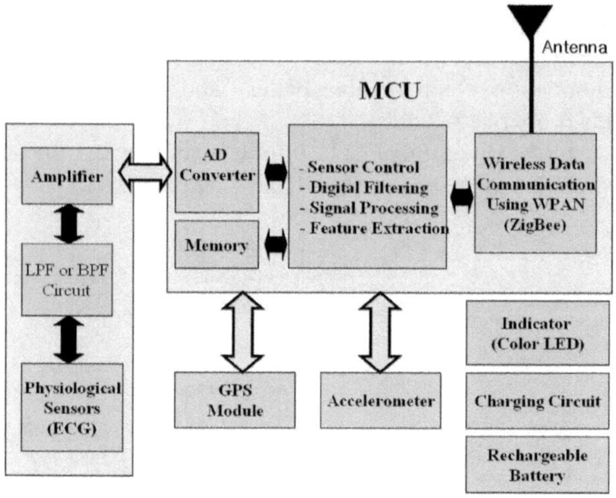

Fig. 3. The Block Diagram of Wearable Healthcare Gadget

3.2 WPAN(ZigBee)

ZigBee network is one of low-powered, low-cost and easy-handled wireless network technologies. Protocol and Application of Zigbee based on the physical and MAC layer is standardized in IEEE 802.15.4.

One of the famous wireless communications is WLAN. The disadvantage of WLAN is high power consumption, so it is hard to adapt to mobile device. Bluetooth is one of low-powered wireless network which has 1Mbps low-speed and 1mW power consumption. Otherwise ZigBee has 250kbps very low-speed and low-powered wireless network which is operated only 3μA in sleep mode. ZigBee provides for high data throughput in applications where the duty cycle is low. This makes ZigBee ideal for home, business, and industrial automation where control devices and sensors are commonly used. In this paper, because the data of Wearable Healthcare Gadget is not very big and the operation time is long, ZigBee is adapted as wireless communication [8].

We adapt ZigBee as the wireless network part of Wearable Healthcare Gadget which provides a low powered wireless data transmission and inherently provides WPAN. Through the ZigBee network, the sensed information can be exchanged among the Wearable Healthcare Gadgets.

Figure 4 shows the prototype of Wearable Healthcare Gadget.

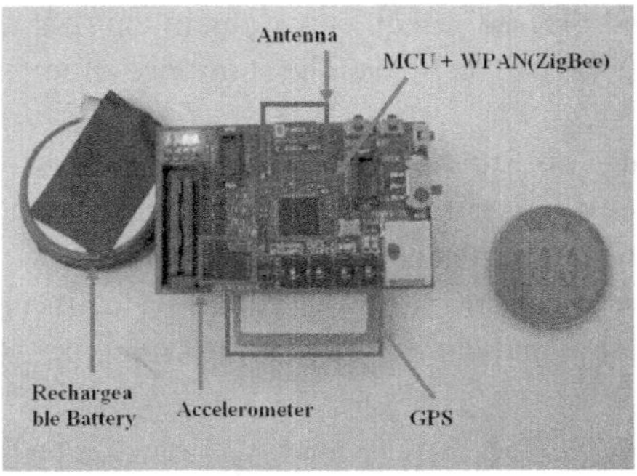

(a) GPS and Accelerometer

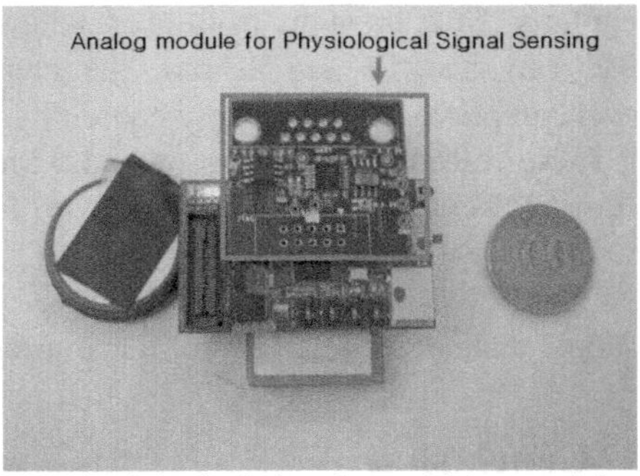

(b) Physiological signal acquisition module

Fig. 4. Wearable Healthcare Gadget Prototype

4 Life-Log Service Using Wearable Healthcare Gadget

In this study, Wearable Healthcare Gadget can provide life-log service using several sensors. Accelerometer can calculate the amount of exercise per day by measuring the number of step. If the amount of exercise is saved in the server and a user compares the amount of exercise everyday, it can give the user a motivation of exercising. Also, as accelerometer gives information of movements and posture, a user can remind what he did.

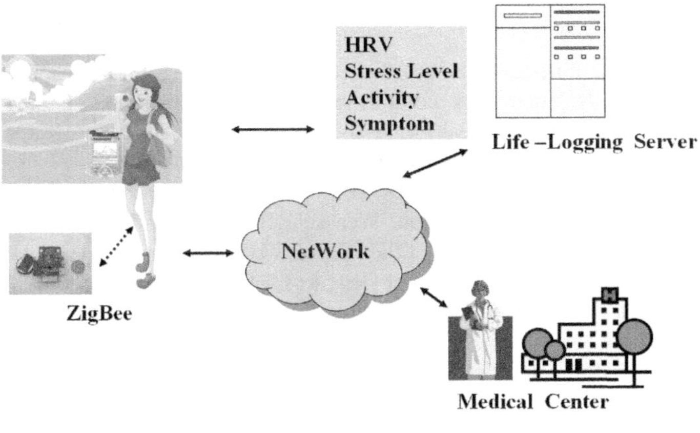

Fig. 5. Concept of Life-Log Service System

From R-R interval of ECG, Wearable Healthcare Gadget can calculate Mean HR. If the Mean HR is saved in the server, experts of physical training can provide the proper prescription of exercising with reference to the recorded Mean HR. Logged HR can calculate HRV and SDRR. From HRV and SDRR, it can monitor the mechanism of homeostasis maintenance of autonomic nervous system. Also HRV and SDRR can be saved in the server to report to the medical center on the network regularly. That prevents from heart attack and disease. Frequency domain analysis of ECG can show LF and HF ratio that can analyze stress level. The inference of stress level can prevent adult disease caused by stress.

These informations synchronized with time information and position information from GPS can be logged in the server. Latter doctors or experts of physical training can retrieve these informations according to time and place.

Figure 5 is a concept of Life-Log Service System using Wearable Healthcare Gadget that can collect physiological information and environmental information.

5 Conclusion

In this paper, we propose a smart object platform called Wearable Healthcare Gadget that has the processing and networking capability, and that can be equipped, carried or embedded into a personal to process various informations. Wearable Healthcare Gadget is able to provide physiological information and environmental information for Life-Log service.

Even though Wearable Healthcare Gadget provides the feasibility of Life-Log for personal healthcare, there have some issues to be solved. Couples of them first come to our minds from the hardware point of view includes the easiness of carrying Wearable Healthcare Gadget and optimization of the power management. Also to measure correctly, motion artifacts from movement should be decreased.

References

1. Franchi, D., Belardinelli, A.: New Telemedicine Approach to the Dynamic ECG and Other Biological Signals Ambulatory monitoring. Comput Cardiol, vol. 25 (1998)
2. Paradioso, R.: A Wearable Health Care System Based on Knitted Integrated Sensors, IEEE TRANS ON Technology in Biomedicine, vol. 9(3) (2005)
3. Asada, H.H., Jiang, H.-H., Gibbs, P.: Active Noise Cancellation Using MEMS Accelerometers for Motion-Tolerant Wearable Bio-Sensors. In: Proceedings of the 26th Annual International Conference of the IEEE EMBS San Francisco, CA, USA (2004)
4. Won, J., Bae, C.: Wearable Inteligent Gadgets for Personalized Services. Submitted on the 1th ICUT 2007, Dubai, UAE (2007)
5. Seong, H.M., Ik, C.D., Kim, S.W., Park, S.J., Kim, C.J., Yoon, Y.R.: The study of Driving Fatigue using HRV Analysis. J. Biomed. Eng. Res. vol. 24(1), pp. 1–8 (2003)
6. Kim, S.Y., Euler, D.E.: Baroreflex Sensitivity Assessed by Complex Demodulation of Cardiovascular Variability. Hypertension 29(5), 1119–1125 (1997)
7. Spiers, J.P., Silke, B., McDermott, U., et al.: Time and frequency domain assessment of heart rate variability: A theoretical and clinical appreciation. Clinical and Autonomic Research 3, 145–158 (1993)
8. Search Mobile Computing homepage http://searchmobilecomputing.techtarget.com/topics/
9. Kitney, RI., Rompelman, O.: The study of Heart Rate Variability. Oxford: Clarendon (1980)
10. Masthie, M.J: Determining Activity using triaxial accelerometer. In: Proceedings of the second joint EMBS conference (2002)

Vision Based Laser Pointer Interaction for Flexible Screens

Nam Woo Kim, Seung Jae Lee, Byung Gook Lee, and Joon Jae Lee

Division of Image Contents, School of Design & IT,
San 69-1, Jurye 2-dong, Sasang-gu, Busan, 617-716
{d5302010,d9003147,lbg,jjlee}@dongseo.ac.kr

Abstract. In recent years high quality interaction devices have become very popular in our environment. The industries are also currently undergoing rapid change and various technologies have been explored to enable these capabilities. Projection systems using beam projectors and laser pointer became the ubiquitous infrastructure for command technology. Group meetings and other non-desk situations require that people should be able to interact at a distance from a display surface. This paper presents new interaction techniques that use a laser pointer to directly interact with display on a large screen. The camera is subsequently used to detect the position of the pointing device (such as a laser pointer dot) on the screen, allowing the laser pointer to emulate the pointing actions of the mouse. The laser pointer will behave as a active point on the projected display where the user can interact. This vision-based system is augmented with a natural interface that enables the user to interactively refine the suggested rectification. This makes it very easy for users to execute fast and continuous commands. The interaction model developed behaves like a "smart interaction system." The vision based interaction system requires no special hardware and runs on a standard computer.

Keywords: Vision-based interaction, determining the mouse interaction, recognize laser spot, camera calibration, nonlinear mapping function.

1 Introduction

Interaction with input devices has always been an important part of computer vision. Traditional methods of controlling computer-based interactions require the user to send commands to the computer using either the keyboard or the mouse. But, the ubiquitous environments of today require that people should be able to interact with the display surface from a distance. Much work has been done on the development of laser pointers as interaction devices. The combination of laser pointers and camera as an interaction systems have become an increasingly active topic in the field of Human Computer Interfaces (HCI) and Computer Vision (CV).

Existing systems for accepting user input include expensive electronic white-boards and pointing devices such as remote mice. Electronic white-boards are not portable and either requires laborious manual calibration and/or forces the use of

J. Jacko (Ed.): Human-Computer Interaction, Part II, HCII 2007, LNCS 4551, pp. 845–853, 2007.

specially coded markers. Remote mice lack of the transparency and immediacy of pointing actions, and suffer from other problems. For instance: infrared mice require the user to point the mouse at a small target; radio mice are subject to interference; mice with long cables are unwieldy.

A single-pointer system for executing more complicated tasks is presented by Olsen and Nielsen [1]. This system has an interaction technique that uses widgets as shown in Figure 1. The selection of widget works well with user interface but requires a feedback procedure. It also projects an alien object on the user interface, which creates distraction.

Fig. 1. The feedback is through an echoing cursor and through the selection mechanism for the widgets. There are four cursor modes.

On the other hand, Sukthankar, Stockton and Mullin's self-calibrating camera-assisted presentation interface incorporates virtual buttons that allow user to select function to be performed [3]. However, the addition of virtual buttons requires user to adapt to the user interface [3,4]. Buntarou Shizuki, Takaomi Hisamatsu, Shin Takahashi and Jiro Tanaka use the four edges of a projected screen as the main goals of crossing, which maximizes the goals and thereby maximizes usability. They presented interaction techniques that use a laser pointer for direct manipulation of systems displayed on a large screen. But, the method requires the use of three types of goal crossings. Lines and filled circles depict a laser spot's trajectory on a projected screen and the spot's current position, respectively [7].

This paper presents a robust and efficient laser interaction for imitating mouse function(e.g. move, click, double click and right button) algorithm that allows and enables the user to directly control the interaction at a distance from the computer using a pointing device such as a laser pointer. Our method works intuitively similar to mouse interaction. The laser pointer spot function like a cursor and there is no change to the user interface. The camera can be placed anywhere in the room such that its field of view contains the presentation area. The projector may also be placed anywhere in the room since distortions due to misalignment are automatically corrected regardless external screen such as flexible wall or fabric material by our nonlinear mapping function. It is also an inexpensive technique as it uses only camera and laser pointer. Our system allows user to use the system under a variety lighting conditions, and helps to reduce the amount of image parsing required to find laser position by the order of magnitude.

2 System Configuration

An overview of vision based interaction system using laser pointer is shown in Figure 2. The system consists of a laser pointer with a toggle button, a USB2.0 camera to capture the movement of the laser spot projected on the screen, and a computer. A beam projector is used for the projection of display image. The laser pointer's function is to interact with the projected image. The camera captures the image projected and obtains the position of laser spot. The computer functions as the processing unit. Software part for the image processing consists of image processing module and coordinate mapping module.

Generally, user must repeatedly go towards the computer to stroke a key in order to flip the slides while doing presentation by using a computer. This distraction to the screen-based explanation interferes with the concentration of both the presenter and the audience. This study investigates and motivates another portable and cheap approach which allows the user to use the laser pointer to control mouse interaction by moving the laser spot and turning the beam on or off. It allows a presenter to point to anywhere on a screen quickly, without concerning the screen size, and the distance of a presenter from the screen.

This makes it very easy for users to run commands, as the vision based interaction enables users to execute fast and continuous commands. System responds correspondingly to various input commands from user.

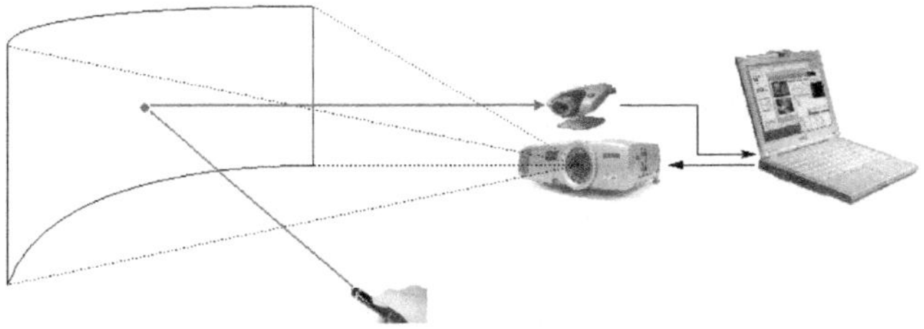

Fig. 2. The vision based interaction system ; The portable LCD projector and USB2.0 camera are placed at the front of the screen, while the user can control the mouse function using laser pointer

The software part of vision based system is divided into three modules as shown in figure 3. Initially, the image processing module detects the laser spot, followed by determining the mouse action by the mouse interaction module and then operating system module maps the coordinates. The laser spot module help to find the laser pointer in input image. The mouse interaction module decides mouse event. The operating system module finds out the position.

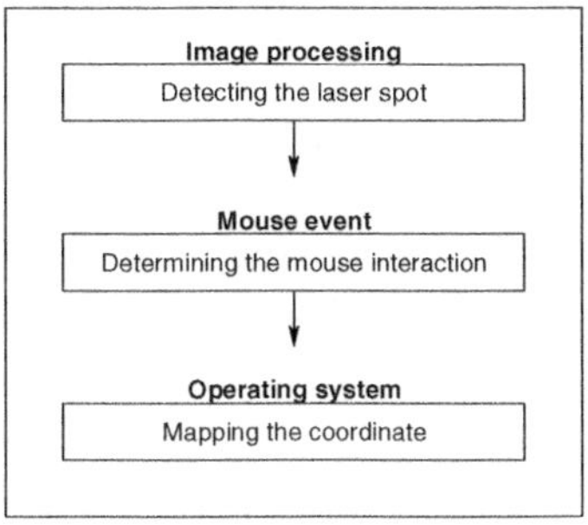

Fig. 3. Flowchart for vision based laser pointer interaction system consisting of image processing, the mouse action and operating system

3 Laser Pointer Interaction

There are three fundamental problems to making this system work.

- Laser pointer detection and recognition
- Interaction function
- Mapping the coordinate

3.1 Laser Pointer Detection and Recognition

The robust algorithm used in the system helps to differentiate between noise and the laser pointer. Therefore it is possible to recognize laser spot regardless to the external environment. Laser pointer calculation involves two steps. The color component of RGB color format is first converted into HSI one. The input image $f(x, y)$ is then segmented by equation (1) that is if $f(x, y)$ is in the predefined laser spot region like Figure 4, it is set as "1" otherwise "0".

$$B(x,y) = \begin{cases} 1, & f(x,y) \in LS \\ 0, & otherwise \end{cases} \tag{1}$$

where

$$LS = \{(H,S,I) \mid \theta_1 < H < \theta_2, \alpha < S, \beta < I\}$$

$$\begin{aligned} f_{(x,y)} &= \{R_{(x,y)}, G_{(x,y)}, B_{(x,y)}\} \\ &= \{H_{(x,y)}, S_{(x,y)}, I_{(x,y)}\} \end{aligned} \tag{2}$$

The currently commercialized colors (red or green) of laser pointer can be used. Furthermore, if we are using the laser filter (which passes the light having wavelength 630nm ~ 650nm in case of red) for spot detection, the efficiency for spot detection is improved by making color range of the laser spot smaller as shown in Figure 4 (b). It is possible to choose the color that user want to detect color for his purpose. Any color can be detected depending on the user requirement. UI controls can recognize each color component value of which users' desire. Then the coordinate mapping module finds the position of spot in projected image, which will be explained in next section. The equipment for laser spot detection consists of a computer attached to a projector and a camera to detect the laser pointer position. The camera used is a USB2.0 camera that can deliver up to 30 frames per second; the algorithms for the image processing involve the color setting module followed by the coordinate mapping module for finding the position.

3.2 Interaction Function

This section describes the key ideas regarding the laser pointer based smart control interaction system. The recognizer communicates with interactive system in terms of

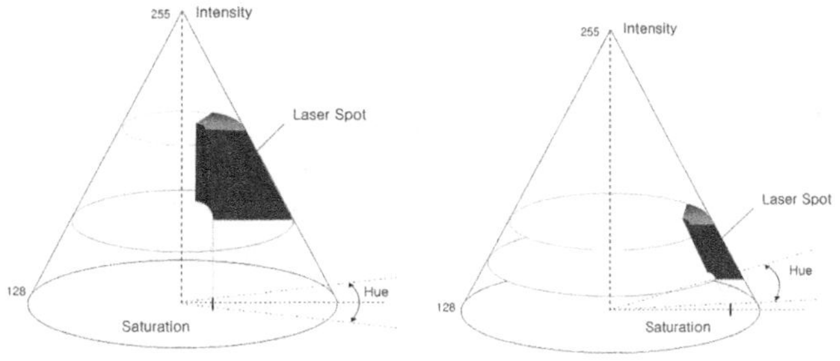

(a) (b)

Fig. 4. The range of laser pointer HSI color model with (a) no band pass filter, (b) band pass filter

four events, namely the mouse move, left button click, double click and right button click. We propose new algorithm that enable the user to directly control the mouse function, at a distance from the computer using just a laser pointer. It is very simple to use and anyone can be trained to use it easily.

Mouse Move. The laser spot detection method has been explained in the upper part. We search for the high intensity red spot. If we cannot find an acceptable spot in that frame, we then search the whole screen in the next frame. Once the laser pointer spot is tracked, we calculate the mapping coordinate of the laser pointer position and return it as the position of the mouse cursor. The fact that cameras, projectors and rooms are all different in their optics and their positioning poses a problem. What is needed is a function that will map a detected laser spot (x, y) position in the camera image to the corresponding position of the mouse cursor in the interactive display. The method is explained in detail at next step. The laser spot is lighted on the display surface when user wants a mouse movement.

The movement is detected when there is difference of coordinate of the laser pointer between two continuous frames. However, we do not want to register this movement as mouse movement because trembling hand can cause minor laser pointer movement. Therefore, a condition to limit the mouse movement only if the laser pointer moves beyond the fixed threshold as follows:

$$\| P_t - P_{t-1} \|_{L_1} > T_d \tag{3}$$

where P_t is the position of the laser point at time T (current frame), P_{t-1} is the position of the point in the previous frame and T_d is the tolerance given.

Mouse Left Button Click. Left mouse button is pressed and then released once if user wants a mouse left click interaction. Likewise, this action is done using laser pointer by turning the laser pointer on and off in less than a few hundreds of milliseconds predefined by setting module. Then laser pointer position (x, y) where the laser pointer light is turned off is recorded.

Mouse Left Button Double Click. Similarly, left mouse button is pressed and released twice if a user wants a mouse left double click interaction. This action is done using laser pointer by turning the laser pointer on and off twice. We consider only the laser pointer position (x, y) where the laser pointer light is turned off for the first time is recorded, the reason of not taking second time the laser pointer is turned on and off is to avoid the laser pointer movement caused by such action twice.

Right Button Click. Mouse right button click action will be activated when the pointer of light is being on for more than a few hundreds of milliseconds on the pointer target. The laser pointer position (x, y) is recorded.

4 Mapping Image to Screen Coordinate

In this section we discuss the process of mapping the coordinate of laser pointer position recorded by the camera named as captured image coordinate (x, y) and the mouse cursor position on the projected screen given by window screen coordinate (u, v). This process is done at the background without the knowledge of the user. In other words, given an observed feature at (x, y) in the camera image (e.g., a laser spot), we would like to know the position (u, v) in the display surface corresponding to (x, y). In this coordinate mapping or calibration process, a check board, as shown in Figure 5, is used.

However, in today's virtual reality environment, curve screen is utilized sometimes instead of a flat screen. Unfortunately, the usual method of linear transformation proposed by Sukthankar, Stockton and Mullin[4], could not be applied in such environment. To deal with that, we proposed a quadratic method for nonlinear environment.

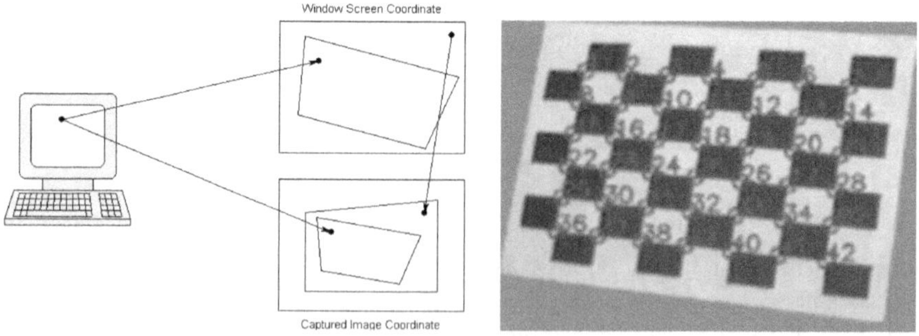

Fig. 5. The relationships between the three frames of reference corresponding to the laptop display (source image frame), camera (camera image frame) and projection screen (projected image frame)

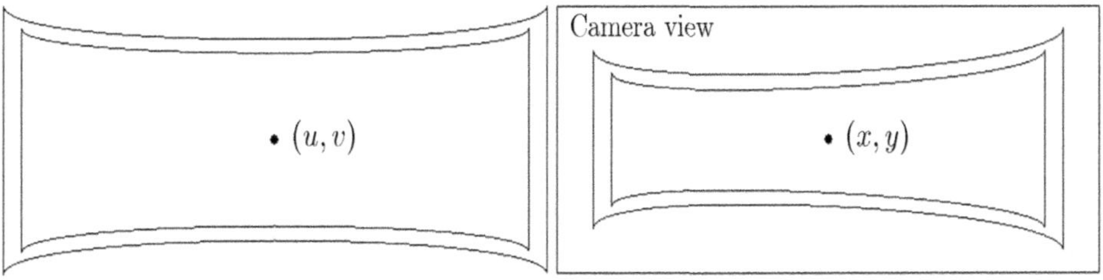

Fig. 6. The application image can be appropriately distorted, using the new mapping algorithm so that it appears nonlinear after projection through a misaligned projector

$$u = \frac{p_1 x^2 + p_2 xy + p_3 y^2 + p_4 x + p_5 y + p_6}{p_{13} x^2 + p_{14} xy + p_{15} y^2 + p_{16} x + p_{17} y + p_{18}}$$

$$v = \frac{p_7 x^2 + p_8 xy + p_9 y^2 + p_{10} x + p_{11} y + p_{12}}{p_{13} x^2 + p_{14} xy + p_{15} y^2 + p_{16} x + p_{17} y + p_{18}}$$

with eighteen degrees of freedom, $\vec{p} = (p_1 \quad p_2 \quad \cdots \quad p_{18})$ constrained by $|\vec{p}| = 1$. The same transform is more concisely expressed in homogeneous coordinates as:

$$\begin{pmatrix} uw \\ vw \\ w \end{pmatrix} = \begin{pmatrix} p_1 & p_2 & p_3 & p_4 & p_5 & p_6 \\ p_7 & p_8 & p_9 & p_{10} & p_{11} & p_{12} \\ p_{13} & p_{14} & p_{15} & p_{16} & p_{17} & p_{18} \end{pmatrix} \begin{pmatrix} x^2 \\ xy \\ y^2 \\ x \\ y \\ 1 \end{pmatrix} \quad (4)$$

$\vec{p}$ can be determined from the obtained corner points from the chess board for calibration.

Given n feature point matches, $\{(x_i, y_i), (u_i, v_i)\}$, let A be the following $2n \times 18$ matrix :

$$\begin{pmatrix} x_1^2 & x_1y_1 & y_1^2 & x_1 & y_1 & 1 & 0 & 0 & 0 & 0 & 0 & 0 & -x_1^2u_1 & -x_1y_1u_1 & -y_1^2u_1 & -x_1u_1 & -y_1u_1 & -u_1 \\ 0 & 0 & 0 & 0 & 0 & 0 & x_1^2 & x_1y_1 & y_1^2 & x_1 & y_1 & 1 & -x_1^2v_1 & -x_1y_1v_1 & -y_1^2v_1 & -x_1v_1 & -y_1v_1 & -v_1 \\ \vdots & \vdots & \vdots & \vdots & \vdots & \vdots & \vdots & \vdots & \vdots & \vdots & \vdots & \vdots & \vdots & \vdots & \vdots & \vdots & \vdots & \vdots \\ \vdots & \vdots & \vdots & \vdots & \vdots & \vdots & \vdots & \vdots & \vdots & \vdots & \vdots & \vdots & \vdots & \vdots & \vdots & \vdots & \vdots & \vdots \\ x_n^2 & x_ny_n & y_n^2 & x_n & y_n & 1 & 0 & 0 & 0 & 0 & 0 & 0 & -x_n^2u_n & -x_ny_nu_n & -y_n^2u_n & -x_nu_n & -y_nu_n & -u_n \\ 0 & 0 & 0 & 0 & 0 & 0 & x_n^2 & x_ny_n & y_n^2 & x_n & y_n & 1 & -x_n^2v_n & -x_ny_nv_n & -y_n^2v_n & -x_nv_n & -y_nv_n & -v_n \end{pmatrix}$$

The goal is to find the unit vector $\vec{p}$ that minimizes $|A\vec{p}|$, and this is given by the eigenvector corresponding to the smallest eigen value of $A'A$. And then using (4) we can get mouse position (u, v) of screen coordinate.

5 Experimental Results

The coordinate mapping of distorted screen is done by using check board to identify whether the distortion area of the screen mapped the coordinate correctly. In some occasions, projector may be placed at the side of the room, where it should not get interfered by anything. By the proposed quadratic transformation, 42 corner points of curved screen is mapped with no distortion as shown in Fig. 7 while by linear transformation the rectangular screen appears as a distorted quadrilateral. Next, we have tested the mouse event of mouse move, left click, left double click, and right click to prove our algorithm on flat and curved screen at various angles. This is started from laser spot detection, followed by other functions, as show in Fig. 8. The other events are determined by the time needed by users to perform the action of turning the pointer light on and off. We found out the average time needed is around 0.3 second to get good results. We conclude that our system is suitable for ubiquitous environment where the mouse event can be control by using laser pointer

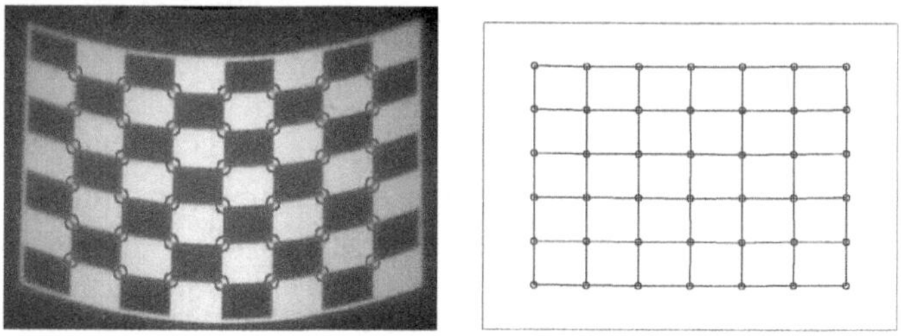

(a) (b)

Fig. 7. Transformation results : (a) shows the curved screen with check board while (b) is the calculated mapping coordinate by nonlinear matrix

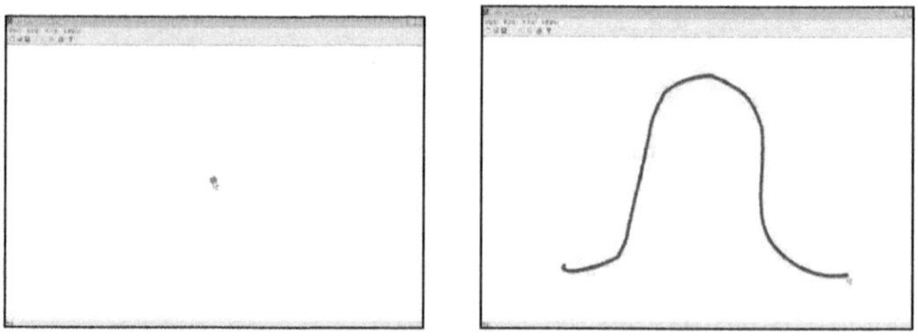

(a) (b)

Fig. 8. Laser spot detection followed by mouse move function according to laser spot movement. (a) is the laser pointer and (b)is the curved made by the mouse pointer as the laser pointer is moved.

6 Conclusions and Future Works

Our system provides a better interface for mouse interaction system by allowing users to place portable projectors anywhere in the room, and any distortion produced will be automatically rectified. Although many studies have examined the use of laser pointers as input devices, they have suffered from bottlenecks resulting from interaction design. For example, methods proposed by stimulating a button press/release event or began manipulation of GUI parts by leaving the laser spot in one location for a certain period. These methods forced users to wait before executing a command. In contrast, our interaction technique does not involve a delay for the user, enabling quick and continuous command execution. The proposed method presents a robust and efficient laser interaction algorithm that allows the user to directly control the interaction with computer from a distance using a pointing device such as a laser pointer. Additionally, the experimental results show that it also works well on curved screen such as flexible wall or fabric material by our proposed nonlinear mapping function. Furthermore, we want our system to be suitable not only for mouse functions but also scalable to support groups of multiple users, capable of supporting social communication for cooperative tasks.

Acknowledgement. This research was supported by the program for the Training of Graduate Students in Regional Innovation which was conducted by the Ministry of Commerce Industry and Energy of the Korean Government.

References

1. Olsen Jr., D.R., Nielsen, T.: Laser pointer interaction. Proceedings of the SIGCHI conference on Human factors in computing systems, vol. 17(11) (2001)
2. Ahlborn, B.A., Thompson, D., Kreylos, O.: A practical system for laser pointer interaction on large displays. In: Proceedings of the ACM Virtual Reality Software and Technology, pp. 1006–1009 (2005)
3. Sukthankar, R., Stockton, R.G., Mullin, M.D.: Self-calibrating camera-assisted presentation interface. In: Proceedings of the International Conference on Control, Automation, Robotices and Vision (2000)
4. Sukthankar, R., Stockton, R.G., Mullin, M.D.: Smarter presentations: exploiting homography in camera-projector systems. In: Proceedings of the International Conference on Computer Vision, vol. 1(247) (2001)
5. Sukthankar, R., Stockton, R.G., Mullin, M.D.: Automatic keystone correction for camera-assisted presentation interfaces. In: Proceedings of the International Conference on Multimedia Interfaces. vol. 1948(2000) pp. 607–614 (October 2000)
6. Dekel, A., Kirkpatrick, S.: Room user interface (RUI) design for laser based interaction. submitted to CHI 2005 (2005)
7. Shizuki, B., Hisamatsu, T., Takahashi, S., Tanaka, J.: Laser pointer interaction techniques using peripheral areas of screens. In: Proceedings of the working conference on Advanced visual interfaces (AVI'06), Venezia, Italy. pp. 95–98 (May 23-26, 2006)
8. Oh, J.-Y., Stuerzlinger, W.: Laser Pointers as Collaborative Pointing Devices. Graphics Interface 2002, AK Peters and CHCCS, pp. 141–149 (May 2002)
9. Vogt, F., Wong, J., Po, B.A., Argue, R.S, Fels, S., Booth, K.S.: Exploring collaboration with group pointer interaction. Proceedings of the Computer Graphics International (CGI'04), vol. 00 (June 16-19, 2004)
10. Raskar, R., Brown, M.S., Yang, R., Chen, W.-C., Welch, G., Towles, H., Seales, B., Fuchs, H.: Multi-projector displays using camera-based registraction. In: Proceedings of the conference on Visualization '99: celebrating ten years (IEEE Visualization), San Francisco, California, United States, pp. 161–168 (1999)

Implementation of Multi-touch Tabletop Display for HCI (Human Computer Interaction)

Song-Gook Kim, Jang-Woon Kim, and Chil-Woo Lee

Department of Computer Engineering, Chonnam National University
Yong-bong Dong 300, Gwang-Ju, Korea
uaini@hanmail.net, lucky418@nate.com , leecw@chonnam.ac.kr

Abstract. In this paper, we describe the development of multi-touch tabletop display system and the classification of hand gesture commands for interacting with our system. And also, we analyze the suitability for interactive tabletop in light of the respective input and output degrees of freedom, as well as the precision and completeness provided by each. Our system is based on FTIR (Frustrated Total Internal Reflection) principle and hand gestures for necessary instructions are predefined using position sensing and tracking of multi-touch points and the number of fingertips. The system consists of two beam-projectors, diffuser film, four infrared cameras and large acrylic screen that attached infrared LED. In recognition process, gesture commands are analyzed by comparing with predefined gesture instructions according to the number of contacted fingertips, Euclidean distance and angles between two bright spots. In this paper, vision based tabletop display system that we proposed provides much advantages understanding human and computer interaction. Also the Efficiency of proposed method can be proved through controlling Google-earth.

Keywords: Multi-touch, Tabletop display, Frustrated Total Internal Reflection (FTIR), human computer interaction.

1 Introduction

Recently, the technology for supporting user friendly and intelligent interaction becomes very important as the computer technology advances and the complexity of information systems grows. Specifically, a lot of world-wide researches have been focused on the input technology using hands and gestures which are the most intuitive tools for human. This technology becomes a core component of the information devices adopting dynamic touch interfaces. In this paper, we develop a hardware platform and its component technologies which are used to manipulate the contents naturally by recognizing the motion of user's hands and the contact between the hands and display. This technology enhances the availability of next generation multimedia contents utilizing the interaction between the user and information system.

One of the benefits of the tabletop display is the natural direct manipulation experience they provide, as well as their potential for more complicated interactions using multiple fingers. It would be desirable to allow more than one user to access the

J. Jacko (Ed.): Human-Computer Interaction, Part II, HCII 2007, LNCS 4551, pp. 854–863, 2007.

display without affecting the work of others. The users of tabletop display can randomly access any point on the display by simply touching the desired location. And also, physical objects can be used for augmented reality. Lastly, the expense of developing the system is not expensive. Ultimately, the system that we developed pursues interaction of four components (human, computer, physical object and displayed objects). Additionally, tabletop display can help cooperative interaction of multi-users as medium of communication.

In this paper, we analyze the suitability for interactive tabletop in light of the respective input and output degrees of freedom, as well as the precision and completeness provided by each. One important point is that we are going to use some gestures to control the system and for interaction. We divided gesture instructions that are used in tabletop display as in following details. The instructions are divided into four major categories; static gesture, spatial dynamic gesture, temporal dynamic gesture, and (spatial+temporal) dynamic gesture.

2 System Overview of the Multi-touch Tabletop Display

2.1 FTIR (Frustrated Total Internal Reflection) Sensing Techniques

FTIR principle used mainly in biometrics community for fingerprint extraction since the 1960, it is also a total reflection obstacle phenomenon that is used in robot sensor technology. Total reflection is a phenomenon that light which have incidence angle more than critical angle is reflected into the medium interiors from medium surface. When an object touches the surface of a waveguide medium, the condition of the total internal reflection is disturbed. Therefore, a scattering occurs along the surface where FTIR happens and we can detect the object's position. Similarly, the system that we developed is based on FTIR technique. And when the finger is touching the surface of the screen, the condition of Total Internal Reflection is disturbed. As a result, we can detect discrete light through infrared camera with attached IR pass filter installed under the screen. We recognize position of homogeneous point that finger is touched.

2.2 Hardware Configuration

We adopted the multi-touch display concept developed by NewYork University using two rows of infrared LED as light sources on the both sides of a acrylic screen, which acts as a waveguide [1]. In our prototype, we used a 1950mm (wide) × 1330mm (high) × 8mm (thick) sheet of acrylic, whose four edges have been polished clearly (Fig. 1). The four edges of the acrylic is lit by infrared LED which is placed directly against the polished four edges to maximize efficiency of the total internal reflection, while the infrared camera with the infrared pass filter is mounted orthogonally to the screen. The screen is covered by a special film in rear-projection configuration that acts as a diffuser and prevents the light from escaping. And also, we used stainless reflector to prevent the spread of the light.

Figure 1 shows the prototype of our table-top display, which includes two short focal-length projector, four infrared cameras attached with the infrared pass filter and infrared LEDs. The infrared camera can capture 320*240 images at 30 frames per second on a Pentium IV 3.0GHz. We connected four infrared cameras which are received screen image on single computer. And then the results are sent to another computer after recognizing hand gestures. Finally, computer projects the screen dividing using two projectors.

We emphasized on the following aspects for developing our table. We want to obtain sufficient screen size in order to offer cooperative space of multi-user. We design the low height table so that user can sit on chair and work. To facilitate transfer, we designed the system so that we can disjoint and assembly the system easily.

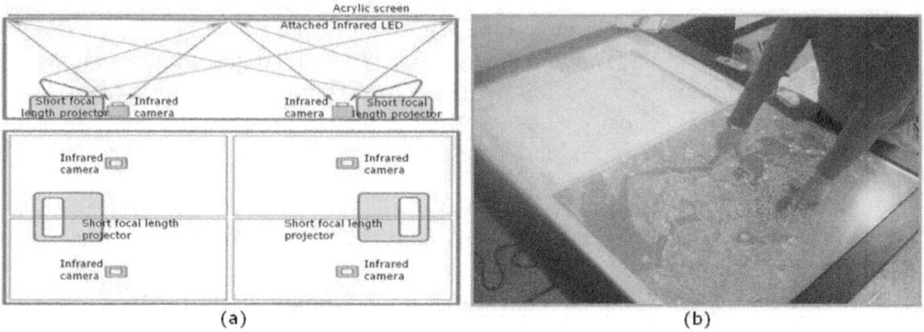

Fig. 1. (a) The cross-sectional view of the tabletop display system, and the configuration of camera and projector. (b) The system control of our tabletop display using both hands.

Fig. 2. The algorithm flowchart of our tabletop display system

3 Algorithm Flowchart for Multi-touch Recognition

The flowchart of the proposed algorithm consists of several steps. First, input video frame is obtained from the infrared camera. Second, the segmentation of detecting touched fingertips. Third, counting and tracking of bright spots. And the last is hand gesture recognition using counting and tracking information (Fig. 2).

Our table-top display is capable of tracking fingertip movement and counting the number of fingertips that the user is using for interaction. Only once calibration is required, in the process the view of the camera has to be adjusted to a quarter of screen size (1950mm*1330mm). The captured image is successively processed through a series of pipelined stages shown in Fig. 2.

3.1 Input Video Frame from Infrared Camera

The RGB color images obtained from infrared camera are converted to the gray scale images. At this time, we used the compact infrared camera with wide angle lenses for covering large screen regions. As a result, barrel distortion can occur in captured image. Accordingly, the barrel distortion effect has to be removed by calibrating the camera and subsequently correcting the input image.

3.2 Segmentation of the Contacted Fingertips

We have to convert BGR image into binary image for extracting the touched fingertips on screen surface. Therefore, we take the appropriate T=70 (threshold value). If the brightness value of pixel is smaller than T, change the value into 0. And the opposite change into 255. We use the image histogram information for choosing the appropriate threshold value. And then we implement the simple morphology techniques for removing noise. Figure 3 shows the case that the area of touched fingertips on screen is not detected because we select the inappropriate threshold value.

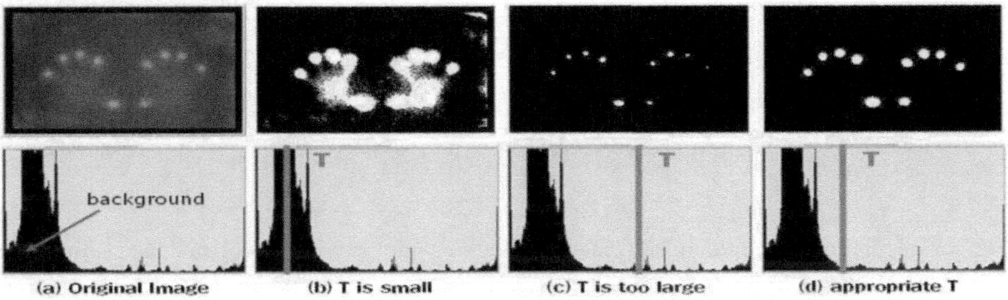

Fig. 3. Separate the touched fingertips from the background using histogram information

3.3 Counting of the Bright Spots

We implement 8-connected neighbor algorithm for counting fingertips on the contacted screen. We can calculate the features of size, position, direction and so on. We can obtain the information for counting the fingertips on the screen that is the number of connected components via these processes. And also, we can acquire the extreme top, bottom, left and right position by making a rectangle for each blob.

3.4 Tracking of the Bright Spots

We can know the location of top, bottom, left and right points by creating the rectangle about detected fingertips. And also, the center of fingertip on the screen can be extracted using coordinate information. The center coordinate value of the first contacted fingertip on the screen is stored to the buffer. And then, we continuously compare the coordinate value stored in the buffer with the current location value of the fingertips. Also, we calculate the Euclidean distance and angle among the initially touched points that it is can be considered estimation means for hand gesture recognition.

3.5 Hand Gesture Recognition

The calculating example of the Euclidean distance and angle is shown in Fig. 4. Coordinate value of the index finger is expressed by C1 (x1, y1) and coordinate of the thumb is expressed by C2 (x2, y2). If tan θ is smaller than 10 degree and larger than -10 degree, we considered the idle state for waiting command (Fig. 4-c). If tan θ is smaller than -10 degree, we performed the command of left-rotation (Fig. 4-b). And also if tan θ is larger than 10 degree, we executed the command of right-rotation (Fig. 4-d). At this time, we can control the rotation command according to the speed and moving direction of the index finger when the thumb is fixed. We stored the distance between C1 and C2 to the buffer; that is the distance of initially touched points of the thumb and the index finger. And then we compared current Euclidean distance with the original distance in the buffer. We performed the zoom-out or zoom-in command according to the variation of current Euclidean distance.

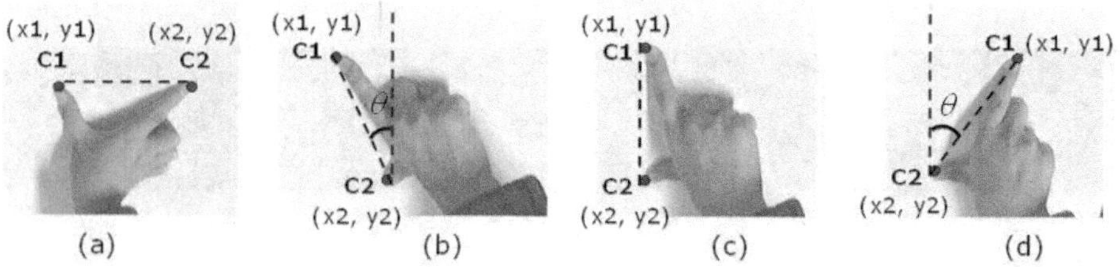

Fig. 4. Calculating of the Euclidean distance and the angle between thumb and index finger. (a) Euclidean distance, (b) tan θ < -10 degree, (c) 10 degree >= tan θ > -10 degree, (d) tan θ > 10 degree.

4 Definition of Gesture Model for Interaction

4.1 Sharing Techniques of the Digital Information

In tabletop display, the biggest advantage is that user can share digital information. To support sharing we introduce four interaction techniques; release, relocate, reorient, and resize. First, the release technique mimics interactions with paper documents. If one user holds an electronic document and another user attempts to take it, then if one user continues to hold the document, another user will come away empty-handed. However, if one user releases his touch from the document, another user will successfully acquire it. Second, the relocate technique for sharing is information transfer. When the document is in one user's private area, it is inaccessible to other users. By moving the document to the center section of the table, it becomes publicly accessible. Third, the reorient technique is used for switching the direction. When one user's document faces him it is not accessible to other users. At this time, one user rotates his document to face the center of the table in order to make it publicly accessible. At last, the resize technique make the document smaller than a threshold size makes it private, while enlarging it opens it to public access. These instructions are frequently used for interaction in tabletop display. We analyze hand gesture and define as following. Defined hand gesture must be able to use even if there is no special training. And also user should be conveniently interacts with each other so the commands should be intuitive. Used gestures are expected to change according to the contents of application program. However, we develop methods to recognize the most used general gestures. Information that is inputted to touch screen does not necessarily agree with the type that is used in real life.

4.2 Definition of the Hand Gesture Model for Rotation and Move and Tilt Technique

In order to better compare the various methods of rotation, tilt and translation, we define several common variables. The following points are used as input to the algorithms used in the interaction techniques for rotation and translation of objects on a direct-touch input device (See the Fig. 5):

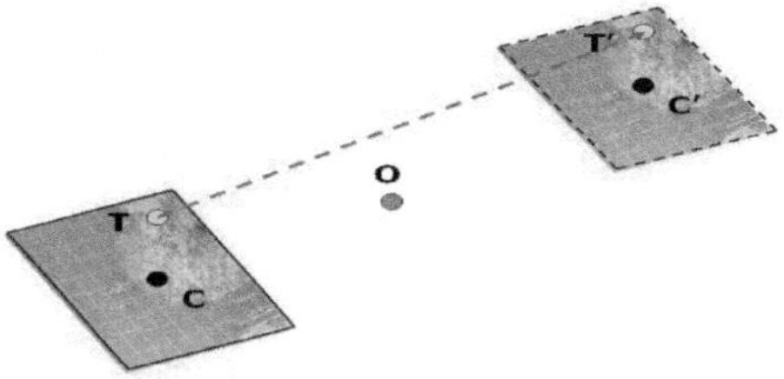

Fig. 5. Input parameters of rotation and translation. This diagram shows an example of translate-only motion.

T – the point of initial input contact
(for multiple points of contact the notation T1, T2, etc. is used)
T'– the point at which the input contact is released
(for multiple points of contact the notation T'1, T'2, etc. is used)
O – the center of the table
C – the center of the object before it is moved and/ or rotated
C'– the center of the object after it has been moved and/ or rotated

The common properties of any rotation and translation algorithm are the center of rotation which is typically one of T, O or C, one or more fixed points on the object that remain independent of the rotation, and the angle of rotation (θ) [2].

We assume that the user is at the outside border of the table. Therefore, the system can automatically orient an object so that its top always faces the center of the table (O) and its bottom faces the outside border of the table. This orientation is easily calculated from the angle component of an object's position in polar coordinates. Because of this simplicity, the resulting interaction is predictable and may, therefore, be understandable to users. However, this simplicity has the consequence that not all rotation and position combinations can be achieved.

The rotation and translation instructions that is used in tabletop display are independent-translation, independent-rotation, automatic-continuous, automatic-discrete, integral-RNT, two-point methods. We adapted the methods of independent translation and continuous rotation by comparing the various methods. In a continuous variation, the object is rotated about O by the angle θ, formed by T, O, and T' and translated along the axis OT' by the difference between OT and OT' (Fig. 6). Therefore, we can control the tilt-up and tilt-down commands according to the speed and moving direction of the index finger of right hand when the fingers of left hand are fixed (Fig. 7). For input, independent translation, continuous automatic rotation, tilt-up and tilt-down use 2 degree of freedom (DOF). For output, independent rotation, tilt-up and tilt-down use 1DOF, continuous automatic rotation use 2DOF (See the Table 1).

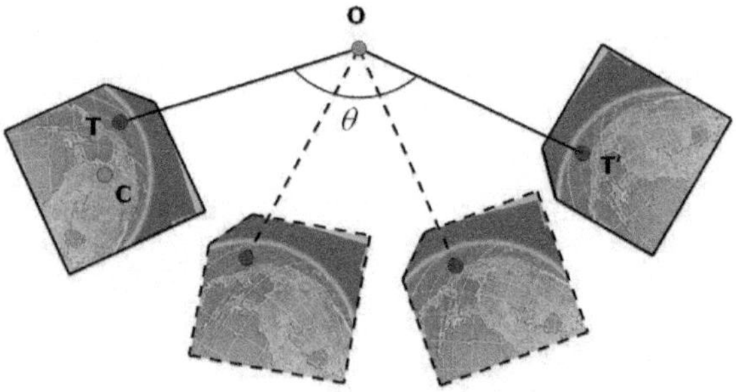

Fig. 6. The continuous automatic rotation. The object is translated so that the initial touch point, T, is moved to the new touch point, T', but the angle of rotation is relative to the center of the table, O.

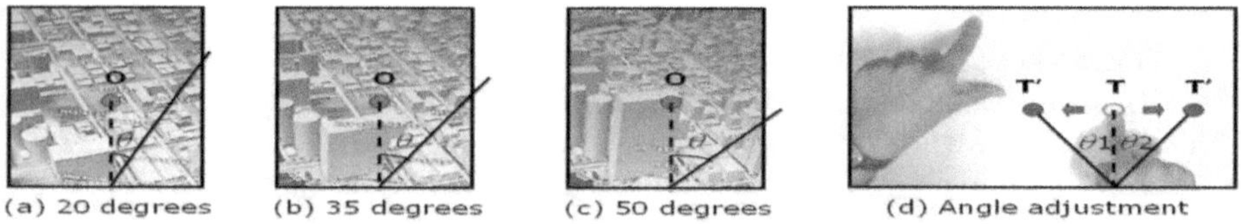

Fig. 7. Operation of tilt-up and tilt-down commands. The scene is tilted so that the initial touch point, T, is moved to the release point, T', but the angle of tilt is relative to the distance between T and T'.

Table 1. Degree of freedom of input and output for the rotation, move and tilt technique. x and y are the two coordinates of T.

	Input	Output
Automatic (table-centric) Orientation	x and y	r and θ
Independent Translation (Move)	x and y	x and y
Tilt-Up, Tilt-Down	x and y	$\theta 1$ and $\theta 2$

5 Experimental Results of the Interaction Techniques

There are Pointing, Move, Left-Rotation, Right-Rotation, Zoom-In, Zoom-Out, Tilt-Up, Tilt-Down instructions for controlling the Google-earth. We have classified the gesture commands for interacting with tabletop display. And also we have defined the hand gesture model by analyzing the degree of freedom of input and output for convenience and the efficiency of communication. The model of hand gesture can be divided into one hand gesture and both hands gesture. Table 2 and Fig. 8 show the control commands for the Google-earth.

5.1 One-Handed Interaction Techniques

In case of using only one hand, a user can use the move, zoom-in, zoom-out, left-rotation, right-rotation instructions for controlling of Google-earth. If the bright spot is one, the click event of left button of mouse happens and acts as role of catch. So, by moving the fingertip to forward, backward, left, right or arbitrary direction the user is able to explore of satellite picture. When the user touches on screen using a thumb and a forefinger, namely it has two touch points; zoom-in and zoom-out instructions are achieved. If the user does not move in the state that the thumb and the forefinger are touched, any reaction will not occur. But if the distance between two fingers becomes closer, the zoom-out instruction is achieved. On the other hand the distance of two fingers become away, the zoom-in instruction is executed. Both left-rotation and right-rotation instructions are also controlled by using the thumb and the forefinger. At this time, the moving index finger indicates rotation amount and direction while the thumb is fixed as principal axis. Figure 9 shows the instruction set of one hand motion.

5.2 Two-Handed Interaction Techniques

In case of using both hands, other instructions; zoom-in, zoom-out, tilt-up, tilt-down, and play-tour, can operate the system depend on the number of fingertips that are contacted on the screen. If the distance of two fingertip spots made by one finger of both hands become away from each other, zoom-in instruction is executed, and in the opposite case, zoom-out instruction is achieved. In this case, we can use faster and more dynamic command than one handed instruction. We detected the center of two fingertips and calculated the Euclidean distance between two bright spots in this case. Also the user can execute tilt-up and tilt-down instruction. For the instruction, the user activate the tabletop display with two fingers of left hand which are fixed on the screen, on the contrast to the fingers, one finger of right hand determines the amount of tilt variation by moving the finger position. To performed instruction predefined information are continuously compared with the calculated information from input image. Figure 10 shows instruction set that consists of using both hands.

Table 2. The control commands for the Google-earth™

Command	Control result of Google-earth™
Move	*Move the viewer in the direction of the arrow.*
Rotate Clockwise	*Rotates the view clockwises. The earth spins counter-clockwise.*
Zoom-In	*Zooms the viewer in.*
Zoom-Out	*Zooms the viewer out.*
Tilt-Out	*Tilts the viewer toward "top-down" view.*
Tilt-Down	*Tilts the viewer toward "horizon" view.*
Play Tour	*Plays the tour mode for all selected items in the places pane.*

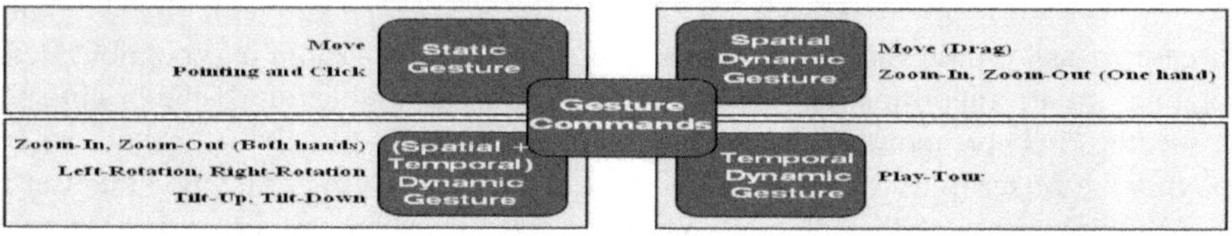

Fig. 8. The classification of gesture commands for interacting with tabletop display

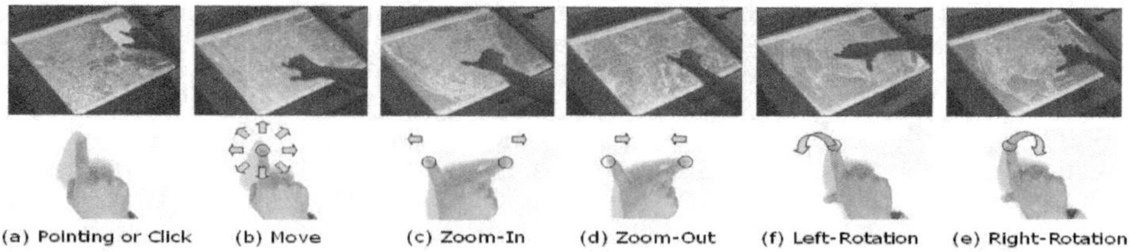

Fig. 9. One handed instruction set (a)Pointing or Click: single point touch. (b)Move: move to arbitrary direction. (c)Zoom-In (d)Zoom-Out (e)Right-Rotation: the thumb is fixed. (f)Left-Rotation: the thumb is fixed.

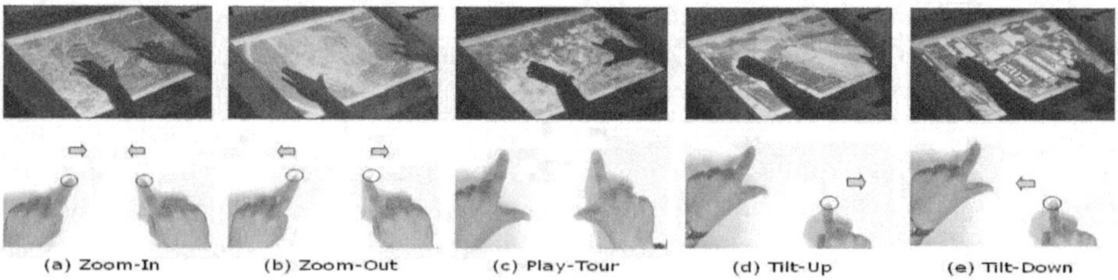

Fig. 10. Two handed instruction set. (a)Zoom-In (b)Zoom-Out (c)Play-Tour: both hands are fixed for a few seconds. (d)Tilt-Up: fingers of left hand are fixed. (e)Tilt-Down: fingers of left hand are fixed.

6 Concluding Remarks and Future Work

In this paper, we explained about a large size table-top display system for embodiment of co-operative interaction. And then we classified interaction gesture into control this system by degree of freedom and degree of convenience. Our study in tabletop that we have developed used a multi touch recognition technology to expand natural interface that mouse and keyboard do not offer. However, this system does not offer various and complex interface. For example, we use interface instruction like one hand touches table surface and other hand takes gestures and hand gesture on table top. Therefore, if we use only multi-touch, it is very limited to construct intelligence interface system. Our research target is to construct intelligence interface system that recognizes human's intention in tabletop environment. So we have to combine hand gesture and our multi-touch table-top display system. In tabletop environment, the background is complex and always changes. Therefore, we have to use IR camera and color camera for detecting the hand region efficiently. Ultimately, we can embody context awareness table top display system that offers various and natural interface than existent multi touch table-top system by using hand gesture instruction, multi-touch instruction and combined hand gesture and multi-touch instruction.

Acknowledgements. This research has been supported by research funding of “Culture Technology Research Institute”, Chonnam National University, Korea.

References

1. Han, J.Y.: Low-Cost Multi-Touch Sensing through Frustrated Total Internal Reflection. In: Proceedings of the 18th Annual ACM Symposium on User Interface Software and Technology, pp. 115–118. ACM Press, New York (2005)
2. Grossman, T., Balakrishnan, R., Kurtenbach, G., Fitzmaurice, G., Khan, A., Buxton, B.: Interaction techniques for 3D modeling on large displays. In: Proceedings of the 2001 symposium on Interactive 3D graphics, pp. 17–23 (2001)

End User Tools for Ambient Intelligence Environments: An Overview

Irene Mavrommati[1,2] and John Darzentas[1]

[1] University of the Aegean, Product & Systems Design Engineering, Syros, Hellas
[2] Computer Technology Institute, Kazantzaki str, University Campus, 26500 Patras, Hellas
mavrommati@cti.gr, idarz@aegean.gr

Abstract. New elements that are introduced by the nature of living and interacting within an Ambient Intelligence (AmI) environment lead to new HCI paradigms. While AmI User Interfaces are moving off the desktop and the GUI paradigm, and become augmented and diffused within the ubiquitous environments, a new generation of User Interface Design Tools to facilitate the design and realization of AmI applications, is emerging. Issues and specific shifts related to Human Computer Interaction in AmI environments, which affect the design of these tools, is outlined in this paper. The high level characteristics of End User Tools that facilitate users to reason as well as manipulate the behavior of the AmI environment are outlined.

Keywords: Human Computer Interaction, Ubiquitous Computing, End User Tools, Ambient Intelligence Environments.

1 Introduction

End User tools aimed at end users within Ubicomp environments stem from the perspective that it does not seem possible in ubiquitous computing environments to cater for all the potential needs of all categories of users [15, 17, 13]; it seems much more reasonable to enable people to cater for some of these needs themselves, and empower them (via provision of appropriate tools) to the creation of ubiquitous applications that fit their own idiosyncratic needs. The development of such tools for people living in Ambient Intelligent Environments (AmI) has to face not only the technological issues that Ubiquitous computing poses, but also the challenges that occur due to the shifts in human computer interaction that owe to the very nature of interaction within AmI environments.

2 Living in AmI Environment and New HCI Paradigms

New elements that are introduced by the nature of living and interacting within an ambient intelligent environment lead to new HCI paradigms. Some of the issues that have an impact in AmI HCI research practice [12] are:

J. Jacko (Ed.): Human-Computer Interaction, Part II, HCII 2007, LNCS 4551, pp. 864–872, 2007.

1. A shift in the nature of interaction

Interaction in Ambient Intelligence Spaces can range from explicit to implicit interaction. Unintended user actions on the environment may result in unintended control and manipulation of the applications. The implicit nature of interaction (achieved in AmI by both sensing and physical action) assumes a seamless human computer relationship where there may often be no conscious interaction. On the other hand, since no system is completely error free, issues of the appropriate level of visibility and transparency to the workings of the system are raised. The possibility of facilitating a degree of transparency (providing upon request some visibility into the workings of the ubiquitous system) is an element that could be considered for End User Tools. [3, 13].

2. Organizational concerns of users

AmI systems may be used by single users, but who may also operate in larger groups [2]. There can be more than one user for an AmI application, working on it simultaneously, from the same or remote locations. The same may also hold as a requirement for Tools aimed for the creation and editing of AmI applications. It may be in the interest of more than one user to co-edit an application that involves them, synchronously or asynchronously, but collaboratively and from different ends.

3. Different interaction channels

In AmI there is a shift in the nature of input and output devices. Interaction becomes multimodal and ubiquitous: many appliances and artifacts within an environment can be used and in many different operations as well as sensing capabilities of the environment; the same applies for the nature of the output devices of the application: speech, gesture, tangible interfaces, biometrics, are a few of the elements into play. A value to this approach could be the replacement of complex command languages with actions from manipulating directly the objects, and making use of multimodal interface combinations to interact with the system. Among the issues to be addressed [2] are the following: how to identify and select a possible interaction object, how to select one action and bind it to the object while voiding unintended selection, how to handle more abstract functions, and how to embody appropriate feedback and direct it to users attention.

4. The role of intelligence

Actors coming into play can be human, or agent software. In the latter case there are risks of unexpected behavior –resulting agent intervention- that may surprise the user. Such kind of surprise must be avoided; visibility on the workings of the agent and the intelligent application and its rationale should be available upon request, as well as an overwrite function for the applications or the agents within them (the overall off switch). Appropriate feedback so that users can be aware of the systems attention has to be considered [13].

5. Visibility. Reversibility of action(s). Error tolerance

Feedback should be provided for actions upon the physical environment that involve the AmI application. Syntactic correctness of sequences of actions has to be checked at all times, in order to appropriately inform users, so as to avoid errors before they are made. To be able to undo actions (reversibility of actions) is also very important in the case of error: a requirement stemming from these is the ability to recover previous state. Visibility, reversibility, and syntactic correctness of actions, can also be dependant on issues of context awareness and compatibility of platforms. In an AmI environment many interoperating platforms may come into play, while the locus and nature of both feedback and of stored actions is distributed. Therefore error prevention, tolerance and reversibility all pose grave but interesting system design challenges [2, 3, 12].

3 End User Tools

In AmI the application and the interface tend to merge into one entity, as it is the augmented artifacts/spaces that are the access points to applications, but may also carry the application functions. As ubiquitous computing develops, prototyping tools for ubiquitous computing applications will be in demand, for developers, but also for end users. Such tools will initially be aimed to application designers so that they can participate in the development of applications that currently requires a high-level of technical expertise [10, 13]. End User Tools can also be appropriated to facilitate users to reason as well as manipulate the behavior of the AmI environment, so that they can supervise and eventually create or modify AmI applications to fit their own idiosyncratic wishes and needs. Emergent functionality in AmI can be the result of niche, but previously unforeseen implementations, created by end users themselves [4, 13]. This new generation of prototyping tools can help shape the future of ubiquitous computing and eventually accelerate the development of next generation ubiquitous applications [10, 13, 1].

What we can consider as tools that facilitate the development of AmI applications are:

- Mental models
- Ontologies
- Application/Software mechanisms

Mental Models

People are an intrinsic part of a Disappearing Computer environment, as it is their actions and behavior, as well as their needs that define the environment. The human element can be catalytic for the whole system: one of things that can create 'emerging' and previously unforeseen functionality is the inherent human creativity and the human capability for problem solving and expression. Nevertheless, this relies on people's adoption of ubiquitous computing, and in turn the technology's understandability and openness for adaptation. Mental models can be considered as End User tools, since they facilitate end users to gain an understanding of the workings of the AmI system, so that they can reason about the AmI applications. Such models need to be suitable to act both as high level technology models as well people's conceptual models.

One such example is the adoption and appropriate adaptation of component models that allows for the recombination of functions [4, 15]. To enable the recombination of elements into new functions, the basic concepts and elements of a component model need to designed in a way that they are capable to be easily communicated to people, so that there is a degree of transparency into the –otherwise invisible- workings of a ubiquitous environment. This can be done by an appropriately designed mental model –that carries along the basic technology concepts that allow for inter-associations of artefacts. An example of a high level programming model that provides a conceptual abstraction that allows end users to describe Ubiquitous scenarios is described in [4]. In fact such model acts as a high level interface for the user within a ubiquitous computing environment; they act as a communication layer, which people can understand, and by having access to it they can manipulate the 'disappearing computers' within their environment. The creation of such models as interfaces, for the broader interaction with ubiquitous computing environments, goes hand in hand with the creation of middleware, that acts as a bridge between core technology layers (such as protocols, communication etc), devices, and people.

To support such mental models, metaphors may be used, that stem from already existing (non-ubiquitous) widely recognizable paradigms that imply interconnectivity. Examples that imply interconnectivity can be appropriate familiar terms (like the verbal term 'Plugs' used in [4] or familiar images like for example a 'Puzzle' [6]) that may be used and transferred into the realm of Ubiquitous Computing.

Ontologies

An ontology can provide a common basis for communication and collaboration between heterogeneous artefacts and AmI environments. The ontology can describe the basic conceptual terms, the semantics of these terms, and define the relationships among them. It is therefore fundamental for the creation of ubiquitous applications, and can be considered as a tool, in the broad sense of the term.

Application/Software Mechanisms

What is generally understood with the term 'Editing tools' in the most commonly used form, are application mechanisms that supports the establishment and management of applications. With a range of external devices, the 'Editors', people can supervise available sources (artifacts, services, etc) and create associations between them, thus making AmI applications. These mechanisms' core structure can be independent of particular modalities [13], so that various point-application editors can be implemented with a variety of multimodal interfaces, and in a variety of devices.

4 Resources and High Level Mechanisms

There are three basic questions that we can ask regarding the software mechanisms for End User Tools for creating AmI applications:

- What is available as resources from the environment to the Tools?
- What should the Tools do upon the environment?
- Which elements that may come into play, that can be considered for these Tools?

Available as resources from the environment to the Tools are [8]:

- Multiple sensor approach
- Ambiguity of input
- Diversity and distribution of computing platforms
- Diversity of contexts of use
- Diversity of users
- Amount of Data
- Interactions available in the environment

The handling of these resources can lead to a number of challenges, the most prominent of which is *context awareness*. Such resources can also provide the input needed for the concept of *computing ahead* the next likely editing stages, so that guidance in editing actions is provided by the software tools.

Context-aware applications are one of the most important forms of next generation interactive systems. As ubiquitous computing develops, prototyping tools for context-aware applications will be in demand. Such tools can also help produce more usable context-aware applications in an efficient way [10]. Context awareness therefore has to be used by editing tools, has to be specified or configured, so that it can be used as a necessary element of the AmI applications that are being created.

Decision making is a related aspect according to which the developer or advanced user may want to dynamically define or change the rules determining an individual artifact or even an application's behavior, in a high level manner. Dynamically defining the parameters for an application is another aspect that can be defined or altered using tools aimed at developers. As [4] reports, a tool providing a GUI for creating or changing rules, can provide the advantage that rules can be dynamically altered in a high level manner, without disturbing the operation of the rest of the system.

Assuming substantially more computing power in the application context of distributed, multimodal sensing and recognition techniques we might want to consider constantly *"computing ahead"* – modeling the user's actions and pre-computing the results along perhaps the five most likely next inputs - as Scott Hudson states in [5]. This can be *used* to provide new kinds of feedback as well as shortcuts for the user, but can also enable proactive pre-fetching from other media. According to Hudson, related to the concept of "computing ahead" is the notion that we should move from the idea of a single state of a system or object of interest, to maintaining multiple alternative states simultaneously. This will be useful both in interesting new interaction techniques which allow "what if" explorations to happen naturally [18] and as basic support for dealing with ambiguity and asynchrony.

Several challenges may arise from this proposed approach that can lead to sophisticated models of probability –which in turn could be based on machine learning approaches for adaptation to users and tasks, and models of ambiguity of inputs so that it is made easier to deal with [14].

5 Tools Interfaces and Metaphors: Some Concepts

Elements that can be considered for the interfaces of AmI editing tools are:

- Automatic interface generation
- Programming by example techniques
- High level abstractions

Several concepts can be borrowed from the report of the Future of User Interface Design Tools workshop [8] at CHI2005, which, although more generally aimed, can provide food for thought in this area.

Automatic Interface Generation

Automatic interface generation requires specific information about the user and the current situation to be incorporated into the design of the user interface. A user interface could be displayed on whatever device the user has available. Another possibility is that the interface could use familiar elements that the user has seen recently, and personalize according to the user's profile. Model-based systems attempt to formally describe the tasks, data, and users that an application will have, and then use these formal models to guide the generation of the user interface [16].

Systems can use this input to automatically design the user interface, or to design assistance to a human. When a user requests an interface to control an appliance, the user's device downloads a functional model from the appliance and uses that model to automatically generate an interface. Although there have been successful developments in limited domains (namely dialog box design and remote controls), it is noted that model-based user interface tools have not become common. [16] Nevertheless, assuming a manageable scope of foreseen interfaces for tools, we should note that those model-based techniques may hold potential for the interface instantiations of AmI tools.

Programming by Example

Programming by example techniques and intelligent agents can help users with routine complex tasks. Nevertheless they can not remedy all cases of application configuration. There are cases that there can not be a task example performed –i.e. because the application splits between different locations, different time periods or in situations that cannot be replicated (for example the application pertaining many people present, or a specific point in time, while the application creator does not need to require the availability for these in order to configure an application for them). Although programming by example provides ease of use for end user programming of AmI applications in specific cases, it can not be generalizable as an interaction form in broader aimed End User tools. Nevertheless, it can prove a useful complement to the tools functions.

High Level Abstractions

In prototyping an AmI application designers and users acting as designers need to explore the large and ubiquitous input space and specify the contexts of use. A design tool can facilitate this task by providing high level abstractions. In Topiary [11] a map abstraction was used to represent spatial relations of entities and thus allowed designers to capture location contexts of interest by demonstrating scenarios. In e-Gadgets on the other hand, a high level conceptual model was used to explain the workings of the system to the users and enable them to make connections.

Metaphors

Metaphors are a commonly used way to facilitate the use of a tools based on existing paradigms that are familiar to the user experience. Various forms of connectible 'puzzles' are metaphors often used in editors user interfaces. A fridge magnet metaphor is used in [9] while a browser approach is used in the Speakeasy system [15] -where components are connected using a visual editor based on file-system browsers. [6] uses a "jigsaw puzzle" metaphor in the Graphical User Interface (GUI). Sensors as well as devices are represented by puzzle piece-shaped icons that the user "snaps" together to build an application. Nevertheless in all the above cases the interactions are simplified to sequential execution of actions and reactions depending on local properties (e.g. sensor events), which limits the potential to express many of the user's ideas [3]. As Drossos et al state in [3] the non existence of emergent properties, and the absence of rule based logic, can result in very simple application behavior.

A high-level mechanism to abstract context, that also allows the rapid construction of ambient computing applications, is presented by [7]; this is complemented by a clear conceptual model for AmI. A well-defined vocabulary is used in this model that tries to map the physical and virtual world to elementary component objects that can be interconnected in order to create AmI applications. The architecture seems to limit the real world's representation to sets of sensors; that in turn restricts the model's scope, as well as the autonomy of the components [19].

The e-Gadgets UbiComp Application Editor is another example of a prototype that realizes a conceptual model. The experiences reported after expert and user trials suggest that an architectural approach where users can compose predefined components seem to be worthwhile [13], however, it is pointed out that further improvement is necessary in the design and interaction of editing tools.

6 Conclusions

Editing tools are required to manage the ubiquity and understand the logic of the AmI environments. Several of these tools are addressed more to the developer or the advanced user rather to an everyday end-user. The purpose of these tools is to configure certain aspects of the system's behavior, and implement certain applications within AmI environments.

Such tools need to allow for utilizing context awareness, but also provide adaptive interfaces to cater for a variety of user profiles. The consideration of modalities (augmented reality, gesture, or speech interfaces for example) poses a number of challenges on the design of editing tools. Robustness and adaptation to changes -different environments and infrastructure-, being able to dynamically define the parameters of an application, providing many perspectives for accessing services, are but a few of the challenges posed.

Further challenges involve developing techniques for providing support for debugging and testing the applications build, providing feed forward, as well as feedback, allow for transparency into the workings of the system, and design and develop the system and the tools so as to prevent errors, minimize them, tolerate them, and recover from them -within the ubiquitous computing infrastructure.

Tools aimed at end users need to be researched in their own merit, as they constituting a very important part of the Ambient Intellience vision. The research community needs to work on defining a roadmap towards appropriate, efficient and effective editing tools for creating of AmI applications.

Acknowledgments. We would like to thank the project ASTRA (FET IST-29266), and the project extrover-Gadgets (FET IST-2000-25240), for providing ground towards the development of end user tools for pervasive environments.

References

1. ASTRA project website: http://www.astra-project.net/
2. Bellotti, V., Back, M., Edwards, W.K., Grinter, R.E., Henderson, A., Lopes, C.: Making Sense of Sensing Systems: Five Questions for Designers and Researchers. In: Proceedings of the Conference on Human Factors and Computing Systems (2002) pp. 415–422 (2002)
3. Dey Anind, K.: End-User Programming: Empowering Individuals to Take Control of their Environments. In: Proceedings of the CHI 2005, workshop on the Future of User Interface Design Tools (2005)
4. Drossos, N., Goumopoulos, C., Kameas, A.: A Conceptual Model and the Supporting Middleware for Composing Ubiquitous Computing Applications. Journal of Ubiquitous Computing and Intelligence (JUCI), special issue on Ubiquitous Intelligence in Real Worlds, vol. 1, pp. 1–13, American Scientific Publishers (2007)
5. Hudson, S.: Leveraging 1,000 and 10,000-Fold Increases: Considering the Implications of Moore's law on Future UI Tools Research. In: Proceedings of the CHI 2005, workshop on the Future of User Interface Design Tools (2005)
6. Humble, J., et al.: Playing with the Bits, User-Configuration of Ubiquitous Domestic Environments. In: UbiComp 2003, pp. 256–263. Springer, Heidelberg (2003)
7. Jacquet, C., Bourda, Y., Bellik, Y.: An Architecture for Ambient Computing. In: The IEE International Workshop on Intelligent Environments (June 2005)
8. Olsen, D., Klemmer, S.: In: proceedings of the CHI 2005, workshop on the Future of User Interface Design Tools (2005)
9. Truong, K.N., Huang, E.M., Abowd, G.D.: CAMP: A Magnetic Poetry Interface for End-User Programming of Capture Applications for the Home. In: Davies, N., Mynatt, E.D., Siio, I. (eds.) UbiComp 2004. LNCS, vol. 3205, pp. 143–160. Springer, Heidelberg (2004)
10. Yang, Li.,Landay, J.A.: Rapid prototyping tools for context aware applications. In: Proceedings of the CHI 2005, workshop on the Future of User Interface Design Tools (2005)
11. Li, Y., Hong, J.I., Landay, J.A., Topiary: A Tool for Prototyping Location-Enhanced Applications. UIST 2004, CHI Letters 6(2), 217–226 (2004)
12. Mavrommati, I., Darzentas, J.: An overview of AmI from a User Centered Design perspective. In: IET Proceedings of IE06, Athens (2006)
13. Mavrommati, I., Kameas, A., Markopoulos, P.: An editing tool that manages device associations in an in-home environment. In: Personal and Ubiquitous Computing. ACM. 8(3-4), pp. 255–263. Springer, Heidelberg (2004)
14. Mankoff, J., Hudson, S., Abowd, G.: Providing integrated toolkit-level support for ambiguity in recognition-based interfaces. In: Proceedings of the SIGCHI conference on Human factors in computing systems, pp. 368–375 (2000)

15. Newman, M., Sedivy, J., Neuwirth, C.M., Edwards, W.K., Hong, J.I., Izadi, S., Marcelo, K., Smith, T.: Designing for serendipity. In: Serious Reflection on Designing Interactive Systems (ACM SIGCHI DIS2002), June 25-28, 2002 London, England. NY, pp. 147–156. ACM, New York (2002)
16. Nichols, J., Faulring, A.: Automatic Interface Generation and Future User Interface Tools. In: Proceedings of the CHI 2005, workshop on the Future of User Interface Design Tools (2005)
17. Rodden, T., Benford, S.: The evolution of buildings and implications for the design of ubiquitous domestic environments. In: Proceedings of the CHI 2003 conference on human factors in computing, Florida, USA, April 5-10, 2003 (2003)
18. Terry, M., Mynatt, E., Nakakoji, K., Yamamoto, Y.: Variation in element and action: supporting simultaneous development of alternative solutions. In: Proceedings of the 2004 conference on Human factors in computing systems, pp. 711–718 (2004)
19. Drossos, N., Mavrommati, I., Kameas, A.: Towards ubiquitous computing applications composed from functionally autonomous hybrid artifact. In: Streitz, N, Kameas, A, Mavrommati, I (eds.) The Disappearing Computer, pp. 161–181. Springer, Heidelberg (2007)

Tangible Interaction Based on Personal Objects for Collecting and Sharing Travel Experience

Elena Mugellini[1], Elisa Rubegni[2], and Omar Abou Khaled[1]

[1] University of Applied Sciences of Western Switzerland, Fribourg
Bd de Pérolles 80, 1705 Fribourg, Switzerland
{elena.mugellini,omar.aboukhaled}@hefr.ch
[2] University of University of Siena, Via dei Termini 6, 53100, Siena, Italy
rubegni@media.unisi.it

Abstract. The paper presents a case study which addresses the design of a system which supports the recollection of memories and the creation of storytelling by combining physical objects with digital resources. The purpose of our research is twofold. The first aim is to investigate the experience of travelling focusing on how objects and information support human activity. The second aim is to explore the Tangible User Interfaces (TUIs) framework and the enabling technology in order to support recalling and sharing of travel experience.

Keywords: human-computer interaction, tangible user interface, travel activity, personal object, souvenir, case study, RFID technology.

1 Introduction

Tangible User Interfaces (TUIs) are emerging as a new paradigm for facilitating user interaction with digital world by providing a mean for integrating physical and digital environments [1]. Interaction with TUIs relies on users' existing skills of interaction with the real world, thereby offering the promise of interfaces that are quicker to learn and easier to use. Recently it has been demonstrated that the use of personal objects as tangible interfaces will be even more straightforward. Those objects are meaningful for the user since they are associated to events to be remembered and they facilitate the comprehension of their usage for memory recollection [5].

According to this perspective this paper presents a case study which aims to support users in sharing and remembering personal experiences through the use of personal objects as tangible interfaces. In particular, we investigated the role of souvenirs in supporting sharing of travel experience. Travelling, as defined also by Bationo et al. [6], is by essence a multi-sensorial experience where all senses and physical manipulation play a key role in interacting with the environment. Souvenirs are connected to the memory of particular events which can be easily evoked by the physical manipulation of object. However with the development of new information and communication technologies travelling activity has evolved towards a more

J. Jacko (Ed.): Human-Computer Interaction, Part II, HCII 2007, LNCS 4551, pp. 873–882, 2007.

substantial collection of and interaction with information in a digital form. Digital information and physical objects concern different aspects of the voyage and they give back two different views of the travel; both can be used for constructing travelling narratives, but because of their different nature they are consumed mostly independently form each other. Therefore the activity of recalling and sharing travel experiences could be enriched by integrating these two dimensions, using souvenirs and personal objects as tangible interfaces to control and interact with digital information.

2 Related Work

The idea of linking physical objects (personal or not) to digital ones has been investigated by several works in different research domains.

Some works concern how people practically link physical and digital objects as TMCS [12], the Paper++ technology and SuperInks [10]. The combination of these two technologies enables people to create "affinity between material document and digital resources" [10]; it creates a reference between paper document and digital resource. The limits of that project are quite obvious considering the context in which every object, and not only paper document, has to be connected with digital resources.

Other works focus on the use of personal objects as tangible user interfaces. In particular the work of Van Hoven in 2005 [5] was the first one that assessed the role of personal objects as ambient intelligent objects for memory recalling. Van Hoven investigated the opportunity of using souvenirs as tangible links to memories. Based on Van Hoven approach, our research work wants to go one step further towards understanding how objects and information are grasped and collected, and also how they can be combined to support sharing of travel experience.

Finally regarding the sharing of pictures and creation of storytelling for sharing experience numerous studies have been done on that direction. Some research studies explored the interaction ways in which people share and collaborate around the collections of photographs both paper-based and digital in order to design an application to support the distributed sharing of photos as Crabtree et alt. [2] and Frohlich et alt. [3].

In our project some of those aspects are integrated in order to improve the creation of storytelling and the sharing of experience combining personal physical objects and digital resources. In this sense some of the relevant aspects of the related works project cited before merge in our project.

3 The Memodules Project

The case study has been developed within a research project called Memodules [7]. Memodules project has the objective of developing, experimenting and evaluating the concept of tangible shortcuts (reminders), facilitating (a) the control of devices in the everyday life and also (b) the information categorization in order to improve information access and retrieval. The project aims at facilitating user interaction with multimedia information by supporting the creation and management of tangible links, called Memodules, to digital content. The process of "remembering" usually consists in associating something with a sensory cue [11]. For example, we may see a picture of a place visited in our childhood and the image recalls memories associated to the same time. It appears that humans easily access and retrieve information when it is linked to other related information or objects [11]. Based on this associative process of remembering, the main objective of our research is to investigate the opportunity of a more complex, combination of, and interaction between, personal objects and multimedia information (e.g. photos, videos, audio files, text documents, web resources, etc.). In particular we decided to focus our research on traveling as a privileged application domain since this activity is strongly related to the concept of souvenirs and memories collection.

The work consisted in studying the activity of travelling in order to understand and point out:

- how personal objects and souvenirs are used and collected,
- how those objects are connected and reminds to memories,
- how we could combine those objects with multimedia content (digital photos, music etc.) to enhance memories recalling and storytelling.

The work we have carried out followed two complementary approaches, user-centered design and technology oriented which feed each other within the process.

User-centred design aims to explore travelling activity in order to elicit users needs and wishes to inform the design process. Travelling activity is revealed as composed by three sub processes: the planning, the travel and the return back home.

Technology-oriented approach aims to explore the opportunity of enabling technology to manage the interaction between physical artefacts and digital information and to provide suitable mechanisms to allow end users to easily create "smart" objects.

In accordance with our design approach the technology-oriented approach has been conducted separately from user-centred design, and then the results achieved within the two have been integrated in the development of a mock-up.

3.1 The User Centred-Design Approach

In order to explore and understand travel activity we conduct the user studies using different methodologies: focus group interview, the analysis of travel diaries (journal written during the travel) and an investigation of the most common habits on sharing travel memories through the Web.

The first investigation was conducted using focus group [4] since it provides us with a great deal of data about current practices of tourists and helps us in understanding how to address to the issue of traveling. The key findings emerged from the focus group helped us to drive further investigation activities. Further study was oriented to elicit information regarding how people document the travel and which are the most common practices to publish and share multimedia data and travel stories. Along the study, travelling has been revealed a quite complex activity articulated into many independent sub-processes. Travelling is moreover a social practice even if a person travels alone the activity of travelling includes numerous of social relations.

To better comprehend the nature of travelling activity, we organized different workshops involving people who represent the users' class such as: independent travellers who arrange their own travel and activities, they are between 25 and 30 years old, with intermediate/advanced technology knowledge. They travel for pleasure for long and short period of time. Focus groups focused on the objects and information people are used to use in planning, during and after the travel.

Outcomes from these activities clarified the basic features and some drawbacks of existing practices and tools which support travelling activities. For example planning a travel requires collecting a number of information from several and different resources, and one of the most common ways to grasp information mostly regarding culture, habits and *bon tuyaux* [1] is through personal contact. Social relations have a key role on planning activity since people are one of the most important resources to gather information: friends, colleague, relatives whom already have been there, native, etc.

Focus groups investigated how users grasp souvenirs and collect information during the travel and how they use them after. For example the objects are grasped, organised, manipulated and consumed by the user in the attempt of fixing memory and remembering the experience of the voyage.

The whole user activity analysis provides us with many interesting elements and several scenarios for guiding the design process. Among the several scenarios, we focused on few of them concerning the activity of sharing experience through story telling, collecting objects which evoke the travel and making personal reflection of the experience.

According with the selected scenarios and related research works, some critical issues emerged:

- Users have difficulties in integrating different media (paper pictures, digital pictures, diary book, objects, etc…) and to exchange file and data,
- People use storytelling as the most natural way of narrate the experience,
- Souvenirs are important for travellers to retrieve events and circumstances; they are tangible cues to memories and good incipit for stories,
- Souvenir sometimes finish hidden somewhere inside home and it is more and more difficult for people to find them as time pass by.

These issues guided our work in the successive step of the design process. Along the concept generation we explored the relationship of object, collected and produced during the voyage, and how they can afford the recollection of memory and the sharing of experience with others.

The concepts developed in this phase are high level; they are inspired by the results of the previous studies. Several concepts have been developed, following we present the one that has been implemented as mock up according with the technology survey results and then evaluated.

People during the travel take note of events emotionally relevant. Actually, as our studies highlighted many people are used to have a diary just to fix some important events and some reflections. In many cases diary holds few objects inside such as tickets, business cards or brochures, grasped during the travel, that remember them

[1] It is a French expression which means good tips.

something. The diary is a kind of "witness" of the travel; people browsing the contents in its pages can remember their travel and narrate it to others.

In this perspective, the ***travelBook*** is a physical journal in which the users can write note and collect small objects that remind them the travel The travelBook aims to support users in the collection and sharing of memories of the travel through the link of physical material (such as written notes, drawings, and other physical object grasped during the voyage.

The travelBook allows the users to create and to recover the connections made during the voyage among physical souvenirs, media (such as pictures, video and audio recording) and notes while narrating. Users bookmark different resources (that could be both physical and digital) and then create connections among them and retrieve these relations through the travel. The notes written on the travelBook and the objects grasped are tagged with Radio Frequency IDentification (RFID) tags[2] and the user can create connection among those. For example, if the user takes a picture of the restaurant in which s/he has been, then that picture can be associated to the business card tag of the restaurant in the travelBook and maybe also to some notes or other tagged objects. Later at home, user can retrieve from the object or the note in the travelBook the pictures and the other resources connected with it.

The travelBook takes the advantages of the physical property of diary and of the consolidated way people use it. At the same time, travelBook improves the way people keep memory of the travel and increases the opportunity for different kinds of resources to be connected.

This concept exploits innovative modality to interact with souvenirs enabling the collection of memory and the sharing of experience.

The concept drove the mock up which focus on supporting travellers in creating a tangible trace of their experience and facilitate the communication and sharing of their experience with others.

3.2 The Technology-Oriented Approach

The main aim of technology-oriented approach is to investigate enabling technology to manage the interaction between physical artefacts and digital information and to provide suitable mechanisms to allow end users to easily create smart objects. The survey focuses on tagging technologies, tangible interface prototyping and smart sensor applications. Within this phase we explored the use of personal objects as tangible interfaces to interact with personal resources: objects with embedded sensors and technology, called Memodules, enhance their capabilities as cues to digital information.

Memodules are the key elements upon which a set of prototypes, called Memodules Framework, has been developed.

The framework is composed by four main components presented in the following paragraphs.

---

[2] RFID is a low-cost identification technology; each RFID tag contains a numeric code that uniquely identifies the object to which it is attached.

In order to associate an object with some multimedia content it is necessary to identify the object: the ***Memodules Lay&Play*** allows for this. It is composed of a webcam and an RFID reader (see figure 1). Once the object is tagged, the webcam takes a picture of the object while the RFID reader identifies the ID and associates it with the picture. The digital representation of the object is available in both Memodules Action Builder and Souvenir and Media Browser (see next paragraphs).

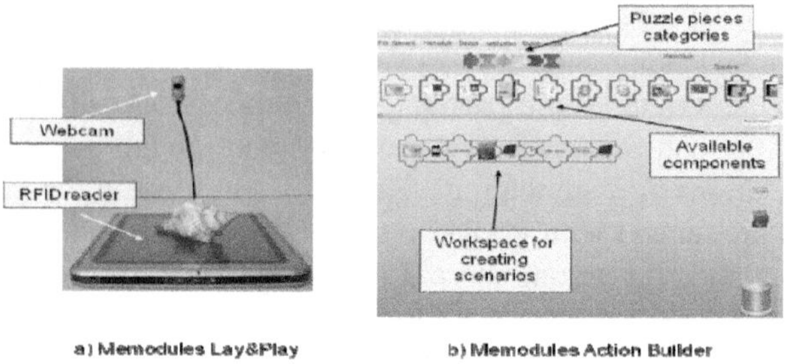

Fig. 1. Memodules Lay&Play and Action Builder

Memodules Action Builder. aims at providing an easy way for users to program and configure Memodules interaction scenarios[3]. Memodules Action Builder is based on the puzzle metaphor. Puzzle pieces represent the different components (e.g. Memodules, multimedia resources, etc.) which are connected through a series of left-to-right couplings (see figure 1) by users to describe interaction scenarios [9].

Memodules Console. investigates the opportunity of integrating RIFD technology with different types of sensors (infrared sensor, touch sensor) and LCD (Liquid Cristal Display) touch screen for playing scenarios associated to Memodules.

The Memodules Console carries out the interaction between the physical and digital environment (see figure 2); it is equipped with several sensors activated through Memodules as well as user's hand and gesture and supports the manipulation of multimedia information. For instance when approaching a physical souvenir to the Console, multimedia content associated to such object is retrieved and displayed on the Souvenir and Media Browser.

The ***Souvenir and Media Browser.*** is the result of a research on visualization techniques for multimedia information display. The Souvenir and Media Browser is an attempt to facilitate the access to and the browsing of data stored on the local PC and available on the pre-defined Web social networks. The figure 2 shows that information associated to a souvenir (the Greek flag, at the center in figure 2) is presented according to two main classifications: "file type" classification, inner circle, which groups all the content in to 4 file types (music, textual document, video and picture) and "time & events" classification, which presents information on a time basis according to main travel events, selected by the user.

[3] Interaction scenario is defined as the process of associating multimedia content to a Memodules (a tagged physical object) and describing how this content is rendered to the user.

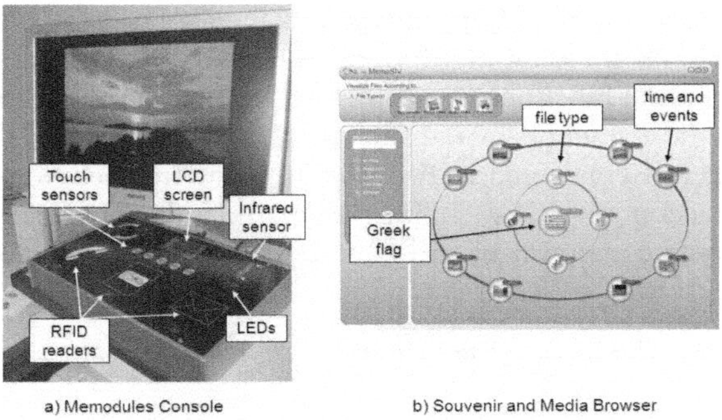

Fig. 2. Memodules Console and Souvenir and Media Browser

These preliminary prototypes are currently under improvement in order to assess the technology and also to support the development of the concepts.

Physical artifacts (souvenirs, train tickets, restaurant business cards, etc.) are tagged and associated to other resources (both physical and digital) through the Memodules Lay&Play and then inserted in the travelBook. Using Memodules Action Builder it is possible to describe how multimedia content is rendered, by the mean of Memodules Console, to the user to support storytelling and memory sharing activities. Finally the Souvenir and Media Browser can be used to visualize and navigate through all content associated to Memodules.

4 The Mock Up: A First Evaluation of Concept

The previous presented concept supports the sharing of travel memories through the connection of physical souvenirs with notes and digital resources produced or grasped during the travel. As the first step of concept assessment and prototyping, we developed a mock up of the travelBook since it could help us to elicit some feedback regarding how people collect and put in relation items and resources. The mock up was a low fidelity prototype, cheap and easy to change, which allows eliciting feedback from the user in a real context of use: with the mock up we aimed to evaluate conceptual model and early design ideas.

In particular, we focused on how the traveler creates his/her travelBook during the voyage. The mock up aims to prototype and evaluate the way people create connection during the travel among physical souvenirs, notes and digital resources. These aspects were the ones pointed out by the user as the most critical during the preliminary scenario-based evaluation session. For example, the actions of bookmarking physical objects, sticking tag on them, and creating connections with other content while traveling emerged to be perceived by users as complex and problematic tasks. While the use of the travelBook as a cue to retrieve connections among resources has been perceived very important and relevant.

The mock up evaluation helped us to explore these issues. The mock up was evaluated using the Wizard of Oz techniques based on a specific scenario of use. Even if the mock up was a low fidelity prototype the Wizard of Oz allowed us to explore design issues and to obtain relevant information for the development of a prototype.

In the mock up some functionality, as the tagging and the connection among items, was simulated by the evaluators by the way of paper screen shots of the user interface.

The evaluation was conducted in Fribourg following a specific scenario in which the user has to accomplish few simple tasks using the physical mock-up of the travelBook that was composed of different elements and associated with a mobile device (see Fig. 3):

- A Mobile phone (P910) used as a mobile device with camera and a RFID card reader,
- A Black Moleskine notebook with a pocket on the back,
- A stripe with adhesive reinforcement rings, in transparent plastic film, which simulate RFID Tag

Fig. 3. A picture of the mock up evaluation set: the mobile device, the moleskine with the adhesive reinforcement rings, a map and a tourist brochure

The user corresponded to the character profile of the scenarios. They received a map of the city and a small guide book. They had to perform few tasks according to a scenario: during the visit of the city if they take note in the travelBook, take picture, make video/audio registration, or grasp objects, they have to bookmark resources that are considered important to help them remember and sharing the experience and create associations among these resources using the id of the tags.

As usual the main feature of the mock-up was presented to the users and the scenario was explained underlining how feedback would be provided to them. When the user reads the tag with the mobile device in order to bookmark an object or a note the Wizard show him/her a screenshot as feedback of the system. The evaluation began and the evaluators followed users visiting the city.

Fig. 4. Some pictures from the evaluation session

The user could stick tags on objects and notes on the travelBook in order to bookmark them and create associations also with digital resources. The main activities user had to perform concern the creation of connection between different kinds of resources both physical and digital. This means to stick a tag on a physical object (as a guide book or a ticket) which reminds something to the user and to create the association between the object and other resources (physical of digital) by the mean of the tag using the mobile device. Evaluators just gave some example regarding how the users could bookmark and tag resources then during the evaluation they were free to explore other modalities of use.

Every evaluation cycle gave us feedback to assess the mock up that changed many times. Feedbacks from users were fundamentals to understand how to implement the system for bookmarking and tagging the resources. Some users perceive two different levels of tagging: a first general level (such as journey in Fribourg), then a second level that corresponds to a more specific issue (such as architecture in Fribourg). This means that every time the user produced a media, the media is automatically linked to the general level tag if is not explicitly required to link it to a specific level tag. Others create different bookmarks for each resource. The visibility of existing connections on the mobile device screen seems to be very important for the user which needs to have a clear idea of the links between resources.

The use of the physical book was quite relevant since, if at first it was used to take notes and associate them with other resources, then it was used as a physical reminder of the connections; the note described the main subject of the connection between resources.

At the end of the evaluation users declared to be satisfied by the mock up; they appreciate the functionality of creating connections on the fly that could help reminding later the experience they had. They gave us many suggestions regarding the improvement of the prototype and they emphasized the importance of using objects as physical reminders.

The travelBook concept was improved by all the suggestions and feedbacks in order to assess a first prototype that is being implemented and will be tested following the same scenario and methodology.

5 Conclusion

This paper presented a case study exploring the opportunity of tangible media and technology for supporting the activity of sharing travel memories and souvenirs. Travelling is by essence a multi-sensorial experience where all senses and physical manipulation play a key role in interacting with the environment.

The main goal of our research activity was to investigate the opportunity of merging physical souvenirs and digital resources for sharing of travel experience. Our research works were articulated into four main steps: travelling activity analysis, concept generation, enabling technology survey and mock-up development and evaluation.

In the next future we are going to explore how the opportunity offered by multimodal systems can support innovative interaction modalities in order to improve human activity towards a multi-sensorial experience.

Acknowledgments. This research has been supported by Hasler Foundation within the framework of Memodules project. Particular thanks to Sandro Gerardi and Maurizio Caporali for their precious help in the mock up evaluation and to the Prof. Rolf Ingold, Dr. Denis Lalanne and all the other people involved in the project for their valuable contributions.

References

1. Ullmer, B., Ishii, H.: Emerging frameworks for tangible user interfaces. IBM Systems Journal 39, 915–931 (2000)
2. Crabtree, A., Rodden, T., Mariani, J.: Collaborating around collections: informing the continued development of photoware. In: Proceedings of the 2004 ACM conference on computer supported cooperative work, Chicago, pp. 396–405. ACM Press, New York (2004)
3. Frohlich, D., Kuchinsky, A., Pering, C., Don, A., Ariss, S.: Requirements for photoware. In: Proceedings of the 2002 ACM Conference on Computer Supported Cooperative Work, New Orleans, Louisiana, pp. 166–175. ACM Press, New York (2002)
4. Krueger, R.A.: Focus Groups: a practical guide for applied research. Sage publications, Newbury Park, Calif (1988)
5. van den H.E.,, Eggen, B.: Personal souvenirs as Ambient Intelligent objects. In: Proceedings of the 2005 Joint Conference on Smart Objects and Ambient intelligence: innovative Context-Aware Services, Usages and Technologies, Grenoble, France, pp. 123–128. ACM Press, New York, USA (2005)
6. Bationo, A., Kahn, J., Decortis, F.: Traveling narrative as a multi-sensorial experience: A user centered approach of smart objects. In: Proceedings of Smart Objects Conference (sOc',2003) pp. 160–163 (2003)
7. Memodules project website http://www.memodules.ch
8. Rodden, T., Crabtree, A., Hemmings, T., Koleva, B., Humble, J., "Akesson, K-P., Hansson, P.: Between the dazzle of a new building and its eventual corpse: assembling the ubiquitous home. In: Proceedings of the 2004 ACM Symposium on Designing Interactive Systems, August 1st-4th, Cambridge, Massachusetts, ACM Press, New York (2004)
9. Mugellini, E., Rubegni, E., Gerardi, S., Abou Khaled, O.: Using Personal Objects as Tangible Interfaces for Memory Recollection and Sharing. In: 1st International Conference on Tangible and Embedded Interaction 2007, TEI'07, Baton Rouge, Louisiana, USA, (February 15-17, 2007)
10. Luff, P.: Touching the Surface: Creating Affinities between Digital Content and Paper. CSCW, Chicago, ACM (2004)
11. van den. H.E.: Graspable Cues for Everyday Recollecting, PhD Thesis, Department of Industrial Design, Eindhoven University of Technology, The Netherlands (2004)
12. Oh, S., Woo, W.: Manipulating Multimedia Contents with Tangible Media Control System. In: Rauterberg, M. (ed.) ICEC 2004. LNCS, vol. 3166, pp. 57–67. Springer, Heidelberg (2004)

Attentive Information Support with Massive Embedded Sensors in Room

Hiroshi Noguchi[1, 2], Taketoshi Mori[2], and Tomomasa Sato[2]

[1] CREST, Japan Science and Technology Agency,
[2] Graduate School of Information Science and Technology, Univesity of Tokyo,
7-3-1 Hongo, Bunkyo-ku, Tokyo 113-8656 Japan
{noguchi,tmori}@ics.t.u-tokyo.ac.jp,
tomomasasato@jcom.home.ne.jp

Abstract. We constructed informational support system based on massive sensor data in a room. In the room, called "Sensing Room", approximate 600 sensors are distributed. Pressure sensors are embedded in a floor, a table, chairs and bed. Switch sensors and electric current sensors are attached on furniture and electric appliances. RFID tag readers are embedded into room planes. The room monitors human activities without restriction of occupants. Information support system includes steerable active projector on the ceiling. The projector displays information on all planes of the room. The occupant watch information wherever he/she exists in the room without restriction. Based on captured activities, information support system decides timing, position and contents fitting the occupants' activities. In this way, massive sensors data achieves attentive support. We demonstrate notification, decision support and navigation by informational support system.

Keywords: Smart Room, Informational Support, Active Projector, Sensing Room, Massive Embedded Sensors.

1 Introduction

Smart room is a remarkable research topic in pervasive computing [1]. In smart rooms, massive sensors and computers are distributed invisibly. The smart rooms monitor occupants' activities and room situations with sensors. The rooms support the habitants attentively with measured situations and captured human activities. Example applications are such home automations as air conditioning fitting the personal preference and automatic collaboration of audio-visual appliances. In the future, the smart room will support the occupants actively. For instance, the room will notify important information with displays and audio devices. Robots in the room will support home tasks (e.g. serving a cup of drink). We target support by displaying information in smart rooms. Displaying the information to occupants realizes decision helps of daily-life action (ex. whether a habitant should bring out an umbrella in going out), notification of important schedule events and navigation to missing objects.

There are two approaches for displaying image to occupants. An approach is displaying to each person with such mobile devices as PDA and mobile phone. The other approach is presentation with displays in rooms (e.g. televisions and PCs).

J. Jacko (Ed.): Human-Computer Interaction, Part II, HCII 2007, LNCS 4551, pp. 883–892, 2007.

Mobile devices can display multiple people fitting their personal preferences. The users can decide to watch information or not. I.e. the users are not forced to watch information. If the devices are missed or put into a pocket, notification is difficult without such other devices as bells and vibrators. The mobile devices have the merit that they are utilized as input devices, sensor for user command. Handling the mobile device in all time is inconvenient and overload for the users. Presentation with installed display devices in the room does not constrict the occupant activity. Displaying with room devices attracts the attention of the occupants. The approach is suit for notification of important information. However, in this approach, it is difficult to measure user input in sync with displayed image. Instead, the user input and other situations are obtained through distributed sensors in the room. Displaying without restriction of the occupants is as important as monitoring without restriction for support in natural daily life. We adopt presentation with displays in the room. A typical application of information displaying support fitting personal activities is "Following Me" application [2]. The application with active badge switches the display monitor as the target user is moving. However, in room environment, number of displays is limited. It is difficult to introduce the display devices into all over the room. We utilize steerable active projector. Steerable active projector is utilized for interactive presentation in real environment [3]. Active projector can present the image on all planes in the room. All planes are regarded as displays.

In displaying the information, it is necessary to determine where to project, what image to project and when to project. To decide these parameters, not only whereabouts of the occupants but also their activities is needed. The smart rooms capture detailed situations of the room and the activities of the habitants with distributed sensors. The several researches construct the smart rooms and capture the human daily activities. Aware Home [4], PlaceLab [5], Gator Tech House [6], Easy Living [7], Ubiquitous Home [8] and LARES [9] construct houses and rooms, with which are embedded cameras, door switches, microphones, RFID Tags etc. These research track positions of the people and detect contexts (e.g. activities of the occupants and surrounding situations) from embedded sensors. MavHome [10] and Vivid Room [11] introduce such simple sensors as switch sensors for room lights and doors into the room. These researches estimate human behaviors from simple sensors and extract daily pattern of human activities. Our laboratory has been developing Robotic Room 2 [12] and Sensing Room [13] for measurement of detail human daily behavior. Sensing Room does not miss the human activity with pressure sensors all over the room. No camera is embedded in the room for reduction of the habitant's psychological stress. The objects in the room are also monitored with RFID tag readers. These features are different from other smart room researches. Our research goal is attentive informational support with active projector based on massive sensed data from Sensing Room.

2 Sensing Room

Sensing Room is developed on assumption of a single rental room in Japan. The room includes all room function except lavatory and bath room. The size of room is 5200mm x 4300mm. Sensing Room contains 600 sensors, which are mainly pressure sensors. Room photo and room layout are illustrated in Fig. 1. Visualized sensor data is shown in Fig. 2.

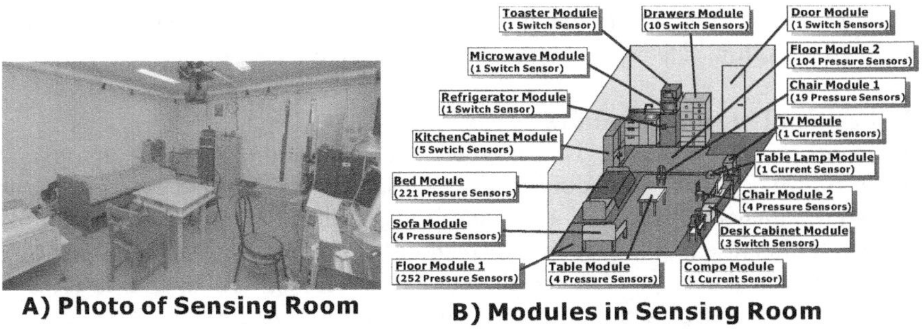

Fig. 1. Photo and Module Layout of Sensing Room

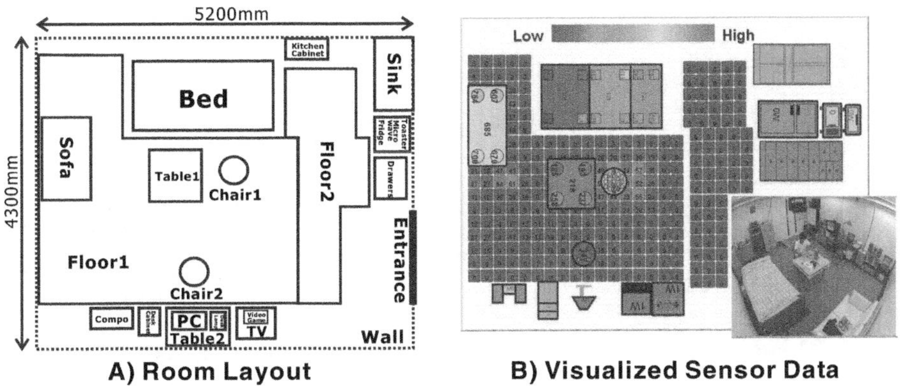

Fig. 2. Room Layout and Visualized Image

2.1 Modules

Sensors in Sensing Room are grouped into modules. Sensors attached on the same objects or the same kinds of sensors are clustered into a module. The grouping policy is based on how sensors are introduced into the rooms. One way is introduction with new appliances and furniture. I.e. when the new appliance comes into the home or when old ones are replaced with new ones, the sensors are embedded in new appliance. Managing sensors attached on the same object as one unit is adaptable to modification of room layout. The other way is embedding sensors into the room beforehand or attaching sensors on the room after building. In this case, single sensor is often meaningless, but bulk of distributed sensors is beneficial. These sensors are often managed with single control box. Examples of the sensor are surveillance cameras, door switches and pyroelectric sensors. Both two type of grouping are regarded as clustering sensors that connect to the same control box into one unit. In Sensing Room, sensors are grouped into 18 modules. Sensors in the module are managed by small board computer. The sampling rate of sensors in Sensing Room is 10 Hz, which is sufficient for human activities.

Sensing Room is developed to measure human activity (e.g. sitting and lying) rather than room environmental data (e.g. temperature and humidity). The room can capture 4 types of properties about human activity: position, posture, operation for devices in the room and object handling. The modules are classified into 4 types. In the following section, sensors in 4 typical modules are explained.

2.1.1 Position Detection Modules

Whereabouts of an occupant is important for estimation of daily activity. For example, if an occupant is standing near the gate of his/her house, his/her outing or returning is estimated. Position of a habitant is also utilized as a hint for support of the occupants. In this research, image is projected based on the positions of habitants.

Floor modules detect positions with pressure sensors (Fig. 3). Pressure sensors, called Force Sensing Register (FSR), cover the room floor in 200mm grid interval. On every 4 sensors, one veneer tile masks. The two modules exist in Sensing Room. They are created at different time and are connected to different controllers. Resolution of pressure value is 8 bit.

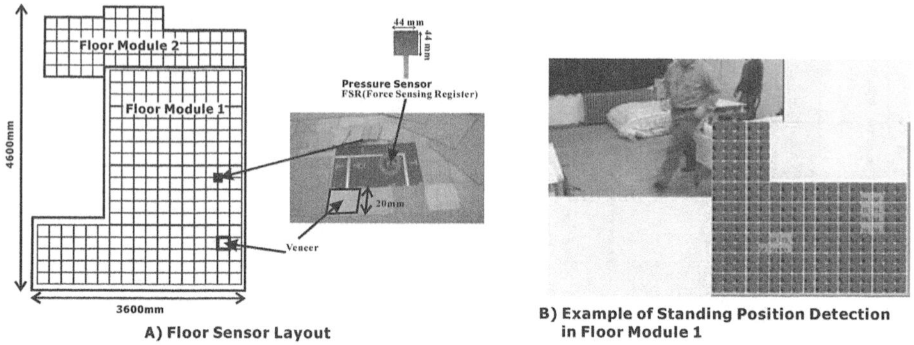

Fig. 3. Sensor Layout and Output Visualization of Floor Modules

Pressure values of the floor module are regarded as grayscale image by averaging the pressure sensor values of each veneer tile. The procedure of standing position estimation is the following. The module subtracts initial pressure values from measured pressure values, eliminates noise data by threshold, labels pressure detected tile and calculates center of the labels. Multiple people are easily distinguished except close case (within 60mm). Since pressure sensors do not output accurate pressure values, identification of people on the floor is difficult. A person walks in the room, at least his/her foot contacts floor surface. The floor module rarely misses the person.

2.1.2 Posture Detection Modules

Behaviors closely related to location are estimated from position of the occupants easily. However, although a occupant exists on the same location, supports are different between sitting case and standing case. Sitting positions moves as the chair moves. Position information is not significant. Sitting state is important. For example, in recognition of relaxing activity near a sofa, information "lying or sitting on the sofa" is more important than the information "near the sofa". Posture detection modules measure the sensor data related to postures of the occupants.

Posture detection modules are bed modules, chair module, table module etc. In the modules, mainly pressure sensors, which are the same type of floor sensors, are embedded. The modules detect contact positions of the habitants. From only contact positions and pressure values, accurate posture is not calculated. However the modules can estimate sitting state, lying state and touch position on the table.

Typical module is the table module (Fig. 4). In the table module, contact state and weight of object on the table are measured with 4 load cells. The pressure values are utilized for estimation of working on the table. The antenna of passive RFID tag is also embedded in the table. The RFID tag is mentioned at Sec. 2.1.4. Resolutions of all pressure sensors in posture detection modules are 10 bit.

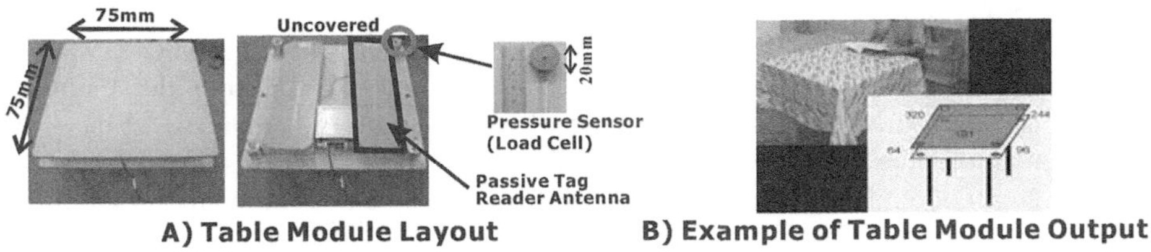

Fig. 4. Sensor Layout and Output Visualization of Table Modules

2.1.3 Operation Detection Modules

In the room environment, the occupants often operate electric appliances and handle furniture. Status of the appliances and furniture and detection of operation are important. The examples are television control, room light status and handling a refrigerator. Closing motion of room door is also regarded as a kind of furniture handling. Operation detection modules capture these operation and status.

The modules include mainly switch sensors for status of doors and devices. As for electric appliances, monitoring of appliance status is easier than detecting operation of appliances. The electric appliances are attached with electric current sensors. Toaster module, microwave module, electric appliance module, refrigerator module and drawers module are shown in Fig. 5. In Sensing Room, total 28 switch sensors including microswitch, reed switch and electric current sensors exist.

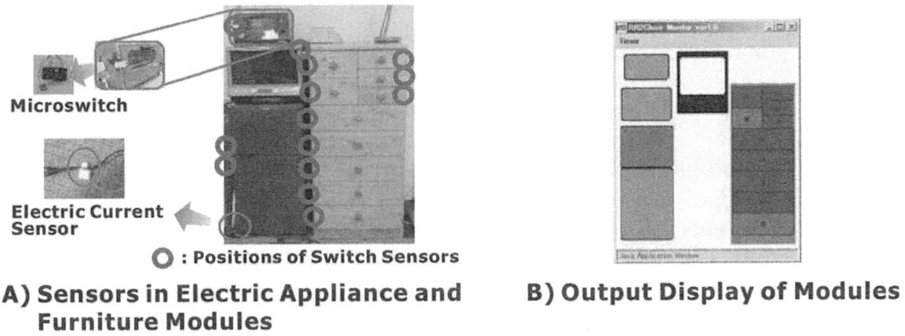

Fig. 5. Sensor Layout and Output Visualization of Toaster Module, Microwave Module, Refrigerator Module and Drawers Module

2.1.4 Object Handing Detection Modules

In the room, the habitants often handle tools and objects as well as they operate the electric appliances. The handling objects are hints for recognition of human activity. In the case of work recognition, if handling object on the table is identified, the activity is estimated. If handing object is a book, the activity is probably reading. If handling object is a cup, the behavior is probably drinking. Discrimination with only table pressure sensor values is difficult. Object handling detection modules helps detailed behavior recognition.

In Sensing Room, only one object handling detection module exists (Fig. 6). The module is passive RFID (Radio Frequency IDentification) tag system. RFID tag system consists of ID tags and tag readers. The tag reader can communicate with ID tags and read data of ID tags within antenna range (Fig. 6-B). Based on the read data, ID tag is identified by matching read data with object database. Since the communication area of the reader is limited, locations of the objects are assumed. ID tags are small enough to be attached with most of all objects in room environment.

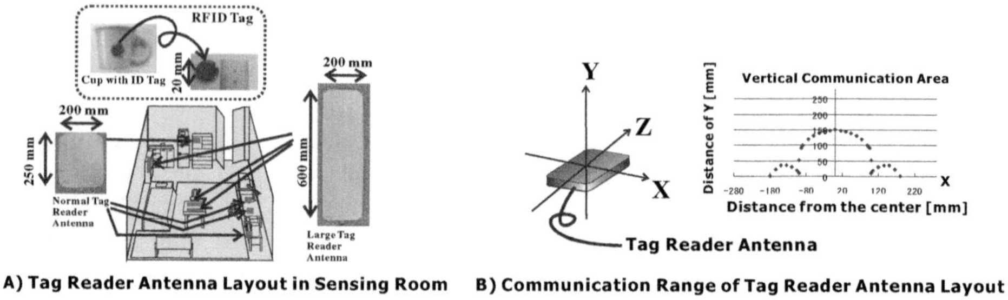

Fig. 6. Location of Tag Readers in Sensing Room and Communication Range of RFID tag

Since the electric wave from tag reader antenna interferes with each other, it is difficult to embed a lot of tag readers in one room. Based on several interference experiments and the room layout, we decided the arrangement of the tag readers as shown in Fig. 9-A.

2.2 Management of Modules

Sensor data is stored in a module unit by accumulation software [14]. The application programs can obtain sensor data through network middleware for sensors in room online [12]. The application programs can treat with both raw sensor data and processed sensor data with the middleware. The middleware provides sensor-processing programs such as noise filtering. Typical programs of sensor data processing in Sensing Room are following. Posture estimation programs calculate sitting posture and lying posture from chair modules and bed modules. Estimation program of person direction calculates direction from recent sequence of standing positions. Program for estimation of handing positions computes handling position from change of electric appliance status and the positions of the appliances in the room. Sensing Room can monitor not only electric appliance and furniture status but also the occupant's posture in the room from both raw sensor data and processed sensor data. Fig. 7 illustrates 3D view of estimated postures in Sensing Room. Although there is no camera in Sensing Room, coarse posture estimation is realized from massive embedded sensors.

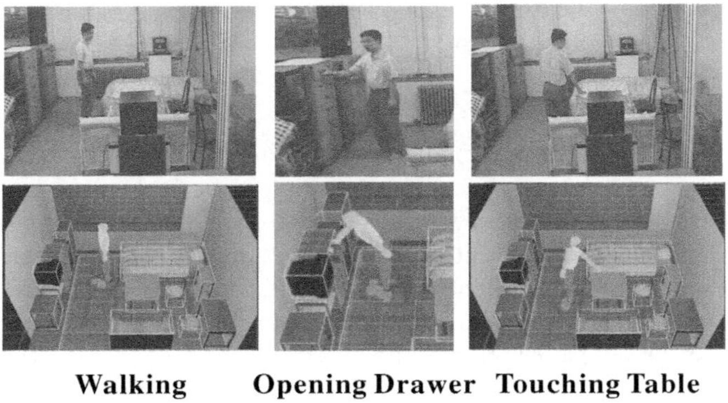

Fig. 7. 3D Visualization of Estimated Postures

3 Information Support with Active Projector

3.1 Active Projector System

As mentioned at Sec. 1, we utilize steerable active projector for information support. Overview of active projector system is shown in Fig. 8. Active projector is installed on the ceiling center of Sensing Room. The projector displays image on all plane of the room except the ceiling (Fig. 8-C). Projector system consists of projector controller, distorted image generator and informational support decider. Informational support decider generates image data for support and determines projection point based on sensor data of Sensing Room. Projector controller calculates pan and tilt parameter of the steerable projector from projection points and plane model created beforehand. The controller sends command to the projector. Distorted image generator contains plane model of the room and calibrated projection model. Given the plane model, the projection model and the projection point, image distortion is calculated. The generator transforms the source image into inverse-distorted image (Fig. 8-B). Combination of 3 parts realizes attentive information support based on sensor data of Sensing Room.

Information support decider calculates 3 properties (timing, position, image of projection) about information support from sensor data of Sensing Room. Timing of projection is decided by matching the rules for support timing with symbolized sensor data (e.g. specific location of standing, status of appliances and sitting status). Position of projection is determined by mapping data between the occupant's status and projection points. The mapping data includes standing position, sitting status and lying status. Images of projection are difficult to be prepared in advance. The images

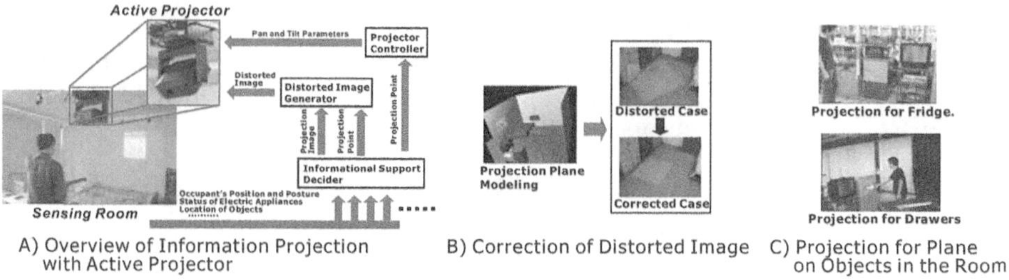

Fig. 8. Overview of Active Projector System

should modify according to current information such as current timestamp, weather, whereabouts of the occupants and schedules. We prepare template image. The decider embeds the information that depends on current status of the room into the template image. The rule, mapping data and template image are related to each other. They are written in Resource Description Framework (RDF) [9,14]. By RDF, relationship among them is easily described. The relationship description adapts the decider to modification of 3 parameters flexibly. For example, if rule related to specific location is modified, the decider calculates projection position based on relationship description about the location without change of mapping data.

3.2 Demonstration of Information Support

We demonstrate several informational supports (Fig. 9). The active projector system notifies weather forecast when the occupant is going out. It informs schedules before habitant's relaxing. Map and the other information about visiting schedule are shown on the wall, when the occupant is relaxing on the sofa. The system navigates to the refrigerator for drinking in the point of entering room and dressing. It recommends a cool drink among the drinks in front of the refrigerator.

This support system is unrealizable without Sensing Room, massive sensor environment. In capturing activity with the only position sensors or vision sensors,

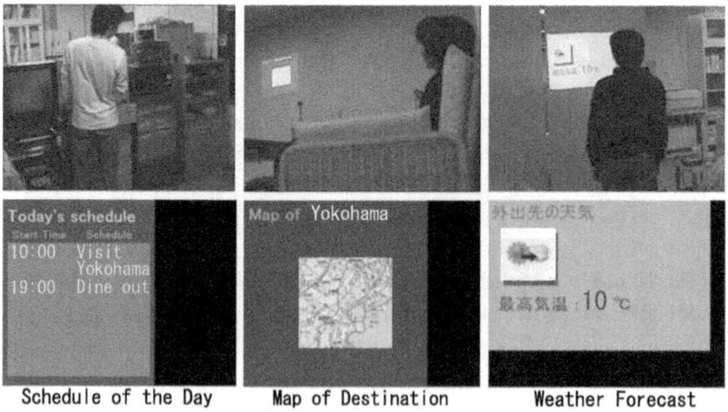

Fig. 9. Image Projection Examples

display position is easy determined. However, it is insufficient to support according to complicated activity such as works on the table. In case of a lot of simple sensors, they are easily installed but recognizable activities are limited and inaccurate. In Sensing Room, form substantive embedded sensors, various accurate activities are obtained. The rich sensor data helps to support the habitant fitting their individual properties.

4 Conclusion

We constructed Sensing Room, a room for monitoring of human daily activity and information support system with steerable active projector. Combination of sensing room and active projector realizes continuous monitoring and support without restraint of the habitants. Sensing Room captures the occupant's position, posture, operation and handling objects with massive embedded sensors. The projector system decides appropriate timing, position and image of the projection with recognized rich activities. We demonstrate example applications of information support.

Currently, support parameters are determined by prepared rules. We challenge to support based on prediction of activities and long patterns of activities.

References

1. Intille, S.S.: Designing a home of the future. IEEE Pervasive Computing 1, 76–82 (2002)
2. Harter, A., Hopper, A., Steggles, P., Word, A., Webster, P.: The anatomy of a context-aware application. Wireless Networks 8, 187–197 (2002)
3. Pinhanez, C., Podlaseck, M.: To frame or not to frame: The role and design of frameless display in ubiquitous applications. In: Beigl, M., Intille, S.S., Rekimoto, J., Tokuda, H. (eds.) UbiComp 2005. LNCS, vol. 3660, pp. 340–357. Springer, Heidelberg (2005)
4. Kidd, C.D., Orr, R.J., Abowd, G.D., Atkeson, C.G., Essa, I.A., MacIntyre, B., Mynatt, E., Starner, T.E., Newstetter, W.: The aware home: A living laboratory for ubiquitous computing research. In: Proceedings of the Second International Workshop on Cooperative Buildings, pp. 191–198 (1999)
5. Intille, S.S., Larson, K., Tapia, E.M., Beaudin, J.S., Kaushik, P., Nawyn, J., Rockinson, R.: Using a live-in laboratory for unbiquitous computing research. In: Fishkin, K.P., Schiele, B., Nixon, P., Quigley, A. (eds.) PERVASIVE 2006. LNCS, vol. 3968, pp. 349–365. Springer, Heidelberg (2006)
6. Helal, S., Mann, W., El-Zabadani, H., King, J., Kaddoura, Y., Jansen, E.: The gator tech smart house: A programmable pervasive space. IEEE Computer, pp. 50–60 (2005)
7. Brumitt, B., Meyers, B., Krumm, J., Kern, A., Shafer, S.: Easyliving: Technologies for intelligent environments. In: Handheld and Ubiquitous Computing, pp. 12–27 (2000)
8. Yamazaki, T.: Ubiquitous home: Real-life testbed for home context-aware service. In: Tridentcom 2005 (First International Conference on Testbeds and Reserch Infrastructures for the DEvelopment of NeTworks and COMmunities) pp. 54–59 (2005)
9. Bien, Z., Park, K., Bang, W., Stefanov, D.: LARES: An intelligent sweet home for assisting the elderly and the hnadicapped. In: 1st Cambridge Workshop on Universal Access and Assistive Technology (CWUAAT). pp. 43–46 (2002)

10. Youngblood, G., Holder, B.L., Cook, D.J.: Managin adaptive versatile environment. In: Proceedings of the 3rd IEEE Int'l Conf. on Pervasive Computing and Communications (PerCom). pp. 351–360 (2005)
11. Nakauchi, Y., Noguchi, K., Somwong, P., Matsubara, T., Namatame, A.: Vivid room: Human intention detection and activity support environment for ubiquitous autonomy. In: Proceedings of the 2001 IEEE/RSJ International Conference on Intelligent Robots and Systems pp.773–778 (2003)
12. Mori, T., Asaki, K., Noguchi, H., Sato, T.: Accumulation and summalization of human daily action data in one-room-type sensing system. In: Proceedings of the 2001 IEEE/RSJ International Conference on Intelligent Robots and Systems pp. 2349–2354 (2001)
13. Mori, T., Noguchi, H., Takada, A., Sato, T.: Sensing room: Distributed sensor environment for measurement of human daily behavior. In: First International Workshop on Networked Sensing Systems (INSS), pp. 40–43 (2004)
14. Noguchi, H., Mori, T., Sato, T.: Network middleware for flexible integration of sensor processing in home environment. In: Proceedings of IEEE International Conference on Systems, Man and Cybernetics, pp. 3845–3851 (2004)
15. Lassila, O., Swick, R.R.: Resource description framework (rdf) model and syntax specification (1999) available at http://www.w3.org/TR/1999/REC-rdf-syntax-19990222

A Novel Infrastructure of Digital Storytelling Theme Museums Based on RFID Systems

Myunjin Park and Keechul Jung

HCI Lab., School of Media, College of Information Technology,
Soongsil University, South Korea
{cooljin,kcjung}@ssu.ac.kr

Abstract. This paper suggests a storytelling service infrastructure using RFID systems for theme museums with relevant multimedia contents providing an active experience space and drawing more interest. The proposed storytelling system uses RFID tags, a wireless LAN, and a mobile device for the theme museum, and relevant technical issues involving an overall architecture of RFID system will be introduced in this paper. Therefore, the proposed storytelling service infrastructure could be further applicable for games and animation to experience the people realistic scene through providing additional story and virtual information related to each object using RFID, a wireless LAN and a remote storytelling server.

1 Introduction

As the progress of the digital technology has been changing ways of delivering information, there have been tremendous changes to the function of a museum. There are some examples that a cyber museum is constructed on the web, or a guide system for viewing using a computer is installed in an exhibition space. But those are not all the digital technology has brought [1]. Thus, the breakthrough on the area of cyber museum lays not on the digital technology itself, but the people visit a museum like they do shopping with family. And they visit the homepage of a museum like they enjoy a computer game. So, it can be said that an online or offline museum competes with a shopping center, a movie theater, a theme park as well as a computer game. To maintain the present status of a museum in this kind of circumstances, a museum has to exhibit objects[1] which can not be seen in a shopping center, provide experiences which a theme park does not give, and have information which can not be given in the web. Now, a museum has to transform a static space to exhibit objects into a culture complex which can give information, interest, and experience simultaneously.[2] Actually, storytelling can be used for combining educational and entertaining function of a museum.

An object exhibited in a museum has its own theme, but people who do not have any advance information might get information from a guiding board installed in a

[1] A museum object is collected for exhibition in a museum. An object means something that has 3 dimensional shape.

[2] A good example is the digital storytelling project of art center 'Nabi' in Korea or a guide system which has a storytelling system in Korean National Museum.

J. Jacko (Ed.): Human-Computer Interaction, Part II, HCII 2007, LNCS 4551, pp. 893–900, 2007.

museum. This simplified explanation through letters halves interest which people have for an object. And a voice guiding system in a museum also has a disadvantage that it is impossible to convey information to people at specific time they want. The most important thing of a storytelling theme museum is harmony between an overall design and new technology. So, it will be possible for people to handle a storytelling service for themselves using games and animation if a museum is equipped with RFID tag, RFID reader, and mobile phone. In terms of a storytelling, people can experience new culture technology [2] through additional story and information related to each object.

This paper introduces a storytelling service which can provide more interesting and active experience using RFID, a wireless LAN and a web storytelling server.

2 The Concept of a Storytelling and a Theme Museum

2.1 Concept of a Storytelling and a Museum

The concept of a museum includes art, history, a science center, an aquarium, a botanical garden, and a nature center [3]. A storytelling museum is a sequential process that a storyteller provides an event and a story to give people a living experience. A museum storytelling is different from a game storytelling or an animation storytelling in that it should be based on a fact. Sometimes it is called non-fiction storytelling. Therefore, the digital storytelling can be deployed on theme museums having its own stories at both online or offline sites.

2.2 Necessity of a Storytelling

Many prototype versions of storytelling museums exist around world such as the British museum[3] providing history quizzes made using Flash for kids, National museum of industrial history[4] showing the process of development of industry since the invention of a steam engine using Flash, and Teddybear Museum parodying Millet's the Angelus and Da Vinci's the Mona Lisa using teddybears. But considering people's fondness, it is hard to say that they meet people's request. For example, National museum of Korea[5] provides the 3D visual information of relics, but it is not enough to draw passive spectator's interest. The 3D visual information of relics is the technique a museum wants to be proud of, not the information spectators want. Most spectators want to experience the story that an exhibit has. So it should be a type of story to draw a concern from spectators. It is the reason storytelling has to be applied to a museum and museum contents. The reason that a storytelling has to be applied lies here.

2.3 A Storytelling Theme Museum

A storytelling theme museum provides people with the stories or animations related to the exhibited objects. The Teddybear Museum[6] available online and offline is a good

---

[3] www. thebritishmuseum.ac.uk
[4] www.nimh.org
[5] www.museum.go.kr
[6] www.teddybearmuseum.com

example. It is called a museum, but it performs totally different functions by reproducing a historical event or person, and parodying Millet's the Angelus and Da Vinci's the Mona Lisa using teddybears. Figure 1 shows examples dealing with the astronauts on the moon and the unity of German. Objects exhibited are not collections but just dolls sold in shopping malls. It provides new interest applying a storytelling to information, rather than gives new information [4].

Fig. 1. Teddy Bear Gallery presenting "Moon Landing" and "German Reunion"

2.4 Designing a Storytelling Museum

Figure 2 shows that one of scenes from a popular TV drama in Korea, "A Palace", is expressed using teddybears. The left picture is the real exhibit in a theme museum. People can experience more than watching if they are provided with interactive contents. It is useless to say that well-organized stories and a supporting system should be behind contents. People can search historical background or historical research related to objects through new contents. They also can get animation which has educational[7] element and take a part in immediately using mobile BBS or a digital camera. Also, connecting fun scenes to a game and providing it interactively can bring about more interesting environment. This sequential process gives people new experiences

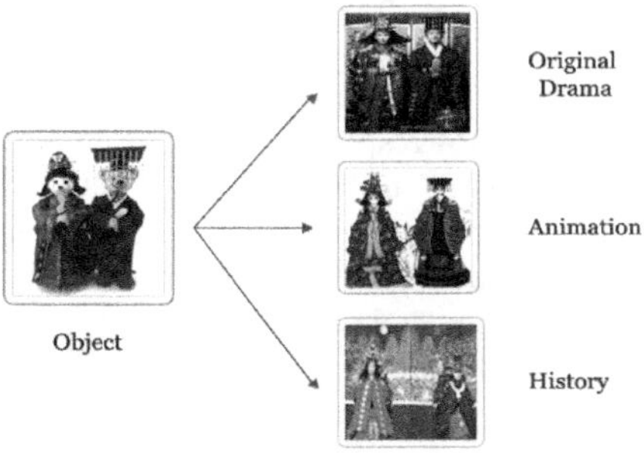

Fig. 2. Examples of multimedia contents related to a certain drama topic represented by using humanized teddy bears

[7] Edutainment is a new word combining education and entertainment. It means new type of education that entertaining element is added to education to induce participation and interest.

accompanied with information and entertainment by connecting a real object with content in cyber space [5, 6]

3 A Storytelling Multimedia System Using RFID and Wireless LAN

3.1 Differences from Existing Multimedia Museums

A storytelling museum presented in the paper gives people a chance to harmonize with objects by providing a story, historical background, animation, or games connected to theme. Museums using RFID or IrDA have already been built in many countries, and most of them are used for giving superficial information. Leeum Museum[8] in Korea (Figure 3), Modern Art Museum in San Francisco and Experience music project in Seattle are good examples. They let people get information through IrDA attached to objects and provide multimedia information stored in PDA.

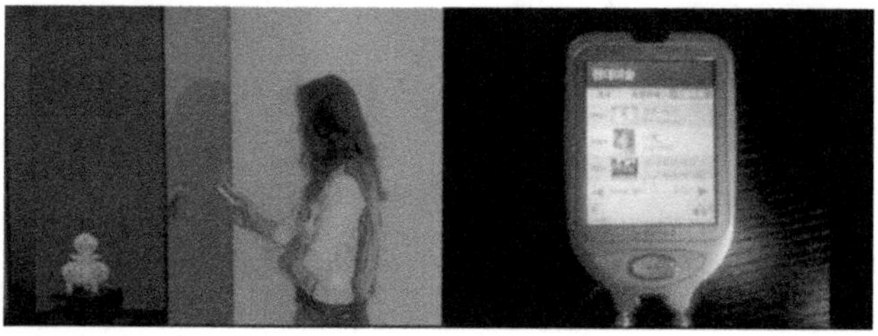

Fig. 3. Example of information guidance system using IrDA and PDA deployed in Leeum Museum, Seoul, Korea

Recently, Electronic Guidebook Forum[9] was founded to manage various project for developing a commercial system or prototype of interactive museums based on wireless communication. Among the projects it performed, Sotto Voce electronic guidebook [7] provides people with a real object and historical image in virtual environment using a wireless unit. That is, they make people feel like they are in front of an exhibit by moving a historical image to the wall a real object attached to. Similar example is a museum[10] which has virtual environment element developed by MIT Media lab. It uses IrDA to monitor a spectator's location and how long he or she stays at a specific exhibit and to provide storytelling information. But it has a disadvantage that people should carry a laptop computer to store a huge amount of multimedia data and process virtual environment.

To solve this problem, HP introduced Cooltown project [7] that uses RFID. But it also has a problem that it needs a PI station separately and it has to be close to an object. A storytelling museum presented in the paper is for getting various contents from a remote storytelling server via electronic product code (EPC)[11] network using

[8] www.leeum.org
[9] www.exploratorium.edu/guidebook
[10] www.archimuse.com/mw2002/papers/sparacino/sparacino.html
[11] http://www.epcglobalinc.org/

RFID system suggested by MIT Auto-ID lab.[12] It is the system that people can get various contents from a storytelling server of local area or a remote storytelling server using RFID tags storing EPC. It is also possible to get web site information using EPC and search more various website via a storytelling server. People can request desired information from a storytelling sever administrator such as story, historical background, game, or animation just using simply a mobile phone. The storytelling server contains lots of classes of multimedia contents such as animations, games, and fiction or nonfiction movies. Since the people only retrieve those contents from either local or remote storytelling server, the user handheld does not have to have high computing power. The handheld simply achieves EPC stored in RFID tag attached ordinary at the object, and transfer it to the storytelling server via internal or external EPC network. Thus, referring to the categories of EPC in the form of web addresses, it is also possible to retrieve relevant information from worldwide existing websites. Therefore, when the user requests more detailed information, the storytelling server as the gateway automatically searches many places to fulfill the user's satisfaction.

3.2 Design of a Storytelling Museum Using RFID and a Wireless LAN

The proposed infrastructure of a storytelling museum comprises of EPC network and a wireless LAN and RFID tags in order to store all information about objects and send

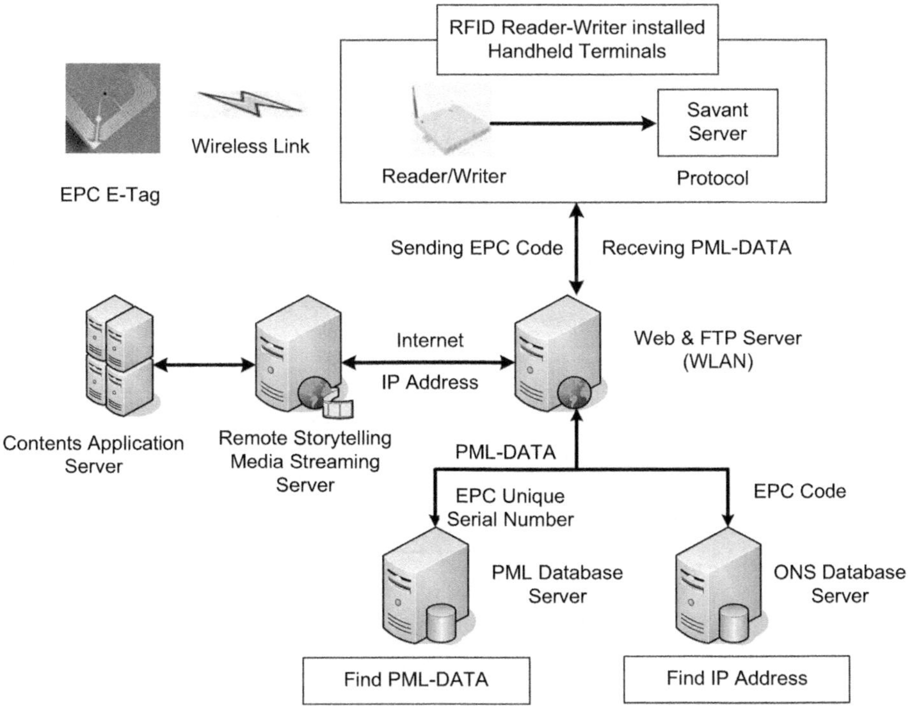

Fig. 4. Procedure of accessing remote storytelling server based on RFID network

[12] http://www.autoidlabs.org

Table 1. Components in RFID network infrastructure

EPC	The globally unique identifier that serves as a pointer for making enquiries about the item it identifies.
RFID Tags	The carrier for the EPC that communicates with the reader.
Reader	The data capture device; portable or fixed(installed), connected to a Savant server or network..
Savant	Servers which act as local repositories for EPCs and associated information, and which support middleware for serving PML queries.
ONS	Object Name Service; the distributed resource that "Knows" where information about EPCs is held(just like DNS)
PML	Physical Markup Language; like XML, with XQL query structure to allow structured querying and reporting concerning EPCs.

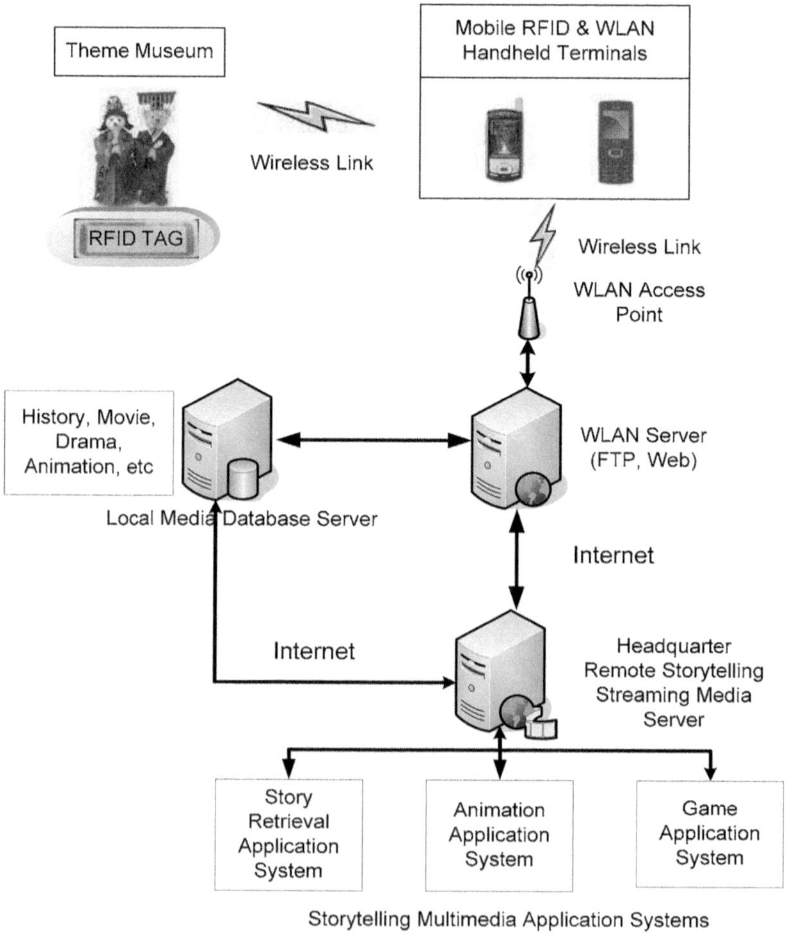

Fig. 5. Overall structure of storytelling information service system using RFID, WLAN and Internet for theme museums

information to the spectators via a handheld when they stop by each object. A handheld has to read RFID tags, have Savant function for storing EPC codes and related information and support a middleware for processing PML data from a PML server later on. Also it has to connect to wireless local area network (WLAN) and sends EPC codes to PML server and object name service (ONS) server included in area of WLAN and gets IP address and PML data from them. After that, it is connected to a remote storytelling server via WLAN using PML data and IP address and search data or brings multimedia data interactively. Figure 4 shows the process of connecting to a remote storytelling server using RFID and a wireless LAN, and Table 1 explains about elements for running RFID.

Figure 5 shows overall system for a theme museum using RFID and a wireless LAN. A storytelling sever consists of three kinds of application softwares, those for running various story, animation software, and game software. Additionally, a mobile device has to have software for running Viscape, Shockwave, Macromedia Flash Player, Blaxxum, Cortona, MGI viewer, and Live Picture. The proposed digital storytelling infrastructure surely upgrades ordinary and cyber museums by transforming objects into synthetic multimedia contents, such as movie, drama, animation and game. More interestingly, a digital storytelling museum could be more revitalized by accompanying with edutainment which is a combinatory field encompassing education and entertainment.

4 Conclusion

This paper suggests the importance of storytelling design, development of theme museum contents and a storytelling theme museum using RFID systems to complement objects which have lack of experience. The paper also designs overall system of RFID and a wireless LAN and discusses necessity of new contents in which a storytelling is applied to provide a huge amount of information of a museum using RFID system. People can get information related to objects on internet instead of printing information and get extra interest from various contents. This paper upgrades an ordinary storytelling museum by transforming objects into synthetic multimedia contents, such as movie, drama, animation and game via internet. If a storytelling museum is accompanied by edutainment which has educational and entertaining function from now on, it can be expected that it is revitalized.

Acknowledgements. This work was supported by grant No.(R01-2006-000-11214-0) from the Basic Research Program of the Korea Science & Engineering Foundation.

References

1. Burcaw, G.E.: Introduction to museum work: 3rd edn. Aaslh Book Series (1997)
2. Lim, C.J., Han, S.Y.: Investigation of a trail characteristic of a museum spectator, a collection of design papers 4th, p. 198 (1999)
3. Falk, J.H., Dierking, L.D.: Learning from museum, pp. 48–49. AltaMira Press, New York (2000)

4. Gang, S.H.: Digital Edutainment Storytelling, Salim (2005)
5. Murray, J.H.: Hamlet on the Holodeck: The future of narrative in cyberspace. The MIT Press, Cambridge, MA (1998)
6. Kinderg, T., Barton, J.: A web-based nomadic computing system, Computer Networks, vol. 35(4), pp. 443–456. Elsevier, North-Holland, Amsterdam (2001)
7. Aoki, P.M., Woodruff: Improving electronic guidebook interface using a task-oriented design approach. In: Proc. 3rd ACM Conf. on Designing Interactive System, New York, August

A Novel Human-Computer Interface Based on Passive Acoustic Localisation

D.T. Pham, Ze Ji, Ming Yang, Zuobin Wang, and Mostafa Al-Kutubi

Manufacturing Engineering Centre, Cardiff University, Cardiff CF24 3AA, UK

Abstract. This paper describes work aimed at developing new tangible computer interfaces that can be created out of almost any surface by detecting the vibrations generated when a user's finger interacts with the surface. Two modes of interaction have been considered: discrete impact and continuous scratching. Two methods for localising the point of impact have been investigated: Time Difference of Arrival (TDOA) and Location Template Matching (LTM). Tracking of the continuous movement of a finger scratching on a surface has been implemented by extending the TDOA method. These methods have been tested using solid objects of different materials and shapes. Experimental results have shown the potential of the presented technologies for real-time impact localisation in this new form of human-computer interfaces.

Keywords: HCI, time reversal, TDOA, Kalman filter, tangible acoustic interfaces.

1 Introduction

There are basically two types of human-computer interfaces, tangible (touchable) and intangible (non-touchable). The vast majority of input interfaces are tangible. Currently, such tangible interfaces include keypads, mice and touch screens which are reliable and easy to use. However, a common problem with these devices is that they restrict the mobility of users, constraining them to be in certain locations during interactions with the computer. An alternative solution would be to convert everyday objects such as table tops, walls and windows into interactive surfaces.

In recent years, various attempts have been made using tangible objects as interfaces for human computer interaction [1, 2]. The advantage of these techniques is that the interaction surface is not limited to a specific size as a touch screen. A passive acoustic technique has been demonstrated by MIT on shop windows for public browsing [2, 3]. A commercial product using shop windows has also been promoted [4]. Those two applications were based on the well-known Time Difference of Arrival (TDOA) principle for localising the impact caused by the user tapping on the surface of a solid object.

In addition to the TDOA method which can be employed to detect the micro impacts generated when the user scratches on a surface, another technique known as

J. Jacko (Ed.): Human-Computer Interaction, Part II, HCII 2007, LNCS 4551, pp. 901–909, 2007.

Location Template Matching (LTM) has also been applied to the problem of impact localisation [5].

This paper first describes the principles of these different methods and then focuses on the implementation of prototype acoustic interfaces and a comparative discussion of the different approaches.

2 Background

2.1 LTM

LTM is based on the time-reversal theory [5]. That theory shows that an acoustic source can be reconstructed at its original location in a scattering medium by recording the received signals then sending back the time reversed version of these signals through the medium [5]. This implies that the received signal carries its source location signature as a result of scattering in the transmission medium and reflections from complex boundaries.

A signal $S(t)$ received by a sensor can be formulated as the convolution between the emitted source $e(t)$ from source position p and the impulse response function $h_{ps}(t)$ of the propagation between the source and the receiver positions

$$S(t) = e(t) \otimes h_{ps}(t) \tag{1}$$

where $\otimes$ denotes the temporal convolution operation. The duration of the emitted source is assumed very short and can be estimated as the Dirac delta function $\delta(t)$, so that

$$S(t) \cong h_{ps}(t) \tag{2}$$

Therefore, equation (2) indicates that the measured signal can be estimated as the impulse function of the propagation between the source and the sensor. The reconstructed signal at the source position p is in fact the convolution between $h_{ps}(t)$ and its time reversed version $h_{ps}(-t)$, and can be understood as the cross-correlation function.

In the LTM approach, the uniqueness of the received acoustic signal, as a function of its source location, which is based on the time-reversal theory, is employed to localise an impact on a tangible object [7]. This is achieved by creating a template of received signals generated from taps at pre-known locations. The source location can then be determined by a cross-correlation analysis from the best similarity match of an unknown signal with a signal in the templates. The principle of the LTM method is illustrated in Fig. 1.

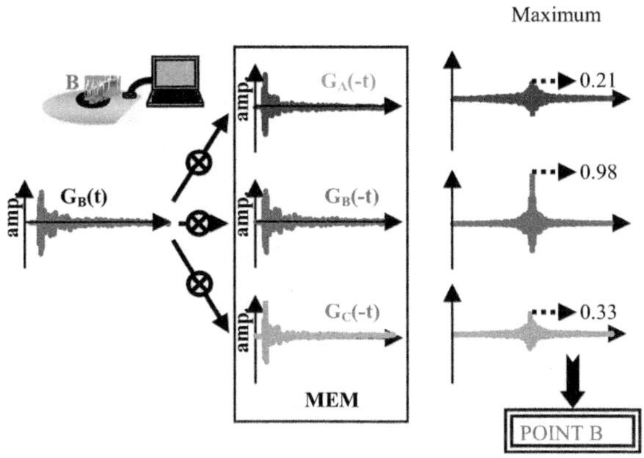

Fig. 1. LTM method flowchart

2.2 TDOA

The principle of the TDOA method is to use the measurement of time differences between arrivals of signals to estimate the source location [6]. These time arrival delays result from the differences in distances from the source to the sensors which are placed at known geometric positions.

Fig. 2 presents a typical TDOA system comprising a plate, four sensors installed at the four corners. The sensor outputs are amplified and filtered, then digitised and finally processed by the PC to obtain the coordinates of the position of the knock.

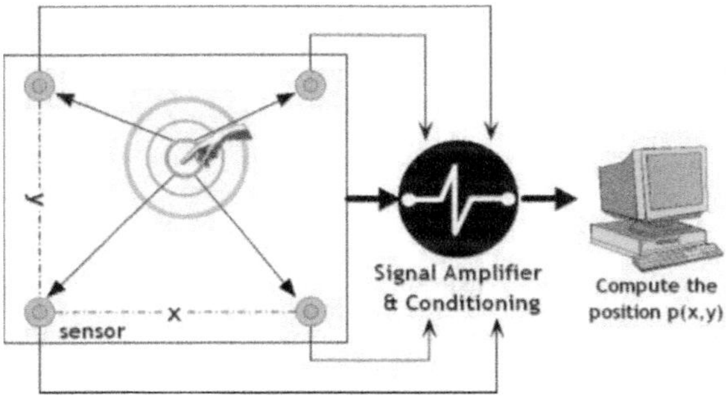

Fig. 2. TDOA hardware block diagram

Theoretically three sensors will be sufficient for localisation, the location at (x, y) has the following relationship with the time differences of the sensor signals:

$$\sqrt{(x-x_1)^2+(y-y_1)^2}-\sqrt{(x-x_3)^2+(y-y_3)^2}=v\Delta t_{13} \tag{3}$$

$$\sqrt{(x-x_2)^2+(y-y_2)^2}-\sqrt{(x-x_4)^2+(y-y_4)^2}=v\Delta t_{24} \tag{4}$$

where (x_1, y_1), (x_2, y_2), (x_3, y_3) and (x_4, y_4) are the coordinates of the four sensor positions. v is the acoustic wave propagation velocity in the plate. Δt_{13} is the measured time difference for the sensor locations (x_1, y_1) and (x_3, y_3), and Δt_{24} is the measured time difference for the sensor locations (x_2, y_2) and (x_4, y_4).

The above equations can be expressed in a general form given below:

$$\Delta d_{i,j} = \sqrt{(x-x_i)^2 + (y-y_i)^2} - \sqrt{(x-x_j)^2 + (y-y_j)^2} \tag{5}$$

where i and j represent the sensor indices. The source location can therefore be calculated by minimising the following expression:

$$E = \sum_{i=2}^{4} (v\Delta t_{1,i} - \Delta d_{1,i})^2 \tag{6}$$

where $\Delta t_{1,i}$ represents the time difference between signal arrivals at the 1st sensor and the i th sensor.

It should be pointed out that the determination of the source location in a plane is based on the hypothesis of acoustic waves travelling in the plate at a constant velocity.

Conventionally, cross-correlation is the most popular method to determine the time difference for sound localisation in air [4, 8]. However, it is not suitable for localisation in solids due to the dependence of propagation velocity on the elastic properties of different materials [6]. Moreover, the result of the cross-correlation can be affected by the multiple reflections of acoustic waves from object boundaries. Time of Flight (ToF) is thus an efficient method to determine the arrival time at which the waveform crosses a threshold level. However, the dispersion and wave attenuation make the ToF less reliable than applications in air. In practice, this method can be improved with a proper pre-filtering and an additional calibration. This method has been applied in this work due to its computational efficiency and accuracy. In addition, it is prone to ambient noises, particularly for weak signals.

2.3 Continuous Tracking

The friction of a finger moving on a surface can generate micro-impacts, and hence produce complicated vibration signals. To overcome the timing uncertainty for continuous signals, two novel approaches for the localisation of an impulsive acoustic source in a solid object have been investigated in this work [9]. First, the Continuous Wavelet Transform (CWT) was utilised to extract different frequency components from the recorded acoustic signals for estimation of the group velocities of the frequencies interested. Then Maximum Likelihood Estimation (MLE) was introduced to overcome problems of ambiguities in time difference estimation. The MLE method searches for a target position over all possible positions in the workspace instead of just looking for the precise time difference of the arrived signals. The highest likelihood determines the target presence.

Tracking a moving object is an application of sequential estimation of its state space. In this work, a Kalman filter was employed for tracking continuous movements. The Kalman filter is an optimal solution to estimate the state $x \in \Re^n$ of a discrete-time controlled process that is governed by a linear differential equation [10]

$$x_k = F_k x_{k-1} + Bu_{k-1} + w_{k-1} \tag{7}$$

where F_k is the state transition model which is applied to the previous state x_{k-1}, B_k is the control-input model which is applied to the control vector u_{k-1}, w_{k-1} is the process noise which is assumed to be zero mean normal distribution with covariance Q_k. The measurement $z \in \Re^n$ is modelled as

$$z_k = H_k x_k + v_k \tag{8}$$

where H_k is the measurement function and v_k is the noise of the observation (measurement) with the same assumption of zero mean normal distribution with covariance R_k.

The goal of the Kalman filter is to compute the a posterior state estimate by a linear combination of the a priori estimate $\hat{x}_k^-$ and a weighted difference between an actual measurement z_k and a measurement prediction $H\hat{x}_k^-$ as shown below

$$\hat{x}_k = \hat{x}_k^- + K(z_k - H\hat{x}_k^-) \tag{9}$$

where the difference of $(z_k - H\hat{x}_k^-)$ is called the measurement innovation, or the residual. The gain K is governed by the following relationships:

$$\begin{aligned}
&\text{State estimate propagation: } \hat{x}_k^- = F_k \hat{x}_{k-1} \\
&\text{Error covariance propagation: } P_k^- = F_k P_{k-1} F_k^T + Q_{k-1} \\
&\text{Kalman gain matrix: } K = P_k^- H_k^T [H_k P_k^- H_k^T + R_k]^{-1} \\
&\text{State estimate update: } \hat{x}_k = \hat{x}_k^- + K(z_k - H_k \hat{x}_k^-) \\
&\text{Error covariance update: } P_k = (I - KH_k) P_k^-
\end{aligned} \tag{10}$$

3 Implementation and Discussion

3.1 LTM

Compared to the TDOA method, the major advantage of the LTM method is its simpler hardware configuration, which requires only a minimum of one sensor. However, two sensors are normally employed in practice to improve reliability of localisation. Another advantage of the LTM method is its adaptability to materials of almost any shape, including inhomogeneous 3-D objects. In contrast to the TDOA method, the sampling rate here was relatively low, because the useful signal energy is concentrated in the audio band.

In practice, a threshold was set to identify the closest match with the template using the cross correlation coefficient as a measure for determination of the degree of similarity. For thin glass plates, a resolution of a few millimetres can be achieved.

Fig. 3 shows an implementation on a normal filter glass plate, which is mounted in front of the screen of a laptop computer. With sufficient points calibrated on the plate in advance, a normal laptop LCD screen can be used as a touch screen. Fig. 4 depicts an example of the conversion of an ordinary globe into a touch sensitive computer interactive interface, showing its applicability to 3-D objects.

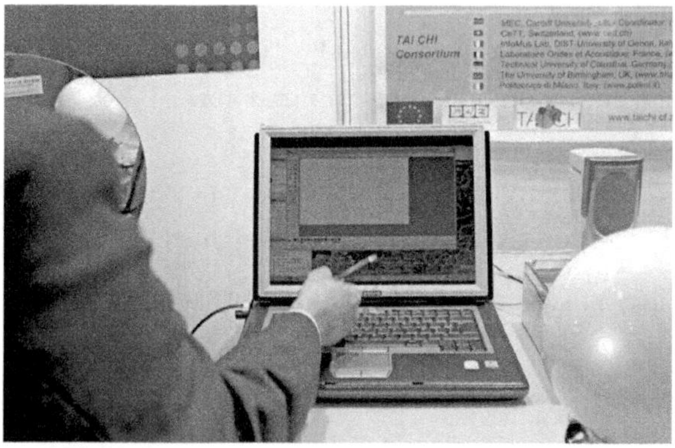

Fig. 3. A conversion of the laptop screen into touch sensitive screen. (IST 2006 exhibition by Tai-Chi project[1])

Fig. 4. A 3-D touch sensitive object (IST 2006 exhibition by Tai-Chi project)

---

[1] Tai-Chi is a European FP6 IST Project "Tangible Acoustic Interfaces for Computer-Human Interaction (TAI-CHI)".

3.2 TDOA and Continuous Tracking

The TDOA method is more versatile but requires more sensors. An advantage of the TDOA method over the LTM method is its ability to localise an impact without the initialisation stage at all points. The ToF method is found to be the most efficient way to locate impacts when distinct wave fronts of the signals are available. This method has been applied to create a virtual piano on a whiteboard with an area of 1200x1000 mm^2 as shown in Fig. 5.

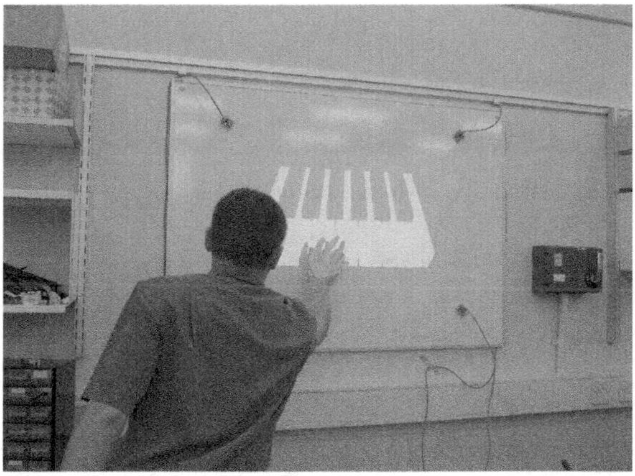

Fig. 5. Virtual piano implemented on a whiteboard with the TDOA method

The image of a piano keyboard was projected onto the whiteboard from a PC. Captured acoustic signals were sampled at a frequency of 100 kHz. Localisation errors were about 28 mm on average, and reduced to 14 mm after calibration.

In order to realise a mouse 'drag-and-drop' function on large surfaces, continuous tracking of the finger's motion needs to be implemented. However as mentioned above, the ToF method is not suitable for tracking continuous movement. Therefore, the MLE based method with proper selection of frequency band in CWT is used to determine the starting position of a continuous movement and the positions can be predicted using a Kalman filter.

The prototype system for tracking a continuous acoustic source is based on a thin Medium Density Fibreboard (MDF) board with dimensions of 1200x900x6 mm^3 shown in Fig. 6. The sensors are placed at the four corners of the central experimental area of 600x400 mm^2. This material was chosen for this work because of its relative rough surface, which provides signals of high enough amplitudes from finger movement. A prototype was implemented to simulate the 'mouse event'. The start and the end of a series of continuous measurement can be used to simulate the pressing and releasing of the left button of the mouse at the corresponding positions. During the movement, the mouse will be simply set to the corresponding finger positions. Thus, this surface can be used as an interactive drawing pad for many applications, such as *paint* on Microsoft® Windows, as shown in Fig. 7.

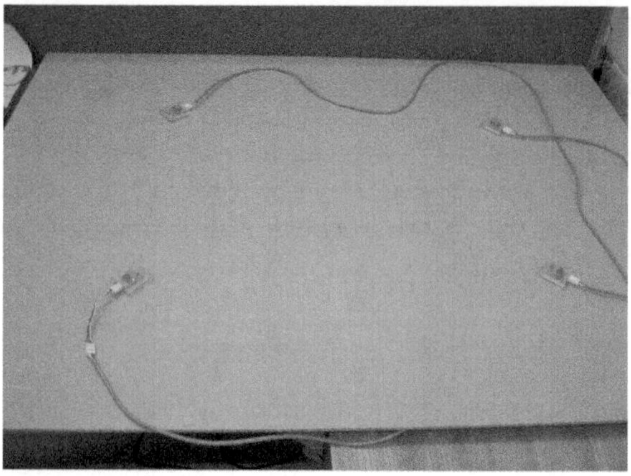

Fig. 6. MDF board with four sensors located at the four corners

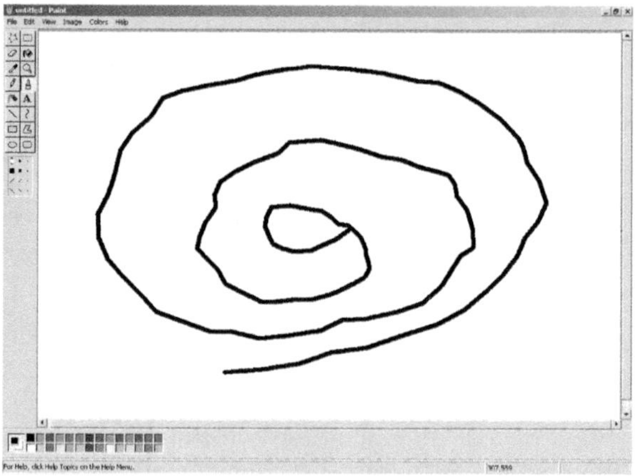

Fig. 7. Screenshot of a drawing produced with the tracking algorithm

4 Conclusion

This paper has presented various approaches for implementing tangible acoustic interfaces. Advantages and disadvantages have been discussed for each method. In summary, the LTM method is simple in hardware requirement, and adaptable to almost any material. However, it requires the prior initialisation at all positions. In contrast, the TDOA method is more useful for large flat surfaces. However, the accuracy of this method is highly reliant on the knowledge of the sound wave velocity for the material. Continuous tracking can be implemented with the Kalman filter calculation and the initial measurement by the MLE based method.

Acknowledgements. This work was financed by the European FP6 IST Project "Tangible Acoustic Interfaces for Computer-Human Interaction (TAI-CHI)". The support of the European Commission is gratefully acknowledged. The authors are members of the EC-funded Network of Excellence on Innovative Production Machines and Systems (I*PROMS).

References

1. Paradiso, J.A., Hsiao, K., Strickon, J., Lifton, J., Adler, A.: Sensor systems for interactive surfaces. IBM Systems Journal 39(3&4), 892–914 (2000)
2. Paradiso, J.A., Leo, C.K., Checka, N., Hsiao, K.: Passive acoustic knock tacking for interactive windows. ACM CHI 2002, Conference, Minneapolis, Minnesota,pp. 20–25 (April 2002)
3. Checka, N.: A system for tracking and characterising acoustic impacts on large interactive surfaces. MS Thesis, MIT (2001)
4. http://www.i-vibrations.com
5. Fink, M.: Time-reversal mirrors. J. Phys. D: Appl. Phys. 26 UK pp. 1333–1350 (1993)
6. Prosser, W.H, Gorman, M.R, Humes, D.H: Acoustic emission signals in thin plates produced by impact damage. Journal of Acoustic Emission 17(1–2), 29–36 (1999)
7. Pham, D.T, Al-Kutubi, M., Ji, Z., Yang, M., Wang, Z., Catheline, S.: Tangible acoustic interface approaches. In: Proceedings of IPROMS 2005 Virtual Conference, pp. 497–502. Elsevier, Amsterdam (July 2005)
8. Knapp, C.H, Carter, G.C.: The generalized correlation method for estimation of time delay. IEEE Transactions on Acoustics, Speech, and Signal Processing, vol.24, pp. 320–327 (1976)
9. Pham, D T, Ji, Z., Yang, M., Wang, Z., Al-Kutubi, M.: Localisation of impacts on solid objects using the Wavelet Transform and Maxmum Likelihood Estimation. In: Proceedings of IPROMS 2006 Virtual Conference, pp. 541–547. Elsevier, Oxford (2006)
10. Welch, G., Bishop G.: An introduction to Kalman filter. http://www.cs.unc.edu/welch/kalman/kalmanIntro.html

Inhabitant Guidance of Smart Environments

Parisa Rashidi[1], G. Michael Youngblood[2], Diane J. Cook[1], and Sajal K. Das[3]

[1] Washington State University, Pullman, WA 99163 USA
{prashidi,cook}@eecs.wsu.edu
[2] University of North Carolina at Charlotte, Charlotte, NC 28221 USA
youngbld@uncc.edu
[3] University of Texas at Arlington, Arlington, TX 76009 USA
das@cse.uta.edu

Abstract. With the convergence of technologies in artificial intelligence, human-computer interfaces, and pervasive computing, the idea of a "smart environment" is becoming a reality. While we all would like the benefits of an environment that automates many of our daily tasks, a smart environment that makes the wrong decisions can quickly becoming annoying. In this paper, we describe a simulation tool that can be used to visualize activity data in a smart home, play through proposed automation schemes, and ultimately provide guidance to automating the smart environment. We describe how automation policies can adapt to resident feedback, and demonstrate the ideas in the context of the MavHome smart home.

1 Introduction

Since the beginning, people have lived in places that provide shelter, basic comfort, and support, but as society and technology advance there is a growing interest in improving the intelligence of the environments in which we live and work. A "smart environment" acquires and applies knowledge about the physical setting and its residents, in order to improve their experience in the setting. A smart environment can be treated as an intelligent agent, which perceives the state of the environment using sensors and acts upon the environment using device controllers in a way that can optimize a number of different goals including maximizing comfort of the inhabitants, minimizing the consumption of resources, and maintaining safety of the environment and its inhabitants.

As the need for automating these personal environments grows, so does the number of researchers investigating this topic. Some researchers are targeting individual devices that provide a useful function, such as programmable appliances. While these devices are novel and useful for limited tasks, they typically do not consider the bigger picture of interacting with the rest of the environment. Others design interactive conference rooms, offices, kiosks, and furniture with seamless integration between heterogeneous devices and multiple user applications in order to facilitate collaborative work environments. Ideas for recognizing environment resident activities [3], for planning environment reminders [5], and for reacting to hazardous situations [4] have been discussed.

J. Jacko (Ed.): Human-Computer Interaction, Part II, HCII 2007, LNCS 4551, pp. 910–919, 2007.

Smart environments have the potential to aid people with mental and physical limitations, to provide resource conservation, and to make our lives more comfortable and productive. The main hindrance to realize this potential is the ease with which smart environment technology can be integrated into the lifestyle of its residents. Our vision is to design a smart environment that adapts to its residents. With our approach, the resident plays a critical role in guiding the enviornment's automation policy.

In this paper we describe an important step toward that goal: design of the ResiSim simulation environment. This environment can be used to visualize daily resident activities and proposed automation schemes. We will explain how it can ultimately be used as a tool for capturing user feedback, and will describe how such feedback can be incorporated into the automation model. We will describe this approach in the context of the MavHome smart home environment.

2 The MavHome Smart Home Environment

The MavHome project treats the smart home environment as an intelligent agent. The home agent perceives the environment using sensors and acts upon the environment using powerline controllers. The MavHome algorithms have been tested in two physical environments, and MavLab workplace environment and the MavPad on-campus apartment. The MavLab (Figure 1 left) contains work areas, cubicles, a break area, a lounge, and a conference room, and is equipped with 54 X10 controllers and sensors for light, temperature, humidity, motion, door usage, and seat usage. The MavPad apartment (Figure 1 right) hosts a full-time volunteer resident and offers additional sensing for leak detection, vent position, smoke detection, CO detection, and window status.

Fig. 1. The MavLab (left) and MavPad (right) smart environments

To automate our smart environment, we collect observations of manual resident activities and interactions with the environment. We mine sequential patterns from this data using a sequence mining algorithm, ED [2]. ED identifies sequences of resident activities that yield a high value using the Minimum Description Length (MDL) principle. The MDL measure prefers that are frequent, long, and periodic (occur at regular intervals).

Next, we predict the resident's upcoming action using a text-based prediction algorithm, ALZ [1]. ALZ parses the history of observed events into substrings and stores them with frequency information in a tree. Relative frequencies from different size contexts (phrase sizes) are combined to generate the probability of each possible action being the next one to occur. The most-likely action is the one reported by ALZ.

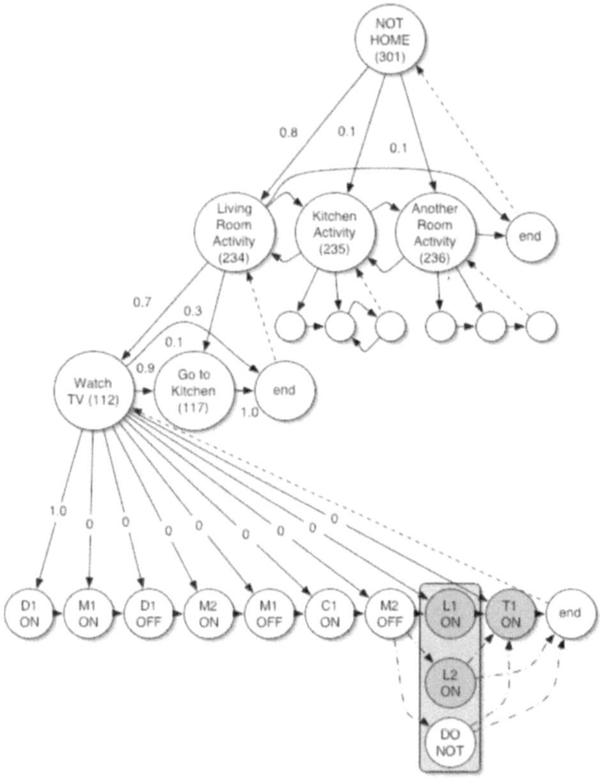

Fig. 2. An example hierarchical Model created from observed resident activities

Finally, a hierarchical Markov model is automatically created from historical event data. Our ProPHeT decision learner uses nodes at the lowest level of the hierarchy to represent raw event information, and uses nodes at the higher levels of the hierarchy to respresent ED-discovered abstract sequences (see Figure 2). ProPHeT use reinforcement learning to generate a policy for this model that will control the environment.

We have implemented a number of case studies in the MavLab and MavPad. The MavLab has been used to automate the activities of a group of six students and the MavPad hosted a succession of three student volunteers. In our case studies, this approach to automation was successful in reducing the number of manual interactions by approximately 75% [7].

3 Simulation of Smart Environments

Simulation is an important tool for performing evaluation and research in many areas. This is particularly true for smart environments, where simulation plays many key roles. First, simulation tools can be used to visualize resident activities, which will in turn provide insights on patterns that can be automated and trends that need to be monitored.

We designed an algorithm, ResiSim, that simulates smart environments as a discrete event simulation. Each object is a self-contained, accurate simulation of an item in the environment and has the ability to be replaced by actual objects, bridging the gap between reality and virtual reality. As in most real-world environments, new objects can be introduced at any time and existing objects can be removed.

Fig. 3. Simulation object types in ResiSim

ResiSim is a Zero Configuration distributed simulator. As such, objects can be of any size and functionality, and are categorized as static, dynamic, simulation, observation, and interface. Static objects simply exist and and do not move. Dynamic objects can move in the environment or change state. Simulation objects provide mathematical support to coordinate interactions between other objects, and observation objects provide a view into the simulation. Interface objects allow either users or other external entities to interact with the simulation. While each object contains attributes and maintains a state, it may also provide functionality in the form of operators. To run a simulation, all that is necessary is to start all of the objects. The static objects make up the environment while the dynamic objects are the key actors. The simulation objects determine the effects of the dynamic objects on each other, causing state changes as necessary. The simulation can be viewed through an observation object that may appropriately display the state of the simulation. User interaction or external information may be channeled through an interface object. Updating is usually event driven, but other types of simulations could be established depending on the core programming of the objects and their defined attributes and operations.

ResiSim consists of three main parts: logical proxy objects, core simulation objects, and user interface objects. Logical proxides are ZeroConf-enabled object processes that are distributed among the available computing assets on the network and represent a physical object (e.g., a lamp or a chair) in the real world. Logical proxies in our work are usually static objects, but could be dynamic if they move around or change state in the environment. Our logical proxies usually take one of two forms — physical or simulated. Physical logical proxies are used to bridge the gap between reality and virtual reality by projecting a logical interface to a real-world object into the simulation environment so that the simulator can actually control the real-world object. For example, we can allow some lights in the real-world to be turned on and off through simulation actions (e.g., a virtual inhabitant can turn on real-world lights). Simulated logical proxies are virtual reality objects that simulate the behavior of the real-world objects they represent.

The core simulation objects include ZeroConf-enabled virtual inhabitant dynamic objects, simulation objects, interface objects, and an observation object. Figure 4 (left) shows an observation object view of the MavLab simulation and Figure 4 (right) shows an interface panel which allows selection of the simulated objects. In our implementation, we aggregate the core simulation objects into the ResiSim Server component. We call this a server because from the simulation core we can serve to clients outside our link-local addresses through IP connections. If the clients are within the link-local network then they participate as ZeroConf objects; otherwise, they must be configured to locate the server on the Internet. The server provides a collecting point for all of the necessary components for a complete simulation; however, all of the constituent components are independent ZeroConf objects. This approach allows for easy dynamic changes in the simulation where any object can be added or removed to the simulation. Removed objects notify ResiSim of their removal through ZeroConf, allowing interacting objects to accommodate the change. Added objects notify ResiSim of their availability and service through ZeroConf, allowing other objects to seek interactions with them. These components comprise a complete Zero Configuration distributed simulation environment.

The ResiSim software architecture is shown in Figure 4. We utilize both real-world and simulated logical proxy objects in our simulation, which allows the decision making function to control either virtual objects in a simulation environment or physical objects in a real-world environment in an identical fashion. This way, the learned policy can be simulated before the policy goes into effect in the physical environment. We have complete 2D and 3D models of the MavLab (containing of 139 modeled objects) and the MavPad (containing 111 modeled objects). These simulations are used to visualize resident activities and learned control policies, which we will discuss next.

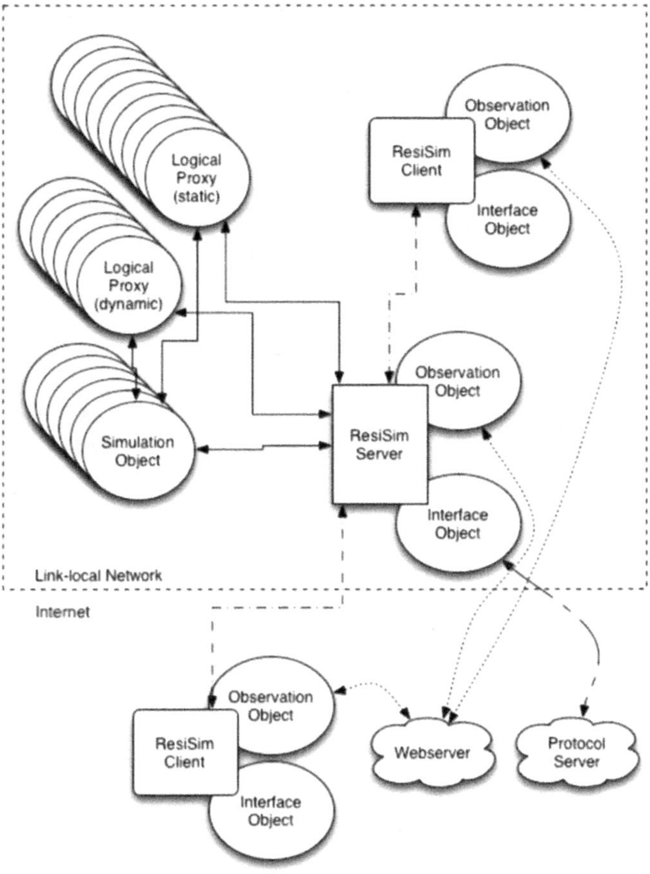

Fig. 4. ResiSim architecture

4 Guiding a Smart Environment

Our initial studies indicate that machine learning technologies can be used to model and predict inhabitant activities, and that a policy can be learned using this information to automate a smart environment. However, what is not investigated here, or in any smart environment project, is how beneficial and pleasing the automation is to the inhabitant. If the environment makes a wrong automation decision, it will be at best an annoyance and at worst a hindrance to accomplishing everyday tasks.

We are investigating techniques for integrating inhabitant feedback and guidance into a smart environment. To do this, the agent's reward signal will now combine feedback from the environment and from the human inhabitant. Designing environments that learn by interacting with everyday people is a neglected topic, although some researchers have investigated human interaction with robots as a teaching mechanism].

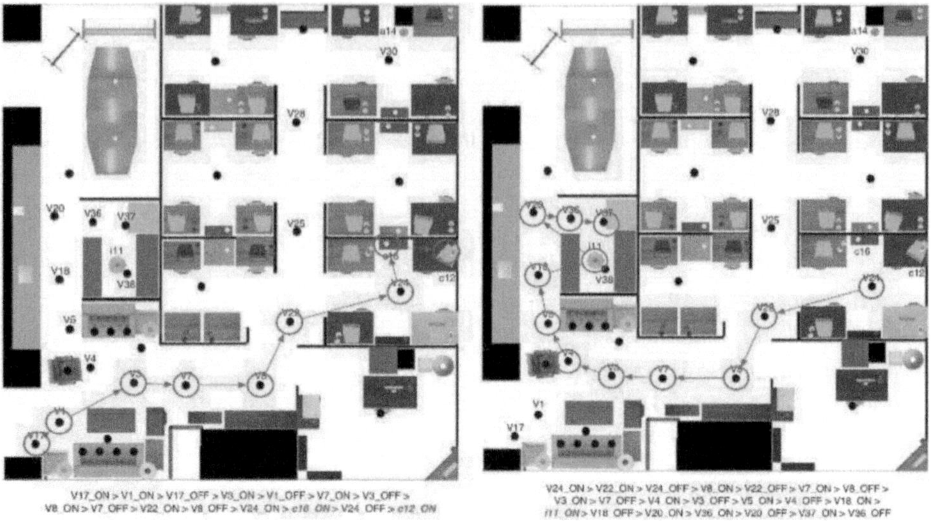

Fig. 5. Visualized MavLab patterns of lab entry to desk (left) and going on break (right). Sensors starting with "V" are motion or door sensors, the rest are X10 powerline controllers.

Inhabitant training of the environment will be based on reactive to inhabitant behavior and on proactively allowing the inhabitant to guide future policy based on simulation. For each approach, we will also need a machine learning algorithm that not only learns an initial model from data, but also refines the model to encompass new actions and alternatives as suggested by the inhabitant.

4.1 Reaction to Inhabitant Feedback

If a smart environment is designed for life-long use, it must have the ability to react to feedback from the inhabitant and adapt to changes in inhabitant lifestyle. An example of reacting to inhabitant feedback is the immediate reversal of an automation action. If the inhabitant immediately turns a light back off that the environment turned on, this constitutes a negative reinforcement for the learner.

A manually-constructed hierarchy will be brittle in the face of such changes. However, our data-driven approach should be able to accommodate these changes, making incremental modifications to the model when appropriate and triggering construction of a new model when needed. Incremental modifications of ProPHeT's hierarchical model will occur based on inhabitant interaction. If Event E is countermanded (reversed within a time threshold from the point at which it was automated) or replaced by an alternative inhabitant action (he prefers light a16 to be on instead of a14), two parallel states are added to the model. The first is a "NO ACT" state. This allows ProPHeT to leave one of the automated actions out given sufficient inhabitant feedback. The second is a state corresponding to the alternative action (in our example, a "a16 ON" state). As shown in Figure 2, these new states connect to all possible downstream states in the Markov chain. Through experience ProPHeT can learn what the appropriate connection should be.

We envision that over time, some of the states in the model may not be needed because they no longer reflect events that actually occur. In order for state space reduction to occur, we will give episodes and individual states a time-to-live counter that is refreshed each time a given part of the hierarchical model is traversed. Unused sections of the HPOMDP will be pruned for increased effciency. This assists in removing unused episodes and clutter inserted from feedback learning that may have been placed without suffcient continued reinforcement. Keeping the model as clean and dynamic as possible promotes fast policy convergence.

Finally, if both the performance of the ProPHeT model degrades steadily over time, this may be an indicator of a drift, or a steady change in inhabitant actions. When this occurs over a period of time, ProPHeT will initiate learning of a new model based on recent data (after the performance started to change). If the new model performs better on recent historic data, a system reboot will be initiated to use the new model.

4.2 Inhabitant Guidance of the Environment

Thomaz and Brezeale [6] show that robots performed better when the human trainer moved beyond reacting to robot actions and guided to the robot to future beneficial tasks. environment. As shown in Figure 5, ResiSim can be run at a real-world pace or sped up to highlight daily activities. Simulation of inhabitant activities in our earlier experiments provides a great deal of information. In the lab setting we can easily observe when the inhabitant arrives, works on the computer, takes a break, interacts with other people in the lab, and leaves. In the apartment setting the observer can tell,

Fig. 6. 3D ResiSim views of the MavLab (top left) and MavPad (bottom left). The reinforcement bars are shown in the upper right of each display, and the lamp object is highlighted in the MavLab. A corresponding interface panel for the lamp appears (right) when the object is selected.

for example, when the inhabitant is cooking, eating, taking a shower, watching television, working, sleeping restfully, and stirring in their sleep.

Using the ResiSim simulator, inhabitants can view past actions and automations. They can also view a simulation of a new policy, by watching the simulated actions play out based on projected inhabitant activities. A feedback bar will be shown on the display (see Figure 6), and the viewer can slide the bar to the appropriate level. The reward signal r is a scalar value in the range [-1,1]. The user can at any point in the simulation click on the interface panel in order to provide reward to the system.

In addition, passing the mouse over individual objects highlights the objects and brings up the corresponding panel. The user can select the desired status of the device (e.g., turn lamp 16 on or off) and a corresponding reward, inputting both pieces of information to the system with a single click. This will guide ProPHeT to introduce a new action at the given point in the policy that has a corresponding reward. For example, a worker may like the lamp on their desk to be illuminated when they first enter the lab. ProPHeT may not include this option in the current model because the inhabitant typically does not perform this activity. However, by highlighting the light object and clicking on a reward, the new possible action will be added to the model and given the corresponding reinforcement.

5 Conclusions and Figure Work

In this paper we discussed a distributed simulator that provides visualization of smart environment resident activities and learned control policies. This simulator will ultimately allow users to provide reactive feedback and proactive guidance to the environment. We anticipate that user guidance of our smart environments will increase satisfaction with automation assistance and promote more wide-spread use of smart environment technologies. Our user interface will be ported to a PDA that the inhabitant can use to provide guidance to the system anywhere, anytime. The PDA interface will also allow the inhabitant to monitor and control the environment remotely. The algorithms will be tested in a smart lab on campus, in a smart apartment on campus with volunteer inhabitants, in a smart apartment of a volunteer elder adult, and in an assisted care facility.

References

1. Gopalratnam, K., Cook, D.: Online sequential prediction via incremental parsing: The Active LeZi Algorithm. IEEE Intelligent Systems, vol. 22(1) (2007)
2. Heierman, E.O., Cook, D.: Improving home automation by discovering regularly occurring device usage patterns. In: Proceedings of the International Conference on Data Mining (2003)
3. Luhr, S.: Recognition of emergent human behavior in a smart home: A data mining approach. Journal of Pervasive and Mobile Computing, vol. 3 (2007)
4. Moncrieff, S.: Multi-model emotive computing in a smart house environment. Journal of Pervasive and Mobile Computing, vol. 3 (2007)

5. Simpson, R., Schreckenghost, D., LoPresti, E.F., Kirsch, N.: Plans and planning in smart homes. In: Augusto, J., Nugent, C. (eds.) AI and Smart Homes, Springer, Heidelberg (2006)
6. Thomaz, A.L., Brezeal, C.: Reinforcement learning with human teachers: Evidence of feedback and guidance with implications for learning performance. In: Proceedings of the National Conference on Artificial Intelligence (2006)
7. Youngblood, G.M., Cook, D.J.: Data mining for hierarchical model creation. IEEE Transactions on Systems, Man, and Cybernetics, Part C (2007)

Application of Tangible Acoustic Interfaces in the Area of Production Control and Manufacturing

Wolfgang Rolshofen, Peter Dietz, and Günter Schäfer

Technical University of Clausthal, Institute of Mechanical Engineering,
Robert-Koch-Str. 32,
38678 Clausthal-Zellerfeld, Germany
{rolshofen,dietz,schaefer,info}@imw.tu-clausthal.de

Abstract. This article explores how physical objects like machine housings can be transformed into natural, seamless, unrestricted touch interfaces. The objective is to design multimodal tangible acoustic interfaces (TAI) that bridge the gap between the virtual and physical worlds. The methods presented are based on the principle that interacting with a physical object modifies its surface acoustic patterns. By visualizing and characterizing such acoustic patterns, it is possible to transform almost any object (for example, a machine, wall, window, table top, giant screen, or arbitrary 3D objects) into an interactive interface. Because of their numerous advantages over other methods, acoustic-based interfaces will have potential for the whole computer and information industry, as well as manufacturing.

Keywords: Tangible Acoustic Interface, Acoustic Source Localization, Production Control, Manufacturing.

1 Introduction

Human beings are able to perceive their physical environment due to their sense organs. Consequently, they can react on it.

Meanwhile, many technical devices have become common standard in everyday life; however, to make full use of them is hardly ever intuitive. At least, not all of human skills could be inserted for Human-Computer-Interaction. At present, communication with the "digital world" takes place through graphical user interfaces (GUI), which are controlled by instruments like keyboard or mouse [1].

Nevertheless, this makes the work already much easier contrary to usage of character user interfaces (CUI) though achievement potential is still unused owing to available features of the human stimuli.

Therefore, an enhancement is constituted by tangible user interfaces (TUI), where digital information is linked with physical objects or at least with areas on their surface. Based on acoustical signals, they are a specialization and they are referred to as tangible acoustic interface (TAI). It is intended to take advantage of originated sound in air or in solids respectively during interaction with any item.

J. Jacko (Ed.): Human-Computer Interaction, Part II, HCII 2007, LNCS 4551, pp. 920–925, 2007.

For instance, this could be machine housings where acoustic sensors detect any interaction on a tangible surface (Fig. 1). Those converted signals are analyzed and induce a machine application.

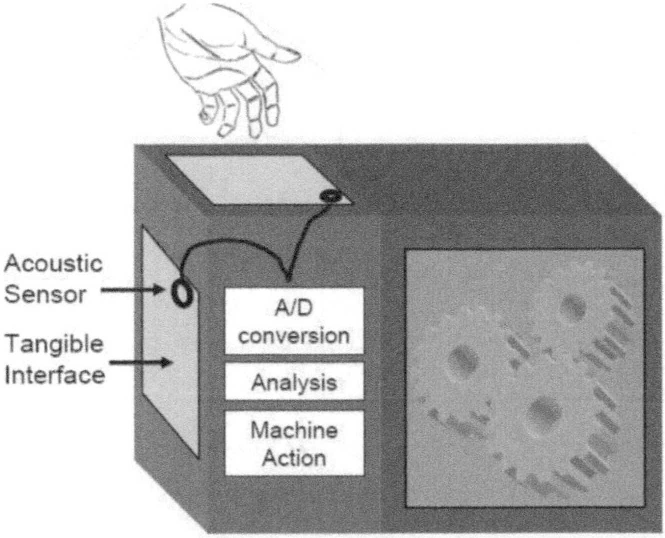

Fig. 1. A user can interact with a machine by touching a tangible interface on its housing. This impact is detected by acoustic sensors. After their signal is converted and analyzed, a machine action can take place.

2 Tangible Acoustic Interfaces for Computer-Human Interaction

For a successful exertion of such interfaces, the knowledge of the place of interaction is necessary. It is for this reason that different methods for localization as well as requisite elements in signal processing are seen from this angle [2,3].

2.1 Acoustic Sensors

To design an object of daily routine as a tangible interface, appropriate sensors are needed. Actions like knocking, tapping or clapping shall be detected. Owing to the vibration of an object as a consequence of interaction, microphones as well as accelerometers are suitable. These are mounted in the space of interest or direct on the surface of the object.

Prevailing conditions like material respectively geometry of tangible interface determine how much sensors and their arrangement are required. Moreover, different localization methods are investigated.

2.2 Source Localization Techniques

Presently, several approaches are investigated with the intention to create TAIs. Subsequent, three basic methods are described.

Comparing with seismology, a state of the art solution is to measure the runtime of the source signal at several sensors. Under the condition of a known propagation velocity the distance between sensor and source position could be calculated. In Fig. 2 four sensors in each corner of the plate detect the acoustic signal which arise at the contact point and spreads out. The time delay of arrival is calculated and refers to the point of interaction.

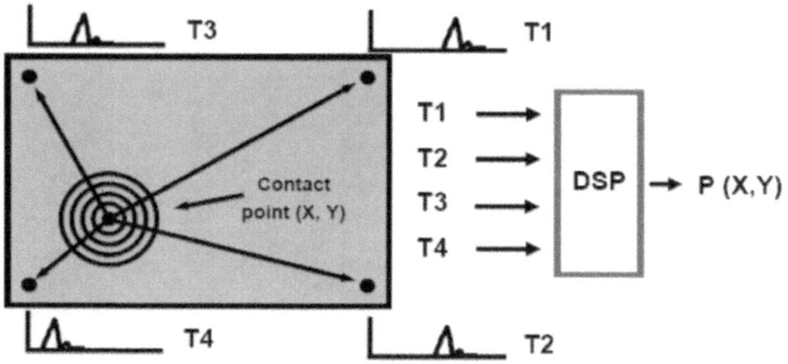

Fig. 2. Time delay of arrival; depending on the source position, signals' propagation time to each sensor position is different. For example, *T4* is the shortest and *T1* the longest duration. The *Digital Signal Processor (DSP)* calculates based on the delay of arrival the source position which is the contact point.

Another method works sufficiently with fewer sensors which is called Time Reversal [4]. During a kind of training, each acoustic wave belonging to a position on the tangible surface is recorded. Then, the time signal is reversed and stored in a database for the following reason. It could be imagined like an echo which is transmitting from the receiving sensor to the source. Each new interaction is compared with these echoes and the best correlation reveals the contact point.

In avoidance of disturbances by surrounding sound, Institute of Mechanical Engineering is investigating a third method based on Acoustic Holography. It is researched if direct contact of sensors on an object's surface is an improvement. For this reason, accelerometers are used in this approach contrary to holography in air. But propagation velocity is not constant in-solids and depends on the material chosen. Therefore, it is essential to pick the most useful frequency for localisation. A suitable criterion will be worked out with more experiments. In spite of numerous boundary effects, Fig. 3 shows that tapping on a steel plate can be found out using this approach for localization. Tap position has been in centre of the plate and is marked by a black circle. Based on colours' intensity, maximum amplitude distribution for a frequency of 1163Hz is in coincidence with it.

Currently, only single impacts can be back-projected [5]. However, in further investigations it is researched if this method is capable to detect multiple acoustic sources simultaneous on various positions.

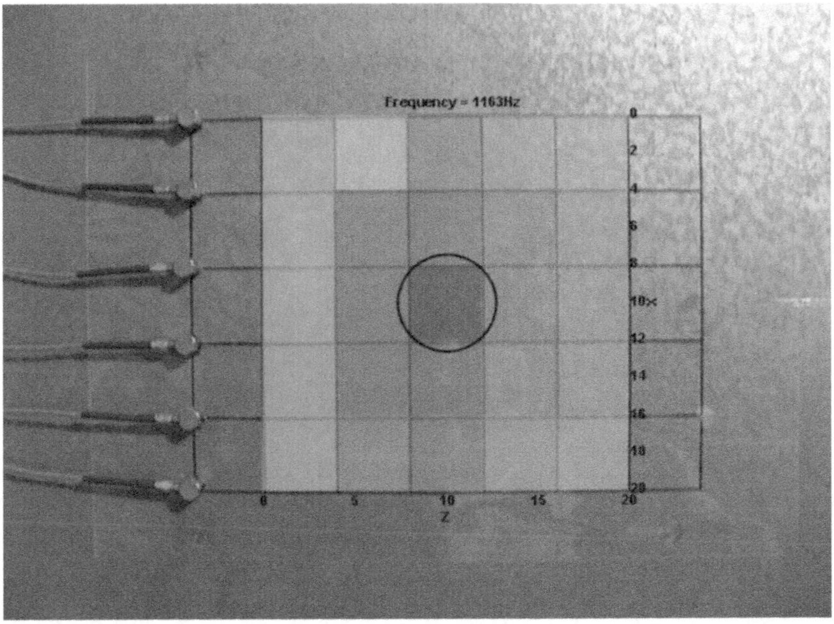

Fig. 3. Representation of a localization result, an approach for in solid Acoustic Holography calculates amplitude distribution for a frequency of *1163Hz* after tapping on a plate of steel in its centre. Position of interaction is marked by a *black circle*.

On the whole, more different localization principles are available and can be applied to design any kind of object in a tangible interface [6,7,8,9].

2.3 Application Scenarios

Doubtlessly, production processes and machines have become more important and complex. Due to this, control about these instruments is going to be more difficult for skilled workers also. Therefore, this increased responsibility has to be taken into account and new ways respectively tools for interaction between human and machine have to be developed. In the European FP6 IST Project "Tangible Acoustic Interfaces for Computer-Human Interaction (TAI-CHI)" new ways for communication have been developed e.g. an interactive ceramic hob (Fig. 4). Correct functionality has been proved by comparing results of calculation on a monitor with tapping positions.

Besides this, potentialities for such interfaces are unlimited also in the range of production control, manufacturing and machine maintenance. Starting from innovative products like low cost desktop keyboards and keypads with no switches, an "invisible mouse" is also possible. It means that users move with their fingers directly on the surface. As well as device-free electronic whiteboards and pointing systems by use of conventional pens or direct by finger can be built. Of course, touch-screens or touch-pads are already available but on the one hand they are expensive and on the other mostly not usable under rough conditions. So, a solution is

Fig. 4. Each control unit can be used by tapping on the ceramic hob. Comparing with the calculation result on the monitor, each interaction can be located successfully. In future a self-adjustable stove could prepare a meal.

appreciated where any surface e.g. machine housing could become an interactive interface. Also, skins for robots or interactive environments in Virtual Reality can be equipped with tangible acoustic interfaces.

3 Prospectus for TAI in Manufacturing

Obviously, such tangible acoustic interfaces enhance the working environment. Machine control is more intuitive and interactive screens are available with reference to worker's education.

Moreover, additional applications for such localization techniques are reachable. Machine tools for punching or perforation need a sophisticated positioning system why not using acoustic sensors and analyze their signals for position determination?

Another scenario is a fully automated production line. Although these machines work autonomous, maintenance or quality assurance work is necessary from time to time. A reason for many accidents is the human factor in such situations, because those machines have to swivel sometimes. In case the worker does not know the next movement or the system does not know his position then crashes are unavoidable. An improvement could be a detection of the worker's position, so that the system stops or at least warns in case of needs.

Acknowledgments

Partly, this work was financed by the European FP6 IST Project "Tangible Acoustic Interfaces for Computer-Human Interaction (TAI-CHI)" and the European Network of Excellence for "Innovative Production Machines and Systems (I*PROMS)". The support of the European Commission is gratefully acknowledged.

References

1. Ishii, H.: Get in Touch – Tangible Bits: Bridging Digital and Physical, Ars Electronica (2001)
2. Reference to the TAI-CHI homepage. URL: http://www.taichi.cf.ac.uk/
3. Crevoisier, A., Polotti, P.: Tangible Acoustic Interfaces and their Applications for the Design of New Musical Instruments, International Conference on New Interfaces for Musical Expression, NIME 2005, Dublin (2005)
4. Ing, R.K., Quieffin, N., Catheline, S., Fink, M.: Time Reversal Interactive Objects. JASA, vol. 5, p. 115 (2004)
5. Rolshofen, W., Dietz, P., Schäfer, G.: Innovative Interface for Human-Computer Interaction. In: Proceedings of the 9th International Design Conference DESIGN 2006, Dubrovnik, Croatia (2006)
6. Xiao, L., Collins, T., Sun, Y.: Acoustic Source Localization for Design of Tangible Acoustic Interfaces. I*PROMS 2006, Virtual Conference, Cardiff (2006)
7. Pham, D.T., Al-Kutubi, M., Yang, M., Wang, Z., Ji, Z.: Pattern Matching for Tangible Acoustic Interfaces. I*PROMS 2006, Virtual Conference, Cardiff (2006)
8. Rovetta, D., Sarti, A., De Sanctis, G., Fabiani, M.: Modelling Elastic Wave Propagation in Thin Plates. European Signal Processing Conference, Florence, Italy (2006)
9. Bornand, C., Camurri, A., Castellano, G., Catheline, S., Crevoisier, A., Roesch, E., Scherer, K., Volpe, G.: Usability Evaluation and Comparison of Prototypes of Tangible Acoustic Interfaces. In: The 2nd International Conference on Enactive Interfaces, Genoa, Italy (2005)

Cyberwalk: Implementation of a Ball Bearing Platform for Humans

Martin Schwaiger, Thomas Thümmel, and Heinz Ulbrich

TU Munich, Institute of Applied Mechanics
schwaiger@amm.mw.tum.de

Abstract. This paper presents an advanced model of a treadmill using balls which are actuated by a belt on a turntable. The platform is able to run at high speeds which are close to normal walking speed and can withstand the load of a 100kg human. Several different tests have been performed to prove the principle on the one hand and to evaluate the upscalability of the system on the other hand. First, a human is walking on the platform at different speeds. The speed is increased until the unit gets instable at about 1.5 m/s. Methods for further stabilization at higher speeds are discussed. Second, a vehicle simulates the movements of a human in an urban environment at a downscaled level. The control recenters the vehicle and the resulting accelerations on the vehicle are calculated and upscaled.

These results are compared to the preliminary results of our partner Max Planck Society Tübingen where the research about the human perception of accelerations is done..

1 Introduction

The development of the virtual world has seen a lot of progress in the last years. One of the big issues is still the goal to enable a person to move freely in the cyberspace without using metaphors which translate gestures or input devices into motion. The most natural way of maneuvering - natural walking - still faces various restrictions. Many innovative approaches can be found such as the Gaiter System [16] which tracks and evaluates the users movements to generate motion in the virtual world without using a specially prepared floor. Thus the real movement is still limited by the room dimensions. The GaitMaster [9] uses footpads which follow the users motion and is able to simulate walking also on uneven terrain but turns are difficult to realize. A foot follower which allows this full turning capabilities is described in a former publication of the author [14]. To enable the user to move into any direction and in any pose he wants (also crawling), solutions were found which set the whole ground underneath the walker in motion with the goal to recenter the user. The energy to move the ground can be either produced by the user itself or with actuators. In the first case, the person stands inside of a sphere or on a spherical calotte. As soon as the person moves, a recentering momentum acts on the sphere which is generated by the force vector of the user which moves out of sphere centre and thus generates a momentum. This principle was realized with the Cybersphere [3] and the Virtusphere

J. Jacko (Ed.): Human-Computer Interaction, Part II, HCII 2007, LNCS 4551, pp. 926–935, 2007.

[10] which both use closed spheres. The Ball-Bearing Disc [4] is an example of a spherical calotte.

In the second case the floor is moved with actuators. The Circula Floor [8] is made up of independent elements which travel from behind the walker to the front and form a new consistent floor. The omnidirectional treadmill (ODT) [2] uses two orthogonal belts which are made up of rolls and thus add the velocities. A different approach, the Torus Treadmill [6] uses several belts which form a complete torus. A completely different system was demonstrated with the BAT [1] whose principle can also be found in a patent application [12]. In this case, balls are aligned in an array which has a belt underneath. This belt can be rotated around the centre of the array. As soon as belt and turntable are actuated, the balls add up the velocities and are able to recenter the person.

An approach using balls to actuate the user shows some very interesting characteristics which predestines the principle for further use in VR environments especially if the person should not be restricted by a harness or rim (except for security reasons). To mention only some advantages, the setup generates only little noise and vibration. By the use of advanced mechanical components and an intelligent control, a very high performance is possible. Moreover the motion is not only limited to walking but includes also crawling and virtually any other motion. Current applications like the BAT [1] only allow very low speeds which are far from walking speed and the platform is not able to bear a human standing on it.

The goal of the cyberwalk project is to build up a system which can bear the weight of a human (100 kg) and has velocities which are near walking speed. Details about the construction itself are published at World Haptics 2007[14]. The size of the prototype which will be presented in this paper is chosen in a way which allows haptic and walking experiments and also a downscaled simulation of a real walker.

2 Principle and Improvements

2.1 Basic Principle

The principle of the platform has been described before (BAT[1], patent application[12], construction[14]) and thus shall only be outlined in brief.

Fig. 1. Platform principle

As seen in figure 1, the platform has two degrees of freedom: a rotational one deriving from the turntable and a linear which is generated by the belt. These two motion vectors are added up by the balls and generate a resulting vector which recenters the person or object on the platform.

The apparatus consists of a turntable which is carried by the frame. This turntable is actuated by a servo motor via a toothed belt. On top of the turntable a conveyor belt is mounted. Within the turntable, a rotational feedthrough transmits the energy and data lines to the conveyor belt system which is also actuated by a servo motor. Thus the surface has two degrees of freedom, namely a linear and a rotational one. On top of the setup, the balls are held in place by a matrix.

Additionally the platform has supporting devices for testing and development. First, two measurement systems are present. One using strings to triangulate the vehicle, another which uses optical, markerless tracking. Second, a vehicle has been developed which moves according to previously recorded GPS motion data of a person.

The current setup provides a ball grid with a diameter of 800mm and contains 4332 balls of 8mm diameter.

Fig. 2. Complete setup of the platform with mechanical position measurement (triangulation)

The Tracker calculates the position of the walker / the vehicle and transmits it to the main control. Here, the actual platform position and speed is computed with the motion data of the vehicle and new speed commands for the platform are generated.

2.2 Improvements

One of the major improvements of the platform can be found in the dynamics of the model. The BAT [1] moving at 0,5 cm/s on its linear axe. The current implementation is now able to generate speeds up to 200 cm/s which is 400 times faster. The acceleration can be up to $5m/s^2$. The rotational degree of freedom is able to rotate at 2 rad/s with an acceleration of $20rad/s^2$. These high values are necessary to handle the requirements of the control when the walker is close to the areas of singularity, lateral to the belt direction from the turntable centre. The achievement of an appropriate speed is very crucial to test the upscalability of the principle.

Moreover the structure is able to carry the dynamic load of an adult person up to 100 kg. The main frame and the conveyor belt support are stiffened with light weight aluminium profiles. The belt material is especially designed for functional grip between belt and balls for secure acceleration of higher loads.

The actuated size of the array is 800mm, formed in a hexagon shape, which is enough to test the platform making small steps with enabled control or normal steps at constant speed.

The matrix itself is one of the most crucial components of the platform. In this case a polymeric structure was chosen as the best solution. An inox steel variant which was manufactured with CNC die cutting showed strong deformations even after special treatment. Moreover the adhesion between steel and belt was quite high and led to slip-stick effects at low speeds. The polymer material had very little friction and independently from any motion speeds or direction did not show slip-stick-effects.

The cylindrical holes were cut using high pressure water cutting. One disadvantage of cylindrical holes is the fact that the balls may be pulled out of the hole as soon as the sole of the foot has enough adhesion when moving up. The solution to this issue are concave shaped holes. They can be manufactured by using a five-axis water cutting machine which creates two plates with cone shaped holes. The balls are placed on one plate, then the plates are glued together. This assembly ensures that the balls stay in place, but the manufacturing process is costly and tends to block balls due to glue and tolerances.

To conclude, the polymer plate with cylindrical holes is an ideal combination which ensures operation on the one hand and feasibility on the other.

3 Experiments and Results

3.1 Walking on the Cybercarpet

One of the most interesting questions is how a human who is walking on the platform will perceive the ground. Our platform has a size of 800 mm in diameter which is sufficient to simulate one whole step of a tall human (figure 3, 1.92 cm tall, 100 kg). The system was accelerated in steps from zero to 1,6 m/s, higher values were unsuitable.

The test person had normal shoes with an almost flat sole. Neither toe nor heel side were specially rounded. When activating the platform, the ground has a very natural feeling according to the test persons. The balls can not be felt because the sole is stable enough to disperse the force over the whole foot in a homogenous way. Immersion is not affected by a foot touching the carpet material. The gap between the 8mm balls is small enough to prevent the shoe to get in touch the carpet material in a way which would be perceivd. Tests with other materials showed that a very stiff sole (plastic plate) was uncomfortable because it rips over the balls when rising and lowering the feet and inhibits the foot to deform in a natural way. A very weak sole on the other hand was not able to withstand the weight. It id deformed until the sole gets in contact with the carpet material, the balls block mostly and started to slide over the belt. Due to the width of the sole, the single balls are not felt by the foot itself.

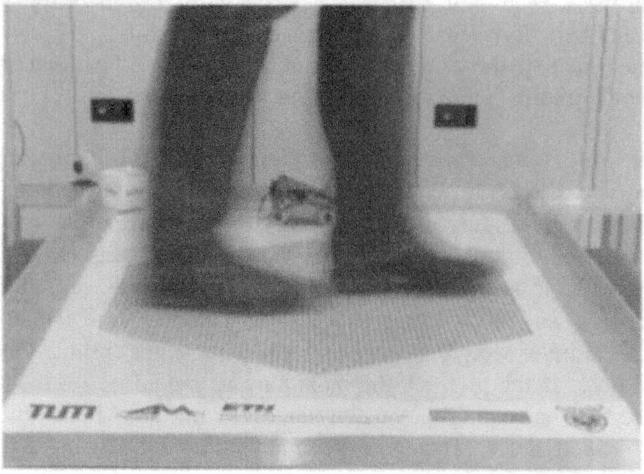

Fig. 3. Human walking on platform

The sole material is exposed to high stress. The balls have only very small contact to the surface in the beginning. As the load rises, they deform the sole within the boundarys of stiffness to enlarge the area of contact. When moving over the platform, a section of the sole is deformed completely each time when it rolls over one ball. This leads to wear on the sole and the wear debris (figure 4) can clearly be seen on the platform.

In the following, the wear debris starts to enter the holes where the balls fit in which leads to blocking of the balls, flip out of balls and degradation of the belt. As a

Fig. 4. Wear debris of the sole

result the sole of the walker has to meet certain criteria, it has to be abrasion-resistant and stiffness must be well chosen.

3.2 Simulating a Downscaled Path on the Cyberwalk

To simulate an environment in a downscaled version, it must be ensured that each element is downscaleable without changing the result in an inappropriate way. The first step is to retrieve representative motion data of a walker in the city. Different scenarios are possible, e.g. a person heading to a named place walking fastly and using the shortest path. A completely different set of motion can be found if the person is strolling around in the city without a direct goal.

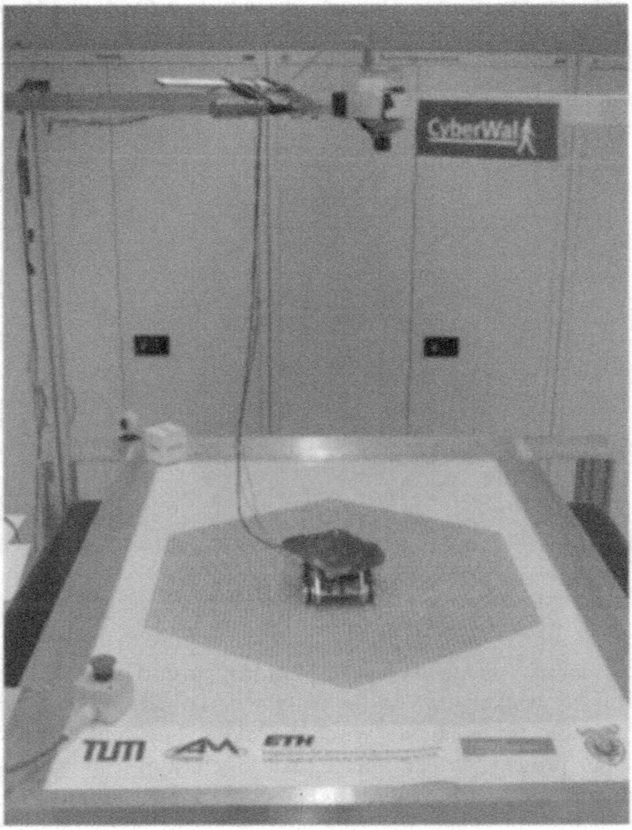

Fig. 5. Platform moving the vehicle

Our Project partner, the Max Planck Society in Tübingen started to research the nature of human behaviour in urban areas. In order to track the human precisely they assembled a backpack which uses GPS and accelerometers to track the path trough e.g. a city including position and orientation. The data is very accurate because of the sensor fusion algorithms which are used. This motion data is now downscaled and transferred into a path which can be used by the control of a non-holonomic vehicle. An analysis of the data showed that the transition of the path from a holonomic to a non holonomic system is not a big problem because the human quite rarely uses his ability to step aside. For the overall control algorithm, small sidesteps e.g. to avoid collision with another person do not change the overall direction of motion and thus do not alter the result of the control in a significant way.

In order to track the position of the vehicle, a markerless tracker is applied. This tracker is provided by pour project partner from the ETH Zürich. The basisc of the tracker are described here [13], the Cybercarpet uses an enhanced version with a flexible ellipse size. The vehicle simulating the human is equipped with an image of a person seen from the top. The combination of the camera's focal width and distance to the platform surface generates the same image as a camera would see from a higher distance on a full scale platform. Another reason to use a venhicle for the small scale platform is the fact that actually available biped robots are not able to reach the required speeds. Nevertheless plans to test the platform with an e-nuvo [5] biped robot exist.

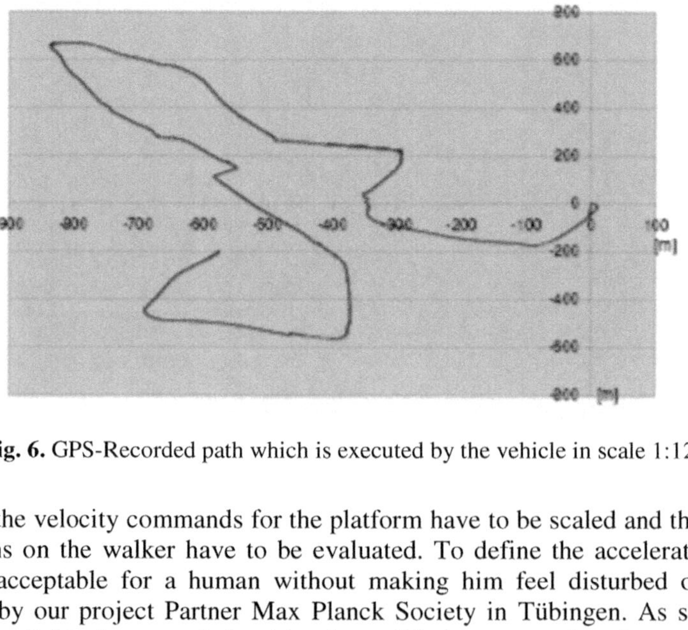

Fig. 6. GPS-Recorded path which is executed by the vehicle in scale 1:12

Finally, the velocity commands for the platform have to be scaled and the resulting accelerations on the walker have to be evaluated. To define the acceleration values which are acceptable for a human without making him feel disturbed or sick are researched by our project Partner Max Planck Society in Tübingen. As soon as the values are available the control algorithm is modified to ensure that the person is only exposed to limited forces. The algorithm itself is developed by our partner UOR [11] and is refined during the whole project.

Figure 6 shows a pathway where a person walks trough a city. The length of the walk was about 32 minutes with a total length of 4 km.

This pathway is downscaled with a ratio of 1:12 and applied to the vehicle. The tracker transmits the coordinates to the control and commands for the platform are generated. The resulting pathway of the vehicle on the platform can be found in figure 7. A diameter of 0.6 meters is used while 0.8 meters would be available. The peak velocity commands are 0.12 m/s for the linear DOF and 0.2 rad/s for the rotational DOF. These values are far below the capabilities of the platform and are caused by the minimization of accelerations on the "body" of the walker - in our case: the vehicle. The peak accelerations on the vehicle stay below $0.1 m/s^2$, this maximum value is an estimation of preliminary results of our project partner, the Max Planck Society in Tübingen.

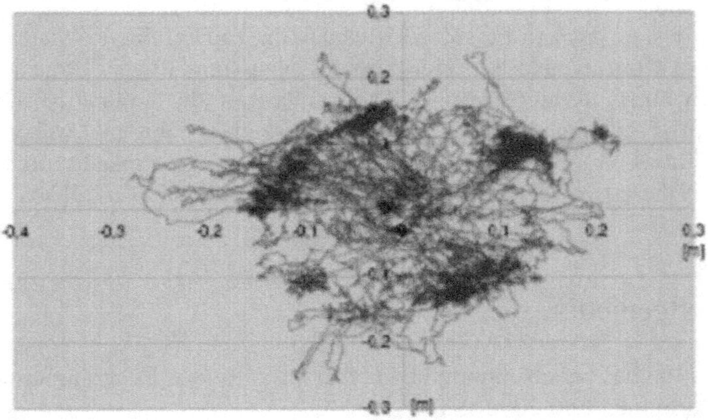

Fig. 7. Recentered track of the vehicle on the platform acquired by the vision system

When the actual velocities are multiplied with the scale of the experiment, the original estimation of the required velocities is prooved.

The results show that the quite high accelerations close to the singularities can be avoided by an intelligent control strategy. It preserves the walker to come close to the singularities and in case it happens takes care that he will be moved out of the singularity smoothly.

4 Further Work

The control algorithm will be jointly refined and the findings respecting the accelerations on the walker will be implemented. Moreover experiments will be conducted with a small biped robot which does not reach downscaled human walking speed but is very vulnerable to inappropriate accelerations. The robot's gyros can moreover be used to evaluate the whole system.

The platform itself will be equipped with an additional interface which allows a command rate of more than 100 Hz - more than the speed of the optical tracker but several methods (Observers, Extrapolation) will be used to predict the steps inbetween.

The shoe of the walker must be researched in detail to find the optimal combination between friction, stiffness and a non-abrasive behavior. The carpet material can moreover be shaped in a way that prevents the balls to flip out of the holes even if debris occurs.

5 Conclusion

The platform has shown an excellent behavior and enables the person standing on it to walk at high speeds without feeling disturbed by the ball carpet. Although the current ball array gets a little bit unstable at speeds above about 1,5 m/s there are many possibilities to overcome this fact. Nevertheless this speed is already perceived as fast walking and the effectively useable speed is still 300 times faster than former implementations. The potential of the principle is massive although several constructive issues have to be solved. Besides the capabilities to bear a real human walker, the platform is able to perform downscaled simulations of tracks which were recorded of walkers in the real world. The results from the application of downscaled tracks are satisfying and show that the whole system is stable and well dimensioned. The accelerations on the body of the walker are within a reasonable limit. Combining the results of these two sectors the base for the construction of a full scale platform is settled.

Acknowledgements

This publication has been supported by Cyberwalk Project, EC-contract number FP6-511092, Action line: Fp6-2002-IST-C-2.3.4.1.

The video tracker was provided by Michael van den Berg, ETH Zürich Computer Vision Lab - Dept. Van Gool.

We were able to use preliminary research results about the human perception by Ilja Frissen, the motion data for the experiments was provided by Manish Sreenivasa, both Max Planck Institute for Biological Cybernetics Cognitive and Computational Psychophysics - Dept. Bülthoff.

The control was implemented together with Paolo Robuffo Giordano, Dipartimento di Informatica e Sistemistica "A. Ruberti Universita' di Roma La Sapienza" - Dept. De Luca.

References

1. Darken, R.P., Cockayne, W.R., Carmein, D.: The omni-directionaltreadmill: A locomotion device for virtual worlds. In: Proc. ACM UIST, pp. 213–221 (1997)
2. Ernst, M., Buelthoff, H.: for Max-Planck-Gesellschaft zur Foerderung der Wissenschaften e.V. Munich GER. Foerdereinrichtung insbesondere fuer ein laufband, Filed, 2004 Published 10-2005. DE 102004 016 429 A1 (2004)
3. Fernandes, K.J., Raja, V., Eyre, J.: Cybersphere: the fully immersive spherical projection system. Commun. ACM 46(9), 141–146 (2003)
4. Huang, J.Y.: Transactions on multimedia. IEEE, vol. 5,1st edn. (March 2003)
5. ZMP Inc. e-nuvo biped robot. http://www.zmp.co.jp/e-nuvo
6. Iwata, H.: Walking about virtual environments on an infinite floor. In: Proc. IEEE Virtual Reality Conference 1999, p. 286 (1999)
7. Iwata, H.: Locomotion interface for virtual environments. In: Proc. 9th Int. Symp. onRobotics Research, pp. 275–282 (2000)

8. Iwata, H., Yano, H., Fukushima, H., Noma, H.: Circulafloor. In: Proc. SIGGRAPH 2004, pp. 3 (2004)
9. Iwata, H., Yano, H., Nakaizumi, F.: Gait master: A versatile locomotion interface for uneven virtual terrain. In: Proc. IEEE Virtual Reality Conference 2001, p. 131 (2001)
10. Latypov, N.N., Latypov, N.N.: The virtusphere (2006) http://www.virtusphere.com
11. De Luca, A., Mattone, R., Giordano, P.R.: Feedback/feedforward schemes for motion control of the cybercarpet. In: Proc. ICRA 2006, pp. 275–282 (2006)
12. Nagamori, A., Wakabayashi, K., Ito, M.: The ball array treadmill: A locomotion inter-face for virtual worlds. In: Workshop on New Directions in 3D User Interfaces (at VR 2005) Bonn, Germany (2005)
13. Nummiaro, K., Koller-Meier, E., Van Gool, L.: An adaptive color-based particle filter (2002)
14. Schwaiger, M., Th"ummel, T., Ulbrich, H.: A 2d-motion platform: The cybercarpet March (2007)
15. Schwaiger, M., Ulbrich, H., Th"ummel, T.: A foot following locomotion device with force feedback capabilities. In: Proceedings of VIII Symposium on virtual Reality, Belem, Brazil pp. 309–321 (2006)
16. Templeman, J.N., Denbrook, P.S., Sibert, L.S.: Virtual locomotion: Walking in place through virtual environments. In: PRSESENCE vol. 8(6), pp. 598–617 (1999)

A Huge Screen Interactive Public Media System: Mirai-Tube

Akio Shinohara[1], Junji Tomita[2], Tamio Kihara[1], Shinya Nakajima[1], and Katsuhiko Ogawa[1]

[1] NTT Cyber Solutions Labs., Nippon Telegraph and Telephone Corp.
1-1 Hikari-no-oka, Yokosuka, Kangawa Japan
[2] NTT Resonant Inc. 1-6-1 Otemachi, Chiyoda, Tokyo, Japan
shinohara.akio@lab.ntt.co.jp, tomita-j@nttr.co.jp, {nakajima.shinya,kihara.tamio,ogawa.katsuhiko}@lab.ntt.co.jp

Abstract. We develop an interaction framework for huge public displays with multiple users in public spaces such as concourses, lobbies in buildings, and rendezvous spots. Based on this framework, we introduce an interactive system for public spaces called Mirai-Tube[1]. This system creates a scalable interactive media space and has a scalable real-time recognizer. A Mirai-Tube system was installed in the underground concourse of Minato Mirai Station in Yokohama. We conducted a demonstration experiment from 1st Feb. to 31st Oct. 2004. This trial represents the world's first experiment in a real public space in terms of its scale and its time period. We evaluate our interactive media system from three points of view: acceptability as a public media, how much attention the public pays to it, and its understandability as an advertising media. This paper describes the features, implementation, and operation of the interactive media system and the results of the evaluation.

Keywords: interactive public displays, ambient displays, interactive advertising, pattern recognition, subtle interaction.

1 Introduction

The purpose of this paper is to establish a new interactive media in public spaces. Information is being provided in various ways in public spaces such as concourses at stations, lobbies in buildings, and rendezvous spots. Recently, the interactive provision of information in public spaces has taken on increased importance. The major reason for this is the relative weakening of TV CMs by the emergence of multi-channel digital broadcasting. Another reason is the wide variation in personal interests and preferences.

The conventional method of providing information in public spaces has been paper-based such as posters, but digital displays are becoming increasingly prevalent in public spaces (see [4]). There are a number of reasons for this. One is that digital displays are becoming larger with much higher definitions. Another reason is that content

[1] Mirai means future in English. Tube is the underground.

J. Jacko (Ed.): Human-Computer Interaction, Part II, HCII 2007, LNCS 4551, pp. 936–945, 2007.

delivery from remote locations has become possible through the use of broadband networks. Public digital displays can change their content by the minute and by the hour. Most public displays are designed for one-to-many broadcast content distribution, and are minimally interactive. Therefore, digital displays fail to grab the attention of the public.

We turn now the content for public displays; most public displays show motion picture content like TV CF. However, such content is not suitable for people moving through concourses, because their movement means that they fail to see the whole motion picture. Under some circumstances, it's good to use freeze-frame pictures like posters and fliers. Current public displays do not work very well from the viewpoint the effective provision of information in public space.

Let us now look at interaction with users. The dominant example is the kiosk machine. Such machines mainly target information services with interactive interfaces. Users choose their item of interest via a touch-panel, and the kiosk machine then displays detailed information of the chosen item. Kiosk machines provide a specific service only to people who are interested in the service. When a kiosk machine is idle, it plays some CM content that no one watches. Furthermore, kiosk machine are designed for single user operation. The proposal made in this paper lies between these two approaches (electric displays and kiosk machines); it is a new interactive media in public spaces that combines mass reach with personal interaction.

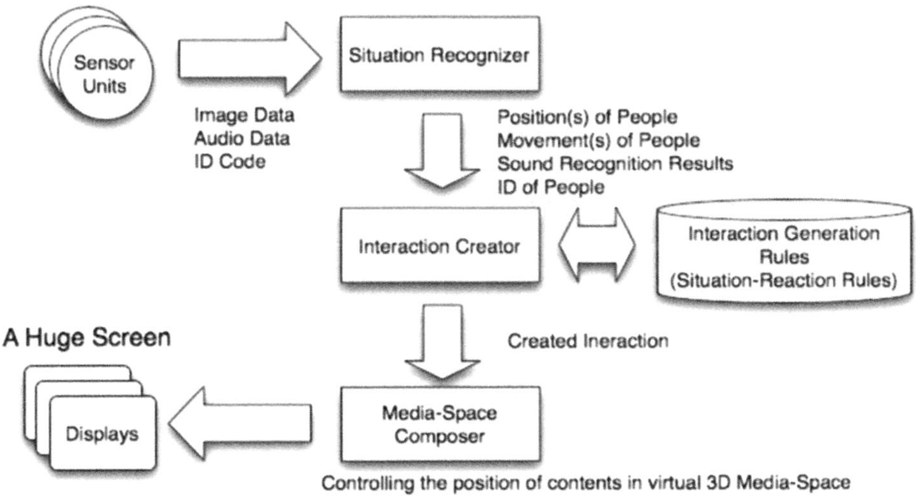

Fig. 1. The Conceptual Structure of Mira-Tube

Many studies on public displays focus on public spaces within organizations. Interactive Public Ambient Display (see [7]) focuses on transitioning from implicit to explicit interaction. The prototype recognized body orientation and user proximity to the display to realize implicit interaction, and recognized hand gestures for explicit interaction. FXPAL's Plasma Posters (see [3]) are large screen, digital, interactive poster-boards to facilitate informal content sharing within teams, groups, organizations and communities. They used a touch panel for interaction, the same as kiosk machines. Opinionizer (see [1]) uses a projector in social gatherings such as book launch parties and welcome parties. The users input information by keyboard and share it via the large display.

Interactive digital art in museums has become popular (see [5]). However, interactive art and entertainment in public spaces are not so popular. Interactive advertising in public spaces is popular as evidenced by the increasing number of public kiosks but interactive advertising with large displays is less well known. Interactive advertising through large displays in public spaces is planned for the Metro in Copenhagen, Denmark (see [2]). This system uses projectors and is planned to be installed at the landings of escalators in a concourse.

These related works focus on public spaces for supporting communities and organizations, not the general public. Few papers have even attempted to support interaction with multiple users.

In this paper, we focus on huge public displays, cinema screen size, in real public spaces such as concourses, lobbies in buildings and rendezvous spots. We implement a system called Mirai-Tube that realizes huge interactive spaces. We evaluate this system as installed in an actual public space.

The next section describes interactive media systems for public spaces. Section 3 describes the demonstration experiment. Section 4 reports the evaluation method and results. The final section gives our conclusions and future work.

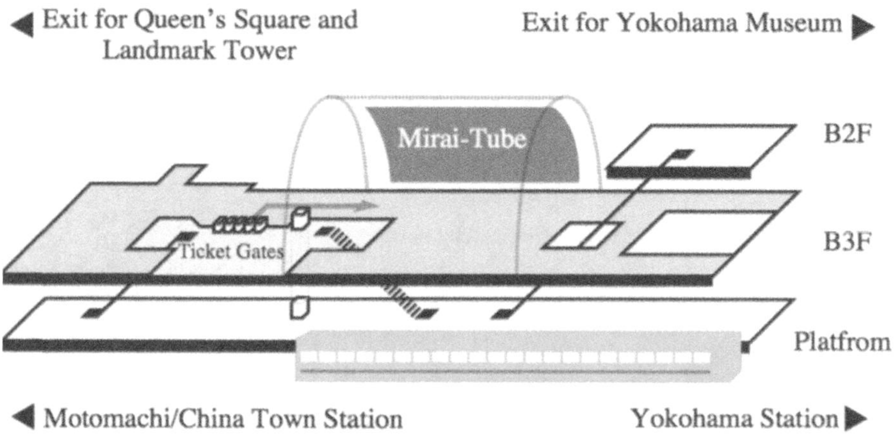

Fig. 2. Map of Minato Mirai station

2 Interactive Media in Public Spaces

Interactivity offers two advantages. The first advantage is on-demand provision of information, i.e. users can request the system to present the items or goods that they are interested in. Another advantage is its higher awareness due to adaptive controls.

Image changes and sound effects can be adaptively controlled according to people's movements or situations, and this increases awareness and/or attention.

To verify the first point, we performed an experiment at 'Shibuya Station' in Tokyo, in 2001 (see [6]). This experiment employed 12 movie promotions and the passers-by could select the movie of interest via their mobile phone's Internet access interface.

This paper focuses on the second advantage. By controlling audio and visual effects, interactive media can realize higher awareness and attention than conventional static displays.

Our system assumes a large public space as a concourse in a station, lobbies in buildings, and rendezvous spots. In such spaces, multiple users can interact simultaneously with the same system. To that end, the screen is large enough to support multiple virtual screens. In addition, considering installations for various locations, the system can be configured flexibly. That means that the system creates a scalable interactive media space and has a scalable real-time recognizer.

We formulated the conceptual structure of a huge screen interactive system (see Fig.1). Situation Recognizer combines information from multiple sensors such as video cameras, RF ID readers, and microphones to recognize the conditions in the space in real time. For example, the video cameras allow the system to recognize the position of people, as well as the speed and acceleration of their movements.

Interaction Creator controls contents scheduling and matches the recognition result with Interaction Generation Rules for controlling content display.

Media-Space Composer creates a continuous virtual media space and controls the synchronized output of several PCs in real time. Any number of these screens can be combined freely either vertically or horizontally, enabling high-resolution image spaces that can be flexibly configured.

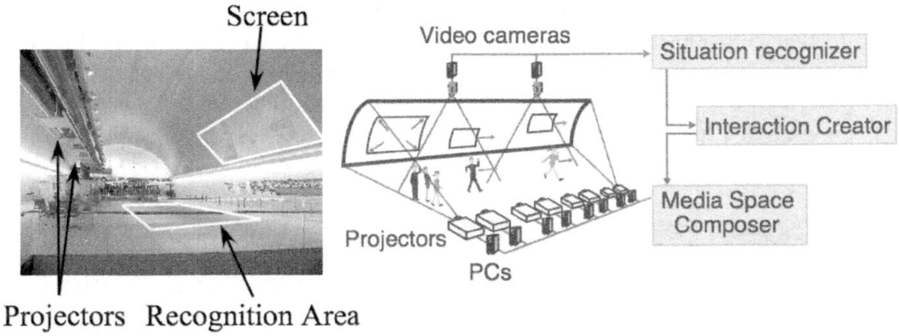

Fig. 3. Mirai-Tube System

3 Mirai-Tube Demonstration Experiment

As the place to implement the experimental system, we selected the Minato Mirai station of the Minato Mirai line. The two key reasons for this choice were that we could set up our experimental system before the station was opened, i.e. we could start our experiments from the start of the line, and the station has a huge public space (20 meters wide by 60 meters long) that combines a passage way with a rendezvous space. Minato Mirai line is a brand-new subway line that opened on 1st Feb. 2004; it runs through the center of Yokohama city. Minato Mirai station is in the middle of the subway line and serves social institutions (an exhibition hall and an art museum), commercial complex, amusement facility, and business offices.

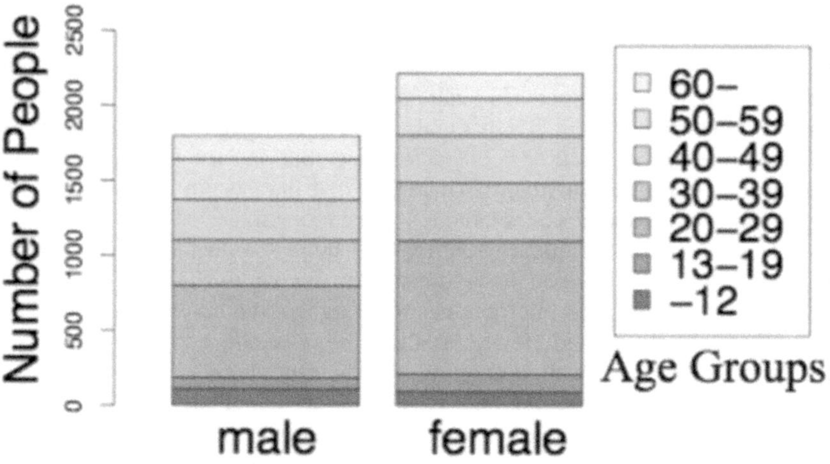

Fig. 4. Number of Passerby in Mirai-Tube

Our demonstration experiment was installed B3F concourse in the station (see Fig. 2). This system uses 2 cameras for recognition and 8 projectors, which were stacked into 4 pairs side by side, forming a massive screen measuring 12 meters long by 3 meters high - the equivalent of a 500-inch screen - on the vaulted wall of the concourse (see Fig.3).

This space is not main aisle. The station sees 14,000 people a day but only 1,000 of them passed through the experiment space (by observation from 10 a.m. to 18 p.m. between 9th and 12th Sep. 2004). Fig. 4 shows a breakdown of the observation results by gender and age group.

Fig. 5. Face Poiesis and Lagrange Game

We conducted a demonstration experiment from 1st Feb. to 31st Oct. 2004. During the experiment, we presented 20 interactive advertisements and 30 interactive digital art works.

As interactive digital art, we employed 'Face-Poiesis'. In 'Face-Poiesis', more than 500 face pictures are generated automatically by a genetic painting technique. When a passerby stops in front of the face pictures, the face at the corresponding position in the screen is zoomed up (see Fig. 5). When the passerby goes away, the face picture vanishes and a new one is displayed.

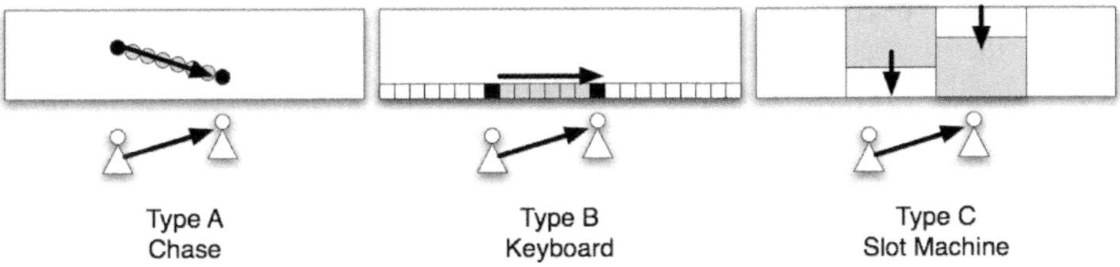

Fig. 6. Interaction Type Evaluated

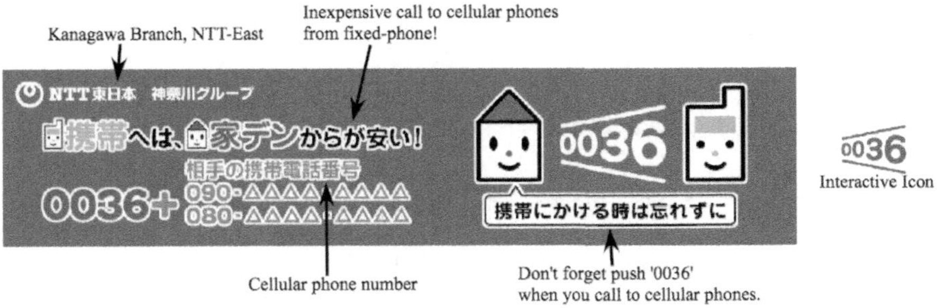

Fig. 7. Evaluation Content

We also employed the interactive game called 'Lagrange Game', which is intended trigger ad-hoc collaboration among people who gather by chance in public spaces. In the Lagrange Game, when three people stand in recognized areas forming a regular triangle, the computer displays something on the screen (see Fig. 5). This game requires the cooperation of three people. During the trials couples would often call to a passing stranger to join the game.

4 Evaluation Experiments

4.1 Goal of the Assessment

We evaluated the system from the following points:

1. For evaluating the Mirai-Tube system as a public media, we surveyed the public's acceptance and impressions of the system.

2. As an advertising service, the public attention and awareness of our system were first investigated.
3. We then surveyed the public's understandability and interest in the Mirai-Tube content.

For evaluating points 2 and 3, we used the following 3 types of interaction (see Fig. 6).

- Type-A '*Chase*': When someone enters the area, an icon appears at the corresponding point on the screen. As he moves, the icon follows him. The system sounds at the beginning and end of the movements.
- Type-B '*Keyboard*': We put 21 square icons on the bottom of the screen. They imitate a sort of keyboard instrument. When someone stands in front of one of the 21 icons, the corresponding icon changes and a specific tone is sounded. Each of the 21 icons has its own tone like a piano keyboard.
- Type-C '*Slot Machine*': The screen and the interactive area are divided into 4 parts. Each part of the screen is shown in different color. When someone enters one of the 4 parts of the area, the corresponding part of the screen scrolls like a slot machine making a rolling sound.

The content used in the evaluation was an advertising film produced by NTT East Corp. that indicated that when calling from a fixed line phone to a mobile phone, the charge could be discounted by dialing '0036' before the number to be called (see Fig. 7).

4.2 Evaluation Results

In this subsection, we describe the evaluation results with regard to acceptability, awareness, and understandability of our system.

Table 1. Impressions of the Interactive Media

Impression (Positive)	Score	Impression (Negative)	Score
Interesting	1.81	Persistent	-0.58
Strong Impact	1.48	Noisy	-0.65
Impressive	1.45	Annoying	-0.94
Conspicuous	1.39	Feeling Bad	-1.32
Easy to understand	0.29	Nuisance	-1.45

Acceptability. We hired 31 subjects, showed them the 3 types of interactive contents and gave them questionnaires. For each impression word, subjects were asked to assign one of five grades; 'exactly yes: 2', 'yes: 1', 'neutral: 0', 'maybe no: -1', and 'no: -2'. The result, average scores for the 31 subjects, is shown in Table 1. As for the positive impressions, the differences between 'interesting' and the others, and those between 'easy to understand' and others, were both significant (bilateral T-Test, $p<0.05$). Hence, our interactive contents are interesting but not easy to understand. For the negative impressions, the joint average score of 'persistent' and 'noisy' differed from that of 'feeling bad' and 'nuisance' significantly (bilateral T-Test, $p<0.05$). Therefore, very few people had impressions of 'feeling bad' or 'nuisance', but there were a few people who felt that it was 'persistent' or 'noisy'. In any case, the result is that our interactive system is interesting and acceptable as a media in public spaces.

Attention. We then evaluated how much attention the paid to the interactive contents. On 10th (Fri) Sep. 2004 and 11th (Sat), 10 a.m. to 6 p.m., each type of interactive content was presented for 15 minutes with one hour interval. We observed 1,956 people who passed (or stopped by) the Mirai-Tube area. We define 'being aware of' as 'glancing at', or 'paying attention' as 'watching the same content for 3 seconds or more'.

The result is shown in Table 2. Roughly speaking, more than half of the public passed through the area without seeing the content. This is because the screen is set 3m high and hence, without looking up, people cannot see the screen. Awareness may improve better as Mirai-Tube becomes more familiar.

Among the 3 types of interactions, Type C, *Slot Machine*, received higher scores for both awareness and attention. This might be somewhat trivial, since Type D interaction offers the most drastic screen movement.

Table 2. Attention paid to Interactive Media

	Being aware of	Paying attention	Number of people
Type A (Chase)	39.9%	17.4%	671
Type B (Keyboard)	42.5%	17.8%	628
Type C (Slot Machine)	45.1%	20.4%	657
Total	42.4%	18.6%	1,956

Interest and Understandability. To assess interest and understandability, 205 passersby were interviewed (46 people for type-A, 54 people for type-B, and 48 people for type-C). Each subject was asked to assign one of 5 levels 'exactly yes: 2', 'yes: 1', 'neutral: 0', 'maybe no: -1', and 'no: -2' to both interest and understandability. The result is shown in Fig. 8.

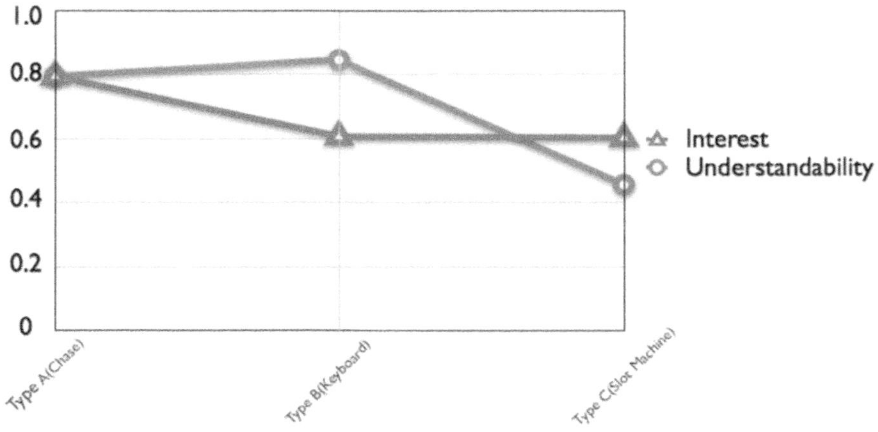

Fig. 8. Interest and Understandability

As for interest, type-C *Keyboard* received the highest score but was not significant (unilateral T-Test, $p>0.1$). From the public interest point of view, there is no drastic difference among the 3 interactive types.

As for understandability, the difference between type A *Chase* and type C *Slot Machine* represented a significant trend (unilateral T-Test, $0.05<p<0.1$). In other words, compared to *Chase*, the *Slot Machine* interaction is difficult to understand. In the interactions other than *Slot Machine*, the picture on the screen is basically stable. On the other hand, the *Slot Machine* interaction splits the screen into 4 parts regardless of the figures or texts on the picture and this rude splitting may reduce understandability.

More generally, the modification created by the interaction should take account of the semantic content of the presentation.

5 Conclusion and Future Work

We have developed an interaction framework for huge public displays with multiple users in public spaces such as concourses, lobbies in buildings, and rendezvous spots. Based on this framework, we introduced an interactive system for public spaces called Mirai-Tube. This system creates a scalable interactive media space and has a scalable real-time recognizer. A Mirai-Tube System was installed in the underground concourse of Minato Mirai Station in Yokohama. We conducted a demonstration experiment from 1st Feb. to 31st Oct. 2004. This paper described the features, implementation, and operation of the interactive media system and the results of the experiment.

We evaluated our interactive media system from three points of view: acceptability as a public media, how much attention the public paid to it, and its understandability as an advertising media. The results confirmed that our system is sufficiently interesting and hence acceptable as a public media. The results of attention and understandability assessments indicated a trade-off. To strengthen attention, the movement or modification created by the interaction should be drastic or radical. To improve understandability, however, minor modifications or modifications that take account of the semantic content are preferable.

As future work, we plan to study how to combine moving pictures and sounds so as to create much more efficient interactive content. We also plan to evaluate the impact of ad hoc collaboration among people who gather by chance in public space with content like the 'Lagrange Game'.

Acknowledgments. This research was carried out as collaborative project among Yokohama Minatomirai Railway Company, NTT-EAST and NTT Cyber Solutions Laboratories. 'Face Poiesis' was designed by Toshihiro ANZAI and Rieko NAKAMURA.

References

1. Brignull, H., Rogers, Y.: Enticing People to Interact with Large Public Displays in Public Spaces. INTERACT Conference, pp. 17–24 (2003)
2. Brooks, T., Kruger, V., Guglielmi, M.: A real-time tracking environment towards cross modal applications in public installations and education. In: Proceedings Computers in Art and Design Education Conference, Copenhagen, Denmark (2004) http://asp.cbs.dk/cade2004/

3. Churchill, E.F., Nelson, L., Denoue, L., Helfman, J., Murphy, P.: Sharing multimedia content with interactive public displays: a case study. In: Proceedings of the 2004 conference on Designing Interactive Systems, Cambridge, MA, USA, pp. 7–16 (2004)
4. Erdelez, S.: Information encountering: a conceptual framework for accidental information discovery. In: Proceedings of an international conference on Information seeking in context, pp. 412–421 (1997)
5. Sparacino, F. (Some) Computer Vision based Interfaces for Interactive Art and Entertainment Installations. INTER_FACE: Body Boundaries, Paris France (2001)
6. Shinohara, A., Nakajima, S.: Shibu-Doco Fair - the electric transit advertising trial with cellular phones. IPSJ SIG Technical Report, 2002-MBL-22, (IN JAPANESE) pp. 39–46 (2002)
7. Vogel, D., Balakrishnan, R.: Interactive Public Ambient Displays: Transitioning from Implicit to Explicit, Public to Personal, Interaction with Multiple Users. In: Proceedings of the 17th annual ACM symposium on User interface software and technology, Santa Fe, NM, USA, pp. 137–146 (2004)

Kitchen of the Future and Applications

Itiro Siio[1], Reiko Hamada[2], and Noyuri Mima[3]

[1] Department of Information Sciences, Ochanomizu University,
2-1-1 Otsuka, Bunkyo-ku, Tokyo 112-8610, Japan
siio@acm.org

[2] Graduate School of Information Science and Technology, The University of Tokyo,
7-3-1 Hongo, Bunkyo-ku, Tokyo 113-8656, Japan
reiko@mtl.t.u-tokyo.ac.jp

[3] School of Systems Information Science, Future University-Hakodate,
116-2 Kamedanakano-cho, Hakodate, Hokkaido 041-8655, Japan
noyuri@fun.ac.jp

Abstract. A kitchen is a place where food is prepared and education and communication activities relating to food are carried out. As it is a place that witnesses more activity when compared to the other parts of the house, there are many potential ubiquitous computing applications that can be installed in a kitchen. We are developing a computer-augmented kitchen environment, the Kitchen of the Future, that incorporates various computing elements into a standard kitchen unit. In this paper, we describe an overview of the Kitchen of the Future system and three applications, that is, recording and replaying of a cooking process, videoconferencing cooking instructions, and interactive cooking navigation.

Keywords: Kitchen of the Future, Ubiquitous computing, computer-augmented kitchen, home computing, computer-aided cooking, remote instruction.

1 Introduction

A kitchen is not just a place of labor. Throughout history, the activity of preparing food has been accompanied by (and even used as an excuse for) social interactions and the development of social bonds. Modern lifestyles and convenience foods have reduced the time and effort required for cooking; however, at the same time, they have reduced opportunities for interactions. We believe that the introduction of computer technology in a kitchen not only improves cooking efficiency but also revitalizes the kitchen as a place of learning and communication. For example, installing support systems such as a system for communicating with friends and family members in remote areas and installing one for storing interactive multimedia contents that can provide guidance on cooking can make cooking an enjoyable experience.

For this purpose, we are developing a computer-augmented kitchen environment with embedded video cameras, displays, microphones, switches, sensors, and a network [6]. This "Kitchen of the Future" allows people to use applications for facilitating communication by placing cooking guides on the Internet, learning

J. Jacko (Ed.): Human-Computer Interaction, Part II, HCII 2007, LNCS 4551, pp. 946–955, 2007.

cooking by using these guides, supporting communication and learning through videoconferencing with kitchens in remote areas, and assisting interactive cooking by using multimedia. In this paper, we will report the benefits of the Kitchen of the Future that was ascertained by actually cooking with the aid of these applications.

2 Kitchen of the Future

The Kitchen of the Future is a computer-augmented kitchen environment that incorporates various computing elements into a standard kitchen unit, as shown in Figure 1. Our kitchen has four workplaces comprising a sink, cooking stoves, and two preparation spaces. In each workplace, we have installed a liquid crystal display (LCD), a camera, a microphone, and a foot switch, and we have connected them to a computer system and the Internet. We have implemented three such kitchens in remote areas and have networked them for the purpose of experimenting with the communication system with regard to activities such as remote cooking support.[1]

Fig. 1. Overview of the "Kitchen of the Future." Video cameras, and microphones, LCDs, and foot switches are installed under the cupboard, on the wall, and on the floor, respectively.

Downward-facing video cameras are installed under the cupboard so that the cooking process can be recorded clearly. Such a position for the cameras is also employed in other systems [7]. These cameras capture only the users' hand movements and not their faces and the interior of their rooms, and therefore invasion of privacy by the video cameras in a house can be avoided. When conducting a remote videoconference using this system, those who desire privacy might prefer such a position for the cameras.

---

[1] Two kitchen counters were installed in Tokyo, and another was installed in Hokkaido.

We have installed foot switches in the lower part of the kitchen counter, as shown in Fig.1. The foot switches are for recording sounds and images that illustrate the cooking process, switching between cameras and displays for remote communication, and controlling the multimedia contents that are used in the cooking process. Since these operations are performed during cooking, i.e., when the user's hands are occupied or wet, they should be performed using a hands-free method. The possible methods include voice recognition, gaze control, and gesture input. There are examples of the use of such methods [2], but we feel that foot switches are appropriate because people can use it without facing a recognition error.

In the following section, we will introduce three applications that are installed in the Kitchen of the Future: a system for recording and replaying a cooking process, a remote cooking support system, and a cooking navigation system.

3 Recording and Replaying of Cooking Process

3.1 Recording and Web Publishing

The Internet has proved popular for the sharing of cooking experiences, and there are recipe-based Web communities[2] with a million users per month. However, in a conventional kitchen where people's hands are occupied most of the time, it is difficult to record images of the cooking process. We believe that the Kitchen of the Future will help in creating web-ready recipes under such a circumstance. Therefore, we developed an application to record cooking in the Kitchen of the Future. The application monitors the operation of the foot switches. When a foot switch is pressed, the application takes a picture of the kitchen counter during cooking and records a five-second voice memo to explain the cooking process.

The images and sound data clip collected are automatically posted on the Internet as a recipe Web page, as shown in Fig.2. In this page, people can browse the images of the cooking process and listen to the voice memo. The Web page also provides editing functions such as the deletion of unnecessary images/sounds or the addition of hand-written notes by clicking on an image.

We actually cooked in the Kitchen of the Future to record the cooking process (Fig.3). Operating the foot switches was easy and we could record the images freely, which was like teaching a person near us how to cook. The total number of images that was taken was 67. The five-second voice memo seemed to be ok a sufficient duration.

3.2 Replaying of Cooking Process

The recipe Web pages mentioned above contain the information on the cameras that are used for recording and on the order of the recording; therefore, they can be used to indicate the cooking process at the appropriate workplaces at different times. This enables users to follow the original cooking process precisely and comprehend the different steps involved; therefore, a user can simultaneously perform two steps such

[2] For example, www.cookpad.com.

Fig. 2. An example of a recipe Web page with pictures and voice memo that show a cooking process. Simple editing functions such as deletion of unnecessary images/sounds or addition of hand-written notes are also provided.

Fig. 3. A user is recording his cooking process using cameras and microphones that are activated by foot switches

as washing vegetables while stewing on the stove. Therefore, we developed an application to show the originally recorded cooking process on four displays installed in the Kitchen of the Future. The application provides images and sounds to illustrate the cooking process on a particular display. When a user presses the foot switch of the workplace after completing an assigned work there, the next cooking process will be shown on the display at the next designated workplace. The user can follow the cooking process by moving between the workplaces and following the instruction on the displays in order.

A subject (24-year-old male) who had little experience in cooking participated in an experiment. He tried to cook by browsing the recorded cooking process on our application (Fig.4) and was subsequently interviewed. Being a novice at cooking, it was beneficial for him to learn how to arrange the cookware and ingredients at each workplace. He mentioned that it was good to understand where to place the pots, pans, and ingredients by observing the images shown on the displays. He pointed out that the foot switches were operable even when his hands were wet, and the operation was not tiring. On the other hand, there were some drawbacks. The quality of some still images was not clear; for example, the image of the pieces of onion on the cutting board was not clear. The subject pointed out the necessity of providing moving images.

Fig. 4. A user is cooking while replaying the recorded pictures and sounds of the cooking process on the LCDs. The images are displayed on one of the four LCDs at the workplace. When he completes the displayed step, he can view the next step by pressing the foot switch.

4 Videoconference for Cooking Instruction

The computer-augmented kitchen allows remote communication. To support communication between kitchens, we conducted an experiment on providing cooking support through a videoconference system installed in a kitchen. If remote communication through videoconferencing is possible, parents, for example, can teach their children residing in remote areas to cook; further, people can learn cooking from a professional cook.

Two pairs of Kitchens of the Future in remote areas are networked and a dedicated videoconference system is installed. The videoconference system relies on the LCDs, microphones, speakers, and foot switches provided in the Kitchen of the Future. The system monitors the state of the foot switches, identifies the workplace where the switch is pressed, and shows the video chat window on a nearby display. As a result, users at both the kitchens can watch the other partner's activity from the same position.

Fig. 5. An expert (upper) and a beginner (lower) who are cooking in the distant kitchens

We conducted the experiment on remote cooking support by networking the kitchens in remote areas using this system (Fig.5). A cooking expert in one kitchen assisted a beginner in the other kitchen via videoconference. The experiment proceeded well in general. It seemed that the expert could assist the beginner as though they were cooking in the same kitchen. During the planning phase of the experiment, we expected that the video screen would help the beginner to understand how the expert cooked. In fact, however, the beginner had to concentrate on the assigned work and was busy listening to the oral instruction rather than looking at the display. The expert, on the other hand, viewed the video screen often to assess the status of the beginner and to give precise instructions. When seasoning, the beginner seemed to be puzzled because he could not understand how to salt the food properly. This kind of problem will be solved if we create a device to provide information on the salinity concentration via the Internet.

5 Interactive Cooking Navigation

5.1 Happy Cooking

Prior to this work, we had developed a multimedia cooking support application called "Happy Cooking" [3]. The input data of Happy Cooking are cooking recipes, movie files of the cooking processes, and index information for each scene of a movie. Using these data, Happy Cooking organizes the cooking process automatically to minimize the cooking time and to complete each dish on time. In the process, it displays the text and images in proper order and guides the users.

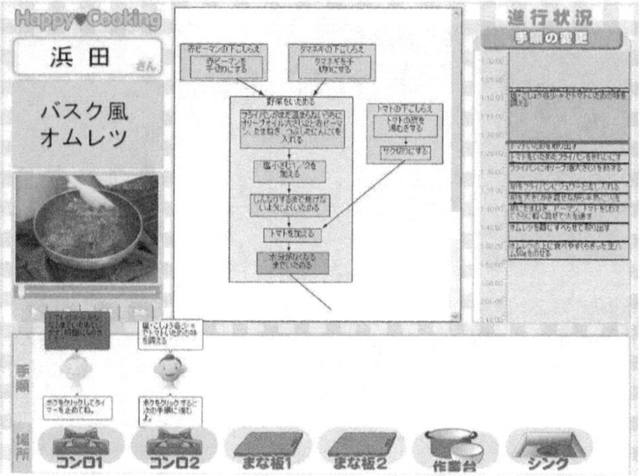

Fig. 6. An example image in the original version of Happy Cooking

Fig.6 shows an example image in the original version of Happy Cooking. The icons appearing at the bottom of the screen represent the instructions that the user must follow, and the movie of the activity is played repeatedly on the left side of the screen. At the same time, users can confirm the cooking process by looking at the flow graph at the top of the screen. When the users click the icon at the bottom of the screen after finishing the assigned work, it shows the next work to be done.

Happy Cooking was generally operated using a pen tablet display. Therefore, users had to place the kitchenware aside to pick up the pen device for operating the display. As a result, users cooking under a time constraint panicked. In addition, when users cooked at a kitchen counter away from the display of Happy Cooking, they had to move back and forth between the kitchen and the display to check the instructions. A cooking support system requires a hands-free interface and the display to be located near the users. It is important for the distance between the users and the system to be minimal.

5.2 Improvement of the User Interface

Happy Cooking is an interactive support system that users rely on during cooking. However, as mentioned earlier, there are various restrictions on the activities in a kitchen. It was found that the existing interface could cause many problems that could seriously affect the usability of the software. Therefore, we installed Happy Cooking in the Kitchen of the Future to make it an interactive cooking support system using multi displays and foot switches.

First, the movement of the users can be minimized by showing the assigned instructions on the displays installed in all the four workplaces of the kitchen. For example, users can be taught cooking by showing them instructions such as "cut an onion into small pieces" on the display near the cutting board or "heat two tablespoons of butter in a pan" on the display near the stove. Replaying the cooking

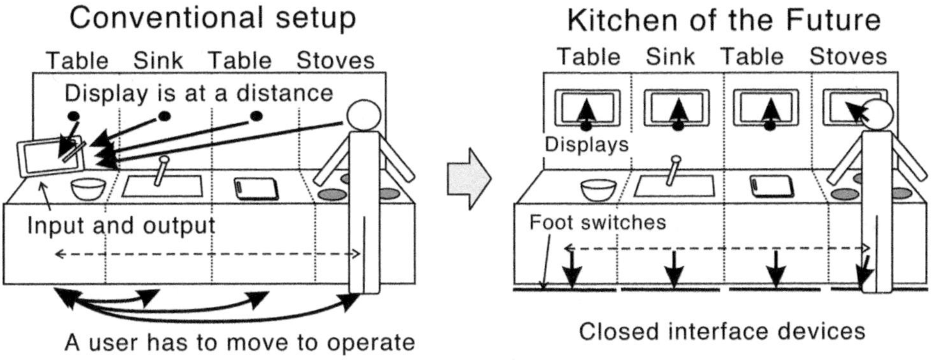

Fig. 7. Original (left) and improved (right) Happy Cooking user interface

image enables the users to imitate the activity and enhances their learning dramatically.

Next, we utilized the foot switches on the floor of all the four workplaces so that users could operate the system comfortably even though their hands were occupied or wet. This enabled the users to operate the system without moving from the workplaces. Since their hands were free and they did not have to change their posture for the operation, the stress level due to the interaction with the system can be considered to be minimal. Fig.7 illustrates the conventional interface and the new user interface that is optimized by the Kitchen of the Future environment.

For the purpose of comparing the conventional user interface with the Kitchen of the Future, three subjects participated in an experiment. Each subject cooked one dish. All of them responded that the foot switches were easily operable when compared to a conventional pen tablet interface. Furthermore, the subjects liked the multi display facility, which enabled them to cook uninterruptedly by displaying the quantity of ingredients in large fonts right in front of their eyes.

6 Related Works

Many conventional computer technologies that are used in offices and factories have the potential of being employed in the kitchen.

Cooks Collage [7] is a memory aid system to help people keep track of a cooking process while being interrupted by everyday events such as conversations with family members, telephone calls, and visitors. Our system, "Kitchen of the Future," focused on the communication and educational aspects in a kitchen environment.

Counter Intelligence [1] displays information in a kitchen environment by using image projection on walls and worktables and uses embedded displays in the handles of the drawers in a kitchen counter. Intelligent Kitchen [5] has a mobile robot that indicates the next action by inferring a user's actions in the kitchen. We adopted stable devices such as LCDs and foot switches to realize a practical cooking support system.

Gaze and voice interfaces that are designed for kitchen use, are installed in some interactive recipe systems such as eyeCOOK [2]. CounterActive [4] projects recipes on the surface of the kitchen counter. We aimed to realize practical recipe browsing in a kitchen environment by using clear on-wall displays and recognition-error-free foot switches.

7 Summary and Future Plan

This paper introduced the Kitchen of the Future, a computer augmented kitchen environment with embedded displays, video cameras, microphones, sensors, switches, and networked remote kitchen counters. We have implemented three kinds of applications in the kitchen, i.e., recording and replaying of a cooking process, videoconferencing for cooking instructions, and interactive cooking navigation.

We are planning to enhance the current applications by adding facilities for motion picture handling, cooking time measurement, and image and voice quality improvement. We are also developing new devices such as a remote salt-sensing system and multifunction foot switches using Radio Frequency Identification (RFID) tag readers.

Acknowledgments

This work was partially supported by the Ministry of Education, Science, Sports and Culture, Japan (Grant-in-Aid for Scientific Research, 17300272, 2005-2008) and the Cleanup Corporation. During the development of the system, we received technical assistance from Hiroshi Miyazawa, Shuichi Sakai, Yukitoshi Suzuki, Jun Okabe, Hidenori Tsuji, and Shinichi Satoh. We also received valuable advice from Takeo Igarashi.

References

1. Bonanni, L., Lee, C.-H., Selker, T.: CounterIntelligence: Augmented Reality Kitchen, Extended Abstracts of Computer Human Interaction (CHI), 2005, pp. 2239–2245. ACM Press, New York (2005)
2. Bradbury, J.S., Shell, J.S., Knowles, C.B.: Hands On Cooking: Towards an Attentive Kitchen, CHI '03 Extended Abstracts on Human Factors in Computing Systems, pp. 996–997. ACM Press, New York (2003)
3. Hamada, R., Okabe, J., Ide, I., Satoh, S., Sakai, S., Tanaka, H.: Cooking Navi: Assistant for Daily Cooking in Kitchen, MULTIMEDIA '05. In: Proceedings of the 13th Annual ACM International Conference on Multimedia, New York, USA, pp. 371–374. ACM Press, New York (November 2005)
4. Ju, W., Hurwitz, R., Judd, T., Lee, B.: CounterActive: An Interactive Cookbook for the Kitchen Counter, CHI '01 Extended Abstracts on Human Factors in Computing Systems, pp. 269–270. ACM Press, New York (2001)

5. Nakauchi, Y., Fukuda, T., Noguchi, K., Matsubara, T.: Intelligent Kitchen: Cooking Support by LCD and Mobile Robot with IC-Labeled Objects. In: Proc. of the 2005 IEEE/RSJ International Conference on Intelligent Robots and Systems (IROS2005), pp. 2464–2469 (2005)
6. Siio, I., Mima, N., Frank, I., Ono, T., Weintraub, H.: Making Recipes in the Kitchen of the Future, Extended Abstracts of the 2004 Conference on Human Factors and Computing Systems, p. 1554. ACM Press, New York (2004)
7. Tran, Q.T., Calcaterra, G., Mynatt, E.D.: Cook's Collage: Deja vu Display for a Home Kitchen. In: Proceedings of HOIT 2005, April 13-15, pp. 15–32 (2005)

A Tangible Game Interface Using Projector-Camera Systems

Peng Song, Stefan Winkler, and Jefry Tedjokusumo

Interactive Multimedia Lab
Department of Electrical and Computer Engineering
National University of Singapore (NUS)
Singapore 117576
{psong,winkler,jefry}@nus.edu.sg

Abstract. We designed and implemented a tangible game interface using projector-camera systems. The system offers a simple and quick setup and economic design. The projection onto a paper board held by the user provides more direct viewing as well as more natural and flexible interaction than bulky HMD's or monitor-based game interfaces. Homography calibration techniques are used to provide geometrically compensated projections on the board with robustness and accuracy.

Keywords: Projector-camera systems, projector-based display, interface design, tilt-board, homography calibration, augmented reality, tangible user interface (TUI).

1 Introduction

With the prevalence of low-cost projectors and cameras, more and more projector-based entertainment systems come into existence. Traditional displays such as CRT monitors and LCD panels are limited by their display size and heavy weight. For large-scale display walls, projectors provide better display quality compared to screens because of the lack of physical seams. However, entertainment activities involving projectors are usually watching movies, playing video games, etc. which only exploit the projector's characteristics in creating large displays. Cameras, if combined with projectors, can enable an intelligent projection system to project certain content and "see" it at the same time. This empowers a projector-camera system to support more complex interactions with the virtual and real world.

A projector's capability of projecting images onto objects or surfaces, combined with a camera's capability of seeing the objects and surfaces, enables the use of projector-camera systems in a variety of augmented reality applications. The early Everywhere Displays [1,2] and iLamps [3] augment the real world with a projector-camera system, but there is very little user interaction. These two systems are mainly designed to help label the real world and simulate the texture/effects on real world objects respectively. The more recent active pursuit tracking projector-camera system [4] is designed to help humans interact with volumetric MRI data, while the handheld projector [5] is aimed at both labeling

J. Jacko (Ed.): Human-Computer Interaction, Part II, HCII 2007, LNCS 4551, pp. 956–965, 2007.

objects and playing games. However, holding a projector in the hand still hinders the user's interaction in spite of the relative lightness of the portable system. Motion-intensive games cannot be played on handheld projectors, which limits the user's gaming experience.

An alternative interaction approach is mixed reality games where users have to wear head-mounted displays (HMD's) or view monitors [6] while moving objects to play the game. HMD's provide 3D views to the user but affect the comfort and flexibility of players. Besides, they are quite expensive and hard to set up in a new environment. Object-handling interactive games such as Magic Cube [7] provide more flexibility to the user, and the cost is also quite low. However, the separation of the display on the monitor from the object held by the user requires good hand-eye coordination and is not intuitive. Other tangible user interface (TUI) applications such as Geniebottles [8] require active sensors, which are more intrusive in terms of setup and use.

We have designed and implemented a new tangible and interactive interface for games using a projector, a camera and a paperboard. Our system has several advantages:

- *Economic design.* Our system comprises a paperboard together with a cheap off-the-shelf webcam and a projector of any type, all of which are readily accessible; no extra devices, such as sensors, HMD's, or cubes are needed.
- *Easy setup.* The setup and calibration are simple and quick. A normal home-user pc is sufficient to run the application, as it is computationally inexpensive.
- *Direct viewing.* The games are directly projected onto a tilt board, which provides real-time undistorted views, unlike traditional mixed reality games, where the display is separate from the object.
- *Natural and flexible interaction.* The interactions include natural manipulations of the tilt board to complete different tasks. Holding and manipulating a lightweight cardboard gives the user comfort and flexibility in playing games.

In Section 2, the design of our system is elaborated, followed by a discussion of the system calibration in Section 3. The implementation and results are presented in Section 4.

2 Interface Design

Projector and camera are mounted on tripods. The cardboard is held in the field of view of the camera and the projector. Since the board is light and can be manipulated easily by the user, this tangible interface provides direct viewing and interactive capability. Users move the board for interaction and watch as the projected content changes accordingly.

As shown in Figure 1, the camera is overlooking the projected content on the cardboard. The geometric distortion is captured by the camera and compensated in real-time such that the game interface shown on the cardboard is always undistorted. The geometric compensation is achieved by homography transformation. Fiducial markers are placed on the paper board for tracking its 3D orientation.

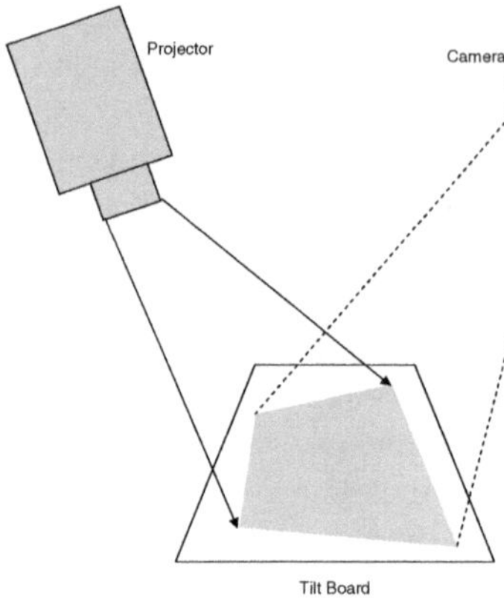

Fig. 1. System design. The projector is mounted above and projecting onto the tilt board. The projection area is observed by the camera. The tilt board acts as the user interface as well as the display.

Our system only requires a cheap commodity projector with an off-the-shelf webcam. Users need not wear or hold any special devices other than a piece of paper to play games ont, hence it provides direct, natural and flexible interactions between the player and the computer.

A single projector-camera pair can be used for single-user games, while multiple projectors and cameras can be used to support multi-player games either in a collaborative or competitive fashion. An example of a multi-player projector-camera setup is shown in Figure 2.

3 Geometric Calibration

While playing the game, users have to tilt the cardboard for interaction, which results in oblique projection from the projector. In order to compute the orientation of tilt board and to compensate for the geometrically distorted content projected on the tilted board, geometric calibration techniques are used. Homography calibration is used to compensate for the geometric distortion caused by oblique projection on to the board, and marker tracking is used for estimating the pose of the board.

3.1 Homography Calibration

In an obliquely positioned projector-camera system setup, the geometric relationship needs to be recovered to correctly display an image for the viewer,

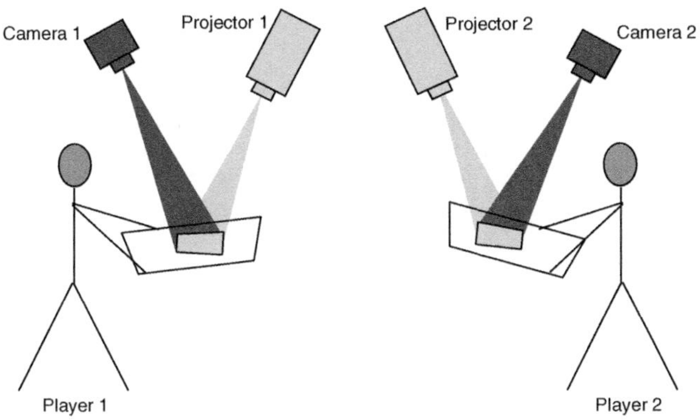

Fig. 2. Multi-player setup. By replicating multiple projector-camera pairs, multi-player games can be played on our interface either in a collaborative or competitive fashion.

otherwise the image shown on the board will be severely distorted, as shown in Figure 3.

As the distortion is predominantly the result of perspective projection, pre-warping the image via a homography can be used to correct for the distortion. The homographies between projector, camera, and the board need to be calibrated prior to pre-warping. Sukthankar *et al.* [9,10] proposed an automatic keystone correction method for the above setup. Assuming that the pinhole model may be used for projectors and cameras, the transforms between the projector, the camera, and the tilt board can all be modeled as 2-D planar homographies:

$$\begin{bmatrix} kx \\ ky \\ k \end{bmatrix} = \begin{bmatrix} t_1 & t_2 & t_3 \\ t_4 & t_5 & t_6 \\ t_7 & t_8 & t_9 \end{bmatrix} \begin{bmatrix} X \\ Y \\ 1 \end{bmatrix} \tag{1}$$

where (x, y) and (X, Y) are corresponding points in either two frames of reference, and $\mathbf{t} = (t_1, ..., t_9)^T$ with $|\mathbf{t}| = 1$ are the parameters of the homography. Thus the homography here only has 8 degrees of freedom and can be recovered from as few as 4 pixel correspondences. If more than 4 pixel correspondences are available, more accurate solutions can be determined by a least-squares method. Given m point correspondences, we can have the following $2m \times 9$ matrix $\mathbf{A}$:

$$\begin{bmatrix} X_1 & Y_1 & 1 & 0 & 0 & 0 & -X_1x_1 & -Y_1x_1 & -x_1 \\ 0 & 0 & 0 & X_1 & Y_1 & 1 & -X_1y_1 & -Y_1y_1 & -y_1 \\ X_2 & Y_2 & 1 & 0 & 0 & 0 & -X_2x_1 & -Y_2x_2 & -x_2 \\ 0 & 0 & 0 & X_2 & Y_2 & 1 & -X_2y_2 & -Y_2y_2 & -y_2 \\ \vdots & \vdots & \vdots & \vdots & \vdots & \vdots & \vdots & \vdots & \vdots \\ X_m & Y_m & 1 & 0 & 0 & 0 & -X_mx_m & -Y_mx_m & -x_m \\ 0 & 0 & 0 & X_m & Y_m & 1 & -X_my_m & -Y_my_m & -y_m \end{bmatrix}$$

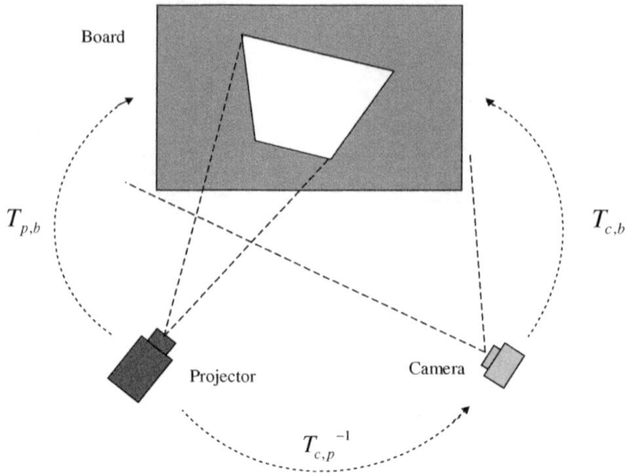

Fig. 3. Homography calibration. Due to misalignment of projector and projection surface, the rectangular display appears as a distorted quadrilateral in the center of the board. This can be compensated by pre-warping using the homographies shown.

Then the unit vector $\mathbf{t}$ needs to be found that minimizes $|\mathbf{At}|$. This can solved by finding the eigenvector corresponding to the smallest eigenvalue of $\mathbf{A}^T\mathbf{A}$.

A simple solution using four feature points correspondences is shown in Figure 3. If a white rectangle is projected onto the board against a high-contrast background, the four corners of the projected quadrilateral in the camera image can be computed. To do this, we extract the contours in the image and check for closed contours with four corners. With the coordinates of the corners known in the projector reference frame, the projector-camera homography $\mathbf{T}_{cp}$ can be recovered. The corners of this quadrilateral completely specify the camera-board homography $\mathbf{T}_{cb}$. The homography between the projector and the board $\mathbf{T}_{pb}$ can be recovered from the following relationship:

$$\mathbf{T}_{pb} = \mathbf{T}_{cp}^{-1}\mathbf{T}_{cb} \tag{2}$$

By applying the inverse transform $\mathbf{T}_{pb}^{-1}$ to pre-warp the original image, a corrected image can be displayed on the tilt board.

3.2 Tilt Board Pose Estimation

Markers are printed on the board to help track its 3D pose [11]. The image of a marker observed by the camera is a projective transformation of the original physical marker, which includes rotation, translation and scaling. An example is shown in Figure 4.

After thresholding the image observed by the camera, lines and corners are extracted using contour detection. The distorted subimage within the square region can be matched with the original marker subimage through normalization after it has been warped using the homography estimated between the camera and the marker.

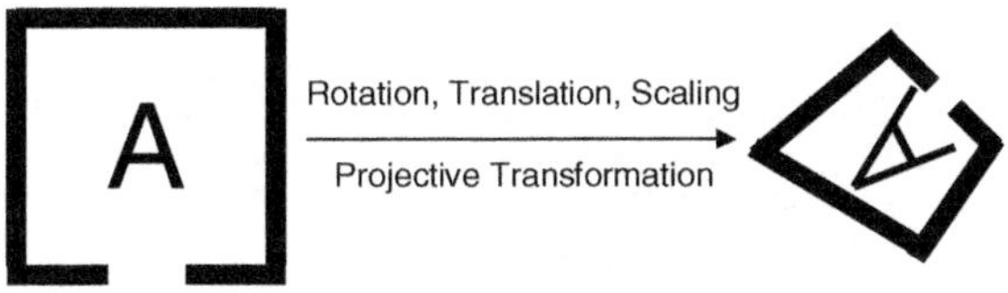

Fig. 4. Projective transformation of a marker. A square marker observed by the camera is a projective transformation of the original marker.

The pose of the marker with respect to the camera can be recovered using camera calibration techniques. A point in camera pixel coordinates (x_c, y_c) and in camera coordinates (X_c, Y_c, Z_c) can be related to its board coordinates (X_b, Y_b, Z_b) as:

$$\begin{bmatrix} hx_c \\ hy_c \\ h \\ 1 \end{bmatrix} = \mathbf{K} \begin{bmatrix} X_c \\ Y_c \\ Z_c \\ 1 \end{bmatrix} = \mathbf{K} \cdot \mathbf{H} \begin{bmatrix} X_b \\ Y_b \\ Z_b \\ 1 \end{bmatrix} \tag{3}$$

where h is an unknown scaling factor. **K** and **H** are the camera intrinsic and extrinsic matrices, respectively:

$$\mathbf{K} = \begin{bmatrix} s_x f & m & x_0 & 0 \\ 0 & s_y f & y_0 & 0 \\ 0 & 0 & 1 & 0 \\ 0 & 0 & 0 & 1 \end{bmatrix}, \quad \mathbf{H} = \begin{bmatrix} R_{11} & R_{12} & R_{13} & T_x \\ R_{21} & R_{22} & R_{23} & T_y \\ R_{31} & R_{32} & R_{33} & T_z \\ 0 & 0 & 0 & 1 \end{bmatrix}$$

where f is the focal length, s_x, s_y are the scale factors of pixel/mm in x and y directions respectively, m is the slant between x-axis and y-axis (normally zero), (x_0, y_0) is the principal point shift of the camera, $(R_{11}, \cdots, R_{33})$ is the rotation matrix, and $(T_x, T_y, T_z)^T$ is the translation vector.

Pairs of (x_c, y_c) and (X_b, Y_b, Z_b) allow us to estimate the matrices **K** and **H** using camera calibration techniques. Since standard camera calibration techniques require special physical patterns, we use the MXR Toolkit [12], which was designed specifically for marker tracking.

4 Implementation and Results

Our system comprises an Optoma EP-739H DLP portable projector, a Logitech webcam and a piece of cardboard with square markers printed on it, which is shown in Figure 5. Geometric calibration results and an exemplary racing-ball game running on our interface are described in the following.

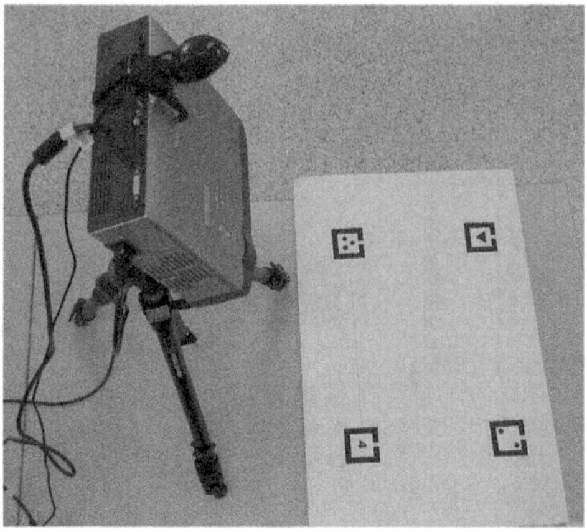

Fig. 5. Tilt board interface using a projector-camera system

4.1 Geometric Calibration Results

In the geometric calibration of our projector-camera system, the projector-board homography $\mathbf{T}_{pb}$ and camera-board homography $\mathbf{T}_{cb}$ will change as the tilt board moves. The projector-board homography can be estimated through observing projected patterns from the camera and extracting the point correspondences between the camera and the projectors. The camera-board homography $\mathbf{T}_{cb}$ is recovered by observing the physical markers attached on the tilt board with the camera. Subsequently, the projector-board homography can be computed through Eq. (2).

As the player is moving the board constantly, these homographies have to be computed in real-time. However, since the projector and the camera are stationary, we can pre-compute projector-camera homography $\mathbf{T}_{pc}$ from several poses of the board in the system initialization once and for all. This is better than computing $\mathbf{T}_{pc}$ real-time in the game, as this may not be accurate due to camera noise. Furthermore, when the projected area intersects with the physical markers, corner extraction may fail, resulting in a wrongly computed projector-board homography $\mathbf{T}_{pb}$, which can be avoided by using the pre-computed homography.

Table 1 shows an example of pre-calibrated and real-time computed $\mathbf{T}_{pc}$, together with the matrix norm differences between the pre-calibrated $\mathbf{T}_{pc,i}$ $(i = 0)$ and each real-time computed $\mathbf{T}_{pc,i}$ $(i = 1, 2, 3, 4)$. The matrix norm differences between 41 and 172. These differences are contributed mostly by the matrix elements in column 3, which are responsible for the translation, so even though these numbers are large, it has little impact on the shape of the image.

The four corners on the tilt board are also computed using $\mathbf{T}_{pc,0}$ and $\mathbf{T}_{pc,i}$. Then we calculate the corner angles of the quadrilateral at each corner. Figure 6 shows the angle differences of the four corners calculated for four arbitrary tilt board poses. Take note that even though pose 1 has the smallest norm difference, it has the largest difference in degree. This is mainly due to the difference between

Table 1. Pre-calibrated and real-time computed $\mathbf{T}_{pc}$

	$\mathbf{T}_{pc,i}$			Matrix Norm (real-time vs. pre-computed)
Pre-computed	1.452257	0.061707	−500.917816	0
	−0.007086	1.234739	−262.956879	
	−0.000012	−0.000341	1	
Real-time Pose 1	1.390219	−0.05998	−462.887207	41.3651
	−0.041811	1.457855	−279.226654	
	0.000046	−0.000807	1	
Real-time Pose 2	1.545433	0.081606	−550.048706	51.719
	0.002831	1.286384	−246.801178	
	−0.000019	−0.000303	1	
Real-time Pose 3	1.606216	0.108573	−571.732544	73.2658
	−0.002608	1.242908	−244.1651	
	0.000018	−0.000133	1	
Real-time Pose 4	1.854606	0.096473	−660.308655	172.5482
	−0.223254	1.434345	−196.871918	
	0.00035	−0.000304	1	

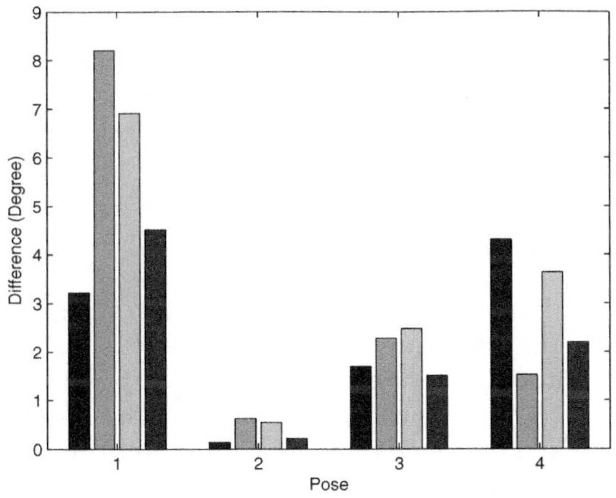

Fig. 6. Differences (in degree) of projected corners using precalibrated vs. real-time computed $\mathbf{T}_{pc}$ for 4 different board poses

elements in column 1,2 of $\mathbf{T}_{pc,1}$ and $\mathbf{T}_{pc,0}$, which are larger compared to other poses. To conclude, pre-calibrated $\mathbf{T}_{pc}$ may not be 100% accurate, but it is more robust and stable when projected corners overlap with physical markers.

4.2 Racing-Ball Game

We implemented a racing-ball game on our system, as shown in Figure 7. The player tilts and slants the board to steer the ball through a maze while avoiding holes and collecting bonus items.

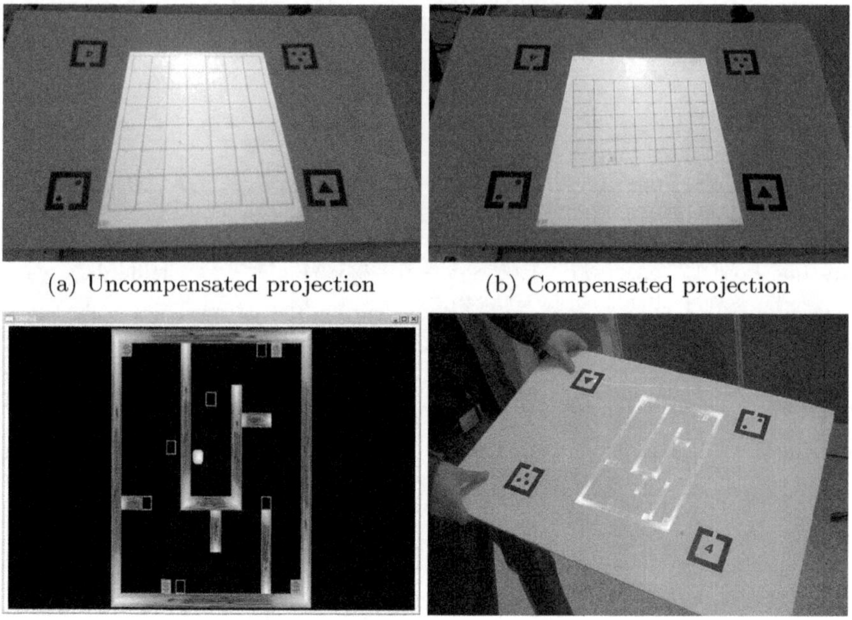

(a) Uncompensated projection (b) Compensated projection

(c) Game screenshot (d) Game projection

Fig. 7. Racing-ball game implementation using cardboard and projector-camera system. (a) geometrically uncompensated projection; (b) geometrically compensated projection; (c) original racing-ball game screenshot; (d) in-game shot of user slanting and tilting the cardboard in the racing-ball game.

5 Conclusions and Future Work

We have designed and implemented a tangible game interface using a projector-camera system. Our interface provides a more direct and natural interaction than HMD's or monitor-based interfaces. Homography calibration and physical marker tracking are used to implement the system. The system setup is simple, easy, quick and economic since no extra special devices are needed.

We are now conducting a usability study to evaluate the system from a user perspective. Furthermore, due to the oblique projection, there are issues such as projection color imbalance and out-of-focus projector blur that need to be investigated.

References

1. Pinhanez, C.: The Everywhere Display Projector: A device to create ubiquitous graphical interfaces. In: Proc. Ubiquitous Computing, Atlanda, GA, pp. 315–331 (2001)
2. Pingali, G., Pinhanez, C., Levas, A., Kjeldsen, R., Podlaseck, M., Chen, H., Sukaviriya, N.: Steerable interfaces for pervasive computing spaces. In: Proc. IEEE International Conference on Pervasive Computing and Communications, Fort Worth, TX, 315 (2003)

3. Raskar, R., Baar, J., Beardsley, P., Willwacher, T., Rao, S., Forlines, C.: iLamps: Geometrically aware and self-configuring projectors. ACM Transactions on Graphics 22(3), 809–818 (2003)
4. Gupta, S., Jaynes, C.: Active pursuit tracking in a projector-camera system with application to augmented reality. In: IEEE International Workshop on Projector-Camera Systems (PROCAMS), pp. 111–119 (2005)
5. Beardsley, P., van Barr, J., Raskar, R., Forlines, C.: Interaction using a handheld projector. IEEE Computer Graphics and Applications 25(1), 39–43 (2005)
6. Cheok, A., Fong, S., Goh, K., Yang, X., Liu, W., Farbiz, F.: Human Pacman: A sensing-based mobile entertainment system with ubiquitous computing and tangible interaction. In: 2nd Workshop on Network and System Support for Games, pp. 106–117 (2003)
7. Zhou, Z., Cheok, A., Pan, J., Li, Y.: Magic Story Cube: An interactive tangible interface for storytelling. In: Proc. ACM SIGCHI International Conference on Advances in Computer Entertainment Technology, Singaproe, pp. 364–365 (2004)
8. Mazalek, A., Wood, A., Ishii, H.: Geniebottles: An interactive narrative in bottles. In: SIGGRAPH Conference Abstracts and Applications, Los Angeles, CA, p. 189 (2001)
9. Sukthankar, R., Stockton, R., Mullin, M.: Automatic keystone correction for camera-assisted presentation interfaces. In: Proc. International Conference on Multimodal Interfaces, Beijing, China, pp. 607–614 (2000)
10. Sukthankar, R., Stockton, R., Mullin, M.: Smarter Presentations: Exploiting homography in camera-projector systems. In: Proc. International Conference on Computer Vision, Vancouver, Canada, pp. 247–253 (2001)
11. Kato, H., Billinghurst, M.: Marker tracking and HMD calibration for a video-based augmented reality conferencing system. In: Proc. 2nd International Workshop on Augmented Reality (IWAR), San Francisco, CA, pp. 85–95 (1999)
12. NUS Mixed Reality Lab:MXR Toolkit `http://mxrtoolkit.sourceforge.net/`

Context-Aware Mobile AR System for Personalization, Selective Sharing, and Interaction of Contents in Ubiquitous Computing Environments*

Youngjung Suh[1], Youngmin Park[1], Hyoseok Yoon[1], Yoonje Chang[2], and Woontack Woo[1]

[1] GIST U-VR Lab., 500-712, S.Korea
{ysuh,ypark,hyoon,wwoo}@gist.ac.kr
[2] GIST CTRC, 500-712, S.Korea
naugulp@naver.com

Abstract. With advances in tracking and increased computing power, mobile AR systems are popular in our daily life. Researchers in mobile AR technology have emphasized the technical challenges involved in the limitations imposed from mobility. They did not consider context-aware service with user-related information annotation, even if in ubiquitous computing environment, various contexts of both a user and an environment can be utilized easily as well as effectively. Moreover, it is difficult to have access to pervasive but invisible computing resources. At the same time, the more smart appliances become evolved with more features, the harder their user interfaces tend to become to use. Thus, in this paper, we propose Context-aware Mobile Augmented Reality (CaMAR) system. It lets users interact with their smart objects through personalized control interfaces on their mobile AR devices. Also, it supports enabling contents to be not only personalized but also shared selectively and interactively among user communities.

Keywords: context-aware, mobile AR, personalization, selective sharing.

1 Introduction

Until now, augmented reality (AR) systems have been developed to faithfully realize the basic concept that they supplement the real world with virtual objects (or information) to enhance the user's perception of and interaction with the real world [1]. Researchers in AR technologies have emphasized the technical challenges involved in accurate augmentation, natural interaction, realistic rendering. With advances in tracking and increased computing power, mobile AR systems are developing. Studies on mobile AR technologies also try to technically improve challenges [2]. They did not consider context-aware service with user-related information annotation, even if in ubiquitous computing environment, various

* This research is supported by the Ubiquitous Computing and Network (UCN) Project, the Ministry of Information and Communication (MIC) 21st Century Frontier R&D Program in Korea.

J. Jacko (Ed.): Human-Computer Interaction, Part II, HCII 2007, LNCS 4551, pp. 966–974, 2007.

contexts of both a user and an environment can be utilized easily as well as effectively. However, uniform provision of such context information using mobile AR technology lets the user fall into utter confusion. Thus, making a bridge between a variety of contexts in ubiquitous computing environment and mobile AR technology, several studies have tried to overcome the limitations that those are restricted to provide uniform information to every person [2][3]. aPost-it[4] was proposed as a context-based information augmentation and sharing system. However, it personalized only media contents through a webpage obtained from an object. It did not deal with personalization in controlling smart objects. In addition, for selective sharing of media contents, through user interfaces in a web page users have to explicitly inform the system of whether they would like to share. However, it is difficult to have access to pervasive but invisible computing resources. At the same time, the more smart appliances become evolved with more features, the harder their user interfaces tend to become to use. Moreover, it is not convenient to explicitly request selective sharing of contents.

Thus, in this paper, we propose Context-aware Mobile Augmented Reality (CAMAR) system. It supports enabling contents to be not only personalized but also shared selectively and interactively among user communities based on mobile user's profile and context in ubiquitous computing environments. Moreover, users can control various kinds of smart objects within the environment in their own personalized manner, once they take pictures of smart objects within the environment with a camera in a mobile AR device. Thus, making a bridge between a variety of contexts in ubiquitous computing environment and mobile AR technologies, the proposed system overcomes limitations in the existing Information Technologies which provide uniform information to every person. Applicable areas of the proposed system could be MAR-enabling applications, such as a meeting system that supports information augmentation to real environment and collaboration, a universal remote controller for controlling various kinds of smart objects, a mobile service agent that utilize user's location and activity to diversify and expand its use for MAR-based services.

This paper is organized as follows. In section 2, overview of the CAMAR system is given. We describe the applicable scenarios in section 3. Section 4 deals with implementations. Finally, we conclude our work and briefly outline a remaining work in Section 5.

2 System Overview

Context-aware Mobile AR system will support personalization, selective sharing, and mobile AR interaction-based collaboration. It supports user-centric monitoring and controlling of smart services as well as personalized contents in ubiquitous computing environments. Personalized UI in a controller of smart services lets AR systems provide intuitive and transparent UI such that let user concentrate on the original task. Also, it supports presenting private information to individuals without fearing that others will see it. As for personalized contents, it allows personalized responsive content to be augmented. It constructs group or community space based on common interests among users in ubiquitous computing environments. Based on the constructed communities in ubiquitous computing environments, selective contents sharing and collaboration will be supported. It specifically enables selective sharing of common knowledge/experience on contents interactively/collaboratively among user communities. **Fig. 1** shows the concept diagram for CAMAR system supporting personalization, selective sharing, and mobile AR interaction-based collaboration in the environment equipped with smart TV, window, table, etc.

Fig. 1. The concept diagram for CAMAR

3 Applicable Scenarios

As a test-bed regarding contents, we model a rich knowledge containing many different types of information on a specific domain, the Unju temple. Our test data, thus, includes cultural heritage information, legendary characters, photos, geographic information, and detailed 3D models of places, characters, and items [7][8].

Fig. 2 shows the conceptual diagram implying scenarios applicable to CAMAR system.

Fig. 2. Visualization of overall scenarios applicable to CAMAR

3.1 Personalized Smart Object Control

"We can control, in a personalized manner, smart objects which we take pictures with a camera in a mobile AR device"

When a user takes a picture of a specific smart object with a camera in a mobile AR device, a personalized controller to the captured smart object could be augmented on the mobile AR device: ubiTV Controller, ARTable Controller, MRWindow Controller, Light Controller [9][10].

Mr. Kang comes home from his work. He becomes aware of the fact that his wife Ms. Lee went to a market in a neighborhood. As soon as he comes into a living room, lighting service prepares a green lighting he prefers at ordinary times. He changes the color of lighting into a blue one since he feels the weather is so hot and wants to make the room refreshing. Then, he approaches ubiTV to watch TV. ubiTV recognizes that Mr. Kang might approach close to it and provides recommendations based on his preference at normal times. Only media contents with a high degree of similarity to his preference are recommended. Mr. Kang selects sports news channel using ubiTV Controller on his PDA and begins to watch TV. Ms.Lee comes back home from a market. After she confirms that Mr. Kang picks up a sports channel to watch TV, she decides to pay a visit of a virtual Unju temple through PDA before watching TV. She moves to MRWindow. First of all, she confirms available service lists from service discovery on her PDA. Then, she is about to enjoy an interesting service searching from service lists. Unfortunately, she forgot how to use services available in MRWindow since she hardly have used them. She gets to have a chance to review how to use MRWindow services through sound guidance from her PDA. She begins to control MRWindow services and navigates a virtual Unju temple. After she enjoys herself in a virtual navigation system to the full, she comes to ubiTV because she recognizes that sports news program Mr. Kang has watched is over. At this time, in MRWindow, there displays a painting she prefers normally. When she is in front of ubiTV, authority transfer button is appeared in Mr. Kang's ubiTV Controller on PDA. Mr. Kang transfers his authority on controlling ubiTV to Ms. Lee. ubiTV recognizes that Ms. Lee gets the authority on ubiTV from Mr. Kang and provides recommendations based on Ms.Lee's preference at normal times. Only media contents with a high degree of similarity to her preference are recommended. Ms. Lee selects cooking channel using ubiTV Controller on her PDA and begins to watch TV. After Ms. Lee moves to the dining room, ubiTV and Light service are automatically turned off.

Fig. 3 shows visualization of the scenario applicable to Personalized Smart Object Controller in ubiquitous computing environments.

3.2 Context-Based Contents Augmentation and Sharing

1) Mr. Kang Got Back from Visiting Unju Temple Last Week . Mr. Kang got back from visiting Unju temple with his family in the last week. He really loves photographing. So, he took a picture of in the precincts of Unju temple. The photos are indexed spatially through GPS-receiver in the mobile device that was used to take the photograph, so that Mr. Kang can later know where a certain photo was shot.

Fig. 3. Visualization of the scenario applicable to Personalized Smart Object Controller in ubiquitous computing environments

Mr. Kang decides to recommend visiting the Unju temple to his friend. Mr. Kang invites his friend Mr. Kim to show the pictures he took in Unju temple. It goes by a week from that time. That's why it is difficult that Mr. Kang remembers he took which scenes at which places and when. Mr. Kang likes to revive the memory of Unju temple through ARTable and navigate a road in virtual Unju temple. He recognizes with a single glance the place he took the pictures through the map displayed on ARTable. Mr. Kang moves UMPC with his hands to a specific region on the map to see again the picture he took in the region. Mr. Kang enjoys the pictures augmented on a screen in UMPC. As an optional service, he got to have a same feeling of one at that time searching all over the region with the enlarged one of the pictures.

2) Mr. Kim Visit Mr. Kang's Home. Mr. Kim has never visited Unju temple. He decides to visit a virtual Unju temple through ARTable, hearing from Mr. Kang that Unju temple gives an unusual impression unlike other temples. The places at which Mr. Kang took the pictures can be indicated through makers displayed on the map in ARTable. "Wabul" in the map is indicated by a distinguished marker. Mr. Kim decides to look into that place moving UMPC with his hands to that one. Mr. Kim feels that is impressive and have a good understanding of that place. He got interested

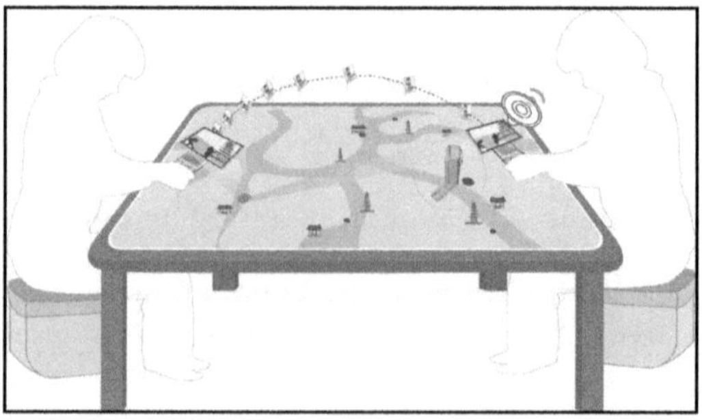

Fig. 4. Visualization of the scenario applicable to Context-based contents augmentation and sharing service

in Unju temple with the help of sound guidance on the tale of the place. Immediately he feels like visiting even "Chilsung" and "Gongsa" rock in Unju temple. He may make a definite promise to visit Unju temple and make a novel experience with his family in next week. Fig. 4 shows visualization of the scenario applicable to Context-based contents augmentation and sharing service.

4 Implementations

We present Context-aware Mobile Augmented Reality (CAMAR) system that supports two main functionalities. One is controlling smart objects with mobile AR devices. The other is enabling contents to be not only personalized but also shared selectively and interactively among user communities. **Fig. 5** shows overall system block diagram.

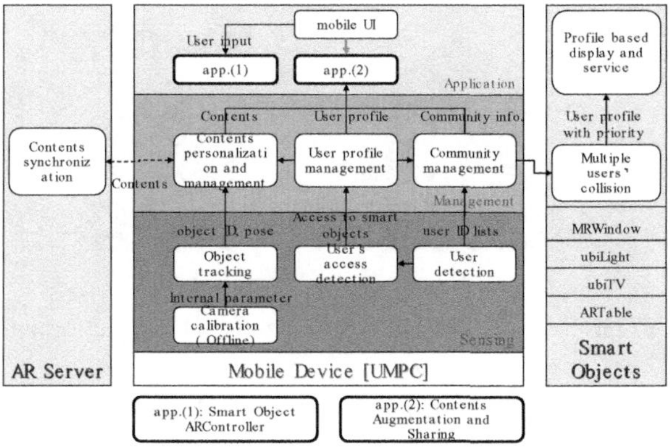

Fig. 5. CAMAR System block diagram

4.1 Smart Object Control: Controlling Smart Objects with Mobile AR Device

The personalized smart object controller system lets users interact with their smart objects through personalized control interfaces on their mobile AR devices. Most mobile devices interact with only one user, making it easy for the mobile device to provide personalized interfaces. For example, a mobile AR device provides interfaces that are consistent with smart object ones that the user is familiar with or preferred. We have designed and implemented a personalized smart object controller to make users control smart objects in their environment through a personalized user interface. When a user wants to control a smart object, the user has only to take a picture of it with a camera attached to mobile AR device. When a user takes a picture of a smart object, the controller device gets a context containing an abstract functional description from the smart object and uses that context of the description to properly generate an interface. We explored developing graphical user interfaces on PDA. The personalized controllers to smart objects augmented on the mobile AR devices are

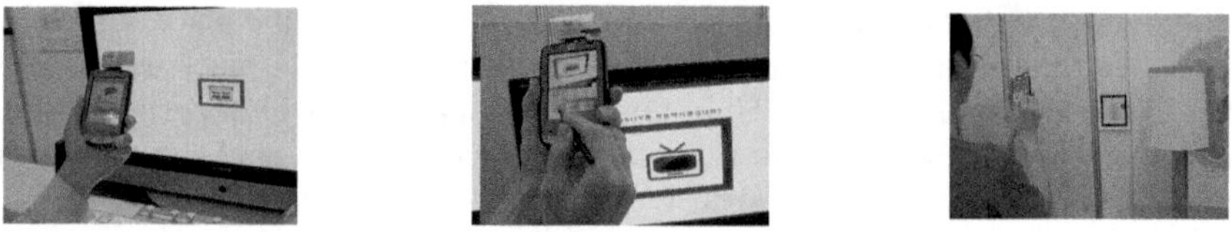

Fig. 6. Smart Object Control with AR Controllers

ubiTV Controller, MRWindow Controller, Light Controller, ARTable Controller [5] [6]. Some of them are shown in Fig. 6.

For prototypes, AR Controller is implemented in PDA and UMPC platforms, respectively. PDA platform has an advantage because it is relatively smaller, cheaper and highly portable. However, UMPC performs better in image processing for pattern matching. For research purpose, we used both platforms interchangeably to develop compatible components for PDA and UMPC alike. **Fig. 7** shows two different versions of AR Controller.

(a) (b)

Fig. 7. AR Controller in (a) UMPC platform and (b) PDA platform, respectively

4.2 Context-Based Contents Augmentation and Sharing

The context-based contents augmentation and sharing system lets users experience the personalized contents and share them with the others who have common interests. To show contents augmentation and sharing with mobile AR technology, we implement an edutainment system that augment and share photos in a site. When we explore a cultural site, we tend to take a picture of cultural assets and save them in our mobile device to treasure up our memory or experience. The context information we can acquire in this aspect might be the time we took a photograph of the cultural assets and the location of the impressive places we took a photograph of. The personal context information such as time, location, etc. is managed in an individual mobile device like UMPC. We made our system to show the different contents to two users depending on whether a user has an experience of visiting Unju temple or not [7][8]. **Fig. 8** shows that the system augments the personalized photo contents and makes them to be shared within a specific site in ARTable[6].

The personal context information such as time, location, etc. is managed in an individual mobile device like UMPC. We assume a user has ever been to Unju temple. Then the pictures he took in several places at Unju temple are saved in his UMPC. When the user looks into a specific AR marker in a map in ARTable with his UMPC in his hands, the pictures he took in that place are augmented. The user can flick through and enlarge the pictures one by one by clicking buttons.

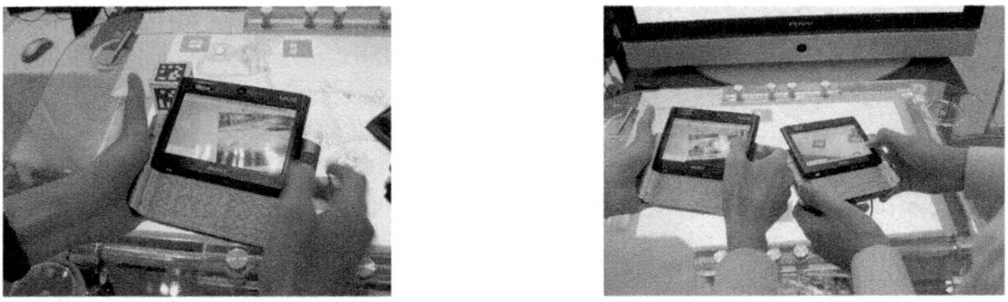

Fig. 8. Context-based AR contents augmentation and sharing

For selective sharing, our system interprets preferences on contents of a user and provides the personalized contents to the user. Additionally, the system generates and manages group context by extracting common preferences after analyzing multiple users' integrated contexts and the relationship. By managing group context, it selectively allows the users who have interests in common to share contents.

5 Conclusion and Future Work

Our work demonstrates the feasibility of personalized smart object AR controllers in ubiquitous computing environments as well as context-based contents augmentation and selective sharing systems in ubiquitous computing environments. It supports enabling contents to be not only personalized but also shared selectively and interactively among user communities based on mobile user's profile and context in ubiquitous computing environments. Moreover, users can control various kinds of smart objects within the ubiquitous computing environments in their own personalized manner, once they take pictures of smart objects within the environment with a camera in a mobile AR device. Thus, making a bridge between a variety of contexts in ubiquitous computing environment and mobile AR technologies, the proposed system overcomes limitations in the existing Information Technologies which provide uniform information to every person. We also plan to conduct user studies to see how our system is interesting and accepted as a novel one to users comparing with the existing other similar systems. Considering compatibility of embodied technology and contents, we will try to find out contents to support concretizing user's experience and sharing something meaningful to family through CAMAR device. Also, to increase satisfaction of embodied technology, we need to show possibility for controlling various smart appliances which users are able to think of as more useful using CAMAR device.

References

1. Höllerer, T., Feiner, S., Pavlik, J.: Situated Documentaries: Embedding Multimedia Presentations in the Real World. In: Prc. ISWC '99 (3rd Int. Symp. On Wearabel Computers), San Francisco, CA, October 18-19, pp. 79–86 (1999)
2. Henrysson, Ollila: UMAR - Ubiquitous Mobile Augmented Reality. To appear at 3rd Mobile Ubiquitous Multimedia 2004, Washington, USA (2004)

3. Reitmayr, G., Schmalstieg, D.: Collaborative Augmented Reality for Outdoor Navigation and Information Browsing (To appear). In: Proc. Symposium Location Based Services and TeleCartography (2004)
4. Oh, Y., Lee, M., Jung, S., Woo, W.: Dynamic Contents Provision of Context-based Information Augmentation & Sharing System, ACM/IEEE ICAT04, pp. 594–597 (2004)
5. Oh, Y., Shin, C., Jung, W., Woo, W.: The ubiTV application for a Family in ubiHome. In: 2nd Ubiquitous Home workshop, pp. 23–32 (2005)
6. Park, Y., Woo, W.: The ARTable. In: Pan, Z., Aylett, R., Diener, H., Jin, X., Göbel, S., Li, L. (eds.) An AR-based Tangible User Interface System. LNCS, vol. 3942, pp. 1198–1207. Springer, Heidelberg (2006)
7. Lee, Y., Oh, S., Lee, B., Park, J., Park, Y., Oh, Y., Lee, S., Oh, H., Ryu, J., Lee, K.H., Kim, H., Lee, Y., Kim, J., Ho, Y., Woo, W.: Responsive Multimedia System for Context-based Storytelling. LNCS (PCM), vol. 3767, pp. 361–372 (2005)
8. Lee, Y., Oh, S., Woo, W.: A Context-based Storytelling with Responsive Multimedia System (RMS), LNCS(ICVS), vol. 3805, pp. 12–21 (2005)
9. Oh, Y., Shin, C., Jung, W., Woo, W.: The ubiTV application for a Family in ubiHome. In: 2nd Ubiquitous Home workshop, pp. 23–32 (2005)
10. Park, Y., Woo, W.: The ARTable: An AR-based Tangible User Interface System, LNCS, vol. 3942, pp. 1198–1207 (2006)

Center or Corner? The Implications of Mura Locations on LCD Displays

Kuo-Hao Tang, Yueh-Hua Lee, and Kuo Hsun Ku

Department of Industrial Engineering and System Management,
Feng Chia University, Taiwan 407
{khtang,p9318667}@fcu.edu.tw

Abstract. With the consideration of Mura area and contrast, SEMI Standard provides a guideline for Mura inspection. However, for an end user, due to different tasks and environments, when interacting with a computer, Mura location on the screen may be an important factor affecting a user's overall satisfaction with the LCD display. Regression analysis from this study showed that both Mura level and Mura location affect the perceived value of an LCD by a user. Further analysis showed that this perceived value may change across different Mura Level ranges. When Mura levels are high, the small correlation coefficient between markdown value of a display due to Mura and Mura location suggests that the display won't be accepted by customers regardless of Mura location. On the other hand, if the Mura level is moderate, a higher correlation can be obtained, which means customers are sensitive to the Mura location.

Keywords: Mura, User evaluation, LCD display, Mura location.

1 Introduction

LCD displays have the largest market share in the flat-panel display (FPD) industry, due to their full-color display capabilities, low power consumption, low radiation and low weight. However, various physical factors, such as non-uniformly distributed liquid crystal material and foreign particles within the liquid crystal, produce a brightness uniformity related problem called Mura in LCDs. Mura refers to the imperfections of a display pixel matrix surface that are visible when the display screen is driven to a constant gray level. Depending on shape and size, Mura defects may be classified as spot-Mura, line-Mura, and region-Mura defects. Mura related quality issues affect not only price, but also the overall satisfaction of end users. Most LCD manufacturers are still using human eyes to inspect Mura levels. However, human inspection is not consistent, both for one inspector at different times, and across multiple inspectors. In addition, human inspection may result in higher costs. In order to cope with this problem, the concept of machine vision is being explored and has a good opportunity to replace human inspectors.

Most researches in this field follow the framework of VESA FPDM [4], which provides a flow chart for processing real images from LCD panels. For different types of Mura, algorithms have been developed to separate the places with uneven

J. Jacko (Ed.): Human-Computer Interaction, Part II, HCII 2007, LNCS 4551, pp. 975–981, 2007.

uniformity from the background [3], and to combine techniques such as thresholding and quality control to identify Mura candidates [1], [2]. In order to avoid over-detecting Muras, that is, detecting Muras beyond the contrast sensitivity of human eyes, Lee and Yoo [2] showed that with considerations of Mura area and Mura contrast following the SEMI Standard of Mura level less than 5.5, Mura could not be detected by human eyes. These research results may suggest a new approach to reduce Mura inspection cost while improving the inspection consistency and efficiency. Although the SEMI Standard provides a guideline for Mura inspection, it operates from the viewpoint of a manufacturer considering only Mura area and contrast. For an end user, due to different tasks and environments when interacting with a computer, Mura location on the screen may be an important factor affecting a user's overall satisfaction with the LCD display. In the pilot test, we verified different Mura properties (e.g., area, contrast, location, etc.) that affect user performance. The second part of experiment explored the possibility of modifying the SEMI Standard to consider Mura location.

2 Pilot Test

The pilot test assessed the importance of factors that might influence user performance. These factors include Mura area, Mura contrast, Mura location, and background brightness. Mura patterns used in this experiment imitated real Mura and were created by using Adobe PhotoShop. There were three levels of Mura area, namely, 43.3 mm^2, 209.6 mm^2 and 6447.7mm^2. Since the viewing distance between subjects and LCD display was 50 cm, spatial frequencies were 0.1, 1.07 and 2.35 cycles per degree respectively. Due to the blurry boundary of the Mura, spatial frequencies can be underestimated. There were 10 Mura contrast levels, including 5 levels of positive polarity and 5 levels of negative polarity. Two levels of gray gradient were chosen as Mura backgrounds.

During the experiment, for each background, Muras of different sizes and contrast levels would randomly appear on 13 locations on the LCD display as shown in Figure 1.

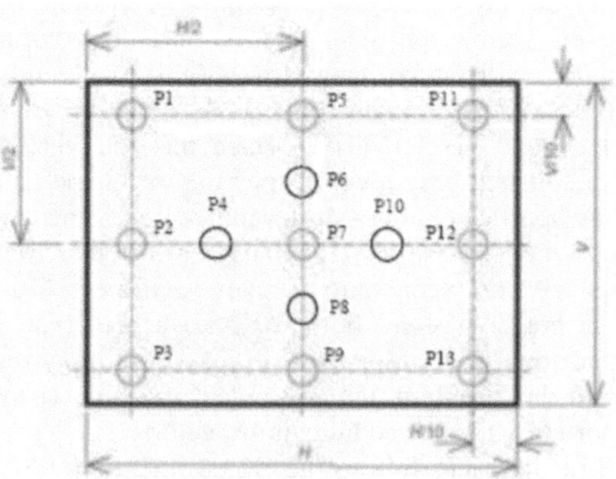

Fig. 1. Mura positions in related to LCD display used for the experiments

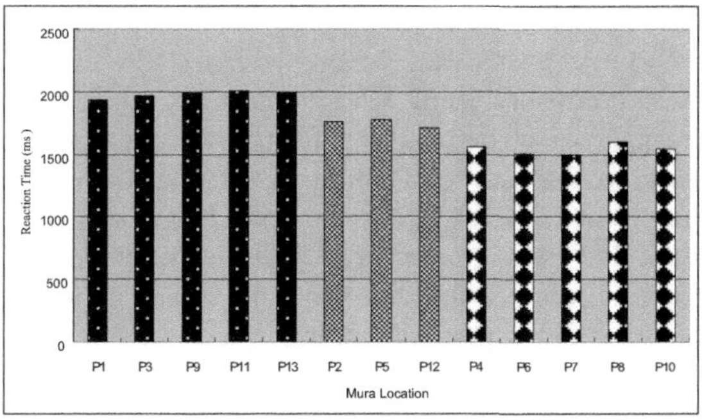

Fig. 2. Mean time taken to detect Muras in milliseconds

Participants were asked to answer yes/no questions for the detection of Mura and to point out the Mura location when answering yes with a mouse click. Reaction time was recorded and accuracy rate was calculated as a dependent variable. The result showed that all main effects and interaction terms were highly significant ($p<0.001$). The results from post hoc testing ($\alpha=0.05$) on Mura locations revealed that the reaction times can be divided into three groups as shown in Figure 2. This result may suggest that Mura locations indeed affect reaction time for Mura detection. The accuracy rate analysis showed similar results. Thus, it can be reasonably assumed that information regarding Mura location may be used for product grading, from the perspective of a customer.

3 Experiment

3.1 Mura Generation

As mentioned above, the present research intends to explore the effect of Mura location on end-users' preferences. Hence the experiment was designed for subjects to evaluate the impact of Mura. For this experiment, 32 Mura figures with different Mura Levels were created. The 32 Mura levels ranged from 0.66 to 16.24. The calculation of Mura Level followed the SEMI Standard that both Mura size and contrast with background must be taken into account.

The Mura figures used for this experiment were imitated from real Mura and were created by Adobe PhotoShop. The experiment program was developed using Microsoft Visual Basic. Figure 3 (a) shows the real Mura from the Paris Academy of Computer Science- SUPINFO Projects, and Figure 3 (b) were the imitation Mura's that were used in this study. Number of Mura figures and Mura Level calculations were provided as below.

3.2 Subject

Twelve paid subjects participated in this study, two subjects were female and ten were male. The average age of the subjects was 26 years old with standard deviation 5.3 years. All subjects had a normal or corrected to normal eyesight.

3.3 Task

Indoor luminance was controlled to 32 lux and subjects sat at a preset work station in order to avoid experimental error resulting from different visual angles. Two LCDs were placed side by side, one as a control panel for interacting with the program and the other as a display that waited to be evaluated. The background of the evaluation display was set to the 155 grey gradient (21.5 nits). The experiment started with the entry of the subject's ID, after which the program would controlled to show a Mura figure on the evaluation LCD with a beep at the time of display.

Subjects were asked to answer the question: "How much should it be marked down due to the existence of Mura in order to have some chance of being bought by a customer if the selling price is NTD 6000." Subjects were instructed to mark down the price based on their subjective preferences.

In order to maintain the consistency of subject's standard, the subjects were encouraged to double-check the grading standard at any time they wanted. After grading 96 Mura showed on the display, the experiment finished. All of related data, including Mura Level, Mura central coordinates, and each grade, were saved for analysis.

3.4 Design

There were 2 independent variables in this experiment, Mura Level and Distance. As described in Section 3.1, a total of 32 Mura's with different Mura Levels were created. Each subject would finish one trial session. For one trial session, one of these 32 Mura's would appear 3 times and the total 96 trials were randomized within each session. And for each trial, the Mura would appear at a random location on the evaluation LCD and the subject would evaluate the markdown value. The markdown value was treated as a dependent variable in this experiment.

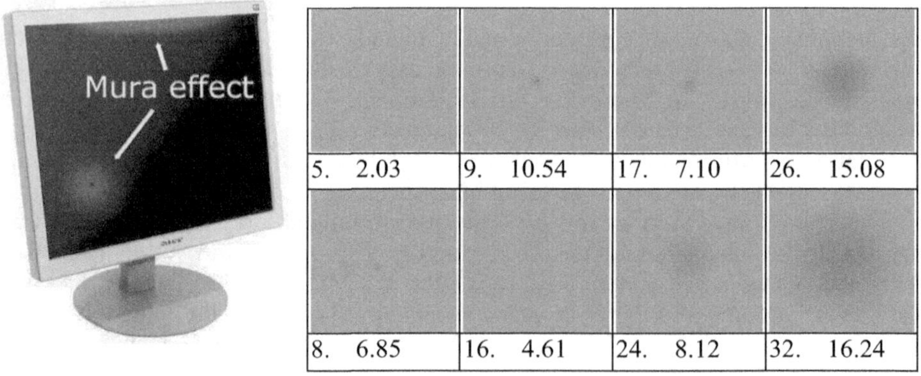

Fig. 3. (a) real Mura from SUPINFO Projects (b) created Mura used in the experiment

4 Results

In order to reveal tendency effects, the Mura Level range (ML_range)variable has been defined: 32 Mura Levels were divided into 4 groups according to magnitude.

ML_range 1 gathers Mura figures with Mura Level less than 2.15, ML_range 2 is Mura Level larger than 2.6 and less than 4.61, ML_range 3 is Mura level between 4.71 to 9.56, and ML_range 4 is between 10.54 and 16.25. Each group contains 8 Mura figures.

There are several results that should be addressed here. First of all, a three-way ANOVA was used to analyze the collected data and revealed three significant main effects: ML_range, $F(3, 33)=34.06$, $P<0.001$; subject, $F(11, 33)=6.78$, $P<0.001$ and Distance $F(1, 1103)=9.07$, $P<0.005$ which was treated as covariance. Distance was defined as the distance from the center of display. Moreover, the interaction term ML_range* subject also showed highly significant effects, $F(33, 1103)=13.82$, $P<0.001$, although it means different Mura levels caused different impacts on subjects but a certain trend still exists to some extent, as Figure 4 shows. As ML_range became larger, subjects tended to have more markdown.

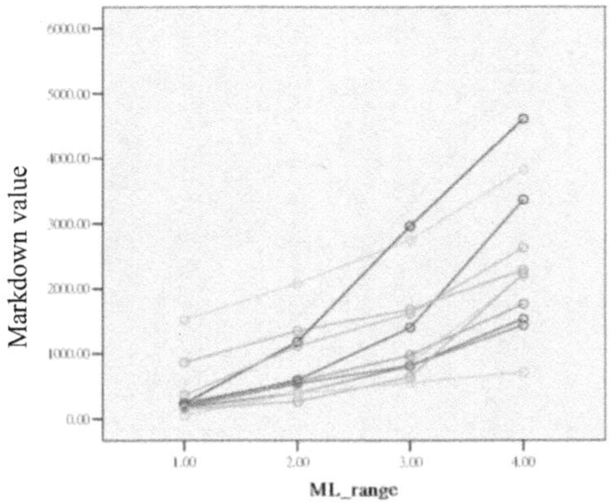

Fig. 4. Subjects' markdown price in difference ML_range

Second, regression was used to estimate the effect of factors. The equation is as below :

$$\text{Markdown value} = 233.432*\text{Mura Level} - 0.564\ \text{Distance},\ R^2=0.514$$

and the model predicting these two parameters has high significance with $F(2,153)=80.93$, $p<0.01$. Subjects' markdown price was positively correlated to Mura Level with parameter 233.43, and negatively correlated to Distance with parameter 0.56. Which means as Mura Level increases 1 level, subjects would markdown NT 233.43 dollars and as the Mura gets 1 pixel closer to the center of display, subjects would markdown NT 0.56 dollars. This result seems to have positive correlation with our common experience.

Before addressing the third point, Distance factor was recoded as another variable named Mura Location, which has two levels: center and corner. If the Distance is less than 130 pixels, the value is "center," and if the Distance is more than 500 pixels, the value is "corner." ANOVA was again used to evaluate the effect on ML_range and Mura Location and reveal two significant main effects: ML_range, $F(3,358)=158.591$,

Table 1. Mean and standard deviation of each Mura Level range under two locations

Mura_Location	ML_range	Mean	Std. Deviation	N
Center	1	484.4444	565.16512	45
	2	1009.3750	804.61807	48
	3	1576.7442	1084.26785	43
	4	3112.9032	1790.11023	31
	Total	1404.4910	1404.24085	167
Corner	1	261.2245	364.75810	49
	2	802.1739	656.33295	46
	3	1358.9286	1294.53773	56
	4	2628.1250	1755.20218	48
	Total	1266.0804	1441.87648	199
Total	1	368.0851	482.03484	94
	2	907.9787	739.23468	94
	3	1453.5354	1206.70433	99
	4	2818.3544	1773.58064	79
	Total	1329.2350	1424.55683	366

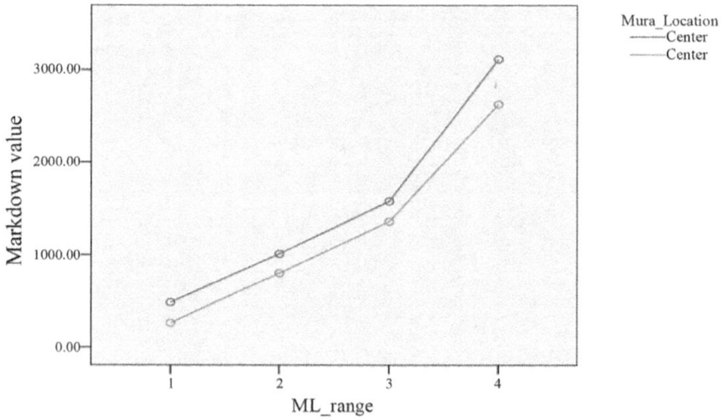

Fig. 5. Correlation between subjects' preference and Distance under different Mura Level range

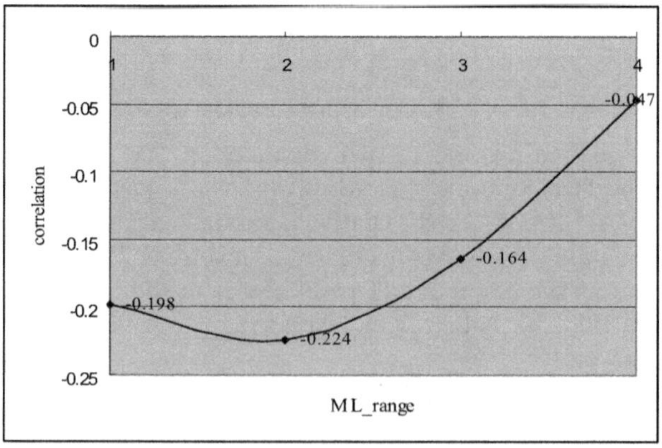

Fig. 6. The interaction term between Mura Level range and Mura Location

P<0.01; and Mura Location, F(1,358)=13.14, P<0.01. There is no significant two-way interaction term. Table 1 shows the mean and standard deviation of each Mura Level range under two locations. A Mura appearing at a corner is always better than one that appears at the center. Figure 5 points out this concept.

5 Conclusion and Future Study

This study focused on the effect of Mura location on an LCD display and was evaluated by participants' subjective markdown values. Though the Distance factor reached statistically significant level, nonetheless the effect was relatively small when compared with other factors such as Mura Level and Mura Level range. There are two implications for this finding.

First, from the experimental design perspective, since the Mura Level dominated the markdown value, any minor deviation of the participant "perceived" Mura Level from the calculated "true" Mura Level can generate biased results which may in turn suppress the Distance effect. An imbalanced experimental design may also create the same problem. Therefore, to ensure the "perceived" and "true" Mura Levels are highly collinear is a key to successfully evaluate Distance effect. More importantly, Figure 6 provides meaningful insights into pricing strategy from a manufacturer's perspective. When Mura levels are high, the small correlation coefficient suggests that the participants were so overwhelmed that no matter the location of the Mura, the markdown value would be large, which means that LCD's with such quality should be scrapped at factory. As the Mura level decrease, the Mura location (Distance) and markdown value becomes more correlated. This suggests that Mura location on the LCD display does affect the perceived value of this display to a certain extent. The decreasing trend from Mura Level range=2 to Mura Level range=1 may suggest that for very minor Mura's, participants can barely detect their existence and therefore the Mura location becomes less relevant to the perceived value. This finding can be used to determine scraping threshold for severe Mura's and marked-down price for moderate Mura's. With this information, the true cost involved in Mura related quality issues thus can be estimated. Following this study, it is reasonable to incorporate Mura location into SEMI standard so that a new standard from end-users' perspective can be developed.

References

1. Kim, W.S., Kwak, D.M., Song, Y.C., Choi, D.H., Park, K.H.: Detection of spot-type defects on liquid crystal display modules. Key Engineering Materials. 270–273, pp. 808–813 (2004)
2. Lee, J.Y., Yoo, S.I.: Automatic Detection of Region-Mura Defect in TFT-LCD. IEICE TRANS. INF. & SYST. E87-D pp. 2371–2378 (2004)
3. Otsu, N.: A threshold selection method from gray-level histograms, IEEE Trans. Syst. Man, Cybern. SMC-9, pp. 62–66 (1979)
4. VESA Flat Panel Display Measurements Standard Ver. 2.0 (2001)
5. Wen, C.H.: FPD standard activities in Taiwan: Measurements for MURA and motion blur. In: Proceeding of The 6th International Meeting in Information Display & International Display Manufacturing Conference (2006)

A Taxonomy of Physical Contextual Sensors

Philippe Truillet

IRIT UMR CNRS
Université Paul Sabatier
118, Route de Narbonne – Toulouse Cedex 4
Philippe.Truillet@irit.fr

Abstract. In this article, we propose to introduce taxonomy of physical contextual sensors. Indeed, applications are now becoming more and more interactive, mobile and pervasive in which context is a big issue. Knowledge from the user and context in which user interacts is crucial in the design. Then, our objective is to help designers to choose best sensors to use from context thy want to collect. We extended and refined taxonomy of context by associating sensors to this taxonomy.

Keywords: physical sensors, taxonomy, design.

1 Introduction

Human Computer Interaction (HCI) is no longer confined to the traditional keyboard, mouse and screen on a fixed desktop. Increasing evolutions of technologies lead to a diversity of interaction techniques. HCI is now focusing on three major aspects:

1. Multimodality, which aims at offering several interaction modalities to enable relevant and efficient communication between a system and a user;
2. Ubiquitous computing, which aims at sensing contextual data to support dynamic adaptation of interactive systems [9, 11];
3. And mixed systems, facilitating human activities by merging the use of every day life physical objects and computers capabilities [10].

Technical and theoretical advances are numerous in these three domains but little attention has been paid to the interconnection of the results of three domains. Researchers have demonstrated exciting examples of physical user interfaces [5, 9, 11]. Nevertheless, programmers can face hurdles when they want to design these ubiquitous interactive systems: how to combine physical sensors or devices with programming languages? How to design such systems? How to describe them?

We propose to develop a conceptual model describing ubiquitous interactive situations and combination of these situations that leads to multimodal ubiquitous mixed interactive systems.

Context awareness is a big issue in HCI, giving meaning to surrounding facts. Knowledge from the user and context in which user interacts is crucial in the design. Choice of context information used in applications is often driven by the acquisition mechanisms available - hardware and software sensors and not by real needs.

J. Jacko (Ed.): Human-Computer Interaction, Part II, HCII 2007, LNCS 4551, pp. 982–989, 2007.

Context is defined by [7] as "any information that can be used to characterize the situation of entities (i.e. whether a person, place or object) that are considered relevant to the interaction between a user and an application, including the user and the application themselves". Entities identified to be relevant are places, people and things.

This paper aims to introduce taxonomy of physical contextual sensors, which can be seen as a bootstrap in design of pervasive systems.

2 Contextual Sensors

Context awareness is an important concept for system usability. Even if research in this field become numerous last years [1, 2, 3; 4, 12], there is no established core methods to take into account the context.

More and more technologies may be considered as physical contextual sensors: RFID, GPS, light sensors, etc. As [13], we define a contextual sensor *as an association between two units*: on one hand, a capture unit and on the other hand calculator unit.

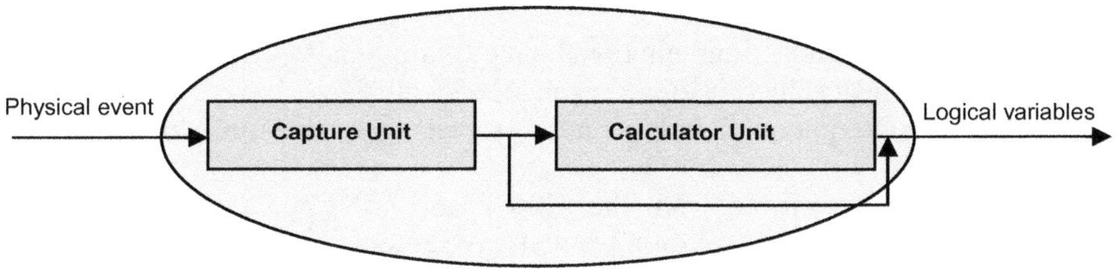

Fig. 1. Contextual sensor architecture

The second unit captures information directly from the physical environment. Then, calculator unit computes the raw information into logical information usable by the system.

In our point of view, a device and a contextual sensor are different. Actually, the information taken from a classical device can be directly interpreted as an "action" from a user. On the other side, information taken from a contextual sensor must be computed (considering the variation of the context) before being interpreted by the system.

3 Taxonomy of Physical Contextual Sensors

Several taxonomies or framework have been proposed in the field of context-awareness [1, 2, 15]. Nevertheless, they seemed to be so much complex to be used. Hence, our taxonomy concerns only physical sensors. Indeed, we think that logical sensors are so much different in terms of characteristics to be taken into account in this phase. We defined some criteria in order to establish this taxonomy. This one is based on and extends the taxonomy of context from [14] (cf. Figure 2.).

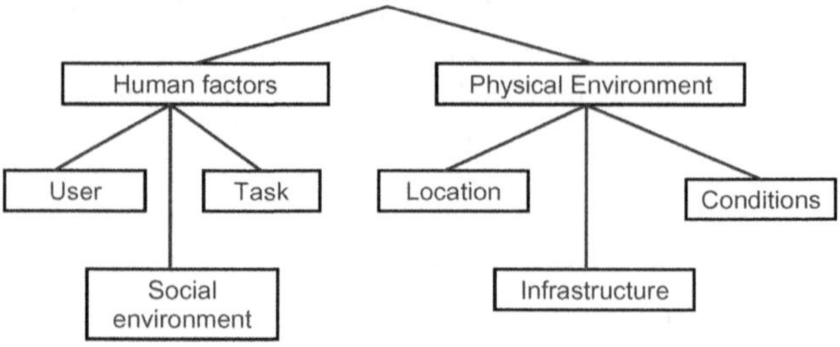

Fig. 2. The Context Feature Space from [14]

The taxonomy of Context Feature Space [14] does not allow designers to identify sensors from context to collect. Our taxonomy permits to establish a link between a "type of context" and corresponding physical contextual sensors able to collect pertinent information. We can note that sensors presented as examples in figures are not limitative and may be various.

The root node of the taxonomy is empty and is subdivided into two branches: the **human factors** (cf. Figure 3) branch and the **physical context** (cf. Figure 4.) branch.

Concerning Human Factors, three categories are identified:

- The User' own context : the emotional state (via psychological and physiological clues), the physical state (position, ...) and the identity
- The Social environment: (i.e. domain and social interaction) in which the user is during the task.
- And the context retrieved from the task: is the task spontaneous, critical, and repetitive? In this branch, we didn't found any sensors eligible to give information on the task. Moreover, we think that this kind of information is only accessible from a task analysis.

Concerning physical context, categories are also identified:

- Conditions e.g. physical values collected by a sensor (temperature, humidity, voltage,). We refined this branch in two sub-categories: natural and artificial conditions, consequence of a human intervention.
- Infrastructure context: indications on the local area and network infrastructure available.
- Localization gives an absolute or relative information on entities available in the area

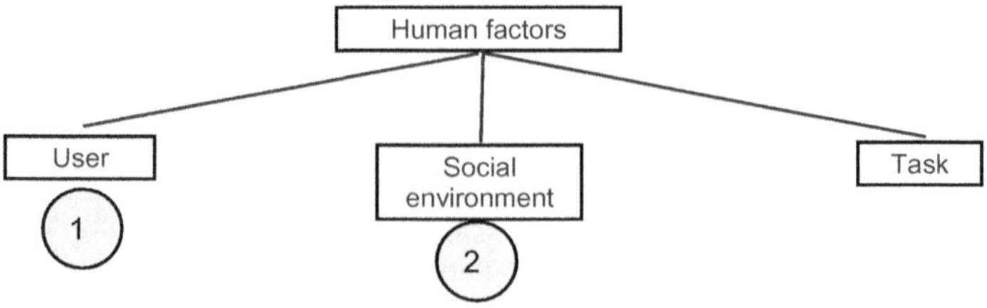

Fig. 3. The Human Factor part of the taxonomy

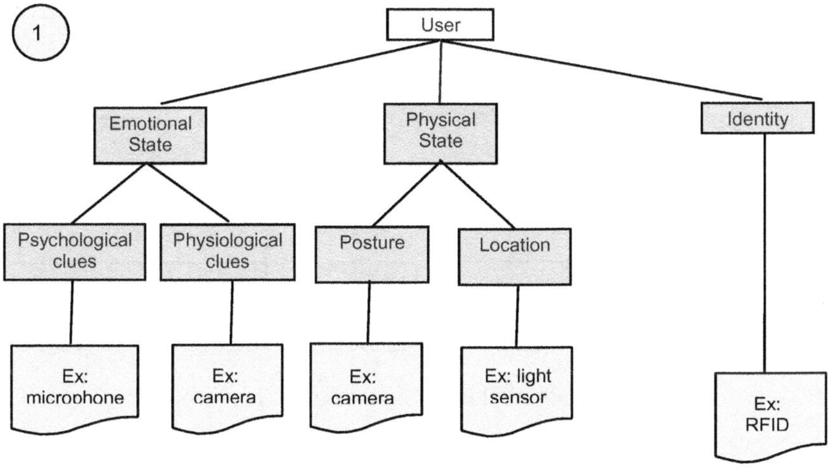

Fig. 3.1. The Human Factor subpart (1) of the taxonomy

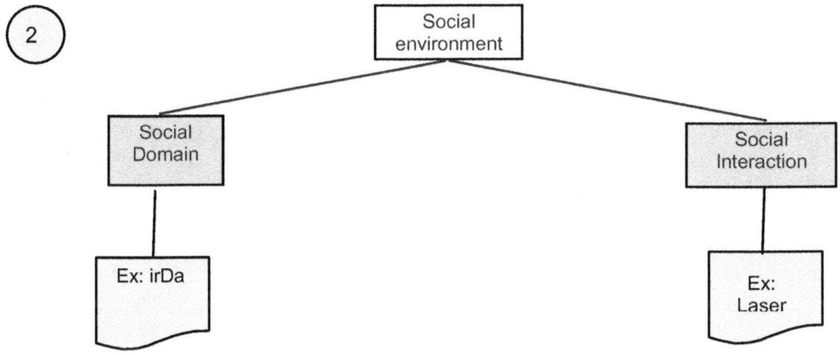

Fig. 3.2. The Human Factor subpart (2) of the taxonomy

These categories are placed on the nodes of our taxonomy. Then, sensors are placed on leaves of the taxonomy.

Redundancy of a physical sensor in different leaves is not really a problem. The designer skims through the graph from the top to the bottom (sensors). Then, there is no ambiguity even a same sensor is placed several times.

Moreover, taxonomy is simple enough to be completed with new sensors.

Sensors are placed on leafs of this tree. For example, a webcam can be a contextual sensor and be used to collect several "types of context" such as physical state or social environment. Redundancy of sensors in the taxonomy is not really a problem. When using the taxonomy, designers examine the graph from root to leaf: hence, there is no ambiguity in choosing the appropriate sensor for desired context.

This taxonomy can be used in a more general architecture model. For example, [8] propose architecture structured in several layers integrating different sensors. More

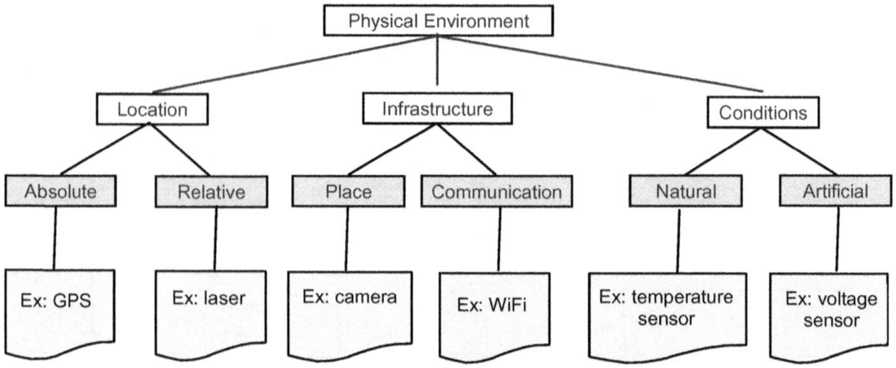

Fig. 4. The Physical Environment part of the taxonomy

recently, [13] described an enhancement of the ARCH model in which sensors are integrated.

In our point of view, our taxonomy may be integrated in the physical layer.

4 Use of the Taxonomy

We designed several pervasive systems with the help of this taxonomy in particular for motor disabled persons. We present in this section two examples of use of the taxonomy.

4.1 Smart Environment for Disabled

In smart environment, we wanted to allow a motor disabled person to open automatically a door and boot automatically his computer (cf. Figure 5.).

Fig. 5. Smart environment for disabled

In the design process, we first precise what we have to collect:

- We must recognize the handicapped person in front of the door. Scanning the taxonomy, we find the *human factor* | *user* | *identity* branch. We choose a camera connected to facial recognition software (cf. Figure 5.)
- Secondly, we must know when the user is in front of his computer. In accordance with our taxonomy, we have to collect a user's context (*Human Factors* branch) and more precisely *location* of the *physical state*. Then, we can choose for example a light sensor among the whole sensors.
- Then, we must identify the user to boot the computer. As the first identification, we scan the *human factor* | *user* | *identity* branch. Finally, we choose the RFID sensor to identify the user.

4.2 Tangible Objects to Interact with Google Earth Environment

We wanted to replace mouse and keyboard devices by a tangible object to allow users to browse in Google Earth software (http://earth.google.com).

Using tangible object implies to collect location of this object and transform it in relative coordinates for Google Earth.

According to our taxonomy, we need to deal with a *relative location* in the *physical environment*. As a solution, we choose a camera to sense this physical context (cf. Figure 6) coupled with the AR Toolkit (http://www.hitl.washington.edu/ artoolkit).

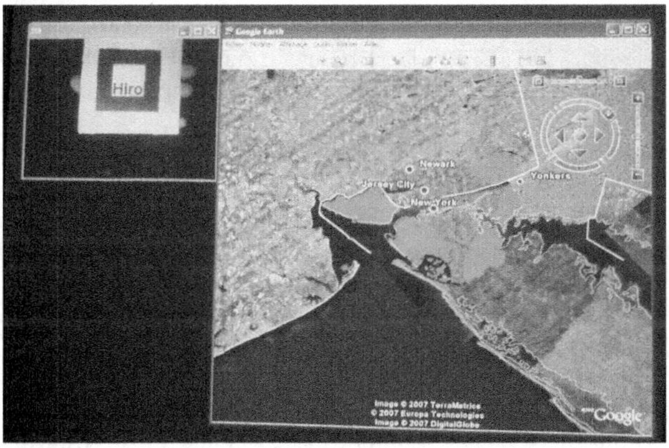

Fig. 6. An example of browsing activity in Google Earth

Even if these examples are simple, this taxonomy allows us to start from needs and determine solutions well-adapted. Moreover, we think that it is to solve more complex problems.

5 Conclusion

The proposed taxonomy is a bootstrap in design of a pervasive system. Its main goal is to allow designers to choose the most adapted sensors for their application.

We have attempted to lay out foundations for the design and development of pervasive systems. Using a variety of applications that we have implemented, we demonstrated how this taxonomy can be used to select sensors.

Nevertheless; this work has to be extended to determine how to merge information provided by sensors and verify consistency between sensors.

We must also define a framework in which this kind of application could be designed. Then, we must evaluate the advantages of using this framework. Finally, this framework must be able to integrate new sensor types.

Acknowledgments. We would like to acknowledge the tireless help of Loïc Chapron and for inspiration he provided for this paper.

References

1. Abowd, G.D., Atkesson, C.G., Brotherton, J.A., Enqvist, T., Gully, P., Lemon, J.: Investigating the capture, integration and access problem of ubiquitous computing in an educational setting. In: Proceedings of CHI'98, pp. 440–447 (May 1998)
2. Boyle, M.: Ubiquitous Awareness Spaces. Report, 2000-682-05, Department of Computer Science, University of Calgary, Alberta, Canada (2001)
3. Chalmers, M.: A Historical View of Context. The. Journal of Collaborative Computing: Computer Supported Cooperative Work. 13(3-4), 223–247 (2004)
4. Chen, G., Kotz, D.: A Survey of Context-Aware Mobile Computing Research, Dartmouth College, Department of Computer Science, UK (November 2000)
5. DeVaul, R., Sung, M., Gips, J., Pentland, A.: MIThril 2003: Applications and Architecture. In: ISWC 2003, 7th IEEE International Symposium on Wearable Computers, New-York, (October 2003)
6. Dey, A.K., Abowd, G.D.: Toward a Better Understanding of Context and Context Awareness. Georgia Institute of Technology, Atlanta, GA, USA (1999)
7. Dey, A.K., Abowd, G.D., Salber, D.: A Conceptual Framework and a Toolkit for Supporting the Rapid Prototyping of Context-Aware Applications. Human-Computer Interaction, Special Issue: Context-Aware Computing, LEA 16(2-4), 97–166 (2001)
8. Gellersen, H.W., Schmidt, A., Beigl, M.: Multi-Sensor Context-Awareness in Mobile Devices and Smart Artifacts. in Mobile Networks and Applications (MONET) 7(5), 341–351 (2002)
9. Greenberg, S., Fitchett, C.: Phidgets: Incorporating Physical Devices into the Interface. In: Newman, M., Edwards, K., Sedivy, J.,(eds.) Proceedings of the Workshop on Building the Ubiquitous Computing User Experience. held at ACM CHI'01, Seattle (2001)
10. Ishii, H., Ullmer, B.: Tangibles bits: Towards seamless interfaces between people, bits and atoms. In: proceedings if ACM CHI'97, pp. 234–241 (1997)
11. Lalis, S., Savidis, A., Stephanidis, C.: Wearable systems for everyday use. ERCIM News, special issue on embedded systems (January 2003)
12. Tapia, M.E., Intille, S., Larson, K.: Activity Recognition in the Home Using Simple and Ubiquitous Sensors. In: Ferscha, A., Mattern, F. (eds.) PERVASIVE 2004. LNCS, vol. 3001, pp. 158–175. Springer, Heidelberg (2004)
13. Rey, G., Coutaz, J.: Le Contexteur: une Abstraction Logicielle pour la Réalisation de Systèmes Interactifs Sensibles au Contexte in IHM'02, Poitiers (France) (Novembre 2002) ISBN 1-58113-615-3/02/0011

14. Schmidt, A., Beigl, M., Gellersen, H.W: There is More to Context Than Location. Computers and Graphics 23(6), 893–901 (December 1999)
15. Tilak, S., Abu-Ghazaleh, N., Heinzelman, W.: A Taxonomy of Wireless Micro-Sensor Network Models. ACM Mobile Computing and Communications Review 6(2), 28–36 (2002)

Human-Robot Interaction in the Home Ubiquitous Network Environment

Hirotada Ueda[1], Michihiko Minoh[1], Masaki Chikama[2], Junji Satake[2], Akihiro Kobayashi[2], Kenzabro Miyawaki[3], and Masatsugu Kidode[4]

[1] Graduate School of Informatics, Kyoto University
Yoshida-Honmachi, Sakyo-ku, Kyoto 606-8501 Japan
[2] National Institute of Information and Communications Technology
3-5 Hikaridai Seika-cho, Soraku-gun, Kyoto 619-0289 Japan
[3] Osaka Institute of Technology,
1-79-1 Kitayama Hirakata, Osaka 573-0196 Japan
[4] Nara Institute of Science and Technology
8916–5 Takayama-cho Ikoma, Nara 630-0192 Japan
{ueda,minoh}@media.kyoto-u.ac.jp, {masaki-c,j-satake, akihiro-k}@nict.go.jp, d1d05a01@info.oit.ac.jp, kidode@is.naist.jp

Abstract. The situation recognition ability of the robot is enhanced by connecting a home ubiquitous network and conversational robots. The situation explanation ability of the robot is also enhanced by acquiring information through the network. The new development of the human robot interaction can be expected in total. In this paper we describe a prototype system that is developed in the experimental house based on such a concept. Then, the study of the actual proof experimental life in the house is discussed.

1 Introduction

The idea to make a residence intelligent has been proposed by installing a sensor in many since the 1980's. After that, the miniaturization, lightening and price reduction of the machine proceed, and the realization of the intelligent smart-home is getting reality. The Aware Home[1] is noteworthy and successful project. We can also enumerate much preceding research in this field[2-4]. However, in spite of so great the efforts, still the advantage of the smart-home is not so clear and no one could find out the killer-application yet. We have to develop a new concept and new frameworks.

There are two important issues, the choice of platform, and the choice of interface[5]. For the former issue, we design a distributed cooperative function platform called "UKARI core," which is named after our project name UKARI: Universal Knowledgeable Architecture for Real-LIfe appliances. For the latter issue, we introduce a compact size conversational robot that can interact with family members via natural language. In our UKARI project we built a real-life test bed in which various sensors, information equipments and household electric appliances are integrated over the network, called the "Ubiquitous Home," for home context aware service experiments. When the sensors and appliances in the home connected by the network provide intelligent functions, the home itself can be just considered an

J. Jacko (Ed.): Human-Computer Interaction, Part II, HCII 2007, LNCS 4551, pp. 990–997, 2007.

invisible robot. We specially paid attention to this point and studied the human-robot relation by combining a visible conversational robot with this invisible robot.

2 Basic concept

One of the basic ideas of the UKARI project is to introduce the two types of robots, i.e. unconscious type robot and visual type robot. It is important to prepare a good mental model to help users deepen their understanding of the system[6]. To this end, we propose a "***Mother-Child*** metaphor," as shown in Fig. 1. The entire house that is composed of networked devices and sensors and autonomously provides services, representing an unconscious robot, can be compared to a ***mother***. This unconscious robot is like a mother who is always at home for the family and naturally gives support whenever family members are in need of it. On the other hand the visible robot, with which the user carries on a dialogue, is compared to a ***child***.

By the restriction of the present technological level, we may give this visible robot the conversation ability of just about a three–years-old child. However the visible robot can be assumed to be a "fanatic" on networks and home appliances in our Ubiquitous Home environment. This ***child*** (visible robot), in collaboration with its ***mother*** (unconscious robot), receives real-time sensor information, internal status information of appliances, information on the present status of the entire system that provides various services, and all history records of these information from the database on the home network. The database also records the users' individual likes and dislikes. Based on all these pieces of information, the ***child*** carries on an appropriate dialogue with the user.

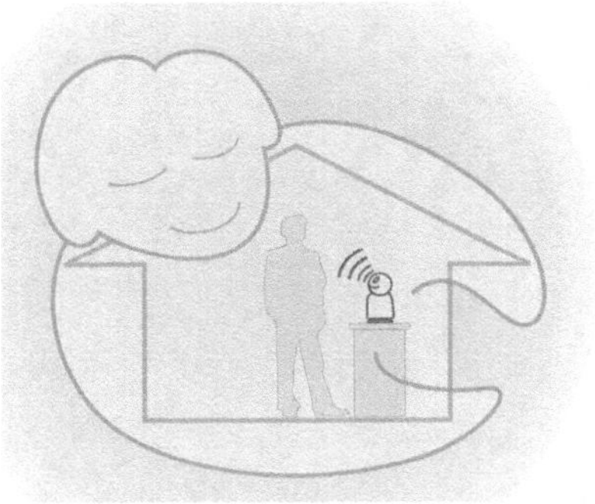

Fig. 1. Mother-Child metaphor

This "Mother-Child" setting eliminates the strange feeling that users of unconscious robots may often have. It provides an explanation in the event of an unexpected or strange systems' autonomous behavior. In a conversation with a user, the ***child*** also can give proper answers to the user's questions by using information obtained from its ***mother***. Furthermore based on a conversation with the user, the ***child*** can request its ***mother*** to provide appropriate services. Thus, this child-mother collaboration system can provide flexible, sophisticated, and careful services to the family members never before achieved.

When a family member talks to the ***child,*** his/her multimodal dialogue (through voice, images, eye-contacts, facial expressions, gestures, etc.) with a three-dimensional robot that actually exists attracts other family members' interests. Thus a topic may be shared by family members and will help solve the problem concerning the isolation of family members. For example, searching for information on the Internet was traditionally done by alone on a PC, but in the Mother-Child setting, it is expected for family members to carry on a dialogue with the robot and search for information on a big-screen TV together in a cheerful manner.

3 Ubiquitous Home

The Floor plan of the Ubiquitous Home is shown in Fig. 2. As the sensors, there are cameras and microphones in the ceiling, floor pressure sensors throughout the flooring, infrared sensors at the important positions. Three types of RFID systems are located over the ceiling of each room, in the corridor and in the furniture. In addition, 113 on-off switch sensors around every door of the house including shelves and every drawer are installed to detect every day events. As the actuators, there are flat panel displays including TV tuners, speakers and networked consumer appliances such as lamps, air-conditioners, a refrigerator, and a washing machine etc. The conversational robots, details are described later, are located in almost every room and they work as sensors as well as actuators because each robot has a camera, three microphones and a speaker.

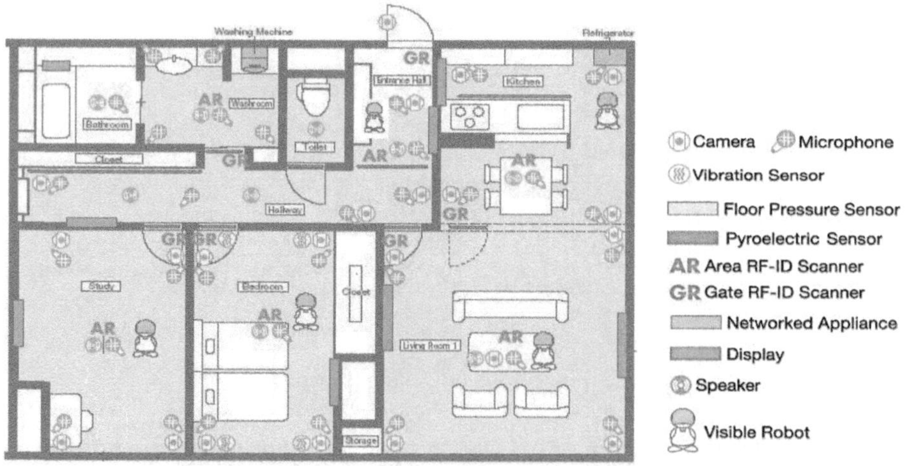

Fig. 2. Floor plan of the Ubiquitous Home

Floor pressure sensors installed throughout the flooring contain 18 cm by 18 cm binary detection units and are used to track the family members. Infrared sensors installed at the top of the entrance door in each room, at foot positions in the kitchen and in the corridor detect infrared sources, so can be used to detect the movement of the family members. The RFID receivers detect the RFID tags held by the family or attached to the objects in the home.

The Ubiquitous Home was constructed in the Research Center building of the National Institute of Information and Communications Technology. However, we tried to make Ubiquitous Home as much as possible that experimenters can collect real-life data as if subjects are living in their own house, not in a laboratory. As shown in Fig. 2, the Ubiquitous Home has a living room, dining room, kitchen, study, bedroom, washroom, bathroom and other utilities necessary to enjoy a comfortable life. Fig. 3 show a view of the living room and the kitchen. Entrance for the subjects is separated from the researchers and any researcher does not try to speak to the subjects when they are running the experimental life in the Ubiquitous Home. All the sensor data and audio-video data gathered in the Ubiquitous Home are stored in the big database. Researchers access those data only if they are really necessary to check for the research purpose.

Fig. 3. Living room and kitchen of the Ubiquitous Home

4 Conversational Robot

Since the family consists of members in various ages, universal interface is absolutely necessary. Natural language speech interface is one of the most preferable universal interfaces. We developed a tiny conversational robot, named Phyno, as a ***child*** of the Mother-Child metaphor. In designing a human interface, affordance is really important[6]. Phyno can freely manipulate home appliances through the network and has a good memory (database) and also knows the family members' situation by the networked sensors, therefore Phyno can strongly support the family's life. However the ability to carry on a dialogue in a natural language is unfortunately not sufficient. We therefore decided to regard Phyno as a three-year-old child. In order to make the "Mother-Child" system work well, it is necessary to make the user understand these matters as a firm mental model.

According to the research of cognitive development[7], a child begins to make inferences about physical phenomena, like falling down a slope, and understands the concept of category to some extent by the age of three or four. It is observed in daily life that a small child tries to interrupt a conversation between adults, catching at a word that the child can understand. The small child, making the best use of ability to associate and infer things, and memories, provides an associated topic that it can hit upon from his/her knowledge and tries to attract the adults' attention towards his/her own topic. When the adults respond, the child tries to continue talking about what he/she knows. The child continues conversation with the adults trying to do something useful for the adult. From the viewpoint of the system, to do something useful means to provide a desirable service.

Phyno has an intension to provide a good service to the family members and it must find what is the desired target service through the conversation. Therefore association is an effective strategy to promote conversation between the Phyno and the family members. Using the association mechanism, we designed Phyno's dialog method to try to lead the conversation to one of its possible services.
Physical design of Phyno was managed by the following basic policy.

- Childlike appearance
- Cute childlike behavior
- Not walk but exist everywhere
- Small size not to be an obstacle

Phyno is shown in Fig. 4. Phyno has is 25cm tall and its neck has three degrees of freedom. Phyno's waist and both hands have each one-degree of freedom. Phyno has a camera and can recognize registered family members faces. Phyno also has three microphones and a speaker

Fig. 4. Conversational robot Phyno

5 Context Aware Services

At the Ubiquitous Home, we introduced a new framework as shown in Fig. 5. Many appliances and many sensors are connected to the home network and data form these devices are gathered into the Environment Action Database. Event analyzer and context analyzer are attached this database. Using those data in the database, the unconscious-type robot (house itself) performs the context aware services. Results of services and actions of family members are also collected and stored in this database. We have implemented several context aware services.

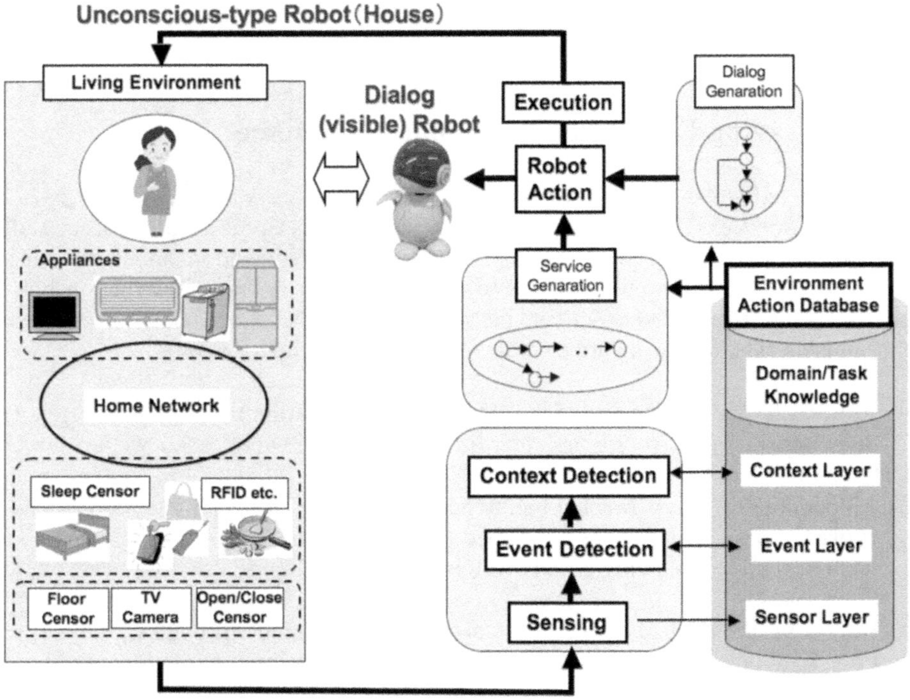

Fig. 5. The framework to carry out context aware services

a) Appliance control service

The family member can control all the appliances, including room lamps, in the house through the conversation with Phyno. Everything what remote controller can do is done.

b) Finishing notice service

The laundry transmits its status information such as "washing" or "drying finish" in the text format to the home network. This message is displayed on the TV or converted into the voice and presented to the speaker, depending on the context where the person who started the laundry is and what he/she is doing now.

c) Wake up service

When the time to wake up has come, the sleeping sensor checks the depth of sleep of the person and Phyno plays music that is suitable to the depth and his/her likes.

d) Check a thing left behind service

When the floor sensor detects an outgoing trajectory, Phyno tells him/her if there are some items left behind. This service is done by comparing his/her going out purpose in his/her schedule database with his belongings.

e) TV program recommendation service

The history of which TV program the family member watches is stored in the database. When the family member comes and turns on the TV, Phyno retrieves the database, and recommend a TV program that may be preferable to him/her.

f) Cooking recipe retrieval service

The family member can find out his/her favorite cooking through the associative conversation with Phyno watching the cooking recipe on the TV screen.

6 Real Living Experiments at Ubiquitous Home

We conducted a real-life experiment in which a family stays at the Ubiquitous Home for about two weeks. Five families lived in the Ubiquitous Home as the subjects. Before starting the experiment we gave the subjects brief explanation about the sensors installed in the Ubiquitous Home. We also give them a short introduction how to communicate with Phyno to activate the services. After the experiment, we interviewed the subjects. The following are a summary of the experimental results.

- Almost all the subjects said that at first they felt the strain because they were aware of the sensors in the rooms and their life was not usual but after 3 days they got used to them.
- All people said that it was not bad to be seen with the camera in the head of Phyno. However, almost all people mentioned that the existence of the ceiling camera gave them the bad feel of being closely watched. (This bad feel is also disappears after the three days)
- Regarding the control of the home appliances and lamps through the dialog with Phyno, about two days were necessary for every subject before he/she got accustomed to the way of talking which was easy to recognize in speech recognition software. At the beginning the recognition rate is as low as 30%, but it rises to more than 90%. Many subjects said, "It is convenient that time to look for a remote controller disappeared and it will be a big welcome if all control is integrated into this robot dialog interface."
- As for the finishing notice service, it was typical impression that the notice was helpful because it wasn't missed even when I was busy.
- We got some interesting reports such as "Phyno of the kitchen came to listen to what I say well, and Phyno of the living room came to listen to what father says well." It is expressed as a robot learned though it is the result that a human being practiced.
- Sixty married couples reported " When we went shopping, we sometimes felt that we had better to come back early because Phyno was waiting." They also reported that they kept on watching the television program recommended by Phyno.

We found many cases that should be analyzed from the viewpoint of the attachment[9] to the robot through this living experiment. There also was a report that a subject lived with Phyno having the question if Phyno is the creature or the inanimate object. These are many future important research themes from the psychological viewpoint as well as to the social science viewpoint.

7 Conclusion

We proposed a concept that a cooperation of a home network, as an invisible unconscious-type robot, and a visible conversational robot produces a new human-robot interaction and realizes intelligent services. The situation recognition ability of the robot is enhanced by connecting a home ubiquitous network and conversational robots. The situation explanation ability of the robot is also enhanced by acquiring information through the network. We conducted a real-life experiment in which a family stays at the Ubiquitous Home for about two weeks. The result acquired through the experiment was reported. The result showed the effectiveness and future possibility of the concept.

References

1. Kidd, C.D., Orr, R.J., Abowd, G. D., Atkeson, C.G., Essa, I.A., MacIntyre, B., Mynatt, E., Starner T.E., Newstetter, W.: The Aware Home: A Living Laboratory for Ubiquitous Computing Research. In: Proc. of the Second International Workshop on Cooperative Buildings - CoBuild'99, (1999)
2. Mori, T., Noguchi, H., Takada, A., Sato, T.: Sensing Room: Distributed Sensor Environment for Measurement of Human Daily Behavior. In: Proc. of First International Workshop on Networked Sensing Systems (INSS2004) pp. 40–43 (2004)
3. Helal, A., Mann, W., Elzabadani, H., King, J., Kaddourah, Y., Jansen, E.: Gator Tech Smart House: A Programmable Pervasive Space. IEEE Computer magazine, pp. 64–74, (March 2005)
4. Lee, J.-S., Park, K.-S., Hahn, M.-S.: WindowActive: An Interactive House Window On Demand. In: 1st Korea-Japan Joint Workshop on Ubiquitous Computing and Networking Systems (UbiCNS 2005), pp. 481–484 (June 2005)
5. Yamazaki, T.: Ubiquitous Home: Real-life Testbed for Home Context-Aware Service. In: the First International Conference on Testbeds and Research Infrastructures for the DEvelopment of NeTworks and COMmunities (Tridentcom 2005), Trento, Italy pp. 54–59 (2005)
6. Norman, D. A.: The Psychology of Everyday Things, New York: Basic Books, Inc. (1988)
7. Inui, Tshiroo (eds.): Ninchi hattatsu to shinka (in Japanese), Tokyo: Iwanami Shoten, pp. 88–93 (2001)
8. Ueda, H., Kobayashi, A., Satake, J., Chikama, M., Sato, J., Kidode, M.: Dialog Strategy for Interactive Robot Interface in Home Network (in Japanese) Trans. Of IPSJ, vol. 47(1), pp. 87–97 (2006)
9. Matsumoto, N., Ueda, H., Yamazaki, T., Tokosumi, A.: The cognitive characteristics of communication with artificial agents. In: Joint Third International Conference on Soft Computing and Intelligent Systems and Seventh International Symposium on Advanced Intelligent Systems (SCIS & ISIS 2006), CD-ROM, pp. 1269–1273 (2006)

Measuring User Experiences of Prototypical Autonomous Products in a Simulated Home Environment

Martijn H. Vastenburg, David V. Keyson, and Huib de Ridder

Delft University of Technology, Faculty of Industrial Design Engineering
Landbergstraat 15, 2628 CE, Delft, The Netherlands
{m.h.vastenburg,d.keyson,h.deridder}@tudelft.nl

Abstract. Advances in sensor technology, embedded processing power, and modeling and reasoning software, have created the possibility for everyday products to sense the environment and pro-actively anticipate user needs. There is however a risk of creating environments in which people experience a lack of control. The aim of this study is to explore the degree in which people are willing to delegate control to a pro-active home atmosphere control system. The findings suggest that participants are willing to delegate control to easy-to-use systems, and they do not want to delegate control to complex and unpredictable systems. It is argued that the willingness to delegate should not be considered as a fixed degree, rather system initiative might depend on the situation at hand or on changes in time. Design research on mixed initiative systems faces a methodological challenge, in terms of measuring user experience of autonomous prototypes in a controlled way, while still preserving the sense of a realistic experience. The paper describes advantages and disadvantages of testing in a simulated home environment versus testing in the field.

Keywords: Smart environments, user studies, intelligent interfaces, mixed initiative, interaction design, user adaptivity.

1 Introduction

Increasingly, people are being confronted with products in the home that can automatically adapt to the context of use. Advances in sensor technology, embedded processing power, and modeling and reasoning software, have enabled everyday products to sense their environment and pro-actively anticipate user needs [13]. For example, stair lights can be activated in the home by movement at night using commercially available domotics systems. Context-aware and autonomous services might eventually automatically anticipate user needs, and accurately fit into domestic routines [1,16]. There is however a risk of creating an environment in which people experience a lack of control [1,3]. In a worst case scenario, instead of feeling understood and supported by the environment, the future home user might feel as if the environment is out of control.

To design controllable and pleasurable semi-autonomous products for the home, designers need to know how prototypes of these products may be experienced by people [4,5,8]. In existing studies, user experiences with autonomous products are

J. Jacko (Ed.): Human-Computer Interaction, Part II, HCII 2007, LNCS 4551, pp. 998–1007, 2007.

sometimes based solely on product descriptions on paper. For example, in a study by Barkhuus and Dey [2] on autonomous applications for mobile phones, participants were asked to imagine using autonomous services based on a written service description. Using a five-day diary, participants indicated how often they would have used the service, and then rated the usefulness of the service. Since the participants had never used autonomous services on their phones before, the degree to which people were able to imagine these services is unknown. The study showed that users are willing to partially give up user control if only the application's usefulness is greater than the cost of limited control. Apparently, the limited user control as implied by product autonomy can be compensated by product advantages. Barkhuus and Dey agree that a logical next step would be to develop and test working prototypes.

Product descriptions on paper also played a central role in a study by Rijsdijk and Hultink [10], which focused on consumer appreciation of autonomous products. Participants were not given the opportunity to actually experience the autonomous products; in the study, only a short description of the product was given. The user experience invoked by the product descriptions might not correspond with the experience of real products. The study reveals that consumers perceive highly autonomous products as more risky and complex than less autonomous products. Relative advantage, i.e., the degree to which an innovation is perceived as superior to the idea that it supersedes [11], was however found to compensate for the negative effect of perceived risk. It would be interesting to see if the user experience changes in time, an aspect which could not be examined in the Rijsdijk and Hultink study.

From an ecological perspective, the home is the obvious place to study and evaluate domestic products and to collect experience-based feedback [1,12]. Current practice is however such that most studies take place in lab environments [6,9]. Many practical obstacles prevent researchers from doing research in the field, including: 1) *time constraints*; it generally takes more time to get the product to the user than vice versa; 2) *deployment issues*; most autonomous products are still under development, and product behavior is often wizard-of-oz based. Deployment in the field would require a huge implementation effort; 3) *controllability issues*; although the living patterns of people would be more natural inside their homes, [e.g., 14,15], creating a controlled environment can help in focusing in on relevant aspects of the product; 4) *ethical issues*, including privacy concerns, make it hard to monitor users at home. Laboratory studies might not suffice, since it can be hard to mimic the natural setting in the lab, and long term product use cannot be studied in the lab. Researchers are faced with a methodological challenge in terms of measuring the user experience of autonomous prototypes in a controlled way, while still preserving the naturalness of the experience. In many cases, however, most relevant aspects of the home situation can be recreated in the lab. In a comparative study, Kjeldskov et al. found that both a lab evaluation and a field evaluation of a context-aware mobile system resulted in the same list of issues [9], thereby demonstrating the practical use of the laboratory for studying autonomous products.

This paper is organized as follows. Section 2 presents a user study, in which the degree of system initiative as preferred by the users was studied in a simulated home environment. The findings of the user study are described in section 3, followed by a discussion and conclusions in section 4, and suggestions for future work in section 5.

2 Methodology

A user study was conducted to find out how much initiative people may be willing to delegate to an atmosphere control system in the living room, and to study to what degree early prototypes of autonomous domestic products can be studied in a simulated home environment. The atmosphere control system used in the experiment made it possible to activate and adjust predefined atmospheres; each atmosphere consists of a combination of music, electronic wall art and light settings [15]. To determine if preferred system initiative depends on the situation at hand or on changes in time, the willingness to delegate will be studied in relation to context (user activities) and user perceived product characteristics (usefulness, confidence, ease of use, user control).

Diary Study. Diary booklets were used to personalize the experiment sessions, thereby creating a sense of attachment and familiarity. Participants were asked to log their activities at home for five evenings prior to the experiment. These logs were used to create realistic activity-based assignments that were used in the experiment.

Previous studies with the atmosphere projection system showed that although generic atmosphere presets can be used as a start, they do not fit the preferences for music, projections and colors of the individual users [15]. In preparation of the present study, participant couples were asked to indicate, for each activity, their music and ambient-color preferences. These preferences were used to create personalized atmosphere presets, i.e., predefined combinations of (colored) light settings, electronic wall art, and music.

Prototype description. A living room setting was created in a lab environment. Participants could use a touch-screen user interface, specifically developed for the experiment, to activate the preset personalized atmospheres and to control the individual lights, electronic wall art, and music separately. The prototype uses a home atmosphere control module that was developed earlier at Delft University of Technology. The atmosphere controller is based on an atmosphere control model, in which functions and features have been clustered based on how people experience their environment. Prior to the experiment, the atmosphere content was personalized according to the participants' preference for music and room light color as stated in their diaries. The predefined atmospheres could not be changed during the experiment. Preset settings of lamps and music volume were defined for selected activities. For example, when activating the activity 'watch TV', lights were dimmed and music was muted. Presets could be temporarily overridden in the user interface by users.

In a separate frame, which was visible at the lower section of the screen at all times, users could select the preferred level of system autonomy (Fig.1). The prototype offered three modes of operation, similar to the three levels of interactivity as defined by Barkhuus and Dey. In the *manual mode*, users had to take initiative to control the atmospheres, activity settings and manual overrides. In the *semi-automatic mode*, the system would suggest a change of setting to the users. The suggestion was presented on the touch screen, which could be viewed from most positions in the room, and a bell sound was played. Suggestions were accepted or rejected by uttering 'yes' or 'no'. In the *automatic mode*, the system would pro-actively change settings; users were still able to override the automatic settings. For example, when a user would pick up a book, in the automatic mode the reading lamp would be switched on automatically, whereas in the semi-automatic mode the system would suggest turning on the reading lamp. Both automatic and semi-automatic system behavior were wizard-of-oz; the operator observed the participants via a camera, and activated settings and suggestions when appropriate.

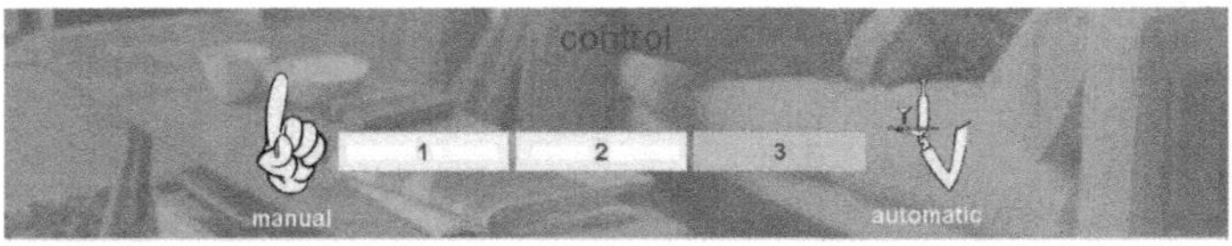

Fig. 1. Using the touch-screen, users could select the preferred level of system autonomy: manual control, semi-automatic, and automatic

Procedure. Data was collected over ten 2.5 hour-sessions. Ten participating couples (10 women, 10 men) aged between 23 and 30 (mean 26.7, SD 1.9) participated in the study. There were 4 students and 16 non-student adults with diverse backgrounds. Participants had no prior experience with the control system used in the experiment. Couples were selected based on their home situation, i.e., household, no children.

One week prior to the experiment, the couples were visited and were given a diary to collect personal data for the experiment. The completed diaries were collected the day before the experiment, and were used to create a personalized atmosphere model, as well as to create eight activity assignments for the experiment.

The study was carried out in the living room laboratory at the Faculty of Industrial Design Engineering at Delft University of Technology. An introduction to the system was given, in which the functional use of the system was demonstrated. Participants were given some time to try out the interface, and were encouraged to ask any questions relating to product usage. Participants were asked to try out the various system initiative settings; they were explicitly told that they could not do anything wrong. During the experiment, the participants were left alone in the living room lab. Each session took approximately three hours per couple.

Eight activity-assignments were given. These activity-assignments were selected from the diaries such that they roughly resembled the activity pattern at home, squeezed into a 2.5 hour session. Some of the activities had to be performed individually, while others were at the couple level. For each assignment, the participants were asked to engage in the activity and to use the central touch screen to select the preferred product autonomy level (a single product autonomy setting for both participants); the autonomy level could be modified at any time during the activity. Participants were given the option of manually changing the room settings to accommodate a given activity whenever they wanted to. After approximately 15 minutes, the experiment supervisor asked to finish the activity and to fill in the evaluation questionnaire, as described in table 1. After finishing the questionnaire, the system was reset, and the participants started their next activity-assignment. At the end of the experiment, participants were asked for general feedback in an exit interview.

Table 1. A paper-based questionnaire was administered to measure the user experiences immediately after each activity-assignment using continuous rating scales. Participants were asked to rate I) their activities, II) their satisfaction with the enviroment settings, III) preferred mode of operation, and IV) perceived product characteristics.

Part I: user activities	**Q1a** concentration level	(low-high)
	Q1b physical effort level	(low-high)
	Q1c social interaction level	(low-high)
Part II: functional and atmosphere settings	**Q2** satisfaction with functional settings	(low-high)
	Q3 satisfaction with atmosphere settings	(low-high)
Part III: willingness to delegate control	**Q4** user preferred system mode of operation	(manual – automatic)
Part IV-a: product scores - initial expectations	**Q5a** confidence level	(low-high)
	Q5b ease of use	(low-high)
	Q5c user control	(low-high)
Part IV-b: product scores – actual experience	**Q6a** confidence level	(low-high)
	Q6b ease of use	(low-high)
	Q6c user control	(low-high)

3 Preliminary Findings

The total number of completed questionnaires was 148; six activity-assignments had to be skipped because the of time constraints. The experiment sessions were limited to 2.5 hours, due to limited lab availability. As a result, five couples completed eight activities, four couples seven, and one couple six.

Correlation analysis. To understand how willingness to delegate control related to the items in the questionnaire, a Pearson correlation analysis was conducted on the questionnaire results. Willingness to delegate was measured by Q4: *user preferred autonomy level*. A significant moderate-positive correlation ($r=.245$, $n=144$, $p<.005$) was found between Q4 and Q6b, being the *ease-of-use* score, taken after each assignment. Apparently, high scores on willingness to delegate control to the system were related to high product scores on confidence, ease of use and user control. Q4 was also positively correlated to the initial expectations product scores Q5a (confidence) ($r=.175$, $n=140$, $p<.05$) and Q5b (ease of use) ($r=.167$, $n=140$, $p<.05$).

General trends in time. Significant correlations were found between the activity-assignment sequence number, i.e., the time-line, and the initial expectations product scores Q5a ($r=.391$, $n=141$, $p<.0005$), Q5b ($r=.292$, $n=141$, $p<.0005$) and Q5c ($r=.306$, $n=141$, $p<.0005$), respectively. As shown in figure 2, on average, participants were neutral at the start of the experiment, and the initial expectations product scores on confidence and ease of use increased over time. It would seem that participants needed some time to familiarize themselves with the idea of product autonomy, and to gain appreciation for the prototype.

User ratings on initial expectations product scores gradually increased in time, whereas the actual experience product scores fluctuated throughout the experiment. A possible explanation would be that the initial expectations scores (Q5) were used to express an overall score in relation to the prototype, whereas the actual experience scores (Q6) were used to give feedback to the prototype performance during the previous activity.

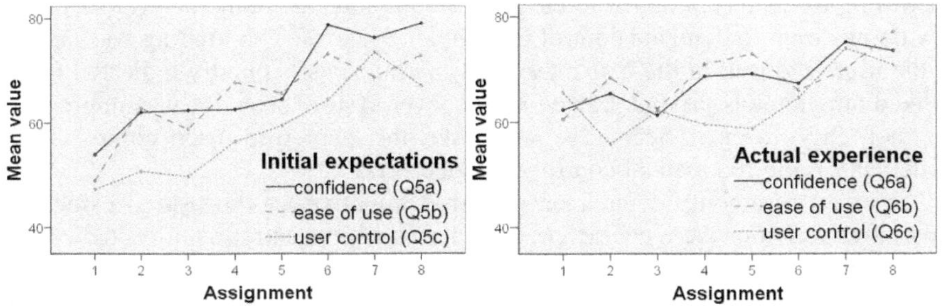

Fig. 2. Mean values for initially expected (left) and actual experienced (right) product scores in time for confidence, ease of use, and user control, on a scale from 0 (low) to 100 (high)

Factor analysis. A factor analysis on the results of the questionnaire resulted in six factors explaining a cumulative 78% of the variance (Table 2). Six factors were selected based on the percentage of variance explained. The factors were labeled 1) ease of use (expected), 2) ease of use (actual), 3) perceived user control, 4) functional lighting score, 5) physical activity, and 6) social activity, considering the factor loadings of the questions. Q4 loads on three factors: FAC1, FAC3 and FAC6, suggesting that ease of use (expected), perceived user control, and social activity contribute significantly to user preferred control.

Table 2. Rotated Principal Component Anaysis, using varimax rotation. All values <.20 suppressed. The table shows the factor loadings of the questionnaire items. User preferred control (Q4) loads on three factors: FAC1, FAC3 and FAC6, suggesting that ease of use (expected), user control, and social activity contribute significantly to user preferred control.

Factor label	ease of use (expect.)	ease of use (actual)	perceived user control	functional lighting score	physical activity	social activity
Component (% of variance)	**1 (28,9%)**	**2 (12,8%)**	**3 (10,8%)**	**4 (9,2%)**	**5 (8,1%)**	**6 (8,0%)**
Q1a concentration				,508	,548	,226
Q1b physical effort					,858	
Q1c social interaction						,916
Q2 functional lighting score				,894		
Q3 atmosphere score	,204	,246		,466	-,453	,465
Q4 user preferred control	,428		-,602			-,217
Q5a confidence (expected)	,837	,201				
Q5b ease of use (expected)	,839	,249				
Q5c control (expected)	,615		,685			
Q6a confidence (actual)	,220	,839	,209			
Q6b ease of use (actual)	,223	,897				
Q6c control (actual)	,235	,441	,745			

User preferred product autonomy. The user scores on Q4 can be visualized using the components of the factor analysis. Q4 has high factor loadings on FAC3 and FAC1. As shown in Figure 3, the willingness to delegate control to the system appears to be related to the perceived ease of use. This might suggest that participants are willing to delegate control to easy-to-use autonomous home control systems, but they do not want to delegate control to complex systems. This finding was confirmed by the user feedback in the exit interviews; participants explicitly indicated that they disliked autonomous product behavior whenever system behavior was unpredictable, i.e., not easy to use. Secondly, whenever the perceived user control is high, participants preferred manual control, and vice versa.

The effect of activity context on preferred initiative was measured using Q1a, b and c; user activities were characterized in terms of concentration, physical effort and social interaction. According to the results of the factor analysis, preferred control (Q4) has a small negative loading on social activity (FAC6), which might suggest that, in the case of autonomous home control systems, people prefer manual control whenever they are involved in social acts. However, no significant correlations were found between user activities and preferred control.

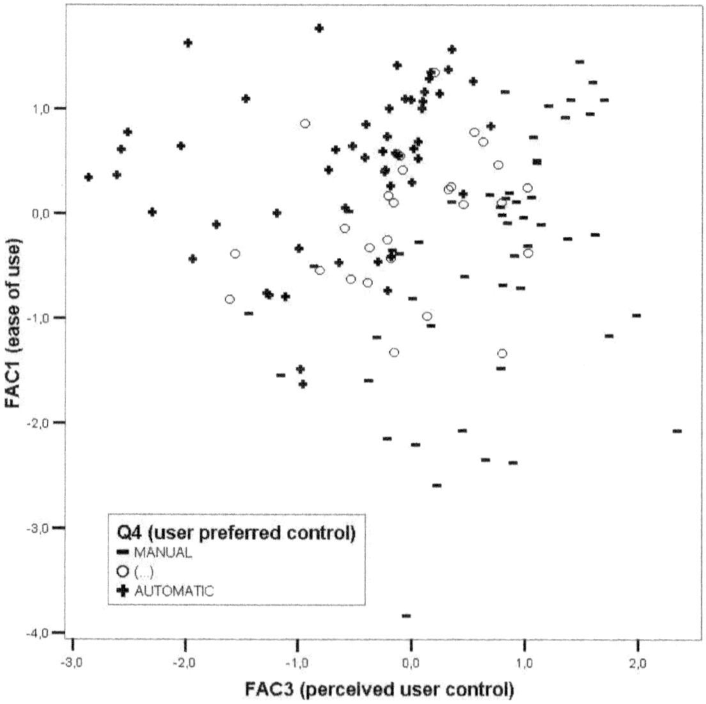

Fig. 3. User ratings of preferred mode of operation plotted against the relevant components of the factor analysis

Observations and user reactions. Participants generally indicated in the exit interview that the experiment session resembled a normal evening at home, although most participants would conduct fewer activities at home. In the exit interview, eight out of ten couples indicated that they would like to have a similar autonomous system in their homes, whereas two couples were neutral. Seven couples indicated they enjoyed using the system.

The sense of being able to predict system actions was found to have a direct impact on confidence in the system. For example, at one point the system switched off a lamp when the participants had not moved for quite some time. The participants did not understand why the system took the initiative to change the setting, and got confused. One participant explicitly indicated that her confidence in the system dropped in reaction to each unpredictable action.

4 Discussion and Conclusions

Willingness to delegate control. Participants were willing to delegate control to the autonomous home control prototype used in the experiment. Participants did need time to familiarize with the prototype and to appreciate the product autonomy. On average, participants were neutral at the start of the experiment, and the product scores improved in time. Apparently, participants changed their expectations and first impressions based on the real experiences they had with the prototype; this issue could not have been studied with paper-based product concepts only.

Ease of use and predictability were found to be fundamental issues in creating acceptable autonomous products for the home. User feedback from the exit interviews suggests that especially the predictability of autonomous system actions needs the attention of designers of autonomous systems for home use; unpredictable system behavior had a negative effect on ease of use, and consequently on the willingness to delegate control. This type of feedback is valuable in the early phases of the design process; the design can then be improved before starting a field study.

Although high system autonomy was found to be related to low user control, the lack of user control does not necessarily have a negative influence on the willingness to delegate control, and consequently to the acceptability of autonomous products in the home. This is in line with results from earlier, similar studies [2].

Being 'at home' in the lab. Considerable time was spent rebuilding a living room in the lab. Also, input from a diary study was used to personalize the course of the experiment, resulting in user driven scenarios instead of scenarios that were fixed for all participants. Since user activities at home varied between subjects, it would not have been natural to enforce default activities. The variations in scenarios between sessions made it hard to compare results between subjects. Despite this limitation, the results do provide insight in trends in time, as well as in general acceptability of autonomous products.

The diaries proved to be a valuable source of information in terms of modeling participants' typical home activities. Activities in the lab did however differ in user experience from activities at home. First, secondary activities, such as 'putting the dishes into the dishwasher', and interruptions, such as incoming phone calls, were not captured by the diary and therefore were not part of the experiment. Subjects generally reported that the experiment session was more relaxing than an evening at home, since many such interruptions were missing. Second, there was no sense of purpose or urgency in the activities in the lab, since there were no deadlines or real consequences. Consequently, participants might have been more relaxed in the lab, resulting in neutral scores on concentration (Q1a). The user study in the lab should however be regarded as a step towards field testing; testing the effect of secondary activities and interruptions in the lab might not be feasible at all.

Personalization of atmosphere content based on the diaries turned out to be a time consuming activity that had to be redone in preparation of every session. In the exit interviews, however, participants did indicate that the personalized atmospheres helped create an experience similar to home.

Experiment design. Participants were explicitly instructed to try out various initiative settings during the experiment. The actual system settings were not consistent with the actual preferred settings, and consequently the system settings as logged in the log file could not be used in the data analysis. In the case that the actual system settings are needed for the data analysis, participants should be instructed to use the system as they would do at home.

Reflections on the methodology. Collecting realistic user feedback in the initial stages of a design process for pro-active home systems remains a challenge. Whereas many studies focus on testing concepts, without working prototypes, a simulated environment can enable researchers to measure realistic user experiences with prototypes. Preparation of the present lab study was however a time-consuming process. In general, however, the user studies in the laboratory setting did provide useful input for the field studies, thereby saving time in later stages of the design process. A flexible design approach is suggested in which early user studies in a lab environment are followed by realistic and longitudinal studies in the field.

5 Future Work

The ideal autonomous home product would probably take into account the actual context of use and adapt the system autonomy accordingly. Based on the results of the current study, autonomous products could lower system initiative whenever the user perceived ease of use is low. For example, when users implicitly show their discomfort with system actions, system initiative should be reduced; this would give the user some time to regain confidence in product behavior.

As a next step, a study is foreseen in which a similar prototype will be tested in the field. Studying the prototype for a longer period of time in the field should result in a more natural user experience, and consequently in a better understanding of the mechanisms underlying acceptability of autonomous products in the home environment. In the view of the methodological challenges as mentioned before, it might still take some time before practical and usable autonomous products find their way to the home.

Acknowledgments. The authors would like to thank the study participants and colleagues for their support in the course of the design and the user study.

References

1. Abowd, G.D., Mynatt, E.D.: Charting past, present, and future research in ubiquitous computing. ACM Trans. Comp.-Hum. Interact 7(1), 29–58 (2000)
2. Barkhuus, L., Dey, A.: Is Context-Aware Computing Taking Control Away from the User? Three Levels of Interactivity Examined. In: Dey, A.K., Schmidt, A., McCarthy, J.F. (eds.) UbiComp 2003. LNCS, vol. 2864, pp. 149–156. Springer, Heidelberg (2003)
3. Edwards, K., Grinter, R.E.: At Home with Ubiquitous Computing: Seven Challenges. In: Proc. of Ubicomp'01, pp. 256–272 (2001)
4. Gaver, B., Martin, H.: Alternatives: exploring information appliances through conceptual design proposals. In: Proc. of SIGCHI Human Fact. in Comp. Syst. (2000)
5. Haines, V., Mitchell, V., Cooper, V., Maguire, M.: Probing user values in the home environment within a technology driven Smart Home project. Pers. and Ubiq. Comp (2006)
6. Hansen, T.R., Bardram, J.E., Soegaard, M.: Moving out of the lab: Deploying pervasive technologies in a hospital. IEEE Perv. Computing 5(3), 24–31 (2006)
7. Hardian, B., Indulska, J., Henricksen, K.: Balancing Autonomy and User Control in Context-Aware Systems - a Survey. In: Proc. of the 3rd Workshop on Context Modeling and Reasoning, 4th IEEE Int. Conf. on Perv. Comp. and Comm. (2006)
8. Intille, S.S., Rondoni, J., Kukla, C., Iacono, I., Bao, L.: A Context-Aware Experience Sampling Tool. In: Proc. of CHI '03 Human Fact. in Comp. Syst, pp. 972–973 (2003)
9. Kjeldskov, J., Skov, M.B., Als, B.S., Hoegh, R.T.: Is it worth the hassle? Exploring the added value of evaluating the usability of context-aware mobile systems in the field. In: Proc. of MobileHCI, pp. 61–73 (2004)
10. Rijsdijk, S.A., Hultink, E.J.: Honey, have you seen our hamster? Consumer evaluations of autonomous domestic products. J. of Product Innovation Mgt. 20(3), 204–216 (2003)
11. Rogers, E.M.: Diffusion of innovations, 5th edn. Free Press, New York (2003)
12. Stewart, J.: The social consumption of information and communication technologies (ICTs): insights from research on the appropriation and consumption of new ICTs in the domestic environment. Cognition, Technology & Work 5(1), 4–14 (2003)
13. Streitz, N.A., Rocker, C., Prante, T., van Alphen, D., Stenzel, R., Magerkurth, C.: Designing smart artifacts for smart environments. Computer 38(3), 41–49 (2005)
14. Vastenburg, M.H., Keyson, D.V., De Ridder, H.: Interrupting People at Home. In: Proc. of IEEE Int. Conf. on Systems, Man and Cybernetics (2004)
15. Vastenburg, M.H., Keyson, D.V., Ross, P.R.: Reducing complexity of home atmosphere control via a user experience based approach. Univ. Access in the Inf. Soc. 6-01 (2007)
16. Weiser, M., Brown, J.S.: The coming age of calm technology. Beyond Calculation: The Next Fifty Years of Computing. Springer, New York (1997)

Evaluation of Tangible User Interfaces (TUIs) for and with Children – Methods and Challenges

Diana Xu[1], Janet C Read[1], Emanuela Mazzone[1], Stuart MacFarlane[2], and Martin Brown[1]

[1] Child-Computer Interaction (ChiCI) Group, Department of Computing, University of Central Lancashire, Lancashire, Preston, PR1 2HE, UK
{yfxu,jcread,emazzone,martinbrown}@uclan.ac.uk
http://www.chici.org/
[2] Independent Consultant
sjmacfarlane@btinternet.com

Abstract. In recent years, creating alternative computer environments, especially Tangible User Interfaces (TUIs) for children, has become increasingly popular. However, up till now, the evaluation of tangible technologies has been rather scarce. This paper focuses on evaluating children's technologies that go beyond the desktop computer. A qualitative case study on our TUI prototype will be presented by using selected methods: Think Aloud (TA), Peer Tutoring (PT) and Drawing Intervention (DI). We found some limitations to the methods and there were lessons that were learnt when the evaluation studies were carried out with children. The research will contribute to the paradigms, such as the design and evaluation of 'the disappearing computer' and 'tangible computing'.

Keywords: Evaluation, Children, Tangible User Interface (TUI), Usability, Fun.

1 Introduction

This paper presents early work on the use of Tangible User Interfaces (TUIs) with children. The work reported is situated in a museum context and was originally inspired by the use of physical items in 'museum loan boxes' [1] in the U.K. These boxes are supplied, on request, by museums to schools, and contain replica objects which can be explored in the school classroom. These replica objects include items of clothing, reports and documents from the particular era, and physical objects, including weapons, household items and toys. As the replica items are very tangible, in the loosest definition of the word, the potential for adding interactivity to them was evident and so, using RFID (Radio Frequency Identification) technology, we designed a prototype application based around the museum objects and used this in several evaluation studies.

In the evaluation studies, the research questions that the project is seeking to answer relate to the effectiveness of several traditional evaluation methods for children's interactive products as well as the potential for new evaluation methods for

J. Jacko (Ed.): Human-Computer Interaction, Part II, HCII 2007, LNCS 4551, pp. 1008–1017, 2007.

children's tangible technology. Three small studies are reported in this paper that collectively investigate:

- Suitable evaluation methods for children's tangible technology,
- Problems in applying the existing evaluation methods on TUIs with children,
- The optimal environment setting for the evaluations, and the best way of conducting the evaluations with children.

The rest of the paper is divided into four sections. Section 2 gives an overview of the related work in this area. Section 3 goes on to describe the prototype and outlines the three research studies. Finally, sections 4 and 5 draw the work together and present some thoughts for future work.

2 Literature

The literature is presented in three parts. The first part outlines the work on TUIs. This is followed by a discussion on the evaluation of interactive products with children, and then the final part provides the literature on the use of tangible technology for children.

2.1 Tangible User Interface

Ulmer and Ishii define TUIs to be systems that use physical artefacts as representations and controls for digital information. One characteristic of a TUI is *'Seamless coupling of everyday graspable objects...with the digital information that pertains to them'* [2]; another characteristic of a TUI is *'physical objects play a central role as both physical representations and controls...for directly manipulating their underlying associations'* [3]. Tangible interfaces rely on a balance between physical and digital representations.

With the traditional desk top Graphical User Interface (GUI) based systems, the screen is merely a window through which we reach into a digital world, with TUIs, the interface blending into the environment and the interactions taking place in the space with the artefacts, users act within and touch the interface itself [4].

Regarding children as the users of TUIs, historically, they learn a variety of skills by playing with physical objects; and they are born with the ability to tangibly manipulate objects with little cognitive effort. herefore, a TUI would appear as a 'natural' form to them. Tangible technology has great educational potential [5, 6]; unlike traditional desktop computers with GUI interfaces, which rely on a limited variety of physical objects and a limited range of human abilities, TUIs offer direct manipulation of physical objects and provide more means of interaction.

2.2 Evaluating Interfaces with Children

In the field of Human Computer Interaction (HCI), growth has occurred in studying children as technology users, which led to efforts to encode methodological knowledge for usability testing with children as test participants [7]. There have been comprehensive *Guidelines for Usability Testing with Children* provided by Hanna et al.

in 1997 [8]. Followed by that, there are a number of studies [9-14] focuses on study of existing Evaluation Methods (EMs) for children and in new methods that are specially designed for children. The common EMs involved in these studies were Think Aloud (TA) protocol [15], Constructive Interaction (also called Co-discovery) [16], Cooperative Evaluation [17] and also new methods include Peer-Tutoring [18] and Problem Identification Picture Cards (PIPC) method [19].

In the majority of these studies, the focus has been on the usefulness of the method for use with children. Studies have tended to report how adult-centred methods need to be adapted for child users and how easy the different methods are for children to use.

2.3 Tangible Interfaces for Children

There have been a number of studies[6] that have described tangible interfaces for children. Several key papers are briefly discussed here. One of the earliest tangible interfaces for children was TICLE [20]. TICLE, created in 1999, was a desktop environment which used a physical tangram[1] consists of 7 pieces on a projected desktop. Using spatiality and connectedness, the physical pieces were represented on a computer screen (environmental embodiment). The game pieces were statically bounded to the information.

Snark [21] uses a room based interface with hand-held devices. It has also been played outdoors and is one of only a few tangible interfaces to have been developed into different aspects. In the room based version, the binding is predominantly static, the game uses spatial and relational interactivity, and the embodiment appears to be local and environmental.

A different sort of interface is Ec(h)o [22]. This is a tangible cube that is used on museum visits. With verb metaphors and nearby embodiment, Ec(h)o is a spatial interface that is statically bound. Ec(h)o is a handheld tangible that is intended for use in wide spaces.

A TUI that appears to have some dynamic binding is Tangible Flags [23]. This is also intended for use in open spaces and uses abstract metaphors and spatial interactions to encourage children in information gathering in a physical space. These few studies highlight the diversity of TUIs.

3 The Research Studies

As has been outlined earlier in the paper, the research studies that have been carried out were intended to collectively answer several questions about the potential for several different evaluation methods for children in relation to TUIs. The three small evaluation studies were carried out with a class of 22 Year 4 (aged 8 to 9) children. We worked with these 22 children and their school teacher in real world contexts: in the classroom and in informal learning contexts, such as playtime outside the classroom.

[1] Tangram is a Chinese puzzle, and a type of dissection puzzle. A tangram consists of 7 pieces, called tans, which fit together to form a shape of some sort.

3.1 The Tangible User Interface (TUI) Prototype

In order to investigate the different evaluation methods, a tangible interface was designed. This interface was a puzzle game that was based on the life of the Romans. The game used a number of different replica objects that were used by the Romans in their dining rooms.

The prototype was designed in a way that the technologies were hidden so that they did not intrude on the interactions. The Roman artefacts were tagged with digital tags and were manipulated in a miniature Roman room that was augmented with an RFID reader. The prototype is described in Figure 1.

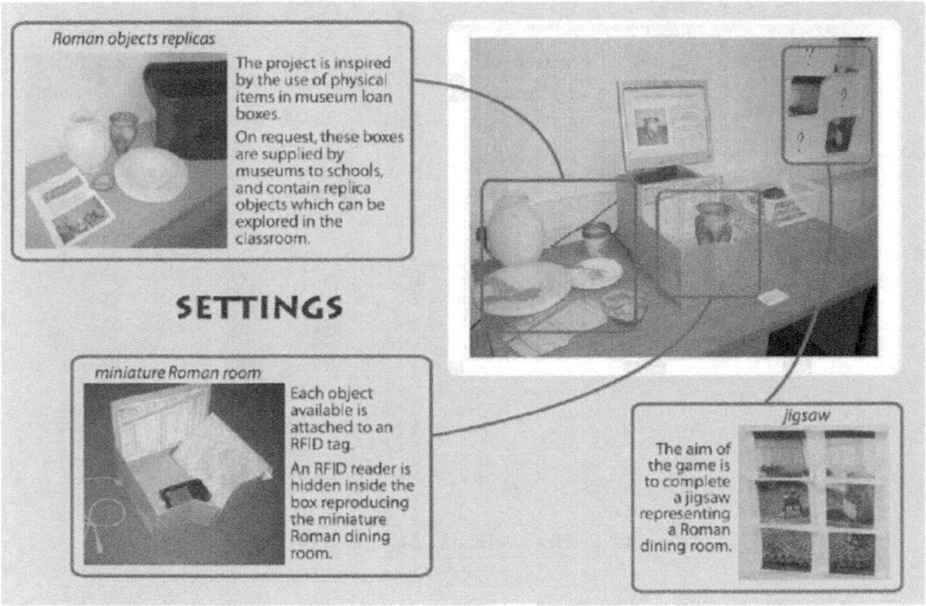

Fig. 1. The TUI Prototype Setting

To play the game, the children selected a Roman item and placed it in the room. On placing the item, information about it was provided in the form of visual and audio feedback. If the selected object belonged in the Roman dining room, the children were given a piece of a jigsaw and instructed to place that piece in the right place. If the selected item did not belong in the dining room the child's turn in the game ended. The game ended when all the jigsaw pieces had been used.

3.2 Choice of Methods

The main evaluation methods used were observation methods. Think Aloud (TA) and Peer Tutoring (PT) were adopted during the observation to elicit verbal comments from children; a newly invented method, Drawing Intervention (DI), was also used; however, as a method it needs further validation. The three methods are described in

Fig. 2. Following the activities a questionnaire was given to the children to inquire about their opinions on the TUI and the activities they did. The questionnaire was especially designed for them with explicit questions and the choices for the answers were represented as picture stickers.

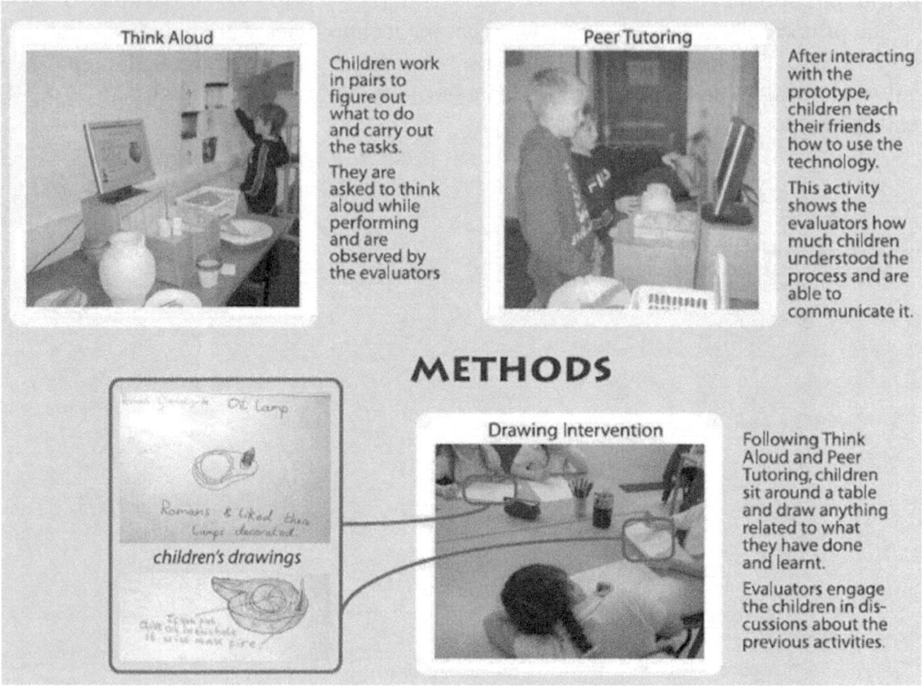

Fig. 2. The Evaluation Methods Used

Thinking Aloud (TA) provides the evaluator with information about the cognition and emotion of a user while the child performs a task or solves a problem. There can be difficulties in applying this method to children, due to their more limited ability to verbalise their thoughts. Studies [9] have demonstrated that children aged 9 to 12 are able to speak about the problems they encounter while performing the tasks, but they often need to be prompted with hints or questions by the evaluators.

In the Peer Tutoring (PT) method, children teach their friends how to use the technology after they have interacted with the product. This technique is useful to see how children have understood the functioning of the product and how they are both able and willing to communicate it to their peers.

Drawing Intervention (DI) is new and more of an informal evaluation method, inspired by the natural school classroom settings. According to it, after the children completed the tasks, we let them sit around a table, and draw anything related to what they have done, and also write a sentence about their drawings. Whilst this was being done, the observer asked questions that were related to the drawings.

3.3 The Three Studies

The research team carried out three major evaluation studies. Each evaluation activity was carefully planned beforehand with the personnel involved, equipment needed, contact with the school, and plan of the timeline and so on. After the evaluation sessions, based on the qualitative data that was collected, analysis was carried out. The evaluation was not concerned with performance measures, such as time to completion, error rates and other quantitative aspects of performance. The tasks were used as a means to get the participants to express themselves and test on the evaluation methods.

Table 1. The Three Studies

Study	Participants	Location	Event
No. 1 (1 hr)	4 children: 4 girls, 2 researchers	***ChiCI Play Lab*** A children's lab, large space with a variety of technologies children could play with.	***ChiCI Open Day*** Children came in small groups and tried out different things in the Lab.
No. 2 (2 hrs)	7 children: 5 boys and 2 girls, 2 researchers	***MSc room*** A medium-sized computer lab, where a space for the TUI evaluation was prepared.	***'Mess Day'*** A large group of children came and did different activities at the different locations in the building.
No. 3 (2 hrs)	11 children: 7 girls and 4 boys, 3 researchers	***School ICT room*** A medium-sized room, where a space for the TUI evaluation was prepared.	***School Visit*** Each time, two or three children were called out during their class to participate the evaluation.

A total of 22 local school children: 9 boys and 13 girls, aged 8-9, from the same school class took part in the evaluation. In the first study, we started testing the evaluation methods with a small number of children, acting as pilots (4 children for the first study), in our ChiCI Play Lab. In the second and the third studies, the numbers increased to 7 and 11 children respectively. The studies took place in the university lab and then in the School ICT (Information Communication Technology) room (Table 1.).

While they collaborated on the tasks, the children's conversation and gestures were observed and recorded on the observation sheet. The data collected for analysis included verbal description and non-verbal data, such as gestures, and their reactions to the TUI.

In the study, firstly, the Think Aloud (TA) method was applied. For the TA method we tried to select the most talkative children in the class; however, we also attempted to encourage the less talkative ones by paring them with a talkative friend. To enable the activities to flow more fluently, we re-introduced the children from the TA to the PT activity by asking the 2 children from the TA to each select one friend to peer-tutor them. By doing this, we were able to reduce the time required to complete the whole set of activities. Finally, to conclude the activities, we applied Drawing Intervention (DI) by putting the children into a large group (4 to 11children) and allowing them to do an activity they were familiar with. This meant that the children were a lot more relaxed and felt less inhibited when talking to each other. The same procedure was adopted for all the three studies.

To avoid the possibility of the children who had already done the evaluation giving hints to the other children we suggested that they were involved in a 'secret mission' and that they shouldn't reveal anything when they went back to the common room. All the children seemed to be excited about this idea and very happily accepted the 'mission'.

From the studies we found that the following issues particularly related to the TUI:

- **Physical Ergonomics:** The TUI has to fit the size of the child and their physical ability should be considered. In our prototype, some of the children had difficulty in manipulating the large heavy Roman artefacts.
- **Affordance:** Provide clear clues about the way the artefacts should be manipulated. The artefacts need to have good affordance. When the children were placing the artefacts, the audio feedback effectively informed the children about what they could do with the system.
- **Playfulness:** In learning or play, the child needs to be able to work out what is happening by playing with the interface.

Also, some interesting findings about the evaluations methods:

- **The location:** The surrounding environment plays a large part on how children behave; the children felt more at ease in their school ICT room and they were more focused on the tasks.
- **The disposition of the space:** i.e. Reading the screen, listening to the audio, looking at the object, completing the jigsaw; also, avoid the researcher being in the middle of the interface.
- **Think Aloud method:** The selection of children is important; not all the children were naturally talkative when they used the product. The evaluator had to encourage them constantly to think aloud, which is very distracting and forcing.
- **Peer Tutoring:** Shy children who did not talk a lot during the Thinking Aloud method showed enthusiasm and engagement in teaching their friends how to use the product and helping them to carry out the same tasks again.
- **Drawing Intervention:** A number of children placed a chosen artefact in front of them to do the drawing. Drawing is a medium for children to express themselves. As children were working in bigger groups, they were a lot more relaxed and felt free to talk to each other while doing the drawings. We were able to discover their real thoughts about the design and their experiences.

4 Discussion

Some useful results were found concerning the usability, fun and educational design of the prototype, which will assist us in refining the prototype. More importantly, the results show how well the evaluation methods we chose performed for children's tangible technology and these results inform us how future evaluations can be designed and carried out.

4.1 Concerning the Evaluation Methods

We found that Think Aloud (TA) is difficult to apply to child users, and is more suitable for expressing feelings and emotions rather than for analyzing actions. Peer Tutoring (PT) has been a successful method with children; however, it is difficult to balance the roles of the children. Our new method, Drawing Intervention (DI), elicited extra information about the TUI from the children that we did not learn through the traditional methods; however, it needs further validation.

4.2 Concerning the Environment Setting and Conducting of the Evaluations

The choice and the setting of the environment are crucial and can be vital to the evaluations. If the evaluation takes place in an unsuitable location, the children will not feel natural or at ease and the whole evaluation can go wrong. Although finding a perfectly controlled environment is very difficult, there are things we can consider and plan ahead for to achieve the optimum results. Generally speaking, a familiar location for children with minimum distraction is ideal, but at the same time we have to consider how to 'plant' the TUI into that location, as interface is embedded in the environment and physical objects.

A few researchers are required to conduct an evaluation: one facilitator, one observer and one camera person, if needed. Children often feel more at ease with their friends in a new environment, so we normally put children in pairs for the evaluation studies.

5 Conclusion and Future Work

The challenges for the future are: evaluating TUI requires not only the evaluation of the digital content, but also the physical form, and their interrelations within hybrid ensembles; therefore, it is a multi-dimensional task. Observation methods are suitable to record exactly what happens in situ in the 3-D space in real time; preferably, the future event is video recorded for looking back and for further analysis.

Future work will carry out in-depth study of evaluation methods which could be beneficial for designing and evaluating TUIs for children, validate the new evaluation methods we proposed and bring about refinements to the prototype. The results will be used for developing design and evaluation guidelines for researchers, policymakers, educational software developers and ICT coordinators.

Acknowledgement. A special thanks to the children and their teacher, Despoina Mitropoulou for helping us with the evaluations and Ian Dewhurst for invaluable comments in the preparation of this paper.

References

1. Lancashire Museums, School Loans Service (2007) [cited 2007 10 February] Available from: http://www.lancashire.gov.uk/education/museums/learning/schoolloans.asp.
2. Ishii, H., Ullmer, B.: Tangible Bits: Towards Seamless Interfaces Between People, Bits and Atoms. In: CHI'97 Conference on Human Factors in Computing Systems, Atlanta GA USA, ACM Press, New York (1997)
3. Ullmer, B., Ishii, H.: Emerging Frameworks for Tangible User Interfaces. In: Carroll, J.M. (ed.) Human-Computer Interaction inthe New Millennium, pp. 579–601. Addison-Wesley, London, UK (2001)
4. Hornecker, E., Buur, J.: Getting a Grip on Tangible Interaction: A Framework on Physical Space and Social Interaction. In: CHI 2006 Conference on Human Factors in Computing Systems 2006, Montreal, Canada, ACM Press, New York (2006)
5. Xu, D., Mazzone, E., MacFarlane, S.: Informant Design with Children - Designing Children's Tangible Technology. In: International Workshop Re-Thinking Technology in Museums, Limerick, Ireland (2005)
6. O'Malley, C., Fraser, D.S.: Literature Review in Learning with Tangible Technologies, NESTA Futurelab (2004)
7. MacFarlane, S., et al.: Tutorial: Evaluating interactive products with and for children. In: Conference of Human Factors in Computing Systems (CHI 2004) Vienna, Austria (2004)
8. Hanna, L., Risden, K., Alexander, K.: Guidelines for Usability Testing with Children. Interactions 5, 9–14 (1997)
9. Donker, A., Markopoulos, P.: A comparison of Think-aloud, Questionnaires and Interviews for testing usability with children. In: The 16th BCS British-HCI 2002. London, UK (2002)
10. Read, J.C., MacFarlane, S.J., Casey, C.: Endurability, Engagement and Expectations: Measuring Children's Fun. In: Interaction Design and Children Workshop, Eindhoven, Netherland (2002)
11. Kesteren, I.E.H.v.,et al.: Assessing usability evaluation methods on their effectiveness to elicit verbal information from children subjects. In: IDC2003, Preston, England, ACM Press, New York (2003)
12. Markopoulos, P., Bekker, M.: On the assessment of usability testing methods for children. Interacting with Computers 15(2), 227–243 (2003)
13. Als, B.S., Jensen, J.J., Skov, M.B.: Exploring verbalization and collaboration of constructive interaction with children. In: Interact, Tenth International Conference on Human-Computer Interaction 2005. Rome, Italy (2005)
14. Baauw, E., Bekker, M.M.: A comparison of two analytical evaluation methods for children's computer games. In: Interact, Tenth International Conference on Human-Computer Interaction 2005. Rome, Italy (2005)
15. Erikson, K.A., Simon, H.A.: Protocol Analysis: Verbal Reports on Data. MIT Press, Cambridge, MA (1984)
16. Miyake, N.: Constructive Interaction and the Iterative Process of Understanding. Cognitive Science 10(2), 151–177 (1986)
17. Monk, A., et al.: Improving your human computer interface: a practical approach. Prentice Hall International, Englewood Cliffs (1993)
18. Hoysniemi, J., Hamalainen, P., Turkki, L.: Using peer tutoring in evaluating the usability of a physically interactive computer game with children. Interacting with Computers 15(2), 203–225 (2003)

19. Barendregt, W., Bekker, M.M.: Development and Evaluation of the Picture Cards Method. In: Interact 2005 Tenth International Conference on Human-Computer Interaction 2005. Rome, Italy (2005)
20. Scarlatos, L.L.: TICLE: using multimedia multimodal guidance to enhance learning Information Sciences—Informatics and Computer Science. An International Journal 140(1), 85–103 (2002)
21. Price, S., et al.: Using tangibles to promote novel forms of playful learning. Interacting with Computers 15(2), 169–185 (2003)
22. Wakkary, R., Hatala, M.: ec(h)o: Situated Play in a Tangible and Audio Museum Guide. In: Designing Interactive Systems 2006, DIS 2006. University Park, Pennsylvania, USA (2006)
23. Chipman, G., et.al.: A case study of tangible flags: a collaborative technology to enhance field trips. In: Proceeding of the 2006 conference on Interaction design and children, Tampere, Finland, ACM Press, New York (2006)

Social Intelligence as the Means for Achieving Emergent Interactive Behaviour in Ubiquitous Computing Environments

Ioannis D. Zaharakis[1] and Achilles D. Kameas[1,2]

[1] Research Academic Computer Technology Institute
N. Kazantzaki str, University Campus,
26500 Patras, Hellas
{jzaharak,kameas}@cti.gr
[2] Hellenic Open University
23 Sahtouri str,
26222 Patras, Hellas

Abstract. This work introduces a framework for modelling the main actors (human, artefacts and services) in a symbiotic Ambient Intelligence environment. It, also, proposes an architectural scheme that associates the social behaviour, which is not an inherent characteristic of the participants, during interaction with the functional behaviour of the participants of a Ubiquitous Computing application. The overall approach is demonstrated by a specific example of application which illustrates its concepts through a more technical point of view.

Keywords: Ambient Intelligence, Emergent Behaviour, Human-Computer Interaction, Social Intelligence, Ubiquitous Environments.

1 Introduction

As computational power diffuses in our living/working environment and the everyday devices that are capable of sensing, processing and communicating continuously grow in number, the potential use of the objects emerges mainly from the interactions of the humans with the digital devices and these interactions are not only time-dependent but also space- or context-dependent. A further consequence is that the nature of the human activities eventually assisted by artefacts is rapidly changing. Execution of tasks involving the use of (collections of) artefacts may become difficult due to the inherent systemic complexity of Ubiquitous Computing (UbiComp) applications, which, among others, results from device incompatibility, and the huge number of interactions among visible and non-visible actors.

There is a pressing need for a design framework that will act as a common referent between designers and users (i.e. ordinary people) of UbiComp applications that exist within an Ambient Intelligence (AmI) environment. This framework should support not only the representation of user's interactions with artefacts or predefined collections of artefacts (such frameworks already exist today, see [8]), but would also

J. Jacko (Ed.): Human-Computer Interaction, Part II, HCII 2007, LNCS 4551, pp. 1018–1029, 2007.

cater for the design of adaptive interactions, as artefact ecologies will be evolving to encompass changing user requirements. Finally, the supported interactions should be people-centred, because with an AmI environment (according to ISTAG vision of AmI [7]) people will be acting as naturally as possible (while now they are interacting with a computer).

In this paper, we provide a new perspective by enabling socially intelligent interactions among people and artefacts and we claim that by subsuming task optimization to social intelligence, people interactions with artefacts will become more natural. This work adopts and extends the framework proposed in [15] which deals with different perspectives of the interrelations developed in symbiotic ecologies where people and artefacts coexist. We propose a subsumption architecture that supports the integration of social behaviour with functional behaviour of UbiComp applications. Our approach is bottom-up, in the sense that it considers social and functional elementary "behaviours" as basic building blocks of complex and emerging UbiComp behaviour.

The main innovation introduced by the proposed framework is that we do not aim simply at autonomous systems; instead, we aim at systems that although consisting of largely reactive parts, they exhibit a pro-active behaviour in a social level. Furthermore, the social behaviour is not an inherent characteristic of the participants but it is a result of the interactions among participants.

The next section details on the proposed framework integrating people, artefacts and services into a symbiotic AmI environment. The section 3 focuses on interaction with UbiComp applications and on how the social and the individual behaviours are reflected by the participating artefacts and the provided services. Finally, the section 4 puts our approach into an example scenario and demonstrates a realisation of the proposed concepts through a more technical portion.

2 Proposed Framework

Technically, the reproduction of social behaviours and the handling of complex tasks with an equal agility as the one exhibited by natural intelligent systems could be achieved by i) considering that all the necessary information lies out the environment and surrounds the participants (according to R. Brooks [2, 3, 4]) and ii) using bio-inspired approaches in designing intelligent systems, in which autonomy, emergence, and distributed functioning are promoted [1, 10].

We propose to distribute the individual physical/computational/cognitive capabilities over the entire ecology and then immerse the ecology into a UbiComp environment, aiming to generate theory and technology for the understanding of the own self and its relation with the surrounding world. We deal with this consideration by i) attributing AmI objects with physical expression (dimensions, shape, texture, colour, plugs, sockets, connectors, etc) and ii) dealing with the provided services as basic behavioural building blocks of the overall system behaviour.

According to our approach, a living/working AmI space is populated of many heterogeneous objects with different capabilities and provided services. All these objects and services are regarded as basic building blocks having an internal part that encapsulates the internal structure and functionality, and an external part that manifests the capabilities and influences the surroundings. Additionally, every basic building block has several pre-defined functions (we call them *basic behaviours*). Some of the basic behaviours are just reactions to external events and some are continuously pursued to be fulfilled. The former type of basic behaviours imitates the reflex actions of the living organisms, while the latter the preservation instincts. The interrelationships between the basic building blocks and the associated environment form an *ecology*. In such ecologies artificial entities coexist unobtrusively with humans and perform collaborative tasks through a continuous evolvable process concerning both their physical and social cognitive growth (we call them "*ambient spheres*"). Similar approaches can be found in a natural ecosystem and have been used in (purely reactive) collective robotics. In addition, we integrate them into another ingredient, called *ambient system* (AmS).

The AmS acts as the "glue" between the tangible and non-tangible basic building blocks of the ecology by providing an Interface Definition Language (IDL) and thus integrating the basic building blocks into a common interoperability framework. One step to this end is the design and implementation of a hierarchy of multi-dimensional ontologies that include both non-functional descriptions, and rules and constraints of application, as well as aspects of dynamic behaviour and interactions. During the ecology life-time a core ontology, open and universally available and accessible, is supplemented with higher-level goal, application and context specific ontologies. These ontologies describing specific application domains can be proprietary. Emerging behaviour, in this context, are considered as a result of interactions among heterogeneous, seemingly incompatible or non pre-defined entities. Additionally, the AmS is responsible for the observation and collection of the interactions between AmI objects, provided services and users. The collected data are used to create best practice ecology configurations that will help the gradual assembly of social memory. Aspects of Social Intelligence are embodied to the ecology configurations as basic social behaviours aiming to regulate the group interactions. These social behaviours are provided as ontological constructions which are also subject to evolution. On the other hand, all the collected information are provided by the AmS as feedback to the members of the ecology (social memory in association to user "perceived quality") favouring the best configurations and implicitly assigning cognition to the whole ecology. It is mentioned that the feedback information is provided to the ecology as another stimulus or stimuli and thus does not require extra (complicated) sensors mounted to the artefacts. Notably, this would require a different modelling and engineering approach comparatively to the one described so far. Instead and along the lines of Swarm Intelligence where the environment is a stimulus for the swarm, we treat the AmS as another (special) basic building block, the environment building block.

The AmS system is realised as a distributed platform that supports the instantiation of ambient spheres, each of which is formed to support human activity. Examples of candidate AmS technologies are the currently available distributed component frameworks and service-oriented architectures. An ambient sphere is an integrated autonomous system realised within AmS as a set of configurations between the AmI objects and their services. In our model of discourse, the end-users are placed inside the ambient sphere, as this allows us to model them as another basic building block that generates events and changes the environment.

Focusing on interaction within such an AmI space, people still have to realize their tasks, ranging from mundane everyday tasks (i.e. studying, cooking etc) to leisure or work related tasks, or even tasks that relate to emergency situations (i.e. home care, accident, unexpected guests etc). To do so, they have at their disposal the objects that surround them. These in fact, are new or improved versions of existing objects, which by using Information and Communication Technology (ICT) components (i.e. sensors, actuators, processor, memory, wireless communication modules) can receive, store, process and transmit information, thus allowing people to carry out new tasks or old tasks in new and better ways. In the following, we shall use the term "artefacts" for this type of augmented objects. Turning an object into an artefact is a process that aims at enhancing its characteristics and properties and abilities so that the new affordances will emerge. In practical terms, it is about embedding in the object the necessary hardware and software modules.

From the interaction point of view, we are mostly concerned with the interface of the artefacts and the collective interface of UbiComp applications. The former shall directly affect or depend upon the physical form and shape of the artefacts. The latter can exist in the "digital space" of a computer, i.e. a PDA that runs specific software representations of the artefact services. Thus, people interact with an AmI environment in order to [9]:

- Engineer a UbiComp application within the environment, as a composition of artefacts, which collectively serve a specific purpose or satisfy a declared set of needs.
- Use an application to satisfy their needs: such an application may be composed by people themselves, or could be bought and installed.

Interaction takes place in two levels:

- Artefact-to-artefact: the objects themselves may form an "underlying" layer of interactions, mainly in order to exchange data and to serve their purpose better. Such interactions may use wired channels or any of the available wireless protocols (in a peer-to-peer or broadcast manner), or even the Internet.
- User-to-application. The user interacts a) with any single artefact b) with a collection of co-operating devices. Moreover one has to consider the case where many users interact with the same application.

The degree of visibility and control that people may have on these interactions may vary depending on people's ability to perceive the system state: any of these two types of interaction may happen either explicitly or implicitly.

An explicit interaction happens under the control of people always provides feedback about its state to them. Although this may seem desirable, it may also become very annoying if one takes into account that there will be hundreds of artefacts in our environment. People interact explicitly with objects or services (or collections of these). In the case of individual objects (or, preferably, services), interaction can be supported by the object affordances. When people interact with a UbiComp application composed of a collection of objects, its "affordances" have to emerge and made explicit.

Implicit interactions are usually under the control of actors other than people; these could be processes, artefacts, intelligent agent mechanisms or even artefact owners. Implicit interactions can only be acceptable if they can be trusted and do not violate privacy or ethics. People need not be directly aware of the communication among objects. Moreover, even certain interactions with UbiComp applications should happen unobtrusively, i.e. people should be made aware of the state changes of the application components without being disrupted from their current tasks.

Finally, one should also consider the context of interaction, which ranges from public to private (with respect to disclosure), from individual to shared (with respect to stakeholders) and from closed to open (with respect to space).

3 Interacting with AmI Spheres

The AmI spheres constitute a dynamic distributed system, composed of artefacts with finite sets of capabilities (services) offered usually through proprietary user interfaces. People have to interact with an AmI sphere in two levels:

- the task level, whereby they will have to use each individual artefact in order to make use of the collective AmI sphere capabilities
- the meta-task level, whereby they will have to compose, decompose or otherwise edit AmI spheres

When interacting with an AmI sphere, people are in fact using the artefacts that compose it (i.e. they are simply acting, not interacting). This is as close as we can get to the notion of calm technology promoted by M. Weiser, who stated that the most profound technologies are those which disappear in the background [14]. This view is directly inspired from Heidegger's theory of "dasein", which states that people are thrown in the world and are always engaged with acting within it to accomplish their tasks. In this view, technological tools disappear in the background in favour of tasks-at-hand; tools only appear when the task accomplishment procedure breaks down, that is, when something goes wrong.

First of all, artefacts have to demonstrate their affordances, both in the physical environment (for people to be able to use them) and to the digital space (so that other artefacts, agents etc will be able to interact with them). Then, the state of each artefact must be made visible / available for the same reasons (although the procedure used to compute the state should be internal to the artefact). AmI spheres introduce two factors that cause the breakdown of the existing task models: people will have to make sure that they can still carry on with ordinary tasks, and they will have to become familiar with the new affordances of the artefacts. In addition to adapting their skills for using artefacts, people will have to develop skills for using the computing properties of their new environments as well [12].

3.1 The GAS Approach

To deal with the above, Gadgetworld Architectural Style (GAS) adopts a layered architecture that transparently supports composing and using AmI spheres (called eGadgetWorlds) from autonomous artefacts (called eGadgets), which can be objects, services or both [8]. To enable composition of AmI spheres, GAS proposes the plug-synapse model: a "plug" is the manifestation of a property, capability or service in a semantically-rich way and a "synapse" is a communication established between compatible plugs. For example, a TV set may offer the display service and a digital camera may establish a synapse in order to output images; a chair may offer the capability to recognize whether a person is seated on it and a table lamp may use it to switch itself on; etc. Plugs are either ingoing (i.e. used as "remote sensors") or outgoing (i.e. used as "remote actuators"). Clearly this concept scales well, as more complex "plugs" can be defined as compositions of simpler "plugs", either at an artefact or sphere level. For example, a "reading plug" for an office AmI sphere may be defined by combining specific plugs from a chair, a table, a lamp and a book (in fact, we refer to their artefact counterparts) in such a way that when someone is seated on the chair and the chair is located close enough to the table and a book is opened on the table, then the lamp is switched on; with the help of the room (considered as an artefact), the system could also recognize who is seated on the chair and switch on automatically his/her reading profile; then, the "reading plug" could be used by the room to redirect phone calls so as not to disturb the user unless necessary.

An interesting case appears when the AmI sphere breaks down. Consider, for example, the case where the desk lamp is broken. Then the system can either inform the user and wait for his/her action, or search for a similar service in the environment (for example, the sphere, with the help of the AmS system, can locate the room lamp and switch it on). In the latter case, it is necessary that all artefacts hold an internal description of their services and goals; and that these descriptions are compatible. GAS includes a multi-layered ontology, which describes artefact "plugs" and rules of usage (i.e. constraints) using a commonly available core ontology of basic terms. The use of ontology makes possible the communication between heterogeneous eGadgets and helps in achieving a shared understanding (as described in [6]). Emergent behaviour of this type is a direct result of the ability of eGadgets to communicate in socially meaningful ways, as described in their hierarchy of basic behaviours.

The above definition supports emerging functionality because (a) artefacts are self-sufficient and their plugs are described in a functionally independent way, (b) not all synapses need to be known from the start, (c) new synapses may be added or existing synapses may be deleted, for example, as an artefact may move outside the sphere (that is, outside the range of the wireless network), and (d) experience may be recorded in local artefact ontologies and appear in the form of higher level plugs (the use of a common core ontology available in the sphere's environment ensures the compatibility of plug definitions).

Plugs and synapses are managed by GAS-OS, a distributed middleware platform that takes care of resource management and communication. Thus, an AmI sphere is defined as a GAS-OS application; all eGadgets in it run GAS-OS; compatible plugs of these eGadgets are engaged in synapses to provide collective sphere functionality.

3.2 Supporting Tasks and Meta-tasks

Within an AmI sphere composed as an eGadgetWorld, a user may perform his/her tasks simply by using the artefacts therein. We do not propose to embed screen-based interfaces on every artefact, or to use a computer as a sphere master, as these would greatly alter the affordances of the artefacts and consequently have a negative effect on people's capacity to form new task models. Another unwanted consequence is that these artefacts would no longer be functionally autonomous.

In the case of AmI spheres, the issues are to conduct a coherent dialogue composed of user actions within the sphere and eGadgets' responses and to preserve a distributed but meaningful dialogue state. To achieve this, each eGadget must be aware of the state of other eGadgets in the sphere. This can be achieved by exchanging information through the synapses that compose the sphere. By processing the combined perception of the states of itself, peer artefacts (connected via synapses) and the environment and then applying its architecture of subsumed behaviours, each artefact is able to locally maintain a dialogue state that is compatible with the AmI sphere dialogue state.

GAS offers a set of tools that support the meta-tasks of creating and editing spheres. These editors run on PDAs and laptops and have been positively evaluated by non-expert users [13].

3.3 The Subsumption Architecture

The proposed conceptual framework extends the GAS approach, by allowing the eGadgetWorld management tasks to be dynamically performed by the AmS (though the direct user involvement is not prohibited) based not only on the available artefacts and services, but also on the observed user habits and the social rules in context. The proposed approach achieves uniformity and coherence, because it uses the notion of basic behaviours to represent both functional and social capacities of eGadgets, thus providing uniform support for individual functionality and "social interactions" between the sphere members (artefacts, agents, and people).

In order to realise this approach, the decision making module of the middleware of each eGadget is composed of two behaviour calculation modules: those that implement its core functionality and those that realize the context of social intelligence. The former use the data gathered by the eGadget sensors to calculate the object's state and to decide a set of (re)actions. The latter use sensor data as well as synapse input to determine context of operation and to select the most appropriate action in the list.

There are different subsumption architectures to choose from. In the simplest one, all basic behaviours are placed in the same hierarchy. To enhance modularity and scalability, one could separate the basic behaviours into two different subsumption schemes: the social and the functional one. In any case, we choose to give social intelligence behaviours greater precedence over functional behaviours, thus allowing the eGadget to realise the most socially intelligent response depending on the situation at-hand. Thus, using the two level selection mechanism, we ensure independence in the determination of local state and response, while we achieve a socially-driven eGadget behaviour.

Examples of functional basic behaviours are: "turn light on", "produce specific sound", "move towards a specific direction", etc. These depend on the actuators and the outgoing plugs of the eGadget and determine the affordances the eGadget offers in physical and digital spaces. This set also contains the basic behaviours "form synapse" and "learn", which ensure that affordances such as composeability and changeability are supported. To deal with possible heterogeneity in data definition, each eGadget uses a local ontology to translate data incoming through synapses.

Regarding social behaviour, we can choose from the basic social behaviours drawn from the social intelligence studies (e.g., benevolence, non-intrusion, altruism, responsibility, antagonism, empathy, emergency, etc), depending on the nature of the UbiComp application. The subsumption scheme contains in a hierarchical structure several degrees of sociality – from non sociality at all in the lower level to high sociality in the top level – as well as the suppression between the social behaviours.

3.4 The GAS Symbiotic Interaction Metaphor

In order to describe our proposed metaphor for interacting with UbiComp applications composed from communicating artefacts (Fig.1), let us first make explicit some basic assumptions:

- User inhabits an AmI space, which contains artefacts, having a physical presence and offering digital services;
- User forms a plan to achieve a goal he has in mind; in this stage, the plan probably consists of steps and sub-goals, some of which may not be conscious at all;
- User tries to realise his plan by combining services offered by the artefacts in his environment; in this endeavour, user can only be aware of the affordances of the artefacts and tries to use them accordingly

First of all, GAS supports the following meta-tasks, using the GAS editor:

- User can query the services and capabilities of each eGadget
- User composes an eGadgetWorld by combining eGadgets capabilities using the plug/synapse model
- User can have an overview of the existing eGadgetWorlds and even edit or delete any of them

Then, we propose the following interaction metaphor:

- The state of each eGadget is communicated using its actuators
- User simply uses each eGadget based on its affordances, directly affecting its local state
- As a consequence, the eGadget communicates the new state to the eGadgets it is connected to via its synapses
- Peer eGadgets calculate new local states (thus user indirectly affects them) and communicate them using their actuators; each eGadget decides the form of communication using its local subsumption architecture, its local state and the context it perceives via its local sensors and peer eGadgets states (via its synapses)
- A new global eGadgetWorld state emerges as a consequence of local state changes of all the eGadgets in the eGadgetWorld
- The new global state is collectively but independently communicated to the user by all eGadgets in the eGadgetWorld

In this approach, we must make a few remarks. Firstly, because this is a symbiotic ecology, there is no centralized decision making component. All eGadgets are considered as peers and each one is responsible for local decision making and acting by taking into account local and global information (here "global" is restricted to

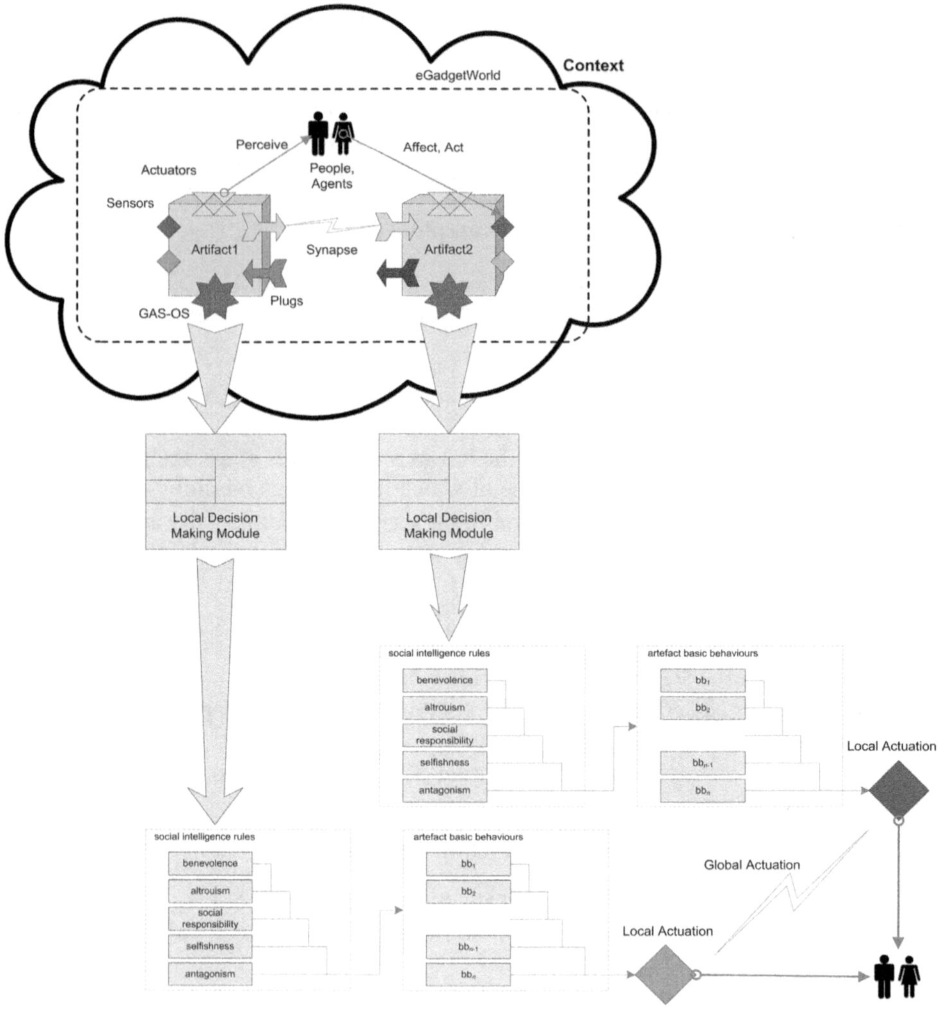

Fig. 1. The proposed architectural scheme supporting the integration of social with functional behaviour of UbiComp applications

those eGadgets in the AmI sphere). However, the eGadgets that compose an eGadgetWorld, if they have this basic behaviour, may choose to elect representatives, that is, eGadgets which will act as eGadgetWorld "leaders". This process is supported by contemporary communication protocols (i.e. Wi-Fi) and ensures that the eGadgetWorld will remain functional even if some secondary or weak eGadgets are not occasionally operating.

Secondly, because the local eGadget state is communicated to other peer eGadgets via the synapses and triggers changes in their local states, which are also communicated to peer eGadgets, there exists the risk of the eGadgetWorld falling in an infinite loop of recursive global state changes. This falls within the scope of our modelling approach and can be avoided using two measures. Firstly, synapses are directed: if a synapse exists from eGadget A to eGadget B, this means that only changes in the state of eGadget A are communicated to eGadget B and not the other way round. In addition, when composing or editing an eGadgetWorld, the GAS tools offer the user the ability to send a "ping" message, which propagates to all eGadgets in the eGadgetWorld, thus helping in discovering if any loops exist.

4 An Example Scenario

Let's consider a scenario of a not so distant future, whereby we can demonstrate the concepts and potential of the proposed approach.

Anna is a single, 36 years old mother, living with her daughter in a modern 3 room apartment in Athens. She is a hard working employee in a private telecommunications company. Despite the demanding job and family requirements, Anna likes to be a calm person. She likes the view from her apartment and the Greek sunlight. She enjoys a warm morning bath while listening to soft rock music. That is why, before she gets up into her overfull daily schedule, she has programmed her apartment to implement a specific routine. In fact, she has created a "wake up" AmI sphere consisting of the following eGadgets: an alarm clock, the bed-mattress, the bedside picture frame, the bathroom mirror, the window blinds, and the room light. The eGadgets in this sphere have plugs through which they offer access to their properties and services. For example, the clock, the blinds and the room light are equipped with light sensors and can produce a light intensity reading through their "luminosity" plug; the clock also uses the "alarm" plug to send a buzzing event; the bed-mattress has weight and pressure sensors and can decide whether there is someone "lying upon" or not; the window blinds can be set to a specific height or angle through their "lift" and "rotate" plugs.; the bedside picture frame and the bathroom mirror can display images or videos that receive through their "content" plug; finally, the room light also offers the plug "light intensity".

Anna has programmed this eGadgetWorld to gradually increase the intensity of light in her bedroom after the alarm has gone off, to start playing nice relaxing music and display pictures from her summer holiday before it starts communicating to her the first news of the day.

She has managed to program the control of light intensity by connecting the "alarm" plug to the blinds "lift" plug, the light "intensity" plug and the frame "content" plug. With manipulation of synapse rules, the AmI sphere can now, once the alarm has gone off, gradually lift the blinds (until the pre-programmed level of light intensity in the room has been reached), display pictures in the frame and use it to play some music (until Anna has got off from bed, as can be communicated by its "lying upon" plug). Then, as she enters the bathroom, the news of the day are displayed in her bathroom mirror using its "content" plug.

This functionality can be implemented using only the functional basic behaviours of the eGadgets. When the social basic behaviours are also used, then this functionality can become adaptive. For example, because of the "selfishness" basic behaviour, all eGadgets try to achieve their local goals, whereas because of the "social responsibility" basic behaviour, in case the window blinds cannot be lifted due to malfunction, the eGadget will try to rotate the blinds or as a final resort, ask the room light to gradually increase its light intensity, to make up for the blocked sunlight. Additionally, because of the "altruism" basic behaviour, only the blinds can be lifted, if the day is bright, but if the day is cloudy, the room light is also gradually turned on, as it senses a low level of luminosity in the room. Also, the bathroom mirror will take over from the frame the task of communicating the news of the day, when Anna enters the bathroom. On the other hand, because of the "non disturbance" basic behaviour, the blinds are slowly rotated or lifted, the room light gradually becomes brighter and the volume of music gradually increases to the specified levels. At last, when the "emergency" basic behaviour is triggered, a picture of Anna's partner pops up in the bathroom mirror instead of the news of the day: it's Valentine's Day and he recorded a tender message for her!

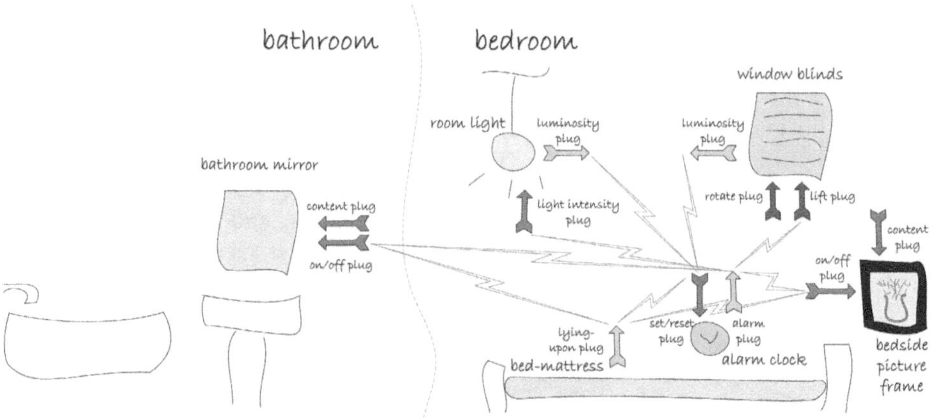

Fig. 2. The "wake-up" AmI sphere

5 Summary

This work examines symbiotic UbiComp environments and deals with the participating actors and the interactions taking part therein through a novel perspective. Especially, participating artefacts and provided services compose AmI spheres supporting several user tasks taking into account both functional properties and social rules of behaviour. The emphasis is given to social behaviour where social rules suppress individual behaviour when applied. The spheres are dynamic in nature ensuring application efficiency and service provision continuity. However, we investigate methods of providing feedback to the spheres aiming at the creation of a kind of social memory. With the embodiment of machine learning and evolution mechanisms into the ambient system, this phenomenon could be exploited to contribute to the creation of systems with self-management properties such as self-configuration, self-healing, self-optimisation, and self-protection.

Acknowledgement. This work was supported in part by a grant from the European Community under the "Information Society Technologies" Programme (01/05/2006-30/04/2009), Project ASTRA IST-29266 (www.astra-project.net).

References

1. Bonabeau, E., Dorigo, M., Theraulaz, G.: Swarm Intelligence: From Natural to Artificial Systems. Oxford University Press, Oxford, UK (1999)
2. Brooks, R.A.: Intelligence without Reason. In: Proceedings of 12th Int. Joint Conf. on Artificial Intelligence, Sydney, Australia, pp. 569–595 (1991)
3. Brooks, R.A.: Intelligence without representation. Artificial Intelligence 47, 139–159 (1991)
4. Brooks, R.A.: Robot: The future of flesh and machines. London: Penguin Books (2002)
5. Calvary, G., Coutaz, J., Thevenin, D.: A unifying reference framework for the development of plastic user interfaces. In: EHCI 2001. LNCS, vol. 2254, pp. 173–192. Springer, Heidelberg (2001)
6. Habermas, J.: The theory of communicative action (Vol I and II) (translator McCarthy, T.) Beacon Press, Boston (1984)
7. IST Advisor Group: Scenarios for Ambient Intelligence in 2010. European Commission Community Research (2001) Available in from http://cordis.europa.eu/ist/istag-reports.htm
8. Kameas, A., Bellis, S., Mavrommati, I., Delanay, K., Colley, M., Pounds-Cornish, A.: An architecture that treats everyday objects as communicating tangible components. In: Proceedings of the First IEEE International Conference on Pervasive Computing and Communications (PERCOM2003), Texas-Fort Worth (2003)
9. Kameas, A., Mavrommati, I., Markopoulos, P.: Computing in tangible: using artifacts as components of Ambient Intelligent Environments. In: Riva, G., Vatalaro, F., Davide, F., Alcaniz, M. (eds.) Ambient Intelligence: The evolution of Technology, Communication and Cognition, pp. 121–142. IOS Press, Amsterdam, Trento, Italy (2004)
10. Kennedy, J., Eberhart, R.: Swarm Intelligence. Morgan Kaufmann, San Francisco (2001)
11. Mavrommati, I., Kameas, A.: The evolution of objects into hyper-objects. Personal and Ubiquitous Computing 779, ACM 7(3-4), 176–181 (2003)
12. Mavrommati, I., Kameas, A.: The concepts of an end user enabling architecture for ubiquitous computing. In: Proceedings of the 2nd International Conference on Pervasive Computing (Pervasive 2004), Vienna (2004)
13. Mavrommati, I., Kameas, A., Markopoulos, P.: An Editing tool that manages device associations in an in-home environment. In: Proceedings of the 2nd International Conference on Appliance Design (2AD), HP Labs, Bristol, UK, May 11-13, 2004 pp. 104–111 (2004)
14. Weiser, M.: Some Computer Science Issues in Ubiquitous Computing. CACM 36(7), 75–84 (1993)
15. Zaharakis, I.D., Kameas, A.D.: Emergent Phenomena in AmI Spaces. In: Proceedings of 1st International EASST-EU Workshop on Future Research Challenges for Software and Services, associated to The European Joint Conferences on Theory and Practice of Software (ETAPS'06), Vienna, Austria, pp. 82–96 (2006)

The Research on Human-Computer Interaction in Ambient Intelligence

Yong Zhang[1], Yibin Hou[1], Zhangqin Huang[1], Hui Li[1], Rui Chen[1], and Haitao Shang[2]

[1] Beijing University of technology, 100 Ping Le Yuan, Chao Yang District, 100022 Beijing, P.R. China
{zhangy,yhou,zhuang,hli,rchen,zhangy}@bjut.edu.cn
[2] LanZhou Commercial College, 418 Duan Jia Tan, Chen Guan District, 730020 Lanzhou, P.R. China
Aatt2002@163.com

Abstract. So far the research on Ambient Intelligence (AmI) has been lunched in Europe and Human-Computer Interaction becomes an important technical aspect of it. AmI is the integration of ubiquitous computing, ubiquitous communications and the application of user interface, and its goal is to design and realize the brand-new intelligent, personalized and connective systems or services. In this paper, we put forward an experimental system, which incarnate the essential characteristics of Ambient Intelligence. The architecture and context-aware mechanisms of this system is discussed briefly and the detail of some Human-Computer-Interaction techniques is expounded. With the building of research platform, some Human-Computer-Interaction techniques are worthy of further study in the future.

Keywords: Ambient Intelligence, Human-Computer Interaction, Context-aware, Agent, Human facial-orientation.

1 Introduction

In recent years the "Ubiquitous Computing" research has been lunched in developed countries in Europe and the United States[1]. In 2001, the European ISTG made a "final report" (Scenarios for Ambient Intelligence in 2010)[2] on Ambient Intelligence: AmI application system could be divided into a number of physical space independent subsystems, these subsystems have the interaction capacity, and a variety of portable equipment can be "transparent" in their movements, thus realizing the target of "Ubiquitous Computing". Ambient Intelligence is the integration of ubiquitous computing, ubiquitous communications and the application of user interface, and its goal is to design and realize the brand-new intelligent, personalized and connective systems or services, and to provide the new interaction way between people and machines environment in the entire existence and thereby greatly improve the quality of life for people [3]. In its overall concept, the important thing is: the user benefit from the various services and applications through the back support of new technology systems, and intelligent user interface become the bridges between front

J. Jacko (Ed.): Human-Computer Interaction, Part II, HCII 2007, LNCS 4551, pp. 1030–1039, 2007.

and back-end system. So far, many renowned foreign universities and research institutions have conducted research related topics, such as Philips Research's HomeLab projects, MIT's Intelligent Room and Oxygen project, Stanford's Interactive Workspace etc. In this paper we would introduce some research harvest about AmI in Beijing University of Technology[4],[5].

2 Design of System Framework and HCI Mechanism

In order to deeply study the technical characteristics and application framework of AmI, and for the purpose of developing some novel Human-Computer Interaction techniques of AmI, we designed and constructed a experimental systems named as "AmI-Space", which is a context-aware application system based on Multi-Agent architecture[5] and possesses the objective scenarios as below:

In a certain physical space, with some intelligent interaction equipment hidden someway from eyeshot, the system users can wear a subminiature electronic-badge to obtain non-contact automatic identification services; by the use of portable devices such as PDA, the user can obtain several services system provide, e.g., control of household appliances or multimedia service. On the other hand, system can also automatically measure some status in order to provide personalized initiative services.

In such an AmI environment, several technical tools are developed to meet the need of intelligent Human-Computer Interaction. According to the scenarios of AmI-Space discussed above, we set time, temperature and humidity of room as the environmental context; set the working status as the equipment context; set PDA-input from user, user's identity, and user's facial orientation etc. as the user context.

As the Fig.1 shown, the system context information is measured by the initial sensor, and then these data is stored and handled by the system in order to be capable

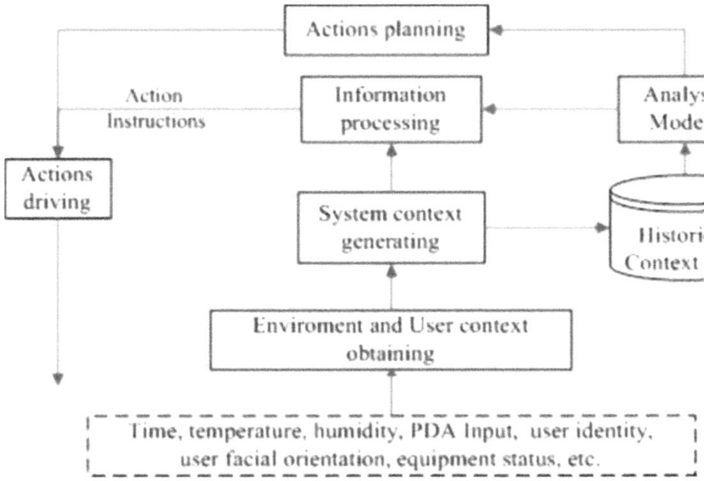

Fig. 1. The DFD analysis of AmI-Space system. There are several processing unit to obtain and process the system context. Therefore, the system can provide intelligent services.

of finding some rules based on historical context data and in order to do some behavior planning according to context. Based on the context-aware DFD analysis, we could easily grasp the overall system by our brains. In addition to the context-aware characteristics, the AmI-Space should first be a distributed and ubiquitous computing system; secondly, this system must have the intelligence and the natural interaction features. Based on analysis and research about some foreign AmI research projects, we adopt the Multi-Agent modeling methods to design the structure and mechanism of our AmI-Space system.

As the Fig.2 shown, in the Interaction tier there is an Aware-Agent-Group is consisted of a number of context-aware agents. By this agent group, the AmI-Space system can access a variety of information from outside. The information traverses those sensors and analyzing processors; then the information is transformed to be some export data or control volume. Those processed data is imported to the Smart Agent which is a control center for further analysis and intelligent behavior planning. Besides, a Interaction tool, PDA-user-operating-agent, is developed for user to get service from the Control-tier.

In the Control tier, the Control-Agent-Group is consisted of the Smart Agent and the Agency agent. The Smart Agent is a kernel controller with some intelligence. First, it handles all messages sent to it. In addition, the Smart-Agent also takes on user's certification authority and issues various service instructions to meet their needs based on the system context. More importantly, it must have some intelligence, namely, it can control or management other agents to fulfill the user's specific needs forwardly. As far as the Agency-Agent is used for construct a wider AmI application group in order to achieve regional collaboration and remote access.

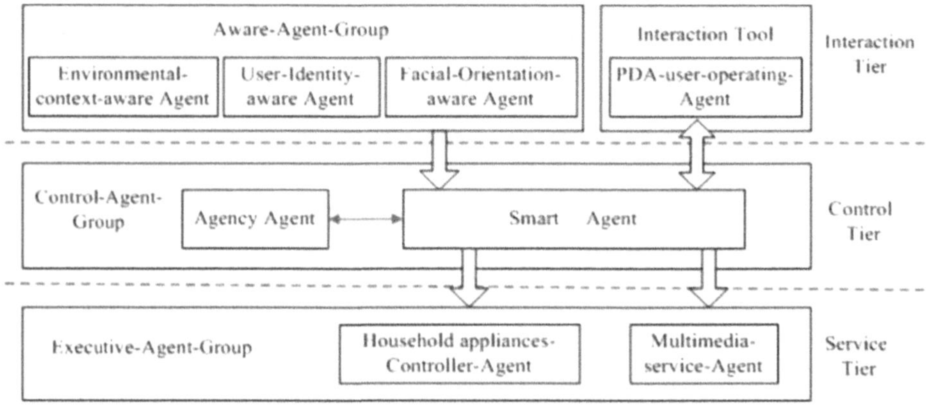

Fig. 2. The AmI-Space is consisted of Aware-Agent-Group, Smart Agent, Excutive-Agent-Group and Interaction Tool. They are divided into three tier: Interaction tier, Control tier and Serice Tier. Every tier involves several agents or units.

Finally, in the Service tier, the Executive-agent-group involves the Household appliances-controller-agent and Multimedia-service-agent. According to the directive issued from Smart-Agent, those agents control some equipment to work incarnating the behaviour of holistic system.

The Figure-3 shows the system realization based on the structure designed above. We established these agents deployed in several different devices, and each agent is a strong autonomist being responsive. Currently, several of these Agents have become some embedded equipment with very small size achieved by FPGA technology[5].

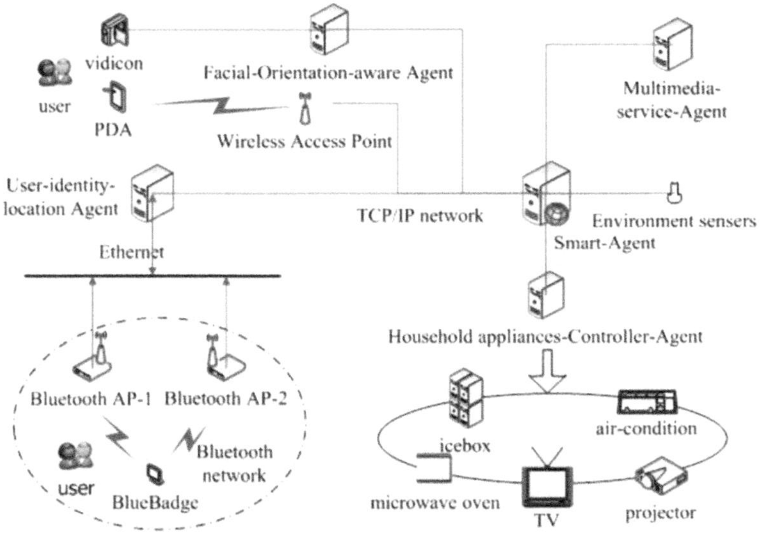

Fig. 3. The physical structure of AmI-Space

To expound the mechanism of AmI-Space and some HCI techniques, we compiled the retral paragraph for discussion.

3 Principles of the Interaction Tier and Service Tier

3.1 The Principles of Some HCI Agent

Now several agents affiliated to AmI-Space system will be expounded in this paragraph.

User-Identity-Aware Agent. It (shown as Fig.4-left) inspects the wireless signals from user's Bluetooth logo in real-time, the signal contains only the user identifier; with the analysis by signal integration algorithms, the user's logo location can be estimated.

The PDA-user-operating-aware Agent. It (shown as Fig.4-right) is embedded in portable device, it accepts the message from PDA's electronic pen and keyboard. After message processing, PDA-user GUI is updated and some information is transmitted to the Smart-Agent to handle (Fig.4).

Environmental-Context-aware Agent. It mainly collects the data of temperature, humidity, pressure, cleanliness of the environment real-time by sensors, and

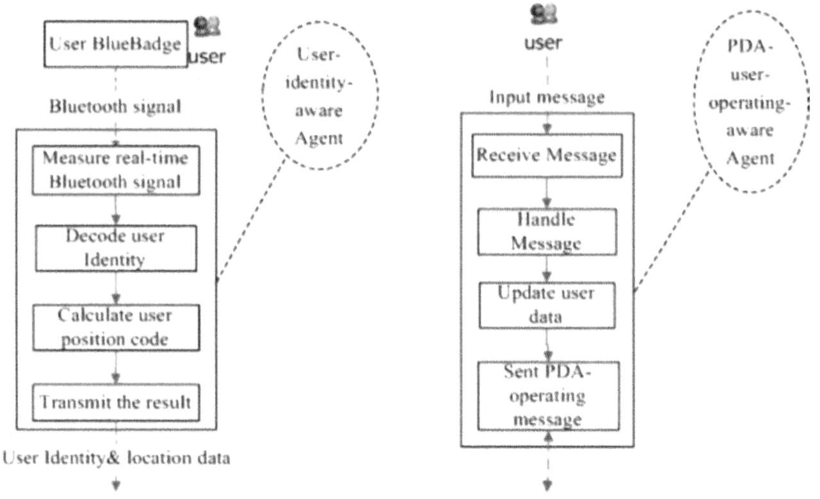

Fig. 4. Mechanism of User-Identity-aware Agent and PDA-User-operating-aware Agent

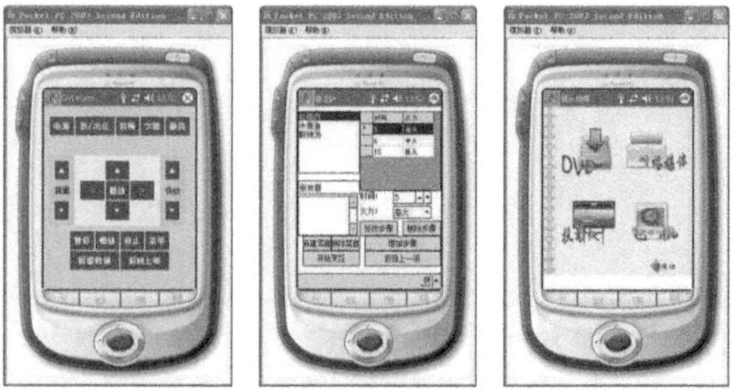

Fig. 5. Example of PDA GUI

calculates some status data. And then these data is transmitted to the Smart-Agent as reference of action planning.

Household appliances-Controller-Agent. It is to some extent independent of management, and is an operational controller of controllable home. It collects real-time work parameters and diagnostic data, stands to monitor the work instructions from the Smart-Agent; furthermore it should generates electrical signals to control equipments to work.

Multimedia-service Agent. It addresses and manages the multimedia resource, and deals with the messages from the user PDA or Smart-Agent: sensing mouse movements conduced by the PDA's pen upon screen, examining the touch stroke for selecting service commands. At last the Multimedia-service-Agent would control broadcast equipment (such as TV or projector) to play the multimedia.

3.2 The Principle of Facial-Orientation-Aware Agent

Facial-Orientation-aware Agent is an independent subsystem [16], its main work is capturing real-time image, image-segmentation, features-extraction and user's facial orientation recognition. Its significance is to achieve the follow-purpose multimedia broadcasting, for example, always controlled projectors to rotate and broadcast multimedia according to the user's facial oriented direction. The awareness of human facial orientation is completed by matching the template of human facial hair model. Therefore, the first problem is how to exactly position the area of the type of human hair and obtain the geometric shape of the hair. However, the partition of human hair will be generated lots of holes for the different texture of the hair lightened, so the noise must be filtered to connect the hair into a whole region.

Wavelet transformation[9] is a space-frequent analyzing method, it can be got a better space resolution in the higher frequent of the image and also got a better frequent resolution in the lower frequency of the image, namely, wavelet is capable to extract the facial localized feature of the image of space and frequency. Here the wavelet analyzing method is adopted to eliminate the noise of facial image for the aim of the whole area of hair.

The image of human face is presented by 2-dimension plan picture, therefore the 2-d concatenation wavelet transformation is used to analyze the human face image. The finger image is a 2-d function as g(x,y) denoted as X coordinate and Y coordinate respectively; if W(x,y) is the basic wavelet of 2-dimension, then φ_{a,b_x,b_y} (x,y) mean the continue wavelet transformation of displacement of the W(x,y) scale flex and the 2-dimension of the image:

$$WT_g(a, b_x, b_y) = \int_{-\infty}^{\infty}\int_{-\infty}^{\infty} g(x, y)\varphi_{a,b_x,b_y}(x, y)d_x d_y \text{ ,} \tag{1}$$

Where,

$$\varphi_{a,b,b_y}(x, y) = \frac{1}{\sqrt{a}}\phi\left[\frac{x-b_x}{a}, \frac{y-b_y}{a}\right] \tag{2}$$

Where a is the scale of the specific basic function, b_x, b_y are the parallel displacement of the degree of 2-dimension. Then, the 2-d continue reverse wavelet transformation is given by,

$$g(x, y) = \frac{1}{c_b}\int_0^{\infty}\frac{da}{\alpha^2}\int_{-\infty}^{\infty}\int_{-\infty}^{\infty} WT_g(a, b_x, b_y)\phi_{a,}b_x, b_y(x, y)db_x db_y \tag{3}$$

Where,

$$C_b = \frac{1}{4\pi^2}\int_{-\infty}^{\infty}\int_{-\infty}^{\infty}\frac{|\varphi(\omega_x, \omega_y)|^2}{|\omega_x^2 + \omega_y^2|}d\omega_x d\omega_y \tag{4}$$

Generally, discreted as the binary data, set $a = 2^j (j \in Z)$, j is called factor of scale. Here, the image signal g(x,y) is divided into lower frequency (V_l) and higher frequency (W_l), during the partition, the information losted by V_l, lower frequency and higher frequency information is partitioned further more, and partition is processed three layers, the details of basic of wavelet is following[10].

First, the sub-space Vj and Wj is token by a new sub-space $U_j^n(n=0,1)$, if set $U_j^0 = V_j, U_j^1 = W_j, j \in Z$, then $V_j = V_{j+1} \oplus W_{j+1}^1$, the partition of U_j^n can be united as:

$$U_j^0 = U_{j+1}^0 \oplus U_{j+1}^1, j \in Z \tag{5}$$

Defined sub-space U_j^{2n+1} is the closed space of $U_{2n+1}(t)$ function, U_j^{2n} is the closed space of function $u_{2n}(t)$, and set Un(t) with the dual scale equation,

$$u_{2n}(t) = \sqrt{2}\sum_{k \in z} h_k u_n(2t-k) \tag{6}$$

$$u_{2n+1}(t) = \sqrt{2}\sum_{k \in z} g_k u_n(2t-k) \tag{7}$$

Where, the coefficient of hk and gk have the relationship,

$$(h_{(k-2l_1)}, h_{(k-2l_2)}) = \delta_{l_1 l_2} \text{ and } (g_{(k-2l_1)}, g_{(k-2l_2)}) = \delta_{l_1 l_2} \tag{8}$$

$$(h_{(k-2l_1)}, g_{(k-2l_2)}) = 0 \text{ , } \sum h_k = \sqrt{2} \text{ and } \sum g_k = 0 \tag{9}$$

In multiple resolution analysis, there are corresponding scalar function $\phi_{(t)}$ and basic wavelet function $\varphi_{(t)}$, they are satisfied dual scale equation,

$$\phi(t) = \sqrt{2}\sum_{k \in z} h_k \phi(2t-k) \tag{10}$$

$$\varphi(t) = \sqrt{2}\sum_{k \in z} g_k \phi(2t-k) \tag{11}$$

When n=0,

$$u_0(t) = \sqrt{2}\sum_{k \in z} h_k u_0(2t-k) \tag{12}$$

$$u_1(t) = \sqrt{2}\sum_{k \in z} g_k u_0(2t-k) \tag{13}$$

U(t) and U1(t) degraded as scalar function $\phi_{(t)}$ and basic wavelet function $\varphi_{(t)}$.

The wavelet of above equation is adopted to conform a wavelet partition three layers, next partition the package of wavelet of human face. The coefficient of wavelet is processed, the coefficient of lower frequency is extended and the coefficient of higher frequency is reduced. Finally, the image is reconstructed with three layer lower and higher frequency coefficients. The processing flow of the algorithm is:

Step-1: Collects the raw image by real time video card;

Step-2: Starts up a thread to copy the raw image and wait for another main thread transform the parameter;

Step-3: Filters the noise of background with difference of frame algorithm, and gets the interesting moving images;

Step-4: Transforms the area of moving image with YUV transformation;
Step-5: Gets the area of human with creating skin model;
Step-6: Expands and erodes the image to get the area of face;
Step-7: Monitors the thread and get the data of human face area;
Step-8: Executes three layers wavelet transformation upon the raw grey image;
Step-9: Enlarges the lower frequency coefficient and reduces the higher frequency coefficient;
Step-10: Resumes the raw image by reverse wavelet transformation;
Step-11: Swells, erodes and deletes the discrete dots;
Step-12: Gets the region of face area by integrating every area of the hair area;
Step-13: Matches the hair region with template model and decides the human face orientation.(the templates is shown as Fig.6).

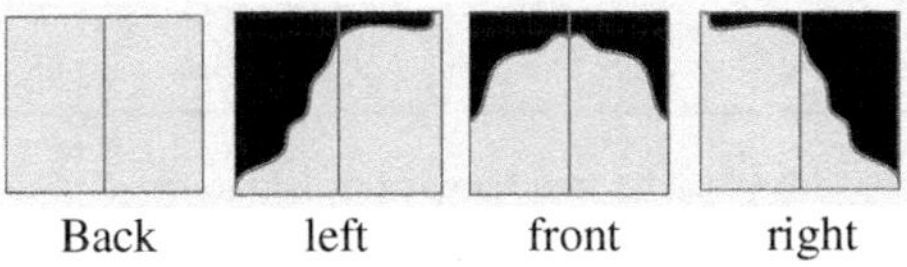

Fig. 6. The templates image of hair for matching

The experiment result shows that the method adopted here is very efficacious, its accuracy can obtain about 90%.

3.3 The Principle of Smart Agent

The Smart-Agent (Fig.7) plays a very important role in the overall control. First, it handles all messages sent to it according to the types of information. In addition, the Smart-Agent also takes on user's certification authority and issues various service instructions to meet their needs based on the system context. More importantly, it must have some intelligence, namely, it can control or management other agents to fulfill the user's specific needs forwardly. For example, according to the user's age, sex, body status and specific user's knowledge, it can adopt various illation models to forecast user's potential need, and generate certain action sequence instructions to drive other agents work for user.

In the structure of Smart-Agent, there is a smart planner unit which is a important section. In this smart planner unit, by the maintenance interface the psychology and physiology models of users and service targets are input. Based on the historical context data, the data miner can also find new knowledge added to the knowledge base about the outside world or users by a analysis algorithms. The service targets set means personalized service objectives which the planner module trying to achieved, and the information can be obtained through the system interface or data excavator to generate and adjust. The information in service targets set may also hold priorities or priority level for different objectives.

The planner module of smart planner is used to create action plans. With the aid of models knowledge and the experienced service targets set, according to current

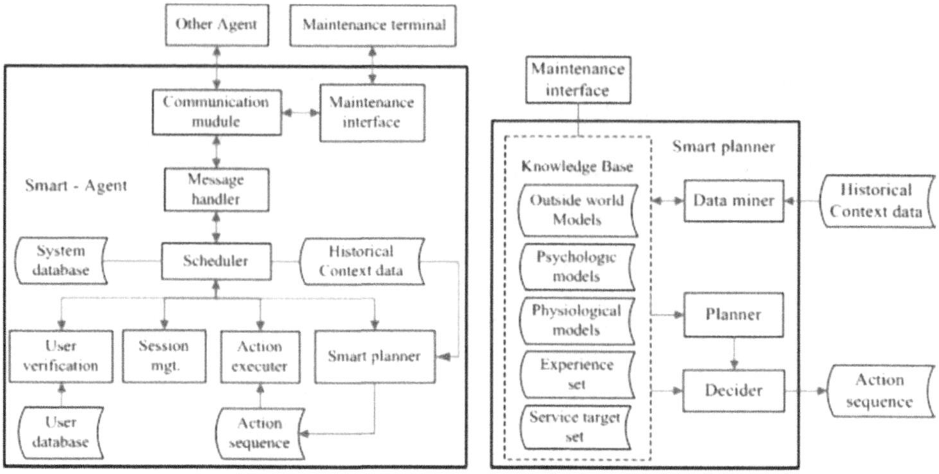

Fig. 7. The mechanism of Smart-Agent

conditions, it would query similar examples and evaluate corresponding solutions from the target set, that is, an old action planning result would be adopted or a new action planning would be created. The main task of decider is coordination: its information source is the planner module, and its main target is conflict detection and elimination to determine the current action sequence.

The planner module of smart planner is used to create action plans. With the aid of models knowledge and the experienced service targets set, according to current conditions, it would query similar examples and evaluate corresponding solutions from the target set, that is, an old action planning result would be adopted or a new action planning would be created. The main task of decider is coordination: its information source is the planner module, and its main target is conflict detection and elimination to determine the current action sequence.

4 Conclusion

In this paper, we put forward a very interesting experimental research system-- "AmI-Space", which incarnate the essential concept and characteristics of Ambient Intelligence. The multi-agent architecture and context-aware mechanisms of this system is discussed briefly and the detail of some Human-Computer-Interaction techniques is expounded. In one word, with the building of research platform, some Human-Computer-Interaction techniques are worthy of further study in the future to improve the quality of life for people.

Acknowledgments. This research is supported by the Research Plan of the National Natural Science Foundation of China under Grant No.90407017; the Natural Science Foundation of Beijing of China under Grant No. KZ200510005006.

References

1. Weber, W. et al.: Ambient intelligence-key technologies in the information age. IEEE International conference on Electron Devices, pp. 11–118 (2003)
2. ISTAG: Scenarios for Ambient Intelligence in 2010, Online http://www.cordis.lu/istag.htm
3. Aarts, E.: Ambient Intelligence: a multimedia perspective. IEEE Multimedia, pp. 12–19 (2004)
4. Yi-min, W., Xu-hui, C., Liang, C., Xue, Q.: Architecture of the smart home network in ambient intelligence. Journal of Computer Engineering and Design, Beijing vol. 5, pp. 38–41 (2005)
5. Zhang, Y., et al.: A Context-aware AmI system Based on MAS model. In: Proceeding of IEEE International conferrence on Interlligent Information Hiding and Multimedia signal Processing, Pasadena, pp. 703–706 (2006)
6. Rui, C., Hui, L.: Facial Orientation Analysis and Application in Human-Computer Interactive system. In: Proceedings of the 8th International Conference for Young Computer Scientists, pp. 553–560. Beijing University of Posts and Telemunications Press, Beijing (2005)
7. Fusheng, Y.: Wavelet tranformation for engineer analysis and application[m]. Science publisher, Beijing (2000)

The Universal Control Hub: An Open Platform for Remote User Interfaces in the Digital Home

Gottfried Zimmermann[1] and Gregg Vanderheiden[2]

[1] Access Technologies Group, Wilhelm-Blos-Str. 8, 72793 Pfullingen, Germany
gzimmermann@acm.org
[2] Trace R&D Center, University of Wisconsin-Madison, USA
gv@trace.wisc.edu

Abstract. This paper describes the application of an international user interface standard in the digital home in a gateway-based approach: The Universal Control Hub. ISO/IEC FDIS 24752 specifies the Universal Remote Console framework, promoting a "user interface socket" and pluggable user interfaces. The Universal Control Hub implements this standard in a way that facilitates the operation of existing controlled devices and controller devices. It retrieves user interfaces for the discovered target devices from resource servers that hold registered resources from multiple parties for any target device. Thus an open platform for user interfaces in the digital home is created that decouples the user interface from the device. This approach is expected to lead to more usable and more accessible user interfaces.

Keywords: Remote user interfaces, task-based user interfaces, digital home, usability, accessibility, Universal Control Hub, Universal Remote Console.

1 Introduction

It is widely acknowledged that complex user interfaces are an impediment for the proliferation of the digital home. A recent CEA study [1] found that “ease of use” is the third most important aspect for home theater owners, only narrowly topped by “video quality” and “sound quality”. Also, “ease of using remotes” is identified as the second most important aspect for these owners that they are not satisfied with, indicated by a low ratio of the percentage of satisfied consumers and the percentage of those rating the attribute as important.

Consumer electronics industry and manufacturers of home appliances need to recognize the importance of solving the usability problem in their very own interest. Philips Electronics North America’s CEO Zeven reports that only 13 percent of Americans believe technology products in general are easy to use [2]. That is why experts have suggested having new products tested by older persons as a litmus test for ease-of-use [3]. The answer to the question “Can grandma figure out how to use it?” is a good hint for a product’s usability in general.

J. Jacko (Ed.): Human-Computer Interaction, Part II, HCII 2007, LNCS 4551, pp. 1040–1049, 2007.

The usability problem has a significant impact on sales numbers. Two out of three Americans have lost interest in a technology product because it seemed too complex to set up or operate [2]. In addition, the manufacturer's profit on actual sales is cut down by a large number of returned products. Den Ouden [4]found out that half of all 'malfunctioning products' returned to stores by consumers are in full working order, but customers cannot figure out how to operate the product.

What is a huge problem if unsolved can be a tremendous opportunity if adequate solutions are found. Bias and Mayhew [5]estimate that companies that excel in usability can improve their return on such investment more than 10,000 times. This number should be reason enough for product manufacturers to increase their efforts in solving the "complexity crisis".

What constitutes an "impediment" for some consumers can be an insurmountable barrier for others. Older people and people with disabilities are often cut off from technological advancements in the home because they are not able to operate modern products. In fact, these user groups would probably benefit the most from recent digital home products if existing usability and accessibility problems would be overcome.

This paper introduces the "Universal Control Hub" architecture as an open user interface platform for the digital home that can facilitate solutions that address current usability and accessibility problems.

Note: In this paper, the term "target" is used for devices and services that are remotely controlled, and the word "controller" for devices used to control targets. A controller is running a "remote user interface" exposed by the target for the purpose of controlling it remotely.

2 State of the Art

For currently available remote user interfaces for the digital home, we identify the following problems:

Problem 1: Remote user interfaces are tied to specific target devices

Traditionally, remote user interfaces, running on a controller, are dedicated to one particular target.

Infrared-based remote controls shipped with and bound to specific target devices are prevalent in today's homes. This results in a large number of remote controls in the digital home, a real usability problem with a growing number of target devices in the average home.

Devices such as network routers and digital media players can be controlled through software dedicated to this target device. The control software may be located on the target device and running inside a Web server (allowing control from any Web browser) or the control software has to be installed on a platform-specific controller such as a PC. In either case, each product again has its own different user interface – except this time they are software based rather than hardware.

UPnP Remote User Interface [6]builds upon the Web server model for remote control, and specifies a protocol for controllers (called "remote user interface clients") to discover a set of user interfaces exposed by a target ("remote user interface server").

Similarly, CEA-2027-B [7] lets a target device (called "logical unit") convey a remote user interface in HTML (called "control frame") to a TV acting as controller (including its remote control).

Because of this 1-to-1 relationship between remote user interfaces and targets, issuers are typically stuck with the user interface provided by the device manufacturer. Often, this does not meet the needs and preferences of a particular user.

Problem 2: Remote user interfaces are controller device dependent

"Universal remote controls" have some success, but are still bound to a particular controller device. Nevertheless, the ability to be programmed or to download infrared codes, based on a user's configuration, eliminates their dependency on specific targets. Some newer models connect to a "master controller" via wireless radio frequency technology, allowing users to control targets even when these are located in a different room. Still, users have to use the user interface that comes with the controller which has been designed by its manufacturer. These remotes are careful to always expose the full functionality of the devices resulting in interfaces that are often even more complex than the individual remotes provided with the products.

Some very high-end universal remote controls are made to be programmed by professional user interface designers, the custom-home installers, using proprietary tools and proprietary protocols. Designing a user interface for one of these controllers is a cumbersome process requiring skills specific to the platform employed. This is a niche market, offering products that are out of reach for most people because of the expensiveness of these custom installation homes. Still, this shows that there is market for custom-made user interfaces, though hampered by cumbersome programming and installation, and high costs.

Besides custom-installation homes, users are left with a very limited choice of controller devices and user interfaces that they can employ to control a particular target device. Oftentimes, users will find the "default" controller unintuitive to use. For some users who have special needs, it may not even be accessible. Speech-based or tactile user interfaces are typically not provided by manufacturers at all.

Abstract user interface specifications have been discussed as a potential remedy for this problem. The idea is that an abstract user interface can be rendered on any device, using whatever input and output modalities are present.

The User Interface Markup Language (UIML) standard [8], developed by OASIS, claims to be such an abstract language. But it is not living up to its promises: It doesn't include a generic vocabulary for abstract widgets, although this has been attempted externally to the standardization effort, for an older version of UIML. Moreover, UIML does not provide a clean separation between content and presentation (see problem 5 below).

XForms [9], a technology for next-generation Web forms, defines a useful set of abstract user interface components (called "XForms form controls"), but its model is based on the typical request-response pattern of Web forms. It cannot be easily applied to digital home control.

Other work on abstract user interfaces includes the Pebbles project [10] at CMU and the SUPPLE project [11] at the University of Washington. Although Pebbles' "Personal Universal Controller" language has been demonstrated to generate visual and auditory user interfaces, it lacks the flexibility of external resources and third-party user interface components. SUPPLE has developed a technology for automatic generation of user interfaces, but is constrained to visual user interfaces.

CEA-2014 [12], which builds upon UPnP Remote User Interface [6], could provide a partial solution to this problem. It facilitates a match-making process for an arbitrary controller device to pick a user interface protocol that is supported by the controller platform and suits the user's preferences. Support for a specific user interface protocol, dubbed "CE-HTML" (an XHTML profile in Web 2.0 style) is mandatory for user interface servers so that at least interoperability is guaranteed for controllers supporting this protocol. However, CE-HTML requires a Web browser with JavaScript support, and is focused on visual user interfaces only.

Problem 3: Remote user interfaces are device-oriented rather than task-oriented

This is a consequence of problem 1 (user interfaces tied to target devices). Since every manufacturer binds users to the user interface that they deliver for their targets, and since there are typically multiple targets from different manufacturers in the home, users end up "juggling" multiple user interfaces, one per target device. Each of these user interfaces reflects the functionality of a single target, and does not directly offer cross-target functionality that would be required for more intuitive and task-oriented user interfaces.

For example, the (simple) task of watching a DVD movie on a typical home theater system involves at least 3 target devices that the user needs to set up in the right way for interoperation: The TV screen must be switched on and accept input from the DVD player; the same holds for the receiver/equalizer; and the DVD player must be switched on and instructed to play the DVD.

This situation is also prohibitive for natural language user interfaces that would allow users to interact with targets in terms of what they want to do rather than how to do it. The fact that users have to operate multiple user interfaces (one per device involved) to achieve a goal is one of the biggest impediments for easy-to-use interfaces in the digital home. This problem becomes worse the more devices are required for a particular task.

An evolving standard on task model representation, CEA-2018, currently being developed by the CEA working group R7 WG12 [13], may help to solve this problem for future generations of devices in the digital home.

Problem 4: Some new devices are network-enabled, but there is no uniform networking platform for the digital home

Network-enabled devices are emerging on the market. These can be controlled remotely by means of standardized networking protocols. Such home networking protocols include, among others: Universal Plug and Play (UPnP) [14], CECED Home Appliances Interoperating Network (CHAIN) [15], HDMI Consumer Electronics Control channel (CEC) [16], HANA [17], and LonWorks [18].

The networked devices allow for *one* controller device being used to control *all* target devices of a particular network protocol. For example, the Siemens serve@Home product line [19], which is built upon the CHAIN standard, includes a touch-screen controller device (called "info display") which can be used to view status information and remotely control all serve@Home products in a home. Another example is the Rudeo Play & Control software [20] which promotes a Pocket PC based PDA to a remote control for any UPnP Media Player in the home network.

However, there is no networking platform today that would encompass the full range of devices in the digital home. Therefore users are still required to cope with multiple controller devices and user interfaces, one for each platform that is being used by a target device in their home. They cannot use the controller device and user interface of their choice, such as PDAs, cell phones or assistive technology devices.

Problem 5: No clean separation between user interface code and networking code

Since existing tools encourage user interface code that is interspersed with networking code, writing user interfaces requires knowledge of protocol stacks for device-to-device communication. Typically, connectivity and network-oriented programmers end up writing user interface code themselves.

The missing separation between user interface code and connectivity code is a major cause for poorly designed user interfaces because no user interface experts were involved in their design. Consequently, unsatisfied customers frequently complain about non-intuitive user interfaces – and manufacturers suffer from high return rates on the retail market.

3 Requirements

To overcome the above problems, a framework for remote user interfaces for the digital home is needed with the following requirements. Note that there are generally no one-to-one correspondences between requirements and problems, but the set of requirements together is designed to address all the problems described above.

Requirement 1: Users can choose the controller device and user interface that suits their needs and preferences

Users should be able to use the controller device and user interface technology they are most familiar with and that suits their needs. For example, one user would like to run a Flash application on a PDA, a second favors a Web 2.0 page in their PC's browser, a third would prefer a very simple remote control with visual feedback on the TV screen, and a fourth wants to use a Braille-based handheld computer.

Users should be able to use one controller and one user interface of their choice for all targets. Even if they transition to a new target device (e.g. because the old target broke) they should still be able to use the same, familiar controller and user interface.

Requirement 2: Third parties can provide user interfaces and user interface components for any target

Obviously, there is no "one-size-fits-all" approach for usable and accessible user interfaces. Open competition in user interfaces will result in more usable and more personally accessible user interfaces over time. Users will be able to pick the user interface that matches best their needs and preferences.

We need an open market for remote user interfaces in which any party, including manufacturers, 3rd party organizations, user groups, and users, can create a user interface for any target. These user interfaces and user interface components should be globally available for any consumer who wishes to use them.

Requirement 3: Facilitate cross-device user interfaces

Many tasks in the digital home require multiple target devices (cf. the DVD movie playing example above). In general, the targets will come from multiple manufacturers. Users want to control these from one user interface, with the devices being transparent to them, or at least allowing for seamless user operations.

Task-based user interfaces that communicate with the user in terms of "what to do" rather than "how to do it" are seen as potential remedy for the user interface complexity problem in consumer electronics. Cross-target user interfaces (rather than strictly target-specific ones) are a prerequisite for task-based user interfaces.

Requirement 4: Middle layer between user interface and target functionality

There needs to be a middle layer, a standardized "connection point", between the functionality of a target (as given by the target device manufacturer) and the user interface created by any party. This is called "user interface socket" in the Universal Remote Console framework[21][22].

Typically, the manufacturer would specify the user interface socket for their target. The user interface socket specifies a target's functionality in terms of abstract user interface elements not bound to any particular device. A user interface socket reflects a target's state at any time, and allows for triggering commands and state changes on the target. If a user interface socket is available for a target, a user interface designer can easily bind their user interface to it, without needing to write code for the specific networking and connectivity platform employed.

Regarding task-based user interfaces, the user interface socket can serve as an "atomic task layer". A task model may specify tasks and their sub-tasks as a multi-level hierarchy, with the sub-tasks of the lowest level being bound to elements of the user interface socket. This makes the task model independent of the underlying networking platform.

4 The Universal Control Hub

The Universal Control Hub (UCH) is a gateway based architecture for implementing the Universal Remote Console (URC) framework [21][22]in the digital home. It reaps the benefits of the URC framework without requiring URC-compliant targets and controllers. The UCH architecture was originally proposed for UPnP based home networks [23], but is also applicable to any other networking platform and any combination of them.

In the UCH architecture, the control hub is the gateway between controllers and targets that would otherwise not be able to talk to each other. It is easy on requirements on targets and controllers in the system, since it handles most of the

URC-related technologies. In fact, all of the URC framework's components are running inside the control hub. In short, the Universal Control Hub exposes pluggable user interfaces to controllers on behalf of targets, based on the URC framework.

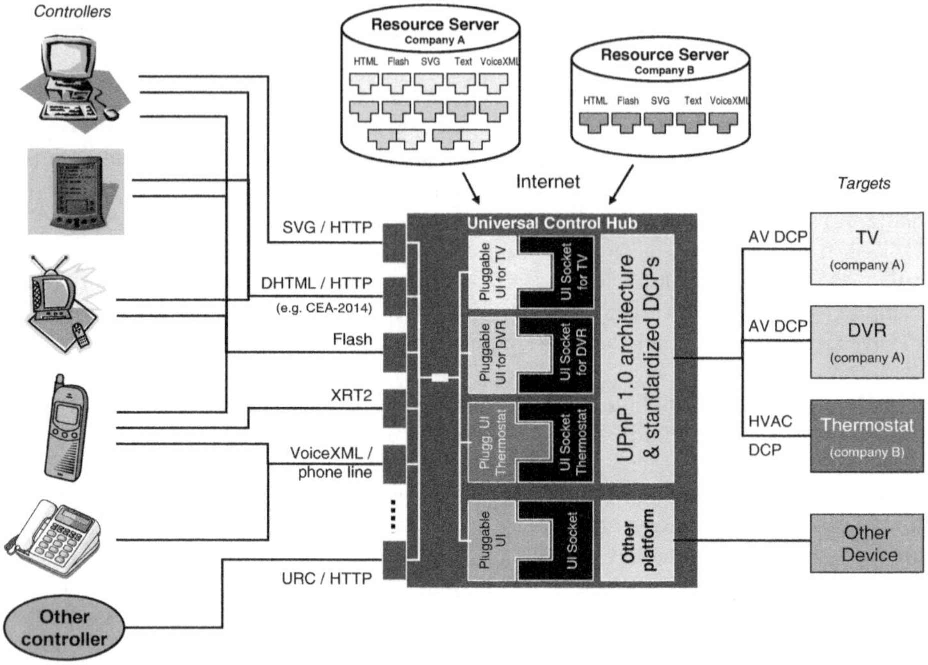

Fig. 1. Universal Control Hub architecture (from [23] with minor modifications). The control hub (in the middle) connects to different controllers (at the left hand) through a variety of user interface protocols (sample protocols shown as gray boxes on the left side of the control hub). The control hub connects to targets (at the right hand) through network-specific code (here as an example the UPnP 1.0 architecture & standardized DCPs). The control hub downloads pluggable user interfaces from resource servers on the Internet (at the top).

Controllers need to discover the control hub and thus get access to the connected targets in the home. CEA-2014 [12] may be used for that purpose. However, this requires a UPnP control point be available on the controllers. Alternatively, users can establish the connection to the control hub manually once and store it for subsequent uses (e.g. as a bookmark in a Web browser).

The remainder of this section describes how various features of the Universal Control Hub architecture meet the requirements described above.

Feature 1: Control hub between targets and controllers.
The hub approach solves the interoperability problem between targets and controllers: It bridges between targets with their control language and controllers with their user interface languages and protocols.

The hub spans multiple targets. This facilitates user interfaces that seamlessly integrate multiple targets and that are structured by tasks rather than by individual targets.

Feature 2: Standard-based user interface socket
The UCH is based on the Universal Remote Console framework defined in ISO/IEC 24752 [22]. This framework allows third parties to provide pluggable user interfaces for targets of other manufacturers, based on a user interface socket description for a target device. This facilitates an open market for remote user interfaces in the digital home.

The user interface socket (short "socket") is the connection point between a target and remote user interface. It reduces the interconnection problem from an n*m problem to an n+m problem (with n=number of controllers and m=number of targets). Note: Actually, this calculation is overly simplistic since it assumes that there is always exactly one user interface per target.

The user interface socket description abstracts platform specific details of networking and connectivity protocols, so that a pluggable user interface does not need to care about that. The user interface socket description can also contain pre- and postconditions as typically used in task models. These dependencies can be used by sophisticated pluggable user interfaces such as intelligent agents to generate more usable user interfaces.

Feature 3: Variety of user interface protocols
The control hub provides a variety of user interface protocols (such as DHTML over HTTP, Flash, VoiceXML, etc.) for controllers. Controllers can pick the most suitable user interface protocol that it supports.

Users can choose their controller and their favorite user interface as long as there is a matching pluggable user interface that runs inside the control hub. The pluggable user interface may be created by the manufacturer of a target device, the manufacturer of a controller, or by a third party.

This provides for a "user interface forward-compatibility" of targets, i.e. one can control the same targets with conventional controllers today, and tomorrow with intelligent agents and natural-language based controllers, once they are mature enough and available for everybody.

If there is no appropriate pluggable user interface available for a specific combination of controller and targets, a controller can fall back to the URC-HTTP protocol which is mandatory for the hub. The URC-HTTP protocol is the basis for a "functional user interface". It provides direct access to the user interface socket and thus allows for generating a user interface on the fly for any modality.

Feature 4: Globally available resource servers
The control hub connects to global resource servers on the Internet to retrieve various user interfaces for the target devices that it discovers. Third parties can create their own user interfaces for any controllers and any targets and register them with any resource server.

Thus a user interface can be updated on the fly (i.e. by having it downloaded to a control hub) without requiring access to or replacing target devices or controller devices. Note that controller and target devices do not need to have Internet access. It is sufficient that the control hub has an Internet connection (which may be temporary) to access resource servers and download the appropriate pluggable user interfaces for the controller and target devices present in the home.

5 Application of the Universal Control Hub Architecture

An implementation of the Universal Control Hub architecture has been developed at the Trace R&D Center, University of Wisconsin-Madison, USA. A recent prototype demonstrates how a variety of mobile devices can be used to remotely control a UPnP-based entertainment system.

The Universal Control Hub is also being applied in the "i2home" project [24], a project funded by the European Research programme IST. The i2home consortium consists of organizations and companies from Germany, Sweden, the Czech Republic, Spain and Portugal.

Organizations interested in the promotion and implementation of the URC standards have formed the URC Consortium (URCC) that provides more information on current projects and tools [25].

Acknowledgment

This work was partially funded by the US Dept of Education, NIDRR, under Grant H133E030012 (RERC on IT Access); and by the EU 6th Framework Program under grant FP6-033502 (i2home). The opinions herein are those of the author and not necessarily those of the funding agencies.

References

[1] Consumer Electronics Association (2006): Home Theater Opportunities - CEA Market Research Report, September 2006 http://www.ebrain.org/crs/crs_arch.asp?crscode=CRS290

[2] Zeven, P.: Do people need the gizmos we're selling? CNET News December 18, 2006 (2006) http://news.com.com/Do+people+need+the+gizmos+were+selling/2010-1041_3-6144335.html

[3] Ogg, E.: Can Grandma figure out how to use it? CNET News October 13, 2006 (2006) http://news.com.com/The+key+to+gadget+buyers+hearts+Simplicity/2100-1041_3-6125477. html

[4] Den Ouden, E.: Developments of a Design Analysis Model for Consumer Complaints: revealing a new class of quality failures. Ph.D. thesis, Technische Universiteit Eindhoven (2006)

[5] Bias, R.G., Mayhew, D.J.: Cost-Justifying Usability: An Update for the Internet Age, 2nd edn. Morgan Kaufmann, San Francisco (2005)

[6] UPnP Remote UI Client and Server V 1.0. UPnP Forum. http://www.upnp.org/standardizeddcps/remoteui.asp

[7] CEA-2027-B. A User Interface Specification for Home Networks Using Web-based Protocols. Consumer Electronics Association (2006) http://ce.org/Standards/2502.asp
[8] OASIS User Interface Markup Language (UIML) Technical Committee http://www.oasis-open.org/committees/tc_home.php?wg_abbrev=uiml
[9] XForms 1.0 (2nd edn.) W3C Recommendation (March 14, 2006) http://www.w3.org/TR/2006/REC-xforms-20060314/
[10] The Pittsburgh Pebbles PDA Project. Human-Computer Interaction Institute, Carnegie Mellon University http://www.pebbles.hcii.cmu.edu/
[11] SUPPLE: Automatic Generation of Personalizable User Interfaces. Department of Computer Science and Engineering, University of Washington http://www.cs.washington.edu/ai/ supple/
[12] CEA-2014. Web-based Protocol and Framework for Remote User Interface on UPnP™ Networks and the Internet (Web4CE). Consumer Electronics Association (2006) http://www.ce.org/Standards/browseByCommittee_2757.asp
[13] CEA R7 WG12, Task-Based User Interface http://www.ce.org/Standards/CommitteeDetails. aspx?Id=000011032608
[14] Universal Plug and Play (UPnP) Forum http://www.upnp.org/
[15] CECED Home Appliances Interoperating Network (CHAIN). European Committee of Domestic Equipment Manufacturers (CECED) http://www.ceced.org/IFEDE/easnet.dll/ ExecReq/WPItem?eas:dat_im=010113&eas:display=CHAIN
[16] High-Definition Multimedia Interface (HDMI) http://www.hdmi.org
[17] High-Definition Audio-Video Network Alliance http://www.hanaalliance.org/
[18] The LonWorks Platform: Technology Overview. Echelon http://www.echelon.com/developers/ lonworks/
[19] Siemens serve@Home http://www.servehome.com/
[20] Rudeo Play & Control for UPnP Devices and Windows Media Player http://www.rudeo.com/ playctrl.htm
[21] ANSI/INCITS 289-2005, 290-2005, 291-2005, 292-2005,293-2005. Information Technology - Protocol to Facilitate Operation of Information and Electronic Products through Remote and Alternative Interfaces and Intelligent Agents. ANSI, (2005) http://myurc.org/obtain-copies.php
[22] ISO/IEC FCD 24752. Information technology - User interfaces - Universal remote console - 5 parts. International Organization for Standardization (ISO) (2006) http://www.iso.org/iso/en/CombinedQueryResult.CombinedQueryResult?queryString=24752
[23] Zimmermann, G., Vanderheiden, G., Rich, C.: Universal Control Hub & Task-Based User Interfaces. URC Consortium, 2006 (2006) http://myurc.org/publications/2006-Univ-Ctrl-Hub.php
[24] Intuitive Interaction for Everyone with Home Appliances based on Industry Standards (i2home) http://www.i2home.org/
[25] URC Consortium http://myurc.org/

Part V

Emerging Interactive Technologies

An Investigation of Usability Evaluation for Smart Clothing

Haeng-Suk Chae[1], Ji-Young Hong[1], Hyun-Seung Cho[2], Kwang-Hee Han[1], and Joo-Hyeon Lee[3]

[1] Cognitive Engineering Lab, Yonsei University, Seoul, Korea
[2] Research Institute of Clothing & Textile Sciences, Yonsei University, Seoul, Korea
[3] Dept. of Clothing and Textiles, Yonsei University, Seoul, Korea
{acechae19,hongcom,hyunseung-cho,khan,ljhyeon}@yonsei.ac.kr

Abstract. The purpose of this paper is to develop usability evaluation for smart clothing. In this paper, we propose evaluation factor and object through user centered evaluation process. The basic idea of this paper is to know the thought from wearable user. Also, we gathered the opinion from expert group. As a result, we adopted evaluation item categories. By examining some empirical data which is obtained from Observation Evaluation (OE) and Wearability Evaluation (WE), we conclude usability evaluation of Smart Clothing. The design process in creating a successful wearable usability is no longer about providing technical success, rather about creating an optimal user experience. Their studies provide guideline on the types of limit process that can affect user's situation in wearable computing. In this paper, usability of smart clothing is described, including improving reinforces of previous studies [2], [4], [5]. In addition, we provide a framework for usability to support new types. First, we were composed of systematic experience factor structure from an extraction factor as qualitative process based on scenario. We made factor-object matrix to check usability factor and wearable object position. Second, we finished developing questions about evaluation domain. Third, we took evaluation by questionnaire as observational and wearable types. Last, we did analysis and structure evaluation. We implemented factor analysis which was possible to access theoretic structure and delete meaningless questionnaire.

Keywords: Smart Clothing, Observation Evaluation (OE), Wearability Evaluation (WE), Wearable Computer, Usability Evaluation, Comport Rate Scale(CRS), Wearablility.

1 Introduction

"Wearable" has been defined as implying the use of the human body as a support for some product [2]. Besides, "Smart clothing" may be an intelligent garment, which is augmented with electrical or non-electrical component, including safety and entertainment [8]. User-centered smart clothing design must be related with user task [10] since smart clothing is constantly with the user's better responds to their needs [6]. We propose a design process based on scenarios for smart clothing. Such

J. Jacko (Ed.): Human-Computer Interaction, Part II, HCII 2007, LNCS 4551, pp. 1053–1060, 2007.

processing is shown to scenario draft, formed between researcher group and general user including early adopter. Interface of smart clothing need the awareness of social situation, environment, and the goal of the user [1]. The ideal of smart clothing is based on social acceptance environment, the space in which human interacts. Our method of designing smart clothing makes it easy to understand user's needs. Our study made a few prototype scenarios whose purpose was to verify the suitability of smart clothing. And the process of scenarios involves many fields. Smart clothing will be intelligent product that provides new platform from the development of innovative application. And it is significant to clarify the design process that needed to be solved before starting the actual smart clothing design. This work needs to determine user requirement.

The purpose of this paper is to investigate usability evaluation for Smart Clothing. In this paper, we present evaluation factor and the basic idea of this process is to know the thought of wearable user. Also, we gathered the opinion from expert group, adding context evaluation. As a result, we adopted evaluation categories. By examining some empirical data which is obtained from Observation Evaluation (OE) and Wearability Evaluation (WE), we performed usability evaluation of smart clothing. The design process in creating a successful usability of smart clothing is no longer about providing technical success, rather about creating an optimal user experience.

2 Related Research

Usability studies with smart clothing are nearly rare in the research areas. According to McCann, the demands of the end-user can be categorized under the topics as Demands of the Body, Demands of the Activity /End-use, Demands of the Culture and Aesthetic considerations [7].

Previous studies show limited results on wearable computing. Gemperle provides a feature for wearability design guideline and satisfaction assessment [2]. Another studies by Knight shows that Comfort Rating Scale(CRS) is needed to be supported [4], [5].

Wearability. Gemperle et al. noted dynamic wearability, which includes the notion of the device being wearable when the body is in motion [2].

CRS. Gemperle et al. studied wearable design formed by asking participants to carry out activities and level of comfort [5]. And they suggested that an assessment of wearable computers should include an element of comfort. Comfort has been evaluated in ergonomics in many areas related with workplace design process. For wearable computer, comfort assessment has been carried out for devices into helmets [9] and for arm-worn devices [11]. Knight measured levels of pain and discomfort with reference to the use of wearable computers such as head and arm posture, the neck, shoulder, upper arm, and forearm [4]. When wearing, comfort can be affected by many of things as the device's size and weight, movement, and pain, whether direct or indirect. As a result, comfort should be measured above a lot of dimensions.

3 Evaluation of the Method

3.1 The Design Process on Scenarios

Smart Clothing environment faces user issue as well as technical problem and its design process differs from computing environment. Though most of smart clothing environment is personal condition, brainstorming through small group interview such as Focus Group Interview (F.G.I) is a more systematic process in smart clothing environment. We describe our process to capture data on human behavior, including interactions with others, and activities, using smart clothing in the future.

We select the task to test among scenarios and adapt the materials of information on smart clothing needs. And we present a briefing note to participants for identifying the target population. And we find that this evaluation is reasonable, well-structured, and free of unexpected mistakes. And then we need modification. We make up evaluation as instruction note, asking the participant to perform response, and we have background material for some task, recording sheet to record observations. We observe the evaluation. And assemble the result. We try to assess strength and weakness after each session. Most of user didn't know smart clothing, so we described smart clothing environment. It is explanation to have a rough idea of scenario such as "Music-prism T-shirt", "Smart jogging buddy", "Beat amplifier", "Ski wear: safety and freedom", "Healthy sleeping suit", "Lovers' glove", "Safety hiking suit" and "A stray child check".

Each scenario gives each participant cues for smart clothing. It conveys a sense of smart clothing to everyday user so that they have the pool of knowledge and experience smart clothing environment in the future. Concept evaluation on scenarios through small group interview was divided into ages which is costume play (age: 13 – 22) and easy and care life style (age: over 35). There is a process such as scenario presentation, free discussion, a structured interview, preference for scenarios, purchase intentions, video recording, voice recording and script extraction. The analysis of this research is three types that are needed to be shown in measurement – life style analysis for ages, strength and weakness in scenarios and ideation in scenarios. And then observed results can be viewed as being Scenario-Needs-Function-Device (SNFD) Analysis. Using the SNFD has good patterns in various situation of smart clothing. This represents qualitative analysis based on scenarios in smart clothing.

To achieve useful measurement, Device-Function Matrix (DFM) including scenarios and opinion of user has been suggested in the measure process. DFM process is to define the concept being measured. In domain, the concept is elaborated in terms of its content. We find some categories in function. And it is divided into 6 functions such as advice, notification of a situation, sensing & monitoring, actuating, communication and customizing. The function given above shows effects of user choice.

3.2 Development of Evaluation Item

To develop evaluation item of smart clothing, we generated a list of specific terms which could be applied to smart clothing. The process was generated using brainstorming discussion including process based on scenario. Scope of smart clothing was used to generate specific terms. Initially, the terms generated were not specific to wearing some device but instead referred to wearing some object on the body. The important point was given to wearable devices that have the ability to see user condition, carrying out this procedure generated 8 main evaluation objects; platform, sensing, light emitting, thermal control, communication, music playing, general and experience satisfaction, including sub-evaluation objects; appearance, material, detector, controller, emitter, generator/cooler, display, headset/speaker, main board and connector.

The evaluation objects are given a definition explaining how to describe wearing and affecting the user. The user is asked to score the device for each of 8 main evaluation objects and execute an analysis of the evaluation of a wearable device. It is essential to apply to use according to smart clothing to a more manageable level.

To construct evaluation items, we produced data from the categorizing evaluation items by generating similarity matrix. The matrix was filled in 5 factors; appearance, wearablility, usefulness, easy to manage and safety.

3.3 Usability Evaluation

Previous studies provide guideline on the types of limit process that can affect user's situation in wearable computing [2], [4], [5]. But in this paper, usability of smart clothing is described, including improving reinforces of previous studies. In addition, we provide a framework for usability to support new types.

First, we were composed of systematic experience factor structure from an extraction factor as qualitative evaluations. We made factor-object matrix to check usability factor and wearable object position. Second, we finished developing questions about evaluation domain. Third, we took evaluation by questionnaire as observational and wearable types. Last, we did analysis and structure evaluation. We implemented factor analysis which was possible to access theoretic structure and delete meaningless questionnaire.

The method was evaluated through empirical data such as Observation Evaluation(OE) and Wearability Evaluation (WE). The main issue of evaluation process in this paper is OE.

3.3.1 Observation Evaluation(OE)

Subjects. 35 students took part in the evaluation. All were undergraduates, Yonsei University, Korea who had taken psychology class.

Experimental Procedures. For the observation evaluation the subjects were given an image stimulus of the method and asked to watch it before making out questionnaire. The evaluation was to select appropriate question. The subjects filled in a questionnaire rating Smart Clothing on a 1–7 scale. Most subjects completed the task in an hour.

Question Screening. The question screening produced by the subjects was assessed for item validity on a 1-4 scale. The One-Sample T-test compares the mean score of a sample to a known value as the known value is a population mean. We have 34 degrees of freedom. There is a significant difference between the two groups (the significance is less than .05). Therefore, we can say that our sample mean is significantly greater than the population mean of 2.5. As a result, 56 question items in 206 questions were selected.

Table 1. Evaluation Code and Qusetion Screening Results

code	N	Mean	StDev	t	df	Sig.(2-tailed)	Mean Diff
pa111-2	35	3	1	2.958	34	0.006	0.5
pa112-1	35	3.14	0.94	4.03	34	0	0.64
pa112-2	35	3.23	0.97	4.431	34	0	0.73
pa121-1	35	2.94	1.03	2.55	34	0.015	0.44
pa121-2	35	2.91	1.04	2.358	34	0.024	0.41
pa131-1	35	3.14	0.88	4.325	34	0	0.64
pa131-2	35	2.89	0.9	2.535	34	0.016	0.39
pa141-1	35	3.26	0.82	5.484	34	0	0.76
pa141-2	35	2.89	0.93	2.448	34	0.02	0.39
pa314-1	35	2.89	0.87	2.633	34	0.013	0.39
pa322-1	35	3.06	0.87	3.778	34	0.001	0.56
pa322-2	35	3	0.8	3.677	34	0.001	0.5
pa322-3	35	3.06	0.8	4.108	34	0	0.56
pa323-1	35	3.17	0.79	5.058	34	0	0.67
pa323-2	35	2.94	1	2.624	34	0.013	0.44
pa326-1	35	2.94	0.97	2.705	34	0.011	0.44
pa512-3	35	3.17	0.98	4.034	34	0	0.67
pm111-1	35	3.46	0.89	6.392	34	0	0.96
pm111-2	35	2.94	0.94	2.795	34	0.008	0.44
le111-1	35	3.4	0.77	6.874	34	0	0.9
le112-1	35	3.4	0.69	7.666	34	0	0.9
le121-1	35	3.26	0.78	5.743	34	0	0.76
le131-1	35	3.37	0.65	7.985	34	0	0.87
le141-1	35	3.54	0.7	8.807	34	0	1.04
le141-2	35	3.43	0.78	7.062	34	0	0.93
le416-2	35	2.89	0.87	2.633	34	0.013	0.39
le511-1	35	3.11	0.9	4.038	34	0	0.61
le512-2	35	3.14	0.97	3.903	34	0	0.64
e111-1	35	3.06	1	3.302	34	0.002	0.56
e111-2	35	3.4	0.81	6.56	34	0	0.9
e112-1	35	3.43	0.85	6.462	34	0	0.93
e121-1	35	3.46	0.78	7.26	34	0	0.96
e121-2	35	3.37	0.81	6.384	34	0	0.87
e121-3	35	3.4	0.69	7.666	34	0	0.9
e131-1	35	3.03	0.86	3.649	34	0.001	0.53
e131-2	35	3.34	0.76	6.52	34	0	0.84
e131-3	35	3.2	0.9	4.596	34	0	0.7
e131-4	35	3.09	0.82	4.237	34	0	0.59
e131-5	35	3.31	1.05	4.584	34	0	0.81
e131-6	35	3.26	0.85	5.257	34	0	0.76
e141-1	35	3.37	0.81	6.384	34	0	0.87
e141-2	35	3.4	0.74	7.238	34	0	0.9
e141-3	35	3.51	0.7	8.551	34	0	1.01
e141-4	35	3.57	0.7	9.079	34	0	1.07
e321-4	35	3.29	0.86	5.405	34	0	0.79
e322-1	35	3	0.91	3.26	34	0.003	0.5
e322-5	35	2.91	0.89	2.764	34	0.009	0.41
e322-6	35	2.97	0.95	2.922	34	0.006	0.47
e326-1	35	2.91	0.92	2.666	34	0.012	0.41
e326-2	35	3.09	1.01	3.428	34	0.002	0.59
e326-3	35	3	0.91	3.26	34	0.003	0.5
e329-3	35	2.86	0.91	2.316	34	0.027	0.36
e329-4	35	2.83	0.89	2.182	34	0.036	0.33
e329-5	35	3.2	0.8	5.196	34	0	0.7
e511-3	35	2.97	0.92	3.021	34	0.005	0.47
e512-2	35	2.86	1.03	2.045	34	0.049	0.36

Results. Varimax rotation is used as factor rotation. The results of the factor analysis indicated that there were 8 factors with eigenvalues greater than 1.0, accounting for 72.52 % of the total variance. By selecting 8 factors in smart clothing environment, we will dynamically create for usability evaluation. We illustrate the actions for users requesting factor as social situation compatibility, easy of use, operational rationality, appearance and durability and danger (body danger), control feeling immediately, the worry regarding the electromagnetic waves and shortening.

Table 2. Factor Analysis (Varimax Rotation)

	Factor							
	1	2	3	4	5	6	7	8
e141-3	0.909							
e141-1	0.869							
e141-4	0.829							
e131-1	0.797							
le121-1	0.775							
e141-2	0.774							
e112-1	0.74							
le141-1	0.717							
pa121-1R	0.715							
le131-1	0.694							
e131-2	0.684							
e111-2	0.682							
e131-6	0.679							
pa131-2	0.671							
e121-3	0.668							
e131-4	0.655							
pa121-2R	0.6							
le112-1	0.586							
e131-3	0.574							
pa131-1	0.55							
e322-1		0.751						
e322-5		0.742						
pa322-2		0.732						
e322-6		0.732						
e326-3		0.701						
pa322-1		0.632						
e326-1		0.615						
pa323-2		0.601						
pa322-3		0.582						
e326-2		0.541						
pa314-1			0.833					
pa141-2R			0.737					
pa323-1			0.592					
e512-2			0.539					
e121-2				0.665				
e121-1				0.636				
pa112-1				0.602				
le111-1				0.563				
pa112-2				0.533				
e111-1				0.522				
le416-2R					0.782			
e511-3R					0.755			
pa326-1					0.562			
le511-1R					0.526			
e329-3						0.82		
e329-5						0.798		
e329-4						0.614		
pa141-1						-0.572		
pa111-2R						0.508		
pa512-3R							0.65	
le512-2R							0.539	
e321-4								0.67

3.3.2 Wearablity Evaluation(WE)

Observation Evaluation (OE) overcomes the limit which is not the possibility of trying on Smart Clothing. But Wearability Evaluation (WE) actually will be able to reflect the opinion of the user more accurately than Observation Evaluation (OE).

11 students took part in the evaluation. All were undergraduates, Yonsei University who had taken psychology class. The subjects put on the smart clothing and participated to a research. Research process was the same as observation evaluation including making out questionnaire. In the result of Question Screening, that our sample mean is significantly greater than the population mean of 2.5 was 126 question items in 206 questions were selected (the significance is less than .05).

4 Discussion

The purpose of this paper has been to describe usability evaluation method that is based on experimental investigations of user. Further contribution has been development of a design process specifically for smart clothing to support the method. The evaluation results showed that was comprehensible and usable and had a positive impact on the quality of smart clothing design. The framework of evaluation provides restricted aspect for use of smart clothing design, however, it presents positive factor in combination with other modalities, leaving the designer to judge their merit. This study has produced some advances in usability evaluation of smart clothing, however, it has not directly demonstrated the effectiveness of evaluation process in real world practice as WE. OE and WE did not test the control condition without any real situation. Further experimental investigations need to demonstrate this aspect of the method. A clear evaluation process informed by user needs the research and development of smart clothing. It is informed and empowered to participate in decision making about new technologies. Smart clothing is originally main issue recently. The impact of modern technology in daily innovation life is increasing.

Acknowledgments. This work was supported by Korea Ministry of Commerce, Industry and Energy (2006-8-1653).

References

1. Dey, A., Ljungstrand, P., Schmidt, A.: Distributed and Disappearing User Interfaces in Ubiquitous computing. A workshop held at CHI 2001. In: Extended Abstracts of Computer-Human interaction(CHI)2001, pp. 487–488. ACM Press, New York (2001)
2. Gemperle, K., Kasabach, C., Stivoric, I., Bauer, M., Martin, R.: Design for wearability. In: The Second International Symposium on Wearable Computer. Los Alamitos, CA:IEEE Computer Society, pp. 116–122 (1998)
3. Kortuem, G., Segall, Z.: Wearable communities: Augmenting social networks with wearable computer. IEEE Pervasive Computing, (2) 1 (January-March 2003)
4. Knight, J.F., Baber, C., Schwirtz, A., Bristow, H.W: The Comfort Assessment of Wearable Computers. In: The Sixth International Symposium on Wearable Computers, pp. 65–72 (2002)

5. Knight, J.F., Baber, C.: A Tool to Assess the Comfort of Wearable Computers. Human Factors; Spring 2005 ProQuest Medical Library vol. 47(1) p. 77 (2005)
6. Lyons, K., Starner, T.: Mobile capture for wearable computer usability testing. In: Proceedings of IEEE International Symposium on Wearable Computing (ISWC 2001), Zurich, Switerland (2001)
7. McCann, J., Hurford, R., Martin, A.: A Design Process for the Development of Innovative Smart Clothing that Addresses End-User Needs from Technical, Functional, Aesthetic and Cultural View Points. In: Proceedings of 9th IEEE International Symposium on Wearable Computers. Osaka Japan, pp. 70–77 (2005)
8. Rantanen, J., Impio, I., Karinsalo, T., Malmivaara, M., Reho, A., Tasanen, M., Vanhala, J.: Smart Clothing Prototype for the Arctic Environment. Personal and Ubiquitous Computing 6, 3–16 (2002)
9. Robinette, K.M.: Fit testing as a helmet development tool. In: New development in mechanics, biomechanics and design aspects of military helmets. Farnborough, UK: Defense Research Agency, Flight Systems Department, pp. 69–73 (1993)
10. Smailagic, A., Siesiorek, D.P.: Modalities of interaction with CMU wearable computers. IEEE Personal Communications 3, 14–25 (1996)
11. Stein, R., Ferrero, S., Hetfield, M., Quinn, A., Krichever, M.: Development of a commercially successful wearable data collection system. In: The Second International Symposium on Wearable Computers. Los Alamitos, CA: IEEE Computer Society, pp. 18–24 (1998)

Textile Touch Visualization for Clothing E-Business

G. Cho[1], S. Jang[1], J. Chae[1], K. Jeong[2], and G. Salvendy[3]

[1] Yonsei University, Seoul, Korea
[2] Purdue University, West Lafayette, IN, USA
[3] Purdue University, West Lafayette, USA and Tsinghua University, Beijing, China

Abstract. The purpose of this study is to investigate the effect of textile touch visualization on e-commerce web site. Two e-commerce web sites (Gap and Anthropology) were selected and 160 female subjects took part in this study. To visualize the tactile sensation, clothing materials of each brand was measured by KES and the values were displayed in bar chart. This visualized tactile information, lightness, and washing method was added on the original web site. Each brand had two web sites (one is with original, the other is modified with added information) and 40 participants answered the questionnaire on each web site. The questionnaire was constructed with two parts which would be answered before and after touch. In results, the modified web sites showed a significant difference between 'no visual information' and 'with visual information' on most of the questions. This may indicate that the modified web sites provide enough tactile information about clothing material to customers more accurately. However, both modified web sites didn't show any significant difference between before and after touching while the original web sites showed significant difference.

Keywords: textile touch visualization, Kawabata evaluation system, mechanical property, primary hand value, converted primary hand value, tactile sensation, visual information, internal consistency, purchasability, return rate, decision making time.

1 Introduction

Through spreading of the internet, the world became smaller and smaller. The internet allows companies to contact and pursue customers at anytime and anywhere. Because of this, companies try to advertise and sell their products through the internet. This phenomenon makes increase the selling rate of products in e-commerce market. Despite of this, the clothing products do not show the increase in selling rate compared to other products such as home appliances, devices of communication, and computers. It can be assumed that the low selling rate of clothing products is affected by peoples' need to make sure the clothing personally. For increasing the selling rate of clothing products, the study of clothing products on web sites is required. In the Hwang, Jung and Salvendy's study (2006), they conducted a study of online shopping preferences among three countries. The result shows that people want accurate and detailed information. Especially, physical contact with the product, which didn't exist

J. Jacko (Ed.): Human-Computer Interaction, Part II, HCII 2007, LNCS 4551, pp. 1061–1069, 2007.

previously, was preferred. So, it can assume that more intuitive and accurate tactile sensation information of clothing product, which doesn't exist before, will lead the increasing selling rated of clothing product or shorten decision making time for purchasing and return rate. Therefore, in this study, after selecting few important tactile sensation variables providing more accurate physical contact information, we visualized the tactile sensation variables on two actual web sites and examined the impact of textile touch visualization on them. By comparing the result between original web site and modified web site, we observed the difference in physical sensation, purchasability and return rate by presenting the textile tactile information. Through this, this study figured out whether the textile touch visualization was effective and helpful enough to customers. Finally, we anticipated that this study would affect the increasing selling rate of clothing product in e-commerce market. The detailed purpose of this study is like this: First, observing the change of purchasing and return rate by giving visual information, second, the effect of actual touching on return rate, third, comparing the overall physical sensation of before and after touching through the presence of visual information.

2 Methodology

2.1 Clothing e-Commerce Web Site and Item Selections

First, we chose two popular internet web sites selling women's casual wear. The brand names were Gap and Anthropology (Gap: www.gap.com, Anthropology: www.anthropology.com). Of two web sites, sweater items having same fabrication method, weft knitting, were selected. Selected two items had different fiber contents-Gap item consisted of 80% of cotton and 20% of angora and Anthropology item consisted of 50% of cotton and 50% of wool.

2.2 Contents of Questionnaire

To examine the effect of visualized textile touch which showed on the selected web sites, the questionnaire was developed. The questionnaire had two parts which were sensation related textile touch before subjects look or touch the real fabrics and after look or touch. In details, the first part can be divided into three categories such as overall satisfaction, content information of textile touch, and purchasability perception of selected items. Each category includes three, five, and two questions. The second part has two categories: Accuracy evaluation and perception of return rate. Total six questions are included in the second part. The specific details are presented in Figure 1. Especially in case of content information of textile touch, we evaluated selected web sites with three variables such as bulkiness, smoothness, and flexibility.

The questionnaire was measured on a 7-point Likert scale ranged from "Strongly disagree" to "Strongly Agree."

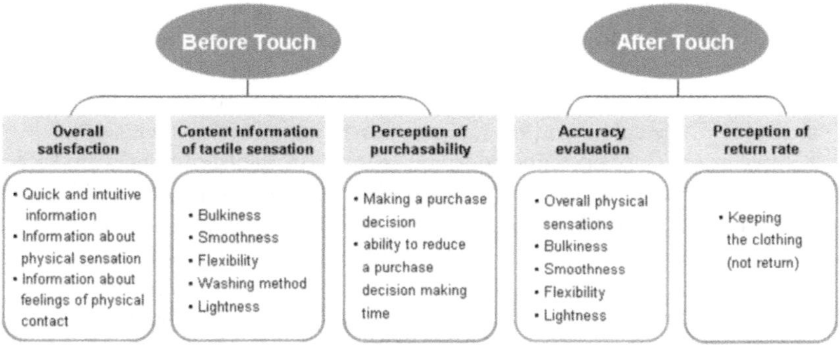

Fig. 1. Evaluation instrument of questionnaire

2.3 Steps for Visualization

To visualize sensation related textile touch of clothing materials on the selected web sites (Gap and Anthropology), we conducted several procedures as shown in Figure 2.

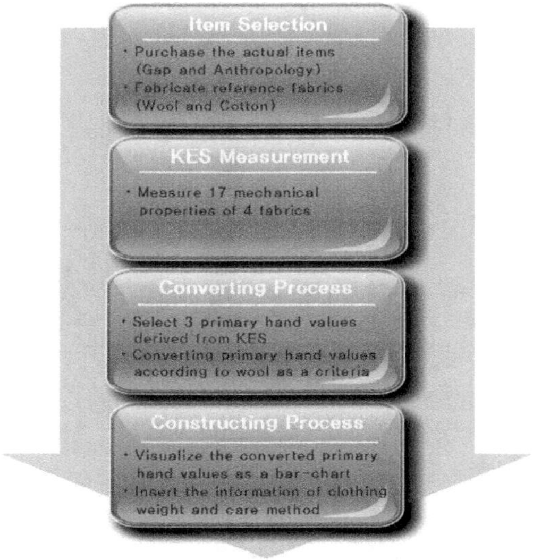

Fig. 2. Flow chart of visualization procedures

First of all, we purchased the actual items sold on the web that we selected. The items were sweaters which had same fabric construction and yarn type. Then, we fabricated 100% wool and 100% cotton with the similar fabric geometry as reference materials for those who were not familiar with the clothing materials. This makes potential customers can obtain more accurate information about sensation related textile touch. Totally four specimen were prepared and cut into 20㎝×20㎝for the next step.

In the second step, we measured mechanical properties of four specimen using 'Kawabata Evaluation System' (KES). The KES is the most common method for objective evaluation of fabric hand developed by Japanese Professor Kawabata (Kawabata, 1980). In the KES, seventeen mechanical properties related to fabric extension, shear, bending, compression, surface friction and roughness were measured. Based on the results from KES measurement, Primary hand value (PHV) and Total hand value (THV) are calculated from regression equations (Kawabata, 1980).

Next, three primary hand values derived from KES measurement were selected as variables for visualization of textile touch. The selected primary hand values were Fukurami (Fullness, another expression of bulkiness), Numeri (Smoothness), and Koshi (Stiffness, opposite meaning of flexibility). In case of Koshi, the primary hand value showed minus numbers so that we took the absolute numbers and renamed flexibility. However, it is still hard to understand non-expert people the degree of primary hand values. Therefore, in order to help people to obtain the degree of textile touch sensation of the clothing materials, the converting procedure was conducted. As a standard value, the primary hand value of 100% wool was converted into one hundred points. Then, the values of other fabrics such as 100% cotton, Gap and Anthropology items were converted into the proportional values to the value of wool. The original primary hand values and converted values of the four specimens are presented in Figure 3.

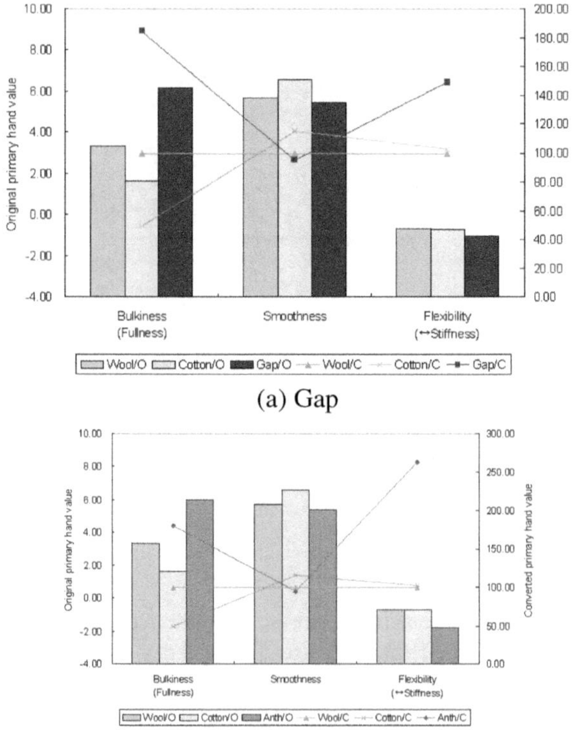

(a) Gap

(b) Anthropology

/C: Converted vaule, /O: Original value

Fig. 3. The original primary hand values and converted values of specimen by KES

The fourth step is constructing visualized textile touch sensation on the selected web sites. Using the converted primary hand values of each fabric, the bar-chart was made and inserted on the web sites of Gap and Anthropology. Additionally, the information of clothing weight (lightness) and care method was also inserted. Thus, both Gap and Anthropology web sites were modified with the visualized variables related textile touch sensation and information of weight and care method. The modified web sites are shown in Figure 4.

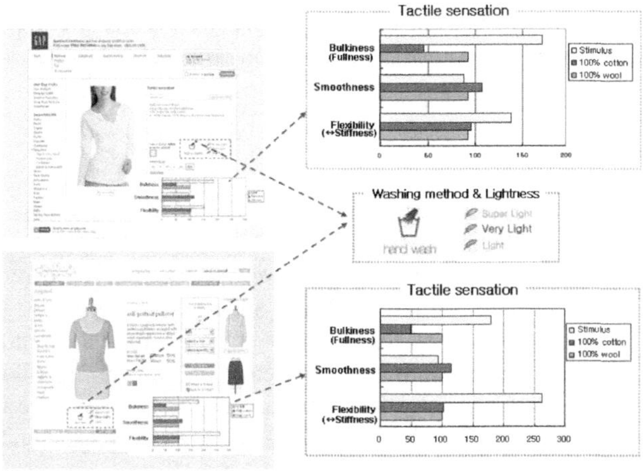

Fig. 4. Visualized information modified on original websites

2.4 Procedures

From 12th to 18th of August, 2006 in Korea, the questionnaire was conducted with female undergraduate or graduate students all in twenties. For using four different web sites as stimuli, 160 participants were randomly divided into four groups, including 40 participants in each group.

The questionnaire process was consisted with three steps. First, before answering the questions in the section of 'tactile sensation before touch', each participant observed the assigned web site only. Second, after answering questions of the first section 'tactile sensation before touch', participants moved to the place where the clothing fabric used for the product in the assigned web site (Gap or Anthropology) is. Then, each participant personally touched and felt it. Last, after returning to the seat, the second section of 'tactile sensation after touch' was answered. This last procedure was to evaluate the accuracy of textile touch visualization on the web site.

2.5 Data Analysis

One-way and between subjects design were used for investigating the effect of visualization of tactile sensation. The independent variables, the offer of visual representations, have two levels: 'With visual information' & 'No visual information'. The dependent variables are the first part of the questionnaire, including overall satisfaction, tactile sensation variables and purchase decision. By using the same experimental design for both e-commerce web sites, the effect of textile touch visualization of clothing is verified further.

3 Results and Discussion

For the data analysis, internal consistency measurement was performed ahead. Then, a comparative analysis between 'no visual representation' and 'with visual representation' of tactile sensation of a clothing product and a comparative analysis between 'before touch' and 'after touch' on overall physical sensation were performed in order.

3.1 Internal Consistency

Above all, verification of internal consistency has to conduct first. To figure out which evaluated measurement items measure the theoretical construct in a constant manner, internal consistency has to evaluate and can be measured by computing the Cronbach's coefficient alpha. Usually 0.7 and above is acceptable (Nunnally, 1978). To see overall internal consistency for the entire dataset, the measured value was .86. In addition to the overall internal consistency, each of four groups (Gap w/ info, Gap, Anth w/ info, Anth) was measured. The value of all four group were higher than .75, values of each group were .77, .81, .88, .75, so the internal consistency turned out to be acceptable.

3.2 Comparative Analysis (No Visual Information vs. with Visual Information)

Both Gap and Anthropology web sites indicated a significant difference between 'no visual information' and 'with visual information' on most of the questions at part 1 which is conducted before touch the real fabrics. This may indicate the modified web sites provide enough information related textile touch sensation. Especially in case of Anthropology, a significant difference between 'no visual information' and 'with visual information' was shown in most questions even in 'after touch(part 2)'. In perception of return rate case, both web sites did not show a significant difference between 'no visual information' and 'with visual information', but the mean values of both web sites were increased. This might imply people want to keep their products more when visual information was given.

Gap

In order to explore the effect of visual information on the Gap, the original web site without visual information and the modified web site with visual information were compared (Figure 5). A statistically significant difference was shown in questions #2 to #9 and #15. That is, the modified web site showed higher agreement on overall physical sensation, overall physical contact information, bulkiness, smoothness, flexibility, washing method, lightness, purchase decision which belong to before touch (part 1) and lightness which belongs to after touch (part2). In case of perception of purchasability(#9, #10), purchase decision(#9) showed a significant difference

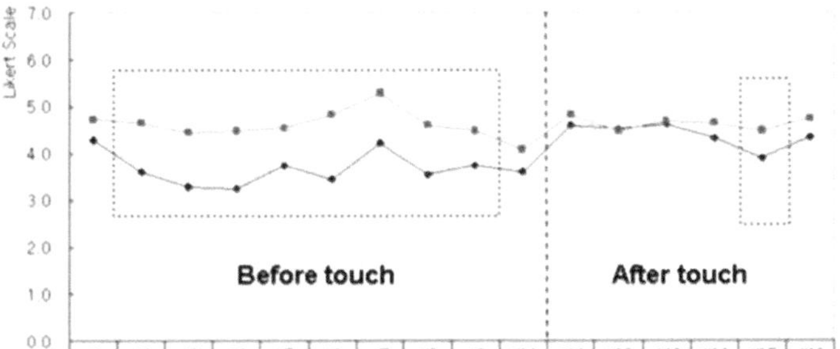

	#1	#2	#3	#4	#5	#6	#7	#8	#9	#10	#11	#12	#13	#14	#15	#16
Gap	4.3	3.6	3.3	3.2	3.8	3.4	4.2	3.6	3.8	3.6	4.6	4.5	4.6	4.3	3.9	4.4
Gap w/ Info	4.7	4.7	4.5	4.5	4.6	4.8	5.3	4.6	4.5	4.1	4.8	4.5	4.7	4.7	4.5	4.8
F value	3.7	14.3	20.0	20.2	8.4	31.3	13.1	14.6	6.4	2.7	0.5	0.0	0.0	1.1	4.0	1.6

$p < .05$

Fig. 5. Comparison (No visual info vs. With visual info) for Gap

while purchase decision making time(#10) was not significant. That is, visualized information of Gap gave enough information for making a purchase decision but did not affect purchase decision making time.

Anthropology

To compare the results of Gap web site modified with visual information, we chose another web site: Anthropology. In Anthropology case, most questions showed statistically significant differences. However, only perception of return rate did not show a significant difference (Figure 6). That is, the modified web site of Anthropology showed higher mean values on overall physical sensation, the individual content variables of physical sensation and purchase decision. This might imply visualized textile sensation added on Anthropology web site had more accurate and precise prediction. Specially, on the question about making a purchase decision, there was significant difference in Anthropology web site. It means that web site with

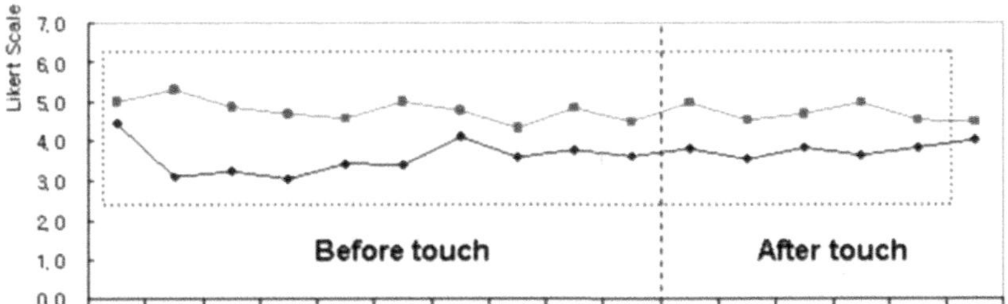

	#1	#2	#3	#4	#5	#6	#7	#8	#9	#10	#11	#12	#13	#14	#15	#16
Anth	4.5	3.1	3.3	3.0	3.4	3.4	4.1	3.6	3.8	3.6	3.8	3.5	3.9	3.7	3.9	4.0
Anth w/ Info	5.0	5.3	4.9	4.7	4.6	5.0	4.8	4.4	4.8	4.5	5.0	4.6	4.7	5.0	4.5	4.5
F value	4.7	69.9	29.5	31.0	15.0	24.7	4.1	7.8	14.5	8.1	12.7	10.8	6.9	19.8	5.6	2.1

$p < .05$

Fig. 6. Comparison (No visual info vs. With visual info) for Anthropology

visual information helps customers purchase, obviously. Even though the return rate didn't show significance in return rate, web site with information had higher mean value than original Anthropology web site. From this, we can expect that giving textile touch information affect on reducing return rate.

3.3 Comparative Analysis (Before vs. After Touch Evaluation)

Overall physical sensation was compared between before and after touching the clothing product textile to evaluate the accuracy of textile touch visualization on the modified web sites. As shown in Figure 7, except 'Anth w/ info', the rest of cases showed that overall physical sensation after touching has higher mean value. However, only both original sites showed significant difference between before and after touching. It means that the information of textile touching visualization on the modified web sites was accurate and enough to describe the real physical contact sensation, so overall physical sensation of before and after touching of both modified web sites has similar mean value.

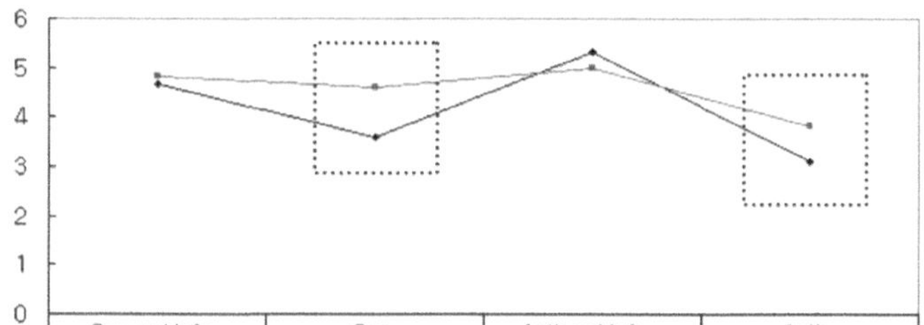

	Gap w/ Info	Gap	Anth w/ Info	Anth
Before(Q2)	4.65	3.6	5.3	3.1
After(Q11)	4.83	4.6	4.98	3.83
F value	0.31	11.89	1.51	5.08

$p < .05$

Fig. 7. Overall physical sensation before touch and after touch

4 Conclusion

The purpose of this study was to reveal the effect of textile touch visualization on e-commerce web site about whether it affect on purchase decision and perception of return rate. For this, after selecting two web sites, the questionnaire about textile touch visualization on web sites was conducted and then analyzed. For comparing the result of modified web sites with original web sites, the degree of people's physical (tactile) sensation about clothing product was increased by adding visual information on the selected web sites (Gap and Anthropology). The result of comparing between 'before and after touch' sensation about accuracy of visualized tactile information was both web sites with visual information wasn't significant. It means that physical sensation obtaining from textile touch visualized information was not different from actual physical sensation after touching the clothing material personally.

In conclusion, this study revealed that textile touch visualization on e-commerce web site is helpful to people's recognition about the clothing materials and, further, it can be assumed that it will affect on shortening decision making time and return rate. However, this study was limited into only one kind of clothing, sweater, and two kinds of textile, wool and cotton. Also, only female university students were participated in this study. To overcome this limitation, the study using more various kinds of items and fabrics is additionally needed and also it should be conducted in different ages and gender of customers. And also, to research the actual impact on financial benefits of textile touch visualized information, further study conducted by business side researchers is required.

References

1. Hsin-Chung, L., Shyong, L.: Applying pattern recognition principles to grading textile yarns, Textile Research Journal 72(4), 320–326 (2002)
2. Hwang, W., Jung, H.S., Salvendy, G.: Internationalization of e-commerce: a comparison online shopping preferences among Korean, Turkish, and US populations (2006)
3. Kawabata, S.: The Standardization and Analysis of Hand Evaluation, 2nd. Textile Machinery Society of Japan, Osaka, Japan (1980)
4. Kawabata, S., Niwa, M.: Fabric Performance in Clothing and Clothing Manufacture. Journal of Textile Institute 80(1), 19–50 (1989)
5. Nunnally, J.C.: Psychometric Theory, 2nd edn. McGraw-Hill, New York (1978)
6. http://www.marriam-webster.com/dictionary/weft+knit

A Development of Design Prototype of Smart Healthcare Clothing for Silver Generation Based on Bio-medical Sensor Technology

Hakyung Cho* and Joohyeon Lee

Dept. of Clothing & Textile, Yonsei University
*passion@yonsei.ac.kr

Abstract. Recently, "Smart Clothing" technology, along with a rapid change of lifestyle and customers' needs, has been studied and developed for various applications such as Entertainment, Business, and Health Care and Sports areas. Among the number of types in "Smart Clothing" technologies, "Smart Clothing" for health care is anticipated as one of the highly demanded products in future market.The demand of "Smart Clothing" based on bio-medical sensor technology will increase due to the entry of an aging society where a high demand of development in both medical industry and medical welfare rises. This trend is related to the new condition of technological and social transition built through the rapid development of Ubiquitous environment. On the view of customers' demand, "Smart Clothing" technology coincides with the macro-flow of customers' general demand on clothing product. In domestic market, however, the research and development of "Smart Clothing" based on a bio-medical sensor technology are insufficient. In this research, with a consideration in clothing suitability and prevalence rate, a prototype of "Smart Clothing" is firstly developed for diagnosing basic vital signs of cardiac disorder and respiratory disease. A prototype of smart healthcare clothing developed in this research, maintaining similar appearance to common clothing, is equipped with textile-based sensors and other devices which senses and transmits vital signs, while keeping comfortable fits of clothing. When a person having it on, sensed vital signals are transmitted to computer in hospital through wireless transaction for a real-time monitoring process. It is also designed to send back alarm command to the wearer's cellular phone when emergent condition is detected in his body. The RFID tag, equipped on the inside of "Smart Clothing," stores wearer's medical history and personal data, so that a rescuer can collect the data in emergency case and send them to hospital for faster and efficient treatment for the rescue. An evaluation on usability and comfort of the firstly derived prototype in this research were evaluated. Based on the result from evaluation on the two aspects, the design prototype of sensor-based smart healthcare clothing was revised.

Keyword: Smart clothing for health care, Design prototype, Bio-medical sensor, Vital signs, Usability.

---

* Corresponding author.

J. Jacko (Ed.): Human-Computer Interaction, Part II, HCII 2007, LNCS 4551, pp. 1070–1077, 2007.

1 Introduction

Since the late 1990s, "smart clothing" has been developed in a various way to meet the need of users and to help people more friendly interact with computing devices embedded in clothing. Recently, various applications of smart clothing concept have been presented by researchers[1]. Among the various applications, smart clothing for daily check-up of health condition with its sensors is expected to gain the highest rate of consumers' demand in future market. Under this circumstance, research and development for this field have been accelerated[7].

In this research, with a consideration in clothing suitability and prevalence rate, a prototype of "Smart Clothing" is firstly developed for sensing basic vital signs of cardiac disorder and respiratory disease.

2 Theoretical Background

2.1 Concept and Recent Situation of Smart Clothing

Recently, "Smart Clothing" technology, along with a rapid change of lifestyle and customers' needs in the market, has been studied and developed for various applications such as Entertainment, Business, and Health Care and Sports areas[1].

Integrating the textile technology with digital, smart clothing has been entered upon the clothing industry and introduced in market since 2001[2].
As the diversified studies on physical factors such as comfort, usability, ergonomics and design for wearer have been examined, the smart clothing has been progressed in diverse aspects [4].

2.2 A Trend of "Smart Clothing" for Healthcare

1. Sensor based Smart clothing by Philips
Philips has developed a prototype of sportswear that put to use listening music and measuring bio-medical signs within a single garment. Several bio-sensors for measurement of heart beat, blood pressure, body temperature and other vital signals are equipped in this garment [9](Figure 1).

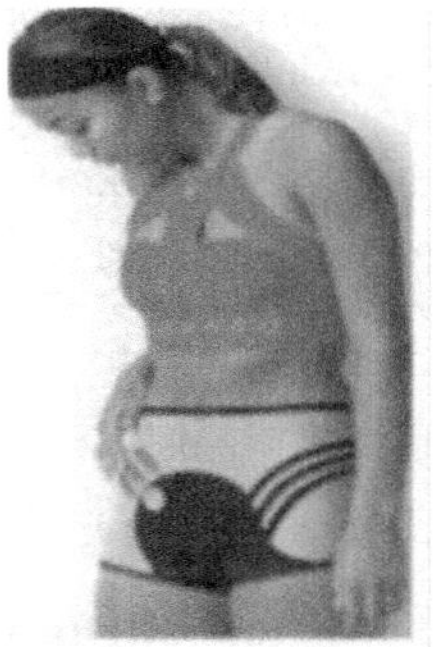

Fig. 1. Sensor-based Sportswear by Phillips

2. Sensor - based Smart sports clothing by Adidas
Adidas, a famous sports brand, has been developed some kinds of smart clothing including sports shoes, sportswear, arm band which measure and transmit the signals of heart rate and amount of workout. By transmitting the vital signals measured in the clothes and shoes to the screen on the wristwatch-typed monitor, it allows users to be able to keep real-time monitoring[7](Figure 2).

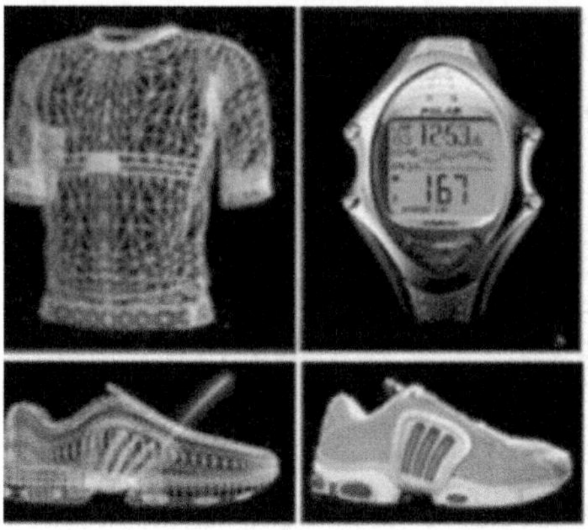

Fig. 2. Sensor based Smart clothing by Adidas

2.3 A Vision of " Smart Clothing" for Healthcare

Among the number of types in "Smart Clothing" applications, health care is anticipated as one of the highly demanded parts in future market. The demand of "Smart Clothing" based on bio-medical sensor technology is expected to tremendously increase due to the entry of an aging society where high demand of medical welfare rises. This trend is related to the new condition of technological and social transition built through the rapid development of Ubiquitous environment.
Smart clothing with a health care system is most likely to gain the highest demand rate in the market. Under this circumstance, research and development for this field have been accelerated .

According to an exploratory survey conducted by Technology Consulting form, VDC(Venture Development Corporation), smart clothing technology is evaluated as one of the most demanded markets in textile industry in near future. Especially, it is expected that the smart clothing based on bio-medical technology will grow significantly and the demand of smart clothing will be increased when smart healthcare clothing is developed with textile-based sensor technology[10].

3 Research Methods

3.1 Definition and Scope of "Smart Clothing" in This Research

In this research, with a consideration in clothing suitability and prevalence rate, a prototype of "Smart Clothing" is firstly developed for sensing basic vital signs of cardiac disorder and respiratory disease.

When a person has it on, sensed vital signals are transmitted to computer in hospital through wireless transaction for a real-time monitoring process. It is also designed to send back alarm to the wearer's cellular phone when emergent condition is detected in his body.

The RFID tag, equipped inside of the smart clothing which stores wearer's medical history and personal data, also help a rescuer collect needed data in emergency case and send them to hospital for faster and efficient treatment for rescue.

3.2 Process in Development of "Smart Clothing"

In this research, with a consideration in characteristic of silver generation and trend of consumer demand, a prototype of smart healthcare clothing for silver generation based on sensor technology was developed through the process presented in Fig 4.

On the basis of review on theoretical background including sensor technology, smart clothing and medical engineering, suitable sensors to be equipped with the clothes were firstly selected. The design of prototype and device of smart clothing in this research is consisted on the basis of analyzing the proceeding research and medical engineering. Based on this, a prototype for healthcare smart clothing was developed (Figure 3).

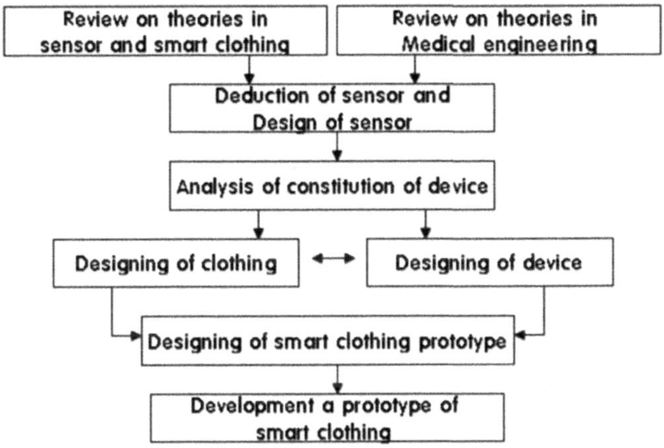

Fig. 3. Flow chart for study

4 Result and Discussion

4.1 Device Part

In this study, the device part consists of electrocardiogram, body temperature. Through this sensor part can measure signal of electrocardiogram, respiration, heart beat, temperature[5].

Main board is consisted of electrocardiogram, battery, RF transaction module and designed for vital sign collection to main board connect with three electrocardiogram electrodes and wire of temperature sensor (Figure 4).

1. Sensor part : This part consists of temperature sensor and electrocardiogram electrode manufactured the width * length, 5*5 size and is designed to 3 parts for exactitude of vital sign measurement.
2. Operation part : This part consists of acceleration sensor, electrocardiogram module and temperature sensor to measure up electrocardiogram with measuring activity by acceleration sensor and body temperature by temperature sensor. Also, this part can measure respiration through electrocardiogram's wave length.
3. wireless transaction part : Sensed vital signs such as Heart beat, respiration, temperature are transmitted to main computer through RF transaction for real time monitoring process.
4. output part :. Output part is designed so that vital signs from perating part are transmitted to cellular phone or main computer.
5. Power part: it is generated by 3.0V battery so that operation part, wireless transaction part are smoothly operated .
6. RFID tag : The RFID tag, storing personal data, medical history, is so durable that it can be equipped on the inside of smart clothing.

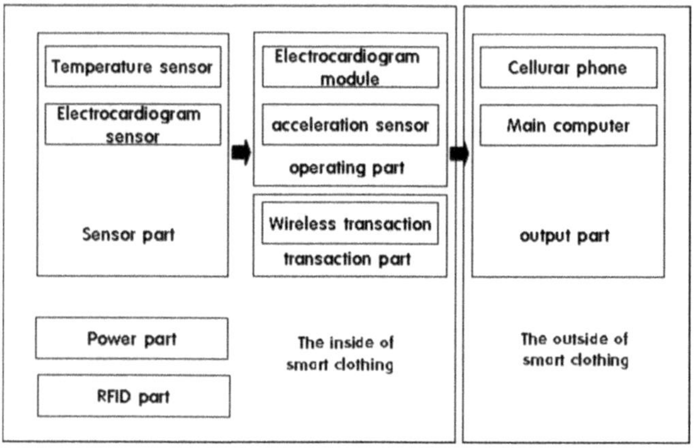

Fig. 4. The conceptual structure for functioning

4.2 Development of Prototype

This prototype consists of a combination of two separate layers, inner layer and outer layer, according to a basic plans of layering system as followed : Inner layer including most parts of sensor and other devices is structured to be compatible with various outer layer, while outer layer with similar appearance to common clothes is invented to be washable and changeable whenever needed.

1. Materials used for the prototype

The material of outer layer is made of "Coolever" which can help to take in the sweat and vapor out so that it help user feel pleasant. For the inner layer, a blend of lycra (the mixture ratio: 11%) is mainly used for measuring up the signal of electrocardiogram sensor and comfort.

Conductive textile material is adopted to convey electronic signal between Electrocardiogram (ECG) electrode and main board, while polyurethane foam is applied to absorb bumping shocks to protect the device parts.

2. Design of outer layer
Outer layer is developed to maintain similar appearance to common sportswear in reference to the customers' demand on preceding researches. Also, outer layer can be compatible with various outer layer, separated inner layer with outer layer(Figure 5).

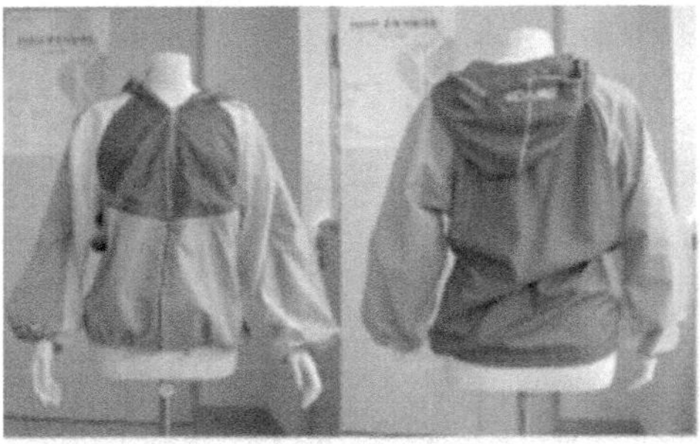

Fig. 5. Design of outer layer

3. Design of inner layer
The newly developed smart clothing in this study appears similar to the previous inventions, but people can feel more comfortable in it with its fabric interaction built in it[3].

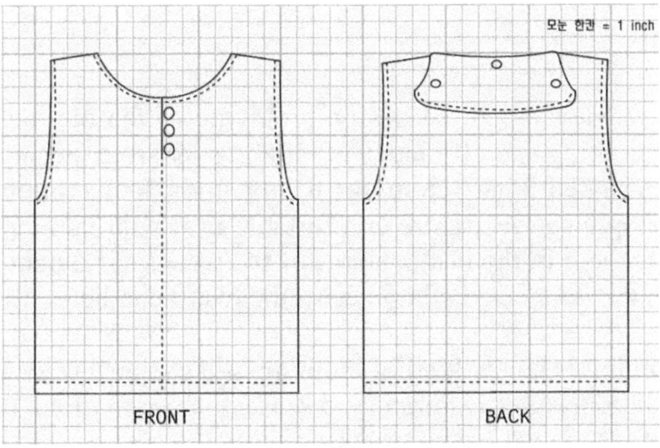

Fig. 6. Design of inner layer

1. Design of device's place
On a result, main board was designed to stick on neck toward the back for wearability[6]. Also, temperature sensor was placed at the armhole for wearability.

Electrocardiogram electrodes constitute three direction electrode which based of theory of medical technology to be obtainable exact signal.

Electrode is placed at the 2.5 cm from the main board to each of the both upper breast and back side of left for movement of each electrode and stability (Figure 6) .

2. Design of textile interconnection
Textile interconnection which can help the electronic signal flow into the textile is applicably reformed for the prototype so that it relieve the discomfort caused by wire(Figure 7).

3. method of sticking and connection
It is designed to put the device into the pocket located on the back side of neck so that the main board can be easily taken off. A hole inside of the pocket is made for protecting the device from the shocks and being stable(Figure 7).

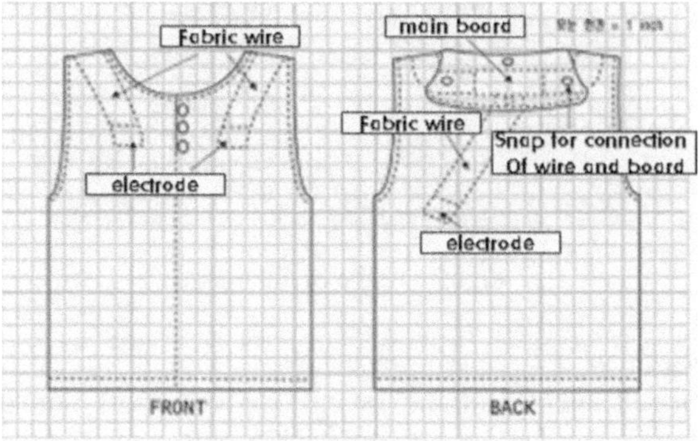

Fig. 7. A draft of inner layer

5 Conclusion

In this research, we developed the design prototype of the bio-medical sensor based healthcare smart clothing and efficiency of clothing for silver generation.

The newly developed smart clothing in this study looks similar to the previous inventions, but people can feel more comfortable in it with its fabric interaction built in it. When people wear it, the health status of the wearers is diagnosed and its signals are transmitted to the connected computer so the result can be easily monitored in real time.

This smart clothing is a new kind of clothing as a supporting system for preventing various cardiac disorder and respiratory diseases using its biometric sensor built-in, and is also an archetype to show how smart clothing can work on the market.

References

[1] Nam, H.J.: Development of Design prototype of intelligent wear for entertainment activity. Master thesis, Yonsei Univ (2004)
[2] Park, S.M.: Development of Design prototype of digital wear for the physically diabled. Master thesis, Yonsei Univ (2004)

[3] sim, B.: Ergonomics of clothing, Seoul: Kyomunsa, Ltd (1996)
[4] woo, S.:inquiring study on clothing type battle jackets for the future battlefield environment. Master thesis, Yonsei Univ (2005)
[5] Association of medical engineering research 1998, medical instrumentation engineering, association of medical engineering research (1998)
[6] Gamperle, F.C., Kasabach, S.J., Bauer, M., Martin, R.: Design for Wearability. In: Digest of Paper Forth International Symposium of Wearable Computer. Los Alamitos, California:IEEE (1998)
[7] http://www.adidas-polar.com
[8] http://www.numitrex.com
[9] www. phllips.com
[10] VDC. The global Market for Wearable Computers. The Quest for Killer Applications (2003)

Design and Evaluation of Textile-Based Signal Transmission Lines and Keypads for Smart Wear

Jayoung Cho[1], Jihye Moon[2], Moonsoo Sung[2], Keesam Jeong[3], and Gilsoo Cho[2]

[1] Research Institute of Clothing and Textile Sciences, Yonsei University, Seoul, Korea
[2] Department of Clothing and Textiles, Yonsei University, Seoul, Korea
[3] Department of Medical Information System, Yong-in Songdam College, Yong-in, Korea
jycho@yonsei.ac.kr, jhmoon@yonsei.ac.kr, mssung@yonsei.ac.kr, ksjeong@ysc.ac.kr, gscho@yonsei.ac.kr

Abstract. The present paper was intended to prove the applications of surface-conductive fabrics as electronic textiles. First, we tested the electrical durability of a Cu/Ni electro-less plated fabric reinforced by PU(polyurethane) sealing. Using the fabric, we constructed textile-based signal transmission lines and textile-based keypads. For performance tests, we compared the output signals between the textile transmission lines and Cu cables and evaluated textile-based keypads by means of operation force and subjective operation feeling. PU sealing was effective to yield electrical durability for surface-conductive fabrics, thus the repeatedly-laundered fabric showed almost identical output signal with that of Cu, successfully operating an MP3 player. Subjective evaluation and operation force measurement identified that the rubber dome switch keypad was preferred due to a low operation force and less pressure on the skin when the keypad-mounted clothing is worn. The paper suggested specific applications and evaluation methods of electronic textiles as essential components for smart wear.

Keywords: electronic textiles, smart wear, electro-less metal plating, conductive fabric, electrical resistance, transmission lines, textile-based keypads, switches, operation force.

1 Introduction

The rapid development of smart wear is accelerating the integration of electrical components into textiles. Various techniques of manufacturing electronic textiles have been explored, and much attention has been paid to the conductive textiles where metal yarns are woven into[1],[2],[3]. However, once a conductive fabric is woven, the electrical passes and tailoring are restricted in weft or warp direction. Compared to this, textile substrates having a conductive surface such as electro-less metal plated fabrics have many advantages. Electro-less metal plated fabrics are potential candidates of electronic textiles, having good characteristics such as good conductivity, flexibility, free tailoring, and easy sewing. These characteristics yield great possibilities to be used in manufacturing the textile-integrated level of smart wear.

J. Jacko (Ed.): Human-Computer Interaction, Part II, HCII 2007, LNCS 4551, pp. 1078–1085, 2007.

Electronic textiles are essential in constructing textile-based input devices, transmission lines, output devices or else. However, issues of practicability remain. The surface-conductive textiles need to maintain durability on the surface so that they can be used as electronic textiles. Also, the performance tests are required for the developed electronic textile products.

As one of the applications of surface-conductive fabrics, textile transmission lines can be suggested. The fabric is electrically conductive in all directions on the surface so that they can be cut into any shape and in any direction. Moreover, the fabric pieces can be directly sewn onto clothing, thus dangling wires or cables often seen inside today's smart wear might disappear. However, the fabric's durability and electrical characteristics remain to be examined for practical situation.

Textile-based input device is another issue in electronic textiles. Switches of keypads attached on clothes are required to suit for the fingers to easily touch. Previous studies[4],[5],[6],[7] have suggested fabric switches made of 100% textile materials. Those fabric switches are flexible and soft but do not give tactile feedback to users and often make malfunction during use. However, textile-based keypads with modified dome switches have advantages such as clear feedback and fewer malfunctions when attached to smart wear.

This paper was intended to (1) examine the possibility of surface-conductive fabrics as electronic textiles by reinforcing electrical durabilty and (2) prove the practicability of the applications for electronic textile products by construction and evaluation of signal transmission lines and input devices.

2 Experimental

2.1 Durability Test of a Cu/Ni Electro-Less Metal Plated Fabric

Specimen. We used a commercially available Cu/Ni electro-less plated polyester fabric as a specimen(Table 1). The thickness of plating on the fabric is about 2μm and the electrical resistance is 0.035Ω/sq.

Table 1. Characteristics of a specimen

Weave	Thickness, *mm*	Weight, g/m^2	Yarn size	Filament density, *5cmX5cm*	Filament count, *5cmX5cm*
Plain	0.12	111.8	Warp: 50D/36F Weft: 75D/54F	4,116X2,496	6,612

Measurement of Electrical Resistance. The electrical resistance was measured by using a multimeter(Agilent 34401A). The samples were prepared into 43cm×1.5cm rectangular strips including contact pads(1.5cm×1.5cm) at both ends.

Surface Reinforcement Using PU-treatment. For surface reinforcement, the metal plated fabric was treated with PU sealing tape(20mm in width and 0.11mm in thickness) on both sides. PU-sealing was done using a hot air welder(Nawon HTM-4100) under 0.2MPa at 330℃and 5㎝/sec.

Laundering Test for Electro-less Metal Plated Fabrics. Samples were prepared in size of 50cm×40cm where PU treated parts were located at regular intervals. The fabrics were laundered up to 10 times using a drum washer(Samsung SEW-5HR120) with 30 RPM, at 20°C of water temperature, and with 70g of detergent for 5Kg of total laundry weight with dummies. A single washing cycle consisted of 10min. washing, 7min. rinsing, and 8min. spin-drying.

2.2 Test for Textile-Based Signal Transmission Lines

In order to examine the applicability of the strips of Cu/Ni electro-less metal plated fabric as transmission line, we measured the I/O signal changes of the textile-based cable over time using an oscilloscope(SoftDSD SDS100A). We connected the output port of an MP3 player to the one terminal of the 40 cm long-fabric strips and then measured the signal on the other end.

Following the transmission line test, we compared the signal transmission characteristics between a conventional Cu cable and the two textile-based ones (unlaundered vs. 10 times laundered). For this, we input a signal($3V_{p\text{-}p}$, 1kHz) by using a function generator(Tektronics CFG253).

2.3 Construction and Evaluation of Textile-Based Keypads

Keypad Construction. In order to develop fabric-based input devices having clear feedback and fewer malfunctions, we developed a keypad consisting of electro-less metal plated fabrics(circuit layer), cotton poplin(insulation layer), and dome switches. The circuit layer was placed between two insulation layers, and the fabric layers were combined with dome switches. Through small holes in the insulation layer, switches are supposed to contact a circuit layer when pressed. We constructed two kinds of keypads using metal dome switches and rubber dome switches(Table 2). The two kinds of switches are commercially available; however, we modified the rubber dome switch by joining with a round metal frame on its upper edge, so that the frame was supposed to touch the conductive layer when pressed. Using the two types of keypads, we additionally prepared two jumpers where the each keypad is mounted.

Table 2. Characteristics of metal dome switches and rubber dome switches

Switch type	Metal dome switch	Rubber dome switch
Image	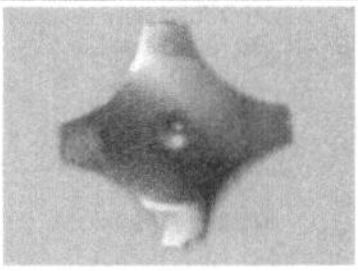	
Height	2.0 mm	6.0 mm
Diameter	13.0 mm	11.0 mm
Weight	0.056 g	0.314 g

Measurement of Operation Force. The operation forces of switches were measured by using a switch feeling tester(Aikoh 1350N with 1015A) applying 200N actuation load. Operation force is the maximum load measured when the dome snaps at compression peak point. The measurement was repeated 10 times.

Subjective Evaluation of Operation Feeling. Switch operation feeling was evaluated to identify the preferred type of switch as a component of smart wear. A total of 30 university students aged between 20 and 29(17 males and 13 females) participated in the subjective evaluation. The four keypads(a metal switch keypad, a metal switch keypad attached on a jacket, a rubber switch keypad, a rubber switch keypad attached on a jacket) were randomly presented to each participants. They were asked to answer the questionnaires including 'easiness of operation,' 'clear feeling,' 'oppressive feeling on the forearm' and 'preference' from not at all(-3) to completely(+3) using a 7-point Likert scale.

3 Results

3.1 Electrical Durability of a Cu/Ni Electro-Less Metal Plated Fabric

The electrical durability of a Cu/Ni electro-less metal plated fabric was measured to identify its usability under repeated laundering. As shown in Table 3, the electrical resistance of untreated fabric(0.311 Ω/sq) became higher than that of PU treated one(0.039 Ω/sq) only after first washing. After 10 launderings, the untreated fabric lost its conductivity while PU sealed fabric maintained excellent electrical durability(0.062 Ω/sq) which is only twice as high as the unwashed one(0.035 Ω/sq). The results show that PU-sealing yields electro-less metal plated fabrics the possibility as electronic textiles in a practical situation.

Table 3. Electrical resistance changes as a function of laundering (unit: Ω/sq)

	Laundering cycles				
	0	1	2	5	10
Untreated	0.035	0.311	5.415	70.154	-
PU-sealed	0.035	0.039	0.040	0.050	0.062

3.2 Performance of the Fabric-Based Transmission Lines

The applicability of electro-less metal plated fabrics as transmission lines was identified by performance test for the textile based cables. When we operated a MP3 player using a PU-untreated fabric by replacing the middle parts of earphone lines, the earphones successfully worked and the sound quality difference was not subjectively perceived. Also, the measurement of input voltage(I) with the output voltage(O) using an oscilloscope showed that the I/O signals were almost identical as presented in Fig. 1.

Moreover, the performance of the 10 times laundered textile transmission lines was compared with that of conventional Cu. When we input a signal by using a function generator, all the output signals were similar to that of Cu(Fig. 2). The results show that surface-conductive fabrics such as electro-less metal plated ones can be one of the good materials as electronic textiles providing many peculiar advantages of their own.

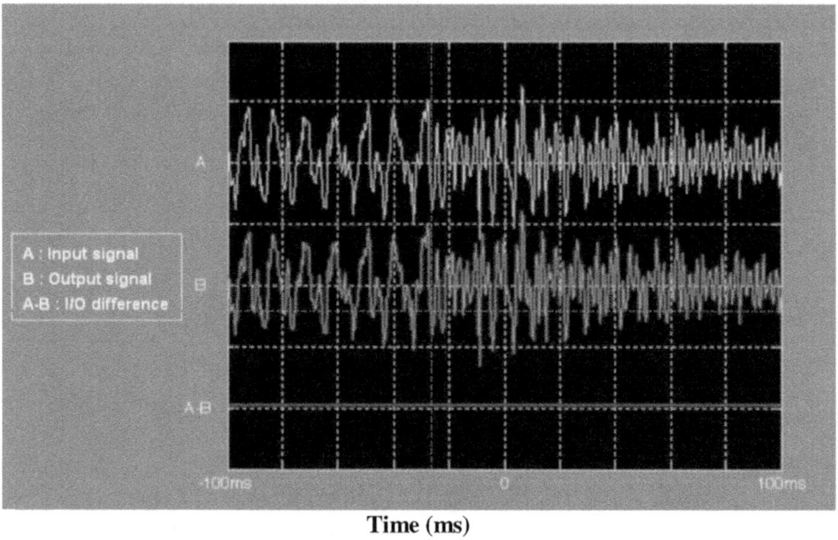

Fig. 1. I/O signals of a textile based cable

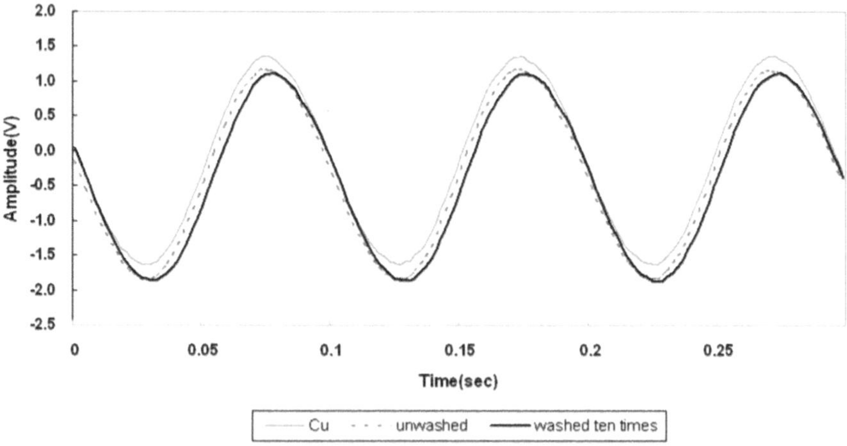

Fig. 2. Comparison of the output signals between Cu and textile based cables

3.3 Performance of Textile-Based Keypads

Operation Force. Operation force was measured to identify the mechanical characteristics of textile-based keypads. The operation force of metal dome was about 5 times higher than that of rubber dome(320 gf vs. 62 gf), which means that rubber dome switches are easily operated.

Operation Feeling. The metal dome keypad showed a big change in operation feeling after mounted on clothing(Table 4). Before mounted on a jacket, the metal dome keypad was preferred to the rubber dome keypad due to clear feeling in spite of higher operation force. However, the metal dome keypad mounted on a jacket gave less clear feeling, increased difficulty, and high oppressiveness on the forearm when pressed. On the contrary, the rubber dome keypad did not make a big change in user response after mounted on clothing, showing easy operation and higher satisfaction than the metal dome keypad.

Table 4. ANOVA analysis results of operation feeling for fabric-based keypads* (n = 30)

	df	*F*	*P*-value	Keypad types			
				M	MC	R	RC
Easiness of operation	3	49.107	<0.000	-0.3^{b} (0.8)	-1.5^{c} (0.9)	0.6^{a} (0.6)	0.8^{a} (1.2)
Clear feeling	3	14.018	<0.000	1.3^{a} (0.8)	0.6^{b} (0.6)	0.4^{bc} (0.8)	0.2^{c} (0.8)
Oppressive feeling on the forearm	1	253.062	<0.000	*N/A*	2.2 (0.7)	*N/A*	-1.2 (0.9)
Preference	3	10.804	<0.000	0.9^{a} (0.8)	-0.1^{c} (0.7)	0.3^{b} (0.5)	0.2^{b} (0.7)

M = A metal switch keypad; MC = a metal switch keypad on clothing.
R = A rubber switch keypad; RC = a rubber switch keypad on clothing.
* SD in parenthesis.
a, b, c; subgroup.

4 Conclusions

This work suggests the possibility of surface-conductive fabrics as electronic textiles by reinforcing electrical durability by PU sealing, and proved the practicability of applications of electronic textiles. The paper applied a Cu/Ni electro-less metal plated fabric for the construction of signal transmission lines and keypads.

PU sealing was found effective for durability improvement for surface-conductive fabrics, protecting both sides of a substrate from external forces such as laundering.

Because surface-conductive fabrics have various advantages including easiness of handling, sewing, and tailoring just as usual textile materials, the fabric would be of use in manufacturing electronic textile products.

We proved that the surface-conductive fabric can be used as signal transmission lines by replacing earphone lines. However, for better practicability of electronic textile products, connection techniques for linking electronic components with textile materials need to be further investigated.

When we tested two different types of textile-based keypads after attaching them on a jacket, rubber dome switches were preferred due to easy operation. Even though rubber dome switches make easy strokes, the protruding dome shape with very low operation force are more likely to cause unwanted strokes. Therefore, optimization of operation forces on the body part needs to be further studied since the electronic textile products are to be worn on the body as a form of smart wear.

In this paper, we constructed input devices using dome switches to give good feedback while previous research on textile-based input devices have focused on mostly 100% fabric-based ones[4],[5],[6],[7]. The results indicated that the metal dome's tactile feedback was preferred by users but decreased sharply on the skin. This implies that the operation characteristics of dome switch keypads need to be tested considering environment condition.

The present study has an implication that we suggested specific applications and evaluation methods of electronic textiles for smart wear using a surface-conductive fabric. More applications and evaluation methods are required for the development of electronic textile products with good performance, reliability, and practicability.

Acknowledgment

The authors would like to thank the Korea MOCIE for funding this effort.

References

1. Cottet, D., Grzyb, J., Kirstein, T., Tröster, G.: Electrical characterization of textile transmission lines. IEEE Transactions on Advanced Packaging 26(2), 182–190 (2003)
2. Dhawan, A., Ghosh, T.K., Seyam, A.M., Muth, J.: Development of Woven Fabric-based Electrical Circuits. In: Symposium Proceedings of the Material Research Society: Electronics on Unconventional Substrates on – Electrotextiles and giant-area Flexible Circuits, December 2-3, 2002, pp.67–72 (2002)
3. Koncar, V., Kim, B., Nebor, E.B., Joppin, X.: FICC(Floatable Intelligent and Communicative Clothing) Project –conductive fibers development. In: Proceedings of Eighth International Symposium on Wearable Computers, October 31-November 3, 2004 pp. 36–39 (2004)
4. Post, E.R., Orth, M.: Smart Fabrics, or Washable Computing. In: Proceedings of First IEEE International Symposium on Wearable Computers, October 13-14, 1997, pp. 167–168 (1997)
5. Post, E.R., Orth, M., Russo, P.R., Gershenfeld, N.: E-broidery: Design and fabrication of textile-based computing. IBM Systems Journal 39(3&4), 840–860 (2000)

6. Softswitch Electronic Fabrics-Applications, Retrieved January 14, 2007 from the World Wide Web (2007) http://www.softswitch.co.uk
7. Wijesiriwardana, R., Mitcham, K., Dias, T.: Fibre-Meshed Transducers Based Real Time Wearable Physiological Information Monitoring System. In: Proceedings of Eighth IEEE International Symposium on Wearable Computers, October 31-November 3, 2004 pp. 40–47 (2004)

Display Button: A Marriage of GUI and PUI

Stanley Chung[1], Jung-Hyun Shim[1], and Changsu Kim[2]

[1] 11th Fl., Joongang Ilbo Bldg., 7, Soonhwa-Dong, Chung-Ku, Seoul 100-759, Korea
UI Research Lab., Corporate Design Center, Samsung Electronics
[2] Computing & Intelligence Lab., Samsung Advanced Institute of Technology
P.O. Box 111, Suwon 440-600, Korea
{stanley.chung, id.shim, cs007.kim}@samsung.com

Abstract. GUI (graphical user interface) output and PUI (physical user interface) input are two major concepts of user interface design for commercial products. GUIs and PUIs have been normally implemented on individual devices such as a screen and sets of buttons, respectively. However, recent researches show several cases of combining GUI and PUI into one user interface module, which can display visual information and collect user inputs simultaneously. With this combination, the expressiveness and flexibility of GUI can compensate impassive face of physical buttons, and the straight-forward and intuitive way of using PUI, like pushing a button, can remedy old tradition of GUI's learnability and memorability issues. This study presents *Display Button*, a modular component combining GUI and PUI with least production cost increase, and surveys its characteristics and merits in several contexts of consumer appliances. Display Button modules were applied in forms of additional components of conventional display and independent components. In order to design user interfaces of mobile phone and digital camera with Display Button modules, pattern-oriented approach is used to ensure smoother migration from traditional user interface to novel use of Display Button. Display Button can be applied to various kinds of consumer electronics with many possible alternative combinations, and hence increase their market competency with both of better end-user experience and less production cost.

Keywords: graphical user interface, physical user interface, display button, usability.

1 Research Background

The commercialization of new user interface not only requires improved usability and some thrill for a new operation method, but also numerous items such as the productivity as a product, manufacturing cost and efficiency of general functions. If a newly developed UI is not able to clearly stand out after challenging the loyal usability of the conventional UI, the users are less likely to part with the conventional UI which they are familiar with and choose the new UI.

Graphical User Interface (GUI), such as menu, icons or cursor on the screen and Physical User Interface (PUI) such as various kinds of buttons or dials are currently the most popular commercialized UI concepts used in various products and even

J. Jacko (Ed.): Human-Computer Interaction, Part II, HCII 2007, LNCS 4551, pp. 1086–1095, 2007.

though numerous alternative UIs have been later proposed, they are considered as the most familiar operation method.

The major characteristic of GUI is its flexible expressivity of representation. Through various visual representations, GUI is able to provide abundant information to the user in an effective, accurate and liberal way but it is also possible for the user to understand differently the designer's intentions of the visual information.

On the other hand, PUI performs only one function written directly on the surface of the product, but enables the user to clearly verify visually and tactually its location and operation method with the most familiar and natural way and enables stable use because the visual and tactile feedback, simultaneous with the operation, confirms the operation output is as intended.

There have been various methods of efforts for reciprocal complementing of these strengths and weaknesses of GUI and PUI. The main method is to operate indirectly through PUI the information represented on the GUI, a method which is used in numerous electronic appliances today. There are two methods in this: method is to assign a directional PUI input, thus the direction keys, with the selection of functions and adjustment of values along with extra operating buttons, and the other is to have the GUI screen adjacent to PUI buttons so that the function written next to the button is operated with the corresponding *soft key*. This type of association is a result of attempting to associate the flexible expressivity of GUI with the stable input of PUI.

However, because GUI and PUI are physically separated in these methods, the user is unable to feel direct operation of the product's functions. One method which enables to directly operate the various functions provided through GUI is the touch screen. Touch screen not only displays information on screen, but also enables the user to designate a specific location on screen by using his/her finger or a stylus. Because touch screen unites the input and output device and enables to select directly the displayed functions, the learning is easy and intuitive. However since it lacks the physical feedback which PUI provides, it is impossible for the user to confirm whether the input was made according to his/her intentions before checking the reaction on the screen, and especially if the layout of the information and the change of the input range on GUI are represented with various combinations, it results in serious user error and confusion.

There are several different approaches in order to complement these disadvantages of the touch screen, especially the tactile feedback when operating. The typical approach is to give vibration feedback when operating the device, and there exist(s) methods from comparatively simple ones such as vibrating the entire product or screen when the user touches the button on the screen, to more complex methods which allow the user to feel the required tactile feedback only on the corresponding area.

However, this method to complement touch screen is focused on the feedback after the operation. In order to prevent user error, it is more effective to tactually notice the user about the layout of buttons and input location before operating rather than merely notifying whether the input is made or not after the operation. Display Button was designed as an alternating solution of the touch screen and is able to present flexible expressivity of GUI and provide PUI feedback before and after operating.

2 Defining D-Button UI = GUI + PUI

In order to provide in one device both tactile feedback before the user operates the system and visual feedback after the operation, Display Button consists of a button input device covering a screen display device. Standard type LCD screen can be used as screen display device and the button input device minimizes physical structure creating input signal and allows viewing the screen display device through a transparent window. The structure of the prototype is shown on the following figure.

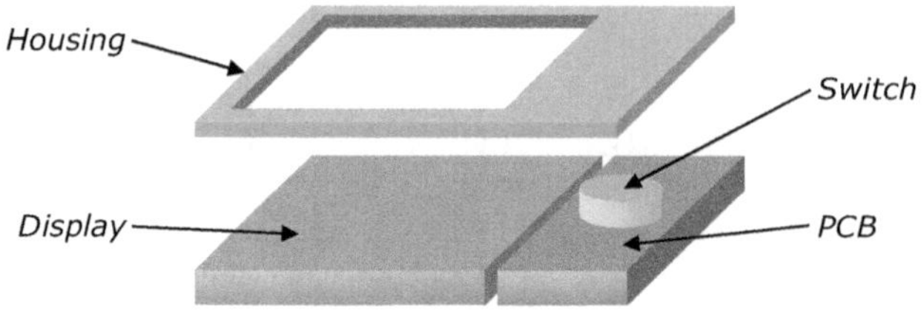

Fig. 1. Structure of Display Button

Display Button can have the screen either entirely or partially covered. In the case of the screen entirely covered, Display Button can be used as several different Display Buttons by dividing properly according to the length and width ratio of the screen and this composition is called the matrix type. In the case of the screen partially covered, button device is laid out in a line mainly to the side or the bottom of the screen and uses the remaining part of the screen as the main display; the composition is called the sidekick type. Both the matrix type Display Button and the sidekick type Display Button can be applied to a product individually or along with other screens.

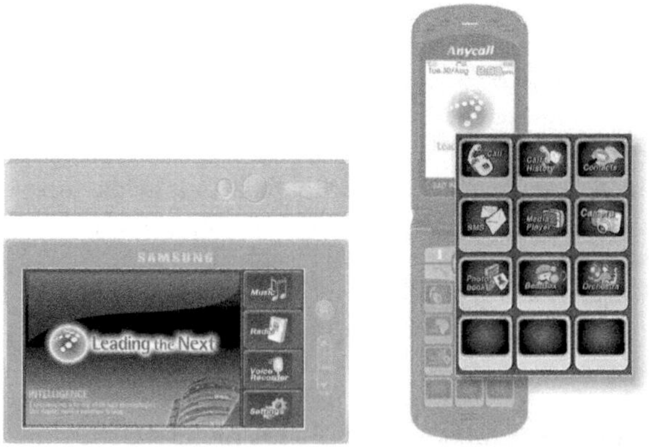

Fig. 2. Layout of Display Button – Sidekick (Left) / Matrix (Right)

It is possible to stably use Display Button through PUI tactile feedback provided before and after the operation as well as offer and select various items according to the context of use by using GUI flexible expressivity provided from the button window. Therefore, PUI disadvantages, mainly indirect operation due to the inability to directly indicate various functions, can be complemented, and possible misunderstanding of the design intentions from the user can be highly reduced since the GUI interaction design possibilities are restrained by the layout of the buttons and operation methods.

Both advantages of the PUI buttons with various and intuitive shapes according to their functions and advantages of the GUI enabling to select freely efficient layouts according to the type of information to be provided are sacrificed in Display Button but it maybe relatively possible to compromise these, compared to the overall advantages acquired from such reciprocal complement between GUI and PUI. The various shapes of PUI buttons can well be substituted to GUI displays of buttons indicated on the screen and the constraints in GUI layout are problems which can be solved in great extent by providing various designs under the given layout of buttons

3 D-Button UI Design Guideline

Display Button's UI is a reciprocal complement of strengths and weaknesses of GUI and PUI as discussed above and it should be designed considering this idea. The main design patterns to be taken into consideration when designing Display Button's module with standard form as described above, are as follow.

3.1 Direct Control

The most basic and straightforward design pattern of Display Button's UI is enabling the user to directly indicate on the button the function to be operated so that the user can immediately find the function he/she wants and use it with consistent usage. This can be applied by indicating on each button the function icons etc. in a navigation situation in which the user is searching for the desired function in the menu, by indicating the corresponding function on the operating icon or option after executing the function, or by listing the visualized items on Display Button.

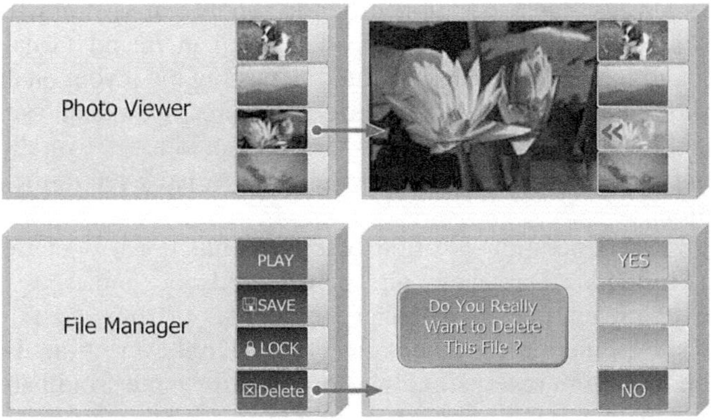

Fig. 3. Examples of Direct Control

The most straightforward application of such Direct Control method would be the push-to-execute mode in which the displayed function is executed when the button is pressed, but there may be several other modified versions. If there are possible options or items listed in a certain Display Button, the user can press the Display Button to select the corresponding item. Or, if the Display Button is displaying the setting of options, the user can press Display Button to toggle the setting. Also, in a mode where Display Button is implemented with touch recognition technology as mentioned above, if the Display Button is held and moved to one side without pressing it, the displayed items on Display Button can be scrolled to that side.

Typical examples of Display Button UI implemented with Direct Control design are shown in Fig. 3.

3.2 Dynamic Information

The greatest characteristic of Display Button is that information is dynamically displayed according to the usage context. Information available on Display Button includes icons or labels to represent the product's functions, options, system settings, index of the contents included in the product and so on.

Identically with other GUI, the graphic representation on Display Button should most of all be designed easy to recognize and understand the related function or item but due to Display Button's characteristics, there may be a few other design guidelines.

First, because Display Button's graphic representations are provided with physically fixed PUI, it should be designed considering the outer part of PUI module such as color or form. Unlike GUI which is provided individually in a PUI device on the product's surface where free modifications are possible within an individual space called image display device, Display Button in which PUI device and GUI display are placed in the same space, harmony with PUI is very important.

Secondly, under the restraint of the button's physical layout, grouping and layout being GUI's long-term subject should be considered into. The order and location of the button's layout should be defined according to the operation directions or relevance and similar functions should be closely located to each other. Because Display Button already has a partitioned button module, it is impossible to use the traditional layout method of GUI but the designer can intend visual grouping by altering the background color of each button or adjusting the layout on the button.

Thirdly, although a device provides various features, it includes similar cases of options provided by each function and for functions used as an overall function such as warning, confirming pop-up etc. are advisable to be displayed in the same position as Display Button.

By instructing the operation position of certain functions, operation learnability which is one of PUI's advantages can be increased and numerous advantages in operating time or preventing errors can be expected. In some cases, however, the position of the same function can intentionally be altered every time. For example, if fatal result such as system reset is likely to occur, error input from habitual behavior can be prevented by locating the confirm button in an arbitrary position.

Lastly, when an option is unable to be used in the corresponding context due to the expressivity of GUI, icons can be displayed as disabled state or emphasize the characteristics of the operation through color or animation. The disabled state can be displayed as a gray image, which is of typical use in GUI. In usage situations such as delete, confirm, etc., Display Button provides flashing animations with them so the user is able to clearly understand the content and operate.

Typical examples of Display Button UI implemented with Dynamic Information design are shown in the following figure.

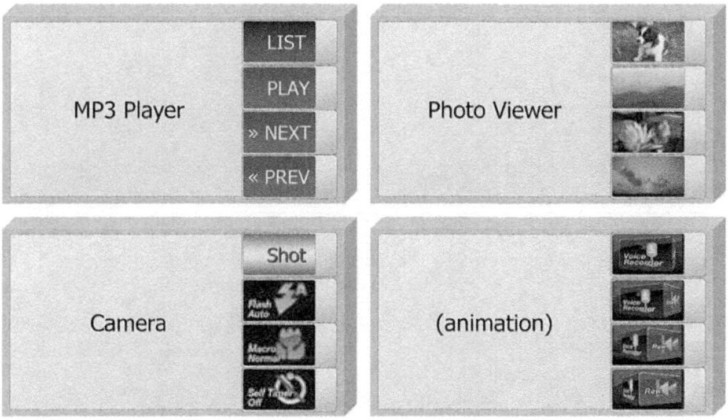

Fig. 4. Examples of Dynamic Information

3.3 Depth Optimization

Display Button can be more effective by being used with a main screen module with traditional shape and functions. Especially with main screen, Display Button can be used complementarily by executing different roles when being used at the same time and the main example would be the fact that the depth of the menu on the information architecture can be more simplified to be optimized.

The reason why effective formation of information structure is imperative to UI design in mobile devices is because only limited information can be displayed on a small screen, it is entirely devoted to the function in process. If the user requires additional functions or wishes to move to other functions, he/she needs a separate screen or pop-up window, and in order to search and select the information he/she needs, he/she has to operate several times and switch screens. Therefore, as a method to select the required items efficiently and yet using the screen to the function in process, hot keys are used. Hot keys are certain buttons on the product's PUI connected to specific items of the function in process, so when pressed the corresponding item is performed. Hot key is provided from the user's customary knowledge of its existence and mapping, or from combining the content written on the button with the connected function on part of the screen displaying the function, and from displaying using a relatively small area.

Hot key's weakest point is that the user finds it difficult to clearly recognize its existence. However, by using Display Button, the user can directly indicate the functions in process on the button, the main screen efficiently provides the contents required to the function, and since all selectable items are directly displayed on the button, the user is able to select items intuitively without worrying about button-function mapping.

Typical examples of Display Button UI implemented with Depth Optimization design are shown in Fig. 5.

Fig. 5. Examples of Depth Optimization

3.4 Direction-Free

It is efficient to arrange various multimedia contents on screen according to their type, especially for mobile device with a small screen which layout is designed with restraints relative to the product's physical design. Therefore, in some cases, the contents are preferred to be displayed on the screen with 90degrees rotation, for example when viewing movie files or TV programs which horizontal lengths are relatively longer on a vertical screen of mobile phones. This type of contents also displays full screen and reduces the space to display UI factors for function operation.

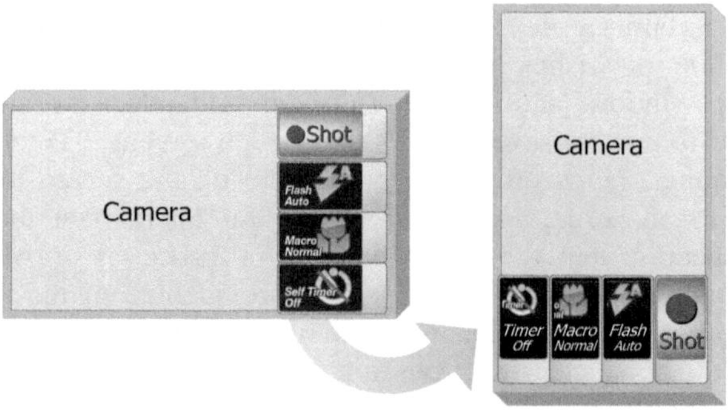

Fig. 6. Examples of Direction-Free

In such case when, in order to display maximum contents, the product is used differently from the usage direction intended at the product development state, the product's PUI layout or displayed graphics are difficult to recognize and result in dramatically poor usability. Display Button not only displays the operation UI required to the corresponding usage context, but also enables optimal usage of each usage scenario by operating the indication directions of the buttons and layout according to the direction of the displayed contents.

Typical examples of Display Button UI implemented with Direction-free design are shown in Fig. 6.

Along with the four representative design patterns as above, there are a few additional GUI developing tips in order to actually develop and apply Display Button. These are caused by characteristics from mechanism designing or from the restraints when arranging Display Button, but because Display Button can be applied differently according to each product design, they will not be mentioned in depth in this research.

4 Method of D-Button UI Design

Display Button has a different feature from UI system of conventional mobile phones because PUI and GUI are combined together, and because of this, UI for Display Button needs a design method different from conventional UI. Conventional UI design method was to build the interaction in a situation in which hardware keys are fixed and GUI changing in the main screen. However, because the button part on Display Button's UI can be varied, it should be designed considering both the main screen and the display button part.

In this research, a method called pattern-oriented approach was used to design a UI accepting conventional UI as well as optimal to Display Button. pattern-oriented approach is a method to deconstruct conventional UI by its functions, organize by giving pattern to UI forms generating at each operation stage on the main screen and design simultaneously the display button part and main screen part using this pattern. With such method, an optimal UI was provided, in which characteristics of Display Button are securely implemented even by maintaining conventional UI system.

This approach maintains the conventional and familiar UI and adds the advantages of Display Button so that it enhances usability in terms of convenience, operation, consistency, efficiency and entertainment without degrading conventional usability. Fig. 7 represents pattern-oriented approach of Display Button on mobile phones.

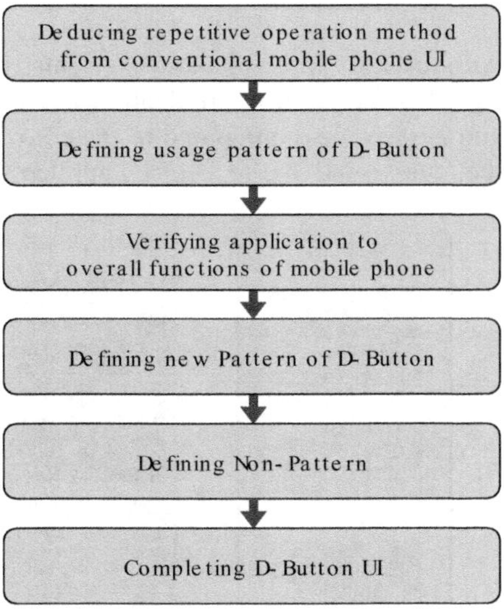

Fig. 7. Design Approach

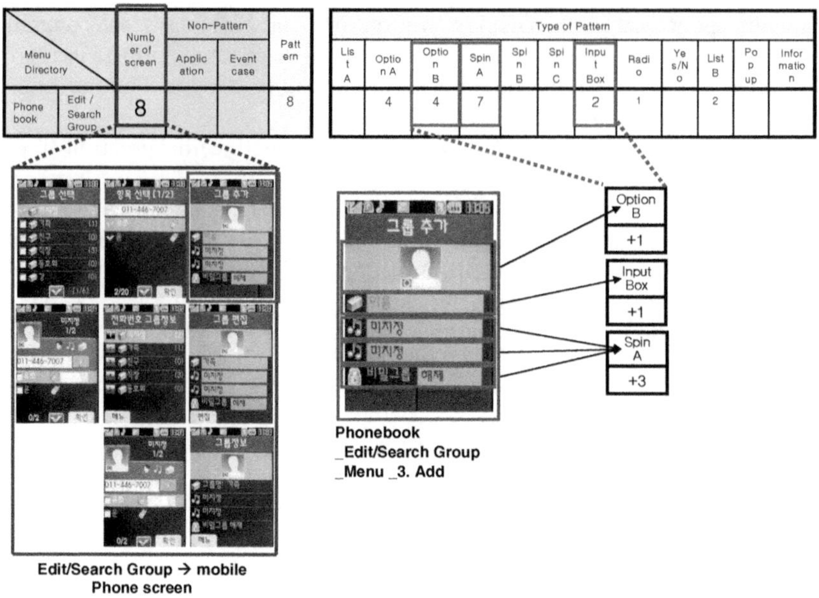

Fig. 8. Analysis of mobile phone screen for verification of pattern application

5 Conclusion

As a result of applying pattern-oriented approach in chapter four, the mobile phone UI with Display Button application reduces operation steps and improves accessibility and intuitiveness compared to the conventional UI. Fig. 9 (a) and (b) are examples of the representative effects of UI applied with Display Button.

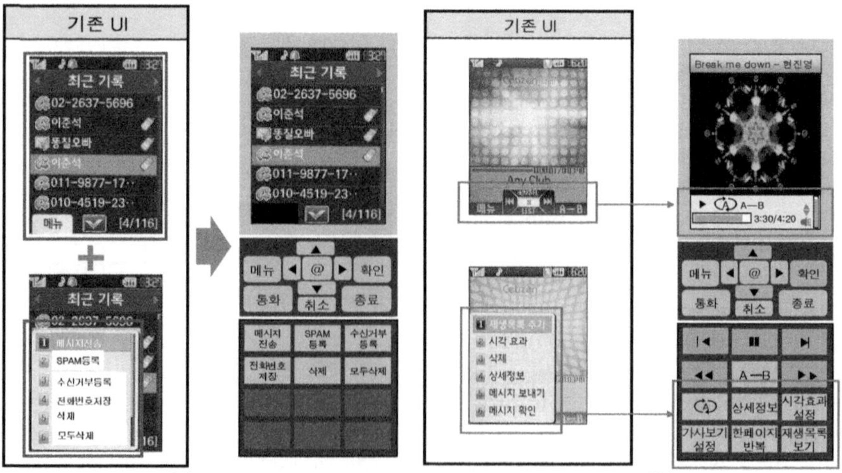

(a) (b)

Fig. 9. Examples of Display Button UI (pattern, Application)

Fig. 9 (a) shows Option B (submenu) which is one of Display Button's characteristics among the twelve patterns and represents best Depth-Free. Option B pattern displays the Option Menu on display button part instead of a pop-up on the main screen as it used to on conventional UI. Concerning operation steps, the primary function or state are displayed on the main screen and the corresponding Option Menu is displayed on the display button part thus displaying two steps in one screen. Enabling to display the related menu simultaneously with the selection of caller, reduced the operation steps and greatly improved accessibility in comparison to prior cases.

Fig. 9 (b) demonstrates the application of Display Button when using MP3 function on Application. When using functions on conventional UI the main screen displays buttons related to operation such as play, stop, view list etc. and maps on the hardware keys related to the navigation of mobile phone. The corresponding menu is displayed as pop-up when the menu button in the lower part of the main screen is selected to play music. However, after applying Display Button to UI, the operation buttons in the display button part and the related menus are displayed simultaneously hence reduce the operation steps, enhance accessibility and enable intuitive operation in comparison to prior cases. Even in confusing situation in which the twelve Display Button's operation buttons and related menu are together, the user is able to intuitively distinguish them by altering colors or images.

It is possible to conclude that the pattern-oriented approach discussed in this research has contributed in maintaining the conventional UI usage method as well as enhancing usability of operational and emotional aspects when designing UI of I/O devices implemented with new technology such as Display Button.

References

1. Nielsen, J.: Non-command user interfaces. Communications of the ACM. 36(4), pp. 83–99. ACM Press, New York (1993)
2. Gray, G.R., Higgins, C.A.: An Introspective Approach to Marking Graphical User Interfaces. In: Proceedings of the 11th annual SIGCSE conference on Innovation and technology in computer science education, vol. 38(3), ACM Press, New York (2006)
3. Raskin, J.: The Humane Interface: New Directions for Designing Interactive Systems. Addison-Wesley, London, UK (2000)
4. Hackos, J.T., Redish, J.C.: User and Task Analysis for Interface Design. Wiley (1998)
5. Preece, J., Rogers, T., Sharp, H.: Interaction Design: Beyond Human Computer Interaction. Wiley (2002)
6. Bergman, E.: Information Appliances and Beyond: Interaction Design for Consumer Products. Morgan Kaufmann, San Francisco (2000)

Construction and Validation of a Neurophysio-technological Framework for Imagery Analysis

Andrew Cowell[1], Kelly Hale[2], Chris Berka[3], Sven Fuchs[2], Angela Baskin[2], David Jones[2], Gene Davis[3], Robin Johnson[3], and Robin Fatch[3]

[1] Pacific National Northwest Laboratory, 902 Batelle Boulevard, Richland, WA
Andrew.Cowell@pnl.gov
[2] Design Interactive, Inc., 1221 E. Broadway, Suite 110, Oviedo, FL
{Kelly,Sven,Angela,David}@designinteractive.net
[3] Advanced Brain Monitoring, Inc., 2850 Pio Pico Drive, Suite A, Carlsbad, CA
{Chris,Gene,Rfatch,Rjohnson}@b-alert.com

Abstract. Intelligence analysts are bombarded with enormous volumes of imagery, which they must visually filter through to identify relevant areas of interest. Interpretation of such data is subject to error due to (1) large data volumes, implying the need for faster and more effective processing, and (2) misinterpretation, implying the need for enhanced analyst/system effectiveness. This paper outlines the Revolutionary Accelerated Processing Image Detection (RAPID) System, designed to significantly improve data throughput and interpretation by incorporating advancing neurophysiological technology to monitor processes associated with detection and identification of relevant target stimuli in a non-invasive and temporally precise manner. Specifically, this work includes the development of innovative electroencephalographic (EEG) and eye tracking technologies to detect and flag areas of interest, potentially without an analyst's conscious intervention or motor responses, while detecting and mitigating problems with tacit knowledge, such as anchoring bias in real-time to reduce the possibility of human error.

Keywords: Augmented Cognition, electroencephalography, eye tracking, imagery analysis.

1 Introduction

Current technology inundates Intelligence Analysts (IAs) with enormous volumes of imagery, which they visually filter through to identify relevant targets that indicate suspicious activity. Interpretation of such data is subject to error due to (1) large data volumes, implying the need for faster and more effective processing, and (2) misinterpretation, implying the need for enhanced analyst/system effectiveness [1]. We must find means to support human processing of DoD imagery intelligence due to the enormous amount of imagery in need of processing as compared to the number of available image interpreters. Attempts to increase the number of image interpreters by hiring more, retaining more, or motivating their performance have not made a significant impact. The unclassified WMD Commission Report indicates "how badly

J. Jacko (Ed.): Human-Computer Interaction, Part II, HCII 2007, LNCS 4551, pp. 1096–1105, 2007.

outgunned our human intelligence collectors are, at precisely the time when the most is expected of them" [1, p. 374]. To support the intelligence community's (IC's) central mission to help the nation avoid strategic surprise, it is essential to provide IAs with tools that can help them focus analytic attention on the most critical information found within massive data.

The Revolutionary Advanced Processing Image Detection (RAPID) system being developed is designed to significantly enhance both image throughput and analysis accuracy by incorporating neurophysiology measurement techniques into a closed-loop system that tracks the imagery analysis process, automatically identifies images of interest as well as specific areas of interest within each image, and also monitors for analysis biases and attempts to mitigate such biases to enhance imagery processing. RAPID incorporates two distinct neurophysiology instruments, specifically electroencephalography event-related potentials (EEG/ERP) and eye tracking technology that together will revolutionize the efficiency and effectiveness of the image analysis process.

2 Background

The human visual system is relied on heavily in the image analysis process, and is designed to provide continuous and rapid processing of a constant barrage of stimuli. When searching for a specific visual stimulus (e.g., area of interest in intelligence imagery), the human visual system uses saccadic eye movements in which sensed images are constantly changing, replaced after each saccade (approximately every 300 ms) [2,3,4] by a totally new image or by an image that is correlated with a previously detected image. During such saccadic processing, an image is thought to be first analyzed via a serial strategy using bottom-up, image-based processing driven by the saliency of stimuli, followed by slower top-down, cognitive-based processing directed by various selection criteria. With conventional displays, the first bottom-up stage of directing attention can be readily accomplished as there are few parameters to focus on (e.g., the color of an active window of information, the position of a menu or icon). Yet, IAs often view open scenes (e.g., high-resolution digital imagery, detailed aerial photographs, wide-angle video feeds), which hinder the bottom-up stage because there are no easy criteria for directing attentional processing [2].

Bottom-up detection of areas of interest is complimented by top-down processing, where analysts' cognitive background (e.g., strategies, heuristics, schemas) give meaning and interpretation to images. However, judgments during top-down processing may be susceptible to assumptions and motivational or cognitive biases [5,6,7]. In the case of Iraq, rejection or ignorance of contrary information due to a prevailing analytic consensus led to "tunnel vision focusing on the Intelligence Community's existing assumptions [i.e., that Iraq had an active WMD program], with little to no consideration of alternative interpretations" [1, p. 162]. Such biases tend to occur because analysts give credence to a given hypothesis by making information consistent with their supposition more available (e.g., through a biased visual search or priming mechanisms) than information that refutes it [8,9]. This is particularly likely to happen when 'hard evidence runs out' [6, p.xxii], i.e. when ambiguity is present.

Neurophysiology measurement approaches, such as electroencephalography event-related potentials (EEG/ERP) and eye tracking technology may be used to realize substantial gains in throughput and accuracy of imagery analysis.

2.1 Electroencephalography (EEG) Technology

EEG/ERP offer excellent temporal resolution and tracking of neural activity representing the flow of information from sensory processing and analysis to initiation of a response (i.e., EEG signals of humans searching for a specific target item in rapidly viewed images can reveal perception of a specific item 130-150 ms post-stimulus, thus before conscious recognition occurs; [8,9,10,11,12,13]. Thus, images that contain areas of interest may be identified using neural signatures, thus eliminating the need for behavioral responses and improving the speed of image throughput. Past research also indicates the feasibility of using EEG/ERP to differentiate between correct responses (i.e., hits and correct rejections), and highly biased responses (e.g., false alarms and misses) [13,14,15], thus supporting the potential for using neurotechnology for enhancing decision accuracy. Another EEG metric for identifying top-down bias is to assess the speed of classification of a particular target. Longer latency and larger amplitude event-related post-processing components (P300, N400) are generally associated with more complex signal analysis and continued search of memory storage to finalize a decision regarding the relevance of a stimulus. Specifically, if a stimulus has been falsely identified as an area of interest as a result of top-down bias influencing the decision, the event-related signature should be very brief as should the reaction time associated with that response. Taken together, these results demonstrate multiple potential opportunities for leveraging neurotechnology to characterize the top-down component of visual image processing (i.e., to capture the analyst's prior or tacit knowledge and determine how these elements are influencing the analytic process).

2.2 Eye Tracking Technology

Eye tracking technology offers a unique methodology for cognitive assessment in that systems can determine exactly what the person has visually perceived, and by adding observation of the user's reactions, direct insight can be gained into cognition, neurological responses and vision capabilities [16]. Eye tracking technology has been used to assess system usability (e.g., user perception and interpretation difficulty) by utilizing metrics such as overall number of fixations and gaze duration mean on each area of interest (AoI) [17,18]. Behavioral differences between novices and experts have been measured by eye tracking search patterns, percentage of time looking at AoI, and fixations [19]. Eye tracking has also delivered promising results as a measure of cognitive load [20], attention level [21], and task difficulty [22]. Additional oculomotor metrics that may be used to evaluate situation awareness (SA; knowledge of ongoing situation) include gaze direction and frequency, frequency/length of saccadic movements, pupil diameter, and eye blink.

3 The RAPID System

Building on the benefits of neurophysiological assessment of imagery processing, the RAPID architecture under development monitors event-related EEG distinctions observed early in the post-stimulus bottom-up processing period, which may reflect a preemptive categorization using simple features or combinations of features that allow a quick match or mismatch to an existing template (i.e., target versus non-target) [9,11]. Eye-tracking is used to complement the EEG signatures to identify specific points in an image that were of interest to analysts, thereby automatically flagging potential targets within images for detailed analysis and/or future reference. In addition, RAPID uses a combination of EEG and eye tracking output to determine the relative amount of time spent in global (overall image pattern) versus local (component parts of an image) bottom-up feature processing and other potential indications of reduced processing attention and/or biased review.

Figure 1 presents a conceptual model of the RAPID System, which identifies images that contain area(s) of interest and those that do not, supports automatic flagging of any image identified as containing an area of interest, as well as localizes

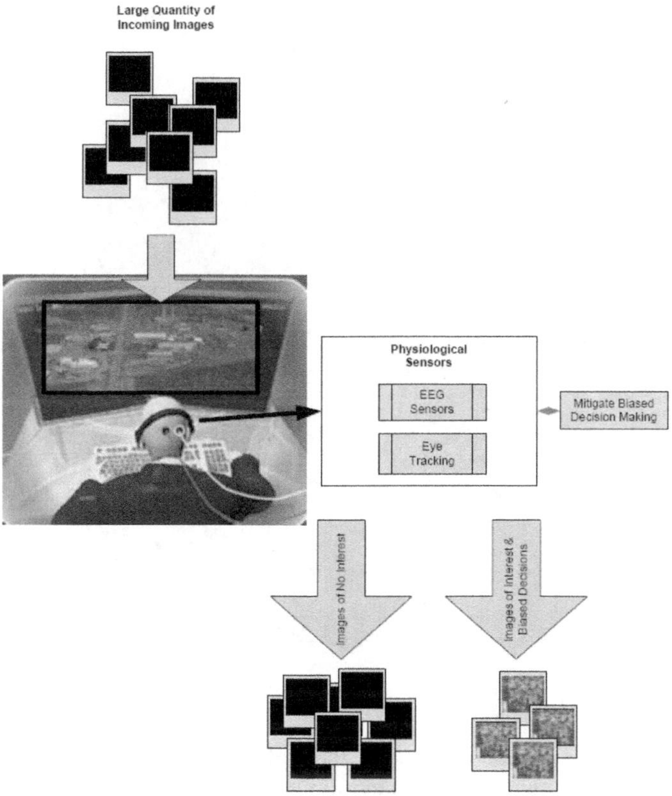

Fig. 1. Conceptual Model of RAPID

specific interest points using eye tracking technology, and saves such imagery with associated metadata for more thorough review (by same or different analyst). By assessing image processing using neurophysiology measurement techniques, images that contain area(s) of potential interest can be quickly and automatically captured and organized for further detailed review separately from those images that are of no interest to the current analyst, thereby creating a system that increases image throughput. Additionally, images that may have been processed with a biased view may be identified and flagged for further analysis/review, thus enhancing accuracy of the analysis process.

RAPID incorporates an integrated hardware and software solution for the acquisition and real-time analysis of EEG and eye tracking developed to facilitate event-locked data extraction. The first hardware component is an easily applied wireless EEG sensor headset suitable for operational applications (Figure 2). The headset made from stretchable fabric fits snugly on the head and houses EEG sensors with sensors located over the right, left and midline frontal, central and paretal-occipital cortical regions. The main electrical component of the Sensor Headset is a battery-powered data acquisition and transmission unit that rests against the back of the head. The Sensor Headset is only used for recording physiological signals and does not introduce energy into the body except for any minor electromagnetic radiation typically emitted by small electronic devices. The sensor headset has been applied and worn by over 1000 human participants.

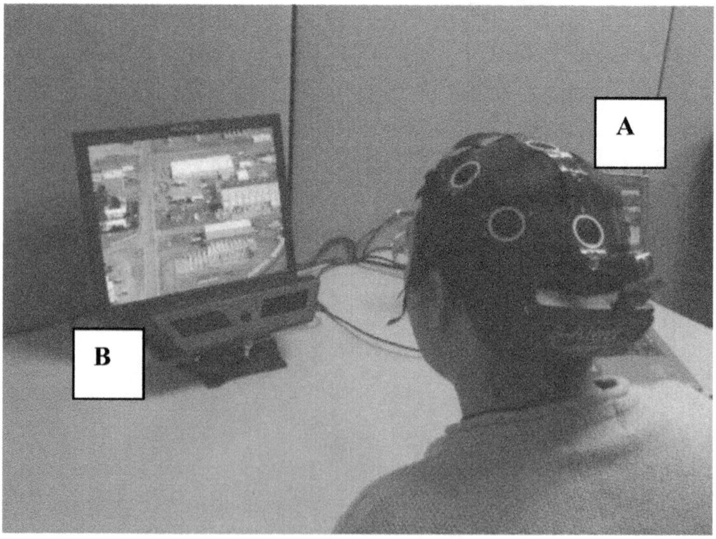

Fig. 2. RAPID System (A: EEG B-Alert Sensor Headset; B: Tobii x50 Eye Tracker)

To capture eye gaze and pupil size, the Tobii x50 eye tracker is included in the RAPID system (Figure 2). This stand-alone unit is completely non-intrusive and utilizes Near-Infrared (NIR) Light-Emitting Diodes (such as used in Camera autofocus systems or remote controls) to generate even lighting and reflection patterns in the eyes of the user. A high-resolution camera is used to capture the reflections. The system collects gaze data simultaneously from both eyes at a frequency of 50 HZ (approximately every 20 msec), which includes horizontal and vertical position of the gazepoint both on a normalized scale and in the camera image for each eye, distance from each eye to the camera, each pupil diameter, and a validity code (accuracy). Gaze data, as well as system-calculated fixation data (gazepoint fixed for specified length of time), are output quantitatively via spreadsheet. Fixation and gazeplot data (a real-time tracing of the person's gaze) are additionally presented qualitatively atop the corresponding images. Areas of interest can be defined pre- or post-stimulus within presented images via a bounding box or polygon, eliciting further system output of fixation data within those specified areas.

A Pentium IV PC drives visual presentation of images to participants on a 17" flat panel monitor. The initial RAPID system collects data in real-time on a single computer with dual monitors. One monitor displays the testbed (i.e., images) to participants, while the second monitor is used to track EEG and eye tracking data capture to ensure minimal loss of signal during testing. The goal of RAPID is to not only collect data in real-time, but also analyze neurophysiology data in real-time and write metadata to images as they are processed.

3.1 RAPID System Output

Initial development of RAPID includes creation of distinct EEG/ERP signature templates that may be used to categorize event-related EEG in real-time into one of four groups: image of interest, image of no interest, potential missed area of interest, potential false alarm. In addition, eye tracking thresholds (e.g., fixation times) need to be defined to categorize area of interest within images. Software has been developed that allows integration of testbed markers and eyetracking data to facilitate algorithm development. This software, the EEG Visualization Application (EVA) includes the flexibility to select multiple signals to present, use tool tips to measure signal changes, auto-scale the presented signals, convert input data to meaningful codes, or apply simple algorithms to specified signals and stripe events that meet the criteria.

Once templates are created, data will be extracted using a real-time, event-based approach, where EEG/ERP signatures and eye tracking metrics are captured for each image that is presented. Figure 3 demonstrates a sample EEG signature that shows a clear distinction in ERPs between targets that were correctly identified and non-targets correctly identified. Targets were 20 predefined images of animals where participants first learned that a subset of 20 out of a group of 100 were the "target" animals. Similar distinct differences are expected when more complex imagery data is reviewed for potential areas of interest. Figure 4 shows eye tracking pilot data from participants viewing images for either 2 seconds or 3 minutes. Highlighted on the screen are fixation points, where the size and color indicate extent of dwell time at any given point (larger space and red color indicate longer fixation points). Based on this data, further pilot testing will be completed to determine the optimal image presentation rate, where participants have sufficient time to scan the entire image and fixate on the areas of interest, yet are not presented images for longer than necessary, as this will result in a slower RAPID system that provides less accurate information

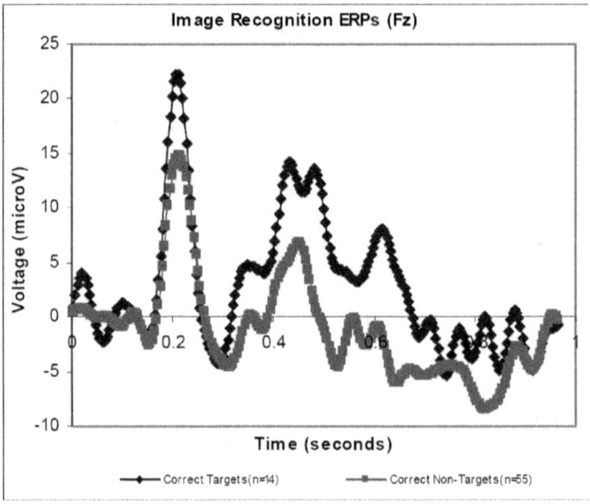

Fig. 3. EEG ERPs for correct identification of 'target' and 'non-target'

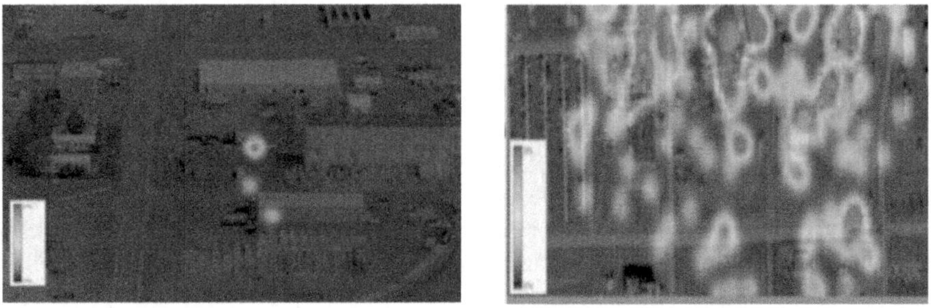

(a) (b)

Fig. 4. Eye tracking fixation point pilot data for (a) 2 seconds and (b) 3 minutes image presentation time

(as longer presentation times may result in a large proportion of the entire image may be identified as fixation points – see Figure 4b).

3.2 Identification of Potential Biases That May Be Mitigated Using RAPID System

Biases are a substantial component in the work of intelligence analysts [23]. The origin of the bias can be twofold – external or internal. *External bias* occurs in information that is received by analysts in an already biased format and where the analyst is not the source of the bias. In contrast, *internal bias* originates directly from the analyst. Objective information assumed, the analyst's perception or interpretation of the data is influenced by underlying mechanisms that skew the analysis results into a direction that is different from the path that a truly objective assessment would take. During a comprehensive literature review, potential internal analyst biases were identified, defined and evaluated for applicability in the RAPID context (Table 1). Three biases highlighted in green in Table 1 were found to be particularly suited for detection and mitigation by the RAPID system.

RAPID will use EEG analysis (i.e., ERP relative positivity, ERP relative negativity, level of cognitive effort, ERP latency and amplitude, reaction time) to capture and interpret IAs unconscious use of prior and tacit knowledge. Specifically, EEG will be used to neurologically detect assumptions and biases during imagery analysis, and thus potentially reduce errors (misses, false alarms). Substantial gains in the accuracy of IAs can then be realized by (1) drawing the analyst's attention to biases (although often this is not enough; c.f. [6]) and (2) offering mitigations to alleviate/avoid biased decisions (e.g., offer alternative views of a situation or suggest a new IA review the data).

Table 1. Biases in Intelligence Analysis

Name	Definition
Confirmation Bias	This bias produces a sort of 'cognitive tunnel vision', in which operators fail to encode or process information that is contradictory to or inconsistent with the initially formulated hypothesis
Vividness Bias	Information that is [vivid, concrete and personal] is more likely to attract and hold our attention
Impact Bias	The tendency to make conservative or risky choice in an ambiguous setting, based on the utility of the outcome
Expectancy Effect	The idea that prior outcomes can influence the outcome of probabilistic events
Emotional Bias	The tendency that decision making is influenced by the current state of mood
Anchoring Bias	A pervasive judgment bias in which decision makers are systematically influenced by random and uninformative starting points
Belief Perseverance	People often maintain beliefs that are based upon information that is eventually shown to be false
Ethnocentrism	Projection of one's culture, ideological beliefs, doctrine, or expectations of others; exaggeration of the casual significance of one's own actions
Hindsight Bias	The tendency for decision makers with outcome knowledge to believe falsely that they would have predicted the outcome
Ignorance	An intentional lack of knowledge that can result from prior-limited priorities or lack of curiosity.
Overconfidence	The tendency to be more confident than is warranted in the correctness of one's hypothesis, so that people will prematurely close off the search for evidence
Pseudo-diagnosticity	The tendency for decision makers to evaluate a hypothesis by considering the likelihood of the evidence given that hypothesis, but neglecting the likelihood of the evidence given an alternative hypothesis

4 Conclusions

The RAPID architecture is expected to lead to significant increases in the amount of imagery reviewed and categorized, as identification and localization of areas of interest within images may occur without an analyst's conscious intervention or motor responses. An additional EEG-based triage designed to identify and classify false positives and misses based on bias or fatigue incorporated into RAPID should reduce the possibility of human error. The vision is that RAPID's neurophysiological technology would one day provide IAs with the ability to rapidly assess massive image data that would otherwise not be viewed due to sheer volume, while ultimately resolving issues of misinterpretation and bias.

Further enhancements to the RAPID system may include detection and measurement of performance-critical issues (e.g., fatigue; cognitive overload), and how these effects can be alleviated by closed-loop real-time mitigation. Follow-on efforts could look at data streams other than images and the collaboration context, particularly with regard to using neurophysiology measurement techniques to direct delegation of incoming information across intelligence analysts.

References

1. WMD Commission. The Commission on the Intelligence Capabilities of the United States Regarding Weapons of Mass Destruction. March 31, 2005, US Government (2005)
2. Ritter, W., et al.: Manipulation of event-related potential manifestations of information processing stages. Science 218, 909–911 (1982)
3. Ritter, W., Simson, R, Vaughan, H.G.: Event-related potential correlates of two stages of information processing in physical and semantic discrimination tasks. Psychophysiology 20, 168–179 (1983)
4. Ritter, W., Simson, R., Vaughan, H.G.: Effects of the amount of stimulus information processed on negative event-related potentials. Electroencephalography and Clinical Neurophysiology 69, 244–258 (1988)
5. Chapman, G.B., Johnson, E.J.: Anchoring, activation, and the construction of values. Organizational Behavior and Human Decision Processes 79(2), 115–153 (1999)
6. Heuer, J.J.R.: Psychology of Intelligence Analysis. Center for the Study of Intelligence Central Intelligence Agency (1999) http://hub.n00bstories.com/csi/books/19104/index.html
7. Meyer, M.A., Booker, J.M., Bradshaw, J.M.: A flexible six-step program for defining and handling bias in knowledge elicitation (1990) http://pages.cpsc.ucalgary.ca/gaines/BooseBradshaw/EKAW90Draft.doc
8. Fabre-Thorpe, M., et al.: A Limit to the Speed of Processing in Ultra-Rapid Visual Categorization of Novel Natural Scenes. Journal of Cognitive Neuroscience 13, 171–180 (2001)
9. Hopf, J.-M., et al.: Localizing visual discrimination processes in time and space. The. American Physiological Society 88, 2088–2095 (2002)
10. Eimer, M.: Does the face-specific N170 component reflect the activity of a specialized eye processor? Neuroreport 9, 2945–2948 (1998)
11. Thorpe, S., Fize, D., Marlot, C.: Speed of Processing in the Human Visual System. Nature 381, 520–522 (June 6, 1996)

12. Bentin, S., et al.: Electrophysiological studies of face perception in humans. Journal of Cognitive Neuroscience 8, 551–565 (1996)
13. Vogel, E.K., Luck, S.J.: The visual NI component as an index of a discrimination process. Psychophysiology, vol. 37 (2000)
14. Yamaguchi, S., Yamagata, S., Kobayashi, S.: Cerebral asymmetry of the top-down allocation of attention to global and local features. The Journal of Neuroscience, 20, RC72 1 of 5 (2000) http://www.ling.uni-potsdam.de/saddy/web%20papers/Yamaguchi%20assymetry%20and %20attention.pdf
15. Sun, Y., Wang, H., Yang, Y., Zhang, J., Smith, J.W.: Probabilistic judgment by a coarser scale: behavioral and ERP evidence (Viewed December 5, 2005) (1994) Available online at: http://www.cogsci.northwestern.edu/cogsci2004/papers/paper187.pdf
16. Tobii Technology. (Viewed January 4, 2007)(2006) Available online at: http://www.tobii.com
17. Fitts, P.M., Jones, R.E., Milton, J.L.: Eye Movement of Aircraft Pilots during Instrument-Landing Approaches. Aeronautical Engineering Review 9, 24–29 (1950)
18. Goldberg, J.H., Kotval, X.P.: Eye Movement-Based Evaluation of the Computer Interface. In: Kumar, S.K. (ed.) Advances in Occupational Ergonomics and Safety, pp. 529–532. IOS Press, Amsterdam (1998)
19. Kurland, L., Gertner, A., Bartee, T., Chisholm, M., McQuade, S.: Using Cognitive Task Analysis and Eye Tracking to Understand Imagery Analysis (2005) Retrieved Nov 14, 2006 from http://www.mitre.org/work/tech_papers/tech_papers_05/05_1365/05_1365.pdf
20. Iqbal, S.T., Zheng, X.S., Bailey, B.P.: Task-evoked pupillary response to mental workload in human-computer interaction. In: Proceedings of the ACM Conference on Human Factors in Computing Systems pp. 1477–1480 (2004)
21. Fukuda, T., Yamada, M.: Quantitative Evaluation of Eye Movements as Judged by Sight-Line Displacements. SMPTE Journal 95, 1230–1241 (1986)
22. Nakayama, M., Takahashi, K., Shimizu, Y.: The Act of Task Difficulty and Eye-Movement Frequency for the Oculo-motor indices. In: Proceedings of the Symposium on Eye Tracking Research & Applications, New Orleans, LA, 2002, pp. 37–42 (2002)
23. Lefebvre, S.: A Look at Intelligence Analysis. Journal of Intelligence and Counter Intelligence 17(2), 231–264 (2004)

A Study on the Acceptance Factors of the Smart Clothing

Ji-Young Hong, Haeng-Suk Chae, and Kwang-Hee Han

Cognitive Engineering Lab. Yonsei University
134, 120-749 Shincheon-dong, Seodaemun-gu, Seoul, Korea
{hongcom,Acechae19,khan}@yonsei.ac.kr

Abstract. This study aims to predict user acceptance of smart clothing. The present research develops and validates new products for smart clothing. Studies suggest that further analysis of the process be undertaken to better establish properties for smart clothing, underlying structures and stability over innovative technologies. The findings reported in this paper should be useful methods which identify user needs. Such findings in now provide a way to explain technology acceptance. Both of qualitative and quantitative methods were applied to this study in order to find out user needs for smart clothing. We are writing scenarios and conducting both focused group interviews and a survey to assess the user's interest. The purpose of the survey is to evaluate the importance of the functions and to evaluate the degree of the participant's feeling and attitude. Furthermore, we explore the nature and specific influences of factors that may affect the user perception and usage.

Keywords: smart clothing, wearable computing, user acceptance factor, SNFD , HCI, user needs.

1 Introduction

Smart clothing is a new type of clothing which incorporates various digital equipments and functions necessary for everyday life. Originally, this term was exclaimed by Steve Mann, who has developed wearable computer as a personal empowerment tool [3]. Generally, wearable computing studies have focused on using useful information anytime, anywhere easily but it is questionable that wearable computer's usefulness would be enough criteria to buy and use these products. A lot of wearable computers were very useful but there is little concerning about social factors as naturalness and aesthetics. Other researchers in this field gradually approach a common consent that wearable computer will be shape to a natural form of ordinary clothes. This concern, however, has been growing rather industry than academic society. Infeneon and Munich design school developed MP3-wear and snowboard wear that has built-in cell-phone switcher and headset [10]. Philips and Apple Company developed the iPod wear [11]. Many clothing products which equipped in digital device have been presented from joint development of electronic and apparel companies.

This trend of industry presents a possibility of new market share, but there are rare studies about what is consumer wants. VDC, the global IT consulting company,

J. Jacko (Ed.): Human-Computer Interaction, Part II, HCII 2007, LNCS 4551, pp. 1106–1112, 2007.

predicted that wearable computing market started to appear in 2002 ~ 2003, in 2004, consumer demands would be established in various market, and then about 2005, the market size would be increased to near 100 percent [9]. Now, however, we are hard to find who wear wearable computer or smart clothes in everyday life. This phenomenon is caused by the lack of effort to consider psychological factors. Consumers may want to natural product as well as functional.

It is important to speculate user's mind, because technologies do not exist for technology itself, but exist for user. Furthermore, design goal could be directed by found acceptance factors. For instance, if users want to more functional product, developers should include various and powerful functions, but if users want to the product which has more natural feature although has limited functionality they should improve it more aesthetic.

So, this study focused to find acceptance factors of smart clothing. Especially, for this goal, we have to review some psychological and sociological theories.

2 Acceptance Factors on Innovative Technology

2.1 Feature of Innovation

Everett Rogers defines diffusion as "the process by which an innovation is communicated through certain channels over time among the members of a social system." [4] He stated four elements that are present in the diffusion of innovation process: Innovation itself, acceptors' feature, communication channels and social system. Innovation itself includes 4 elements also. : *Relative advantage*, *compatibility*, *complexity*, *trialability*, *observability*. *Relative advantage* means the degree that acceptor perceived advantage comparative to usual idea. *Compatibility* means the degree of appropriateness to acceptor's value. *Complexity* means the degreed of hard to understand. *Trialability* means the degree that latent acceptors can try the innovative method. *Observability* means the degree that a technology could be seen to non-acceptors. Acceptor's feature means the degree that the acceptor's risk accepting behavior. Communication channel means the channel to diffuse the innovation. Social system means it has good structure to diffuse the innovation.

2.2 Perceived Risk

According to Rogers, Perceived Risk will influence to acceptance of innovation. Zirkmund classified Perceived Risk to 7 categories: financial risk , functional risk, physical risk, psychological risk, social risk, loss of time and loss of future chance [6]. It is reasonable to assume that user worried about social risk as well as physical risk.

2.3 Technology Acceptance Model (TAM)

Davis [2] proposed TAM(Technology Acceptance Model) from TRA(Theory of Reasoned Action) [12] . His research showed that perceived usefulness and perceived ease of use influence to user acceptance of technology. This model is more explanative than TRA.

2.4 Need for Uniqueness

Need for uniqueness defined non-adaptive individual need to present distinctive one's uniqueness [5]. People usually express by external behavior. Consuming behavior is proper field to present one's need for uniqueness because could be satisfied need for uniqueness without social disadvantages. Need for Uniqueness may adopted a possible factor for acceptance of smart clothing because of it has novelty in the nature.

2.5 A Model Derived from Literature

We can sum up some factors based the literature reviewed above.

1) Social Acceptability: It means the degree of appropriateness to social common value. It is derived from Rogers' compatibility.
2) Novelty: We can easily predict smart clothing's novel features give support to the needs for uniqueness of user.
3) Perceived Usefulness: This factor is derived from Roger's relative advantage and Davis' TAM.
4) Perceived Ease of use: Perceived Ease of use is derived from Davis' TAM as well as many HCI researchers have considered it as a major factor of usability.
5) Perceived Risk (or Safety): The mechanical feature of the smart clothing, physical harm may be occurred as a result of functional error.

3 A Qualitative Analysis of Acceptance

3.1 Scenario Based Focus Group Interview

There are a lot of users who have experienced using mobile computing devices, but few of them have tried wearing clothes equipped with digital functions. In order to find out those users' needs, we formulated several virtual scenarios in which people engage in a variety of activities such as jogging, hiking, skiing, partying, sleeping, and dating with wearing specially designed clothes equipped with computing devices

We presented the scenarios featured in a series of pictures and illustrations to six small groups of users, and then conducted interviews asking their opinions and preferences concerning the situations in the scenarios. We chose this method because a scenario can explicitly visualize users' activities and provide the researchers with useful information about the situations of use. Generally, a scenario consists of actors, objects and a context [1]. Our scenarios include describing users' characteristics, functionality of the clothes and the social contexts.

3.2 Methods

Participants: Thirty-two participants were recruited for F.G.I. Study. They are over the age of 7 to less than 35.

Scenarios: We wrote 21 scenarios that can be occurred when wearing various smart clothes, and then, we reduced the scenarios to 8 stories: "Music-prism T-shirt",

"Smart Jogging Buddy", "Beat Amplifier", "Ski Wear: Safety and Freedom", "Healthy Nightwear", "Lovers' Gloves", "Safety Hiking Jacket" and "A stray child check"(Table 1).

F.G.I. and Data Gathering: The scenarios were shown to the participants and then they were asked to discuss freely many features of the situations. Their conversations were recorded and transcribed.

Analysis: A qualitative analysis was conducted based on *SNFD* method which was specially devised for the present research. *SNFD* stands for Scenario Needs Function Device, a method that elicits users' needs from the responses to the scenarios [7] [8]. From the identified user needs, main function categories are derived which help decide on the specific devices necessary for the particular contexts.

Table 1. Outlines of Scenarios

Title	*Outlines of Scenarios*
Music-Prism T-shirt	A few Girls wear shirts that have modules of changing color by response to ambient sound. They are dancing in clubs with more exciting.
Smart Jogging Buddy	The boys who are usually running for health everyday wear smart-buddy wear which checks their health information and give some advice and networking function for reducing tediousness.
Beat Amplifier	There is a student wears a motion-response jacket. It describes the situation that he tries to playing some music by moving his limbs.
Ski-wear	A Clothes that equipped with functions of phone, MP3 Player,
Healthy Nightwear	A Nightwear for Checking health information such as body temperature and heartbeat rate was described.
Lover's glove	A couple of lover communicate easily and various ways such as gesture
Safety Hiking Jacket	It is a hiking jacket which able to inform one's location and to alarm to rescuers when a hiker meet with a disaster.
A stray child check	The jackets be worn by children inform their location information to their parents.

3.3 Result

We classified comments from participants based on their intention. The scenarios that "Music-Prism T-shirt" and "Beat Amplifier" could be grouped into entertainment focused smart clothing situation, participants' comments show they mainly interested with emotional, social and amusement feature. For the scenarios that "Smart Jogging Buddy", "Healthy Nightwear", could be grouped into sports and leisure concept, participants mainly commented about the importance of health. "Safety Hiking Jacket" and "A stray child check" were the everyday security concept, participants worried about the risk caused by overconfidence of technology as well as agreeing the importance of security.

We derived four main needs from this study, which were entertainment, social satisfaction, health and security. According to those needs, functions were also classified into six categories: advice, notification of a situation, sensing and monitoring, actuating, communication, and customizing. In addition, the participants' main interest factors about the scenarios were analyzed: personal needs, social needs, novelty, joyfulness, perceived feasibility, usefulness in everyday life, comfort, ease of use, safety, and reliability of the information provided.

4 A Quantitative Analysis of Acceptance Factors

4.1 Purpose and Method

The goal of survey is to evaluate the importance of the functions featured in the scenarios. Forty nine undergraduate students taking an introductory psychology course participated in this survey. Ten of the participants were female and the others were male. The mean age of participants was 19.5 years (*stdev.* 1.4 years). The survey consists of two sessions. First, the scenarios were shown to the participants in the form of the pictures and illustrations. Second, the participants were asked to fill out a paper-format 7-point *Likert* scale questionnaire including 144 questions about their preferences of the functions featured in the scenarios as well as the feelings about and attitudes toward them.

4.2 Results

The scenarios that generated the most positive responses about common interests from the participants were 'Healthy Nightwear' and 'Smart Jogging Buddy'. In the

Table 2. Mean Rating Score for Common Interests

Common Interests	Mostly High Rated Scenario rated Highest	Mean Rating Score
1. Personal Needs	Health Nightwear	4.92
2. Social Needs	Smart Jogging Buddy	5.26
3. Novelty	Smart Jogging Buddy	5.69
4. Joyfulness	Smart Jogging Buddy	5.42
5.Perceived feasibility	Health Nightwear	4.41
6.Usefulness to everyday life	Health Nightwear	5.63
7. Comfort	Health Nightwear	4.59
8. Ease of Use	Health Nightwear	5.08
9. Risk	Health Nightwear	3.80
10.Trust to information	Smart Jogging Buddy	4.51
	Healthy Nightwear	4.50

'Healthy Nightwear' scenario, the participants rated highly on personal needs,perceived feasibility, usefulness to everyday life, comfort, ease of use, safety, and reliability. In 'Smart Jogging Buddy', they rated highly on social needs, novelty, joyfulness, and reliability.

As to the preferred functions, the most highly rated function in 'Healthy Nightwear' was the automatic emergency call and sending out healthful substances like vitamin or aroma. In 'Smart Jogging Buddy', cooling functions was rated the most highly.

5 Discussion

This paper proposed a methodology for deriving factors related smart clothing. By reviewing sociological, psychological literature, we preview some possible factors that able to influence acceptance for smart clothing. Interviewing technique and quantitative and analysis are also important, because speculating user's mind leads to instruct orientation of developing smart clothing products. In this article, we described qualitative result by conducting a survey. Although the survey does not realize all of the factors predicted in literature review, it is worth to elaborate toward frames of predicting user acceptance of smart clothing. In order to make smart clothing usable and attractive to users, this type of approach will be needed more and more.

Acknowledgments. This work was supported by Korea Ministry of Commerce, Industry and Energy (2006-8-1653).

References

1. Carroll, J.M.: Five reasons for scenario-based design. Interacting with Computers 13, 43–60 (2000)
2. Davis, F.D.: A technology acceptance model for empirically testing new end-user information systems: theory and results (Doctoral dissertation, Sloan School of Management, Massachusetts Institute of technology) (1986)
3. Mann, S.: Smart Clothing: Wearable Multimedia Computing and personal imaging to restore the technological balance between people and their environments. In: Proceedings of the fourth ACM international conference on multimedia (1997)
4. Rogers, E.M.: Diffusion of Innovations, 4th edn. The Free Press, New York (1995)
5. Snyder, C.R., Fromkin, H.I: Abnormality as a positive characteristic: the development and validation of a scale measuring need for uniqueness. Journal of Abnormal Psychology 86, 518–527 (1977)
6. Zirkmund, W.G.: Business Research Methods, 6th edn. The Dryden Press, Fort Worth (2000)
7. Chae, H.S., Hong, J.Y., Jeon, H.Y., Yim, S.W., Yoo, S., Kim, M.J., Lee, S.Y., Cho, H.S., Han, K.H., Lee, J.H.: The Design process based on Scenarios for Smart Clothing. In: Proceedings of The 6th Japan-Korea International Symposium on Kansei Engineering (2005)

8. Hong, J.Y., Chae, H.S., Cho, H.S., Jeon, H.Y., Yim, S.W., Yoo, S., Kim, M.J., Lee, S.Y., Han, K.H., Lee, J.H.: Investigating User Needs for Smart Clothing. In: Proceedings of The 6th Japan-Korea International Symposium on Kansei Engineering (2005)
9. Shea, T., Christine, A.: The global market for wearable computers: The Quest for Killer Applications, Venture development corporation, Massachusetts (2002)
10. http://www.infineon.com
11. http://www.philips.com
12. Fishbein, M., Ajzen, I.: Attitudes and voting behaviour: An application of the theory of reasoned action. In: Stephenson, G. M., Davis, J. M. (eds.) Progress in applied social psychology vol. 1, pp. 95–125 (1981)

A Wearable Computing Environment for the Security of a Large-Scale Factory

Jiung-yao Huang[1] and Chung-Hsien Tsai[2]

[1] National Taipei University, Dept. of CSIE
jyhuang@mail.ntpu.edu.tw
[2] National Central University, Dept. of CSIE
comple@csie.ncu.edu.tw

Abstract. This paper studies the issue of using the wearable computer as a remote sensing device of a large-scale factory. The infrastructure of ubiquitous security environment to realize the remote sensing capability for the security guard is presented in this paper. This paper also scheme out a wearable computing scenario for the security guard under such a ubiquitous security environment. That is, through the help of the wearable computer, the security guard can remotely sensing the security status of each building when he is patrolling a large-scale factory. To achieve a seamless remote sensing environment, we use the wireless AP (Access Point) as the relay between static sensor networks installed inside each building and the mobile sensing device worn on the security guard. The AP enable the wearable computer to seamless receive security status of each building and upload the wearer status to the security control center at the same time. Furthermore, this research adopts the technology of embedded Linux to design a middleware for the wearable computer. The proposed architecture of the wearable computer is scalable, flexible and modular for the mobile computing system. Finally, this paper elaborates a seamless connection approach for the wearable computer within a ubiquitous security environment.

Keywords: Wearable computer, Mobile Computing, Remote sensing, Ubiquitous security environment.

1 Introduction

Pervasive Computing has already become the computing trend of the next century and, hence, the research of wearable computer has attracted significant attention. The famous propaganda slogan of Nokia Company - Connecting People (science and technology come from the human nature all the time) proclaim the interaction among the scientific and technological products and the people. Due to the immature development of the scientific and technological products in the past, there are passive operational relations between the computer and people. With the progress of relevant technology in the semiconductor, the development trend of computer becomes smaller, cheaper and more quickly, even more intelligent[1]. Steve Mann[2] considered the mobile computing as:" it belongs to the personal space, controlled by

J. Jacko (Ed.): Human-Computer Interaction, Part II, HCII 2007, LNCS 4551, pp. 1113–1122, 2007.

the users, and operated interdynamic continuation at the same time (constancy)". In other words, it is "always on and always accessible". The computer that supports this characteristic is called "wearable computer".

2 Related Works

The major technologies to achieve a ubiquitous security environment are the sensor network, the seamless communication, and the wearable computing. This section will briefly outline previous researches on these issues.

Recent researches on Seamless network[3][4] proposed a "fast handoff" and a "smooth handoff" model to accommodate mobility across heterogeneous networks that uses standard protocol (i.e. IP). These researches attempt to seamlessly and automatically handoff the user information from one access point to another. They also minimize handoff-related delays and packet loss, so that the network session can be persistence among different access points. An important application of the seamless communication technology is the sensor network environment. Ardizzone et al.[5] successfully deployed large amount of powerful wireless sensor networks and use the standard IEEE 802.11 (Wi-Fi) radio channel to monitor transient events in physical environments. Ryan et al.[6] uses high level control to cooperate several small UAVs(unmanned aerial vehicles) with sensors to form a mobile sensor network for remote sensing. Their research goal is to execute tasks such as obtaining sensory measurement, border patrol, search and rescue, surveillance, communications relaying, and mapping of hostile territory over a large area. Akyildiz and Kasimoglu[7] proposed a Wireless Sensor and Actor Networks (WSANs) to achieve seamless communication among distributed static sensor networks. WSANs is a group of sensors and actors linked by wireless medium to perform distributed sensing and actuation tasks. In such a network, sensors gather information about the physical world, while actors take decisions and then perform appropriate actions upon the environment, which allows a user to effectively sense and act at a distance.

The wearable computing is the last ingredient of a ubiquitous security environment. As pointed out in[8], a wearable computer should possess the following features: "Portable while operational", "Hands-free use", Sensors, "Proactive", and "Always on, always running". Among these features, "Portable while operational" is the essential distinction between the wearable computer and the legacy computer, such as desktop computer and the laptop. The wearable computer can be used while the wearer is on the move. Hands-free requirement is emphasize on avoid holding any input device while operation. However, some wearable computing applications may use special input devices that tie on user's hand, such as chording-keyboards, dials, and joysticks. For example, Australian Institute of Marine Science (AIMS) designed a so called WetPC[9] underwater computer for research divers to perform underwater activities. To facilitate the diver to manipulate the WetPC, a five buttons KordPad is specially designed for it. The wearable computer may equip with sensors to perceive surrounding information for the user. For example, DeVaul et al.[10] designed MIThril 2003 wearable computing research platform which equipped wide range of body sensors, such as pulse oximetry, respiration, blood pressure, EEG, blood sugar, humidity, and CO2 sensors etc., to monitor wearer's physiological status for biomedical or social network research applications. In 1998, IBM Japan announced a wristwatch computer, called Linux Watch[11], which looks like an ordinary watch but runs Linux, features X11 graphics, and offers Bluetooth wireless connectivity. Linux Watch also embodies accelerometer and vibrator sensors to detect wearer's motion. Bauer et al. present a collaborative wearable system, called NETMAN[12], with remote sensing capability for network maintenance. Their work has proven that remote sensing capability can significantly improve communication and cooperation of highly mobile computer technicians.

The work presented in this paper is similar to NETMAN[13]. However, we go a step further by adapting the concept of WSANs[7] to design the ubiquitous security environment for a large-scale factory. This research use wireless access points to play the role of sensor nodes and the wearable computer is model as the actor of such environment. In the following sections, the feasibility of using the wearable computing technique for the security of a large-scale factory is discussed first. The architecture of the digital security guard system is then presented. Finally, the seamless communication technique to build a Remote Sensing security environment is elaborated last.

3 The Mobile Surveillance Environment

The security of a large-scale factory is an important task to ensure the safety of the employees and goods. With the increasing complexity of the security scenario in the recent years, the security industry has moved towards professionalism nowadays. A large-scale factory always has blind spots of security no matter how many surveillant cameras are installed inside the factory. The security guard always is the ultimate defense of security.

Due to various uncertain conditions on the incident or crime scene, the security guard may himself trap into a dangerous situation when he arrive the scene. When that happens, his professional skill and reaction capability maybe are the only solution for his own safety. If the security guard can acquire a live coverage of the scene before his arrival, he then can has enough time to properly protect himself from any possible injury. As illustrated in Figure 2, the traditional security system only allows the Security-Service Center to collect security messages from the installed sensors on the scene. When an event occur, the guarder in the Security Service center is then responsible for report received messages to the security guard who is rushing to the scene. This architecture may cause serious information delay which, in turn, may consequently put the security guard into a hazard scenario due to the insufficient information.

To solve this problem, this paper proposes a mobile digital surveillance system to provide a pervasive security environment. The proposed architecture integrates installed intelligent security sensors, wireless and wired networks inside the factory, the wearable computer for the security guard, and the Security-Service Center to reduce limitations of the traditional security system. As depicted in Figure 3, with the help of the wireless communication capability, the security guard can acquire live sensors data before he arrive the event scene.

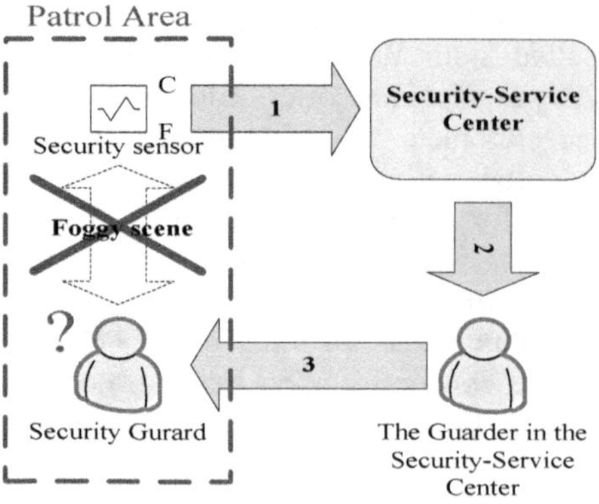

Fig. 1. Information flow of the traditional security system

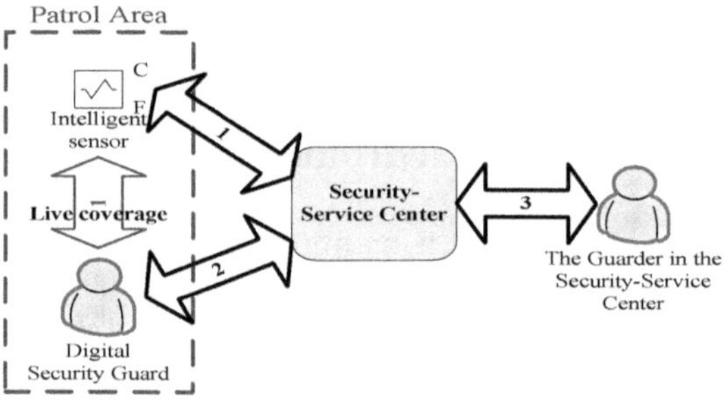

Fig. 2. Information flow of the mobile surveillance system

The proposed system enables the security guard to continuously receive live messages of various sensors from his wearable computer while he is patrolling the factory. Since the security guard always receive live coverage of factory's status, the security guard can have proper response immediately when an event occurred. Furthermore, since the factory is covered with wireless access points, the wearable computer can send the status of the security guard back to the Security-service center in real-time through these wireless/wired networks. By this way, the information delay between the Security-Service Center and the security guard is significantly reduced. In the traditional system, the Security-Service Center and the security guard often have misleading cognition on the event scene due to vocal misinterpretation and insufficient live information. The proposed architecture present in the following sections can solve this problem by providing a pervasive security environment.

4 Digital Security System Architecture

This paper presents architecture of information live exchange between the security guard and the Security-Service Center so that the security guard can response to any event in the factory promptly and safely. It enables the security guard and the Security-Service Center always online while the security guard is patrolling. Meanwhile, the Security-Service Center can aware the location of the security guard at all time. The proposed digital security guard system for a large-scale factor is as illustrated in Figure. 4.

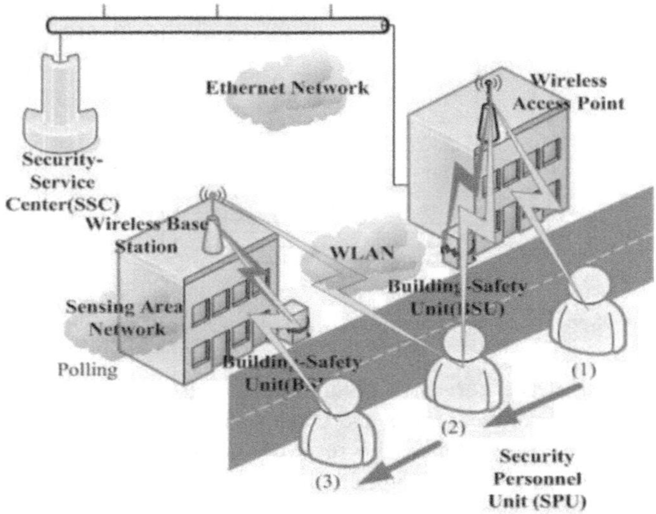

Fig. 3. Scenario of the pervasive security environment

The digital security system mainly composed of three parts: Building-Safety Unit (BSU), Security Personnel Unit (SPU) and Security-Service Center (SSC). Among them, SPU is a wearable computer which equips active communication devices to interact with SSC and BSU in real-time. The SPU constantly transmit the location and status information of the security guard to SSC. The BSU of each building will continuously collect data from various sensors installed inside the building. Meanwhile, BSU will periodically detect if a SPU is entering the coverage of wireless signal of its access point installed outside the building.

As the security guard wearing a SPU approaching a building, his SPU will actively communicate with BSU of that building to obtain detailed security information of that building. At the same time, SPU will also convey the status information of security guard to the SSC through BSU of that building. Hence, BSU of a building play two roles in this scenario. It will transmit the collected security sensors messages of that building to SSC in the background at all time. When it detect a SPU is within the range of its wireless communication, it not only download the security sensors information to SPU but also upload the status information from SPU. The uploaded data is then forward to SSC through wired network between BSU and SSC. That is, BSU act as a relay station between SPU and SSC. Hence, the information flow among SPU, BSU, and SSC can be depicted in Figure 5.

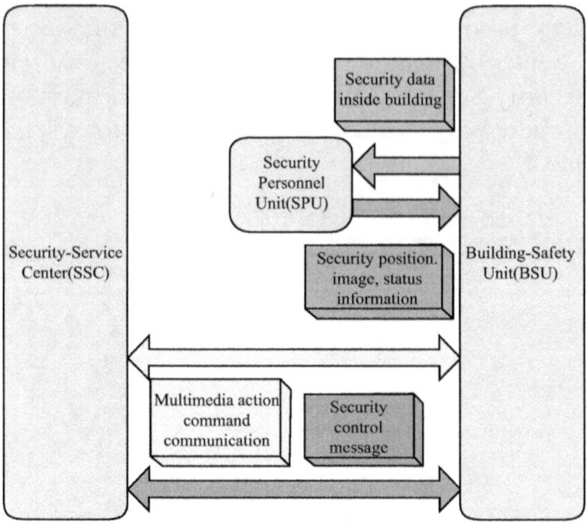

Fig. 4. The message flow of the pervasive security environment

As the research of the pervasive computing has grown vigorously in the recent years, the required sensor techniques and context awareness methodology has already studied[13][14] extensively. Hence, the reset of the paper only focus on the mobile computing of the outdoor environment and present a seamless communication algorithm to provide a pervasive security environment in a large-scale factory.

5 Seamless Communication Network

As illustrated in Figure 4, when the security guard wearing a SPU enters the signal coverage of the Access Point of a building, a message channel will be automatically established among SPU, the Access Point, and BSU. The proposed pervasive security networking environment is based on WLAN (i.e. 802.11a/b/g)[15]. In addition, based upon IEEE 802.11b specification, we define the linking distance between SPU and the Access Point is within 50 meters of signal limitation.

In order to realize the Remote Sensing capability for SPU and SSC, a seamless communication environment is the essential requirement. To achieve this need, both SPU and BSU are designed as multi-thread systems. Furthermore, SPU contains two connection threads, which are Linking Thread and Data Thread, as depicted in Figure 6 and Figure 7. The algorithms for the Linking thread and Data Thread are outlined as follows.

1. Linking Thread: Its functions include detect a potential link, establish a link, and perform handover protocol between SPU and the Access Point, as discussed follows.

   (1) Link detection phase

   This phase will determine which network domain it can carry out the linking? By detecting and examining the signal strength of a access point, SPU can confirm if it is within a signal coverage of a wireless network. When a linking

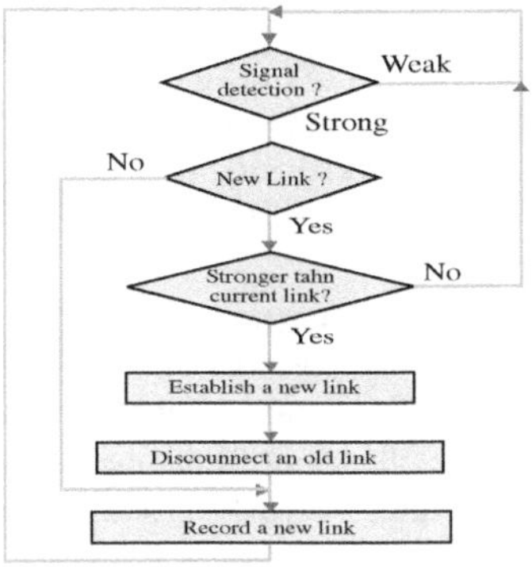

Fig. 5. Linking thread

signal is detected, the linking protocol is then executed. If the signal strength is lower than a predefined strength, it will give up that link. Otherwise, SPU will check whether the received signals come from existing linked access point or not? If not, further check the received signal is stronger than existing one? Follow this procedure, SPU can detect if the security guard is walking away the building of an existing link and moving close to a wireless signal of another building. If SPU detects and approaches another access point, it then begins to establish a new connection link.

(2) Link connection phase

When SPU enters the coverage of an access point, this access point will identify its SSID authentication first. If SPU is an authorized user, this access point will begin to set up a communication channel with SPU.

(3) Handover phase

The foundation of a pervasive security environment is a persistent connection between WLAN and the wearable computer. To achieve this fundamental requirement, we adopt the handover/handoff adaptive technology from CDMA to realize signal handshaking. The handover/handoff mechanism is the key of whether SPU can obtain event alarms in real time. The communication channel switching procedure is divided into two cases: roaming and handover/handoff. Among them, roaming procedure has already defined by IAPP (Inter Access Point Protocol) between a client and the access point. This mechanism allows a client to keep new and old connections simultaneously while switching between two access points. It also maintains the best linking status before switching to ensure not influence client's transmission quality. That is, client can freely move in a large-scale factory within coverage of different access points.

While SPU lost connection to an old access point and establish new connection with another access point, the soft handover or hard handover mechanism is required to accomplish the task. The hard handover approach belongs to Break-Before-Make and its connection feature is easier to be cut off. On the other hand, the soft handover protocol switch communication links under the same frequency, so it can set up a new connection before cut off previous one. Hence, soft handover approach consumes less power but is difficultly to cut off. However, Lin[16] has shown that the performance of the soft handover is better than the hard handover. Rajiv et al.[17] gave the following suggestions to pinpoint delay and improve handover performance:

i. Speed up RA (Router Advertisement).
ii. Increase client-base Caching of RA.
iii. Use soft handover.

Our research adopts soft handover technique to guarantee a persistent communication for SPU to send/receive messages while patrolling among buildings.

2. Data Thread: It is responsible for data exchange between SPU and BSU as shown in Figure. 7. The BSU server has a polling mechanism which provides a robust link with SPU to upload and download status data and security messages, respectively.
   The procedure of the Data Thread can be classified into three phases, which are polling mechanism, Download data, and Upload data.

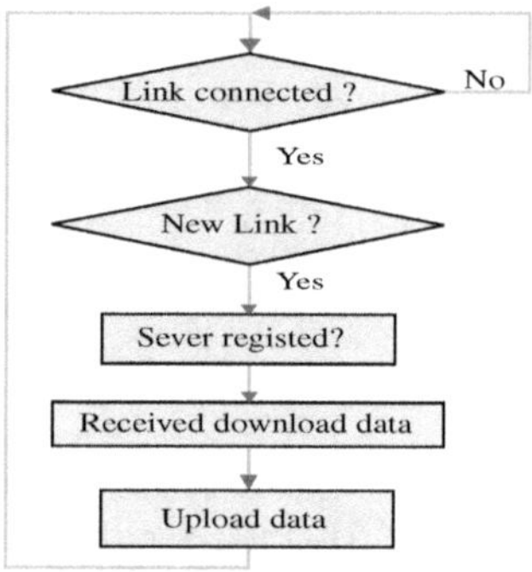

Fig. 6. Data thread

(1) Polling mechanism:
The BSU provides a polling procedure to monitors and communicates its access point. When a SPU is detected and connected, it then tries to assist SPU to login the server.

(2) Download Data:
After SPU login BSU server, server downloads three types of data to SPU. The first one is the detailed security messages of the building. The second type is other buildings' brief security information. Finally, the last one is the control command from SSC. By this way, the security guard can obtain the security status of all buildings within a factory while keep contact with SSC at the same time. In addition, the study of this research combine the specification of IEEE 802.11 MAC (Medium Access Control) PCF (Point Coordination Function) with polling mechanism to provide Real-time Multimedia Downlink[18] capability. The effectiveness of this approach had already proved by Wu[19]. In addition, Guo[20] proposed Connection Manager (CM) and Virtual Connectivity Mechanism to offer Quality of Service (QOS) for End-to-End Operations, connection maintenance, and Subscription/Notification service. The

research by F. Cali et al.[21] pointed out that the available bandwidth is B_0-λL where B_0 is total bandwidth and L is a mean frame size.

(3) Upload Data:
SPU upload the status data of the security guard to BSU, which then forward received data to SSC. This phase enable SSC to fully aware the status of the security guard.

In summary, SPU is a mobile computing device on such pervasive security environment. The seamless communication network enable SPU to actively "talk" to BSUs of each building for its security information while the security guard is patrolling the factory. From this perspective, SPU becomes a seamless communication device in this pervasive environment.

6 Conculsion

The research goal of this paper is to design a pervasive security environment of a large-scale factory. In addition, this paper solves the seamless communication problem of such a pervasive security environment. The proposed system structure integrates the advantage of WLAN, wired network, and the polling mechanism, to achieve a Pervasive, Proactive, Mobility, and Wearable security environment. This research creates a human-centric wearable computing environment to assist user to deal with information that are related to the environment. The presented architecture can significantly improve working efficiency as well as safety of the security guard. Finally, the paper provides a complete solution to integrate the wearable computer into a large-scale factory to achieve the goal of "any time" and "anywhere" complete secure environment.

References

1. Rhodes, B.J.: The wearable remembrance agent: a system for augmented memory. In: First International Symposium on Wearable Computers, pp. 123–128 (1997)
2. Mann, S.: Humanistic Intelligence: WearComp as a new framework for Intelligent Signal Processing. In: Proceedings of the IEEE, vol. 86(11), pp. 2123–2151, (November 1998)
3. Mohammad, A., Chen, A.: Seamless mobility requirements and mobility architectures, Global Telecommunications Conference, 2001. GLOBECOM '01. IEEE, vol. 3, pp. 1950–1956, (November 25-29, 2001)
4. Badache, N., Tandjaoui, D.: A seamless handoff protocol for hierarchical Mobile IPv4. In: 4th International Workshop on Mobile and Wireless Communications Network, pp. 651–655, (September 9-11, 2002)
5. Ardizzone, E., La Cascia, M., Lo Re, G., Ortolani, M.: An integrated architecture for surveillance and monitoring in an archaeological site. In: Proc. ACM Workshop on Video Surveillance and Sensor Networks, pp. 79–86 (2005)
6. Ryan, A., Zennaro, M., Howell, A., Sengupta, R., Hedrick, J.K.: An overview of emerging results in cooperative UAV control. In: Proc. IEEE Conf. on Decision and Control, Atlantis, Paradise Island, Bahamas, December 14-17, 2004 pp. 602–607 (2004)
7. Akyildiz, I.F., Kasimoglu, I.H.: Wireless Sensor and Actor Networks: Research Challenges. Ad. Hoc. Networks Journal (Elsevier) 2(4), 351–367 (2004)

8. Starner, T.: The challenges of Wearable Computing. Part. 1 and 2, Micro, IEEE 21(4), 44–67 (2001)
9. WetPC, [Accessed online 02/07/2007] Available at http://wetpc.com.au/html/technology/wearable.htm
10. DeVaul, R., Sung, M., Gips, J., Pentland, A.:MIThril 2003: Applications and Architecture. In: The 7th IEEE International Symposium on Wearable Computers(ISWC'03), pp. 4–11 (2003)
11. Narayanaswami, et al.: IBMs Linux Watch: The Challenge of Miniaturization, IEEE Computer, pp. 33–41 (January 2002)
12. Bauer, M., Heiber, T., Kortuem, G., Segall, Z.: A Collaborative Wearable System with Remote Sensing. In: Proceedings Second International Symposium on Wearable Computers (ISWC'98) Oct 19-20, 1998 Pittsburgh, PA. pp. 10–17 (1998)
13. Richards, B., Brodersen, R.W.: InfoPad: The Design of a Portable Multimedia Terminal. In: Proceedings of the Mobile Multimedia Conference-2 (April 1995)
14. Dey, A.K., Salber, D., Abowd, G.D.: The Conference Assistant: Combining Context Awareness with Wearable Computing. In: IEEE Third International Symposium on Wearable Computers, pp. 21–28 (1999)
15. P802.11-Wireless LAN Medium Access Control (MAC) and Physical Specifications, IEEE, June 1997[Accessed online 01/18/2005] Available at http://grouper.ieee.org/groups/802/11/index.html
16. Lin, Y.B., Pang, A.C.: Comparing Soft and Hard Handoffs. IEEE Transactions on vehicular technology 49(3), 792–798 (May 2000)
17. Chakravorty, R., Vidales, P., Subramanian, K., Pratt, I., Crowcroft, J.: Performance Issues with Vertical Handovers - Experiences from GPRS Cellular and WLAN Hot-spots Integration. In: Proceeding of the Second IEEE Annual Conference on Pervasive Computing and Communications (PERCOM' 04). [Accessed online 01/23/2005]Available at http://www.cl.cam.ac.uk/coms/
18. Sobrinho, J.L., Krishnakumar, A.S.: Real-Time Traffic over the IEEE 802.11 Medium Access Control Layer, Bell Labs Technical Journal Autumn, pp. 172–187 (1996)
19. Guo, C., Guo, Z., Zhang, Q., Zhu, W.: A seamless and Proactive End-to-End Mobility Solution for Roaming Across Heterogeneous Wireless Net works. IEEE Journal on selected areas in communications 22(5), 834–848 (June 2004)
20. Wu, B.E., Yang, C.S.: Improving the Heterogeneous traffic Performance over wireless LAN IEEE 802.11, Institute of Computer and Information Engineering, National Sun Yat-sen University (2000)
21. Cali, F., Conti, M., Gregori, E.: Dynamic tuning of the IEEE 802.11 protocol to achieve a theoretical throughput limit. IEEE/ACM Trans. on Networking 8, 785–799 (December 2000)

Modification of Plastic Optical Fiber for Side-Illumination

Min Ho Im[1], Eun Ju Park[1], Chang Heon Kim[1], and Moo Sung Lee[2]

[1] Department of Photonics Engineering, Chonnam National University, Gwangju 500-757, Sourth Korea
[2] Faculty of Applied Chemical Engineering and Center for Photonic Materials and Devices, Chonnam National University, Gwangju 500-757, Sourth Korea
imh@moiza.chonnam.ac.kr, jjpeunju@nate.com, moosung@chonnam.ac.kr

Abstract. In this study, we investigated the effect of solvent etching and physical treatment on the sidelighting of POF, even qualitatively. Even though the two were effective in making sidelight POF, the tensile properties of POF were decreased as a result of surface damaged during the treatment. We also investigated how to overcoat side-illuminating POF in order not to be broken during weaving process to make side-illuminating POF fabric. In the view of clarity and interfacial adhesion with POF, AC-100 based on acrylic polymer was chosen for overcoating material. However, tensile strength of notched POF was rather decreased even after overcoating, maybe due to toluene used as diluent, which is also solvent for the core of POF, i.e., PMMA.

Keywords: plastic optical fiber, POF, sidelight, overcoating.

1 Introduction

Plastic or polymer optical fiber (POF) is a fiber type optical waveguide and can transmit optical signal up to several kilometers. Since optical signal is propagated along the fiber by total internal reflection, POF has sheath (or cladding)-core structure and refractive index of cladding should be lower than that of core, i.e., $n_{cladding} < n_{core}$. Usually, poly(methyl methacrylate) (PMMA, n = 1.49) and fluoropolymers with n ~ 1.35 to 1.43 are used as core and cladding polymers, respectively[1,2].

Compared to silica used as core material for glass optical fiber, PMMA is very ductile and cheap. Therefore, it is possible to make optical fiber with large core size, which is easy to connect. Although POF has such advantages, the use of POF in data communication is rather restricted to the automotive field, mainly due to very high optical loss of POF at the telecommunication wavelength range of 1300 ~ 1600 nm. This is originated from the chemical structure of PMMA, which contains C-H bonds. Their harmonic waves are a main cause for the loss.

The main role of optical fibers including POF is to transmit light or optical signal to a specified spot. However, if we apply physical or chemical treatment to cladding of POF, the light leaks out from damaged spot and we can use such sidelight POF for decorations or lighting[3,4,5].

J. Jacko (Ed.): Human-Computer Interaction, Part II, HCII 2007, LNCS 4551, pp. 1123–1129, 2007.

In this study, as a preliminary work on the development of illuminating POF fabric, we investigated the effect of physical surface abrasion and solvent etching of POF on the side-illumination. Also, we investigated how to overcoat side-illuminating POF in order not to be broken during the weaving process to make the side-illuminating POF fabric.

2 Experimental

2.1 Materials

The POFs used in this study were a step index type with the diameter of 1.0mm and 0.25mm and obtained from Nuvitech Co., Ltd, Korea. The core and cladding materials of them are PMMA and a fluoropolymer, respectively, but the details on the cladding have been unknown.

Etching solvents for the chemical treatment are chosen from the solubility test of POF. First, POF was immersed in various solvents for specified periods and then changes in the weight were monitored. Ethyl acetate (EA) was chosen as an etchant, because the weight loss of POF in it was most significant.

Three different types of coating agents were chosen as overcoating materials. They are based on silicone (S-830), acrylic (AC-100) and urethane (UC-100) polymer, respectively and obtained from Nambang CNA Co., Ltd., Korea. Diluents for them were toluene, but their concentration has been unknown.

Poly(vinylidene fluoride-co-hexafluoropropylene) (PVdF-co-HFP) were obtained from Aldrich and used as model polymer for evaluating the interfacial adhesion between POF and overcoating materials.

2.2 Chemical/Physical Treatment of POF

Chemical etching of POF was done by spraying EA two times at 20-minutes intervals. Physical treatments of POF were done by two different methods: by mechanically notching or by gently rubbing with sandpaper. Mechanical notches were applied at intervals of 0.5 cm on bare POF.

2.3 Characterization

The degree of damage applied on the surface of POF was monitored using a field-emission scanning electron microscope (FE-SEM, Hitachi S-4700, Japan) at 15.0 kV or an optical microscope. The intensity of the leak light was measured using a photo detector (Advantest Q8221 optical multi power meter, Japan). A laser diode with the wavelength of 650nm was used as the light source.

Tensile properties of POF, bare or chemically and/or physically treated, were measured using an AGS-500D mechanical tester (Shimadzu Co., Ltd., Kyoto, Japan). The grip distance of the equipment and the elongation speed were fixed at 100 mm and 100 mm/min, respectively. At least five specimens were tested and average values were used for discussion.

The adhesion of overcoating materials with PVdF-co-HFP was determined according to a cross hatch cut tape test (ASTM D3359-02). The specimens for the adhesion test were prepared as follows. First, PVdF-co-HFP substrates with the thickness of 1 mm were prepared using a Carver press at 200°C and then melt-annealed at 170°C for 30 min in order to smoothen the surface. Overcoating solutions were directly spin-coated on the PVdF-co-HFP substrates. The thickness of overcladding was controlled to be 5 μm by adjusting rpm of the spin coater.

3 Results and Discussion

Figure 1 shows the variation in the degree of dissolution of bare POF with the type of the solvent and immersion time. In contrast to chloroform and acetone which are good solvents for PMMA, the dissolution rate of POF in EA is almost linear with immersion time. Moreover, boiling point of EA is 77°C and higher than 66°C of THF. Considering the solubility and volatility, EA is chosen as the etchant for chemical treatment in this study.

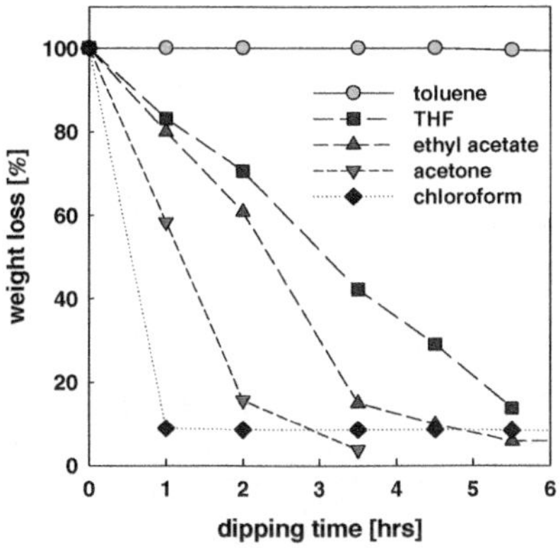

Fig. 1. Etching rate of POF in various solvents. The diameter of POF is 1.0mm.

Figure 2 shows SEM images of POFs, physically and/or chemically treated for the sidelight. As shown in Figure 2(b), core as well as cladding was damaged by rubbing with sandpaper. When the damaged surface was sprayed with EA, the surface was smoothened and the roughness of the surface was reduced, but the cladding layer was not affected by EA sprayed. This indicates that EA is solvent only for PMMA and thus selectively dissolves core. The selective solubility of EA is clearly seen in Figure 2(c). Although cladding layer was not dissolved by EA, the interface between core and cladding was delaminated by EA infiltrated into the interface through cracks. It is expected that the light propagated along core will be emitted at the area damaged by the physical and/or chemical treatment.

Figure 3 is the images of side-illuminating POF arrays. In order to make the light be emitted at specified area, a part of the array was masked before treatments. As expected, the light was emitted at the unmasked area. However, as shown in Figures 3(c) and 3(d), in the case of being sprayed with EA the boundary of the leak light was

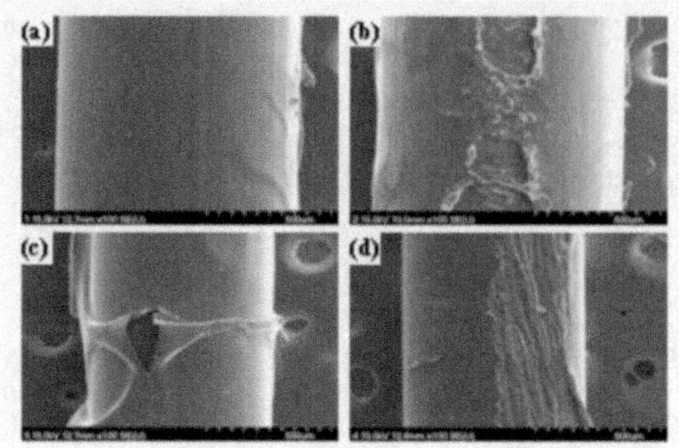

Fig. 2. SEM images of POFs: (a) bare; (b) physically rubbed with sandpaper; (c) etched with EA; (d) physically scratched and then solvent-etched, respectively

not sharp compared to Figure 3(b). This is because the solvent sprayed flows along the fiber during drying and makes the boundary unclear. It is noteworthy that chemically treated POF shows smoother side-illuminating effect than physically scratched one.

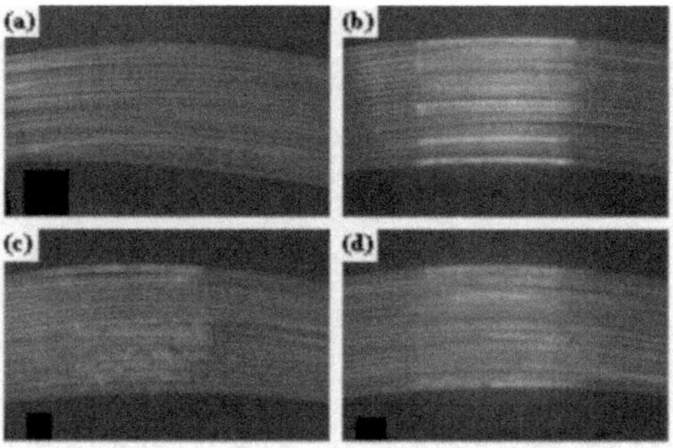

Fig. 3. POF arrays showing sidelighting effect: (a) bare; (b) physically rubbed with sandpaper; (c) etched with EA; (d) physically scratched and then solvent-etched, respectively

Although the methods applied in this study, even though only qualitatively, were effective in making sidelight POF or POF fabrics, physical, especially mechanically properties of POF are dramatically reduced by the damage. In some cases, it is impossible to make POF fabrics with the damaged POF, because it cannot endure the tension applied to the POF during weaving. As shown in Figure 4, surface-treated POFs have lower tensile strength than bare one and show brittle fracture. POF rubbed with sandpaper and then sprayed with EA shows the lowest value. For the POF physically damaged, the scratches applied on the surfaces act as stress concentrator and thus cracks are propagated from them, making ductile bare POF brittle. This result clearly shows the need to enhance the mechanical properties of surface-treated POF as tough as it can endure the tension during manufacturing the POF fabric.

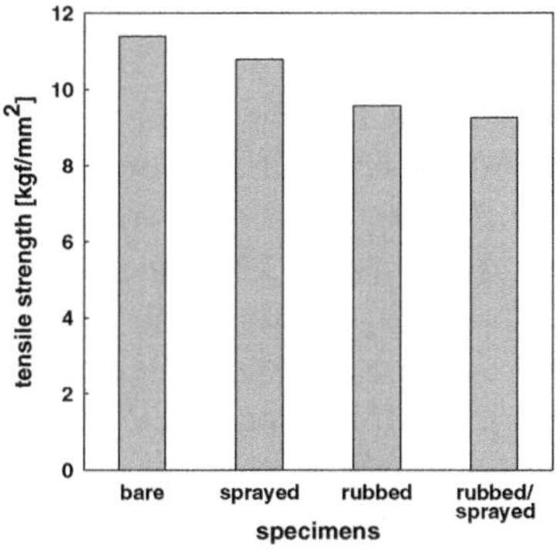

Fig. 4. Tensile strength of surface-treated POFs

As one of the strategies for enhancing mechanical properties of sideligt POF, we attempted to overcoat surface treated POF with coating agents, which have been used for adhesives[6]. As prerequisites for the purpose, they should have good adhesion with POF, especially with cladding, and change fracture mechanism of surface-treated POF from brittle to ductile fracture. Preliminary results on the interfacial adhesion between coating materials chosen as overcoating candidates and PVdF-co-HFP as the model polymer for cladding of POF are shown in Figure 5.

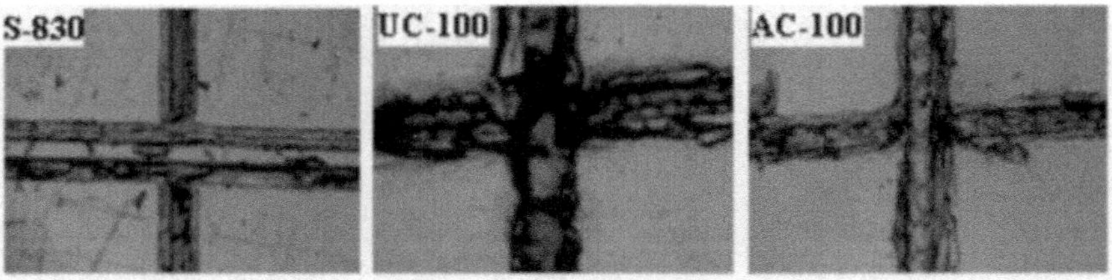

Fig. 5. Optical micrographs showing the interfacial adhesion between the coating materials and PVdF-co-HFP

From the cross-hatched test area, UC-100 based on urethane polymers has graded to show the lowest adhesion to PVdF-co-HFP and thus was eliminated from candidates. From the extent of the side-illumination of overcoated POF (Figure 6), it

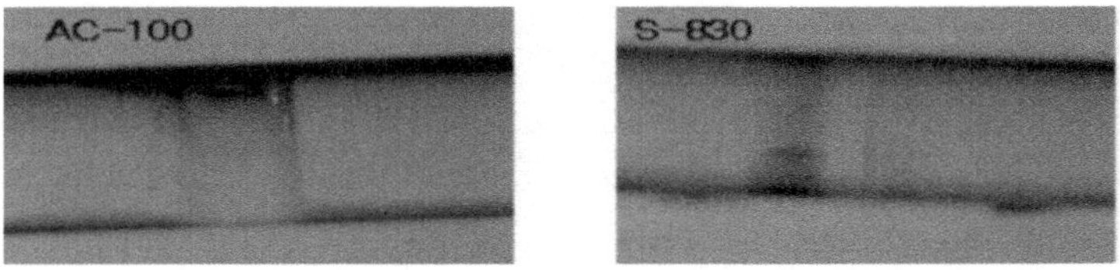

Fig. 6. Optical micrographs of sidelight POFs, overcoated with AC-100 and S-830

is found that S-830 do not offer the sufficient side-illumination, maybe due to turbidity.

The tensile strength of overcoated POFs is shown in Figure 7. Contrary to the expectation, the tensile strength of notched POF was rather slightly decreased after overcoating with AC-100 or S-830. There are two possibilities for the unexpected results. First, overcoating material should be penetrated into cracks of notched area and completely fill the cracks during coating. The conditions applied in this study may not be appropriate for such coating steps. Second, toluene used as dilluent of coating materials is solvent for PMMA, not for PVdF-co-HFP. Since the depth of crack is deeper than the thickness of the cladding layer, toluene dissolves partially core of PMMA during overcoating and thus makes overcoated POF brittle, similarly to the results of Figure 4. The work on overcoating using non-solvent of PMMA for diluent is in progress and the results will be reported within near future.

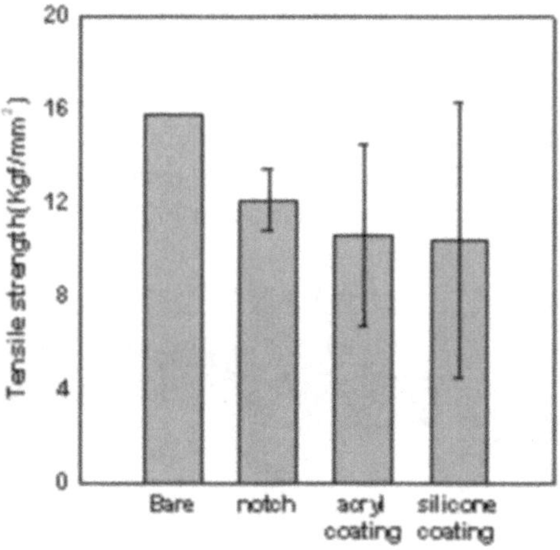

Fig. 7. Tensile strength of overcoated POF

4 Summary

In this study, we investigated the effect of solvent etching and physical treatment for the sidelighting of POF. Event though the two were effective in making sidelight POF, the tensile properties of POF were decreased as a result of the surface damaged during the treatment. In the view of the clarity and the interfacial adhesion with POF, AC-100 based on acrylic polymer was chosen for the overcoating material. However, the tensile strength of notched POF was rather decreased even after overcoating.

Acknowledgments. The authors thank the Ministry of Commerce, Industry, and Energy (MOCIE), Korea for financial support.

References

1. Marcou, J., Robiette, M., Bulabois, J.: Plastic Optical Fibers: Practical Applications. John Wiley & Sons, New York (1997)
2. Daum, W., Krauser, J., Zamzow, P.E., Ziemann, O.: POF: Polymer Optical Fibers for Data Communication. Springer, Berlin (2002)
3. Harlin, A., Myllymaki, H., Grahn, K.: Polymeric Optical Fibers and Future Prospects in Textile Integration, AUTEX Research J. 2(3), 132–143 (2002)
4. Harlin, A., Makinen, M., Vuorivirta, A.: Development of Polymeric Opticl Fibre Fabrics as Illumination Elements and Textile Displays, AUTEX Research J. 3(1), 1–8 (2003)
5. Koncar, V.: Optical Fiber Fabric Displays, Optics & Photonics News, April, pp. 40–44 (2005)
6. Rayss, J., Wibomski, J., Luzinow, I., Voronow, A., Minko, S.: Effect of Polyacrylate Binding Layers on Adhesion of UV-Cured Epoxyacrylate Protective Coating on Optical Fibers, J. Appl. Polym. Sci. 67(11), 1913–1923 (1997)

Exploring Possibilities of ECG Electrodes for Bio-monitoring Smartwear with Cu Sputtered Fabrics

Seeun Jang[1], Jayoung Cho[1], Keesam Jeong[2], and Gilsoo Cho[1]

[1] Department of Clothing and Textiles, Yonsei University, Seoul 120-749, Korea
{seeun,jycho,gscho}@yonsei.ac.kr
[2] Department of Medical Information System, Yong-in Songdam College, Yong-in 449-710, Korea
ksjeong@ysc.ac.kr

Abstract. This article deals with a way of developing E-textiles using sputtering method and their possibilities as ECG electrodes for a bio-monitoring smartwear. As the market of smartwear is growing, researches toward E-textiles become more important. Among various ways of providing conductivity on textiles, we selected sputtering technology. Through the sputtering, we developed E-textiles deposited with thin Cu layer on the surface of the fabrics with thickness of about 2 micrometer. Then we measured the electrical resistances, examined their performances as ECG(electrocardiogram) electrodes and compared ECG signal measured with general AgCl electrodes. In result, ECG signals from Cu sputtered electrodes showed big potentials as textile-based electrodes by showing little difference in its signals compared with commonly used AgCl electrodes.

Keywords: bio-monitoring, smartwear, E-textiles, sputtering, Electro-cardiogram (ECG).

1 Introduction

In the last decade, personal computing technologies are pervasive in western society. As technologies are developed rapidly, electronic devices become increasingly mobile, portable, and accessible [1]. This makes people want to carry digital applications in everywhere at anytime by integrating them into clothing. We call this kind of clothing as smartwear.

In present time, the demand for smartwear increases in various fields such as military, medical, entertainment and daily life purposes. Among them, bio-monitoring is used fairy extensively in research and in medical field. However, aside from pure medical applications, bio-monitoring provides a method to observe unconscious physiological changes [1], so the users can get their physiological signals constantly not just in a certain moment.

Through high-technology in textile field, the development of E-textiles (Electronic textiles) is accelerated, giving a new additional value to the traditional textile industry

J. Jacko (Ed.): Human-Computer Interaction, Part II, HCII 2007, LNCS 4551, pp. 1130–1137, 2007.

[1]. E-textiles, which have electrical characteristics and textile properties simultaneously, are considered as a new concept of higher value-added textiles. Therefore, for developing smartwear, using E-textiles are inevitable.

As a way of developing E-textiles, there are several ways to produce them. Textiles can have conductivity through metallic and optical fibers, conductive yarns, fabrics and coatings [2]. The most common way to make E-textiles is to use metallic yarns made of copper, nickel or silver through weaving or knitting conductive yarns while they are fabricated [3]. However, this has several defects such as limitation on tailoring it because of the restricted electrical pass and difficulties in using general sewing machines.

To overcome these problems, conductive coating technology is used in this study. Through the sputtering process, textile materials can have good conductivity without significantly altering existing substrate properties such as density, flexibility, and handle [2]. Sputtering process, which is widely used in semi-conductor industry, is a vacuum process used to deposit very thin metal films on substrates. By sputtering, fabric substrates can have an even coating layer with good adhesion [4]. However, so far very few studies on sputtered fabrics with metal ingredients have been done.

Therefore, the aim of this paper is first, to propose a way to make highly conductive textiles by metal sputtering and second, to measure their electrical performance for transmission lines and finally, to explore possibilities as ECG (electrocardiogram) electrodes for bio-monitoring smartwear.

2 Experimental

2.1 Specimen

As specimen, commercially available nylon fabrics were selected. On the back of the specimen, Polyurethane (PU) layer is treated. PU treatment, extensively used in water-resistant or water-repellent treatment for sportswear, was considered to give a better surface condition for metal deposition by covering its bumpy construction. Therefore, a thin metal layer was expected to be attached uniformly on the fabric substrate. The specimen is cut into the size of 10cm X 10cm in order to meet the dimension of the sputter's chamber. The characteristics of specimen are shown in Table 1.

Table 1. Characteristics of specimen

Composition	Nylon 100%
Finishing	PU Laminating
Fabric construction	Plain weave
Thickness, *mm*	0.117
Weight, g/m^2	101
Yarn size	Warp: 40D, Weft: 40D
Fabric count, $inch^2$	126 X 115

2.2 Sputtering Method

Sputtering is a physical process whereby atoms in a solid target material are ejected into the gas phase due to impact of the material by energetic ions [5]. During the sputtering, the coating material which is called target is ejected atom by atom and is collected in the surface of the fabric, creating a thin metal layer. A wide range of textile substrates can be coated in this manner. In addition, different metals, alloys, or oxides can be mixed or layered in a single application to create specialized coatings for specific applications [6].

For manufacturing highly conductive fabrics, sputtering was performed in a vacuum chamber by applying a high voltage across a low-pressure argon gas. During sputtering, energized ions stroked Cu target, and a textile substrate can get conductivity creating a thin Cu layer by coating with Cu atoms. Figure 1 shows a coating process by sputtering.

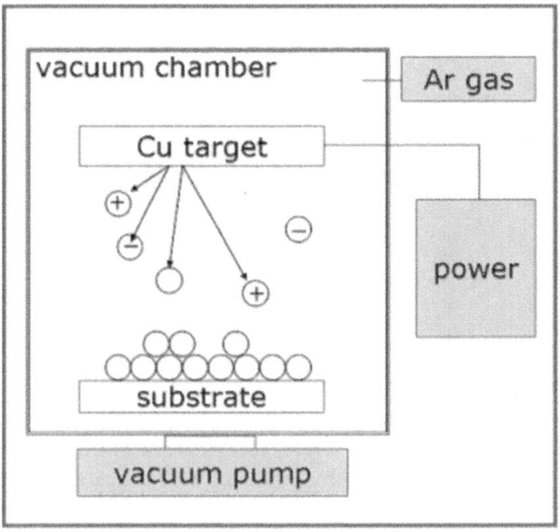

Fig. 1. Diagram of sputtering process

However, because textiles have much different characteristics compared with commonly used substrates in sputtering process, the condition of experiments such as discharge power, processing time as well as temperature should be set suitably for the fabrics. Therefore, before performing sputtering on the textiles, several matters should be considered in order to obtain desirable outcomes. If not, the fabric substrates are sometimes burned due to temperature or discharge power and losing their flexibilities due to the thickness of deposition layer. After several pretests, we set the experimental conditions as below.

Table 2. Conditions of the experiments

Target	Cu
Discharge gas	Ar
Discharge power	300W
Vacuum discharge	10^{-3} Torr
Discharge time	20 min
Discharge temperature	40℃

2.3 Measurement of Electrical Resistance

To investigate the performance of developed E-textile, the electrical resistance was measured by a Multimeter (Agilent 34401A, U.S.A.). Rectangular pieces sized by 9cm X 3cm were taken from sputtered specimen, and then the electrical resistances were measured from both ends of the taken pieces. We measured the electrical resistance of each sample three times and then averaged it.

2.4 SEM Analysis

For observing and comparing the appearance of the specimen before and after sputtering, SEM(scanning electron microscope) analysis was performed. SEM images were taken with magnifications of 300 by HITACHI S-4200, Japan.

2.5 ECG Test

In order to explore the possibility as ECG electrodes for bio-monitoring smartwear, we compared ECG signals obtained from the sputtered electrodes with commercially available AgCl electrodes (Biopac EL503, U.S.A). Before the ECG test, a subject rested for 5 minutes while sitting on an armchair. Then, the electrodes were placed onto both wrists and one right ankle with two kinds of electrodes, sputtered and AgCl ones. The right-ankle electrode was used as a reference. To minimize the difference of signals between electrodes, AgCl electrodes were attached right next to the sputtered ones.

The ECG signals from two kinds of electrodes were simultaneously acquired. The data of ECG signals was collected by Biopac MP150 (U.S.A.) and analyzed by AcqKnowledge V 3.7.3.

3 Results

3.1 Surface Observation

Before SEM analysis, we observed the surfaces of specimen before and after sputtering. As shown in Figure 2, we found that the specimen laminated with PU layer before sputtering (Figure 2, left) was deposited with Cu on the surface of specimen(Figure 2, right) through their color changes from colorless to Cu's own color, metallic pinkish red.

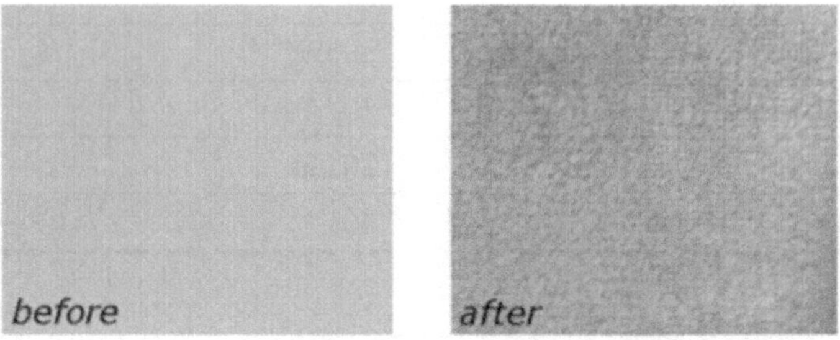

Fig. 2. Optical images of specimen before and after sputtering

For the detailed observation, cross-sectional images were taken by SEM. As shown in Figure 3, the specimen before sputtering (Figure 3, left) was deposited with a thin Cu layer quite evenly on the surface of PU laminating layer (Figure 3, right). Figure 4 showed a more detailed image of deposition status. Because most fabrics were made by crossing weft and warp, the surfaces of the fabrics are uneven. By covering bumpy construction of the fabric with PU laminating layer, even coating layer can be archived, making a flat geometric surface. The thickness of Cu layer was about 2μm

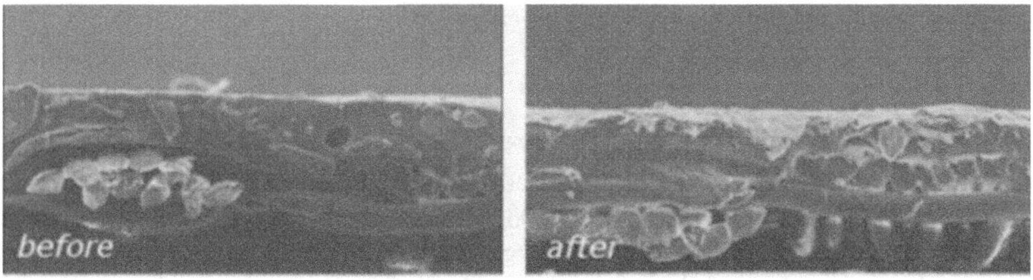

Fig. 3. SEM images of the fabric before and after sputtering X 300

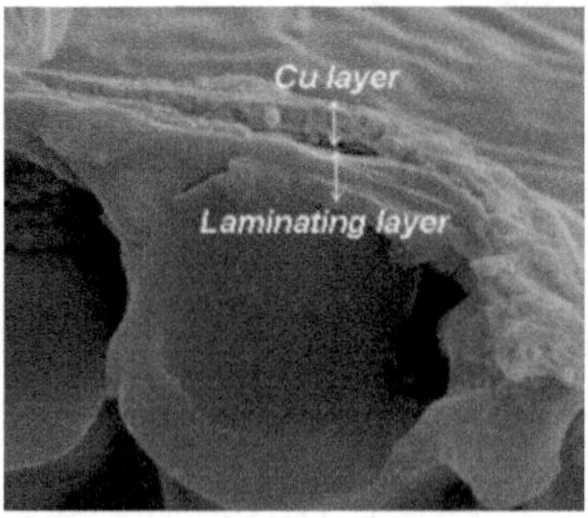

Fig. 4. Detailed SEM images of the specimen X 3,000

Flexibility of the sputtered fabric was also investigated. As a simple test, we just rolled the sputtered fabric around a pencil. As presented in figure 5, we found Cu coated fabric through sputtering process was very flexible.

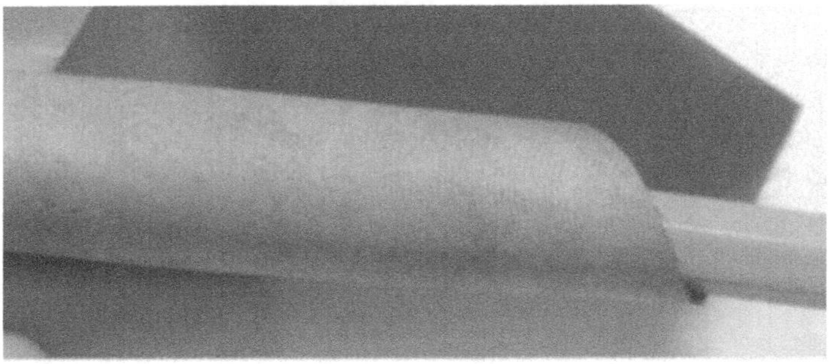

Fig. 5. Flexibility of sputtered fabrics

3.2 Electrical Resistances of the Cu Sputtered Fabric

For investigating the performance of developed E-textile, we measured the electrical resistance of the sputtered sample. Generally, the higher electrical resistance represents, the lower conductivity shows. We measured the electrical resistance of developed E-textile three times, and then averaged it. The average resistance of specimen was 0.316Ω/sq. According to the J. Cho's study [7], which was investigated about performances of elecrolessly Cu/Ni plated polyester fabric as E-textiles, the output signals of the textile-based transmission lines were almost the same as the one of Cu cables even with the resistance of 5.063Ω/sq. Because the lower electrical resistance means the better conductivity, it can be inferred conductive textiles obtained from sputtering process have potentials to be used as simple transmission lines.

3.3 A Test for the Application of Cu Sputtered Fabrics as ECG Electrodes

To explore the performances of developed E-textiles for textile electrodes, ECG signal was collected. From the ECG signal test, the acquired signals of both AgCl and the Cu sputtered textile electrodes represented similar wave patterns as shown in Figure 6. However, the Cu sputtered electrodes showed wider range of voltage than the AgCl electrodes did. This is attributable the adhesion area of the textile electrodes was larger than the AgCl electrodes which were 1cm in diameter while textile ones were 1.5cm X 3cm. In addition, this is perhaps that Cu layers of the sputtered electrodes were directly contacted to the skin while AgCl ones had sponges which might increase contact resistance between skin and electrodes.

4 Conclusion

As a way of developing E-textiles for bio-monitoring smartwear, we investigated sputtering technology and explored the performances of sputtered fabrics. After

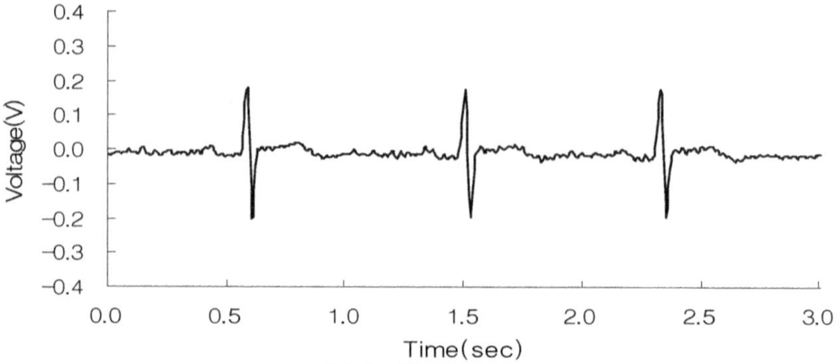

(a) AgCl electrodes

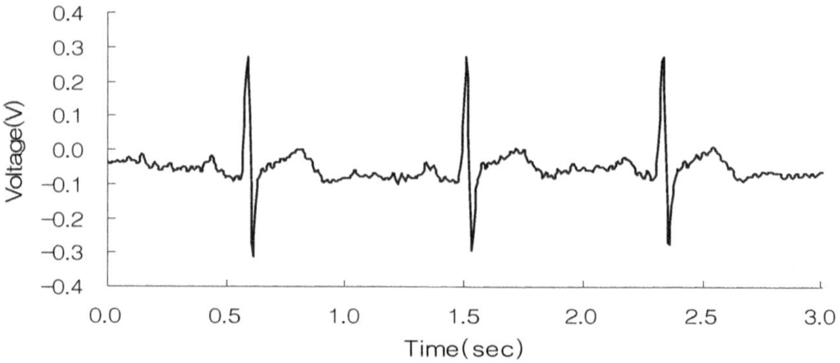

(b) Cu sputtered textile electrodes

Fig. 6. Comparison of ECG signal with AgCl and textile electrodes

sputtering Cu on a fabric substrate, we examined the appearance, electrical performance, and applications as ECG electrodes. Consequently, we found that the surfaces of textiles were uniformly covered with a thin layer of Cu because PU laminating treatment was covered uneven surfaces of fabrics. The color of sputtered fabric was metallic pink which is Cu's own color. Moreover developed fabric had flexibilities also. As a result of compared with prior study, the electrical resistances showed the capability for simple transmission lines. In addition, their performance as ECG electrodes represented the potential substitute as E-textiles for bio-monitoring smartwear.

This paper suggests a strong implication of a new way of manufacturing flexible and highly conductive textiles and applications as textile electrodes for bio-monitoring smartwear. However, durability issues remain to be explored more deeply. Furthermore, coating material beside Cu also needs to be considered for intimateness to the human body.

For further studies, different substrates and deposition methods such as evaporation or ion plating as well as other metal ingredients need to be considered to develop conductive textiles for various purposes' applications. Furthermore, if the patterning methods are to be introduced in sputtering process, fully textile-based bio-monitoring smartwear will be developed in near future which electrodes and circuits are constructed with all fabrics.

Acknowledgements. The support of Korea MOCIE for funding is gratefully acknowledged.

References

1. Dunne, L.E.: The Design of Wearable Technology Addressing the Human-device Interface through Functional Apparel Design, Master Thesis of Cornell University (2004)
2. Meoli, D., May-Plumlee, T.: Interactive Electronic Textile Development: A Review of Technologies. Journal of Textile and Apparel Technology and Management 2(2), 1–12 (2002)
3. Merritt, C.R., et al.: Electrical Characterization of Transmission Lines on Nonwoven Textile Substrates, Material Research Society Symposium Proceeding (2005)
4. Cho, J., Moon, J., Jeong, K., Cho, G.: An Exploration of Electrolessly Cu/Ni Plated Polyester Fabrics as E-Textiles. In: Proceedings of the 9th International Symposium on Wearable Computers, pp. 206–207 (2005)
5. http://en.wikipedia.org/wiki/Sputtering
6. Siefert, W.: Anodic Arc Evaporation-A New Vacuum-Coating Technique for Textiles and Files. Journal of Coated Fabrics 23, 31 (1993)
7. Lekpittaya, P., Yanumet, N., Grady, B.P., O'Rear, E.A: Resistivity of Conductive Polymer-Coated Fabric. Journal of Applied Polymer Science 92, 2629–2636 (2004)
8. Scilingo, E., et al.: Performance Evaluation of Sensing Fabrics for Monitoring Physiological and Biomechnical Variables. IEEE Transactions on Information Technology in Biomedicine 9(3), 345–352 (2005)
9. De Rossi, D., Carpi, F., Lorussi, D., Mazzoldi, A., Paradiso, R., Pasquale, E.: Electroactive Fabrics and Wearable Biomonitoring Devices. AUTEX Research Journal 3(4), 180–185 (2003)

Development of Educational Program for Quick Response System on Textile and Fashion E-Business

Kyung-Yong Jung[1], Jong-Hun Kim[2], Jung-Hyun Lee[2], and Young-Joo Na[3]

[1] School of Computer Information Engineering, Sangji University
kyjung@sangji.ac.kr
[2] Department of Computer Science & Engineering Inha University
jhkim@hci.inha.ac.kr, jhlee@inha.ac.kr
[3] Department of Clothing and Textiles, Inha University
youngjoo@inha.ac.kr

Abstract. It is normal to develop fashion product through predicting purchase needs of consumers in Textile and Fashion industry. If failed in the prediction, that is, if consumers would not purchase the product, there comes problems that discount sale is inevitable or stock increases tremendously. Otherwise, Quick Response System allows that the company observes the consumer's needs consistently and establishes manufacture schedule rapidly so that they could prohibit the products unnecessarily stocked. Consumer's preference is collected and analyzed through the data generated by POS system, and this is provided to the related manufacturer through network in real time, so that the manufactures could merchandise rapidly, produce and deliver the products according to the consumer's need. Thus, this study developed POS system-education program; the merchandising of apparel product by prediction and confirmation and shorten product-lead time; the cooperative system among apparel company, retailers and manufacturer, through Internet Technology in Textile and Fashion Industry.

Keywords: Quick response system, Consumer's needs, POS-educational program, Textile and fashion e-business.

1 Introduction

It is necessary for us educators to show students 'computerization of Fashion and Textile industry' and 'Quick response system' in correspondence with IT era. This is not only educating 'handling computers' but also 'growing the QR manager or the integrating director' in 21st century multi-media and IT fashion-textile industry. They would understand the change of time and speed, and feel world market's needs[1]. Academic school have followed far behind the IT fashion-textile industry in terms of non-practical works or focusing only principles. But today classes need to follow the rapid changes of the environment of industry, help students to adapt to versatility power according to the needs of contemporary society and technology. They need to know the QR and IT connection between fashion- textile companies, B to B, or P to P, P to B, Etc. The world has widened the global sourcing, e-business and QR system

J. Jacko (Ed.): Human-Computer Interaction, Part II, HCII 2007, LNCS 4551, pp. 1138–1146, 2007.

which became the must-have asset. The students have a lot of knowledge, technique, theory, but they are weak in creating a new system, prospective view on the industry and prediction. Thus, this program benchmarks 'educating experts + establishing global SCM' not only the education of CAD/CAM skills. This program contains the upstream–downstream multi works which are the processes among 4 companies: apparel company, textile company, sewing company, and retailers. Thus this study is aimed to the development of the educational program of QR system of fashion and Textile industry. This is multimedia tool for them to work with at the lab. They would understand the mechanism, relationships, processes and steps, communications, and forms and works in detail of textile fashion industry.

2 Process of the Quick Response System

The life cycles of the fashion-textile products are very short. However, lead-time from planning to production and sales is very long. And all produced products seem to be sold or unsold. Therefore the apparel industry increases the production that can actively cope with consumers' responses, which is called the market responses, and diminishes the burden of inventories. Figure 1 demonstrates the process of the Quick Response System proposed in this study.

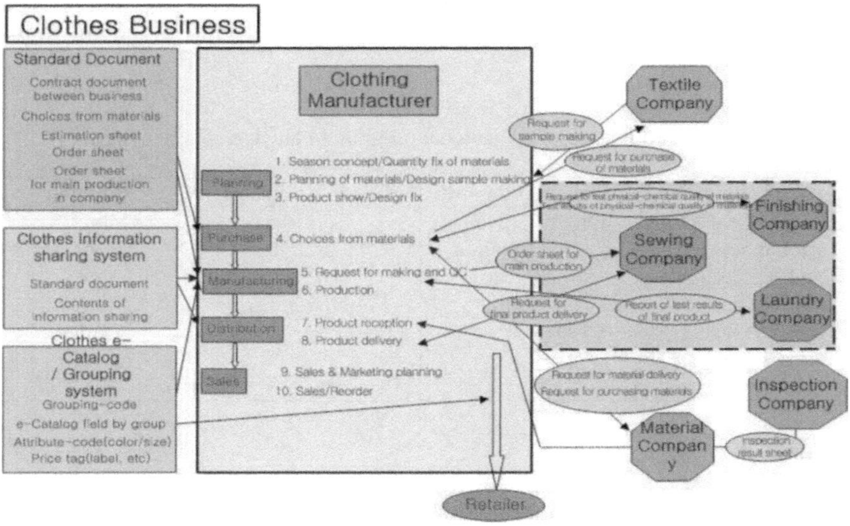

Fig. 1. Process of the quick response system

As a production process, a Web based production management system that can efficiently identify such processes as textile procurement, warehousing, stocking, and production progress is needed. This system enables suppliers, manufacturers, distributors, and retailers to share information, beyond the limitation as individual companies, and even allows small and medium sized companies to conduct international trading with their clients. The proposed quick product planning system consists of server and client module. The computer uses the IBM eServer X206, 2.8GHz, 512MB RAM, 80GB, and the algorithms use MS-Visual Studio C++ 6.0, ASP (IIS 10.0), MS-SQL Server 2000.

The user who has an access to the quick product planning system saves information in each table of database by processing the concerned session. The saved information can be modified and deleted using the administrator's tool. By making the saved designs database by each item, they can contain various and essential information related to the plans of new fashion designs. The database of the designs can be valuable for new idea conception in the process of being built up and observed each year. When the designs adequately created in line with fashion trends by apparel companies, sewing factories, and textile companies are diagramed and made database by item, not only time to design new products and expense is saved, but design quality and level can also be rapidly improved.

3 Quick Product Planning System

The proposed quick product planning system in this study includes the processes ranging from merchandising, production plan, production, logistics, to sales. The proposed system has been suitably configured to enhance the understanding of process. And the use of the system became visually convenient by reorganizing it into an apparel company, a sewing company, a textile company, and stores. Table 1 exhibits the composition as an apparel company, a sewing company, a textile company, and stores.

Table 1. Four steps of educational program in quick response system

Apparel Company	Sewing Company	Textile Company	Stores
Confirm Final Styles Request for sample making Process Status Cost Account Store Management	Order for Main Cost Estimation Product List Inspection Delivery	Confirm Final Styles Textile List Production Cost	Store A Store B Store C Store D Outlet

3.1 Apparel Module

The apparel module can be classified into such sub-domains as a product show, final styles, request for sample making, cost account, process status, and outlet store management. Here, domains have their own screen pages, respectively. All these are organically connected as well. In a real product show, merchandisers and designers select the designs to be produced as samples among many designs in several occasions of meetings. However, the proposed system in this study enables a user to enter his/her ID/password, go directly to the product show page, and enter evaluation scores for each style. Also, the evaluation for each style becomes possible online from a long distance. Figure 2 shows the page of confirm stage in the item of shirt styles and the order sheet for main production in the apparel module.

As shown in Figure 2 (left), online voting is allowed in the limited score range from 1 to 5 in the product show page concerning the evaluation of each style, since there are liberal or conservative people in relation to the evaluation scores. The design styles that received more than average score are selected as the final styles. All the participants select "Enter" in the participant's selection section, and enter their names. Then they give evaluation scores by clicking on "Evaluation" button. If the concerned PC's IP and evaluator's name are the same, the system takes a measure not to build up evaluation with dual evaluation. When an evaluator completes evaluation and clicks on "Finish," the evaluator is automatically logged out. The page of the product show is arranged by item (skirt, slacks, one- piece dress, jumper, jacket, shirt, blouse, etc.), by year (2006, and 2007), by season (spring, summer, autumn, and winter), by gender, and all these are reconfigured with new windows.

In the job instruction for final styles shown in Figure 2(right), item number, order number, material, quantity, factory, work period, style diagram (main label, care label), raw and subsidiary material use sections (dimensions of material code name, required quantity per session, loss, delivered quantity) are entered. While drawing up job instruction for each style, the instruction can be reconfirmed by another worker. When a user clicks on the concerned page, it is opened repeatedly. In other words, the drawn up job instruction can be opened again in order to confirm it.

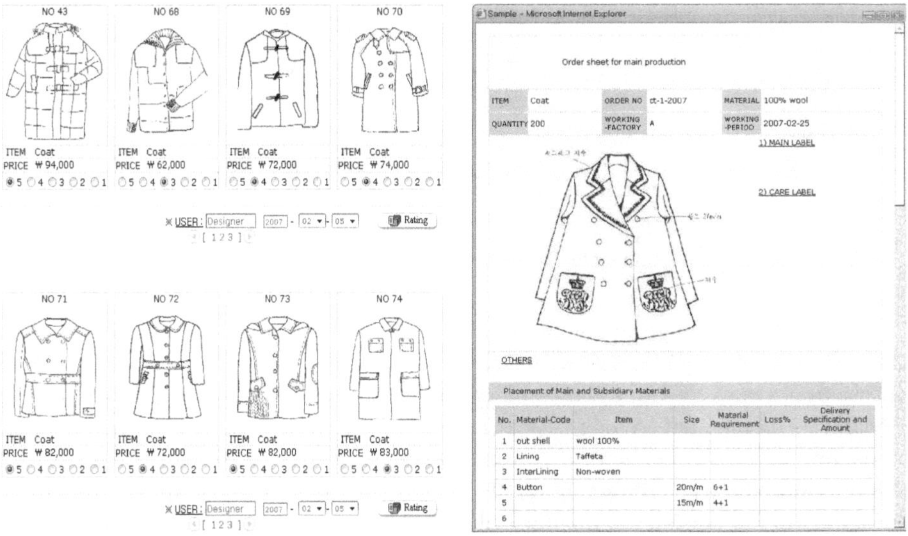

Fig. 2. Page of confirm stage in the shirt styles, order sheet for main production

The page which shows the processing status - the page showing the current location of the process - enables to confirm the current process status regarding the final styles. The point in time of process status indicates the current location of an apparel company, a sewing factory, and stores; concretely, it is demonstrated by time zone, and the following steps are included: drawing up a job instruction → sending the job instruction → drawing up a cost account → sending the cost account to head office → modification of the cost account → completion of an approval of the cost account → under production → sending the product to product inspection → completion of product inspection → warehousing to the head office → delivering to stores → warehousing to stores.

3.2 Sewing Module

The cost account, textile estimate, product list, product inspection, and delivery function were included in the sewing module under the close cooperation with an apparel company, and all these have each screen page.

Figure 3 shows the page of production status in the sewing process and the inspection page for sewing defects.

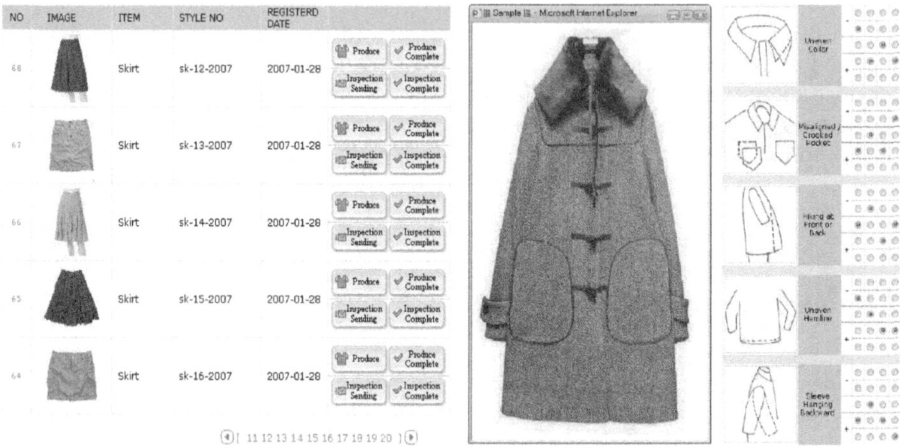

Fig. 3. Page of production status in the sewing process, inspection page for sewing defects

The product list page shown in Figure 3 (left) is connected with the apparel module and the textile module. In the sewing module, textile is cut, based on the job instruction received from the apparel module, sewed by a seamstress, and then apparel is completed. When a textile purchase request is placed by an apparel company in a sewing factory, a textile estimate list is drawn up to purchase the concerned textile. The drawn up textile estimate list is sent to the apparel module and an approval is requested. Apparel product is mass produced in the sewing module according to the approved textile estimate. When apparel is produced using the approved textile in the sewing factory, and when the production is finished, and when a user clicks on "Production," the produced apparel's image is uploaded through scanning. For product inspection, when a user clicks on "Sending to Inspection," the produced apparel is sent to the product inspection. The product inspection page in Figure 3 (right) is carried out focusing on a production request, and size specifications. The content to be inspected is different according to the kinds of apparel, but raw and subsidiary materials, sewing process, size consistency, finishing touch, and box confirmation are included in general. After a problem is caused, there is almost no problem solving method; therefore, the concept of quality focuses on company-wide quality control in improving work efficiency, while it is concerned with diminishing problems ranging from product design to production process. Accordingly, defect rate in sewing is automatically calculated through this system.

3.3 Textile Module

The textile module can be classified into such sub-domains such as textile shows, final textile styles, textile lists, and textile estimate list functions. All of them have their own screen pages, respectively. The textile module is organically connected with the apparel module and sewing module, and judgment of job progress situation, through which jobs are confirmed in each module and an approval process is included in the textile module. The textile show page is demonstrated to include colors (Dyeing and printing), textile tissue (Woven and knit), and post-processing (finishing, embossing, etc.) in terms of textile. Generally, textile designers should be professionals who can design using computers, and be fully aware of technical aspect in a textile producing factory. The textile designers can precisely direct to actually print and apply it to textile design, after experimenting the colors and textile tissues.

Figure 4 shows the page of confirm stage in the converter company. Figure 5 shows the page of request for textile sample making and the page of confirming textile samples from a textile company.

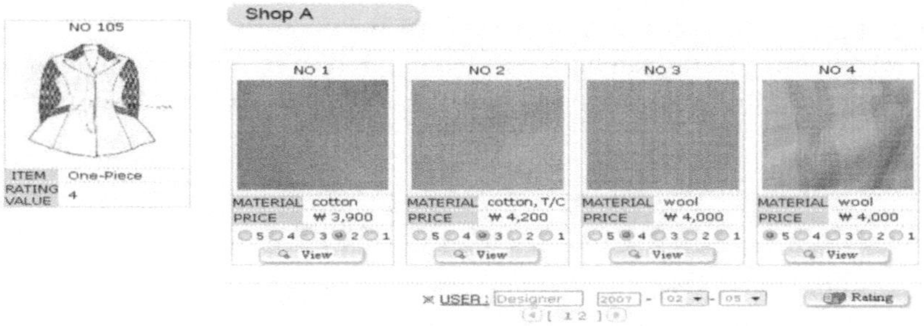

Fig. 4. Page of confirm stage in the converter company

In the page for a request for textile sample making demonstrated in Figure 5 (left), material of the textile, texture, yarn, textile tissue, colors, patterns, and main use can be entered and modified. When a user clicks on the appropriate textile, the textile image is zoomed in. Figure 5 (right) shows only the textile that gained 3 points or higher among the evaluated textile fabrics in the textile show. When an approval is made here, it is sent to the approval list of textile list, and textile estimate can be drawn up and modified for each approved textile. The drawn up textile estimate list is sent to the sewing module, and waits for the approval. When the textile estimate is approved in the sewing module, textile is produced in mass production and supplied in the textile module.

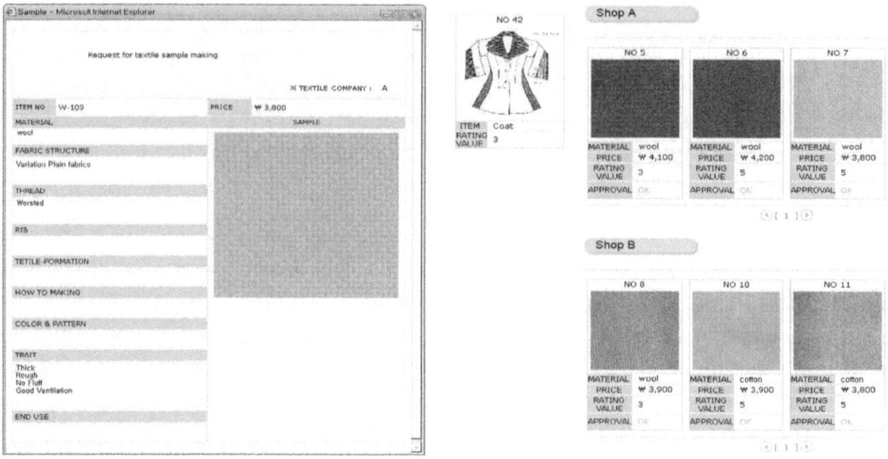

Fig. 5. Page of request for textile sample making, page of confirming textile samples from textile company

3.4 Store Module

The store stages are composed of four stores and outlet stores. In each store, the products are arranged by each item, and thus composed of skirts, slacks, one-piece dresses, jumpers, jackets, shirts, blouses, and so on. This is also arranged by each year again, and the data concerning these products are built up each year. Figure 6 shows the page of product style list in A shop and B shop.

The warehousing status can be confirmed by product in Figure 6. In doing so, the screen concerning the status of inventory at the head office (Y/N), current status, total

Fig. 6. Page of product style list in A shop and B shop

quantity in the current store, sales volume, and sales ratio (%), popularity (high, intermediate, low)is displayed. All these data are required to identify product inventory level in the store. When warehousing confirmation is made in the store module, an automatic notification regarding completion is delivered to the appropriate apparel company. When a user selects a modification in the warehousing status screen, sales volume and target sales can be modified. In general, if a store clings to target sales, more than needed purchase can be made, and consequently, a mistake keeping too many inventories can be made. If inventories are more than sales amount, it will deteriorate fund situation, and store image can be degraded, due to long-time displays of the same products. This may lead to price reduction in the end. Conversely, if inventories are too low, it may be easy to lose many customers. Indeed, inventory levels as well as sales should be strictly controlled. To control inventory level, the beginning inventory of each month and price reduction scale has to be set in general.

4 Conclusion

Quick Response System allows that the companies observe their consumer's needs consistently and design products and establish manufacture schedule rapidly so that they could prohibit the products to be unnecessarily stocked. Consumer's preferences are collected and analyzed through the data generated by POS system, and this is provided to the related manufacturer through network in real time, so that the manufactures could merchandise, produce and provide the products according to the consumer's need. Thus, this study developed POS system (education program), that is, the merchandising of apparel product, product by prediction, retailer, purchase behavior, reduction in stock inventory and product lead-time, cooperative system between apparel company and retailer, and conformation to the consumer's needs are included in this program, through binding the new technology in textile and fashion industry for the purpose of Quick Response system.

We developed the demonstration software program for quick response system of apparel industry in order to educate the students to get used to its expert system and computerized environment of this field. Merchandizing-Sourcing-Production-Retail shop chain of the processes in apparel company is the main pages in web, to show the students majoring clothing and textiles through the multimedia classroom. Up and down stream in the long process of apparel industry needs to shorten the process time that include the communication and instruction form letters between apparel companies, textile companies, sewing companies and shops.

Apparel companies have the pages and functions of online confirmation among designers and MDs, making samples of order sheet, cost accounting sheet, and other worksheets. Textile companies have textile list, confirmation of textiles and estimation sheet. Sewing companies have sewing order sheet, production cost, manufacture process status and delivery order status. Four stage companies are connected each other and can share, receive or send the data generated in each manufacturing process. This system can improve the understandings of the students through displaying the whole process of apparel industry and testing each related tasks with many worksheets.

References

1. Cho, K.W.: Direction of Fashion Education for Globalization of Domestic Fashion Industry in 21C. KOFOTI, vol. 14 (1996)
2. Ko, E.J.: Transactions: A Study of the Model Development of Korean Quick Response System (Part 1)-Focused on the Adoption Situation and the Factors related to the Adoption. Journal of the Korean Society of Clothing & Textiles 23(7), 1052–1063 (1999)
3. Oh, H.N.: Internet Usage for the Implementation of Quick Response as Supply Chain Management across B2B Electronic Commerce in Textile and Apparel Industry. The. Research Journal of Costume Culture 9(1), 100–110 (2001)
4. Jo, J.S., Lee, J.Y.: Transactions: The Essential Information Items to be included in the E-catalogues for B2B Commerce of Textile Materials. Journal of the Korean Society of Clothing and Textiles 26(9-10), 1366–1377 (2002)
5. Kim, S.H., Lee, S.J.: The Present Situation of the Apparel CAD Education in Clothing Departments in Domestic Colleges. Journal of the Korean Society for Clothing Industry 1(1), 26–33 (1999)
6. Kwon, H.S.: Review: The Spread of Role from Changed in the Paradigm of POP (Point of Purchase). Journal of the Korean Society for Clothing Industry 4(1), 1–4 (2002)
7. Lee, J.S., Han, G.H.: A Study to Improve the Rinkage between Apparel Industry and University Education on Clothing construction -Focus on Process of Pattern making-. The Research Journal of Costume Culture 7(6), 972–984 (1999)
8. Segawa, K.: Information of Fashion Education and Database. Journal of the Korean Society for Clothing Industry 2(2), 101–104 (2000)
9. Kim, J.Y.: 3-D Trimming System for Bias-Cut Apparels. Korean Journal of the Science of Emotion and Sensibility 7(2), 157–161 (2004)
10. Jung, K.Y., Na, Y.Z.: Program Deveopment of Quick Product Developing in Textile and Fashion Industry. Journal of the Korea Contents 6(10), 163–173 (2006)

Preparation of Conductive Materials for Smart Clothing: Doping and Composite of Conducting Polymer

Jooyong Kim* and Nowoo Park

Department of Textile Engineering, Soong sil University,
1-1, sangdo-5 Dong, Dongjak-Gu, Seoul, 156-743, Korea
jykim@ssu.ac.kr

Abstract. Polyaniline(PANI) is a conjugated conducting polymer which can be doped by either protonation with a protonic acid or by charge transfer with an oxidation agent. The p-type polyaniline was obtained by a protonic acid doping while the n-type polyanilne was produced by doping a strong reductant. The p-type polyaniline was stable in moisture at the room temperature unlike the n-type polyaniline. In spite of CNTs excellent capability in electrical and mechanical improvements, it has been repeatedly pointed out that the phase separation between the polymer matrix and CNTs leads to very limited applications. In this research, CNTs were pre-treated by a concentrated nitric acid which produced carboxylic acid groups at the defect sites for improving the dispersion ability in the PANI matrix.

Keywords: polyaniline, carbon nanotube, doping.

1 Introduction

Smart clothing necessarily requires flexible yarns with a high level of conductivity. Although many different techniques such as covering, sputtering and power mixing have been researched, the conductive yarns proper for wiring in smart clothing has yet to be developed. Use of conductive polymers, polyaniline (PANI), poly-pyrrole(PPy), carbon black(CB), carbon nanotubes(CNTs) as conductive additives in the thermoplastics industry have been limited mainly due to lack of processing techniques. However polyaniline(PANI) is one of the most popular polymer studied owing to its easy chemical synthesis and its high stability towards environmental exposition.[1,2] It is the conjugated conducting polymer that can be doped either by protonation with a protonic acid or by charge transfer with an oxidation agent.[3] The p-type doped PANI is obtained by doped with protonic acid, hydrochloric acid, camphorsulfonic acid, dodecylbenzenesulfonic acid while the n-type doped PANI is generated by strong reductant, sodium hydride, potassium hydride. In general the p-type conducting polymer is stable in moisture at the room temperature but n-type conducting polymer is not like that. The CNTs added into a polymer matrix improve the electrical conductivity and the mechanical properties of the original polymer matrix. However, past reports indicated that strong points of the polymer/CNTs

* Corresponding author.

J. Jacko (Ed.): Human-Computer Interaction, Part II, HCII 2007, LNCS 4551, pp. 1147–1154, 2007.

composites are restricted due to the phase separation between the polymer matrix and the CNTs. Accordingly the CNTs should be treated with a concentrated nitric acid. The pre- treated CNTs are produced carboxylic acid groups at the defect sites and thus improved the dispersion ability of the CNTs that contained carboxylic groups in the polymer matrix.[4] This study describes the synthesis and characterization of doped polyaniline and PANI/CNT composites.

2 Experimental

2.1 Materials

The multi-walled carbon nanotubes used in this study was CM-95 supplied by Iljin Nnotech co.,Ltd.(Korea). Aniline monomer, ammonium hydroxide, ammonium peroxydisulfate(APS), m-cresol, dimethyl sulfoxide(DMSO) camphorsulfonic acid (CSA), sodium hydryde were purchased from Aldrich Chemical Co. Concentrated sulfuric acid, dodecylbenzenesulfonic acid (DBSA) nitric acid, 1M hydrochloric acid were used as received.

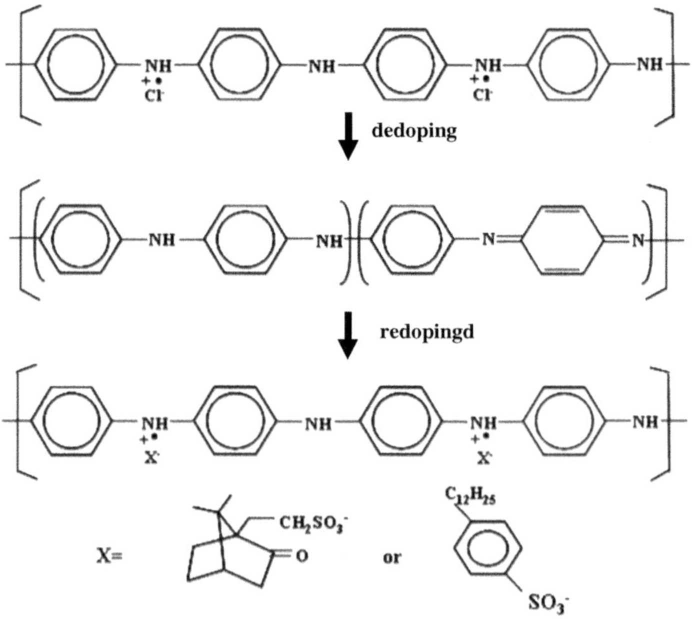

Fig. 1. Structure of polyaniline by the p-type doping

2.2 Synthesis of p-Type Doped PANI

The polyaniline emeraldine base was synthesized via in situ chemical oxidation polymerization. 10 ml aniline monomer was dissolved in 150 ml, 1.0 M HCl solutions, and then transferred into a 500ml four-neck flask with an ice-bath. A 100 ml 1.0 M HCl solution containing 0.125M ammonium peroxydisulfate (APS) was slowly added dropwise into aniline monomer with constant mechanical stirring at a reaction temperature of 0–5 °C for 3 h. The reaction mixture was stirred for a further 2 h at 0–5 °C, and then the resulting green suspension. The suspension was rinsed several times with distilled water and methanol then filtered under the vacuum. The filter cake was dissolved in ammonium hydroxide solution(500ml, 1M)and stirred for 15h. This ammonium hydroxide solution was filtered and dried under vacuum oven at 60 °C for 24h to transform emeraldine salt form of polyaniline(doped with HCl) into the emeraldine base form of polyaniline. The emeraldine base form of PANI was dissolved in a m-cresol after completed doping by camphorsulfonic acid(CSA) or dodecylbenzenesulfonic acid(DBSA)(Figure 1). These mixtures were ultrasonicated for 10 min, then stirred for 1h. The resulting solutions were cast onto flat boards (8×8cm) and dried at 70 °C for 24 h.

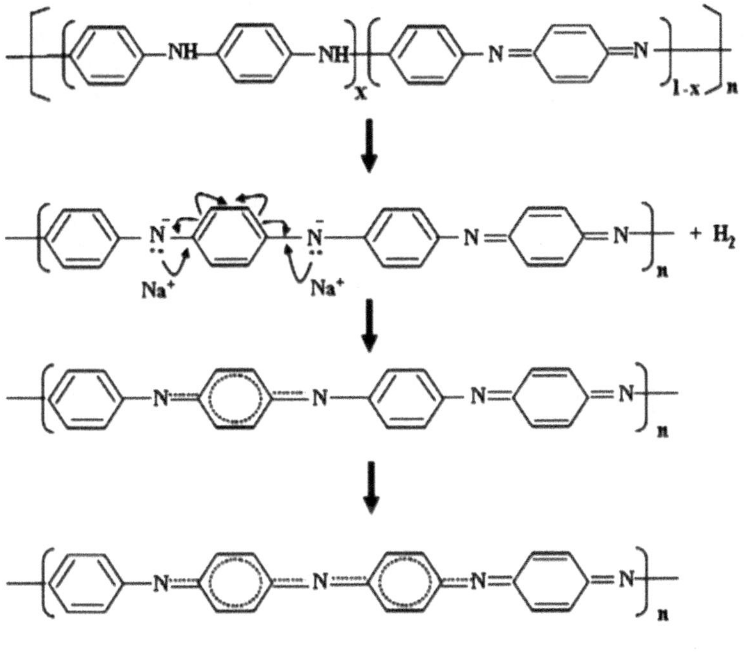

Fig. 2. Structure of polyaniline by the n-type doping

2.3 Synthesis of n-Type Dope PANI

The PANI emeraldine base was dissolved in 50 mL of dimethyl sulfoxide(DMSO). The solution was filtered to remove undissolved PANI and sodium hydride (mole ratio NaH/PANI of amine unit, 1/1, 10/1, and 30/1) were added into the solution in a drybox. These mixtures were stirred for 5 min. The resulting solutions were cast onto flat boards (8×8cm) and dried at 70 °C for 24 h. The structure of n-type doped PANI is shown in Fig.2.

2.4 Modification of the Multi-wall Carbon Nanotubes(MWNTs) Surfaces

In order to modify the surfaces of multi-wall carbon nanotubes(MWNTs), the MWNTs were treated with a concentrated nitric acid in a ultrasonic bath for 2h and stirred for 2h at 100 °C, MWNTs were filtered using a micro filtration assembly. Then MWNTs(designated as c-MWNTs) were rinsed with distilled water and this process was repeated several times to get the neutralized MWNTs. The neutralized MWNTs were filtered and dried under the vacuum freeze drying for 24h.

2.5 Synthesis of PANI/c-MWNT Composites

The composite of c-MWNTs and polyaniline were synthesized via in situ chemical oxidation polymerization. 20ml aniline monomer and various weight ratio of c-MWNTs were dissolved in 300ml 1.0M HCl solutions, then transferred into a 500ml four-neck flask with an ice-bath. A 200ml 1.0M HCl solution containing 0.125M ammonium peroxydisulfate(APS) was slowly added dropwise into aniline monomer with constant mechanical stirring at a reaction temperature of 0–5°C for 3h. The reaction mixture was stirred for a further 2h at 0–5 °C, and then the resulting green suspensions contained c-MWNTs. These solutions are doped by same method of p-type doped PANI.

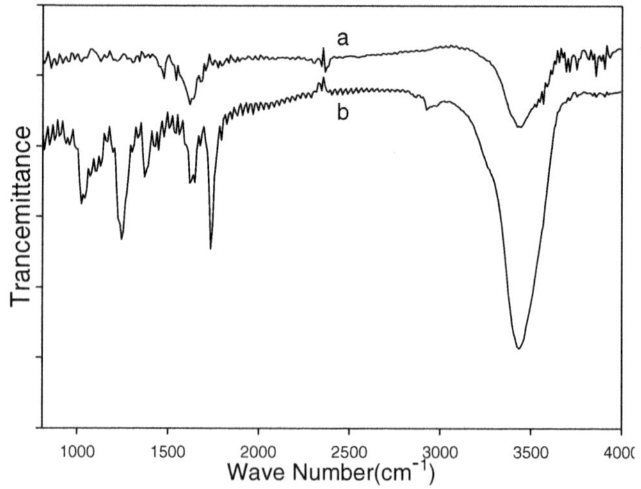

Fig. 3. FTIR spectroscopy of MWNTs and c-MWNT

3 Results and Discussion

The MWNTs were treated with a concentrated nitric acid in a ultrasonic bath for 2h and then stirred for 2h at 100 °C, which produced carboxylic acid groups a the defect sites and thus improved the solubility of the MWNTs that contained carboxylic acid groups (designated as c-MWNTs). Figure 3 shows the ATR-FTIR spectrum of the c-MWNTs and MWNTs.

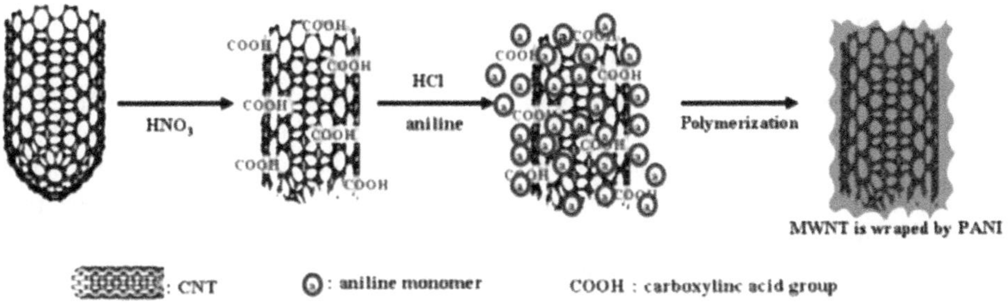

Fig. 4. Form of PANI/c-MWNT composites

The peaks at around 1728, 1254, 3400 cm^{-1} correspond to C=O, C–O, O–H stretching modes and 1602 and 1475 cm^{-1} peak are related to C=C stretching modes of the c-MWNTs. When PANI/c-MWNT composites were synthesized, the carboxylic acid groups of c-MWNT were caused by hydrogen bond interaction between the carboxyl groups of c-MWNT and the amino groups of aniline monomers. So the polyaniline polymerization was encapsulated at the surface of the c-MWNT. (Figure 4)[4]

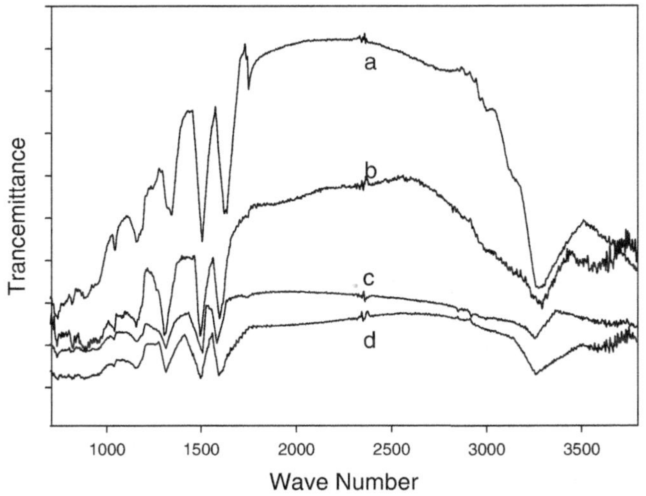

Fig. 5. FT-IR spectroscopy of (a)0wt%c-MWNT contained, (b)1wt% c-MWNT contained, (c)2wt% c-MWNT contained, (d)5wt% c-MWNT contained c-MWNT/PANI–EB composites.

Figure 5 shows the ATR-FTIR spectrum of the c-MWNTs/PANI-EB composites. The peaks at around 1313, 1500, 1593cm-1 attributed to C–N, N–C–N, N=Q=N stretching modes and 1160cm-1 peak is related to a C–H bending mode of the c-MWNTs/PANI-EB composites. The c-MWNTs contents of MWNTs/PANI-EB composites are different from each other, but composites spectra peaks are similar.

This result reveals that although the c-MWNTs contents of composites are increased, the c-MWNTs contents hardly have an effect on structures of the composites.

The TGA curves were conducted to identify the thermal stability of c-MWNT/PANI composites. Figure 6 presents the TGA curves of c-MWNT/PANI composites. The sudden weight loss is occurred in a temperature interval of 500-580°C, slope of c-MWNT contained composites (b, c, d) are gentler than the pure PANI- EB(a). This result indicated that some c-MWNTs can improve thermal stability of composite. The c-MWNT can retard the onset of decomposition of the composites. The retardation is likely to be a result of absorption, by the activated carbon surface, of free radicals generated during polymer decomposition.[5]

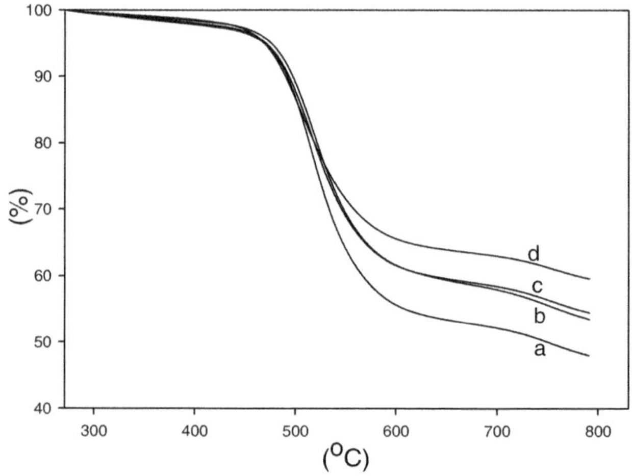

Fig. 6. TGA curves of (a)0wt% c-MWNT contained, (b)1wt% c-MWNT contained, (c)2wt% c-MWNT contained, (d)5wt% c-MWNT contained c-MWNT/PANI-EB composites

The electrical conductivity of CSA, DBSA doped-PANI/c-MWNTs composites were measured by the four point probe method. (Table 1) The electrical conductivity of c-MWNTs/PANI composites was higher than that of pure PANI. This also indicated that the high conductivity of the composites is contributed to c-MWNTs in composites. And the electrical conductivity of the composites doped with CSA was higher than that of the composites doped with DBSA at same the contents of c-MWNTs. It can be explained with the solvation effect which relates with the acidity of dopants and the polarity of organic solvent. In case of the composites doped with CSA and DBSA in each solve to m-cresol which is a polarity solvent, the composites doped with CSA are solved composites doped with DBSA than well due to CSA more polarity than DBSA. This solvation of composites affected on the crystallinity and electrical conductivity.[6]

Figure 7 shows the electric resistance of n-type PANI as time(mole ratio NaH/PANI of amine unit). The electric resistance of PANI doped with NaH was much higher than PANI doped with protonic acid. PANI doped with NaH shows the

Table 1. Electrical resistance of the composites doped with CSA and DBSA

Contents of c-MWNTs	Solvent	Dopant	
		CSA	DBSA
0(%)	m-cresol	13.76(Ω/□)	14.2(Ω/□)
1(%)	m-cresol	8.57(Ω/□)	11.49(Ω/□)
2(%)	m-cresol	4.21(Ω/□)	6.67(Ω/□)
5(%)	m-cresol	2.54(Ω/□)	

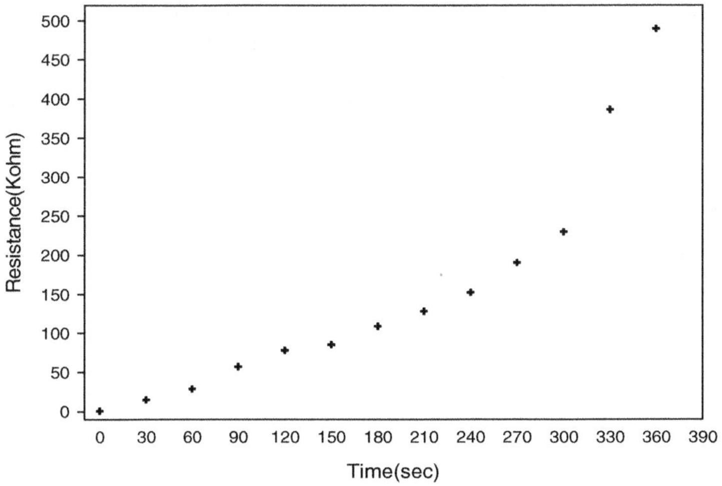

Fig. 7. Electrical resistance of n-doped PANI as time (mole ratio NaH/PANI of amine unit, 30/1)

dramatic increases of resistance above 300 second due to n-type PANI is very instable in moisture. It can be undoped by adding deionized water.[3]

4 Conclusions

The c-MWNTs/PANI composites were synthesized by in-situ polymerization. The c-MWNTs could be randomly dispersed in doped-PANI matrix and thus improved thermal stability of composites by a way of retarding the onset of decomposition. The electrical conductivity of MWNTs/PANI composites was higher than that of pure PANI. Electrical conductivity of the composites doped with CSA was higher than that of the composites doped with DBSA at the same level of c-MWNTs. Electrical resistance of n-type doping PANI showed a dramatic increase of electrical resistance mainly due to rapid undoping by moisture.

Acknowledgments. The authors of this paper would like to thank the Korea Science and Engineering Foundation (KOSEF) for sponsoring this research through the

SRC/ERC Program of MOST/KOSEF (R11-2005-065). This work was supported by Soongsil University Research Fund.

References

1. Macdiarmid, A.G., Chiang, J.C., Richter, A.F., Epstein, A.J.: Polyaniline: a new concept in conducting polymers. Synthetic Metals 18, 285–290 (1987)
2. Ghosh, P., Siddhanta, S.K., Chakrabarti, A.: Characterization of poly(vinyl pyrrolidone) modified polyaniline prepared in stable aqueous medium. Eur. Polym J 35, 699–710 (1997)
3. Hua, M.-Y., Hwang, G.-W., Chuang, Y.-H., Chen, S.-A.: soluble n-doped polyaniline: synthesis and characterization. Macromolecules 33, 6235–6238 (2000)
4. Wu, T.-M., Lin, Y.-W., Liao, C.-S.: Preparation and characterization of polyaniline/multi-walled carbon nanotube composites. carbon 43, 734–740 (2005)
5. Shaffer, S.P., Windle, A.H.: Fabrication and Characterization of Carbon Nanotube/Poly(vinyl alcohol) Composites. adv mater 11, 937–941 (1999)
6. MacDiarmid, A.G., Epstein, A.J.: Secondary doping in polyaniline. Synthetic Metals 69, 85–92 (1995)

A Feasibility Study of Sixth Sense Computing Scenarios in a Wearable Community

Seunghwan Lee, Hojin Kim, Sumi Yun, and Geehyuk Lee

School of Engineering, Information and Communications University,
119,Munji-ro,Yuseong-gu, Daejeon, Korea
{rigelsh,eruhkim,tosumi,geehyuk}@icu.ac.kr

Abstract. We propose a communication method for more abundant interaction using a sixth sensory channel for diffusion of multimedia files in a wearable computing environment. We suggest applications connecting people with their possessing media files as the most suitable applications for introduction of the wearable computer to the public. Sixth sense computing is a name that we use for the study of new possibilities that will be enabled by a wireless multimedia channel between wearcomp users. Scenarios enabled by sixth sense computing are developed and implemented in a wearable computer platform. We demonstrate possible requirements for new types of interaction style, an interface for a wearable computer application, and dynamic variation of society by varying system parameters such as the media selection method for diffusion.

Keywords: Wearable computer, ubiquitous computing, wearable community, sixth sense computing, new interaction style.

1 Introduction

There have been two parallel flows in the evolution of small computers. One is the cell phone, which, starting as a communication device, has begun to evolve into a full-fledged computer. The other flow is the PDA, which is evolving into basically the same form but started as a digital assistant device. Despite having the same ultimate destination, the two paths taken by the two different devices shows significant contrast: the cell phone has been the incomparably dominant flow. The main difference lies in their main applications: connecting people vs. augmenting people.

A wearable computer is still in its infancy, and is expected to take similar paths as the cell phone and the PDA. The main application of wearable computer thus far has been augmenting people, while it has played a relatively minor role in connecting people. The history of small computers tells us that the wearable computer should adopt a right application timely, and we believe such an application is connecting people. A right application will enable early entrance of the wearable computer into the consumer electronics market, which in turn will fuel its further accelerated evolution.

We have been exploring new possibilities of the wearable computers as a communication device. In particular, we are interested in new modes of communication with the "Six-sensory channel (SS)" enabled by the network of

J. Jacko (Ed.): Human-Computer Interaction, Part II, HCII 2007, LNCS 4551, pp. 1155–1164, 2007.

wearable computers, as illustrated in figure 1. People may "wear" pictures, music, and movies. A bench may become older with multimedia "stains". People may "infect" family with news. All these new scenarios raise many new questions about a new interaction model, new multimodal interfaces, and new information dynamics. These aspects are being studied under the name of Sixth Sense Computing (SSC), and we report here some early results including a few scenarios and their implementations with Ubiquitous Fashionable Computers (UFC) [1].

2 Proximity-Based Communication

Some researchers have proposed proximity-based communication for computer-supported cooperative work for enhancing work efficiency. Others have suggested the concept of an 'aura' in a short ranged network connection providing a digital communication link in face-to-face encounters, or enhancement of social networks [2, 3, 4]. The sixth sensory channel that connects UFC wearers is basically the same as the short-ranged network connection described in these earlier studies. In SSC, however, the use of the channel is generally not implemented for work efficiency or information sharing but more for changing communication, e.g., transforming strangers to friends and for experience diffusion between generations. Also, the new channel is not only between people but also between people and ubicomp devices.

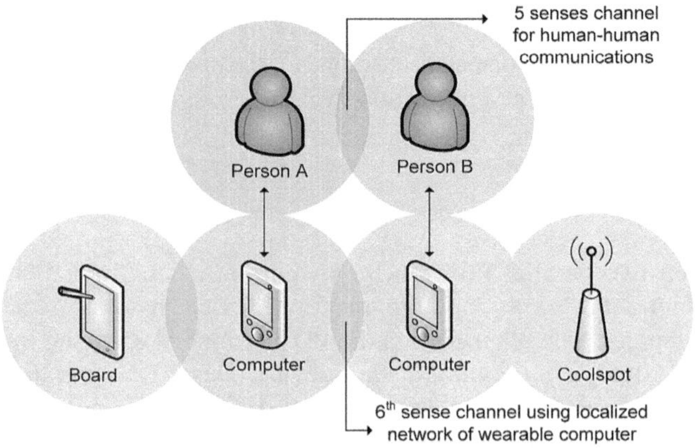

Fig. 1. In addition to the existing 5 senses for communication between people, there is a 6th sense channel that makes possible communication with others, various devices, and the environment around UFC wearer

3 SSC Scenarios

We have developed nine scenarios - SS Media, SS Fashion, SS Tag, SS Vision, SS graffiti, SS Couple, SS Coolspot, SS Commercial, and SS Says - that can be enabled by SS with a localized network, and three have been implemented and studied by a computer simulation.

We can use SS to spread multimedia contents representing ourselves, such as tags, music, photos, and news for better communication, to people nearby much like we wear perfume. The scenario where SS serves such purposes is called "SS Fashion."

The next is about spots where people come and go and/or spend time together. Such a spot may serve multimedia contents, and these may be selected from multimedia worn by people in or near the spots. With a suitable algorithm for selecting representative items from a media pool gathered from the people, the spot can develop its identity autonomously. Such a spot and the scenario are called "SS Coolspot."

The last means is a more large-scale scenario that can be expected in a wearable community. With SS, a multimedia file can migrate from person to person just like a rumor or a cold spreads. As suggested by many marketers' research about WOM [5, 6], SS can play an important role to popularize media items reflecting social distances between people. If some people spend more time together, there is more chance to exchange experiences, e.g., photos, music, or news they like and/or possess. The scenario of information diffusion by SS is called "SS Says."

Fig. 2. People who wear UFC can show their media items to people nearby (*upper figure*). The media files carried by people can be accumulated at a Coolspot; a bench in a park, a coffee shop, or a bus stop can be a Coolspot (*left figure*). Media diffusion is possible through Sixth Sense Computing (*right figure*).

4 Implementation

We implemented the first two scenarios, SS Fashion and SS CoolSpot, on a wearable computer platform (UFC). The last scenario SS Says is studied by a computer simulation as it requires long-term investigation via a large-scale experiment with a large amount of wearable computers, and the current UFC platform could not support the scale required for SS Says. This chapter shows the system design and initial system implementation on the UFC platform.

4.1 Platform

UFC[1], a wearable computer platform developed by the present authors, is an ARM-based computer that supports multi-mode network connection: WLAN, Bluetooth, and Zigbee. It has a LCD display, a camera, a microphone, earphones, and a 3 × 4 keypad, and the computing modules are weaved into clothes as shown in figure 3. The location information of all wearable computers is provided by a multi-modal network, and is utilized to find other wearable computers in proximity. The wearable computer as well as the network infrastructure is illustrated in figure 3.

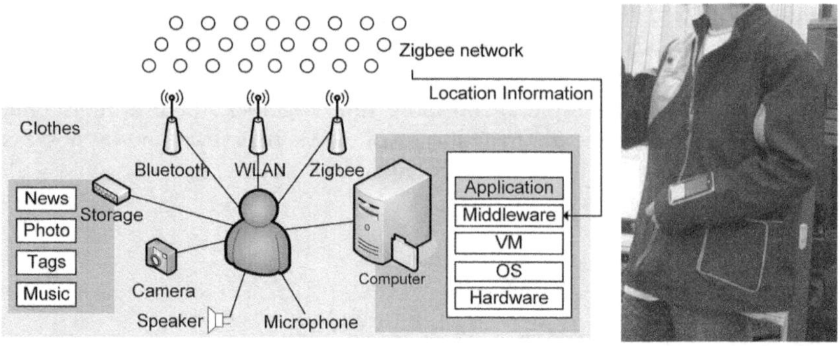

Fig. 3. The scenarios, SS Fashion and SS Coolspot, are implemented as an application on the UFC platform, and a bundle running on middleware. All the items in the outside gray rectangle are included in the UFC clothes (*left figure*). The main computing module is located on the wearer's wrist and other devices are connected to WearNet, the device network in the clothes.

4.2 SS Fashion

The wearcomp has a 320 × 240 display on the wrist and a VGA output for HMD. As a person approaches others, his/her display shows neighbors' name tags, favorite news, and saved or taken photos, as shown in figure 4, and one of the songs owned by

1 Tag	2 Up	3 Music
4 Prev	5 Play	6 Next
7 News	8 Down	9 Photo
* Reset	0 Quit	# Hold

Fig. 4. Screenshot of UFC display that contains tags, news, photos, music list (*left figure*) and the method to see all items using 4-direction buttons (*key 2,4,6,8 in 3 × 4 keypad*). The mode selection among 4 different modes is possible with keys on the corner (*key 1,3,7,9 in 3 × 4 keypad*).

neighbors will be played on the earphones. When a person meets a new neighbor, a whole tag item is delivered and one of his/her multimedia files are selected and transferred. For multimedia file selection, the probability of transmission is assigned to multimedia files linearly according to their rank. Multimedia files are piled on a stack as people move around, and the wearer can select one of 4 display modes or see all items using a keypad. Because function selection with a small pointer or menu navigation with an arrow key can occupy the user's intention too much [7], 4 buttons are directly matched to the position of each media arrangement, i.e., each corner of the display.

4.3 SS Coolspot

SS Coolspot tracks neighbors and collects multimedia data; specifically, only music data in the current version. While collecting music from neighbors, it forms the most representative cluster using a spherical k-means algorithm, where a music item is represented by an n-dimensional feature vector. As shown in figure 5, the music item at the center of the largest cluster is selected and played as background music, and one of the items in the largest cluster are selected and passed to neighbors with regard for individual musical taste.

The more detailed algorithm of Coolspot is as follows. Coolspot collects N music items until the N music items develop a certain distribution in the feature space. Coolspot then identifies 'k' clusters in the collected music distribution with the spherical k-means algorithm. In a pilot experiment, 56 music items were collected and each of them was represented as an 80-dimensional binary vector with genre, artist, year, and mood attributes. Classified 'k' clusters have k centers, and thus N music items are labeled as the nearest center of the clusters. From this point, Coolspot continuously collects music items and those items are temporally labeled as soon as

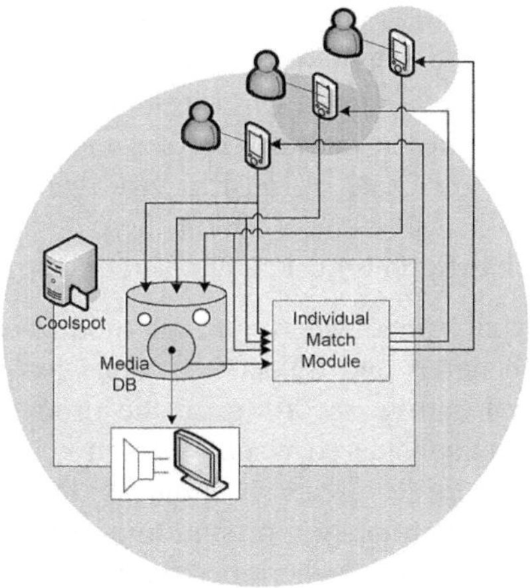

Fig. 5. The music item that is nearest to the center of the largest cluster is selected and played as background music, and items in the largest cluster are selected with individual match modules and passed to neighbors of Coolspot

they are collected in media database as the cluster having the nearest center. When every M music items is collected in the database, the centers of clusters are reconfigured reflecting the effects from temporally added music items. The next step is the same as the step of finding convergence in the k-means algorithm – all music items are re-labeled with reconfigured k centers until the centers of clusters are converged and stable. After convergence of clusters, a music item that is closest to the center of largest cluster is selected as the most representative music for that moment.

The implemented Coolspot algorithm has been running in a virtual 3-D environment in which people can experience the communication enabled by SSC. The Coolspots gather music from visitors and serve selected music from the accumulated music pool.

4.4 SS Says

We designed a series of computer simulations for studying the dynamics of information flow in a community linked by SS. We anticipated the results will depend on the algorithm for music selection as well as many other parameters reflecting individual characters and geometric constraints. Although this is a simplistic simulation, we attempted to make it as realistic as possible with various features of the person model, space model, and interaction methods.

Person Design. Each person has a musical taste that is expressed by a 3-dimensional vector – we can choose the three most influential, quantitative attributes in finding music from existing commercial systems. Each attribute is matched to red, green, and blue values, and thus one person is expressed by a color point representing musical taste. Like a person's musical taste, each music item is expressed in the space with unique color according to its musical characteristics. At the initial state, musical taste is allocated to people, and they start to move around with initial music items that are similar to their musical taste, as shown in the right side of Figure 6. As people gather music from other people nearby, they add different kinds of music from neighbors to the music list. Sometimes they delete music items that are very far from their musical taste, maintaining a minimum number of music items. Also, in a longer period, they tend to adapt their musical tastes partially toward the average color of their music lists. Each model has their own rate of musical taste variation, frequency of musical taste variation and music list adjustment. With these variable parameters, we could make various models with different musical characteristics.

Space Design. The virtual space where virtual models with music items live is modeled as a graph with nodes and links. Each node has transition probabilities to adjacent nodes, and people move according to the probabilities given to the node. Also, typical time to stay is considered when a person is willing to stay, not just pass by the node. We attempted to create a more realistic space with this simple probabilistic space model. The transition probabilities give characteristic to each node as a place in which people crowd or where people pass by. For example, the duration of time people spend in a lecture room, cafeteria, and dormitory is generally long, whereas the space in front of a vending machine or in a lobby can be a place to meet friends, where people spend several minutes. With observations on numerous simulation runs, we found that this simplistic space model similarly reproduces real

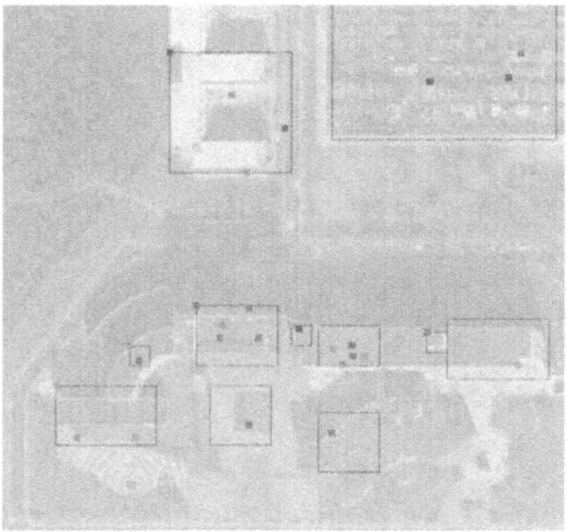

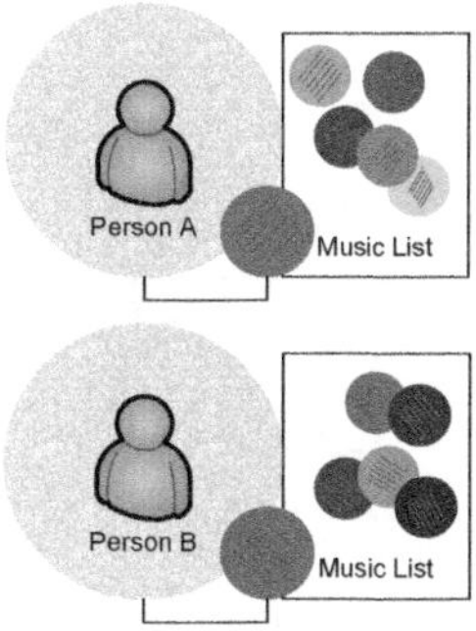

Fig. 6. Several principal places in the university campus are expressed as linked nodes (*left figure*) admitting people who are expressed by their musical taste (*right figure*)

world daily life. The left side of figure 6 shows a screenshot of virtual space with people expressed as color points. The distribution of people in the campus space imitates the real world.

Interaction Design. The simulation results can be affected by the interaction algorithm parameters including the range of communication, the frequency to adjust the music list, the music selection algorithm, and so on. We expected that the simulation results can be diversified according to various parameter values, which are selectable before each run. First, we devised three kinds of algorithms to select music for neighbors: selecting music with some probabilistic formula that reflect the ranks of music items, selecting random music among all music items, and selecting only top ranked music items. Other system parameters were suggested as a reference for this kind of system/service designer. There are two kinds of parameter groups: parameters for interaction and parameters for music list revision. In interaction parameters, the range of communication was fixed within 10, 20, 35 pixels in the 750 × 750 space. Another interaction parameter is connection frequency, which means waiting time for the next music file transmission after one transmission when people stay in the same node. The waiting time is selected among 5, 20, and 70 minutes; for example, the number of sending music items to neighbors changes 12 times, 3 times, and 1 time in a node where people usually spend 60 minutes. For parameters for music list revision, we defined two kinds of deletion range for music items that do not match peoples' musical taste, and three different frequencies for music list revision. The people model starts the simulation with a specified initial number of file lists, and then adjusts the music lists with initial music and gathered music. The time between every revision is selected among 30 minutes, 1hour, and 2 hours. The longer the revision period, the higher the probability of maintaining various music items. Number of files to be deleted among n files is random, between 0 to n – (initial list) × k when k is 1 or 2. Hence, when k is 1, the file list guarantees the number of initial music. In the case of k is 2, twice the number of initial music with gathered music is guaranteed after every music list revision.

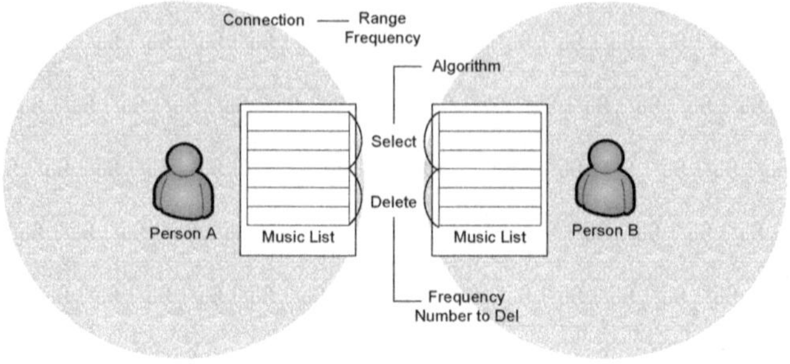

Fig. 7. Interaction parameters include parameters for connection, music selection algorithms on encounter, and policy of periodical music deletion

Hypothesis. Before SS Says simulation, we expected that media diffusion will be influenced by physical distance or shared time in near proximity, and musical taste matching as people who share more time can acquire more information in the real world. Moreover, the musical taste will be reflected in the music list gathered from neighbors, and people can get more diverse music than they would from their own closed music list. The consequence of this service is expected to be different with different music selection algorithms; probabilistic selection brings music diffusion reflecting physical distance and musical taste distance, random selection brings broader music diffusion in the whole space, and we speculate that delivery of only top-rank items cannot bring music diffusion.

5 Simulation Results

The music list of a random person at a random point during the simulation was checked to assess the effect of music diffusion with various selection algorithms. Figure 8 shows normalized values of musical taste difference (orange, the brightest line in black-and-white print), the number of times a multimedia file is received (red, the darkest line in black-and-white print), and the time shared with people (blue). The shape of the graph is similar to the expected result that reflects both individual characters and geometric constraints, which are expressed in time in the communication range. In figure 8, the left-side figures are sorted by musical taste difference in descending order, and thus the person at the rightmost is the person who has the most similar musical taste. The number of media transmissions is negatively related to the musical taste difference, and thus tends to be high for a person who has similar musical taste except people whom one could not meet with.

To assess the correlation among number of music transmissions, shared time, and musical taste difference, we designed the correlation function as follows:

$$Correlation(Time\ in\ the\ comm.range, Number\ of\ survived\ music)$$

As figure 8 shows, the file list after file transmission with each selection algorithm shows different correlation values for the four groups of people who have ascending musical taste similarity; people from 1 to 29 are grouped into 4 groups, and the fourth

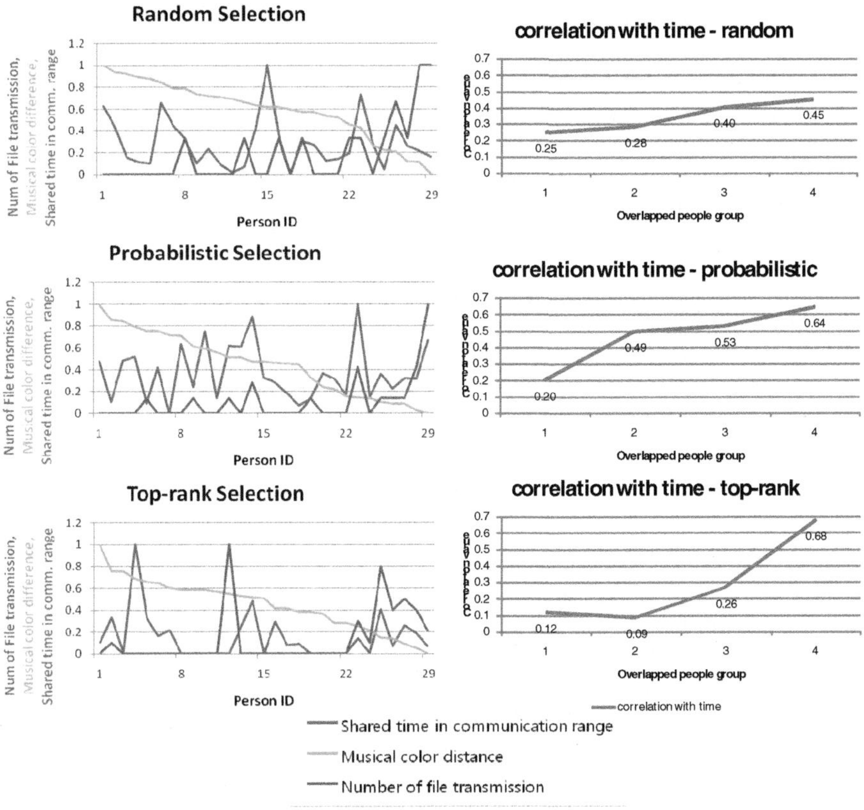

Fig. 8. The music list lineups with three different selection algorithm (*left figure*) and variation of correlation values according to musical taste similarity (*right figure*)

group has the highest musical similarity. Random selection shows no considerable change of correlation for people who have high musical taste similarity and low similarity, and hence the slope is gentle. On the other hand, the top-rank selection algorithm shows a sudden increase of slope for the people who have high musical taste similarity. A person with the top-rank selection algorithm can gather highly matched music items to his/her musical taste at the end of the simulation, and another person who uses the random selection can gather music items with almost equal probability from people whom they have met. The former experiences 'music recommendation' from the SS Says service while the latter experiences 'mood reminder' from the same service with different system parameters. The probabilistic selection algorithm used in this simulation is a linearly assigned probabilistic model – the top-ranked music has the highest probability to be sent, and the bottom in the list has the lowest probability as the sum of probability of music items is maintained at 100%. Other probability model shapes including exponential or logarithm shapes are expected to bring variety of service provided by top-rank selection and random selection.

6 Conclusion and Future Research

In order to explore new modes of communication that may be enabled by SS in the future wearable community, we developed nine SS scenarios, and studied three of them either by physical implementations or computer simulation. The two implementations using the UFC platform provided tools for studying new interaction styles with SS including a user interface for wearcomp and a representative music selection algorithm, and the simulation results guided the subsequent, physical realization of the scenario.

The authors plan to refine the user interface for use in many types of wearcomp as well as the Coolspot algorithm with a real wearcomp platform, UFC. Also, more simulation results with various system parameter combinations are expected to clarify the possible services that can be applicable to cell phone based service with WPAN in the near future.

References

1. Lee, J., Lim, S.-H., Yoo, J.-W., Park, K.-W., Choi, H.-J., Park, K.H.: A Ubiquitous Fashionable Computer with an i-Throw Device on a Location-based Service Environment. In: Second IEEE International Symposium on Pervasive Computing and Ad Hoc Communications (2007)
2. Terry, M., Mynatt, E.D., Ryall, K., Leigh, D.: Social net: using patterns of physical proximity over time to infer shared interests, CHI '02 extended abstracts on Human factors in computing systems, Minneapolis, Minnesota, USA (2002)
3. Schneider, J., Kortuem, G., Preuitt, D., Fickas, S., Segall, Z.: Auranet: Trust and Face-to-Face Interactions in a Wearable Community, Technical report http://www.cs.uoregon.edu/research/wearables/papers.html
4. Eagle, N., Pentland, A.: Social Serendipity: Mobilizing Social Software. IEEE Pervasive Computing 4, 28–34 (2005)
5. Kjima, K., Hirata, H.: Diffusion of Word-of-Mouth in Segmented Society: Agent-Based Simulation Approach. AIS (2004) pp. 198–206 (2004)
6. Delre, S.A, Jager, W., Janssen, M.A.: Diffusion dynamics in small world networks with heterogeneous consumers. NAACSOS conference, Annual Conference of the North American Association for Computational Social and Organizational Science, Notre Dame, Indiana, USA (2005)
7. Blaskó, G., Feiner, S.: A Menu Interface for Wearable Computing, In: Proc. 6th IEEE International Symposium on Wearable Computers (ISWC 2002) Seattle, WA, USA pp. 164–165 (2002)

Wearable Computers IN the Operating Room Environment

Qi Ma[1,*], Peter Weller[1,*], Gerlinde Mandersloot[2], Arjuna Weerasinghe[3], and Darren Morrow[4]

[1] Center of Health Informatics, City University, London, UK
[2] Royal London Hospital, London, UK
[3] St. Bartholomew's Hospital, London, UK
[4] Norfolk and Norwich University Hospital, Norwich
{q.ma-1,p.r.weller}@city.ac.uk

Abstract. High technology is a common feature in the modern operating room. While this situation enables a wide range of patient related data to be collected and analysed, the optimal viewing of this information becomes problematic. This situation is particularly acute in a busy operating theatre or while the clinician is moving around the hospital. The WINORE (Wearable computers IN the Operating Room Environment) project is a possible solution to this dilemma. It uses wearable computers and head mounted displays to provide an enhanced delivery of patient information, wirelessly collected from a range of devices, to surgeons, anaesthetists, and supervising clinicians. A crucial dimension to the project is how the clinicians interface with the system given the restrictions of sterile conditions and reduced dexterity due to operating procedures. In this paper we present the WINORE project concept, the background ideas and some findings from our trials.

Keywords: Wearable Computer, Operating Room, Head Mounted Display.

1 Introduction

A variety of medical devices are used in the operating room to support and protect the patient and to assist the work of the surgical team. Clinicians need information from these devices to achieve a best decision regarding the patient's problem in the quickest time. For example, during the operation, the surgeon may need to look at patient data and X-Ray/MRI images while operating, especially during some complex procedures. The problem is exasperated if the patient's condition deteriorates and constant observation is required during treatment. Meanwhile, the anaesthetist would benefit from: instant access to real time test results, such as blood tests, to help them prevent any unstable status of the patient during the operation; monitoring patient data while moving around the hospital, to improve their performance.

One possible solution to this dilemma is to use a wearable computer together with a head mounted display. The Wearable Computer can interact with the user anytime,

* Corresponding author.

J. Jacko (Ed.): Human-Computer Interaction, Part II, HCII 2007, LNCS 4551, pp. 1165–1172, 2007.

anywhere and according to the situation [1], [2]. Based on wearable computer technology, a portable system can provide the clinicians not only with rapid access to data, but also with visualised medical images (e.g. angiography, CT or MRI scans) projected to a head up display to be viewed at the same time as looking at patients. This portable system can help to provide continuous patient care and to improve the clinicians' reaction time during the operation.

The WINORE project (Wearable computers IN the Operating Room Environment), aims to develop and evaluate such a system. The ultimate goal of this project is to provide a practical wearable computer system platform that can be conveniently worn, easy and comfortable to interact with (input or output data and command), and dedicated to the medical environment. The platform is designed to integrate seamlessly with the existing hospital information systems to allow a real-time information updating, and also implement other applications to ease and enhance the clinicians' work, such as: X-Ray/MRI image displaying and remote patient monitoring.

Another goal for this project is to explore the best input and output devices for a wearable computer system for the clinicians. While there are a variety of input devices available, limitations in the nature of the operating room environment, such as hands-free requirement or sterile condition, make many commercial devices unsuitable for use by clinicians. Evaluation must be undertaken to find out which one is the most suitable. Modification or design work may be required if no suitable product is available. Output devices should also be considered, though fewer limitations are imposed by the clinical environment.

Usability evaluation of the system in real operating room environment is also required to determine if this concept is suitable for a long duration wearing; how much this system can improve their performance and if it will cause any additionally problems.

In this paper, some initial results from our work will be presented. We will first discuss the requirements from the clinicians in the operating room environment. After that, a general description of the system design will be given. Finally, we will introduce some aspects that need to be considered for using a wearable computer in the operating room environment.

2 Requirements of the Clinicians

As the system is intended to be used in a modern operating theatre, it was necessary to understand the problem domain including the details of the possible intended use of the system by surgeons and anaesthetists. The operating theatres of a London teaching hospital were visited. A range of surgical procedures were observed, ranging from simple dental to complicated neck tumor removal. The problems, requirements and limitations that were identified during that visit are highlighted here.

Problems addressed

- The surgeon has to frequently leave the patient to study X-Ray and MRI images, which is a big distraction that breaks the concentration and continuity of care.
- The anaesthetist must sit beside the working station, observing the patient monitor, to report any problems regarding the patient's status. Replacement cover must be

provided if the anaesthetist needs to leave the theatre for a while to attend to other tasks such as sending out some samples from the patient for further tests.
- Data communication can only be achieved via conversation between the surgeon and the anaesthetist. It is quite difficult to exchange complicated information such as images of the patient's condition or the results of blood testing.

Requirements addressed

- The surgeon would benefit from seeing clear relevant images together with patient's status, while he/she is operating.
- The anaesthetist would like to be able to monitor more than one patient at a time or be able to leave the operating theatre and maintain contact with the operation.

Limitations identified

- Major electrical interference sources in the operating theatre, such as diathermy.
- Sterile gloves are worn by the surgeons and so they can not use either their hands to interact with the wearable computer during the procedure.
- The surgeons need to keep their body stable during the operation. Foot actions will disturb it.
- Operation may last several hours, so the battery life of a wearable computer may be a problem.
- The sterile environment of the operating theatre requires additional protection of wearable computer and peripherals.

In addition to field observations, discussions were held with some surgeons and anaesthetists to collect ideas and feedbacks for this project. A detailed questionnaire has been developed as part of an MSc project [3]. The general feeling of the surgeon's and anaesthetist's view can be summarised as follows:

- They really think this system can ease their work and would like to use it. Especially for the surgeons when they want to access X-Ray and MRI images
- For the anaesthetists, there is a need for central/remote monitoring.
- Not all procedures would benefit from the system. However in those operations that are complex and require continuous intensive attention, this system could be of assistance.
- It is very important that the system should be comfortable to wear and easy to interact with, especially for the surgeon.

3 System Design

With the output from the previous analysis process and investigations on related technologies and available products, such as commercial wearable computer products, wireless communication methods, head mounted display devices, a system design is proposed for this project, as shown in Figure 1.

The main ideas of this system block design are:

- The whole system is easy to install, using a portable computer as a server and the wearable computers as clients.
- Seamless integration with existing devices in the operating theatre: using a VGAtoUSB converter to utilize the existing VGA port in the patient monitor to capture a high quality display image; a webcam can be used to capture views of other interested areas.
- A wireless communication that not only provides long range communication, but also provides enough bandwidth to allow the exchange of high volume data like images. The intention is that it should be usable over a wide range of patient monitoring.
- The whole system should be easily implemented using existing resources to minimize affect on current clinical practice. It should also allow updating or extension in a component level, such that a change of one component will not affect others.

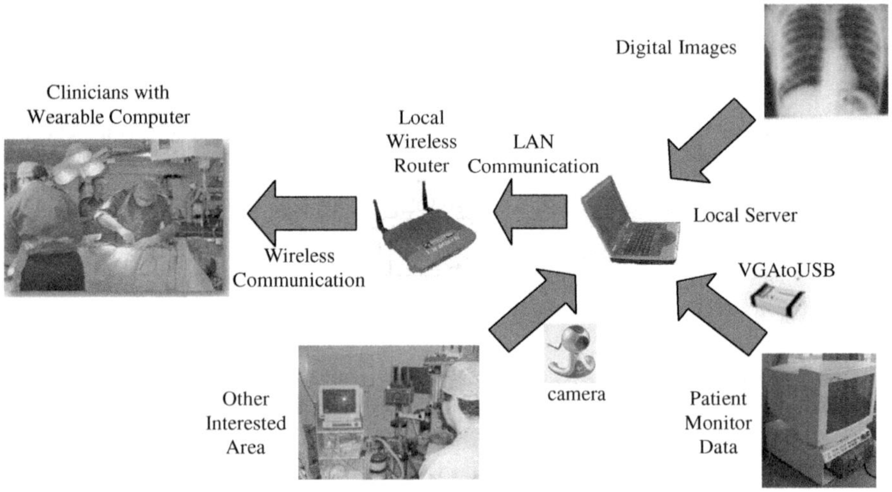

Fig. 1. Block view of the WINORE system

4 Demonstration System

A commercial wearable computer, a head mounted display and other peripherals were obtained with the help of a City University pump priming fund grant. A demonstration program, using Java (j2sdk1.4.2_01) was developed to integrate all components. Major functions of the program are listed below.

Server Side Program

- Collect the image stream from USB web camera.
- Display the captured stream to allow monitoring.

- Process the stream with defined rules.
- Provide an interface to allow the user to adjust the display.
- Communicate with the client side program to distribute the processed stream.

Client Side Program

- Communicate with the server side program to receive the video stream.
- Read in local images, such as MRI or X-Ray images, to be displayed.
- Display local images together with the received stream.
- Provide image viewing functions such as: zoom in/out of the local displayed image, change display location of the received stream in the window.

Figure 2 shows a sample user overlay with this system.

Fig. 2. Viewing at Head Mounted Displayer

Initial evaluations were conducted with the collaborating clinicians wearing this demonstration system to walk around the lab while watching the information from patient monitor and X-Ray image. They all gave positive feedback. Some interface improvements are being implemented according to their suggestions. A formal ethical approval is being sought for use in hospital environment.

5 Discussions

5.1 Methods of Data Input

Based on the results from the previous problems addressing process, it is found that the needs of surgeons and anaesthetists are different. For the surgeons, in the most of time they only require data to be displayed but not need to interact with it. On the other hand, the anaesthetists need to frequently interact with the system.

A variety of input methods have been investigated in the initial phases, such as virtual reality glove, touch pad, hip mouse, foot mouse and wrist keyboard. According to the initial trials, touch pad or hip mouse, together with wrist keyboard can be acceptable for the anaesthetists. However virtual reality glove and foot mouse will be too rigid for both anaesthetists and surgeons to use.

Considered the limitations of the surgeons to use hand or foot to input data or command, speech recognition is the most likely candidate as an input method for the surgeons. However, speech recognition can not provide a 100% accurate recognition rate, especially the work will be required to be carried on the medical words and the recognition problems in that context. A secondary backup method must be provided to avoid an emergency situation.

5.2 Method of Display

To provide an anytime-anywhere information display, head mounted displayer (HMD) is used. One major consideration for the clinicians is the eye strain problem. Some initial evaluations have been undertaken to find the optimal position of the data screen to ensure that under most normal tasks both eyes are using their central vision and to ensure a good binocularity most of the time and minimise any chance of eyestrain. Table 1 is a questionnaire that is used during the evaluations.

Table 1. Eye Strain Evaluation Questionnaire

The task to be performed	
The duration of wearing	
The display has been placed in front of which eye?	R [ ] L [ ]
Description of the position of the data screen	
Has your normal vision seemed clear whilst wearing the display?	Yes [ ] No [ ]
Is the display itself blurred on occasions?	Yes [ ] No [ ]
Have you noticed any double vision?	Yes [ ] No [ ]
If so are the images A. side by side or, B one above the other?	A [ ] B [ ]
Have you suffered any form of headache?	Yes [ ] No [ ]
If YES, whereabouts on the head	Brows/forehead[ ] Side [ ] Top [ ] Back [ ]
Was there any ache, tiredness, or 'pulling' from either eye?	Yes [ ] No [ ]
If YES which eye?	R [ ] L [ ]
Did either eye feel strained?	Yes [ ] No [ ]
If YES which eye?	R [ ] L [ ]

This project also raises a new problem: how to seamlessly integrate a head mounted viewer device with the medical loupe (Figure 3). Initial trials were conducted with the wearing the head mounted viewer together with the medical loupe. It was found that a surgeon can get used to switching between two devices in a short time. It is acceptable to wear these devices together for a short duration, however it is not evaluated what will happen for a long duration and in the real operating room environment. It may still be required to undertake a mechanical redesign of a normal head mounted viewer device.

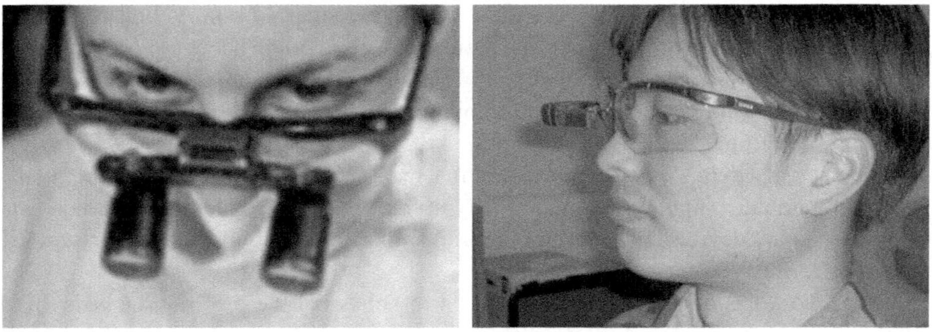

Fig. 3. Wearing a Medical Loupe [4] or a HMD device

5.3 Interference Test

Although some work has been reported on the interference from wireless communication to medical devices [5], [6], there is no report which shows a systematic test of the interference from a medical device to wireless communication, especially for 802.11g, the wireless communication standard applicable for this project.

During previous work investigating the operating theatre environment, the diathermy unit was found to be the worst source of electrical interference in the theatre. A diathermy device could be used to approximately simulate the environment in the operating theatre and the interference on wireless communication measured. The aim of this test is to provide a first approximate picture of how the communication will be affected. A further in-field test in the real operating theatre should be undertaken to ensure that this kind of wireless communication can be sustained in the real setting.

5.4 Power Supply

Many operations can last several hours. This raises the critical problem of battery life. To make the wearable system comfortable to wear for a long time, the weight of the battery can not be too heavy. However this results in a smaller capacity unit with limited battery life.

Hotswaping of batteries could be a possible solution to this problem. The system should have two battery slots allowing a backup battery to be plugged in and removal of the spent unit. During this process, the system should keep working normally. This is quite similar to the hotswap between battery and cabled power supply. However, it will enable the system to maintain the strong point of being wireless.

Although some commercial wearable computer products already provide this hotswap mechanism, the position of the battery slot is not convenient for the changing of batteries even with the help of another person. In this case, some mechanic modifications in the power supply may be required if a commercial system is ultimately used.

6 Conclusions

The modern operating theatre is a quite complex environment with a variety of devices being used to monitor the patient and support the clinicians. Modern operations, such as heart surgery, require a close cooperation among clinicians. Wearable computing could provide a step forward in improving the overall performance by providing continuous monitoring of critical vital signs on the patient or by providing access to pre-processed information in real-time manner that helps to assist in decision making. The healthcare system can also benefit from wearable computing by its capabilities of allowing remote central monitoring.

The special environment of the operating theatre causes many new problems for using a wearable computer system, not only in traditional fields like input methods and head-up display devices, but also in other fields like electrical interference on wireless communication.

Some work has been undertaken in the initial phase of the project. Analysis of the clinicians' requirements in relation to the specific environment was undertaken to identify the detailed problems and specific limitations. Some in-field visits and in-person interviews were carried out for this purpose. A technology feasibility study was also undertaken to determine what is currently available. A system block design has been proposed and its modular design idea was shown to be successful. Demonstration programs have been developed to show software feasibility and also the general functions of the whole system.

However, there is still lot of work to be done by way of further research to deliver a practical system. The wearable computer itself may need a modified design in the power supply system or even a redesign of its base unit to make it suitable for use in the operating theatre environment. Input/output devices need a lot of modification and evaluation work to select the best one from the variety of available options.

References

1. Mann, S.A: first Step Toward Personal Imaging, Computer 30, 25–32 (1997)
2. Bass, L., Kasabach, C., Martin, R., Siewiorek, D., Smailagic, D., Stivoric, J.: The Design of a Wearable Computer. In: Proceedings of CHI'97 (1997)
3. Nyampila, S.: User Requirements Analysis of Wearable Computer. In: The Operating Room Environment (WINORE), MSc in Health Informatics, City University (2005)
4. Corbis Corporation and/or its media providers (2000) http://cache.corbis.com/CorbisImage/thumb /13/16/55/13165521/RF4473831.jpg
5. Høgetveit, J.O.: Technical aspects of wireless trans-mission of data, Rikshospitalet University Hospital (2005)
6. Åkansson, P., Marve, T., Whether medical devices in a hospital environment were affected by the RF exposure from new wireless technologies like GPRS, UMTS and WLAN, Karolinska Institutet, M.Sc Project (2002)

Coupling the Digital and the Physical in Therapeutic Environments

Patrizia Marti and Leonardo Giusti

Communication Science Dept., University of Siena, Via Roma 56, 53100 Siena, Italy
marti@unisi.it, giusti@media.unisi.it

Abstract. The Multi-sensory Room is an ongoing project aiming to develop non pharmacological therapeutic protocols and IT solutions for the treatment of dementia in institutionalized contexts. The project exploits the potential of ambient technologies and tangible media for developing a therapeutic environment to stimulate patients' residual cognitive, behavioral and physical abilities. The Multi-sensory room is currently used in an Italian Home Care. Initial trials and preliminary results are described in the paper.

Keywords: Ambient technologies, Tangible media, Dementia Care, Therapeutic environments.

1 Introduction

The Multi-sensory Room is an ongoing project aiming to develop non pharmacological therapeutic protocols and IT solutions for the treatment of dementia in institutionalized contexts. In particular, the Multi-sensory Room has been developed as a therapeutic environment to stimulate patients' cognitive abilities, to contribute to patients' psycho-behavioural wellness, to reduce isolation and promote social interaction and communication exchange, to ease motor abilities and finally to allow therapists to design different therapeutic activities by reconfiguring the environment according to the patients' specific needs.

Beyond the setting of a rehabilitation space, the project aims at exploring interaction design issues related to the use of IT by people with cognitive or physical impairments. In this respect design for inclusion, acceptability and appropriateness of IT solutions, engagement and motivation are fundamental research topics.

The paper is organised along four parts: an introduction about dementia and the current practices of therapeutic treatment; a design framework describing the challenges we faced in designing for dementia affected subjects; the description of the devices and the ambient technologies we developed; the description of the preliminary assessment of the environment. Discussion and conclusions will address interaction design issues in specific contexts like the one described in the paper.

2 The Dementia Syndrome and Non Pharmacological Treatments

2.1 Dementia Affected Subjects

The target user group was represented by elderly people affected by mild or moderate dementia.

J. Jacko (Ed.): Human-Computer Interaction, Part II, HCII 2007, LNCS 4551, pp. 1173–1182, 2007.

Dementia is a clinical term to designate an acquired permanent neurodegenerative disorder that implies the impairment of intellectual faculties, affecting several cognitive domains, and it is sufficiently severe to impair competence in daily living, occupation, or social interaction [1].

In relation to the progression of cognitive impairments, dementia affected subjects experience an increasing difficulty in making sense of the external world, since they loose the ability to retain and process complex stimuli. Their perceived competence decreases together with their ability to take initiative or to explore autonomously novel situations.

At an early stage of the disease (mild or moderate), patients with dementia realize their diminished cognitive capabilities; as the interviews with therapists revealed, this causes them to refrain from engaging in interaction with unfamiliar objects or situations, in order to avoid frustrating experiences.

From a social relations point of view this often causes a voluntary isolation that results in serious relation difficulties. With the progressing of the disease, the isolation process is accentuated due to the growing loss of autonomy and the appearance of more severe behavioral symptoms such as depression, apathy, loneliness and an increasing loss of social and communication skills. [2]

All these factors contribute to make difficult the involvement of dementia affected subjects in therapeutic activities.

In order to limit frustrating experiences, therapists try to define individual therapeutic pathways starting from situations whereby the patient is familiar; furthermore, the progression of dementia is different for every single patient [3]. These are the reasons why different therapeutic protocols are required depending on the different degree of impairment.

2.2 Therapeutic Activities

There is no treatment that can prevent arrest or heal neuronal degeneration associated with dementia related illnesses. Existing pharmacotherapy can only provide modest symptomatic benefit to patients. At present it is generally accepted that a multi-factorial approach, which includes both pharmacological and non-pharmacological interventions, is important to optimize cognition, affect and global functioning in patients [4].

Non pharmacological treatments are characterized by two major trends related to the specificity of the interventions: Aspecific therapies which focus on the global stimulation of the patients through their involvement in meaningful activities (arts and crafts, housekeeping, entertainments and relaxing occupations); Specific therapies targeted at specific impairments (cognitive, behavioural and physical), that aim to adapt and compensate severe acquired damages [5].

Aspecific therapies. Aspecific therapies are based on the general principle "use it or lose it" referred to patients' residual abilities. They are carried out through a global stimulation of the subject who is involved in various activities (arts and crafts, housekeeping, entertainments and relaxing occupations). Amongst aspecific interventions one can include occupational therapy, music therapy, art therapy, and multi-sensory stimulation. Despite the fact that such techniques are quite commonly adopted in elderly care institutions, there is no clear scientific evidence of their efficacy, though this is partly due to the great difficulty of controlling the huge number of variables at stake [5].

Specific therapies. The theoretical foundation of specific therapeutic intervention is represented by cerebral plasticity, that is to say the ability of the adult brain to adapt and compensate severe acquired damages [5].

Specific therapeutic protocols are characterized by a precise control of the stimulus targeted to the specific loss and the actual level of neuropsychological decay of the treated subject. This implies a stark structure that prevents the patient's from making choices and limits him/her to the solution of the proposed task (cognitive intervention) or to answer to specific questions (behavioural interventions). Specific therapies are techniques for the stimulation of explicit memory (spaced-retrieval, vanishing cues and visual imaginary) or for the stimulation of implicit memory (external memory cues and errorless learning) and techniques for personal orientation (reality orientation therapy and validation therapy), only to cite the ones that address cognitive disorders. They are conducted by the therapist who provides the patient with instructions to accomplish a task. Specific therapies are claimed of experimental confirmation of their results and they are nowadays trusted techniques to face dementia cognitive decline. In this kind of therapies, patient's motivation, his/her subjective emotional background and experience are not considered as relevant features, even though they are considered very important in particular in case of memory rehabilitation [4].

3 The Design Framework

Both aspecific and specific protocols present points of strength and weakness in the treatment of dementia affected patients. On the one hand, the aspecific protocol creates the conditions for the emergence of engagement, intrinsic motivation, active participation and personal meaning elaboration, key elements for actively and successfully involving the patients in the activity. The patient is stimulated at different levels but it is difficult to control every single stimulus since many variables are at stake. On the other hand, specific protocols enable the therapist to maintain an optimal stimulation level but are less effective to engage the patients and to elicit personal meanings during the activity.

The main purposes of the Multi-sensory Room project is to design a flexible, adaptable and relaxing therapeutic environment, augmented with forefront technologies, that allows the therapist to engage the patient in the therapy without renouncing to the stimuli control and fine tuning.

A one year field study focused on the analysis of the users target group and the therapeutic activities currently adopted, significantly contributed to the definition of the design framework of the multi-sensory room and the vision of the project:

- To provide the therapist with a **flexible and adaptable environment** that can be configured in order to support different therapeutic activities (specific and aspecific) and assuring an optimal level of stimulation tailored for the different degree of dementia.

- To stimulate dementia affected subject to interact with the system offering an **engaging**, meaningful and immersive environment.

In order to achieve this vision, the Multi-sensory Room has been equipped with ambient technologies and tangible media, specifically conceived to create an immersive experience and raise the patient's interest. Furthermore, the system has been designed to be flexible enough to allow the therapist to dynamically modify the configuration of stimuli in relation to different activities, therapeutic objectives and the patient's need.

In order to design such a re-configurable system we got inspiration from two main design paradigms: ambient technologies [6,7] and tangible media [8]. These paradigms represent a remarkable opportunity for the development of novel interactive technologies that can overcome the limitation of the current computer-based technologies constrained to screen, mouse and keyboard interaction.

From one side ambient technologies represent a vision of the future where people are surrounded by electronic artefacts and environments, sensitive and responsive. Such systems can allow to achieve interoperability of devices and integration of new services through available tools; and to orchestrate devices and entities to support and enhance human activities. On the other side, tangible media research is focused on the development of seamless interaction with physical information processing systems. They are designed in a way to amplify human physical skills by giving physical form to digital information, seamlessly coupling the dual worlds of bits and atoms.

Following these paradigms a number of qualities of the multi-sensory room have been designed to engage dementia affected subjects in meaningful and pleasant activities and to enable the therapist to tailor the stimulation to the different patients' needs:

- *Natural and familiar interaction modalities:* augmented objects able to stimulate consolidated and familiar interaction patterns in order to encourage dementia affected subjects to interact with the system.
- *Dynamic environment:* the possibilities to control the ambient properties to dynamically produce and move stimuli from the background to the foreground, driving the patient attention only on relevant stimuli and considerably reducing the disturbing effect of the irrelevant ones.
- *Modularity:* the space is composed of modular and inter-operable components [10] that can be assembled in different ways, enabling the therapist to adapt the system in relation to the needs of each single patient by using the same set of tools and services.

4 The Multi-sensory Room

4.1 Ambient Technologies

The Multi-sensory room environment is a 4*4*3 meters booth equipped with ambient technologies and robotic devices [9]. It has been painted with a neutral shade (white walls, ceiling and floor) in order to reduce the amount of undesired stimuli. A projector is mounted on the ceiling to project videos and images on the front wall.

Lighting (designed by Targetti S.p.a) is provided by modular components controlled by a PC unit; lighting can be static or dynamic with a selection of 16 millions of colours and fading effects. By means of a specific software the therapist can control the light modules. The therapist can set the colour of the light or program (through a GUI) dynamic scenes as for example the day light cycle from the down to the sunset. The lighting system can be used standalone or can be connected to two different kinds of tools: the Rolling Pins and the Light&Sound Cylinders. Both the patient and the therapist can modify the ambient light by manipulating such devices.

Sound is diffused through high definition loud speakers. A smell system is also integrated in the environment and controlled through a PC unit that diffuses pre-selected smells.

Furthermore, the room is equipped with a system of two re-configurable desks. They can be positioned in 4 different configurations, in order to adapt the furniture to the different therapeutic activities (see Fig.1).

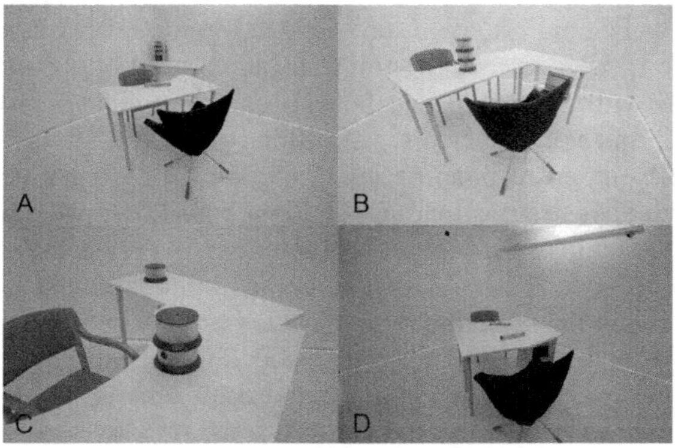

Fig. 1. Desks configuration

The configuration D, for example, provides the therapist and the patient with a wide surface, necessary to roll two Rolling Pins (see section 3.3); the configuration A can be adopted when working with a single Rolling Pins; the configuration B provides the therapist with a direct access to the PC; the configuration C provides a wide surface to interact with several Light&Sound Cylinders at the same time.

4.2 Tangible Media

Two kinds of tools have been implemented: the Light&Sound Cylinders and the Rolling Pins (see fig. 2). These have been designed to exploits the patients' residual skills, in particular the motor procedural memory, which is longer conserved.

Procedural memory contains sensory-motor patterns, which are activated by specific configurations of stimuli. By evoking consolidated sensory-motor patterns, like rolling, grasping, shaking, piling objects one on top of another, patients can start interacting with the tools. Natural interaction modalities trigger a behavioural answer, but there is a need to engage the patients in meaningful activities to generate an intrinsic motivation to participate. To this aim, simple but unfamiliar artefacts, pleasurable to manipulate, with different kinds of feedback (visual, audio, tactile, smell) and with local or environmental output have been designed.

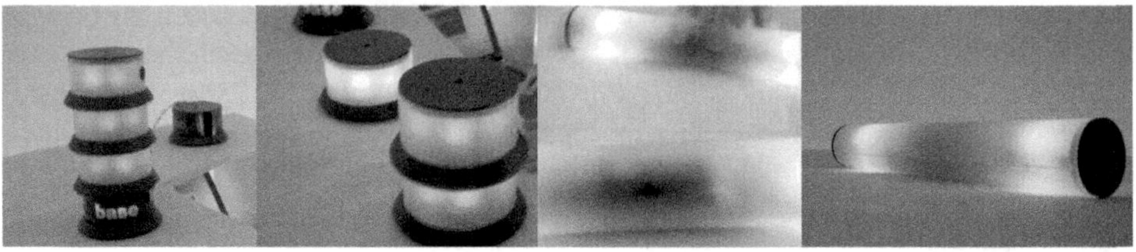

Fig. 2. On the left, two images of the Light&Sound cyliders; on the right two images of the Rolling Pins

Light&Sound Cylinders. A basic light & sound cylinder system consists of three types of units: a PC unit, a base unit and a number of Light & Sound Units (LSUs)[10]. Each LSU consists of a semi transparent plastic tube of 150 mm diameter and 75mm height with solid top and bottom caps, weighting 1100 gram including batteries. The PC unit is connected to an ordinary PC. It contains a radio module to communicate with the corresponding radio module in the base unit. This base unit serves as a remote base to download applications into LSUs when they are placed on top: the base unit contains an infrared (IR) module in the top cap to communicate with LSUs. Each LSU has two IR windows: one at the bottom and one at the top. So, LSUs can communicate with the base unit below as well as with neighbouring LSUs.

Through the PC software the therapist selects an application to use in the session. Once the software is downloaded into LSUs, each unit is autonomous and works independently from the PC.

The patient interacts with the LSUs only. S/he can pile up LSUs in different configurations, obtaining different local visual and audible feedback. Visual feedback is given by six RGB LEDs embedded in each LSU that are able to generate any kind of colour. A loudspeaker in the LSU is used for audible feedback, such as short tunes. The therapist can decide prior to and also during the activity to remove or add one or more LSU in order to modify the stimulation complexity, without compromising the system functioning.

According to the selected application different therapeutic activities and tasks can be supported like *Mixing Colour:* it allows mixing the colours of the stacked cylinders; *Colour Match*: the patient is asked to identify two units with the same colour and pile them up. If the configuration is correct, both units start blinking. Otherwise they become grey. *Sequence Match*: it checks if the LSUs are assembled in a correct sequence (e.g. increasing or decreasing numbers or squares of different size). When the units are correctly assembled the application activates a feedback (e.g. colour blinking, sounds or ambient feedback).

All the different applications of the LSCs have been designed to stimulate the short term memory and reinforce abstract thinking. At the same time, they aim at activating exploratory and proactive behaviours, favouring the emergence of patient's intrinsic motivation [9].

Rolling Pins. A Rolling Pin (RP) consists of a semi transparent plastic tube with solid end caps of black sandblasted plastic. All the electronic components are placed on one large PCB inside the tube (see figure 1). The RP has a length of 300 mm, a diameter of 50 mm, and a total weight of 350 gram including batteries [10].

The RPs are capable of measuring their orientation and the speed of their rotation to activate a visual, tactile or auditory feedback. A gyroscope is used for measuring the speed and direction of the rotation and two axes accelerometers are used for measuring the orientation of the RP. One of the accelerometers is mounted vertically on the PCB, so all three axis can be measured.

The RPs have three types of feedback: RGB light (four RGB leds capable of generating any colour), sound and vibration.

The peculiarity of the RPs is that they are able to communicate with each other or with other devices equipped with the same radio communication technology. The RPs are usually used in pair, since the local feedback of each RP can be dynamically set depending not only on its own speed and orientation, but also on the speed and the orientation of the peer RP. For example, the local feedback of each RP can be a function of the sum of the speed rotation of both RPs; potentially, it can be a function of any other operation between the speed rotations (and orientations) of two RPs.

Furthermore, since each RP runs its own software, each of them can generate its own feedback in relation to rules that are different from the rules of the other one.

The software framework for the RPs allows the applications to run autonomously in the objects, while providing also the possibility for communication with a host PC. The PC software is responsible for controling the application selection; thus allowing the therapist to select an application for usage. A GUI has been designed in order to enable the therapist to modify the sensorial stimuli by selecting different combinations of visual, aural, and tactile feedback. The tactile stimulation can be produced either by the physical surface of the RP (that can be covered by different scabbards) or generated by the vibration actuator. Furthermore, the therapist can also select different "communication rules" between the RPs. In sum, the therapist can adapt the complexity of the interaction to the specific needs of each patient, the therapeutic objectives and the specific therapeutic protocol.

The RPs were specifically designed to scaffold dialogic relationships between the therapist and the patient, providing them with the opportunity to establish a dialogue based on visual, aural, tactile and sensory-motor interaction modalities. Different applications of the RPs have been designed. For example, in the "mirror" application a RP can vibrate whenever it moves at a different speed of its peer. The task of the patient is to imitate the therapist's movement matching the therapist's rotation speed to stop the vibration. The therapist can choose the vibration as a single feedback or to reinforce the output with a visual or aural feedback or both. The particularity of this task consists in its dynamic nature: the therapist can decide to slow down the rotation speed in order to facilitate the patient in the synchronization or can decide to make the task more difficult to execute, by deliberately challenging the synchronization, moving the pin at different speeds and rotation patterns. In other words, the therapist can adapt the task complexity during the task itself. The opportunity to continuously adapt the difficulty of the task to the skill of the patient is fundamental to create an optimal experience and to maintain the patient's attention.

Software architecture. The software framework [10] for the Light&Sound Cylinders and the Rolling Pins (the tools) allow the applications to run autonomously in the tools, while providing the possibility for communication with a host PC. The PC software is responsible for controlling the application selection; thus allowing the user to select an application for usage. This implies that the application itself is controlled in a distributed manner by the tools. Each tool contains no identification thus enabling maximum freedom in the assembly – each cylinder (or pin) can be replaced by another cylinder (or pin). The advantages of this solution is that a program can run without the presence of the PC: the same program code can be loaded into all cylinders (or pins), the program can be made independent of the number of cylinders (or pins), less wireless radio communication is needed, and there will be faster a information flow.

The PC side of the application consists of an easy to use graphical user interface (GUI) which has the capabilities to plug in the different applications.

5 Preliminary Evaluations and Discussion

The Multi-sensory Room is currently under evaluation at the nursing home Casa Protetta Albesani, an institution located in northern Italy (Castel S. Giovanni, Piacenza) that gives hospitality to 150 elderly people with different degrees of cognitive and behavioural diseases.

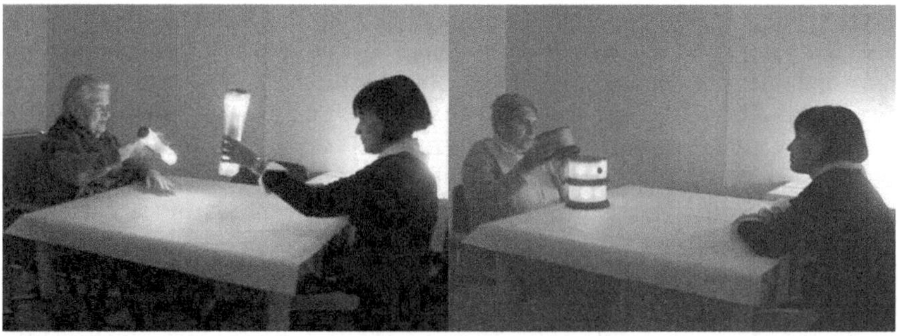

Fig. 3. On the left a trial with the Rolling Pins; on the right a trial with the Light and Sound Cylinders

Different trials (see fig.3) and assessment of the Multi-sensory Room have been performed to collect qualitative feedback on the configurability and flexibility of the system, the acceptance of the system by therapists and patients, and the usability of the environment [9]. The trials were video recorded, and after each session the therapist was interviewed. In general the therapists reported to be satisfied with the flexibility of the environment, and in particular with the opportunity to tune the stimulation before the execution of the task. In same trials, the room was set as a dark and silent environment to focus on the coloured lights of the tools to allow the patients with attention disturbances to be more focused on the task and to reduce unrelated talk.

In other cases, when the environment resulted to be uncomfortable for the patient (for someone it was scaring), the therapist could slightly change the setting to overcome the initial embarrassment.
Usually the manipulation of the tools engaged the patients and the easiness of the task and the constant feedback encouraged them to go on.

Also a controlled experiment [11] on the use of the Rolling Pins has been carried out. As said above, the therapeutic objective in using the RPs is to counteract social isolation that can result in dementia through the loss of social skills. The experiment addressed the effectiveness of the therapeutic intervention using the RPs under two conditions: 1) with the RPs communicating each other (dialogic condition); 2) with the RPs used as single devices, fully interactive but not communicating each other (individual condition). The results suggest that in the dialogic condition, differently from the individual one, the patients participated to the activity without additional verbal instructions; furthermore, in the dialogic condition, the patients coordinated their behaviour with the therapist longer than in the individual condition, imitating the same interaction patterns generated by the therapist. This is a particularly remarkable result since different studies [12] confirm the importance of imitation in facilitating and maintaining people with communication problems in the social world.

In light of these results, we can say that the contribution of our research concerns a re-articulation of the concepts of ambient technology and tangible media in a delicate and almost unexplored domain such as the use of IT for dementia care.

This paper shows that ubiquity, transparency, tangibility and modularity are fundamental feature for embedding technologies in every day objects. However, when design addresses delicate contexts like the one described in this paper, than a deep and accurate understanding of the domain peculiarities is necessary. Indeed, gaining a comprehensive understanding and a perspicuous view on user requirements in the domain of dementia care, and more in general the domain of disability, poses a number of interesting methodological challenges for inclusive design. Countering design exclusion indeed, is not merely about the design itself but also the methods we adopt for informing design. It is not only that many of the important ethical and deployment issues concerning the development, deployment and evaluation of real systems remain unexplored, but that methods for eliciting needs in such a complex setting are relatively under-developed. In this project we have undertook observational studies of the work of the staff as well as more 'lightweight' ethnographic studies with patients. However, the precise nature and value of the ethnographic input into design is controversial. It may be that we require significant shifts in our investigative techniques as well as in our understanding of design, to consider how technology relates to 'care' settings.

The problem is that research in these contexts is often regarded as not merely difficult but often inappropriate and intrusive. The deeply personal nature of care activities and the difficulties in involving patients with cognitive impairments in the design process limit just what can be investigated, as well as how it can be investigated, and reporting the interactional elements in a range of activities and contexts is often difficult. These and other delicate issues represent potentially obdurate problems and methodological responses have to be explored.

References

1. Logiudice, D.: Dementia: an update to refresh your memory. internal medicine journal 32(11), 535–540 (2002)
2. Silvestri, A., Rosano, G., Zannino, G., Ricca, F., Maragliano, V., Fini, M.: Behavioural disturbances in Alzheimer disease: non pharmachological therapeutic approach. In: Arch. Gerontol. Geriatr. Suppl. 9 379–386 (2004)
3. Trabucchi, M.: Le Demenze. UTET scienze mediche, Torino (1998)
4. De Vreese, L.P., Neri, M., Fioravanti, M., Belloi, L., Zanetti, O.: Memory rehabilitation in Alzheimer's disease: a review of progress. International Journal of Geriatric Psychiatry 16(8), 794–809.5 (2001)
5. Zanetti, O., Cotelli, M., Lussignoli, G.: Gli interventi riabilitativi nei pazienti con deficit cognitivi. In: Le demenze. M. Trabucchi. UTET Scienze Mediche, Torino (1998)
6. Weiser, M.: The Computer for the Twenty-First Century. In: Scientific American, pp. 94–10 (1991)
7. Marti, P., Lund, H.H.: Scaling Ambient Intelligence. In: Remagnino, P., Foresti, G.L., Ellis, T. (eds.) Ambient Intelligence: A Novel Paradigm, Springer, New York (2004)
8. Ishii, H., Ullmer, B.: Tangible Bits: Towards Seamless Interfaces between People, Bits and Atoms. In: Proceedings of Conference on Human Factors in Computing Systems CHI '97, pp. 234–241. ACM Press, New York (1997)
9. Marti, P., Lund, H.H., Bacigalupo, M., Giusti, L., Mennecozzi, C.: A multi-sensory environment for the treatment of dementia affected subjects. In: International Journal of Gerontechnology vol. 6(1) (2007)
10. Lund, H.H., Marti, P., Derakhshan, A., Beck, R., Kiltbo, T., Nielsen, J.: Modular Robotics for Novel Tools in Dementia Treatment. In: Proceedings of Ro-Man 2006 IEEE International Workshop on Robots and Human Interactive Communications, University of Hertfordshire, Hatfield, United Kingdom UK (2006)
11. Marti, P., Giusti, L.: Dialogues beyond words. Submitted to: Journal of Interaction Studies (2007)
12. Astell, A.J., Ellis, M.: The Social Function of Imitation in Severe Dementia. Infant and Child Development 15, 311–319 (2006)

Functional Brain Imaging for Analysis of Reading Effort for Computer-Generated Text

Erin M. Nishimura[1], Evan D. Rapoport[1], Benjamin A. Darling[2], Jason P. Cervenka[2], Jeanine K. Stefanucci[3], Dennis R. Proffitt[2], Traci H. Downs[1], and J. Hunter Downs III[1]

[1] Archinoetics, LLC, 700 Bishop St, Ste 2000, Honolulu, HI 96813
[2] Dept. of Psych., University of Virginia, P.O. Box 400400, Charlottesville, VA 22904
[3] Dept. of Psych., College of William & Mary, P.O. Box 8795, Williamsburg, VA 23187

Abstract. This paper discusses two functional brain imaging techniques, functional magnetic resonance imaging (fMRI) and functional near-infrared (fNIR) imaging, and their applications for quantitative usability analysis. This application is demonstrated through a two-phase study on reading effort required for varying degrees of font degradation. The first phase used fMRI to map cortical locations that were active while subjects read fonts of varying quality. The second phase used fNIR imaging, which showed higher levels of activity (and thus greater cognitive effort) in the visual processing area of the brain during a reading task with text presented in degraded fonts. The readability analysis techniques demonstrated in this study also generalize to applications requiring an objective analysis of interface usability.

Keywords: quantitative usability analysis, functional brain imaging, functional magnetic resonance imaging (fMRI), functional near-infrared (fNIR).

1 Introduction

This paper introduces a method for quantitative usability analysis through functional brain imaging. The functional brain imaging techniques used in these studies monitor local hemodynamic (blood flow) changes caused by cognitive activity to detect localized brain activations in the areas of the brain being used. These techniques are applied to determine 1) the areas of the brain being used and 2) the level of activation in those areas during the performance of given tasks. By imaging the user during controlled use of an interface, functional brain imaging offers an objective method for evaluating human-computer interfaces based on required levels of cognitive effort.

This method of quantitative usability analysis through functional brain imaging is presented through a two-phase study on readability analysis in which cognitive activations are measured using functional magnetic resonance imaging (fMRI) and functional near-infrared imaging (fNIR), while reading complexity is manipulated by degrading the quality of the text. Degrading the text quality is expected to degrade its perceptual features and increase reading difficulty. Using functional brain imaging techniques to analyze reading effort as modulated through font degradation introduces a potential tool for objective and quantitative usability analysis in reading interfaces,.

J. Jacko (Ed.): Human-Computer Interaction, Part II, HCII 2007, LNCS 4551, pp. 1183–1192, 2007.

The first phase of this study used fMRI for a global view of brain activations associated with varying degrees of effortful reading. The results of this phase provided a basis for selecting sensor locations for the second phase, which used fNIR sensors in an analysis of the selected cortical locations.

1.1 Reading Processes

The analysis of reading effort through functional brain imaging requires an understanding of the cognitive processes associated with reading, which involves several stages [13]. In the initial stage of reading, perceptual features inherent in the displayed letters are extracted and associated with potential matching letters, processed by the visual cortex and ventral streams projecting into the temporal cortical lobe.

Several previous imaging studies have identified neural correlates of increased reading effort by varying the difficulty of high-level reading processes. During sentence comprehension, higher computational demand from increased syntactic complexity resulted in activation in the left-hemisphere language areas, Wernicke's and Broca's, and to a lesser extent, in these locations in the right hemisphere [8]. An fMRI study of contextual sentence integration [1] found increased activation in these areas instead by increasing the complexity of semantic integration. These studies examine whether degrading the perceptual features of text results in similar activations and if additional areas, such as the visual cortex, also show increased activation.

1.2 fMRI Technology

Functional magnetic resonance imaging (fMRI) has been used extensively for mapping brain activity in studies of cognitive function [2]. By recording a rapid sequence of brain scans while participants engage in a set of cognitive and control tasks, fMRI can generate high-resolution three-dimensional images showing areas of activation over the entire brain volume.

In localizing brain activity, the fMRI scanner does not measure the activity of the neurons directly, but instead measures the local hemodynamic (blood flow) changes that occur in response to neuronal activity [14]. fMRI detects this process using a blood oxygen level dependent (BOLD) measurement. When the neurons in an area are activated in response to a cognitive task stimulus, oxygen is consumed in that region. Oxygenated blood flows into the region to replenish the oxygen supply. This influx exceeds the amount of oxygen consumed [5], lowering the relative concentration of deoxygenated hemoglobin in the region. Deoxygenated hemoglobin is paramagnetic, so the decrease in its concentration results in localized magnetic changes that can be measured by the magnetic resonance imaging scanner [11].

1.3 fNIR Technology

Functional near-infrared (fNIR) technology uses the known scattering response of near-infrared (NIR) light in human tissue to non-invasively monitor relative oxy- and deoxy-hemoglobin concentrations [3]. Multiple wavelengths of NIR light are emitted by the sensor through the tissue; the detected intensities are used to determine the concentrations of oxy- and deoxy-hemoglobin based on the distinct absorption spectra of the NIR wavelengths used [10].

This imaging technique essentially measures the same physiologic signal as fMRI to detect the onset of cognitive tasks and determine levels of activity through local hemodynamic responses. However, fNIR is much smaller, less costly, and less restrictive than fMRI, allowing more natural usage.

The OTIS-2 fNIR system [10], developed by Archinoetics, LLC, was used as the continuous-wave, three wavelength fNIR imager for the second phase of this study (Fig. 1, below). OTIS consists of a small enclosure with an attached set of up to two sensors that are placed on the head. Each sensor has an emitter with up to eight detachable detectors.

Fig. 1. The OTIS-2 system, developed by Archinoetics, LLC

2 Phase I: fMRI Analysis of Usability

The first phase of the study used fMRI for whole-head imaging analysis to identify areas of cortical activation during reading tasks while modulating the font qualities.

2.1 Methods

Twelve right-handed adults participated; all had normal or corrected-to-normal vision. Text was displayed to participants using MRI-compatible video goggles, manufactured by Resonance Technologies Inc. (MRVision 2000 system, http://www.mrivideo.com) and composed of two video screens, one for each eye, with a resolution of 180,000 pixels and a 30 degree field of view along the diagonal.

E-Prime v1.1 (Psychology Software Tools, Inc.) was used to program the stimulus presentation. The stimuli were generated on a laptop computer set to a video resolution of 800 x 600 pixels and sent to a scan converter for conversion to the NTSC signal used by the MRI-compatible goggles. Screen font edge smoothing was turned off to ensure degradation.

Response data was collected using MRI-compatible button box systems (MRI Compatible Joystick, Resonance Technologies, Inc.; Rowland USB Response Box, Rowland Institute). fMRI imaging data was acquired using a whole body 1.5 T Siemens Sonata scanner. An echo planar (EPI) pulse sequence with TR = 2000 ms, TE = 40 ms, and flip angle = 90° was used for functional imaging.

2.1.1 Reading Tasks

Brain imaging data and behavioral measures were collected while the participant engaged in a reading comprehension task, derived from Gugerty et al [7] with sentence content adapted from Gugerty et al. and Federmeier and Kutas [4]. Participants were shown pairs of sentences and asked to judge whether the two sentences fit together plausibly. An example is shown below in Fig. 2.

A) Plausible Sentence Pair:	B) Implausible Sentence Pair:
Drew picked up the starfish from the sea floor. *He was very happy to be scuba diving again.*	*Drew picked up the starfish from the sea floor.* *He was very happy to be sky diving again.*

Fig. 2. Examples of a plausible and implausible sentence pair

Sentences were presented one at a time, each for a fixed duration (6s) to allow synchronization of stimulus presentation with the brain imaging data. Responses were accepted during the display of the second sentence of each pair. Participants were instructed to answer quickly without losing accuracy. After the second sentence was displayed, a '***' symbol appeared for two seconds to warn participants that their time to respond was nearly finished.

Response times and accuracy were recorded for behavioral analysis. Responses made after the response warning ended were not accepted. Only the first response for each sentence pair was accepted. No feedback was given to the subject.

2.1.2 Varying Font Readability

The different levels of degraded fonts used in the study are shown below in Fig. 3.

Verdana	Drew picked up the starfish
Middle	Drew picked up the starfish
xLow	Drew picked up the starfish

Fig. 3. Fonts used in first phase of study

Each session of the fMRI study consisted of three separate runs per person (Fig. 4). Each run alternated between different fonts when presenting the sentence pairs with rest periods in between (the shorter period in runs two and three maximized the design efficiency and the chances of detecting a font-related activation difference).

Run	Fonts	Rest	Pairs / Font
1	Verdana, Middle, xLow	16s	8
2	Verdana, Middle	2s	6
3	Verdana, xLow	2s	6

Fig. 4. Fonts, rests, and number of sentence pairs used for each run

2.1.3 Analysis

Behavioral data analysis determined the effect of font degradation on performance of the reading comprehension tasks. Performance was quantified in terms of response time and accuracy in recognizing the plausibility of the sentence pairs, and was statistically compared between font qualities.

Data analysis on the fMRI data was performed using SPM99 (Wellcome Department of Imaging Neuroscience, University College London, London, UK) running in the MATLAB environment (The Mathworks, Inc., Natick, MA). The volumes from each participant were first corrected for slice timing and then realigned to correct for motion artifacts and normalized to a canonical brain template in the Montreal Neurological Institute (MNI) space. The volumes were smoothed with a Gaussian kernel (FHWM = 8 mm).

Statistical analysis was performed using SPM99, which performs a univariate statistical test (t-test) for each voxel of the brain volume to assess whether one condition in a contrast produces a greater level of activation than another at that location. If the results of the t-test on the voxel meet a specified significance level (p value), the voxel is identified as active for that contrast. Often a threshold value of $p = 0.0001$ (uncorrected) is used, though a more lenient threshold ($p = 0.005$) was used in this study when performing random effects analyses. When using the more lenient p-value threshold, a minimum cluster size of 10 voxels was required; a minimum cluster size of 5 voxels was used for the p-value of 0.001.

2.2 Results

Behavioral analysis showed highly accurate responses in all conditions (80%, 90%, and 86.5% for xLow, Middle, and Verdana, respectively). A repeated measures ANOVA showed that the effect of font quality was not significant, $F(2,22) = 2.12$, $p = 0.14$ suggesting that participants understood the sentences' meanings. Mean response time did increase, however, as font quality was reduced (2975 msec, 3057 msec, and

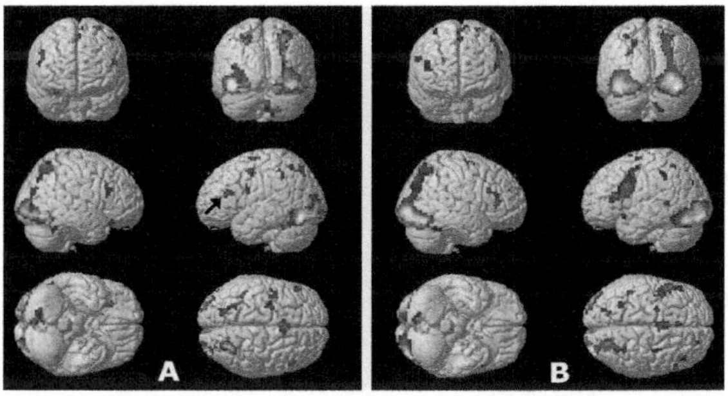

Fig. 5. (A) Surface rendering of activation for xLow > Verdana (rand. eff., p = 0.005). Strong, large clusters of activation are present bilaterally in the occipital lobe. A small, weaker activation was found near Broca's area (indicated by the arrow). (B) Surface renderings of activation for xLow > Verdana (fix. eff., p = 0.001). This more sensitive analysis shows a larger cluster near Broca's area, though the activation is still not as strong as in the occipital cortex (as indicated by the brighter, yellow coloring of occipital activation). A small cluster of activation in the temporal gyrus, near Wernicke's area, was also found in this case.

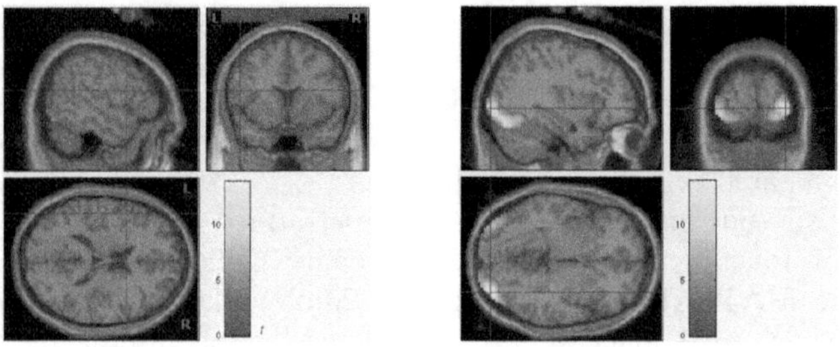

Fig. 6. Left, cross sectional views of the data from Fig. 6B show the large cluster of activation at Talairach coordinates [-50 12 16]. Broca's area (BA 44) makes up the inferior portion of this cluster of activation. Right, the cross sectional views show the strong activation in BA 18 in the occipital cortex near Talairach coordinates [36 -90 2].

4037 msec for Verdana, Middle, and xLow, respectively). A repeated measures ANOVA showed an overall effect of font, $F(2,22) = 8.33$, $p = 0.002$.

Imaging analysis of the fMRI data showed a significant activation when comparing the lowest quality font (xLow) to the highest quality font (Verdana) using random effects analysis, revealing substantial occipital activation and some frontal activation (Fig. 5). Small clusters of activation were detected in the left inferior and middle frontal gyri (BA 6/46) and in the right hemisphere. Using fixed effect analysis to compare xLow to Verdana (Fig. 5 and 6), large areas of activation were again found bilaterally in the occipital cortex. A larger activation was found in the left frontal cortex that included Broca's Area and extended from the inferior gyrus to the middle frontal gyrus and precentral gyrus (BA 6, 9, 44, 47). The fixed effects analysis can be more sensitive to activation than random effects, but is not as statistically rigorous.

2.3 Discussion

Varying the level of font degradation affects the visual characteristics of the text, so it is not surprising that the most robust activations were found in the occipital cortex, which is associated with low-level visual processing. Occipital activation was found for all three contrasts (Middle > Verdana, xLow > Middle, xLow > Verdana), with the largest clusters found for the xLow > Verdana contrast.

Though language area activations were not as robust as the occipital activations, clusters were found near Broca's area and Wernicke's area. These are of interest because previous reading studies showed them to activate when varying cognitive demand through manipulation of other factors, namely syntactic complexity [8], complexity of semantic integration [1], and both lexical and syntactic complexity [9].

Based on the results of the fMRI phase of study, the inferior and middle frontal gyrus (near Broca's area) and the occipital cortex were selected as the most promising regions for further investigation in the fNIR portion of the study.

3 Phase II: fNIR Analysis of Usability

The second phase of the study focused on activation levels in Broca's area and the visual cortex as areas of interest identified by the first phase of the study.

3.1 Methods

Twelve right-handed adults participated; all had normal or corrected-to-normal vision. Text was displayed to participants using a high quality visual display with a 124 DPI resolution (1400x1050 on a 14.1" diagonal). Stimulus presentation software was developed in C#.NET. Screen font edge smoothing was turned off ensure degradation. Response data was collected using the display laptop.

The OTIS-2 system was used for fNIR imaging with its sensors secured to the subjects' head using the commercially available Mark Easy 10-20 cap. This provided assistance in correctly placing the sensors on the scalp over Broca's area and the visual cortex as well as holding the sensors in place comfortably and reliably.

3.1.1 Reading Tasks

The reading tasks, presentation timing, and response scoring used were the same as in the first phase. Response times and accuracy were recorded for behavioral analysis.

3.1.2 Varying Font Readability

This phase of the study compared ClearType font (sub-pixelated Verdana) to Verdana and the extremely degraded xLow. Samples of the fonts used is shown in Fig. 7.

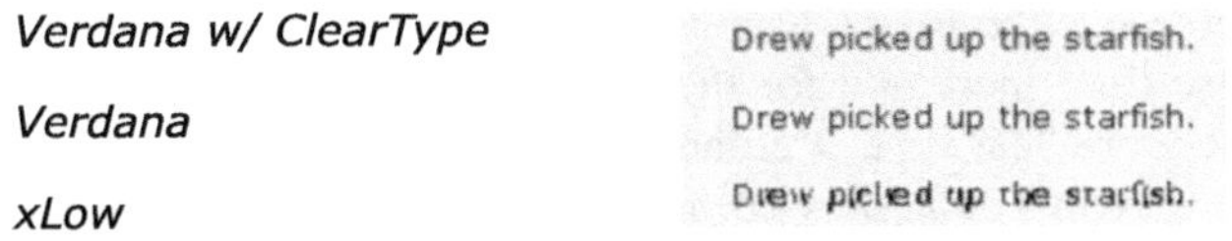

Fig. 7. Fonts used in this phase of the study

The ClearType condition used Verdana text rendered with Microsoft ClearType (http://www.microsoft.com/typography/ClearTypeInfo.mspx), which is a software technology designed to improve readability of fonts on LCD screens. ClearType is a sub-pixel rendering technique that is available in Microsoft Windows.

Each session consisted of three runs per person, with each run consisting of two font conditions and eight sentence pairs for each of the two fonts. The font order was alternated within a run following a 30 second fixation period in which a cross-hair was displayed on the screen to gather baseline data for the oxygenation calculations.

3.1.3 Analysis

Raw fNIR values were converted to relative oxy-hemoglobin concentrations using a modified Beer-Lambert equation [6]. This oxygenation data was smoothed through a low-pass Butterworth filter (f_c = 0.3Hz) then normalized to the mean and standard deviation of the filtered oxygenation signal over each run. Random-effects analysis was used to analyze and compare levels of activation between font states. This is a technique commonly used in functional imaging studies involving multiple subjects and has been adapted to be used with the single-point, time-course fNIR data [12].

This random-effects analysis assessed differences in brain activations related to font degradation using a multiple regression comparing oxygenation data to the modeled time course of each font condition. The canonical hemodynamic response function represents the mathematical model of the expected oxygenation time course due to cognitive activity in the imaged area. This was used as the modeled time course for analysis and was created from the fMRI data analysis package SPM99 (Wellcome Dept of Imaging Neuroscience, University College London, London, UK).

The modeled time courses for each font condition were used as predictors in a general linear model to determine how strongly the occurrence of each font predicted changes in the recorded subject data throughout the run. The regression coefficients, β_i, for each font were found and used to calculate a contrast value for each subject on each run. To test the hypothesis that the oxygenation response to the more degraded font is greater than the response to the less degraded font, the contrast ($\beta_{more\_degraded} - \beta_{less\_degraded}$) was used. A single-sample, one-tailed *t*-test was then performed on the contrast values across subjects for each run, testing for a greater activation in the more degraded font condition.

The behavioral analysis was identical to that used in the first phase of the study.

3.2 Results

Behavioral analysis showed highly accurate responses in all font conditions (90%, 89%, and 93% for xLow, Verdana, and ClearType, respectively). Similar to the behavioral results of the first phase, despite the differences in accuracy as font legibility increased, the effect was not great. As with the results of the first phase, mean response time increased for the highly degraded font (2937 msec, 2764 msec, and 3421 msec for ClearType, Verdana, and xLow, respectively).

The fNIR imaging data showed a significantly higher cognitive activation in the visual cortex when comparing the lowest quality font (xLow) to each of the higher quality fonts, ClearType and Verdana, using random effects analysis. In the trial comparing xLow to ClearType, the random-effects analysis resulted in $t = 1.8$, $p = 0.0494$, indicating higher visual cortex activations when reading xLow text. Similar results were found in the random-effects analysis of the trial comparing xLow to Verdana ($t = 1.9$, $p = 0.0419$). The random-effects analysis showed no significant difference in the visual cortex during the processing of sentence pairs presented in Verdana compared to ClearType, indicating less of a difference in visual processing activation. The analysis also showed no significant difference in the processing of sentence pairs for any fonts in the imaging of Broca's area.

4 Discussion

The results of the analysis indicate statistically significant differences in cognitive activation levels in the visual processing cortex when comparing the processing of xLow and both Verdana and ClearType conditions. These activation differences indicate a higher workload requirement for reading and processing degraded fonts, thus quantitatively verifying the increase in readability as font quality is improved.

The lack of significant differences in the activation levels in Broca's area between font qualities in the second phase of the study using fNIR may be due to the tasks the subjects performed. Although subjects were given six seconds to read each sentence, response times were within the 2-4 second range, so language processing may not have been constant throughout the duration of the six-second sentence display. Future studies will focus on more common and natural reading tasks to determine if these effects persist and will require longer and more consistent reading task blocks to determine the effects, if any, on language processes in the imaging of Broca's area.

The results of this study showed that there are some significant differences in the brain when a subject is reading fonts of varying qualities that can be quantified using fNIR imaging. While the fMRI study mapped areas of the brain that showed significant differences in activity when reading fonts of varying quality, the fNIR device offered a portable and wearable technique for neural imaging. Therefore, fNIR allows readability analysis through cognitive activity monitoring in natural work environments. Given the increasing amount of time spent reading on monitors and devices with LCDs, such as PDAs and phones, the quantitative analysis validation of increased effort required by degraded fonts is significant.

The approach described in this study may also apply more generally for usability analysis to determine the cognitive processes required in performing various tasks, such as with a new software application or electronic device. Following these protocols may provide further insight into the strategies that subjects adopt without relying on self-reports, which can be subjective and potentially biased. This study therefore demonstrates a multi-step process for evaluating interfaces that could become standard practice in user studies and usability engineering.

Acknowledgements

These studies were funded by Microsoft Advanced Reading Technologies. The initial development of the fNIR system used was funded by DARPA under the Augmented Cognition program.

References

1. Baumgaertner, A., Weiller, C., Buchel, C.: Event-related fMRI reveals cortical sites involved in contextual sentence integration. NeuroImage 16, 736–745 (2001)
2. Cabeza, R., Nyberg, L.: Imaging cognition II: An empirical review of 275 PET and fMRI studies. Journal of Cognitive Neuroscience 12, 1–47 (2000)
3. Cope, M.: The development of a near-infrared spectroscopy system and its application for non-invasive monitoring of cerebral blood and tissue oxygenation in the newborn infant, Ph.D. Thesis, Dept. of Medical Physics and Bioengineering, University College London (1991)
4. Federmeier, K.D., Kutas, M.: Right words and left words: electrophysical evidence for hemispheric differences in meaning processing. Cognitive Brain Research 8, 373–392 (1999)
5. Fox, P. T., Raichle, M. E.: Focal physiological uncoupling of cerebral blood flow and oxidative metabolism during somatosensory stimulation in human subjects. In: Proc. Natl. Acad. Sci. USA. vol. 83 pp. 1140–1144 (1986)

6. Franceschini, M.A., Boas, D.A., Zourabian, A., Diamond, S.G., Nadgir, S., Lin, D.W., Moore, J.B., Fantini, S.: Near-infrared spiroximetry: noninvasive measurements of venous saturation in piglets and human subjects. J. Appl. Physiol. 92, 372–384 (2002)
7. Gugerty, L., Tyrrell, R.A., Aten, T.R., Edmonds, K.A.: The effects of subpixel addressing on users' performance and preferences during reading-related tasks. ACM Transactions on Applied Perceptions 1, 81–101 (2004)
8. Just, M.A., Carpenter, P.A., Keller, T.A., Eddy, W.F., Thulborn, K.R.: Brain activation modulated by sentence comprehension. Science 274, 114–116 (1996)
9. Keller, T.A., Carpenter, P.A., Just, M.A.: The neural bases of sentence comprehension: a fMRI examination of syntactic and lexical processing. Cerebral Cortex 11, 223–237 (2001)
10. Nishimura, E.M., Stautzenberger, J., Robinson, W., Downs, T.H., Downs, J.H.III.: A New Approach to fNIR: OTIS. IEEE Engineering in Medicine and Biology Magazine (in press 2007)
11. Ogawa, S., Lee, T.M., Kay, A.R., Tank, D.W.: Brian magnetic resonance imaging with contrast dependent on blood oxygenation. In: Proc. Natl. Acad. Sci. USA. vol. 87, pp. 9868–9872 (1990)
12. Penny, W.D., Holmes, A.J.: Random-Effects Analysis. In: Human Brain Function, 2nd edn. Elsevier, Amsterdam (2004)
13. Pugh, K.R., Shaywitz, B.A., Shaywitz, S.E., Constable, R.T., Skudlarski, P., Fulbright, R.K., Bronen, R.A., Shankweiler, D.P., Katz, L., Fletcher, J.M., Gore, J.C.: Cerebral organization of component processes in reading. Brain 119(4), 1221–1238 (1996)
14. Savoy, R.L.: History and future directions of human brain mapping and functional neuroimaging. Acta Psychologica 107, 9–42 (2001)

Smart Furoshiki: A Context Sensitive Cloth for Supporting Everyday Activities

Ryo Ohsawa, Kei Suzuki, Takuya Imaeda, Masayuki Iwai, Kazunori Takashio, and Hideyuki Tokuda

Keio University, Graduate School of Media and Governance,
5322 Endo, Fujisawa, Kanagawa, 252-8520 Japan
{ryo,suzuk,che,tailor,kaz,hxt}@ht.sfc.keio.ac.jp
http://smart-furoshiki.com/

Keywords: Furoshiki, Smart Cloth, RFID, Context Awareness.

1 Introduction

This paper introduces a novel system for supporting everyday activities. Recent researches have proposed the embedding of computers and sensors in user environments so as to provide assistance in certain scenarios [1]. However, it is difficult for users to make the environments. Our goal is to develop a technology that will enable novice users to create such environments easily. In order to achieve this goal, we have developed a sensorized cloth called ``Smart Furoshiki."

Fig. 1. Furoshiki: Japanese Traditional Wrapping Cloth [2]

Furoshiki, which is a type of traditional Japanese cloth used to wrap merchandise, is large, square-shaped, and flexible. It is also used as a tablecloth and as a cloth to cover or wrap different objects. The Smart Furoshiki can identify objects that are covered by it or placed on it and recognize user actions such as wrapping, covering, and bending. Based on these user contexts, applications can assist users. Researches aimed at realizing a smart carpet or smart tablecloth that is capable of identifying objects placed on it have been conducted in the past [3] [4]. The Smart Furoshiki, in

J. Jacko (Ed.): Human-Computer Interaction, Part II, HCII 2007, LNCS 4551, pp. 1193–1199, 2007.

comparison to the abovementioned cloths, can change its shape with greater flexibility. Therefore, users can use the Smart Furoshiki both as a carpet and as a tablecloth.

2 Concept: A Context Sensible Cloth

An advantage of furoshiki is its ability in assisting in the wrapping of various objects such as a box, bottle, fruit, etc. The method employed for wrapping a box with a furoshiki is shown in Fig.2. Further, a furoshiki is also used as a table cloth, cover, etc. The Smart Furoshiki concept involves obtaining user contexts and providing support in daily life. In order to obtain user contexts, the Smart Furoshiki can detect a user's operations on it and identify objects placed on it.

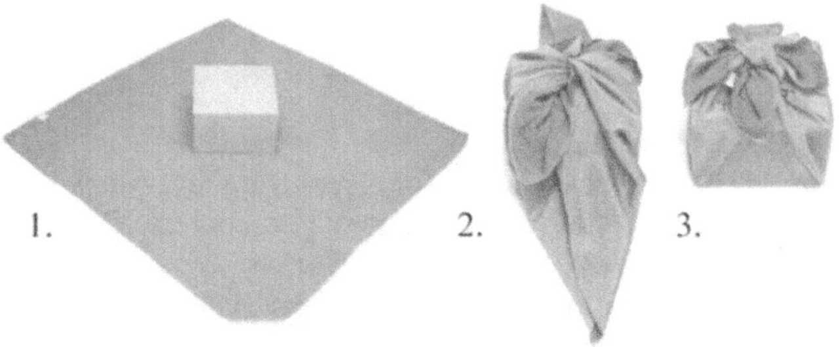

Fig. 2. An example of furoshiki's usage [2]

3 Method

The prototype of the Smart Furoshiki is shown in Fig.3. The antenna of the Smart Furoshiki is made of conductive fabrics [5] so that it can be bent in a flexible manner. The antenna connects an RF reader with a battery. The RF reader also has a Bluetooth module to enable it to communicate with appliances.

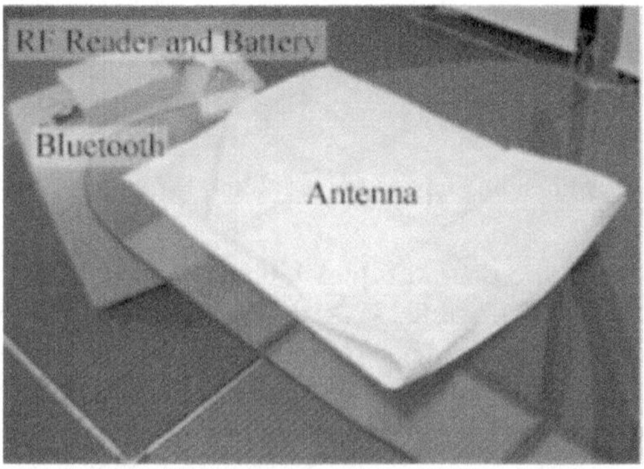

Fig. 3. The prototype of Smart Furoshiki

The Smart Furoshiki has two features. One is that it can identify objects that are placed on it or are covered by it. The other feature is its ability to recognize human actions such as wrapping, covering, and bending. The surface of the Smart Furoshiki can recognize RFID tags, thereby enabling it to identify objects placed on it.

Fig. 4. The Smart Furoshiki contains eight embedded RFID antennas and is capable of recognizing its own shape

This prototype contains eight embedded RFID antennas (in Fig.4), and it can recognize 13.56 MHz passive RFID tags. The RFID reader uses the eight antennas based on a timesharing system in order to prevent radio wave collisions between the antennas. The reading distance ranges from 0 to 180 mm according to the tag size. Since the Smart Furoshiki uses 13.56 MHz radio frequency, it is influenced by metals. Therefore, the range of the Smart Furoshiki would change depending on the environment that it is located in. In order to solve this problem, a calibration algorithm was implemented in the Smart Furoshiki. Furoshiki is used for various purposes. The Smart Furoshiki can recognize user actions such as laying, covering, and hanging. In order to detect these actions, the Smart Furoshiki should be capable of recognizing its own shape. In our approach, tiny RFID tags are embedded in the Smart Furoshiki. The image on the left of Fig.4 shows the antenna and tag layout of the Smart Furoshiki. According to this image, antenna 1 usually reads tag 1. However, if the Smart Furoshiki is folded, as shown in the image on the right, antenna 1 reads tag 4, thereby recognizing its folded form.

4 Applications

This section discusses the effectiveness of the proposed system in actual applications supporting daily activities; some examples are depicted by the images in Fig.5. We start off by explaining three applications. Each application detects different user actions and the shape of the Smart Furoshiki in each of them is different. We assume that objects of everyday use are attached with RFID tags so that the Smart Furoshiki can detect their presence.

4.1 Smart Desk

Smart Desk is a desk covered with the Smart Furoshiki. In one application of this desk, the Smart Furoshiki supports collaboration between media and actuators placed on it (the image one in Fig.5). When a user wishes to watch a movie on a PDA, he/she places the PDA as well as a DVD media, positioned near the PDA, on the Smart Furoshiki. In this application, the PDA is able to detect the DVD media and play the corresponding media content. In another application, when a user leaves his/her work desk and covers objects placed on the desk with the Smart Furoshiki, he/she can lock the objects to prevent other people from using them (the image two in Fig.5). If an unauthorized person uncovers the Smart Furoshiki, a security system immediately sets off an alarm. In order to uncover the Smart Furoshiki, the user's identifying object must be placed on it.

Fig. 5. 1: Smart Desk, 2: Security Cover, 3: Smart Wrapping, 4: Smart Wall

4.2 Smart Wrapping

Since the Furoshiki is essentially used for wrapping objects, the Smart Furoshiki is equipped to recognize wrapped objects and their shape. Nowadays, sensor RFID tags are equipped with additional devices to aid vendors; for instance, RFID tags could be equipped with an acceleration sensor [6] or a temperature sensor [7]. When such tags are embedded in the Smart Furoshiki, the user is able to determine the characteristics of the wrapped object (the image three in Fig.5). For example, if a user wishes to carry a bottle of wine wrapped in the Smart Furoshiki, he/she will be able to determine the characteristics of the bottle and therefore, handle it with care.

4.3 Smart Wall

Another useful application can be realized by hanging the Smart Furoshiki on a wall, like tapestry (the image four in Fig.5). In an office, people often pin memos on the wall in order to remember them easily. In this application, when a user writes a memo with an electronic pen [8]} and pins it on a Smart Furoshiki hung on the wall, the memo appears on a PC or a mobile device. In Fig.5, the Smart Furoshiki is separated into 4 areas based on the priority of the task, such as ``Emergency task'' and ``Pending task.''

4.4 Historical Data Analysis

In order to determine user context from historical data, we use a middleware called ``OreDesk [9]." OreDesk calculates the ``relation index" and ``active index" values for each object based on user operations. The relation index indicates how closely one object is related to another. For conveying the relation index, the Smart Furoshiki reminds users about objects left behind on it. The active index indicates a user's interest in an object. For conveying the active index, the Smart Furoshiki extracts a user's preference from his/her daily behavior in the real world.

5 Experiments

We have conducted two experiments on the Smart Furoshiki prototype. First, in order to evaluate its basic performance, its sensing area is measured in three dimensions. Second, we have conducted a feasibility test in typical scenarios.

5.1 Sensing Area Measurement

The result of a measurement is shown in Fig.6. The left image of the figure indicates a horizontal sensing area. The blue line indicates an antenna embedded into the Smart Furoshiki. The antenna, which is a 200 × 200 (mm^2) square, can identify the RFID tag that is placed on an orange area. In the case when an antenna is in the neighborhood of another one, the sensing area is more spread on account of electromagnetic induction. In the case of the figure, the right, left, and front areas are more spread than the back area. The right image in Fig.6 is a vertical sensing area extending from A to B in the left image. The center of an antenna has the largest sensing area. On account of electromagnetic induction, the sensing area is widely spread across the antenna line.

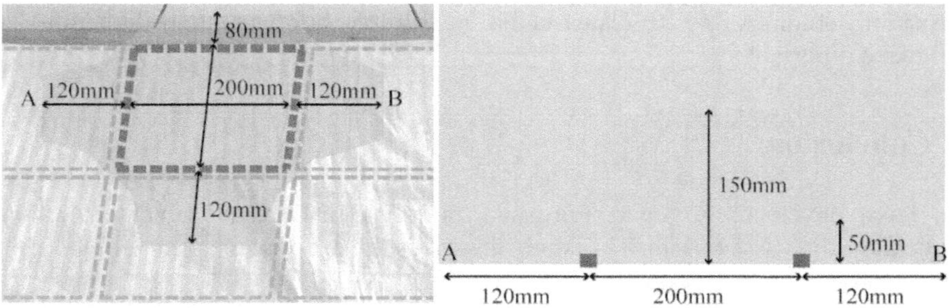

Fig. 6. Left: Horizontal Sensing Area; Right: Vertical Sensing Area

5.2 Feasibility Test in Typical Scenarios

We have conducted a feasibility test in typical scenarios. In one scenario, users lay the Smart Furoshiki on an office desk. In another one, the Smart Furoshiki is used on a dining table. We selected objects that are often used in these situations and experimented to ascertain which objects the Smart Furoshiki can recognize. We used a square 45×76 mm^2 Tag-it RFID tag that is shaped like a business card [10]. We attached these tags both above and under an object. In order to attach them to metal materials, On-Metal tags were prepared. The results of our experiments are shown in Table 1. The 13.56 MHz radio signal that the Smart Furoshiki emits is strongly influenced by aluminum and metal materials. Using the On-Metal Tag, the influence on the Smart Furoshiki by such materials becomes negligible. However, when a large metal object such as a PC and a display covers an object, the Smart Furoshiki cannot recognize it.

Table 1. Sensing accuracy of the objects

	Office Desk								
	Laptop PC	Display	PDA	Cell Phone	Keyboard	DVD	Book	Wallet	Mirror
Under	×	×	×	×	○	○	○	○	○
Under (On-Metal Tag)	×	×	○	○	○	○	○	○	○
Above	×	×	×	×	○	○	○	○	○

	Dining Table								
	Plate			Drink				Package	
				Bottle		Can			
	Ceramic	Wooden	Glass	PET	Glass	Steel	Aluminum	Plastic	Aluminum
Under	○	○	○	○	○	×	×	○	×
Under (On-Metal Tag)	○	○	○	○	○	○	○	○	○
Above	○	○	○	○	○	×	×	○	×

6 Future Work

The Smart Furoshiki prototype that we proposed should enable connecting an RF reader, which is too big for users to carry easily. We are developing the next Smart Furoshiki version. A tiny RF reader and a small li-ion battery are embedded in it. This will make it portable.

7 Conclusion

We have developed a Smart Furoshiki prototype and have implemented many applications that assist users. This study describes the experimentation with this Smart Furoshiki prototype.

References

1. Muller-Tomfelde, C., Konomi, S., Streitz, N., Tandler, P.: Roomware: Towards the next generation of human-computer interaction based on an integrated design of real and virtual worlds. In: Carroll, J.(ed.) Human Computer Interaction in the New Millenium, pp. 553–578. Addison-Wesley
2. Japan furoshiki association http://furoshiki.homepage.jp/

3. Fukumoto, M., Shinagawa, M.: Carpetlan: A novel indoor wireless networking and positioning system. In: Beigl, M., Intille, S.S., Rekimoto, J., Tokuda, H. (eds.) UbiComp 2005. LNCS, vol. 3660, pp. 1–18. Springer, Heidelberg (2005)
4. Post, E.R., Orth, M., Russo, P.R., Gershenfeld, N.: E-broidery: design and fabrication of textile-based computing. IBM Syst. J. 39(3-4), 840–860 (2000)
5. Tanaka, M., Jang, J.-H.: Wearable microstrip antenna for satellite communications. IEICE Transaction on Communications, (August 2004)
6. OMRON Corporation http://www.omron.co.jp/
7. Ltd Oki Electric Industry Co http://www.oki.com/jp/Home/JIS/New/OKINews/2006/04/z06005.html
8. Pentel. Pentel airpen http://www.airpen.jp/
9. Ohsawa, R., Takashio, K., Tokuda, H.: Oredesk: A tool for retrieving history data based on user's operations. In: Proceedings of IEEE International Symposium on Multimedia 2006 (ISM2006), vol. 12 (2006)
10. Texas Instruments Inc. Tag-it. IEICE Transaction on Communications (August 2004) http://www.ti.com/

Information Display of Wearable Devices Through Sound Feedback of Wearable Computing

Park Young-hyun and Han Kwang-hee

Cognitive Engineering Lab., Department of Psychology, University of Yonsei, Korea
ohitsme@yonsei.ac.kr

Abstract. Functions in wearable devices came to be various and specialized during the developmental process of wearable computing. However, such surfacing of new functions made it difficult and time-consuming for the devices to display the condition of their status, such as whether they are turned on or off. Moreover, mere dependency on visual display could lead to an overload of users' visual cognition. In this research, sounds were used for relaying information feedback of the status of wearable devices. We first verified the usefulness of adding sound feedback, and next, the effect of each device-specific sound was confirmed as a sound feedback.

Keywords: wearable computing, information display, sound feedback, auditory icon, earcon.

1 Introduction

Wearable computing researches go with the ideal for customized personal computer. Today's personal computer supports nearly same functions and same features whoever the user is. This means that personal computer is not so personal [10]. Wearable computing, however, has been developed to customized form signaling danger to user by checking the body conditions [14], giving an affective reaction by sensing the physiological status [11], informing the schedule or empowering the personal ability (personal empowerment) [8][9]. At an initial developing process, the use of wearable computer was limited to specific work area like warehouse work and combat situation due to the physical size and economical problems rather than everyday life use. But nowadays, wearable computer is becoming common use device combining with sports industries, entertainment industries, telecommunication industries and so on [12].

Increased personal or industrial expectation made a number of functions and the more wearable devices became necessary. Smart Clothing researches in Yonsei University [2] has a conceptual model of smart wear supports mp3 music playing, mobile communication, body and atmosphere sensing (temperature, humidity, ultraviolet, body heat, body acidity, etc.), heating, and light emitting. And these functions can be supported by each specific device. At this point, some problems reveals.

The common problematic issue starts from the fact that an information display is dependent just upon vision. The type of visual display can be various, for example,

J. Jacko (Ed.): Human-Computer Interaction, Part II, HCII 2007, LNCS 4551, pp. 1200–1209, 2007.

the Head-Mounted Display (HMD) [13], or wrist attaching screens, but these types of display have a physical limitation of size for an amount of information. And, when the wearable computers support the specific workplace tasks, the user's cognitive load should be minimized doing tasks. Because wearable computer has a property of "wears", it must not interfere with the user's movement owing to vision capture [5]. If one's eyes are engaged just in display screen, it is possible to have accidents due to the absence of visual attention.

This study started to overcome the limitation of an information display of wearable computer by auditory display. Although the vision takes a main role in perceiving many objects and their environments, adding the sense of audition and touch makes the process of visual information more fast and accurate [3]. Especially in audition, it is possible to convey considerable information for itself. Up to now, auditory information display has been considered as an assistant to visual displays, for an example of feedback in telephone button press. However auditory display can take a main role in small screen or moving situation like wearable computing and will be indispensable for conveying information.

The effect we would verify in this study is first, adding auditory information display will be benefit rather than interference to information display, secondly audition can convey information about the identity and the conditions of device in wearable computing situation even though the visual display is not possible to use, thirdly this auditory display can get the benefit of not only efficiency, but also subjective satisfaction and perceived usability. In this study, participants were asked to report the name of current functioning device and the condition of device using audio-visual information, and we checked the reaction time (RT) for verifying the efficiency of auditory displays.

Experimental situation assumes that visual information is combined and displayed to one small screen in wearable computer.

2 Experiment 1

Concerns about adding auditory information to visual display are whether it becomes interferences rather than helps with performing other tasks. Actually inadequate redundant information can make the user annoying. So the aim of first experiment is verifying and quantifying the beneficial effect of auditory information in the vision-based wearable computing environment.

2.1 Participants and Apparatus

Ten undergraduate students participated in this experiment and they got academic credits as compensation for participation. Six flexible buttons connected to PC were attached to participant's both sides of shoulder and waist and outer side of knees as a representation of wearable devices. And if participant press theses buttons, experimenters can check which button is pressed. We regard the button pressing as 'participant perceived the current device'.

17-inch CRT Monitor used as a visual display screen, and the stimulus displayed here were 6 x 12cm size pictures representing participant. In this picture, there were

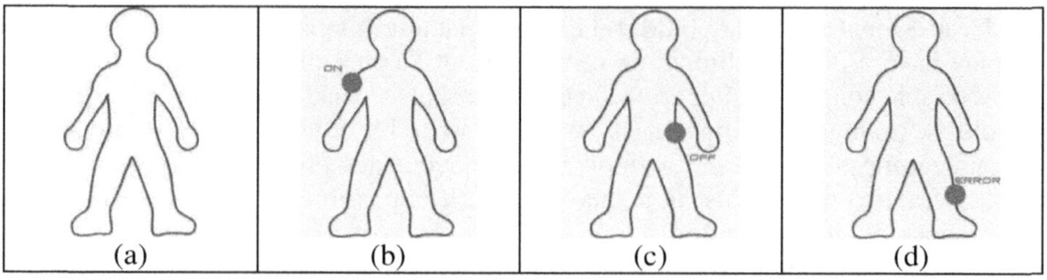

Fig. 1. Examples of visual stimuli used in Experiment. Based on the picture (a), red circle was placed in both side of shoulder, waist and outer side of knees, and "ON", "OFF", "ERROR" was also written in each picture.

red circles at the same positions of participant's body with text (font face "Xirod", font size "16") describes the device conditions.

Including (b), (c), (d) in figure 1, devices were categorized to six through the position and the names of devices were not determined. Conditions were condensed into "ON", "OFF", "ERROR" which every device support. Auditory displays were presented through the earphone and sound stimuli have an Electrical Piano (EP) timbre. Through the experimental conditions, sound was played into left, right or both ears all, and musical tone and structure of sounds were various.

2.2 Procedures

Before the beginning of experiment, experimenter showed the picture stimuli and played the sound stimuli for making them familiar to stimuli and to know what they mean. Task was to press the button attached to the body position expressed to visual and auditory display and to say the condition of device selected.

There are four kinds of experimental conditions, and on all over the conditions, visual display presents after auditory display. At first condition, stimuli are 1000ms of G_4 tone, and this sound presents both sides of ears simultaneously. This has no spatial information and just acted as a notice for the visual stimulus (condition1). Sound in second condition has a spatial (left or right) information (condition2), and if the device now functioning is attached to left side of body in the basis of medial sagittal plane, sound presents just on the left side of the earphone and vice versa. While the sounds have just left or right spatial information in condition 2, elevation information is included to sound stimulus in addition to the sound used in third condition (condition3). Sound for devices attached to the upper part of body has G_6, the mid part of body has G_4, and down part of body has G_6 musical tone. Although sound used to fourth experimental condition is different from the sounds used in other conditions, it consists of two kinds of musical tones which is C-G being mapped to "ON", G-C to "OFF", G-G to "ERROR" (condition4). The way conveying spatial information is same with that of condition2, 3, and elevation information is represented by the octave differences. We call this kind of non-speech sounds as earcon [1]. For example, if the condition of device attached to the right side of shoulder is "ON", sounds consist of C_6-G_6 presented to right side of the earphone and if the condition of device attached to the left side of waist is "OFF", sounds consist of G_4-C_4 presents to

Table 1. Differenct kinds of information in each condition. This was added to the information of Fig.1.

Condition	Left, Right info	Up, Down info	Condition info
1	X	X	X
2	o	X	X
3	o	o	X
4	o	o	o

left side of the earphone and if the condition of device attached to outer side of right knee is "ERROR", sounds consist of G_6-G_6 presents to right side of the earphone.

After participants came to know where the button is, they exercised with training block consist of six trials in each conditions. And in main experimental blocks, participants exposed to four blocks consist of 18trials and the orders of trials and blocks were counterbalanced. And the reaction time was checked from the start point of visual display present.

2.3 Result

Like the figure 2 describes, RT differences among conditions were significant. $F(3, 27) = 69.93$, $p = .00$. Post hoc test showed significant differences in each condition except between condition3 and condition4. (condition1 vs. condition2. $t(9)=4.75$, $p=.001$; condition2 vs. condition3. $t(9)=11.02$, $p=.00$; condition3 vs. condition4. $t(9)=.94$, $p>.05$) This result demonstrates the efficiency of auditory displays and device condition information can be conveyed by sound without loss of performance.

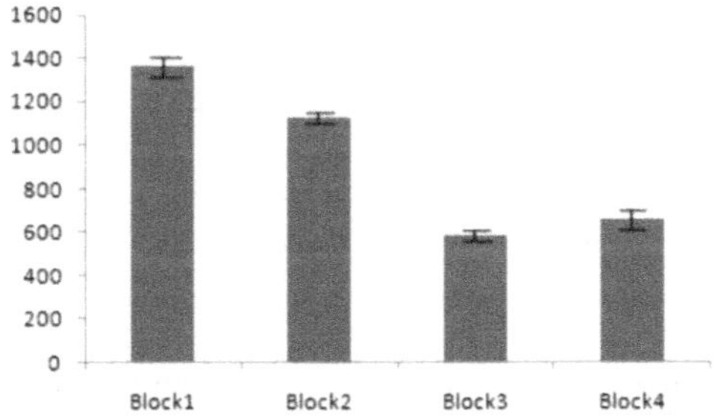

Fig. 2. Distribution of RT in each condition of Experiment1

3 Experiment 2

Based on the result of experiment 1, experimental situation changed to more applicable settings in experiment 2. The differences of situation of experiment 1 comparing to real-world setting are that the position of device was not natural and users had to perceive the devices based on their physical position. So the positions of devices are rearranged in experiment 2 based on the concept models of Yonsei Smart Clothing. And device-specific sounds were used instead of device position sounds for describing device identity in auditory displays. Moreover, methodological problems were revised in experiment 2. Because the visual display was presented after the auditory display, participants had enough time to prepare to react upon visual display and interferences of sound could not exist in this experimental feature. And this situation had less validity than real-world situations. So auditory and visual display presented simultaneously in the experiment 2 for enhancing the external validity.

3.1 Participants and Apparatus

21 undergraduate students participated in this experiment and they got an academy credits as compensation for participation. And we decided to use the trekking wear for the experiment platform among the many smart cloths (trekking wear, jogging wear, party wear, everyday life wear, etc..) developed by Yonsei Smart Clothing. Other devices were removed for experimental use, and flexible buttons used in experiment 2. And the kinds of devices applied to this experiment were also determined based on the concepts of Yonsei Smart Clothing. In addition to the MP3 music player, heating plate, humidity sensor included in trekking wear, light emitting in party wear and GPS transmitter, mobile communication device were supplemented. Device conditions were determined to "ON", "OFF", "ERROR" like the experiment 1.

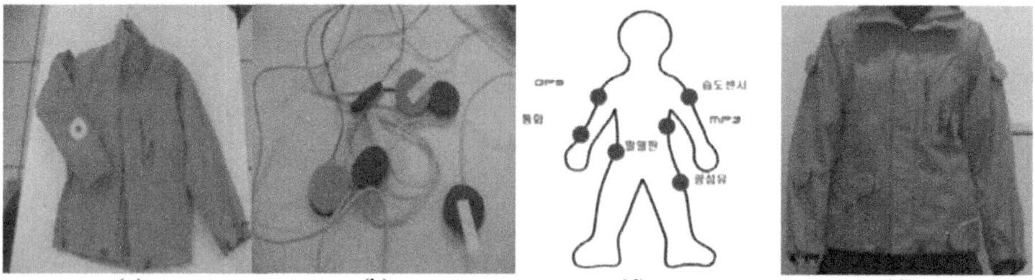

(a) (b) (d) (d)

Fig. 3. Materials used in experiment2 and their arrays. (a) is trekking wear, (b) is picture flexible buttons, (c) is arrays of (b), and (d) is feature of experimental platform which is attached buttons.

Feature of visual display was also modified from picture type to text type. Although picture was intuitive to recognize, participants had to rotate the picture mentally for mapping the picture to their own body. This can make a surplus time or errors to determine the spatial position of devices. In this time, we used text as a visual stimulus which has no problematic factors in spatial decision. Font face was "Xirod" and font size was "16" in the 17-inch CRT monitor.

Sounds were presented through the earphone, and its timbre used as a device condition sound was EP same with experiment 1. However each device-specific sounds has various timbre and we call this kind of non-speech sounds as auditory icon [4]. Lyon (2000) used feedback sounds consisted of ambient sounds, sound effect, narrator's voice for expressing the augmented reality [7]. This study also used an auditory icon and earcon as an ambient sounds and sound effect like Lyon's way.

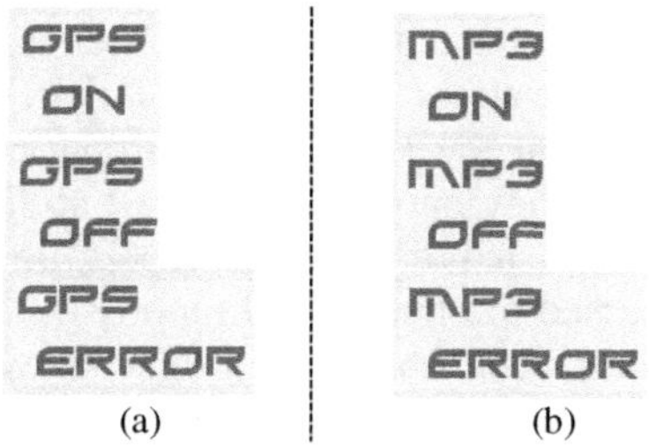

Fig. 4. Examples of visual stimuli used in experiment2. (a) is display for GPS condition, (b) is for MP3 player. Visual display presented like this way.

3.2 Procedure

Task was to press the button attached to the body position which expressed by visual and auditory display and to say the condition of device selected. There are four kinds of experimental conditions, and first two conditions (condition 1, condition 2) are same with condition 1, 2 in experiment 1 except the fact that visual stimulus changed to text type. Auditory stimulus used to third condition consist of device condition sound and device-specific sound, here device-specific sound (auditory icon) presents as a background sound and simultaneously, device condition sound (earcon) presents (condition 3). Duration time is 200ms and device condition sound presents in a 50ms after the device-specific sound presented.

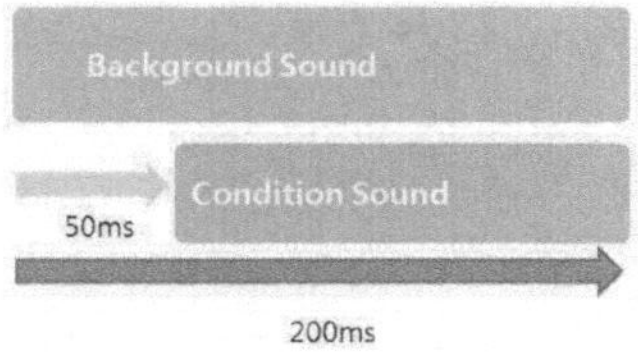

Fig. 5. The way that background sound and device condition sound present. Auditory icon represents device identity present first and earcon represents device condition presents overlapped to auditor icon after 50ms.

So many sounds were made by Reason 3.0, a sequencing application or many downloaded effect sounds modified device by experimenter for representing each. Selected sounds by prior ratings were used as device-specific sounds, and participants heard these sounds two times and were asked to remember the device identity represented by sound. According to the comments of participants for the sound used on experiment 1, musical tone “E” included between the two tones of device condition sound. So “ON” sound consist of “C-E-G”, “OFF” sound consist of “G-E-C”. And “ERROR” sound changed to buzzer sound. These device condition sounds also exposed to participants before the beginning of training blocks and participants were tested whether they recognize the sound as device condition and device identity well. Visual display was removed in fourth condition (condition 4).

Monitor was place to the front-left side of the participant in the degree of 45°, and participant was asked to gaze at the front side at first. If the sound presents on earphone, they asked to look at the screen and to confirm the device identity and device condition. After that, they should press the button represents device which informed by the auditory and visual display, and report the condition of the device. In condition 4, participant pressed the button and reported the device condition without looking at the screen. Each block has 18 trials and these four conditions' blocks formed one session. Three sessions performed for confirming the learning effect in experiment 2.

3.3 Results

Result showed that the difference among three sessions was significant in RT ($F(2, 38)=110.90$, $p=.00$), and interaction effect between conditions and sessions was revealed significantly $F(6, 114)=3.36$, $p<.005$.

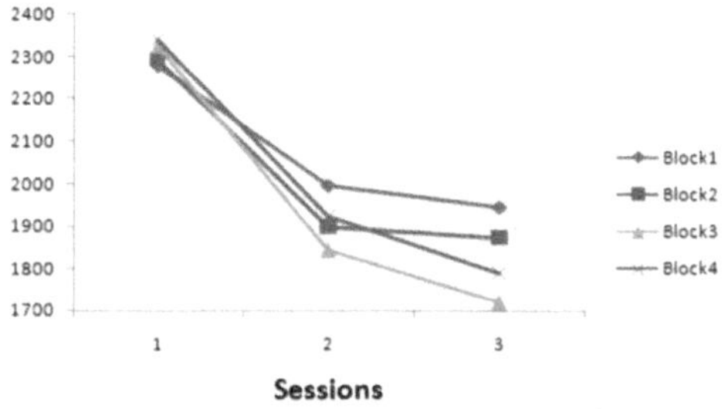

Fig. 6. The distribution of RT according to the condition and session. This shows that RT difference at each condition in one session and RT is becoming shorter as the session flows.

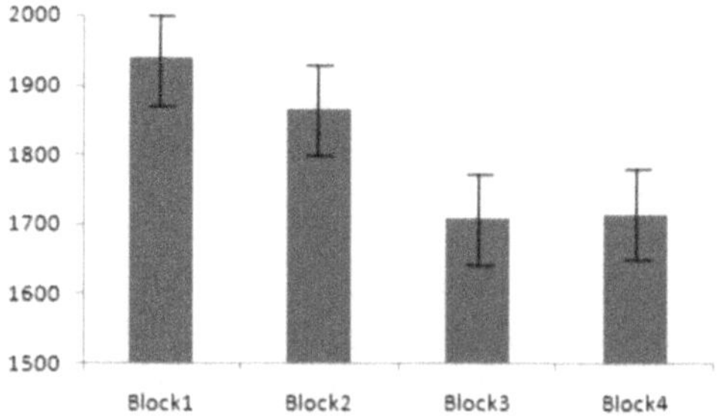

Fig. 7. Examples of visual stimuli used in experiment2. (a) is display for GPS condition, (b) is for MP3 player. Visual display presented like this way.

Based on the interaction effects between the conditions and sessions, the difference in RT among conditions was analyzed separately. There was RT difference significantly among each condition in result of session3 $F(3, 79)=5.39$, $p<.005$. Post hoc test was executed for clarifying the detailed relations among conditions. There were significant differences in each condition except condition 1 vs. condition2 and condition3 vs. condition4 (condition1 vs. condition3, $t(20)$=8.04, p=.00; condition2 vs. condition3-, $t(20)$=4.44, p=.00; condition1 vs. condition4, $t(19)$=3.67, p<.005; condition2 vs. condition4, $t(19)$=2.39, p<.05).

4 Subjective Rating

4.1 Procedure

At the end of each session, participants rated the sound subjectively. They answered to five scaled questionnaires which evaluate the convenience, perceived efficiency, annoyance, learnability, perceived appropriateness, assurance and ease of memorizing. Questions are below.

Table 2. Factors and questions evaluated in subjective rating

Number of Question	Measuring factors	Questions
1	Convenience	This sound is easy to hear.
2	Perceived Efficiency	This sound is helpful for me to use this system.
3	Annoyance	This sounds made me annoying.
4	Learnability	There was not necessary to learn to use this system.
5	Perceived Appropriateness	These sounds are appropriate to this system in my opinion.
6	Assurance	These sounds give me the assurance.
7	Ease of Memorizing	These sounds are easy to memory.

4.2 Result

The result of rating is described to figure 2. T-test showed that there was significant difference between condition 1 and condition 3 in question 1 ($t(17)$=2.38, p<0.5). And the condition 3 was rated significantly higher ($t(17)$=4.592, p=.00; $t(17)$=3.319, p<.01; $t(17)$=2.853, p<.05; condition 2 vs. condition 3) than condition 1 and 2 in question 2, 5, 6 which represents convenience, perceived efficiency, perceived appropriateness and assurance. According to these T-test results, we can conclude that sound used to condition 3 rated higher in convenience, efficiency, appropriateness and assurance than other sounds used in condition 1, 2.

5 Discussion

The results of two experiments show that wearer recognizes more quickly what the device is and how the device is when auditory information display was added to the

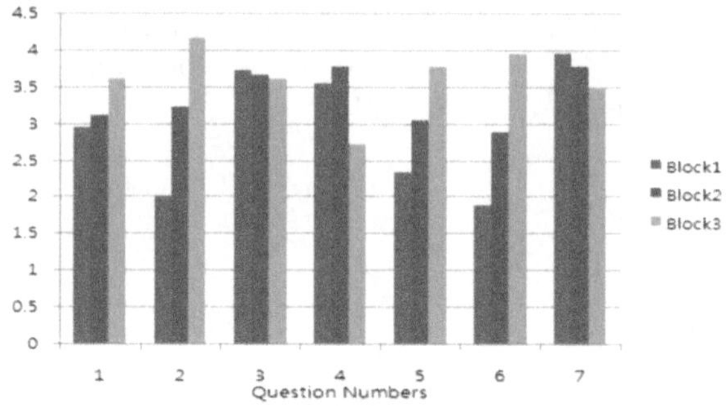

Fig. 8. Result of rating on each question

visual display. And result of continuing subjective rating shows that the effect of auditory display is not only simply limited in effectiveness but also is positive in subjective factors. We can induce next three conclusions by the results.

First, auditory information display is helpful to wearble computing, and information display using sounds can facilitate the performance of information acceptance. This effect originated from the information redundancy using vision and audition.

Second, as the wearer becomes familiar to their own wearable computer, they can recognize the device identity and device condition better using just auditory displays. Wearable computer has high coherence to the individual because they are designed to customized system which is able to perceive the physiological characters and support tasks and personal scheduling. Since the familiarity was assumed like this, the fact that it is possible to convey enough information without visual display, as the number of trial increases, is significant because it is linked to overcoming the physical limitation of screen size.

Third, it is more significant in the applied area that the fact which RT in conditions using background sounds for device identity was shorter and rated higher also in subjective evaluation. Leplatre (2004) emphasized the needs for the aesthetical consideration on the way of auditory display [8]. And there is study that the perceived aesthetic is correlated to the usability [15]. Since the background sounds are made for experiment, its aesthetic factors are not considered here. If the sounds are developed in the sense of aesthetics, it is enough to enhance the satisfactions of wearable computing.

Auditory information display has been studied in itself, and there are so many guidelines of sound design. However, in this study we applied the auditory display to the wearable computing and tested the usefulness and subjective merits. Earcon and auditory icon were used to conveying the wearable device identity and condition information in these two experiments. And there is additional meaning of this study that we applied the notion of earcon and auditory icon to wearable computing and tested its usefulness with quantified way.

Acknowledgments. Korea Ministry of Commerce, industry and Energy supported this work under the Product Planning of Smart Clothing (2006-8-1653). We would like to express our thanks to all the undergraduate students at the University of Yonsei who participated in this experiment. We would also like to thank our colleagues, Chae Haeng-Suk and Hong Ji-Young for their comments on earlier versions of this paper.

References

1. Blattner, M.M., Sumikawa, D.A., Greenberg, R.M.: Earcons and icons: Their structure and common design principles. Human-Computer Interaction 4, 11–44 (1989)
2. Chae, H.S., Hong, J.Y., Lee, S.R., Park, Y.H., Kim, J.H., Cho, H.S., Han, K.H.: Use context analysis for criteria development on usability evaluation of smart clothing. In: 2006 Spring Conference of KOSES & The 7th Korea-Japan Joint Symposium on Emotion & Sensibility (2006)
3. Cohen, P., McGee, D., Clow, J.: The efficiency of multimodal interaction for a map-based task. In: Proceedings of the sixth conference on Applied natural language processing (2000)
4. Gaver, W.W.: Auditory icons: Using sound in computer interfaces. Human-Computer Interaction 2, 167–177 (1986)
5. Knight, J.F., Baber, C., Schwirtz, A., Bristow, H.W.: The comfort assessment of wearable computers. In: The Sixth International Symposium on wearable Computers (2002)
6. Leplatre, G., McGregor, I.: How to tackle auditor interface aesthetics? Discussion and case study. In: International Conference on Auditory Display, Sydney, Australia (2004)
7. Lyon, K., Gandy, M., Starner, T.: Guided by Voices: An Audio Augmented Reality System. In: International Conference on Auditory Display, Atlanta, GA (2000)
8. Mann, S.: Smart Clothing: Wearable Multimedia and Personal Imaging to restore the balance between people and their intelligent environments. In: Proceedings of the forth ACM International Conference on Multimedia 96, ACM Press, New York (1996)
9. Mann, S.: Wearable computing as means for personal empowerment. Keynote Address International Conference on Wearable Computing (1998) http://wearcomp.org/wearcompdef.html
10. Norman, D.A.: The invisible computer. MIT Press, London (1998)
11. Picard, R., Healey, J.: Affective Wearable. In: Proceeding of First International Symposium on Wearble Computers (1997)
12. Shea, T.: The global market for wearable computers: The Quest For Killer Application, Venture Development Corporation, Massachusetts (2002)
13. Sutherland, I.: A head-mounted three-dimensional display. AFIPS Conference Proceedings, vol. 33, pp. 757–764 (1968)
14. Teller, A.: A platform for wearable physiological computing. Interacting with Computers 16(5), 917–937 (2004)
15. Tractinsky, N.: Aesthetics and apparent usability: Empirically assessing cultural and methodological issues. In: Proceedings of CHI'97, Atlanta GA, USA (1997)

An Evaluation Framework for the Design Concepts of Tangible Interface on New Collaborative Work Support System

Youngbo Suh[1], Cheol Lee[2,*], Joobong Song[2], Minjoo Jung[2], and Myung Hwan Yun[2]

[1] Korea Institute for Defense Analyses, Seoul, Korea
[2] Department of Industrial Engineering, Seoul National University
Seoul, 151-742 Korea
iehis@snu.ac.kr

Abstract. This study aims to suggest a systematic evaluation framework to evaluate design concepts of a new product at the conceptual design phase based on users' requirements and tasks, development trends of relevant technologies, and the CPV. The proposed framework to evaluate design concepts of a new product consists of three phases. In phase 1, we identify and analyze users' needs, functional requirements and their expected tasks by utilizing user scenario-based analysis and hierarchical task analysis. In phase 2, by deploying a relevant technology roadmap, we investigate technology alternatives for satisfying the user needs or functional requirements. In phase 3, we evaluate the design concepts using evaluation checklist, which is based on functional requirements derived from relationships analysis, utilizing CPV attribute for a quantifiable measure. A case study was demonstrated to evaluate the design concepts of a new CSCW-based tangible interface that was recently designed to support group decision making activities.

Keywords: Conceptual Design, Concept Evaluation, CPV, Technology Trends Analysis, Scenario, HTA.

1 Introduction

In conceptual design phase, it is required to generate physical solutions to meet design specification and evaluate them to choose one solution [1]. Through concept evaluation process, especially, it is possible to verify and supplement the current design concept to enhance the feasibility of the desired product [2, 3, 4, 5]. If the desired product is a non-existing product, it is difficult to identify users' implicit needs or requirements and related tasks which could be utilized as a basis of concept evaluation [6]. It is also difficult to assess users' perceived value on design concepts of the product since the product is not finalized but also intangible.

This study aims to suggest a systematic framework to evaluate design concepts of a new product at the early stage of product design process. Especially we focused on

* Corresponding author.

J. Jacko (Ed.): Human-Computer Interaction, Part II, HCII 2007, LNCS 4551, pp. 1210–1219, 2007.

the evaluating design concepts based on users' requirements and tasks that are implicit, development trends of relevant technologies, and the users' perceived value relating to the functionality of design concepts.

In this study, we elicited user needs and functional requirements through scenario-based analysis and hierarchical task analysis (HTA). By exploring the state-of-the art technologies and deploying a relevant technology roadmap, we identified technology alternatives that enable users to accomplish the required tasks in terms of effectiveness and efficiency, and to satisfy the user needs or functional requirements. For a quantifiable evaluation measure, we utilized the customer-perceived value (CPV) attributes to evaluate both benefits and costs of current design concepts.

2 Background

2.1 Design Concept Evaluation Methods

Dhillon [2] proposed a procedural approach to evaluate design concept while it may not be useful since specific guidelines for each evaluation phase were not specified. Design review [7], which could be executed after the design specification is determined, makes it possible to verify current design concepts in terms of whether the design concept fully considers initial design alternatives. However, it cannot detect whether the design concept includes all kinds of requirements that users actually need [8]. Concept selection matrix or concept scoring [3] might be quickly performed and easily understandable. There are some limitations in that aforementioned methods cannot verify whether the design concept can support users' expected tasks. In fact, a majority of studies on design concept evaluation mainly dealt with MADM (Multi-Attribute Decision Making) problems. In this context, it is still required to develop a systematic design concept evaluation methodology that enables to capture users' implicit requirements considering multiple attributes of the target product.

2. 2 Analyzing Users' Requirements

Identification of users' needs or requirements is crucial in the product design process. We proposed a procedure to identify and analyze users' requirements and their expected tasks by utilizing scenario-based analysis and hierarchical task analysis among various methods. Scenario can be regarded as a set of use cases having common features that can be occurred in the middle of system or product usage [9]. The reason why scenario-based approaches are useful is that scenarios could deal with specific situations [10].

Hierarchical task analysis is another powerful method to collect, classify, and analyze the data about user performances [11]. Task analysis usually begins with deciding the goals of product development. Next, task transcript including user performance based on task hierarchy is prepared. Based on the task transcript, activity list, which shows every task to be executed as a list, is described. With help of the list, it is possible to identify correlated tasks since components of each task in the list are positioned under the correlation of each task. Accordingly, detailed analysis might be iteratively performed to supplement task hierarchy and activity list so that confirmed task model is obtained.

2.3 Technology Trends Analysis

There are a number of techniques used for technology trends analysis [12]. In this study we utilized technology roadmap for technology trends analysis. Technology roadmap is a method that helps selecting the appropriate technology alternatives in accordance with the trends of technology development. It could be a technology strategy for uncertain future so that so it helps taking technology initiatives [12, 13]. In the era of information technology, technology trends analysis is inevitable for new product development in order to catch a vision of future environment for product usage as well as to take the technology initiatives for mid-to-long term period [13].

2.4 CPV Approaches in New Product Development

From the perspective of new product development, delivering superior value to customers means meeting target customers' needs and enhancing customer satisfaction [14]. In fact, the value concept is considered as one of the most popular and useful constructs among academia and industry [15, 16]. In this context, CPV has recently gained much attention from researchers since it play important role in achieving sustainable competitive advantage [16, 17].

The most common definition of value is the ratio or trade-off between quality and price, which is a value-for-money conceptualization [15, 16, 18]. Another operational definition of CPV is a consumers' overall assessment of the utility of a product based on perceptions of what is received and what is given [17]. According to the definition of Miller and Swaddling [15], CPV is the result of the customers' evaluation of all the benefits and all the costs of an offering as compared to the customers' perceived alternatives, which is the basis on customers' buying decision making. In this study, we utilized CPV in order to comprehend customers' acceptance of design concepts of a new product and their values.

3 Evaluation Framework

We developed a systematic evaluation scheme to assess the design concepts of a new product. The proposed evaluation framework consists of three phases as shown in Fig. 1.

3.1 Identifying Users' Task

The phase 1 is designed to elicit use cases based on scenarios described situation that is available to apply the design concepts of a target product. First, we describe a problem to be solved by design in scenarios. Then we identify various use cases in scenario, and perform claims analysis of effect that use cases could influence customers' tasks. Namely, we analyze trade-off between positive and negative effects that could be induced by functions of a new product [19]. '+ (pros)' represents

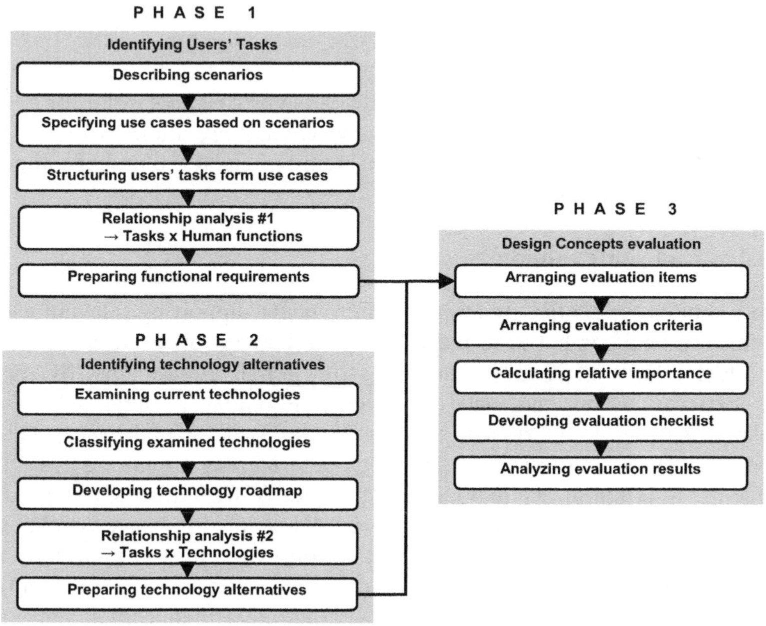

Fig. 1. The proposed framework for evaluation of design concepts

positive effects of related use cases to customers' behavior and '– (cons)' represents negative effects. Claims analysis is appropriate to develop scenarios in various ways based on every use cases in scenario so that it can be utilized to create new functions of the target product. Then, resulting use cases are transformed as users' tasks which are decomposed into sub-tasks and then structured through HTA technique. HTA is a methodology that divides one behavior to different task and its sub-tasks in order to identify hierarchical structure of the task [20]. These sub-tasks are supposed to be correlated with various human functions using relationship matrix analysis. Consequently, it is expected to identify users' functional requirements considering human capabilities, limitations, and characteristics related with the expected tasks.

3.2 Identifying Technology Alternatives

In the phase 2, we perform extensive survey to investigate technologies relevant to specified users' tasks in holistic perspective. It involves survey of product or technology that is already introduced in the market and could be developed in near future since long-range technology trends for 10 or 20 years time span is very chancy. After doing technology survey, we analyze recently available technology developing trends. Examined technologies are classified into several categories based on similarity between functional characteristics of each technology. Each of them would be further analyzed to estimate development trends. Based on the results, a technology roadmap is deployed by expert panel including domain specialists. Commonly, an axis of technology roadmap is market, product, technology or R&D while we focus on technological characteristics rather than market environment. The process of technology roadmapping in this study is adopted from technology roadmapping process by Bray & Garcia [12].

With help of the technology roadmap, it is expected to evaluate whether a technology applying to a design concept reflects the prospective trends or not. Finally, relationship analysis between users' tasks and technology alternatives derived from the technology roadmap, it is expected to identify which technology alternative is appropriate for supporting users' tasks.

3.3 Design Concept Evaluation

The phase 3 aims to identify functional requirements supporting relevant users' tasks by relationship analysis between users' task and human function, and to investigate effective technology alternatives satisfying functional requirements by relationship analysis between users' task and technology alternatives. The result of the first relationship analysis is utilized to evaluate design concepts and the second result is expected to identify appropriate technology alternatives support users' functional requirements. In addition, we extract sub-attributes of CPV through literature survey [21, 22, 23, 24], and make a list of them so as to develop an evaluation checklist. The evaluation checklist is developed using the following three criteria; 1) selection criteria: whether it can used to evaluate on the stage of conceptual design or not, 2) integration criteria: whether there is a similar or duplicated concept or not, 3) deletion criteria: whether it included users' subjective affection. Finally, relative importance of each CPV attribute is determined by analytic hierarchy process (AHP).

4 Case Study

The proposed evaluation scheme was demonstrated using a case study of design concepts of a new CSCW-based tangible user interface that was designed to support group decision making activities such as business meetings and ideations. The case study was conducted in accordance with each phase of the proposed framework.

In phase 1, we developed three representative scenarios based on representative types of meeting activities derived from the published studies [25, 26] on group decision making processes. The three scenarios consists of 1) meeting for schedule planning, 2) meeting for proposing new ideas, and 3) meeting for deciding the optimal solution between various alternatives. Use cases that each scenario implies were also identified and the pros and cons of each of them were further analyzed. Users' tasks and sub-tasks such as 'show schedule', 'enumerate discussion issues', and 'record individual opinions' were specified and structured by HTA. As a result, 8 tasks and 47 sub-tasks were derived.

In phase 2, extensive literature survey was conducted on the state-of-the art technologies in the area of tangible interface technologies. We browsed 124 tangible interface technologies and classified them into control-related technology group and display-related technology group, and further organized each group by date of introduction.

Based on the results of classification, we further analyzed development trends of each group in terms of functionality. For example, 'screen-based control' has improved its controllability by employing pucks in its execution. Accordingly, we developed a technology roadmap showing the prospective trends of tangible interface technologies as shown Fig. 2. Each technology alternative was listed and correlated with users' tasks from the phase 1.

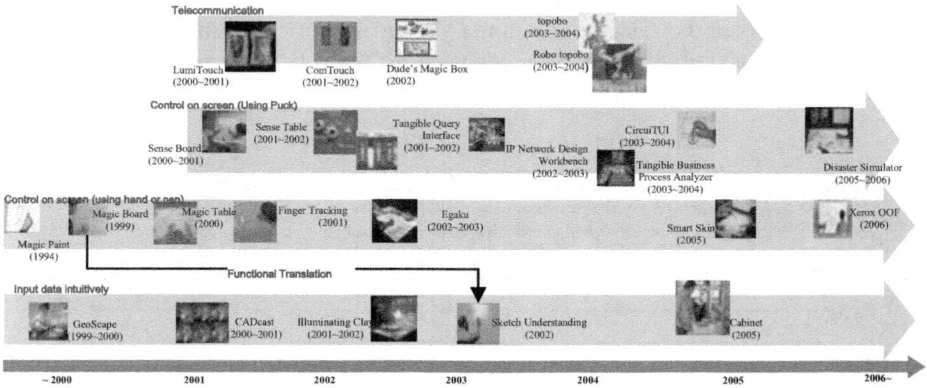

Fig. 2. Technology roadmap of tangible interface technologies

In Phase 3, we evaluated the design concepts of a CSCW-based tangible interface using the evaluation checklist. The evaluation items of the checklist were based on functional requirements that were derived from relationships analysis. Through relationships analysis, each task was correlated with human functions which enabled us to specify users' functional requirements corresponding to the meeting activities.

For the development of an evaluation checklist, we evaluated the degree of which design concepts of a new product supports functional requirements. We selected the

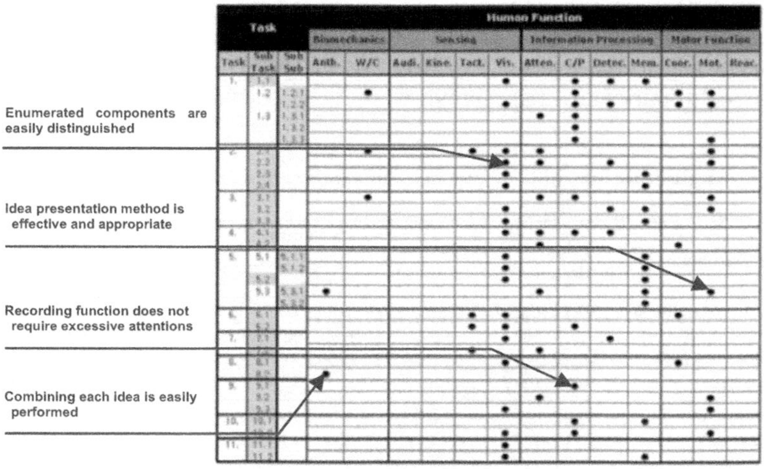

Fig. 3. Human functions – Task relationships analysis

following five tasks, which its degree of support is above half; among 8 tasks and 47 sub-tasks. The selected tasks are as follows; understanding, meeting summary, explaining meeting main topics, idea brainstormings, comparison of alternatives was selected for the case study.

The evaluation of design concepts was performed using the evaluation criteria derived from detailed CPV attributes. The CPV attributes were chosen by pair-wise comparison between the selected task and CPV attributes. Consequently, four benefit attributes and four cost attributes were selected for the following evaluation checklist as shown in Fig. 4.

TITLE Page Numbers

Date		Evaluator		Confirmation	
Functional Requirements	Users' functional requirements required to be satisfied			Rating	
				Relative importance	
Current Functionality	Functionality provided to be intended to support the above requirement (required to be written by evaluator) * If not supported, remain as a blank			1 = not supported 2 = partially supported 3 = fully supported	/ 3
Evaluation Criteria		Weights		Rating scale	Ratings
Benefit	Benefit Attributes I-1			1 Low ← 5 Medium → 9 High	/9
	Benefit Attributes I-2			1 Low ← 5 Medium → 9 High	/9
	:	:		:	:
Cost	Cost Attributes II-1			1 Low ← 5 Medium → 9 High	/9
	Cost Attributes II-2			1 Low ← 5 Medium → 9 High	/9
	:	:		:	:

Fig. 4. An example of evaluation checklist

For the experimentation of CPV evaluation, a total of ten participants, who have experienced business meetings over 1 year, were employed to compare two types of meeting situations. Situation A was a typical meeting process without the support of tangible interface technologies. Situation B was simulated as supported by design concepts of a CSCW-based tangible interface which was recently developed. Participants were asked to evaluate each situation and rate CPV attributes using a 9-point likert-type scale, respectively.

Table 1 shows the average score of CPV attributes relating to the five types of tasks. According to the results, it is revealed that there is a considerable difference among benefit attributes. Especially, there is a considerable difference between

Table 1. Results of CPV evaluation (standard derivation in parenthesis)

CPV Attributes		Task Understanding	Meeting summary	Explaining meeting main topics	Idea brain storming	Comparison of alternatives	Avg.
Benefit	Automatedness	6.6 (1.830)	7.6 (1.048)	7.8 (1.077)	7.1 (1.868)	6.8 (1.077)	7.18
	Simplicity	4.8 (2.112)	N/A	6.6 (1.800)	4.2 (1.711)	5.5 (2.012)	5.28
	Time Saving	6.1 (1.989)	7.7 (1.062)	7.7 (1.193)	6.7 (2.128)	6.2 (1.077)	6.88
	Freshness	7.1 (1.204)	7.5 (0.866)	N/A	7.5 (1.162)	7.5 (0.922)	7.40
Cost	Worrying	5.7 (2.193)	5.1 (1.459)	4.9 (1.879)	5.7 (2.128)	5.0 (1.871)	5.28
	Instructions	6.2 (1.621)	5.6 (1.604)	5.6 (1.685)	6.8 (1.661)	6.2 (1.558)	6.08
	Manual Entry	4.4 (1.652)	4.5 (1.658)	3.4 (1.562)	5.4 (2.059)	5.0 (1.789)	4.54
	Accuracy	5.3 (1.345)	5.7 (1.418)	5.3 (1.512)	6.2 (1.806)	4.9 (2.119)	5.48

simplicity and other factors. This fact indicated that users cannot feel much convenience from the use of design concept. There is also a considerable difference among cost attributes. In fact, higher score of cost attribute is regarded as a negative effect of the design concepts.

In order to calculate overall CPV, which was the ratio of benefit and cost as shown in the below equation, we performed AHP analysis to determine relative weight of each CPV attribute.

$$CPV = \frac{Benefit}{Cost} = \frac{\sum_{i}^{n} Wb_i \times Rb_i}{\sum_{i}^{m} Wc_i \times Rc_i}$$

Where,
Wb_i = Each benefit attribute weight
Rb_i = Each benefit attribute score
Wc_i = Each cost attribute weight
Rc_i = Each cost attribute score
n = Number of benefit attribute
m = Number of cost attribute

According to the result as shown in table 5, task of 'comparison of alternatives' marked the highest score (1.266) among tasks. That is, the design concepts of the tangible interface may deliver superior value to customers when they are performing the task of 'comparison of alternatives'.

Table 2. Overall customer perceived value of design concepts of a tangible interface

Task	Benefit Score	Cost Score	CPV Score
Task understanding	6.070	5.117	1.186
Meeting summary	5.131	5.082	1.010
Explaining meeting main topics	4.845	4.514	1.073
Idea brainstorming	6.171	5.860	1.053
Comparison of alternatives	6.471	5.113	1.266

5 Conclusion

In this study, we proposed an evaluation framework to evaluate design concepts of a new product at the conceptual design phase based on users' requirements and tasks, development trends of relevant technologies, and the CPV. In addition, various methods such as scenario-based analysis, hierarchical task analysis, technology roadmap, and CPV as a quantifiable measure were systematically utilized to develop the proposed evaluation framework to evaluate design concepts of a new product. Finally, a case study was successfully demonstrated to evaluate the design concepts of a new CSCW-based tangible interface that was recently designed to support group decision making activities. From the user-centered design perspective, it is expected that the proposed evaluation framework would be effective at the early stage of product design process.

Acknowledgments. This work was supported by KIST, and in part by the Second Stage of Brain Korea 21 Project in 2006. The authors are grateful to the Research

Institute of Engineering Science at Seoul National University for administrative assistance.

References

1. Al-Salka, M.A., Cartmell, M.P., Hardy, S.J.: A framework for a generalized computer-based support environment for conceptual engineering design. Journal of Engineering Design 9(1), 57–88 (1998)
2. Dhillon, B.S.: Engineering Design: A Modern Approach. Time Mirror Higher Education Group Inc. Company (1996)
3. Pugh, S.: Total Design. McGraw-Hill Companies Inc (1995)
4. Huang, G.Q.: Web-based Support for collaborative product design review. Computers in Industry 48, 71–88 (2002)
5. Ulrich, K.T., Eppinger, S.D.: Product Design and Development. McGraw-Hill, New York (2005)
6. Suri, R., Monroe, K.B.: The effects of time constraints on consumer's judgments of prices and products. Journal of Consumer Research 30(1), 92–104 (2003)
7. Schoonmaker, S.J.: ISO 9001 for Engineering and Designers. McGraw-Hill Companies Inc, New York (1996)
8. Huang, G.Q.: Design for X: Concurrent Engineering Imperatives. Chapman & Hall. Design and Manufacturing (1996)
9. Carroll, J.M.: Making Use - Scenario based design of human computer interaction. MIT Press, Cambridge (2000)
10. Maguire, M.: Methods to support human-centered design. International Journal of Human-Computer Studies 55, 587–634 (2001)
11. Diaper, D., Stanton, N.A.: The handbook of task analysis for human-computer interaction. Lawrence Erlbaum, Mahwah (2004)
12. Bray, O.H., Garcia, M.L.: Technology Roadmapping: The Integration of Strategic and Technology Planning for Competitiveness. Sandia National Laboratories, pp. 25–28 (1997)
13. Albright, R.E., Kappel, T.A.: Roadmapping in the Corporation. Research Technology Management 46(2), 31–59 (2003)
14. Porter, M.E.: Competitive advantage: Creating and sustaining superior performance. The Free Press, New York (1985)
15. Miller, C., Swaddling, D.C.: Focusing NPD research on customer perceived value. In: Belliveau, P., Griffin, A., Somermeyer, S.M. (eds.) PDMA toolbook for new product development, pp. 87–114. John Wiley & Sons, Inc, New York (2002)
16. Ulaga, W., Chacour, S.: Measuring Customer-Perceived Value in Business Markets. Industrial Marketing Management 30, 525–540 (2001)
17. Zeithaml, V.A.: Consumer perceptions of price, quality and value: A means-end model and synthesis of evidence. Journal of Marketing 52, 2–22 (1998)
18. Sweeney, J.C., Soutar, G.N.: Consumer perceived value: The development of a multiple item scale. Journal of Retailing 77, 203–220 (2001)
19. Nielson, J.: Paper versus computer implementations as mock up scenarios for heuristic evaluation. Human-Computer Interaction Interact'90. Amsterdam: North-Holland, pp. 315–320 (1991)
20. Diaper, D., Stanton, N.A.: The handbook of task analysis for human-computer interaction. Lawrence Erlbaum, Mahwah (2004)

21. Bitner, M.J., Faranda, W.T., Hubbert, A.R., Zeithaml, V.A.: Customer contributions and roles in service delivery. International Journal of Service Industry Management 12(5), 423–450 (1997)
22. Curran, J.M., Meuter, M.L., Surprenant, C.F.: Intentions to user self-service technologies: a confluence of multiple attitudes. Journal of Service Research 5(3), 209–224 (2003)
23. Parasuraman, A.: A multiple-item scale for measuring consumer perceptions of service quality. Journal of Retailing 64(1), 12–40 (1998)
24. Suri, R., Monroe, K.B.: The effects of time constraints on consumer's judgments of prices and products. Journal of Consumer Research 30(1), 92–104 (2003)
25. DeSanctis, G., Gallupe, B.: A foundation for the study of group decision support system. Management Science 33(5), 589–609 (1987)
26. Poole, M.S., DeSanctis, G.: Understanding the use of group decision support systems: The theory of adaptive structuration. Sage Publications (1989)

The Research of Using Image-Transformation to the Conceptual Design of Wearable Product with Flexible Display

Yung-Chin Tsao, Li-Chieh Chen, and Shaio-Chung Chan

Department of Industrial Design, Tatung University, No. 40, Chung Shan North Rd., Sec 3
Taipei, Taiwan, 104
tsao@ttu.edu.tw, lcchen@ttu.edu.tw, nsw92jc@seed.net.tw

Abstract. Wearable computer offers job-critical information to people whose hands must be free for other works. By adopting the flexible electronic technology, designs of such apparatus provide the features of highly mobility and durability. This paper takes the duties of the police as a case study. By analyzing the activities of the police and the problems of currently used apparatus, thirty-three problems were elicited. A Quantification Method Type IV and a cluster analysis were employed to analyze the problem's structure and six groups of problems were highlighted. The design specifications were derived from the previous studies. Four conceptual designs of wearable computers were proposed by transferring the soft and wearable images in the design processes. Developing and evaluating the experimental prototypes will be undertaken for further analysis.

Keywords: flexible display, wearable computer, image-transformation.

1 Introduction

Flexible electronics is the technology to fabricate micro electronics on plastics or thin metals. With the slim, bendable features and the benefits of light weight, durability and low cost, the flexible electronic technology can be implemented wildly in different fields, especially for the mobile devices.

According to the recommendations from the STAG (Science & Technology Advisory of the Group) of Taiwanese Government in 2005, the development of the flexible electronic technology should be one of the priority missions for the Government in next decade. The STAG also suggested the industries develop not only on the productivity of the core technology but also on the commercialization of its applications.

Special service crews, such as medical services, rescue teams, news press, police, firefighters and soldiers, gradually rely on mobile computing apparatus to accomplish their tasks. However, due to the complexity of their duties, some of crew members have to stay mobile and keep hands free for handling unanticipated conditions at the same time. In such circumstance, a wearable and foldable apparatus will be suitable for their needs.

J. Jacko (Ed.): Human-Computer Interaction, Part II, HCII 2007, LNCS 4551, pp. 1220–1229, 2007.

This paper utilized the duties of the police as a case study to explore the opportunities of adopting the flexible electronic technology in practice.

The main objectives for this study are:

1. To utilize the flexible electronic technology in practice.
2. To consider the difference between the professionals and propose custom design solutions to fulfill their needs.
3. To recommend the design methodology in this study, in order to be adopted by other related products and professionals.

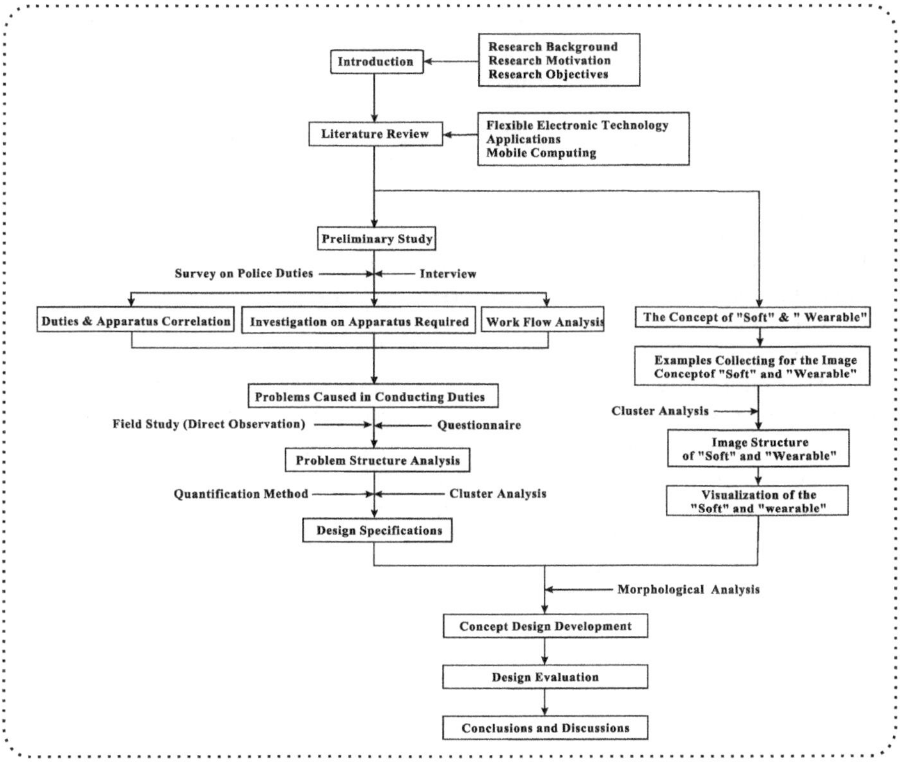

Fig. 1. The research flow chart

2 Literature Review

There were a lot of studies regarding the technical development and applications on the wearable computers. However, most of the studies reported either the development of the state-of-the-art or the software applications for the devices. The interaction designs regarding the usability were seldom investigated.

Lewis et al., (1998) introduced two types of wearable displays developed by Honeywell. The body-worn display was a wrist-type display with a wireless interface while another see-through display, looked like a pair of binoculars, was a handhold device and could be worn around the neck.

IBM integrated and released its prototype for wearable computer in 2000 (Ditlea, 2000). Combined with a walkman-like CPU, wrist-wearing keyboard, HUD, earphone and wrist-wearing touch panel, this unit provided information in helping users to check the inventory and to maintain facilities.

With light beams sensing fingertips and motion sensors tracking hand movement, the “Lightgolve” was an experimental apparatus (Howard and Howard, 2001). This inexpensive design offered a solution for virtual typing and pointing system. However, some of the technical issues needed further explorations.

In terms of the latest development of the personal WLAN, the size of the wireless networking chipset had reduced as a ring (Fishkin et al., 2002). Conjoined with a PDA, a CPU, and a wrist-wearing display, the basic system architecture was established.

Narayanaswami and Raghunath (2000) addressed the challenges in designing a wrist watch computing platform in terms of the packaging, hardware design, power management and embedded software. Applications and interacting design for the proposed wrist watch were also discussed.

The eSleeve', introduced by Randell and Muller (2002), is a wearable wrist computer with position and heading sensors. Coupled with a user interface employing speech recognition and a small display, this device provided audio and visual output based on the position and orientation of the user.

For the applications on medical service, Lukowicz et al. (2002) proposed a wearable, watch-like device to monitor the high risk patients. In emergency, this device can promptly provide the physiological conditions of the patient to doctors and appropriate first aids could be arranged. Hsu (2003) developed a wearable biomedical health-care system which incorporated the wearable computing technology with multi-agent software architecture. Connected with various sensors, this device could sense the patients’ vital signs such as electrocardiogram (ECG), body temperature, and body humidity.

Considering ergonomics as a key to success, Lin and Kreifeldt (2001) proposed a wearable computer design through an ergonomic approach to ensure an appropriate interface relationship between computers and their users.

Cho et al., (2002) and (Kim et al., 2004) compared four types of "body-based" interfaces with different applications and associated tasks. The performance and preference for testing those four devices were recorded. It was suggested that, for applications with many associated tasks, a careful division of tasks was necessary to design the most performing body-based interface.

3 Preliminary Study on the Police’s Duties

In order to understand the basic duties and used apparatus, interviews of the police officers and investigations on police service rules were undertaken. Three police officers from XinJuang, LuJou and NanKang bureaus in Taipei metropolis were invited.

Eleven questions were asked in related to three major fields:

1. How many kinds of duties they had to be performed?
2. What kind of apparatus currently used? and
3. Are there any demands for the new equipments, which will be useful to enhance the performance?

According to the police handbook, major duties for the primary-level policemen were "patrol", "on-site inspection", "road blocking", "touring around the responsibility areas", "swing shift", "on guard" and "standby". Among those missions, "patrol", "on-site inspection" and "road blocking" were the duties in which most of the apparatus were used. And some of the apparatus were repeatedly used in different tasks.

4 Investigations on the Problems Experienced During the Duties Performed

An open questionnaire was designed based on the previous study and 22 policemen from Taipei metropolis were requested to fill-in the questionnaire.

Before the questions were requested, 3 flow-charts, regarding the duties of "patrol", "on-site inspection" and "road blocking", were reproduced and presented to the subjects as references. The subjects were requested to describe the problems experienced in performing their duties referred to those check-points in each work flow.

The questionnaire was divided into three sections. The first section consists of 10 questions about the problems caused during the patrol. The second section consists of 10 questions about the problems caused when conducting on-site inspection. The third section consists of 13 questions about the problems caused when conducting the mission of road blocking. All questions were open-end questions and, for each question, the subjects were requested to describe the problems experienced in using current apparatus and their suggestions on the improvement. According to the responses of the subjects, 33 problems or complains were elicited.

5 Investigation on the Problem Structure

In order to find out the problem structure, a Quantification Method and a cluster analysis were employed at this stage. A correlation matrix was produced based on the 33 problems drawn from the previous study. The correlation between each problem set was evaluated by giving a score from 1 to 10 ("1" means null-correlated while "10" means complete-correlated between the two variables).

The average scores drawn by focus group members were analyzed by using the Quantification Method. The problem structure could be categorized into two dimensions. The first dimension could be explained as the issue of "the apparatus and the working procedures", the horizontal axis, while the second dimension could be explained as the issue of "security concerns", the vertical axis.

To classify these 33 problems into groups, a cluster analysis was employed. The result of the cluster analysis was showed as Fig. 2. and six groups of problems were highlighted. The plot of each group was illustrated in Fig. 3.

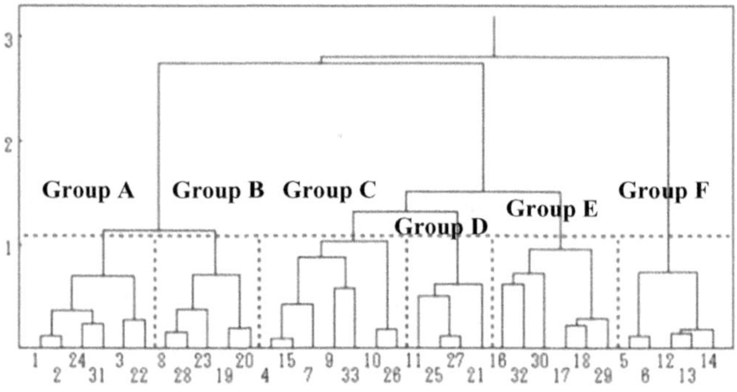

Fig. 2. Tree diagram of the cluster analysis

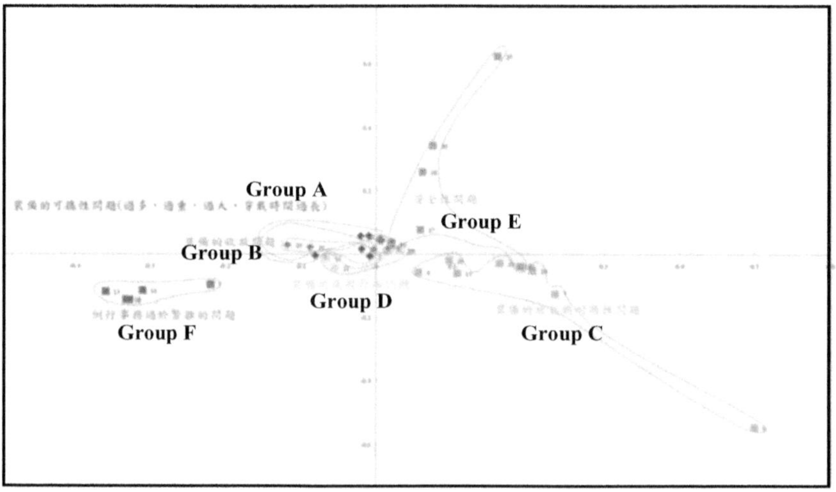

Fig. 3. Illustration of the plots for each group in problem structure space

Group A

In this group, problems included (P01), (P02), (P24), (P31), (P03), and (P22). It can be interpreted as the "problems of portability".

(P01) There are so many apparatus have to be worn.

(P02) Some apparatus, such as the radio and PDA, are too heavy.

(P24) Some apparatus, such as the radio and PDA, are easily pulled off accidentally.

(P31) Inconvenient in using the alcoholmeter (too bulky and not east to hold).

(P03) The police might feel uncomfortable after long-lasting wearing the apparatus.
(P22) The sizes of some apparatus do not fit for everyone.

Group B

In this group, problems included (P08), (P28), (P23), (P19) and (P20). It can be categorized as the "problems of accessibility".

(P08) The size of the radio is bulky.
(P28) Some apparatus, such as radio and PDA, are unable to extract rapidly. Thus, it might threaten the safety of the personnel.
(P23) The police might feel confusion while handling their equipment and events simultaneously (e.g. report to the head quarter while chasing the suspects).
(P19) Not easy to inscribe data while using hands for other events.
(P20) No space to hold the ID collected.

Group C

In this group, problems included (P04), (P15), (P07), (P09), (P33), (P10) and (P26). These problems were related to the usability of the apparatus and can be explained as the "problems of durability and efficiency".

(P04) There is no effective backup plan if some apparatus, such as the radio and PDA, are damaged or suddenly mal-functioned.
(P15) No physically protecting features, such as waterproof, anti-shaking and breakage-proof, for the apparatus.
(P07) Poor radio signal reception.
(P09) Limited battery life of radio.
(P33) Police might feel exhausted after tracking suspects for a long time.
(P10) Limited radio reception coverage.
(P26) Police are unable to locate themselves promptly in unfamiliar environment.

Group D

In this group, problems included (P11), (P25), (P27) and (P21). It can be interpreted as the "problems of usability".

(P11) The operating procedures of some apparatus, such as the radio and PDA, are complicated.
(P25) Specifications are different from model to model.
(P27) The operating procedures vary from model to model.
(P21) Data in Police's PDA is not sufficient and cannot be updated promptly (e.g. unable to distinguish the true or false of the ID)

Group E

In this group, problems included (P16), (P32), (P30), (P17), (P18) and (P29). Some problems were related to safety concerns for a individual police while other problems were related to the use of the apparatus. In general, it can be interpreted as the "problems of security concerns".

(P16) There is no effective backup plan if some apparatus are lost.
(P32) Data transmission is not secured and there is a possibility of revealing confidential information.

(P30) The alcoholmeter provides incorrect data and lags for printout.
(P17) Fighting with the suspects might put the police in danger.
(P18) Without the authorization, police are unable to check whether there are prohibited items hidden in a vehicle or not?
(P29) Insufficient illumination at night.

Group F

In this group, problems included (P05), (P06), (P12), (P13) and (P14). It can be interpreted as the "problems of annoying and complicated paper works".

(P05) Short of receiving apparatus due to carelessness of checking items before go on the duty.
(P06) It is time consuming in receiving apparatus before go on the duty.
(P12) It is time consuming in data entry and filing.
(P13) Massive data cannot be organized easily and timely.
(P14) Complicated procedures for handing over and might make mistakes easily.

Highlighted from the results of the cluster analysis, it is suggested that the six groups of problems were the most critical issues and have to be resolved when developing new apparatus for the police.

6 Investigation on the Image Structure of Wearable and Soft

In order to understand the image structure of "wearable" and "soft", a focus group with design background was organized to discuss the incidents or examples which were related to the images of "wearing" and "soft" in our daily life.

After exploring and sorting, 23 examples of "wearing" and 18 examples of "soft" were acquired. For each image set, the correlations between examples were evaluated by giving a score from 1 to 10 ("1" means null-correlated while "10" means complete-correlated between the two variables). The means of the results were classified by using cluster analysis and shown as below.

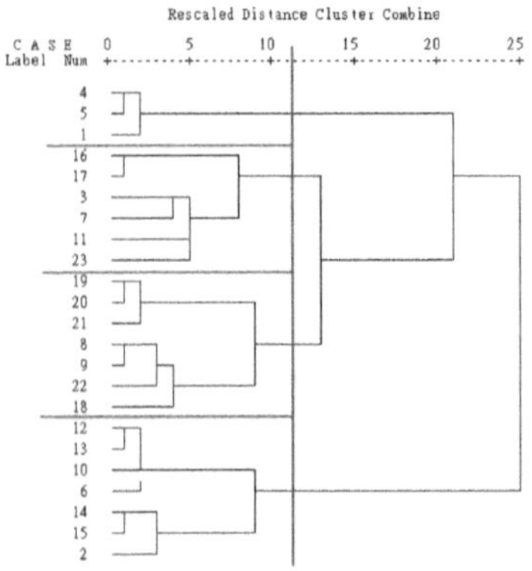

Fig. 4. Cluster analysis for image of "wearing"

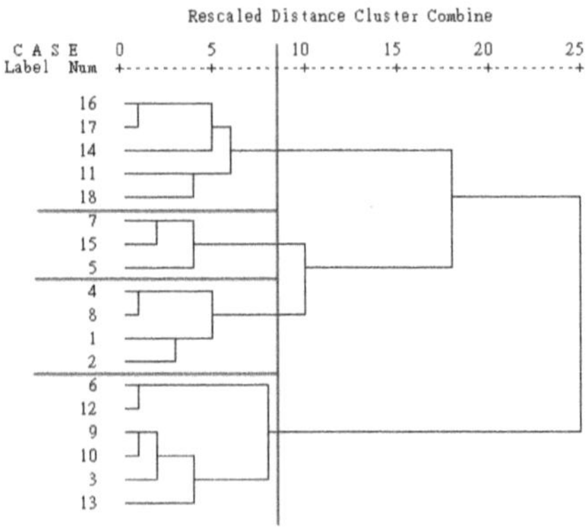

Fig. 5. Cluster analysis for image of "soft"

7 Design Development

Based on the design requirements and product images derived from previous study, a morphological analysis was employed to explore the design solutions. The diagram of the morphological analysis was showed in Table 1.

Table 1. Diagram of the Morphological Analysis

Requirements	*Solutions (Implementation of the flexible electronics)*	
(A) Portability	A-1	Integrate unit combined with data transmission and information query system.
	A-2	Separate unit with modulized design.
(B) Easy to Access	B-1	On the shoulder.
	B-2	On waist
	B-3	In front of the chest.
(C) Durability and Efficiency	Restore the unit to prevent collision	
(D) Ease to Use	Adopt the touchable flexible display (by finger or use stylus)	
(E) Security Concerns	Add-on fingerprint reader and personalized GPS system	
(F) Simplify the Paper Works	Integrate IC and USB interface into the apparatus for data processing and transmission.	
(G) Wearable Image (examples)	G-1	Insert something into the packet in front of the chest.
	G-2	Put on the headset, glasses, hearing aids.
	G-3	Put on the protective gear.
	G-4	Put on the life jacket or vest.
(H) Soft Image (examples)	H-1	Something loses its tension.
	H-2	Rocking jelly or pudding.
	H-3	Breezed hair or prairie
	H-4	The bug or worm wriggles along.

Design A integrates the data transmission unit and information query mechanisms into one set and this flexible unit can be attached around the shoulder. Police can easily access the information through the head-up display unit without holding any apparatus in hand.

Similar to the integrated concept of design A, design B can be worn in from of the chest. The flexible display, built in rubber housing, can be folded when not use. Police can access and restore the device easily.

Design C separates the PDA with the other transmitting apparatus. This flexible PDA can be folded and restored inside the pocket of the vest.

Concept D is a waist-type design. The flexible display can be pulled out from the protective cage and interact with finger or using a stylus. The radio and transmission unit were separated and attached on the shoulder for easy accessibility.

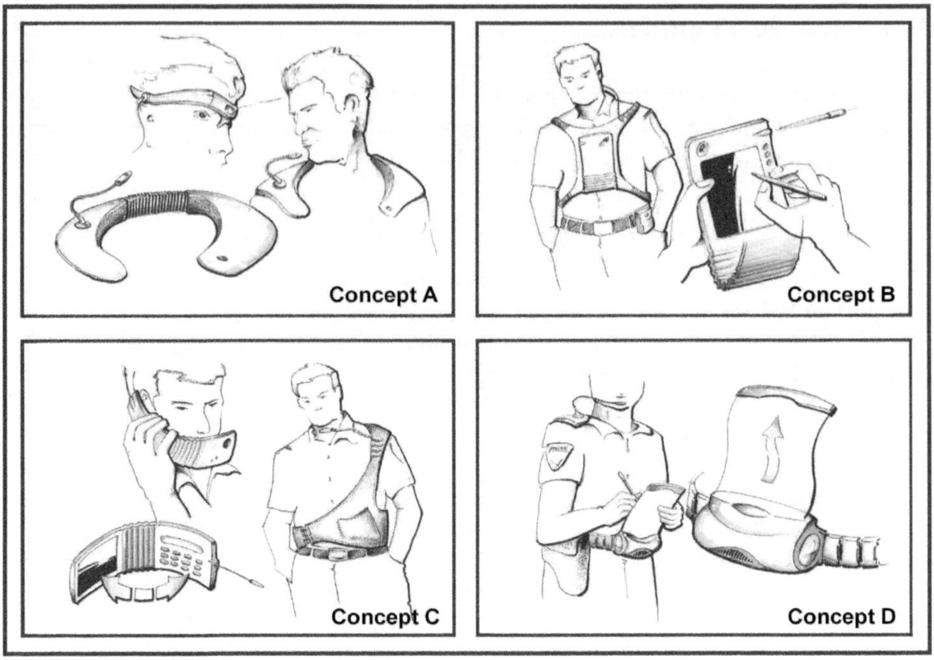

Fig. 6. Illustrations of four design concepts

8 Conclusions and Discussions

This paper demonstrates a design model for wearable computer by adopting the approach of image-transformation. Four conceptual designs integrated the flexible electronic technology and other add-on-value features present design alternatives in different forms of wearing and the current usage problems were well-resolved. It is expected that the design approach and applications summarized in this paper will serve as guidelines for future development.

Detail modifications on the design will be undertaken and experimental prototypes on both hardware and software will be developed coordinately to evaluate the usability for each design proposal in the further study.

Acknowledgements. Financial support of this research by National Science Council, Taiwan, R.O.C. under the grant of General Research Project NSC95-2221-E-036-015 is gratefully acknowledgement.

References

1. Cho, C., Yang, H., Kim, G.J., Han, S.H.: Body-based Interfaces. In: Proceedings of the Fourth IEEE International Conferences on Multimodal Interfaces, October 14-16, 2002 Seoul, Korea pp. 466–472(2002)
2. Ditlea, S.: The PC goes ready-to-wear, IEEE Spectrum 37(10), 34–39 (2000)

3. Fishkin, K.P., Partidge, K., Chatterjee, S.: Wireless user interface components for personal area networks, IEEE Pervasive Computing 1(4), 49–55 (2002)
4. Howard, B., Howard, S.: Lightglove: wrist-worn virtual typing and pointing. In: Proceedings of the Fifth International Symposium on Wearable Computers,October 8-9, 2001, Zurich Switzerland pp. 172 –173(2001)
5. Lewis, S.A., Havey, G.D., Hanzal, B.: Handheld and Bodyworn Graphical Displays. In: Proceedings of the Second International Symposium on Wearable Computing, October 19-20, 1998, Honeywell Technology Center, USA. pp. 102–107 (1998)
6. Lin, R., Kreifeldt, J.G.: Ergonomics in wearable computer design. International Journal of Industrial Ergonomics 27(4), 259–269 (2001)
7. Lukowicz, P., Anliker, U., Ward, J., Troster, G., Hirt, E., Neufelt, C.: AMON: a wearable medical computer for high risk patients. In: Proceedings of the Sixth International Symposium on Wearable Computers 2002 (ISWC 2002), October 7-10, 2002, Wearable Comput. Lab, Eidgenossische Tech. Hochschule, Zurich, Switzerland pp. 133–134 (2002)
8. Narayanaswami, C., Raghunath, M.T.: Application design for a smart watch with a high resolution display. In: Proceedings of the Fourth International Symposium on Wearable Computers, October 16-17, 2000 Atlanta, GA USA pp. 7–14 (2000)
9. Randell, C., Muller, H.L.: The eSleeve: a novel wearable computer configuration for the discovery of situated information. In: Proceedings of the 22nd International Conference on Distributed Computing Systems Workshops,July 2-5 2002, Dept. of Comput. Sci. Bristol Univ. UK pp. 793–796 (2002)
10. Hsu, L.P.: Development of a Wearable Biomedical Health-Care System, Master Dissertation, Department of Mechanical Engineering, National Taiwan University, Taipei, Taiwan (2003)

User Interaction Design for a Wearable and IT Based Heart Failure System

Elena Villalba, Ignacio Peinado, and Maria Teresa Arredondo

LifeSupporting Technologies, E.T.S.I Telecomunicación,
Ciudad Universitaria s/n, 28040, Madrid, Spain
{evmora,ipeinado,mta}@lst.tfo.upm.es

Abstract. In Europe, Cardiovascular Diseases (CVD) are the leading source of death, causing 45% of all deaths. Besides, Heart Failure, the paradigm of CVD, mainly affects people older than 65. In the current aging society, the European MyHeart Project was created, whose mission is to empower citizens to fight CVD by leading a preventive lifestyle and being able to be diagnosed at an early stage. This paper presents the design of the user interaction of a Heart Failure Management System, based on daily monitoring of Vital Body Signals, with wearable and mobile technologies, for the continuous assessment of this chronic disease. The user interaction in such systems plays a role of major importance, enabling the usage of technical solutions which motivate people to adopt healthy lifestyles.

Keywords: user interaction, usability test, wearable systems, health monitoring, personalized applications, personas, goal-oriented design.

1 Introduction

Heart Failure (HF) is a relatively common chronic disorder and is considered the paradigm of cardiac chronic diseases. This disorder mainly affects people older than 65 [1]. The increase on the life expectancy in the developed countries has resulted in an increase in the number of hospitalizations due to chronic diseases, as well as in a potential decrease in the quality of life of the aging population.

The Heart Failure Management System (HFMS) makes use of the latest technologies to monitor heart condition, both with wearable garments (to measure ECG and Respiration); and portable devices (such as Weight Scale and Blood Pressure Cuff) with Bluetooth capabilities.

HFMS aims to decrease the mortality and morbidity of the HF population. The system also focuses on improving the efficiency of the healthcare resources, maximizing the cost-benefit rate of the heart failure management.

Heart Failure Management System consists of three main elements: The Front-end, the User Interaction System and the Back-end. The Front-end is composed of the different garments, textile sensors and electronics for the recording of the vital signals that are required by the application (ECG, Respiration and Activity). The User Interaction System (UIS), which is based on a personal digital assistant device that

J. Jacko (Ed.): Human-Computer Interaction, Part II, HCII 2007, LNCS 4551, pp. 1230–1239, 2007.

receives data from the monitoring devices, processes it and encourages the patients in the daily care of their heart. Besides, it enables the communication and synchronization with the Backend. The last element of the global System, the Back-end, which includes the processing server and the databases, manages all patients' data daily gathered. Professionals can visualize and manage all data through a web access provided by a portal.

The following figure (Fig. 1) sketches the global system:

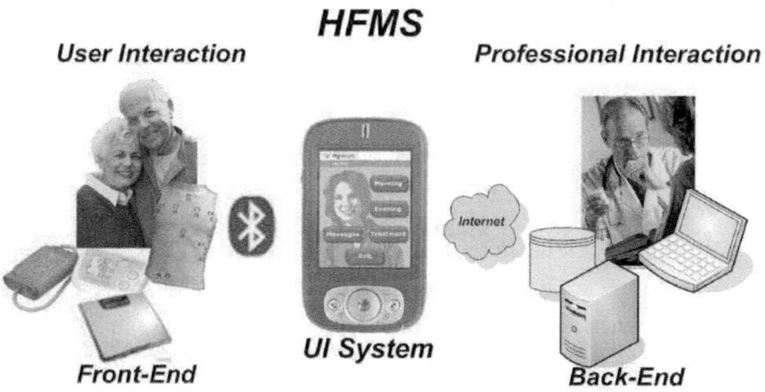

Fig. 1. This figure sketches the HFMS overview with all devices that interact for allowing the personalized monitoring

All the daily routine data are processed and used in the detection of functional capacity, heart failure worsening and other complications. The timing tendency of data is automatically assessed in order to enable an early detection of: a) possible clinical decompensations (clinical destabilization warning signs), b) continuous "out of hospital" arrhythmia risk stratification and, c) evaluation of the HF progression. On the other hand, motivation strategies must be taken into account in order to provide patients with pertinent and relevant information, according to their physical and psychological status.

Since the user interaction plays an enormous role in the success of such systems, the design was carefully performed, adapting the goal-directed methodology to wearable and mobile systems for monitoring chronic diseases. The subsequence sections explained this methodology as well as the results obtained for a particular case: the Heart Failure System.

2 User Interaction Design

The methodology applied is based on Goal-Directed Design [2]. The whole process is divided into seven iterative phases: Research, Modeling, Requirement Definition, Framework Definition, Design, Development and Validation, as shown in the following figure:

Fig. 2. This figure sketches the methodology used in the design and implementation for HFMS. It is based on goal-directed design, but with the last two phases added.

2.1 Research Phase

In order to determinate the right direction to design and develop the user interaction for the HFMS, a preliminary mock-up system was implemented and used in a set of interviews to the main stakeholders.

During the research phase, interviews to the main stakeholders (i.e. HF population, medical specialists, such as cardiologist and nurses; and business managers related to the chronic disease area of hospitals), were carried out.

Within these interviews a preliminary mock-up system (specially implemented for the aim of this research) was thoroughly validated during three months. The validation was based on open and close-ended questions followed by a system demonstration in order to allow the users to assess the usability and comfort of the system. In total 26 people were interviewed: 10 end users (9 men and 1 woman, 80% of them above 60 years), 6 business managers and 10 cardiologists [3]. These interviews were designed by Philips Design Eindhoven in the remit of the MyHeart Project.

Each interview consisted of 5 sections: introduction, storyboard, tangible, conclusion and closure. Within the storyboard section the interviewer presented the global system and asked the interviewees open questions about their impressions and doubts. Once the basics of the system were grasped, the tangible section started, in which wearable garments, electronics, different user devices or the web-portal was presented. Thus, the user was able to determine which PDAs, smart phones and TVs were more suitable for him.

During the conclusion section, the interviewer asked for the overall impression. In addition, the interviewee filled up a scoring sheet with 10 closed questions rated from

1 to 5, which provides a quantitative result. The time for each interview varied from 60 minutes for the professionals to about 120 minutes for the end users.

The overall attitude towards the system was very positive. Most interviewees found it useful and a good solution for the long term treatment of chronic disease. They addressed the need of mobility so the system has to be implemented in a PDA that is both mobile and can be used in an intuitive way through a touch screen.

The system provides a sense of security and confidence in people with HF. Nevertheless some issues where addressed as weakness. For instance, the system needs the user interaction with a technical device, which reduces the number of people that could be incorporated to the follow up of the program.

Besides it forces the users to follow a fixed routine considered as a burden to their lifestyles. Hence, the system should be designed to incorporate a higher modularity, being able to offer different solutions to a diverse range of users, in function of their necessity and capabilities.

2.2 Modeling Phase

Once the Research phase was completed, the modeling phase generated both domain and user models, taking as input the results from the previous phase. Domain models included workflow diagrams. User models, or personas [2], are user archetypes that represent behavior patterns, goals and motivations.

The persona of HFMS is Carlos Gómez, 72 years old. He is retired. He is aware of his heart condition and he is proactive to take a better care. Furthermore, he is able to handle an electronic device, following a very intuitive system. He does not have any special need in terms of accessibility (e.g. blind people).

He used to smoke more than 20 cigarettes per day. 2 years ago he suffered ischemia, and that obliged him to retire. His father died due to a stroke when he was 19, so he was really worried. Visiting his cardiologist very three months is not enough for him. Thus, he decided to join a special program that could help him to manage his health status and communicate with his doctor and other health professionals.

Within his main goals, the most important one is the reassurance and confidence when performing his daily routine. He really needs to feel under control and to loss his fear to die because of a sudden death.

He also aims to be in control of his own health evolution, self managing his health care being independent.

But he does not want to be remained every day he is a chronic patient, so it is of vital importance to give him a system that is not intrusive and no-one notices that he is under treatment.

2.3 Requirements Phase

The requirements phase employed scenario-based design methods. End users were prompted to follow a daily routine divided into morning, exercise and before sleeping contexts.

A context is a set of tasks (also named activities) to be performed together by the user at the same temporary term. For instance, a task or activity is the measurement of the blood pressure. And it can be done together with the weight measurement and the morning questionnaire during the morning. Thus, they all together can form up the morning context.

The scenarios detected within this system are two. They consist of a set of measurements, making use of the wearable garments and portable devices at home. Besides, the user answers two questionnaires defined by the medical team. These two contexts form the indoors scenario. The exercise scenario or context proposes a short walk to promote a healthy lifestyle and to improve cardiovascular capacity, which composes the outdoors scenario. The professional will check the status of all patient though the portal. For the aim of this user design, only the scenarios for the final user are developed.

Carlos wakes up at 8:00 a.m. every morning. He decided together with his cardiologist to perform all daily activities during the morning context. Thus he answers a short questionnaire, and then he measures his weight and blood pressure. Afterwards, he puts on his garment to measure his ECG and respiration. He has to wait then 2 hours before exercising. Hence, he performed other personal tasks until the PDA informs him that it is time to do the exercise. Then, he prepares and goes for a short walk under control. The remaining day he does not need to use the system, so he feels he is free but under control. Before going to sleep he answers a short questionnaire about his general wellbeing during the day.

Once the scenarios were addressed, the main user requirements were detected. The interaction has to be:

- Very simple and intuitive to start when needed
- Easy to use
- Very fast to perform daily activities and always ready when needed
- Adaptable to personal routines
- Need of guide for use, for measurements and help functionalities
- Error prevention and recovery

2.4 Framework Phase

After the description of the main functionality, data and functional elements of the interaction were defined. They represent every data and functionality required to complete a successful interaction. Data and functional elements with similar characteristics were grouped into more complex structures known as functional groups. In HFMS, 4 functional groups were defined: a "header area" that describes the context and activity ("where"), an "information area" that informs the user about the status of the system ("what"), an "instructions area" that tells the user which actions he/she can perform ("how") and a "navigation area" that allows the user to perform the fore mentioned actions, moving through the screens flow. Once the functional groups had been defined, they were used to outline the interaction framework. In HFMS, the different functional groups are displayed as in the following figure:

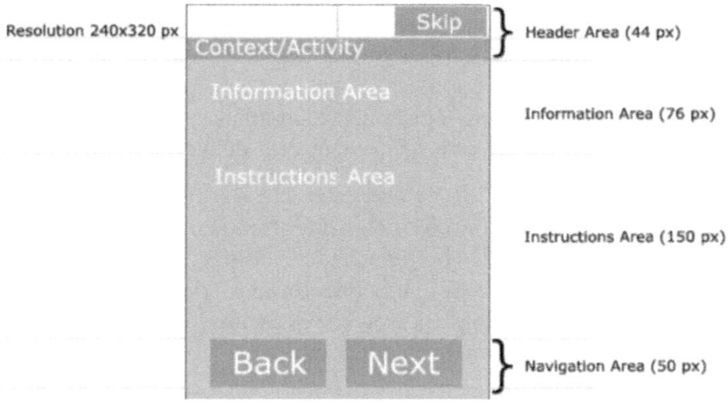

Fig. 2. This figure sketches how the functional groups were organized in the interface, taking into account the lack of space since the PDA has a small screen

From the framework and scenario definition, a key path scenario was defined. Key path scenarios describe, in a task level, the paths through the interface more frequently used. Key paths act as "best case scenarios", describing the user interaction under the assumption that there are no system or user errors. In HFMS, 5 key paths were defined, one for each activity to be performed during the day. From the PDA point of view, weight measurement and blood pressure measurement require the same task sequence, so they share a common key path. Next, a key path for the chest measurement scenario is shown:

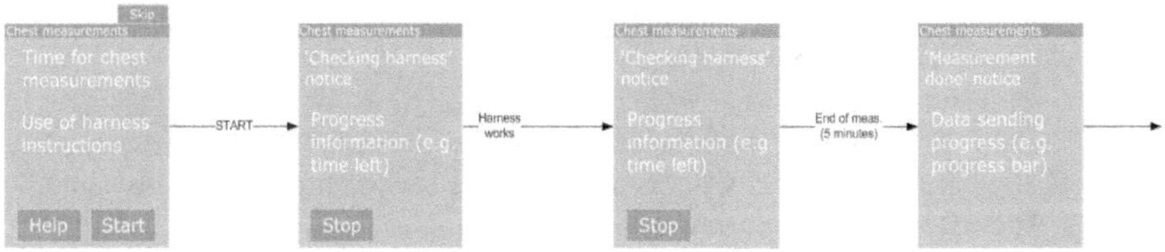

Fig. 3. This figure illustrates the key path for the chest measurement, which is the measurement with the garment of the ECG and respiration

2.5 Design Phase

The "look and feel" defines the graphical aspect and the behavior of the data and functional elements through the whole application. In HFMS, interaction is held by labeled buttons. 3 types of buttons were defined according to the average user's mental model, each one of them representing a different kind of interaction:

- Green buttons. Green buttons will allow the user to move backwards and onwards through the key path screens.

- Grey buttons. Gray buttons are used to give support to the user, giving the user access to the "Help" functionalities and letting the user skip whole activities.
- Red buttons. Red buttons represent exceptional actions, such as stopping the system in the middle of a measurement or a data sending. It is recommended not to push these buttons.

The "look and feel" definition considers the graphical aspect of every functional element, such as progress bars, button shapes, colors and fonts. In HFMS, two different kinds of screens were defined: one for the "device interaction" scenario, where the user interacts with the different devices and other for the help scenario, where the user looks for information to complete a given task. Following figure illustrates both screens:

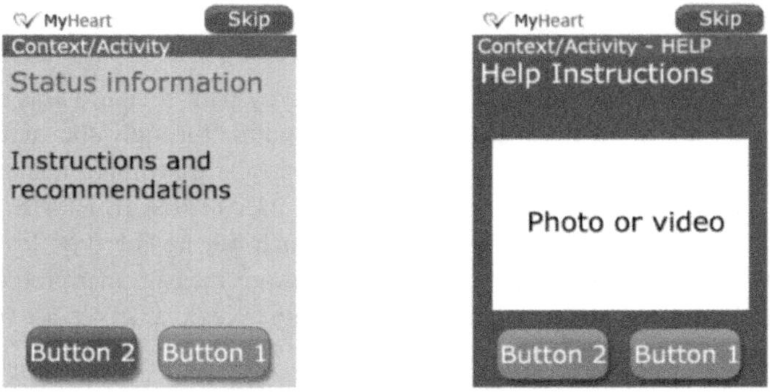

Fig. 4. This figure illustrates two examples of the interface, showing the colors, buttons and position of the main interaction elements

Once the key paths had been defined, the variants to the key-path were considered. In HFMS, the variants to the key paths are associated with hardware failures and help look-ups. The secondary paths were defined according to the following guidelines:

- A user can only skip whole activities. Once the user has started an activity, the system will prevent the user from skipping it, making the "skip" buttons less visible or suggesting through color codes and messages the inconvenience of skipping the activity.
- Every secondary flow has a help support.
- The system asks for confirmation every time the user tries a critical action, such as skipping an activity or stopping a measurement or a data sending.
- Every button is labeled with a text that explains the action it performs, instead of using metaphors. The "Instructions area" displays an explanation of the consequences of pushing each button.

As an example, the complete workflow for the chest measurement scenario is shown in the next figure:

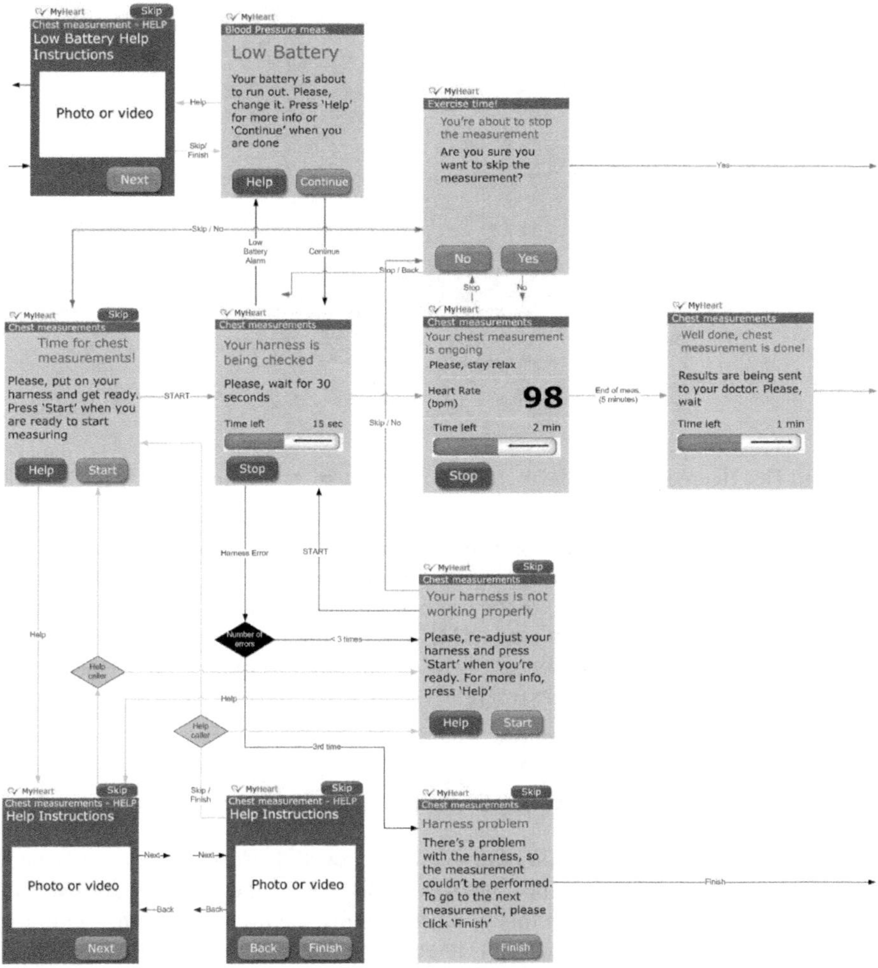

Fig. 5. This figure illustrates the whole flow for the chest measurements, showing all secondary flows when an error occurs or the help function is invoked

3 User Interaction Development

The User Interaction System addresses all the requirements for the user interaction, the communication needs for the sensors readings and the sending of all data to the back-end. Besides, this system implements the daily routine to be performed by users in order to adherent to their heart failure care protocol.

Thus, the user interaction system was divided into four main areas:

In order to provide a good portability among the different mobile devices, the application has been developed under Microsoft .NET framework [6] which is widely compatible with many Pocket-PC compliant devices. The programming language is C-Sharp with Compact Framework version 2 for better compatibility.

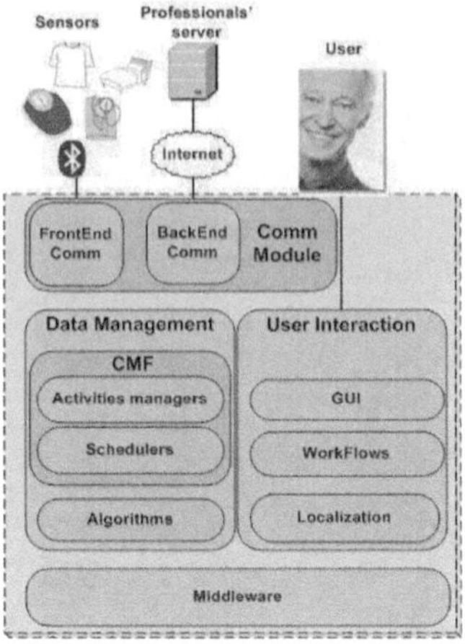

Fig. 6. This figure illustrates the user interaction system that addressed all requirements

The User Interaction module comprises all interfaces and workflows to be invoked that satisfy the use cases. One of the main requirements was the personalization of the tasks to be performed in the daily routine. To achieve it, the user interaction implements a workflow that invokes XML files in the data management module to run in execution time the activities and a particular sequence. This sequence is defined by the user and his professional together at the hospital; and it is downloaded from the Back-end into the user interaction system.

4 User Interaction Validation

As far as now, a heuristic evaluation [7] has been performed, detecting a lack of control during the whole routine. To solve this issue, the skip functionality was implemented, as well as the help functionality, giving the users clear information.

During November 2006, 5 users have been interviewed in Eindhoven, The Netherlands. This validation was performed in 2 rounds with 3 users, following a protocol similar to the one explained in the research phase. All users were over 65 and had some chronic illness related to cardiovascular pathologies or rheum. A woman was interviewed in both rounds, showing a great evolution in the understanding of the interaction. Although all users were able to handle the device, they had some problems in understanding the instructions, especially when there was a metaphor or symbol. Thus, there are no metaphors or icons in the interface and all instructions are given in text in a very explicit way.

A next step comprises a global validation in Madrid, Spain and Basel, Switzerland with 20 patients using the system for 1 or 2 weeks. The design of this validation is currently ongoing.

5 Discussion and Conclusion

As far as the system has been validated, the positive results encourage us to continue with our work and development. Current work focuses on improvement of usability and minimizing interaction requirements giving the system more and more contextual awareness.

The preliminary results show promising in terms of the interaction modality implemented. However, a detailed analysis in order to enhance individuals experience and incorporate this system into their routine is still lacking. This entails an in depth study of diverse behaviour components towards e-health in order to create a tailored communication framework, which boosts motivation of patients to use such systems and truly incorporate them to their daily activities. A framework to be followed considers the analysis of different variables [8].

Finally, in the new paradigm of Ambient Intelligence, we strongly believe that in the future this kind of systems will represent an important part of the daily activity of this sort of patients, supporting a better quality of life and helping to prevent and to treat chronic diseases.

Acknowledgments. This work has succeeded thanks to the close collaboration with Hospital San Carlos of Madrid, Spain and ITACA, Valencia, Spain. We would also like to thank the team of Medtronic, Madrid, Spain and the team from Philips Research Laboratories in Aachen, Germany, as well as the one from Philips Design, Eindhoven, The Netherlands. The Heart Failure Management System described within this paper is an integrated product of the MyHeart project, "Fighting Cardiovascular Diseases by prevention and early diagnosis" (IST-2002-507816); partly funded by the European Commission.

References

1. World Health Organization. The Atlas of Heart Disease and Stroke. Mackay, J., Mensah, G. (eds.) (2004)
2. Cooper, A.: About Face 2.0 The Essentials of Interaction Design. Edited by Wiley Publishing, Inc. (2003) ISBN: 0-7645-26413
3. Villalba, E.: Preliminary Results for acceptability evaluation of a Heart Failure Monitoring System based on wearable and information technologies. presented at ICADI 2006, January 2006 p. 301 (2006) ISBN 0-9754783-0-4
4. Deliverable 6, 7: Application concepts and Technical Progress, MyHeart IST-2002-507816 (January 2005)
5. Zwick, C., Schmitz, B., Kuehl, K.: Designing for Small Screens. Edited by AVA publishing SA, (2005) ISBN: 2-940373-07-8
6. Rubin, E., Yates, R.: Microsoft.NET Compact Framework. Edited by Sams Publising, (2003) ISBN: 0-672-32570-5
7. Dumas, J.S., Redish, J.C.: A practical guide to usability testing. Edited by Intellect Books, (1999) ISBN: 1-84150-020-8
8. del Hoyo-Barbolla, E., Arredondo, M.T., Ortega, M., Fernández, N., Villalba-Mora, E.: A new approach to model the adoption of e-health. In: Proceedings. 13th IEEE Mediterranean Electrotechnical Conference. Benalmádena (Spain) (May 2006) ISBN: 1-4244-0088-0

VortexBath: Study of Tangible Interaction with Water in Bathroom for Accessing and Playing Media Files

Jun-ichiro Watanabe

Hitachi Human Interaction Laboratory, Hitachi Ltd, Tokyo, Japan
junichiro.watanabe.ws@hitachi.com

Abstract. We describe an interface for places where people use water, such as the kitchen, toilet, or bathroom. We developed a prototype that can be operated by users by tangibly interacting with water. It enables image files and movie files to be browsed by projecting the images onto water, it plays music files with album jacket images, and it reads out information from the Internet using speech-synthesis technology. We also describe a demonstration of how users can access their media files by tangibly interacting with water, which is different from conventional way such as pressing buttons on a remote control.

Keywords: Water interaction, ambient display, tangible interaction, content browsing.

1 Introduction

The bathroom in the home is one of the few spaces where we can feel truly relaxed. Soaking one's body in a tub full of hot water literally washes away the fatigue accrued throughout the day. There are many ways of increasing this sense of relaxation, and we have recently been able to watch TV or listen to music in the bathroom. Because the displays or speakers are water-proof, we do not even need to be concerned about splashing. However, these devices are still operated the same way they are in the living room. That is, we have to push buttons to turn them on and off, to change channels, and to control the volume.

The objective of our research was to discover a new way of accessing digital content in the places where people use water, such as a bathroom or a kitchen, that is different from the way this is currently being done in the living room. We explored the possibility of using water itself as a medium to access the content.

2 Related Work

Some studies regarding water interaction techniques have already been conducted. In the field of water installation, various work regarding games and entertainment using water has been done [1], [2]. In these studies, users can play with water while getting feedback on sound, light, or changing the shape of the water. Studies regarding using water as a display have also been conducted [3], [4], [5]. They attempted to allow users to control the water drops or bubbles in the water and use them to draw pictures

J. Jacko (Ed.): Human-Computer Interaction, Part II, HCII 2007, LNCS 4551, pp. 1240–1248, 2007.

or letters in/on the water. One study tested applying real water surface movement in virtual reality applications. They used four sensors that can detect the movement of the water surface [6]. Another study developed and tested a system that can allow users to draw letters or pictures by controlling waves on the water [7], [8]. The system they developed can control the waves on the water using element wave makers. That is, it can control the shape on the water surface. Another study focused on using water as an ambient information terminal [9]. Studies have also been conducted on areas of water usage in the home in regards to security issues [10], [11]. In our study, we made an ambient display with water. The display can be operated tangibly by playing with the water. Furthermore, we made the system without using expensive devices, for example, multiple cameras. Instead, we used a simple sensor to detect the movement of the water.

3 Interface Design

We used people's tangible interaction with water to enable digital media content to be accessed in the bathroom. Ripples appear when we move in this aqueous medium. For example, a vortex appears when we stir it, and when we sprinkle it on our bodies with our hands, waves are created on its surface.

Our basic ideas were to use these interactions with water as triggers to access media information in the bathroom and, at the same time, to use the water surface as a display (Fig. 1).

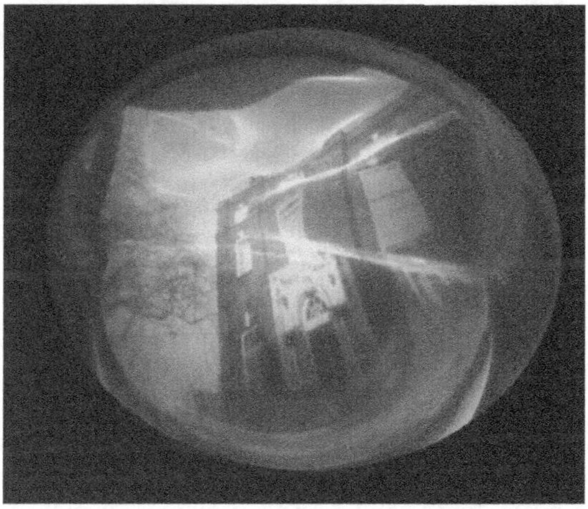

Fig. 1. Interaction with water for accessing digital content

We designed and developed our prototype to play music, display still or movie images, read out text information, and change the ambient color of the tub. It is initiated by the users interacting with the water. When they stir it, the system detects the existence of a vortex or ripples created by this action and begins to do tasks such as playing music or movies.

4 Implementation

4.1 Prototype

We developed a small prototype of a real bathtub for our initial experiments and used a half-transparent acryl bowl 50 cm in diameter to hold the water (Fig. 2 (a)). The bowl was placed on a frame, and images can be projected from below onto its surface. We covered the frame using a box to hide devices such as a PC, projector, or the sensor (Fig. 2 (b)).

(a) Half-transparent bowl and the frame to hold it.

(b) Appearance of the prototype.

Fig. 2. Prototype. (a) Water container and frame to hold it. (b) Photograph of the entire prototype.

The system we developed consists of a sensor to detect water surface movement, a half-transparent acryl bowl to hold the water and to be used as a screen, a projector to display the images, and a PC to receive signals from the sensor and to transmit images to the projector (Fig. 3). An application on the PC received the values from the sensor through a serial cable and executed tasks such as playing music or projecting image slide shows according to these values. The projector displayed images on a half-transparent acryl bowl that holds the water. As a result, the user could clearly see the image through the water.

4.2 Sensor

We used two means to detect the movement of the water. First, we used a fluid flow sensor (Fig. 4) to determine the rate of flow, which was achieved by counting the

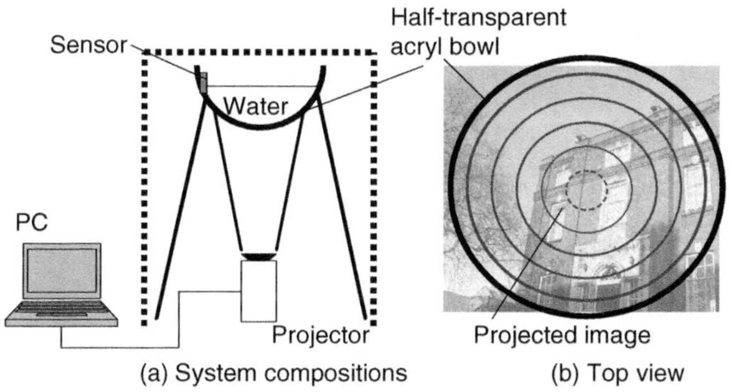

Fig. 3. (a) System compositions. (b) Image seen through water in the bowl.

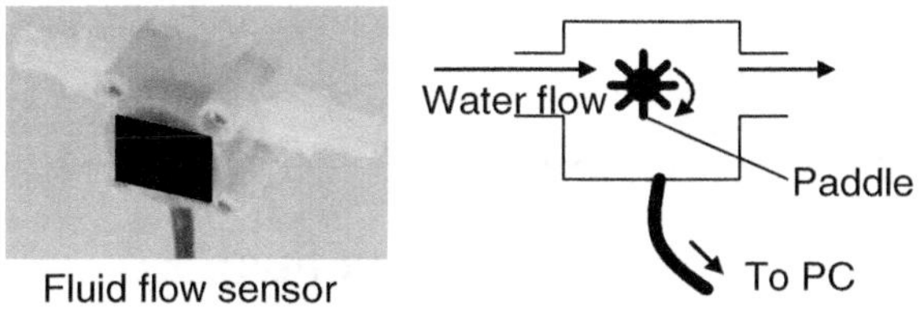

Fig. 4. Detection of water movement with fluid flow sensor

number of rotations a paddle made inside it. The number was transmitted as a frequency to the PC through a serial cable. We found that the paddle rotated when users stirred the water vigorously. Actually, we found that it works well when we tested it in a bathtub, where we can stir the water vigorously and make the liquid move quickly.

Second, we used a floating accelerometer (Fig. 5) to detect acceleration, i.e., gravitational force. We obtained parameters such as tilt angle (θ) and acceleration (g-force) and used these to detect water movement. No acceleration was detected when the surface of the water was calm. However, the accelerometer detected acceleration and the tilt angle when a user stirred the water. Therefore, we could detect water movement more accurately.

In this study, we used the second method. That is, we used the accelerometer because we can use our prototype, a small sized bathtub, and a user did not have to stir the water so vigorously. Also, we used only 1 axis in this initial study, though the sensor we used has the ability to detect 2-axis tilting. The movement on the second axis can be used to detect more complicated movement of the water, such as the shapes of waves. This is also part of our future work.

Using the accelerometer, we can get information on not only whether the water is moving or not, but also on how vigorously it is moving. We can also get the direction and the speed of the liquid by calculating the difference in the tilt angle at any point in time.

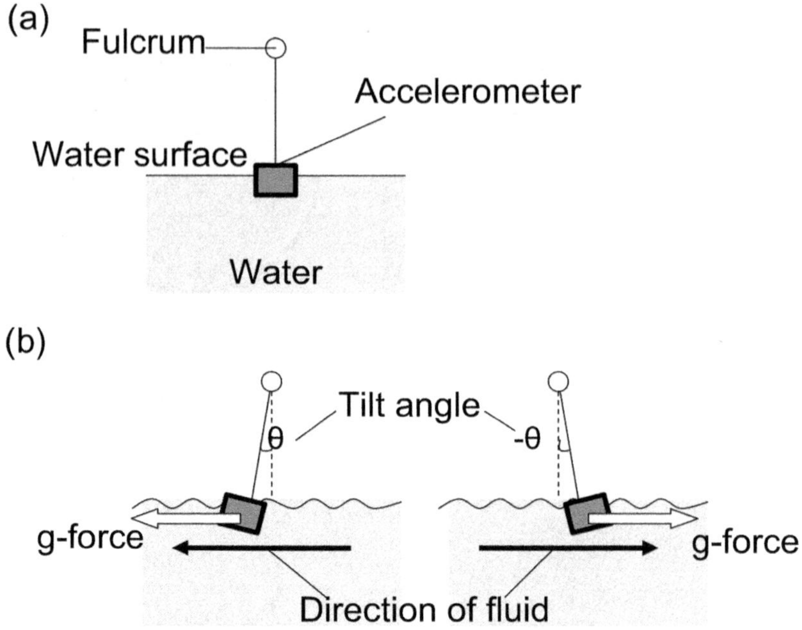

Fig. 5. Detection of water movement using accelerometer. (a) When no water movement exists. (b) When a user stirs the water.

5 Applications

We developed several applications for the prototype.

5.1 Music Player

When a user stirs the water in the bowl, the system starts to play music and display the image from the CD jacket projected onto the surface of the water (Fig. 6).

When a user starts stirring the water, sound turns on and gradually increases, and the image starts to appear. Then, the sound volume and the brightness of the CD jacket image increases as the speed of the water flow increases. If a user wants to change the music, he/she can do that by wiping the image on the water. The old image and sound fade out, and the new music with its linked CD jacket image will fade in gradually.

5.2 Photo Viewer

In this application, we tried to use the direction of fluid as the direction for scrolling photo images. Figure 7 (a) is a photograph of the application. The photo images are arranged horizontally (Fig. 7 (b)), and can be seen through water (Fig. 7 (c)). When the surface of the water is calm, images do not scroll. When a user stirs the water, the

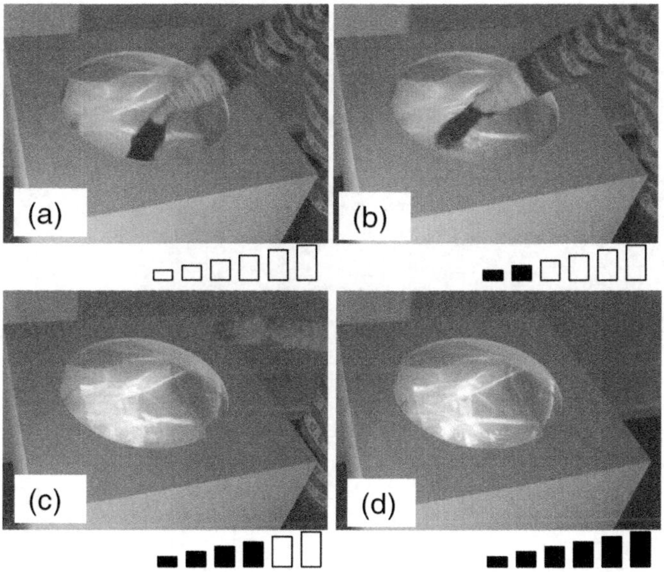

Fig. 6. Music player. (a) User starting to stir water: No image and no sound. (b) Stirring water more vigorously. (c) CD jacket image appearing. (d) Full image brightness. Sound volume levels at each phase are also indicated below the figures.

images scroll with the direction of the rotation of the vortex. That is, if a user makes a rightward vortex, the images are scrolled to the right. If a user stirs the water in the opposite way, the images are scrolled to the left (Fig. 7 (d)).

5.3 Movie Content Viewer

A user, while spending time in the bathroom, may want to watch visual content, such as a TV show or movie stored in a HDD in a home networked device. The movies are projected on the surface of the water. A user can change the movie by stirring the water (Fig. 8).

5.4 News Reader

Our system reads out text information such as Web news. The user can access information from the internet in this way. For example, Internet news headlines with photos can be accessed, and the article can be read out by speech synthesis. Just like with other applications, the user can get access to other items by stirring the water again.

5.5 Changing Bathtub Ambient Color

One of the applications we developed, just out of whimsy, can change the color of the bathtub water by stirring the water. As long as the water is moving, the color changes. When the water is calm, the color stays the same (Fig. 9). The faster the speed of the liquid is, the more quickly the color changes. The application is mildly entertaining.

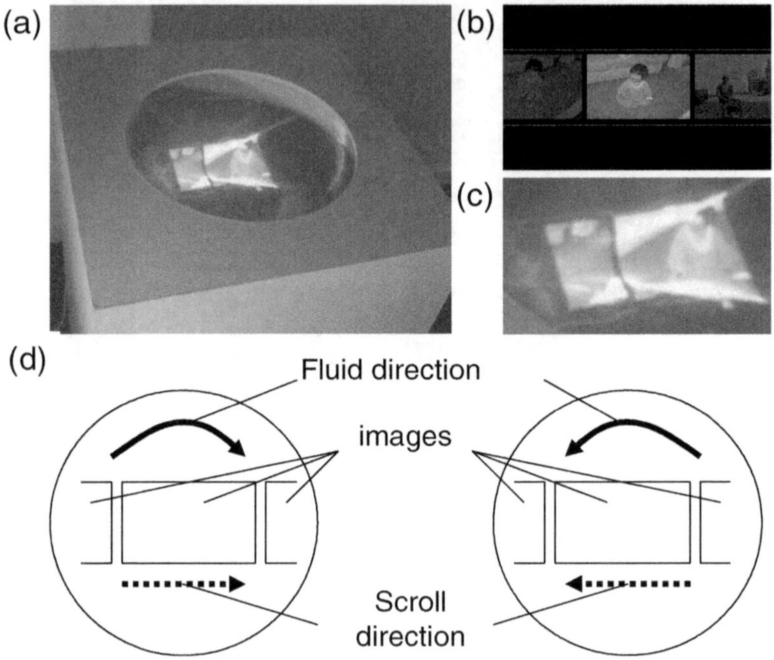

Fig. 7. Photo viewer. (a) Photograph of application displayed in prototype. (b) Images arranged and scrolled horizontally (on PC screen). (c) Images seen through water. (d) Images scrolling with direction of liquid. When a user stirs the water in a rightward/leftward, the images scroll in the corresponding direction.

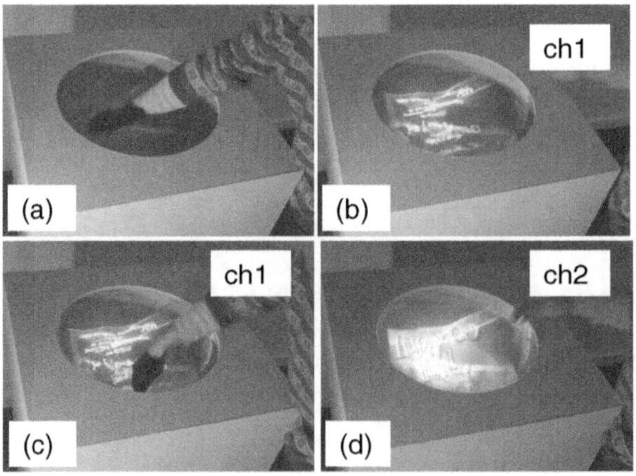

Fig. 8. Movie viewer. (a) User starting to stir water. (b) A channel being shown. (c) Stirring water again. (d) Another channel being shown.

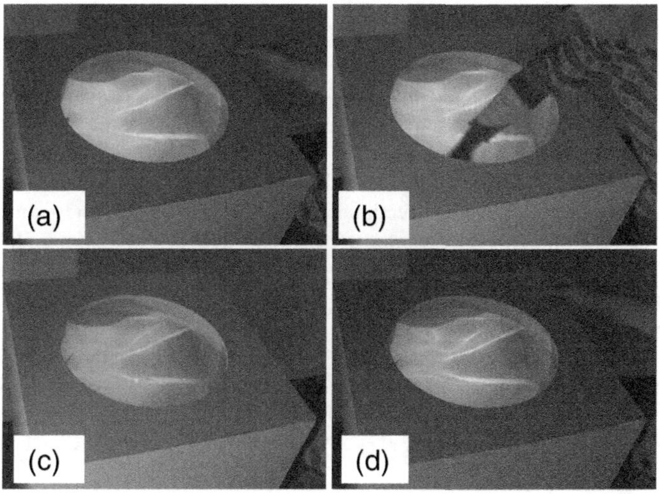

Fig. 9. Changes in ambient color. (a) Calm water with no change in color. (b) User starting to stir water. (c) Water changing while sensor detects liquid movement. (d) Water after final change in color.

6 Experimental Results and Future Work

We got some feedback from participants of a simple test of the developed prototype and the applications for it. First, operating digital media files by tangibly interacting with water gives users a completely new feeling compared to the one they experience with existing devices such as remote controls with numerous buttons. Wiping out or scrolling the images projected on the water tangibly gave the feeling of touching the content directly. Second, the style of information browsing itself may change from active to passive. Actually, the image projected on the water is not as clear as that of in the television in the living room. The image seen through water can be an ambient image, which makes the user feel more relaxed in the bathroom. In future work, we plan to find out how many kinds of vortex or ripple patterns can be distinguished and apply these as commands. We also plan to make a real-size bathtub to apply the interaction technique we have created.

7 Conclusion

We developed a prototype that can be operated by users by tangibly interacting with water and that can be used as a display at the same time. Tests on some applications for the prototype revealed some advantages of using water as a medium to access digital content in the places where people use water.

Acknowledgments. This work was supported in part by the Royal College of Art, London, UK. We wish to thank Prof. Anthony Dunne, Tom Hulbert, and students at the college for their useful advice and comments on this project.

References

1. Dietz, P.H., Han, J.Y., Westhues, J.: Submerging Technologies. Emerging Technologies Sketch, SIGGRAPH (2006) http://www.siggraph.org/s2006/main.php?f=conference&p=etech&s=submergin
2. Parés, N., Durany, J., Carreras, A.: Massive flux design for an interactive water installation: water games. In: Proceedings of the, ACM SIGCHI International Conference on Advances in Computer Entertainment Technology ACE '05, pp. 266–269 (2005)
3. Eitoku, S., Hashimoto, K., Tanikawa, T.: Controllable water particle display. In: Proceedings of the 2006 ACM SIGCHI International Conference on Advances in Computer Entertainment Technology, No. 36 (2006)
4. Heiner, J.M., Hudson, S.E., Tanaka, K.: The information percolator: ambient information display in a decorative object. In: Proceedings of the 12th annual ACM symposium on User Interface Software and Technology UIST '99, pp. 141–148 (1999)
5. Pohflepp, S.: Eavesdripping: water as physical display. ACM SIGGRAPH, Sketches SIGGRAPH '06, No. 109 (2006)
6. Pier, M.D., Goldberg, I.R.: Using water as interface media in VR applications. In: Proceedings of the, Latin American Conference on Human-computer Interaction CLIHC '05, pp. 162–169 (2005)
7. Mitsui engineering & shipbuilding Co., Ltd. http://www.mes.co.jp/Akiken/whatsnew/new20060724.html
8. Okuyama, E.: Technology for Drawing Letters on Water Surface by Element Absorbing Wave Maker, Mitsui technological report, No. 188, (in Japanese) (June 2006) http://www.mes.co.jp/Akiken/whatsnew/pdf/188_03.pdf
9. Dahley, A., Wisnesky, C., Ishii, H.: Water lamp and pinwheels: Ambient projection of digital information into architectural space. CHI 98 Conference Summary on Human Factors in Computing Systems, pp. 269–270 (April 1998)
10. Bonanni, L., Arroyo, E., Lee, C.-H., Selker, T.: Smart sinks: real-world opportunities for context-aware interaction. CHI '05 extended abstracts on Human Factors in Computing Systems CHI '05, pp. 1232–1235 (2005)
11. Arroyo, E., Bonanni, L., Selker, T.: Waterbot: exploring feedback and persuasive techniques at the sink. In: Proceedings of the SIGCHI conference on Human Factors in Computing Systems CHI '05, pp. 631–639 (2005)

Author Index

Lecture Notes in Computer Science

For information about Vols. 1–4505

please contact your bookseller or Springer

Vol. 4611: J. Indulska, J. Ma, L.T. Yang, T. Ungerer, J. Cao (Eds.), Ubiquitous Intelligence and Computing. XXIII, 1257 pages. 2007.

Vol. 4610: B. Xiao, L.T. Yang, J. Ma, C. Muller-Schloer, Y. Hua (Eds.), Autonomic and Trusted Computing. XVIII, 571 pages. 2007.

Vol. 4605: D. Papadias, D. Zhang, G. Kollios (Eds.), Advances in Spatial and Temporal Databases. X, 479 pages. 2007.

Vol. 4602: S. Barker, G.-J. Ahn (Eds.), Data and Applications Security XXI. X, 291 pages. 2007.

Vol. 4600: H. Comon-Lundh, C. Kirchner, H. Kirchner, Rewriting, Computation and Proof. XVI, 273 pages. 2007.

Vol. 4598: G. Lin (Ed.), Computing and Combinatorics. XII, 570 pages. 2007.

Vol. 4597: P. Perner (Ed.), Advances in Data Mining. XI, 353 pages. 2007. (Sublibrary LNAI).

Vol. 4596: L. Arge, C. Cachin, T. Jurdzinski, A. Tarlecki (Eds.), Automata, Languages and Programming. XVII, 953 pages. 2007.

Vol. 4595: D. Bošnački, S. Edelkamp (Eds.), Model Checking Software. X, 285 pages. 2007.

Vol. 4592: Z. Kedad, N. Lammari, E. Métais, F. Meziane, Y. Rezgui (Eds.), Natural Language Processing and Information Systems. XIV, 442 pages. 2007.

Vol. 4591: J. Davies, J. Gibbons (Eds.), Integrated Formal Methods. IX, 660 pages. 2007.

Vol. 4590: W. Damm, H. Hermanns (Eds.), Computer Aided Verification. XV, 562 pages. 2007.

Vol. 4589: J. Münch, P. Abrahamsson (Eds.), Product-Focused Software Process Improvement. XII, 414 pages. 2007.

Vol. 4588: T. Harju, J. Karhumäki, A. Lepistö (Eds.), Developments in Language Theory. XI, 423 pages. 2007.

Vol. 4587: R. Cooper, J. Kennedy (Eds.), Data Management. XIII, 259 pages. 2007.

Vol. 4586: J. Pieprzyk, H. Ghodosi, E. Dawson (Eds.), Information Security and Privacy. XIV, 476 pages. 2007.

Vol. 4585: M. Kryszkiewicz, J.F. Peters, H. Rybinski, A. Skowron (Eds.), Rough Sets and Intelligent Systems Paradigms. XIX, 836 pages. 2007. (Sublibrary LNAI).

Vol. 4584: N. Karssemeijer, B. Lelieveldt (Eds.), Information Processing in Medical Imaging. XX, 777 pages. 2007.

Vol. 4583: S.R. Della Rocca (Ed.), Typed Lambda Calculi and Applications. X, 397 pages. 2007.

Vol. 4582: J. Lopez, P. Samarati, J.L. Ferrer (Eds.), Public Key Infrastructure. XI, 375 pages. 2007.

Vol. 4581: A. Petrenko, M. Veanes, J. Tretmans, W. Grieskamp (Eds.), Testing of Software and Communicating Systems. XII, 379 pages. 2007.

Vol. 4580: B. Ma, K. Zhang (Eds.), Combinatorial Pattern Matching. XII, 366 pages. 2007.

Vol. 4578: F. Masulli, S. Mitra, G. Pasi (Eds.), Applications of Fuzzy Sets Theory. XVIII, 693 pages. 2007. (Sublibrary LNAI).

Vol. 4577: N. Sebe, Y. Liu, Y. Zhuang (Eds.), Multimedia Content Analysis and Mining. XIII, 513 pages. 2007.

Vol. 4576: D. Leivant, R. de Queiroz (Eds.), Logic, Language, Information, and Computation. X, 363 pages. 2007.

Vol. 4575: T. Takagi, T. Okamoto, E. Okamoto, T. Okamoto (Eds.), Pairing-Based Cryptography. XI, 408 pages. 2007.

Vol. 4574: J. Derrick, J. Vain (Eds.), Formal Techniques for Networked and Distributed Systems – FORTE 2007. XI, 375 pages. 2007.

Vol. 4573: M. Kauers, M. Kerber, R. Miner, W. Windsteiger (Eds.), Towards Mechanized Mathematical Assistants. XIII, 407 pages. 2007. (Sublibrary LNAI).

Vol. 4572: F. Stajano, C. Meadows, S. Capkun, T. Moore (Eds.), Security and Privacy in Ad-hoc and Sensor Networks. X, 247 pages. 2007.

Vol. 4570: H.G. Okuno, M. Ali (Eds.), New Trends in Applied Artificial Intelligence. XXI, 1194 pages. 2007. (Sublibrary LNAI).

Vol. 4569: A. Butz, B. Fisher, A. Krüger, P. Olivier, S. Owada (Eds.), Smart Graphics. IX, 237 pages. 2007.

Vol. 4566: M.J. Dainoff (Ed.), Ergonomics and Health Aspects of Work with Computers. XVIII, 390 pages. 2007.

Vol. 4565: D.D. Schmorrow, L.M. Reeves (Eds.), Foundations of Augmented Cognition. XIX, 450 pages. 2007. (Sublibrary LNAI).

Vol. 4564: D. Schuler (Ed.), Online Communities and Social Computing. XVII, 520 pages. 2007.

Vol. 4563: R. Shumaker (Ed.), Virtual Reality. XXII, 762 pages. 2007.

Vol. 4562: D. Harris (Ed.), Engineering Psychology and Cognitive Ergonomics. XXIII, 879 pages. 2007. (Sublibrary LNAI).

Vol. 4561: V.G. Duffy (Ed.), Digital Human Modeling. XXIII, 1068 pages. 2007.

Vol. 4560: N. Aykin (Ed.), Usability and Internationalization, Part II. XVIII, 576 pages. 2007.

Vol. 4559: N. Aykin (Ed.), Usability and Internationalization, Part I. XVIII, 661 pages. 2007.

Vol. 4553: J.A. Jacko (Ed.), Human-Computer Interaction, Part IV. XXIV, 1225 pages. 2007.

Vol. 4552: J.A. Jacko (Ed.), Human-Computer Interaction, Part III. XXI, 1038 pages. 2007.

Vol. 4551: J.A. Jacko (Ed.), Human-Computer Interaction, Part II. XXIII, 1253 pages. 2007.

Vol. 4550: J.A. Jacko (Ed.), Human-Computer Interaction, Part I. XXIII, 1240 pages. 2007.

Vol. 4549: J. Aspnes, C. Scheideler, A. Arora, S. Madden (Eds.), Distributed Computing in Sensor Systems. XIII, 417 pages. 2007.

Vol. 4548: N. Olivetti (Ed.), Automated Reasoning with Analytic Tableaux and Related Methods. X, 245 pages. 2007. (Sublibrary LNAI).

Vol. 4547: C. Carlet, B. Sunar (Eds.), Arithmetic of Finite Fields. XI, 355 pages. 2007.

Vol. 4546: J. Kleijn, A. Yakovlev (Eds.), Petri Nets and Other Models of Concurrency – ICATPN 2007. XI, 515 pages. 2007.

Vol. 4545: H. Anai, K. Horimoto, T. Kutsia (Eds.), Algebraic Biology. XIII, 379 pages. 2007.

Vol. 4544: S. Cohen-Boulakia, V. Tannen (Eds.), Data Integration in the Life Sciences. XI, 282 pages. 2007. (Sublibrary LNBI).

Vol. 4543: A.K. Bandara, M. Burgess (Eds.), Inter-Domain Management. XII, 237 pages. 2007.

Vol. 4542: P. Sawyer, B. Paech, P. Heymans (Eds.), Requirements Engineering: Foundation for Software Quality. IX, 384 pages. 2007.

Vol. 4541: T. Okadome, T. Yamazaki, M. Makhtari (Eds.), Pervasive Computing for Quality of Life Enhancement. IX, 248 pages. 2007.

Vol. 4539: N.H. Bshouty, C. Gentile (Eds.), Learning Theory. XII, 634 pages. 2007. (Sublibrary LNAI).

Vol. 4538: F. Escolano, M. Vento (Eds.), Graph-Based Representations in Pattern Recognition. XII, 416 pages. 2007.

Vol. 4537: K.C.-C. Chang, W. Wang, L. Chen, C.A. Ellis, C.-H. Hsu, A.C. Tsoi, H. Wang (Eds.), Advances in Web and Network Technologies, and Information Management. XXIII, 707 pages. 2007.

Vol. 4536: G. Concas, E. Damiani, M. Scotto, G. Succi (Eds.), Agile Processes in Software Engineering and Extreme Programming. XV, 276 pages. 2007.

Vol. 4534: I. Tomkos, F. Neri, J. Solé Pareta, X. Masip Bruin, S. Sánchez Lopez (Eds.), Optical Network Design and Modeling. XI, 460 pages. 2007.

Vol. 4533: F. Baader (Ed.), Term Rewriting and Applications. XII, 419 pages. 2007.

Vol. 4531: J. Indulska, K. Raymond (Eds.), Distributed Applications and Interoperable Systems. XI, 337 pages. 2007.

Vol. 4530: D.H. Akehurst, R. Vogel, R.F. Paige (Eds.), Model Driven Architecture- Foundations and Applications. X, 219 pages. 2007.

Vol. 4529: P. Melin, O. Castillo, L.T. Aguilar, J. Kacprzyk, W. Pedrycz (Eds.), Foundations of Fuzzy Logic and Soft Computing. XIX, 830 pages. 2007. (Sublibrary LNAI).

Vol. 4528: J. Mira, J.R. Álvarez (Eds.), Nature Inspired Problem-Solving Methods in Knowledge Engineering, Part II. XXII, 650 pages. 2007.

Vol. 4527: J. Mira, J.R. Álvarez (Eds.), Bio-inspired Modeling of Cognitive Tasks, Part I. XXII, 630 pages. 2007.

Vol. 4526: M. Malek, M. Reitenspieß, A. van Moorsel (Eds.), Service Availability. X, 155 pages. 2007.

Vol. 4525: C. Demetrescu (Ed.), Experimental Algorithms. XIII, 448 pages. 2007.

Vol. 4524: M. Marchiori, J.Z. Pan, C.d.S. Marie (Eds.), Web Reasoning and Rule Systems. XI, 382 pages. 2007.

Vol. 4523: Y.-H. Lee, H.-N. Kim, J. Kim, Y. Park, L.T. Yang, S.W. Kim (Eds.), Embedded Software and Systems. XIX, 829 pages. 2007.

Vol. 4522: B.K. Ersbøll, K.S. Pedersen (Eds.), Image Analysis. XVIII, 989 pages. 2007.

Vol. 4521: J. Katz, M. Yung (Eds.), Applied Cryptography and Network Security. XIII, 498 pages. 2007.

Vol. 4519: E. Franconi, M. Kifer, W. May (Eds.), The Semantic Web: Research and Applications. XVIII, 830 pages. 2007.

Vol. 4517: F. Boavida, E. Monteiro, S. Mascolo, Y. Koucheryavy (Eds.), Wired/Wireless Internet Communications. XIV, 382 pages. 2007.

Vol. 4516: L. Mason, T. Drwiega, J. Yan (Eds.), Managing Traffic Performance in Converged Networks. XXIII, 1191 pages. 2007.

Vol. 4515: M. Naor (Ed.), Advances in Cryptology - EUROCRYPT 2007. XIII, 591 pages. 2007.

Vol. 4514: S.N. Artemov, A. Nerode (Eds.), Logical Foundations of Computer Science. XI, 513 pages. 2007.

Vol. 4513: M. Fischetti, D.P. Williamson (Eds.), Integer Programming and Combinatorial Optimization. IX, 500 pages. 2007.

Vol. 4511: C. Conati, K. McCoy, G. Paliouras (Eds.), User Modeling 2007. XVI, 487 pages. 2007. (Sublibrary LNAI).

Vol. 4510: P. Van Hentenryck, L. Wolsey (Eds.), Integration of AI and OR Techniques in Constraint Programming for Combinatorial Optimization Problems. X, 391 pages. 2007.

Vol. 4509: Z. Kobti, D. Wu (Eds.), Advances in Artificial Intelligence. XII, 552 pages. 2007. (Sublibrary LNAI).

Vol. 4508: M.-Y. Kao, X.-Y. Li (Eds.), Algorithmic Aspects in Information and Management. VIII, 428 pages. 2007.

Vol. 4507: F. Sandoval, A. Prieto, J. Cabestany, M. Graña (Eds.), Computational and Ambient Intelligence. XXVI, 1167 pages. 2007.

Vol. 4506: D. Zeng, I. Gotham, K. Komatsu, C. Lynch, M. Thurmond, D. Madigan, B. Lober, J. Kvach, H. Chen (Eds.), Intelligence and Security Informatics: Biosurveillance. XI, 234 pages. 2007.

GPSR Compliance

The European Union's (EU) General Product Safety Regulation (GPSR) is a set of rules that requires consumer products to be safe and our obligations to ensure this.

If you have any concerns about our products, you can contact us on ProductSafety@springernature.com

In case Publisher is established outside the EU, the EU authorized representative is:

Springer Nature Customer Service Center GmbH
Europaplatz 3
69115 Heidelberg, Germany

Batch number: 10830941

Printed by Printforce, the Netherlands